Federal and State Taxation of Limited Liability Companies

2019 Edition

David J. Cartano

Barton, Klugman & Oetting LLP
Los Angeles, CA

This title is current through June, 2018

Wolters Kluwer

Editorial Staff

Editor . . . . Barbara L. Post, Esq.

Production . . . . Jennifer Schencker, Gokiladevi Sashikumar, Anbarasu Anbumani

ISBN: 978-0-8080-5010-0

Printed in the United States of America

Highlights of the 2019 Edition

This 2019 Edition of *Federal and State Taxation of Limited Liability Companies* covers all of the tax laws applicable to limited liability companies. It analyzes every revenue ruling, private letter ruling, revenue procedure, tax advisory memorandum, IRS notice, Treasury regulation, and federal court case dealing with the tax laws applicable to limited liability companies.

The 2019 Edition of *Federal and State Taxation of Limited Liability Companies* brings you up to date on the latest developments and includes the following updates and enhancements:

- The book was completely revised and updated for changes made to the partnership and LLC tax laws under the 2017 Tax Cuts and Jobs Act (Trump tax act), the proposed and final partnership regulations issued by the IRS in December 2017 and in January 2018, and the Consolidated Appropriations Act of 2018.

- ¶409 discusses the tax consequences of an LLC's acquisition of stock in an S corporation under the 2017 rulings.

- ¶508.08 was updated regarding the rulings in 2017 on late classification elections.

- ¶604.02 was updated regarding the tax consequences of issuing a membership interest to a service partner under the 2017 Trump tax act, including the new three-year holding period for long-term capital gain allocated to a profits interest member.

- ¶702 was added regarding the 20 percent deduction under the Trump tax act that members may take in an LLC for their allocable share of the LLC's qualified business income, including the limitations on the deduction based on the taxable income of the member and the W-2 wages paid by the LLC, and the elimination of the deduction for certain service LLCs if the member's taxable income exceeds a phaseout range.

- ¶703.03 was updated regarding the new limits under the 2017 Trump tax act on pass-throughs of charitable deductions by an LLC, and the basis limitations on charitable deductions.

- ¶703.08 added a new section on business expense deductions under the 2017 Trump tax act, including the limitations on investment management services and the elimination of miscellaneous itemized deductions for tax years between 2018 and 2025.

- ¶703.06 discusses the new expensing limitations and repair regulations under the 2017 Trump tax act.

- ¶703.08 discusses the new limits on investment interest expense, which must be separately stated, and business interest expense, which may not be separately stated, under the 2017 Trump tax act, and the limitations on the deductibility and pass-through of business interest expenses which is now limited to 30 percent of the LLCs adjusted taxable income beginning in 2018.

- ¶703.10 discusses the changes in the domestic productions activity deduction for LLCs under the 2017 Trump tax act.

- Chapter 8 discusses the 2017 rulings by the IRS on special allocations, including the ruling which determined that an LLC which did not comply with any of the requirements for substantial economic effect could make special allocations of losses in accordance with the operating agreement provided the LLC did not allocate losses to the members in excess of their positive capital accounts.

- ¶803.03 was updated regarding the requirements for allocations under the economic effect equivalence test.

- ¶804.02 discusses the impact of LLC liabilities on basis and capital accounts.

- ¶804.06 updates the rules on minimum gain chargebacks which allows a member of an LLC to take tax deductions in excess of the member's capital account balance.

- Chapter 9 discusses the basis adjustments to a membership interest that must be made as a result of changes made under the 2017 Trump tax act, including basis adjustments for excess business interest allocated to the member, guaranteed payments, charitable contribution allocations, and foreign tax credit allocations.

- Chapter 11 was updated regarding the rulings in 2017 and 2018 on the numerous types of reorganizations involving an LLC, including changes in classification, conversions from one type of entity to another, and mergers and acquisitions.

- ¶1203 was added regarding the elimination of the technical termination rule under the 2017 Trump tax act in the event of a sale or transfer of more than 50 percent of the membership interests in an LLC.

- ¶1305 was added regarding the prohibition on pass-through of excess business losses from an LLC to the members for tax years between 2018 and 2025 under the 2017 Trump tax act.

- ¶1306.04 was updated regarding the cases in 2017 limiting the pass-through of losses to members of an LLC.

- ¶1402 was updated regarding the new rules on guaranteed payments under the 2017 Trump tax act, including the disqualification of guaranteed payments for the 20 percent qualified business income deduction under Code Sec. 199A.

- ¶1405 was updated regarding the differences between guaranteed payments and distributive shares of income under the 2017 Trump tax act.

- ¶1406.01 now includes a section on the tax consequences of self-insured medical and health insurance plans for LLCs.

- ¶1509.01 was updated regarding the mandatory downward basis adjustment in LLC assets following a transfer under the 2017 Trump tax act whenever the transferee member would receive a loss allocation of more than $250,000 if the LLC sold its assets for cash at fair market value immediately after the transfer.

- ¶1513 was updated regarding when a member may sell the membership interest on the installment basis.

- ¶1517 was added regarding the taxes on transfers to and by foreign members under the 2017 Trump tax act, including gain recognition on the sale of membership interest by foreign persons, and gain recognition on the transfer of membership interest by a U.S. person to a foreign corporation.

- ¶1603 discusses the new like-kind exchange rules under the 2017 Trump tax act, the 2017 rulings regarding reverse like-kind exchanges, and the holding period requirement for relinquished property.

- ¶1603.07 discusses the methods of cashing out minority LLC members prior to or after a like-kind exchange.

- ¶1701 was revised regarding the requirements to use the accrual or cash methods of accounting for LLCs under the 2017 Trump tax act, including the new laws on applicable financial statements, the AFS conformity rule, the $25 million rule allowing LLCs that sell inventory to use the cash method of accounting, and when the accrual method is required.

- ¶1702.01 was updated regarding the new tax laws applicable to long-term contracts, short-term construction contracts, and the percentage of completion method under the 2017 Trump tax act.

- ¶1801.02 was revised regarding the participation exemption system under the 2017 Trump tax act for foreign tax credits, dividends received deductions, and income allocations to an LLC that is a shareholder in a foreign corporation.

- ¶1902.04 was updated regarding the taxation of a foreign member who sells an interest in an LLC that owned real estate.

- ¶1902.05 and ¶1907 were updated regarding the 2017 cases on the taxation of a foreign member who sells an interest in an LLC that is engaged in a U.S. trade or business.

- ¶1902.06 was updated regarding the branch profits tax applicable to corporate members of an LLC.

- ¶2001 was added regarding the tax consequences of investment income and investment expenses of an LLC, including the NII tax rules, interest limitation rule, the passive loss rules, miscellaneous itemized deduction rules, and gain on sale rules that apply to investment income and investment expenses of an LLC.

- ¶2004 was added regarding the requirements for a security partnership and the permissible allocation methods.

- ¶2102.12 was added regarding the gift and estate taxes payable on gifts of LLC membership interests within three years prior to the date of death.

- ¶2104.03 was updated regarding the cases in 2017 discussing the availability of minority or marketability discounts under Code Sec. 2036.

- ¶2104.08 discusses the withdrawal by the IRS in 2017 of the valuation discount regulations under Code Sec. 2704(a).

- ¶2104.09 discusses the withdrawal by the IRS in 2017 of the valuation discount regulations under Code Sec. 2704(b).

- ¶2104.10 discusses the withdrawal by the IRS in 2017 of the valuation discount regulations under Code Sec. 2704(b)(4).

- ¶ 2203 was updated regarding the regulations issued by the IRS in December 2017 regarding the filing of amended returns and administrative adjustment requests for an LLC.

- ¶2203.03 was added regarding liability for taxes on an amended return and the procedures for an LLC to make a pushout election. The section also discusses the differences between payment of additional taxes (referred to as imputed underpayments) on the amended return and payment of the additional taxes if the imputed underpayments result from an IRS audit.

- ¶2702.02 was updated regarding the liability of members of an LLC for self-employment taxes under the 2017 rulings.

- Chapter 28 includes all the changes to the partnership tax laws regarding tax audit procedures, statute of limitations, assessment of taxes and tax filing procedures made by the Consolidated Appropriation Act of 2018.

- Chapter 28 discusses the regulations issued by the IRS in December 2017 regarding the statute of limitations on assessment of taxes, the procedures that the IRS must follow in audits of LLC tax returns, the liability of members for LLC tax liabilities, interest and penalties.

- ¶2803 was updated regarding the default audit procedures for LLCs classified as partnerships under the 2018 final and proposed regulations.

- ¶2804 was added regarding the groupings and netting of adjustments that are required under the 2017 proposed regulations if there is a deficiency assessment.

- ¶2808 was updated regarding the 2017 proposed regulations on the pushout election allowing an LLC to avoid paying any tax deficiency at the entity level on an amended return or as a result of audit.

- ¶2808.06 was added regarding the proposed regulations issued by the IRS in December 2017 regarding the audit of tiered LLCs and partnerships.

- ¶2810 was updated regarding the final IRS regulations issued in 2018 on the right of an LLC with 100 or fewer members to elect out of the default audit rules and assessment procedures.

- ¶2811 was updated regarding the statute of limitations for filing amended returns and for IRS assessments under the 2017 proposed regulations.

About the Author

David J. Cartano was admitted to the bar in California in 1976. He graduated from the University of Washington in 1972, magna cum laude. He received a J.D. from Cornell University in 1976 and a Masters in Taxation from the University of Southern California in 1989, where he had the highest GPA in the history of the tax program.

Mr. Cartano is a partner in the Los Angeles law firm of Barton, Klugman & Oetting. He has been with the firm since his graduation in 1976. He works in all areas of domestic and international taxation.

Mr. Cartano is the author of *Taxation of Compensation and Benefits* and *Taxation of Individual Retirement Accounts*, both published by CCH, a Wolters Kluwer business. He is a contributor to three other books, including *Limited Liability Partnerships, Formation, Operation and Taxation*, published by John Wiley and Sons, Inc. He was one of the first persons to publish a book on taxation on the Internet, published by Internet Publications, Ltd. He is the author of numerous articles, including "The Tax Benefit Rule in Corporate Liquidations," *The Journal of Corporate Taxation*, Autumn, 1983; "Incentive Stock Options—The Sequential Exercise Restriction," *TAXES—The Tax Magazine*, August, 1982; "ESOPs and Restricted Securities," *Journal of Pension Planning and Compliance*, November, 1977; "Meeting the New IRS Requirements," *Financial Operations*, Fall, 1987. He is a frequent speaker on taxation at bar association meetings and for the California Continuing Education of the Bar.

Preface

Wyoming was the first state to authorize limited liability companies in 1977. The LLC is now authorized in all 50 states. It is one of the most popular forms of business organization primarily because of the tax benefits and the limited liability of members. The taxation of LLCs depends on whether the LLC is classified as a corporation, partnership or disregarded entity. Most LLCs that have two or more members are classified as partnerships for federal tax purposes. There is a single level of tax at the member level, subject to exceptions.

Federal and State Taxation of Limited Liability Companies is designed as a comprehensive guide to all aspects of LLC taxation, including the organization and contribution of property to an LLC, taxation of LLC income, special allocations, inside and outside tax basis, distributions, reorganizations, terminations, loss limitations, payments and benefits to members, transfer of membership interests, sales and exchanges of assets, accounting methods and procedures, estate and gift tax planning, self-employment taxes, and international tax.

The book explains the different tax treatment for LLCs classified as partnerships, corporations and disregarded entities. The book also explains when the tax rules applicable to general and limited partnerships do not apply to limited liability companies classified as partnerships.

The laws of all 50 states are summarized in Chapter 23 (state tax laws), Chapter 24 (asset protection, charging orders, creditors' rights), and Chapter 25 (series LLCs). The federal and state tax filing requirements are discussed in Chapter 22.

In 2018, the book was completely revised to take account of all of the numerous partnership and tax law changes in the 2017 Tax Cuts and Jobs Act.

June 2018

Summary of Contents

Table of Contents

5

Classification of LLCs

6

Contributions

11

Reorganizations

12

Terminations

13

Loss Limitations

14

Payments and Benefits to Members

22

Federal and State Filing Requirements

23

State Tax Laws

24

Asset Protection, Charging Orders, Creditors' Rights

28

Tax Audit Procedures

1

Introduction

¶101   History of LLCs
¶102   Terminology Used

¶101 HISTORY OF LLCs

There are nine principal forms of business organizations: sole proprietorship, C corporation, S corporation, general partnership, limited partnership, limited liability company (LLC), limited liability partnership (LLP), limited liability limited partnership (LLLP), and low profit LLC (L3C).[1]

The LLC is a relatively new form of business organization. Wyoming was the first state to authorize LLCs in 1977. It wanted to provide an organization that had the tax benefits of a partnership and the limited liability benefits of a corporation. During the next 12 years, Florida was the only other state that enacted LLC laws. Other states were reluctant to enact LLC laws because there was too much uncertainty regarding the tax consequences of an LLC.

The Internal Revenue Service (IRS) at first proposed to tax LLCs as corporations because none of the owners had unlimited liability, as they do in a partnership. It issued proposed regulations to that effect in 1980.[2] The proposed regulations received little support and were later withdrawn in 1983.[3] After a six-year study of the limited liability issue, the IRS announced in 1988 that an entity could be taxed as a partnership even if none of the owners were personally liable.[4] Later that year it issued a ruling that a Wyoming LLC would be classified as a partnership for federal tax purposes.[5]

After the 1988 ruling, the other states enacted laws authorizing LLCs. Two states enacted LLC laws in 1990; four states enacted LLC laws in 1991; ten states enacted LLC laws in 1992. All of the states and the District of Columbia now have LLC laws.

---

[1] The low-profit LLC is discussed in Chapter 26.

[2] Prop. Reg. § 301.7701-2, 45 Fed. Reg. 75709 (Nov. 17, 1980).

[3] IRS News Release IR-82-145 (Dec. 16, 1982).

[4] IRS Ann. 88-118, 1988-38 IRB 26.

[5] Rev. Rul. 88-76, 1988-2 CB 360.

In 1996, the Treasury issued final regulations permitting almost all LLCs with two or more members to be classified as partnerships.[6] They were issued in response to the numerous state limited liability statutes that blurred the distinction between corporations and partnerships. The regulations are referred to as the "check-the-box" regulations because they permit LLCs and most other unincorporated entities to select classification as a proprietorship, partnership, or corporation by checking the applicable box on an IRS form. The regulations removed much of the uncertainty regarding the tax consequences of forming an LLC.

In 1995, the National Conference of Commissioners on Uniform State Laws approved and recommended for enactment in all of the states the Uniform Limited Liability Company Act.[7]

In 2002, LLCs became the most prevalent form of partnership, constituting 42.2 percent of all partnerships in existence during that year.[8]

LLPs are similar to LLCs with several exceptions. An LLP is a general partnership in which the partners have limited personal liability. In most states, the partners are not personally liable for LLC debts, contract obligations, torts or other liabilities unless the partner personally guaranteed the debt or the debt arose from the partner's own negligence or wrongful act. Some states provide that a partner is only shielded from liability for the torts, negligence or other wrongful acts of other partners, but not for contractual obligations. An existing general partnership may become an LLP by filing a statement of registration or qualification with the Secretary of State or other governmental agency. There is no new entity created or transfer of partnership assets. In some states, an LLP may be a newly formed general partnership. Each state now allows LLPs. Most states allow LLPs to conduct any type of business. California provides that an LLP may only engage in the business of architecture, accounting, engineering, land surveying, or law.[9] LLPs must maintain a registered agent with the state and file annual reports. The LLP is taxed in the same manner as a general partnership, and in a similar manner to an LLC that is classified as a partnership.

A growing number of states permit the formation of limited liability limited partnerships (LLLP). This entity is a limited partnership, unlike an LLP that is a general partnership. The LLLP statutes extend liability protection to the general partner. The general partner has the same protections against personal liability as partners in an LLP.

---

[6] T.D. 8697 (Dec. 18, 1996), enacting final regulations under Reg. § 301.7701.

[7] A free copy of the Act may be obtained from the following address: Uniform Law Commissioners, 211 East Ontario Street, Suite 1300, Chicago, Illinois 60611; or http://www.uniformlaws.org/Act.aspx?title=Limited%20Liability%20Company%20(2006)%20(Last%20Amended%202013).

[8] IR-2005-5.

[9] Cal. Corp. Code §§ 16101(8)(a), 16101(6)(a), 16951–16952.

¶ 102 TERMINOLOGY USED

The basic terminology for LLCs is as follows:

> **Articles of organization**: The articles of organization are filed with the secretary of state in order to form the LLC. This document is analogous to the articles of incorporation for corporations and the certificate of limited partnership for limited partnerships.
>
> **Certificate of formation**: Some states, such as Delaware, refer to the articles of organization as the certificate of formation.
>
> **Economic interest**: An economic interest is the right of a member or nonmember to receive an allocable share of income, gain, loss, deductions, and credits in the LLC. An economic interest does not include the right to vote or participate in management. Normally, a member may transfer an economic interest in an LLC without the consent of the other member unless the organizational documents otherwise provide. However, transfer of the economic interest normally transfers only the member's right to share in distributions and profit and loss allocations. It does not transfer the member's voting and management rights without the consent of the other members (as specified in the operating agreement).
>
> **Limited liability company agreement**: Some states, such as Delaware, refer to the operating agreement as the limited liability company agreement.
>
> **Managers**: Managers are the persons designated by the members to manage the LLC. Most state laws allow members to designate managers. If there are no designated managers, all members normally manage the LLC in accordance with their proportionate interests in the LLC. Managers are analogous to the officers and directors in a corporation and the general partners in a limited partnership.
>
> **Members**: Members are the owners of an LLC.
>
> **Membership interest**: A membership interest is all of a member's ownership rights in an LLC. A membership interest includes the member's right to vote and participate in management and the member's economic interest in the LLC. A membership interest is analogous to the shares of stock in a corporation and the partnership units in a limited partnership.
>
> **Operating agreement**: The operating agreement sets forth the rules regarding the operation of the LLC and the rights and obligations of the members. It is similar to the bylaws in a corporation and the partnership agreement in a partnership.

2

Summary of LLC Laws

¶ 201 INTRODUCTION

LLC laws vary from state to state. The principal features of LLC laws concern the following issues:

- Formation
- Purposes for which LLCs may be formed
- Membership interests
- Duration of LLCs
- Management
- Rights of members

- Limited liability
- Restrictions on transfer
- Withdrawal of members

In 1995, the National Conference of Commissioners on Uniform State Law (NCCUSL) enacted a model statute for LLC state laws. The model statute is called the Uniform Limited Liability Company Act (ULLCA). The 2011 and 2013 amendments to the ULLCA, enacted as part of the Harmonization of Business Entity Acts project, updated and harmonized the language in the Act with similar provisions in other uniform and model unincorporated entity Acts.

On July 19, 2017, the Uniform Law Commission approved the Uniform Limited Liability Company Protected Series Act (ULLCPSA) at its annual meeting. Series LLCs are discussed in Chapter 25.

The following chart sets forth the citations to the LLC laws in each state. These may be accessed without charge via the Internet:[1]

Citations to State LLC Laws

State	LLC Act
Alabama	Ala. Code § 10A-5A-1.01 *et seq.*
Alaska	Alaska Stat. §§ 10.50.010 to 10.50.995
Arizona	Ariz. Rev. Stat. Ann. §§ 29-601 to 29-857
Arkansas	Ark. Code Ann. §§ 4-32-101 to 4-32-1401
California	Cal. Corp. Code §§ 17701.01 to 17713.13 (effective January 1, 2014)
Colorado	Colo. Rev. Stat. Ann. §§ 7-80-101 to 7-80-1101
Connecticut	Conn. Gen. Stat. Ann. §§ 34-100 to 34-200
Delaware	Del. Code Ann. tit. 6, §§ 18-101 to 18-1109
D.C.	D.C. Code Ann. §§ 29-801.01 to 29-810.01
Florida	Fla. Stat. Ann. §§ 605.0101 to 605.1108
Georgia	Ga. Code Ann. §§ 14-11-100 to 14-11-1109
Hawaii	Haw. Rev. Stat. §§ 428-101 to 428-1302
Idaho	Idaho Code §§ 30-6-101 to 30-6-1104
Illinois	805 ILCS 180/1-1 to 180/60-1
Indiana	Ind. Code Ann. §§ 23-18-1-1 to 23-18-13-1
Iowa	Iowa Code Ann. §§ 489.101 to 489.1304
Kansas	Kan. Stat. Ann. §§ 17-7663 to 17-76142
Kentucky	Ky. Rev. Stat. Ann. §§ 275.001 to 275.540
Louisiana	La. Rev. Stat. Ann. §§ 12:1301 to 12:1369
Maine	Me. Rev. Stat. Ann. tit. 31, §§ 1501 to 1693
Maryland	Md. Code Ann., Corps. & Assns. §§ 4A-101 to 4A-1303
Massachusetts	Mass. Gen. Laws Ann. ch. 156C, §§ 1-72

---

[1] https://www.law.cornell.edu/states.

State	LLC Act
Michigan	Mich. Comp. Laws Ann. §§ 450.4101 to 450.5200
Minnesota	Minn. Stat. Ann. §§ 322B.01 to 322B.960
Mississippi	Miss. Code Ann. §§ 79-29-101 to 79-29-1201
Missouri	Mo. Ann. Stat. §§ 347.010 to 347.740
Montana	Mont. Code Ann. §§ 35-8-101 to 35-8-1307
Nebraska	Neb. Rev. Stat. §§ 21-2601 to 21-2653
Nevada	Nev. Rev. Stat. Ann. §§ 86.011 to 86.590
New Hampshire	N.H. Rev. Stat. Ann. §§ 304-C:1 to 304-C:85
New Jersey	N.J. Stat. Ann. §§ 42:2C-1 to 42:2C-70
New Mexico	N.M. Stat. Ann. §§ 53-19-1 to 53-19-74
New York	N.Y. L.L.C. Law §§ 101 to 1403
North Carolina	N.C. Gen. Stat. §§ 57C-1-01 to 57C-10-07
North Dakota	N.D. Cent. Code §§ 10-32-01 to 10-32-156
Ohio	Ohio Rev. Code Ann. §§ 1705.01 to 1705.58
Oklahoma	Okla. Stat. Ann. tit. 18, §§ 2000 to 2060
Oregon	Or. Rev. Stat. §§ 63.001 to 63.990
Pennsylvania	15 Pa. Cons. Stat. Ann. §§ 8101 to 8998
Rhode Island	R.I. Gen. Laws §§ 7-16-1 to 7-16-75
South Carolina	S.C. Code Ann. §§ 33-44-101 to 33-44-1207
South Dakota	S.D. Codified Laws Ann. §§ 47-34A-101 to 47-34A-1207
Tennessee	Tenn. Code Ann. §§ 48-249-101 to 48-249-1133
Texas	Tex. Rev. Civ. Stat. Ann. art. 1528n, 1.01-11.07
Utah	Utah Code Ann. §§ 48-2c-101 to 48-2c-1902
Vermont	Vt. Stat. Ann. tit. 11, §§ 3001-3162
Virginia	Va. Code Ann. §§ 13.1-1000 to 13.1-1123
Washington	Wash. Rev. Code Ann. §§ 25.15.005 to 25.15.902
West Virginia	W. Va. Code §§ 31B-1-101 to 31B-13-1306
Wisconsin	Wis. Stat. Ann. §§ 183.0102 to 183.1305
Wyoming	Wyo. Stat. §§ 17-15-101 to 17-15-144

¶ 202 FORMATION OF LLCs

The LLC is an organization separate and apart from its owners. It can sue and be sued, sign contracts, buy property, and take other action in its own name.

The founders must file articles of organization with the secretary of state or other designated government agency. The articles of organization contain information similar to articles of incorporation for corporations. Most states require the articles of organization to include the name of the LLC, the period of duration, the purpose of the LLC, and the name and address of the registered agent. Other states also require provisions in the articles of organization dealing with the following issues:

- Membership interests
- The right to admit additional members[2]
- The names and addresses of the members or designated managers[3]
- Whether the LLC will have separate series.[4]

In addition to the articles of organization, there is usually an operating agreement. The operating agreement governs the rights, duties, and obligations of members and managers except as otherwise stated in the articles of organization or required by state law. The operating agreement is similar to corporate bylaws or a partnership agreement. The operating agreement may be verbal or in writing.[5]

The members of an LLC may be individuals, corporations, partnerships, other LLCs, trusts, estates, and associations. There are no restrictions on membership except as provided in the organization documents.

The company name must ordinarily contain "limited liability company," "limited company," or "LLC" at the end of the name. The name may not conflict with other registered names.

¶ 203 PURPOSES FOR WHICH LLCs CAN BE FORMED

.01 Generally

An LLC can be formed for any lawful purpose,[6] subject to certain restrictions in some states. For example, some states provide that an LLC may not engage in the following activities:

---

[2] *See* Fla. Stat. Ann. § 608.407; Kan. Stat. Ann. § 17-7607; Nev. Rev. Stat. Ann. § 86.161.

[3] *See* Kan. Stat. Ann. § 17-7607; Utah Code Ann. § 48-2b-116; Wyo. Stat. § 17-15-107.

[4] *See* Chapter 25.

[5] *See, e.g.,* Cal. Corp. Code § § 17000(ab), 17050(a).

[6] Ala. Code § 10-12-3; Alaska Stat. § 10.50.075(2); Ark. Code Ann. § 4-32-106; Cal. Corp. Code § 17701-04(b); Colo. Rev. Stat. Ann. § 7-80-103; D.C. Code Ann. § 29-1003; Ga. Code Ann. § 14-11-201(a); Idaho Code § 30-6-104(2); Ind. Code Ann. § 23-18-2-1(a); Iowa Code § 490A.201.1; Kan. Stat. Ann. § 17-7668(a); Ky. Rev. Stat. Ann. § 275-005; La. Rev. Stat. Ann. § 12:1303; M.G.L.A. ch. 156C, § 6(a); Me. Rev. Stat. Ann. tit. 31, § 611; Mich. Comp. Laws Ann. § 450.4203(1)(b); Miss. Code Ann. § 79-29-108(1); Mo. Rev. Stat. § 347.039.1(2); Neb. Rev. Stat. § 21-2602(1); Nev. Rev. Stat. Ann. § 86.141; N.H. Rev. Stat. Ann. § 304-C:7.I; N.J. Stat. Ann. § 42:2B-8.a; N.Y. LLC § 201; N.C. Gen. Stat. § 57C-2-01(a); N.D. Cent. Code § 10-32-04; Ohio Rev. Code Ann. § 1705.02; Or. Rev. Stat. § 63.074(1); 15 Pa. Cons. Stat. § 8922(a); R.I. Gen. Laws § 7-16-3; S.C. Code Ann. § 33-44-112; S.D. Codified Laws Ann. § 47-34A-112(a); Tenn. Code Ann. § 48-249-104; Tex. Rev. Civ. Stat. Ann. art. 1528n, 2.01.A; Utah Code Ann. § 48-2c-105; Vt. Stat. Ann. tit. 11, § 3012(a); Va. Code Ann. § 13.1-1008; Wash. Rev. Code § 25.15.030(1); W. Va. Code § 31B-1-112(a); Wis. Stat. § 183.0107; Wyo. Stat. § 17-15-103(a).

- Operating a homestead or building and loan association.[7]
- Engaging in the banking, insurance, or trust company business[8] Pennsylvania enacted legislation effective in 2014 permitting an LLC to be formed for banking and for operating a health maintenance organization.[9]
- Engaging in a profession.[10]
- Engaging in any other business or activities to the extent limited by the articles of organization.[11]

.02 Charitable Purposes

An LLC may be formed for charitable purposes. The main types of charitable LLCs are (a) a low-profit LLC (also known as an "L3C"), (b) a tax-exempt Section 501(c)(3) LLC, (c) a subsidiary LLC wholly owned by a tax-exempt organization, and (d) a joint venture LLC between a tax-exempt organization and a for-profit LLC. These are discussed in Chapter 26.

.03 Cooperative Housing Corporations

Tenant-shareholders may contribute their shares in a cooperative housing corporation to an LLC in exchange for membership interests on a tax-free basis.[12] A cooperative housing corporation may transfer shares of stock in commercial units in residential and commercial buildings to an LLC, and distribute the membership interests in the LLC to its shareholders on a tax-free basis.[13]

A tenant-stockholder in a cooperative housing corporation may deduct interest and taxes paid or accrued by a cooperative housing corporation during the tax year. The amount of the deduction is equal to the tenant-stockholder's proportionate share of the taxes and interest. In order to qualify for this favorable tax treatment, the cooperative housing corporation must meet various requirements. One of the requirements is that 80 percent or more of the gross income of the cooperative housing corporation for the tax year must be received from tenant-stockholders.[14]

---

[7] *See, e.g.,* La. Rev. Stat. Ann. § 12:1302.

[8] *See, e.g.,* Ariz. Rev. Stat. Ann. § 29-609; Cal. Corp. Code § 17701-04(b); Conn. Gen. Stat. Ann. § 34-119; Del. Code Ann. tit. 6, § 18-106; 805 ILCS § 180/1-25; Kan. Stat. Ann. § 17-7668(a); La. Rev. Stat. Ann. § 12:1302; Md. Corps. & Ass'ns Code Ann. § 4A-201; Mont. Code Ann. § 35-8-106(2); Neb. Rev. Stat. § 21-2602(1); Nev. Rev. Stat. Ann. § 86.141; N.H. Rev. Stat. Ann. § 304-C:7.I; Okla. Stat. Ann. tit. 18, § 2002; 15 Pa. Cons. Stat. § 8911(a); Vt. Stat. Ann. tit. 11, § 3012(b); Wash. Rev. Code § 25.15.030(1); Wyo. Stat. § 17-15-103(a).

[9] H.B. 1575, Laws 2014, effective September 8, 2014.

[10] *See* ¶ 203.04 *infra* regarding professional LLCs.

[11] D.C. Code Ann. § 29-1003; Ga. Code Ann. § 14-11-201(b); Haw. Rev. Stat. Ann. § 428-111; Ind. Code Ann. § 23-18-2-1(a); Iowa Code § 490A.201.1; Utah Code Ann. § 48-2c-105.

[12] Ltr. Rul. 200801038.

[13] Ltr. Ruls. 200533005, 200515011.

[14] Code Sec. 216(b)(1)(D).

The tenant-stockholders may contribute some of their shares to an LLC. Income that the cooperative housing corporation receives from the LLC in its capacity as a tenant-shareholder qualifies as income derived from the tenant-shareholders for purposes of the 80 percent rule.[15] The LLC must be classified as a partnership for federal income tax purposes. All of the stock in the LLC must be freely transferable and not stapled to any stock in the cooperative housing corporation.

.04 Professional Organizations

Most states permit an LLC to engage in a profession, subject to certain conditions.[16] For example, some states provide that an LLC does not protect members from professional malpractice.[17] Other states permit professional LLCs if the LLC obtains malpractice insurance,[18] complies with additional provisions governing professional LLCs,[19] or complies with the separate laws regulating the profession.[20]

California prohibits an LLC from engaging in any profession.[21]

---

[15] Ltr. Ruls. 200701027, 200636092, 200324004, 200125013, 9802047. *See also* Ltr. Rul. 200244013 regarding a partnership of two LLCs, and Ltr. Rul. 200636092 regarding a cooperative's distribution of LLC interests and issuance of cooperative stock relating to nonresidential units.

[16] Ala. Code § 10-12-4(s); Alaska Stat. § 10.50.015; Ariz. Rev. Stat. Ann. § § 29-841 to 29-847; Ark. Code Ann. § § 4-32-102(13), 4-32-106, 4-32-1401; Colo. Rev. Stat. Ann. § 7-80-103; Conn. Gen. Stat. Ann. § § 34-119(b), 34-133; D.C. Code Ann. § § 29-101(25), 29-1014(c) 29-1075; Fla. Stat. Ann. § 608.403; Idaho Code § § 30-6-201A; 53-615; Ind. Code Ann. § 23-18-2-1(b); Iowa Code § § 490A.1501 to 490A.1519; Kan. Stat. Ann. § 17-7668; Ky. Rev. Stat. § 275.005; M.G.L.A. ch. 156C, § 6(b), (c); Me. Rev. Stat. Ann. tit. 31, § 611; Md. Corps. & Ass'ns Code Ann. § § 4A-101(p), 4A-203.1, 4A-301.1; Mich. Comp. Laws Ann. § § 450.4901 to 450.4910; Miss. Code Ann. § § 79-29-901 to 79-29-933; Mont. Code Ann. § § 35-8-1301 to 35-8-1307; Neb. Rev. Stat. § § 21-2426, 21-2632; Nev. Rev. Stat. Ann. § 86.555; N.Y. LLC § § 1201-1216, 1301-1309; N.D. Cent. Code § § 10-31-01.7, 10-31-07.1, 10-31-02.2; Ohio Rev. Code Ann. § § 1705.01(L), 1705.04(C); Or. Rev. Stat. § 63.074(2); 15 Pa. Cons. Stat. § § 8908, 8922(b), 8995-8998; R.I. Gen. Laws § 7-16-3.1; S.D. Codified Laws Ann. § 47-34A-112(a); Tenn. Code Ann. § § 48-249-1101 to 48-249-1133; Tex. Rev. Civ. Stat. Ann. art. 1528n, 11.01 to 11.07; Utah Code Ann. § § 48-2c-602(5)(a), (b), 1501 to 1513; Va. Code Ann. § § 13.1-1100 to 1123; Vt. Stat. Ann. tit. 11, § 3012(C); Wash. Rev. Code § 25.15.045; W. Va. Code § § 31B-13-1301 to 31B-13-1306; Wyo. Stat. § 17-15-103(b).

[17] Ala. Code § 10-12-45; Conn. Gen. Stat. Ann. § 34-133; D.C. Code Ann. § 29-1014(c); Idaho Code § 53-615(3); Iowa Code § 490A.1507; Md. Corps. & Ass'ns Code Ann. § 4A-301.1; Mont. Code Ann. § 35-8-1306(1); Tenn. Code Ann. § 48-218-406; Tex. Rev. Civ. Stat. Ann. art. 1528n, 11.05.A; Utah Code Ann. § 48-2c-602(5); Wyo. Stat. § 17-15-103(b).

[18] R.I. Gen. Laws § 7-16-3.3.

[19] Ariz. Rev. Stat. Ann. § § 29-841 to 29-847; Iowa Code § § 490A.1501 to 490A.1519; Kan. Stat. Ann. § 17-7668; Mich. Comp. Laws Ann. § § 450.4901 to 450.4910; Miss. Code Ann. § § 79-29-901 to 79-29-933; Mont. Code Ann. § § 35-8-1301 to 35-8-1307; N.Y. LLC § § 1201-1216 (New York LLCs), 1301-1309 (LLCs from other states); Tenn. Code Ann. § § 48-249-1101 to 48-249-1133; Tex. Rev. Civ. Stat. Ann. art. 1528n, 11.01 to 11.07; Va. Code Ann. § § 13.1-1100 to 1123; Vt. Stat. Ann. tit. 11, § 3012(C); Wash. Rev. Code § 25.15.045.

[20] Alaska Stat. § 10.50.015; Ark. Code Ann. § 4-32-1401 (medical and dental LLCs); Colo. Rev. Stat. Ann. § 7-80-103; Conn. Gen. Stat. Ann. § 34-119(b); Fla. Stat. Ann. § 608.403; Idaho Code § 30-6-201A(3); 805 ILCS § 180/1-25(3), (4) (medical and dental LLCs); Ind. Code Ann. § 23-18-2-1(b); M.G.L.A. ch. 156C, § 6(b), (c); Neb. Rev. Stat. § 21-2646 (law LLCs); N.H. Rev. Stat. Ann. § 304-D:1; N.C. Gen. Stat. § 57C-2-01(c); S.D. Codified Laws Ann. § 47-34A-112(a); Vt. Stat. Ann. tit. 11, § 3012(C); Wyo. Stat. § 17-15-103(b).

[21] Cal. Corp. Code § 17701-04(e).

.05 State and Governmental Organizations

A state or other governmental organization may form an investment LLC. Memberships must be limited to a state, a political subdivision of a state, or another entity that may exclude its income under Code Sec. 115(1). The gross income from the LLC allocable to the members qualifies for the exclusion under Code Sec. 115(1).[22]

.06 Nonbusiness Purposes

In some states, an LLC may be formed for nonbusiness purposes. For example, an LLC may be formed in Alabama to hold title, for estate planning purposes, and for purposes other than carrying on a business.[23]

¶204 MEMBERSHIP INTERESTS

Members may contribute property, services, or almost anything else of value to the LLC in exchange for membership interests. Some states prohibit issuance of membership interests in exchange for services[24] or promissory notes.

Membership interests may be treated as securities subject to state registration or notification requirements, particularly if members are passive investors. Most states permit division of membership interests into different classes or groups.

¶205 DURATION OF LLCs

Unlike corporations, LLCs are, in most states, of limited duration. Upon termination and dissolution, the LLC must pay its creditors, distribute its remaining assets to members, and make a filing with the secretary of state or other designated government agency.

An LLC typically terminates and dissolves after a fixed period, by the consent of the members, upon withdrawal of one or more members, or by involuntary dissolution.

.01 Fixed Period

An LLC may terminate after the expiration of the period fixed in the articles of organization or by statute. An LLC may also be terminated in most states upon the

---

[22] Ltr. Rul. 200243023.

[23] *See BNA Daily Tax Report*, No. 59, p. H-1 (Mar. 27, 2014) referring to the analysis by the Alabama Law Institute of the Alabama Limited Liability Company Law 2014, H.B. 2.

[24] *See, e.g.*, Fla. Stat. Ann. § 608.4211; Wyo. Stat. § 17-15-115.

happening of other events specified in the articles of organization or operating agreement.[25]

.02 Consent

An LLC may dissolve by the consent of the members. In some states, the consent must be unanimous.[26] In other states, the consent must be by a majority in interest.

.03 Withdrawal of Member

An LLC normally dissolves at the death, retirement, resignation, expulsion, or bankruptcy of a member unless the remaining members agree to continue the LLC. The consent to continue the LLC is made by a majority in interest, by unanimous consent,[27] or as otherwise provided in the LLC agreements.

Some states also permit members to pre-approve continuation at the loss of a member. Such a statute typically provides that the LLC may be continued at the loss of a member by unanimous consent of the members or under a right to continue stated in the articles of organization of the LLC.

.04 Involuntary Dissolution

An LLC may be terminated involuntarily in most states. There are different grounds for involuntary dissolution. These include the following:

- Failing to pay minimum franchise taxes imposed on LLCs
- Failing to maintain a registered agent[28]
- Obtaining a certificate of organization through fraud[29]
- Abusing its authority or powers[30]
- Carrying on illegal activities[31]
- Undergoing judicial dissolution where it is no longer practical for the LLC to carry on its business in accordance with its operating agreement

---

[25] See, e.g., Del. Code Ann. tit. 6, §18-801; Iowa Code Ann. §490A.1301; Okla. Stat. Ann. tit. 18, §2037.

[26] See, e.g., Ariz. Rev. Stat. Ann. §29-781; Okla. Stat. Ann. tit. 18, §2037; W. Va. Code §31-1A-35.

[27] Iowa Code Ann. §490A.1301; Md. Code Ann., Corps. & Assns. §4A-904; Okla. Stat. Ann. tit. 18, §2037; Va. Code Ann. §13.1-1046.

[28] Colo. Rev. Stat. Ann. §7-80-808; Fla. Stat. Ann. §608.448; Nev. Rev. Stat. Ann. §86.271; R.I. Gen. Laws §7-16-41; Wyo. Stat. §17-15-112.

[29] Colo. Rev. Stat. Ann. §7-80-808; Fla. Stat. Ann. §608.448; Kan. Stat. Ann. §17-7629; Minn. Stat. Ann. §322B.843; R.I. Gen. Laws §7-16-41; Utah Code Ann. §48-2b-142.

[30] Colo. Rev. Stat. Ann. §7-80-808; Fla. Stat. Ann. §608.448; Kan. Stat. Ann. §17-7629; Minn. Stat. Ann. §322B.843; R.I. Gen. Laws §7-16-41; Utah Code Ann. §48-2b-142.

[31] Colo. Rev. Stat. Ann. §7-80-808; Fla. Stat. Ann. §608.448; Kan. Stat. Ann. §17-7629; Minn. Stat. Ann. §322B.843; R.I. Gen. Laws §7-16-41; Utah Code Ann. §48-2b-142.

¶206 MANAGEMENT OF LLCs

The members of an LLC may participate in management without personal liability. Typically, the members designate one or more managers to handle day-to-day operations. The manager is not liable for LLC debts or obligations by virtue of that position. The manager's functions are similar to those of a general partner or president of a corporation.

Management may be vested in designated managers, in all of the members, or as otherwise provided in the LLC agreements. Some states require LLCs to designate managers.[32]

Three states provide for management by governors and a board of governors, rather than managers.[33]

¶207 RIGHTS OF MEMBERS

LLC statutes give members various rights. These rights typically include the right to inspect certain LLC records, such as the articles of organization, operating agreement, names and addresses of other members, tax returns, and other relevant records.[34]

¶208 LIMITED LIABILITY

.01 General

Members of an LLC have limited liability similar to that of shareholders in a corporation. They are not liable for the tort liabilities, debts, and other obligations of the LLC.[35] Agents and managers of an LLC are also not personally liable for LLC debts and obligations. However, certain states provide that members may be liable for the following:

---

[32] *See, e.g.*, Colo. Rev. Stat. Ann. §7-80-401 (LLC must be managed by one or more managers).

[33] Minn. Stat. §§322B.03, 322B.606 to 322B.666; N.D. Cent. Code §10-32-69; Tenn. Code Ann. §§48-239-101 to 48-239-116.

[34] Cal. Corp. Code §§17704.10, 17708.08; Del. Code Ann. tit. 6, §18-305(a), (e); Nev. Rev. Stat. Ann. §86.271; R.I. Gen. Laws §7-16-41; Wyo. Stat. §17-15-112.

[35] Alaska Stat. §10.50.265; Ariz. Rev. Stat. Ann. §29-651; Ark. Code Ann. §4-32-304; Colo. Rev. Stat. Ann. §7-80-705; Ind. Code Ann. §23-18-3-3; Idaho Code §30-6-304; 805 ILCS 180/10-10(a); Iowa Code §§490A.601, 490A.603; Ky. Rev. Stat. Ann. §275-150; Kan. Stat. Ann. §17-7688(a); M.G.L.A. ch. 156C, §22; Md. Corps. & Ass'ns Code Ann. §4A-301; Mich. Comp. Laws Ann. §450.4501(2); Miss. Code Ann. §79-29-305(3); Mont. Code Ann. §35-8-304(1); Neb. Rev. Stat. §21-2612(1); Nev. Rev. Stat. Ann. §86.371; N.H. Rev. Stat. Ann. §304-C:25; N.J. Stat. Ann. §42:2B-23; N.M. Stat. Ann. §§53-19-13, 53-19-16; N.C. Gen. Stat. §57C-3-30; N.Y. LLC §609(a); N.D. Cent. Code §10-32-29.1; Or. Rev. Stat. §63.165(1); Okla. Stat. Ann. tit. 18, §2022; R.I. Gen. Laws §7-16-23; S.C. Code Ann. §33-44-303(a); S.D. Codified Laws Ann. §§47-34A-201, 47-34A-303(a); Tenn. Code Ann. §48-249-114; Tex. Rev. Civ. Stat. Ann. art. 1528n, 4.03.A; Utah Code Ann. §48-2c-601; Vt. Stat. Ann. tit. 11, §3043(a); Va. Code Ann. §13.1-1019; Wash. Rev. Code §25.15.155(1); W. Va. Code §31B-3-303; Wis. Stat. §183.0304(1); Wyo. Stat. §17-15-113.

- Debts personally guaranteed by the member. All states permit members to guarantee or to agree to be personally liable for the LLC's debts.[36]

- Wrongful acts committed by the member.[37]

- Amounts that the member promised to contribute to the LLC.[38] A member may be relieved of an obligation to contribute if all other members consent. However, the member may still be liable to creditors. For example, a member in certain states is liable to creditors who relied on the promised contribution in extending credit to the LLC.[39] In Nevada and Wyoming, members are liable to creditors who extend credit after the articles of organization are filed.[40]

- Amounts treated as wrongful distributions under state law.[41] These distributions include distributions while the LLC is insolvent. Members and managers are liable for a specified number of years after the wrongful distribution.[42]

- Sales taxes not remitted,[43] the trust fund portion of employment taxes not paid,[44] or any other tax liabilities of the LLC.[45]

- Transactions under which the member received an improper personal benefit.[46]

- Violations of criminal laws.[47]

---

[36] Cal. Corp. Code § 17703.04(c), Ga. Code Ann. § 14-11-303(b); Haw. Rev. Stat. Ann. § 428-303(c); 805 ILCS 180/10-10(d); Kan. Stat. Ann. § 17-7688(b); Stat. Ann. § 275-150(2); Me. Rev. Stat. Ann. tit. 31, § 645.4; Miss. Code Ann. § 79-29-305(3); Mont. Code Ann. § 35-8-304(3); N.Y. LLC § 609(b); 15 Pa. Cons. Stat. § 8922(e); S.C. Code Ann. § 33-44-303(c); S.D. Codified Laws Ann. § 47-34A-303(c); Tex. Rev. Civ. Stat. Ann. art. 1528n, 4.03.A; Utah Code Ann. § 48-2c-603; Vt. Stat. Ann. tit. 11, § 3043(b); W. Va. Code § 31B-3-303(c).

[37] Cal. Corp. Code § 17703.04(c); Fla. Stat. Ann. § 608.4228(1)(b)(5); Ind. Code Ann. § 23-18-3-3(a); Iowa Code § 490A.603.3; N.M. Stat. Ann. § 53-19-13; Tenn. Code Ann. § 48-217-101(a)(3); Vt. Stat. Ann. tit. 11, § 3043(a); Wash. Rev. Code § 25.15.155(1); Wis. Stat. § 183.0304(1).

[38] Ala. Code § 10-12-27; Alaska Stat. § 10.50.280; Colo. Rev. Stat. Ann. § 7-80-502; Haw. Rev. Stat. Ann. § 428-402(b); La. Rev. Stat. Ann. § 12:1322.C; R.I. Gen. Laws § 7-16-25(d)(2); Vt. Stat. Ann. tit. 11, § 3052(b).

[39] Colo. Rev. Stat. Ann. § 7-80-502; R.I. Gen. Laws § 7-16-25(d)(2).

[40] Nev. Rev. Stat. Ann. § 86.391; Wyo. Stat. § 17-15-121.

[41] Cal. Corp. Code § 17704.05; Del. Code Ann. tit. 6, § 18-804(c); D.C. Code Ann. § § 29-1029, 29-1030; Fla. Stat. Ann. § 608.428; Idaho Code § 30-6-406(3); Iowa Code § 490A.808; M.G.L.A. ch. 156C, § 35; Minn. Stat. § 322B.56; N.M. Stat. Ann. § 53-19-27; N.D. Cent. Code § 10-32-65; Ohio Rev. Code Ann. § 1705.23; R.I. Gen. Laws § 7-16-32; S.C. Code Ann. § 33-44-407; Tenn. Code Ann. § § 48-249-306, 307; Utah Code Ann. § § 48-2c-602(b), 1006; Vt. Stat. Ann. tit. 11, § 3057; W. Va. Code § 31B-4-407.

[42] Cal. Corp. Code § 17704.06 (four years); Iowa Code Ann. § 490A.808 (five years); Va. Code Ann. § 13.1-1036 (six years); W. Va. Code § 31-1A-30 (four years).

[43] Cal. Rev. & Tax. Code § 6829; Tenn. Code Ann. § 48-217-101(d).

[44] Any person who is a "responsible person" is potentially liable if employment taxes are not paid.

[45] Ga. Code Ann. § 14-11-303(a); Neb. Rev. Stat. § 21-2612(2); S.D. Codified Laws Ann. § 10-45-55 (sales and use, motor fuel and telecommunications taxes).

[46] Fla. Stat. Ann. § 608.4228(1)(b)(2); Wash. Rev. Code § 25.15.155(2); Wyo. Stat. § 17-15-103(b).

[47] Fla. Stat. Ann. § 608.4228(1)(b)(1).

- Malpractice claims in states that permit professional LLCs, including negligence and misconduct by another person under the professional's direct supervision and control.[48]

- Any other liabilities to the extent provided in the articles of organization.[49]

.02 Applicability of Piercing the Corporate Veil Doctrine to LLCs

The applicability of the piercing the corporate veil doctrine to LLCs is discussed in Chapter 24.

.03 Differences between Partnerships and LLCs

There are several differences between the liability of members in an LLC and that of partners in a partnership. In a general partnership, all partners are liable. In a limited partnership, the general partner is liable. In an LLC, none of the members are liable. The Treasury Department at one time believed that an LLC could not be taxed as a partnership unless at least one member was personally liable, as in a limited partnership. The Treasury Department later determined that an LLC could be taxed as a partnership even though no member was personally liable. The current IRS classification regulations do not consider the liability of members in determining classification except for foreign LLCs.[50]

Another difference between LLCs and partnerships concerns participation in management. Limited partners are liable if they participate in the management of the partnership, subject to certain exceptions under state law. LLC members are not liable if they participate in management or become designated managers.

¶ 209 RESTRICTIONS ON TRANSFER

An LLC membership involves two basic rights. The first is a right to receive a share of profits, gain, and other compensation from the LLC. This is referred to as the member's "economic interest." Generally, this right is freely transferable unless otherwise provided in the operating agreement.

The second membership right is a right to vote and participate in management. This right is not freely transferable. State law provides that this right may not be

---

[48] Ala. Code § 10-12-45; Conn. Gen. Stat. Ann. § 34-133; D.C. Code Ann. § 29-1014(c); Idaho Code § 30-6-201A(3); Iowa Code § 490A.1507; Md. Corps. & Ass'ns Code Ann. § 4A-301.1; Mont. Code Ann. § 35-8-1306(1); Tenn. Code Ann. § 48-218-406; Wyo. Stat. § 17-15-103(b).

[49] Fla. Stat. Ann. § 608.4227; Haw. Rev. Stat. Ann. § 428-303(c); 805 ILCS § 180/10-10(d).

[50] *See* ¶ 501 *infra.*

transferred without the consent of a majority[51] or all[52] of the other members or as otherwise provided in the LLC agreements. The state laws were adopted at a time when the IRS regulations required restrictions on transfer in order for the LLC to be classified as a partnership. The current IRS regulations on entity classification no longer require restrictions on transfer.[53] 15 Pa. Cons. Stat. §8924(a)

¶210 WITHDRAWAL OF MEMBERS

The articles of organization or operating agreement may specify the terms and conditions for a member's withdrawal.[54] In some states, a member has a right to withdraw from the LLC and receive the fair market value of his membership interest unless otherwise provided in the operating agreement. Other states require at least six months' notice of withdrawal.[55] A member is ordinarily entitled to receive only cash upon withdrawal even though he has contributed property to the LLC.[56] No member can be compelled to accept a distribution of any asset in kind in lieu of a proportionate distribution of money made to other members.[57]

---

[51] Conn. Gen. Stat. Ann. §34-172(a); Ky. Rev. Stat. Ann. §275.265(1); Neb. Rev. Stat. §21-2621; Nev. Rev. Stat. Ann. §86.351.1; N.Y. LLC §604; Okla. Stat. Ann. tit. 18, §2035.A.2; Or. Rev. Stat. §63.245(2)(a), (b); Utah Code Ann. §48-2b-131; Va. Code Ann. §13.1-1040.

[52] Ala. Code §10-12-22; Alaska Stat. §10.50.165(a); Ariz. Rev. Stat. Ann. §29-731.B.2; Ark. Code Ann. §4-32-706; Cal. Corp. Code §17704.01(c)(3); Colo. Rev. Stat. Ann. §7-80-701; Del. Code Ann. tit. 6, §18-702; D.C. Code Ann. §29-1032(b); Fla. Stat. Ann. §608.432; Ga. Code Ann. §14-11-505(b); Haw. Rev. Stat. Ann. §428-503(a); 805 ILCS §180/30-10(a); Ind. Code Ann. §§23-18-6-1(a)(1), 23-18-6-4.1(b); Idaho Code §53-640; Iowa Code §490A.903.1; Kan. Stat. Ann. §17-76,114; La. Rev. Stat. Ann. §12:1332.A(1); Me. Rev. Stat. Ann. tit. 31, §687.1.B; Md. Corps. & Ass'ns Code Ann. §4A-601(b)(1); M.G.L.A. ch. 156C, §§39(a)(1), 41(a)(1); Mich. Comp. Laws Ann. §450.4506(1); Minn. Stat. §322B.313, subd. 2; Miss. Code Ann. §79-29-301(2)(a); Mo. Rev. Stat. §347.113.2; Mont. Code Ann. §35-8-707(2); N.H. Rev. Stat. Ann. §§304-C:23.II(a), 304-C:46.I(a), 304-C:48.I(a); N.J. Stat. Ann. §42:2C-46.a(1); N.M. Stat. Ann. §§53-19-33.A, 53-19-36.A(1); N.C. Gen. Stat. §§57C-3-01(b)(1), 57C-5-04(a); N.D. Cent. Code §10-32-32.2; Ohio Rev. Code Ann. §1705.20(a)(2); R.I. Gen. Laws §7-16-36; S.C. Code Ann. §33-44-503(a); S.D. Codified Laws Ann. §47-34-21; Tenn. Code Ann. §48-249-501(b); Tex. Rev. Civ. Stat. Ann. art. 1528n, 4.07, 4.07A; Utah Code Ann. §§48-2c-703(1), 1104; Vt. Stat. Ann. tit. 11, §3073(a); Va. Code Ann. §13.1-1040; Wash. Rev. Code §25.15.260(1)(a); W. Va. Code §31B-5-503; Wis. Stat. §183.0706(1); Wyo. Stat. §17-15-122.

[53] *See* Chapter 5 *infra*.

[54] *See, e.g.,* Del. Code Ann. tit. 6, §§18-306, 18-603.

[55] *See, e.g.,* Kan. Stat. Ann. §17-7616; Md. Code Ann., Corps. & Assns. §4A-606.

[56] Cal. Corp. Code §17704.04(c).

[57] Cal. Corp. Code §17704.04(c).

3

Advantages and Disadvantages of LLCs

¶ 301 OVERVIEW

An LLC is designed to incorporate the most favorable aspects of corporations, general partnerships, limited partnerships, and other entities. It provides a single tax at the shareholder level. Losses may pass through to the owners. The LLC may make special allocations of income, gain, loss, credit, and deductions to members. A member may increase his basis in the membership interest by the amount of LLC debt. The members, owners, and managers of the LLC receive the same limited liability protection as shareholders, officers, and directors of a corporation. Overall, the LLC is the most flexible vehicle for a business.

Nevertheless, there are some serious drawbacks to the LLC. Many states prohibit professional LLCs or place restrictions on professional LLCs. Most states prohibit an LLC from conducting certain types of business, such as the banking or trust company business.

Venture capitalists normally prefer a corporation rather than an LLC. Venture capitalists know that 51 percent ownership in a corporation gives them control of the business, whereas it may not in an LLC. Venture capitalists normally provide funding on the hope that they can take the business public. The membership interests in an LLC may not be publicly traded.

Corporations give more certainty. There is a large body of case law that has developed over many years for corporations. Most businesses, lenders, and investors are comfortable with a corporation. On the other hand, many owners, lenders, and investors may not know what a manager is or how an LLC operates. Banks, title companies, lenders, and third parties may impose greater due diligence requirements on LLCs because of their lack of familiarity.

Many states impose a franchise or entity-level tax on LLCs.[1] For example, California imposes an $800 minimum tax and a gross receipts tax up to $11,790. The tax applies even if the LLC has no income.

At one time, the Treasury Department proposed regulations making all managers of LLCs liable for self-employment taxes on their distributive shares of LLC income. Congress then passed legislation temporarily preventing the Treasury Department from implementing regulations on self-employment taxes for LLCs. The ability to reduce or eliminate self-employment taxes for employees of an S corporation is often the principal reason that a business will choose to operate as an S corporation rather than an LLC.[2]

The use of a limited partnership may in some cases be more favorable from a negotiating standpoint to promoters of a new business venture. For example, the promoters can advise limited partner investors that they cannot have voting or management rights in the business (except in limited cases permitted by state law),

---

[1] *See* ¶ 2301 *infra* for a listing of the entity level taxes for each state.
[2] *See* ¶ 404 *infra* for a more detailed discussion.

since voting and management rights would make them personally liable as general partners. If an LLC were used instead, the promoters could not use this argument. The passive investors could demand full voting rights and management authority without subjecting themselves to unlimited liability.

It may also be easier for the promoters to keep the profits in a corporation than an LLC. A corporation may accumulate profits at a lower graduated tax rate. There is no double taxation if the corporation never distributes its profits as dividends. An LLC, on the other hand, has more pressure to distribute profits to investors, who are taxed on those profits each year whether or not distributed.

¶ 302 ADVANTAGES OVER C CORPORATIONS

.01 Single Level of Tax

There is no corporate-level tax for an LLC. There is a single tax at the member level. This is similar to the tax treatment of partnerships and S corporations. A C corporation, conversely, is subject to double taxation. The corporation is first taxed on its earnings and profits. The shareholders are then taxed when the corporation distributes the earnings and profits to the shareholders as a nondeductible dividend. A C corporation may be able to avoid double taxation by reducing its income to zero through payments to shareholders of deductible salary, interest, and rents. However, wages are subject to FICA and FUTA taxes.

A C corporation may also avoid double taxation by not distributing the income in the corporation. Most corporations need some permanent level of working capital. Beginning in 2018, the corporate tax rate is 21 percent, which is significantly below the maximum individual tax rate of 37 percent. Thus, a C corporation may be more advantageous if the owners plan to keep profits inside the entity.

Practice Note: Most accountants advise their clients never to put real estate into a C corporation because it is difficult to get the property out of the corporation without double taxation on the appreciation. Instead, the owner of the real estate should lease the property to the corporation or contribute the property to an LLC, general partnership, or limited partnership.

.02 Pass-Through of Losses

LLCs may pass through losses to investors.[3] These losses may offset other taxable income earned by the members. Conversely, shareholders in a C corporation may not deduct corporate losses or excess deductions on their personal income tax returns. The losses may be used only to offset corporate profits, if any.

---

[3] There are limits on the deductibility of LLC losses. *See* Chapter 7 *infra*.

.03 Capital Contributions

Members in an LLC that is classified as a partnership for tax purposes do not recognize gain or loss on property contributed to the LLC in exchange for membership interests.[4]

Shareholders may contribute appreciated property to a corporation on a tax-free basis only when the transferee-shareholders own at least 80 percent of the total combined voting power of all classes of stock entitled to vote and at least 80 percent of the outstanding shares of all classes of stock. Thus, a new shareholder is taxed on contributions of appreciated stock unless the 80 percent requirement is met. This rule often limits contributions by new shareholders to cash or other unappreciated property.

The LLC is more flexible because it can add members who contribute capital at any time on a tax-free basis for any percentage ownership interest in the LLC. No gain or loss is recognized to the LLC or its members upon the contribution of capital.

.04 Special Allocations

An LLC may make special allocations of income, gain, deductions, credits, and loss.[5] The special allocations may be made at any time prior to the due date of the return (not including extensions).[6] A corporation may not make special allocations to shareholders.

.05 No Personal Holding Company Tax

There is no personal holding company tax on an LLC that is classified as a partnership for federal tax purposes. An LLC may be used as an investment vehicle.[7] For example, an LLC may be used in place of a family limited partnership to hold family investments, to facilitate gifts from parents to children, and to help protect assets from creditors. There is no personal holding company tax even if all of the passive income is retained in the LLC.[8] C corporations that have investment and passive income exceeding 60 percent of adjusted gross income are potentially liable for the penalty tax on undistributed personal holding company income.[9] The penalty tax is in addition to the regular corporate income tax and the dividend tax on shareholders.

---

[4] Code Sec. 721.

[5] *See* Chapter 8 *infra*.

[6] Code Sec. 761(c).

[7] *See* Chapter 8 *infra*.

[8] Ltr. Rul. 9330009.

[9] Code Secs. 541–547.

.06 Debt Increases Members' Bases

One of the advantages of an LLC is that liabilities incurred by the LLC increase a member's basis in the LLC.[10] In an S corporation[11] and a C corporation, liabilities incurred by the corporation do not increase a shareholder's basis.

Basis is important for several reasons. A member's basis in a membership interest determines the amount of gain or loss upon the sale of the membership interest. Losses may be deducted only to the extent of a member's basis in the membership interest.[12] Distributions of money in excess of basis result in taxable gain.

.07 Election to Step Up Basis of Assets under Section 754

An LLC may step up the basis of its assets upon the death of a member or the sale of membership units if the LLC makes an election under Code Sec. 754.[13] There is no step-up in basis of assets in a corporation upon the death of a shareholder or the sale of stock.

Normally, there is a tax advantage to making the election if the underlying assets have a fair market value in excess of their basis (e.g., because of tax depreciation). However, many LLCs do not want to make this election because of the resulting accounting problems. Once the election is made, the LLC must make the basis adjustment any time a member sells membership units, a member dies, or distributions are made to members that result in taxable gain or loss. If the LLC has many members, then each asset could have many different bases. There is an adjustment of basis only with respect to the interest of the purchasing member or the estate of the deceased member in the underlying assets.

In the case of a purchase, the total basis adjustment by the LLC is the difference between the price the member pays for the membership units and the member's share of the adjusted basis of LLC property at the time of purchase. There is an upward adjustment in basis if the purchase price is greater than the member's share of the adjusted basis of LLC property. There is a downward adjustment in basis if the purchase price is less than the member's share of the adjusted basis of LLC property. The adjustment results in the member's basis in the LLC being equal to the adjusted basis of the member's share of the underlying LLC assets.

---

[10] Code Sec. 752.

[11] Code Sec. 1367.

[12] However, nondeductible losses may be carried over to years in which the member has basis in the LLC. Code Sec. 704(d).

[13] *See* ¶ 1508 *infra.*

.08 *Receipt of Membership Interests by Employees*

An LLC may issue membership interests to employees as options or otherwise. There are no withholding taxes upon receipt of the membership interests unless any of the following apply:

- The member receives a capital interest in the LLC, or a profits interest that relates to a substantially certain and predictable stream of income from LLC assets;

- Within two years of receipt, the member disposes of the profits interest; or

- The profits interest is characterized as a limited partnership interest in a publicly traded partnership.[14]

An employee who receives stock in a corporation in exchange for services is subject to income and employment taxes under Code Sec. 83 unless the stock is subject to a substantial risk of forfeiture or subject to the claims of the employer's creditors.[15]

.09 *Distributions and Liquidations*

There are ordinarily no adverse tax consequences to an LLC or its members when the LLC distributes appreciated assets to members.[16] The distribution of appreciated property to a member is not a taxable event.

It is very difficult to get appreciated property out of a C corporation without double taxation. The corporation recognizes gain on the appreciation.[17] The shareholders recognize dividend income to the extent of the corporation's current or accumulated earnings and profits. Upon liquidation, the shareholders recognize capital gain to the extent the value of property distributed exceeds their basis in the stock.[18]

---

[14] Rev. Proc. 93-27, 1993-2 CB 343.

[15] Reg. §§ 1.61-2(d)(4), 31.3401(a)-1(a)(4). *See also Weaver v. Comm'r*, 25 TC 1067 (1956). The value of stock, when made available without restrictions, is wages subject to withholding. Rev. Rul. 79-305, 1979-2 CB 350. Stock transferred by a major shareholder to employees for services rendered is also compensation. It is treated as a contribution of stock to the capital of the corporation followed immediately by a transfer of the stock from the corporation to the shareholder. The value of the stock is taxable compensation to the employee and is deductible by the corporation. Reg. § 1.83-6(d)(1); Ltr. Rul. 9004003.

[16] Code Sec. 731.

[17] Code Sec. 311.

[18] Code Secs. 311(b), 336(a).

.10 Other Benefits

Corporations are subject to the accumulated earnings tax in addition to income and other taxes.[19] LLCs are not subject to the accumulated earnings tax. An LLC is a pass-through entity that does not have accumulated earnings and profits.

A C corporation may be denied a tax deduction for unreasonable compensation paid to officers and shareholders. The excess compensation may be taxed as a dividend. Members of an LLC are not subject to the unreasonable compensation problem, since a member's share of income is taxed as salary, a guaranteed payment, or a distributive share of income.

The favorable tax accounting methods available to LLCs may not be available to corporations. For example, C corporations may not use the cash receipts and disbursement method of accounting, subject to certain exceptions.[20]

¶ 303 ADVANTAGES OVER S CORPORATIONS

The advantages of operating a business as an LLC rather than an S corporation are discussed at ¶ 405. The disadvantages are discussed at ¶ 404.

¶ 304 ADVANTAGES OVER PARTNERSHIPS

.01 Limited Liability

There is limited liability for all members of an LLC. In a limited partnership, the general partner is personally liable. In a general partnership, all partners are personally liable. The problem of personal liability can be overcome to some extent in a limited partnership by using a corporate general partner.

.02 Participation in Management

Limited partners in a limited partnership may not participate in management without becoming personally liable. Members in an LLC may participate in management of the LLC without becoming personally liable. For tax purposes, LLC members must "materially participate" in the business of the LLC in order to avoid the passive loss rules.[21]

---

[19] Code Secs. 531–537.
[20] Code Sec. 448.
[21] The material participation and passive loss rules are discussed in ¶ 1304 *infra*.

¶ 305 DISADVANTAGES OF LLCs

.01 State Taxes and Fees

Some states impose significant taxes and fees on LLCs in addition to the tax on a member's shares of distributable income.[22] The state franchise taxes and fees are listed at ¶ 2301.

.02 Restrictions on Transfer of Interests

There may be restrictions on transfers of LLC membership interests under state law. The state laws were adopted at a time when the IRS regulations required restrictions on transfer in order for the LLC to be classified as a partnership. The IRS regulations on entity classification no longer require restrictions on transfer.[23]

.03 Public Trading

Generally, membership interests in an LLC may not be publicly traded. The LLC may be taxed as a corporation if its interests are publicly traded unless at least 90 percent of its income is specified passive income and certain other requirements are met.[24]

.04 Formalities

A general partnership may be formed in any state by an agreement between the parties. No charter from the state is required. An LLC, on the other hand, must generally file articles of organization with the state and pay the filing fees.

.05 Fiscal Year

An LLC may not ordinarily have a fiscal year. It must use the tax year of members having a majority interest in the LLC, or the tax year of all principal members if there is no majority interest. The LLC must use a calendar year if all of the members of the LLC are individuals.[25]

---

[22] *See* ¶ 2301 *infra* for a listing of states that impose taxes and the amount of these taxes.

[23] *See* Chapter 5 *infra.*

[24] Code Sec. 7704. *See* Chapter 20 *infra.*

[25] *See* ¶ 1703 *infra.*

.06 Members' Withdrawal Rights

Some states allow members to withdraw from the LLC and receive the fair market value of their membership interests unless the operating agreement otherwise provides. Other states provide different protections for withdrawing members.[26]

.07 Automatic Dissolution

An LLC may dissolve upon the loss of a member unless a majority or all of the remaining members agree to continue the business of the LLC. This makes LLCs unattractive for large organizations with many investors. Many states permit the operating agreement to provide for automatic continuation upon the loss of a member.

.08 Self-Employment Taxes

Managers may be subject to self-employment taxes on their distributive shares of income, whether or not distributed.[27] Conversely, limited partners are not subject to self-employment taxes except for guaranteed payments for services to the LLC. In addition, S corporation shareholders do not pay self-employment taxes on dividends. They pay the self-employment tax only on salary payments, provided they receive reasonable compensation for their services.

The extent to which LLC members must pay self-employment taxes is sometimes unclear. However, it is generally believed that an S corporation can save a substantial amount of self-employment taxes in many cases.

.09 Complicated and Expensive Setup and Operation

LLCs are often more complicated and expensive to set up. The partnership tax rules that apply to LLCs are intricate and arcane. The LLC operating agreements are more complicated than the standard boilerplate bylaws for a corporation. Moreover, LLCs typically have more complicated management structures, restrictions on sales of membership interests, and special allocation provisions.

The LLC offers more flexibility than a corporation. However, owners of an LLC that take advantage of this flexibility may incur additional accounting and attorney fees in establishing and operating the LLC.

---

[26] *See* ¶ 210 *supra.*
[27] *See* Chapter 16 *infra*; Prop. Reg. § 1.1402(a)-2; Code Sec. 1402(a)(13).

.10 Fringe Benefits

Members of an LLC are *ineligible* for certain fringe benefits available to employees in a corporation. The types of eligible and ineligible fringe benefits are discussed in Chapter 14.[28]

.11 Tax-Free Reorganizations

Shareholders in a corporation may sell the stock or assets in the corporation in a tax-free reorganization under Section 368 of the Internal Revenue Code. Members of an LLC that is classified as a partnership may not participate in a tax-free reorganization.[29]

An LLC, however, may use the tax-free reorganization provisions by electing to be taxed as a corporation.[30] However, the change in classification from a partnership to a corporation immediately prior to a reorganization may disqualify the reorganization.[31]

A corporation may also merge into a disregarded LLC owned by an acquiring corporation in a tax-free merger if certain requirements are met.[32]

The merger of a corporation into an LLC that is classified as an S corporation will not adversely affect the LLC's status as an S corporation.[33]

.12 Single-Member LLCs

All states now permit LLCs to have one member. A single-member LLC must be classified as a corporation or a single-member disregarded entity.[34] An individual owner of a single-member disregarded LLC must report all income and other items on Schedule C of IRS Form 1040, rather than as a pass-through from Schedule K-1 of the partnership return. This increases the audit risk. C corporations and S corporations may have one shareholder.

.13 Stock Sales

Owners of certain C corporations may exclude 50 percent of their gain upon the sale of original issue stock. The exclusion applies mainly to manufacturing and sales

---

[28] *See* ¶ 1406 *infra.*

[29] Reg. § § 301.7701-2(b), 301.7701-3(a); Ltr. Rul. 201138015.

[30] *See, e.g.,* Ltr. Rul. 200005016 (acquisition of membership units in an LLC that has elected to be classified as a corporation qualifies as a tax-free C reorganization).

[31] *See* ¶ 1106.12 *infra.*

[32] *See* ¶ 1123 *infra.*

[33] Ltr. Rul. 200248023.

[34] *See* ¶ 504 *infra.*

companies. The shareholder must own the stock for at least five years.[35] This tax advantage is not available to members of an LLC.

.14 Reinvesting Profits

Some C corporations may save taxes by keeping earnings in the corporation rather than distributing the earnings to shareholders as deductible salary, rent, or interest. The corporate tax rate is a flat 21 percent tax rate which is less than the maximum individual tax rate of 37 percent. The corporation and the shareholders also avoid paying FICA and FUTA taxes on salary to shareholders by keeping the money in the corporation.

Members of an LLC do not have this flexibility. Members must pay taxes on income that is retained by the LLC to meet working capital, expansion, or other business needs. They are taxed at their individual tax rates on their allocable share of income, whether or not distributed.

.15 Stock Options

A corporation may compensate an employee with stock options. There is no tax on the grant of the option, and there is no tax on the exercise of the option if the option qualifies as an incentive stock option under Section 422 of the Internal Revenue Code.

A member of an LLC that is classified as a partnership recognizes compensation income upon the receipt of a membership interest in exchange for services subject to certain exceptions.[36] This may be a significant disadvantage, especially for small start-up companies that need stock options to hire and retain qualified employees.

.16 Uncertainty in the Law

There is some uncertainty regarding how various laws will be applied to LLCs, since the LLC is a new form of legal entity. For example, there is uncertainty regarding special allocations for tax purposes and the liability of members under CERCLA for environmental liabilities. In some states, it is uncertain when the LLC "veil" can be pierced, thus imposing liability on the individual members. Members may not always have the same limited liability as corporate shareholders, especially in single-member LLCs.

---

[35] Code Sec. 1202.
[36] *See* ¶ 604 *infra.*

¶ 306 COMPARING BUSINESS ENTITIES

The following table summarizes the main differences among LLCs, C corporations, S corporations, and partnerships.

Entity Comparison Chart

Item	Entity	Comparison
Tax rate	LLC	There is no federal tax to the LLC on LLC income. All items of income, gain, and loss pass through and are taxed to the members.
	C corporation	Flat tax rate of 21 percent on all corporate income.
	S corporation	There is no tax to the S corporation except for the built-in gains tax under Code Sec. 1374, the tax on passive investment income under Code Sec. 1375, the LIFO recapture tax under Code Sec. 1363(d), and the investment tax credit recapture under Code Sec. 1371(d)(2).
	Partnership	There is no tax to the partnership on partnership income. All items of income, gain, and loss pass through and are taxed to the partners.
Eligible owners	LLC	There are no restrictions on eligible owners.
	C corporation	There are no restrictions on eligible owners.
	S corporation	An S corporation may not have more than 100 shareholders. It may not have nonindividual shareholders, subject to certain exceptions.
	Partnership	There are no restrictions on eligible owners.
Types of ownership interests	LLC	Membership interests. There may be different classes of membership interests.
	C corporation	Stock. There may be different classes of stock.
	S corporation	Stock. There may be only one class of stock. However, there may be voting and nonvoting common stock.

Item	Entity	Comparison
	Partnership	General and limited partnership units. There may be different classes of ownership interests.
Special allocations	LLC	Special allocations are permitted if the allocations have substantial economic effect.
	C corporation	Special allocations are not permitted. Dividends must be paid based on stock ownership.
	S corporation	Special allocations are not permitted. Income, gain, and loss pass through to the shareholders based on stock ownership.
	Partnership	Special allocations are permitted if the allocations have substantial economic effect.
Liability of owners	LLC	There is limited liability for owners and managers.
	C corporation	There is limited liability for shareholders, officers, and directors.
	S corporation	There is limited liability for shareholders, officers, and directors.
	Partnership	All partners in a general partnership are personally liable. The general partner in a limited partnership is personally liable. There is limited liability for the limited partners in a limited partnership.
Transferability of ownership interests	LLC	There may be restrictions on transfer under state law.
	C corporation	Shares may be freely transferred.
	S corporation	Shares may be freely transferred only to eligible S corporation shareholders.
	Partnership	Partnership interests may be transferred in accordance with the terms of the partnership agreement. Ordinarily, a general partnership interest may not be transferred without the consent of the other partners.

Item	Entity	Comparison
Duration	LLC	An LLC dissolves at the time specified in the operating agreement or upon the loss of a member unless the other members agree to continue the LLC.
	C corporation	A C corporation continues indefinitely.
	S corporation	An S corporation continues indefinitely.
	Partnership	A partnership terminates at the time specified in the partnership agreement or when there is more than a 50 percent change in partnership interests during any 12-month period.
Management	LLC	Managed by all members or designated managers. Members who participate in management are not personally liable.
	C corporation	Managed by directors and officers.
	S corporation	Managed by directors and officers.
	Partnership	Managed by general partners. Limited partners who participate in management are personally liable.
Liabilities and basis	LLC	Liabilities incurred by the LLC increase a member's basis in his membership interest.
	C corporation	Liabilities incurred by the corporation do not increase a shareholder's basis in her stock.
	S corporation	Liabilities incurred by the corporation do not increase a shareholder's basis in his stock.
	Partnership	Liabilities incurred by the partnership increase a partner's basis in the partnership interest.
Pass-through of losses	LLC	Losses of an LLC may be passed through to and deducted by members, subject to certain restrictions (basis, at-risk, and passive loss limitations).
	C corporation	Losses of a C corporation may not be passed through to and deducted by shareholders.

Item	Entity	Comparison
	S corporation	Losses of an S corporation may be passed through to and deducted by shareholders, subject to certain restrictions (basis, at-risk, and passive loss limitations).
	Partnership	Losses of a partnership may be passed through to and deducted by partners, subject to certain restrictions (basis, at-risk, and passive loss limitations).
Fringe benefits	LLC	Members are ineligible for certain fringe benefits.
	C corporation	Shareholder-employees are eligible for most fringe benefits.
	S corporation	Two percent shareholders are ineligible for certain fringe benefits.
	Partnership	Partners are ineligible for certain fringe benefits.
Fiscal year	LLC	Must use the tax year of members having a majority interest in the LLC or the tax year of all principal members if there is no majority interest.
	C corporation	May use any fiscal year. Personal service corporations must use a calendar year, subject to certain exceptions.
	S corporation	Must use the calendar year, subject to certain exceptions.
	Partnership	Must use the tax year of partners having a majority interest in the LLC or the tax year of all principal partners if there is no majority interest.
Tax upon sale or distribution of appreciated assets	LLC	There is a single tax at the member level upon the sale of appreciated assets. Generally, there is no tax upon the distribution of appreciated assets.
	C corporation	There is potential double taxation. There is a corporate-level tax upon the sale or distribution of appreciated assets. There is a potential dividend or capital gains tax upon the distribution of sale proceeds to shareholders.

Item	Entity	Comparison
	S corporation	There is a single tax at the shareholder level upon the sale of appreciated assets. There is also a potential built-in gains tax at the corporate level if the corporation had appreciated property at the time of conversion from a C corporation to an S corporation.
	Partnership	There is a single tax at the member level upon the sale of appreciated assets. Generally, there is no tax upon the distribution of appreciated assets.
Tax to entity upon liquidation	LLC	There is no tax to the LLC upon the sale or distribution of assets.
	C corporation	The corporation is taxed on appreciation in assets upon the sale or distribution of assets.
	S corporation	There is no tax to the corporation except for a potential built-in gains tax if a C corporation was converted to an S corporation in the prior ten years.
	Partnership	There is no tax to the partnership upon the sale or distribution of assets. Gain upon the sale of assets passes through to the partners.
Tax to owners upon liquidation	LLC	Gain upon a liquidating sale of appreciated assets by the LLC passes through to the members. No gain is recognized upon a distribution except to the extent that the money distributed exceeds the member's basis in his membership interest.
	C corporation	Gain is recognized to extent that the fair market value of property distributed exceeds the shareholder's basis in the stock.
	S corporation	Gain is recognized to the extent that the property distributed exceeds the shareholder's basis in his stock.

Item	Entity	Comparison
	Partnership	Gain upon a liquidating sale of appreciated assets by the partnership passes through to the partners. No gain is recognized upon a distribution of appreciated or other assets except to the extent that the money distributed exceeds the partner's basis in the partnership interest.

4

Special Issues Regarding S Corporations and LLCs

¶401 PASSIVE INCOME RECEIVED BY S CORPORATION FROM LLCS

.01 Subchapter S Rules

A corporation's election as an S corporation is terminated if the corporation has subchapter C earnings and profits at the close of each of three consecutive taxable years and if more than 25 percent of the gross receipts for each such year is passive investment income.[1] There is also a tax on the income of an S corporation if the corporation has subchapter C earnings and profits at the close of the year and if more than 25 percent of the gross receipts is passive investment income.[2]

Whether income is active or passive is determined at the LLC level rather than the S corporation level. For example, an S corporation's distributive share of LLC gross receipts attributable to an active trade or business is not passive income, even if the LLC is a passive investor in the S corporation.[3]

The receipt by an S corporation of a distributive share of rental income from an LLC is not passive income for these purposes if the employees of the S corporation[4] or the LLC provide significant services or incur substantial costs in the rental business.[5]

The distributive share of income is normally passive income if the LLC rents the property on a triple net lease basis.[6] However, the rents received by the S corporation from the LLC under a triple net lease may be characterized as active trade or business income in exceptional cases. For example, the rental income will be trade or business income if the LLC rents property used in a franchise in which it is a limited partner and performs significant services or incurs significant costs in monitoring the franchise operations.[7]

EXAMPLE 4-1

An S corporation is a member of an LLC that is classified as a partnership. The LLC leases property to tenants under leases that are not net leases. The S corporation employs full-time employees who directly perform services relating to the properties. The S corporation and the LLC also contract with independent contractors to provide various services related to the rental properties, including property inspection, common area maintenance and repair, carpeting and painting; janitorial and cleaning services; maintenance and repair of building structural components, including roofs and facades; upkeep and repair of building systems (heating, air conditioning, plumbing, water and sewer, electrical and lighting); parking lot maintenance; landscape maintenance; snow removal; trash collection; pest control; providing security personnel; approval and supervision of capital improvements, purchasing and developing new properties, negotiating and drafting individual leases, showing properties to prospective tenants, and hiring and supervising personnel assigned to

---

[1] Code Sec. 1362(d)(3)(A)(i).

[2] Code Sec. 1375(a).

[3] Ltr. Rul. 200102024, ruling under Code Sec. 1375.

[4] Ltr. Rul. 200538025.

[5] Ltr. Ruls. 201738011, 201118011, 200651010 (*citing* Reg. §1.1362-2(c)(5)(ii)(B)), 200647026, 200638007, 200218033, 9536008, 9536007, 9615025.

[6] Ltr. Ruls. 9536008, 9536007.

[7] Ltr. Ruls. 9536008, 9536007.

perform the property management functions. The rental income received by the S corporation from the LLC is not passive income.[8]

.02 Section 469 Rules

The receipt by an S corporation of a distributive share of rental income from an LLC is passive income under the passive activity loss limitation rules,[9] unless an exception applies. The rule applies even of the rental income is not passive income under the rules that provide for termination of an S corporation election when passive investment income exceeds 25 percent of the gross receipts for three consecutive tax years and the corporation has accumulated earnings and profits.[10]

¶ 402 S CORPORATION OWNERSHIP OF LLC

An S corporation may own membership interests in an LLC that is classified as:

- single-member disregarded LLC;[11]
- partnership;[12] or
- corporation. Prior to 1997, an S corporation was prohibited from owning 80 percent of an LLC that was classified as a corporation.[13]

EXAMPLE 4-2

An S corporation owns all of the stock in another S corporation that is a qualified Subchapter S subsidiary. The qualified Subchapter S subsidiary is the sole owner of an LLC that is classified as a disregarded entity. The LLC owns a general partnership interest in a limited partnership. The parent S corporation is treated as the general partner in the limited partnership since both the qualified Subchapter S subsidiary and the LLC are disregarded entities.[14]

The distribution by an S corporation to its shareholders of membership interests in a wholly owned LLC is treated as a sale of the assets of the LLC at fair market

---

[8] Ltr. Rul. 201118011.

[9] Code Sec. 469.

[10] Code Sec. 1362(d)(3).

[11] Ltr. Rul. 200143012.

[12] Ltr. Rul. 9637033.

[13] Ltr. Ruls. 9532008, 9433008; Code Sec. 1361(b)(2)(A) prior to amendment in 1996.

[14] Ltr. Rul. 200143012.

value. The corporation recognizes gain under Section 311(b) on the deemed sale of appreciated assets owned by the LLC.[15]

¶ 403 LLC OWNERSHIP OF S CORPORATIONS

.01 Permissible Stock Ownership

An S corporation may not have shareholders other than individuals, estates, and certain trusts, financial institutions, tax-exempt qualified retirement trusts, and tax-exempt charitable organizations.[16] Nonresident aliens may not be shareholders.[17]

An LLC may own stock in an S corporation if all of the following conditions apply:[18]

- The LLC is a single-member LLC;
- The LLC is disregarded as an entity separate from its owner (rather than classified as a corporation) under the federal check-the-box regulations; and
- The owner of the LLC is a permitted S corporation shareholder.

For example, an LLC owned by an individual may own stock in an S corporation.[19] The sole shareholder of an S corporation may transfer the stock to a single member disregarded LLC.[20] Each of the shareholders in an S corporation with multiple shareholders may transfer their shares to a single-member disregarded LLC.[21]

A trust may own an LLC that owns stock in an S corporation if the trust is the sole owner of the LLC, the trust is a disregarded entity, and the trust is one of the six types of trusts that is an eligible S corporation shareholder.[22] The six types of eligible trusts are:[23]

- A grantor trust, such as a revocable living trust for estate planning purposes, that is treated as wholly owned by a single individual.[24] A husband and wife in a community property state may also transfer their interests in an LLC that owns S corporation stock to a living trust for estate planning purposes.[25]

---

[15] Ltr. Rul. 200910030.

[16] Code Sec. 1361(b)(1)(B).

[17] Code Sec. 1361(b)(1)(C).

[18] Ltr. Ruls. 200816004, 200816003, 200816002, 200339026, 200303032, 200107025, 200008015, 9745017, 9739014.

[19] Ltr. Ruls. 200927014, 200303032, 9745017, 9739014.

[20] Ltr. Ruls. 200816004, 200816003, 200816002.

[21] Ltr. Rul. 200927014.

[22] Ltr. Ruls. 200339026, 200303032, 9745017.

[23] Code Sec. 1361(c)(2), (d), (e).

[24] Code Sec. 1361(c)(2)(A)(i).

[25] Ltr. Rul. 200339026.

- A voting trust that exercises the voting power for eligible S corporation shareholders.[26]
- A Section 678 trust that is owned by a person other than the grantor because the person has the sole power to vest the entire principal or income in himself. A *Crummey* trust that gives the beneficiary the power to withdraw principal contributions for a limited period of time is a Section 678 trust. A marital deduction trust that gives the surviving spouse a general power to appoint principal or income during life or at death is a Section 678 trust.
- An eligible post-death trust that continues to be an S corporation for up to two years after the death of the individual owner.[27]
- A Qualified Subchapter S Trust (QSST).[28] The trust qualifies if (1) the trust has only one current income beneficiary who is a U.S. is a resident, (2) principal distributions during the income beneficiary's life are made only to the beneficiary, (3) all trust income is, or is required to be, distributed to a single individual, (4) the beneficiary's income interest terminates on the earlier of the beneficiary's death or the trust's termination, (5) all the assets of the trust must be distributed to the current income beneficiary if the trust terminates during the life of the beneficiary, and (6) the income beneficiary makes a timely election to have the trust treated as a QSST. For example, a QSST may own a single-member disregarded LLC that owns shares in an S corporation.[29]
- Electing Small Business Trust (EBST).[30] The trust qualifies if (1) the trust beneficiaries are individuals, estates or certain charitable organizations, (2) the interests in the trust are not acquired by purchase, (3) the trustee makes an election to be treated as an EBST, and (4) the trust is not a QSST trust. For example, an ESBT may own a single-member disregarded LLC that owns shares in an S corporation.[31]

An S corporation may own stock in another S corporation only if it owns 100 percent of the stock in the S corporation subsidiary and files an election with the IRS.[32] The parent S corporation may own stock in the S corporation subsidiary indirectly through a disregarded LLC owned by the parent corporation.[33] The parent S corporation may transfer some or all of the stock in the S corporation subsidiary to an LLC if the parent corporation owns the LLC, and if the LLC is classified as a disregarded entity for federal tax purposes. The transfer of the stock to the subsidiary will not cause the termination of the parent corporation's qualified Subchapter S subsidiary election.[34]

---

[26] Code Sec. 1361(c)(2)(A)(iv).

[27] Code Sec. 1361(c)(2)(A)(ii), (iii).

[28] Code Sec. 1361(d).

[29] Ltr. Rul. 9745017.

[30] Code Sec. 1361(e).

[31] Ltr. Rul. 200303032.

[32] Code Sec. 1361(b)(3).

[33] Reg. § 1.1361-2(d), Example (2).

[34] Ltr. Rul. 200107018.

.02 Impermissible Stock Ownership

An LLC that is classified as a partnership for federal tax purposes may not own stock in an S corporation.[35] Such an LLC's acquisition of stock in an S corporation will terminate the S corporation election.

The IRS may grant relief from inadvertent termination as a result of an LLC's acquisition of stock in an S corporation if all of the following apply:[36]

- The S corporation's election was terminated because the corporation ceased to be a small business corporation or had excessive passive investment income;[37]
- The IRS determines that the termination was inadvertent;
- The parties take steps to make the corporation a qualifying S corporation no later than a reasonable period of time after discovery of the events resulting in the termination; and
- The corporation and each person who was a shareholder of the corporation at any time after termination and prior to corrective steps agree to make adjustments required by the IRS consistent with the treatment of the corporation as an S corporation (in those cases, the corporation is treated as continuing to be an S corporation during the period specified by the IRS).

In the normal case, the LLC would take corrective steps by distributing the stock in the S corporation to its members immediately after it determines that the LLC may not own stock in the S corporation. The S corporation must then apply to the IRS for a ruling that the termination was inadvertent and that the S corporation should be treated as an S corporation throughout the period notwithstanding the disqualified shareholder.[38]

In granting relief, the IRS normally requires that the LLC be treated as the owner of the stock during the period of ownership, and that it include in income its pro rata share of the S corporation's separately and nonseparately computed items,[39] make adjustments to stock basis,[40] and take into account any distributions made by the S corporation to the LLC,[41] as provided in Code Sec. 1368.

---

[35] Ltr. Ruls. 201145002, 201129012, 201129011, 201129010, 201129009, 201016025, 200851008, 200847009, 200841007, 200834007, 200827029, 200822014, 200822009, 200813012, 200813011, 200813010, 200810006, 200809028, 200809022, 200752015, 200748009, 200744009, 200737016, 200736021, 200733005, 200728028, 200724022, 200721003, 200713022, 200710002, 200703028, 200703027, 200701028, 200652035, 200633022, 200629017, 200603010, 200537007, 200448003, 200250008, 200250007, 199904008, 9750004-9750008.

[36] Code Sec. 1362(f); Ltr. Ruls. 201016025, 200851008, 200847009, 200841007, 200834007, 200827029, 200822014, 200822009, 200813012, 200813011, 200813010, 200752015, 200751018, 200751017, 200751016, 200748009, 200744009, 200737016, 200736021, 200733005, 200728028, 200724022, 200721003, 200713022, 200710002, 200703028, 200703027, 200701028, 200652035, 200633022, 200629017, 200603010, 200537007, 200448003, 200318023, 200250008, 200250007, 199904008, 9750004-9750008.

[37] Code Sec. 1362(d)(2), (3).

[38] Rev. Proc. 2013-30, 2013-36 IRB 173.

[39] See Code Sec. 1366.

[40] See Code Sec. 1367.

[41] See Code Sec. 1368.

¶404 ADVANTAGES OF S CORPORATIONS OVER LLCS

The main advantage of an S corporation over an LLC is that a shareholder's distributive share of income from the S corporation is not subject to self-employment taxes.[42] Generally, all of a member's share of trade or business income from an LLC is subject to self-employment taxes unless the member is classified as a "limited partner" and the payments are not guaranteed payments for services rendered.

The self-employment taxes are significant. For 2018, the self-employment taxes are the sum of: (i) 12.40 percent OASDI tax on income up to the taxable wage base of $128,400; (ii) 2.90 percent Hospital Insurance tax on income up to the Additional Medicare Tax threshold amounts ($200,000 of self-employment income for a single person, $250,000 of combined self-employment income on a joint return, and $125,000 for a married person filing a separate return);[43] and (iii) 3.80 percent Hospital Insurance tax on income above the Additional Medicare Tax threshold amounts.[44] An S corporation shareholder may avoid the self-employment taxes by recharacterizing earned income as pass-through income from the S corporation rather than wages for services rendered.

The IRS sometimes determines that a shareholder's distributive share of S corporation income should be recharacterized as earned income subject to the self-employment taxes if the amount of wages paid to the shareholder for services rendered is unreasonably low.[45]

To avoid IRS audit problems, the shareholders of the S corporation should normally pay themselves at least some wages or salary each year. The IRS is more likely to audit a shareholder's return if the S corporation pays the shareholder only a nominal salary or no salary at all. The S corporation can also minimize audit problems by not making distributions of cash to a shareholder in excess of the amount declared as wages or salary by the shareholder during the taxable year.

The ability to reduce or eliminate self-employment taxes for an S corporation is often the principal reason that a business will choose to operate as an S corporation rather than an LLC.

---

[42] *See* ¶302 *supra.*

[43] Code Secs. 1401(a), 1401(b).

[44] Code Sec. 1401(b).

[45] Rev. Rul. 74-44, 1974-1 CB 287 (S corporation distributions can be reclassified as wages where uncompensated services are performed by the shareholders); *Joseph M. Grey Public Accountant, P.C. v. Comm'r*, 119 TC 121 (2002); *Spicer Accounting Inc. v. United States*, 918 F.2d 90 (9th Cir. 1990); *Esser v. United States*, 750 F. Supp. 421 (D. Ariz. 1990); *Radtke v. United States*, 712 F. Supp. 143 (E.D. Wis. 1989); *C.D. Ulrich, Ltd. v. United States*, 692 F. Supp. 1053 (D. Minn. 1988); *Paula Constr. Co. v. Comm'r*, 58 TC 1055 (1972); D. Spradling, "Are S Corp Distribution Wages Subject to Withholding?," 71 *J. Tax'n* 104 (Aug. 1989); Ltr. Rul. 7949022.

¶405 ADVANTAGES OF LLCS OVER S CORPORATIONS

The main advantages of an LLC over an S corporation are as follows:

.01 Number of Owners

An S corporation may have only 100 shareholders.[46] An LLC may have an unlimited number of members.

.02 Types of Owners

An S corporation may not have shareholders other than individuals, estates, certain trusts, financial institutions, tax-exempt qualified retirement trusts, and tax-exempt charitable organizations.[47] Nonresident aliens may not be shareholders.[48] Generally, there are no restrictions on eligibility for LLC membership.

.03 Special Allocations

An LLC may make special allocations of income, deductions, gain and loss items if the allocations have substantial economic effect.[49] An S corporation may not make special allocations to shareholders. Because of the one-class-of-stock rule for S corporations,[50] the items of income, gain, loss, deduction, and credit of an S corporation cannot be separately allocated to a particular shareholder. Instead, they are taken into account by all of the shareholders on a per-share, per-day basis.

.04 Ownership Interests

LLCs may issue different ownership interests. An S corporation may issue only one class of stock.[51] Advances by shareholders to the corporation[52] or buy-sell agreements among shareholders[53] may create a second class of stock that disqualifies an S corporation election. No such restrictions apply to LLCs.

.05 Borrowings Increase Basis

S corporation shareholders and LLC members may deduct company losses on their individual tax returns to the extent of basis and the amount at-risk. In addition, LLC members may increase the basis of their membership interests for loss deduction purposes when the LLC borrows money, even when the debt is nonrecourse. S

---

[46] Code Sec. 1361(b)(1)(A).
[47] Code Sec. 1361(b)(1)(B).
[48] Code Sec. 1361(b)(1)(C).
[49] Code Sec. 704(a), (b).
[50] Code Sec. 1361(b)(1)(D).
[51] Code Secs. 1361(b)(1)(D), 1361(c)(4).
[52] Reg. § 1.1361-1(l)(4).
[53] Reg. § 1.1361-1(l)(2)(iii).

corporation shareholders may not increase the basis of their stock when the corporation borrows money from third parties or when the shareholders guarantee a corporate loan. An S corporation shareholder may increase the basis of stock only by the direct loans made by that shareholder to the corporation.[54]

.06 Distribution of Refinancing Proceeds

It is easier to distribute the proceeds of refinanced property in an LLC than in an S corporation. In both cases, distributions are normally taxable to the extent that the cash distributed exceeds the owner's basis in the LLC or S corporation. In an LLC, loans increase a member's basis in the LLC.[55] The proceeds from cash borrowings against LLC property can usually be distributed to members without tax because of the basis increase when the money is borrowed against LLC property. In an S corporation, the cash proceeds from refinanced loans are more likely to result in tax to shareholders, since the corporate loan does not increase a shareholder's basis.

.07 Contributions and Distributions of Appreciated Property

Contributions of debt-encumbered appreciated property to an LLC are generally nontaxable. Contributions of appreciated property to an S corporation are taxed to the extent that debt encumbering the property exceeds the basis of the property.[56]

The distribution of appreciated property by an S corporation to a shareholder is treated as a taxable sale of the property.[57] The rule applies to dividends, redemption of shares, and liquidations.[58] The gain equals the difference between the fair market value of the property and the LLC's adjusted basis in the property. The gain passes through and is taxable to the shareholders on a per-share, per-day basis[59] and increases a shareholder's adjusted basis in his shares. The shareholder who receives the distribution then reduces his basis by the fair market value of the distributed property and receives a fair market value basis in the property.[60]

By contrast, an LLC's distribution of appreciated property to a member is generally not treated as a taxable sale of the property.[61] There is no tax unless the money distributed exceeds the member's basis in the LLC interest or the LLC makes a disproportionate distribution of unrealized receivables or substantially appreciated inventory.[62]

---

[54] Code Sec. 1366(d)(1)(B).

[55] *See* ¶ 903 *infra.*

[56] Code Sec. 357(c).

[57] Code Secs. 311, 336, 1371(a)(1).

[58] Code Secs. 302, 331, 1371(a)(1). *See also* Joint Committee on Taxation Staff Review of Selected Entity Classification and Partnership Tax Issues (JCS-6-97), at 23 (Apr. 8, 1997).

[59] Code Sec. 1366.

[60] *See* Joint Committee on Taxation Staff Review of Selected Entity Classification and Partnership Tax Issues (JCS-6-97), at 23 (Apr. 8, 1997).

[61] Code Sec. 731.

[62] Code Secs. 731, 752(b).

.08 Other Tax Benefits

LLCs are not subject to certain penalty taxes that apply to S corporations that were formerly C corporations, such as the built-in gains tax[63] and the excess passive income tax.[64]

An S corporation may not adjust the basis of its assets upon the death of a shareholder or the sale of stock by a shareholder. An LLC may elect to step up the basis of its assets upon the death of a member or the sale of a membership interest.[65] Therefore, if a shareholder in an S corporation dies, the heirs will receive a step-up in basis for the stock.[66] If the corporation thereafter sells appreciated assets, the gain will flow through and be taxed to the inheriting shareholders even though the appreciation occurred before the shareholder's death. The same problem arises for a person who purchases stock in an S corporation that has appreciated assets.

The S corporation has advantages over the LLC in certain cases. A C corporation may obtain pass-through tax treatment by converting to an S corporation. The conversion does not result in taxation of appreciated assets or other adverse tax consequences, subject to four main exceptions.[67] A C corporation may also obtain pass-through treatment by converting to an LLC. However, the conversion is usually taxable. It is treated as a liquidation of the corporation, taxable both to the corporation and to its shareholders.[68]

The tax-free rules for mergers and other reorganizations apply to S corporations. For example, an S corporation may merge into a C corporation on a tax-free basis. Similar rules do not apply to combinations of LLCs and corporations.[69]

¶ 406 ELECTION AND REVOCATION BY LLC TO BE CLASSIFIED AS S CORPORATION

An LLC that elects to be classified as an S corporation on Form 2553 is automatically classified as a corporation. After 2003, an LLC is no longer required to make a

---

[63] Code Sec. 1374.

[64] Code Sec. 1375.

[65] Code Sec. 754. *See* ¶ 1508 *infra.*

[66] Code Sec. 1014.

[67] Upon conversion, there is a corporate-level tax on (1) the recapture of LIFO benefits under Code Sec. 1363(d) (the amount by which the FIFO value of inventory exceeds the LIFO value) and the adjustment of basis of inventory to account for the recapture, (2) certain built-in gain recognized within ten years after the conversion under Code Sec. 1374, and (3) certain passive investment income earned while the corporation retains its former C corporate earnings and profits under Code Sec. 1375. There is also a loss of carryforwards except to reduce built-in gain.

[68] *See* Chapter 12 *infra.*

[69] *See* Joint Committee on Taxation Staff Review of Selected Entity Classification and Partnership Tax Issues (JCS-6-97), at 24-25 (Apr. 8, 1997).

separate election to be classified as a corporation if it makes a timely and valid S corporation election.[70]

An LLC may make a late election to be classified as a corporation and as an S corporation, subject to approval by the IRS.[71] An LLC must make the late election by following the procedures set forth under Revenue Procedure 2013-30.[72]

The LLC must retain the same employer identification number after it elects to be classified as an S corporation.[73]

An LLC that is classified as a partnership may make an election to be classified as an S corporation for its first tax year. The election will not be invalidated merely because the LLC (an eligible S corporation shareholder) momentarily receives the stock in the S corporation prior to the election.[74]

An LLC that previously filed an election to be classified as an S corporation may request a letter ruling from the IRS to retroactively revoke the S corporation election.[75]

¶407 SECOND CLASS OF STOCK

An S corporation may not have more than one class of stock.[76] The operating agreement of an LLC typically provides that members have different rights, preferences and privileges. Different rights, preferences and privileges may constitute a second class of stock that will disqualify the S corporation election.[77]

The IRS will issue private letter rulings that the operating agreement of an LLC does not constitute a second class of stock if (i) all items of income and loss are allocated among the members pro rata in accordance with the members' percentage interest in the LLC, and (ii) all distributions (both liquidating and nonliquidating) are made in accordance with the members' percentage interests in the LLC.[78]

Distributions from an LLC that take into account varying interests in the LLC during a tax year do not result in a second class of stock.[79]

Distributions from an LLC that are not based on each member's percentage interest in the LLC may cause a termination of the S corporation election. However, there will be no termination in such case if the shareholders eliminate the capital

---

[70] Reg. § 301.7701-3(c)(1)(v). *See also* Ltr. Ruls. 200321004, 200240048, 9853045 for prior law in which an LLC was required to make an election to be classified as an S corporation and a separate election to be classified as a corporation.

[71] Ltr. Ruls. 201251007, 201247007, 201225001, 201226017, 201228006, 201016010, 200917017, 200914008, 200908010, 200849010, 200843028, 200839003, 200837011, 200829025, 200827025, 200820007, 200818017, 200816009, 200810009, 200809021, 200701022, 200701015, 200638005, 200634009, 200548006, 200537028, 200537004.

[72] Rev. Proc. 2013-30, 2013-36 IRB 173.

[73] Reg. § 301.6109-1(h).

[74] Rev. Rul. 2004-59, 2004-1 CB 1050.

[75] INFO 2016-0065.

[76] Code Sec. 1361(b)(1)(D).

[77] Ltr. Ruls. 201136004, 201132013.

[78] Ltr. Ruls. 200802011, 200719007, 200548021, 200505010, 200326025, 200326024, 200326023.

[79] Reg. § 1.1361-1(l)(2)(iv).

account disparity resulting from the disproportionate distributions on a current basis.[80]

Buy-sell agreements among members, agreements restricting the transferability of membership interests, and redemption agreements are normally disregarded in determining whether the membership interests of an LLC confer identical distribution and liquidation rights.[81]

¶ 408 SUBSIDIARY LLC FOR NONQUALIFIED S CORPORATION SHAREHOLDERS

An S corporation may want to issue stock or equity interests to third-party investors who are not qualified S corporation shareholders. The issuance of stock to nonqualified investors will result in a termination of the S election and the tax benefits of the S corporation (e.g., single tax at the shareholder level). Normally, the S corporation may not convert to an LLC since the S corporation would be treated as selling all of its assets to the shareholders for fair market value in a taxable transaction.[82]

There are several ways of accommodating non-qualified third-party investors and retaining the S election of the corporation:

- The S corporation may drop down certain of its assets or liabilities into an LLC that is classified as a partnership. The LLC may then issue membership interests to the S corporation and to the third-party investor. The drop-down of assets and liabilities into an LLC is nontaxable under Section 721 of the Internal Revenue Code.[83] There is an exception to the rule if there is a net decrease in liabilities that exceeds the contributing member's tax basis in the assets transferred.[84] There would be net debt relief to the extent that LLC nonrecourse debt was allocated to third-party investors.[85] There would be a disguised sale taxable to the shareholders of the S corporation to the extent that the LLC distributed cash proceeds received from the third-party investor to the S corporation. However, there would be no tax to the extent that the S corporation retained membership interests in the LLC in exchange for the drop-down of assets.[86]

- The shareholders of the S corporation may form a new S corporation, and contribute their stock in the old S corporation to the new corporation. The new S corporation may then make a QSub election for the old S corporation, in which case the old S corporation would be classified as a disregarded entity

---

[80] Ltr. Rul. 200709051.

[81] Reg. § 1.1361-1(l)(2)(iii)(A).

[82] *See* ¶ 1108 *infra.*

[83] Ltr. Rul. 9640010.

[84] Ltr. Ruls. 9604014, 9313009.

[85] The general rule is that nonrecourse debt must be allocated to all members of an LLC in proportion to their profits interest in the LLC.

[86] Reg. § 1.707-3(f), Examples 1 and 2.

owned by the new S corporation.[87] The formation of the S corporation holding company and QSub election would be treated as an F reorganization.[88] The old S corporation (as a disregarded entity owned by the new S corporation) may then convert on a tax-free basis into a single-member disregarded LLC. The conversion would be treated as an F reorganization.[89] The LLC may then issue membership interests to the third-party investors on a tax-free basis, in which case the LLC would be reclassified as a partnership.[90] If the LLC retained the cash proceeds of sale in the LLC, there would be no tax to the LLC or the S corporation holding company.[91] If the LLC distributed all or part of the cash proceeds to the S corporation holding company, then the S corporation holding company would have taxable gain that would pass through to its shareholders. The S corporation would be treated as selling a pro rata share of each asset of the LLC in a taxable sale.[92]

- The shareholders of the S corporation may form a new S corporation, and contribute their stock in the old S corporation to the new corporation. The old S corporation may then convert into a single-member LLC without making a QSub election. After the transaction, the shareholders would own the new S corporation holding company which would own the disregarded LLC. This transaction would be treated as an F reorganization.[93] The LLC may then issue membership interests to the third-party investors on a tax-free basis, in which case the LLC would be reclassified as a partnership.[94] Alternatively, the S corporation holding company could sell membership interests in the disregarded LLC to the third-party investor. The sale of the membership interests by the S corporation holding company would be treated under Revenue Ruling 99-5 as (i) a purchase by the third-party of a pro rata portion of each of the assets of the LLC, (ii) with the S corporation holding company retaining the remaining pro rata portion of such assets of the Company, (iii) followed immediately by a nontaxable contribution by the third-party investor and the S corporation holding company of such respective assets to a newly formed partnership pursuant to Code Sec. 721.

---

[87] Rev. Rul. 2008-18, 2008-1 CB 674.

[88] Rev. Rul. 2008-18, 2008-1 CB 674.

[89] Ltr. Ruls. 200201005, 201115016; Rev. Rul. 96-29, 1996-1 CB 50; Reg. § 1.1361-5(b)(3), Example 2. Related events that precede or follow the potential F reorganization will not cause the F reorganization to fail to qualify as an F organization. Reg. § 1.368-2(m)(3).

[90] Rev. Rul. 99-5, 1999-5 IRB 8, Situation 2.

[91] Reg. § 1.1361-5(b)(3), Example 2; Rev. Rul. 99-5, 1999-1 CB 434, Situation 2.

[92] Reg. § 1.1361-5(b)(3), Example 2; Rev. Rul. 99-5, 1999-1 CB 434, Situation 1.

[93] *See* Ltr. Ruls. 200201005, 201115016; Rev. Rul. 96-29, 1996-1 CB 50; Reg. § 1.1361-5(b)(3), Example 2. Related events that precede or follow the potential F reorganization will not cause the F reorganization to fail to qualify as an F organization. Reg. § 1.368-2(m)(3).

[94] Rev. Rul. 99-5, 1999-5 IRB 8, Situation 2.

- Following the F reorganization under the prior two cases, the LLC (now owned by the newly formed S corporation holding company) may instead merge into another entity with third-party investors.[95]
- The S corporation may form a single-member disregarded LLC, and merge a QSub subsidiary into the LLC. The merger causes the termination of the QSub election. The S corporation parent company may then sell a percentage interest in the LLC to an unrelated company for cash. The formation of the LLC and the transfer of assets to the LLC pursuant to the merger are disregarded. The sale of the percentage interest to the unrelated third party is treated as a sale of an undivided interest in each of the LLC's assets. Immediately thereafter, the S corporation parent company and the unrelated party are treated as contributing their respective interests in those assets to a partnership in exchange for ownership interest in the partnership. The S corporation recognizes gain or loss from the deemed sale of its percentage interest in each of the assets of the LLC. No gain or loss is recognized by the S corporation or the unrelated party as a result of the deemed contribution of their respective interests in the assets to the LLC in exchange for ownership interests in the LLC.[96]

The first method is used if the parties can easily drop-down the assets, liabilities, licenses, permits, and contracts into a new LLC in which the third party invests. The other methods may be used if the parties want to retain all of the assets, liabilities, licenses, permits, and contracts in the existing entity (the S corporation that converts to an LLC with no drop-down of assets and liabilities).

In either case, the shareholders of the S corporation would retain the tax benefits of the S corporation. There would be a single tax at the shareholder level on the S corporation's allocable share of income earned by the LLC.

¶ 409 LLC PURCHASE OF S CORPORATION STOCK/BASIS STEP UP

An LLC that purchases the stock of an S corporation may treat the stock purchase as an asset purchase if the S corporation and its shareholders make an election under Code Sec. 336(e).[97] This will allow the LLC to step up the basis of the assets in the corporation, and receive higher depreciation and amortization deductions.

The LLC, S corporation and S corporation shareholders must take the following steps in order to make the Section 336(e) election:[98]

---

[95] Ltr. Rul. 200201005.
[96] Reg. § 1.1361-5(b)(3), Example 2.
[97] Ltr. Ruls. 201733003, 201730005, 201730004, 201721011.
[98] Ltr. Ruls. 201733003, 201730005, 201730004, 201721011.

- There must be a qualified stock disposition (QSD). A qualified stock disposition includes any transaction or series of transactions in which an LLC acquires at least 80 percent of the voting and value of the S corporation stock during a 12-month period.[99]

- The S corporation and the S corporation shareholders, including the shareholders who do not sell their stock, must sign an agreement on or before the due date of the federal tax return, including extensions, to make the Section 336(e) election.[100]

- The S corporation must retain a copy of the written agreement.[101]

- The S corporation must attach a Section 336(e) election statement to its timely filed tax return for the tax year that includes the disposition date.[102] The election statement must use the wording prescribed by the regulations.[103]

- A Section 338(h)(10) election may not be available. A Section 338(h)(10) election is similar to a Section 336(e) election, except that it applies only if there is a single corporate purchaser. The election under Code Sec. 338(h)(10) is not available if the LLC is classified as a partnership or disregarded entity. If the LLC is classified as a corporation, a Section 338(h)(10) election may be available, in which case, the LLC must make the Section 338(h)(10) election rather than the Section 336(e) election.

The LLC's acquisition of stock in the S corporation may terminate the S corporation election if the LLC is not a qualified S corporation shareholder.

¶410 OTHER SUBCHAPTER S ISSUES

Other special issues concerning S corporations and LLCs include the following:

- Conversion of an S corporation into an LLC.[104]

- Foreign members and shareholders.[105]

- Merger of a Qualified Subchapter S Subsidiary (QSUB) into a disregarded LLC.[106]

---

[99] Reg. § 1.336-1(b)(6).

[100] Reg. § 1.336-2(h)(3)(i).

[101] Reg. § 1.336-2(h)(3)(ii).

[102] Reg. § 1.336-2(h)(3)(iii).

[103] Reg. § 1.336-2(h)(5).

[104] See ¶1108 *infra*.

[105] See ¶1906 *infra*.

[106] See ¶1108.04 *infra*.

5

Classification of LLCs

¶ 501 OVERVIEW

On December 17, 1996, the IRS issued final regulations on the classification of LLCs and other entities for federal tax purposes.[1] The regulations are referred to as the "check-the-box" regulations because they permit most unincorporated entities to select classification as a proprietorship, partnership, or corporation by checking the applicable box on an IRS form.

Under the default classification rules, an LLC will be classified as follows unless it makes election on Form 8832 to be classified as a corporation:

- *Single-member LLC.* A single-member LLC is classified by default as a disregarded entity. All items of income, gain, credit, loss, and deduction pass through and are taxed to the member.[2] Generally, a single-member LLC is a proprietorship if owned by an individual, a division if owned by U.S. corporation, and a branch (subject to the branch profits tax) if owned by a foreign corporation.[3]

- *Multiple member LLC.* An LLC with two or more members is classified by default as a partnership.[4]

- *Foreign LLC.* A foreign LLC with at least two members of which at least one member does not have limited liability for some or all of the LLC's debts is classified as a partnership. A foreign LLC whose members all have limited liability is classified as a corporation. A foreign LLC with a single member that is liable for some or all of the LLC's debts is classified as a disregarded entity.[5]

- *Publicly traded LLC.* A publicly traded LLC is classified as a corporation.[6]

---

[1] TD 8697 (Dec. 18, 1996), enacting final regulations under Reg. § 301.7701.

[2] *See* ¶ 504.02 *infra.*

[3] *See* ¶ 504.02 *infra.*

[4] *See* ¶ 502 *infra.*

[5] *See* ¶ 505 *infra.*

[6] *See* ¶ 506 *infra.*

- *Spousal LLC.* An LLC may be classified as a single-member disregarded entity in a community property state even though both spouses own membership interests in the LLC.[7] Under current IRS rules, an LLC jointly owned by a husband and wife may not elect to be classified as a "qualified joint venture" owned separately by the spouses.[8]
- *C corporation classification.* Eight types of LLCs and other business entities are automatically classified as corporations. These entities include banks, insurance companies, and certain foreign limited liability companies.[9] An LLC that is classified as a partnership or disregarded entity under the default rules may elect to be classified as a corporation by filing Form 8832.
- *S corporation classification.* An LLC with eligible S corporation members may elect to be classified as an S corporation.[10]
- *Low-profit LLC.* A low-profit LLC is a cross between a nonprofit organization and a for-profit corporation. The classification of a low-profit LLCs is discussed in Chapter 26.

No IRS filings or elections are required for LLCs that choose to be classified under the default rules, which are the desired classifications in most cases.

¶ 502 PARTNERSHIP CLASSIFICATION

.01 General Rule

An LLC with two or more members is by default classified as a partnership. However, an LLC with two or more members is not classified as a partnership if:[11]

- The LLC is a foreign LLC that does not meet the requirements for classification as a partnership.[12]
- The LLC was classified as a corporation on the effective date of the IRS regulations and does not elect to be classified as a partnership.[13]
- The LLC is a publicly traded LLC.[14]
- The LLC elects to be classified as a C corporation.[15]
- The LLC elects to be classified as an S corporation.[16]
- The LLC is (i) an organization formed under federal or state law that refers to itself as incorporated or as a corporation; (ii) a joint-stock company or joint-

---

[7] See ¶ 507.01 *infra.*

[8] Instructions to Form 1065, p. 2. See ¶ 503.01 *infra.*

[9] See ¶ 503 *infra.*

[10] See ¶ 407 *supra.*

[11] Reg. § 301.7701-3(a).

[12] See ¶ 505 *infra.*

[13] Reg. § 301.7701-3(b)(3)(i). The transition classification rules are discussed at ¶ 510 *infra.*

[14] See ¶ 506 *infra.*

[15] See ¶ 503.02 *infra.*

[16] See ¶ 407 *supra.*

stock association; (iii) certain banks; (iv) an organization wholly owned by a state or local government; (v) certain publicly traded partnerships; (vi) a tax-exempt organization; (vii) a real estate investment trust; or (viii) an organization classified as a trust under IRS regulations.[17]

For tax purposes, it is usually advisable for an LLC with two or more members to be classified as a partnership. There is a single level of tax at the member level. All items of LLC income, gain, loss, deduction, and credit pass through to the members.

The final regulations eliminate the four-factor test that was previously used to determine whether an LLC was a corporation or a partnership for tax purposes.[18]

.02 Sham Partnerships and Members Not Treated as Partners

An LLC with two or more members will not be classified as a partnership for federal tax purposes unless two or more parties "in good faith and acting with a business purpose intend to join together in the present conduct of the enterprise."[19]

A member of an LLC that is classified as a partnership will not be treated as a partner if the member does not have the benefits and burdens of ownership. The member must have a meaningful stake in the success or failure of the LLC. The taxpayer may be treated as a secured lender rather than as a partner if the taxpayer's membership interest is unaffected by the LLC's success or failure.[20] The IRS will no longer issue rulings on matters relating to the validity of an LLC as a partnership, or whether a member is treated as a partner in the LLC.[21]

EXAMPLE 5-1

A company made an equity contribution of $16 million in an LLC in exchange for a three percent return and Code Sec. 47 historic rehabilitation tax credits for costs to rehabilitate an historic landmark. The LLC was classified as a partnership for federal tax purposes. The member had no real investment risk or upside potential because it was not required to make capital contributions until the LLC completed renovations required to generate the tax credits. The transaction was reclassified as a sale of tax credits. The taxpayer was denied the tax credits since it was not a bona fide member of the LLC.[22]

---

[17] IRS Publication 541, p. 2 (rev. Dec. 2010).

[18] The four-factor test is discussed at ¶ 513 *infra*.

[19] *Historic Boardwalk Hall, LLC v. Comm'r*, 694 F.3d 425 (3d Cir. 2012), *cert. denied*, 569 U.S. 1004 (2013).

[20] *Historic Boardwalk Hall, LLC v. Comm'r*, 694 F.3d 425 (3d Cir. 2012), *cert. denied*, 569 U.S. 1004 (2013).

[21] Rev. Proc. 2017-3, 2017-1 IRB 130, § 3.01(85).

[22] *Historic Boardwalk Hall, LLC v. Comm'r*, 694 F.3d 425 (3d Cir. 2012), *cert. denied*, 569 U.S. 1004 (2013).

.03 Classification of Members

If an LLC is classified as a partnership, then the LLC may need to classify each of its members as a general partner or limited partner for purposes of certain Code provisions. Members who are classified as general partners or limited partners are treated differently for the following tax purposes:

- Liquidating distributions to retiring or deceased members (¶ 1010.02);
- Passive losses (¶ 1304.03);
- Pension and profit-sharing contributions (¶ 1406.03);
- Cash method of accounting for syndicates (¶ 1701.07); and
- Self-employment taxes (¶ 2702.02).

There is no clear definition in the Code or regulations on the classification of LLC members as general or limited partners.

¶ 503 CORPORATION CLASSIFICATION

.01 Automatic Classification as Corporation

The regulations automatically classify eight types of business entities as corporations for federal tax purposes.[23] The following LLCs are always classified as corporations and may not be classified as a partnership or flow-through entity:

- A European public limited liability company, referred to as a *Societas Europaea* or *SE*.[24] Under European regulations, this form of LLC may be formed after October 8, 2004, and has legal effect in all Member States of the European Economic Area.
- Limited liability companies organized in foreign countries that are on the "(b)(8) list." The IRS has designated over 80 limited liability entities on this list that are automatically classified as corporations.[25]
- Dual chartered LLCs that are classified as a corporation in either the United States or a foreign country.[26] Dual chartered LLCs are also classified as domestic entities even though they retain their charter in a foreign country.[27]

---

[23] Reg. § 301.7701-2(b). These include (i) a business entity organized under federal or state law if the statute describes or refers to the entity as incorporated, a corporation, body corporate, or a body politic, (ii) an association, (iii) a business entity organized under state law if the statute describes or refers to the entity as a joint-stock company or joint-stock association, (iv) an insurance company, (v) a federally insured state-chartered bank, (vi) a business entity wholly owned by a state or any political subdivision of the state, (vii) a publicly traded entity taxable as a corporation, and (viii) certain foreign business entities.

[24] IRS Notice 2004-68, 2004-2 CB 706; Reg. § 301.7701-2(b)(8)(i).

[25] Reg. §§ 301.7701-2(b)(8), 301-7701-3(a) (first sentence).

[26] Reg. § 301.7701-2(b)(9).

[27] Reg. § 301.7701-5.

For example, if a Barbados limited company files a certificate of domestication as a single member Delaware LLC, it will automatically be classified as a corporation. It may not elect classification as a disregarded entity because it remains organized as a Barbados limited company, and a Barbados limited company is always classified as a corporation on the "(b)(8) list."[28] The dual chartered LLC will also be treated as a domestic U.S. corporation even though it is also chartered in a foreign country.[29]

- An insurance company.[30]
- A bank.[31]

Under proposed regulations, a domestic disregarded LLC that is owned by a foreign entity is classified as a domestic corporation for purposes of reporting, records maintenance, and compliance requirements that apply to a 25 percent foreign-owned domestic corporation under Code Sec. 6038A.[32] The reporting requirements are discussed at ¶ 1904.01.

.02 Reasons for Electing Classification as a Corporation

Any LLC may elect to be classified as a corporation for federal tax purposes. An LLC may want to elect classification as a corporation, rather than accept the default classification as a partnership or disregarded entity, for one of the following reasons:

- A corporation that owns an LLC in a foreign state may be treated as doing business in and subject to corporate and franchise taxes in the foreign state if the LLC is a partnership[33] or disregarded entity.[34] The parent corporation may

---

[28] Reg. § 301.7701-5(b), Example (1).

[29] Reg. § 301.7701-5(a).

[30] Reg. § 301.7701-2(b)(4).

[31] Reg. § 301.7701-2(b)(5); *BNA Daily Tax Report*, No. 140, p. G-6 (July 22, 2004).

[32] Prop. Reg. §§ 1.6038A-1(c)(1), 1.6038A-2(b)(3)(xi), 1.6038A-2(b)(9), Examples 1 and 2.

[33] Cal. FTB Legal Ruling 2014-01 (July 22, 2014); *Sahi USA Inc. v. Massachusetts Comm'r of Revenue*, No. C262668, Massachusetts Appellate Tax Board (2006); Michigan Revenue Administrative Bulletin 2014-5 (Jan. 29, 2014), Example 12; Secretary of Revenue Decision No. 2007-28, North Carolina Department of Revenue (Sept. 14, 2007) (an out-of-state corporation that owned a membership interest in a North Carolina LLC classified as a partnership was treated as doing business in North Carolina for corporate income tax purposes, and its income from the LLC was apportionable business income for purposes of determining its North Carolina corporate income tax liability); Corporation Tax Opinion, Pennsylvania S Corporation Filing Responsibilities, Pennsylvania Department of Revenue (Feb. 2, 2000) (the Ohio corporate owners of an Ohio LLC that was doing business in LLC were subject to the Pennsylvania corporate net income tax because the income and activity of the LLC doing business in Pennsylvania flowed through to the corporate members, but the corporate members were not subject to the Pennsylvania capital stock and franchise tax).

[34] Taxpayer Information Ruling LR11-01, Arizona Department of Revenue (Feb. 8, 2011), with an exception for a foreign state insurance company that does business in Arizona through a disregarded LLC; Legal Ruling 2011-01, Franchise Tax Board (Jan. 11, 2011); 103 KAR 16:300E, Secs. 2, 3, Kentucky Department of Revenue (a corporation that owned a single-member disregarded LLC doing business in Kentucky was treated as doing business in Kentucky, and the corporate owner and single-member LLC was treated as one corporation in determining taxable income and the applicable apportionment factor); Massachusetts Department of Revenue Ltr. Rul. LR 00-9 (June 9, 2000) (a Georgia corporation

avoid paying taxes in the foreign state if it elects to classify the LLC as a corporation. In that case, the taxes payable by the LLC in the foreign state are separately determined based on the LLC's income, deductions, and credits, rather than under the allocation and apportionment formulas of the foreign state's tax laws. Some states have determined that a foreign company is not subject to state taxes as a result of its ownership of a domestic LLC classified as a partnership[35] or disregarded entity.[36]

- A corporation that owns an LLC in a foreign state may be required to apportion income of the LLC in the state of incorporation, even if the LLC has no business or other contacts with the state of incorporation.[37] The apportionment rules may not apply if the LLC elects classification as a corporation.

- If the LLC has foreign members, the LLC may want to avoid withholding taxes on undistributed income. Foreign members are subject to a withholding tax on their allocable share of trade or business income earned by the LLC, whether or not the income is distributed.[38]

(Footnote Continued)

was subject to Massachusetts taxation when it acquired a Massachusetts LLC that was classified as a disregard entity; the Georgia corporation was treated as doing business in Massachusetts based on its ownership of the membership units in the LLC; and the Georgia corporation was entitled to apportion its income in accordance with the provisions of Georgia law in determining the taxable income allocable to Massachusetts); Louisiana Department of Revenue, Revenue Information Bulletin Nos. 04-003 (2004), and 02-018 (2002) (the corporate owner of a single-member LLC doing business in Louisiana was subject to Louisiana tax laws, and if either the corporation or the single-member LLC owned by the corporation had a nexus in Louisiana, both would have nexus for Louisiana tax purposes).

[35] In *Express Scripts, Inc. v. Commissioner of Revenue*, Minnesota Tax Court, No. 8272R (Aug. 20, 2012), the Minnesota Tax Court determined that an out-of-state corporation was not required to file a unitary tax return or apportion its income to Minnesota as a result of its membership interest in a Minnesota LLC.

[36] The Texas Comptroller of Public Accounts ruled that a foreign corporation is not subject to the Texas franchise tax as a result of its ownership of a disregarded LLC doing business in Texas. Letter No. 200606695L, Texas Comptroller of Public Accounts (June 1, 2006); Letter No. 200606694L, Texas Comptroller of Public Accounts (June 1, 2006). A Michigan court determined that a single-member disregarded LLC owned by a corporation could file a separate tax return under the state's single business tax act, and would not have to file as part of a combined return with the parent corporation. *Kmart Michigan Property Services LLC v. Michigan Treasury Department*, 283 Mich. App. 647 (2009). Under 2010 legislation, a subsidiary disregarded LLC is not required to file a separate return in Michigan. MCL §205.27a. In *Riverboat Development, Inc. v. Department of Revenue*, Indiana Tax Court No. 49T10-0506-TA-52 (Feb. 22, 2008), the Indiana Tax Court determined that the income allocated by an Indiana LLC to an out-of-state corporate member was not subject to withholding because the foreign corporation was not domiciled in Indiana, and derived its income from the membership interest which was tangible personal property.

[37] See Mich. Comp. Laws §206.661, effective January 1, 2012, which provides that a corporate taxpayer with a direct or indirect ownership interest or beneficial interest in a flow-through entity in a foreign state must apportion its business income directly attributable to the business activity of the flow-through entity, even if the flow-through entity has no business activity in the state of incorporation of the corporate owner.

[38] Code Sec. 1446. *See* ¶ 1902 *infra*.

- The classification of an LLC as a corporation may be necessary in order to obtain financing in a public offering.[39] An LLC must be classified as a corporation if its membership units are publicly traded.[40]

- The classification of an LLC as a corporation will permit the LLC to engage in tax-free corporate reorganizations, such as mergers, reincorporations, and liquidations of subsidiary LLCs into parent corporations or parent LLCs.[41]

- If a corporation owns an LLC, the corporate owner may want to file a consolidated tax return that includes the LLC as a separate entity rather than a disregarded entity. An LLC that is owned by a member of a control group and that is classified as a disregarded entity is treated as part of the control group for consolidated tax purposes.[42] The tax consequences of including the subsidiary on the consolidated return may be more favorable than treating the LLC as a separate disregarded entity. For example, the corporate parent of a single-member LLC may not increase its basis in the LLC membership units by the income that passes through from the LLC to the parent corporation. Since the LLC is disregarded as an entity, the parent corporation is treated as selling all the underlying assets on sale of the LLC to a third party.

- The LLC may want to keep its profits inside the business and take advantage of the lower corporate tax rates for corporations that are not personal service corporations (e.g., 15 percent on the first $50,000 of income).

- An LLC may elect to be classified as an S corporation if it files Form 2553.[43] In certain cases, an S corporation provides more favorable tax benefits.[44] For example, the owner of a single-member disregarded LLC may want to file an S corporation election in order to avoid reporting self-employment income on Schedule C (which is an audit risk factor) and to minimize self-employment taxes (S corporation distributions of earnings are not subject to employment taxes).

- An LLC that is taxed as a corporation may adopt certain employee benefits that are not available to partnerships.[45]

- A corporation may want to convert to an LLC that is classified as a corporation in order to obtain the non-tax benefits available to an LLC under state law. For example, a corporation may not under the laws of some states repurchase stock or make distributions to shareholders unless it has sufficient retained earnings or legally available funds. An LLC is not normally subject to such restrictions. A corporation may be able to avoid the restrictions on stock

---

[39] Ltr. Rul. 200151039.

[40] *See* ¶ 2003 *infra.*

[41] Ltr. Ruls. 200248023, 200204004, 200119016.

[42] Ltr. Rul. 200111053.

[43] *See* ¶ 406 *supra.*

[44] Ltr. Rul. 9853045.

[45] *See* ¶ 1406 *infra.*

repurchases and distributions to shareholders by converting to an LLC that is classified as a corporation.[46]

.03 S Corporation Classification

An LLC may elect to be classified as an S corporation. The S corporation election is discussed at ¶¶ 4.06 and 4.07.

¶ 504 SINGLE-MEMBER DISREGARDED ENTITY CLASSIFICATION

.01 State Laws

Prior to the issuance of the check-the-box regulations, it was generally believed that an LLC should have at least two members in order to be classified as a partnership. All states now permit single-member LLCs, since the federal regulations permit single-member LLCs to achieve pass-through tax treatment.

.02 Classification of Single-Member LLC

A single-member LLC is disregarded as an entity separate from its owner[47] unless it makes an election to be classified as a corporation.[48] A single-member disregarded LLC cannot be classified as a partnership.[49] If a single-member LLC does not elect to be classified as a corporation, it is taxed as follows:

- A single-member LLC owned by an individual is taxed as a sole proprietorship.[50] The owner of the LLC must file a Schedule C to IRS Form 1040 to report the income and expenses of the LLC.[51]
- A single-member LLC owned by a U.S. corporation is taxed as a division.[52] The consolidation rules, such as deferred intercompany gain and excess loss accounts, do not apply. All intercompany transactions are disregarded for federal tax purposes.
- A single-member LLC owned by a foreign corporation is taxed as a branch for U.S. tax purposes.[53] The LLC is subject to the branch profits tax.[54]

---

[46] Ltr. Rul. 200119016.

[47] Reg. § 301.7701-3(b)(1)(ii). *See also* Reg. § 301.7701-2(a), (c)(2).

[48] Reg. § 301.7701-3(a).

[49] CCA 201221015.

[50] Reg. § 301.7701-2(a).

[51] IRS Publication 334, Tax Guide for Small Businesses; Reg. § 301.7701-2(a).

[52] Reg. § 301.7701-(2)(a); Ltr. Rul. 200111053.

[53] Reg. § 301.7701-2(a); Ltr. Rul. 200720010.

[54] Ltr. Rul. 200720010. *See* ¶ 1902.05 *infra.*

A bank may not treat a wholly owned non-bank LLC as a disregarded entity for purposes of applying the special rules of the Code applicable to banks.[55]

.03 Related Members

An LLC may be treated as owned by two or more members even if the members are related. The determination of whether an organization has more than one owner is based on all the facts and circumstances. The fact that some or all of the owners of an LLC are under common control does not require the common parent to be treated as the sole owner.[56] For example, an LLC may be classified as a partnership if the membership interests are owned by any of the following:

- Two corporations that are wholly owned subsidiaries of the same parent corporation.[57]
- A parent and a wholly owned subsidiary corporation.[58]
- An individual and a corporation wholly owned by the same individual.[59]

An LLC may be treated as a single-member LLC and classified as a disregarded entity if an individual and a grantor trust owned by the same individual own the LLC.[60]

.04 Multiple-Member LLCs Treated as Single-Member LLCs

An LLC with more than one member may be treated as a single-member LLC and classified as a disregarded entity for federal tax purposes if:

- One of the members of the LLC has no interest in profits and losses,[61] does not manage the LLC, and has only limited voting rights.[62] The LLC cannot be classified as a partnership if the members have not entered into an agreement to share profits and losses from the operation of a business.[63]
- One of the members of an LLC is a disregarded entity that is owned by the other member of the LLC. For example, an LLC cannot be classified as a partnership if it has two members, one of which is a corporation, and the other which is a single-member disregarded LLC owned by the corporate member.[64]

---

[55] Reg. § 301.7701-2(c)(2)(ii).

[56] TD 8697, Part B, Discussion of Comments on the General Approach and Scope of the Regulations (Dec. 18, 1996) (*citing* Rev. Rul. 93-4, 1993-1 CB 225).

[57] Ltr. Rul. 9520036 (Texas LLC owed by two foreign subsidiaries of a foreign parent corporation); Ltr. Ruls. 9510037, 9520036 (Texas LLC owed by two subsidiaries of a parent corporation); Rev. Rul. 93-4, 1993-1 CB 225 (German GmbH owned by two wholly owned U.S. subsidiaries of a common parent).

[58] Ltr. Rul. 9507004.

[59] Ltr. Rul. 9321070.

[60] Ltr. Rul. 200102037.

[61] CCA 200501001.

[62] Ltr. Ruls. 200201024, 199914006, 199911033.

[63] Ltr. Ruls. 199914006, 199911033.

[64] Rev. Rul. 2004-77, 2004-2 CB 119.

.05 Tax Consequences

LLC Disregarded for Tax Purposes

The single member of an LLC that is classified as a disregarded entity is treated as the owner of the underlying assets of the LLC. This means that:

- There is no gain or loss on the transfer of assets and liabilities by a corporation or other entity to the LLC.[65]
- A charitable contribution to an LLC owned by a tax-exempt organization is treated as a tax-deductible contribution to the charitable organization. The tax-exempt organization is not required to file an application for exemption for the LLC owned by it.[66]
- The LLC may own stock in an S corporation if the member of the LLC is a qualified S corporation shareholder.[67]
- The owner may use the LLC to engage in a like-kind exchange or involuntary conversion of property.[68]
- The member's sale of membership units is treated as a sale of the underlying assets subject to state sales taxes.[69]
- The owner and the LLC must file federal tax returns as a sole proprietor.[70]
- The merger of an LLC into a corporation is treated as if the owner of the LLC transferred all of the assets to the corporation. The merger of a corporation into an LLC is treated as if the owner of the LLC acquired all of the assets of the corporation. Neither merger qualifies as a tax-free merger under Code Sec. 368(a)(1)(A).[71]
- The merger of a subsidiary corporation into an LLC owned by the parent corporation is treated as a tax-free liquidation of the subsidiary into the parent.[72]
- The employees of the LLC may participate in a qualified pension or profit sharing plan, Section 401(k) plan, Section 403(b) annuity plan,[73] employee

---

[65] Ltr. Rul. 200132014.

[66] Ltr. Rul. 200134025.

[67] See ¶ 403 *supra*.

[68] See ¶ ¶ 1505, 1506 *infra*.

[69] See ¶ 1501 *infra*.

[70] IRS Publication 334, Tax Guide for Small Businesses.

[71] Prop. Reg. § 1.368-2(b)(1). *See also* Ltr. Rul. 200102038, involving the merger of a subsidiary corporation into an LLC that was wholly owned by the parent corporation.

[72] Ltr. Rul. 200129024.

[73] Ltr. Rul. 200334040.

stock ownership plan,[74] or other qualified retirement plan of the corporate owner of the LLC. If the corporate owner maintains an employee stock ownership plan, the employees of the LLC may participate in an employee stock ownership plan of the corporate owner of the LLC. The stock in the corporate owner or another member of the controlled group of corporations constitutes qualifying employer securities for the employee stock ownership plan adopted by the LLC.[75]

- The employees of the LLC may participate in a Section 423 employee stock purchase plan of the corporate owner of the LLC.[76] If the corporate owner of the LLC is a subsidiary of a parent corporation, the employees of the LLC may receive stock of the parent corporation under a Section 423 stock purchase plan or an incentive stock option plan.[77]

- The owner of the LLC may not deduct rent paid to the LLC to lease real property owned by the LLC. The LLC is not taxed on the rental income received.[78]

- The owner of the LLC is entitled to any Section 29 synthetic fuel credit attributable to the single-member LLC.[79]

LLC as Separate Entity for Tax Purposes

A single-member disregarded entity is treated as a separate entity for tax purposes in the following cases:

- *Employment taxes.* Beginning January 1, 2009, a single-member disregarded LLC is treated as a corporation for employment tax purposes. The LLC is liable for all withholding and employment tax obligations for non-member employees of the LLC.[80]

- *Tax collection and tax liens.* A single-member LLC is treated as a separate entity for IRS tax collection and tax lien purposes if the LLC is a legal entity separate from its member, and if the member has no transferable interest in property of the LLC, under state law. The LLC is not normally liable for the federal tax liabilities of its owner during periods in which it is a disregarded entity.[81]

- *Sales taxes.* An LLC that is a disregarded entity for income tax purposes is not a disregarded entity for sales tax purposes in some states. In New York, for example, the lease or sale of tangible personal property by the owner of an LLC to the LLC constitutes a retail sale subject to sales tax even though the

---

[74] Ltr. Ruls. 201124030, 200116051.

[75] Ltr. Rul. 200116051.

[76] Ltr. Rul. 200046013.

[77] Ltr. Rul. 200112021.

[78] Ltr. Rul. 200102037.

[79] Ltr. Rul. 200316003.

[80] Reg. § 301.7701-2(c)(2)(iv)(A). *See* ¶ 1603.02 *infra.*

[81] *See* ¶ 2405 *infra.*

LLC is a disregarded entity.[82] Other states have reached the opposite conclusion.[83]

- *Excise taxes.* A single-member disregarded entity is treated as a corporation for certain excise taxes reported on Forms 11-C, 637, 720, 730, 2290 and 8849.[84]

.06 Default Classification of Single-Member LLCs Existing Before January 1, 1997

A single-member LLC in existence before January 1, 1997, will be disregarded as an entity separate from its owner under the default rules. The partnership classification of a single-member LLC may be respected for periods before January 1, 1997, under transition rules, but not for periods after that date.[85] Thus, a single-member LLC that claimed partnership status for periods before January 1, 1997, will be classified as a proprietorship, branch, or division on January 1, 1997, unless it elects to be classified as a corporation.

.07 Single-Member LLC Owned by Foreign Entity

Under proposed regulations, a domestic disregarded LLC that is owned by a foreign entity is classified as a domestic corporation for purposes of reporting, records maintenance, and compliance requirements that apply to a 25 percent foreign-owned domestic corporation under Code Sec. 6038A.[86] The reporting requirements are discussed at ¶ 1904.01.

¶ 505 FOREIGN LLC

.01 Default Classification

The classification of a foreign LLC depends on the number of members and whether the members have limited liability under local law. If the foreign LLC does not make an election, it will be classified as follows:[87]

- The LLC will be classified by default as a partnership if it has two or more members and if at least one member has unlimited liability.[88] A member has

---

[82] Advisory Opinion, Department of Revenue, TBS-A-99(7)S (Jan. 28, 1999).

[83] *See, e.g.,* Rev. Rul. 98-005, Ala. Dept. of Rev. (June 18, 1998). In that ruling, the Alabama Department of Revenue determined that because a single-member LLC was a disregarded entity for federal income tax purposes, it should also be treated as a disregarded entity for sales tax purposes.

[84] Instructions to IRS Form 720; Reg. § § 1.1361-4(a)(8), 301.7701-2(c)(2)(iv), (v).

[85] Reg. § 301.7701-3(b)(3).

[86] Prop. Reg. § § 1.6038A-1(c)(1), 1.6038A-2(b)(3)(xi), 1.6038A-2(b)(9), Examples 1 and 2.

[87] Reg. § 301.7701-3(b)(2)(i).

[88] Reg. § 301.7701-3(b)(2)(i)(A).

unlimited liability if he is personally liable for any or all of the debts of or claims against the LLC, by reason of being a member, based solely on the statute or law pursuant to which the entity is organized.[89] A member has personal liability if creditors of the entity may seek satisfaction of debts of or claims against the LLC from the member as such.[90] If a taxpayer is uncertain whether there is limited liability in a particular case, it may file an election to secure the desired classification.

- The LLC will be classified by default as a corporation if all members have limited liability under the laws of the foreign country.[91] A member has limited liability if the member has no personal liability for the debts of or claims against the LLC by reason of being a member. This determination is based solely on the statute or law of the foreign country under which the LLC is organized.[92] The presence of any member with personal liability for any of the debts of or claims against the LLC will cause the LLC to be classified by default as a partnership. The LLC may instead elect classification as a proprietorship if the LLC has a single member, or as a partnership if the LLC has two or more members and is otherwise eligible for partnership classification.[93]

- The LLC will by default be classified as a proprietorship or entity separate from its owners if it has a single member with unlimited liability.[94]

If a foreign LLC's classification is determined under the default rule, changes in any member's liability will not affect the tax classification of the LLC.[95] Therefore, if a foreign LLC is classified as a partnership when the LLC's classification first becomes relevant because one of the members has personal liability, the subsequent elimination of the member's personal liability will not cause the LLC to be classified as a corporation.

For tax purposes, it is usually advisable for a foreign LLC to be classified as a partnership or disregarded entity.[96]

.02 Per Se Classification

The IRS has designated over 80 foreign limited companies and other entities that are always classified as corporations.[97] This is referred to as the "(b)(8) list" or the "per se list." For example, a U.K. Public Limited Company and a French *Societe Anonyme* are always classified as corporations. The IRS will update the list in notices

---

[89] Reg. § 301.7701-3(b)(2)(ii).

[90] *Id.*

[91] Reg. § 301.7701-3(b)(2)(i)(B); Ltr. Rul. 200315009.

[92] Reg. § 301.7701-3(b)(2)(ii); Ltr. Rul. 200315009.

[93] Reg. § 301.7701-3(a).

[94] Reg. § 301.7701-3(b)(2)(i)(C).

[95] *Id.*

[96] *See* Chapter 18 *infra*.

[97] Reg. §§ 301.7701-2(b)(8), 301.7701-3(a) (first sentence).

of proposed rulemaking on a prospective basis only.[98] The foreign entities on the per se list are listed in the instructions to IRS Form 8832.

The per se list is designed to simplify classification elections for foreign entities. A foreign entity may be classified as a partnership disregarded entity if it is not on the per se list. These classifications may be made either under the default rules or by an elective classification. For example, a foreign LLC with one member may be classified as a disregarded entity if it is not on the per se list. A foreign LLC with two or more members may be classified as a partnership if it is not on the per se list.

.03 *Elective Classification*

A foreign LLC that does not want to be classified under the default rules may elect classification under the following rules:

- An LLC with one or more members that is by default classified as a partnership or disregarded entity may elect classification as a corporation.[99] For example, a single-member LLC with unlimited liability that is classified as a proprietorship, branch or division under the default rules may elect classification as a corporation.[100]
- An LLC that is by default classified as a corporation may elect classification as a disregarded entity (LLC with a single member) or as a partnership (LLC with two or more members) if it is not on the per se list.[101] For example, an LLC with two or more members, with no member having unlimited liability, that is classified as a corporation under the default rules may elect classification as a partnership if it is not on the per se list.[102]
- An LLC that was classified as a corporation prior to the effective date of the IRS classification regulations (January 1, 1997)[103] may elect classification as a partnership, proprietorship, branch or division, if certain requirements are met.[104]

A foreign LLC that does not want to be classified under the default rules must make the election within 75 days after the triggering event for filing Form 8832. As a rule of thumb, a foreign LLC should make the election on Form 8832 within 75 days after (i) the LLC enters into a business transaction in the United States, (ii) the LLC receives U.S. source income, or (iii) a U.S. taxpayer first acquires an ownership interest in the LLC.[105]

---

[98] TD 8697, Notice 97-1, Part B, Discussion of Comments on the General Approach and Scope of the Regulations (Dec. 18, 1996).

[99] Reg. § 301.7701-3(a).

[100] Reg. §§ 301.7701-3(a), 301.7701-3(b)(2)(i)(C).

[101] Reg. §§ 301.7701-3(a), 301.7701-3(b)(2)(i)(B).

[102] Reg. § 301.7701-3(b)(2)(i)(B).

[103] Reg. § 301.7701-3(b)(3).

[104] Reg. § 301.7701-3(b)(3)(ii).

[105] *See* D. Schwartz, "Stay Ahead of the Curve When Choosing Desired Tax Treatment," *Los Angeles Daily J.*, p. 7 (Apr. 15, 2014).

.04 Hybrid Classification

An LLC that is classified by a foreign country as a corporation and by the United States as a partnership or disregarded entity is a hybrid entity.[106] An LLC that is classified by a foreign country as a partnership or disregarded entity and by the United States as a corporation is a reverse hybrid entity. A foreign hybrid LLC is sometimes used to achieve tax savings related to Subpart F income and foreign tax credits.[107]

A U.S. hybrid LLC is also used to achieve tax savings. The tax consequences of a U.S. hybrid LLC are discussed at ¶ 1908.

.05 Disregarded LLCs

Disregarded LLCs are treated as persons under the anti-conduit financing regulations.[108] The purpose of the regulation is to prevent companies from obtaining the benefits of the U.S. Tax treaty or avoiding withholding on portfolio interest by using a disregarded LLC as a conduit entity in a foreign country. The IRS may disregard the LLC as the intermediate entity, and recharacterize the transaction as occurring between the remaining parties.[109]

A financing arrangement for purposes of the regulations is a series of transactions by which a person advances money or other property to another person through one or more intermediate entities or other persons.[110]

.06 Mistaken Election Relief

The IRS will provide election relief to:[111]

- *Disregarded LLC.* A foreign LLC that made a check-the-box election to be classified as a partnership under a reasonable but mistaken assumption that it had more than one member. The IRS will treat the original election as an election to be a disregarded LLC. The LLC's single owner or purported owners as of the election date must file original or amended returns consistent with the treatment of the LLC as a disregarded entity for any tax year that would have been affected if the election had been made to treat the LLC as a disregarded entity. The LLC must file all required amended returns before the close of the Section 6501 limitation period for assessments for any relevant tax year. The member must file Form 8832 with the Internal Revenue Service

---

[106] *See* Notice 95-14, 1995-1 CB 297.

[107] *See* Notice 95-14, 1995-1 CB 297; Mullis, K, "Check-the-Box and Hybrids: A Second Look at Elective U.S. Tax Classification for Foreign Entities," Tax Notes International, p. 371 (Oct. 31, 2011).

[108] Reg. § 1.881-3(a)(2)(i)(C).

[109] Reg. § 1.881-3(a)(1), (3); TD 9562 (2011).

[110] Reg. § 1.881-3(a)(2).

[111] Rev. Proc. 2010-32, 2010-36 IRB 320.

Center and attach a copy to the member's amended returns for the tax year during which the original election was made.

- *Partnership LLC.* A foreign LLC that made a check-the-box election to be classified as disregarded entity under a reasonable but mistaken assumption that it had only one member. The IRS will treat the original election as an election to be a partnership. The LLC's members as of the election date must file original or amended returns consistent with the treatment of the LLC for any tax year that would have been affected if the election and been made to treat the LLC as a partnership. The LLC must file all required amended returns before the close of the Section 6501 limitation period for assessments for any relevant tax year. The members must file Form 8832 with the Internal Revenue Service Center and attach a copy to the LLC's amended return for the tax year during which the original election was made.

.07 *Default Classification of Foreign LLCs Existing Before January 1, 1997*

A foreign LLC existing before January 1, 1997, may keep its same classification under the default rules only if it is a "foreign eligible entity" and the claimed classification affected the liability of any person for U.S. tax or information purposes at any time during the five years before January 1, 1997.[112]

Foreign LLCs on the per se list[113] are not foreign eligible entities and may not elect partnership classification. However, under grandfather rules, foreign LLCs that claimed classification as a partnership, branch, or division before January 1, 1997, may continue to be classified as a partnership, branch, or division after January 1, 1997, if six requirements are met.[114]

- The LLC was in existence on May 8, 1996 (or formed thereafter under a written binding contract in effect on that date).
- The LLC's claimed classification was relevant[115] to any person for U.S. tax purposes on May 8, 1996.
- Neither the LLC nor any member for whom U.S. classification was relevant treated the LLC as a corporation for purposes of filing U.S. tax returns, information returns, and withholding documents for the tax year that included May 8, 1996.
- Any change in the LLC's claimed classification during the 60 months before May 8, 1996, occurred solely as a result of a change in the organizational documents of the LLC, and the LLC and all of its members recognized the federal tax consequences of any change in the LLC's classification during the 60 months before May 8, 1996.

---

[112] *Id.*

[113] Reg. § 301.7701-2(b)(8). *See* ¶ 503.01 *supra.*

[114] Reg. § 301.7701-2(d).

[115] Reg. § 301.7701-3(d)(1).

- There was a reasonable basis for treating the LLC as other than a corporation.

- The LLC was not under tax audit with respect to the classification on May 8, 1996.

A foreign LLC on the per se list that qualifies under these transition rules may instead elect to be classified as a corporation. However, after making that election, it may not later elect classification as a partnership or branch. The grandfather status of an entity on the per se list will end upon a termination of the LLC caused by either the sale or exchange of 50 percent or more of the interests in the LLC's capital or profits within a 12-month period,[116] a division of the LLC into two or more LLCs,[117] or when one or more persons were not owners of the LLC as of November 29, 1999, become owners of 50 percent or more of the equity interests in the LLC.[118] The successor entity will thereafter be permanently treated as a corporation.

¶ 506 PUBLICLY TRADED LLCs

A publicly traded LLC is normally classified as a corporation for federal tax purposes.[119] A publicly traded LLC is an LLC whose interests are traded on an established securities market or are readily traded on a secondary market.[120] There are the following exceptions:

- The LLC has fewer than 100 investors and the membership units are sold in a private placement or other offering not requiring SEC registration.[121]

- The sum of capital and profits interests sold or disposed of during the year is less than two percent of the total capital or profits interests of the LLC.[122]

- At least 90 percent of the LLC's income is qualifying passive income.[123] Qualifying passive income includes interest; dividends; real property rents; gain from the sale of real property; income and gains relating to minerals and natural resources; gains from the sale of a capital asset or certain trade or business property held for the production of the foregoing types of income; capital gains from the sale of stock; income from holding annuities; income

---

[116] Code Sec. 708(b)(1)(B). However, the LLC's grandfather status will not end in the case of a termination caused by the sale or exchange of membership interests in an LLC described in Reg. § 301.7701-2(d)(2) if the sale or exchange is to a related person within the meaning of Code Secs. 267(b) and 707(b) and occurs no later than 12 months after the date the LLC is formed. Reg. § 301.7701-2(d)(3)(ii).

[117] Code Sec. 708(b)(2)(B).

[118] Reg. § 301.7701-2(d)(3)(i)(D).

[119] Code Sec. 7704; Reg. § 1.7704-1.

[120] Code Sec. 7704; Reg. § 1.7704-1.

[121] Reg. § 1.7704-1(h)(1).

[122] Reg. § 1.7704-1(j)(1).

[123] Code Sec. 7704(c). *See* Ltr. Rul. 9751048 in which the IRS ruled that an LLC would not be a publicly traded partnership since its income consisted entirely of interest, dividends and gains from the sale of stock or securities with the meaning of Code Sec. 7704.

from a notional contract; and other substantially similar income from ordinary and routine investments to the extent determined by the Commissioner.[124]

¶ 507 LLCS OWNED BY SPOUSES

.01 *Community Property Ownership*

An LLC that is owned by a husband and wife may elect to be classified either as a partnership or disregarded entity if:[125]

- The LLC is wholly owned by a husband and wife as community property under the laws of a state, a foreign country, or a U.S. possession.
- No person other than one or both of the spouses is an owner for tax purposes.
- The LLC is not classified as a corporation for federal tax purposes.

Normally, a husband and wife will want to treat the LLC as a partnership rather than a disregarded entity since there is a higher audit risk for tax returns with Schedule C items.

.02 *Qualified Joint Venture*

Spouses in non-community property states may also elect to treat an LLC as a disregarded entity or partnership if the LLC is a "qualified joint venture." An LLC is qualified joint venture if:.[126]

- the husband and the wife are the only members of the LLC;
- both spouses materially participate in the business;
- the business is a trade or business and not a mere joint ownership of property; and
- both spouses elect to treat the LLC as a qualified joint venture.

If the spouses do not make the election, the LLC is classified as a partnership. If the spouses make the election, the LLC is classified as a disregarded entity, and the spouses are not required to file a partnership return. Instead, all items of income, gain, loss, deduction and credit are divided between the spouses in accordance with their respective interests in the joint venture,[127] and are reported on Schedule C of Form 1040.

The IRS informally determined that an LLC owned jointly by a husband and wife may not make the election.[128]

---

[124] Code Sec. 7704(d); Reg. § 1.7704-3.

[125] Rev. Proc. 2002-69, 2002-45 IRB 831; CCA 200851102.

[126] Code Sec. 761(f)(2); CCA 201411035.

[127] IRC §§ 761(f)(1)(B), 761(f)(1)(C).

[128] IRS Publication 541, Partnerships, under the heading, "Qualified Joint Venture Election."

¶ 508 CLASSIFICATION ELECTION

.01 Generally

An LLC may file an election regarding its classification for federal tax purposes. However, LLCs normally do not need to file an election.[129] The default classification rules are designed to provide most LLCs with the classification that they would likely choose without requiring them to file an election.

Absent an election, an LLC with a single member is classified as a proprietorship or entity separate from its owner.[130] A domestic LLC with two or more members is classified as a partnership.[131] Partnership classification is usually the preferred classification.

An election should be filed in the following three cases:

1. The LLC wants initially to be classified differently than under the default rules.
2. The LLC wishes to change its previous classification.
3. There is doubt about the proper classification. The uncertainty is more likely to arise for foreign LLCs where the rules are more complex.[132]

.02 Manner of Election

An LLC must file an election on Form 8832, Election Classification. The election must specify the name, address, and taxpayer identification number of the LLC; the chosen classification; whether the election results in a change in classification; and whether the LLC is a domestic or foreign LLC.[133] An election will not be accepted unless all information on the form is completed.

The election must be signed by all members of the LLC or by any officer, manager, or member who is authorized to make the election. Any such authorized officer, manager, or member must represent under penalty of perjury that he is authorized to sign on behalf of the LLC.[134] The LLC may attach an unsigned copy of the form to its tax or information return for tax years beginning in 2003 in order to facilitate electronic filings.[135]

---

[129] Reg. § 301.7701-3(a).

[130] Reg. § 301.7701-3(b)(1)(ii).

[131] Reg. § 301.7701-3(a).

[132] For example, there may be uncertainty concerning the member's liability under the law of a foreign jurisdiction, which may affect the default classification. The preamble to the check-the-box regulations states that protective elections are not prohibited. In those cases, Form 8832 should state that the election is protective.

[133] Reg. § 301.7701-3(c)(1)(i).

[134] Reg. § 301.7701-3(c)(2).

[135] Reg. § 301.7701-3(c)(1)(ii).

.03 Effective Date of Election

The election is effective on the date specified on the election or on the date filed if no date is specified.[136] The effective date specified may not be more than 75 days prior to or 12 months after the date on which the election is filed. Thus, an election may be retroactive to a date up to 75 days before the date of the election. If an election is effective for any period before the filing date, each person who was an owner between the effective date and the filing date and who is not an owner at the time the election is filed must also sign the election.[137]

If an election specifies an effective date more than 75 days before the date on which it is filed, it will be effective 75 days before the filing date. If an election specifies an effective date more than 12 months after the date on which the election is filed, it will be effective 12 months after the filing date.[138]

No election may be effective for a period before January 1, 1997.

.04 Filing Requirements

There are two filing requirements for Form 8832. First, Form 8832 must be filed with the IRS Service Center in Philadelphia. Second, a copy of the form must be attached to the LLC's federal tax return for the year in which the election is made.[139] If the LLC is not required to file a return for that year, a copy of Form 8832 must be attached to the federal income tax or information return of each direct and indirect owner of the LLC for the tax year of the owner that includes the date on which the election was effective. An otherwise valid election will not be invalidated if the LLC or its owners fail to attach a copy of Form 8832 to the federal tax return as required. However, the nonfiling party may be subject to penalties.[140]

.05 Duration of Classification

If an LLC changes its classification, it may not elect to change its classification again during the 60-month period after the effective date of the election.[141] However, an LLC may change its classification during the 60-month period in the following cases:

- More than 50 percent of the ownership interests in the LLC as of the effective date of the subsequent election are owned by persons who did not own any interest in the LLC on the filing date or on the effective date of the LLC's prior

---

[136] Reg. § 301.7701-3(c)(1)(iii).
[137] Reg. § 301.7701-3(c)(2).
[138] Reg. § 301.7701-3(c)(1)(iii).
[139] Reg. § 301.7701-3(c)(1)(ii).
[140] *Id.*
[141] Reg. § 301.7701-3(c)(1)(iv).

election. The Commissioner must consent to the change in classification.[142] The 60-month limitation does not apply if an LLC sells its assets to another entity.[143] The transferee may make a new election at any time consistent with the regulations.

- The LLC makes no election on the date of organization and is therefore classified under the default rules. The 60-month limitation applies only to changes in elections.
- The LLC makes an election effective on the date of formation to be classified other than under the default rules. This is not considered a change in classification.[144]
- The classification of the LLC changes as a result of a change in the number of members. A change in the number of members does not result in a new entity for purposes of the 60-month limitation on elections.[145] However, a classification election that is made at the time that the classification of the LLC would automatically change because of a change in the number of members is treated as an election classification for purposes of the 60-month rule.

EXAMPLE 5-2

Member A forms an LLC in which she is the sole member. The LLC is classified as a disregarded entity under the default classification rules. However, Member A wants the LLC to be classified as a corporation. She makes an election to be classified as a corporation when the LLC is formed. Member A may make an election to change the classification at any time. She is not restricted in making an election classification change for 60 months because the initial election was effective on the date of formation. An initial election is not considered a change in classification even though it changes the classification that would otherwise apply under the default classification rules.[146]

EXAMPLE 5-3

Member A is the sole owner of an LLC that is classified as a disregarded entity. On January 1, 2000, Member B acquires a 50 percent interest in the LLC. Under the regulations, the LLC is automatically classified as a partnership when the number of members of an LLC that is classified as a disregarded entity is increased from one to two. However, the members

---

[142] Reg. § 301.7701-3(c)(1)(iv). Ltr. Ruls. 200906018, 200905022, 200535016, 200426012.

[143] TD 8697, Part C, Discussion of Comments Relating to the Elective Regime (Dec. 18, 1996).

[144] Reg. § 301.7701-3(c)(1)(iv).

[145] Reg. § 301.7701-3(f)(3).

[146] Reg. § 301.7701-3(c)(1)(iv).

want to be classified as a corporation rather than a partnership. They make an election on January 1, 2000, to be classified as a corporation. The election is a change in classification. Therefore, the LLC may not change its classification by election during the next 60 months.[147]

EXAMPLE 5-4

Member A and Member B form a foreign LLC on April 1, 2000. The LLC is treated as the corporation under the default classification rules. The LLC does not make an election to be classified as a partnership. Member A subsequently purchases all of the membership interests of Member B. Under the regulations, the LLC continues to be classified as a corporation. However, the LLC may elect at any time to be a disregarded entity. The 60-month limitation on new classification elections does not prevent the LLC for making an election because it has not made a prior election.[148]

EXAMPLE 5-5

Member A and Member B form an LLC on January 1, 1998. The LLC is a foreign LLC that is classified as a corporation under the default classification rules for foreign LLCs. On January 1, 1999, the LLC elects to be classified as a partnership for federal tax purposes. On June 1, 2000, Member A purchases the entire membership interest of Member B. After the purchase, the LLC can no longer be classified as a partnership since there is only one member. The LLC is automatically classified as a disregarded entity when Member A becomes the only member of the LLC. The LLC may not elect at that time to be classified as a corporation because it made a classification election within the prior 60 months. The LLC is not treated as a new entity for purposes of the 60-month rule as a result of a change in the number of members. As a result, the 60-month limitation period continues to apply to the LLC until January 1, 2004 (60 months after January 1, 1999, the effective date of the election by the LLC to be classified as a partnership). Thus, the LLC may elect to be classified as a corporation on or after January 1, 2004.[149]

---

[147] Reg. § 301.7701-3(f)(4), Example 1.
[148] Reg. § 301.7701-3(f)(4), Example 2.
[149] Reg. § 301.7701-3(f)(4), Example 3(ii).

.06 Change in Classification

Types of Elective Changes

The following four elective changes in classification are permitted under the final check-the-box regulations:[150]

1. *A partnership elects to be taxed as a corporation.* If a partnership elects to be taxed as a corporation, the partnership is deemed to contribute all of its assets and liabilities to the corporation in return for stock in the corporation. The partnership is then deemed to have liquidated by distributing the stock in the corporation to its partners.[151] The tax consequences of the conversion are discussed at ¶ 1106.
2. *A corporation elects to be taxed as a partnership.* If a corporation elects to be taxed as a partnership, the corporation is deemed to liquidate by distributing its assets and liabilities to its shareholders. The shareholders are then treated as having contributed all of the assets and liabilities to the partnership.[152]
3. *A corporation with a single member elects to be disregarded as an entity for tax purposes.* If a corporation with a single member elects to be disregarded as an entity separate from its owner, the corporation is deemed to liquidate by distributing its assets and liabilities to its sole shareholder.
4. *A disregarded entity elects to be taxed as a corporation.* If a disregarded LLC with a single member elects to be classified as a corporation, the owner of the LLC is deemed to have contributed all of the assets and liabilities of the disregarded LLC to the corporation in exchange for stock in the corporation.[153]

An entity that is designated as a corporation in its articles of incorporation cannot elect classification as a partnership or disregarded entity. The entity is automatically classified as a corporation under the per se rules.[154] An LLC that is classified as a corporation (either under the default rules for foreign LLCs or by an election for a domestic LLC) may elect to be classified as a partnership if it otherwise meets the requirements for classification as a partnership.

Timing of Elections

The election to change the tax classification occurs at the start of the day for which the election is effective. Any transactions that are deemed to occur because of a

---

[150] Reg. § 301.7701-3(g).

[151] The Treasury Department stated in the preamble to the proposed regulations that the regulations would not affect Rev. Rul. 84-111, 1984-2 CB 88, in which the IRS ruled that it would respect the particular form undertaken by the taxpayer when a partnership converts to a corporation.

[152] The Treasury Department pointed out that this characterization is consistent with Rev. Rul. 63-107, 1963-1 CB 71. *See* TD 8697, Part A, Summary of the Regulations (Dec. 18, 1996) regarding conversions from corporations to partnerships.

[153] Reg. § 301.7701-3(g); Ltr. Rul. 200843024 (First Reincorporation).

[154] *See* ¶ 503.01 *supra.*

¶ 508.06

change in classification are treated as occurring immediately before the close of the day before the effective date of the election.[155]

EXAMPLE 5-6

An LLC is classified as a corporation. It elects to be classified as a partnership on January 1, 2000. The LLC is treated as having distributed all of its assets and liabilities to its shareholders in liquidation of the LLC immediately before the close of the day on December 31, 1999. The shareholders are treated as having contributed all of the distributed assets and liabilities to a newly formed LLC that is classified as a partnership immediately before the close of the day on December 31, 1999. The members must report both transactions on December 31. Thus, the last day of the corporate LLC's tax year is December 31, and the first date of the partnership LLC's tax year is January 1.[156]

The owners of the LLC when the election is effective may be different from the owners of the LLC when the conversion transactions are deemed to occur. The election must be signed by every owner on the date of the deemed conversion transactions, even though the persons are not owners on the effective date of the change in classification.[157] The rules are designed to insure that the taxpayers who recognize the tax consequences of a conversion election approve the election. Therefore, purchasers who wish to make a classification election effective as of their first day of ownership must obtain the consent of the previous owners.

Changes in Number of Members

A change in the number of members of an LLC has the following effects on the classification of the LLC:[158]

- The change in the number of members of an LLC classified as a corporation does not affect the classification of the LLC as a corporation.
- If an LLC classified as a partnership subsequently has only one member, the LLC will be disregarded as an entity separate from its owner unless the LLC elects to be classified as a corporation.[159]
- If a single-member LLC that is disregarded as an entity separate from its owner subsequently has more than one member, the LLC will be classified as a partnership as of that date.

---

[155] Reg. § 301.7701-3(g)(3).
[156] Reg. § 301.7701-3(g)(3).
[157] Reg. § 301.7701-3(c)(2)(iii).
[158] Reg. § 301.7701-3(f).
[159] Ltr. Ruls. 200813011, 200518039.

The tax consequences of a change in the number of members are discussed in Chapter 11.[160]

Tax Consequences of Elective Change

The tax treatment of an elective change in classification is based on all the relevant provisions of the Internal Revenue Code and general principles of tax law, including the step transaction doctrine.[161] The tax consequences of an elective change are identical to the tax results that would have occurred if the taxpayer had actually taken the deemed steps specified by the regulations.

For example, an LLC that changes its classification from a partnership to a corporation is subject to Code Sec. 351, which deals with transfers to a corporation controlled by the transferor. Normally, there are no adverse tax consequences unless the liabilities exceed the basis of the assets at the time of conversion.[162] The tax consequences of the election to be classified as a corporation are discussed in Chapter 11.[163]

The change in classification of an LLC from a corporation to a partnership is a deemed liquidation resulting in gain or loss to the corporate LLC and the members.[164] Gain or loss is not generally recognized on the deemed transfer back to the partnership LLC.[165] There is no gain or loss recognized if a subsidiary corporation makes an elective classification change to a partnership or disregarded entity.[166]

Retroactive Change in Classification

After an LLC has filed an election to be classified in a certain manner, it may not make a retroactive election to be classified in a different manner. For example, an LLC that elects to be classified as a corporation may not make a retroactive election to be classified as a partnership. The IRS will not issue private letter rulings granting the LLC an extension of time to make a retroactive election.[167]

---

[160] *See* ¶¶ 1117, 1118 *infra.*

[161] Reg. § 301.7701-3(g)(2).

[162] Code Sec. 357(d).

[163] *See* ¶ 1106.06 *infra.*

[164] Code Secs. 336, 331.

[165] Code Sec. 721.

[166] Reg. § 301.7701-3(g)(2)(ii); REG-110659-00, IRS Proposed Regulations on Amending Check-the-Box Regulations for Subsidiary Corporations. The change in classification by the subsidiary corporation is treated as a tax-free liquidation under Code Sec. 332 even though the parent corporation does not adopt a formal plan of liquidation.

[167] INFO 2003-0199.

.07 Employer Identification Number

An LLC that does not have a taxpayer identification number at the time of an election must apply for one on Form SS-4.[168] An LLC whose classification changes as a result of an elective change or a change in the number of members retains the same employer identification number.[169] There are the following exceptions:

- An LLC classified as a partnership that becomes a single-member LLC must use its owner's Social Security number or taxpayer identifying number.[170]
- A single-member LLC disregarded as an entity separate from its owner that is later classified as a corporation or partnership must use the employer identification number of the LLC prior to the change in classification. However, if the LLC did not have a separate employer identification number apart from the Social Security number or taxpayer identification number of the single member, then it must obtain a new employer identification number.[171]

A single-member disregarded LLC must ordinarily use the Social Security number of the individual owner rather than a separate employer identification number for the LLC, unless the LLC hires employees.[172]

.08 Late Elections

An LLC that fails to file a timely classification election on Form 8832 may request the IRS to approve a late classification election by (i) by following the procedures set forth in Revenue Procedure 2009-41, or (ii) requesting a private letter ruling.

An LLC may request a late classification election under Revenue Procedure 2009-41 if:[173]

- The LLC files the request within three years and 75 days of the requested effective date for the initial classification or change in classification.
- The LLC failed to obtain the requested classification solely because it failed to file Form 8832 on a timely basis.
- The LLC either (i) did not file a federal tax return for its first tax year in which the election was intended because the due date had not passed for that year, or (ii) timely filed all federal tax returns and information returns consistent with the requested classification for the applicable tax years.
- There was reasonable cause for failure to make a timely election.

---

[168] Reg. § 301.7701-3(c)(1)(i).

[169] Reg. § 301.6109-1(h).

[170] Reg. § 301.6109-1(h)(2)(i).

[171] Reg. § 301.6109-1(h)(2)(ii).

[172] Instructions to Form SS-4. *See also* TD 8844, Preamble to IRS Final Regulations on Treatment of Changes in Elective Entity, 64 Fed. Reg. 66,580 (Nov. 29, 1999), which pointed out that Notice 99-6, 1999-3 IRB 1, provides guidance on the limited circumstances under which a disregarded entity may use its own employer identification number.

[173] Rev. Proc. 2009-41, 2009-2 CB 439, § 4.01.

- The LLC files the request on Form 8832. The LLC must (i) write "Filed Pursuant to Revenue Procedure 2009-41" across the top of Form 8832, (ii) attach a declaration to the form stating that the requirements under Section 4.01 of Revenue Procedure 2009-41 have been satisfied and (iii) attach a statement to the form explaining the reasons for failure to file on a timely basis. There are no user fees for filing the application.

An LLC may request a private letter ruling for late classification election if it does not qualify for relief under Revenue Procedure 2009-41. The procedures for requesting a private letter ruling are set forth in Revenue Procedure 2009-41[174] and Revenue Procedure 2017-1 (and its successor rulings).[175] The IRS will grant private letter rulings for late classifications as a partnership,[176] corporation,[177] or disregarded entity.[178]

¶ 509 TERMINATION OF LLC

An LLC that is classified as a partnership terminates if there is a sale or exchange of 50 percent or more of the total interests in the LLC's capital and profits within a 12-month period.[179] The LLC is treated as transferring its assets to a new LLC. The new entity is classified as a partnership, but may elect to change its classification thereafter.[180]

¶ 510 TRANSITION RULES

An LLC's claimed classification for periods before January 1, 1997 will be respected, notwithstanding provisions in the regulations prohibiting that classification, if all of the following requirements are met:[181]

1. The LLC is not one of the business entities described in regulations that are per se corporations;[182]
2. The LLC had a reasonable basis[183] for its claimed classification (for example, if the LLC claimed classification as a partnership, it should have a reasonable argument that it lacked at least two of the four corporate characteristics under the four-factor test of the prior regulations);

---

[174] Rev. Proc. 2009-41, 2009-2 CB 439, §§ 3.03, 4.04.

[175] Rev. Proc. 2017-1, 2017-1 IRB 1, § 5.03(5), (6).

[176] Ltr. Ruls. 201216024, 201216014, 201126024.

[177] Ltr. Ruls. 201414008, 201328021, 201222023, 201215001, 201213009, 201144012, 201138010, 201137003.

[178] Ltr. Ruls. 201744012, 201636012, 201608004, 201224022, 201224021, 201215003, 201215002, 201116011.

[179] Code Sec. 708(b)(1)(B). See ¶ 1203 *infra*.

[180] Reg. § 301.7701-3(e).

[181] Reg. § 301.7701-3(f)(2).

[182] Reg. § 301.7701-2(b)(1), (3), (4), (5), (6), (7).

[183] Reasonable basis is determined under Code Sec. 6662.

3. The LLC and all members of the LLC recognized the federal tax consequences of any change in the LLC's classification during the 60 months
   before January 1, 1997; and

4. The LLC's classification was not under audit on May 8, 1996, the date the
   regulations were proposed.

There are special transition rules for foreign LLCs.[184]

¶ 511 RULING REQUESTS

The IRS issued the check-the-box regulations on the classification of LLCs so that
ruling requests will generally not be necessary. However, it will still issue classification rulings under the check-the-box regulations.[185]

¶ 512 STATE TAX CLASSIFICATION

The following chart summarizes the state tax classification of limited liability
companies.[186]

Summary of State Tax Classification of LLCs

State	Follows Federal	Always Taxed as Corporation	Always Taxed as Partnership	Determination Based on State Law
Alabama	x			
Alaska				
Arizona	x			
Arkansas	x			
California	x			
Colorado	x			
Connecticut	x			
Delaware	x			
D.C.	x			
Florida	x			Taxed as a corporation prior to July 1, 1998

---

[184] *See* ¶ 505.02 *supra.*
[185] *See, e.g.,* Ltr. Rul. 200214016.
[186] *See* Chapter 23 *infra* for discussion of state tax classification.

State	Follows Federal	Always Taxed as Corporation	Always Taxed as Partnership	Determination Based on State Law
Georgia	x			
Hawaii	x			
Idaho	x			
Illinois	x			
Indiana	x			
Iowa	x			
Kansas	x			
Kentucky	x			An LLC was classified as a corporation and required to pay the corporate franchise tax for the 2005 and 2006 tax years.
Louisiana				LLC is classified for state income tax purposes in the same manner that the LLC is classified under federal law. LLC is classified for all other state tax purposes, including the franchise tax, as a limited partnership.
Maine	x			
Maryland	x			
Massachusetts	x			
Michigan	x			
Minnesota	x			
Mississippi	x			
Missouri	x			
Montana	x			
Nebraska	x			
Nevada				No state income tax

State	Follows Federal	Always Taxed as Corporation	Always Taxed as Partnership	Determination Based on State Law
New Hampshire				An LLC is taxed as a separate legal entity regardless of its classification for federal tax purposes. If the LLC has foreign members, then there is an apportionment formula. Members of the LLC are not taxed on their distributive shares of income.
New Jersey	x			
New Mexico	x			
New York	x			
North Carolina	x			
North Dakota	x			
Ohio	x			
Oklahoma	x			
Oregon	x			
Pennsylvania				x
Rhode Island	x			Taxed as a corporation for purposes of the annual $500 Business Corporation Tax
South Carolina	x			
South Dakota				No state income tax
Tennessee				LLC subject to franchise tax
Texas		x		LLC subject to margins tax
Utah	x			
Vermont	x			
Virginia	x			
Washington				LLC subject to Business and Occupations Tax

State	Follows Federal	Always Taxed as Corporation	Always Taxed as Partnership	Determination Based on State Law
West Virginia	x			LLC subject to franchise tax
Wisconsin	x			
Wyoming				No state income tax

¶ 513 LAW BEFORE 1997

Before 1997, LLCs received the favorable tax status of partnerships[187] and were not taxed as corporations unless they possessed more corporate characteristics than noncorporate characteristics.[188] A corporation had the following characteristics:[189]

- Associates
- Objective to carry on business and to divide the gains from the business
- Continuity of life
- Centralization of management
- Limited liability
- Free transferability of interests

The corporate characteristics of associates and an objective to carry on business and divide the gains were disregarded because they were also characteristics of a partnership.[190] The four other characteristics were common to corporations, but not to partnerships.

Therefore, the determination of whether an LLC was taxed as a corporation or a partnership depended on whether there was continuity of life, centralized management, limited liability, and free transferability of interests. The LLC was taxed as a partnership if it possessed only one or two of these characteristics. It was taxed as a corporation if it possessed three or four of these characteristics.[191]

Almost all LLCs had the corporate characteristic of limited liability, since LLC members were not personally liable for the debts and obligations of the LLC. Therefore, the LLC had to lack two of the remaining three corporate characteristics to be taxed as a partnership.

The Treasury Department proposed regulations regarding the classification of LLCs in 1980.[192] These proposed regulations were later withdrawn.[193] The Service issued a revenue procedure in 1995 regarding the classification of an LLC for ruling

---

[187] The main tax benefit is that income, gain, and losses pass through to the members. There is a single tax at the member level. There is no corporate or LLC tax.

[188] Reg. § 301.7701-2(a)(3).

[189] Id.

[190] Reg. § 301.7701-2(a)(2).

[191] Rev. Rul. 93-38, 1993-1 CB 233.

[192] Prop. Reg. § 301.7701-2, 45 Fed. Reg. 75,709 (Nov. 17, 1980).

[193] IRS News Release IR-82-145 (Dec. 16, 1982).

purposes.[194] The revenue procedure based its analysis on the traditional four-factor tests.

Before 1997, there were two main types of statutes relating to the classification of LLCs. These were commonly referred to as "bulletproof" and "flexible" statutes. In a state with a bulletproof statute, an LLC was always classified as a partnership for federal tax purposes regardless of the optional provisions chosen by the LLC in the articles of organization or operating agreement. In a state with a flexible statute, the organizers could draft the organizational documents so that the LLC was classified as a corporation for federal tax purposes.

Some states had flexible bulletproof or default bulletproof statutes. The laws in such states contained default provisions that could be varied by agreement among the members. The LLC was automatically classified as a partnership if the default provisions were chosen. The LLC was classified as a corporation if the default provisions were modified by the members.

The IRS issued the following revenue rulings and private letter rulings on the classification of LLCs under the old law before issuance of the check-the-box regulations.

IRS Rulings on LLC Classification

State	Rev. Rul.	Pvt. Ltr. Rul.	IRS Tax Classification
Alabama	94-5		Partnership or corporation depending on tax attributes
Alaska	None	None	
Arizona	93-93		Partnership or corporation depending on tax attributes
		9321047	Partnership
California	None	None	
Colorado	93-6		Partnership
Connecticut	94-79		Partnership or corporation depending on tax attributes
		9611041	Partnership
Delaware	93-38		Partnership or corporation depending on tax attributes

---

[194] Rev. Proc. 95-10, 1995-1 CB 501.

State	Rev. Rul.	Pvt. Ltr. Rul.	IRS Tax Classification
		9308027	Partnership
		9335032	
		9415005	
		9416025	
		9416026	
		9507004	
		9602012	
		9609029	
District of Columbia	None	None	
Florida	93-53		Partnership or corporation depending on tax attributes
		8937010	Partnership
		9010027	
		9029019	
		9030013	
		9119029	
		9443018	
Georgia	None	None	
Hawaii	None	None	
Idaho	None	None	
Illinois	93-49		Partnership or corporation depending on tax attributes
		9325039	Partnership
		9333032	
Indiana		9422034	Partnership
		9647028	
		9647029	
		9647030	
		9647031	
Iowa		9644059	Partnership
Kansas	94-30		Partnership or corporation depending on tax attributes

State	Rev. Rul.	Pvt. Ltr. Rul.	IRS Tax Classification
		9625013	Partnership
		9625014	
		9625015	
		9625016	
		9625017	
		9625018	
		9625023	
		9625024	
Kentucky	None	None	
Louisiana	94-5		Partnership or corporation depending on tax attributes
		9404021	Partnership
		9409014	
		9412030	
		9419016	
		9606006	
		9622007	
Maine	None	None	
Maryland		9501033	Partnership
Massachusetts	None	None	
Michigan	None	None	
Minnesota	None	None	
Mississippi	None	None	
Missouri	None	None	
Montana	None	None	
Nebraska	None	None	
Nevada	93-30		Partnership or corporation depending on tax attributes
		9227033	Partnership
New Hampshire	None	None	
New Jersey	94-51		Partnership or corporation depending on tax attributes
New Mexico	None	None	

State	Rev. Rul.	Pvt. Ltr. Rul.	IRS Tax Classification
New York	None	None	Partnership or corporation depending on tax attributes
North Carolina	None	None	
North Dakota		9425013	Partnership
Ohio	None	None	
Oklahoma	93-92		Partnership or corporation depending on tax attributes
Oregon	None	None	
Pennsylvania	None	None	
Rhode Island	93-81		Partnership or corporation depending on tax attributes
South Carolina	None	None	
South Dakota	95-9		Partnership
Tennessee	None	None	
Texas		9210019	Partnership
		9218078	
		9242025	
		9510037	
		9520036	
		9520046	

State	Rev. Rul.	Pvt. Ltr. Rul.	IRS Tax Classification
Utah	93-91		Partnership or corporation depending on tax attributes
		9210019	Partnership
		9218078	
		9219022	
		9226035	
		9242025	
		9313009	
		9320019	
		9320045	
		9321070	
		9325048	
		9443024	
Vermont	None	None	
Virginia	93-5		Partnership
Washington	None	None	
West Virginia	93-50	9308039	Partnership
Wisconsin	None	None	
Wyoming	88-76	8106082	Partnership
Jurisdiction Not Identified		8304138	Corporation
		8828022	
		9215009	
		39798	Partnership
		6707214880A	
		7817129	
		7935051	
		8003072	
		8004010	
		8012080	
		8104129	
		8304138	
		9001018	
		9010028	
		9029019	
		9035041	
		9038027	

State	Rev. Rul.	Pvt. Ltr. Rul.	IRS Tax Classification
		9052039	
		9119029	
		9147017	
		9210039	
		9216004	
Brazilian *Limitada*		7817129	Partnership
		8003072	
		8019112	
		8401001	
		9526029	
		7814012	Corporation
		7828063	
		7831021	
		7928063	
		7941054	
		8019112	
Chilean *Limitada*		7936050	Corporation
Columbian SRL		35294	Corporation
French SAS		9524022	Partnership
German GmbH	77-214	8221136	Partnership
		8309062	
		9010028	
		9341018	
	93-4	7908004	Corporation
		7937054	
		7952027	
		8114095	
		7747089	Proprietorship
		8436030	No opinion expressed
Greek LLC		7843006	Corporation
Hong Kong LLC		7935046	No opinion expressed
Italian SRL		7841008	Corporation
Mexican *Limitada*		7108110470A	Partnership
Portuguese LLC		7826023	Corporation

State	Rev. Rul. Pvt. Ltr. Rul.	IRS Tax Classification
Saudi Arabian LLC	7921079 8006068 8007029	Partnership
	7926034	Corporation
Spanish *Limitada*	8106082	Partnership
U.K. LLC	9002056 9152009 9306008	Partnership

As a result of the check-the-box regulations, the IRS determined that 37 revenue rulings and one revenue procedure issued prior to 1995, a majority of which dealt with the entity classification of LLCs, are now obsolete.[195]

---

[195] Rev. Rul. 98-37, 1998-32 IRB 5.

6

Contributions

¶ 601 CONTRIBUTIONS TO LLC CLASSIFIED AS PARTNERSHIP

.01 *Gain or Loss Recognition*

An LLC and its members do not recognize gain or loss when the members contribute property to the LLC in exchange for membership interests[1] unless any of the following apply:

- The LLC would be treated as an investment company if incorporated.[2] The investment company rules are discussed in Chapter 20.
- There is a net decrease in liabilities of a member exceeding that member's basis in the assets transferred.[3]
- There is a disguised sale.[4]
- The member contributes services to the LLC in exchange for a capital interest[5] or a profits interest that does not meet IRS guidelines.[6]
- A creditor receives a membership interest in exchange for unpaid rent, royalties or interest.[7]
- The member acts other than in his capacity as a partner in a transaction with the LLC.[8]
- The LLC acquires stock of a corporate member in exchange for property.[9]
- The member receives property other than a membership interest (boot) in exchange for the contribution.[10]
- U.S. persons transfer appreciated property to a domestic or foreign LLC. The built-in gain is immediately taxed if (i) a related foreign person is a member of

---

[1] Ltr. Ruls. 200125013, 200123035, 9713007, 9701032, 9409016, 9409014, 9404021, 9331010, 9321047, 9313009, 8106082 (*citing* Code Sec. 721(a)).

[2] Ltr. Ruls. 9751048, 9331010 (*citing* Code Sec. 721(b)).

[3] Ltr. Ruls. 9604014, 9313009 (*citing* Code Sec. 752 and Reg. § 1.752-1(f)). *See* ¶ 601.02 *infra*.

[4] Code Sec. 707(a)(2)(B). This is likely to result if a member contributes appreciated property to an LLC and within two years thereafter receives cash or other non-like-kind property from the LLC. *See* ¶ 605 *infra*.

[5] Reg. § 1.721-1(b)(1). *See* ¶ 604.01 *infra*.

[6] Rev. Proc. 93-27, 1993-1 CB 343. *See* ¶ 604.02 *infra*.

[7] Reg. § 1.721-1(d)(2).

[8] *See* ¶ 1403

[9] Notice 89-37, 1989-1 CB 679.

[10] The receipt of property other than a membership interest is treated as a distribution under Code Sec. 731, or as consideration received in a disguised sale under Code Sec. 707(a)(2)(B).

the LLC, and (ii) the U.S. transferor and one or more related persons own more than 80 percent of the membership interests in the LLC.[11]

The contribution of a long-term leasehold interest to an LLC in exchange for a membership interest is nontaxable.[12] No gain or loss is recognized if a member contributes only cash to the LLC in exchange for a membership interest.[13]

.02 Contribution of Property Subject to Liabilities

A member recognizes gain on the contribution of property to an LLC subject to liabilities in excess of basis if the net liability shift to the other members exceeds the contributing member's basis in the property.[14]

Code Sec. 752(a) treats an increase in a member's share of LLC liabilities as a contribution of money by the member to the LLC.[15] The deemed money contribution increases the member's basis in membership interest.[16] Code Sec. 752(b) treats a decrease in a member's share of LLC liabilities as a distribution of money to the member.[17] The deemed distribution decreases the member's basis in the membership interest.[18]

The member's share of liabilities before and after the contribution are netted against each other.[19] For example, a net decrease in the member's share of liabilities as a result of the contribution is treated as a money distribution and a reduction in the member's tax basis in the membership interest.[20] A money distribution in excess of basis results in taxable gain.[21] A shift in liabilities from a contributing member to a noncontributing member also increases the noncontributing member's tax basis in his or her membership interest.

There is no gain to the contributing member unless the net decrease in liabilities as a result of the contribution exceeds the contributing member's basis in membership units.[22]

---

[11] *See* ¶ 1903 *infra.*

[12] Ltr. Rul. 199915040.

[13] Ltr. Ruls. 201123035 (Ruling 2), 9713007 (*citing* Code Sec. 721).

[14] Reg. § 1.752-1(f), (g), Example 1; Ltr. Rul. 9751048.

[15] Reg. § 1.752-1(b).

[16] Code Sec. 722.

[17] Reg. § 1.752-1(b).

[18] Code Sec. 733(1).

[19] Reg. § 1.752-1(f).

[20] Reg. § 1.752-1(f).

[21] Code Sec. 731(a)(1).

[22] Reg. § 1.752-1(f), (g), Example 1.

EXAMPLE 6-1

Member B contributes a building to an LLC with an adjusted basis of $1 million. The property is subject to recourse debt of $10 million. The LLC agrees to pay the debt in full. However, the member remains personally liable for repayment to the bank if the LLC defaults. Member B receives an initial basis in the LLC of $1 million equal to the adjusted basis of property contributed to the LLC. Member B's individual liabilities decrease by $10 million. This is treated as a money distribution. At the same time, however, Member B's share of LLC liabilities increases by $10 million. The LLC must allocate the entire recourse liability to Member B for basis purposes since Member B is personally liable to the bank. This is treated as a money contribution. The net amount of the money contribution and distribution is zero. Therefore, Member B's initial basis in the LLC is equal to the $1 million basis for the contributed property.[23] There is no taxable gain as result of the contribution since there is no net money distribution to Member B in excess of his basis in the membership units.

The member may also recognize gain under the disguised sales rules on the contribution of encumbered property to an LLC if the member encumbers the property within two years prior to the date of contribution.[24]

.03 Member's Basis in Membership Interest

A member's basis in the membership interest is determined under one of the following methods:

- general method;
- asset method; or
- capital account and liabilities method.

These basis rules are discussed in detail in Chapters 9 and 15.[25]

.04 LLC Basis in Contributed Assets

The LLC's basis in the contributed assets equals the members' adjusted bases in the assets immediately prior to the contribution.[26] The LLC takes a transferred basis in the contributed assets. The liabilities assumed by the LLC have no effect on the basis as a result of the Tax Reform Act of 1984 which repealed the last part of Code Sec. 723, and provided the basis would only be increased by the amount of gain

---

[23] Reg. § 1.752-1(g), Example 1.

[24] *See* ¶ 605.01 *infra.*

[25] *See* ¶¶ 901, 902, 903, 1503 *infra.*

[26] Ltr. Ruls. 200125013, 9720008–013, 9719015, 9719019–029, 9331919, 9331010, 8106082 (*citing* Code Sec. 723).

recognized by the member under Code Sec. 721(b) on contribution of assets to the LLC.

There is potential double taxation if a member contributes appreciated property to the LLC. First, the member may recognize gain on the sale of the membership interest reflecting the difference between the fair market value of the contributed property and the member's carryover basis in the membership interest. Second, the LLC may recognize gain on the sale of the property. This gain flows through to the contributing member.[27]

An LLC may avoid double taxation resulting from the contribution of appreciated property if the LLC makes an election under Code Sec. 754 to step up the basis of its assets on the transfer of a membership interest[28] or on the distribution of property to a member.[29] However, an LLC may not step up the basis of its assets under Code Sec. 754 as a result of a contribution of property or money to the LLC.[30]

The LLC's basis in its assets is generally referred to as the "inside basis." The member's basis in the membership interest is generally referred to as the "outside basis." Upon formation of the LLC, the inside basis is generally equal to the outside basis, since the LLC receives a carryover basis for the assets and the member receives a basis in the membership interest equal to the cash and adjusted basis of assets contributed. The inside basis and outside basis may become different under a number of circumstances.[31]

An LLC does not receive any basis in contributed property that has no value on the date of contribution.[32]

An LLC must make a special basis adjustment if a member contributes property to an LLC with a built-in loss. The built-in loss rules are discussed at ¶ 806.

An LLC must adjust the inside basis of its assets when it distributes assets to a member, or when a member transfers a membership interest. These rules are summarized at ¶ 904.

.05 Holding Period

LLC's Holding Period in Assets

The LLC's holding period in the contributed assets includes the member's holding period in the assets prior to contribution.[33]

---

[27] *See* ¶ 805 *infra.*

[28] *See* ¶ 1508 *infra.*

[29] *See* ¶ 1006 *infra.*

[30] Reg. § 1.743-1(a).

[31] *See* ¶ 901.02 *infra.* The LLC and the members may eliminate the disparity between inside and outside basis in such cases by making an election to adjust the basis of LLC assets under Code Sec. 754.

[32] *Santa Monica Pictures, LLC v. Comm'r*, TC Memo 2005-104 (2005); FSA 200242004.

[33] Rev. Rul. 99-5, 1999-1 CB 434, *citing* Code Sec. 1223(2).

Member's Holding Period in Membership Interest

The holding period of a membership interest acquired in exchange for a contribution of capital assets or Section 1231 assets includes the holding period of such assets.[34]

The holding period of a membership interest acquired in exchange for cash, and property other than capital assets and Section 1231 assets, commences on the day after the contribution.[35] There is no tacking on the holding period in such cases.

A member will have a split or fragmented holding period if the member contributes a combination of assets.[36] The holding period for each fractional portion of the membership interest is determined by the relative fair market value of the assets associated with that fractional portion of the membership interest.[37]

There is also a split holding period if the member contributes to the LLC at different times. A member receives a new holding period on the date of each new contribution for a percentage of the membership interest based on the amount of the new contribution compared to the fair market value of the membership interest immediately after the contribution.[38] Capital contributions that increase the fair market value of a membership interest will cause the member to report some of the gain on a subsequent disposition of a membership interest within one year as short-term capital gain. The member may avoid the split-holding period by recharacterizing the capital contribution as a loan.

EXAMPLE 6-2

A contributes $5,000 of cash and a nondepreciable capital asset that A has held for two years to PRS LLC for a 50 percent interest in PRS. A's basis in the capital asset is $5,000, and the fair market value of the asset is $10,000. After the exchange, A's basis in A's interest in PRS is $10,000, and the fair market value of the interest is $15,000. A received one-third of the interest in PRS for a cash payment of $5,000 ($5,000/$15,000). Therefore, A's holding period in one-third of the interest received (attributable to the contribution of money to the LLC) begins on the day after the contribution. A received two-thirds of the interest in PRS in exchange for a capital asset ($10,000/$15,000). Accordingly, pursuant to Section 1223(1), A has a

---

[34] Code Secs. 723, 1223(2); Reg. §§1.723-1, 1.1223-3; Let. Rul. 9701032 (*citing* Rev. Rul. 84-52, 1984-1 CB 157).

[35] Reg. §§1.1223-1(a), 1.1223-3(f), Example (1).

[36] Reg. §§1.1223-3(a)(2), 1.1(h)-1(f), Example 5(iv).

[37] Reg. §1.1223-3(b)(1).

[38] Reg. §1.1223-3(b), (c), (f). The fair market value of each additional membership interest acquired at a different time is compared to the fair market value of the total membership interests determined after each additional acquisition of an additional membership interest to determine the percentage of the interest allocable to each such interest.

¶601.05

two-year holding period in two-thirds of the membership interest received in PRS.[39]

.06 Depreciation and Depreciation Recapture

The LLC is required to use the same method and period of depreciation for contributed property as used by the contributing member.[40] If the contributed property is personal use property, the LLC must determine annual depreciation deductions by using depreciation rules in effect on the date the property was converted to business use property.[41]

There is no depreciation recapture income when a member contributes Section 1245 or 1250 recapture property to an LLC unless the contributing member recognizes gain under Code Sec. 731(a)(1) as a result of the contribution.[42] The member's adjusted basis in the property and the potential for depreciation recapture carries over to the LLC.[43] The property is subject to depreciation recapture when the LLC sells or disposes of the property at a later date.[44] When the LLC sells the depreciated property, the ordinary income recapture amount will be allocated to the contributing member under Code Sec. 704(c). The member's share of depreciation recapture on sale of the property is equal to the lesser of (a) the member's share of total gain from the disposition of the property under the normal provisions of the operating agreement, or (b) the member's share of depreciation that was previously allocated to the member, including any depreciation allowed or allowable to the member before the property was contributed to the LLC. The LLC must allocate to the other members any depreciation recapture that cannot be allocated to a member because his share of gain from the disposition of the property is less than his share of depreciation recapture. This additional depreciation recapture is allocated among such other members in proportion to their relative shares of total gain from the disposition of the property.[45]

---

[39] Reg. § 1.1223-3(f), Example 1.

[40] Code Sec. 168(i)(7).

[41] Reg. § 1.168-2(j)(1).

[42] Code Secs. 1245(b)(3), 1250(d)(3); Reg. § § 1.1245-1(c)(1), (4), Examples (2)-(3), 1.1250-3(c)(1), (2)(vi).

[43] Code Sec. 723.

[44] Reg. § § 1.1245-1(c)(2), 1.1250-3(c).

[45] Reg. § 1.1245-1(e)(2)(i)-(iii). *See also* Reg. § 1.1245-1(e)(2)(iii), Example (3) regarding allocation of depreciation recapture on sale of property in which there was both pre-contribution and post-contribution depreciation.

.07 Investment Tax Credit Recapture

There is no recapture of investment tax credits on a contribution to an LLC of property for which an investment credit was taken (currently the rehabilitation credit, the energy credit, and the reforestation credit) if the following conditions are met:[46]

- the LLC retains the property as investment credit property in its trade or business; and
- the contributing member retains a substantial interest in the LLC.

.08 Accounts Receivable

A member is not taxed on the transfer of accounts receivable to an LLC.[47] The LLC will recognize taxable income when it collects the receivables. The taxable income is equal to the amount collected, less the basis for the receivables (which is zero in the case of a contributing member using the cash method of accounting). The LLC must allocate all of the taxable income to the contributing member to the extent that the value of the receivables on the date of contribution exceeds the member's basis in the receivables.[48] The value of the receivables is likely to be far less than their face value, especially if there is a long period of time between the billing and collection dates or if there are collection problems associated with the receivables.

The LLC receives a basis in the receivables equal to the contributing member's basis at the time of the contribution.

.09 Personal Use Property

A member's contribution of personal use property to an LLC is nontaxable. The LLC receives a basis in the property equal to the lower of the property's fair market value at the time of contribution or the contributing member's adjusted basis.[49]

.10 Patent Rights

The holder of a patent may transfer patent rights to an LLC that is classified as a partnership. Each contributing inventor is treated as a partner of the LLC for purposes of Code Sec. 1235. Thus, each partner retains his or her status as a "holder" under Code Sec. 1235. Each inventor's share of any gain recognized by the LLC on disposition of an interest in the patent qualifies under Code Sec. 1235 as long-term capital gain, provided the other requirements of Code Sec. 1235 are met.[50]

---

[46] Code Sec. 50(a)(4) (flush paragraph).

[47] Rev. Rul. 80-198, 1980-2 CB 133.

[48] Code Sec. 704(c).

[49] *Au v. Comm'r*, 40 TC 264 (1964), *aff'd per curiam*, 330 F.2d 1008 (9th Cir. 1964).

[50] Ltr. Ruls. 200506019, 200506009, 200506008, 200135015, *citing* Reg. § 1.1235-2(d)(2).

.11 Installment Obligations

The contribution of an installment obligation to an LLC is not a disposition resulting in taxable gain to the member.[51] However, the contribution is taxable if the LLC issues a membership interest in satisfaction of installment obligation to the contributing member.[52]

The LLC must continue to report the gross profits on the installment method as payments are received.[53] The LLC must allocate to the contributing member the deferred gain and any accrued interest as of the date of the contribution.[54] The LLC may allocate to all of the members in accordance with the operating agreement the interest income earned on the note while held by the LLC. Gain will be accelerated if the installment note is distributed to a member other than the contributing member within seven years, or if the contributing member receives property other than the contributed note within seven years the contribution.[55]

.12 Contribution of Debt for Membership Interest

The contribution by a creditor of recourse or nonrecourse debt owed by the LLC in exchange for a membership interest in the LLC is not a taxable event.[56] However, this nonrecognition rule does not apply to the transfer of the membership interest to a creditor in satisfaction of the LLC's debt for unpaid rent, royalties or interest on debt.[57]

.13 Federal, State, and Local Subsidies and Grants

Federal, state and local subsidies, grants and other payments by nonowners to an LLC are taxable. There is no exclusion from income under Code Sec. 118 or common law doctrines.[58]

---

[51] Reg. §§ 1.453-9(c)(2), 1.453B-1(c); Prop. Reg. §§ 1.453B-1(c)(1)(i)(B), 1.721-1(a).

[52] Prop. Reg. § 1.453B-1(c)(1)(ii)(B).

[53] Reg. §§ 1.721-1(a), 1.453-9(c)(2).

[54] Code Sec. 704(c).

[55] Code Secs. 704(c), 737.

[56] Prop. Reg. § 1.721-1(d)(1).

[57] Prop. Reg. § 1.721-1(d)(2).

[58] IRS Position Paper, LMSB-4-0908-047 (2008).

¶ 602 CONTRIBUTIONS TO LLC CLASSIFIED AS CORPORATION

.01 Member's Recognition of Gain or Loss

Members do not recognize gain or loss upon the contribution of property to the LLC, whether or not additional shares are issued.[59] The contributing members must have 80 percent control of the LLC and otherwise comply with the requirements of Code Sec. 351. The same rule applies to foreign LLCs, subject to certain requirements and restrictions.[60] The shareholders do not recognize gain or loss when the corporation assumes liabilities if the liabilities do not exceed the basis of assets contributed.[61] Gain is recognized if the shareholders receive cash or other nonstock property in the exchange.[62]

.02 Member's Basis in Membership Interest

A member's basis in his membership interest is the same as the basis of the assets transferred to the LLC in exchange, decreased by the amount of liabilities assumed by the LLC[63] and the liabilities to which the transferred assets are subject,[64] and increased by the amount of any gain recognized if the shareholder receives cash or other nonstock property in the exchange.[65] If an LLC shareholder already owns stock and makes an additional capital contribution, the basis in the stock is increased by the basis of property contributed to the capital of the LLC.[66]

.03 Member's Holding Period

A member's holding period in the stock includes the period during which the shareholders held the assets prior to the transfer, provided the assets were held as capital assets or Code Sec. 1231 assets on the date of the exchange.[67]

---

[59] Ltr. Ruls. 8029031, 8011038, 7937054, 7821084 (*citing* Code Sec. 351(a)). If no shares are issued, the capital contribution to the LLC is treated as a contribution in constructive exchange for additional shares under Code Sec. 351.

[60] Ltr. Ruls. 8029031, 8023029, 7935046, 7843099, 7833112 (*citing* Code Sec. 367(a)); Ltr. Ruls. 8029031, 8011038 (*citing* Code Sec. 367(c)(2) and Rev. Rul. 77-449, 1977-2 CB 110).

[61] Ltr. Rul. 7937054 (*citing* Code Sec. 357).

[62] Ltr. Rul. 7935046 (*citing* Code Sec. 351(b)).

[63] Ltr. Ruls. 7937054, 7843099 (*citing* Code Sec. 358(a), (d)).

[64] Ltr. Rul. 7833112 (*citing* Code Sec. 358(a)(1)).

[65] Ltr. Rul. 7935046 (*citing* Code Sec. 358(a)(1)).

[66] Ltr. Ruls. 8029031, 80111038 (*citing* Code Sec. 358(a)).

[67] Ltr. Ruls. 7937054, 7935046 (*citing* Code Sec. 1223(1)).

.04 *LLC Gain Recognition*

The LLC does not recognize gain upon the contribution to capital in exchange for the issuance of stock, or if no stock is issued.[68]

.05 *LLC Basis in Contributed Property*

The LLC's basis in the contributed property is the same basis that the LLC shareholders had in the property immediately prior to the capital contribution.[69]

.06 *LLC Holding Period for Contributed Property*

The LLC's holding period for the property received includes the period during which it was held by the shareholders.[70]

¶ 603 CONTRIBUTION TO LLC CLASSIFIED AS DISREGARDED ENTITY

There are no federal tax consequences on the transfer of property by a taxpayer to an LLC that is classified as a single-member disregarded LLC.[71] The LLC must continue to use the same accounting methods used by the taxpayer prior to the transfer.[72]

¶ 604 CONTRIBUTION OF SERVICES

A member may recognize compensation income upon the contribution of services to an LLC in exchange for an LLC interest. Code Sec. 721 provides that a member does not recognize gain or loss upon the contribution of property to an LLC that is classified as a partnership. However, this nonrecognition provision does not apply, since a contribution of services is not a contribution of "property."

The tax consequences are different depending on whether a member receives a capital interest or a profits interest in exchange for the contribution of services.

.01 *Contribution of Services for a Capital Interest*

A member recognizes compensation income upon receipt of an interest in the capital of an LLC in exchange for services if (i) the other members in the LLC give up

---

[68] Ltr. Ruls. 8029031, 8011038, 7937054, 7843099 (*citing* Code Sec. 1032(a)).

[69] Ltr. Ruls. 8029031, 8011038, 7937054, 7843099 (*citing* Code Sec. 362(a)).

[70] Ltr. Rul. 7937054 (*citing* Code Sec. 1223(2)).

[71] Ltr. Rul. 200423016.

[72] Ltr. Rul. 200423016.

any part of their interest in capital,[73] and (ii) the person receiving the membership interest has a right to a share of proceeds if the LLC's assets are sold at fair market value and then distributed in complete liquidation of the LLC.[74] The service member's basis in the membership interest is the amount includable in the member's income.[75]

The date of recognition is the date that the property is substantially vested. A membership interest is substantially vested when it is transferable or is no longer subject to a substantial risk of forfeiture.[76] The capital interest is subject to a substantial risk of forfeiture and is not taxable when issued if the member is required to perform substantial additional services in order to receive the capital interest.[77]

The amount of income recognized is the fair market value of the capital interest.[78] There are several methods used to determine the value of a capital interest, including the following:

- determining the fair market value by the prices of comparable interests in the LLC sold near the time of the transfer;[79]
- determining the value of the interest received by reference to the value of the services performed;[80]
- determining the amount the contributing member would receive upon liquidation.[81]

A member who receives a capital interest that is subject to a substantial risk of forfeiture may make an election under Code Sec. 83(b) of the Internal Revenue Code to be taxed immediately. The compensation income recognized is equal to the value of the membership interest received, without reduction in value for the risk of forfeiture or other restrictions on transfer except those that never lapse. The election must be made within 30 days after receipt of the interest. It may be made only if the membership interest has a readily ascertainable fair market value.

A service member who receives a capital interest is not a partner or member of the LLC for tax purposes until the membership interest vests,[82] or the member makes an election under Section 83(b).[83]

---

[73] Reg. § 1.721-1(b)(1); *Mark IV Pictures, Inc. v. Comm'r*, 969 F.2d 669 (8th Cir. 1992); *ZuHone v. Comm'r*, 55 TCM 533 (1988); *Larson v. Comm'r*, 55 TCM 1637 (1988); *Hensel Phelps Constr. Co.*, 74 TC 939 (1980), *aff'd*, 703 F.2d 485 (10th Cir. 1983); Schneider and O'Conner, "LLC Capital Shifts: Avoiding Problems When Applying Corporate Principles," 92 J. Tax'n 1, 13 (Jan. 2000).

[74] *Crescent Holdings LLC v. Comm'r*, 141 TC 477 (2013).

[75] Cost basis under Code Sec. 1012.

[76] Reg. § 1.83-1(a); *Hensel Phelps Construction Co.*, 74 TC 939, 954 n.6 (1980), *aff'd*, 703 F.2d 485 (10th Cir. 1983); *Schulman v. Comm'r*, 93 TC 623 (1989).

[77] Code Sec. 83(c).

[78] Reg. § 1.721-1(b)(1).

[79] *Larson, Thomas E.*, TC Memo 1988-387.

[80] *Hensel Phelps Constr. Co. v. Comm'r*, 74 TC 939 (1980), *aff'd*, 51 AFTR2d 83-1006, 703 F.2d 485, 83-1 USTC (10th Cir. 1983).

[81] McKee, Nelson, Whitmire, Federal Taxation of Partnerships and Partners (1998).

[82] Reg. § 1.83-1(a)(1).

[83] *See Crescent Holdings LLC v. Comm'r*, 141 TC 477 (2013).

.02 Contribution of Services for a Profits Interest

Vested Interest at Date of Issuance

Some courts have determined that a contribution of services for a vested profits interest is taxable.[84] Other courts have reached the opposite conclusion.[85] The IRS no longer treats the contribution of services for a vested profits interest as a taxable event unless one of the following is true:[86]

- The profits interest relates to a substantially certain and predictable stream of income from LLC assets (e.g., the LLC owns only triple net lease property);
- The member disposes of the profits interest within two years of receipt;
- The profits interest is a limited partnership interest in a publicly traded LLC;
- The services are performed in the capacity of an employee rather than as a partner;[87]
- The party performing services for an LLC waives the fees for services, and another related party receives an interest in future profits the value of which approximates the amount of the waived fees;[88] or
- The LLC issues the profits interest in conjunction with the member foregoing payment of an amount that is substantially fixed for the performance of services. This would include the issuance of a profits interest in exchange for a guaranteed payment or payment in a non-partner capacity.[89]

Nonvested Interest at Date of Issuance

The issuance of a nonvested profits interest in an LLC is nontaxable, both at the date of grant and at the date of vesting, if:[90]

- The LLC and the service provider treat the service provider as the owner of the membership interest from the date of grant.
- The service provider takes into account the distributive share of membership income, gain, loss, deduction, and credit associated with the membership interest for the entire period during which the member has the interest.

---

[84] *Diamond v. Comm'r*, 492 F.2d 286 (7th Cir. 1972).

[85] *Campbell v. Comm'r*, 943 F.2d 815 (8th Cir. 1991); *Kobor v. Comm'r*, 88-2 USTC ¶9477 (C.D. Cal. 1987); *Hale v. Comm'r*, 24 TCM 1497 (1965). *See also St. John v. United States*, 84-1 USTC ¶9158, 53 AFTR2d 84-718 (C.D. Ill. 1983); S. Frost, "Receipt of Capital and Profits Interests Continues to Have Uncertain Tax Consequences," 75 *J. Tax'n* 38 (July 1991).

[86] Rev. Proc. 93-27, 1993-2 CB 343.

[87] CCA 201348012.

[88] REG-11545214, Preamble to Proposed Regulations on Disguised Payments for Services.

[89] REG-11545214, Preamble to Proposed Regulations on Disguised Payments for Services.

[90] Rev. Proc. 2001-43, 2001-34 IRB 191, Sec. 4.

- On grant of the interest and when the interest becomes substantially vested, neither the LLC nor the member deducts any amount as wages, compensation, or otherwise for the fair market value of the interest.
- All other conditions of Revenue Procedure 93-27 discussed above are satisfied.

A member who receives an interest in profits in exchange for services is not required to make an election under Code Sec. 83(b), even if the profits interest is substantially nonvested.[91] However, it may still be advisable to make a Code Sec. 83(b) election on the date of grant, showing the value of the profit interest as zero consistent with Revenue Procedure 93-27. If there is a disposition of the interest within two years after the date of grant, the taxpayer would presumably recognize ordinary income rather than capital gain. However, if the member made a Code Sec. 83(b) election on the date of grant, then the gain on disposition would be capital gain.[92]

Carried Interest

Under general partnership tax laws, long-term capital gain recognized by an LLC on the sale or exchange of its assets is treated as long-term capital gains in the hands of the member to whom such gain is allocated, regardless of the member's holding period for the membership interest. The gain is taxed at the lower long-term capital gains tax rate.

Beginning in 2018, there is a three-year holding period for certain net long-term capital gain allocated to a profits interest member.[93] The LLC must hold the assets for at least three years in order for the member's share of such gain to be taxed at the lower long-term capital gains tax rate. If the LLC does not hold the assets for at least three years prior to sale, then the entire gain allocated to the profits interest member is treated as short-term capital gain taxed at up to the ordinary income tax rate.

The three-year holding period requirement applies to an "applicable partnership interest." An applicable partnership interest is an interest in a partnership transferred to a partner in connection with the performance of substantial services in an applicable trade or business.[94] An applicable trade or business is any activity conducted on a regular or continuous and substantial basis that consists of (i) raising or returning capital, and (ii) investing in, disposing of or developing specified assets,[95] including securities, commodities, real estate held for rental or investment and certain other enumerated assets.[96]

---

[91] Rev. Proc. 2001-43, 2001-34 IRB 191, Sec. 3.

[92] *See* Blake Rubin and Shane Orr, "Recent Developments in Partnership Taxation from Congress, Treasury, and Courts," *BNA Daily Tax Report* No. 82, p. J-1, pt. II.B.4 (Apr. 29, 2002) for a detailed discussion of the advantages and disadvantages of making a Code Sec. 83(b) election.

[93] Code Sec. § 1061.

[94] Code Sec. § 1061(c)(1).

[95] Code Sec. § 1061(c)(2).

[96] Code Sec. § 1061(c)(3).

An applicable partnership interest does not include a membership interest held by a corporation. It also does not include a capital membership interest that provides the member with the right to share in LLC capital commensurate with the amount of capital contributed or the value of the interest included in income under Code Sec. 83 on receipt or vesting of the interest.[97]

If a profits interest in an LLC is not an applicable partnership interest, then its tax treatment will continue to be governed by guidance previously issued by the IRS.[98]

Deferred Compensation

Until the IRS issues additional guidance, the issuance of a profits interest or an option to acquire a profits interest in exchange for services is not a deferred compensation plan subject to the requirements of Code Sec. 409A.[99]

Disguised Payment for Services

Certain LLC arrangements are treated as disguised payment for services rather than a distributive share of income when the member's performance of services is related to the LLC's distribution of income. The result is that the income received from the disguised payment for services is treated as compensation taxed as ordinary income rather than a distributive share of LLC income taxed as capital gain in certain cases. The IRS was mainly concerned with fee waivers by managers of private equity funds. However, proposed regulations on disguised payment of services apply much more broadly than to private equity fund managers. Disguised payments for services are discussed at ¶ 1410, *infra*.

.03 Income Distributions Prior to Vesting

Distributed Amounts

A service member who receives actual distributions of income prior to vesting of a membership interest receives additional compensation income equal to the income received. The rule applies whether the member receives a capital interest or a profits interest in the LLC.[100]

---

[97] Code Sec. § 1061(c)(4).

[98] *See* Rev. Proc. 93-27, 1993-2 CB 343; Rev. Proc. 2001-43, 2001-34 IRB 191; Prop. Reg. REG-105346-03.

[99] IRS Notice 2005-1, Q&A-7, 2005-2 IRB 274.

[100] *Crescent Holdings LLC v. Comm'r*, 141 TC 477 (2013), *citing* Reg. § 1.83-1(a)(1).

Undistributed Amounts

A service member is not taxed on undistributed income prior to vesting or the date of a Section 83(b) election if the member receives a capital interest in the LLC. Instead, the income attributable to the nonvested membership interest must be reallocated on a pro rata basis to the other members of the LLC.[101]

It is unclear if undistributed income attributable to a membership interest is includable in the service member's gross income prior to vesting if the interest is a profits interest.[102]

.04 2005 Proposed Regulations

In 2005, the IRS issued proposed regulations governing the issuance of a membership interest for services. The regulations apply Section 83 to all membership interests, including a profits interest, a capital interest, or an option to acquire a membership interest.[103] The IRS does not believe that there is a substantial basis for distinguishing among membership interests for purposes of Section 83.[104]

However, the regulations provide that a member will not be taxed on receipt of a profits interest in exchange for services if the LLC makes a valuation safe-harbor election. Under the valuation safe-harbor rules, a membership interest is valued at its cash liquidation value. Thus, a membership interest with a zero initial capital account is valued at zero, resulting in no compensation income to the member receiving an LLC interest in exchange for services.

The IRS issued these regulations so that a member could not receive a large initial capital account as part of a membership interest issued in exchange for services, and then claim that the capital account had almost no value as a result of minority, marketability, and liquidity discounts. The IRS will agree not to tax a member on receipt of the profits interest only if the member agrees to pay tax on the full amount of any capital account received in the exchange (less any amount paid by the member for the membership interest).

If the LLC makes a valuation safe-harbor election and an allocation safe-harbor election, then the rules are as follows:

- *Vested membership interest.* A member is not taxed on receipt of a profits interest in exchange for services. A member is taxed on receipt of a capital interest in exchange for services. The capital interest is valued at its liquidation value, without any valuation discounts.

- *Nonvested membership interest, no Section 83(b) election.* A service provider is not treated as a member in the LLC with respect to a nonvested membership

---

[101] *Crescent Holdings LLC v. Comm'r*, 141 TC 477 (2013).

[102] *See* discussion in *Crescent Holdings LLC v. Comm'r*, 141 TC 477 (2013).

[103] Prop. Reg. § 1.721-1(b)(1) (second sentence).

[104] REG-105346-03, IRS Partial Withdrawal of Proposed Rules, Proposed Regulations, and Hearing Notice on Partnership Equity Transfers for Services (May 24, 2005).

interest prior to the date of vesting.[105] The LLC may not allocate items of LLC income, gain, loss, deduction, or credit to the member prior to vesting.[106] Distributions to the member prior to vesting are compensation income. Amounts allocated to the member's capital account on the date of vesting, less amounts paid by the member for the membership interest, are compensation income to the member at that time.[107]

- *Nonvested membership interests, Section 83(b) election.* A member may make an election under Section 83(b) to recognize income on the date of issuance of a nonvested membership interest, rather than on the date of vesting. In such case, the member is not taxed on receipt of a profits interest in exchange for services. The member is taxed on the receipt of a capital interest, less the amount paid for the membership interest. The LLC may treat the member as a partner in the LLC on the date of issuance, and allocate items of income, gain, loss, deduction, and credit to the member commencing on that date. Under the allocation safe-harbor election, the LLC must allocate offsetting items of income, gain, loss, and deduction to the member if the member subsequently forfeits the membership interest. The member may not take a loss deduction on forfeiture that would reverse the gain recognized by member when the Section 83(b) election was made.

¶605 CONTRIBUTIONS TREATED AS DISGUISED SALES

.01 Purpose of Rules

Under traditional partnership tax rules, taxpayers could sell appreciated property without recognizing taxable gain by making a disguised sale through an LLC. The three principal types of disguised sales are (a) a contribution of money, property, or services to an LLC followed by a related distribution of money or property to the contributing member within two years after the contribution, (b) a contribution of appreciated property to an LLC by one member followed by a distribution of that property to another member within seven years after the contribution, and (c) a contribution of appreciated property to an LLC followed by a distribution of other property to the contributing member within seven years after the contribution.

Congress enacted Code Secs. 707(a)(2)(B), 704(c)(1)(B), and 737 to prevent these disguised sales. The rules are sometimes referred to as the disguised sales rules or the mixing bowl rules. The rules cover many different types of disguised sales, and are sometimes overlapping. The most common disguised sales covered by the rules are as follows:

---

[105] Prop. Reg. § 1.761-1(b).
[106] IRS Notice 2005-43, Section 6(4), Example 4, 2005-24 IRB 1221.
[107] IRS Notice 2005-43, Section 6(4), Example 4, 2005-24 IRB 1221.

- Code Sec. 707(a)(2)(B)—A member contributes appreciated property to an LLC, and the LLC distributes money to the member within two years thereafter (other than distributions of normal operating profits).
- Code Sec. 737—A member contributes appreciated property to an LLC, and the LLC distributes non-cash property to the contributing member within seven years thereafter.
- Code Sec. 704(c)(1)(B)—A member contributes appreciated property to an LLC and the LLC distributes that property to another member within seven years thereafter.

Any taxes owed under the disguised sales rules as a result of an IRS audit are payable by the LLC, rather than the member, under the IRS audit guidelines effective in 2018.[108]

.02 Distributions That Are Related to a Contribution—Code Sec. 707(a)(2)(B)

Disguised Sale of Property

The first type of disguised sale is a contribution of money, property, or services to an LLC followed (or preceded) by a related distribution of money or property to the contributing member within two years after the contribution.[109] The most common disguised sale is a contribution of appreciated property to an LLC followed by a distribution of money from the LLC to the contributing member.[110] Under traditional partnership tax laws, the distribution to the member was treated as a nontaxable return of capital rather than a taxable payment of the purchase price.

EXAMPLE 6-3

Mary owned a condominium in Aspen. Her basis in the condominium is $400,000. The fair market value is $800,000. Mary needs to sell a one-half interest in the condominium to pay for her retirement expenses. A management company is willing to pay her $400,000 cash for a one-half interest in the condominium. However, the sale would result in taxable gain of $200,000 ($400,000 cash payment, less $200,000 basis in the one-half interest). To avoid taxation, the parties form an LLC. Mary contributes her property to the LLC. The management company contributes $400,000 in cash. The LLC distributes the $400,000 cash to Mary one week later. The $400,000 cash payment reduces Mary's basis in her membership interest from $400,000 to zero. Under traditional partnership tax rules,

---

[108] Prop. Reg. § 301.6221(a)-1(b)(1)(i)(H). *See* ¶ 2802.
[109] Code Sec. 707(a)(2)(A), (B); Reg. § 1.707-3.
[110] CCA 200513022.

there is no taxable gain, since distributions are taxable only if the cash distribution exceeds the member's basis in the membership interest.

Code Sec. 707(a)(2)(B) now provides that a contribution of money or property to an LLC followed by a distribution of money or property from the LLC to the member is a disguised sale of property, and not a contribution, if the following tests are met:[111]

- The distribution would not have been made but for the contribution, and
- If the transfers are not made simultaneously, the member's right to the distribution does not depend on the success of LLC's operations.

All facts and circumstances are considered in determining if there is a disguised sale. The regulations list ten facts and circumstances in determining whether there is a disguised sale of property.

If the contribution and distribution occur within two years of each other, the transfers are presumed to be a disguised sale unless the facts clearly indicate that the transfers are not a sale. If the contribution and distribution occur more than two years apart, the transfers are presumed not to be a disguised sale unless the facts clearly indicate that the transfers are a sale.[112]

If there is a disguised sale, then the member will be treated as selling to the LLC a portion of each contributed property. The portion deemed sold will be the same proportion as the amount of money received bears to the fair market value of the contributed property. The member then recognizes gain in the amount by which the money received exceeds the member's basis in the portion of the property sold.[113]

EXAMPLE 6-4

A transfers property to AB LLC in exchange for an interest in the LLC. At the time of the transfer, the property has a fair market value of $4,000,000 and an adjusted tax basis of $1,200,000. Immediately after the transfer, the LLC transfers $3,000,000 in cash to A. Assume that the transfer is treated as a sale of property to the LLC (disguised sale). Because the amount of cash A receives does not equal the fair market value of the property, A is considered as having sold a portion of the property with a value of $3,000,000 to the LLC in exchange for cash. Accordingly, A must recognize $2,100,000 of gain, which is the $3,000,000 amount realized less $900,000 adjusted basis ($1,200,000 multiplied by $3,000,000/4,000,000). Assuming A receives no other consideration for the sale of the property, A is considered to have contributed to the LLC, in A's capacity as a partner, $1,000,000 of the fair market value of the property with an adjusted basis of $300,000 ($1,200,000 less $900,000).[114]

---

[111] Reg. § 1.707-3(b)(1); CCA 200513022; F.S.A. 199936011.

[112] Reg. § 1.707-3(c).

[113] Reg. §§ 1.707-3(a)(2), 1.707-3(f), Example (1).

[114] Reg. § 1.707-3(f), Example 1.

Disguised Sale of Membership Interest

Code Sec. 707(a)(2)(B) also applies to a disguised sale of a membership interest between members.[115] The transfer by a purchasing member of money, property or other consideration to an LLC, and a related transfer of consideration by the LLC to the selling member, are merged and treated as a single disguised sale of the selling member's membership interest to the purchasing member.

In 2004, the IRS issued proposed regulations on disguised sales of membership interests. The IRS withdrew the proposed regulations in 2009 because of technical difficulties. Under the proposed regulations, the transfer of money, property or other consideration by a purchasing member to an LLC, and a related transfer of consideration by the LLC to the selling member, were merged and treated as a single disguised sale of the selling member's membership interest to the purchasing member. The transfers were related if, based on all the facts and circumstances,[116] the LLC would not have made the transfer to the selling member "but for" the transfer of consideration to the LLC by the purchasing member.[117] There was a presumption that transfers within two years of each other were a disguised sale of a membership interest, and that transfers more than two years apart were not a disguised sale of a membership interest.[118]

Cost Basis of Assets to LLC

The LLC obtains a cost basis in the assets that it is deemed to have purchased in the disguised sale.[119]

EXAMPLE 6-5

Two persons form an LLC. Member A contributes cash in exchange for a 50 percent interest. Member B contributes assets in exchange for a 50 percent interest. Since the assets have a slightly greater value than the cash contribution, the LLC makes an adjusting payment of cash to Member B in order to equalize the members' contribution values. The LLC has a cost basis in the assets that it is deemed to have purchased with the payment to Member B.[120]

---

[115] The rules applicable to a disguised sale of membership interest are addressed in Prop. Reg. § 1.707-7.

[116] Prop. Reg. § 1.707-7(b)(2).

[117] Prop. Reg. § 1.707-7(b)(1).

[118] Prop. Reg. § 1.707-7(c), (d).

[119] FSA 199936011.

[120] *Id.*

Exceptions

The regulations set forth several distributions that may be made to a contributing member within two years after the date of the contribution without triggering the disguised sales rules. The basic rule is that a property distribution that is a return *on* capital does not cause a disguised sale, whereas a property distribution that is a return *of* capital (i.e., results in a withdrawal of the member's capital) does result in a disguised sale. Distributions that are treated as bona fide distributions (returns on capital) and that do not result in a disguised sale include the following:[121]

- Guaranteed payments for use of a member's capital, that are reasonable in amount (defined below) and determined without regard to the LLC's income.[122]
- A preferred return or preferential distribution of cash flow with respect to capital contributed by a member, which is reasonable in amount.[123]
- Reimbursement of LLC organization and syndication costs incurred by the contributing member during the two years preceding the contribution of property to the LLC.[124]
- Operating cash flow distributions to the member.[125]
- Cash reimbursements to the member for preformation capital expenditures. The capital expenditures must have been incurred during the two years before the contribution to the LLC. The reimbursements must be for capital costs incurred with respect to property contributed by the member to the LLC. The capital costs may not exceed 20 percent of the fair market value of the contributed property. The 20 percent rule does not apply unless the fair market value of the contributed property is at least 120 percent of the member's adjusted basis in the contributed property at the time of contribution. The 20 percent test and the 120 percent test apply on a property-by-

---

[121] Reg. § 1.707-4 (with respect to a disguised sale of property); Prop. Reg. § 1.707-7(e) (with respect to a disguised sale of a membership interest).

[122] Reg. § 1.707-4(a)(1). *See, e.g.*, Ltr. Rul. 199915010, in which an LLC contributed cash to a partnership to be used for renovations and the other partner contributed property and received a guaranteed payment. The IRS determined that there was no disguised sale, since the guaranteed payment was reasonable in amount.

[123] Reg. § 1.707-4(a)(2).

[124] Reg. § 1.707-4(d).

[125] Reg. § 1.707-4(b).

property basis, subject to limited exceptions.[126] The member must not have incurred debt for the capital expenditures in anticipation of the transfer.[127]

- Loan repayments from the LLC to the member and guaranteed payments for services.[128]

- Distributions of money in liquidation of a member's interest.[129]

- Transfers resulting from a termination of a partnership by a discontinuance of the LLC's business or sales and exchanges of more than 50 percent of the membership interests in the LLC.[130]

Reasonable Requirement for Preferred Returns and Guaranteed Payments

A guaranteed payment or preferred return is considered reasonable, and not a disguised sale, if:

- the transfer is made to the member pursuant to a written provision in an operating agreement that provides for payment for the use of capital in a reasonable amount;

- the payment is made for the use of capital after the date on which that provision is added to the operating agreement;[131] or

- the sum of any preferred return and any guaranteed payment for capital that is payable for that year does not exceed the amount determined by multiplying the safe-harbor interest rate for that year by (i) the member's unreturned capital at the beginning of the year, or (ii) the member's weighted average capital balance for the year.[132] The safe-harbor interest rate is 150 percent of the highest "applicable federal rate" in effect at the time that the right to payment is first established pursuant to a binding written agreement.[133]

---

[126] Reg. §§ 1.707-4(d)(1)(ii)(B), 1.707-4(d)(6), Example; Prop. Reg. § 1.707-4(d)(1)(ii)(B). Aggregation is permitted to the extent that (i) the total fair market value of the aggregated property (of which no single property's fair market value exceeds one percent of the total fair market value of such aggregated property) is not greater than the lesser of 10 percent of the total fair market value of all property, excluding money and marketable securities, transferred by the member to the LLC, or $1,000,000; (ii) the member uses a reasonable aggregation method that is consistently applied; and (iii) the aggregation of property is not part of a plan to avoid the disguised sales rules. Reg. § 1.707-4(d)(1)(ii)(B)(1).

[127] Reg. § 1.704-4(d); Ltr. Ruls. 9914006, 9829027.

[128] *See* T.D. 8439 (Sept. 15, 1992).

[129] Prop. Reg. § 1.707-7(e).

[130] Reg. § 1.707-3(a)(4).

[131] Reg. § 1.707-4(a)(3)(ii).

[132] Reg. § 1.707-4(a)(3)(ii).

[133] Reg. § 1.707-4(a)(2).

Loans Prior to Contribution

A member may not avoid the disguised sales rules by obtaining a loan against the property immediately before contributing it to the LLC. The contribution of the property to the LLC results in debt relief to the member. The net debt relief is treated as a money distribution. The money distribution is a disguised sale payment if the liability is a nonqualified liability. The money distribution is not a disguised sale payment if the liability is a qualified liability.[134]

LLC Assumption of Qualified Liabilities

An LLC's assumption of a qualified liability does not cause the contribution of property to an LLC to be treated as a disguised sale (assuming that the contribution is not otherwise considered a disguised sale).[135]

A "qualified liability" is one that was not incurred in anticipation of the contribution to the LLC. A qualified liability includes the following:[136]

- Liabilities incurred by the member more than two years prior to the earlier of the contribution or agreement to contribute the property. There is a conclusive presumption that these liabilities are qualified liabilities. The liabilities are considered "old and cold." The transferred liability must encumber the property.
- Liabilities incurred by the contributing member within two years prior to the earlier of the contribution or the agreement to contribute, but not incurred in anticipation of the contribution of the property to the LLC.[137] The transferred liability must encumber the property. A liability incurred by a member within two years of the transfer and assumed by the LLC (or taken subject to) is presumed to be incurred in anticipation of the transfer unless the facts and circumstances clearly established that the liability was not transferred in anticipation of the transfer.[138] The member must disclose such liabilities to the IRS.[139]
- Liabilities incurred by the contributing member within two years of the transfer if the proceeds were used to acquire or improve the contributed property (capital expenditures).
- Liabilities incurred in the ordinary course of the trade or business in which property transferred to the LLC was used or held if all the material assets related to that trade or business are contributed to the LLC. This rule covers trade payables and other liabilities whose purpose is not to cash out the contributing member's interest in the LLC.

---

[134] Reg. § 1.707-5(a)(5).
[135] Reg. § 1.707-5(a)(5)(i).
[136] Reg. § 1.707-5(a)(6)(i).
[137] Reg. § 1.707-5(a)(6)(i)(B).
[138] Reg. § 1.707-5(a)(7).
[139] Prop. Reg. § 1.707-5(a)(7)(ii).

LLC Assumption of Nonqualified Liabilities

The LLC's assumption or taking property subject to a nonqualified liability may result in a disguised sale. The LLC is treated as transferring consideration to the contributing member to the extent that the liability assumed by the LLC exceeds the member's share of the liability after the assumption.[140] The portion of the nonqualified liability shifted from the contributing member to the other members constitutes payment for a disguised sale.

A nonqualified liability is a liability other than a qualified liability. It is a liability that is incurred in anticipation of transferring the property to the LLC and that is used as a device by the member to cash out his or her investment in the contributed property. There is a presumption that a liability incurred less than two years before the contribution of property to an LLC is a nonqualified liability.[141]

EXAMPLE 6-6

A & B form AB LLC. A transfers $500,000 in cash to AB and B transfers an office building. At the time of the transfer, the building has a basis of $400,000 and a fair market value of $1,000,000. The building is encumbered by a $500,000 non-recourse liability that is not a qualified liability. In accordance with the operating agreement, B's share of the liability is 50 percent or $250,000. The LLC's taking of the building subject to the liability is treated as a transfer of $250,000 to B ($500,000 less B's $250,000 share of the liability). B is treated as having sold 25 percent of the fair market value of the office building ($250,000/$1 million) to the LLC in exchange for the assumption of the debt. This results in $150,000 gain to B [$250,000 less the $100,000 basis allocated to the sale portion (25% × $400,000)].[142]

For purposes of the disguised sales rules, all liabilities (including recourse and nonrecourse liabilities) are treated as nonrecourse liabilities, and each member's share of recourse liabilities is based on the member's share of LLC profits.[143] The IRS plans to modify this rule in future regulations.[144] .

---

[140] Reg. § 1.707-5(a)(1).

[141] Reg. § 1.707-5(a)(7)(i).

[142] Reg. § 1.707-5(f), Example 1.

[143] Temp. Reg. § 1.707-5T(a)(2).

[144] BNA Daily Tax Rept. No. 30, p. 10 (Feb. 13, 2018).

Services

Prior to the enactment of Code Sec. 707(a)(2)(A), an LLC could convert certain nondeductible payments for services to a contractor into deductible payments by making the contractor a member. For example, an LLC must capitalize payments for services on a construction project. It may not deduct such payments to the extent they constitute capital expenditures. In order to obtain the deduction, the LLC would make the contractor a member and give that member a distributive share of income rather than a nondeductible payment for services. The distributive share of income would be similar to a deduction for the LLC since it would reduce the taxable income of the other members. The contractor would not care how the payments were characterized since a distributive share of income and a payment for services are both taxable as ordinary income.

Prior to the enactment of Code Sec. 707(a)(2)(A), members of an LLC, such as hedge fund managers, could convert service income taxed as ordinary income into capital gains by waiving fees for services and instead receiving a distributive share of capital gain income.

Code Sec. 707(a)(2)(A) now allows the IRS to recharacterize the transaction as taxable compensation and a nondeductible capital expense if the performance of services, and the payments to the member or contractor for those services, are related to each other.[145] The purpose of this rule was to prevent partnerships from receiving a deduction for capital expenditures and to prevent partners from converting ordinary income into capital gain.[146]

The disguised sales rules do not apply to every situation in which a member obtains a membership interest by contributing services or property to the LLC. Instead, Code Sec. 707(a)(2)(A) applies to allocations that are related to the contribution of property or services that have the economic effect of payment for the property or services.[147]

Purchases of Property from Outsiders

Code Sec. 707(a)(2)(B) prevents an LLC from obtaining a deduction for payments to a nonmember for property purchased by the LLC. Prior to the enactment of Code Sec. 707(a)(2)(B), a person who was not a member would sell land or other property to an LLC. The LLC would not receive a deduction for the payment of the sales price, since it would be a capital expenditure. Certain capital expenditures could be amortized. However, if raw land was purchased, the LLC would not be entitled to

---

[145] *See, e.g.,* IRS Market Segment Specialization Program, Partnerships, Audit Technique Guide, under the heading, "Capital Item Shown as a Deduction or Distribution," in which the IRS determined that a partnership could not deduct brokerage fees to an outside broker by making the broker a partner, and treating the commissions as a distributive share of income. *See also* ¶1403.04 *infra* regarding a discussion of when payments to a member for services are treated as guaranteed payments or payments to a person other than in his or her capacity as a member.

[146] S. Rep. No. 169, 98th Cong., Vol. 1 p. I-225 (1984).

[147] S. Rep. No. 169, 98th Cong., Vol. 1 p. I-226 (1984).

depreciation or amortization. To obtain a deduction, the LLC would make the selling party a temporary member, and allocate income to that member up to the sales price. The distributive share of income would be similar to a deduction for the LLC, since it would reduce the taxable income of the other members. The selling party would receive ordinary income rather than capital gain. However, the selling party would not care if the selling party were a dealer in property, in which case all proceeds from the sale of the property would be taxable as ordinary income.

Code Sec. 707(a)(2)(B) now allows the IRS to recharacterize the transaction as a sale if the sale of property, and the payment to the member, are related to each other.

Distribution of Loan Refinancing Proceeds (Leveraged Transactions)

Code Sec. 707(a)(2)(B) places limits on the distribution of loan proceeds to a member who contributes appreciated property to an LLC. This is referred to as an *Otey* transaction. Prior to enactment of Code Sec. 707(a)(2)(B), a member would contribute appreciated property to an LLC. The LLC would borrow money secured by the property. The borrowings would increase the member's basis in the LLC. The LLC would then distribute the loans proceeds to the contributing member in reduction of the member's basis. The LLC would receive a carryover basis in the property. All gain on a subsequent sale would be allocated to the contributing member under Code Sec. 704(c). However, the contributing member could defer taxation until the date of a subsequent sale of the property by receiving a distribution of basis from the LLC rather than receiving consideration from the sale of property.

Code Sec. 707(a)(2)(B) now allows the IRS to recharacterize such transactions as a sale if the contribution of property, and the distribution of loan proceeds to the member, are related to each other.

A contributing member may receive a distribution of refinancing loan proceeds (or other loan proceeds secured by the contributed real property) without gain recognition if the money distribution does not exceed the member's allocable share of the LLC liabilities, including any liability amount guaranteed by the member. The LLC must make the distribution within 90 days after the LLC obtains the loan.[148] The LLC must distribute actual loan proceeds, rather than other LLC funds.[149]

Beginning in 2017, IRS regulations limit the amount of loan refinancing proceeds that the contributing member may receive in a leveraged transaction. For purposes of the disguised sales rules, all liabilities (including recourse and nonrecourse liabilities) are treated as nonrecourse liabilities, and each member's share of recourse liabilities is based on the member's share of LLC profits.[150] A member does not receive additional tax basis or an additional deferral of gain for disguised sales purposes by guaranteeing LLC debt.

---

[148] Reg. § 1.707-5(b)(1), (c).

[149] Reg. § 1.707-5(f), Example 10. The distribution amount must be traced under Reg. § 1.163-8T to the separately segregated loan refinancing proceeds.

[150] Temp. Reg. § 1.707-5T(a)(2).

EXAMPLE 6-7

(*Rules prior to 2017*) A member contributes property to an LLC in which the member owns a 25 percent interest. The property has a basis of $200,000 and fair market value of $1 million. The LLC receives a carryover basis of $200,000. The LLC borrows $800,000 on nonrecourse basis in the following year, which the member personally guarantees. This increases the member's basis to $1 million. The LLC distributes the $800,000 refinancing proceeds to the member. Because the member personally guaranteed the LLC debt, the debt is recourse to the member, and the member's allocable share of that debt is $800,000. The distribution decreases the member's basis to $200,000. There is no taxable gain to the member because of the debt-financing distribution exception to the disguised sales rules for tax years prior to 2017. The distribution of the debt refinancing proceeds does not exceed the member's allocable share of the LLC liabilities encumbering the property. The member has effectively liquidated his interest in the property without taxable gain.

EXAMPLE 6-8

(*Current Rules*) In the same example, the recourse liability is treated as nonrecourse for disguised sales purposes beginning in 2017. Thus, the member's share of LLC liabilities is $200,000 (25% × $800,000). The member's basis increases from $200,000 to $400,000. The distribution is treated as a disguised sale since it is made within two years after the contribution of the property to the LLC. The distribution results in taxable gain of $400,000 ($800,000 distribution minus $400,000 tax basis).

.03 Distributions of Contributed Property to Another Member—Code Sec. 704(c)(1)(B)

Prior to 1989, it was relatively easy for a person to avoid gain on the sale of appreciated property by forming a partnership with the buyer. The seller would contribute the appreciated property to the partnership. The buyer would contribute the cash purchase price to the partnership. The partnership would then make a liquidating distribution of the appreciated property to the buyer. The seller would not recognize gain since the seller would remain a partner in the partnership and not receive a distribution within two years after the contribution. The buyer would receive a step-up in basis for the appreciated property equal to the cash purchase price contributed to the partnership. The partnership would continue as an investment partnership with one or more minority partners.

Section 704(c)(1)(B) now provides that if a member contributes built-in gain or loss property to an LLC, and if the LLC distributes that property to another member within seven years from the date of contribution, the contributing member recognizes gain or loss equal to the lesser of (a) the built-in gain or loss inherent in the property at the time of contribution, or (b) the gain or loss that would have been allocated to the contributing member if the LLC had sold the property to the distributing member for its fair market value.[151] If the property was contributed prior to June 9, 1997, the recognition period is five years.

The fair market value of the distributed property is the price at which the property would change hands between a willing buyer and a willing seller at the time of distribution, neither being under any compulsion to buy or sell and both having reasonable knowledge of the relevant facts. The fair market value assigned by an LLC to the distributed property is regarded as correct, provided that the value reflects an arm's-length negotiation and the members have sufficiently adverse interests.[152]

The contributing member's basis in the membership interest is increased by the gain and decreased by the loss recognized by the member.[153] The LLC must also increase or decrease the inside basis of the property by the gain or loss. The basis adjustment is made immediately prior to the distribution to the non-contributing member.[154] Other members are not affected by the deemed sale. Any increase or decrease in basis is therefore taken into account in determining the distributee member's adjusted tax basis in the distributed property under Code Sec. 732.[155]

EXAMPLE 6-9

Biotech Corporation, Giant Pharmaceuticals Inc. and Venture Capital Inc. form an LLC. Biotech contributes a patent with a basis of $2 million and fair market value $10 million. Giant Pharmaceuticals and Venture Capital Inc. each contribute $10 million cash. The LLC then distributes the patent to Giant Pharmaceuticals 15 days later in complete liquidation of its interest. Biotech has in substance sold its patent for $10 million cash. The disguised sales rules under IRC Section 707 do not apply in this case because Biotech did not receive a distribution. However, Biotech realizes a gain of $8 million under Section 704(c)(1)(B) because the LLC distributed built-in gain property within seven years after the date of contribution to a member other than the contributing member. Biotech's capital account increases by the $8 million gain. The LLC must increase its basis in the patent by that amount. Thus, Giant Pharmaceutical's basis in the distributed patent would be $10 million under Section 732 rather than $2 million. Section 704(c)(1)(B) thus prevents the income shifting of built-in gain from Biotech to Giant Pharmaceuticals, and also prevents the defer-

---

[151] Code Sec. 704(c)(1)(B)(i), (ii); Reg. § 1.704-4(a)(1).

[152] Reg. § 1.704-4(a)(3).

[153] Reg. § 1.704-4(e)(1).

[154] Reg. § 1.704-4(e)(2).

[155] Reg. § 1.704-4(e)(2).

ral of gain. If Section 704(c)(1)(B) were not in effect, the LLC could use the patent indefinitely, and the gain might never be taxed.[156]

The gain or loss recognized by the contributing member has the same character as the gain or loss that would have resulted if the distributed property has been sold by the LLC to the distributee member at the time of the distribution.[157] Therefore, any gain or loss is ordinary to the contributing member if (i) the distributing member holds more than a 50 percent interest in the LLC, and (ii) the property is not a capital asset in the hands of the distributing member.[158]

EXAMPLE 6-10

Steve and Diane form an equal LLC. Diane contributes $200 cash. Steve contributes Beach Lot and Desert Lot. Both lots have a tax basis of $40 and a fair market value of $100. The LLC uses the cash to subdivide the property. After three years, the Beach Lot is worth $150. The LLC then distributes Beach Lot to Diana. Steve as the contributing member must recognize gain equal to the lesser of:

(a) $60, which is the property's built-in gain at the time of contribution; and

(b) $85, which is the amount that Steve as the contributing member would recognize if the LLC had sold the property at fair market value (built-in gain of $60 plus one-half of the $50 gain that accrued in the hands of the LLC after the date of contribution).

Thus, Steve recognizes $60 of gain on the distribution. The gain increases his outside basis by $60. It also increases the basis of Beach Lot immediately prior to its distribution. Thus, Diane's basis in Beach Lot is $100.[159]

No gain or loss is recognized if the property is distributed to the contributing member.[160] The rules requiring recognition of gain or loss on distributions of contributed property do not apply to deemed distributions resulting from partnership terminations.[161]

---

[156] IRS Market Segment Specialization Program, Partnerships, Audit Technique Guide, Chapter 4, Example 4-10.

[157] Reg. § 1.704-4(b)(1).

[158] Reg. § 1.704-4(b)(2); Code Sec. 707(b)(2)(A).

[159] IRS Market Segment Specialization Program, Partnerships, Audit Technique Guide, Chapter 4, Example 4-11.

[160] Reg. § 1.704-4(c)(2).

[161] Reg. § 1.704-4(c)(3).

When a member sells a membership interest, the transferee member inherits the Section 704(c) taint, and is treated as the contributing member.[162] Code Sec. 704(c)(1)(B) does not apply if:

- The LLC distributes the contributed property back to the contributing member or the member's successor in interest.[163]
- The distribution of the contributed property to another member occurs more than seven years after the date of its contribution.
- There is a distribution of like-kind property under Code Sec. 1031 to the contributing member not later than the earlier of the 180th day after the date of distribution of the contributed property to another member or the due date for the contributing member's tax return for the year in which the distribution was made.[164]
- The LLC distributes non-contributed property to the contributing member.

.04 Distributions of Other Property to the Contributing Member—Code Sec. 737

General

The third type of disguised sale is when a member contributes appreciated property to an LLC, and the LLC distributes non-cash property[165] to the contributing member.

Prior to 1992, a member could circumvent the disguised sales rules by contributing appreciated property to an LLC, waiting two years, and then receiving a distribution of other property from the LLC. The LLC could purchase the replacement property selected by the member, and distribute that property to the member on a tax-free basis. There was no gain under Section 707(a)(2)(B) for distributions more than two years after the date of contribution. Section 731(a) did not apply either since there was no distribution of money in excess of the member's basis in the LLC.

Section 737 now provides that a member who contributes appreciated property to an LLC recognizes the precontribution gain if the LLC distributes property other than money to the member with a value exceeding the member's basis in the membership interest. The distribution must occur within seven years after the member contributes property to the LLC. Section 737 applies whether or not the member's interest in the LLC is reduced as a result of the distribution.

---

[162] Reg. § 1.704-4(d)(2).

[163] Code Sec. 704(c)(1)(B); Reg. §§ 1.704-4(c)(2)(i), 1.704-4(c)(6).

[164] Code Sec. 704(c)(2).

[165] Other property does not include properties that the member previously contributed to the LLC. This property is not taken into account in determining the amount of the excess distribution or the member's net precontribution gain. Other property also does not include unrealized receivables or substantially appreciated inventory items if the distribution is treated as a sale or exchange. *See* IRS Publication 541, Partnerships, under the heading "Net Precontribution Gain."

Gain Recognized

A member recognizes gain, but not loss, if the LLC distributes property other than money to the member within seven years after the member contributes appreciated property. Section 737 assumes that the LLC sold any appreciated property that was contributed during the previous seven years.

A cash distribution that is made at the same time as a Section 737 property distribution is taxed under Code Sec. 731 to the extent the cash distribution exceeds the member's basis in the membership interest. Gain recognized under Section 737 is in addition to gain recognized under Section 731.[166] The member must first compute gain under Section 731.[167]

The gain recognized under Section 737 is the lesser of:[168]

- The amount by which the fair market value of the property received in the distribution exceeds the member's basis in the membership interest immediately prior to the distribution, reduced (but not below zero) by any money received in the distribution,[169] or
- The member's net precontribution gain.[170] This is the net gain that the member would recognize if all of the property contributed by the member within seven years of the distribution, and held by the LLC immediately before the distribution, were distributed to another member other than a member who owned more than 50 percent of the LLC.[171] In the case of depreciable or amortizable property, the LLC must reduce the disparity between the property's book value and tax basis under Code Sec. 704(c) by allocating more depreciation to the noncontributing members.[172] Thus, the amount of net precontribution gain declines over time as more depreciation is shifted away from the contributing member.[173]

EXAMPLE 6-11

John contributes land to an LLC with a basis of $50,000 and a fair market value of $100,000. He contributes a building with a basis of $80,000 and a fair market value of $120,000. Five years later, his tax basis in the member-

---

[166] Code Sec. 737(a)(2) (last sentence).

[167] IRS Market Segment Specialization Program, Partnerships, Audit Technique Guide, Chapter 4, Examples 4-14, 4-19.

[168] Reg. § 1.737-1(a)(2).

[169] Reg. § 1.737-1(b).

[170] Reg. § 1.737-1(c).

[171] IRS Publication 541, Partnerships, under the heading "Net Precontribution Gain." The special rules applicable to the computation of gain and loss on sales between LLC and a more than 50 percent member, discussed at ¶ 1403.03 *infra*, are ignored in determining the amount of net precontribution gain.

[172] See ¶ 805 *infra*.

[173] IRS Audit Technique Guide—Partnerships, Chapter 4, under the heading, "Amount of Gain."

ship interest is reduced to $30,000 as a result of losses. The LLC distributes to John at that time cash of $40,000 and a warehouse valued at $300,000.

John must first compute taxable gain under Section 731. This is $10,000 (the $40,000 cash distribution in excess of John's $30,000 tax basis in the membership interest). John's tax basis is reduced by $10,000 to $30,000.

John's precontribution gain is $90,000 ($50,000 from the land contribution and $40,000 from the building contribution). The value of the distributed warehouse exceeded his outside basis by $270,000 ($300,000 fair market value less $30,000 tax basis). Thus, John's Section 737 gain is $90,000 (the lesser of the precontribution gain or the value of the distribution in excess of basis). John's total gain is $100,000 ($10,000 Section 731 gain and $90,000 Section 737 gain).[174]

Character of Gain

The character of the gain recognized depends on the character of net precontribution gain. Precontribution gains and losses are first netted according to their character. The character of a net negative amount is disregarded.[175]

EXAMPLE 6-12

Judy, a real estate developer, contributes Parcel A, Parcel B, and Pacific Inc. common stock to an investment LLC. Parcel A has a tax basis of $10,000 and a fair market value of $20,000. Parcel B has a tax basis of $10,000 and a fair market value of $5,000. The common stock has a tax basis of $50,000 and a fair market value of $5,000.

The real estate parcels are inventory in Judy's hands prior to contribution. Parcel A has a built-in gain of $10,000, and Parcel B has a built-in loss of $5,000. Therefore, Judy has $5,000 of net ordinary precontribution gain. The $45,000 of built-in loss from the common stock is disregarded since it is a net negative amount. Therefore, the character of any distribution to Judy to which Section 737 applies is ordinary income.[176]

---

[174] IRS Market Segment Specialization Program, Partnerships, Audit Technique Guide, Chapter 4, Example 4-15.

[175] Reg. § 1.737-1(d).

[176] IRS Market Segment Specialization Program, Partnerships, Audit Technique Guide, Chapter 4, Examples 4-14, 4-19.

Basis Adjustment

A member's adjusted basis in his or her membership interest is increased by the amount of gain recognized under Section 737. The basis increase is treated as occurring immediately prior to the distribution of property.[177] The basis increase is not taken into account in determining the gain recognized under Section 731 on the same transaction.[178] It is, however, taken into account in determining the basis of the property received. The basis of the distributed property is determined under the normal rules.[179]

The LLC must increase the basis of eligible property[180] by the gain recognized by the member under Section 737.[181] The basis increase is allocated among the eligible properties in the order in which they were contributed to the LLC. Starting with the first contributed property, basis is allocated in an amount equal to the difference between the property's fair market value and adjusted basis at the time of distribution.

A member's adjusted basis in his membership interest is increased by the amount of gain recognized under Code Sec. 737. The basis increase is treated as occurring immediately prior to the distribution of property.[182]

The LLC may increase the basis of the contributed appreciated property by gain that the member recognizes under Code Sec. 737.[183]

.05 Overlap of Disguised Sales Rules

Overlap of Sections 707(a)(2)(B) and 737

Section 707(a)(2)(B) provides that there is a disguised sale if there is a contribution of money, property or services to an LLC followed (or preceded) by a related distribution of money or property to the contributing member within two years after the contribution. Section 737 provides that a member who contributes appreciated property recognizes gain if the LLC distributes other property to the contributing member within seven years after the contribution.

Section 707(a)(2)(B) is similar in purpose to Section 737. However, there is no overlap between the two sections. Once the IRS determines that a disguised sale has taken place under Section 707(a)(2)(B), gain is recognized under that section, and Section 737 does not apply. The reason is that any disguised sale under Section 707(a)(2)(B) is deemed to have taken place at the time of a member's initial convey-

---

[177] Code Sec. 737(c)(1).

[178] Reg. § 1.737-1(b)(3).

[179] *See* Code Sec. 732(a), 732(b).

[180] Eligible property is defined in Reg. § 1.737-3(c)(2). It includes a property that entered into the calculation of the member's net precontribution gain.

[181] Code Sec. 737(c)(2).

[182] Code Sec. 737(c)(1).

[183] Code Sec. 737(c)(2).

ance of property to an LLC.[184] The contributing member is treated as receiving a right to a payment of cash or property from the LLC in exchange for the sale of property. Any related distribution of cash or property to the member within two years before or after the disguised sale is treated as a payment obligation rather than a distribution. Section 737 cannot apply since the LLC is not making a "distribution" of property to the member.

There are other differences between the two sections. The major differences include the following:

- Section 737 applies if the LLC distributes property other than money to the contributing member.[185] Section 707(a)(2)(B) applies if the LLC distributes property or money to the contributing member.

- Section 737 applies if the LLC makes a distribution within seven years after the date of a contribution. Section 707(a)(2)(B) applies if the LLC makes a distribution within two years after the date of a contribution.

- Section 737 applies if the LLC makes a distribution to the member in his or her capacity as a member.[186] Section 707(a)(2)(B) applies if the LLC makes a distribution to a member other than in his or her capacity as a member.[187] The contribution and related distribution of property under Section 707(a)(2)(B) are treated as a sale or exchange with a person other than in his capacity as a member.

- The IRS is not required to show that the distribution is related to a contribution under Section 737. The IRS must show that a contribution of money, property or services to an LLC is related to a distribution of money or property to the contributing member under Section 707(a)(2)(B).

- A member may recognize gain, but not loss, under Section 737. A member may recognize gain or loss under Section 707(a)(2)(B).

Overlap of Sections 704(c)(1)(B) and 737

Section 737 is the "mirror image" of Section 704(c)(1)(B). Section 704(c)(1)(B) provides that a member who contributes appreciated property recognizes gain if the LLC distributes that property to another member within seven years after the date of contribution. Section 737 provides that a member who contributes appreciated property recognizes gain if the LLC distributes other property to the contributing member within seven years after the contribution.

The two sections will overlap if the LLC distributes precontribution gain property to the contributing member, and if such property was originally contributed to the LLC by another member. The contributing member who receives a distribution will recognize gain under Section 737, and the other member who contributes

---

[184] Reg. § 1.707-3(a)(2).

[185] Code Sec. 737(a)(1); Reg. § 1.737-1(a)(1).

[186] Reg. § 1.737-1(a)(2).

[187] Code Sec. 707(a)(2)(B) (last sentence).

appreciated property to the LLC that is distributed within seven years will recognize gain under Section 704(c)(1)(B).

Overlap of Sections 704(c)(1)(B) and 707(a)(2)(B)

Section 707(a)(2)(B) provides that there is a disguised sale if there is a contribution of money, property or services to an LLC followed (or preceded) by related distribution of money or property to the contributing member within two years after the contribution. Section 704(c)(1)(B) provides that a member who contributes appreciated property recognizes gain if the LLC distributes that property to another member within seven years after the date of contribution.

There is no overlap between the two sections. Once the IRS determines that a sale has occurred under Section 707(a)(2)(B), the contributing member recognizes gain, and all of the pre-contribution gain is eliminated. The sale is deemed to have occurred at the outset of the initial transfer of the property to the LLC.[188] Thus, there is no pre-contribution gain under Section 704(c)(1)(B), and no gain is recognized under Section 704(c)(1)(B) on distribution of the property to the other member.

Overlap of Sections 731, 737, and 751(b)

Section 731 provides that gain is recognized to the extent that money distribution exceeds the member's outside basis in his membership interest immediately prior to the distribution. Gain recognized under Section 737 is in addition to any gain recognized under Section 731. A distribution could result in gain recognized under both Section 731 and Section 737.[189]

Section 751(b) applies if a member receives a disproportionate distribution of hot assets and cold assets. Section 737 does not apply to a distribution to the extent that Code Sec. 751(b) applies. Section 751(b) applies before Section 737 if the distribution is disproportionate.[190]

¶606 REPORTING REQUIREMENTS

An LLC and its members are subject to the following reporting requirements for contributions to an LLC:

---

[188] Reg. § 1.707-3(a)(2). The contributing member is deemed to have received a payment right, rather than a partnership interest, at the time of the initial contribution of property to the LLC, and any subsequent related distribution of cash or property to the member is characterized as a payment in satisfaction of the LLC's obligation to make a payment in exchange for the sale (and not a distribution).

[189] IRS Audit Technique Guide—Partnerships, Chapter 4, under the heading, "Effect of IRC Section 751 and IRC Section 731."

[190] Reg. § 1.737-1(a)(2).

- An LLC must report on Item M of Schedule K-1 for each member whether the member contributed property with built-in gain or loss. If the LLC checks the "Yes" box, then the LLC must attach a statement.
- An LLC must report capital contributions by the member during the year on Item L of Form Schedule K-1.
- A member must attach Form 8275, Disclosure Statement (or other statement) to his or her return if the member contributes property to an LLC and, within two years before or after the contribution, the LLC transfers money or other consideration to the member.
- An LLC must attach Form 8275 (or other statement) to its return if it distributes property to a member and, within two years before or after the distribution, the member transfers money or other consideration to the LLC. The LLC may also file Form 8594, Asset Acquisition Statement, to its return.
- A member who incurs liabilities within two years prior to the contribution of property to an LLC, and claims that the liabilities were not incurred in anticipation of the transfer, must disclose such liabilities to the IRS on Form 8275.[191] These are liabilities assumed by the LLC or taken subject to, and that the member treats as "qualified liabilities."
- If a member contributes property to an LLC with built-in losses, the LLC must make a special basis adjustment for the contributing member. The LLC must attach a statement to the partnership return for the year of the contribution setting forth the name and taxpayer identification number of the contributing member, the basis adjustment, and the property with the built-in loss.[192] The mandatory basis adjustment rules under Code Sec. 704(c)(1)(C) are discussed at ¶806.
- United States persons who contribute property to a foreign LLC must file a report with the IRS on Form 8865.[193] United States persons who contribute built-in gain property to a domestic or foreign LLC with foreign members must file Schedule O of Form 8865.[194]

---

[191] Reg. §§ 1.707-5(a)(7)(ii), 1.707-8.
[192] Prop. Reg. § 1.704-3(f)(3)(vi).
[193] See ¶ 1806.02 *infra*.
[194] See ¶ 1903 *infra*.

7

Taxation of LLC Income

¶ 701 TAXABLE INCOME

An LLC that is classified as a partnership is subject to the partnership tax rules under subchapter K of the Internal Revenue Code.[1] The taxable income of the LLC is determined under Code Sec. 703(a). The LLC does not pay taxes at the entity level.[2] It is a pass-through entity. All items of income, gain, credit, loss, and deduction pass through to the members.[3] The members report their distributive shares on their personal tax returns, whether or not the income or other amounts are distributed.[4]

An LLC must compute its taxable income for reporting purposes even though it is not a taxpaying entity.[5] The LLC reports its taxable income on IRS Form 1065, which is an annual information return. It reports each member's distributive share on Schedule K-1. Schedule K-1 is filed as part of IRS Form 1065 and sent to each member. The LLC must file the return for each year that it receives income or incurs expenditures allowable as deductions.[6]

The taxable income, loss, credit, and deductions of an LLC are determined on the last day of its tax year.[7] Each member must report such items on his return for the tax year coinciding with the LLC's tax year, or for the tax year immediately following such year if the member has a different tax year.[8] Thus, if an LLC has a tax year

---

[1] Code Secs. 701-761.

[2] Code Sec. 701; Reg. § 1.701-1.

[3] Code Sec. 702(a).

[4] Code Sec. 706(a); Reg. § 1.702-1(a).

[5] Code Sec. 703.

[6] Reg. § 1.6031(a)-1(a)(1).

[7] Code Sec. 706(a); Reg. § 1.705-1(a).

[8] Code Sec. 706(a).

ending on April 30, 2009, an individual member must report the distributive share of income and other items on the member's tax return for the year ending December 31, 2010.

The taxable income is computed in the same manner as for an individual, subject to certain exceptions.[9] The Schedule K-1 that the LLC sends to each member is designed to resemble Form W-2 so that the member will know exactly where to report the LLC income, gain, loss, and deduction on his or her Form 1040.

The LLC must account for or report the following items on Form 1065 and Schedule K-1:

1. Items that must be separately stated.[10]

2. Nondeductible amounts.[11]

3. All other items of income and expense that are grouped together as "ordinary income (loss) from trade or business activities." The net amount of such items is the "bottom line" taxable income or loss of the LLC.[12] These are the items of income from operations, expenses, depreciation, and other items that are not separately stated because they do not affect each member differently.

4. Special allocations and each member's distributive share of income. A member's distributive share of income, gain, loss, credit, and deduction is determined in accordance with the operating agreement.[13] However, special allocations to members are not respected unless the allocations have substantial economic effect.[14]

Each member must take into account his or her distributive share of taxable income, the separately stated items, and the disallowed amounts.[15]

---

[9] Code Sec. 703. Code Sec. 703(a) provides:

The taxable income of a partnership shall be computed in the same manner as in the case of an individual except that (1) the items described in section 702(a) shall be separately stated, and (2) the following deductions shall not be allowed to the partnership: (A) the deductions for personal exemptions provided in section 151, (B) the deduction for taxes provided in section 164(a) with respect to taxes, described in section 901, paid or accrued to foreign countries and to possessions of the United States, (C) the deduction for charitable contributions provided in section 170, (D) the net operating loss deduction provided in section 170, (E) the additional itemized deductions for individuals provided in part VII of subchapter B (sec. 211 and following), and (F) the deduction for depletion under section 611 with respect to oil and gas wells.

[10] Code Sec. 702(a). *See* ¶ 703 *infra*.

[11] Code Sec. 703(a)(2). *See* ¶ 704 *infra*.

[12] Code Sec. 702(a)(8); Reg. § 1.704-1(b)(1)(vii).

[13] Code Sec. 704(a).

[14] *See* Chapter 8 *infra*.

[15] Reg. § 1.702-1(a)(9).

¶ 702 20% QUALIFIED BUSINESS INCOME DEDUCTION

.01 General

For tax years after 2017 and before 2026, non-corporate taxpayers may deduct 20 percent of:

- qualified business income;[16]
- qualified cooperative dividends;[17]
- REIT dividends;[18] and
- qualified publicly traded partnership income.[19]

This means that owners of an LLC and other pass-through businesses are taxed on only 80 percent of their pass-through income (or at only 80 percent of the normal tax bracket rate on all their business income) if the deduction can be fully utilized. The maximum effective pass-through tax rate in such case is 29.6 percent (80% × 37% maximum tax rate for individuals). However, the deduction is subject to numerous limitations and requirements, which will usually limit the maximum benefit for pass-through business owners and sole proprietors. The principal limits are:

- overall limit on deduction, based on the "combined qualified business income amount" and taxable income in excess of net capital gains;[20]
- qualified business income definition, which limits the types of LLC income qualified for the deduction;
- wage limit for owners of LLCs with taxable income in excess of a threshold amount;
- elimination of deduction for owners of service LLCs with taxable income in excess of a wage limit phase-in range;
- below-the-line deduction limits; and
- pass-through losses from prior years that limit the qualified business income (QBI) deduction in the current year.

Most LLCs do not have qualified cooperative dividends, REIT dividends, or qualified publicly traded partnership income. Thus, only the rules related to QBI are discussed below.

---

[16] Code Sec. 199A(a)(1).
[17] Code Sec. 199A(a)(2).
[18] Code Sec. 199A(b)(1)(B).
[19] Code Sec. 199A(b)(1)(B).
[20] Code Sec. 199A(a)(1).

.02 Overall Limit on Deduction

The QBI deduction may not exceed the lesser of (i) the taxpayer's combined qualified business income amount, or (ii) 20 percent of the taxpayer's income in excess of net capital gains.[21]

The combined qualified business income amount is not an income amount, but is instead a deduction amount. It is equal to 20 percent of the taxpayer's qualified business income from each LLC or other qualified trade or business carried on by the taxpayer.[22] The deduction is computed on a trade-by-trade basis. The sum of the 20 percent deductions from each separate trade or business is the combined QBI amount.

EXAMPLE 7-1

Peter earned $100,000 of qualified business income. He reports $70,000 of taxable income on his tax return after applicable deductions, which includes $10,000 of capital gain. His QBI deduction is $12,000, which is the lesser of (i) 20 percent of qualified business income ($20,000), or (ii) 20 percent of taxable income in excess of capital gain ($12,000).

.03 Qualified Business Income

The deduction is limited to 20 percent of QBI. QBI is the net amount of income, gain, loss and deductions for a taxpayer's trade or business. It is the ordinary income, less ordinary deductions, that a taxpayer earns from a sole proprietorship, S corporation, partnership, or LLC.[23] If the net amount of qualified income, gain, loss and deduction for the qualified trade or business is less than zero for any tax year, then such amount is treated as a loss from a qualified trade or business in the succeeding taxable year.[24]

Wages of an employee are not qualified business income, whereas self-employment income of an independent contractor is qualified business income.

QBI does not include any of the following:

- Reasonable compensation payable to the taxpayer for services rendered in the trade or business.[25] The reasonable compensation rule applies to shareholders in an S corporation, but may not apply to members in an LLC classified as a partnership. There is not yet a reasonable compensation standard for LLCs

---

[21] Code Sec. 199A(a)(1).

[22] Code Sec. 199A(b)(1)(A).

[23] Code Sec. 199A(c).

[24] Code Sec. 199A(c)(2).

[25] Code Sec. 199A(c)(4)(A).

classified as partnerships because partnership income is not subject to double taxation and is usually subject to self-employment taxes. The IRS is considering a reasonable compensation requirement for LLCs classified as partnerships that are disregarded entities for purposes of the 20 percent deduction;[26]

- Guaranteed payments to a member or partner for services rendered in the trade or business;[27]

- Payments to a partner other than in his capacity as a partner in the LLC for services in the trade or business of the LLC to the extent provided in IRS regulations;[28]

- Investment income.[29] This includes short-term capital gain or loss, long-term capital gain or loss, dividend income, and interest income; or

- Income attributable to foreign business activities. Qualified business income must be effectively connected with the conduct of a U.S. trade or business.[30]

.04 Wage Limits on Deduction

If the taxpayer's income is below a threshold amount, the QBI deduction is 20 percent of qualified business income. The threshold amounts for 2018 are $157,500 for individuals and $315,000 for married couples filing jointly (indexed annually for inflation).[31]

If the taxpayer's income is above a threshold level but within a phase-in range, the deduction is limited based on the taxpayer's share of W-2 wages paid by the LLC. The wage limit phases in as taxable income increases within the phase-in range.[32] The phase-in ranges for 2018 are between $157,500 and $207,500 for a single person, and between $315,000 and $415,000 on a joint return. The wage limit phase-in computations are discussed at ¶702.06.

If the taxpayer's income exceeds phase-in range, the QBI deduction is limited to (i) 50 percent of W-2 wages,[33] or (ii) 25 percent of W-2 wages plus 2.5 percent of the unadjusted basis of qualified business property.[34]

The QBI deduction for owners of LLCs, other than service LLCs, can be summarized as follows:

---

[26] BNA Daily Tax Report, No. 29, p. 6 (Feb. 12, 2018).

[27] Code Sec. 199A(c)(4)(B).

[28] Code Sec. 199A(c)(4)(C).

[29] Code Sec. 199A(c)(3)(B).

[30] Code Sec. 199A(c)(3)(A)(i).

[31] Code Sec. 199A(e)(2).

[32] Code Sec. 199A(b)(3).

[33] Code Sec. 199A(b)(2)(B)(i).

[34] Code Sec. 199A(b)(2)(B)(ii).

Taxpayer's income is less than the threshold	QBI deduction is the lesser of: (a) 20% of qualified business income for each qualified trade or business; (b) 20% of taxable income in excess of net capital gains.
Taxpayer's income exceeds the threshold and is within phase-in range	QBI deduction is the lesser of: (a) 20% of qualified business income, (b) a wage limit phase-in amount (¶ 702.06), or (c) 20% of taxable income in excess of net capital gains.
Taxpayer's income is above the phase-in range	QBI deduction is the lesser of: (a) 20% of qualified business income, (b) the greater of (i) 50% of W-2 wages, or (ii) 25% of W-2 wages plus 2.5% of the unadjusted basis of qualified property, or (c) 20% of taxable income in excess of net capital gains.

EXAMPLE 7-2

A single-member disregarded LLC operates a repair shop which has $10 million of revenue, $6 million of profits, and $1 million of W-2 wages. It has no qualified property. The owner of the repair shop has $7 million of taxable income from all sources. Since the owner has taxable income above the phase-out range, the deduction is $500,000, which is the lesser of:

1. 20 percent of qualified business income (20% × $6 million = $1,200,000),
2. 50 percent of W-2 wages paid to employees (50% × $1 million = $500,000), or
3. 20 percent of taxable income in excess of net capital gains (20% × $7 million = $1,400,000).

EXAMPLE 7-3

Betty purchases a $2 million office building and earns $1 million in rental income through her single-member disregarded LLC. She pays no W-2 wages. Her QBI deduction is $50,000, which is the lesser of:

1. 20 percent of qualified business income ($200,000),
2. 25 percent of W-2 wages ($0) plus 2.5 percent of the $2 million initial depreciable cost basis of the building ($50,000), or
3. 20 percent of taxable income in excess of net capital gains ($200,000).

¶ 702.04

EXAMPLE 7-4

Steve owns a single-member LLC that earns $400,000 of qualified business income. He pays no W-2 wages and reports all of his income on Schedule C of IRS Form 1040. He has no qualified property. His QBI deduction is zero since he pays no W-2 wages and has no qualified property.

EXAMPLE 7-5

Mary owns an engineering LLC that is classified as an S corporation. She pays herself $50,000 in W-2 wages and earns an additional $105,000 in qualified business income that passes through to her as S corporation income. Her taxable income is $155,000, which is less than the threshold amount of $157,500. Therefore, she may deduct 20 percent of $105,000. The wage limits do not apply. The deduction would be less if the IRS determined that the LLC failed to pay reasonable salary to Mary for her engineering services.

The W-2 wages for purposes of the computations mean wages for federal income tax withholding purposes, Code Sec. 3401(a), elective deferrals under Section 402(g)(3), deferred compensation under Section 457, and designated Roth contributions under Section 402A.[35]

If there are multiple owners of an LLC, then each member receives an allocable share of the Form W-2 wages. The owners of disregarded LLCs receive 100 percent of any Form W-2 wages paid to employees for QBI deduction purposes. The allocation must follow the allocation of expenses to the members related to the wages.

.05 Wage Limits–Qualified Property

Capital-intensive businesses with few employees, such as real estate investors and factories, will normally use the 25 percent wage limit test instead of the 50 percent wage limit test. The deduction under the 25 percent wage limit test is the lesser of:[36]

1. 20 percent of qualified business income,
2. 25 percent of W-2 wages plus 2.5 percent of the unadjusted basis of qualified property, or
3. 20 percent of taxable income in excess of net capital gains.

---

[35] Code Sec. 199A(b)(4).
[36] Code Sec. 199A(b)(2)(B)(ii).

Qualified property is tangible, depreciable property, including depreciable real estate. It does not include inventory. The qualified property must meet the following requirements:[37]

- The property must be held and available for use in the business at the close of the tax year.
- The property must be used at any point during the tax year in the production of qualified business income.
- The depreciable period for the property must not have ended before the close of the tax year. The depreciable period for the property begins on the date that the property was first placed in service by the taxpayer and ends on the later of ten years after such date or the last day of the full year in the applicable recovery period under Code Sec. 168. Any asset that was fully depreciated before 2018 will not count towards basis unless it was placed in service after 2008.

The LLC must take into consideration the basis of the property "immediately after acquisition" in determining the unadjusted basis of the property.[38] It is unclear whether the step-up in basis on death counts as an acquisition for QBI deduction purposes.

.06 Wage Limits Phase-in Computations

If a member's income is above the threshold level and within the phase-in range discussed above, then the wage limits are phased in as a member's income increases within the phase-in range. The computations are made as follows:

1. Determine the deduction without the wage limitation. This is 20 percent of qualified business income.
2. Determine the deduction with the wage limitation, which is the lesser of (a) 20 percent of qualified business income, or (b) the greater of (i) 50 percent of W-2 wages, or (ii) 25 percent of W-2 wages plus 2.5 percent of the unadjusted basis of qualified business property.
3. Determine the benefit that the taxpayer would receive if the wage limit did not apply. This is the amount in Step 2 subtracted from the amount in Step 1.
4. Determine the member's taxable income in excess of the threshold amount. This is the excess taxable income.
5. Determine the wage limit phase-in percentage. This is the excess taxable income from Step 4 divided by the total phase-in range. The total phase-in range is $50,000 for a single person and $100,000 for a married person filing jointly.
6. Determine the wage limit dollar amount. This is the wage limit phase-in percentage from Step 5 multiplied by the member's taxable income in excess of the threshold amount.

---

[37] Code Sec. 199A(b)(6).
[38] Code Sec. 199A(b)(2)(B)(ii).

7. Determine the final deduction by reducing the deduction amount determined without the wage limit in Step 1 by the wage limit dollar amount under Step 6.

EXAMPLE 7-6

A married couple's allocable share of income from an LLC is $300,000. Their allocable share of W-2 wages paid by the LLC is $60,000. Their share of the unadjusted basis of qualified property held by the LLC is zero. One spouse earns an additional $75,000 in W-2 wages. The deduction is computed as follows:

1. The deduction without the wage limit is $60,000 (20 percent of the member's allocable share of LLC qualified business income).

2. The deduction with the wage limit is $30,000. This is the lesser of (a) 20 percent of qualified business income ($60,000), and (b) the greater of (i) 50 percent of W-2 wages ($30,000), or (ii) 25 percent of W-2 wages ($15,000) plus 2.5 percent of the unadjusted basis of qualified business property ($0).

3. The difference between the amounts in Step 1and Step 2 is $30,000.

4. The taxable income in excess of the threshold amount is $60,000 ($375,000 of taxable income less threshold amount of $315,000 for a married person filing jointly).

5. The wage limit phase-in percentage is 60 percent (excess taxable income of $60,000 divided by the total phase-in range $100,000).

6. The wage limit dollar amount is $36,000 (taxable income of $60,000 in excess of the threshold amount multiplied by the wage limit phase-in percentage of 60 percent).

7. The final deduction amount is $24,000 (deduction without the wage limit of $60,000 from Step 1 reduced by the wage limit dollar amount of $36,000 from Step 6).

.07 Partnerships and S Corporations

The QBI deduction applies at the member, partner or shareholder level for LLCs, partnerships and S corporations.[39] In order to compute the deduction, members of an LLC must take into account their allocable share of:

---

[39] Code Sec. 199A(f)(1)(A)(i).

- Each item of an LLC's income, gain, loss and deduction.[40]
- W-2 wages of the LLC.[41] A member's allocable share of wages paid by the LLC is determined in the same manner as his or her share of the LLC's wage deduction.[42] Wages are normally deducted from Line 1 ordinary income on Schedule K-1. Thus, if a member of an LLC receives 20 percent of Schedule K-1, Line 1 ordinary income items, then the member must be allocated 20 percent of the LLC's W-2 wage expenses regardless of any other special allocations or capital account contributions.
- LLC's basis of tangible depreciable property if the LLC is using the second alternative wage limit test to determine the deduction (25 percent of W-2 wages plus 2.5 percent of basis). A member's allocable share of basis is determined in the same manner as allocations of depreciation expense.[43] Thus, if a member receives a special allocation of 80 percent of depreciation from LLC property, then the member's allocable share of basis of that property is 80 percent, even though the member receives a different allocation of other items of income, gain, loss and deduction.

Each member of an LLC calculates his or her own QBI deduction based on the member's allocable share of LLC income, gain, loss, deductions and W-2 wages. Thus, lower-paid members may still be eligible for the QBI deduction even if the higher paid members are not.

Self-employed individuals will have a lower effective tax rate than employees doing substantially similar work. This will provide an incentive for employees to recharacterize their working relationship from an employee to an independent contractor or form a separate business entity that contracts back to the employer for their prior work. This tax planning will not work for employees working in "specified service trades or businesses" with income in excess of the phase-in range (¶702.08 and ¶702.09). In addition, the self-employed person will have to pay his or her share of self-employment taxes (15.30 percent up to the taxable wage base and 2.90 percent on earnings above the taxable wage base).

.08 Service Trades or Businesses

The deduction is phased out for service trades or businesses if taxable income is above a threshold amount and within a phase-out range. The deduction is completely eliminated if taxable income is above the phase-out range. The threshold amounts and phase-out ranges are the same for other businesses, which are as follows for 2018:

- single person return: threshold amount of $157,500 and phase-out range from $157,500 to $207,500;
- joint return: threshold amount of $315,000, and phase-out range from $315,000 to $415,000.

---

[40] Code Sec. 199A(f)(1)(A)(ii).
[41] Code Sec. 199A(f)(1)(A)(iii).
[42] Code Sec. 199A(f)(1)(A) (last paragraph).
[43] Code Sec. 199A(f)(1)(A) (last paragraph).

The phase-out rules differ in two important respects for service companies. First, there are different rules regarding the phase-out of the deduction for taxpayers with income in the phase-out range. There is both a wage limit phase-in and a qualified business income phase-out. For regular companies, there is only a phase-in of the wage limit. The phase-in and phase-out rules for service companies are discussed at ¶ 702.09.

The second difference is that the deduction is completely eliminated for service companies if the service provider has taxable income in excess of the phase-out range. The QBI deduction for members of regular LLCs with taxable income in excess of the phase-out range is the lesser of (a) 20 percent of qualified business income, or (b) the greater of (i) 50 percent of W-2 wages, or (ii) 25 percent of W-2 wages plus 2.5 percent of the unadjusted basis of qualified property.

Specified service trades or businesses subject to the reduced QBI deduction include:

- Any trade or business described in Code Sec. 1202(e)(3)(A) other than engineering and architecture companies.[44] Under that definition, specified service trades or businesses include businesses in the fields of accounting, health, law, consulting, athletics, financial services, and brokerage services;

- Any business where the principal asset of the business is the reputation or skill of one or more of its employees;[45] and

- A business involving the performance of investment and investment management services, trading, or dealing in securities, partnership interests or commodities.[46]

The QBI deduction for members of a specified service LLC can be summarized as follows:

Taxpayer's income is less than the threshold	QBI deduction is the lesser of: (a) 20% of qualified business income for each qualified trade or business; (b) 20% of taxable income in excess of net capital gains.
Taxpayer's income exceeds the threshold and is within phase-in range	QBI deduction is the lesser of: (a) 20% of qualified business income, (b) a wage limit phase-in and phase-out amount (¶ 702.09), or (c) 20% of taxable income in excess of net capital gains.
Taxpayer's income is above the phase-in range	No QBI deduction

---

[44] Code Sec. 199A(d)(2)(A).

[45] Code Secs. 199A(d)(2)(A), 1202(e)(3)(A).

[46] Code Sec. 199A(d)(2)(B).

.09 Phase-Out Rules for Service Businesses

The QBI deduction is phased out for members of LLCs that are specified service businesses if the member's taxable income is above a threshold level and within a phase-out range. There are two types of phase-outs for service businesses:

1. First, the QBI deduction must be determined after multiplying the member's allocable share of qualified business income, W-2 wages and basis by an "applicable percentage." The applicable percentage is based on the amount by which the taxpayer's taxable income exceeds the threshold amount within the phase-out range. For example, on a joint return, the phase-out range is $100,000. If the taxpayer earns $80,000 above the threshold level, then the taxpayer's share of qualified business income, W-2 wages and basis is reduced by 80 percent, ($80,000 divided by $100,000). The applicable percentage is the remaining 20 percent representing the share of qualified business income, W-2 wages and basis that the taxpayer should be allowed to keep.[47]

2. Second, the wage-limit phase-in reductions are applied in the same manner as for non-service businesses, except that the computations are made using the taxpayer's adjusted share of qualified business income, W-2 wages and basis.

EXAMPLE 7-7

A married couple has taxable income of $375,000, consisting of $300,000 of qualified business income from an accounting firm LLC, and $75,000 of W-2 wages earned by one spouse in a separate business. The member's share of W-2 wages paid by the LLC is $40,000. The member's share of the unadjusted basis of qualified property of the LLC is zero. The QBI deduction is $14,400, computed as follows:

A. Determine Applicable Percentage. The applicable percentage is 40 percent, determined as follows:

1. Determine taxable income in excess of the threshold amount. This is $60,000 (taxable income of $375,000 less threshold of $315,000 for a joint return).

2. Divide the excess taxable income by the total phase-in range. This is 60 percent ($60,000 divided by phase-in range of $100,000 for a joint return, expressed as a percentage).

---

[47] Code Sec. 199A(d)(3)(B).

    3. Determine the "applicable percentage." This is 40 percent (100 percent less the 60 percent determined under Step B).

B. Determine Adjusted QBI Deduction. The member is only allowed to deduct 20 percent of qualified business income, after qualified business income is reduced by the applicable percentage (40 percent). The adjusted QBI deduction is $24,000, determined as follows:

    1. Determine qualified business income under the regular rules. This is $300,000.

    2. Multiply qualified business income by the applicable percentage. This $120,000 (40 percent of $300,000).

    3. Multiply the amount in Step 2 by 20 percent. This is $24,000.

C. Determine Adjusted Wage Limit Deduction (Without the Wage Phase-in Limits). The member is only allowed to take into account the applicable percentage of his allocable share of W-2 wages paid by the LLC. The adjusted wage limit deduction is $8,000, determined as follows:

    1. Determine the member's allocable share of the W-2 wages paid by the LLC. This is $40,000.

    2. Multiply the member's allocable share of W-2 wages by the applicable percentage. This is $16,000 (40% × $40,000).

    3. Determine the wage limit deduction without regard to the W-2 wage phase-in limits. This is $8,000, which is the greater of (i) 50 percent of the member's adjusted W-2 wages (50% × $16,000 = $8,000), or (ii) 25 percent of adjusted W-2 wages (25% × $16,000 = $4,000) plus 2.5 percent of basis ($0).

D. Determine the Tentative Deduction. This is $8,000, which is the lesser of:

    1. 20 percent of the $120,000 adjusted qualified business income ($24,000); or

    2. the greater of (i) 50 percent of the $16,000 adjusted W-2 wages ($8,000), or (ii) 25 percent of the $16,000 adjusted W-2 wages ($4,000) plus 2.5 percent of basis ($0).

This tentative deduction is based on the following applicable percentage amount:

Item	Allocable share	Applicable percentage (40%)
Qualified business income	$300,000	$120,000
W-2 wages	$40,000	$16,000
Basis in assets	$0	$0

E. <u>Determine the Phase-In Wage Limit Deduction</u>. The adjusted W-2 wage limit in Step D does not apply if the member's taxable income on a joint return is less than $315,000. The adjusted W-2 wage limit is phased in if the member's taxable income is within the phase-out range of $315,000 to $415,000 in 2018. The member's taxable income in the example is $375,000, so the wage limit is phased in as follows:

1. Determine the member's taxable income in excess of the threshold amount. This is $60,000 ($375,000 of taxable income less threshold amount of $315,000 for a married person filing jointly).

2. Determine the wage limit phase-in percentage. This is 60 percent (excess taxable income of $60,000 divided by the total phase-in range of $100,000 for a married person filing jointly).

3. Determine the deduction without the wage limitation, but after reducing the member's share of qualified business income by the applicable percentage. This is $24,000 from Step B (20 percent of the $120,000 adjusted qualified business income).

4. Determine the deduction with the wage limitation, after reducing the member's share of qualified business income, W-2 wages, and basis by the applicable percentage, but without reduction for the phase-in wage limitation. This is $8,000 from Step D.

5. Determine the total benefit that the member would receive without a phase-in wage limitation. This is $16,000 ($24,000 without the wage limitation less $8,000 with the wage limitation.

6. Multiply the $16,000 wage limit benefit by the phase-in percentage of 60 percent. This is $9,600 and represents the wage limit phase-in amount that applies to the member.

F. <u>Determine the Final QBI Deduction</u>. The final QBI deduction is $14,400, which is:

20 percent of adjusted qualified business income	$24,000
Wage limit reduction in QBI deduction because the member's income exceeds the threshold amount of $315,000	($9,600)
Final QBI deduction	$14,400

.10 Below-the-Line Deduction

The QBI deduction is not an above-the-line deduction in computing adjusted gross income, and is not an itemized deduction. It does not reduce a taxpayer's self-employment income. Instead, it is a below-the-line deduction that reduces taxable income.[48] Taxpayers who claim the standard deduction may also claim the deduction for qualified business income.

EXAMPLE 7-8

John earns $100,000 in net business income from a single-member disregarded LLC. He also deducts $3,000 for health insurance, $7,065 for self-employment taxes, and $5,000 for a SEP IRA contribution. These are adjustments on Form 1040 in calculating adjusted gross income rather than business deductions. Therefore, the QBI deduction is the lesser of 20 percent of $100,000 (net business income) or 20 percent of his taxable income. John must pay self-employment taxes on $100,000 of net business income, without reducing the net business income by the QBI deduction.

The QBI deduction is the same for alternative minimum tax purposes as for regular tax purposes.[49]

.11 Losses and Loss Carryforwards

Losses from a sole proprietorship, partnership, LLC or S corporation reduce the amount of QBI income eligible for the deduction in the current year. The sum of all income and losses for the separate trades and businesses are netted, and the maximum deduction is 20 percent of the net amount.

EXAMPLE 7-9

Jennifer is the sole member of three LLCs that own rental properties. Two of the LLCs have net incomes of $10,000 and $15,000. One of the LLCs has losses of $5000. Jennifer may deduct 20 percent of $20,000.

If the taxpayer has net losses in one year from QBI activities, those losses carry forward to the next year and reduce the QBI income in the subsequent year solely for the purposes of computing the 20 percent QBI deduction.[50] This carryforward applies

---

[48] Code Sec. 62(a), as added by 2017 Tax Cuts and Jobs Act Sec. 11011(b).
[49] Code Sec. 199A(f)(2).
[50] Code Sec. 199A(b)(6).

even if the taxpayer offset the losses in the prior year against wages or other income for regular income tax purposes.

EXAMPLE 7-10

A member of an LLC has net losses of $300,000 in 2018. There is no QBI deduction because there is a loss rather than qualified business income. If the member's allocable share of qualified business income from the LLC is $400,000 in 2019, then that amount must be reduced by the $300,000 loss from 2018. The maximum QBI deduction in 2019 is 20 percent of $100,000 rather than 20 percent of $400,000.

.12 Real Estate Businesses

A last-minute change to the 2017 Tax Cuts and Jobs Act permits some real estate investment companies to take the 20 percent deduction from an investment LLC, partnership or S corporation. The House version of the 2017 Tax Act would have substantially reduced the deduction for real estate investment pass-through entities since the deduction under the House Bill was limited to the lesser of 20 percent of qualified business income or 50 percent of the total wages paid to employees (with no wage limits for taxpayers with income of less than $157,500 for individuals or $350,000 for joint filers). Real estate investment pass-through entities, which generally have few employees and large capital investments, would have received almost no benefit because of the 50 percent wage limit.

However, the final version of the tax Act offered an alternative limit on the deduction, which is 25 percent of wages paid plus 2.5 percent of the purchase price of tangible depreciable property. Tangible depreciable property includes housing complexes, apartment buildings, office buildings and shopping centers. This alternative limit allows real estate investment companies to take a deduction up to the lesser of (i) 20 percent of qualified business income, or (ii) 2.5 percent of the unadjusted basis of depreciable real estate plus 25 percent of W-2 wages.

The 20 percent deduction is substantially limited for real estate brokerage companies. The reason is that the deduction is reduced for owners of "specified service providers" if income exceeds income thresholds of $207,500 for a single person and $415,000 for a joint return in 2018. A real estate brokerage company is a specified service provider, and is thus subject to the phase-in of the deduction.

.13 Rental Businesses

It is unclear whether rent from a single rental property constitutes qualified business income. Code Sec. 199A(c)(1) requires that a qualified business income be earned in a qualified trade or business of the taxpayer. Under Code Sec. 162, a trade or business is a business that is regular, continuous and substantial. Thus, rental income from a single triple net lease may not constitute qualified business income eligible for the 20 percent deduction.

.14 Trusts, Estates, Tiered Entities and Other LLC Owners

Trusts and estates[51] and tiered entities[52] that own an interest in an LLC may also take the deduction.

.15 Penalties

There is normally an accuracy related penalty if taxes are underpaid by 10 percent or more. However, if the taxpayer claims the deduction under Code Sec. 199A, the penalty tax applies if taxes are understated by five percent or more. The rule applies regardless of the size of the deduction claimed under Code Sec. 199A.[53] The penalty tax may be as high as 20 percent of the unpaid tax.

.16 Choice of Entity

In some cases, it may be advisable for an LLC to elect classification as a corporation or to convert to a C corporation because of the lower 21 percent corporate tax rate. This is less than the maximum individual tax rate on flow-through income from an LLC or S corporation. The lower tax rate will be most advantageous if the corporate owners keep the profits in the corporation. However, a C corporation has the following disadvantages:

- If the C corporation distributes profits as a dividend to shareholders, then the combined corporate tax rate and dividend tax rate will normally be higher than the single pass- through rate from an LLC or S corporation after the 20 percent deduction. The maximum tax on dividends is 23.8 percent (top 20 percent tax rate for qualified dividends plus a 3.8 percent net investment income tax).
- There is a 20 percent accumulated earnings tax on closely held C corporations that hold liquid assets in excess of the reasonable needs of the business.
- There is 20 percent personal holding company tax on undistributed passive income earned in a closely held C corporation.
- Losses in a C corporation do not pass through to the owners. Losses in an LLC pass through to the owners and can offset other income, subject to limits discussed in Chapter 13.
- If a C corporation is planning to sell the company in the near future, it may be more advantageous to stay a C corporation which is easier to sell than an LLC. Gain on the sale of stock in a C corporation is taxed at the capital gains rate. The maximum capital gains tax rate is 23.8 percent (top 20 percent tax rate for capital gains plus the 3.8 percent net investment income tax). The owners may also be eligible for the 50 -100 percent exclusion of gain if the

---

[51] Code Sec. 199A(f)(1)(B).
[52] Code Sec. 199A(f)(4)(B).
[53] Code Sec. 6662(d)(1)(C).

stock has been held for more than five years and otherwise meets the requirements for qualified business stock under Code Sec. 1202. Gain on the sale of a membership interest in an LLC is taxed in part as ordinary income.[54]

- A C corporation recognizes gain on the distribution of appreciated property to the shareholders in kind.[55]
- The conversion to a C corporation will trigger taxable gain to the extent that the amount of business debt assumed by the corporation is greater than the adjusted basis of the assets.[56]

¶703 SEPARATELY STATED ITEMS

The LLC must separately state certain items of income, gain, loss, deduction, and credit rather than aggregating these amounts into the taxable income figure. The separately stated items are items that could have potentially varying tax consequences to particular members.[57] The LLC must also separately state each member's share of nontaxable income and nondeductible expenditures. These items are necessary for basis computation purposes. The separately stated items include the following:[58]

.01 Capital Gains and Losses

Capital gains and losses and Section 1231 gains and losses must be separately stated.[59] Special allocations of capital gains and losses are not reported on Schedule D.

EXAMPLE 7-11

An LLC has a long-term capital gain that is specially allocated to a member and a net long-term capital gain reported on line 15 of Schedule D that must be reported on line 9a of Schedule K. Because specially allocated gains or losses are not reported on Schedule D, the LLC must report both the net long-term capital gain from Schedule D and the specially allocated gain on line 9a of Schedule K. Box 9a of the Schedule K-1 for the member must include both the specially allocated gain and the member's distributive share of the net long-term capital gain from Schedule D.[60]

---

[54] See ¶1507 infra.

[55] Code Sec. 311(b).

[56] Code Sec. 357(c).

[57] Code Secs. 702(a), 703(a)(1).

[58] Reg. § 1.702-1(a)(1) to (9).

[59] Code Secs. 703(a)(1), 702(a)(1)-(3); Reg. § 1.702(a)(1)-(3).

[60] Instructions to Form 1065 under the heading, *Special Allocations.*

An LLC must attach a statement to Form 1065 identifying the various items of gain sourced at the member level. The statement must (i) identify gains on the sale of personal property other than inventory, depreciable property, and certain intangible property on which a foreign tax of ten percent or more was paid or accrued, (ii) identify losses on the sale of such property if the foreign country would have imposed a ten percent or higher tax had the sale resulted in a gain, and (iii), separately identify the amounts of such gains or losses within each separate limitation category that are long term capital gains and losses.[61]

The rules regarding capital gains and losses are discussed at ¶ 1601.

.02 Ordinary Business Income

The LLC's ordinary business income is reported as a net amount on page 1 of Form 1065. The specific income and deductions for each separate trade or business activity must be reported on a statement attached to Form 1065 and on a supplemental information schedule attached to each Schedule K-1. The reason is that each member must determine if the member materially participated in an activity for purposes of the passive loss rules.[62] The passive loss rules are discussed at ¶ 1304.

The LLC's ordinary business income allocated to each member is reported in Item 1 of Schedule K-1. Each member's allocable share of the income and deductions from each trade or business activity must also be reported on the statement attached to Schedule K-1.[63]

.03 Charitable Contributions

An LLC must separately state charitable contributions.[64] The LLC may not deduct charitable contributions.[65] However, the members may deduct charitable contributions on their individual tax returns. Each member is treated as having paid his distributive share of a charitable contribution paid by the LLC within its tax year ending within or with the member's tax year.[66] Members must add their individual charitable contributions to their distributive shares of LLC contributions, and apply

---

[61] Instructions to Form 1065 under the heading, *Line 16c. Gross Income Sourced at Partner Level (Code C).*

[62] Instructions to Form 1065 under the heading, *Trade or Business Activities.*

[63] Instructions to Form 1065 under the heading, *Trade or Business Activities.*

[64] Code Secs. 703(a)(1), 702(a)(4); Reg. § § 1.702-1(a)(4), 1.703-1(a)(2)(iv).

[65] Code Sec. 703(a)(2)(C).

[66] Reg. § 1.703-1(a)(2)(iv).

the percentage limitations[67] to the total amount.[68] Each member's basis in the membership interest is reduced by the member's share of cash or LLC basis in property donated by the LLC to the charity.[69]

Beginning in 2018, a member may not deduct the member's allocable share of charitable contributions in excess of the member's tax basis in the membership interest.[70] The basis limitation does not apply to the excess of the contributed property's fair market value over its adjusted basis.[71]

The LLC must attach a statement to Schedules K and K-1, indicating by amount the charitable contributions that are subject to the 20, 30, and 50 percent limitations.

A member may not deduct charitable contributions passed through from an LLC for contributions in excess of $250, unless the LLC obtains a written acknowledgement from the charitable organization. The written acknowledgement must show the amount of cash contributed, describe the property contributed, and give an estimate of the value of any goods or services provided in return for the contribution. The LLC must obtain the acknowledgement by the due date, including extensions, for the LLC return or any earlier date that the LLC files its return. The LLC is not required to attach a copy of the acknowledgement to its return.[72]

The LLC must complete Form 8283 if it makes noncash charitable contributions in excess of $500. The LLC must give a copy of the form to every member if the charitable deduction for an item or group of contributed property exceeds $5,000. If it is less than $5,000, the LLC must still give the form to each member, and each member must complete his or her own Form 8283.[73]

A member's charitable contribution of a membership interest will be treated as a part-gift part-sale transaction if the charity is allocated any LLC liabilities as a result of the gift. The member will receive a charitable contribution deduction under Code Sec. 170 equal to the fair market value of the membership interest less the member's share of liabilities at that time.[74] The member will also recognize gain equal to the difference between the amount realized and the member's basis in the membership interest. The amount realized equals the member's share of LLC liabilities that are allocated to the charity after the transfer. The member's basis for determining gain is equal to the total basis multiplied by a fraction, the numerator of which is the member's allocable share of debt and the denominator of which is the fair market value of the membership interest.[75] If the LLC has no unrealized receivables or appreciated inventory items, the gain will be capital gain.[76]

---

[67] Code Sec. 170(b).

[68] Reg. § 1.702-1(a)(4).

[69] Rev. Rul. 96-11, 1996-1 CB 140.

[70] Code Sec. § 704(d)(3)(A).

[71] Code Sec. § 704(d)(3)(B).

[72] Instructions to Form 1065.

[73] *Id.*

[74] Rev. Rul. 75-194, 1975-1 CB 80.

[75] Code Sec. 1011(b); Reg. § 1.1011-2.

[76] Rev. Rul. 75-194, 1975-1 CB 80.

.04 Investment Income and Expenses

An LLC must separately state investment income and non-business production of income investment expenses.[77] The LLC must report the gross investment income on line 20a of Schedule K and the investment expenses on line 20b of Schedule K. Investment income is reported on Schedule K-1, Box 20, using Code A. Investment expenses are reported on Schedule K-1, Box 20, using Code B. This information is necessary so that the member can compute the investment interest expense limitation.[78] The information is also necessary for the member to compute the deductibility limits at the member level for miscellaneous itemized deductions other than investment interest.[79]

Beginning in 2013, an LLC must separately state on Schedule K-1 each member's share of the LLCs net investment income. Net investment income is reported on Schedule K-1, Box 20, using Code Y. The member's share of net investment income from the LLC and all other sources is subject to the 3.8 percent NII tax. The NII tax is discussed at ¶ 708.

Investment income and expenses are discussed in Chapter 20.

.05 Dividends

An LLC must separately state qualified dividends that are passed through to individual members and taxed at a maximum 20 percent tax rate.[80] Qualified dividends are reported on Line 6b of Schedule K-1. Qualified dividends include dividends received from:

- *Domestic corporations.* Dividends received by an LLC from domestic corporations are qualified dividends except for (i) dividends that the LLC received on shares held for less than 61 days during the 121-day period that began 60 days before the ex-dividend date, (ii) dividends attributable to periods totaling more than 366 days that the LLC received on any share of preferred stock held for less than 91 days during the 181-day period that began 90 days before the ex-dividend date, (iii) dividends that relate to payments that the LLC is obligated to make with respect to short sales or positions in substantially similar or related property, (iv) dividends paid by a regulated investment company that are not taxed as qualified dividend income under Code Sec. 854, and (v) dividends paid by a real estate investment trust that are not treated as qualified dividend income under Code Sec. 857(c).[81]
- *Qualified foreign corporations.* Dividends received from a qualified foreign corporation are qualified dividends if the foreign corporation is (i) incorpo-

---

[77] Reg. § 1.702-1(a)(8)(i); Rev. Rul. 84-131, 1984-2 CB 37.

[78] Instructions to Form 1065.

[79] Code Sec. § 67(c)(1); Reg. § § 1.67-2T(b)(1), 1.67-2T(b)(2), Example; Lender Management, LLC v. Comm'r, TC Memo 2017-246.

[80] Code Secs. 703(a)(1), 702(a)(5); Reg. § 1.702-1(a)(5).

[81] *See* Instructions to Form 1065; Code Sec. 1(h)(11); IRS Publication 550.

rated in the possession of the United States, or (ii) eligible for treaty benefits under a comprehensive income tax treaty with United States that includes an exchange of information program, or (iii) any other foreign corporation if the stock associated with the dividend is readily tradable on an established securities market in the United States. Qualified dividends do not include dividends paid by a passive foreign investment company.[82]

.06 Section 179 Expenses and Repair Regulations

Section 179 Expenses

An LLC must separately state Section 179 expenses. The maximum amount of Section 179 expenses is $1 million for property purchased and placed in service in 2018, indexed for inflation.[83] The $1 million limitation is reduced on a dollar-for-dollar basis (but not below zero) by the cost of Section 179 property placed in service during the 2018 tax year that exceeds $2.5 million, indexed for inflation.[84]

The $1 million limitation applies at both the LLC and member level.[85] The member's own Section 179 expense and distributive share of LLC Section 179 expense cannot exceed the annual limit. However, a member does not include the cost of Section 179 property purchased by the LLC during the year in determining whether the $2,500,000 investment limit for the member was exceeded.[86]

The member must reduce his basis in the LLC by his distributive share of Section 179 expense even if the member cannot currently deduct the expense.[87] The member's basis for determining gain or loss on sale of the membership interest is increased by any outstanding carryover Section 179 expense allocated from the LLC.

The LLC must reduce the basis of its Section 179 property by the amount of the deduction even if the member cannot deduct his allocable share because of the limits on deduction at the member level.[88]

An LLC may not allocate Section 179 expense deductions to its members in excess of the LLC's taxable income for the year.[89] The Section 179 expense deduction may not create a net trade or business loss at either the LLC or member level.[90] The deduction may not exceed the LLC's net active trade or business taxable income from all sources, or the member's active trade or business taxable income from all sources. The limitation is applied first at the LLC level and then at the member level.

---

[82] *See* Instructions to Form 1065; Code Sec. 1(h)(11)(C); IRS Notice 2011-64, 2011-37 IRB 231.

[83] Code Sec. 179(b)(1).

[84] Code Sec. 179(b)(2).

[85] Code Sec. 179(d)(8); Reg. §§ 1.179-2(b)(3), 1.179-3(g).

[86] Reg. § 1.179-2(b)(3).

[87] Reg. § 1.179-3(g)(2).

[88] Reg. § 1.179-1(f)(2).

[89] Reg. § 1.179-2(c)(2).

[90] Code Sec. 179(b)(3); Reg. § 1.179-3(g)(1).

The LLC may carry over amounts that are not deductible because of the active trade or business income limit.[91] The LLC may not carry over amounts that are not deductible (i) because of the annual dollar limits on property placed in service, or (ii) because the LLC made no Section 179 election or made an election in an amount less than the maximum allowable deduction.[92]

A member that receives a Schedule K-1 from an LLC must report the sale, exchange or other disposition of property for which a Section 179 expense deduction was previously claimed and passed through to its members on Form 4797, 4684, 6252, or 8824.[93]

Repair Regulations

An LLC may expense materials, equipment, and supplies in excess of the Section 179 limits by making the de minimis safe-harbor election under the Section 263 regulations.[94] The de minimis safe harbor rule allows taxpayers to deduct property repair expenses or amounts paid for the acquisition and production of new property that otherwise must be capitalized under Section 263. Unlike the Section 179 expense election, there is no aggregate annual dollar limit on the amount that an LLC can expense under the de minimis safe-harbor election. The regulations give an example of a company expensing $6,250,000 for computer equipment in a single year.[95]

An LLC may make the election if the following requirements are met:

- The LLC produces or acquires a "unit of property" (UOP), or acquires materials or supplies during the tax year. The LLC may not make the election for inventory property, land, or certain rotable, temporary or standby emergency spare parts.

- At the beginning of the tax year, the LLC has written accounting procedures treating the amount paid for property costing less than a specified dollar amount, or with an economic useful life of 12 months or less, as an expense for non-tax book purposes.

- The LLC treats the amount paid for the property as an expense on its applicable financial statements, or on its books if it has no applicable financial statements. The applicable financial statements include SEC financial statements, certified audited financial statements, or financial statements provided to federal or state government or agency other than the SEC or IRS.

- The maximum amount paid for a UOP may not exceed $5,000 per unit as substantiated by an invoice if the LLC has applicable financial statements, or $2,500 per unit if the LLC does not have applicable financial statements.[96]

---

[91] Code Sec. 179(b)(3)(B); Reg. § 1.179-3(b)(1).
[92] Reg. § 1.179-3(b)(1).
[93] Instructions to IRS Form 4797.
[94] Reg. § 1.263(a)-1(f).
[95] Reg. § 1.263(a)-1(f)(7), Example 3.
[96] IRS Notice 2015-82, 2015-50 IRB 859.

- The LLC makes the de minimis safe-harbor election to expense all UOPs, materials and supplies as an expense for tax purposes in the same manner as for book purposes (book-tax conformity). The LLC must make the election by attaching a statement to a timely filed tax return for the year.

.07 Depreciation

Depreciation expenses are not separately stated unless there is a special allocation of depreciation. In such event, it is separately stated only to the extent of the special allocation. Depreciation does not otherwise affect the members differently.

Depreciation of LLC property is subject to numerous provisions in the Code and regulations, including the following:

- *Contribution to the LLC.* The LLC must use the same method and period of depreciation for contributed property as used by the contributing member. The member's tax basis in the property carries over to the LLC for depreciation purposes, subject to the exceptions noted below. The depreciation rules and the depreciation recapture rules are discussed at ¶ 601.06.

- *Tax allocations for contributed property.* An LLC must allocate depreciation with respect to contributed property among the members so as to take account of the difference between the tax basis and the fair market value of the property at the time of contribution. The allocations must be made for tax purposes, not book or capital account purposes. There are three methods of making depreciation allocations: the traditional method; the traditional method with curative allocations; and the remedial allocation method. These depreciation methods are discussed at ¶ 805.

- *Safe-harbor rules for book allocations.* Under the safe-harbor regulations for book allocations, an LLC must depreciate property for capital account purposes based on the fair market value of the property at the time of contribution, and must depreciate property for tax purposes using the cost basis of the property. The amount of depreciation taken for book purposes must be based on the tax depreciation multiplied by a fraction, the numerator of which is the book value of the assets on the date of contribution, and the denominator of which is the tax basis. The safe-harbor rules for book depreciation are discussed at ¶ 804.02.

- *Contribution of built-in loss property.* If a member contributes built-in loss property to an LLC, the LLC must write down the tax basis of the property to the fair market value as of the date of contribution. The LLC must list as an asset in its financial statements the built-in loss component of the contributed property (carryover tax basis less fair market value on the date of contribution). It must depreciate the asset using the same method and remaining term of depreciation as used by the contributing member for the property prior to the contribution. It must make a special allocation of the depreciation to the contributing member for tax purposes only.[97] The depreciation rules for built-in loss property are discussed at ¶ 806.

- *Distributions to member.* A member who receives depreciable property in a distribution must use the same method and period of depreciation or amortization for the property used by the LLC prior to the distribution. If the member receives a higher basis in the property than the LLC's basis prior to the distribution, the property is treated as newly acquired property for depreciation purposes to the extent of the excess basis. The member will have a bifurcated basis for depreciation purposes. An LLC's distribution of depreciable property to a member does not trigger depreciation recapture. The depreciation rules on distribution to a member are discussed at ¶ 1003.06.

- *Depreciation and bifurcated basis after Section 754 distribution.* If the basis of property is increased as a result of a Section 754 election after the LLC distributes property to a member, then the increased portion of the basis must be taken into account as if it were newly purchased recovery property placed in service when the distribution occurs. Consequently, the LLC may use any applicable recovery period and method to determine the depreciation for the increased portion of the basis. However, there is no change in determining the depreciation period for the portion of the basis for which there is no increase. If the basis of the property is decreased as a result of a Section 754 election, then the decrease in basis must be accounted for over the remaining depreciation period of the property beginning with the depreciation period in which the basis is decreased.[98] The depreciation rules after a Section 754 distribution are discussed at ¶ 1006.01.

- *Depreciation and bifurcated basis after Section 754 transfer.* If the basis of property is increased as a result of a Section 754 election after a member transfers a membership interest in an LLC, then the increased portion of the basis must be taken into account as if it were newly purchased recovery property placed in service when the transfer occurs. Consequently, the LLC may use any applicable recovery period and method to determine the depreciation for the increased portion of the basis.[99] There is no change in the depreciation method or recovery period for the portion of the basis that has not been increased.[100] The LLC must separately list the Section 754 asset on its schedule of depreciable assets, and show the depreciation for the Section 754 asset. It must make a special allocation of the depreciation to the transferee member for tax purposes, and not for capital account purposes. During the years following the transfer, the transferee must receive a tax allocation of the member's share of common basis depreciation, and all of the tax depreciation on the increased

---

[97] Prop. Reg. § 1.704-3(f)(3)(ii)(D)(2), Example.

[98] Code Sec. 731(a)(1).

[99] Reg. § 1.743-1(j)(4)(i).

[100] Reg. § 1.743-1(j)(4)(i)(B)(1). There are special rules if the LLC uses the remedial allocation method with respect to depreciable property. Reg. § 1.743-1(j)(4)(i)(B)(2).

¶ 703.07

basis.[101] The depreciation rules after a Section 754 transfer are discussed at ¶1508.03.

- *Tax-exempt and non-U.S. members.* If the LLC has a tax-exempt member or a non-U.S. member, the LLC must use different depreciation schedules. It must depreciate buildings over a 40-year recovery period (rather than a 27 $^1/_2$-or 39-year recovery period). It must depreciate personal property over 12-year recovery periods rather than a seven-year recovery period using the straight-line method of depreciation to the extent of its tax-exempt members. If property owned by the LLC is treated as "tax-exempt use property" under Code Sec. 168(h), it must depreciate the property using the straight-line method over 40 years in the case of real property, and over a longer period than the MACRS cost recovery periods for tangible personal property that is not tax-exempt use property.[102]

EXAMPLE 7-12

An LLC offers membership interest to qualified plans, IRAs and certain foreign members. To the extent that their share of LLC income and gain from depreciable property owned by the LLC is not taxable to them as unrelated business taxable income (UBTI) under Code Sec. 511, their allocable share of LLC depreciable property may be treated as tax-exempt use property under Code Sec. 168(h). Any adjustments to the LLC's cost recovery deductions, and any tax-exempt use losses incurred by the LLC due to the presence of tax-exempt members in the LLC, are normally allocated under the operating agreement to those tax-exempt members only.

.08 Interest Income and Expense

Reporting

An LLC must separately state each member's share of LLC investment interest expense.[103] Investment interest expenses are reported on Schedule K-1, Box 13, using Code H. The member must report the investment interest expense on Form 4952, Parts I and III.

The rule is different for business interest expense which may not be separately stated.[104]

---

[101] Reg. § 1.743-1(j)(4(i)(C), Example 1.

[102] Code Sec. 168(h)(5), (6).

[103] *See* Code Sec. 67(c).

[104] Code Sec. 163(l)(4)(A) (last sentence).

Investment Interest Expense

The members of an LLC may not deduct investment interest in excess of net investment income.[105] The members must compute the investment interest limitations on IRS Form 4952, Investment Interest Expense Deduction.

Investment interest is interest allocable to investments by an LLC that do not generate passive income.[106] For example, if an LLC trades in securities for its own account, and not for customers, a member's share of interest incurred on LLC debt is investment interest.[107]

The members must aggregate investment interest expenses from the LLC with their own investment interest expenses in computing the limitations on the investment interest deduction.[108] An individual member may deduct investment interest expenses, including a member's allocable share investment interest expenses incurred by the LLC,[109] only to the extent of "net investment income."[110] Prior to 1982, the limits on investment interest expense were determined at the LLC level.

Business Interest Expense

Business interest is interest paid or accrued on debt allocable to the LLC's trade or business. It does not include investment interest.[111] An LLC's business interest deduction may not exceed the sum of:[112]

1. The LLC's business interest income;
2. Thirty percent of the adjusted taxable income[113] of the LLC for the tax year. Adjusted taxable income is intended to resemble EBITDA (earnings before interest, taxes, depreciation and amortization) for 2018 through 2021 and EBIT (earnings before interest and taxes) for subsequent taxable years. Adjusted taxable income cannot be a negative amount,[114] so if an LLC has a loss for the year, then the business interest is deductible up to the sum of business interest income and any floor plan financing; and
3. Floor plan financing (e.g., auto dealership financing interest).[115]

---

[105] Ltr. Rul. 201505010, *citing* Code Sec. 163(d)(1).

[106] Ltr. Rul. 201505010, *citing* Code Sec. 163(d)(4)(B).

[107] Rev. Rul. 2008-12, 2008-10 IRB 520; FSA 200111001.

[108] Reg. § 1.702-1(a)(8)(iii); Rev. Rul. 84-131, 1984-2 CB 37.

[109] Code Sec. 67(c).

[110] Code Sec. 163(d)(1).

[111] Code Sec. 163(j)(5).

[112] Code Sec. 163(j)(1).

[113] Code Sec. 163(j)(8)(A)(v). Adjusted taxable income is taxable income before (a) the deduction for net interest expense, (b) the deduction for nonbusiness items, (c) the deduction for net operating losses, (d) the 20 percent deduction for pass-through income, and (e) depreciation, depletion and amortization deductions. Beginning with tax years in 2022, adjusted taxable income is after the depreciation deductions, which lowers adjusted taxable income and the interest expense deduction.

[114] Code Sec. 163(j)(1) flush paragraph.

[115] Code Sec. 163(j)(1).

EXAMPLE 7-13

An LLC has $3 million of taxable income, which includes $200,000 of business interest income, $2 million of interest expense, and $200,000 of depreciation. The adjusted taxable income is $5 million ($3 million − $200,000 + $2 million + $200,000). The overall limitation is $1.7 million (30% × $5 million of adjusted taxable income plus $200,000 of business interest income). Thus, the LLC may deduct only $1.7 million of the $2 million of interest expense. Beginning with tax years in 2022, adjusted taxable income would be $4.8 million since adjusted taxable income would be computed after (rather than before) depreciation.

The deduction limits do not apply to:

- LLCs with $25 million or less in average annual gross receipts for the prior three years.[116] The gross receipts of all related businesses are aggregated in determining average annual gross receipts.[117] The aggregation rules are determined under Code Sec. 52 (which is based on the aggregation rules in Code Sec. 1563) and Code Sec. 414.[118]

- An electing real property trade or business.[119] LLCs in a real property trade or business[120] may elect out of the business interest limitation.[121] However, the LLC must in such case depreciate real property using the alternative depreciation system (ADS),[122] which is straight depreciation over 40 years for non-residential rental property, 30 years for residential rental property, and 20 years for qualified improvement property.[123] In addition, the LLC will not

---

[116] Code Sec. 163(j)(3), which makes reference to the $25 million amount in Code Sec. 448(c).

[117] Code Sec. 163(j)(3).

[118] Code Sec. 448(c)(2).

[119] Code Sec. 163(j)(7)(A)(ii). Code Sec. 167(j)(7) provides that electing real property trade or business is not a trade or business for purposes of Section 163(j). Code Sec. 163(j)(5) provides that the business interest expense subject to the limitation on deductibility is interest paid or accrued on debt allocable to a trade or business. Thus, there is no limit on the deductibility of business interest under Code Sec. 167(j) for an electing real property trade or business.

[120] A real property trade or business has the meaning under Code Sec. 469(c)(7) which includes leasing, construction, development, acquisition, operation, management or brokerage of real property.

[121] Code Sec. 163(j)(7)(A)(ii).

[122] Code Secs. 163(j)(10)(A), 168(g)(1)(E), 168(g)(7), 168(g)(8).

[123] The regular depreciation lives are 39 years for non-residential rental property, 27.5 years for residential rental property, and 15 years for qualified improvement property. Due to a technical oversight and drafting error in the 2017 Tax Cuts and Jobs Act, the tax writers forgot to designate qualified improvement property for the 15-year life (which was the recovery period under the prior law until qualified leasehold property, qualified restaurant property, and qualified retail improvement property were consolidated into a single "qualified improvement property" category to be

be eligible to claim 100 percent bonus depreciation on qualified improvement property because those assets will be depreciated using the ADS depreciation method.[124]

- An electing farming business.[125] If an electing farming business elects out of the business interest limitation, then the farming business must use straight-line depreciation under ADS for any assets with a life of ten or more years.[126] In addition, the LLC will not be eligible to claim 100 percent bonus depreciation on qualified improvement property because those assets will be depreciated using the ADS depreciation method.[127]

- Furnishing or selling certain types of energy.[128]

The deduction limits are applied at the LLC level.[129] An LLC's business interest expense does not pass through to the members as a separately stated item except for the disallowed portion of the business interest. Instead, the business interest is taken into account in determining the non-separately stated taxable income or loss of the LLC.[130]

However, the deduction limits are applied at the member level under certain circumstances. In calculating a member's annual deduction for business interest, a member may not include the member's share of LLC business interest income for the tax year except to the extent of the member's share of the excess of LLC business interest income over business interest expense.[131]

The deduction limits are also applied at the member level if the member has other income. The member may deduct the business interest expense up to 30 percent of the member's own adjusted taxable income. The member's adjusted taxable income in such case does not include the member's distributive share of LLC income, gain, loss or deduction[132] except for "excess taxable income" (defined below)[133] after the member has fully offset the member's excess business interest expense from the LLC, for all tax years, against excess taxable income from the LLC.[134]

(Footnote Continued)

assigned a 15-year recovery period under Code Sec. 168). As a result, qualified improvement property falls under a default recovery period of 39 years until the drafting error is corrected.

[124] Code Sec. 168(k)(2)(D). An LLC that makes this election may still take bonus depreciation for assets with a life of 20 years, or a life other than for leasehold improvements.

[125] Code Sec. 163(j)(7)(A)(iii).

[126] Code Secs. 163(j)(10)(B), 168(g)(1)(G).

[127] Code Sec. 168(k)(2)(D).

[128] Code Sec. 163(j)(7)(A)(iii).

[129] Code Sec. 163(j)(4)(A)(i).

[130] Code Sec. 163(j)(4)(A)(i).

[131] Notice 2018-28, 2018-16 IRB 492, Sec. 7.

[132] Code Sec. 163(j)(4)(A)(ii)(I).

[133] Code Sec. 163(j)(4)(A)(ii)(II).

[134] Code Sec. 163(j)(4)(B)(ii)(II).

EXAMPLE 7-14

An LLC has $200 of business income and $90 of business interest expense. The LLC may deduct only $60 of the interest (30% × $200). The LLC allocates $55 of the net income to Mary (50% of $200-$90) and $15 of the excess business interest expense to Mary. Mary has a $20 business interest expense from a sole proprietorship that is deductible up to 30 percent of the Mary's adjusted taxable income. Mary has no taxable income other than her distributive share of income from the LLC. Mary cannot deduct the $20 of business interest expense from the sole proprietorship against her distributive share of income from the LLC since her adjusted taxable income is determined without regard to her distributive share of LLC income. She may deduct the $15 of excess business interest expense from the LLC in the next succeeding tax years in which she receives an allocation of excess taxable income from the LLC, but only to the extent of such excess taxable income.[135]

An LLC must allocate any disallowed business interest expense to the members.[136] The disallowed business interest is allocated to the LLC members in the same manner as non-separately stated taxable income or loss.[137] Each member may then deduct the excess business interest in the next succeeding tax years in which the member receives an allocation of excess taxable income[138] from the same LLC, but only to the extent of such excess taxable income.[139] A member may not deduct the disallowed interest against other taxable income that it might generate outside of the LLC.

The LLC's excess taxable income is the LLC's total taxable income, multiplied by a fraction. The numerator of the fraction is the actual business interest deduction by the LLC and the denominator is the maximum allowable business interest deduction.[140] The member's share of the LLC's excess taxable income is the same as the member's distributive share of the LLC's non-separately stated taxable income or loss.[141] A member may use the excess taxable income from an LLC to deduct the member's own interest expense not coming from the LLC, but only after the member

---

[135] Code Sec. 163(j)(4)(B)(ii)(I) provides that "if a partner is allocated any excess business interest from a partnership under clause (i) for any taxable year—(I) such excess business interest shall be treated as business interest paid or accrued by the partner in the next succeeding taxable year in which the partner is allocated excess taxable income from such partnership, but only to the extent of such excess taxable income ... "

[136] Code Sec. 163(j)(4)(B)(i)(II).

[137] Code Sec. 163(j)(4)(B)(i)(II).

[138] Code Sec. 163(j)(4)(C).

[139] Code Sec. 163(j)(4)(B)(ii).

[140] Code Sec. 163(j)(4)(C).

[141] Code Sec. 163(j)(4)(A)(ii).

has fully deducted any carryover disallowed interest from the LLC against excess taxable income from the LLC.[142]

EXAMPLE 7-15

An LLC has $200 of business income and $40 of business interest expense. The LLC may deduct the full $40 of interest since it is less than the maximum allowable amount of $60 (30% × $200). The LLC allocates $80 the net income to Mary (50% of $200-$40). Mary has a $30 business interest expense from a sole proprietorship that is deductible up to 30 percent of the Mary's adjusted taxable income. Mary has no taxable income other than her distributive share of income from an LLC. The LLC has excess taxable income of $66.67. This is equal to the $200 of business income multiplied by a fraction, the numerator of which is the $40 actual business interest deduction divided by the $60 maximum allowable business expense deduction. Mary's $1/2$ share of the excess taxable income is $33.33. This is counted as her adjusted taxable income. She may deduct $10 of the interest from her separate business (30% × $33.33 of adjusted taxable income). She may not deduct the remaining $20 of business interest expense in the current year.

EXAMPLE 7-16

A member receives an $11,000 allocation of carryover interest from the LLC in 2019. In the following year, the member has $9,000 of its own business expense and receives an allocation of $12,000 of excess taxable income from the LLC. The member must first deduct the $11,000 of carryover interest from the LLC against the $12,000 of excess taxable income from the LLC. The member can then deduct $1,000 of its own $9,000 of interest expense against the remaining $1,000 of excess taxable income from the LLC.

The member's adjusted basis in the membership interest is reduced by the amount of disallowed business interest allocated to the member.[143] Thus, the member is required to reduce basis in the membership interest even if the member cannot deduct the disallowed interest. The member does not reduce basis a second time if the member deducts the interest in a future year as a result of excess taxable income allocated from the LLC to the member. If an LLC has losses in the same year as the disallowed interest, the member may deduct the losses only to the extent of basis in the membership interest, with basis computed after the reduction for the disallowed

---

[142] Code Sec. 163(j)(4)(B)(ii)(II).
[143] Code Sec. 163(j)(4)(B)(iii)(I).

interest. If a member transfers, donates or otherwise disposes of a membership interest, the adjusted basis in the membership interest is increased immediately prior to the disposition by the amount of remaining disallowed business interest.[144] No deduction is allowed to the transferee or transferor for any disallowed business interest resulting in a basis increase.[145]

Passive Loss Rules

The passive loss rules that apply to interest income, interest expense, and self-charged interest are discussed at ¶ 1304.05.

NII Tax

The NII tax on interest income and expense through an LLC is discussed at ¶ 708.05.

Refinanced Loans

Interest expense on refinanced loans may be deductible by the members depending on the LLC's use of the refinancing proceeds. If the LLC distributes the refinancing proceeds to the members, then the LLC may characterize the debt in one of two ways.[146] First, it may characterize the debt based on how the members use the debt proceeds. This will result in a disallowed interest deduction if the members use the debt proceeds for personal purposes. Alternatively, the LLC may allocate refinancing debt to expenditures made by the LLC during the same tax year as the distribution of the refinancing proceeds, but only to the extent that the debt proceeds have not been otherwise allocated to such expenditures. If the amount of the distributed debt proceeds exceeds the amount of the expenditures, the excess debt must be allocated based on how the member uses the debt proceeds.

Allocation of Interest Expense

Individual members of an LLC who are classified as general partners or who own ten percent or more of the membership interest in the LLC must first classify their distributive shares of LLC interest expense as interest incurred in the active conduct of trade or business, passive interest, or investment interest. The members must then apportion their interest expense (including the distributive share of LLC interest expense) among U.S. source and foreign source income.[147] The interest

---

[144] Code Sec. 163(j)(4)(B)(iii).
[145] Code Sec. 163(j)(4)(B)(iii)(II).
[146] IRS Notice 89-35, 1989-1 CB 675.
[147] Reg. § 1.861-9(e)(3).

expense allocated to foreign sources reduces foreign source income and the amount of foreign tax credits that the taxpayer may receive.

A corporate member that is classified as a general partner or that owns ten percent or more of the membership interests must apportion its distributive share of LLC interest expense at the partner level using the asset method described in the regulations, which includes the member's percentage interest in LLC assets.[148] A corporate member may value its assets using the fair market value, tax book value, or alternative tax book value.

There are separate rules for allocations of interest expense for members who are classified as limited partners and own less than ten percent of the membership interests.[149]

.09 Cancellation of Indebtedness Income

General Rules

An LLC must separately state cancellation of indebtedness income.[150] The COD income is reported on Schedule K-1, Box 11, using Code E. The determination of the existence or amount of COD income, and the amount of sale/exchange gain or loss, are determined at the LLC level.[151] The taxation of that income and the eligibility for an exclusion are determined at the member level.[152]

Items Constituting COD Income

An LLC has cancellation of indebtedness income if a creditor of the LLC cancels or reduces a debt owed by the LLC.[153] The following items do not constitute COD income:

- Discharge of a recourse or nonrecourse debt owed by the LLC in exchange for a membership interest with a fair market value equal to the debt canceled. However, the members must include in income the amount of canceled debt exceeding the fair market value of the membership interest.[154] The fair market value depends on all the facts and circumstances.[155] Under a safe-harbor rule, the fair market value of the membership interest is the liquidation value immediately after the debt discharge if certain requirements are met.[156]

---

[148] Reg. § 1.861-9(e)(2), (6)(iv).

[149] Reg. § 1.861-9(e)(4).

[150] Rev. Rul. 92-97, 1992-2 CB 124.

[151] IRS Market Segment Specialization Program, Partnerships, Audit Technique Guide, Chapter 8, under the heading, "Issue: Cancellation of Indebtedness–IRC Sections 108 and 1017."

[152] *See* ¶ 703.09 under the heading, "Taxation of Member" *infra*.

[153] Code Sec. 61(a)(12).

[154] Reg. § 1.108-8(a).

[155] Reg. § 1.108-8(b)(1).

[156] Prop. Reg. § 1.108-8(b)(2).

- Reduction in seller financed debt for a solvent LLC. The reduction is treated as a purchase price reduction. It is not COD income.[157] A bankrupt or insolvent LLC may also treat a reduction in a purchase money note as a purchase price adjustment.[158] The LLC must reduce the basis of the property securing the debt.[159] A debt reduction by a third-party lender is not a purchase price adjustment, and the COD exemption does not apply.[160]
- Discharge of an amount that would have given rise to a deduction.[161] For example, there is no COD income if a creditor cancels a cash basis LLC's obligation to pay an expense.[162] There is no COD income if the creditor cancels unpaid interest that was added to loan principal, and then forgiven, if the forgiven interest could have been deducted had it been paid.
- Nonrecourse debt, if the LLC does not retain the property. The special rules for recourse and nonrecourse debt are discussed below.

Taxation of Member

A member is taxed on his or her distributive share of COD income.[163] COD income is passive income to the extent allocated to passive activity expenditures at the time of the debt discharge.[164] A member may exclude COD income under Section 108 if:[165]

- *Bankruptcy.* The discharge occurs in a Title 11 bankruptcy case.[166] The bankruptcy exception applies at the partner level if the LLC is classified as a partnership.[167] The bankruptcy exception applies at the member level if the LLC is classified as a disregarded entity.[168] Thus, if there is cancellation of debt for a single-member disregarded LLC, the bankruptcy exception will not apply unless the member files for bankruptcy. The IRS announced its non-acquiescence in four Tax Court cases, each of which held that a partner who guaranteed the debt of a partnership in his individual capacity, and who was not in bankruptcy, may exclude from gross income under Code Sec. 108(a) partnership debt canceled in a partnership Title 11 case.[169]

---

[157] Code Sec. 108(e)(5).

[158] Rev. Proc. 92-92, 1992-2 CB 505; Ltr. Rul. 200336032.

[159] Rev. Proc. 92-92, 1992-2 CB 505.

[160] Rev. Proc. 92-92, 1992-2 CB 505.

[161] Code Sec. 108(e)(2).

[162] IRS Audit Technique Guide—Partnership, Chapter 8, under the heading, "Issue: Cancellation of Indebtedness—IRC Sections 108 and 1017."

[163] Rev. Rul. 92-97, 1992-2 CB 124; Code Sec. 61(a)(12).

[164] Rev. Rul. 92-92, 1992-2 CB 103.

[165] Code Sec. 108(a)(1).

[166] Code Sec. 108(a)(1)(A).

[167] Code Sec. 108(d)(6); Reg. § 1.108-9(b).

[168] Reg. § 1.108-9(a).

[169] *See* Action on Decision 2015-001 (Feb. 5, 2015) and cases cited therein.

- *Insolvency.* The member is insolvent.[170] The COD exclusion is limited to the amount by which the member is insolvent.[171] The insolvency exception applies at the partner level if the LLC is classified as a partnership.[172] The insolvency exception applies at the member level if the LLC is classified as a disregarded entity.[173] Thus, if there is cancellation of debt for a disregarded LLC, the insolvency exception will not apply except to the extent that the member is insolvent.

- *Qualified farm indebtedness.* The debt is qualified farm indebtedness.[174] The person discharging the debt must be a "qualified person" who is unrelated to the LLC and who is actively engaged in the lending business.[175] The member must have sufficient tax attributes.[176]

- *Qualified real property business indebtedness.* The debt is qualified real property business indebtedness (QRPBI), the member is not a C corporation, and the member elects to reduce the basis in depreciable real property.[177] The determination of whether cancelled debt is QRPBI is made at the LLC level. The debt cancelled must be secured by real property used in the trade or business and incurred before January 1, 1993, or be "qualified acquisition indebtedness." The debt may also be secured by a member's interest in a single-member disregarded LLC that holds the real property, in which case the lender in a foreclosure proceeding takes ownership of the LLC interest rather than the real property.[178] This form of security is sometimes used in mezzanine financing where the lender is in second position. The excluded COD income cannot exceed the member's share of the difference between (i) the outstanding principal amount of debt (before discharge) and the fair market value of the real property (reduced by the outstanding principal amount of any other QRPBI secured by such property), and (ii) the member's total adjusted bases of depreciable real property. The outstanding principal amount includes the prior year's accumulated accrued and unpaid interest.[179]

The insolvency and bankruptcy exceptions apply at the owner level if the LLC is classified as a single-member disregarded LLC.[180] Therefore, if an LLC is insolvent or

---

[170] Code Sec. 108(a)(1)(B). Insolvency is the amount by which the member's liabilities exceed the fair market value of the member's assets immediately prior to the discharge. *Merkel v. Comm'r,* TC Memo 1954-82 (1954). The member may not include contingent liabilities (guarantees) in the insolvency computations. *Merkel v. Comm'r,* 109 TC 463 (1997), *aff'd,* USTC ¶99-2 USTC ¶50,848, 84 AFTR 2d 99-6119 (9th Cir. 1999).

[171] Code Sec. 108(a)(3).

[172] Code Sec. 108(d)(6); Reg. § 1.108-9(b).

[173] Reg. § 1.108-9(a).

[174] Code Sec. 108(a)(1)(C).

[175] Code Sec. 108(g)(1).

[176] Code Sec. 108(g)(3).

[177] Code Sec. 108(a)(1)(D).

[178] Rev. Proc. 2014-20, 2014-9 IRB 614; Ltr. Rul. 200953005.

[179] Reg. § 1.108-6(a).

[180] Reg. § 1.108-9(a).

bankrupt at the time of debt cancellation, the insolvency and bankruptcy exceptions are available only if the owner is insolvent or bankrupt.

The insolvency and bankruptcy exceptions apply at the member level if the LLC is classified as a partnership.[181] Therefore, if an LLC is insolvent or bankrupt at the time of debt cancellation, the insolvency and bankruptcy exceptions are available only to the members who are insolvent or bankrupt at that time.

The insolvent or bankrupt member may exclude the debt discharge from taxable income only if the member reduces net operating loss carryforwards and other tax attributes.[182] A member may elect to reduce the basis in depreciable property owned by the member instead of reducing tax attributes.[183] The member must make the election on Form 982. A member may also reduce the basis in the membership interest instead of reducing tax attributes, if the LLC makes a corresponding basis reduction in LLC depreciable property with respect to that member. There are detailed regulations regarding this election.[184]

Members of an LLC sometimes attempt to avoid gain on foreclosure of LLC property by claiming that the LLC liability continues to exist. The LLC files tax returns for many years after the foreclosure showing the outstanding debt on the balance sheet, even though the LLC has no significant business activities. The IRS refers to these LLCs as "zombie partnerships."[185] If the liability does not in fact exist at the end of the year, it will be treated as a Section 752(b) cash distribution for that year.[186]

Special Allocations

An LLC must allocate cancellation of indebtedness income from nonrecourse debt to the members in accordance with their interests in the LLC if the operating agreement does not comply with the safe-harbor regulations on book allocations. The LLC may not make special allocations of COD income if it does not comply with the safe-harbor regulations.[187]

There are limitations on the ability of an LLC to make special allocations of COD income to insolvent or tax neutral members.[188]

---

[181] Reg. § 1.108-9(b); Code Sec. 108(d)(6); Rev. Rul. 99-43, 1999-42 IRB 506; Rev. Rul. 92-97, 1992-2 CB 124.

[182] Code Sec. 108(b).

[183] Code Secs. 108(b)(5), 1017; Reg. §§ 1.108-4, 1.1017-1.

[184] Reg. § 1.1017-1(g).

[185] IRS Audit Technique Guide—Partnerships, Chapter 8, under the heading, "Issue: Capturing Phantom Gain in Zombie Partnerships."

[186] *Id.*

[187] FSA 200131013.

[188] Rev. Rul. 92-97, 1992-2 CB 124.

Nonrecourse Debt—Property Sold or Abandoned

There is no COD income when an LLC disposes of property that secures a nonrecourse debt.[189] The rule applies to any disposition, including a sale, foreclosure, deed in lieu of foreclosure or abandonment.[190] Gain is recognized to the extent that the amount realized exceeds the LLC's basis in the property. The amount realized is the greater of the outstanding debt on all loans immediately before the foreclosure or the fair market value of the property plus the proceeds received from the foreclosure (e.g., relocation payment from the lender).[191]

Nonrecourse debt is debt for which no member or related person bears the economic risk of loss, even though the debt may be recourse to the LLC.[192] The determination of whether LLC debt is recourse or nonrecourse is made at the LLC level.[193] This is a factual determination based on the operating agreement, loan documents and any relevant state law.[194] The regulations under Code Sec. 752 do not determine whether an LLC debt is recourse or nonrecourse to the member for purposes of determining whether the LLC has cancellation of indebtedness income.[195] Thus, an LLC liability may be nonrecourse for COD purposes, even though one or more of the members have personally guaranteed the debt and even though the debt is recourse under the Section 752 regulations.[196]

EXAMPLE 7-17

Facts:

Sales price of the property	$200,000
Basis	50,000
Nonrecourse liability	300,000

---

[189] CCA 201525012; Rev. Rul. 76-111, 1976-1 CB 214.

[190] CCA 201525012.

[191] Real Estate Property Foreclosure and Cancellation of Debt Audit Technique Guide, Chapter 2 (Mar. 11, 2015).

[192] *See Great Planes Gasification Associates v. Comm'r*, 92 TCM 534 (2006) in which the court applied Section 752 principles in determining that a debt was nonrecourse to the partners, even though the debt was recourse to the partnership. The court cited Reg. §1.752-1(a)(2) which provides that, for purposes of allocating partnership liabilities among partners, "A partnership liability is a nonrecourse liability to the extent that no partner or related person bears the economic risk of loss for the liability." Commentators have pointed out that it is unclear whether debt is recourse or nonrecourse to the members for other purposes (such as cancellation of LLC debt) where the debt is only recourse to the LLC. *See* BNA Daily Tax Report No. 87, p. G-6, "Difference Between Recourse, Nonrecourse Debt Unclear In Law, Conference Panel Says" (May 6, 2013).

[193] CCA 201525012.

[194] CCA 201525012.

[195] CCA 201525012.

[196] CCA 201525012.

Computation of gain:

Amount realized (nonrecourse debt)	$300,000
Basis	(50,000)
Gain on sale of property	$250,000

* IRS Market Segment Specialization Program, Partnerships, Audit Technique Guide, Chapter 8, Example 8-1.

The result of the classification of LLC debt as nonrecourse debt is that the members will not be able to exclude the gain from tax under Code Sec. 108, since there is no COD income when the nonrecourse debt is canceled.[197]

The gain recognized is capital gain,[198] unless part or all of the gain is treated differently due to one of the following provisions:[199]

- *Code Sec. 1245.* All depreciation on Section 1245 property is recaptured as ordinary income.
- *Code Sec. 1250.* Excess depreciation above straight-line depreciation prior to 1987 is recaptured as ordinary income.
- *Unrecaptured Section 1250 gain.* For sales of depreciable property after May 7, 1997, depreciation not recaptured under Section 1250 as ordinary income (straight-line depreciation) is taxed at a maximum 25 percent tax rate.[200]
- *Unrecaptured Section 1231 losses.* Any current Section 1231gain, that would otherwise be characterized as capital gain, is treated as ordinary income to the extent of non-recaptured net Section 1231 losses. Non-recaptured net Section 1231 losses are the aggregate amount of net Section 1231 losses for the five most recent preceding tax years reduced by any amount already recaptured in prior year.
- *Code Sec. 111.* Under the tax benefit rule, members recognize ordinary income to the extent of accumulated unpaid accrued interest expense and real estate taxes that are not paid on disposition of real estate financed by nonrecourse debt.

Nonrecourse Debt—Property Retained

There is COD income if (i) the LLC retains the property, (ii) the creditor reduces the nonrecourse debt in a loan modification, and (iii) the nonrecourse debt is greater than the fair market value of the property.[201]

---

[197] CCA 201525012.

[198] Code Sec. 1231.

[199] IRS Market Segment Specialization Program, Partnerships, Audit Technique Guide, Chapter 8, under the heading, "Issue: Disposition of Property Subject to Non-Recourse Debt and Unpaid Interest."

[200] Code Sec. 1(h).

[201] Real Estate Property Foreclosure and Cancellation of Debt Audit Technique Guide, Chapter 2 (Mar. 11, 2015); Rev. Rul. 2012-14, 2012-24 IRB 1012; Rev. Rul. 91-31, 1991-1 CB 19 (nonrecourse debt reduced); *Gershkowitz v. Comm'r*, 88 TC 984 (1987) (nonrecourse debt canceled); Rev. Rul. 99-43, 1999-4 CB 506. Rev. Rul. 2012-14, 2012-24 IRB 1012; Rev. Rul. 91-31, 1991-1 CB 19; Rev. Rul. 99-43, 1999-4 CB 506.

EXAMPLE 7-18

Nonrecourse debt before reduction*	$300,000
Nonrecourse debt after reduction	(200,000)
COD income	$100,000

* IRS Market Segment Specialization Program, Partnerships, Audit Technique Guide, Chapter 8, Example 8-2; Rev. Rul. 2012-14, 2012-24 IRB 1012.

An LLC may avoid cancellation of indebtedness income in such case if the property is rental property (other than triple net lease property) or other real property used in a trade or business, and the member elects[202] to reduce the basis of depreciable property by the amount of COD income.[203]

Recourse Debt—Property Sold or Abandoned

If the LLC disposes of the property in a foreclosure sale, and the recourse debt is discharged, then there is a bifurcation of the transaction.[204] Part of the gain or loss is capital gain or loss, and the other part is COD income.

In the first part of the transaction, the LLC recognizes capital gain or loss. The gain or loss is the amount realized plus any proceeds received from the foreclosure (e.g., relocation payment from the lender) minus the adjusted basis of the property immediately before the foreclosure sale. The amount realized is the lesser of the fair market value[205] of the property or outstanding debt balance.[206]

In the second part of the transaction, the LLC realizes COD income to the extent that the debt discharged exceeds the fair market value of the property.[207] This COD

(Footnote Continued)

CB 506. Rev. Rul. 2012-14, 2012-24 IRB 1012; Rev. Rul. 91-31, 1991-1 CB 19; Rev. Rul. 99-43, 1999-4 CB 506.

[202] The election must be made by the member pursuant to Code Sec. 703(b)(1).

[203] *See* Code Sec. 108(c) which provides an exclusion for the discharge of qualified real property business indebtedness. In order to qualify for the exclusion, the real property must be used in a trade or business. Rental property normally constitutes a trade or business. CCA 200919035. For example, multi-tenant property rental property normally constitutes a trade or business where the taxpayer provides substantial services in connection with the management and operation of the property. Ltr. Ruls. 9426006 to 9426019, 9840026. Triple net lease property ordinarily does not constitute trade or business property. Rev. Rul. 73-522, 1973-2 CB 226; TAM 835008; *Neill*, 46 B.T.A. 197 (1942).

[204] CCA 201525012; Rev. Rul. 90-16, 1990-1 CB 12; *Frazier v. Comm'r*, 102 TC 784 (1994), *citing* Reg. § 1.1001-2(a)(2).

[205] Absent clear and convincing proof to the contrary, the sale price of property at a foreclosure sale is presumed to be its fair market value. *See Community Bank v. Comm'r*, 79 TC 789, 792 (1982), *aff'd*, 819 F.2d 940 (9th Cir.1987); Real Estate Property Foreclosure and Cancellation of Debt Audit Technique Guide, Chapter 2 (Mar. 11, 2015).

[206] Real Estate Property Foreclosure and Cancellation of Debt Audit Technique Guide, Chapter 2 (Mar. 11, 2015).

[207] CCA 201525012; Real Estate Property Foreclosure and Cancellation of Debt Audit Technique Guide, Chapter 2 (Mar. 11, 2015); Rev. Rul. 90-16, 1990-1 CB 12; Reg. § 1.1001-2(c), Example (8).

income may be excludable from the member's taxable income under Code Sec. 108(a)(1)(B) if the member is insolvent.[208] There is no COD income if the recourse debt is equal to or less than the fair market value/sales price of the property.

If the member is insolvent, the member will normally want to show that the fair market value of the foreclosed property is very low (e.g., less than the sales price at the foreclosure sale). This will increase the amount of COD income that is excludable under Section 108(a)(3), and decrease the amount of taxable capital gains that is not excludable under Section 108.[209]

EXAMPLE 7-19

*Facts:**

LLC gives a building back to the lender. The building is subject to a recourse debt.

Fair market value of property	$100,000
Recourse debt	200,000
Tax basis	$ 75,000

Computation of gain:

Fair market value of property	$100,000
Basis of property	(75,000)
Taxable gain on sale of property	$25,000

Computation of COD income:

Discharge of recourse debt	$200,000
Fair market value of property	(100,000)
COD income	$100,000

* IRS Market Segment Specialization Program, Partnerships, Audit Technique Guide, Chapter 8, Example 8-3.

An LLC may avoid cancellation of indebtedness income in such case if the property is rental property (other than triple net lease property) or other property used in a trade or business, and the member elects[210] to reduce the basis of depreciable property by the amount of COD income.[211]

---

[208] CCA 201525012.

[209] *Frazier v. Comm'r*, 102 TC 784 (1994).

[210] The election must be made by the member pursuant to Code Sec. 703(b)(1).

[211] *See* Code Sec. 108(c) which provides an exclusion for the discharge of qualified real property business indebtedness.

If the property is abandoned, and the debt is recourse debt, there are no immediate tax results. Instead, the LLC reports income when the lender forecloses on the property.

If COD income is derived in connection with a trade or business and is reported on a Schedule C or F, then it is self-employment income and subject to self-employment tax. If an exception applies to exclude COD income from gross income, then there is no self-employment tax.[212]

Recourse Debt—Property Retained

The entire debt canceled is COD income if (i) the LLC retains the property, (ii) the creditor reduces the recourse debt in a loan modification, and (iii) the recourse debt is greater than the fair market value of the property.[213]

EXAMPLE 7-20

Recourse debt before reduction*	$300,000
Recourse debt after reduction	(200,000)
COD income	$100,000

* IRS Market Segment Specialization Program, Partnerships, Audit Technique Guide, Chapter 8, Example 8-4.

An LLC may avoid cancellation of indebtedness income in such case if the property is rental property (other than triple net lease property) or other property used in a trade or business, and the member elects[214] to reduce the basis of depreciable property by the amount of COD income.[215]

Basis in Membership Interest

The cancellation of indebtedness income increases a member's basis in the membership interest. The relief of debt decreases basis by a corresponding amount (assuming no special allocations).[216]

---

[212] Real Estate Property Foreclosure and Cancellation of Debt Audit Technique Guide, Chapter 2 (Mar. 11, 2015).

[213] Rev. Rul. 92-97, 1992-2 CB 124.

[214] The election must be made by the member pursuant to Code Sec. 703(b)(1).

[215] *See* Code Sec. 108(c) which provides an exclusion for the discharge of qualified real property business indebtedness.

[216] *See* Rev. Rul. 92-97, 1992-2 CB 124 which states, "When the COD income is properly allocated, the outside bases of A and B are increased under section 705(a)(1)(A) of the Code by $90x and $810x, respectively, for their distributive shares of the partnership's COD income. Under section 108(d)(6), A and B individually determine if any portion of their distributive shares is excluded from gross income. Under section 705(a)(2), the outside bases of A and B are decreased by $90x and $810x,

EXAMPLE 7-21

An LLC has two equal members. The LLC owns an office building with a fair market value of $7,000. The office building is subject to a nonrecourse debt of $10,000. The lender agrees to reduce the debt by $3,000 in a workout arrangement. Each member has a basis of $4,000 in his membership interest (which includes each member's $5,000 share of nonrecourse liabilities). The debt reduction is cancellation of indebtedness income to the LLC. The income is allocated to each member equally and is taxable at the member level. The income allocation increases each member's basis by $1,500 from $4,000 to $5,500. The $3,000 debt reduction also decreases each member's share of liabilities for basis purposes, thus reducing the $5,500 basis for each member back down to $4,000.[217]

Issuance of Membership Interest to Creditor

An LLC recognizes cancellation of indebtedness income when it issues a capital or profits interest to a creditor in satisfaction of a recourse or nonrecourse debt.[218] The LLC is treated as having satisfied the debt with money equal to the fair market value the membership interest. The fair market value is the liquidation value if certain conditions are met.[219] The liquidation value does not take into account the minority interest discount, lack of liquidity discount, or other discounts that would reduce the value of the membership interest. As a result of the higher value, the amount of cancellation of indebtedness income is reduced. The LLC must allocate any COD income to the members immediately prior to the transfer.

(Footnote Continued)

respectively, for their distributions of money under section 752(b) resulting from the cancellation of the debt. A and B recognize no gain under section 731 in year 6 because the distributive shares of COD income provide an outside basis increase for each partner sufficient to cover the distribution of money to that partner. Because of the integral relationship between the COD income and the section 752(b) distribution of money from the cancelled debt, section 1.731-1(a)(1)(ii) of the regulations treats the distribution of money to each partner from the cancellation of the debt as occurring at the end of AB's taxable year as an advance or drawing against that partner's distributive share of COD income." *See also* Rev. Rul. 72-205, 1972-1 CB 37.

[217] Rev. Rul. 92-97, 1992-2 CB 124; Rev. Rul. 94-4, 1994-1 CB 195.

[218] Code Sec. 108(e)(8).

[219] Reg. § 1.108-8, the conditions are that (i) the LLC must maintain capital accounts for members in accordance with the safe-harbor regulations, (ii) the creditor, the LLC and its members must treat the fair market value of the debt as equal to the liquidation value of the membership interest, (iii) the debt-for-equity exchange must be an arm's-length transaction, and (iv) the LLC may not redeem the membership interest, and related parties may not purchase the membership interest, with the principal purpose of avoiding the COD income by the LLC.

Cancellation of Loan to Member

The cancellation of a loan by an LLC to a member is treated as a distribution of money to the member. Gain is recognized to the extent that the deemed distribution exceeds the adjusted basis of the member's interest in the LLC immediately before the distribution.[220]

.10 Domestic Production Activities

The domestic production activity deduction is repealed for tax years after 2017.[221] Prior to that date, an LLC classified as a partnership was required to separately state each item of income, gain, loss, and deduction attributable to domestic production activities.[222]

Prior to 2018, the deduction for domestic production activities was applied at the member level. Each member was required to compute the deduction separately. The LLC could specially allocate items of income, gain, loss and deduction attributable to qualified production activities if the allocations had substantial economic effect.[223] The member then aggregated his or her share of such items from the LLC with domestic production activity items from other sources.

.11 Passive Income and Expenses

In order to allow each member to correctly apply the passive activity limitations, the LLC must report income, loss and credits separately for each of the following:[224]

- Trade or business activities. The LLC must report the specific income and deductions for each separate trade or business activity on a statement attached to Form 1065. The LLC must also report each member's allocable share of income and deductions from each trade or business activity on a statement attached to Schedule K-1.
- Rental real estate activities.
- Rental activities other than real estate.
- Portfolio income.

The IRS listed 14 different items that an LLC must identify on the statement attached to the return in connection with passive activities conducted through an LLC that is classified as a partnership.[225]

The passive loss rules are discussed at ¶ 1304.

---

[220] Ltr. Rul. 201314004; Reg. § 1.731-1(c)(2).

[221] Code Sec. 199, repealed by 2017 Tax Cuts and Jobs Act § 13305(a).

[222] Reg. § 1.199-5(b)(i).

[223] IRS Notice 2005-14, 2005-1 CB 498, ¶ 4.06(1)(a)(i).

[224] Instructions to Form 1065, under the heading, "Passive Activity Limitations."

[225] Instructions to Form 1065, under the heading, "Passive Activity Reporting Requirements."

.12 Nonbusiness Expenses

Nonbusiness expenses must be separately stated.[226] These are expenses incurred in connection with investments, and the production and conservation of income and capital, but which do not rise to the level of a trade or business. These expenses are not deductible by the LLC.[227] However, they must be separately stated, and are deductible by members. The only possible exception would be for corporate members, since the heading of Code Sec. 212 states that such nonbusiness expenses are deductible only by an individual. To avoid this problem, the Section 212 expenses should be listed as Section 162 expenses for a corporate member.

.13 Rental Income and Expenses

Reporting

An LLC must separately report income, loss and credits with respect to rental real estate activities and rental activities other than real estate. The purpose is to allow each member of the LLC to correctly apply the passive activity limitations.[228]

Self-Rental Income and 3.8 Percent NII Tax

An LLC may deduct rent paid to a member for property leased from the member. The rent received by the member is called "self-rental income." The rental income is treated as net investment income subject to the 3.8 percent NII tax unless an exception applies. The main exception is for a member's lease of property to an LLC for use in a trade or business activity in which the member materially participates.

EXAMPLE 7-22

A member leases a building to an LLC. The LLC uses the building in a trade or business activity in which the member materially participates. The LLC pays the member $50,000 per year in rental income. The rental income is not subject to the 3.8 percent NII tax because of the self-rental exception.

The 3.8 percent tax on net investment income is discussed at ¶ 708.

---

[226] Reg. § 1.702-1(a)(8).
[227] Code Sec. 703(a)(2)(E).
[228] Instructions to Form 1065, under the heading, "Passive Activity Limitations."

Foreign Members

There is a 30 percent withholding tax on rental income allocated to foreign members in an LLC. The tax is on gross rental income without any deductions or credits. Alternatively, the LLC may withhold taxes at a 35 percent rate on net rental income after deductions. The rental income rule for foreign members is discussed at ¶1902.04.

Tax-Exempt Organizations

Rental income received by a tax-exempt organization from an LLC may be unrelated business taxable income if the property is debt-financed or the rental income is unrelated to the organization's tax-exempt functions. These rules are discussed at ¶2607.04.

S Corporation

Rental income received by an S corporation from an LLC may be treated as passive income, which may adversely affect the corporation's election as an S corporation. These rules are discussed at ¶401.01.

Passive Loss Rules

If the LLC leases property to other companies, the leasing business is a passive activity subject to the passive loss rules. The passive loss rules are discussed at ¶1304.02.

If a member leases property to an LLC in which the member materially participates, the lease is subject to the self-rental income rules for passive loss deductions. These rules are discussed at ¶1304.02 and ¶1403.02.

.14 Other Items

An LLC must separately state any other items of income, gain, loss, deduction, or credit to the extent provided in IRS regulations.[229] The IRS has specified numerous additional items that must be separately stated.[230] These items include the following general classes:

- Items that the LLC specially allocates to members under the operating agreement.[231]
- Items that an LLC must separately state in all cases, such as medical expenses and insurance premiums for members and employees, dependent care ex-

---

[229] Code Secs. 703(a)(1), 702(a)(7).
[230] Reg. § 1.702-1(a)(8).
[231] Reg. § 1.702-1(a)(8)(i) (last clause).

penses for members and employees, taxes and interest paid to cooperative housing corporations, intangible drilling and development costs, exploration expenditures, and certain mining expenditures.[232]

- Items that an LLC must separately state only if the allocation would result in income tax liability for a member that is different from that which would result if the member did not take the item into account separately.[233] These items include earned income for a member who is a *bona fide* resident of a foreign country; pensions annuities, interest, rents, dividends, and earned income for a member who qualifies for the retirement income credit; and all losses for a member if the business of the LLC constitutes a hobby loss for the member.

¶704 NONDEDUCTIBLE ITEMS

An LLC may not deduct the following items in determining LLC income:[234]

- taxes paid or accrued to foreign countries and to possessions of the United States;[235]
- charitable contributions;[236]
- capital expenditures, including expenses incurred in connection with property acquisitions and real estate development;[237]
- standard deduction;[238]
- personal exemptions;[239]
- net operating loss deduction carrybacks and carryforwards;[240]
- capital loss carryovers;[241]
- depletion with respect to oil and gas wells;[242]
- additional itemized deductions for an individual set forth in Code Sec. 211 *et seq.* For example, the LLC may not deduct medical expenses under Code Sec.

---

[232] Reg. § 1.702-1(a)(8)(i).

[233] Reg. § 1.702-1(a)(8)(ii).

[234] Code Sec. 703(a)(2).

[235] Code Sec. 703(a)(2)(B). This item must be separately stated and is deductible by the members. Code Secs. 703(a)(1), 702(a)(6); Reg. § 1.703-1(a)(2)(iii). Each member must add his distributive share of taxes paid by the LLC to foreign countries or possessions of the United States to any such taxes paid or accrued by him. The member may then elect to use the total amount either as a credit against taxes owed or as a deduction from income. Reg. § 1.703-1(b)(2)(i).

[236] Code Sec. 703(a)(2)(C). This item must be separately stated and is deductible by the members. Code Secs. 703(a)(1), 702(a)(4); Reg. § 1.703-1(a)(2)(iv).

[237] *FRGC Investment, LLC v. Comm'r*, 84 TCM 508 (2002).

[238] Reg. § 1.703-1(a)(2)(i).

[239] Code Sec. 703(a)(2)(A); Reg. § 1.703-1(a)(2)(ii).

[240] Code Sec. 703(a)(2)(D); Reg. § 1.703-1(a)(2)(v).

[241] Reg. § 1.703-1(a)(2)(viii).

[242] Code Sec. 703(a)(2)(F); Reg. § 1.703-1(a)(2)(vii).

213, alimony under Code Sec. 215, moving expenses under Code Sec. 217, and IRA deductions under Code Sec. 219;[243]

- syndication fees;[244] and
- organization expenses[245] and start-up expenses,[246] unless the LLC makes an election to amortize such expenses over 180 months.

The LLC must separately state the nondeductible items. In most cases, the member is treated as having paid the nondeductible amounts directly. For example, the member may deduct charitable contributions if the aggregate charitable contributions by the member and the member's allocable share of LLC contributions do not exceed the percentage limitations under Code Sec. 170(b).[247]

The member's basis in the membership interest is reduced by the member's share of certain nondeductible items.[248]

¶705 AGGREGATION RULE

Unless otherwise provided in the Code, a member must aggregate the amount of separately stated deductions and exclusions passed through to the member from the LLC with the member's own deductions and exclusions in determining the amount of allowable deductions and exclusions for which a limitation is imposed.[249] For example, the member must aggregate the following items in applying limitation amounts and the elections under the Code for those items:

- mining exploration expenditures;[250]
- income received by a nonresident alien from the LLC related to real property located in the United States;[251]
- charitable contributions;[252]
- taxes paid or accrued by the LLC to foreign countries or possessions of the United States;[253]
- qualified production activity expenses under Section 199;[254]
- miscellaneous itemized deductions for purposes of the two percent floor on deductibility for such items. Between 2018 and 2025, a taxpayer may not deduct miscellaneous itemized deductions;[255]

---

[243] Code Sec. 703(a)(2)(E); Reg. § 1.703-1(a)(2)(vi).

[244] *See* ¶707.02 *infra.*

[245] *See* ¶707.03 *infra.*

[246] *See* ¶707.01 *infra.*

[247] *See* ¶703.03 *supra.*

[248] *See* ¶902.03 *infra.*

[249] Reg. § 1.702-1(a)(8)(iii).

[250] Reg. § 1.703-1(b)(2)(ii).

[251] Reg. § 1.703-1(b)(2)(iii).

[252] Reg. § 1.702-1(a)(4).

[253] Reg. § 1.703-1(b)(2)(i).

[254] Reg. § 1.199-5(b).

[255] Code Sec. § 67(g), as amended by 2017 Tax Cuts and Jobs Act § 11045(a).

- Section 179 expenses;[256]
- long-term and short-term capital gains and losses;
- Section 1231 gains and losses;
- investment interest expense; and
- a member's distributive shares of income, losses, and credits that are passive to the member. These LLC items are combined with the taxpayer's passive income and losses for purposes of determining the tax attributable to passive activities, whether passive losses may be deducted, and whether passive credits may be taken.

¶706 ELECTIONS REGARDING INCOME, DEDUCTIONS, AND CREDITS

.01 Elections by LLC

The LLC must make most elections regarding its income, deductions, and credits.[257] For example, it must elect the following:[258]

- Accounting methods.[259]
- Depreciation and cost recovery methods.[260]
- Nonrecognition of gain on an involuntary conversion.[261]
- Expensing the cost of certain depreciable property.[262]
- Amortization of organization and start-up costs.[263]
- Adjustments to basis.[264]
- Amortization of cost of pollution control facilities.
- Choice of inventory method. The contribution by members of LIFO inventory to an LLC that is classified as a partnership does not trigger recapture of the LIFO reserve. However, the LLC must file IRS Form 970 and comply with Code Sec. 472 in order to adopt the dollar-value LIFO inventory method.[265] Any LIFO inventory contributed to the LLC is Code Sec. 704(c) property. Thus, any built-in gain or loss attributable to the inventory must be allocated to the contributing member for tax purposes when the inventory is sold.[266] On approval by the IRS, the LLC may treat the items included in its opening

---

[256] Code Sec. 179(d)(8).

[257] Code Sec. 703(b); Reg. § 1.703-1(b)(1).

[258] Reg. § 1.703-1(b)(1).

[259] Id.

[260] Reg. § 1.703-1(b)(1); Prop. Reg. § 1.168-5(e)(7); Rev. Rul. 81-261, 1981-2 CB 60.

[261] Fuchs v. Comm'r, 80 TC 506 (1983).

[262] See Code Sec. 179.

[263] Code Sec. 709(b).

[264] See Code Sec. 754.

[265] Ltr. Rul. 200124030.

[266] Id.

inventory as having been acquired at the same time, and determine their cost by the average cost method as provided under Code Sec. 472(b)(3).[267]

- Reinvestment of involuntary conversion proceeds. If gain is realized, the LLC must reinvest in similar or related property.[268]
- Election not to use the installment method of reporting.[269]
- Election under Code Sec. 754 to adjust the basis of LLC assets under Code Secs. 734 and 743 on the transfer of membership interests or on distributions from the LLC.[270]
- Treatment of income from discharge of indebtedness.[271]
- Expensing of assets under Code Sec. 179.[272]
- Treatment of soil and water conservation expenditures.[273]
- Deferral of gain under Code Sec. 1042 on the sale of stock to an employee stock ownership plan.[274]
- Expensing of film production costs under Code Sec. 181.[275]
- Cost allocation method for LLCs using the simplified method of determining a member's share of W-2 wages and qualified production activities income for purposes of computing the Section 199 domestic production activities deduction.[276]

.02 *Elections by Members*

The members rather than the LLC must make certain elections regarding LLC income, deductions, and credits. These elections include the following:

- Basis reduction related to discharge of debt.[277]
- Deduction and recapture of certain mining exploration expenditures.[278]
- Optional ten-year write-off of certain tax preferences.[279]
- Use of the foreign tax credit, rather than deduction, for taxes paid to foreign countries in United States possessions.[280]

---

[267] *Id.*

[268] *T.K. McManus v. Comm'r*, 65 TC 197 (1975), *aff'd*, 575 F.2d 1177 (6th Cir. 1978); *M. Demirjian v. Comm'r*, 457 F.2d 1 (3d Cir. 1972).

[269] Reg. § 15a.453-1(d)(1), (d)(3)(i); Rev. Rul. 79-92, 1979-1 CB 180. However, an LLC that is required to use the accrual method of accounting may not use the installment method of reporting.

[270] Code Sec. 754; Reg. § 1.754-1; *Atlantic Veneer Corp.*, 85 TC 1075, *aff'd*, 812 F.2d 158 (4th Cir. 1987).

[271] Code Sec. 703(b)(1).

[272] Code Secs. 179(c), (d)(8); Reg. § 1.179-1(h).

[273] Reg. § 1.703-1(b)(1).

[274] Ltr. Rul. 200243001.

[275] Reg. § 1.181-2(b).

[276] Rev. Proc. 2007-34, 2007-23 IRB 1345.

[277] Code Sec. 703(b)(1); Ltr. Rul. 201432009.

[278] Code Sec. 703(b)(2).

[279] Code Sec. 59(e).

[280] Code Sec. 703(b)(3).

- Election by nonresident alien individuals and foreign corporations to treat gross income from real property that is not trade or business income as if it were trade or business income.
- Election to carry back net operating losses, including a member's allocable share of trade or business losses passed through from the LLC.[281]
- Election under Code Sec. 732(d). Under that section, a member who purchased a membership interest without the benefit of a Section 754 election in effect, and within two years after the purchase receives a distribution of property from the LLC, may elect to treat the LLC's tax basis of the distributed property as the tax basis that the property would have had if the LLC had made a Section 754 election. This election is discussed at ¶ 1007.
- Election regarding preproductive expenses.[282]

¶ 707 ORGANIZATION, SYNDICATION, AND START-UP EXPENSES

.01 Start-Up Expenses

The general rule is that an LLC may not deduct start-up expenses.[283] However, an LLC may elect to deduct start-up expenses up to $5,000 in the year in which the LLC begins business, reduced by the amount by which the start-up expenses exceed $50,000.[284] The LLC may amortize the remaining start-up expenses ratably over a 180-month period beginning with the month in which the LLC begins business.[285]

There are three types of startup expenses:[286]

1. *Investigation expenses.* Expenses paid or incurred in connection with investigating the creation or acquisition of an active trade or business are startup expenses. Investigatory expenses include costs incurred in the general search for new business. Investigatory expenses also include costs incurred in the review of a prospective business before the LLC makes a decision to acquire the business.[287] Costs incurred to actually purchase a specific business are capital expenditures that are not amortizable.

2. *Creating an active trade or business.* Expenses paid or incurred in connection with creating an active trade or business are startup expenses. These expenses are sometimes called preopening expenses. These expenses include advertising expenses, salaries and wages for training employees, and travel expenses for obtaining prospective distributors, suppliers or customers. The

---

[281] Code Sec. 703(a)(2)(D).

[282] Code Sec. 263A(d).

[283] Code Sec. 195(a).

[284] Code Sec. 195(b)(1)(A); Reg. § 1.195-1(a).

[285] Code Sec. 195(b)(1)(B); Reg. § 1.195-1(a).

[286] Code Sec. 195(c)(1)(A).

[287] Rev. Rul. 99-23, 1999-20 CB 3.

startup expenses must be expenses that would be currently deductible if they had been incurred after actual business operations began. Startup expenses do not include the cost of expanding an existing business.

3. *Anticipatory expenses.* Expenses paid or incurred in connection with an activity engaged in for profit or for the production of income before the active trade or business begins, in anticipation of such activity becoming an active trade or business, are startup expenses. These expenses are similar to pre-opening expenses.

Ordinary and necessary business expenses of an ongoing trade or business are not disallowed as start-up expenses merely because the taxpayer later converts part of the business into a separate LLC.[288]

.02 Syndication Expenses

An LLC may not deduct syndication expenses.[289] The expenses must be capitalized,[290] and may not be amortized over any period. The LLC may not deduct syndication expenses even if the syndication is unsuccessful. Syndication costs that the member pays increase the member's outside basis in the membership interest.[291]

Syndication expenses are expenses to sell or to promote the sale of membership interests in an LLC.[292] Syndication expenses include brokerage fees, underwriting commissions, registration fees, printing costs connected with issuing and marketing membership interests in an LLC, legal fees of the underwriter and issuer for securities and tax advice relating to the adequacy of tax disclosures in the prospectus or private placement memorandum, accounting fees for preparation of materials included in the prospectus or private placement memorandum, cost of tax opinion included in the prospectus, due diligence costs, and other selling and promotional material.[293]

---

[288] *Toth v. Comm'r*, TC Memo 2007-14 (2007).

[289] Code Sec. 709(a); Reg. § 1.709-1(b)(2).

[290] Reg. § 1.709-2(b).

[291] IRS Market Segment Specialization Program, Partnerships, Audit Technique Guide, Chapter 2, under the heading, "Outside Basis—A/B of a Partner's Interest."

[292] Code Sec. 709(a); Reg. § 1.709-2(b).

[293] Code Sec. 709(a); Reg. § 1.709-2(b); Rev. Rul. 85-32, 1985-1 CB 186 (fees for a tax opinion used in partnership prospectus were not deductible); *Collins v. Comm'r*, 53 TCM 873 (1987) (legal and accounting fees incurred shortly after formation were recharacterized in part as syndication expenses); *Egolf v. Comm'r*, 87 TC 34 (1986) (syndication costs paid to a partner as a disguised management were not deductible); *Finoli v. Comm'r*, 86 TC 697 (1986) (amounts paid for preparation of a tax opinion to promote the sale of partnership interests, and commissions and consulting fees were nondeductible syndication expenses); *Surloff v. Comm'r*, 81 TC 210 (1983) (fees for preparation of a tax opinion letter used in the prospectus were nondeductible syndication expenses).

.03 Organization Expenses

The general rule is that an LLC may not deduct organizational expenses.[294] However, an LLC may elect to deduct organizational expenses up to $5,000 in the year in which the LLC begins business, reduced by the amount by which the organizational expenses exceed $50,000.[295] The LLC may amortize the remaining organization expenses ratably over a 180-month period beginning with the month in which the LLC begins business.[296]

Organization expenses are expenses that are (a) incurred to create the LLC, (b) are properly chargeable to a capital account, and (c) are not syndication expenses or startup expenses.[297] Examples of organization expenses include legal costs for preparing the organization documents and accounting fees incident to the organization of LLC. The organization expenses must be incurred during a time period that begins a reasonable period of time before the LLC begins business and ends on the due date (not including extensions) for filing the LLC return for the tax year in which the LLC commences business.[298]

.04 Election Requirements

After August 16, 2011, an LLC is deemed to have made an election to deduct start-up expenditures[299] and organizational expenses[300] for the tax year in which it begins its active trade or business. An LLC is no longer required to file a separate election statement to deduct such amounts or to specifically identify the deducted amounts as start-up expenditures or organizational expenses for the election to be effective.

An LLC may choose to forego the deemed election by capitalizing the start-up expenditures[301] and organizational expenses[302] on a timely filed federal income tax return (including extensions). The election to capitalize must be made in accordance with the forms and instructions used by the LLC to file its federal income tax return. An election to deduct or capitalize start-up expenditures[303] and organizational expenses[304] is irrevocable and applies to all start-up expenditures and organizational expenses that are related to the active trade or business.

---

[294] Code Sec. 709(a).

[295] Code Sec. 709(b)(1)(A); Reg. § 1.709-1(b)(1).

[296] Code Sec. 709(b)(1)(B); Reg. § 1.709-1(b)(1).

[297] Code Sec. 709(b)(2); Reg. § 1.709-2(a).

[298] Reg. §§ 1.709-1(b)(1), 1.709-2(a).

[299] Reg. § 1.195-1(b).

[300] Reg. § 1.709-1(b)(2).

[301] Reg. § 1.195-1(b).

[302] Reg. § 1.709-1(b)(2).

[303] Reg. § 1.195-1(b).

[304] Reg. § 1.709-1(b)(2).

¶ 708 NII TAX

.01 Overview

Beginning in 2013, there is a tax on a member's share of net investment income from the LLC and from all other sources. The tax is called the net investment income tax (NII tax), also known as the unearned income Medicare contribution tax.

The tax is 3.8 percent of the lesser of (i) net investment income, or (ii) the amount by which modified adjusted gross income (MAGI) exceeds the threshold amounts. The threshold amounts are $200,000 for individuals, $250,000 for married couples filing joint returns, and $125,000 for married couples filing separate returns.[305]

The NII tax applies only to individuals, trusts and estates.[306] It does not apply to LLCs. However, income passed through to the individual members of the LLC may be subject to the net investment income tax depending on whether the member is actively involved in the LLC's business.

There are three categories of net investment income subject to the tax:[307]

1. Income from interest, dividends, annuities, royalties and rents, other than income which is derived in the ordinary course of a trade or business. Rental income is included in the determination of net investment income whether or not derived from a trade or business.[308]

2. Other income derived from a trade or business if the business is a passive activity under Code Sec. 469 or involves the trading in financial instruments or commodities. Net investment income does not include income from a trade or business in which the member materially participates.

3. Gain attributable to the disposition of property other than property held in a trade or business that is not a passive activity and is not a financial instrument/trading business. This category includes income from the sale of property that is used in a passive activity and any asset not used in a trade or business.

EXAMPLE 7-23

A, an unmarried individual, is a member in PRS, an LLC that is classified as a partnership. The LLC is engaged in a trade or business that does not involve a rental activity. A does not materially participate in the LLC within the meaning of Reg. §1.469-5T(a), and so the trade or business of the LLC is a passive activity with respect to A for NII tax purposes. A's $500,000 allocable share of PRS's income consists of $450,000 of gross

---

[305] Code Sec. 1411(b).

[306] Code Sec. 1411(a).

[307] Code Sec. 1411(c)(1)(A); Reg. §1.1411-4(a)(1).

[308] Reg. §1.1411-5(b)(3), Example 1.

income from a trade or business and $50,000 of gross income from dividends and interest that is not derived in the ordinary course of the trade or business of PRS. A's $450,000 allocable share of PRS's income is included in the calculation of NII because it is gross income from a trade or business that is a passive activity. A's $50,000 allocable share of PRS's income from dividends and interest is included in the calculation of NII because such income is not derived in the ordinary course of a trade or business.[309]

.02 LLC Payments Subject to the NII Tax

In addition to the general categories of allocable net investment income subject to the NII tax (discussed at ¶708.01), the following payments by the LLC are subject to the NII tax:

- *Section 731 distribution gains.* Section 731 gains are treated as net investment income subject to the NII tax if the LLC's trade or business is a passive activity with respect to the member.[310] Section 731 distribution gains are actual distributions of money or marketable securities in excess of a member's outside basis. These amounts are treated as received from the sale or exchange of a membership interest.

- *Guaranteed payments.* Guaranteed payments for capital are net investment income because the payments are similar to interest, which is one of the taxable categories of net investment income. Guaranteed payments for services are not net investment income.[311]

- *Section 736(a)(1) payments.* Section 736(a)(1) payments of LLC income to a retiring or deceased member are treated as net investment income if the LLC is a passive activity with respect to the member at the time of liquidation of the membership interest.[312] The determination of whether the member materially participated in the LLC's trade or business prior to death or retirement, and whether the LLC activities are passive or non-passive with respect to the member, are made under the rules of Code Sec. 469 and regulations thereunder.[313]

- *Section 736(a)(2) payments.* Section 736(a)(2) payments of LLC income to a retiring or deceased member for unrealized receivables and goodwill are treated as guaranteed payments. The payments are not net investment income if the payments are made to the retiring or deceased member for services. The

---

[309] Reg. § 1.1411-5(b)(3), Example 5.

[310] *See* S. Starr and R. Prillaman, "Net Investment Income Tax and Pass-through Entity: New Proposed Rules," BNA Daily Tax Report No. 246. p. J-1 (Dec. 23, 2013).

[311] Prop. Reg. § 1.1411-4(g)(10).

[312] Prop. Reg. § 1.1411-4(g)(11)(ii).

[313] Prop. Reg. § 1.1411-4(g)(11)(ii)(B).

payments are net investment income if the payments are made to the retiring or deceased member for capital.[314]

- *Section 736(b) payments.* Section 736(b) payments to a retiring or deceased member for the member's interest in the LLC are treated as net gain subject to the NII tax if the LLC's trade or business is a passive activity with respect to the member.[315]

- *Installment payments to retiring or deceased member.* The determination of whether liquidating payments to a retiring or deceased member made over a period of years are subject to the NII tax is made at the time of liquidation of the member's interest.[316]

.03 Transfer of Membership Interest

Net gain from the sale of a passive interest in an LLC is subject to the NII tax. Net losses are deductible against other net investment income. Net gain or loss from the sale of an active interest in an LLC is not subject to the NII tax.[317]

Under proposed regulations, the net gain or loss attributable to a sale of a passive interest in an LLC is the net gain or loss that the selling member would take into account if the LLC sold all of its Section 1411 property for fair market value immediately prior to the disposition of the interest.[318] Section 1411 property is property that, if disposed of by the LLC, would result in net investment income to the selling member. These assets include (i) property held in a trade or business activity in which the member does not materially participate, (ii) property not held in a trade or business such as marketable securities, and (iii) property held in the business of trading in commodities or financial instruments.[319]

There are two methods for determining the passive activity gain or loss: the primary method and the simplified method. Under the primary method, the passive activity gain subject to the NII tax is the lesser of (i) the member's total gain on sale of the membership interest, or (ii) the amount of gain that the LLC would have allocated to the member if the LLC had sold all of its passive activity assets immediately prior to the sale of the membership interest.[320] The passive activity loss is the lesser of (i) the member's total loss on sale of the membership interest, or (ii) the amount of loss that the LLC would have allocated to the member if the LLC had sold all of its passive activity assets immediately prior to the sale of the membership interest.[321] The gain or loss is determined on an activity-by-activity basis. The LLC must value each of its activities at the time of sale, and then back out the basis of the assets used

---

[314] Prop. Reg. § 1.1411-4(g)(11)(iii).

[315] Prop. Reg. § 1.1411-4(g)(11)(iv).

[316] Prop. Reg. § § 1.1411-4(g)(11)(v), (ii)(B), Example 1, 1.469-2(e)(2)(iii).

[317] Code Sec. 1411(c)(4); Prop. Reg. § 1.1411-7.

[318] Prop. Reg. § 1.1411-7(a)(1).

[319] Prop. Reg. § 1.1411-7(a)(2)(iv).

[320] Prop. Reg. § 1.1411-7(b)(1)(i).

[321] Prop. Reg. § 1.1411-7(b)(1)(i).

in that activity, in determining the net gain or loss allocable to the selling member for his or her interest in each activity.

EXAMPLE 7-24

A owns a one-half interest in LLC, a calendar year LLC classified as a partnership. In Year 1, A sells his interest for $200,000. A's adjusted basis for the interest is $120,000. Thus, A recognizes $80,000 of gain from the sale. LLC is engaged in three trade or business activities, X, Y, and Z, none of which are trading in financial instruments or commodities. LLC also owns marketable securities. For Year 1, A materially participates in activity Z. A does not materially participate in activities X and Y. The fair market value and adjusted basis of the assets used in the LLC's activities are as follows:

Activity	Adjusted basis	Fair market value	Gain/loss	A's share of gain/loss
X (passive as to A)	136,000	96,000	(40,000)	(20,000)
Y (passive as to A)	60,000	124,000	64,000	32,000
Z (non-passive as to A)	40,000	160,000	120,000	60,000
Marketable securities	4,000	20,000	16,000	8,000
Total	240,000	400,000	160,000	80,000

A's allocable share of gain from the LLC's Section 1411 property is $20,000 ($20,000 loss from X + $32,000 gain from Y + $8,000 gain from the marketable securities). The gain from the sale of the membership interest subject to the NII tax is $20,000 (the lesser of the $20,000 gain from the sale of Section 1411 property and A's $80,000 total gain from the sale of the membership interest).[322]

Under the simplified reporting method, the amount of gain on sale of a membership interest subject to the NII tax is based on a percentage of assets within the LLC that are passive with respect to the transferor.[323] There is a look-back period that includes the current year and the preceding two years to determine the LLC's net

---

[322] Prop. Reg. § 1.1411-7(b)(2), Example (1).
[323] Prop. Reg. § 1.1411-7(c).

investment income as a percentage of its overall pass-through entity items. For example, if five percent of the income reported on the member's Schedule K-1 is passive income based on historic distributive share amounts during the look-back period, then ten percent of the member's gain on sale of the membership interest would be subject to the NII tax. The seller of the membership interest must meet either or both of two tests in order to use the optional simplified method.[324] Under the first test, the net gain or loss from the disposition of the membership interest may not exceed $5 million. The sum of the separately stated items of income, gain, loss and deduction allocable to the member on Schedule K-1 that are taken into account in determining net investment income must be five percent or less of all separately stated items of income, gain, loss and deduction allocated to the member during the disposition year and the two prior tax years. Under the second test, (i) the gain or loss may not exceed $250,000, (ii) the member must have held the membership interest for at least 12 months, and (iii) the member may not be one of the specified types of members that are prohibited from using the optional simplified method.

.04 Reporting Requirements

The net investment income is reported on Schedule K-1, Box 20, using Code Y.

An LLC must disclose additional information to a member if it knows or has reason to know that (i) the member transferred an interest in the LLC, (ii) the member materially participated in one or more trades or businesses of the LLC, and (iii) the member did not qualify for the optional simplified reporting method discussed above associated with the transfer of membership interest. Generally, the LLC must in such case provide the member with his or her distributive share of the net gain and loss from the deemed sale for fair market value of the LLC's property, other than property that relates to the trades or businesses in which the member materially participated.[325]

.05 Self-Charged Interest

When the member makes a loan to an LLC, the member receives interest income and an allocable share of the LLC's interest expense deduction on the loan. This is called "self-charged interest." The interest income is included in net investment income for purposes of the NII tax. Absent a special rule, the member's allocable share of interest expense deduction would not reduce the net investment income if the interest expense was generated in an LLC in which the member materially participated. However, there is a special rule for self-charged interest from a nonpas-

---

[324] Prop. Reg. § 1.1411-7(c)(2).

[325] Instructions to Form 1065, under the heading, "Net Investment Income Tax Reporting Requirements."

sive activity. The member may exclude from net investment income the member's allocable share of the LLC's interest deduction.[326]

EXAMPLE 7-25

A member loans $10,000 to an LLC in which the member materially participates. The member owns a 90 percent interest in the LLC. The LLC pays $700 in interest to the member during the year. The member's allocable share of the interest expense deduction is $630 (90% × $700). The member may exclude $630 of the interest income from the computation of net investment income. The member must include the remaining $70 of interest income in net investment income subject to the NII tax.

¶ 709 CHARACTER OF GAIN OR LOSS

The character of any item of income, gain, loss, deduction, or credit is normally determined at the LLC level rather than at the member level.[327] The pass-through items retain the same character after the allocation and distribution to the members.[328] For example, if the LLC sells a depreciable business asset at a gain, the gain is Section 1231 gain or depreciation recapture even though the member is not engaged in a trade or business.

The character of gain or loss to the LLC is determined at the member level for the following three types of contributed assets:[329]

1. *Unrealized receivables.* Gain or loss on receivables contributed by a member to an LLC is ordinary income or loss to the LLC.[330] This would normally be the rule in the absence of a specific Code section.

2. *Inventory items.* Inventory that a member contributes to an LLC will result in ordinary income if the LLC sells the property within five years after the contribution by a member, even if the property is investment property in the hands of the LLC.[331] The rule is designed to prevent a member from converting ordinary income items into capital gains by contributing the property to an LLC. This is the reverse of Code Sec. 735(a)(2), which provides that inventory coming out of an LLC will result in ordinary income if sold by the member within five years after the date of distribution.

---

[326] Reg. § 1.1411-4(g)(5).
[327] Code Sec. 702(b); Reg. § 1.702-1(b).
[328] Code Sec. 702(b).
[329] Code Sec. 724.
[330] Code Sec. 724(a).
[331] Code Sec. 724(b).

3. *Capital loss property.*[332] Loss recognized by the LLC on a sale or disposition of property for a period of five years after the contribution is treated as a capital loss (up to the amount of built-in loss on the date of contribution) even though the property is inventory in the hands of the LLC. Any loss attributable to post-contribution depreciation may be characterized as ordinary loss by the LLC if the property is inventory in the hands of the LLC or is otherwise ordinary loss property.

If the LLC has losses, the members may deduct the losses on their individual tax returns, subject to the passive loss rules. The LLC may not carry back or carry forward the losses to other years as a net operating loss. However, the members may use those losses as net operating loss carrybacks and carryovers on their individual returns.

---

[332] Code Sec. 724(c).

8

Allocations

¶ 801 GENERAL RULES

An LLC that is classified as a partnership does not pay taxes except in limited cases.[1] The income and losses of the LLC pass through to and are allocated to the members.[2] A member must take into account separately the member's distributive share of each class or item of LLC income, gain, loss, deduction, or credit, whether or not distributed.[3]

The members can decide what amount of income, gain, loss, deduction or credit will be allocated to each of the members. The LLC is not required to make the allocations in proportion to each member's capital account or percentage ownership interest in the LLC. For example, the LLC may provide that all depreciation will be allocated to one of the members, or that certain members will receive all the cash distributions until they have received back their initial capital contributions. The ability to make special allocations to members is one of the principal benefits of an LLC.

¶ 802 DIFFERENCES BETWEEN BOOK AND TAX ALLOCATIONS

Book allocations are allocations of income, gain, loss and deduction to a member's capital account. The capital accounts reflect each member's economic interest in the LLC. The allocations are debits and credits to the capital accounts and affect the amount that the member receives on liquidation of the LLC or liquidation of the

---

[1] For example, the LLC is subject to state and local taxes in some jurisdictions.

[2] Code Sec. 701.

[3] Ltr. Rul. 8003072 (*citing* Reg. § 1.702-1).

member's interest. The amount of book allocations to the member's capital accounts is determined under the operating agreement, not the Internal Revenue Code. However, some operating agreements provide that the book allocations will be made in accordance with the safe-harbor rules for book allocations under the Section 704 regulations.

Tax allocations are allocations made on a member's Schedule K-1, and are reported on the member's income tax return. The tax allocations do not affect a member's economic interest in the LLC.

For many LLCs, tax allocations and book allocations are the same. The LLC may keep its books on a tax basis, and report tax allocations that are the same as book allocations.

The rules for making book and tax allocations can be summarized as follows:

- *Book allocations.* An LLC must first make allocations of income, gain, loss and deduction as determined by the operating agreement.[4] The allocations are book allocations, not tax allocations. The allocations are made to each member's capital account. The capital account balance determines the amount that the member will receive on withdrawal as a member or liquidation of the LLC. Liquidating distributions must normally be made in accordance with positive capital account balances. The required order of book allocations under the safe-harbor regulations is discussed at ¶ 804.09.

- *Tax allocations.* After an LLC makes the book allocations, it must convert those book allocations into tax allocations. The general rule is that tax allocations must follow book allocations.[5] However, book allocations and tax allocations are not the same if there is a disparity between the book value and tax basis of the assets. The methods of converting book allocations into tax allocations are discussed at ¶ 804.10

- *Special allocations.* Special allocations are allocations of one or more items of income, gain, loss or deduction to a member that differ from the member's percentage interest in capital, or percentage interest in profits and losses. These allocations are book allocations, not tax allocations. Tax allocations will follow the book allocations in such case if the book allocations have "substantial economic effect."[6] If the book allocations do not have substantial economic effect, then the tax allocations will instead be made in accordance with each member's interest in the LLC.[7] The requirements for special allocations are discussed at ¶ 803.07.

- *Contributed property.* The LLC must allocate income, gain, loss, deductions, and credits with respect to contributed property so as to take account of any

---

[4] Code Sec. 704(a), (b)(2).

[5] Code Secs. 704(a), (b) provide that tax allocations will follow book allocations under the operating agreement if the book allocations have substantial economic effect. If the book allocations do not have substantial economic effect, or if the operating agreement is silent, then tax allocations will be made in accordance with each member's economic interest in the LLC based on all the facts and circumstances.

[6] Code Sec. 704(b)(2); Reg. § 1.704-1(b)(1)(vii).

[7] Code Sec. 704(b)(2).

difference between the tax basis and the fair market value of the property on the date of contribution. There are three principal ways of making the allocations: the traditional method; the traditional method with curative allocations; and the remedial allocation method. The allocations are made for tax purposes only. The tax allocations do not follow book allocations. The allocation methods for contributed property are discussed at ¶805.

- *Built-in loss items after transfer or liquidation.* If a member contributes built-in loss property to an LLC, the LLC may take the built-in loss into account only in allocating tax items to the contributing member. Built-in loss is the excess of the adjusted bases of the property to the contributing member over its fair market value at the time of contribution to the LLC. The basis of the contributed property is treated as equal to the fair market value of the property at the time of contribution for purposes of allocations to other members.[8] This rule denies built-in loss tax allocations to a transferee member after sale of the contributing member's interest, and to the remaining members after liquidation of the contributing member's interest.[9] The built-in-loss rules are discussed at ¶¶806, 1307, and 1509.

- *Varying interest rule.* Under the varying interest rule, an LLC must take into account the varying interests of the members in the LLC during the tax year in making allocations of income, gain, loss and deduction. The main methods of allocations are the closing of the books method and the proration method. The varying interest rule is discussed at ¶807.

- *Gifts and sales to family members.* A taxpayer may not assign income that the taxpayer earns through an LLC to a family member. The family partnership rules require special allocations of LLC income to the family members after a gift or sale of a membership interest. Family allocations are discussed at ¶808.

- *Retroactive allocations.* An LLC cannot allocate items to new members that are attributable to periods prior to the time that such persons became members in the LLC. Retroactive allocations are discussed at ¶809.

- *Extraordinary items.* Extraordinary items must be prorated to the members in proportion to their interests in the LLC at the time of day on which the extraordinary item occurred. Extraordinary items may not be prorated using the proration method or the interim closing of the books method. Extraordinary items are discussed at ¶807.08.

---

[8] Code Sec. 704(c)(1)(C)(ii).

[9] This rule supplements the rule that built-in gains and losses for contributed property must be allocated to the contributing member. *See Santa Monica Pictures, LLC v. Comm'r*, TC Memo. 2005-104, fn. 81 (2005) in which the court noted that, prior to the American Jobs Creation Act of 2004, if a contributing member of an LLC transferred his membership interest, built-in gain or loss was allocated to the transferee member to the same extent it would have been allocated to the transferor member pursuant to Reg. § 1.704-3(a)(7).

¶803 PERMISSIBLE BOOK ALLOCATION METHODS

.01 Overview

The allocations under the operating agreement are book allocations, not tax allocations. The book allocations are made to each member's capital account. The positive capital accounts determine the amount that the members will receive on withdrawal as a member or on liquidation of the LLC. An LLC may make book allocations in any manner that it wants, and is not required to follow the safe-harbor regulations on book allocations under Code Sec. 704.[10]

Tax allocations will follow book allocations[11] if the book allocations meet any one of the following tests:[12]

- The allocations have substantial economic effect.
- The allocations have economic effect equivalence.
- The allocations are made in accordance with each member's interest in the LLC.
- The allocations meet one of the special rules tests in the regulations.

If the book allocations do not meet one of the four tests above, or if the operating agreement does not provide for the allocation of income, gain, loss, deduction, or credit to a member, then LLC's taxable income, gain, loss, deduction, and credit will be reallocated in accordance with each member's interest in the LLC.[13]

Practice Note

Most operating agreements specify how income will be allocated, without specifying whether the allocation is a book or tax allocation. These agreements should be interpreted to mean that (i) the allocations are book allocations to each member's capital account, and (ii) tax allocations will

---

[10] The IRS determined that an LLC or partnership should not be "unduly concerned" with the complexities of the safe-harbor regulations if the LLC makes straightforward and consistent allocations of income, gain, loss and deduction to the members in accordance with their percentage ownership interests in the LLC. IRS Market Segment Specialization Program, Partnerships, Audit Technique Guide, Chapter 6, under the heading, "Introduction." *See also* IRS Audit Technique Guide—Partnerships, Chapter 6, under the heading, "INTRODUCTION," which states, "Because of the flexibility inherent in Subchapter K, partnership agreements can be written to reflect whatever economic sharing arrangement and risk sharing arrangement the parties wish to execute." In CCA 201741018, IRS determined that an LLC which did not comply with any of the requirements for substantial economic effect could make special allocations of losses in accordance with the operating agreement provided the LLC did not allocate losses to the members in excess of their positive capital accounts.

[11] Code Sec. 704(a).

[12] Reg. § 1.704-1(b)(1).

[13] Reg. § 1.704-1(b)(1)(i).

follow the book allocations as required by Code Sec. 704(a).[14] Some operating agreements actually specify how tax allocations will be made. These tax allocations will be respected if the tax allocations follow book allocations and if the book allocations have substantial economic effect.

.02 Substantial Economic Effect Test

The first permissible test for book allocations is the substantial economic effect test. Tax allocations will follow book allocations if the book allocations have substantial economic effect.[15] The substantial economic effect test is a two-part test. First, the allocation must have "economic effect." Second, the economic effect of the allocation must be "substantial."[16] Generally, an allocation has economic effect if the allocation affects the amount that the member will receive on withdrawal of the member or liquidation of the LLC.[17] The economic effect of the allocation is substantial if the allocation has meaningful non-tax consequences.[18]

The Treasury Department issued safe-harbor regulations setting forth when the substantial economic effects test will be met. The safe-harbor regulations are discussed in detail at ¶804. Under the regulations, allocations will have substantial economic effect if:[19]

- The LLC maintains capital accounts in accordance with the regulations.[20] The capital accounts track each member share of the book value of LLC assets, net of liabilities.
- The LLC makes liquidating and cash-out distributions in accordance with the members' positive capital account balances.[21]
- Each member is unconditionally obligated to restore any deficit in his capital account on liquidation of the membership interest. However, the members are not required to restore deficits in their capital accounts if (i) the LLC complies with an alternate economic effect test, (ii) the members contribute a personal promissory note to the LLC, or (iii) the members are unconditionally obligated to make subsequent contributions to the LLC other than pursuant to a promissory note.[22]
- The economic effect of such allocations is substantial.[23]

---

[14] However, the tax allocations will be made in accordance with each member's interest in each item of income, gain, loss and deduction if the book allocations do not have substantial economic effect. Code Sec. 704(b)(2).

[15] Code Sec. 704(a), (b)(2); Reg. § 1.704-1(b)(1)(i).

[16] Reg. § 1.704-1(b)(2)(i).

[17] Reg. § 1.704-1(b)(2)(ii).

[18] Reg. § 1.704-1(b)(2)(iii).

[19] Reg. § 1.704-1(b)(2)(ii)(b).

[20] See ¶ 804.02 infra.

[21] See ¶ 804.03 infra.

[22] See ¶ 804.04 infra.

[23] See ¶ 804.05 infra.

An LLC does not need to comply with the safe-harbor regulations if it makes pro rata allocations instead of special allocations. The IRS informally determined that an LLC or partnership should not be "unduly concerned" with the complexities of the safe-harbor regulations if the LLC makes straightforward and consistent allocations of income, gain, loss and deduction to the members in accordance with their percentage ownership interests in the LLC.[24] State taxing authorities, interpreting federal law, have also determined that an LLC does not need to comply with the safe-harbor regulations if there are no special allocations.[25]

The substantial economic effect test does not apply to allocations of (i) nonrecourse deductions that cause the book value of property to decline below the outstanding loan balance encumbering the property, (ii) tax credits, or (iii) creditable foreign tax expenditures. Instead, these items must be allocated in accordance with each member's interest in the LLC, or under one of the safe-harbor special rules for such items.[26]

Practice Note

Most LLCs do not fully comply with the safe-harbor regulations because of the complexities of the regulations. Book allocations will normally have substantial economic effect without compliance with the safe-harbor regulations if the LLC (i) maintains capital accounts, (ii) allocates income, gain, loss and deductions to each member's capital account, (iii) makes liquidating distributions to the members in accordance with positive capital accounts, and (iv) distributes amounts in excess of positive capital accounts to the members in accordance with their percentage ownership interests in the LLC. Tax allocations will follow book allocations in such case.[27] The IRS seldom challenges the tax allocations under such circumstances because if it reallocates more taxable income to some of the members (resulting in more taxes), it must reduce the taxable income of other members (resulting in tax refunds).

---

[24] IRS Market Segment Specialization Program, Partnerships, Audit Technique Guide, Chapter 6, under the heading, "Introduction."

[25] *See, e.g.*, California Franchise Tax Board, Partnership Technical Manual ¶1180, which explains: "Note that the principal purpose of the substantial economic effect tests is to prevent abuses regarding special allocations of certain partnership items of income or deduction. If the allocations are not 'special,' then whether or not the requirements under the economic effect are contained in the partnership agreement does not make any difference."

[26] *See* Reg. §1.704-2(b)(1) (allocation of nonrecourse deductions); Reg. §1.704-1(b)(4)(ii) (allocation of tax credits); Reg. §1.704-1(b)(4)(viii)(a) (allocation of creditable foreign taxes).

[27] IRS Market Segment Specialization Program, Partnerships, Audit Technique Guide, Chapter 6, under the heading, "Introduction."

.03 Economic Effect Equivalence Test

The second permissible test for book allocations is the economic effect equiva-lence test. Tax allocations will follow book allocations if the book allocations have economic effect equivalence.[28] The IRS refers to this test as the dumb-but-lucky rule.[29] Under this test, the LLC must show that a liquidation of the LLC at the end of the year in which the allocation takes place (or at the end of any future year) would produce the same results that would occur under the safe-harbor regulations.

The determination of what a member would receive on liquidation is sometimes made as follows:

- First, determine the proceeds that the LLC would receive if it liquidated at the end of the tax year by selling its assets for book value.

- Second, deduct from this amount all outstanding liabilities shown on the LLC's tax balance sheet at the end of the tax year. In the case of land and improvements encumbered by nonrecourse debt, deduct liabilities only up to the book value of the encumbered assets. The lender bears the risk of loss on liquidation for nonrecourse debt in excess of the book value of the property.[30]

- Third, determine the distribution amount that each member would receive on liquidation under the operating agreement, and the corresponding reduction in each member's capital account.

- Fourth, increase each member's capital account by the member's share of partnership minimum gain. Partnership minimum gain is the amount by which nonrecourse debt exceeds the tax basis of the property securing the debt.[31] It is equal to the tax gain that the LLC would realize if it abandoned or sold the property for no consideration other than the purchaser's assumption of nonrecourse debt. If there is a difference between the tax basis and the book value of the property, then the LLC must use book value in determining partnership minimum gain.[32] Partnership minimum gain is allocated to the capital accounts of the members who received the deductions that caused the book value of the assets to decline below the debt encumbering the assets.

- Fifth, allocate book income (and a corresponding amount of tax income) from the current year to the members so that if the LLC made liquidating distribu-tions to the members under the terms of the operating agreement, each member would have a zero capital account at the end of such tax year.

This rule is designed to protect allocations based on unsophisticated but nonabu-sive operating agreements that would otherwise fall outside of the safe-harbor regulations.

---

[28] Reg. § 1.704-1(b)(2)(ii)(i).

[29] IRS Market Segment Specialization Program, Partnerships, Audit Technique Guide, Chapter 6, under the heading, "Economic Effect Equivalence."

[30] The regulations assume that the book value of the property is equal to the fair market value.

[31] Reg. § 1.704-2(b)(2).

[32] Reg. § 1.704-2(d)(3).

EXAMPLE 8-1

Joe and Sarah form an LLC to operate an apartment building. Sarah contributes $100,000 in cash to be used as working capital and guarantees LLC debt of $500,000. Joe contributes nothing and manages the apartment building. Joe and Sarah want to reduce expenses, so they write their own operating agreement without consulting an attorney or accountant. They agree to divide all profits and losses equally. They do not include any of the safe-harbor provisions in their partnership agreement. At the end of five years, the LLC has cumulative losses of $50,000 which are allocated to Sarah. The LLC liquidates, repays the lender, and distributes $50,000 to Sarah. The allocations are valid because they produce the same results that would apply under the safe harbor regulations.[33]

Practice Note

A typical provision in an operating agreement that is designed to comply with the economic equivalence test is as follows:

After giving effect to the special allocations set forth above, and except as may otherwise be provided in this Operating Agreement, Net Profits or Net Losses (and to the extent necessary individual items of gross income, gain, loss or deduction) shall be allocated such that the Capital Account balances of each Member, immediately after making such allocations, are as nearly as possible equal to (i) distributions that would be made to the Member on liquidation if the LLC were dissolved, its assets sold for their respective Book Values, its liabilities satisfied in accordance with their terms (limited with respect to each Nonrecourse Liability to the Asset Value of the assets securing such liability), and the net assets distributed to the Members in accordance with liquidation provisions of this Operating Agreement, minus (ii) such Member's share of LLC Minimum Gain and Member Nonrecourse Debt Minimum Gain, computed immediately prior to the hypothetical liquidation of the LLC. An allocation of Net Losses shall not be made to the extent that it would create or increase an Adjusted Capital Account Deficit for a Member at the end of any tax period. The intent of the foregoing allocation is to comply with the economic effect equivalence test under Treas. Reg. § 1.704-1(b)(2)(ii)(i).

---

[33] IRS Market Segment Specialization Program, Partnerships, Audit Technique Guide, Chapter 6, Example 6-3.

.04 Member's Interest in the LLC Test

The third permissible test for book allocations is the member's interest in the LLC test.[34] Under the basic allocation rules discussed above, tax allocations will follow book allocations if the book allocations (i) have substantial economic effect, (ii) have economic effect equivalence, (iii) are made in accordance with each member's interest in the LLC, or (iv) meet one of the special rules tests in the regulations. If the book allocations do not meet one of these tests, or if the operating agreement does not provide for the allocation of income, gain, loss, deduction, or credit to a member, then LLC taxable income, gain, loss, deduction, or credit will be reallocated in accordance with each member's interest in the LLC.[35]

The members' interests in the LLC are based on "the manner in which the members have agreed to share the economic benefit or burden (if any) corresponding to the income, gain, loss, deduction, or credit (or items thereof) that is allocated."[36] The purpose of this test is to make sure that a member who is economically enriched by items of LLC income or gain bears the associated tax burden, and that a member who is economically hurt by items of LLC loss is allocated the tax benefit of the loss. The tax allocations must conform to the economics of the LLC's book allocations.[37]

The starting point for determining each member's interest in the LLC is the "partnership agreement."[38] The term "partnership agreement" is very broad and includes any oral or written agreement that has an impact on the economic sharing arrangement among the members or between one or more of the members and the LLC.[39] It includes the operating agreement, loan and credit agreements, assumption agreements, indemnification agreements, subordination agreements, correspondence with the lender concerning terms of a loan, and guarantees.[40]

There is a presumption that all members have an equal interest in the LLC, determined on a per capita basis.[41] Either the taxpayer or the Service may rebut this presumption by establishing facts and circumstances which show that the members' interests in the LLC are not equal. All of the facts and circumstances are considered.[42] The facts and circumstances include the following:[43]

---

[34] Code Sec. 704(b); Reg. § 1.704-1(b)(1)(i), (b)(3).

[35] Code Sec. 704(b)(2); Reg. § 1.704-1(b)(1)(i); CCA 201741018.

[36] Reg. § 1.704-1(b)(3)(i).

[37] IRS Audit Technique Guide—Partnerships, Chapter 6, under the heading, "INTRODUCTION."

[38] IRS Audit Technique Guide—Partnerships, Chapter 6, under the heading, "Partner's Interest in the Partnership Test."

[39] Reg. § 1.704-1(b)(2)(ii)(h).

[40] IRS Audit Technique Guide—Partnerships, Chapter 6, under the heading, "Partner's Interest in the Partnership Test."

[41] Reg. § 1.704-1(b)(3).

[42] Code Sec. 704(b); Reg. § 1.704-1(b)(1)(i).

[43] Reg. § 1.704-1(b)(3)(ii).

- the members' relative contributions to the LLC;
- the interest of the members in economic profits and losses (if different from taxable income or loss);
- the interest of the members in cash flow and other non-liquidating distributions; and
- the rights of the members to distributions of capital upon liquidation.

This test is a "subjective test." Unlike the safe-harbor rules, this test is not governed by lengthy or detailed regulations. It is a short, simple and subjective test. The safe-harbor rules are normally a more appropriate test in large LLCs where tax opinions may be required. This test is appropriate in smaller, more informal partnership arrangements.[44]

The LLC is not required to allocate losses to the members on a pro rata basis under the members' interest in the LLC test.[45] The reason is that the references in the Code and regulations to a partner's interest in the partnership signify the manner in which the partners have agreed to share the economic benefit or burden corresponding to the income, gain, loss, deduction or credit that is allocated.[46] The members of an LLC may thus decide in the operating agreement to make special allocations to one or more of the members under the members' interest in the LLC test.

In practice, an LLC has considerable flexibility under the "members' interest in the LLC test," provided the LLC does not specially allocate losses to members in excess of their positive capital accounts. For example, in a 2017 ruling, a group of domestic and foreign corporations formed an LLC. The LLC did not comply with any of the requirements for substantial economic effect under the safe-harbor regulations. Thus, the IRS determined that LLC losses should be allocated in accordance with the members' interest in the LLC, reflecting the manner in which the members agreed to share the economic burden corresponding to that loss. Applying this principle, the IRS determined that (i) the LLC could make a special allocation of the losses to two of the members up to the amount of their positive capital account balances since these members bore the economic burden of the losses to the extent of their positive capital accounts, and (ii) any additional losses should be allocated to the other members of the LLC with positive capital accounts.[47]

.05 Special Rules Test

The fourth permissible test for book allocations is the special rules test. An allocation will be respected for tax purposes if it is made under one of the special rules in Reg. § 1.704-1(b)(4). These are allocations that cannot have substantial economic effect because the allocations do not affect the amount that the member will receive on liquidation of the LLC or cash-out of the membership interest. There are safe-harbor rules for several items, including the following:

---

[44] IRS Audit Technique Guide—Partnerships, Chapter 6, under the heading, "Partner's Interest in the Partnership Test."

[45] CCA 201741018.

[46] Reg. § 1.704-1(b)(3)(i).

[47] CCA 201741018.

- *Nonrecourse deductions.* These are deductions that cause the book value of property secured by nonrecourse debt to decline below the outstanding loan balance. The allocation of nonrecourse deductions cannot have substantial economic effect because only the lender bears the risk of loss if the LLC defaults on the nonrecourse loan. Nonrecourse deductions must be allocated in accordance with each member's interest in the LLC, or under the safe-harbor rule for nonrecourse deductions.[48] The safe-harbor rule for nonrecourse debt is discussed at ¶ 804.06.

- *Tax credits.* Most tax credits cannot have substantial economic effect because the tax credits do not affect the members' capital accounts. The tax credits only affect the taxes owed by the members. Tax credits must be allocated in accordance with each member's interest in the LLC, or under the safe-harbor rule for tax credits.[49] The safe-harbor rule for tax credits is discussed at ¶ 804.07.

- *Foreign tax expenditures.* Creditable foreign tax expenditures must be allocated in accordance with each member's interest in the LLC, or under the safe-harbor rule for foreign tax expenditures.[50] The safe-harbor rule for foreign tax expenditures is discussed at ¶ 804.08.

.06 Alternative Allocation Methods

General Rules

There are many alternative methods of book allocations. An LLC may make book allocations in any manner that it wants.[51] It is not required to follow the safe-harbor regulations. If the alternative book allocations have substantial economic effect or comply with one of the other permissible book allocation rules discussed above, then tax allocations will be made in accordance with each member's interest in the LLC.[52]

Target Allocations

Some LLCs use the target method of allocation if the LLC gives members a preferential return on capital and a preferential distribution of capital on liquidation. The LLC makes allocations so that each member will have a capital account equal to

---

[48] Reg. § 1.704-2(b)(1).

[49] Reg. § 1.704-1(b)(4)(ii).

[50] Reg. § 1.704-1(b)(4)(viii)(a).

[51] *See, e.g.,* IRS Audit Technique Guide—Partnerships, Chapter 6, under the heading, "INTRODUC-TION," which dates, "Because of the flexibility inherent in Subchapter K, partnership agreements can be written to reflect whatever economic sharing arrangement and risk sharing arrangement the parties wish to execute."

[52] Code Sec. 704(b).

the targeted capital account balance that the member is entitled to receive on liquidation of the LLC or buyout of the member's interest.

EXAMPLE 8-2

An LLC has two members. Member A contributes $100,000 to the LLC and Member B contributes $50,000 to the LLC. Member A is entitled to a six percent preference distribution each year on contributed capital. Member A is also entitled to receive back his $100,000 capital contribution before any distribution to Member B. Member B is then entitled to receive back his $50,000 capital contribution. Thereafter, capital account balances are distributed equally on liquidation.

The LLC earns income of $30,000 during the first year, and has total assets of $180,000 (initial capital accounts plus income) at the end of the year. The target capital account balances are $118,000 for Member A and $62,000 for Member B. This is computed as follows: First, Member A is entitled to receive back his $100,000 capital contribution and an additional $6,000 representing the six percent preference return on contributed capital. Second, Member B is entitled to the next $50,000 of capital. Third, the members split the remaining $24,000 of capital.

The LLC must allocate $18,000 of income to Member A and $12,000 of income to Member B so that their capital accounts are equal to the hypothetical target capital account that each member is entitled to receive on liquidation.[53]

This allocation method does not follow the safe-harbor regulations. However, the regulations give some authority for target allocations under the economic effect equivalence test.[54] The IRS informally approved the target allocation method, and may issue guidance to assist taxpayers in using the target allocation method.[55]

Target allocations are a common method of allocating LLC items of income, gain, loss, deductions and credits, but are frequently misused due to a lack of clear IRS guidance.[56]

---

[53] This example is from *Top Federal Tax Issues for 2018*, ¶ 813, Wolters Kluwer, 2018.

[54] The regulations provide that allocations which do not have economic effect under the safe-harbor regulations will nevertheless be treated as having economic effect if, at the end of each tax year, the liquidation of the LLC would produce the same economic results to the members as would occur under the safe-harbor regulations (economic effect equivalence rule). Reg. § 1.704-1(b)(2)(ii)(i). The regulations also provide that allocations must be made in accordance with each member's interest in the LLC if the LLC does not comply with the safe-harbor regulations. Reg. § 1.704-1(b)(1)(i). The target allocation method basically makes distributions and allocations in accordance with each member's interest in the LLC.

[55] *BNA Daily Tax Reports*, No. 132, p. G-1 (July 13, 2010).

[56] *See* "AICPA Draft Rev. Rul. Urges IRS to Issue Guidance on Targeted Allocations," *BNA Daily Tax Report* No. 23, p. G-4 (Feb. 19, 2014).

Tracking and Schedular Allocations

Some LLCs track particular assets and allocate the income, gain, loss, deduction and credit from those assets in a particular way. Tracking allocations are commonly found in series LLCs that separate all of the assets of the LLC into separate series for the benefit of the members of each series.

An LLC may make special allocations, which include tracking and scheduler allocations. However, if an LLC completely divides up its assets among separate members so that there is no common sharing of profits and losses, then the IRS may treat the separate groups of assets and liabilities as separate partnerships for federal tax purposes.[57]

Tiered Allocations

LLCs commonly provide for tiered allocations. Net profits are divided first according to some preferential formula, and then in accordance with each member's interest in the LLC. For example, an LLC may provide for distributions of net profits first to the members in an amount equal to the net losses allocated to the members in prior years in excess of the net profits allocated to such members. LLCs sometimes provide for preferential distributions to investing members in an amount equal to their initial capital account.

Tiered allocations can usually be structured to comply with the safe-harbor regulations on allocations having substantial economic effect.

Fill-Up Allocations

Fill-up allocations are used for a member who receives a cash distribution in excess of basis. The member recognizes capital gain on the excess amount.[58] The LLC makes a special allocation of capital gain income to the member in an amount equal to the capital gain that the member will recognize on the distribution. This reduces the capital gain that must be allocated to the other members. The member who receives the fill-up allocation does not recognize any additional capital gain income as a result of the allocation.

The tax consequences of fill-up allocations are uncertain, and are not addressed in the regulations.

.07 Special Allocations

An LLC may make special allocations of income, gain, loss and deduction to members under the operating agreement. These are book allocations since they affect

---

[57] *See* discussion under ¶ 2503 *infra* regarding the tax consequences of a series LLC. *See also* Rev. Rul. 55-39, 1955-1 CB 403.

[58] *See* ¶ 1006.02 *infra*.

the member economically. The tax allocations must follow the book allocations in such case if the book allocations meet one of the permissible tests for book allocations discussed at ¶ 803.01. The most common test is the substantial economic effect test.[59]

EXAMPLE 8-3

Al and Kay form an LLC. Al and Kay contribute $1,000 and $99,000 in cash, respectively. Due to Al's expertise in management and his daily participation in the LLC's business, the operating agreement provides that Al will be allocated 20 percent of the LLC taxable income and one percent of the LLC loss. Thus, although Al owns only one percent in the LLC capital, his profit sharing ratio is 20 percent. This tax allocation between Al and Kay is respected as long as the distribution of economic benefits between the two is also in the same ratio (i.e., 20 percent to Al and 80 percent to Kay).[60]

If the special allocations do not have substantial economic effect, then the IRS may reallocate tax items to members in accordance with the members' economic interest in each item of income, gain, loss or deduction.[61] The IRS may not reallocate book income, capital accounts, distributions, or the amount that members are entitled to receive on liquidation under the operating agreement. These are economic items. The IRS may only reallocate tax items.

¶ 804 SAFE-HARBOR RULES FOR BOOK ALLOCATIONS

.01 *Overview*

Normally, an LLC that is classified as a partnership wants its tax allocations to follow book allocations. Tax allocations will follow book allocations if the book allocations have substantial economic effect. If the book allocations do not have substantial economic effect (or do not meet one of the other permissible tests for book allocations), then the IRS may reallocate tax items to members in accordance with the members' economic interest in each item of income, gain, loss or deduction.[62]

An LLC must disclose its method of book allocations on Schedule K-1. There are four checkboxes for: (i) GAAP; (ii) Tax Basis; (iii) Section 704(b) Book (safe-harbor allocations); and (iv) Other.

---

[59] Code Sec. 704(b)(2); Reg. § 1.704-1(b)(2).

[60] Example 2 from California Franchise Tax Board, Partnership Technical Manual ¶ 1110, which states: "There has been some misunderstanding that a 'special allocation' similar to the one described in Example 2 is an abuse of the tax law. However, the law generally respects such allocations provided the tax allocations correspond to the economic arrangements."

[61] Code Sec. 704(b); Reg. §§ 1.704-1(b)(1)(i), 1.704-1(b)(3).

[62] Code Sec. 704(b); Reg. §§ 1.704-1(b)(1)(i); 1.704-1(b)(3).

The IRS issued comprehensive safe-harbor regulations under Code Sec. 704 discussing when book allocations have substantial economic effect.[63] Under the safe-harbor regulations, book allocations have substantial economic effect if:[64]

- the LLC maintains capital accounts;[65]
- the LLC makes liquidating distributions and cash-out distributions in accordance with the members' positive capital account balances;[66]
- each member is unconditionally obligated to restore any deficit in his capital account on liquidation of the membership interest. However, the members are not required to restore a deficit in their capital accounts if (i) the LLC complies with an alternate economic effect test, (ii) the members contribute a personal promissory note to the LLC, or (iii) the members are unconditionally obligated to make subsequent contributions to the LLC other than pursuant to a promissory note;[67] and
- the economic effect of such allocations is substantial.[68]

There are special safe-harbor rules for allocations that cannot have substantial economic effect. The allocations of these items are not analyzed under the substantial economic effect test.[69] Instead, these items must be allocated in accordance with each member's interest in the LLC,[70] or under one of the safe-harbor rules for such items. There are special safe-harbor rules for (i) nonrecourse deductions discussed at ¶ 804.06, (ii) tax credits discussed at ¶ 804.07, and (iii) foreign tax expenditures discussed at ¶ 804.08.

.02 Capital Accounts

Overview

The first requirement under the safe-harbor regulations is that the LLC must maintain capital accounts.[71] The capital accounts must be maintained in accordance with Section 704 of the regulations.[72] The capital accounting under the regulations is not based on generally accepted accounting principles, tax accounting, or other normal methods of accounting. Instead, there is a completely separate type of accounting invented by the drafters of the regulations. The capital accounts are

---

[63] Reg. § 1.704-1(b).

[64] Reg. § 1.704-1(b)(2)(ii)(b).

[65] See ¶ 804.02 infra.

[66] See ¶ 804.03 infra.

[67] See ¶ 804.04 infra.

[68] See ¶ 804.05 infra.

[69] Reg. § 1.704-1(b)(1)(i).

[70] Reg. § 1.704-2(b)(1) (allocation of nonrecourse deductions); Reg. § 1.704-1(b)(4)(ii) (allocation of tax credits); Reg. § 1.704-1(b)(4)(viii)(a) (allocation of creditable foreign taxes).

[71] Reg. § 1.704-1(b)(2)(ii)(b)(1).

[72] Reg. § 1.704-1(b)(2)(iv).

sometimes referred to as Section 704(b) capital accounts. The accounting method is sometimes referred to as Section 704(b) accounting.

Special allocations will not be respected for tax purposes if the allocations are not reflected in the members' capital account.[73]

If there are discrepancies between the members' actual capital accounts and the capital accounts determined under Treas. Reg. § 1.704-1(b)(2)(iv), these discrepancies will not adversely affect the validity of an allocation, provided the discrepancies are minor and are attributable to good faith errors by the LLC.[74]

Increases in Capital Accounts

A member's capital account is increased by the following items under the safe-harbor regulations:[75]

1. the amount of money contributed to the LLC;
2. the fair market value of the property contributed to the LLC, net of any encumbering liabilities assumed by the LLC;
3. the member's distributive share of LLC income and gain, including income exempt from tax;
4. the book (not tax) income and gain with respect to property whose adjusted tax basis differs from its fair market value; and
5. unrealized income with respect to accounts receivable and other accrued but unpaid items.

Decreases in Capital Accounts

A member's capital account is decreased by the following items under the safe-harbor regulations:[76]

1. the amount of money distributed by the LLC to the member;
2. the fair market value of property distributed by the LLC to the member, net of any encumbering liabilities assumed by the distributee member;
3. the member's distributive share of LLC losses and deductions and LLC expenditures that are neither deductible by the LLC in computing taxable income nor properly chargeable to capital accounts (such as syndication costs, and expenditures incurred in generating tax-exempt income);
4. book (not tax) losses and deductions with respect to property whose adjusted tax basis differs from its fair market (book) value;
5. unrealized deductions with respect to accounts payable and other accrued but unpaid items; and
6. excess percentage depletion regarding depletable property.

---

[73] *Miller v. Comm'r*, TC Memo 1984-336 (1984).

[74] Reg. § 1.704-1(b)(2)(iv)(p).

[75] Reg. § 1.704-1(b)(2)(iv)(b).

[76] Reg. § 1.704-1(b)(2)(iv)(b).

The increases and decreases are determined at the LLC level.

Contributions of Property

A member's capital account must be increased by the fair market value of the property contributed to the LLC on the date of contribution.[77] The fair market value, rather than the tax basis, is used to prevent the shifting of pre-contribution gain or loss to the members other than the contributing member. The fair market value must be reasonable and agreed to by the members in arm's-length negotiations.[78]

EXAMPLE 8-4

There are two equal members in an LLC. One contributes $10,000 in cash. The other contributes land with a tax basis of $2,000 and a fair market value of $10,000. Both members receive an initial capital account of$10,000.

If a member contributes encumbered property to the LLC, the LLC must credit the member's capital account with the fair market value of the property less liabilities encumbering the property that the LLC assumes or takes subject to.[79]

EXAMPLE 8-5

John purchases a building for $100,000. He pays no cash down and gives the seller a promissory note. The promissory note provides for interest only for ten years with a balloon payment after ten years. John receives $80,000 of depreciation on the building, which reduces his tax basis from $100,000 to $20,000. The fair market value of the property increases to $125,000. John contributes the property to the LLC in exchange for a 25 percent interest in the LLC. The LLC assumes the $100,000 debt on the property. The following capital account and basis adjustments must be made:

- The LLC must credit John's capital account with $25,000. This is the fair market value of the property, less the debt encumbering the property.
- The LLC's book value for the property is equal to the $125,000 fair market value. Its basis in the property is $20,000, which is John's basis in the property prior to the contribution.

---

[77] Reg. § 1.704-1(b)(2)(iv)(d).
[78] Reg. § 1.704-1(b)(2)(iv)(h).
[79] Reg. § 1.704-1(b)(2)(iv)(b).

- John has net debt relief of $75,000. Prior to the contribution, he owed the lender $100,000. After the contribution, his share of the liability assumed by the LLC is $25,000 (25 percent of the $100,000 debt). The net debt relief is treated as a money distribution to John.[80]

- The deemed money distribution of $75,000 to John first reduces his basis in the LLC. John's initial basis in the LLC is $20,000, which is the basis of the property contributed to the LLC. The deemed money distribution reduces this basis to zero. The $55,000 money distribution in excess of John's basis is taxable gain to John.[81]

- If the LLC makes an election under Section 754, it may increase the tax basis of the contributed property by $55,000, which is the gain that John recognizes upon the contribution to the LLC.[82]

- If John sells his membership interest for $25,000 cash, equal to his capital account of $25,000 (fair market value of equity contributed to the LLC), then John recognizes an additional taxable gain of $50,000. This is equal to the amount realized of $50,000 upon the sale ($25,000 cash, plus $25,000 debt relief), less the zero basis in his membership interest.

- John's total gain after the sale is $105,000. This is equal to the $55,000 gain upon the contribution of the property to the LLC and the $50,000 gain upon the sale of the membership interest for $25,000 in cash. This $105,000 of gain is the same gain that John would have recognized if he had sold the property himself for the fair market value of $125,000 rather than contributing it to the LLC. His gain would have been the amount realized of $125,000 ($25,000 cash, plus $100,000 debt relief), less his $20,000 basis in the property.

EXAMPLE 8-6

Same facts as in Example 8-5, except that John does not sell his membership interest or the land. After John contributes the land to the LLC, the LLC sells the land for its fair market value of $125,000. The purchase price consists of $25,000 cash and assumption of the $100,000 debt by the buyer. The capital account and tax consequences are as follows:

---

[80] Code Sec. 752.
[81] Code Sec. 731(a)(1).
[82] Code Sec. 734(b)(1)(A).

- There is no book gain that is allocated to the members' capital accounts. The LLC's book value prior to the sale is the $125,000 fair market value on the date of contribution. The amount realized from the sale is also $125,000, resulting in zero book gain.
- The LLC realizes $105,000 of tax gain. This is equal to the amount realized of $125,000, less the $20,000 carryover basis for the property when John contributed the property to the LLC. The $105,000 of tax gain must be allocated entirely to John. When contributed property is sold, the built-in gain or loss must be allocated entirely to the contributing member.[83] John now has a total taxable gain of $160,000. This is equal to the $55,000 of gain upon the contribution of the property to the LLC, plus the $105,000 of gain that must be allocated to him under Section 704(c) when the LLC sells the property.
- If the LLC makes an election under Section 754, then it may step up the basis in the contributed property by $55,000, equal to the gain recognized by John upon the contribution of the property to the LLC.[84] In that case, the LLC would step up the basis of the contributed property from $20,000 to $75,000. The amount of gain upon the sale would be only $50,000 ($125,000 amount realized, less $75,000 basis). Again, the entire $50,000 of built-in gain would be allocated to John.
- The total gain recognized by John in this case would be $105,000 (assuming that the LLC makes an election under Section 754). This would be equal to the $55,000 gain recognized upon the contribution of the property to the LLC, plus the $50,000 of gain allocated to him under Section 704(c) when the property is sold. This gain would be exactly the same as if John had sold the property directly to the buyer without first contributing it to the LLC ($125,000 purchase price, less $20,000 basis in the property).
- John increases the basis in his membership interest by $25,000 after the sale by the LLC (assuming that the LLC makes an election under Section 754). The $50,000 gain allocated to John increases his basis by that amount. The $25,000 debt relief (25% × $100,000 of debt assumed by the buyer) decreases John's basis. The net basis increase of $25,000 increases his basis in the LLC from $20,000 to $45,000.

Sale of Contributed Property

When the property is sold, the book gain or loss (difference between the sales price and the capital account value of the asset) must be allocated to the member's capital accounts in accordance with their percentage interest in the LLC. The book

---

[83] Code Sec. 704(c).
[84] Code Sec. 734(b)(1)(A).

gain and the tax gain are normally the same if the LLC originally purchased the property from a third party.

Operating agreements sometimes provide that each member's capital account will be increased by the member's share of taxable income and gain. However, this formula produces an incorrect result if a member contributes appreciated or depreciated property to an LLC, and the LLC later sells the property. The member's capital account would be adjusted twice by the amount of built-in gain or loss. The initial capital account would include the increase or decrease in fair market value of the asset on the date of contribution. There would be a second adjustment for the same amount on the date of sale since the amount of built-in gain or loss must be allocated to the contributing member for tax purposes when the property is sold.[85] As a result, only the book gain or loss on sale of property should be allocated to the contributing member's capital accounts.[86]

EXAMPLE 8-7

A member contributes land to an LLC with a tax basis of $2,000 and a fair market value of $10,000 in exchange for a 25-percent membership interest. The member receives a basis in the membership interest of $2,000 equal to the tax basis of the contributed property. The LLC receives a carryover basis of $2,000 in the property. However, the LLC must credit the member's initial capital account under the safe-harbor rules with $10,000, equal to the fair market value of the contributed property.

If the LLC sold the property in the following month for $11,000, it would have $1,000 of book gain ($11,000 sales price less $10,000 book value) and $9,000 of tax gain ($11,000 sales price less $2,000 tax basis). The LLC must allocate the $1,000 of book gain and a corresponding amount of tax gain to the members in accordance with their percentage interest in the LLC.[87] Thus, the contributing member's capital account should be increased by $250 (representing 25 percent of the book gain) to $10,250. Under Section 704(c)(1)(A), the LLC must allocate the remaining $8,000 of tax gain to the contributing member representing the built-in gain (difference between fair market value and tax basis of the land on the date of contribution). However, it should not increase the member's capital account by the built-in tax gain.

If the LLC increased each member's capital account by the taxable income allocated to the member, the contributing member would receive an extra $8,000 increase in his capital account on sale of the property representing the built-in gain allocated to the member for tax purposes. The member's capital account would then be $18,250, rather than $10,250.

---

[85] *See* ¶ 805 *infra.*

[86] Reg. § 1.704-1(b)(2)(iv)(g)(1), 1.704-1(b)(5), Example (14).

[87] *See* ¶ 805.02 *infra.*

This would not make economic sense since the member's capital account would be credited twice with the $8,000 of built-in gain.

Distributions of Property

Distributed assets must be revalued for book purposes to fair market value whenever there is a distribution (other than a de minimis amount).[88] The capital account of the member receiving the distribution must be reduced by the fair market value of the distributed property, whether in a liquidation or otherwise.[89] The LLC is treated as having sold the property for fair market value and recognizing gain or loss for capital account purposes. The gain or loss is allocated to the members' capital accounts. However, there is no gain or loss for tax purposes, since the distribution of property to a member is not a taxable event.[90]

EXAMPLE 8-8

An LLC has four equal members. Member A has a 25 percent interest in the LLC. Her capital account is $10,000. The adjusted basis of her membership interest is $8,000. One of the assets of the LLC is a building that the LLC purchased for $100,000. There is $90,000 of depreciation on the building. The LLC's tax basis and adjusted book value in the property are $10,000. The property has a fair market value of $30,000. The LLC distributes the property to Member A, who retains her 25 percent interest in the LLC after the distribution. The distribution has the following consequences:

- The distribution is treated as a sale of the property to Member A at its fair market value of $30,000. The LLC has book gain of $20,000, equal to the fair market value, less its $10,000 book value for the property. There is no tax gain, since a distribution of property to a member is not a taxable event.
- The $20,000 book gain is allocated to the four members equally for capital account purposes. Therefore, $5,000 of book gain is allocated to Member A.
- Member A's capital account is a negative $15,000, computed as follows:

Initial capital account prior to distribution	$ 10,000
Plus book gain upon distribution	5,000

---

[88] *See also* Prop. Reg. § 1.751-1(b)(2)(iv) regarding required valuations for distributions if the LLC has unrealized receivables or inventory items.

[89] Reg. § 1.704-1(b)(2)(iv)(a).

[90] Reg. § 1.704-1(b)(2)(iv)(e).

Less distribution of property at fair market value	(30,000)
Ending capital account	$(15,000)

- Member A's tax basis in the property is $8,000. Normally, a member receives a carryover basis in property in a nonliquidating distribution.[91] However, the basis of the distributed property cannot exceed the member's adjusted basis in her membership interest immediately before the distribution.[92] Therefore, Member A receives a step-down in basis for the property from $10,000 to $8,000.

- Member A's $8,000 adjusted basis in her membership interest is reduced to zero. The basis is reduced by the $8,000 basis that the member receives in the distributed property.[93]

- The LLC may increase the basis of its remaining assets by $2,000, the amount of step-down in the basis of the asset to the member, if the LLC makes an election to adjust the basis of its assets under Section 754 of the Internal Revenue Code.[94]

- If the LLC sells its remaining property and liquidates, the proceeds must be distributed to the members according to the ending positive capital account balances after the above adjustments are made.

If the LLC distributes encumbered property to a member, the LLC must reduce the member's capital account by the fair market value of the property, less the debt encumbering the property that the member assumes or takes subject to.[95] The LLC must also treat the distribution as a sale resulting in book gain or loss that is allocated to all of the members.

EXAMPLE 8-9

An LLC has four equal members. The LLC distributes a building to Member A in a nonliquidating distribution. The financial statements of the LLC show the following:

---

[91] Code Sec. 732(a)(1).
[92] Code Sec. 732(a)(2).
[93] Code Sec. 733(2).
[94] Code Sec. 734(b)(1)(B).
[95] Reg. § 1.704-1(b)(2)(iv)(b).

Fair market value of building distributed	$100,000
Book value of building (original purchase price, less book depreciation)	$ 80,000
Liabilities encumbering the building assumed by Member A in the distribution	$ 70,000
LLC's tax basis in the property	$ 40,000
Member A's tax basis in LLC	$ 20,000
Member A's capital account determined under Code Sec. 704(b)	$ 20,000

The nonliquidating distribution of the building to Member A has the following capital account and tax consequences:

- The LLC must treat the distribution as a sale. The sale results in book gain of $20,000. This is equal to the fair market value of $100,000, less the book value of $80,000. There is no taxable gain on the distribution, since a distribution of property to a member is not a taxable event.

- The $20,000 of book gain must be allocated to the four members for capital account purposes. Therefore, the LLC allocates $5,000 of the book gain to Member A.

- Member A is treated as receiving a capital account distribution of $30,000. This is equal to the $100,000 fair market value of the property, less the $70,000 in liabilities assumed by Member A.

- The distribution results in a negative capital account for Member A of $5,000, determined as follows:

Beginning capital account	$ 20,000
Plus 1/4 share of book gain upon the sale of the property	5,000
Less capital account distribution (fair market value of property, less liabilities)	(30,000)
Ending capital account balance	$(5,000)

- Member A has an ending adjusted tax basis in his membership interest in the LLC after the distribution of $2,250, determined as follows:

Beginning basis	$ 20,000
Plus net increase in Member A's share of liabilities as a result of the distribution. The net increase is treated as a contribution of money by Member A to the LLC. The net increase is equal to $30,000 of liabilities assumed by Member A, less Member A's $7,500 relief from LLC liabilities (1/4 share of the $30,000 of LLC liabilities prior to the distribution).	22,500
Less basis in property distributed to Member A	(40,000)
Ending tax basis	$ 2,250

- The property distributed to Member A has a tax basis of $40,000, which is equal to the tax basis that the LLC had in the property prior to the distribution.

Depreciation

Depreciation at the LLC level reduces LLC income that is reflected in the members' capital accounts. The depreciation basis for book purposes is the fair market value of the property. This is the same as the cost basis of the property if the LLC purchases property. However, if a member contributes property to the LLC, the LLC must depreciate the property for capital account purposes based on the fair market value of the property at the time of contribution, and must depreciate the property for tax purposes using the cost basis of the property.

The amount of depreciation taken for book purposes under the safe-harbor regulations must be based on tax depreciation multiplied by a fraction. The numerator of the fraction is the book value of the assets on the date of contribution, and the denominator is the tax basis. If the property has a zero adjusted tax basis, the book depreciation, depletion, or amortization may be determined under any reasonable method selected by the LLC.[96]

EXAMPLE 8-10

Property contributed to an LLC has an adjusted tax basis of $200 and a fair market value of $500 and is subject to three-year cost recovery deductions in the amounts of $60 (30 percent), $100 (50 percent), and $40 (20 percent). The corresponding book depreciation deductions are $150, $250, and $100.[97]

Investment Tax Credits

The members of an LLC must reduce the tax basis in their membership interests when the LLC takes the investment tax credit. The LLC must make a corresponding reduction in the member's capital account at that time.[98]

The members of an LLC must increase the tax basis in their membership interests if there is a recapture of the investment tax credit (such as a sale or disposition within

---

[96] Reg. § 1.704-1(b)(2)(iv)(g)(3).

[97] From Example, California Franchise Tax Board, Partnership Technical Manual ¶1460.

[98] Reg. § 1.704-1(b)(2)(iv)(j).

five years). The LLC must make a corresponding increase in the members' capital accounts at that time.[99]

Members of an LLC must reduce the basis in their membership interests by 100 percent of the investment tax credit taken by the LLC for rehabilitation property[100] and by 50 percent of the investment tax credit taken by the LLC for energy credit property.[101] The LLC must make a corresponding reduction in the member' capital account at that time.[102]

Optional Revaluation of LLC Property

An LLC may elect to revalue the book value of its assets immediately prior to any of the following events:[103]

- the contribution of money or other property to an LLC, other than a de minimis amount, by a new or existing member as consideration for the issuance of a membership interest;
- the liquidation, dissolution, winding up, or insolvency of the LLC or a distribution of money or other property by the LLC, other than a de minimis amount, to a retiring or continuing member as consideration for an interest in the LLC;
- the issuance of a membership interest for services;
- under generally accepted accounting practices, provided that all of the LLC's property other than money consists of stock, securities, commodities, options, warrants, futures or similar instruments that are readily tradable on an established securities market; or
- whenever the members agree to change how they share any item or class of items under the operating agreement, other than a de minimis change.[104]

The allocations that the LLC makes with respect to the revalued property are referred to as "reverse Section 704(c) allocations."

The LLC must use the following procedures in making revaluations:

- The LLC must adjust the book value of LLC property to fair market value on the date of the adjustment. The revaluation must be on a property-by-property basis.[105] There is no adjustment to the tax basis of property.
- The revaluation must take into account Code Sec. 7701(g), which provides that the fair market value of property must be at least the amount of any nonrecourse debt to which such property is subject.[106]

---

[99] Reg. § 1.704-1(b)(2)(iv)(j).
[100] Code Sec. 50(c)(1), (5).
[101] Code Sec. 50(c)(3), (5).
[102] Reg. § 1.704-1(b)(2)(iv)(j).
[103] Reg. § 1.704-1(b)(2)(iv)(f), (g); Ltr. Rul. 200448024.
[104] Prop. Reg. § 1.704-1(f)(5)(v).
[105] Reg. § 1.704-1(b)(2)(iv)(h).
[106] Code Sec. 7701(g); Reg. § 1.704-1(b)(2)(iv)(f)(1).

- There must be a corresponding adjustment to the members' capital accounts equal to the book up or book down in the value of assets. The LLC is treated as selling the property and recognizing gain or loss for capital account purposes. The amount of gain or loss is the difference between the fair market value of the property and the LLC's capital account value for the property immediately prior to the revaluation. There is no tax gain, since the revaluation of the property is not a taxable event. The book gain or loss allocated to each member's capital account is normally based on the member's share of profits and losses in the LLC, or based on the amount of built-in gain or loss that must be allocated to the contributing member under Code Sec. 704(c).[107]

- After the revaluation, the members' distributive shares of depreciation, depletion, amortization, gain or loss for tax purposes must be determined so as to take account of the variation between the adjusted tax basis and book value (FMV) of the contributed property. The LLC may use the traditional method, the traditional method with curative allocations, or the remedial allocation method. These rules are discussed at ¶ 805.

- After the revaluation, if the LLC uses the safe-harbor regulations, the LLC must allocate book depreciation, amortization, depletion, and book gain or loss for the revalued property in accordance with the safe-harbor regulations discussed above. For example, the amount of depreciation taken for book purposes must be based on tax depreciation multiplied by a fraction, the numerator of which is the book value of the assets on the date of contribution and the denominator of which is the tax basis.

Mandatory Revaluation of LLC Property

Under proposed regulations, an LLC must revalue its assets immediately prior to distribution if (i) the LLC maintains capital accounts in accordance with the safe-harbor regulations, (ii) the LLC distributes money or other property to a member, and (iii) the LLC owns Section 751 property (unrealized receivables or inventory) after the distribution. If the LLC does not maintain capital accounts in accordance with the safe-harbor regulations, the LLC must compute the members' shares of Section 751(b) gain or loss immediately prior to the distribution as if the LLC sold all of its assets for cash in a fully taxable transaction. The LLC must then account for each member's share of built-in gain or loss under the traditional method, the traditional method with curative allocations, or the remedial allocation method.[108]

An LLC that does not own Section 751 property immediately after the distribution may still revalue its property, but is not required to do so under the proposed regulations.

---

[107] Reg. § 1.704-1(b)(2)(iv)(f).
[108] Prop. Reg. § 1.751-1(b)(2)(iv).

Capital Account Table

The following table lists the main items that must be taken into account for capital account purposes under the safe-harbor regulations:

Capital account items	Notes
Allocations of items not deductible in computing LLC income and that are not properly chargeable to capital	These items decrease capital accounts. Reg. § 1.704-1(b)(2)(iv)(b). Examples of such items include (i) life insurance premiums that are nondeductible under Code Sec. 264; (ii) interest and other expenses related to the production of tax-exempt income that are nondeductible under Code Sec. 265; (iii) foreign taxes that may be deductible by the member but that are not deductible by the LLC; (iv) Section 179 expenses, whether or not the member may deduct all or part of such expenses on his or her individual return; (v) losses disallowed on the sale of LLC property under Code Secs. 267(a)(1) and 707(b)(1); and (vi) charitable contributions equal to the donated cash and adjusted basis of LLC property.
Built-in gains and losses	Section 704(c) allocations of income, gain, loss and deductions do not affect capital accounts, and are made for tax purposes only. Reg. § 1.704-1(b)(2)(iv)(g)(1), 1.704-1(b)(5), Example (14). A member receives an increase in his or her capital account equal to the fair market value of the property when the member contributes property to the LLC.
Cash contributions	Cash contributions increase capital accounts. Reg. § 1.704-1(b)(2)(iv)(b).
Cash distributions	Cash distributions decrease capital accounts. Reg. § 1.704-1(b)(2)(iv)(b)
Deficit restoration obligation	An LLC may allocate book losses to a member that create a deficit capital account balance if there is a deficit restoration obligation. The member must be unconditionally obligated to restore the deficit capital account balance by the later of the end of the tax year or 90 days following the liquidation or cash out of the member's interest. See ¶ 804.04.

Disallowed losses	Disallowed losses decrease capital accounts. Reg. § 1.704-1(b)(2)(iv)(i)(3). If a loss incurred in connection with the sale or exchange of LLC property is disallowed to the LLC under Code Sec. 267(a)(1) (related party transaction) or Code Sec.707(b) (transactions with respect to controlled partnerships), the disallowed loss will be treated as a Section 705(a)(2)(B) expenditure that reduces the members' capital accounts.
Excess distributions at fair market value over LLC's tax basis	Reg. § 1.704-1(b)(2)(iv)(e). The LLC has book income or loss when it distributes property to a member with a fair market value that differs from tax basis. Prior to the distribution, the capital accounts of the members must first be adjusted to reflect the manner in which the unrealized book income, gain, loss and deduction inherent in such property accounts would be allocated among all the members if there were a taxable disposition of such property for fair market value. Normally, 100 percent of the book gain or loss is allocated to the capital account of the member receiving the distribution.
Fair market value of property contributed during the year, net of liabilities assumed by the LLC or taken subject to	Capital account contributions are booked at the fair market value of contributed property as agreed to by the members, rather than at the cost basis that is used in determining the outside basis of the member's LLC interest. Reg. § 1.704-1(b)(2)(iv)(d).
Fair market value of property distributed to the member, net of liabilities assumed by the member or taken subject to	Capital accounts are reduced by such items. Reg. § 1.704-1(b)(2)(iv)(b).
Guaranteed payments	Reg. § 1.704-1(b)(2)(iv)(o). Guaranteed payments do not change the recipient member's capital account except to the extent of the member's distributive share of any LLC deduction, loss or other downward capital account adjustment resulting from such payment.

Income and gain allocations under the operating agreement, including tax-exempt income and gain	Reg. § 1.704-1(b)(2)(iv)(b). These are allocations of book income and gain, rather than taxable income, unless the LLC keeps its books on a tax basis. The LLC may reduce the amount of income allocations to the member by the amount of special allocations under the LLC minimum gain chargeback, the member minimum gain chargeback, and the qualified income offset if permitted by the operating agreement.
Investment tax credit reduction	Capital account must be reduced by all or part of the ITC taken in the year in which the property is placed in service (50 percent for ITC for energy credit property). For example, eligible costs for solar equipment qualify for a 30 percent investment tax credit. Code Sec. 48. There must be a 15 percent reduction in the members' outside basis in their membership interests (50% × 30% × eligible costs). Code Sec. 50(c)(3), (5). The LLC must make a corresponding reduction in the members' capital accounts. Reg. § 1.704-1(b)(2)(iv)(j).
Investment tax credit recapture	Capital accounts must be increased by the members' allocable share of ITC recapture. Code Sec. 50(c); Reg. § 1.704-1(b)(2)(iv)(j). There is a 20 percent reduction for each year that the LLC owns ITC property for fewer than five years after property is placed in service. Code Sec. 50(a)(1).
IRS tax audit	If an IRS tax audit results in tax adjustments, the adjustment year members' capital accounts and the LLC's book value in property must be adjusted to what they would have been if the adjustments were made in the reviewed year to the reviewed-year members and property and then modified to take into account the amount by which the assessed tax deficiency would increase a partnership item for any intervening year (e.g., amortization or depreciation of property). REG-136118-15, Preamble to proposed regulations on Centralized Partnership Audit Regime (2017).

Liabilities	Reg. § 1.704-1(b)(2)(iv)(c). LLC liabilities do not increase or decrease capital accounts. However, a member's capital account is increased by LLC liabilities assumed by a member that are treated as a contribution of money by the member to the LLC. The member's capital account is not increased with respect to liabilities secured by property distributed by the LLC to the member, to the extent the fair market value of the property is reduced by the amount of those liabilities. Instead, the member's capital account is reduced by the net fair market value of the property distributed. A member's capital account is also decreased by the amount of any member's liabilities assumed by the LLC that are treated as a distribution of money to the member.
LLC minimum gain chargeback	The minimum gain chargeback applies if there is a decrease in the amount of partnership minimum gain. See ¶ 804.06. In such case, the LLC must make a special allocation of book income to the members in an amount equal to the minimum gain reduction. This is the highest priority allocation of book income. Each member receives a special allocation in proportion to the amount of deductions allocated to the member that caused the book value of the property to decline below the outstanding loan balance. Reg. § 1.704-2(j).
Loss allocations and deductions under the operating agreement	Reg. § 1.704-1(b)(2)(iv)(b). These are allocations of book losses and deductions, rather than taxable losses, unless the LLC keeps its books on a tax basis.
Member minimum gain chargeback	The member minimum gain chargeback applies if there is a decrease in the amount of partner minimum gain. See ¶ 804.06. In such case, the LLC must make a special allocation of book income to the member who made a loan to the LLC in an amount equal to the member minimum gain reduction. This is the second highest priority allocation of book income. See ¶ 804.06.

Minimum gain increases	Minimum gain increases do not affect capital accounts. Partnership minimum gain is the amount by which nonrecourse debt exceeds the tax basis of the property securing the debt. It is equal to the tax gain that the LLC would realize if it abandoned or sold the property for no consideration other than the purchaser's assumption of nonrecourse debt. If there is a difference between the tax basis and the book value of the property, then the LLC must use book value in determining partnership minimum gain. Reg. § 1.704-2(b)(2), (g)(1).
Money contributed during the year	Money contributions increase capital accounts. Reg. § 1.704-1(b)(2)(iv)(b).
Organization and syndication fees (amounts paid to organize the LLC or to promote the sale of membership interests)	Such items decrease capital accounts, whether or not deductible. Reg. § 1.704-1(b)(2)(iv)(i)(2).
Qualified income offset	The qualified income offset applies if the LLC makes an "unexpected distribution" to a member that creates a negative capital account after adjusting for minimum gain. The LLC must then make a special allocation of book income to the members as quickly as possible in order to eliminate the deficit capital account balance. The income must consist of a pro rata portion of each item of LLC income and gain for the year. This is the third highest priority allocation of book income. Reg. § 1.704-1(b)(2)(ii)(d)(6) (flush paragraph). See ¶ 804.04.
Remedial allocations	Reg. § 1.704-3(d)(4). If the LLC uses the remedial allocation method to account for built-in gain and loss, the remedial items are notional tax items created by the LLC solely for tax purposes and do not affect the members' capital accounts.

Revaluations of LLC property	The LLC may make upward or downward revaluations of property and corresponding adjustments in each member's capital accounts on the date of contributions, distributions, liquidations, or issuance of a membership interest in exchange for services. Reg. § 1.704-1(b)(2)(iv)(f).
Stop loss reallocation	If the ending interim adjusted account balance is negative, then losses allocated to the member up to the deficit adjusted capital account are reallocated to the other members. The reallocated amounts are taken into account in determining the other members' taxable income. Under the safe-harbor regulations, the LLC may not allocate book losses or deductions to a member to the extent that such losses or deductions create a deficit capital account balance for the member in excess of (i) the deficit amount that the member is required to pay back to the LLC on liquidation or cash out, or (ii) the member's share of partnership minimum gain as reflected in the adjusted capital account. Reg. § 1.704-1(b)(2)(ii)(d)(3) (flush paragraph under subparagraph (3)).
Tax adjustments resulting from tax audit or amended return, and LLC pays taxes at entity level	Prop. Reg. § 301.6225-4(a)(2). If there are tax adjustments as a result of the tax audit or amended return, and the LLC pays the taxes at the entity level, it must create notional items reflecting the items of income, gain, loss, deduction or credit. The notional items must be allocated to the members and reflected in the members' capital accounts.
Transfer of membership interest	The capital account of the transferor carries over to the transferee, subject to several adjustments. See ¶ 1510.

.03 *Liquidating Distributions*

The second requirement under the safe-harbor regulations is that distributions on liquidation of the LLC or liquidation of a member's interest in the LLC[109] must be made in accordance with positive capital account balances.[110] The capital account balances are determined after taking into account the revaluations and adjustments referred to above for the year in which the liquidation or cash-out occurs.

Planning Note

Liquidating distributions are not always equal to the members' positive capital account balances. There are certain circumstances under the safe-harbor regulations in which distributions may exceed positive capital account balances. The operating agreement should provide that distributions will be made in accordance with the members' positive capital account balances, and that distributions in excess of positive capital account balances will be made in accordance with each member's percentage interest in the LLC (or based on the number of membership units owned by each member compared to the number of membership units owned by all members).

The LLC must make the liquidating distributions by the later of (a) the end of the LLC tax year in which the LLC is liquidated, or (b) within 90 days after the date of the liquidation.[111]

Special allocations will not be respected for tax purposes if liquidating distributions are based on ownership percentages rather than on capital account balances.[112]

.04 *Restoration of Deficits*

Overview

The third requirement under the safe-harbor regulations is that a member must be unconditionally obligated to restore any deficit capital account balance following the liquidation of his interest. The obligation to restore the negative capital account must be expressly provided in the operating agreement, and cannot be based on similar requirements under state or local law.

The deficit capital account balance is determined after taking into account all capital account adjustments during the liquidating year. The tax year of the LLC is determined without regard to Code Sec. 706(c)(2)(A), which provides that the LLC's

---

[109] Reg. § 1.704-1(b)(2)(ii)(g).

[110] Reg. § 1.704-1(b)(2)(ii)(b)(2).

[111] *Id.*

[112] *Goldfine v. Comm'r*, 8 TC 843 (1983); *Miller v. Comm'r*, TC Memo 1984-336 (1984).

¶ 804.03

tax year closes with respect to a member who sells or exchanges his entire interest in the LLC.

The deficit account must be restored by the later of the end of the tax year or 90 days following the liquidation.[113] Any member who has a negative capital account balance on liquidation must contribute sufficient cash to the LLC to restore the capital account to zero.[114]

An allocation will be treated as having economic effect even though a member is not required to restore deficits in his capital accounts if:[115]

- the member contributes a personal promissory note to the LLC;
- the member is unconditionally obligated to make subsequent contributions to the LLC other than pursuant to a promissory note; or
- the LLC complies with the alternate economic effect test.

Contribution of Note

A member who is not obligated to restore a deficit in his or her capital account will be treated as obligated to restore the deficit balance to the extent of the outstanding principal balance of a promissory note of which the member is the maker that is contributed by the member to the LLC.[116] The note must be satisfied no later than the end of the LLC's tax year in which the member's interest is liquidated or within 90 days after the date of such liquidation. In lieu of actual satisfaction, the following requirements may be met:

- the note is negotiable;
- the LLC retains such note; and
- the member contributes to the LLC the excess, if any, of the outstanding principal of such note over its fair market value at the time of liquidation.

EXAMPLE 8-11

Upon the formation of an LLC, Paul contributes his negotiable promissory note with a $10,000 principal balance. The note unconditionally obligates Paul to pay $10,000 to the LLC (i) at the end of the LLC's fifth tax year, or (ii) at the end of the year that Paul's membership interest is liquidated. Paul is considered obligated to restore up to $10,000 of his deficit capital account balance to the LLC. Thus, if the LLC allocates losses that cause a deficit up to $10,000 in Paul's capital account, such an allocation has substantial economic effect.[117]

---

[113] Reg. § 1.704-1(b)(2)(ii)(b)(3).

[114] *See* Reg. § 1.704-1(b)(5), Example (1)(vii).

[115] Reg. § 1.704-1(b)(2)(ii)(c).

[116] Reg. § 1.704-1(b)(2)(ii)(c)(1).

[117] California Franchise Tax Board, Partnership Technical Manual ¶ 1130, Example 1.

If the note is not legally enforceable or the facts and circumstances otherwise indicate a plan to circumvent such obligation, the member will not have satisfied the requirement to restore his deficit capital account.[118]

Unconditional Obligation to Make Subsequent Contributions

A member who is not obligated to restore a deficit in his or her capital account will be treated as obligated to restore the deficit balance to the extent the member has an unconditional obligation to make subsequent contributions to the LLC other than pursuant to a promissory note.[119] The obligation must be satisfied no later than the end of the LLC's tax year in which the member's interest is liquidated or within 90 days after the date of such liquidation.

The amount of the unconditional obligation may be imposed under the operating agreement or by State or local law.

EXAMPLE 8-12

Same facts as in the prior example, except Paul's obligation to restore his negative capital account is not evidenced by a promissory note. Instead, the LLC operating agreement imposes upon Paul the obligation to make an additional contribution of $10,000 at the earlier of (i) the end of the LLC's fifth tax year, or (ii) the end of the LLC tax year in which Paul's interest in the LLC is liquidated. Paul is considered to have satisfied his deficit capital account restoration obligation up to $10,000.[120]

Alternate Economic Effect Test

If the operating agreement does not provide a deficit restoration obligation, or if a member is required to restore only a limited dollar amount of such deficit balance, an allocation may still be treated as having economic effect if it complies with the alternate economic effect test. An allocation meets the alternate economic effect test if:[121]

1. the LLC maintains capital accounts in accordance with the safe-harbor regulations;
2. liquidating and cash-out distributions are made in accordance with the members' positive capital accounts;
3. the operating agreement contains a qualified income offset;

---

[118] Reg. § 1.704-1(b)(2)(ii)(c).

[119] Reg. § 1.704-1(b)(2)(ii)(c)(2).

[120] *See* Reg. § 1.704-1(b)(5), Example (1)(x).

[121] Reg. § 1.704-1(b)(2)(ii)(d).

4. the allocation does not cause or increase a deficit balance in the member's capital account as of the end of the LLC tax year to which such allocation relates; and

5. the members' capital accounts are reduced by three special adjustments.

The first two requirements are the same requirements that apply under the regular safe-harbor rules for LLCs that have a deficit restoration obligation. The remaining three requirements are discussed below.

Qualified Income Offset

The first additional provision that an LLC operating agreement must contain under the alternative economic effects test is a qualified income offset.[122] An operating agreement contains a qualified income offset if it provides that a member who "unexpectedly" receives an adjustment, allocation, or distribution described in Treas. Reg. § 1.704-1(b)(2)(ii)(d)(4), (5), or (6) that causes a deficit capital account balance must receive an allocation of income and gain in an amount sufficient to eliminate such deficit balance as quickly as possible.[123] An unexpected adjustment, allocation, or distribution during the current year is an adjustment, allocation, or distribution that was not reasonably expected as of the end of the prior tax year.[124]

The three items of adjustments, allocations, and distributions referred to in the regulations include the following:

1. reasonably expected future depletion allowances for oil and gas depletion;

2. reasonably expected future allocations of loss or deduction mandated by certain Code provisions that may override Section 704(b). These include the required allocations under the family partnership rules,[125] the varying interest rules,[126] and the Section 751 collapsible partnership rules;[127] and

3. reasonably expected future distributions that, as of the end of the year, exceed reasonably expected increases in the member's capital account,[128] other than expected gain from the sale of LLC assets.[129]

The allocation of income must consist of a pro rata portion of each item of LLC income, including gross income and gain for such year.

---

[122] Reg. § 1.704-1(b)(2)(ii)(d)(3).
[123] *See* Reg. § 1.704-1(b)(2)(ii)(d) (last flush paragraph).
[124] *See* Reg. § 1.704-1(b)(5), Example (1)(vi).
[125] Code Sec. 704(e)(2).
[126] Code Sec. 706(d).
[127] Reg. § 1.751(b)(2)(ii).
[128] Reg. § 1.704-1(b)(2)(ii)(d)(6).
[129] Reg. § 1.704-1(b)(2)(ii)(d).

The qualified income offset must be made only if the member has a deficit capital account balance in excess of the member's share of minimum gain[130] and any deficit amount that the member is required to pay back to the LLC on liquidation.[131]

The qualified income offset is an allocation of book income, not tax income.[132] The income allocation is made to the member's capital account.

The operating agreement may provide that a member who receives a special allocation of income under the qualified income offset rules will receive a reduced allocation of other income. The purpose of this provision is to ensure that the total income allocated to the member is to the extent possible equal to what the member would have received if there had been no qualified income offset.

Some practitioners take the position that the qualified income offset rarely, if ever, applies because of drafting errors in the regulations. The qualified income offset applies if the member receives an "unexpected" adjustment, allocation, or distribution described in subparagraph (4), (5), or (6) of the regulations referred to above. The items described in subparagraph (4), (5), or (6) are adjustments, allocations, or distributions that "reasonably are expected to be made." Thus, the qualified income offset technically applies only when a member *unexpectedly* receives an adjustment, allocation, or distribution that is *reasonably expected*. The IRS has not yet issued guidance regarding what is unexpected, when the determination of unexpected is made, how unexpected the item must be, and how the member can unexpectedly receive something that is reasonably expected.

EXAMPLE 8-13

Member A has a $100,000 capital account balance at the beginning of 2018. Member A receives a loss deduction of $100,000 in 2018, which reduces her capital account balance down to $0. Member A receives a distribution of $10,000 during 2018. The distribution creates a $10,000 negative capital account balance. The distribution is an "unexpected" distribution, assuming that the LLC did not reasonably expect such distribution to exceed the member's capital account balance as of the last day of the prior tax year. Under the qualified income offset rule, Member A must receive a special income allocation of $10,000 during 2018 (or as soon as practical thereafter) in order to eliminate the negative capital account balance.

---

[130] A member's share of minimum gain and partner nonrecourse debt minimum gain is treated as a deficit restoration obligation for such purpose. Penultimate sentences of Reg. § 1.704-2(g)(1), 1.704-2(i)(5). *See* ¶ 804.06 *infra* for the definition of minimum gain.

[131] Reg. § 1.704-1(b)(2)(ii)(d)(3) (flush paragraphs at the end of subparagraph (3) and subparagraph (6)).

[132] However, tax allocations must follow book allocations, and book allocations must have substantial economic effect. The method of converting book allocations into tax allocations is discussed below at ¶ 804.08.

Stop Loss Reallocation

The second provision that an LLC operating agreement must contain under the alternative economic effects test is a stop loss reallocation provision. The LLC may not allocate losses or deductions to a member to the extent that such losses or deductions create a deficit capital account balance for that member[133] in excess of (i) any deficit amount that the member is required to pay back to the LLC on liquidation,[134] and (ii) the member's share of minimum gain.[135] Any loss not allocated to a member as result of this restriction must be allocated to the other members (to the extent such other members are not also limited with respect to loss allocations).[136]

Nonrecourse deductions are not subject to this rule. The reason is that nonrecourse deductions that create a negative capital account also result in partnership minimum gain that is added back to the member's "adjusted capital account" for purposes of the rule.[137]

If all members of the LLC have a deficit capital account balance, then losses are allocated to the members in accordance with their interests in net taxable losses. The determination of the members' interest in net taxable losses is made by comparing how distributions (and any required contributions by members) would be made at the end of the prior tax year and at the end of the current tax year if the LLC sold the property at its adjusted tax basis and liquidated at the end of each such tax year. The LLC must allocate tax losses to the members who would bear the economic risk of loss as a result of the liquidations.[138]

In the most common cases, the qualified income offset provisions and the loss limitations rules work as follows:

- At the end of each tax year, the LLC must reduce the member's capital account by adjustments, allocations, or distributions that are reasonably expected in the following year. Under the loss limitation rules,[139] the LLC may not allocate losses to the member in excess of the member's capital account as so adjusted.

- During the following tax year, all adjustments, allocations, and distributions that were not reasonably expected in the prior tax year are treated as "unexpected" adjustments, allocations, and distributions. If any such adjustments, allocations, or distributions create a negative capital account, then the LLC must make a special allocation of income to the member as quickly as possible

---

[133] *See* Reg. § 1.704-1(b)(2)(ii)(d)(3) (flush clause under subparagraph (3)).

[134] Reg. § 1.704-1(b)(2)(ii)(d)(3) (flush paragraph at the end of subparagraph (3)).

[135] A member's share of minimum gain and partner nonrecourse debt minimum gain is treated as a deficit restoration obligation for such purpose. Penultimate sentences of Reg. § 1.704-2(g)(1), (i)(5). *See* ¶ 804.06 *infra* for the definition of minimum gain.

[136] *See* Reg. § 1.704-1(b)(5), Example (1)(iv).

[137] *See* ¶ 804.06.

[138] Reg. § 1.704-1(b)(5), Example (15)(ii).

[139] *See* ¶ 804.04 under the heading, "Adjusted Capital Account and Adjusted Capital Account Deficit" *supra*.

in order to eliminate the deficit capital account. The income must consist of a pro rata portion of each item of LLC income and gain for the year.[140]

- The LLC is not required to make a special allocation of income to eliminate a deficit if the deficit is caused by a downward revaluation of assets.

Special Adjustments

The third provision that an LLC operating agreement must contain under the alternative economic effects test is a special adjustments provision. The LLC must reduce the members' capital accounts by the following three special adjustments:[141]

1. reasonably expected future depletion allowances for oil and gas depletion;

2. reasonably expected future allocations of loss or deduction mandated by certain Code provisions that may override Section 704(b). These include the required allocations under the family partnership rules,[142] the varying interest rules,[143] and the Section 751 collapsible partnership rules;[144] and

3. reasonably expected future distributions that, as of the end of the year, exceed reasonably expected increases in the member's capital account,[145] other than expected gain from the sale of LLC assets.[146] This is the most important adjustment and the only adjustment that will apply for most LLCs. The practical effect of this rule is to prevent an LLC from delaying a scheduled distribution during the current year until the beginning of the following year so that the member will have a sufficient capital account in the current year to absorb a loss allocation.

An LLC may allocate nonrecourse deductions to a member even though the allocation creates a deficit capital account in excess of the member's obligation to restore that deficit. The reason is that the deductions result in a corresponding amount of partnership minimum gain that is added back to the capital account for purposes of the alternate economic effect test. Nonrecourse deductions are deductions that cause the book value of property to decline below the outstanding nonrecourse loan balance secured by the property.[147] The minimum gain must be allocated to the member who received the nonrecourse deductions that caused the book value of the property to decline below the outstanding loan balance. The member's share of minimum gain is treated as a deficit restoration obligation that is satisfied when the

---

[140] Reg. § 1.704-1(b)(2)(ii)(d)(6) (flush paragraph).

[141] Reg. § 1.704-1(b)(2)(ii)(d)(3) (flush paragraph at the end of subparagraph (3)).

[142] Code Sec. 704(e)(2).

[143] Code Sec. 706(d).

[144] Reg. § 1.751(b)(2)(ii).

[145] Reg. § 1.704-1(b)(2)(ii)(d)(6).

[146] Reg. § 1.704-1(b)(2)(ii)(d).

[147] See ¶ 804.06 infra.

LLC allocates income to the member under the minimum gain chargeback in reduction of the minimum gain.[148]

The IRS gave the following example of how the third special adjustment works under the alternate economic effect test:[149]

> Steve and Jerry form an LLC that is used to buy depreciable personal property. The operating agreement provides that Steve and Jerry will have an equal share of LLC taxable income and loss (computed without regard to depreciation deductions) and that all depreciation deductions will be allocated to Steve. The agreement further provides that the members' capital accounts will be maintained in accordance with Treas. Reg. § 1.704-1(b)(2)(iv), and that liquidating distributions will be made in accordance with the members' positive capital accounts. There is no requirement that a member with a negative capital account restore the negative capital account balance. The operating agreement contains a qualified income offset. At the end of the first tax year, the members have the following capital account balances:
>
> | | |
> |---|---|
> | Steve | $20,000 |
> | Jerry | $50,000 |
>
> In the second tax year, the LLC has operating income equal to its operating expenses, and has an additional $20,000 of depreciation deductions that it allocates entirely to Steve under the operating agreement. Normally, without any special adjustments, Steve would be able to deduct the full $20,000 of depreciation deductions because the deductions would not cause a negative capital account balance.
>
> However, at the end of the second year, the members reasonably expect that the LLC, during the third tax year, (i) will have operating income equal to its operating expenses and no depreciation deductions, (ii) will borrow $10,000 (recourse) and distribute the amount equally to Steve and Jerry, and (iii) will sell the personal property equal to its adjusted tax basis, repay the $10,000 loan, and liquidate.
>
> In determining if the special allocation of the $20,000 cost recovery deduction to Steve in year two meets the alternate economic effect test, the fair market value of the property is presumed to be equal to its adjusted tax basis. Thus, there will be no gain on the sale of the property and there can be no reasonable expectation that there will be any increases to Steve's capital account in the third tax year that will offset the expected $5,000 distribution to Steve.
>
> Therefore, the expected distribution of the loan proceeds in year three must reduce Steve's capital account in year two under the alternate economic effect test. Under these circumstances the allocation of $20,000 cost recovery deduction to Steve in year two satisfies the alternative

---

[148] Penultimate sentences of Reg. § 1.704-2(g)(1), (i)(5).
[149] *See* Reg. § 1.704-1(b)(5), Example (1)(vi).

economic effect test only to the extent of $15,000. The remaining $5,000 of the cost recovery deduction must be allocated to Jerry.

The results in this example would be the same if the operating agreement provided that the gain on the sale of the property would be allocated to Steve to the extent of the cost recovery previously allocated to him, and that at the end of the second year the members were confident that the gain on the sale of the property in year three would be sufficient to offset the expected $5,000 distribution to Steve.

Adjusted Capital Account and Adjusted Capital Account Deficit

Some operating agreements define "Adjusted Capital Account" and/or "Adjusted Capital Account Deficit" to comply with the alternate economic effect test. One of the requirements of the alternate economic effect test is that the LLC may not allocate losses or deductions to a member to the extent that such losses or deductions create a deficit capital account balance for that member.[150] The capital account deficit for such purposes (defined in the operating agreement as the Adjusted Capital Account Deficit) is the negative amount, if any, determined by:[151]

1. starting with the member's capital account determined under the Section 704(b) regulations;[152]
2. increasing the member's capital account by any amount that the member is obligated to restore under the operating agreement or by operation of law;
3. increasing the member's capital account by any amounts that the member is treated as obligated to restore under Treas. Reg. §§1.704-2(g)(1) and 1.704-2(i)(5), including the member's share of partnership minimum gain; and
4. decreasing the member's capital account by the items described in Treas. Reg. §§1.704-1(b)(2)(ii)(d)(4), (5) and (6) (adjustments, allocations, and distributions which, as of the end of each tax year, are reasonably expected to be made in the next tax year).

The operating agreement then provides that no member will receive an allocation that creates an Adjusted Capital Account Deficit.

EXAMPLE 8-14

At the end of year two, Patrick has a capital account in the LLC of $27,000. In year three, the LLC allocates to Patrick net losses of $13,500 (excluding nonrecourse deductions), and nonrecourse deductions of $63,000, resulting in a negative capital account of $49,500. The nonrecourse deductions

---

[150] *See* Reg. §1.704-1(b)(2)(ii)(d)(3) (flush clause under subparagraph (3)).
[151] Reg. §1.704-1(b)(2)(ii)(d).
[152] Reg. §1.704-1(b)(2)(iv)(b).

are deductions that cause the book value of property secured by nonre-course debt to decline below the outstanding loan balance secured by the property. This creates partnership minimum gain since the LLC would be required to recognize taxable gain equal to the nonrecourse debt if it sold the property for no consideration other than the assumption of the debt (amount realized equal to debt relief less tax basis of property). Patrick's share of partnership minimum gain is $63,000 equal to the nonrecourse deductions allocated to him. The LLC must allocate this minimum gain to Patrick on the sale of the property under the minimum gain chargeback rules discussed below. Patrick's Adjusted Capital Account after the allo-cation is $13,500 (equal to his negative capital account of $49,500 plus his $63,000 share of partnership minimum gain). This means that in the succeeding year, the LLC could allocate to Patrick an additional $13,500 of LLC deductions and losses, other than nonrecourse deductions.[153]

Reallocation Rule

If the LLC maintains capital accounts in accordance with the Section 704 regula-tions, and makes liquidating distributions in accordance with positive capital ac-counts, but fails to comply with the deficit restoration obligation (or the alternate economic effect test), then LLC income, gain, loss, and deductions must be reallo-cated as follows:[154]

- *Step 1*: Compute the difference between (a) the proceeds that the member would receive (or contribution he would be obligated to make) if, immedi-ately at the end of the year to which the allocation in question relates, all LLC property were sold for its book value and the LLC was then liquidated, and (b) the proceeds that the member would receive (or the contribution he would be obligated to make) if, immediately at the end of the year preceding the year to which the allocation in question relates, all LLC property were sold for its book value and the LLC was then liquidated. These amounts must be ad-justed for the items described in Treas. Reg. §1.704-1(b)(2)(ii)(d)(4), (5), and (6).

- *Step 2*: Determine the member's portion of the allocation that has economic effect and subtract this amount from the amount computed in Step 1. The remainder represents the member's share of the portion that has no economic effect.[155]

---

[153] Reg. §1.704-2(m), Example (1)(i).

[154] Reg. §§1.704-1(b)(3)(iii), 1.704-1(b)(5), Example (15); California Franchise Tax Board, Partnership Technical Manual ¶1630, Example.

[155] Reg. §1.704-1(b)(3)(iii)(b).

EXAMPLE 8-15

Steve and Jerry form an LLC. Each contributes $50,000 that is used by the LLC to buy depreciable personal property for $100,000. The operating agreement provides that Steve and Jerry will have equal shares of LLC taxable income and loss (computed without regard to cost recovery deductions such as depreciation deductions) and that all cost recovery deductions will be allocated to Steve. The operating agreement further provides that the members' capital accounts will be maintained in accordance with Treas. Reg. § 1.704-1(b)(2)(iv), and that distributions in liquidation will be made in accordance with the members' positive capital account balances throughout the term of the LLC. There is no requirement that a member restore a negative capital account balance. The operating agreement contains a qualified income offset. As of the end of each LLC tax year, there are no adjustments, allocations, or distributions that are reasonably expected to cause or increase a deficit balance in Steve's capital account.[156]

In the LLC's first tax year, it recognizes operating income equal to its operating expenses and has an additional $30,000 cost recovery deduction that is allocated entirely to Steve.

Capital Accounts	*Steve*	*Jerry*
Beginning of the first year	$50,000	$50,000
Less: cost recovery deduction	(30,000)	0
End of the first year	$20,000	$50,000

In Year Two, the LLC recognizes operating income equal to its operating expenses and has a $30,000 cost recovery deduction that is allocated entirely to Steve according to the operating agreement.

Capital Accounts	*Steve*	*Jerry*
Beginning of the second year	$20,000	$50,000
Less: cost recovery deduction	(30,000)	0
End of the second year	($10,000)	$50,000

The allocation of $30,000 cost recovery deduction to Steve has economic effect up to $20,000. The remaining $10,000 that lacks economic effect must be reallocated as follows:

- *Step 1*: If the LLC sold its property at the end of Year 2 for $40,000 (its book value and adjusted tax basis: cost $100,000 less depreciation of $60,000 in Years 1 and 2), Steve would receive none of the proceeds because his capital account at the end of Year 2 is negative. If the LLC sold its property at the end of the *preceding* year to which the allocation in question relates (Year 1) for $70,000 (its book value and adjusted tax basis: cost $100,000 less deprecia-

---

[156] California Franchise Tax Board, Partnership Technical Manual, ¶ 1630, Example.

tion of $30,000 in Year 1), Steve would receive $20,000 based on his positive capital account balance. Thus, the difference between Years 1 and 2 is $20,000.

- *Step 2*: Determine the portion that has economic effect: The amount determined in Step 1 with regard to Steve is $20,000. Thus, the $30,000 cost recovery deduction allocated to Steve has economic effect up to $20,000. When this amount ($20,000, the portion that has economic effect) is subtracted from the amount determined in Step 1 (which is also $20,000), the remainder is zero. This means that with regard to the $10,000 that must be reallocated, Steve has no interest in it.

If the above calculation is performed with regard to Jerry, it will show that Jerry has an interest in the reallocated $10,000 and that this amount is allocated entirely to him.

The allocation of the $30,000 depreciation deduction to Steve satisfies the alternate economic effect test only to the extent of $20,000. Therefore, only $20,000 of the $30,000 allocation has economic effect. The remaining $10,000 must be reallocated in accordance with the members' interest in the LLC (which is 50/50). However, under the general principle that the member who is allocated LLC losses must bear the economic risk of loss with regard to the loss, it is necessary to determine who actually bears the economic risk of loss with regard to this $10,000 loss. If the LLC sells the property immediately at the end of the LLC's second tax year for $40,000 (its adjusted tax basis: total cost of $100,000 less depreciation of $60,000), the entire $40,000 proceeds will be allocated to Jerry pursuant to the operating agreement (liquidation distribution in accordance to members' positive capital accounts). Since Jerry's total investment is $50,000 and he receives only $40,000 in the hypothetical liquidation distribution, he bears the economic risk of loss of $10,000. Thus, the remaining $10,000 of the $30,000 cost recovery deduction must be reallocated to Jerry because he bears the economic burden corresponding to such amount.[157]

.05 Substantiality of Economic Effect

The fourth requirement under the safe-harbor regulations is that the economic effect of such allocations must be "substantial." The economic effect of an allocation is substantial if there is a reasonable possibility that it will affect substantially the dollar amount that the members receive from the LLC, independent of tax consequences.[158]

---

[157] California Franchise Tax Board, Partnership Technical Manual ¶ 1630, Example.

[158] Reg. § 1.704-1(b)(2)(iii)(a). Even if the dollar amount is substantially affected, the economic effect will not be considered substantially affected if at the time the allocations become part of the operating agreement, (i) the after-tax economic consequences of at least one member may be enhanced compared to the consequences if the allocations were not in the operating agreement, and (ii) there is

The regulations contain one affirmative test and three negative tests for determining substantiality. The affirmative test (the general rule) states that an allocation is substantial if it has a pre-tax dollar effect. The allocation must affect the amount of money that a member will receive independent of tax consequences. If the capital accounts do not change after an allocation, then the allocation may be insubstantial. If a tax savings occurs for one or more of the members in an LLC, and the economic sharing arrangement is unaltered, then the allocation probably lacks substantiality.[159]

There are three negative tests for substantiality.[160] The economic effect of an allocation is not substantial in the following cases:

- *"Some help, no hurt" allocations.* The allocation enhances one member's after-tax economic position, but is not likely to substantially diminish another member's after-tax economic position.[161] The rule is known as the overall tax-effect rule. The IRS refers to these allocations as "some help, no hurt" allocations.[162] For example, an allocation would be insubstantial if the LLC amended the operating agreement each year to allocate the taxable income only to the members with net operating losses or other pass-through losses who could absorb the special allocations of income. The allocations would not be respected because they exploit the different outside tax profiles of the members in order to give an after-tax benefit to some members without hurting the other members.[163]

- *Shifting character allocations.* These allocations shift tax consequences among the members within a single year without substantially altering economic consequences.[164] The shifting allocations reduce the members' overall tax liabilities in a given year without altering their capital account balances. The members may be allocated the same amount of income or loss, but the members' attempt to select the character that will interact in the most favorable manner with their own individual tax profiles. For example, an allocation would be insubstantial if an LLC allocated all of the tax-exempt interest to a member in a high tax bracket, and allocated the same amount of ordinary income items to a member with a large net operating loss carry forward.[165]

(Footnote Continued)

a strong likelihood that the after-tax economic consequences will not be diminished for any member compared to the consequences if the allocations were not in the operating agreement.

[159] Reg. § 1.704-1(b)(2)(iii)(a).

[160] Reg. § 1.704-1(b)(2)(iii)(b). *See also* Rev. Rul. 99-43, 1999-2 IRB 506.

[161] Reg. § 1.704-1(b)(2)(iii)(a).

[162] IRS Market Segment Specialization Program, Partnerships, Audit Technique Guide, Chapter 6 Partnership Allocations, Example 6-4.

[163] IRS Market Segment Specialization Program, Partnerships, Audit Technique Guide, Chapter 6 Partnership Allocations, Example 6-4.

[164] Reg. § 1.704-1(b)(2)(iii)(b).

[165] IRS Market Segment Specialization Program, Partnerships, Audit Technique Guide, Chapter 6 Partnership Allocations, Example 6-4.

- *Transitory allocations.* These allocations are temporary due to the likelihood of a subsequent offsetting allocation.[166] Transitory allocations occur over two or more years. An allocation is transitory when an original allocation is offset by a reversing allocation in the future, and there is a tax savings for one or more of the members. The allocations taken as a whole produce a wash in the capital accounts.[167] For example, an allocation is transitory if an LLC decides not to give a member a loss allocation in a particular year because the member has loss carry forwards and cannot immediately benefit from an allocation of losses, but agrees to give the member makeup losses in future years when the member can use the losses.[168] If there is a strong likelihood that the offsetting allocations will not be made within five years of the original allocation, the transitory allocation will usually be respected.[169]

.06 Nonrecourse Debt and Minimum Gain Chargeback

Overview

Members of an LLC may receive allocations of losses in excess of their capital accounts if the allocations are nonrecourse allocations and if the LLC has a minimum gain chargeback. The minimum gain chargeback is designed to ensure that the members will not leave the LLC with a negative capital account.

Nonrecourse deductions are deductions financed by nonrecourse borrowing which cause the book value of property securing a nonrecourse loan to decline below the outstanding loan balance[170] If the nonrecourse loans to the LLC are made or guaranteed by a member or related person, the nonrecourse debt is treated as "partner nonrecourse debt."[171]

The nonrecourse debt regulations are based on the assumption that the book value of the property represents the fair market value of the property. Thus, when an LLC purchases property with nonrecourse debt, the members of the LLC bear the risk of loss with respect to their investment as reflected in the book value of the property. The lender bears the risk of loss with respect to the loan amount in excess of the book value of the property. Nonrecourse deductions cannot have substantial economic effect because the lender (or the guaranteeing member in the case of partner nonrecourse debt) bears the economic burden corresponding to those allocations. Thus,

---

[166] Reg. § 1.704-1(b)(2)(iii)(c).

[167] IRS Market Segment Specialization Program, Partnerships, Audit Technique Guide, Chapter 6 Partnership Allocations, Example 6-5.

[168] IRS Market Segment Specialization Program, Partnerships, Audit Technique Guide, Chapter 6 Partnership Allocations, Example 6-6.

[169] Reg. § 1.704-1(b)(2)(iii)(c).

[170] Reg. § 1.704-2(b)(3).

[171] Reg. § 1.704-2(b)(3).

nonrecourse deductions must be allocated in accordance with each member's interest in the LLC.[172]

In order for allocations of nonrecourse deductions to be deemed in accordance with the members' interests in the LLC, the LLC operating agreement must meet a set of requirements provided in Treas. Reg. § 1.704-2(b)(e). If those requirements are not satisfied, then the members' distributive shares of nonrecourse deductions will be determined in accordance with the members' overall economic interests in the LLC.[173]

Requirements for Allocation of Nonrecourse Deductions

Allocations of nonrecourse deductions are deemed to be in accordance with the members' interests in the LLC only if all of the following requirements are satisfied:[174]

1. Throughout the full term of the LLC, the LLC satisfies the economic effect requirements under Treas. Reg. § 1.704-1(b)(2)(ii)(b). Under those regulations, (i) the LLC must maintain capital accounts in accordance with the Section 704(b) regulations, (ii) liquidating distributions must be made in accordance with the members' positive capital account balances, and (iii) members with deficit capital accounts must have an unconditional obligation to restore the deficit balances or the LLC operating agreement must satisfy the alternate economic effect test.[175]

2. Beginning in the first tax year of the LLC in which there are nonrecourse deductions and thereafter throughout the full term of the LLC, the operating agreement provides that allocations of nonrecourse deductions will be made in a manner that is reasonably consistent with the allocations that have some other significant partnership items. These "significant partnership items" are items that have substantial economic effect and are attributable to the property securing the nonrecourse liabilities.[176] Some operating agreements provide that nonrecourse deductions will be allocated to the members pro rata in accordance with the membership interest held by each member.

3. The operating agreement contains a minimum gain chargeback provision (discussed below).[177]

4. All other material allocations and capital account adjustments under the operating agreement must have substantial economic effect.[178]

---

[172] Reg. § 1.704-2(b)(1).
[173] Reg. § 1.704-2(b)(1).
[174] Reg. § 1.704-2(e).
[175] Reg. § 1.704-2(e)(1).
[176] Reg. § 1.704-2(e)(2).
[177] Reg. § 1.704-2(e)(3).
[178] Reg. § 1.704-2(e)(4).

Minimum Gain Chargeback Requirement

The operating agreement must contain a minimum gain chargeback provision applicable to the first tax year in which the LLC has nonrecourse deductions or makes a distribution of proceeds of a nonrecourse liability allocable to an increase in partnership minimum gain,[179] and thereafter throughout the full term of the LLC.[180]

The minimum gain chargeback rule is the vehicle which allows a member of an LLC to take tax deductions for property secured by nonrecourse debt in excess of the member's capital account balance. Under the safe-harbor regulations, an LLC may not allocate losses to a member with a negative capital account. Under the minimum gain chargeback rules, the nonrecourse deductions result in minimum gain which is added back to the members' capital accounts, eliminating the negative account balance caused by the nonrecourse deductions. Thus, the LLC may allocate nonrecourse deductions to the members even though such loss allocations would otherwise create a negative capital account.

The LLC must take the following steps to comply with the minimum gain chargeback requirement:[181]

1. Determine if the LLC has partnership minimum gain.
2. Determine if there is a net increase or decrease in partnership minimum gain.
3. Determine the amount of nonrecourse deductions.
4. Allocate the nonrecourse deductions to the members.
5. Determine each member's share of partnership minimum gain.
6. Determine each member's share of any net decrease in partnership minimum gain.
7. Make the partnership minimum gain chargeback if there is a net decrease in partnership minimum gain.
8. Make the partner minimum gain chargeback if there is a net decrease in partner minimum gain.

The steps are discussed below.

Partnership Minimum Gain

The first step in applying the minimum gain chargeback rules is to determine whether the LLC has partnership minimum gain. Partnership minimum gain is the amount by which nonrecourse debt exceeds the tax basis of the property securing the

---

[179] An LLC makes a distribution of proceeds of a nonrecourse liability allocable to an increase in partnership minimum gain to the extent the increase results from encumbering LLC property with aggregate nonrecourse liabilities that exceed the property's adjusted tax basis. Reg. § 1.704-2(h)(1).

[180] Reg. § 1.704-2(e)(3).

[181] The steps are discussed in detail in California Franchise Tax Board, Partnership Technical Manual, interpreting federal law, available at https://www.ftb.ca.gov/aboutFTB/manuals/audit/ptm/ptm.pdf.

¶ 804.06

debt.[182] It is equal to the tax gain that the LLC would realize if it abandoned or sold the property for no consideration other than the purchaser's assumption of nonrecourse debt. If there is a difference between the tax basis and the book value of the property, then the LLC must use book value in determining partnership minimum gain.[183]

EXAMPLE 8-16

An LLC purchases property for $500,000 with $100,000 cash and an interest-only nonrecourse loan of $400,000. The LLC takes depreciation deductions of $200,000, reducing the tax basis from $500,000 to $300,000. The partnership minimum gain is $100,000 (nonrecourse debt of $400,000 less adjusted tax basis of $300,000). The partnership minimum gain is also the amount of tax gain that the members would recognize on transfer of the property back to the lender for no consideration (amount realized equal to debt relief of $400,000, less tax basis of $300,000).

The concept of minimum gain arose out of a 1983 Supreme Court case, *Commissioner v. Tufts*.[184] In that case, the lender foreclosed on an apartment building whose fair market value had declined below the outstanding debt secured by the property. The borrower surrendered the property to the lender in exchange for debt relief. The taxpayer argued that the amount realized was limited to the fair market value of the property. The court determined that the amount realized included the full amount of nonrecourse debt (which was higher than the fair market value).

As a result of the *Tufts* case, a taxpayer recognizes gain on abandonment of property equal to the difference between the outstanding amount of nonrecourse debt and the basis in the property if lower. This potential gain is referred to as minimum gain. In an LLC, there will be minimum gain and potential taxes owed by the members whenever the tax basis of LLC property is less than the outstanding amount of nonrecourse debt secured by the property.

After the *Tufts* case, the IRS decided to use minimum gain as the mechanism to allow investors to deduct losses in excess of their equity investment, to the extent that the losses were funded by nonrecourse debt. It also used minimum gain and "minimum gain chargeback" as the mechanisms to track when the investor must repay the IRS for the extra tax losses. The IRS allowed investors to deduct excess losses because the investor would eventually be required to recognize additional taxable income when the nonrecourse debt was repaid.

Partnership minimum gain is a rough approximation of the amount of tax losses and deductions taken by the members in excess of their equity investment.

The aggregate partnership minimum gain is determined by first computing for each LLC nonrecourse liability any gain the LLC would realize if it disposed of the

---

[182] Reg. § 1.704-2(b)(2).

[183] Reg. § 1.704-2(d)(3).

[184] *Comm'r v. Tufts*, 461 U.S. 300 (1983).

property subject to that liability for no consideration other than full satisfaction of the liability, and then aggregating the separately computed gains.[185]

Increases and Decreases in Minimum Gain

The second step in applying the minimum gain chargeback rules is to determine whether there is a net increase or decrease in partnership minimum gain during the tax year. The net increase or decrease in partnership minimum gain is determined by comparing the partnership minimum gain on the last day of the current tax year with the partnership minimum gain on the last day of the immediately preceding tax year.[186]

Minimum gain is created or increases in the following ways:

- Depreciation and other deductions attributable to property secured by nonrecourse debt cause the adjusted tax basis of the property to decline below the outstanding loan balance.[187]
- The LLC refinances the property, which increases the amount of nonrecourse debt.
- The LLC incurs additional liabilities with respect to encumbered property.[188]
- The LLC converts recourse debt to nonrecourse debt.

A net increase in minimum gain for a member is not a taxable event and does not affect current book or tax allocations.

Minimum gain is reduced in the following ways:

- The LLC repays principal on nonrecourse debt. Minimum gain is at its highest point when the LLC uses up all of its depreciation deductions for the property, assuming that there are no further increases in nonrecourse debt or refinancing of the property. Thereafter, minimum gain will decrease on a dollar-for-dollar basis as principal on the nonrecourse debt is repaid.
- The LLC sells property secured by nonrecourse debt, resulting in a cancellation or repayment of the nonrecourse debt.
- The LLC abandons property secured by nonrecourse debt.
- The LLC converts nonrecourse debt into recourse debt.
- The LLC makes capital improvements to the property secured by nonrecourse debt.

An LLC may not decrease partnership minimum gain by increasing members' capital accounts in a revaluation. If the members' capital accounts are increased to reflect a revaluation of LLC property subject to a nonrecourse liability, the net increase or decrease in partnership minimum gain for the tax year of revaluation is determined by (i) first calculating the net decrease or increase in partnership mini-

---

[185] Reg. § 1.704-2(d)(1).
[186] Reg. § 1.704-2(d)(1).
[187] Reg. § 1.704-2(b)(1).
[188] Reg. § 1.704-2(h), (j), (k).

mum gain using the current year's book values and the prior year's partnership minimum gain amount, and (ii) then adding back any decrease in minimum gain arising solely from the revaluation.[189]

If the members' capital accounts are decreased to reflect a revaluation, the net decrease or increase in partnership minimum gain is determined in the same manner as in the year before the revaluation, but by using book values rather than adjusted tax bases. The fair market value of the revalued property cannot be less than the outstanding nonrecourse liability secured by such property.[190]

If there is a net decrease in minimum gain for a member, the LLC must allocate additional taxable income to the members equal to the net decrease under the minimum gain chargeback rules discussed below.

Computation of Nonrecourse Deductions

The third step in applying the minimum gain chargeback rules is to determine the amount of nonrecourse deductions. The amount of nonrecourse deductions for each tax year is:[191]

- the net increase in partnership minimum gain during the year,
- reduced (but not below zero) by the aggregate distributions made during the year of the proceeds of a nonrecourse liability that are allocated to an increase in partnership minimum gain.

Generally, nonrecourse deductions consist first of certain depreciation deductions or cost recovery deductions and then, if necessary, a pro rata portion of other LLC losses, deductions, and Section 705(a)(2)(B) expenditures for that year.[192] The nonrecourse deductions may be less than, equal to, or more than the LLC's taxable loss during the year.

If the nonrecourse deductions exceed the LLC losses during the year, the excess amount is carried over as an increase in partnership minimum gain in the succeeding tax year.[193]

EXAMPLE 8-17

An LLC has no partnership minimum gain at the beginning of its tax year. It has rental income of $95,000, operating expenses of $10,000, interest expense of $80,000 and depreciation deductions on property subject to a nonrecourse debt of $90,000, resulting in a net taxable loss of $85,000. The LLC borrows an additional $200,000, secured by a nonrecourse mortgage on the property, which it uses for working capital. At the end of the tax

---

[189] Reg. § 1.704-2(d)(4).
[190] Code Sec. 7701(g).
[191] Reg. § 1.704-2(c).
[192] Reg. § 1.704-2(c).
[193] Reg. § 1.704-2(h)(4).

year, the amount by which the outstanding nonrecourse loan balance exceeds the tax basis of property securing the debt is $290,000. Because the LLC did not distribute the loan proceeds during the year, the potential amount of partnership nonrecourse deductions for the year is $290,000. This is equal to the increase in partnership minimum gain for the year. Because the total nonrecourse deductions of $290,000 for the year exceed LLC deductions, all of the LLC's deductions for the year ($180,000) are treated as nonrecourse deductions, and the $110,000 of excess nonrecourse deductions are treated as an increase in partnership minimum gain during the following tax year.[194]

EXAMPLE 8-18

Same facts as in the prior example, except that the LLC distributes the $200,000 of refinancing proceeds of the nonrecourse debt during the year. The nonrecourse debt deduction is $90,000 ($290,000 increase in minimum gain for the year less the $200,000 distribution of the proceeds of the nonrecourse refinancing). Under the ordering rules discussed above, all of the $90,000 in depreciation deductions would be treated as a nonrecourse deduction.[195]

Allocation of Nonrecourse Deductions to Members

The fourth step in applying the minimum gain chargeback rules is to allocate the nonrecourse deductions to the members. A member who is allocated nonrecourse deductions is subject to the minimum gain chargeback. An LLC must allocate nonrecourse deductions to the members as follows:

1. First, the LLC must allocate losses to the members in accordance with the operating agreement.
2. Second, the LLC must allocate nonrecourse deductions to the members in accordance with the operating agreement and consistent with the allocation of "other significant partnership items attributable to the property that have substantial economic effect."

EXAMPLE 8-19

An LLC has no partnership minimum gain at the beginning of its tax year. At the end of the tax year, the amount by which the outstanding nonre-

---

[194] Reg. § 1.704-2(m), Example 1(m)(6).
[195] Reg. § 1.704-2(m), Example 1(m)(6).

course loan balance exceeds the tax basis of property securing the debt is $7,000. The total LLC tax loss for the year is $8,500 which includes $7,000 of nonrecourse deductions and $1,500 of losses (without nonrecourse deductions). The LLC allocates the $1,500 loss 90 percent to Lori and ten percent to Gary in accordance with the operating agreement. The LLC also allocates the nonrecourse deductions 90 percent to Lori and ten percent to Gary. The allocation of the nonrecourse deductions to the parties is respected since it is consistent with the allocation of other significant LLC items attributable to the property that have substantial economic effect (which in this example are taxable losses of $1,500).[196]

Members' Shares of Partnership Minimum Gain

The fifth step in applying the minimum gain chargeback rules is to determine each member's share of partnership minimum gain. A member's share of partnership minimum gain at the end of any tax year equals the sum of:[197]

1. nonrecourse deductions allocated to that member (and to that member's predecessors in interest),

2. plus, the distributions made to that member (and to that member's predecessors in interest) of the proceeds of a nonrecourse liability allocable to an increase in partnership minimum gain (i.e., to the extent the increase results from encumbering LLC property with aggregate nonrecourse liabilities that exceed the property's adjusted tax basis),

3. less the member's (and the member's predecessor in interest) aggregate share of the net decreases in partnership minimum gain,

4. less the member's (and the member's predecessor in interest) aggregate share of decreases resulting from revaluation of LLC property subject to one or more LLC nonrecourse liabilities.

In the typical case, a member's share of partnership minimum gain is equal to the member's percentage interest in the LLC multiplied by the amount by which nonrecourse debt exceeds the book value of property securing the debt.

A member's share of partnership minimum gain is important for two reasons. First, as discussed below, there is a minimum gain chargeback whenever there is a decrease in the member's share of partnership minimum gain. Second, the member's share of partnership minimum gain is added back to member's capital account, thereby allowing the LLC to make additional loss allocations to the member under the safe-harbor regulations without creating a deficit capital account.[198]

---

[196] *See* Reg. § 1.704-2(m), Example 1(i)
[197] Reg. §§ 1.704-2(g)(1), 1.704-2(m)(1)(i) and (3)(i), Examples.
[198] Reg. § 1.704-2(g)(1)(ii). This rule is discussed at ¶ 804.04.

Members' Shares of Net Decrease in Partnership Minimum Gain

The sixth step in applying the minimum gain chargeback rules is to determine each member's share of any net decrease in partnership minimum gain. A member's share of the net decrease in partnership minimum gain is determined by multiplying the total net decrease in partnership minimum gain by the member's percentage share of partnership minimum gain at the end of the prior tax year.[199]

EXAMPLE 8-20

There are two equal members in an LLC. At the end of Year 2, the LLC allocates $20,000 of depreciation deductions to the members that causes the book value of the property to decline by $7,000 below the outstanding nonrecourse loan balance secured by a mortgage on the property. The partnership minimum gain is $7,000, which is the taxable amount that the LLC would recognize if it sold the property for no consideration other than the assumption of the debt. Each member's share of the partnership minimum gain is $3,500 (which is equal to the nonrecourse deductions allocated to each member). If the LLC sold the property in Year 3, there would be a $7,000 reduction in partnership minimum gain. Each member's share of the net decrease in partnership minimum gain would be $3,500 (equal to the total net decrease multiplied by each member's percentage share of partnership minimum gain at the end of the prior tax year).

Net decreases in partnership minimum gain as a result of revaluations of LLC property are ignored. A member's share of any decrease in partnership minimum gain equals the increase in partner's capital account attributable to the revaluation to the extent the reduction in minimum gain is caused by the revaluation.[200]

Minimum Gain Chargeback

The seventh step in applying the minimum gain chargeback rules is to allocate income to the members through a minimum gain chargeback. If there is a net decrease in partnership minimum gain during any tax year, the minimum gain chargeback requirement applies and the LLC must allocate to each member income and gain for that year equal to the member's share of the net decrease in partnership minimum gain.[201] The result is that the income and gain are allocated to the members

---

[199] *See* California Franchise Tax Board, Partnership Technical Manual ¶ 3120 (interpreting federal law).

[200] *See* California Franchise Tax Board, Partnership Technical Manual ¶ 3120 (interpreting federal law).

[201] Reg. § 1.704-2(f)(1).

who received the nonrecourse deductions that caused the book value of the property to decline below the outstanding debt on the property.

The main idea behind the minimum gain chargeback is that a member who receives tax deductions in excess of the member's equity investment from property financed by nonrecourse debt should at some future date recognize taxable income in the same amount. The IRS decided that the appropriate time for income recognition should be when the LLC repays the nonrecourse debt, or when the amount of minimum gain is otherwise reduced as discussed above.

The minimum gain chargeback is an allocation of book income, not tax income.[202] The allocation is made to the member's capital account. The effect of the allocation is to reverse the prior book allocations of nonrecourse deductions.

The minimum gain chargeback is also called an "income shift" since it shifts book income from other members of the LLC to the members with a net decrease in minimum gain during the year. It is the highest priority allocation. The LLC must make this book allocation before any other allocations under the operating agreement.[203] The LLC must allocate book income under the chargeback first from book gain on the disposition of property subject to the nonrecourse debt, and then if necessary, from a pro rata portion of the LLC's other items of income and gain for the year.[204]

If the LLC has insufficient income or gain for the tax year to satisfy the minimum gain chargeback, the difference carries over to future years.[205]

If the LLC has excess income after making the minimum gain chargeback, the LLC may make a special allocation of income to the other members. The offsetting allocations are made so that each member's capital account and allocable share of income, gain, loss and deduction are to the extent possible equal to the share that the member would have had if there had been no minimum gain chargeback. These special allocations are called "curative allocations," which are different from the curative allocations under the ceiling rule for contributions of appreciated property.[206] The operating agreement typically provides that the managers may make the offsetting allocations in whatever manner they determine appropriate.

An LLC should not attempt to reverse nonrecourse deductions with allocations of operating income, because nonrecourse deductions will be reversed again by allocations under the minimum gain chargeback rules. A special allocation of operating income to reverse prior nonrecourse deductions would then result in a double chargeback.

A member is not subject to the minimum gain chargeback requirement to the extent the member contributes capital to the LLC that is used to repay the nonrecourse liability or to increase the basis of the property subject to the nonrecourse

---

[202] However, tax allocations must follow book allocations, and book allocations must have substantial economic effect. The method of converting book allocations into tax allocations is discussed at ¶ 804.10 *infra*.

[203] Reg. § 1.704-2(j).

[204] Reg. § 1.704-2(j)(1).

[205] Reg. § 1.704-2(f)(6).

[206] See ¶ 805.03 *infra*.

liability, provided that the member's share of the net decrease in partnership minimum gain results from the repayment of debt or an increase in basis.[207]

Partner Minimum Gain Chargeback

The eighth step in applying the minimum gain chargeback rules is to determine the partner minimum gain chargeback. The partner minimum gain chargeback rules are similar to the partnership minimum gain chargeback rules.

A member rather than the LLC bears the economic risk of loss on debt that is nonrecourse to the LLC if (i) the member (or person related to the member) loans money to the LLC or guarantees LLC debt, (ii) the debt is secured by LLC property, and (iii) LLC deductions cause the book value of the property to decline below the outstanding loan balance.[208] The deductions that cause the book value of such property to decline below the outstanding loan balance are called "partner nonrecourse deductions."[209]

The LLC must allocate partner nonrecourse deductions to the lending or guarantor member who bears the economic risk of loss. If more than one member bears the economic risk of loss for a partner nonrecourse liability, any partner nonrecourse deductions attributable to that liability must be allocated among the members according to the ratio in which they bear the economic risk of loss.[210]

The LLC may allocate depreciation and other deductions to all of the members in accordance with the operating agreement if the book value of the property exceeds the outstanding loan balance of nonrecourse debt securing the loans made or guaranteed by a member. These deductions are not treated as partner nonrecourse deductions because all members of the LLC bear the economic risk of loss when the book value exceeds the outstanding loan balance.

There is "partner nonrecourse debt minimum gain" if depreciation and other deductions cause the book value of the property to decline below the debt securing the property.[211] This is the amount of gain that the LLC would realize if the LLC sold the property for no consideration other than the purchaser's assumption of the nonrecourse debt.

If there is a net decrease in partner nonrecourse debt minimum gain, then the LLC must make a "partner nonrecourse debt minimum gain chargeback."[212] The net decrease is determined by comparing the lending or guaranteeing member's share of partner nonrecourse debt minimum gain at the end of the current year to the member's share at the end of the prior tax year.

The chargeback is an allocation of income to the lending or guaranteeing member who received the deductions in prior years that caused the book value of

---

[207] Reg. § 1.704-2(f)(3).
[208] Reg. § 1.704-2(b)(4).
[209] Reg. § 1.704-2(i)(1), (2).
[210] Reg. § 1.704-2(i)(1).
[211] Reg. § 1.704-2(i)(3).
[212] Reg. § 1.704-2(i)(4).

LLC property to decline below the nonrecourse debt secured by the property. The effect of the allocation is to reverse the prior allocations of deductions to the member bearing the economic risk of loss with respect to such debt. The LLC must allocate (or charge back) book income and gain to the member that is at least equal to the member's share of the net decrease in LLC minimum gain. The allocation is called a "partner nonrecourse debt minimum gain chargeback."[213] If the LLC has insufficient income or gain for the tax year to satisfy the chargeback requirement, the difference carries over to future years.[214]

A net increase in minimum gain for a member is not a taxable event and does not affect current book or tax allocations.

The LLC may take into account any special allocations under the member minimum gain chargeback rules in computing subsequent allocations of income, gain, loss, and deduction. The offsetting book allocations are made so that each member's capital account and allocable share of income, gain, loss, and deduction are to the extent possible equal to the share that the member would have had if there had been no member minimum gain chargeback.

EXAMPLE 8-21

An LLC borrows $100,000 from Member B in 2016 (interest-only loan for ten years) to buy property for $120,000. The loan is nonrecourse to the LLC. The first $20,000 of depreciation may be allocated to all of the members in accordance with the LLC operating agreement. The remaining depreciation that causes the book value of the property to decline below the nonrecourse debt encumbering the property must be allocated to Member B, who is then the only member who bears the risk of loss if the loan is not repaid.

EXAMPLE 8-22

Same facts as in the prior example. In 2020, the property has an adjusted basis and book value of $40,000. The outstanding loan balance is $60,000. Therefore, the partner nonrecourse debt minimum gain is $20,000 (outstanding loan balance in excess of book value). This is the amount of tax gain that the LLC would recognize if the LLC sold the property for no consideration other than the assumption of the debt. All of this minimum gain must be allocated to the lending or guaranteeing member. The allocation is not a taxable event and does not affect such member's capital account.

---

[213] Reg. § 1.704-2(i)(4).
[214] Reg. § 1.704-2(i)(4).

¶ 804.06

EXAMPLE 8-23

Same facts as in prior example. During 2021, the LLC repays the loan in full. There is a decrease in member minimum gain of $20,000, since the amount of liabilities in excess of book value has been reduced from $20,000 to $0. Therefore, the LLC must make a special allocation of $20,000 of income or gain to Member B during 2021 under the member minimum gain chargeback rules before any other allocations.

Reasonable Consistency Requirement

Allocations of nonrecourse deductions under the safe-harbor regulations must satisfy the reasonable consistency test. This means that the allocation of nonrecourse deductions must be made in a manner similar to the allocation of other items which do have substantial economic effect.[215] For example, if the LLC splits all items of income, gain, loss, and deduction equally between two members, it would be inconsistent to allocate to one member 90 percent of the LLCs nonrecourse deductions.[216]

An LLC will meet the reasonable consistency requirement if it allocates nonrecourse deductions to members in accordance with their percentage interest in profits and losses. If the LLC has a more complex arrangement, the LLC may allocate nonrecourse deductions within a certain range and still meet the consistency requirement. The regulations give an example of a partnership with an initial profit-sharing arrangement between the partners of 90:10, which changes to a 50:50 split when the partnership breaks even. Nonrecourse deductions may be allocated in such case in any ratio between 90:10 and 50:50. However, an allocation of 99:1 would be inconsistent with other items that have substantial economic effect.[217]

.07 Tax Credits

Overview

Tax credits cannot have substantial economic effect since the credits do not impact the member's capital accounts, or the corresponding amount that the members receive on liquidation of the LLC. As a result, tax credits must be allocated according to the member's interests in the LLC.

---

[215] IRS Market Segment Specialization Program, Partnerships, Audit Technique Guide, Chapter 6, under the heading, "Allocations Attributable to Non-recourse Deductions."

[216] *Id.*

[217] Reg. § 1.704-2(m)(ii)-(iii).

The LLC's tax basis of ITC property must be reduced by the full amount of the investment tax credit (or 50 percent of the investment tax credit for renewable energy property).[218] This is designed to reduce the double benefit from the investment tax credit and the allowable depreciation deductions. The members must reduce their basis in the membership interests by the LLC's tax credit tax basis reduction.[219]

There are many different types of tax credits under the Code. The two most common tax credits for an LLC or partnership are the low-income housing credit under Section 42 and the rehabilitation tax credit under Section 47.[220] The rehabilitation credit is part of the investment credit. The investment credit and the low-income housing credit fall under Code Sec. 38, General Business Credit. The safe-harbor rules for the rehabilitation credit are treated differently from the other credits.

There is no specific, mechanical or safe-harbor for allocating tax credits. The regulations provide that if an expenditure gives rise to a tax credit and an allocation of a loss or deduction, then the credit should be allocated in the same manner as the loss or deduction. The same principles apply to credits that arise from gross receipts of the LLC.[221]

Investment Tax Credit and Rehabilitation Tax Credit

The regulations treat the allocation of the investment tax credit (which includes the rehabilitation tax credit) differently from other tax credits. The reason is that the rehabilitation tax credit (unlike the low housing credit) has an impact on the members' capital accounts and the amount that they will receive on liquidation. The LLC must reduce the basis of depreciable property by the amount of the rehabilitation tax credit.[222] The members must also reduce their capital accounts by their ratable share of the rehabilitation tax credit.[223]

The general rule is that each member's share of the rehabilitation costs is based on the general profit ratio of the LLC.[224] The IRS issued safe harbor guidelines under which the IRS will not challenge LLC allocations of Code Sec. 47 rehabilitation credits by an LLC to its members.[225]

An LLC may not specially allocate items generated by the same property. The LLC may not separate the depreciation and tax credits from other items of deduction or income generated by the same rehabilitation tax credit property. All items of income, gain, loss of deduction from a particular property must be allocated together.

---

[218] Code Sec. 50(c).

[219] Code Sec. 50(c)(5); Reg. § 1.704-1(b)(2)(iv)(j).

[220] IRS Market Segment Specialization Program, Partnerships, Audit Technique Guide, Chapter 6, under the heading, "Allocation of Tax Credits."

[221] Reg. § 1.704-1(b)(4)(ii).

[222] Code Sec. 50(c)(1).

[223] Reg. § 1.704-1(b)(2)(4)(j).

[224] Reg. § 1.46-3(f)(2).

[225] Rev. Proc. 2014-12, 2014-3 IRB 415.

EXAMPLE 8-24

A real estate professional and a venture capitalist form an LLC to rehabilitate and renovate historic buildings. The venture capitalist also lends money to the LLC. The venture capitalist receives 99 percent of the depreciation deductions and 99 percent of the rehabilitation credit. All other profits and losses are split equally between the two members. The LLC complies with all other requirements for special allocations under the safe-harbor regulations. The LLC maintains capital accounts, distributions on liquidation are made in accordance with positive capital accounts, and the operating agreement contains an unlimited deficit restoration agreement. The debt is recourse debt. The allocation of the tax credit will not be respected in this case because (i) the allocation is not made in accordance with the general profit-sharing ratio of the LLC, and (ii) the income, gain, loss and deductions are not allocated in the same manner. As a result, the credit will be reallocated 50 percent to each member.[226]

.08 Foreign Tax Expenditures

An LLC normally bears legal liability for taxes under foreign law. If the foreign country treats the LLC as a fiscally transparent entity, the foreign country taxes the members on their shares of LLC income as determined under the tax laws of the foreign country. In either case, the LLC must allocate the tax expenditures to the members. Members who are U.S. taxpayers may claim a dollar for dollar credit against their federal income tax for their allocable share of income taxes paid to the foreign country. The maximum foreign tax credit may not exceed the U.S. income tax imposed on the member's foreign source taxable income (determined under IRS regulations). The foreign tax credit limitation is applied separately to different categories or baskets of income to prevent tax reduction through cross-crediting or averaging of high taxed foreign source income with low taxed foreign source income. A member of an LLC may elect to deduct the member's allocable share of foreign tax expenditures instead of receiving a credit for the foreign taxes.

Allocations of creditable foreign tax expenditures (CFTE) do not have substantial economic effect and must be allocated in accordance with each member's interest in the LLC.[227] Under a safe-harbor rule, allocations are treated as made in accordance with each member's interest in the LLC if (i) the LLC allocates the CFTE in proportion to the members' distributive shares of income to which the CFTE relate, and (ii) the LLC complies with the regular safe-harbor rules for substantial economic effect (i.e., capital account maintenance, liquidations according to capital account, and either the deficit restoration obligation or qualified income offset).

---

[226] IRS Market Segment Specialization Program, Partnerships, Audit Technique Guide, Chapter 6, Example 6-12.

[227] Reg. § 1.704-1(b)(4)(viii).

Under final regulations issued in 2006 and temporary regulations issued in 2016, an LLC that complies with the safe-harbor rules must:[228]

- Determine the categories of CFTE paid by the LLC. The net income from all activities of the LLC is included in a single category, unless the allocation of net income or loss from one activity differs from the allocation of net income or loss from other categories. The allocations may differ if certain foreign income receives preferential tax treatment or if the LLC conducts business in more than one location or through more than one entity or branch.
- Determine the LLC's net income in each CFTE category.[229]
- Allocate the CFTE to each category of activities. A CFTE is related to a category of CFTE income if the income is included in the base on which the foreign tax is imposed. If the foreign tax is assessed on an item that would be income in another year under U.S. tax rules, the foreign tax is allocated to the CFTE category for the year in which the foreign tax is imposed. An LLC that is classified as a partnership must allocate CFTE to each CFTE category in proportion to allocations of LLC net income to that category.

.09 Required Order of Book Allocations

An LLC allocates income, gain, loss and deductions to the members based on each member's percentage interest in the LLC or in such other manner specified in the operating agreement. These allocations are book allocations, not tax allocations. The allocations are made to each member's capital account. The allocations affect the members economically since liquidating and cash-out distributions are normally made in accordance with positive capital accounts. Book allocations are the same as tax allocations only if the LLC keeps its books on a tax basis.

Most LLCs do not follow the safe-harbor regulations on book allocations because of the complexity of the regulations. However, if the LLC decides to comply with the safe-harbor regulations, then book allocations must be made in the following order:[230]

1. *LLC minimum gain chargeback.* This is the highest priority allocation. The LLC must make this book allocation before any other allocation under the operating agreement. Minimum gain arises when the book value of property secured by nonrecourse debt is less than the amount of nonrecourse debt. The LLC must allocate additional book income to a member who received nonrecourse deductions with respect to the property, when there is a decrease in the amount of minimum gain.[231]

2. *Member minimum gain chargeback.* Member minimum gain arises when a member loans money to the LLC, or guarantees debt, that is used to buy LLC property. There is member minimum gain when the book value of the

---

[228] Reg. §§ 1.704-1(b)(4)(viii), 1.704-1T.

[229] Reg. § 1.704-1(b)(4)(viii)(c)(3).

[230] Reg. § 1.704-2(j).

[231] *See* ¶ 804.06 *supra.*

property is less than the amount of the debt. The LLC must allocate additional book income to the member who loaned the money or guaranteed the debt if there is a decrease in the amount of member minimum gain.[232]

3. *Qualified income offset.* An LLC must make a special allocation of income to a member who receives an unexpected distribution, adjustment or allocation that causes a deficit capital account balance.[233] The income allocation is equal to the deficit capital account. This provision rarely applies.

4. *Operating agreement allocations.* The LLC must allocate the remaining book income, gain, loss, and deductions to the members' capital accounts in accordance with the operating agreement.

Many operating agreements provide that each member's capital account will receive a priority allocation of income to the extent of net losses allocated to the member's capital account in prior years. This will result in a double gain chargeback if there is LLC minimum gain or member minimum gain attributable to LLC property secured by nonrecourse debt. The first gain chargeback will be under the operating agreement, and the second gain chargeback will be under the minimum gain chargeback rules. The operating agreement should provide that there will be no priority allocation of book income to a member to the extent that the member may receive a future mandatory minimum gain chargeback for the same amount.[234]

Book allocations are important because they affect the amount credited to a member's capital account, which in turn determines the amount that the member will receive on liquidation of the LLC.

.10 Converting Book Allocations into Tax Allocations

After an LLC has made book allocations of income, gain, loss, and deduction to each member's capital account, it must then convert the book allocations into tax allocations. The LLC must report the tax allocations on a Schedule K-1 for each member. The conversion is made as follows:

- *Tax allocations follow book allocations.* The general rule is that tax allocations must follow book allocations.[235] Many LLCs keep their books on tax basis so that book and tax allocations are the same. If the LLC makes a special allocation of book income to a member for capital account purposes, it must normally allocate the same amount of income to the member for tax purposes. Tax allocations will not be respected if the LLC allocates all of the book income and proceeds of sale to the members in accordance with their percent-

---

[232] *See* ¶ 804.06 *supra.*

[233] *See* ¶ 804.04 *supra.*

[234] *See* Reg. § 1.704-1(b)(2)(iv)(g)(1), 1.704-1(b)(5), Example (14).

[235] Code Sec. 704(b); Reg. § 1.704-1(b)(1)(vii); IRS Market Segment Specialization Program, Partnerships, Audit Technique Guide, Chapter 2, under the heading, "Books/Tax Differences—Contributed Property."

age interest in the LLC, and then allocates all the taxable income to members with net operating losses or to members in a lower tax bracket.[236]

- *Difference between book value and tax value.* There will be a difference between book income and tax income if the LLC determines capital account values based on fair market value rather than tax basis. The methods of converting book income into tax income when there is a book-tax disparity is determined under Code Sec. 704(c). The LLC must allocate income, gain, loss, and deduction with respect to the contributed property for tax purposes in a manner that takes account of the variation between the book value and the tax basis of the property at the time of the contribution (or at the time of revaluation).[237] The LLC may use the traditional method, the traditional method with curative allocations, or the remedial allocation method. These methods are discussed below.[238]

- *Regulatory allocations and reallocations.* There are a series of Code Sections and regulations that override the general tax allocation rules. For example, the LLC may be required to reallocate tax income under (a) Section 704(e)(2) for family allocations, (b) Section 482 for income and other tax attributes between commonly controlled entities, (c) Section 706(d) if the members have varying interests in the LLC during the tax year, (d) Section 1.751-1(b)(2)(ii) of the Treasury regulations concerning collapsible partnerships, and (e) the assignment of income doctrine.

¶ 805 ALLOCATIONS RELATED TO CONTRIBUTED PROPERTY

.01 Overview

An LLC must allocate taxable income, gain, loss, and deductions with respect to contributed property among the members so as to take account of the difference between the tax basis and the fair market value of the property at the time of contribution.[239] The mandatory allocation rules apply to Section 704(c) property. Section 704(c) property is property that a member contributes to an LLC in exchange for a membership interest if, at the time of contribution, the book value of the property for capital account purposes is greater or less than the contributing member's adjusted tax basis.[240]

The allocations must be made for tax purposes, not book (accounting) purposes. This differs from the regulatory allocations for minimum gain and qualified income offset that are made for book purposes, not tax purposes.[241]

---

[236] *Goldfine v. Comm'r,* 8 TC 843 (1983); *Miller v. Comm'r,* TC Memo 1984-336 (1984); *Martin Magaziner v. Comm'r,* TC Memo 1978-205 (1978).

[237] Code Sec. 704(c).

[238] *See* ¶ 805 *infra.*

[239] Code Sec. 704(c)(1)(A).

[240] Reg. § 1.704-3(a)(3)(i), (a)(5).

[241] *See* ¶ 804.08 *supra.*

There are two basic rules that apply to Section 704(c) property:

1. If the LLC sells Section 704(c) property and recognizes gain or loss, the built-in gain or loss must be allocated to the contributing member.
2. If the Section 704(c) property is subject to amortization, depletion, depreciation, or other cost recovery, the LLC must, to the extent possible, allocate the tax deductions to the noncontributing members in an amount equal to their share of book deductions for the Section 704(c) property. Any remaining amount of tax deductions for the Section 704(c) property may be allocated to the contributing member.

On December 21, 1993, the IRS issued final regulations on contributed property.[242] Under the regulations, the LLC may use one of the following four methods for making allocations for contributed property:

1. The traditional method.
2. The traditional method with curative allocations.
3. The remedial allocation method.
4. Any other reasonable method that takes into account the built-in gains and losses so that the contributing member receives the tax burdens and benefits of any built-in gain or loss.

The allocation method applies on a property-by-property basis.[243]

An LLC may use different methods with respect to different items of contributed property, provided that the LLC and the members consistently apply a single reasonable method for each item of contributed property, and that the overall method or combination of methods is reasonably based on the facts and circumstances and consistent with the purposes of Code Sec. 704(c). For example, it may be unreasonable to use one method for appreciated property and another method for depreciated property.[244]

.02 Traditional Method

Summary of Rule

The first method of allocation for contributed property is the traditional method.[245] This is the most common method. The traditional method requires that when an LLC has income, gain, or loss attributable to Section 704(c) property, it must allocate to the contributing partner the built-in gain or loss associated with the property to avoid shifting the tax consequences.[246] An LLC makes this allocation by (i) allocating tax gain or loss from the sale of property to the noncontributing member

---

[242] Reg. § 1.704-3; T.D. 8500 (Dec. 21, 1993).
[243] Reg. § 1.704-3(a)(2).
[244] Reg. § 1.704-3(a)(2).
[245] Reg. § 1.704-3(b).
[246] Reg. § 1.704-3(b)(1).

equal to that member's share of book gain or loss, (ii) allocating tax depreciation to the noncontributing member equal to that member's share of book depreciation, and (iii) allocating the remaining tax gain or loss from the sale of property and the remaining tax depreciation to the contributing member.

Sale of Property

An LLC must allocate the built-in gain or loss to the contributing member when the property is sold.[247] The allocation of gain or loss is made for tax purposes, not book purposes. Any gain or loss other than the built-in gain or loss is allocated to all of the members in accordance with the operating agreement.

The built-in gains and losses are determined on a property-by-property basis rather than on an aggregate net basis.[248] There is a limited exception for securities LLCs. If the book value and tax basis are the same at the time of sale, then each member's share of book gain and tax gain will be the same.

The computations under the traditional method are made as follows:

- First, the LLC must calculate the amount of book gain or loss and tax gain or loss from the sale of each property. The book gain or loss is the difference between the sales price and the capital account value. The tax gain or loss is the difference between the sales price and adjusted tax basis.
- Second, the LLC must allocate the book gain or loss to the members in accordance with the operating agreement.
- Third, the LLC must allocate tax gain or loss to the noncontributing member in an amount equal to that member's share of book gain or loss.
- Finally, the LLC must allocate the remaining tax gain or loss to the contributing member. The special allocation of tax gain does not increase the member's capital account since the member previously received an increase or decrease in capital account for the built-in gain or loss when the property was contributed to the LLC.[249]

EXAMPLE 8-25

An LLC has two equal members. Member A contributes land to the LLC with a $10,000 tax basis and $17,000 fair market value. Member B contributes $17,000 in cash to the LLC. Each member receives an initial capital account of $17,000. The LLC sells the property two years later for $19,000. The LLC recognizes $2,000 of book gain ($19,000 sales price less $17,000 book value) and $9,000 of tax gain ($19,000 sales price less $10,000 tax basis). The LLC must allocate the $2,000 of book gain equally to the

---

[247] Reg. § 1.704-3(b)(1). The built-in gain is the difference between the property's book value and the member's tax basis in the property on the date of contribution. Ltr. Rul. 200123035.

[248] Reg. § 1.704-3(a)(2).

[249] *See* Reg. § 1.704-1(b)(2)(iv)(g)(1), 1.704-1(b)(5), Example (14).

members in accordance with the operating agreement ($1,000 to each member). This increases each member's capital account from $17,000 to $18,000. The LLC must allocate $1,000 of tax gain to Member B (the noncontributing member) equal to his allocable share of book gain. The LLC must allocate the remaining $8,000 of tax gain to Member A. The result is that Member A receives an allocation of tax gain equal to the built-in gain ($7,000) plus his one-half share of book gain ($1,000).

Under the ceiling rule, the total amount of tax gain or loss allocated to a member for a tax year cannot exceed the total LLC tax gain or loss with respect to the property for the tax year.[250] The ceiling rule applies if the book gain or loss from the sale of the property exceeds the tax gain or loss.

EXAMPLE 8-26

An LLC has two equal members. Member A contributes land to the LLC with a $10,000 tax basis and $17,000 fair market value. Member B contributes $17,000 in cash to the LLC. Each member receives an initial capital account of $17,000. The LLC sells the land for $15,000. The LLC has a book loss of $2,000 (sales price of $15,000 less book value of $17,000), and a tax gain of $5,000 (sales price of $15,000 less tax basis of $10,000). The LLC must allocate the book loss equally between the members in accordance with the operating agreement. This decreases each member's capital account by $1,000 from $17,000 to $16,000. The LLC cannot allocate any tax loss to Member B (the noncontributing member) since it has no tax losses. It must allocate all of the $5,000 tax gain to Member A (the contributing member).[251] The LLC cannot allocate any tax gain to Member B as the noncontributing member since Member B received no allocation of book income.

Depreciation

If the contributed or revalued property is depreciable property, then the noncontributing member first receives tax depreciation deductions equal to book depreciation deductions.[252] The contributing member receives any remaining tax depreciation deductions. The result is that the contributing member receives less depreciation deductions over the remaining life of the property. The computations are made as follows:

---

[250] Reg. § 1.704-3(b)(1).

[251] *See* Reg. § 1.704-3(b)(2), Example 1(iii).

[252] Reg. § 1.704-3(b)(2), Example 1(ii).

- First, the LLC must calculate the amount of book depreciation and tax depreciation for each property with a book-tax difference. The book depreciation is normally based on the book value of the property and the property's remaining useful life. Under the safe-harbor rules for special allocations, book depreciation must be based on tax depreciation multiplied by a fraction. The numerator of the fraction is the book value of the assets on the date of contribution, and the denominator is the tax basis.[253] The tax depreciation is normally based on the accelerated cost recovery system (ACRS).

- Second, the LLC must allocate the book depreciation to the members in accordance with the operating agreement.

- Third, the LLC must allocate tax depreciation to the noncontributing member equal to that member's allocable share of book depreciation. The LLC must allocate any remaining tax depreciation to the contributing member.

EXAMPLE 8-27

An LLC has two equal members. Member A contributed a depreciable building to the LLC with an adjusted tax basis of $80,000 and a fair market value of $100,000. Member B contributed $100,000 of cash to the LLC. Each member has an initial capital account of $100,000. The LLC depreciates the building for book and tax purposes over a period of ten years on a straight-line basis. Thus, the book depreciation is $10,000 per year and the tax depreciation is $8,000 per year. The LLC must allocate $5,000 of book depreciation each year to the members in accordance with the operating agreement. This decreases each member's capital account at the end of the first year from $100,000 to $95,000. The LLC must then allocate $5,000 of tax depreciation to Member B (the noncontributing member) equal to his allocable share of book depreciation. The LLC must allocate the remaining $3,000 of tax depreciation to Member A (the contributing member).

Under the ceiling rule, the tax depreciation allocated to the noncontributing member may not exceed the total amount of tax depreciation with respect to such property. If there is insufficient tax depreciation, then the LLC must first allocate the available tax depreciation to the noncontributing member up to the member's share of book depreciation and then allocate any remaining tax depreciation to the contributing member.[254]

---

[253] Reg. § 1.704-1(b)(2)(iv)(g)(3).
[254] Reg. § 1.704-3(b)(1).

EXAMPLE 8-28

An LLC has two equal members. Member A contributed a depreciable building to the LLC with an adjusted tax basis of $4,000 and a fair market value of $10,000. Member B contributed $10,000 of cash to the LLC. Each member has an initial capital account of $10,000. The LLC depreciates the building for book and tax purposes over a period of ten years on a straight-line basis. Thus, the book depreciation is $1,000 per year and the tax depreciation is $400 per year. Ordinarily, the LLC would be required to allocate to Member B (the noncontributing member) $500 of tax depreciation equal to Member B's allocable share of book depreciation. However, there is only $400 of tax depreciation. Therefore, only $400 of tax depreciation is allocated to Member B, and no tax depreciation is allocated to Member A.[255]

The amount of built-in gain or loss that must be allocated to the contributing member on sale of the property is reduced each year if the property is subject to depreciation, amortization or other cost recovery deductions. The built-in gain or loss at the end of each tax year is a difference between the book value (as adjusted for book depreciation) and the tax basis (as adjusted for tax depreciation).[256]

EXAMPLE 8-29

An LLC has two equal members. Member A contributed a depreciable building to the LLC with an adjusted tax basis of $4,000 and a fair market value of $10,000. Member B contributed $10,000 of cash to the LLC. Each member has an initial capital account of $10,000. The LLC depreciates the building for book and tax purposes over a period of ten years on a straight-line basis. Thus, the book depreciation is $1,000 per year and the tax depreciation is $400 per year. The built-in gain on the date of contribution is $6,000 ($10,000 book value of the building less $4,000 adjusted tax basis). The built-in gain at the end of the first year is $5,400 ($9,000 adjusted book value less $3,600 adjusted tax basis).[257] There is no reduction in Member A's outside tax basis since Member B received no allocation of tax depreciation. Member B's outside tax basis is decreased from $10,000 to $9,600 as a result of the $400 allocation of tax depreciation.

---

[255] Reg. § 1.704-3(b)(2), Example 1(ii).
[256] Reg. § 1.704-3(b)(2), Example 1(ii).
[257] Reg. § 1.704-3(b)(2), Example 1(ii).

.03 Traditional Method with Curative Allocations

The second method of allocation for contributed property is the traditional method with curative allocations.[258] This method is the same as the traditional method, except that the LLC allocates additional items of income or loss to the members to make up for the limits on allocations required by the ceiling rule under the traditional method.

Under this method, the LLC first determines the amount of taxable gain or loss that cannot be allocated to the noncontributing member because of the ceiling rule. The LLC then looks at the tax items that it has generated for the year, and searches for one that is of the same character as the item limited by the ceiling rule. If the LLC has such an item, it "borrows" that item and allocates it to the noncontributing member up to the amount limited by the ceiling rule.[259] The contributing member receives a corresponding reduction in the same tax item.

The curative allocation is made for tax purposes only and does not affect the book capital accounts. For example, if a non-contributing member is allocated less tax depreciation than book depreciation with respect to built-in gain property, the LLC may make a curative allocation to that member by allocating tax depreciation from another item of LLC property to make up the difference (although the corresponding book depreciation of that other item is still allocated to the contributing member).[260]

The result is that the noncontributing members and the contributing members are allocated offsetting tax items. The noncontributing member receives a gain or loss reduced from what he would normally have received, and the contributing member receives the mirror opposite.[261]

The purpose of the curative allocation is to eliminate the difference in the capital account and outside tax basis for the noncontributing member. The curative allocation normally increases the book/tax disparity for the contributing member.

Curative allocations for built-in gain property may be made in one of the following two ways:[262]

- Allocate additional items of tax deduction or loss to the noncontributing member to substitute for a deduction or loss that is not available to the member as a result of the ceiling rule; or

- Allocate additional amounts of taxable income or gain to the contributing member equal to the deduction or loss that is not available to the noncontributing member as a result of the ceiling rule.

---

[258] Reg. § 1.704-3(c).

[259] IRS Market Segment Specialization Program, Partnerships, Audit Technique Guide, Chapter 3, under the heading, "Traditional Method with Curative Allocations."

[260] Reg. § 1.704-3(c)(1).

[261] IRS Audit Technique Guide—Partnerships, Chapter 3, under the heading, "Traditional Method with Curative Allocations."

[262] Reg. § 1.704-3(c)(3)(iii), (4), Examples 1 and 2.

Similar rules apply for built-in loss property. The LLC would allocate additional taxable income and gain to the noncontributing member or additional tax deductions and loss to the contributing member.

EXAMPLE 8-30

An LLC has two equal members. Member A contributes $2,800 cash to the LLC. Member B contributes Building 1 to the LLC. The property has a tax basis of $800 and a fair market value of $2,800. The LLC depreciates the property over a period of four years. Thus, there is $700 of book depreciation each year (1/4 × $2,800) and $200 of tax depreciation (1/4 × $800). The LLC must allocate $350 of book depreciation on the property to each member in accordance with the operating agreement. This allocation reduces each member's capital account by $350. Under the traditional method, the LLC would be required to allocate $350 of tax depreciation to Member A. This is equal to the book depreciation that Member A, as the noncontributing member, receives from the property. However, the LLC may allocate only $200 of tax depreciation to Member A under the ceiling rule because there is only $200 of tax depreciation.

EXAMPLE 8-31

Same facts as in prior example, except that the LLC elects to make curative allocations under Regulations Section 1.704-3(c), using depreciation on other property owned by the LLC. The LLC also owns Building 2 that generates $400 of book and tax depreciation each year that is allocated equally to the members ($200 each). Thus, $150 of the $200 tax depreciation that would otherwise be allocated to Member B under the traditional method must be reallocated to Member A under the traditional method with curative allocations.[263] The book depreciation is not affected by the curative allocations and is allocated equally between the members.

A LLC may limit curative allocations to allocations of one or more particular tax items (e.g., only depreciation from a specific property or properties), even if the allocation of those available items does not fully offset the effect of the ceiling rule.[264]

The LLC must be consistent in its application of curative allocations with respect to each item of built-in gain or loss property from year to year.[265]

---

[263] Reg. § 1.1245-1(e)(2)(iii), Example 3(iii).
[264] Reg. § 1.704-3(c)(1).
[265] Reg. § 1.704-3(c)(2).

An LLC that uses the traditional method with curative allocations must depreciate contributed property for book purposes over the same method and rate that it uses for tax purposes.[266]

The curative allocation must be made within a reasonable period of time. The LLC operating agreement must provide for the curative allocation for the year of contribution or revaluation. Curative allocations may be made in the current year to offset the effect of the ceiling rule in prior years, provided that the current year's curative allocations are made over a reasonable period of time and are provided for under the operating agreement.[267]

The curative allocation may be made only to the extent necessary to avoid the distortion created by the ceiling rule.[268] The items used for the curative allocations must have the same character (e.g., capital or ordinary) as the items affected by the ceiling rule.[269] If the LLC does not have a sufficient amount of like character items to make the curative allocation in a particular year, the LLC may not make catch-up curative allocations in succeeding years,[270] subject to two exceptions.[271]

.04 Remedial Allocation Method

General Requirements

The third method of allocation for contributed property is the remedial allocation method.[272] The purpose of remedial allocations is to eliminate the difference in the capital account and outside tax basis for the noncontributing member caused by the ceiling rule.

This method is similar to the curative allocation method with one important difference. Curative allocations can only be made if the LLC has another item of the same amount and character as the item limited by the ceiling rule. The LLC cannot make curative allocations if it does not have similar tax items during the current year. Remedial allocations can be made even though the LLC does not have another item of the same amount and character as the item limited by the ceiling rule. The LLC

---

[266] Reg. § 1.704-1(b)(2)(iv)(g)(3).

[267] Reg. § 1.704-3(c)(3)(ii).

[268] Reg. § 1.704-3(c)(3)(i).

[269] Reg. § 1.704-3(c)(3)(iii)(A).

[270] Reg. § 1.704-3(c)(3)(i).

[271] Under the first exception, catch-up curative allocations are permitted on disposal of the property. Reg. § 1.704-3(c)(3)(iii)(B). Under the second exception, catch-up curative allocations are permitted if they are made in subsequent years over a reasonable period of time, such as the property's economic life, and the membership agreement in effect for the year of contribution provides for the catch-up curative allocations. Reg. § 1.704-3(c)(3)(ii). *See also* Reg. § 1.704-3(c)(4), Example 3(ii)(C), in which there were sufficient curative items in a subsequent year, but use of the full catch-up amount in such year would have been an unreasonable use of the curative method. The curative allocations would have been reasonable if made over the property's economic life of ten years rather than over the property's remaining depreciation recovery period of one year.

[272] Reg. § 1.704-3(d).

may simply make up whatever tax items that the noncontributing member needs in order to eliminate the book/tax disparity caused by the ceiling rule.

The character of the remedial allocations of income, gain, loss, or deductions to the non-contributing member is determined with reference to the items limited by the ceiling rule. For example, if the item limited by the ceiling rule is depreciation from rental property, the remedial allocation to the non-contributing member is depreciation from property used in a rental activity and the offsetting remedial allocation to the contributing member is ordinary income from that rental activity. Each member then applies Code Sec. 469 to the allocation at his or her level as appropriate.[273]

The LLC makes remedial allocations by creating pairs of tax items.[274] In the case of built-in gain property, the LLC creates an income or gain item to the contributing member, and an offsetting deduction or loss item for the noncontributing member. In the case of built-in loss property, the LLC creates a deduction or loss item for the contributing member, and an offsetting income or gain item to the noncontributing member. These items do not really exist. They are notional or artificial tax items made up by the LLC. The aggregate taxable income or loss of the LLC remains the same because the income or gain item created by the LLC always equals the offsetting deduction or loss item created by the LLC.

The LLC creates the remedial allocation items only to the extent necessary to eliminate the disparity between book and tax allocations for the noncontributing member caused by the ceiling rule. The LLC makes a remedial allocation of tax items to the noncontributing member equal to the full amount of the disparity between book and tax allocations for the noncontributing member caused by the ceiling rule. The LLC then allocates the offsetting remedial item to the contributing member.

Unlike the curative allocation method, the remedial allocation method does not force the LLC to look for tax items that actually exist. However, remedial allocations are real for tax purposes in spite of their purely fictitious origin. Remedial items have the same effect as actual tax items on a member's tax liability and on the member's adjusted tax basis in the membership interest. For example, if an LLC makes a remedial allocation of $500 of gain to Member A on the sale of LLC property, then Member A must recognize an additional $500 of taxable income, and his adjusted tax basis in the LLC increases by the same amount, in the year of allocation.[275]

Remedial items do not affect the LLC's computation of its taxable income under Code Sec. 703 and do not affect the LLC's adjusted tax basis in its property.[276]

---

[273] Reg. § 1.704-3(d)(3).

[274] Reg. § 1.704-3(d)(1).

[275] Reg. § 1.704-3(d)(4).

[276] California Franchise Tax Board, Partnership Technical Manual ¶ 2340.

Mechanics of Remedial Allocations

The remedial allocations are made as follows:[277]

1. The LLC must first determine book allocations, and each member's share of book allocations. The book allocations are based on capital account values, rather than the adjusted tax basis of LLC property. The LLC must compute book allocations in accordance with special rules under the remedial allocation method. The main differences between regular book allocations and remedial book allocations concern depreciation, as discussed below.
2. The LLC then allocates the corresponding tax items to the members using the traditional method.
3. If the book allocations and tax allocations of an item are different for the noncontributing member because of the ceiling rule, then the LLC must create a remedial item of income, gain, loss, or deduction equal to the full amount of the difference, and allocate that to the noncontributing member. The LLC does not borrow the item from the contributing member as under the traditional method with curative allocations. Instead, it creates a fictional item with the same tax attributes as the tax item that it is designed to replace.[278]
4. The LLC must simultaneously create an offsetting remedial item in an identical amount, and allocate that to the contributing member.
5. The remedial items do not affect the LLC's computation of taxable income or the adjusted tax basis of its property.[279] The remedial items are "notional tax items" that the LLC creates only for tax purposes. They do not affect the members' capital accounts.[280] They have the same effect as actual tax items on a member's tax liability and on the member's adjusted basis in the LLC membership interest.[281]

EXAMPLE 8-32

An LLC has two equal members. Member A contributed depreciable property to the LLC with a tax basis of $60,000 and a fair market value of $100,000. Member B contributed $100,000 of cash to the LLC. The LLC has no items of income, gain, loss, deduction, or credit other than depreciation. It has $20,000 of book depreciation, which it allocates equally between Member A and Member B in accordance with the operating agreement. It has $6,000 of tax depreciation. Normally, the LLC would be

---

[277] Reg. § 1.704-3(d)(2).

[278] Reg. § 1.704-3(d)(3).

[279] Reg. § 1.704-3(d)(4)(i).

[280] IRS Market Segment Specialization Program, Partnerships, Audit Technique Guide, Chapter 3, under the heading, "Remedial Allocation Method."

[281] Reg. § 1.704-3(d)(4)(ii).

required to allocate $10,000 of tax depreciation to Member B as a noncontributing member, since that is the amount of book depreciation that was allocated to Member B for capital account purposes. However, because of the ceiling rule, the LLC can allocate only $6,000 of tax depreciation to Member B and no tax depreciation to Member A. The LLC cannot use the traditional method with curative allocations, since it has no other items of tax depreciation from other property to allocate to Member B. Under the remedial allocation method, the LLC creates $4,000 of additional tax depreciation, which it allocates to Member B. It also creates an additional $4,000 of ordinary income, which it allocates to Member A as the contributing member. The result is that Member B receives $10,000 of tax depreciation, equal to the $10,000 of book depreciation (even though the LLC has only $6,000 of tax depreciation). Member A recognizes $4,000 of taxable ordinary income (even though the LLC has no taxable income).

Depreciation

If an LLC has depreciable property and uses the remedial allocation method, the LLC must compute book depreciation using a split depreciation scheme. The LLC must bifurcate the book basis of the contributed property into two portions. The portion equal to the adjusted tax basis in the property is depreciated in the same manner as the adjusted tax basis in the property is depreciated (i.e., generally over the remaining recovery period under Code Sec. 168(i)(7) or other applicable sections). The portion of the book basis in excess of the adjusted tax basis is recovered using any depreciation period and method available to the LLC for newly purchased property.[282]

EXAMPLE 8-33

Peter and Jane are equal members in an LLC. Peter contributes equipment with a fair market value of $100 and an adjusted basis of $20. The equipment is ten-year Section 1245 property with a five year remaining straight-line depreciation life. Jane contributes $100 cash. The LLC receives a carryover tax basis in the property of $20. The LLC uses the remedial allocation method. The LLC has no income during its first year of operations. The LLC makes the remedial allocations as follows:[283]

    (a) The LLC must first compute book and tax depreciation. The LLC may depreciate the tax basis of $20 over the equipment's remain-

---

[282] Reg. §1.704-3(d)(2); IRS Audit Technique Guide—Partnerships, Chapter 3, under the heading, "Remedial Allocation Method."

[283] IRS Market Segment Specialization Program, Partnerships, Audit Technique Guide, Chapter 3, Example 3-7.

ing five-year life ($4 per year). There is $4 of book depreciation each year equal to this tax depreciation. The LLC also has book depreciation for the $80 fair market value of the property in excess of the tax basis. This excess book value is depreciated as if it were newly purchased property. In this example, it is depreciated over ten years ($8 per year). Thus, the LLC has $4 of tax depreciation and $12 of book depreciation.

(b) The LLC must then allocate the book depreciation to the members. It must allocate $6 of book depreciation to each member in accordance with the operating agreement since the members share book profits and losses equally.

(c) Finally, the LLC must allocate the tax depreciation to the members. The LLC must allocate $6 of tax depreciation to Jane as the noncontributing member equal to the amount of the book depreciation allocated to her. However, the LLC only has $4 of tax depreciation. Therefore, it must make up $2 of tax depreciation and a corresponding $2 of ordinary income. It must allocate the $2 of made-up depreciation to Jane and the $2 of made-up ordinary income to Peter.

(d) The remedial allocation eliminates the difference between Jane's capital account and her outside tax basis. The computations are summarized as follows:

| | *Peter* | | *Jane* | |
	Tax basis in membership interest	*Capital account*	*Tax basis in membership interest*	*Capital account*
Initial tax basis and capital account	20	100	100	100
Traditional allocation of depreciation	(0)	(6)	(4)	(6)
Balance	20	94	96	94
Remedial allocation of made-up depreciation and income	2	0	(2)	0
Adjusted tax basis and capital account after first year	22	94	94	94

.05 Other Reasonable Methods

The LLC may use any other reasonable method of allocation for contributed property that takes into account the built-in gains and losses so that the contributing member receives the tax benefits and burdens of the built-in gains and losses.[284] An allocation method or combination of methods is not reasonable if the contribution of property and corresponding tax allocations are made for the purpose of shifting the tax consequences of built-in gain or loss among the members in a manner that substantially reduces the present value of the members' aggregate tax liability.[285]

.06 Which Method to Choose

The most common allocation method is the traditional method.

The contributing member normally wants the traditional method if the member contributes appreciated property to the LLC. Under the traditional method, the LLC simply allocates tax depreciation to the noncontributing member equal to what the tax depreciation would have been if the contributed property had a tax basis equal to fair market value. If there is insufficient tax depreciation to allocate to the noncontributing member, then the noncontributing member receives only the actual amount of tax depreciation. The contributing member receives less in depreciation tax deductions.

The noncontributing member normally wants the remedial allocation method. If there is insufficient tax depreciation, then the LLC must create additional phantom tax depreciation to allocate to the noncontributing member. This could be very costly to the contributing member who must receive an equal amount of phantom ordinary income.

A member who contributes appreciated property to an LLC should request that the LLC include the following provisions in the operating agreement:

- The LLC will use the traditional method. The traditional method is used in most cases because of the adverse tax consequences to the contributing member of the remedial allocation method.
- The LLC will not sell or exchange the appreciated property, or drop the appreciated property into a subsidiary,[286] without reimbursing the contributing member for any resulting tax liability. Alternatively, the member may require the LLC to reimburse the member for any tax liability as a result of the sale or exchange of the appreciated property within a certain number of years after the date of contribution. If the LLC sells the property, any taxable built-in gain on the date of contribution must be allocated to the contributing member.[287]
- The LLC will not make a distribution of the appreciated property to another member that causes the disguised sales rules to apply. The distribution of appreciated property to another member within seven years after the date of contribution may be treated as a disguised sale that is taxable to the contributing member.[288]

---

[284] Reg. § 1.704-3(a)(1).

[285] Reg. § 1.704-3(a)(10).

[286] The contribution of the property to a subsidiary LLC that is classified as a partnership will permit the subsidiary to elect its own distributive share method under Code Sec. 704(c)(1)(A) (e.g., traditional method, curative method, or remedial allocation method).

[287] See ¶ 805.02 *supra*.

[288] See ¶ 605 *supra*.

.07 Forward and Reverse Section 704(c) Revaluations

An LLC may elect to revalue its property to fair market value on the date of contribution by a new member, distribution to a member, or liquidation. The revaluation procedures are discussed at ¶804.02.[289]

The capital accounts are revalued so that gain or loss inherent in LLC property since the date of contribution will be allocated among the members in the same manner as if the LLC made a taxable disposition of the property for fair market value. The allocations that the LLC makes with respect to the revalued property are referred to as "reverse Section 704(c) allocations."[290]

The book-up or book-down in capital accounts creates two layers of Section 704(c) built-in gain or loss. The built-in gain or loss on the date of contribution is commonly referred to as "forward Section 704(c) gain or loss." The additional built-in gain or loss on the date of revaluation is commonly referred to as "reverse Section 704(c) gain or loss."

The same principles that apply to forward Section 704(c) gain or loss must be applied to reverse Section 704(c) gain or loss.[291] In the case of reverse Section 704(c) gain or loss, the existing members of the LLC whose capital accounts are revalued are treated as the "contributing members," and the new members who contribute cash (or property with a fair market value equal to its tax basis) are treated as the "non-contributing members."

.08 Small Disparities

If there is a small disparity between the fair market value and the adjusted tax basis of a contributed property, the LLC may account for the difference between book value and tax basis in one of the following ways:[292]

- use a reasonable Section 704(c) method (traditional method, traditional method with curative allocations, or remedial allocation method);
- disregard the application of Section 704(c) to the property; or
- defer the application of Section 704(c) to the property until the disposition of the property.

There is a small disparity if (i) the difference between the book value and the basis of all properties that a member contributes to the LLC during the same tax year

---

[289] *See* ¶804.02 *supra*, under the heading, "Optional Revaluation of LLC and Property."
[290] Reg. §1.704-3(a)(6)(i).
[291] *See* Reg. §1.704-3(a)(6).
[292] Reg. §1.704-3(e)(1)(i).

is not more than 15 percent of the basis for such properties, and (ii) the total gross difference between book value and basis does not exceed $20,000.[293]

.09 Distribution of Property

If an LLC distributes built-in gain or loss property to a member within seven years from the date of contribution to the LLC, the contributing member must recognize gain or loss equal to the lesser of (a) the built-in gain or loss inherent in the property at the time of contribution, or (b) the gain or loss that would have been allocated to the contributing member if the LLC had sold the property to the distributing member for its fair market value.[294] If the property was contributed prior to June 9, 1997, the recognition period is five years.

The fair market value of the distributed property is the price at which the property would change hands between a willing buyer and a willing seller at the time of distribution, neither being under any compulsion to buy or sell and both having reasonable knowledge of the relevant facts. The fair market value assigned by a LLC to the distributed property is regarded as correct, provided that the value reflects an arm's-length negotiation and the members have sufficiently adverse interests.[295]

.10 Transfers of Membership Interests

If a contributing member transfers a membership interest, the built-in gain or loss associated with the contributed property must be allocated to the transferee member in the same manner that it would have been allocated to the transferor member.[296]

¶ 806 ALLOCATIONS WITH RESPECT TO BUILT-IN LOSS PROPERTY

.01 General Rules

There are two rules that are designed to prevent members from shifting built-in losses from the contributing member to noncontributing members. The first rule is Code Sec. 704(c)(1)(A) which provides that built-in losses must be allocated to the contributing member while that person is a member of the LLC. This rule is discussed at ¶ 805. The second rule is Code Sec. 704(c)(1)(C) which provides that

---

[293] Reg. § 1.704-3(e)(1)(ii).
[294] Code Sec. 704(c)(1)(B)(i), (ii); Reg. § 1.704-4(a)(1).
[295] Reg. § 1.704-4(a)(3).
[296] Reg. § 1.704-3(a)(7).

built-losses may not be allocated to noncontributing members after the contributing member ceases to be a member in the LLC.

Prior to the American Jobs Creation Act of 2004, an LLC and its members could take double losses on the same property. The member would first contribute built-in loss property to the LLC. The member would receive a basis in the membership interest equal to the basis of the contributed property. The LLC would receive the same carryover basis in the contributed property. Immediately thereafter, the member could sell the membership interest at a loss. The LLC could at a later date sell the high-basis property at a loss and allocate those losses to the transferee members.[297] An LLC and its members could also take double losses if a member contributed built-in loss property to an LLC, and then received a liquidating distribution of other property.[298]

Code Sec. 704(c)(1)(C) now prohibits double losses. It provides that if a member contributes built-in loss property to an LLC, the built-in loss may be taken into account only in determining the amount of items allocated to the contributing member. It also provides that, in determining the amount of items allocated to other members, the LLC's basis in contributed property is equal to its fair market value at the time of the contribution. Built-in loss means the excess of the adjusted basis of the property over its fair market value at the time of contribution.[299]

The fair market value rule means that the built-in loss is eliminated when the contributing member's interest is transferred or liquidated. LLC allocations to the remaining members after the date of transfer or liquidation must be based on the lower fair market value of the property on the date of contribution rather than the higher carryover basis.

EXAMPLE 8-34

Larry contributes to an LLC a note receivable with a fair market value of $100,000 and a basis of $200,000. Donna contributes $100,000 cash. Larry subsequently sells his membership interest to Bob for $100,000 and recognizes a $100,000 loss (the difference between his $200,000 outside basis and the $100,000 amount realized on sale of the membership interest). If the LLC does not have a Code Sec. 754 election in place, the LLC could sell the note receivable and recognize the same $100,000 loss again. Code Sec. 704(c)(1)(C)(ii) prevents this by treating the LLC's basis in the built-in

---

[297] Code Sec. 704(c)(1)(A) requires the partnership to allocate items of partnership income, gain, loss, and deduction with respect to contributed property among the partners so as to take into account any built-in gain or built-in loss in the contributed property. This rule is intended to prevent the transfer of built-in gain or built-in loss from the contributing partner to other partners. If a partner contributes built-in gain or built-in loss property to a partnership and later transfers the interest in the partnership, Reg. § 1.704-3(a)(7) provides that the built-in gain or built-in loss must be allocated to the transferee partner as it would have been allocated to the transferor partner.

[298] *See* discussion in the preamble to IRS proposed regulations under Code Sec. 704(c)(1)(C), REG-144468-05 (2014).

[299] Code Sec. 704(c)(1) (last sentence); Prop. Reg. § 1.704-3(a)(3)(ii).

loss property as equal to its fair market value at the time of contribution to the LLC ($100,000), thereby eliminating the built-in loss for the noncontributing members.[300]

.02 Proposed Regulations

Proposed regulations create the concept of a "Section 704(c)(1)(C) basis adjustment." The Section 704(c)(1)(C) basis adjustment is initially equal to the built-in loss associated with the contributed property at the time of contribution, and is then adjusted in accordance with the regulations. When an LLC receives contributed property with a built-in loss, the LLC's tax basis in the property with respect to the noncontributing members is the fair market value the property. The LLC's tax basis in the property with respect to the contributing member is the fair market value the property plus the Section 704(c)(1)(C) basis adjustment. Thus, the basis adjustment is unique to the contributing member. The basis adjustment does not affect the member's capital accounts or the LLC's computation of any tax items under Code Sec. 703.

EXAMPLE 8-35

A contributes property to an LLC with a fair market value of $6,000 and an adjusted basis of $11,000. A has a Section 704(c)(1)(C) basis adjustment of $5,000. The LLC's basis in the property with respect to the noncontributing members is $6,000. The LLC's basis in the property with respect to A is $11,000 ($6,000 fair market value plus the $5,000 Section 704(c)(1)(C) basis adjustment). A's basis in the membership interest is $11,000, which is equal to the basis of the property contributed to the LLC.[301]

The mandatory basis adjustment under the proposed regulations has the following tax consequences:[302]

- *Computation of LLC income.* The LLC must compute book items of income, deduction, gain or loss at the LLC level in the normal manner without taking account of the special basis adjustment. It must then allocate those items to the members in accordance with the operating agreement and adjust the members' capital accounts accordingly. The LLC must then allocate tax items to the members on Schedule K-1. Normally, tax allocations must follow book allocations. However, the LLC must adjust the distributive shares of taxable income reflected on Schedule K-1 to reflect the special basis adjustment for the contributing member. Generally, this means that the member who contrib-

---

[300] IRS Audit Technique Guide—Partnerships, Chapter 3, Example 3-14.

[301] Example from preamble to IRS proposed regulations under Code Sec. 704(c)(1)(C), REG-144468-05 (2014).

[302] Prop. Reg. § 1.704-3(f)(3).

uted the built-in loss property will have less taxable gain on sale of the contributed property,[303] or more taxable depreciation[304] and other deductions. The special tax adjustments do not affect the contributing member's capital account.[305]

- *Sale of contributed property.* If the LLC sells the contributed property, the contributing member receives a reduced allocation of gain or an increased allocation of loss equal to the basis adjustment.[306]

- *Exchange of contributed property in nonrecognition transaction.* If the LLC exchanges the property in a nonrecognition transaction, the contributing member retains the Section 704(c)(1)(C) basis adjustment in the replacement property.[307]

- *Transfer of membership interest.* If the contributing member sells the membership interest, the LLC's basis adjustment for the contributed property is eliminated.[308] For example, if a member sells a 20 percent interest in an LLC, the member recognizes an outside loss with respect to that 20 percent interest, and 20 percent of the member's basis adjustment for each property contributed to the LLC with built-in loss is eliminated.[309] The result is that only the member recognizes the built-in loss on sale or other disposition of the membership interest. Transferee members do not receive the benefit of the Section 704(c)(1)(C) basis adjustment.

- *Distribution to noncontributing member.* If the LLC distributes built-in loss property to a noncontributing member, the Section 704(c)(1)(C) basis adjustment for that property is eliminated. However, the contributing member keeps the Section 704(c)(1)(C) basis adjustment by reallocating it to other LLC property.[310] This rule prevents an LLC from shifting precontribution losses to noncontributing members by distributing the built-in loss property to noncontributing members.

- *Liquidation of interest of contributing member.* If the LLC liquidates the interest of a contributing member, the adjusted basis of LLC property distributed to the member includes the Section 704(c)(1)(C) basis adjustment. The LLC must reallocate any Section 704(c)(1)(C) basis adjustment for property retained by the LLC to distributed property of like character. If there is no distributed property of like character, then the remaining Section 704(c)(1)(C) basis ad-

---

[303] *See* Prop. Reg. § 1.704-3(f)(3)(iii)(C), Example 3(iii).

[304] Prop. Reg. § 1.704-3(f)(3)(ii)(D)(2), Example.

[305] Prop. Reg. § 1.704-3(f)(3)(ii)(B).

[306] *See* Prop. Reg. § 1.704-3(f)(3)(iii)(C), Example 3(iii).

[307] Prop. Reg. § 1.704-3(f)(3)(iv)(A).

[308] Prop. Reg. § 1.704-3(f)(3)(iii)(A).

[309] Example from preamble to IRS proposed regulations under Code Sec. 704(c)(1)(C), REG-144468-05 (2014).

[310] Prop. Reg. § 1.704-3(f)(3)(v)(B). The Section 704(c)(1)(C) basis adjustment is reallocated to other LLC property in accordance with the rules set forth in Reg. § 1.755-1(c).

¶ 806.02

justment is treated as a positive adjustment under Code Sec. 734(b).[311] The Code Sec. 734(b) adjustments are discussed at ¶1006.

EXAMPLE 8-36

A contributes Property to an LLC on January 1, 2015 with a tax basis of $12,000 and a fair market value of $5,000. B contributes $5,000 to the LLC. Prior to the contribution, A depreciated Property under Code Sec. 168 over ten years using the straight-line method and the half-year convention. On the contribution date, Property has 7.5 years remaining in its recovery period. Property is Code Sec. 704(c)(1)(C) property, and A's Section 704(c)(1)(C) basis adjustment is $7,000. The LLC's basis in Property is $5,000 (fair market value). In accordance with Code Sec. 168(i)(7), the depreciation is $667 per year ($5,000 divided by 7.5 years), which is shared equally between A and B. A's $7,000 Section 704(c)(1)(C) basis adjustment is subject to depreciation of $933 per year in accordance with Code Sec. 168(i)(7) ($7,000 divided by 7.5 years), which is taken into account by A for tax purposes.[312]

The Section 704(c)(1)(C) basis adjustment is similar to the mandatory basis adjustment under Code Secs. 734 and 743. There are certain differences. Code Sec. 704(c)(1)(C) applies if the member contributes built-in loss property to an LLC. Code Sec. 734 applies if an LLC makes a distribution of property resulting in a substantial basis reduction with respect to the distribution. Code Sec. 743 applies if an LLC has a substantial built-in loss immediately after the transfer of a membership interest. The mandatory basis adjustment under Code Sec. 734 is discussed at ¶1009. The mandatory basis adjustment under Code Sec. 743 is discussed at ¶1509.

¶807 VARYING INTEREST RULE

.01 Overview

Under the varying interest rule, an LLC must take into account the varying ownership interests of the members in the LLC during the tax year in making allocations of income, gain, loss and deduction.[313] An LLC may not make retroactive allocations to a member of income, gain, loss, deduction, or credit that was received or incurred before that member joined the LLC.

An LLC must normally use one of the following methods to account for the members' varying interests in the LLC:

---

[311] Prop. Reg. § 1.704-3(f)(3)(v)(C).
[312] Prop. Reg. § 1.704-3(f)(3)(ii)(D)(2), Example.
[313] Code Sec. 706(d)(1); Reg. § 1.706-1(c)(4).

- interim closing of the books method (discussed at ¶ 807.04);
- proration method (discussed at ¶ 807.05);
- cash method for allocable cash-basis items (discussed at ¶ 807.06);
- proration method for tiered partnerships and LLCs (discussed at ¶ 807.07); or
- time-of-day method for extraordinary items (discussed at ¶ 807.08).

.02 Steps for Applying Varying Interest Rule

There is a ten-step process for making allocations under the varying interest rule when the LLC uses the proration method or the interim closing of the books method:[314]

1. Determine if the varying interest rule does not apply because (a) the change in allocations is among contemporaneous members (and not attributable to capital contribution to the LLC or distributions to a member), or (b) the LLC is a service partnership in which capital is not a material income-producing factor.
2. Determine if any of the items are extraordinary items, such as tort liabilities or sales of assets other than in the ordinary course of business. These items must be prorated to the members in proportion to their interests in the LLC item at the time of day on which the extraordinary item occurred, subject to a small item exception. Extraordinary items are discussed at ¶ 807.08.
3. Determine whether to use the interim closing of the books method or the proration method. The LLC must use the interim closing of the books method absent an agreement among the members to use the proration method. The interim closing of the books method is discussed at ¶ 807.04. The proration method is discussed at ¶ 807.05.
4. Determine when a member's interest in the LLC changes during the year as a result of the admission of a new member, the reduction of the membership interest, or the disposition of a partial or complete membership interest. The regulations refer to these changes in interest as "variations." The LLC may use the calendar date convention, the semi-monthly convention, or the monthly convention in determining when changes in membership interests occur. The various conventions are discussed at ¶ 807.03.
5. Determine whether the members agreed to perform regular monthly or semi-monthly interim closings. If so, the LLC must perform an interim closing of its books at the end of each month (or at the end and middle of each month) regardless of whether any variations occur. Absent an agreement of the members to perform regular monthly or semi-monthly interim closings, the LLC must use the actual time of occurrence of any change in membership interests for the interim closing of the books method.
6. Divide the tax year into segments if the LLC is using the interim closing of the books method. The first segment commences at the beginning of the tax

---

[314] Reg. § 1.706-4(a)(3).

year and ends at the time of the first interim closing. Any additional segment commences immediately after the closing of the prior segment and ends at the time of the next interim closing, or at the end of the tax year for the last segment.

7. Apportion each item of LLC income, gain, loss and deduction for the year into segments if the LLC is using the interim closing of the books method. The LLC must treat each segment as a separate distributive share period. For example, an LLC may compute a capital loss for the first segment of the tax year even though the LLC has net capital gain for the entire tax year.

8. Determine the proration periods if the LLC is using the proration method. Each proration period begins immediately after the close of the prior proration period and ends at the time of the next variation for which the LLC selects the proration method. If the LLC is using the proration method for some variations and the closing of the books method for other variations, the LLC must first divide its tax year into segments, and then divide each segment into proration periods. The segments are the periods of the LLC tax year created by the interim closing of the books method, and the proration periods are the portions of a segment created by the proration method. The first proration period within each segment begins at the beginning of a segment, and ends at the time of a variation for which the LLC uses the proration method. The next proration period begins immediately after the close of the prior proration period and ends at the time of the next variation. Each proration period within a segment may end no later than the close of a segment.

9. Prorate the items of income, gain, loss, deduction and credit in each segment among the proration periods within the segment if the LLC is using the proration method for some variations and the closing of the books method for other variations.

10. Determine the members' distributive shares of LLC items under Code Sec. 702(a) by taking into account the members' interests in such items during each segment and proration period.

An LLC may use the interim closing method for certain variations and the proration method for other variations in the same tax year, subject to restrictions issued in future IRS guidance.[315]

An example of allocations under the interim closing of the books method is discussed at ¶807.04. An example of allocations under the proration method is discussed at ¶807.05.

---

[315] Reg. §1.706-4(a)(3)(iii).

.03 Conventions

An LLC may use one of the following conventions in applying the proration method or the interim closing of the books method:[316]

- Calendar day convention. Under the calendar day convention, each variation is deemed to occur at the end of the day on which the variation occurs. An LLC that uses the proration method must use the calendar day convention.[317]
- Semi-monthly convention. Under the semi-monthly convention, each variation occurring during the first 15 days of the calendar month is deemed to occur at the end of the last day of the immediately preceding calendar month, and each variation occurring from the 16th through the end of the calendar month is deemed to occur at the end of the 15th day of the calendar month.
- Monthly convention. Under the monthly convention, each variation occurring during the first 15 days of the calendar month is deemed to occur at the end of the last day of the immediately preceding calendar month, and each variation occurring from the 16th through the end of the calendar month is deemed to occur at the end of the last day of that calendar month.

All variations within a taxable year must occur no earlier than the first day of the tax year and no later than the close of the tax year.

.04 Interim Closing of the Books Method

The first method of allocation for varying interests is the interim closing of the books method. This is the default method. An LLC must use this method unless the members agree to use the proration method.[318] Under this method, the LLC closes its books whenever there is a change in ownership interest. The LLC allocates items of income, gain, credit, and deduction incurred before and after the change to the members based on their membership interests in the LLC before and after the change.[319]

EXAMPLE 8-37

ABC LLC has three equal members. On August 6, 2018, Member B sells one-half of her membership interest to D. The LLC has $75,000 of ordinary income for the year. There are no extraordinary items. The LLC accepts the default interim closing of the books method. Capital is a material income producing factor, so the regular interim closing of the books rules apply. If the LLC selects the semi-monthly convention, then the change in

---

[316] Reg. § 1.706-4(c)(1).

[317] Reg. § 1.706-4(a)(4), Example (iii).

[318] Reg. § 1.706-4(a)(3)(iii).

[319] Reg. § 1.706-4(c)(1).

ownership would be deemed to occur at the end of the day on July 31, 2018. Since the LLC does not perform semi-monthly or monthly closings, the LLC will have only one interim closing for 2018 occurring at the end of the day on July 31. The LLC must divide its tax year into two segments. The first segment is from January 1 until the end of the day on July 31. The second segment is from August 1 until December 31. If the LLC earned $60,000 of ordinary income during the first segment, then it would allocate the income from that segment equally to Members A, B, and C ($20,000 each). The LLC would allocate the remaining $15,000 of ordinary income to the members based on their ownership interest during the second segment ($5,000 to each of Members A and C, and $2,500 to each of Members B and D).[320]

An LLC may use the interim closing of the books method for some changes in ownership and the proration method for other changes in ownership. In such case, the LLC must follow the ten steps discussed at ¶ 807.02 to determine allocations. The LLC must divide its tax year into segments with respect to each interim closing of the books and into proration periods within each segment for the proration period.[321] Normally, an LLC should choose either the proration method or the interim closing of the books method for all changes in ownership during the tax year in order to simplify accounting.

.05 Proration Method

The second method of allocation for varying interests is the proration method. Under this method, the LLC must allocate each item of income, deduction, credit, and loss among the members in proportion to the number of days each person was a member during the year. The LLC must use the calendar day convention if it uses the proration method. A change in ownership is treated as occurring at the end of the day in which the ownership change occurs.[322] The LLC may use the proration method only if there is an agreement among the members.[323]

EXAMPLE 8-38

ABC LLC has three equal members. On April 16, 2018, Member A sells one-half of her membership interest to D. The LLC has $75,000 of ordinary income for the year. There are no extraordinary items. The members agree to use the proration method rather than the default interim closing of the books method. Capital is a material income producing factor, so the

---

[320] *See* Reg. § 1.706-4(a)(4), Example.

[321] Reg. § 1.706-4(a)(4), Example.

[322] Reg. § 1.706-4(a)(4), Example (iv).

[323] Reg. § 1.706-4(a)(3)(viii).

regular proration rules apply. The LLC must use the calendar day convention since it has selected the proration method. There are two proration
periods. The first proration period is from January 1 until April 16, 2018
containing 106 days. The second proration period is from April 17, 2018
until December 31, 2018 containing 259 days. Thus, the LLC must first
allocate 106/365 of the tax items to the first proration period ($21,781 of
ordinary income) and 259/365 of the tax items to the second proration
period ($53,219 of ordinary income). The LLC must then allocate the items
within each proration period to the members in accordance with their
percentage interests during that proration period. Thus, it must allocate
the $21,781 of ordinary income during the first proration period equally to
Members A, B, and C ($7,260 to each) since they were equal members in
the LLC during that period. The LLC must allocate the remaining $53,219
of ordinary income 1/6th to each of Members A and D, and 1/3rd to each
of Members B and C based on their percentage ownership interests
during the second proration period.[324]

An LLC may use the proration method for some changes in ownership and the
interim closing of the books method for other changes in ownership. In such case, the
LLC must follow the ten steps to determine allocations discussed at ¶807.02. The
LLC must divide its tax year into segments with respect to each interim closing of the
books and into proration periods within each segment for each proration period.[325]
Normally, an LLC should choose either the proration method or the interim closing
of the books method for all changes in ownership during the tax year in order to
simplify accounting.

.06 Cash-Basis Items

Prior to the Tax Reform Act of 1984, an LLC could in effect make retroactive
allocations by adopting the cash method of accounting, using the interim closing of
the books method, and deferring the payment of deductible expenses until the end of
the LLC's tax year. A person who became a member in the LLC at the end of the year
could then receive an allocable share of expense deductions attributable to the period
prior to becoming a member. Code Sec. 706(d)(2) was added in 1984 to prevent this
abuse. It provides that certain "allocable cash-basis items" must be prorated over the
period to which they are attributable.[326]
Cash basis items include interest, taxes, payments for services or for use of
property, and any other items specified in IRS regulations.[327] Under proposed regulations, cash basis items include any item of income, gain, loss or deduction that

---

[324] *See* Reg. § 1.706-4(a)(4), Example (x).

[325] Reg. § 1.706-4(a)(4), Example.

[326] Code Sec. 706(d)(2); Reg. § 1.706-2.

[327] Code Sec. 706(d)(2)(B).

accrues over time and that would, if not allocated as a cash basis items, result in a significant misstatement of a member's income.[328]

There is a two-step process for allocating cash-basis items. First, the cash-basis items are assigned to each day during the tax year in which the items accrued.[329] Second, the cash-basis items are assigned to each member in proportion to his or her membership interest at the close of each day.[330]

EXAMPLE 8-39

An LLC has four equal members. The LLC earns interest income during the calendar year of $4,000. The interest income was attributable to a bank deposit on December 1 of the year. Member A became a member of the LLC on December 1. The $4,000 of interest must be assigned to the month of December, when it was earned. Since Member A was a 25 percent member of the LLC during the entire calendar month of December, the LLC must allocate to Member A $1,000 (25% × $4,000) of the interest income.

EXAMPLE 8-40

Same facts as in the above example, except that the $4,000 of interest income received in December was interest on a promissory note that was outstanding for the entire calendar year. The LLC must allocate to Member A $83.33 of interest income (1/12 × 25% × $4,000).

An LLC must allocate cash-basis items attributable to periods before the current tax year to the first day of the year.[331] These items are then allocated to the persons who were members during the prior period to which the cash-basis items were attributable based on their varying interests in the LLC during that period. The LLC must capitalize that portion of the cash-basis items that is allocated to persons who are no longer members in the LLC on the first day of the tax year in which the items are taken into account.[332] Capitalized expenses are allocated to the basis of LLC assets under Section 755 of the Internal Revenue Code.[333]

---

[328] Prop. Reg. § 1.706-2(a)(2). This could include, for example, cash advances, prepaid expenses, insurance premiums, and refund payments.

[329] Code Sec. 706(d)(2)(A)(i).

[330] Code Sec. 706(d)(2)(A)(ii).

[331] Code Sec. 706(d)(2)(C).

[332] Code Sec. 706(d)(2)(D)(ii).

[333] Code Sec. 706(d)(2)(D)(i).

An LLC must allocate cash-basis items attributable to periods after the current tax year to the last day of the tax year.[334] If an LLC pays cash-basis expenses after the close of the fiscal year to which such expenses are attributable, then such expenses are treated as paid on the first day of the fiscal year.[335] The amounts are then allocated among the persons who were members in the LLC during the period in the prior fiscal year to which the expenses were allocable in accordance with each member's varying interest in the LLC during such period.

If the LLC allocates cash-basis items to a person who is no longer a member in the LLC on the first day of the fiscal year, then such amount must be capitalized and allocated to the remaining assets under Code Sec. 755. This gives the remaining members a deduction or reduced share of income to the extent it is allocable to depreciable items, inventory or other items that offset the gain.

If there are prepaid items of interest, taxes, rent, or payment for services, then such items are assigned to the last day of the tax year.[336]

.07 Tiered Partnerships

Prior to the Tax Reform Act of 1984, an LLC could in effect make retroactive allocations through a tiered partnership arrangement. The LLC would own an interest in a subsidiary partnership or LLC. When a new member acquired an interest in the LLC, the LLC would use the interim closing-of-the-books method. It would then claim that the LLC realized its allocable share of income, gain, loss and deduction from the subsidiary LLC on the last day of the subsidiary's tax year. Thus, the new member in the LLC was entitled to a full share of losses from the subsidiary (including losses attributable to the subsidiary's tax year before the member acquired an interest in the LLC). Code Sec. 706(d)(3) was added in 1984 to prevent this abuse. It provides that an LLC which is a partner in another LLC or partnership must treat the income of the subsidiary partnership as earned pro rata over the tax year.

.08 Extraordinary Items

Extraordinary items may not be prorated using the proration method or the interim closing of the books method. Extraordinary items must be prorated to the members in proportion to their interests in the LLC item at the time of day on which the extraordinary item occurred.[337] Extraordinary items include the following items,[338] subject to a small item exception:[339]

---

[334] Code Sec. 706(d)(2)(C).

[335] Code Sec. 706(d)(2)(C)(i).

[336] Code Sec. 706(d)(2)(C)(ii).

[337] Reg. § 1.706-4(e)(1).

[338] Reg. § 1.706-4(e)(2).

[339] Reg. § 1.706-4(e)(3).

- any item from the disposition or abandonment of a capital asset, a Section 1231(b) asset, and certain Section 1221 assets (other than dispositions in the ordinary course of business);
- any item from the disposition of assets under an applicable asset acquisition under Code Sec. 1060(c);
- any item resulting from a change in accounting method initiated by the filing of an appropriate form after variation occurs;
- any item from the discharge or retirement of indebtedness;
- any item from the settlement of a tort or similar third party liability or the payment of a judgment;
- any tax credit to the extent it arises from activities or items that are not ratably allocated, such as the rehabilitation tax credit;
- any item if the members agree to consistently treat such item as an extraordinary item;
- any item that would, in the opinion of the IRS, result in a substantial distortion of income if ratably allocated; and
- certain other items specified in the regulations.

EXAMPLE 8-41

An LLC uses the interim closing of the books method to account for varying interest of the members in the LLC. The LLC settles a tort claim for $500,000 at 3:15 PM on December 7, 2015. On December 12, 2015, a member in the LLC disposes of his entire interest in the LLC. There is no termination of the LLC under Code Sec. 708 during 2015. There are no other extraordinary items, and the small item exception does not apply. The LLC must allocate the loss attributable to the tort liability in accordance with the members' interests in the LLC in the extraordinary item as of 3:15 PM on December 7, 2015. The remaining partnership items of the LLC must be allocated in accordance with the interim closing of the books method.[340]

¶ 808 FAMILY ALLOCATIONS

.01 In General

The family partnership rules restrict taxpayers from shifting income to family members through gifts and sales of membership interests.[341] A family member for such purposes is a spouse, ancestor, lineal descendant, or trust established for the

---

[340] Reg. § 1.706-4(e)(2), Example 1.
[341] Code Sec. 704(e); Reg. § 1.704-1(e).

primary benefit of such person.[342] If the LLC does not comply with the family partnership rules, the donee will not be recognized as a member for tax purposes, and the IRS may reallocate the donee's distributive share of income to the donor.[343]

The original focus of Section 704(e) was to prevent taxpayers from splitting income among family members, and shifting income to younger family members in a lower tax bracket. This rule is now much less important because of the reduction in marginal tax rates, and the "kiddie tax" which taxes the unearned income of children at their parents' highest marginal tax rate.[344] The emphasis is now shifting to exploiting family partnerships to reduce estate and gift taxes, which is discussed in Chapter 21.

Under Section 704(e), restrictions on allocations to family members depend on whether capital is a material income-producing factor.

.02 Capital Is Material

Capital is a material income-producing factor if a substantial part of the gross income of the LLC comes from the use of capital. Capital is ordinarily an income-producing factor if the operation of the LLC requires substantial inventories or investments in plants, machinery, or equipment.[345]

If capital is a material-income-producing factor, then the IRS will respect to allocations of income to family members who acquired their interest by gift or purchase from another family member if:

- The family member acquired the capital interest in a bona fide transaction, actually owns the membership interest, and actually controls the membership interest.[346] The family member may be treated as a member in the LLC in which capital is a material income-producing factor whether or not such interest was obtained by purchase or gift, and whether or not the interest was acquired from another family member.[347] If the family member is not a bona fide member, then LLC income must be allocated to the real owner of the membership interest.[348]

- The LLC allocates to a donor family member an amount representing the reasonable value of the donor's services.[349]

- The donee member's distributive share of income attributable to donated capital is not proportionally greater than the donor's share attributable to the

---

[342] Reg. § 1.704-1(e)(3).

[343] Reg. § 1.704-1(e)(3)(i)(b).

[344] Code Sec. 1(g).

[345] IRS Publication 541, under the heading, "Family Partnerships."

[346] IRS Publication 541, under the heading, "Family Partnerships."

[347] Code Sec. 761(a).

[348] IRS Audit Technique Guide—Partnerships, Chapter 11, under the heading, "Capital Is a Material Income Producing Factor."

[349] Reg. § 1.704-1(e)(3)(i)(a).

retained capital.[350] The fair market value of the purchased interest is considered donated capital.

- The LLC is a bona fide partnership in which the members have joined together with the purpose of conducting an active trade or business.[351]

Members of a family for such purposes include only spouses, ancestors and lineal descendents, or trusts primarily for the benefit of such persons.[352]

EXAMPLE 8-42

A father sold 50 percent of his membership interests in an LLC to his son. During 2007, the LLC had profits of $60,000. Capital is a material income-producing factor. The father performed services worth $24,000, which is reasonable compensation, and the son performed no services. The LLC must allocate $24,000 to the father as compensation. Of the remaining $36,000 in profits due to capital, the LLC must allocate at least 50 percent, or $18,000, to the father since he owns a 50-percent capital interest. The son's share of LLC profit cannot be more than $18,000.[353]

.03 Capital Is Not Material

If capital is not a material income-producing factor, the family member will be recognized as a partner only if all of the members join together in good faith to conduct a business, agree that contributions of each entitle them to share in the profits, and each contribute some capital or service to the LLC.[354] If capital is not a material income producing factor, and the member performs no services, then LLC income must be allocated to the other members who perform the services.[355]

Capital is not a material income-producing factor if the income of the business consists principally of fees, commissions, or other compensation for personal services performed by members or employees of the partnership.[356]

.04 Judicial Doctrines

The IRS may reallocate income and disregard an LLC under the economic substance doctrine and the sham transaction doctrine if the main purpose of the LLC

---

[350] Reg. § 1.704-1(e)(3).

[351] Code Sec. 761(b).

[352] IRS Publication 541, under the heading, "Family Partnerships."

[353] Example from IRS Publication 541, under the heading, "Family Partnerships."

[354] IRS Publication 541, Partnerships, under the heading "Family Partnership."

[355] IRS Audit Technique Guide — Partnerships, Chapter 11, under the heading, "Capital Is Not a Material Income-Producing Factor."

[356] IRS Publication 541, under the heading, "Family Partnerships."

is to reduce tax liabilities and to allocate income to family members who are not involved in services that generate the taxable income.[357]

¶ 809 RETROACTIVE ALLOCATIONS

An LLC may not allocate items to new members that are attributable to periods prior to the time that such persons became members in the LLC.[358]

However, an LLC can decide after the end of the tax year how to allocate income, gains, losses, deductions, and credits to the members for the prior year. The LLC may amend the operating agreement regarding allocations at any time prior to the due date (not including extensions) for filing of its tax return for the prior year. The amendment must be approved by all the members of the LLC or must otherwise be in accordance with the operating agreement.[359]

An LLC may achieve the same result as a retroactive allocation of losses to newly admitted members, without violating the varying interest rule, by making special allocations of losses to new members for the period after they become members.[360]

---

[357] *Walker v. Comm'r*, TC Memo 2012-5 (2011).

[358] Code Sec. 706(d).

[359] Code Sec. 761(c).

[360] *Ogden v. Comm'r*, 84 TC 871 (1985).

9

Basis and Member's Share of Debt

¶ 901 GENERAL

.01 Importance of Basis

Basis in a membership interest is important for the following reasons:

- A member's basis in a membership interest determines the amount of gain or loss on sale,[1] liquidation,[2] or other disposition of the membership interest.
- Losses may be deducted only to the extent of a member's basis in the membership interest.[3] Losses in excess of basis are suspended and may be carried over to years in which the member has basis in the LLC.[4] If the member sells the membership interest, any unused losses disappear and cannot be used to offset any gain on the disposition.[5]
- Distributions of money in excess of basis result in taxable gain.[6]
- The basis of property distributed in liquidation of a membership interest is equal to the member's basis in the membership interest, reduced by any money distributed.[7] The basis of property in a nonliquidating distribution cannot exceed the member's basis in the membership interest, reduced by any money distributed in the same transaction.[8]

.02 Inside and Outside Basis

A member's basis in the membership interest is referred to as the "outside basis." An LLC's basis in its assets is referred to as the "inside basis." The inside and outside basis are initially the same when the members contribute property on formation of an LLC, subject to certain exceptions. There is a carryover basis for the assets that a member contributes to the LLC. The inside and outside basis may become different under the following circumstances:

- The member incurs legal, accounting, tax, and other expenses in connection with the acquisition of a membership interest. The expenses must be capitalized and added to the basis of the membership interest. These capitalized expenses do not give rise to inside basis.
- The member sells a membership interest at a price that is different from the basis in the membership interest. The purchasing member's basis in the

---

[1] See ¶ ¶ 1502 and 1503 *infra* for discussion of basis and gain computation on sale of a membership interest.

[2] See ¶ 1003.02 *infra*.

[3] Code Sec. 704(d). See ¶ 1302 *infra* for discussion of basis limitations on loss pass-through to members.

[4] Code Sec. 704(d); Reg. § 1.704-1(d)(2).

[5] Code Sec. 704(d).

[6] Code Sec. 731(a)(1).

[7] Code Sec. 732(b).

[8] Code Sec. 732(a)(2).

membership interest is the purchase price, rather than the selling member's basis.

- The member dies. The estate of the member receives a step up or step down in basis of the membership interest to fair market value as of the date of death or six months after the date of death.

- The LLC makes a nonliquidating money distribution to the member in excess of the member's basis in the membership interest. The member's outside basis is reduced to zero, and the money distribution in excess of basis is taxable gain.[9]

- The LLC makes a liquidating distribution to a member. The basis of property (other than money) distributed to the member is equal to the member's interest in the LLC prior to the distribution, reduced by any money distributed.[10] The inside and outside basis for the remaining members in the LLC will be different to the extent that the money and the adjusted basis of the property distributed by the LLC are different from the distributee member's adjusted basis in the membership interest immediately prior to the distribution.

- The LLC receives money for the grant of an option. The grant of the option is not taxable income to the LLC, but will increase the inside basis, since the LLC has received money. The members' outside basis will not increase, since the option money is not taxable income and is not income exempt from tax. It is merely deferred income.

- The member contributes to the LLC worthless property with a tax basis. An LLC does not receive a carryover basis in contributed property that has no value or only a speculative value on the date of contribution.[11]

The LLC may keep the inside and outside basis the same in most of these cases by making an election under Section 754 of the Code.[12] Section 754 elections are discussed below.[13]

.03 Differences between Capital Account and Basis

A member's basis is not the same as the member's capital account. There are the following differences:

- The capital accounts keep track of the members' contributions, distributions, and allocations. It shows each member's equity in the LLC and how much the member is entitled to receive on liquidation of the LLC or withdrawal by the

---

[9] Code Sec. 732(a)(2).

[10] Code Sec. 732(b).

[11] *Santa Monica Pictures, LLC v. Comm'r*, TC Memo. 2005-104 (2005).

[12] *See* ¶1006 *infra* regarding the Section 754 election in connection with distributions, and ¶1508 regarding the Section 754 election in connection with transfers.

[13] *See* ¶1006 *infra* with respect to distributions and ¶1508 *infra* with respect to transfers of membership interests.

member. The capital account is separate and distinct from the member's adjusted basis in the membership interest.[14] The member's outside basis determines how much tax gain or loss the member will recognize if the member sells his or her membership interest.

- Capital accounts are kept using book accounting. Basis is kept using tax accounting.

- The capital account is based on the fair market value of the property as determined by the members. The LLC may adjust the fair market value of property for capital account purposes on the occurrence of certain events, including contributions, distributions, and sales of membership interests. The tax basis of property is based on the cost of the property, adjusted for tax depreciation, amortization, and depletion.

- A member's capital account is initially the cash and the value of the property contributed to the LLC. A member's outside basis is initially the cash and the cost basis of the property contributed to the LLC. When a member contributes additional property to an LLC, the basis of the membership interest is increased by the adjusted basis of the property contributed. The capital account is increased by the fair market value of property contributed.[15]

- Basis includes a member's share of LLC liabilities. The capital account does not include LLC liabilities.[16]

- The capital account and basis for individual members will differ as a result of depreciation if a member contributes appreciated property to the LLC. Under Code Sec. 704(c), the LLC may allocate the book depreciation to the members in accordance with their percentage interest in the LLC, but must allocate all of the tax depreciation to the noncontributing members up to the amount of depreciation they would have received if the property had been contributed with a basis equal to fair market value. On sale of property, the LLC may allocate the book gain to the members in accordance with their percentage interests in the LLC, but must allocate all of the pre-contribution tax gain to the contributing member.[17]

- When a member sells a membership interest, the new member receives a basis equal to the purchase price of the membership interest. The new member receives a capital account equal to the capital account of the selling member.[18]

- The basis and capital account can each fluctuate in amount independently. For example, an LLC may revalue its property to fair market value for capital account purposes when members contribute additional property to the LLC.[19] The revaluation does not change the members' bases in their membership interests. Likewise, the death of a member results in a step up or step down in

---

[14] Reg. § 1.705-1(a)(1).

[15] Reg. § 1.704-1(b)(2)(iv)(b).

[16] Reg. § 1.704-1(b)(2)(iv)(c).

[17] *See* ¶ 805 *supra*.

[18] Reg. § 1.704-1(b)(2)(iv)(l).

[19] Reg. § 1.704-1(b)(2)(iv)(f).

basis of the membership interest to fair market value. The adjustment to basis on death does not result in an adjustment to the capital account for the estate of the deceased member.

- Both the tax basis and capital account restrict the amount of losses that the LLC may allocate to a member. A member may not deduct tax losses in excess of basis. An LLC that complies with the safe-harbor rules may not allocate losses to a member that would create a negative capital account,[20] subject to exceptions.

- The LLC may depreciate its assets for book purposes based on the fair market value and useful lives of the assets. The LLC must depreciate assets for tax purposes under one of the methods permitted by the Code.

- Organization expenses reduce the members' capital accounts (but not basis) in the year incurred, unless the LLC makes an election to amortize such expenses over 60 months.[21]

Many LLCs keep capital accounts on a tax basis.[22] In such case, the main difference between capital accounts and basis is that basis includes a member's share of LLC liabilities, and capital accounts do not.

The determination of capital accounts under the safe-harbor rules is discussed at ¶ 804.02.

¶ 902 BASIS OF MEMBERSHIP INTEREST (OUTSIDE BASIS)

.01 Initial Basis

A member's initial basis in a membership interest depends on how the member acquired the membership interest, as follows:

- *Contribution.* The initial basis of a member who acquires a membership interest in exchange for contributions to the capital of an LLC is the sum of (i) the cash contributed, (ii) the adjusted basis of property contributed, and (iii) any gain recognized under Code Sec. 721 (regarding transfers of property to an LLC classified as an investment partnership).[23]

- *Contribution of encumbered property.* If a member contributes encumbered property to an LLC, the LLC is treated as having assumed the liabilities encumbering the property to the extent that the liabilities do not exceed the fair market value of the property at the time of contribution.[24] The member's basis

---

[20] *See* ¶ 804.04 *supra.*

[21] Reg. § 1.704-1(b)(2)(iv)(i)(2). The capitalized portion of organization expenses do not reduce basis. Code Sec. 705(a)(2)(B).

[22] The LLC must specify in Item N on Schedule K-1 whether it maintains each member's capital account on a tax basis, Section 704(b) book basis, GAAP basis, or some other basis.

[23] Code Sec. 722; Reg. § 1.722-1. A member may recognize gain on contribution of property to an LLC only in very limited circumstances. *See* ¶ 601.01 *supra.*

[24] Reg. § 1.752-1(e).

includes the member's share of LLC liabilities after the contribution, less the liabilities assumed by the LLC on transfer of assets to the LLC.[25] Thus, a member's basis in the LLC is decreased to the extent there is a net decrease in the member's share of liabilities.[26] The contributing member may be required to recognize taxable gain on the contribution if the deemed cash distribution exceeds the contributing member's basis in the membership interest.[27] Gain recognized upon a contribution of encumbered property does not result in an increase in the contributing member's basis in the LLC, since the gain results only from a deemed cash distribution to the member in excess of his or her basis in the LLC.[28]

- *Promissory note.* The initial basis of a member who acquires a membership interest in exchange for a promissory note is zero since a promissory note has a zero basis.[29] The member acquires basis, and is treated as contributing capital to the LLC, when the member makes payments on the promissory note to the LLC.[30] The principal amount of a promissory note does not increase the member's capital account under the safe-harbor regulations until there is a taxable distribution of such note by the LLC or when the member makes principal payments on the note.[31]

- *Purchase.* The initial basis of a member who acquires a membership interest by purchase from another member is the purchase price.[32]

- *Gift.* The initial basis of a member who acquires a membership interest by gift is the sum of (a) the donor's adjusted basis for the membership interest,[33] and (b) gift taxes paid attributable to the fair market value of the property on the date of the gift in excess of the donor's basis.[34] However, if the basis exceeds the fair market value at the time of the gift and the property is subsequently sold at a loss, then the basis for determining loss is the fair market value on the date of the gift.[35] If the membership interest is encumbered by debt, the basis to the donee is the greater of the donor's basis at the time of the gift or the amount of debt assumed by the donee.[36] A membership interest is encumbered by debt if the LLC allocated any portion of its recourse or nonrecourse liabilities to the donor member (usually reflected on Schedule K-1). If the debt

---

[25] *See* ¶ 903 *infra.*

[26] Code Sec. 733.

[27] Code Secs. 731(a)(1), 741.

[28] Rev. Rul. 84-15, 1984-1 CB 158.

[29] *VisionMonitor Software, LLC v. Comm'r*, TC Memo 2014-182 (2014); CCA 201326014.

[30] TC Memo. 2014-182; Rev. Rul. 80-235, 1980-2 CB 229; *Levy v. Comm'r*, 732 F.2d 1435 (9th Cir. 1984); *Irvin J. Bussing v. Comm'r*, 88 TC 49 (1987).

[31] Reg. §§ 1.704-1(b)(2)(iv)(d)(2), 1.704-1(b)(2)(iv)(e)(2).

[32] Code Secs. 742, 1012; Reg. § 1.742-1.

[33] Code Secs. 742, 1015.

[34] Code Sec. 1015(d)(6).

[35] Code Sec. 1015(a).

[36] IRS Market Segment Specialization Program, Partnerships, Audit Technique Guide, Chapter 7, under the heading, "Gift of a Partnership Interest Encumbered by Debt."

assumed by or allocated to the donee exceeds the donor's basis in the property, then the donor has taxable gain equal to the amount realized (debt assumed or allocated to the donee) less the donor's basis in the membership interest.[37] The donee's basis in the membership interest in such case is the sum of (i) the greater of the amount paid by the donee, including assumption of debt, or the donor's adjusted basis in the property at the time of the gift, and (ii) the amount of gift taxes paid attributable to the fair market value of the property on the date of the gift in excess of the donor's basis in the property.[38] Suspended passive activity losses of the donor are added to the donee's basis in the membership interest immediately prior to disposition,[39] subject to special rules.[40] If the donee pays the gift taxes, the donor has taxable income.[41]

- *Inheritance.* The initial basis of a member who acquires a membership interest by inheritance is the fair market value of the membership interest as reported for estate tax purposes.[42] Fair market value is normally determined as of the date of death. However, if the estate of the decedent is obligated to pay estate taxes, the estate may elect the alternate valuation date that is six months after the decedent's death.[43] The basis is increased by the successor's share of LLC liabilities on that date and reduced by items constituting income in respect of a decedent.[44]

- *Loan by member to LLC.* Amounts loaned by the member to the LLC increase the member's basis if no other member is personally liable for repayment of the debt.[45]

- *Multiple acquisitions.* A member who acquires interests in an LLC in multiple transactions must combine those interests and maintain a single adjusted tax basis for those interests. If the member sells or otherwise disposes of less than all of the membership interest, a portion of the tax basis must be allocated to the interest sold using an "equitable apportionment" method.[46] However, the portion of the member's basis attributable to LLC liabilities is taken into account only to the extent that the member's share of LLC liabilities is reduced.

- *Lender's cancellation of debt.* A lender who receives a membership interest in exchange for canceling an unpaid balance of indebtedness has a basis in the

---

[37] Reg. § 1.1001-1(e).

[38] Reg. § 1.1015-4(a).

[39] Code Sec. 469(j)(6)(A).

[40] *See* ¶ 2102.07 *infra.*

[41] *Diedrich v. Comm'r,* 457 U.S. 191 (1982).

[42] Code Secs. 742, 1014(a); Reg. § 1.742-1.

[43] Code Secs. 2031, 2032.

[44] Reg. § 1.742-1.

[45] Reg. § 1.752-2(c)(1). The loan is treated as a recourse loan. The liability is then allocated to the member who made the loan. The allocation of the recourse liability to the lending member increases that member's basis. The loan by the member to the LLC also increases the member's at-risk basis under Code Sec. 465. Prop. Reg. § 1.465-7(a).

[46] Rev. Rul. 84-53, 1984-1 CB 159.

LLC equal to fair market value of the membership interest.[47] However, where the lender cannot establish a fair market value for the membership interest because of the financial condition of the LLC, his or her basis is zero.[48]

.02 Increases in Basis

A member's initial basis in a membership interest is increased by the following items:[49]

- Additional cash that the member contributes to the LLC;[50]

- The member's adjusted basis in additional property contributed to the LLC;[51]

- The member's allocable share of taxable income from the LLC, whether or not distributed;[52]

- The member's allocable share of tax-exempt income and tax-exempt receipts[53] (e.g., life insurance proceeds), whether or not distributed;[54]

- The member's allocable share of deductions for depletion to the extent the deductions exceed the basis of LLC property subject to depletion:[55] There is an exception if the property is oil or gas wells whose basis has been allocated to the members.

- Any increase in the member's share of LLC liabilities;[56]

- Gain recognized by the member on the contribution of property to an LLC that is classified as an investment partnership.[57]

- Cancellation of indebtedness income which results in LLC taxable income and a corresponding increase in the adjusted basis of a member's interest in the LLC. There is a basis increase even if the member excludes the cancellation of debt income under Code Sec. 108(a)(1).[58]

---

[47] *Sargent v. Comm'r*, TC Memo 1970-214 (1970).

[48] *Shaheen v. Comm'r*, TC Memo 1982-445 (1982).

[49] Code Sec. 705(a)(1); Reg. § 1.705-1(a)(2).

[50] Reg. § 1.705-1(a)(2).

[51] Reg. § 1.705-1(a)(2).

[52] Code Sec. 705(a)(1)(A).

[53] Reg. § 1.705-1(a)(2ii).

[54] Code Sec. 705(a)(1)(B).

[55] Code Sec. 705(a)(1)(C); Reg. § 1.705-1(a)(4).

[56] Code Sec. 752(a) provides that an increase in a member's share of LLC liabilities is treated as a contribution of money by the member to the LLC. Code Sec. 722 provides a member's basis in an LLC is increased by the amount of money contributed to the LLC.

[57] Reg. § 1.722-1.

[58] *See* ¶ 703.09 under the subheading, Basis in Membership Interest.

.03 Decreases in Basis

A member's initial basis in a membership interest is decreased by the following items:[59]

- The amount of cash that the LLC distributes to the member.[60]
- The LLC's adjusted basis of property distributed to the member.[61]
- The member's allocable share of taxable losses from the LLC, including capital losses.[62] Distributions reduce basis first before the member's share of allowable pass-through losses are considered.[63] Losses in excess of basis are suspended, and may be deducted in future years when the member has basis.[64] Losses reduce basis even though the losses are not deductible by the member under the at-risk rules.[65]
- The member's allocable share of nondeductible LLC expenses that are not capital expenditures.[66] The nondeductible expenses that reduce the member's basis in the membership interest include (i) life insurance premiums that are nondeductible under Code Sec. 264; (ii) interest and other expenses related to the production of tax-exempt income that are nondeductible under Code Sec. 265; (iii) foreign taxes that may be deductible by the member but that are not deductible by the LLC; (iv) Section 179 expenses, whether or not the member may deduct all or part of such expenses on his or her individual return;[67] (v) losses disallowed on the sale of LLC property under Code Secs. 267(a)(1) and 707(b)(1);[68] and (vi) charitable contributions equal to the donated cash and adjusted basis of LLC property.[69]
- The member's allocable share of depletion deductions for oil and gas property owned by the LLC to the extent such share does not exceed the proportionate share of the adjusted basis of such property allocated to the member;[70]
- Any decrease in the member's share of LLC liabilities.[71] If a member contributes property to an LLC that is subject to indebtedness, or if the LLC assumes

---

[59] Code Sec. 705(a)(2); Reg. § 1.705-1(a)(3), (4).

[60] Code Sec. 733(1); Reg. § 1.705-1(a)(3).

[61] Code Sec. 733(2); Reg. § 1.705-1(a)(3).

[62] Code Sec. 705(a)(2)(A).

[63] Rev. Rul. 66-94, 1966-1 CB 166.

[64] Code Sec. 704(d); Reg. § 1.704-1(d)(2).

[65] Prop. Reg. § 1.465-1(e).

[66] Code Sec. 705(a)(2)(B); Rev. Rul. 96-10, 1996-1 CB 138; Rev. Rul. 96-11, 1996-1 CB 140.

[67] Rev. Rul. 89-7, 1989-1 CB 178.

[68] Rev. Rul. 96-10, 1996-1 CB 138; Reg. § 1.704-1(b)(2)(iv)(i)(3).

[69] Rev. Rul. 96-11, 1996-1 CB 140.

[70] Code Sec. 705(a)(3).

[71] Code Sec. 752(b) provides that a decrease in a member's share of LLC liabilities is treated as a distribution of money by the LLC to the member. Code Sec. 773(1) provides that a distribution by an LLC to a member reduces the member's adjusted basis in the membership interest (but not below zero) by the amount of money distributed.

liabilities of the member, the member's basis must be reduced by the portion of the debt allocated to the other members.[72]

- A member's share of certain investment tax credits.[73] The basis of a member's membership interest must be reduced by the investment tax credit. When the investment tax credit is recaptured on sale of the property, the recaptured amount is added back to basis.[74] The adjustments to tax basis is 50 percent of the investment tax credit or recapture amount in the case of renewable energy tax credits.[75] For example, an LLC may claim a solar tax credit up to 30 percent of qualifying solar equipment. The LLC must reduce the tax basis of the solar equipment by one-half of that amount, or 15 percent. The LLC may pass through the 30 percent solar tax credit to the members who must reduce their tax basis in the membership interests by the 15 percent basis adjustment to LLC property. There is no additional adjustment made under Code Sec. 705(a)(2)(B).[76] The basis adjustments must be shared among the members in the same proportion as the adjusted tax basis or cost of (or the qualified investment in) the ITC property is allocated among the members.[77]
- The member's share of the LLC's basis in property or cash donated by the LLC to a charity.[78]

EXAMPLE 9-1

An LLC has two equal members. Member A contributes $5,000 cash to the LLC, and property with a basis of $10,000 and a fair market value of $7,000. The LLC borrows $10,000 to purchase depreciable equipment. During the first year of operations, the LLC earns $4,000 of income. It distributes $1,000 to Member A at the end of the year. Member A's adjusted basis in her membership interest at the end of the year is $18,000, computed as follows:

Cash contributed to LLC:	$ 5,000
Adjusted basis of property contributed to LLC:	$ 7,000
One-half share of $10,000 LLC liabilities (treated as cash contributed to LLC):	$ 5,000
One-half share of LLC income:	$ 2,000
Distribution:	($ 1,000)
Ending adjusted basis:	$18,000

---

[72] Reg. § 1.722-1.

[73] Code Sec. 50(c)(1), (c)(5). The basis of a rehabilitated building must be reduced by 100 percent of the rehabilitation credit. The basis of energy credit property must be reduced by 50 percent of the allowed credit. Code Sec. 50(c)(3).

[74] Code Sec. 50(c)(5).

[75] Code Sec. 50(c)(5); Reg. § 1.704-1(b)(2)(iv)(j).

[76] Reg. § 1.704-1(b)(2)(iv)(j).

[77] Reg. § 1.704-1(b)(2)(iv)(j).

[78] Rev. Rul. 96-11, 1996-1 CB 140.

¶ 902.03

.04 Items That Do Not Affect Basis

The following items do not change a member's outside basis in his or her membership interest:

- Distributions in excess of outside basis. Distributions cannot cause a negative basis in the member's membership interest. The member must report taxable gain to the extent of distributions in excess of basis.[79]

- Tax loss allocations in excess of outside basis. Tax loss allocations on Schedule K-1 cannot cause a negative basis in the member's membership interest. Instead, the losses are suspended and may be deducted in subsequent years when the member has positive basis.[80] This rule is different from the rule for capital accounts. Under the safe-harbor rules, the LLC must have a stop loss reallocation provision under which book losses causing a negative capital account in excess of minimum gain and any deficit restoration obligation are reallocated to the other members.[81]

.05 Table of Basis Adjustments

The IRS provided a worksheet for determining the basis of a member's interest in an LLC in the Instructions to Schedule K-1.

The following table shows the most common adjustments to a member's basis in his or her membership interest:

Item	Notes
Initial basis	The initial tax basis is the amount of cash and adjusted basis of contributed property. The initial basis for a member who acquires a membership interest by purchase from another member is the purchase price. The initial basis for a member who acquires the interest by gift is the donor's adjusted basis in the membership interest plus gift taxes paid attributable to the fair market value of the property on the date of the gift in excess of the donor's basis. The initial basis for a member who acquires the interest by inheritance is the fair market value of the membership interest as reported for estate tax purposes. See ¶ 902.01.

---

[79] See ¶ 902.06 *infra.*
[80] Code Sec. 704(d).
[81] See ¶ 902.06 *infra.*

Allocable share of income.	Code Sec. 705(a)(1)(A). The allocable share of income increases basis, whether or not distributed.
Allocable share of tax-exempt income and receipts.	Code Sec. 705(a)(1)(B). The allocable share of tax-exempt income increases basis, whether or not distributed.
Cash contribution	Reg. § 1.705-1(a)(2). Basis is increased by the cash contribution.
Cash distributions	Code Secs. 705(a)(2), 733(1). Cash distributions decrease basis.
Charitable contributions	Rev. Rul. 96-11, 1996-1 CB 140. Member's basis in membership interest is decreased by the donated cash and adjusted basis of LLC property. Beginning in 2018, a member may not deduct charitable contributions in excess of the member's tax basis in the membership interest. The basis limitation does not apply to the excess of the contributed property's fair market value over its adjusted basis. Code Sec. 704(d)(3).
Death of member.	Code Sec. 1014(b)(6). There is a basis step-up or down to fair market value on death of the non-owner spouse in community property states
Depletion.	Code Sec. 705(a)(1)(C). The excess of deductions for depletion over the basis of property subject to depletion increases basis.
Depreciation	A member's allocable share of depreciation reduces basis. If there is a disparity between book and tax basis for contributed property, the member contributing cash must receive tax depreciation deductions equal to book depreciation deductions. See ¶ 805.
Foreign taxes	Beginning in 2018, a member may not deduct the member's allocable share of foreign taxes in excess of the member's tax basis in the membership interest. Code Sec. 704(d)(3).
Guaranteed payment	A guaranteed payment does not affect a member's basis in the LLC. CCA 201741018.
Interest	A member's adjusted basis in the membership interest is reduced by the amount of excess business interest allocated to the member. Code Sec. 163(j)(4)(B)(iii)(I). If a member transfers or disposes of a membership interest, the adjusted basis in the membership interest is increased immediately prior to the disposition by the amount of remaining excess business interest. No deduction is allowed to the transferee or transferor for any excess business interest resulting in a basis increase. Code Sec. 163(j)(4)(B)(iii)(II).

Investment tax credits	Code Sec. 50(c)(1), (3), (5). The member's basis is reduced by 50 percent of the tax credits for energy credit property and by 100 percent of the tax credits for rehabilitation property. For example, tax basis is reduced by 15 percent for qualified solar equipment (50 percent of maximum 30 percent tax credit for qualified solar equipment).
Investment tax credit recapture	The outside basis must be increased by the member's allocable share of investment tax credit recapture. Code Sec. 50(c); Reg. § 1.704-1(b)(2)(iv)(j).
IRS tax audits	If an IRS tax audit results in tax adjustments, the adjustment year members' outside bases and the LLC's basis in property must be adjusted to what they would have been if the adjustments were made in the reviewed year to the reviewed year members and property and then modified to take into account the amount by which the assessed tax deficiency would increase a partnership item for any intervening year (e.g., amortization or depreciation of property). REG-136118-15, Preamble to proposed regulations on Centralized Partnership Audit Regime (2017).
Liabilities.	A member's share of LLC nonrecourse liabilities, recourse liabilities, and qualified nonrecourse liabilities as reported on Schedule K-1 increase basis, but do not increase the member's capital account. A decrease in a member's share of liabilities is treated as a money distribution and decreases basis.
Loss allocations	Code Sec. 705(a)(2)(A). Loss allocations decrease basis. Tax loss allocations in excess of basis cannot create a negative outside basis. These losses are suspended and may be deducted in future years when the member has positive tax basis in the membership interest. Code Sec. 704(d).
Nondeductible expenditures	Code Sec. 705(a)(2)(B). Nondeductible expenditures not properly chargeable to capital account decrease basis. See ¶ 902.03.
Property contributions	Reg. § 1.705-1(a)(2). Basis is increased by the adjusted basis in contributed property.
Property distributions	Code Secs. 705(a)(2), 733(2). The general rule is that the adjusted basis of distributed property decreases basis. Distributions that create a negative amount in the basis calculation should be added back. This rule is different from the rule for capital account purposes in which distributions may create a negative capital account.

Suspended losses recovered from prior years	When the member has positive basis in subsequent years, the member may deduct the disallowed losses that exceeded tax basis in prior years. The member's outside basis must be reduced when the member uses the suspended losses.
Tax adjustments resulting from tax audit or amended return, and LLC pays taxes at entity level	Prop. Reg. § 301.6225-4(b)(6)(iii). If there are tax adjustments as a result of a tax audit or amended return, and the LLC pays the taxes at the entity level, it must create notional items reflecting the items of income, gain, loss, deduction or credit. The notional items must be allocated to the members and reflected in the members' tax basis in the membership interest.

.06 Alternative Methods of Determining Basis

There are two alternative methods of determining a member's adjusted basis.[82] The alternative methods may be used if it is impractical or impossible to determine basis under the normal rules, or if the IRS determines that the alternative methods will not produce a substantially different result.

Assets Method

Under the first alternative method, a member's basis is the member's share of the LLC's basis in its assets.[83] This is the basis of LLC property that would be distributed to the member on termination of the LLC. Generally, it is equal to the LLC's inside basis in its assets multiplied by the member's percentage interest in the LLC. Liabilities are ignored since they are taken into account in determining basis when an asset is purchased.

EXAMPLE 9-2

An LLC has three equal members. The members and the LLC do not keep track of the basis of the membership interests. The LLC has assets with a basis of $300,000 and a fair market value of $400,000. The LLC has liabilities of $150,000. Under the alternative rule for determining basis, Member A's basis in her membership interest is $100,000 ($1/3 × $300,000).[84]

---

[82] Code Sec. 705(b); Reg. § 1.705-1(b).

[83] Code Sec. 705(b); Reg. § 1.705-1(b); IRS Publication 541, Partnerships, under the heading, "Alternative rule for figuring adjusted basis."

[84] Reg. § 1.705-1(b), Example (1).

EXAMPLE 9-3

Three equal members each contribute $110 to an LLC. The LLC purchases property for $360. Member A sells his membership interest to Member D for $80 who receives and $80 basis in the membership interest. Member D's share of the inside basis of LLC assets is $110 ($1/3 \times$ $360) even though its outside basis in the LLC is less than the outside basis of the other members.[85]

There are several problems with the alternative method of determining basis. First, the member must have access to the books and records of the LLC showing the tax basis in each of the LLC's assets. It is not always possible for the member to obtain access to the current books and records of the LLC.

Second, the member must make adjustments in determining basis. There are significant discrepancies that result from the contribution of property, transfers of membership interests, or distributions of property to members. For example, the member must make an adjustment if one or more of the members contribute property to the LLC with a tax basis different than its capital account value. The basis adjustment in this case is the difference between the member's percentage share of basis in LLC assets and the member's actual basis in the membership interest at the time of contribution.

EXAMPLE 9-4

There are three equal members in an LLC. Two of the members contribute $30,000 in cash to the LLC. The other member contributes property with an adjusted basis of $10,000 and a fair market value of $30,000. Each member has a $33^1/3$ percent interest in the total adjusted basis of LLC assets ($70,000). However, one-third of the adjusted basis for each member would be $23,333. This would be $6,667 too low for the members contributing cash and $13,333 too high for the member contributing the appreciated property. Thus, the basis of the member's interest in the LLC under the alternative method is determined each year by multiplying the member's percentage interest by the adjusted basis of LLC property, and then increasing that amount by $6,667 for the members contributing cash and decreasing that amount by $13,333 for the member contributing appreciated property.

A member who acquires a membership interest by purchase must also make an adjustment to basis under the alternative method. The amount of the adjustment is

---

[85] Rev. Rul. 87-115, 1987-2 CB 163.

the difference between the purchase price and the member's percentage share of basis in LLC assets at the time of purchase.[86]

EXAMPLE 9-5

There are three equal members in an LLC. Each member contributes $100 in cash. Each member has a basis of $100 in his membership interest. The LLC buys property for $300, which appreciates in value to $600. Member A sells his membership interest to Member D for $200. Member D has a basis of $200 in his membership interest equal to the purchase price. However, his one-third share of basis in LLC assets is only $100. That understates his basis by $100. Therefore, Member D must increase his basis by $100 under the alternative method of determining basis.

After ten years of operations, the LLC has a basis in its assets of $6,000. Member D's basis is $2,100 (his one-third percentage share of basis in LLC assets plus the $100 adjustment).

Capital Account and Liabilities Method

Under the second alternative method (which is more commonly used), a member's basis is equal to the member's capital account plus his share of LLC liabilities. This method may be used if the LLC maintains its books and records on a tax basis (or makes annual adjustments for the difference between book and tax basis capital accounts).[87]

This method is normally easier to apply than the first alternative method. The member does not need access to the LLC books and records. The member can obtain the necessary information from the Schedule K-1 that the member receives from the LLC each year. The member's capital account is set forth in Item L of the form. The member's share of debt is set forth in Item K.

There are also fewer adjustments that must be made in applying the second alternative method. The member does not need to make an adjustment for the difference between the basis and fair market value of contributed assets since the actual tax basis of contributed assets is reflected in the member's capital account.

---

[86] Reg. § 1.705-1(b), Example (2).

[87] Code Sec. 705(b); Reg. § 1.705-1(b), Example (3). The IRS explained this rule as follows: "The Schedule K-1 does not compute the outside basis. However, a quick test for outside basis can be done by adding the ending capital account and the liabilities reflected on the Schedule K-1. This should result in a positive figure. The result may be distorted when the tax return reflects the book value capital accounts at FMV and adjusted basis. If the tax return is prepared using the tax capital account basis, which is reflected at adjusted basis, then it is easier to make a better 'best guess' estimate because outside basis is also based on adjusted basis." IRS Market Segment Specialization Program, Partnerships, Audit Technique Guide, Chapter 2, under the heading, "Quick Test or Computing Outside Basis."

The second alternative method is different from the first alternative method in one other respect. The first alternative method disregards debt in determining basis. The second alternative method adds a member's share of LLC debt to the member's capital account in determining basis.

EXAMPLE 9-6

There are three equal members in an LLC. Member C wants to sell her membership interest in the LLC to Member D. Member C will be taxed on the difference between the sales price and her basis in the membership interest. The LLC has been in existence for many years. It is impossible for Member C to determine her tax basis under the general rule for determining basis. The LLC maintains its books and records on a tax basis. Thus, Member C may use the capital account method for determining basis. The balance sheet of the LLC is as follows:

Assets	Tax basis per books	Fair market value
Cash	$3,000	$3,000
Receivables	4,000	4,000
Depreciable property	5,000	5,000
Land held for investment	18,000	30,000
Total	30,000	42,000

Liabilities and capital accounts

Liabilities	6,000
Capital accounts	
Member A	4,500
Member B	4,500
Member C	15,000
Total liabilities and capital	30,000

Members C's basis in the membership interest determined under the capital account method is $17,000. This is equal to her tax-basis capital account of $15,000 plus her one-third share of LLC liabilities.[88]

A member's basis in the membership interest under this alternative method must be adjusted to reflect discrepancies between a member's share of the adjusted basis of

---

[88] Reg. § 1.705-1(b), Example (3).

LLC property and the LLC's adjusted basis in its property at the time of any prior transfers, contributions, or distributions.[89]

EXAMPLE 9-7

Member D pays $17,500 for the membership interest. Member D's capital account at the time of purchase is $15,000 and her one-third share of liabilities is $2,000. Member D paid $500 more for the membership interest than her original capital account and share of liabilities. Thus, if Member D uses the capital account method and liabilities method for determining basis in future years, Member D must increase her basis by $500.[90]

Other Methods

A member who does not keep proper records may not establish basis by uncorroborated oral testimony regarding contributions and loans to the LLC in prior years.[91]

.07 Negative Capital Accounts and Basis

A member may not have a negative basis in a membership interest.[92] Loss allocations to the member in excess of basis are suspended and may be deducted in subsequent years when the member has positive basis.[93] Cash and marketable securities distributions in excess of basis are generally taxed at the capital gains rate.[94] The member is not taxed on property distributions in excess of basis, and takes a zero basis in the distributed property.[95]

A member may have a negative capital account. On sale or disposition of the membership interest, the gain recognized is generally equal to the negative capital account plus any cash received.[96]

If the LLC follows the Section 704(b) safe-harbor regulations on book allocations, then the members may not have negative capital accounts except in the following cases:

---

[89] Reg. § 1.705-1(b).

[90] *Id.*

[91] *Namen v. Comm'r*, TC Memo 2017-24 (2017).

[92] Code Secs. 705(a)(2), (3), 733.

[93] Code Sec. 704(d).

[94] *See* ¶ 1002 *infra.*

[95] *See* ¶ 1003 *infra.*

[96] IRS Market Segment Specialization Program, Partnerships, Audit Technique Guide, under the heading, "Overview, Liquidation/Termination."

- *Qualified income offset.* If the LLC makes an "unexpected" distribution that causes a deficit capital account balance, the LLC must allocate items of income and gain to that member as quickly as possible in order to eliminate the deficit balance.[97]

- *Deficit restoration obligation.* An LLC may allocate losses to a member that create a deficit capital account balance if there is a deficit restoration obligation. The member must be unconditionally obligated to restore deficit capital account balance by the later of the end of the tax year or 90 days following the liquidation or cash out of the member's interest.[98] Members typically limit the amount of the deficit restoration obligation to a fixed dollar amount, such as 10 percent to 20 percent of the total investment.

- *Minimum gain chargeback.* A member may have a deficit capital account if there is a minimum gain chargeback. Minimum gain is the amount by which nonrecourse debt deductions cause the book value of debt-financed property to decline below the outstanding loan balance. The LLC must allocate the minimum gain to the members who received the deductions that caused the book value to decline below the outstanding loan balance. The minimum gain is added to the member's capital account, resulting in an adjusted capital account balance. Allocations of losses that create a negative capital account are permissible as long as the allocations do not cause a deficit in the adjusted capital account balance that includes the minimum gain.[99]

- *Stop loss reallocation.* Loss allocations to members with deficit capital accounts are permissible if all members have deficit capital accounts. Under the safe-harbor regulations, the LLC may not otherwise allocate losses or deductions to a member to the extent that such losses or deductions create a deficit capital account balance for the member in excess of (i) the deficit amount that the member is required to pay back to the LLC on liquidation or cash out, and (ii) the member's share of minimum gain as reflected in the adjusted capital account.[100] The LLC must restore the capital account through reallocations of losses or cash away from the member with the deficit to the other members.

.08 Timing of Basis Adjustments

The timing and order in which basis adjustments are made is important in applying the loss limitation rules and determining the amount of gain or loss on distributions. The following timing rules apply to basis adjustments:[101]

---

[97] *See* ¶ 804.04 *supra.*

[98] *See* ¶ 804.04 *supra.*

[99] *See* ¶ 804.06 *supra.*

[100] Reg. § 1.704-1(b)(2)(ii)(d)(3) (flush paragraph under subparagraph (3)).

[101] *See* California Franchise Tax Board, Partnership Technical Manual ¶ 5060 (interpreting federal law).

- Basis adjustments are made before calculating the loss limitation.[102]
- Basis is computed at the end of the LLC's tax year. However, if a member transfers, withdraws, or liquidates his or her interest in the LLC, the basis is adjusted as of the date of transfer or withdrawal, even though the distributive share of income or loss has not yet been determined.
- Income or loss is taken into account at the end of the LLC year.
- Contributions increase a member's basis at the time of contribution.
- Distributions decrease basis at the time of distribution. Basis immediately before a distribution is the relevant basis for determining gain or loss on the distribution.
- Advances or draws of money or property against a member's distributive share of income are treated as current distributions made on the last day of the LLC's tax year.[103]
- Deemed distributions resulting from a decrease in the member's share of LLC liabilities is treated as if it is made on the last day of the LLC tax year.[104]

.09 Required Basis Computations

A member of an LLC is only required to compute the basis in a membership interest if the computation is necessary for the determination of his or her tax liability.[105] Ordinarily, a basis computation is necessary in the following circumstances:[106]

- to determine the deductibility of the member's share of a loss from an LLC;
- upon liquidation or disposition of a member's interest, in order to determine the amount of gain or loss;
- upon the distribution of cash or property to a member, in order to determine the basis of the property received or the taxability of the cash distribution.

¶ 903 EFFECT OF LIABILITIES ON OUTSIDE BASIS

.01 General

One of the advantages of an LLC is that a member's share of LLC liabilities increases the member's basis in his or her membership interest. In an S corporation[107] and a C corporation, liabilities incurred by the corporation do not increase a shareholder's basis.

---

[102] Rev. Rul. 66-94, 1966-1 CB 166.

[103] Reg. § 1.731-1(a)(1)(ii).

[104] Rev. Rul. 94-4. 1994-1 CB 195.

[105] Reg. § 1.705-1(a)(1).

[106] California Franchise Tax Board, Partnership Technical Manual ¶ 5010 (interpreting federal law).

[107] Code Sec. 1367.

EXAMPLE 9-8

Two equal members of an LLC each contribute $10,000 cash to the LLC. The LLC borrows $80,000 to purchase land for $100,000. Each member has a capital account of $10,000, which is the amount of the member's contribution to the LLC. Each member has a basis in his membership interest of $50,000, consisting of the $10,000 cash contribution, plus the one-half share of LLC liabilities allocated to the member.

A member's share of LLC liabilities must be determined whenever it is necessary to determine the tax liability of the member or any other person.[108]

Code Sec. 752(a) treats an increase in a member's share of LLC liabilities as a contribution of money by the member to the LLC. The deemed money contribution increases the member's basis in his membership interest.[109] This allows the member to take tax deductions passed through from the LLC in excess of the cash and property that the member contributes to the LLC.[110]

Section 752(b) treats a decrease in a member's share of LLC liabilities as a distribution of money to the member. The deemed money distribution decreases the member's basis in his membership interest.[111] A money distribution in excess of basis results in taxable gain, but does not result in negative basis. A member's basis cannot be reduced below zero.[112]

If a member contributes property to an LLC that is subject to a liability, then there is a netting process. The liabilities assumed by the LLC, less the member's share of those liabilities after the contribution, are treated as a cash distribution to the member and reduce the member's basis in the LLC.[113]

The deemed money contributions and distributions can arise in a number of different circumstances, including contributions of encumbered property to an LLC, distributions of encumbered property by an LLC, assumption of debt by an LLC, and refinancing or payment of debt. In each case, any increase or decrease in the member's share of LLC liabilities results in a basis adjustment.

EXAMPLE 9-9

An LLC has two equal members, Member A and Member B. Each member contributes $500 in cash to the LLC. Each member has a basis in her membership interest and a capital account of $500. The LLC admits Member C to the LLC as an equal one-third member. Member C contrib-

---

[108] Reg. § 1.752-4(d).

[109] Code Sec. 752(a); Reg. § 1.752-1(b).

[110] The tax deductions are also limited by the at-risk rules, the passive loss rules, and related parties rules discussed in Chapter 13 *infra*.

[111] Code Sec. 733(1).

[112] Code Secs. 733(1), 731(a)(1).

[113] Reg. § 1.752-1(f).

utes property worth $800, subject to a nonrecourse debt of $300 (net equity of $500 in the property) in exchange for the one-third interest in the LLC. The LLC assumes the $300 debt on the property. Member A's and Member B's bases in their membership interests increase by $100, to $600, as a result of the contribution. Each has a one-third share of the $300 in liabilities assumed by the LLC. Their allocations of $100 in additional LLC liabilities are treated as cash contributions by them, which increase their bases in their LLC membership interests from $500 to $600. Member C's basis in her membership interest is also $600. Her initial basis was $800, which is the adjusted basis of the property contributed to the LLC. The basis in her membership interest had to be reduced by $200, which is her net debt relief as a result of the property contribution. Before the contribution, Member C was liable for $300 in debt. After the contribution, she was liable for only $100 (one-third share of $300 in liabilities assumed by the LLC).

The amount of liabilities that are allocated to each member for basis purposes depends on the type of liability. There are two types of liabilities, recourse debt and nonrecourse debt.

.02 Allocation of Recourse Liabilities

General Rules

Recourse debt is allocated to the members who bear the economic risk of loss for that liability.[114] The economic risk of loss concept is used to distinguish recourse from nonrecourse liabilities, and to determine a member's share of such recourse liabilities.

Recourse debt is debt for which one or more LLC members bear the economic risk of loss.[115] A member bears the economic risk of loss if the member, or a person related to the member,[116] would be obligated to make a payment to the LLC's creditor or a contribution to the LLC with respect to the liability if the LLC liquidated at that time on a zero asset value basis.[117] Thus, the economic risk of loss test consists of two steps: (i) a hypothetical constructive liquidation of the LLC, and (ii) the determination of each member's obligations to make payments or to contribute to the LLC as a result of the constructive liquidation.

Step 1: Constructive Liquidation

The first step in the determination of a member's economic risk of loss is a hypothetical liquidation of the LLC in which all of the following events are deemed to occur simultaneously:[118]

---

[114] Reg. § 1.752-2(a).

[115] Reg. § 1.752-1(a)(2).

[116] *See IPO II v. Comm'r*, 122 TC 295 (2004); Reg. §§ 1.752-1(a)(3), 1.752-4(b)(1).

[117] Reg. § 1.752-2(b)(1).

[118] Reg. § 1.752-2(b)(1).

1. All of the liabilities of the LLC become payable in full.
2. All of the LLC's assets, including cash, have a zero value except for property contributed to the LLC to secure an LLC liability.
3. The LLC disposes of all of its assets in a fully taxable transaction for no consideration (except for relief from liabilities where the creditors' repayment rights are limited to one or more assets of the LLC).
4. All items of income, gain, loss, and deduction are allocated among the members in accordance with the operating agreement.
5. The LLC liquidates.

The determination of the deemed gain or loss in parts 3 and 4 of this step is computed in accordance with the following rules:

- If the creditor's right to repayment of an LLC liability is limited solely to one or more assets of a LLC, gain or loss is recognized in an amount equal to the difference between the amount of the liability that is extinguished by the deemed disposition and the tax basis in those assets (or book value if there is a difference between the book value and tax basis).[119]
- A loss is recognized equal to the remaining tax basis of the LLC's assets (or book value if there is a difference between the book value and tax basis).[120]

Step 2: Determination of Each Member's Obligations

The second step is to determine each member's obligations to make payments or to contribute to the LLC as a result of the constructive liquidation. The determination of the extent to which a member or a related person has an obligation to make a payment is based on the facts and circumstances at the time of the determination. All statutory and contractual obligations relating to the LLC liability are taken into account for the purposes of the determination, including:[121]

- Contractual obligations outside the operating agreement such as guarantees, indemnification, reimbursement agreement, and other obligations running directly to creditors, to other members, or to the LLC.
- Obligations to the LLC that are imposed by the operating agreement, including the obligation to make a capital contribution and to restore a deficit capital account upon liquidation of a LLC.
- Payment obligations (whether directly to another member or to the LLC) imposed by state law including the governing state LLC statute.

The net effect of these two steps is to create a hypothetical situation in which all of the LLC's assets are deemed worthless or lost. The constructive losses are then allocated among the members, which cause their capital accounts to be negative. Each member's negative capital account is a measure of the net amount (obligation) that he or she must pay to satisfy LLC creditors or pay to the members with positive capital accounts. This net amount represents each member's "economic risk of loss"

---

[119] Reg. § 1.752-2(b)(2)(i).
[120] Reg. § 1.752-2(b)(2)(ii).
[121] Reg. § 1.752-2T(b)(3).

regarding LLC liabilities. The share of LLC recourse liabilities among the members is based on this economic risk of loss.

EXAMPLE 9-10

An LLC has two members, Member A and Member B, who share equally in profits and losses. Member A contributes $300 to the LLC, and Member B contributes $500 to the LLC. The LLC borrows $1,000 and purchases property for $1,800. The members personally guaranteed the note. The LLC operating agreement provides that all LLC debts will be paid with LLC assets, and that members will be personally liable for the recourse debt to the extent of their negative capital accounts if LLC assets are insufficient to repay the recourse debt. Under the five-step zero asset value liquidation method, the allocation of recourse debt is made as follows:[122]

1. The $1,000 debt is treated as payable in full.
2. The $1,800 of LLC assets have a zero value.
3. The LLC is treated as selling all of its property in a fully taxable transaction for no consideration. Therefore, the LLC has a tax loss of $1,800 (zero consideration, less $1,800 adjusted basis in the property).
4. The $1,800 of tax losses are allocated among the members in accordance with the operating agreement. Therefore, $900 of tax losses are allocated to Member A, and $900 of tax losses are allocated to Member B.
5. The LLC liquidates. Upon liquidation, Member A has a negative $600 capital account (initial capital contribution of $300, less $900 in tax losses). Member B has a negative $400 capital account (initial capital contribution of $500, less $900 of tax losses). Since all the LLC assets have a zero value and were deemed sold in a taxable transaction for no consideration, the members of the LLC are personally liable for repayment of the $1,000 debt. In accordance with the terms of the operating agreement, Member A is liable for repayment of $600 of the debt, and Member B is liable for repayment of $400 of the debt based on their negative capital accounts as of the date of the hypothetical liquidation. Therefore, $600 of the recourse liability is allocated to Member A, and $400 of the recourse liability is allocated to Member B.

---

[122] *See* IRS Audit Technique Guide—Partnership, Chapter 1, under the heading, "Partner's Share of Recourse Liabilities."

EXAMPLE 9-11

Tom and Jerry form an LLC with each contributing $100 in cash. The LLC purchases a building from an unrelated party for $1,000, paying $200 in cash and signing a note to the seller for the balance of $800. The note is a general obligation of the LLC. Both Tom and Jerry are personally liable for repayment on the note. The operating agreement provides that all items are allocated equally, except tax losses, which are specially allocated 90 percent to Tom and ten percent to Jerry. Member's capital accounts are maintained in accordance with the Code Sec. 704(b) regulations, including the obligation to restore a deficit capital account on liquidation.

In a constructive liquidation, the $800 liability becomes due and payable immediately. All of the LLC's assets (which is the building) are deemed to be worthless. The building is deemed to be sold for a zero value, which causes a loss of $1,000 (LLC's cost basis in the building of $1,000 less sales price of $0). The loss is allocated to Tom and Jerry. Their capital accounts are adjusted to reflect the hypothetical disposition, as follows:

	Tom	Jerry
Initial contribution	$100	$100
Loss on disposition	(900)	(100)
Ending capital account	($800)	$0

There are no other contractual obligations between the members except the obligation to satisfy the creditor of the LLC ($800). The $800 liability, therefore, is classified as a recourse liability. The liability is allocated entirely to Tom since he is the only one with a positive capital account ($800) and bears the full economic risk of loss if the LLC liquidates under the zero asset value liquidation test.[123]

In this example, the computation of the loss on the deemed disposition is based on the LLC's tax basis in the building. The creditor's right to repayment is not limited solely to the building of the LLC because the note is a general obligation of the LLC (members are personally liable for repayment as stated in the Example).

Contingent Obligations

If a payment obligation is subject to contingencies that, based on all facts and circumstances, make it unlikely that the obligation will ever be discharged, the obligation is disregarded. If a payment obligation would arise at a future time after the occurrence of an event that is not determinable with reasonable certainty, the obligation is ignored until the event occurs.[124]

---

[123] Reg. § 1.752-2(f), Example (1).
[124] Reg. § 1.752-2(b)(4).

Reimbursement Rights

If a member or related person is entitled to reimbursement from another member (or a related person of the other member), the payment obligation is reduced by the amount of reimbursement.[125]

Loan by Member to LLC

If a member or related person makes a nonrecourse loan to the LLC, the loan will normally be treated as recourse for tax purposes.[126] However, the loan by a member or related person to an LLC will be treated as a nonrecourse liability for basis allocation purposes if (i) the member owns ten percent or less of each item of LLC income, gain, loss, deduction or credit, (ii) there are no guarantees of interest by the member or related person, and (iii) the loan constitutes qualified nonrecourse financing secured by LLC real property under the at-risk rules.[127]

Pledge of Property as Security

If a member or a related person pledges his or her separate property (other than a direct or an indirect interest in the LLC) as security for the LLC liability, then he is considered to bear the economic risk of loss for the LLC liability to the extent of the value of the pledged property.[128]

If a member indirectly pledges property by contributing property to the LLC solely for the purpose of securing an LLC liability, the member is considered to bear the economic risk of loss to the extent of the value of the contributed property. A property is not considered as contributed solely for the purpose of securing an LLC liability unless substantially all of the items of income, gain, loss, and deduction attributable to the contributed property are allocated to the contributing member. This allocation is generally greater than the member's share of other significant items of LLC income, gain, loss, or deduction.[129]

Guarantee by Member

An LLC liability guaranteed or assumed by a member or related person may be treated as recourse debt if (i) the member is personally liable for the debt; (ii) the creditor knows that the liability was assumed or guaranteed by the member or related person; (iii) the creditor can demand payment from the member or related person; and (iv) no other member or person related to another member will bear the economic risk of loss for that liability immediately after the assumption or guarantee by the member.[130]

---

[125] Reg. § 1.752-2(b)(5).

[126] Reg. § 1.752-2(c)(1).

[127] Reg. § 1.752-2(d), (e).

[128] Reg. § 1.752-2(h)(1).

[129] Reg. § 1.752-2(h)(2).

[130] Reg. § 1.752-2(f), Examples 3-7; IRS Publication 541, Partnerships, under the heading, "Family Partnership."

If one or more members or related persons guarantee the payment of more than 25 percent of the total interest that will accrue on an LLC nonrecourse liability over its remaining term, and it is reasonable to expect that the guarantor will be required to pay substantially all of the guaranteed future interest if the LLC fails to do so, then the LLC liability is treated as two separate LLC liabilities. The member or related person that provides the guarantee is treated as bearing the economic risk of loss for the liability to the extent of the present value[131] of future interest payments. The remainder of the stated principal amount of the LLC liability constitutes a nonrecourse liability.[132] In February 2016, the IRS issued a ruling that partnership obligations were recourse liabilities allocable to the partner who guaranteed them, even though the guarantee only applied when the partnership committed certain bad acts, such as the voluntary filing of a petition in bankruptcy.[133] The ruling was "quite troubling" to the real estate industry which believed that bad-boy guarantees should not affect basis and loss deductions taken by the other partners because the guarantees were merely designed to discourage bad behavior by the borrower.[134]

In April 2016, the IRS reversed its position. It determined that the events described in the typical bad boy guarantee would not cause nonrecourse debt to be treated as recourse debt on the part of the guaranteeing partner. The reason is that the events in a typical bad-boy guarantee are remote since a guarantor would not ordinarily act against its self-interest by voluntarily committing those bad acts.

If two or more members of an LLC personally guarantee an LLC debt, then the LLC debt is allocated to those members for basis purposes based on a fraction, the numerator of which is the liability of each member, and the denominator of which is the sum of the liabilities of all members.

EXAMPLE 9-12

A and B are unrelated equal members of an LLC that is classified as a partnership for federal tax purposes. The LLC borrows $1,000 from the bank. A guarantees payment for the entire amount of the LLC's 1,000 liability, and B guarantees payment for $500 of the liability. Both A and B waive their rights of contribution against each other. The aggregate amount of A's and B's economic risk of loss ($1,500) exceeds the LLC's liability ($1,000). Thus, the LLC's liability must be allocated between the members. A's economic risk of loss is $667 ($1,000 × $1,000/$1,500). B's economic risk of loss is $333 ($1,000 × $500/$1,500).[135]

---

[131] The present value of the guaranteed future interest payments is computed using the discount rate equal to (i) the interest rate stated in the loan document, or (ii) the applicable federal rate if the interest rate is imputed under either § 483 or § 1274, compounded semiannually. Reg. § 1.752-2(e)(2).

[132] Reg. § § 1.752-2(e)(1), 1.752-2(f), Example 5.

[133] CCA 201606027.

[134] BNA Daily Tax Rep't No. 75, p. G-3 (Apr. 19, 2016).

[135] Reg. § 1.752-2(f), Example 9.

Bottom dollar guarantee

A bottom dollar guarantee is not considered in determining whether a liability is a recourse liability, subject to limited exceptions.[136] The guaranteed debt is treated as a nonrecourse debt that is allocated to all of the members in the LLC. There is a limited exception if the member guarantees at least 90 percent of the initial payment obligation. A bottom dollar guarantee is a guarantee where the member agrees to repay LLC debt only if the lender collects less than the guaranteed amount from the LLC. For example, if an LLC borrows $100,000, and the member signs a bottom dollar guarantee for $10,000, the member must satisfy the guarantee only if the lender cannot collect at least $10,000 from the LLC. In a normal guarantee, the guarantor is liable for any and all amounts of the debt left unsatisfied by the LLC up to the stated guarantee amount.[137]

.03 Allocation of Nonrecourse Liabilities

General Rules and Principles

Nonrecourse debt is debt for which no member or related person bears the economic risk of loss.[138] Nonrecourse debt is allocated to the members under a three-tier system. Each member's share of nonrecourse debt is the sum of the following three different categories of debt allocations:[139]

1. member's share of Code Sec. 704(b) partnership minimum gain;

2. member's share of taxable gain that would be allocated to the member under Code Sec. 704(c); and

3. member's share of excess nonrecourse debt based on the member's share of profits.

Each of the categories has its own computational rules. The nonrecourse debt allocation rules under Code Sec. 752 are coordinated with the income and expense allocation rules under Code Sec. 704(b). The three categories are designed to make sure that each member has sufficient outside basis so that the nonrecourse deductions (depreciation, depletion and amortization) generated by the property will not be disallowed under Code Sec. 704(d).[140]

---

[136] Reg. § 1.752-2T(b)(3)(ii).

[137] Reg. § 1.752-2T(f), Example 10.

[138] Reg. § 1.752-1(a)(2).

[139] Reg. § 1.752-3(a); Rev. Rul. 92-97, 1992-2 CB 124; Rev. Rul. 95-41, 1995-1 CB 132.

[140] IRS Audit Technique Guide—Partnerships, Chapter 1, under the heading, "Partner's Share of Nonrecourse Liabilities."

Tier 1—Member's Share of Section 704(b) Partnership Minimum Gain

Under the first tier, nonrecourse liabilities are allocated in proportion to each member's share of Code Sec. 704(b) partnership minimum gain.[141]

Partnership minimum gain is the amount by which nonrecourse debt exceeds the tax basis of the property securing the debt.[142] It is equal to the tax gain that the LLC would realize if it abandoned or sold the property for no consideration other than the purchaser's assumption of nonrecourse debt. If there is a difference between the tax basis and the book value of the property, then the Section 704(b) minimum gain is based on the book value.[143]

EXAMPLE 9-13

An LLC purchases depreciable property for $1,100,000 which is financed with $1 million of nonrecourse debt, interest only for ten years. The LLC takes a $300,000 depreciation deduction, reducing the basis of the property to $800,000. The minimum gain is $200,000. This is the amount by which the $1 million nonrecourse debt exceeds the $800,000 basis in the property. The $200,000 of minimum gain equals the $200,000 of nonrecourse deductions.[144] The LLC must allocate nonrecourse debt to the members under the first tier in proportion to the amount of tax deductions received by each member that caused the book value of LLC property to decline below the outstanding loan balance securing the property. The first $100,000 of depreciation does not create minimum gain, and is not treated as a "nonrecourse deduction," because it does not reduce the basis of the property below the outstanding loan balance.

EXAMPLE 9-14

A and B formed an LLC in 2017. A contributed $10,000 and B contributed $90,000. The operating agreement provides that losses will be allocated ten percent to A and 90 percent to B. The LLC bought depreciable property in 2017 for $1,000,000, paying $100,000 in cash, with the balance financed through a nonrecourse loan. As of December 31, 2019, the LLC's adjusted basis in the property was $800,000 (due to depreciation of $200,000), and the loan balance was $950,000. Assuming the LLC disposed of the building for no other consideration except to satisfy the nonrecourse loan, the LLC would realize $150,000 in minimum gain (loan

---

[141] Reg. § 1.752-3(a)(1); Rev. Rul. 95-41, 1995-1 CB 132.

[142] Reg. § 1.704-2(b)(2).

[143] Reg. § 1.704-2(d)(3).

[144] IRS Audit Technique Guide—Partnerships, Chapter 1, Example 1-9.

balance in excess of tax basis). Under the "minimum gain chargeback" rule, this gain would normally be allocated ("charged back") to the members who took the (depreciation) deductions that caused the book value to decline below the outstanding loan balance, thus creating the minimum gain. Therefore, an amount of nonrecourse liability equal to the minimum gain of $150,000 is allocated to A and B in accordance with their share of depreciation deductions on the property, which is ten percent and 90 percent, respectively.[145] The remaining $800,000 of the nonrecourse liability is allocated under Tier 3 according to the members' profit ratio (see discussion of Tier 3 allocations below). There is no allocation under Tier 2 (see discussion of Tier 2 allocations below) because the book value of the property is the same as the tax basis.

Tier 2—Member's Share of Code Sec. 704(c) Taxable Gain

Under the second tier, nonrecourse liabilities are allocated based on the amount of taxable gain that would be allocated to the members under Code Sec. 704(c) if the LLC sold in a taxable transaction all LLC property subject to one or more nonrecourse liabilities in full satisfaction of the liabilities and for no other consideration.[146]

Section 704(c) property is property contributed to an LLC with a fair market value for capital account purposes that is different from its tax basis on the date of contribution. Section 704(c) property also includes property that is revalued for capital account purposes as a result of a contribution, distribution, admission, or withdrawal of a member. The amount by which the fair market value of the contributed or revalued property exceeds the tax basis of the property is referred to as Section 704(c) gain, or built-in gain.[147] If the LLC sold the built-in gain property for no consideration other than the debt relief, the tax gain would equal the debt relief less the tax basis of the property. This is the amount of nonrecourse debt that must be allocated to the members under the second tier.

EXAMPLE 9-15

Tim and Beverly are equal members in an LLC. Tim contributes a building with a fair market value of $200,000 and a tax basis of $100,000. The property is encumbered by nonrecourse debt of $150,000. Beverly contributes $50,000 cash to the LLC. The LLC has no nonrecourse debt to allocate under Tier 1 because the LLC was just formed and no depreciation was allocated to the members that caused the book value of the property to decline below the outstanding loan balance. The LLC must allocate

---

[145] Reg. § 1.704-2(m), Example (1).

[146] Reg. § 1.752-3(a)(2); Rev. Rul. 95-41, 1995-1 CB 132.

[147] Built-in gain is discussed at ¶ 805.

$50,000 of nonrecourse debt to Tim under Tier 2. This is the difference between the liability encumbering the property ($150,000) and the property's tax basis ($100,000).[148]

This second tier is designed to ensure that a contributing member whose property is encumbered with a nonrecourse liability in excess of its tax basis will not incur gain under Code Sec. 731.

Tier 3—Member's Share of Excess Nonrecourse Debt

Under the third tier, any additional nonrecourse liabilities (referred to as "excess nonrecourse liabilities") are allocated to the members in accordance with one of the following methods:[149]

- *Significant item method (profits method).* The excess nonrecourse liabilities may be allocated in accordance with each member's profits interest in the LLC. A member's share of profits is determined by reference to all the facts and circumstances. An operating agreement may specify the members' share of LLC profits for this purpose if the share is reasonably consistent with allocations having substantial economic effect or some other significant item of LLC income or gain. The allocation of excess nonrecourse liabilities in accordance with each member's profits interest is the most common method of allocation.
- *Alternative method.* Excess nonrecourse liabilities may be allocated among the members in the manner that deductions attributable to those liabilities are reasonably expected to be allocated.
- *Additional method.* The LLC may first allocate an excess nonrecourse liability to a member up to the amount of built-in gain allocable to the member on Section 704(c) property where such property is subject to a nonrecourse liability to the extent that such built-in gain exceeds the Tier 2 gain.

Under proposed regulations, the significant item method and the alternative method are deleted. Instead, excess nonrecourse liabilities under the third tier must be allocated in accordance with the members' interest in LLC profits, provided that such interests are in accordance with the members' liquidation value percentages.[150] The liquidation value of a member's interest is the amount of cash that the member would receive if the LLC sold all of its assets for cash equal to the fair market value of such property (taking into account Code Sec. 7701(g)),[151] satisfied all of its liabilities (other than those described in Reg. § 1.752-7), paid an unrelated third party to assume all of its § 1.752-7 liabilities in a fully taxable transaction, and then liquidated.[152]

---

[148] IRS Audit Technique Guide—Partnerships, Chapter 1, Example 1-10.

[149] Reg. § 1.752-3(a)(3); Rev. Rul. 95-41, 1995-1 CB 132.

[150] Prop. Reg. § 1.752-3(a)(3).

[151] Code Sec. 7701(g) provides that the fair market value of the property may not be less than the amount of nonrecourse debt to which such property is subject.

[152] Prop. Reg. § § 1.752-3(a)(3), 1.752-3(c), Example 2.

EXAMPLE 9-16

Tim and Beverly are equal members in an LLC. Tim contributes land with a fair market value of $200,000 and a tax basis of $100,000. The property is encumbered by nonrecourse debt of $150,000. Beverly contributes $50,000 cash to the LLC. The LLC has no nonrecourse debt to allocate under Tier 1 because there are no depreciation deductions on land that could cause the book value of the property to decline below the outstanding loan balance. The first $50,000 of debt is allocated to Tim under Tier 2. This is the amount of built-in gain that would be allocated to Tim as the contributing member if the LLC sold the land for no consideration other than debt relief (amount realized equal to debt relief of $150,000 less tax basis of $100,000). The remaining $100,000 of nonrecourse debt is allocated equally between the members under Tier 3 in accordance with their equal interests in the profits. Tim and Beverly's basis in the LLC is thus computed as follows:[153]

Outside basis items	Tim	Beverly
Adjusted basis of contributed property	$100,000	
Nonrecourse debt assumed by the LLC, treated as a distribution of money by the LLC to the member under Code Sec. 752(b)	(150,000)	
Cash contribution		50,000
Tier 1 liabilities	0	0
Tier 2 liabilities	50,000	0
Tier 3 liabilities	50,000	50,000
Outside basis in membership interest	$50,000	$100,000

.04 §1.752-1 and §1.752-7 Liabilities

The final regulations in 2005 classified liabilities as one of two types: §1.752-1 liability,[154] and §1.752-7 liability.[155] A §1.752-1 liability is a liability to the extent that it:[156]

---

[153] IRS Audit Technique Guide—Partnerships, Chapter 1, Example 1-10.
[154] Reg. §1.752-1(a)(4)(i).
[155] Reg. §1.752-7(b)(3).
[156] Reg. §1.752-1(a)(4).

- creates or increases the basis of any of the obligor's assets;
- gives rise to an immediate deduction by the obligor; or
- gives rise to an expense that is not deductible in computing the obligor's taxable income and is not properly chargeable to capital.

A § 1.752-1 liability is a fixed or contingent obligation (other than a § 1.752-1 liability) to make payment without regard to whether the obligation is otherwise taken into account for tax purposes. Obligations include debt obligations, environmental obligations, tort obligations, contract obligations, pension obligations, obligations under short sales, and obligations under derivative financial instruments such as options, forward contracts, and future contracts and swaps.[157]

These two types of liabilities, and the basis consequences of classifying a liability as a § 1.752-1 liability or a § 1.752-7 liability, are discussed at ¶ 1308.

.05 Assumption of Liabilities

A member's assumption of LLC liabilities, or an LLC's assumption of a member's personal liabilities, is treated as a cash contribution to or cash distribution from the LLC.[158]

The general rule is that a person is considered to assume a liability only to the extent that he is personally obligated to pay the liability. If a member or a related person assumes an LLC liability, the creditor must know of the assumption and be able to enforce payment of the liability. In addition, no other members or persons related to the other members may bear the economic risk of loss with respect to the liability immediately after the assumption.[159]

There is an exception to the general rule for contributions and distributions of encumbered property. The transferee is treated as having assumed the liability, to the extent that the amount of liability does not exceed the fair market value of the property at the time of the contribution or distribution.[160] There is no requirement in such case that the creditor know of the assumption of the liability.

EXAMPLE 9-17

A contributes property with an adjusted basis of $5,000 to an LLC in exchange for an interest in the LLC. At the time of contribution, the property is subject to recourse debt of $1,000 and has a fair market value in excess of $1,000. The LLC does not have any other outstanding liabilities. After the contribution, A remains personally liable to the creditor. None of the other members bears the economic risk of loss for the liability under state law or otherwise. Under the rule stated above, the LLC is treated as having assumed the $1,000 liability. Therefore, A's individual

---

[157] Reg. § 1.752-7(b)(3), *referring to* Reg. § 1.752-1(a)(4)(ii).

[158] Code Sec. 752.

[159] Reg. § 1.752-1(d).

[160] Reg. § 1.752-1(e).

liability decreases by $1,000. At the same time, however, the entire $1,000 LLC liability is allocated to A because he bears the economic risk of loss. Accordingly, A's initial basis in the LLC interest is $5,000.[161]

.06 Partner Nonrecourse Debt

If a member or related person makes a nonrecourse loan to the LLC, the nonrecourse loan will be characterized as a recourse loan.[162] The reason is that the lender-member is deemed to bear the economic risk of loss if the LLC defaults on the loan.

Nonrecourse loans made by a member or related person to the LLC are referred to as "Partner Nonrecourse Debt" under the Section 704 regulations dealing with allocations.[163] For allocation purposes, a debt that is treated as a partner nonrecourse debt must be allocated to the lending member since he or she bears the economic risk of loss. The other members may not include any portion of this loan in their basis.

EXAMPLE 9-18

A and B are equal members in an LLC AB. A and B each contributes $500 cash to the LLC in 2018. The LLC purchases a rental property for $100,000 from C, an S corporation of which B is 100 percent shareholder. The LLC paid C $1,000 in cash and signs a promissory note for $99,000. The note is secured by the property. Neither A nor B is personally liable for the note. Even though the note is nonrecourse, it is treated as recourse because it is made by a related person to B. B is considered to bear the entire economic risk of loss with regard to the note. As a result, the note liability is allocated 100 percent to B.[164]

There are two de minimis exceptions to these rules. A loan from a member or related person will not be recharacterized as recourse debt if:

- *Member as lender.* The member as a lender meets both of the following requirements: (i) the lender member or related person's interest in each item of LLC income, gain, loss, deduction, or credit for every taxable year is ten percent or less, and (i) the loan made to the LLC constitutes "qualified non-recourse financing" within the meaning of Code Sec. 465(b)(6) (determined without regard to the type of activity financed).[165] To be a qualified nonre-

---

[161] Reg. § 1.752-1(g), Example.

[162] Reg. § 1.752-2(c)(1).

[163] Reg. § 1.704-2(b)(4).

[164] Example from California Franchise Tax Board, Partnership Technical Manual ¶ 5491 (interpreting federal law).

[165] Reg. § 1.752-2(d).

course loan under Code Sec. 465, the loan must be from a qualified lending institution, or if from a related person, it must be commercially reasonable. For purposes of computing the ten percent interest in the LLC, both direct and indirect ownership of the LLC through one or more LLCs, including the interests of any related person, are taken into consideration.

- *Member is guarantor.* The member as a guarantor meets both of the following requirements: (i) the member meets the same ten percent ownership requirement, and (ii) the member guarantees a loan that would otherwise constitute a qualified nonrecourse financing within the meaning of Code Sec. 465(b)(6) if the guarantor had made the loan to the LLC.

.07 Accounts Receivable

If the LLC uses the cash accounting method, the accrual basis liabilities (i.e., accrued, unpaid expenses and accounts payable) are not considered LLC liabilities because they are not deductible by a cash basis LLC until they are paid.[166]

¶ 904 BASIS OF LLC PROPERTY (INSIDE BASIS)

An LLC's basis in its property is referred to as the inside basis. An LLC's basis in LLC property is determined under the following rules:

- *Purchase.* The basis of LLC property acquired by purchase is the purchase price of the property.[167]
- *Contribution of property to LLC.* The basis of LLC property that a member contributes to an LLC is the carryover basis, subject to exceptions.[168] An LLC does not receive basis in contributed property that has no value on the date of contribution.[169] The basis rules for contributions are discussed at ¶ 601.04.
- *Personal use property.* If a member contributes personal use property to an LLC that will be used by the LLC for business use, the LLC's basis for the property for purposes of determining gain or loss is the lesser of its value at the time of the contribution or its adjusted basis in the contributing member's hands.[170] The special basis rule applies only for losses and depreciation purposes. Therefore, an LLC may have to maintain a second basis record for an asset to determine the amount of any gain realized on the sale of the asset.[171]
- *Contribution of built-in loss property.* An LLC must make a mandatory basis adjustment if a member contributes property to an LLC with a built-in loss. The LLC's tax basis in the property with respect to the noncontributing

---

[166] Rev. Rul. 88-77, 1988-2 CB 129.

[167] Code Sec. 1012.

[168] Code Sec. 723.

[169] *Santa Monica Pictures, LLC v. Comm'r*, TC Memo 2005-104 (2005); FSA 200242004.

[170] Reg. § § 1.165-9(b), 1.167(g)-1.

[171] California Franchise Tax Board, Partnership Technical Manual 4620 (interpreting federal law).

members is the fair market value of the property on the date of contribution. The LLC's tax basis in the property with respect to the contributing member is the fair market value plus the built-in loss.[172] For example, if A contributes property to an LLC with a fair market value of $6,000 and an adjusted basis of $11,000, the LLC's basis in the property with respect to the noncontributing members is $6,000. The LLC's basis in the property with respect to A is $11,000. A's basis in the membership interest is $11,000.[173] The upward basis adjustment for the contributing member does not affect the computation of taxable items under Code Sec. 703. The built-in loss rules are discussed at ¶806.

- *Section 754 transfers.* An LLC must adjust the basis of its assets under Code Sec. 743(b) if the LLC makes an election under Code Sec. 754, and a member transfers a membership interest. The basis adjustment applies only to the transferee. The basis adjustment on transfer is discussed at ¶1508.

- *Transfer when the LLC has built-in loss property.* An LLC must make a mandatory basis adjustment to its property if (i) the LLC has not made a Section 754 election, (ii) a member sells or exchanges a membership interest or dies, and (iii) the LLC has built-in loss property of $250,000 or more at that time, or the transferee member would receive a loss allocation of more than $250,000 if the LLC sold its assets for cash at fair market value immediately after the transfer. The LLC must in such case make a negative basis adjustment in the transferee member's basis of LLC assets. The mandatory basis adjustment is discussed at ¶1509.01.

- *Transfer by member who contributed built-in loss property.* If a member contributes built-in loss property to an LLC and then transfers the membership interest, the LLC's special basis adjustment for the contributed property under Code Sec. 704(c)(1)(C) is eliminated.[174] The basis adjustment at the time of contribution of built-in loss property to the LLC and subsequent transfer of the membership interest is discussed at ¶806.

- *Section 754 distributions.* An LLC must adjust the basis of its assets under Code Sec. 734 if the LLC makes an election under Code Sec. 754 and distributes property to a member. The basis adjustment on distribution is discussed at ¶1006.

- *Distributions to member who acquired membership interest when LLC had built-in losses.* An LLC must make a mandatory basis adjustment to its property if (i) the LLC makes a distribution to a member, (ii) the LLC had not made a Section 754 election at the time that a member acquired a membership interest, (iii) the fair market value of LLC property other than money exceeded 110 percent of the LLC's adjusted basis of its assets at the time that the member acquired the membership interest, and (iv) the LLC makes a distribu-

---

[172] Code Sec. 704(c)(1)(C)(i).

[173] Example from preamble to IRS proposed regulations under Code Sec. 704(c)(1)(C), REG-144468-05 (2014).

[174] Prop. Reg. §1.704-3(f)(3)(iii)(A).

tion to that member. The basis adjustment must be made at the time of distribution to reflect the basis that the distributed property would have received if the LLC had made a Section 754 election at the time that the member acquired the membership interest. The basis adjustment is discussed at ¶ 1008.

- *Distribution within two years after acquisition of membership interest.* Under Code Sec. 732(d), a member who purchased a membership interest without the benefit of a Section 754 election in effect, and within two years after the purchase receives a distribution of property from the LLC, may elect to treat the LLC tax basis of the distributed property as the tax basis that the property would have had if the LLC had made a Section 754 election. This election is discussed at ¶ 1007.

- *Distribution of built-in loss property to a member.* An LLC must make a mandatory basis adjustment to its property if the member receives a substituted basis in distributed property that is at least $250,000 more than the LLC's basis in the property. The mandatory basis adjustment is discussed at ¶ 1009.01.

- *Disproportionate distributions.* An LLC must adjust the basis of its assets if it makes the disproportionate distribution of "hot assets" and "cold assets" to members. Disproportionate distributions are discussed at ¶ 1005.

- *Depreciation.* The LLC's basis in its assets is reduced by depreciation. The Section 754 basis-step up for each asset is listed as a separate asset on the balance sheet and treated as a newly acquired asset for depreciation purposes. The depreciation must be specially allocated to the transferee member.

¶ 905   MEMBER'S BASIS IN DISTRIBUTED PROPERTY

.01 Nonliquidating Distributions

In a nonliquidating distribution, a member's basis in distributed property is equal to the LLC's adjusted basis in the property immediately preceding the distribution.[175] However, the basis in distributed property is limited to the member's adjusted basis in the membership interest immediately preceding the distribution (decreased by any money distributed in the same transaction).[176]

EXAMPLE 9-19

On January 1, 1996, Member A has a $20,000 adjusted basis in his membership interest. During the year, the LLC distributes in a non-liquidating distribution, $10,000 cash and property with a fair market

---

[175] Code Sec. 732(a)(1); Reg. § 1.732-1(a).
[176] Code Sec. 732(a)(2); Reg. § 1.732-1(a).

value of $15,000 and an adjusted basis to the partnership of $12,000. A's basis in his membership interest is first reduced to $10,000 ($20,000 adjusted basis less $10,000 distribution). A's adjusted basis in the distributed property is limited to $10,000, the adjusted basis in his membership interest. The $10,000 distribution of property further reduces the adjusted basis in his membership interest to $0 ($10,000 adjusted basis after cash distribution less $10,000 property distribution).[177]

.02 Liquidating Distributions

A member's basis in property received in a liquidating distribution is equal to the member's basis in the membership interest immediately before a liquidating distribution and after any money distribution.[178] Since a liquidating distribution is a distribution in complete liquidation of a member's interest, there is no need to determine the member's adjusted basis in the membership interest after the distribution.

EXAMPLE 9-20

Member B has a $20,000 adjusted basis in her membership interest. During 2016, the LLC makes a liquidating distribution to B of $5,000 cash, and a building with a fair market value of $75,000 and an adjusted basis of $40,000. B's distribution of cash first reduces her basis to $15,000 ($20,000 adjusted basis less $5,000 cash distribution). B's basis in the building is $15,000 which is the adjusted basis of her membership interest after the cash distribution. There is no gain or loss reported on this transaction.[179]

¶906 REPORTING

An LLC must report the following items in connection with LLC liabilities:

- *Share of liabilities.* An LLC must report each member's share of liabilities on Item K of Schedule K-1, including recourse liabilities, nonrecourse liabilities, and qualified nonrecourse financing liabilities.
- *Bottom-dollar payment obligations.* Bottom dollar payment obligations must be reported on Form 8275, Disclosure Statement. The form must be attached to

---

[177] Example from California Franchise Tax Board, Partnership Technical Manual ¶5220 (interpreting federal law).

[178] Code Sec. 732(b); Reg. § 1.732-1(b).

[179] Example from California Franchise Tax Board, Partnership Technical Manual ¶5230 (interpreting federal law).

the LLC return for the tax year in which the bottom dollar payment obligation is undertaken or modified. Bottom-dollar payment obligations are discussed at ¶ 903.02.[180]

---

[180] Reg. § 1.752-2T(b)(3)(ii)(D).

10

Distributions

¶ 1001 GENERALLY

An LLC that is classified as a partnership does not recognize gain on the distribution of money or other property to a member.[1]

The distributee member does not recognize gain or loss on the distribution of LLC property subject to the limited exceptions noted below. Any gain or loss recognized is capital gain or loss unless otherwise provided under the rules relating to unrealized receivables and substantially appreciated inventory.[2]

¶ 1002 MONEY DISTRIBUTIONS

The most common type of distribution is a cash distribution. A cash distribution first reduces a member's adjusted basis in his or her membership interest. The member recognizes gain only if the distribution exceeds his or her basis in the membership interest immediately before the distribution.[3]

There are five types of money distributions:

1. Cash.
2. Relief of debt. A member is treated as having received money when the member is relieved of his share of LLC debt as a result of the sale of a

---

[1] Code Sec. 731(b).

[2] Reg. § 1.731-1(a)(3); Code Sec. 741(a).

[3] Code Sec. 731(a); Reg. § 1.731-1(a)(1)(i).

membership interest, the assumption of the member's liability by the LLC, the payment by the LLC of liabilities allocated to the member, or a liquidating distribution.[4] This is referred to as a "deemed money distribution."

3. Marketable securities, subject to an adjustment.[5]

4. The member's share of ordinary income assets when the member receives a disproportionate distribution.[6]

5. Property that the LLC acquires for distribution to the member in a liquidating distribution. The member is treated as receiving a money distribution equal to the amount that the LLC paid for the property.[7]

EXAMPLE 10-1

There are four equal members in an LLC. Member A has a basis in his membership interest of $1,000. The LLC incurred $1,000 of nonrecourse debt. The LLC makes a liquidating distribution of $1,000 cash to Member A. Member A recognizes $250 of gain. This is equal to the money distribution of $1,250 ($1,000 cash, plus relief of a one-fourth share of the LLC's nonrecourse debt), less the member's basis of $1,000.

A member recognizes capital gains to the extent the money distribution exceeds the member's basis in the LLC.[8] However, a portion of the gain is ordinary income if there is a disproportionate distribution of the member's share of LLC unrealized receivables and inventory.[9]

A member does not recognize a loss on a nonliquidating cash distribution.[10] The cash distribution merely reduces the member's adjusted basis in his membership interest. A member may recognize a loss on a liquidating cash distribution.[11] Loss is

---

[4] Code Sec. 752(b); Reg. § 1.752-1(c).

[5] *See* ¶ 1004 *infra.*

[6] *See* ¶ 1005 *infra.*

[7] CCA 200650014. In that case, a partnership formed an LLC that it used to acquire a house in which the departing partner intended to live. The partnership then distributed the LLC membership interests to the partner in liquidation of the partner's interest in the partnership. The partner took the position that there was no tax on the liquidating distribution because the partner had not received a money distribution in excess of basis. Instead, the partner received property with a basis equal to the partner's outside basis in the partnership interest immediately prior to the distribution. The IRS disagreed with this position. It ruled that the distribution was really a money distribution under the anti-abuse regulations, the step-transaction doctrine, and a variety of other theories.

[8] Code Sec. 731(a)(1); Reg. § 1.731-1(a)(1)(i).

[9] *See* ¶ 1005 *infra.*

[10] Code Sec. 731(a)(2).

[11] A member may not recognize a loss upon a liquidating distribution if property other than cash, receivables or inventory is distributed in the liquidation. Code Sec. 731(a)(2).

recognized to the extent of the member's adjusted basis in the membership interest over the money distributed (including debt relief).[12]

The member's basis in the membership interest is reduced by the amount of money distributed in the nonliquidating distribution.[13]

¶1003 PROPERTY DISTRIBUTIONS

Different rules apply when the LLC distributes property other than or in addition to cash. The tax consequences depend on whether there is a liquidating or nonliquidating distribution, whether the LLC has elected to adjust the basis of distributed assets under Section 754, and whether the member is required to adjust the basis of distributed assets.

.01 Nonliquidating Distributions

Taxation

Distributions of property to members are generally tax-free. The member does not recognize gain[14] unless

(1) the member receives a money distribution in excess of the member's basis in the membership interest,[15]

(2) the member receives a marketable securities distribution,[16]

(3) the member receives a disproportionate distribution of hot assets and cold assets,[17]

(4) the distribution is a guaranteed payment or distributive share of income to a retiring or deceased member,[18] or

(5) the distribution is part of a disguised sale.[19] A member never recognizes loss on a nonliquidating distribution.[20]

The LLC does not recognize gain or loss in a nonliquidating distribution.[21]

---

[12] *Id.*

[13] Code Sec. 733.

[14] Code Sec. 731(a).

[15] *See* ¶1002 *supra.*

[16] *See* ¶1002 *supra.*

[17] *See* ¶1004 *infra.*

[18] *See* ¶1010 *infra.*

[19] *See* ¶605 *supra.*

[20] Code Sec. 731(a)(2).

[21] Code Sec. 731(b).

Order of Distributions

Distributions are treated as made in the following order:[22]

- *Money.* The member first reduces his outside basis by the amount of any money received in the distribution.[23] A member is taxed on any distribution of money in excess of outside basis.[24] The gain recognized is capital gain,[25] except as provided under Code Sec. 751.[26]

- *Accounts receivable and inventory items.* The member next reduces his outside basis by the LLC's pre-distribution basis in unrealized receivables and inventory distributed to the member.[27] The member receives a carryover basis in such property,[28] up to the member's remaining outside basis.[29]

- *Other distributed property.* The member next reduces his outside basis by the LLC's pre-distribution basis in other property distributed to the member.[30] The member receives a carryover basis in such property,[31] up to the member's remaining outside basis.[32] Once the basis is reduced to zero, the member may not receive any more basis in the distributed property. There is no tax to the member even if the LLC's basis in the distributed property exceeds the member's remaining outside basis.[33]

- *Encumbered property.* Liabilities assumed by the member on distributions of encumbered property are treated as a money contribution and increase basis.[34] Liabilities that a member is relieved of on distribution of property are treated as a money distribution and decrease basis.[35] There is a netting process. A member recognizes gain only if the net debt relief exceeds the member's outside basis. Increases and decreases in liabilities on distribution of property are treated as occurring simultaneously for purposes of determining gain or loss.[36]

---

[22] IRS Market Segment Specialization Program, Partnerships, Audit Technique Guide, Chapter 4, under the heading, "Basis of Distributed Property in Current Distributions."

[23] Code Sec. 733(1).

[24] Code Sec. 731(a).

[25] Code Secs. 741, 731(a) (last sentence).

[26] *See* ¶ 1005 *infra.*

[27] Code Sec. 732(c)(1)(A)(i).

[28] Code Sec. 732(a)(1).

[29] Code Sec. 732(a)(2).

[30] Code Sec. 733(2). The property's basis includes any Section 743(b) basis adjustment related to the member who receives the distribution. Reg. § 1.743-1(g)(2)(i). The LLC must reallocate Section 743(b) basis adjustments to the distributed property to other members of the LLC if the basis adjustments were related to other members of the LLC who did not receive a distribution. Reg. § 1.743-1(g)(2)(ii). The Section 743(b) basis adjustment is discussed in ¶ 1006 *infra.*

[31] Code Sec. 732(a)(1).

[32] Code Sec. 732(a)(2).

[33] Code Sec. 731(a).

[34] Code Sec. 752(a).

[35] Code Sec. 752(b).

[36] Reg. § 1.752-1(f); Rev. Rul. 87-120, 1987-2 CB 161.

EXAMPLE 10-2

A member has a basis of $2,000 in her membership interest in an LLC. The LLC distributes property to the member having a basis of $1,000. The member receives a carryover basis of $1,000 in the property and must reduce her basis in the membership interest by $1,000.

EXAMPLE 10-3

A member has a basis of $2,000 in her membership interest in an LLC. The LLC distributes property to the member with an adjusted basis of $2,500 in a nonliquidating distribution. The member's basis in the distributed property is $2,000, since the carryover basis cannot exceed the member's basis in her membership interest. The member must reduce her basis in the membership interest from $2,000 to zero as a result of the distribution.

EXAMPLE 10-4

Emily has a basis in her membership interest of $30,000. She receives a nonliquidating cash distribution of $4,000 and property with a $20,000 basis to the LLC. Her basis in the property is $20,000. She must reduce the basis in her membership interest by $24,000 to $6,000.[37]

EXAMPLE 10-5

Steve has a basis in his membership interest of $10,000. He receives a nonliquidating cash distribution of $4,000 and property with an $8,000 basis to the LLC. His basis in the distributed property is limited to $6,000 ($10,000 − $4,000 cash). He must reduce his basis in the membership interest by $10,000 to $0.[38]

---

[37] *See* IRS Publication 541, Partnerships, under the subheading, "Assumption of liability."

[38] *See* IRS Publication 541, Partnerships, Example 2, under the heading, "Partner's Basis for Distributed Property."

Basis

A member's basis in his membership interest is reduced by the amount of money and the basis of property distributed in a nonliquidating distribution.[39]

A member's basis in distributed property in a nonliquidating distribution is the lesser of the LLC's basis in the distributed property or the member's basis in the LLC interest (after reduction by any money distributed to the member).[40]

.02 Liquidating Distributions

A liquidating distribution is the termination of a member's entire interest in an LLC by means of a distribution, or a series of distributions. A series of liquidating distributions may span more than one tax year.[41]

Liquidating distributions to members are subject to the following rules:

- *Gain recognition.* A member does not recognize gain unless (i) the member receives a money distribution in excess of basis in the membership interest,[42] (ii) the member receives a marketable securities distribution,[43] (iii) the member receives a disproportionate distribution of hot assets and cold assets,[44] (iv) the distribution is a guaranteed payment or distributive share of income to a retiring or deceased member,[45] or, (v) the distribution is part of a disguised sale.[46]

- *Assumption of Liabilities.* A member who would otherwise recognize gain on receipt of a money distribution in excess of basis may decrease the recognized gain by assuming liabilities. The assumed liabilities are treated as an increase in basis immediately prior to the money distribution.[47]

- *Loss recognition.* A member does not recognize loss on a distribution unless three conditions are met. First, the member must receive only cash, unrealized receivables, or inventory. Second, the member must receive a liquidating distribution of his entire membership interest. Third, the adjusted basis of LLC assets distributed to the member must be less than the member's basis in his membership interest. The loss recognized is the amount by which the basis

---

[39] Code Sec. 733.
[40] Code Sec. 732(a).
[41] Reg. § 1.761-1(d).
[42] *See* ¶ 1002 *supra.*
[43] *See* ¶ 1002 *supra.*
[44] *See* ¶ 1004 *infra.*
[45] *See* ¶ 1010 *infra.*
[46] *See* ¶ 605 *supra.*
[47] Code Sec. 752(a).

in the membership interest exceeds the money and the LLC's basis in unrealized receivables and inventory items distributed to the member.[48]

- *Character of gain or loss.* The gain or loss recognized is capital gain or loss,[49] except as provided under Code Sec. 751.[50]
- *Substituted basis.* The member receives a substituted basis in the distributed property. The basis in the property is the same as a member's basis in the membership interest immediately prior to the distribution, reduced by any money received.[51] This differs from the basis rule for a nonliquidating distribution in which the member receives a carryover basis rather than a substituted basis.
- *Basis in membership interest.* The member's outside basis in the membership interest must be zero after a liquidating distribution.

EXAMPLE 10-6

An LLC distributes land with a basis and fair market value of $100,000 to Member A in a liquidating distribution. Member A has a basis of $2,000 in her membership interest. Member A receives a basis of $2,000 in the land, equal to her basis in the membership interest prior to the distribution.

EXAMPLE 10-7

Same facts as in above Example, except that the LLC distributes property to the member with a basis and fair market value of $500. The member receives a basis of $2,000 in the distributed property.

.03 Allocation of Basis to Multiple Properties

General Rule

If an LLC distributes more than one asset in kind, and the member receives a substituted basis in the property rather than a carryover basis, the member must allocate the member's outside basis in the membership interest among the distributed properties in determining the substituted basis for each property.

A substituted basis is a basis for distributed property that is measured by reference to the member's outside basis in the membership interest, rather than by

---

[48] Code Sec. 731(a)(2).

[49] Code Secs. 741, 731(a) (last sentence).

[50] *See* ¶ 1005 *infra.*

[51] Code Sec. 732(b).

the LLC's basis in the distributed assets. A member receives a substituted basis for distributed property in a liquidating distribution, and in a nonliquidating distribution if the member's basis in the membership interest is less than the LLC's basis in the distributed property.

Basis Divided Among Properties

If there is a substituted basis, the member must allocate the member's outside basis to the distributed properties in the following order:[52]

1. Reduce the outside basis by the money received in the same transaction.[53]

2. If the member's remaining basis in the membership interest is greater than the LLC's basis in inventory and unrealized receivables, the LLC's basis in inventory and unrealized receivables is carried over to the distributee, and the distributee's basis in his membership interest is reduced accordingly. If the member's remaining basis in the membership interest is less than the LLC's basis in distributed unrealized receivables and inventory items, the remaining basis is allocated among the unrealized receivables and inventory items in proportion to the bases of such assets in the hands of the LLC.[54] In that event, any other class of property distributed along with the unrealized receivables and inventory receives a basis of zero.

3. If the distributee's basis in the membership interest is not completely absorbed by the cash, unrealized receivables and inventory items distributed, then the other distributed properties receive an initial tax basis equal to the LLC's tax basis prior to the distribution.[55] If the member's allocable outside basis exceeds the total of such assigned bases (liquidating distributions only), increase the assigned bases by the amount of excess. If the total of the assigned bases exceeds the member's allocable outside basis, decrease the assigned bases by the amount of the excess.[56]

4. Allocate any basis increase required under rule 3 first to properties with unrealized appreciation to the extent of unrealized depreciation. If the basis increase is less than total unrealized appreciation, allocate basis increase among those properties in proportion to their respective amounts of unrealized appreciation. Allocate any remaining basis increase among all the properties in proportion to their respective fair market values.

5. Allocate any basis decrease required under rule 3 first to items with unrealized appreciation to the extent of the unrealized depreciation. If the basis decrease is less than the total unrealized appreciation, allocate basis decrease among those properties in proportion to their respective amounts of unreal-

---

[52] Code Sec. 732(c). *See also* IRS Publication 541, Partnerships, under the heading, "Partner's Basis for Distributed Property."

[53] Code Sec. 733; Reg. § 1.733-1.

[54] Code Sec. 732(c)(1); Reg. § 1.732-1T(c)(1)(i).

[55] Code Sec. 732(c)(1)(B)(i); Reg. § 1.732-1T(c)(1)(ii).

[56] Code Sec. 732(c)(1)(B)(ii); Reg. § 1.732-1(c)(2).

ized appreciation. Allocate any remaining basis decrease among all the items in proportion to their respective assigned basis amounts after such decrease.[57]

The member has a capital loss to the extent of the remaining outside basis if (i) there is a liquidating distribution, (ii) the member's outside basis in the membership interest is more than the LLC's adjusted basis for the unrealized receivables and inventory items distributed to the member in the complete liquidation, and (iii) the LLC distributes no other property to which the member can apply the member's remaining outside basis. There is no capital loss in a nonliquidating distribution.

Basis Increase Example

Jill's basis in her membership interest is $55,000. The LLC distributes to her in a complete liquidation Properties A and B, neither of which is inventory or unrealized receivables. Property A has an adjusted basis to the LLC of $5,000 and fair market value $40,000. Property B has an adjusted basis to the LLC of $10,000 and a fair market value of $10,000.

Jill must first assign bases of $5,000 to Property A and $10,000 to Property B equal to their adjusted bases to the LLC. This leaves an additional $40,000 of basis that must be allocated to the properties ($55,000 outside basis less the $15,000 initially assigned bases). Jill must allocate $35,000 of this excess amount to Property A equal to its unrealized appreciation. She must allocate the remaining $5,000 between the properties based on their fair market values. She must allocate $4,000 ($40,000/$50,000) to Property A and $1,000 ($10,000/$50,000) to Property B.

Jill's basis in Property A is $44,000 ($5000 + $35,000 + $4,000). Her basis in Property B is $11,000 ($10,000 + $1,000).[58]

Basis Decrease Example

Judy's basis in her membership interest is $20,000. The LLC distributes to her in a complete liquidation Properties A and B, neither of which is inventory or unrealized receivables. Property A has an adjusted basis to the LLC of $15,000 and fair market value $15,000. Property B has an adjusted basis to the LLC of $15,000 and a fair market value of $5,000.

Judy must first assign bases of $15,000 to Property A and $15,000 to Property B equal to their adjusted bases to the LLC. There must then be a $10,000 basis decrease in these properties since the assigned bases exceeds Judy's outside basis in her membership interest by $10,000 ($30,000 of assigned bases less the $20,000 outside basis). Judy must allocate the entire $10,000 basis decrease to Property B (its unrealized depreciation).

---

[57] Code Sec. 732(c)(3); Reg. § 1.732-1(c)(2)(i).

[58] *See* IRS Publication 541, Partnerships, Example under the heading, "Partner's Basis for Distributed Property."

¶ 1003.03

Judy's basis in Property A is $15,000. Her basis in Property B is $5,000 ($15,000 − $10,000).[59]

.04 Holding Period

A member may tack the LLC's holding period to the member's holding period of distributed property,[60] unless the property is inventory or unrealized receivables. The member is allowed to tack the holding period if the member receives a carryover basis[61] or a substituted basis in the distributed property.[62]

.05 Subsequent Sale by Member

A member who receives a distribution of property from an LLC recognizes gain or loss upon a subsequent sale of the property. The amount of gain or loss is the difference between the amount realized upon sale and the member's basis in the property. The character of the gain or loss is capital or ordinary depending on the member's use of the property. The gain or loss is capital if the asset is a capital gain asset in the hands of the member and ordinary income or loss if the asset is an ordinary income asset in the hands of the member.

A member's sale or other disposition of an asset received from an LLC results in ordinary gain or loss to the member without regard to his personal use of the property in the following cases:

1. The property is an unrealized receivable.[63]
2. The property is inventory and is sold by the member within five years after the distribution from the LLC.[64] After the five-year time period has elapsed, the character of the distributed property is based on its character in the hands of the distributee at the time of the sale.[65]
3. The property is Section 1245 property. The member will recognize ordinary depreciation recapture income on sale of the property up to the lesser of the gain recognized or the recomputed basis adjustment. The recomputed basis adjustment includes the amount of depreciation recapture that the LLC would have recognized if the LLC had sold the property for fair market value immediately prior to the distribution.[66] Similar rules apply to Section 1250 property to the extent the LLC took depreciation in excess of straight-line depreciation prior to 1987.

---

[59] *See* IRS Publication 541, Partnerships, Example under the heading, "Partner's Basis for Distributed Property."

[60] Code Sec. 735(b); Reg. § 1.735-1(b); Ltr. Rul. 200204005.

[61] Ltr. Ruls. 200204005, 9816024, citing Code Sec. 1223(2).

[62] Ltr. Ruls. 9816024, 9724013, citing Code Sec. 1223(1).

[63] Code Sec. 735(a)(1); Reg. § 1.735-1(a)(1).

[64] Code Sec. 735(a)(2); Reg. § 1.735-1(a)(2).

[65] Reg. § 1.735-1(a)(2).

[66] *See* ¶ 1003.06 *infra*. The recomputed basis adjustment will also include any depreciation that the member took on the property after the date of distribution.

.06 Depreciation

Depreciation Basis and Method

A member who receives depreciable property in a distribution is bound by the LLC's period and method of depreciation or amortization with respect to the LLC's basis in the property prior to the distribution.[67]

A member may receive a basis in the property that is higher than the LLC's basis in the property if the member's outside basis in the membership interests exceeds the LLC's basis in the property.[68] The property will be treated as newly acquired property for depreciation purposes to the extent of the excess basis. Thus, the member will have a bifurcated basis for depreciation purposes.

Depreciation Recapture

An LLC's distribution of depreciable property to a member does not trigger depreciation recapture.[69] The potential depreciation recapture inherent in the property carries over to the member. The member recognizes ordinary income for the recapture amount on resale of the property. The Code accomplishes this result by defining two additional terms: "recomputed basis" for Section 1245 property; and "additional depreciation" for Section 1250 real property.

Generally, the member's initial basis in Section 1245 property distributed from the LLC is the member's outside basis in the membership interest, reduced by any cash received in the distribution.[70] The member's recomputed basis is the member's basis on distribution, increased by the amount of depreciation recapture that the LLC would have recognized if it had sold the Section 1245 property for fair market value immediately prior to distribution.[71] In subsequent years, the member's recomputed

---

[67] Code Sec. 168(i)(7).

[68] *See* ¶ 1003.02 *supra.*

[69] Code Sec. 1245(b)(3) and Code Sec. 1250(d)(3) state that there will be no depreciation recapture in a distribution by an LLC under Code Sec. 731 if the member's basis in the property is the same as the LLC's basis in the property on the date of distribution. Code Sec. 1245(b)(6)(A) and Code Sec. 1250(d)(6)(A) provide that a member's basis in property distributed by LLC is the same as the LLC's basis in the property immediately prior to the distribution (even though the basis may actually be different under the substituted basis rules).

[70] *See* ¶ 1003.01 *supra.*

[71] Code Sec. 1245(b)(5)(B)(i); Reg. § 1.1245-4(f)(2). The recomputed basis is reduced to the extent that the LLC recognizes depreciation recapture income on distribution of the property. Code Sec. 1245(b)(5)(B)(ii). This would apply if the LLC made a disproportionate distribution of depreciable assets and other hot assets to the member. The LLC in such case would be treated as making a proportionate distribution of other assets (cold assets), and then selling the excess depreciable assets to the member for the additional cold assets that the member would have received in a proportionate distribution. The LLC would recognize depreciation recapture income on the deemed distribution and sale. Tax practitioners largely ignore this provision.

basis is the member's adjusted basis, increased by the amount of depreciation on the property taken by the member, plus the amount of depreciation recapture that the LLC would have recognized if it had sold the Section 1245 property for fair market value immediately prior to distribution.

When the member sells the Section 1245 property, the member recognizes ordinary income recapture up to the lesser of the gain realized or the amount by which the recomputed basis exceeds the member's adjusted basis.[72]

EXAMPLE 10-8

Member A has a basis of $75,000 in her membership interest. The LLC distributes Section 1245 property to the member in complete liquidation of her membership interest. The LLC originally purchased the property for $110,000 and took $25,000 of depreciation, resulting in an adjusted basis of $85,000. The property has a fair market value of $100,000 at the time of distribution. Member A receives a basis of $75,000 in the property on distribution equal to her outside basis in the membership interest. Member A's recomputed basis is $90,000. This is the basis of $75,000 on distribution plus the $15,000 of depreciation recapture that the LLC would have recognized if it sold the property for fair market value immediately prior to the distribution ($100,000 fair market value less the LLC's $85,000 adjusted basis).

If Member A sells the asset one month later for $103,000 prior to taking any additional depreciation deductions, then Member A would recognize $15,000 of Section 1245 gain (depreciation recapture income) equal to the $103,000 amount realized less the $90,000 recomputed basis. The remaining $13,000 of gain would be Section 1231 gain, assuming that the aggregate holding period of the property for the LLC and Member A was more than one year.

If Member A instead sells the asset one month later for $80,000, then Member A would recognize $5,000 of depreciation recapture income. The amount of depreciation recapture cannot exceed the gain realized by Member A on sale of property (amount realized of $80,000 less adjusted basis of $75,000).[73]

---

[72] Code Sec. 1245(a)(1).

[73] Example from S. Rep. No. 1881, 87th Cong., 2d Sess. (1962), reprinted in 1962-3 CB 94.

.07 Investment Tax Credit Recapture

An LLC's distribution of investment credit property to a member before the close of its estimated useful life used in computing the investment credit triggers recapture for all members, including any nondistributee members.[74]

.08 Installment Obligation Distributions

The distribution of an installment note or obligation is not a taxable transaction (except as provided under Code Secs. 704(c)(1)(B), 736, 737, and 751(b)).[75] The deferred gain continues to be deferred in the hands of the distributee member.[76] The members recognize gain or loss as payments are received or when there is a disposition of the installment obligation.[77]

.09 Debt Distributions/Cancellations

If an LLC distributes a member's promissory note or debt, or cancels the debt as part of the distribution, the tax consequences vary depending on the type of debt:

1. *Direct loan.* If an LLC loans money to a member and the loan is subsequently canceled, the member whose debt was canceled will be treated as having received a distribution of money or property at the time of cancellation.[78] The LLC will not recognize gain or loss.[79] The member will not recognize gain or loss unless the amount of money, including debt relief, received in the distribution exceeds the basis of the membership interest.[80] If the distributee member recognizes a gain or loss and the LLC made a Section 754 election, the basis of LLC assets must be increased or decreased in accordance with Code Sec. 734(b).[81]

2. *Member debt acquired from third parties.* A distribution of a member's debt that has been acquired by an LLC from a third party is considered a property distribution.[82] No gain or loss is recognized by the LLC. The transaction is divided into two parts.[83] First, the LLC is deemed to have distributed the debt to the member, who acquires a basis in the distributed debt pursuant to the rules of Code Sec. 732. Second, after the member receives the distributed

---

[74] Reg. § 1.47-6(a)(2).

[75] Prop. Reg. § 1.453B-1(c)(1)(i)(C).

[76] Ltr. Rul. 9853013, citing Reg. § 1.453-9(c)(2).

[77] Ltr. Rul. 9853013.

[78] Reg. § 1.731-1(c)(2).

[79] Code Sec. 731(b).

[80] Code Sec. 731(a)(1).

[81] California Franchise Tax Board, Partnership Technical Manual ¶ 6561 (interpreting federal law).

[82] Rev. Rul. 93-7, 1993-1 CB 125.

[83] Rev. Rul. 93-7, 1993-1 CB 125.

debt, the debt is treated as canceled for an amount equal to its fair market value. The member realizes cancellation of indebtedness income measured by the difference between the fair market value of the distributed debt and its basis.[84]

3. *Member debt contributed in exchange for membership interests.* If a member contributes a promissory note to an LLC in exchange for a membership interest, the note does not increase the member's basis in the LLC until actual payments are made.[85] When an LLC distributes the note to a member, it is treated as a deemed distribution of money if it causes a reduction in the member's share of LLC liabilities.

4. *Transfer of property in exchange for deferred payments.* If a member enters into a deferred payment obligation to pay an LLC for property purchased from the LLC and the obligation is cancelled, the obligor member will have a deemed distribution of money.[86] The member will be taxed to the extent the money distribution exceeds the member's tax basis in the membership interest.

.10 Encumbered Property Distributions

A distribution of encumbered property may result in gain to the member receiving the distribution, or to any other member whose share of LLC liabilities is reduced as a result of the distribution, if the reduction in the member's liabilities as a result of the transaction exceeds the member's basis in the LLC immediately before the distribution.[87] The member's assumption of an LLC liability is treated as a constructive contribution of money to the LLC.[88] The distribution of encumbered property results in a decrease in LLC liabilities allocated to the members, and is treated as a distribution of money to the extent of each member's share of such liabilities immediately prior to the distribution.[89]

When LLC property subject to a liability is distributed to a member, the transferee members are treated as having assumed the liability.[90]

Increases and decreases in a member's share of LLC liabilities can both occur when property subject to a liability is distributed. When this happens, the increases and decreases in liabilities are netted in order to determine whether a member will be treated, overall, as having made a contribution or as having received a distribution as a result of the transaction.[91] If more than one encumbered property is distributed as part of a single transaction, the increases and decreases in liabilities resulting from all

---

[84] Code Sec. 61(a)(12).

[85] *Vision Monitor Software, LLC v. Comm'r*, TC Memo 2014-182 (2014); CCA 201326014.

[86] S. Rep. No. 1622, 93d Cong., 2d Sess. 30 (1954); Reg. § 1.731-1(c)(2).

[87] Code Secs. 731(a), 752(b).

[88] Code Sec. 752(a).

[89] Code Sec. 752(b).

[90] Reg. § 1.752-1(e).

[91] Reg. § 1.752-1(f).

of the distributions will be offset in determining the overall result for the partners.[92] If the constructive money distribution exceeds the member's basis in the membership interest, the member will recognize gain in the same manner as a member receiving an actual cash distribution.[93]

Adjustments to a member's basis caused by an increase or decrease in the member's share of LLC liabilities are made before the property distribution is taken into account.[94] If the member's net decrease in liabilities exceeds his basis in the LLC immediately before the property is distributed, the member will recognize gain in the amount of the excess, and the member's basis in the distributed property will be zero.

EXAMPLE 10-9

G and T are equal members in GT LLC. G has a basis of $1,000 in his membership interest. The LLC distributes property to G (other than Section 751 property). The property has a basis to the LLC of $2,000, and is subject to a liability of $1,600. As a result of the distribution, G's basis in his membership interest is increased by $1,600 to reflect his assumption of the liability. At the same time, his basis is also decreased by $800 to reflect the reduction in G's share of LLC liabilities (50 percent of the $1,600 liability). The net result of these adjustments is an increase of $800 to G's basis in his membership interest ($1,000 original basis plus $1,600 liability less G's $800 share of liability = $1,800). G's basis in the distributed property is $1,800, the lesser of (i) the LLC's $2,000 basis in the distributed property immediately prior to the distribution, or (ii) G's $1,800 basis in his membership interest immediately prior to the distribution but after the net adjustment for liabilities. G does not recognize gain as a result of the distribution.[95]

¶1004 MARKETABLE SECURITIES DISTRIBUTIONS

.01 Generally

A member recognizes gain to the extent that a money distribution exceeds the member's basis in the LLC. The term money includes marketable securities.[96] The amount treated as a money distribution is the fair market value of the securities

---

[92] Rev. Rul. 79-205, 1979-2 CB 255.

[93] Code Sec. 731(a)(1).

[94] Code Secs. 732(a)(2), 732(b).

[95] Example from California Franchise Tax Board, Partnership Technical Manual ¶6580 (interpreting federal law).

[96] Code Sec. 731(c).

distributed to the member,[97] reduced (but not below zero) by the excess of (a) the member's share of unrealized gain in the marketable securities held by the LLC immediately prior to the distribution,[98] over (b) the member's share of unrealized gains in the marketable securities held by the LLC immediately after the distribution.[99] The reduction amount is equal to the deferred gain that the member must recognize on a subsequent resale of the securities.

EXAMPLE 10-10

ABC LLC holds 300 shares of X Corporation common stock (a marketable security) and other assets. A owns a 1/3 interest in ABC. The stock has a basis of $10 a share and a value of $100 a share. A has a $5,000 basis in his membership interest. ABC distributes all of the stock in X to A in liquidation of his membership interest. Under the rule treating marketable securities as a cash distribution, A is treated as receiving $3,000 in cash (300 shares × $100 per share). The amount is reduced by $9,000, the amount that A would have recognized if the LLC had sold the securities ($30,000 fair market value less $3,000 adjusted basis, divided by his 1/3 interest which equals $9,000). Therefore, A is treated as receiving a cash distribution of $21,000 ($30,000 less $9,000). The end result is that A recognizes a gain of $16,000 on this transaction ($21,000 distribution less $5,000 adjusted basis in his membership interest).[100]

EXAMPLE 10-11

An LLC has four equal members. Each member has a basis of $5,000 in her membership units. The LLC owns 20,000 shares of publicly traded stock with a basis of $80,000 and a fair market value of $100,000. The LLC makes a liquidating distribution to one of the members of 5,000 shares of stock with a basis of $20,000 and a fair market value of $25,000. The amount treated as a money distribution is $20,000. This is the $25,000 fair market value of the shares distributed to the member, less $5,000 determined as follows:

---

[97] Code Sec. 731(c)(1)(B).

[98] This is the member's distributive share of gain that would be recognized if the LLC sold all of its marketable securities at their fair market value immediately before the transaction resulting in the distribution.

[99] Code Sec. 731(c)(3)(B); Reg. § 1.731-2(b)(2); Ltr. Ruls. 200223036-200223045.

[100] H.R. 826, 103d Cong., 2d Sess. 192.

Member's share of unrealized appreciation in the securities owned by the LLC before the distribution (1/4 of $20,000 total unrealized appreciation)	$5,000
Less member's share of unrealized appreciation in securities owned by the LLC after the liquidating distribution	0
Reduction amount	$5,000

Consequently, the member recognizes gain of $15,000, which is the amount of securities treated as money distributed ($25,000 − $5,000 = $20,000), less the member's $5,000 basis in her membership interest immediately prior to the distribution.

The member receives a $20,000 basis in the distributed shares equal to the member's outside basis immediately prior to the distribution, plus gain recognized. Consequently, the member would recognize an additional $5,000 of capital gain if the member immediately resold the securities for the $25,000 market value.

.02 Definition of Marketable Securities

The term "marketable securities" is defined broadly. It includes the following type of actively traded financial instruments:[101]

- Stocks
- Equity interests
- Debt
- Options
- Forward and futures contracts
- Notional principal contracts
- Derivatives
- Interests in actively traded precious metals and other financial instruments
- Other financial instruments and foreign currency that are actively traded within the meaning of the straddle provisions of Section 1092(d)(1) of the Internal Revenue Code
- An interest in any other entity if more than 90 percent of the value of the entity is attributable to marketable securities.[102]

---

[101] Code Sec. 731(c)(2).

[102] Ltr. Ruls. 200223036-200223045; Code Sec. 731(c)(2)(B)(v).

.03 Excluded Transactions

The following distributions of marketable securities do not result in gain recognition:[103]

- The member who received the distribution of the security contributed the security to the LLC.[104]

- The LLC acquired the security in a nonrecognition transaction. The value of the marketable securities and money exchanged by the LLC in the nonrecognition transaction must be less than 20 percent of a value of all assets exchanged by the LLC in the nonrecognition transaction. The LLC must distribute the security within five years after either the date of acquisition, or, if later, the date on which the security became marketable.[105]

- The security was not a marketable security on the date of acquisition. The entity that issued the security must not have marketable securities at the time of acquisition by the LLC. The security must be held by the LLC for at least six months before the security becomes marketable. The LLC must distribute the security within five years after the date that the security becomes marketable.[106]

- The LLC is an investment partnership, and the member is an eligible partner. An investment partnership includes an LLC that has never engaged in a trade or business if substantially all of its assets are investment assets as specified in the Internal Revenue Code and regulations. An LLC is not engaged in a trade or business for such purposes as a result of its activities as an investor, trader, or dealer in investment assets. An eligible partner includes any member of the LLC who before the date of distribution did not contribute any property other than specified investment assets.[107]

.04 Basis in Distributed Securities

The member's basis in the distributed securities is the LLC's adjusted basis in the securities immediately prior to the distribution, increased by the amount of gain recognized by the member on the distribution.[108] The gain is allocated to the securities in proportion to the amount of unrealized appreciation in the securities.[109]

---

[103] Code Sec. 731(c)(3)(A), (C).

[104] Reg. § 1.731-2(d)(1)(i).

[105] Reg. § 1.731-2(d)(1)(ii).

[106] Code Sec. 731(c)(3)(A)(ii); Reg. § 1.731-2(d)(1)(iii).

[107] Code Sec. 731(c)(3)(A)(iii); Reg. § 1.731-2(e)(1).

[108] Code Sec. 731(c)(4); Reg. § 1.731-2(f)(1)(i).

[109] Code Sec. 731(c)(4)(B).

EXAMPLE 10-12

N is a 50 percent member in NB LLC. She has a basis in her membership interest of $100. NB distributes Security X to N, with a basis of $90 and fair market value of $120. The distribution of Security X is treated as a $105 money distribution ($120 fair market value of the stock less N's one-half share of the $30 unrealized appreciation in the stock prior to the distribution). The result is that N must recognize $5 of gain on the distribution ($105 money distribution less basis of $100). N's adjusted basis in Security X is $95 ($90 adjusted basis of Security X plus $5 of gain recognized by N).[110]

.05 Basis in Membership Interest

The member's basis in his membership interest is the basis immediately prior to the distribution, decreased by the LLC's adjusted basis in the securities. The basis in the membership interest is not decreased by the fair market value of the securities distributed or the deemed money distribution under Code Sec. 731(c). Thus, the gain recognized under that section does not affect the member's basis in his membership interest.

.06 LLC's Basis in Its Assets

The LLC's adjusted basis in its remaining assets is not affected by the distribution of the marketable securities. There is no basis adjustment for the distributed securities under Code Secs. 754 and 734(b). The LLC may not adjust the basis of its assets as a result of the gain recognized by the member on the distribution.

EXAMPLE 10-13

An LLC owns various assets, including 20,000 shares of common stock with a basis of $4 per share and a fair market value of $5 per share ($1 appreciation per share). The LLC files an election under Section 754 to adjust the basis of its assets upon transfers of membership interest and distributions to members. Member A has a basis in her membership interest of $5,000. The LLC makes a nonliquidating distribution to the member of 2,000 shares of the common stock with an aggregate basis of $8,000 and a fair market value of $10,000. Member A is a 25 percent owner of the LLC before and after the distribution. The distribution of the common stock is treated as a money distribution to the member. The initial amount of the money distribution is the fair market value of the

---

[110] Reg. § 1.731-2(j), Example 5.

securities of $10,000. However, the deemed money distribution is reduced by $500, from $10,000 to $9,500, as follows:

Member A's share of unrealized appreciation in the common stock immediately prior to the distribution (1/4 × 20,000 shares × $1 appreciation per share)	$ 5,000
Less member A's share of unrealized appreciation in the marketable securities immediately after the distribution (1/4 × 18,000 shares × $1 per share)	(4,500)
Reduction in the fair market value of securities that is treated as a money distribution	$ 500

Consequently, Member A's gain on the nonliquidating distribution is $4,500. This is the amount by which the deemed money distribution of $9,500 exceeds Member A's basis in her membership interest. Member A's basis in her membership interest is reduced to zero. Her basis in the common stock is $24,500. This is the LLC's adjusted basis of $20,000 in the distributed stock (5,000 shares × $4 per share), plus the member's $4,000 gain upon the distribution of the securities. Even though the LLC has made an election under Section 754, it may not adjust the basis of its remaining assets as a result of the gain recognized by the member. Therefore, the adjusted basis of its remaining assets stays the same, and the overall basis for its assets is reduced by the $20,000 basis in the distributed stock.

¶1005 DISPROPORTIONATE DISTRIBUTIONS

.01 Characterization of Gain

A member ordinarily recognizes capital gain if the member receives a distribution from an LLC of money in excess of the member's basis in his membership interest. The capital gain is equal to the amount of money in excess of the member's basis in his membership interest. A member recognizes capital loss if the member receives a liquidating distribution consisting only of cash, inventory, and/or unrealized receivables, and the basis to the LLC of the distributed property is less than the member's basis in the LLC interest.[111]

However, a portion of the gain or loss is recharacterized as ordinary income or loss if the member receives a disproportionate distribution of "hot assets" or "cold assets." The determination of each member's proportionate share is based on the fair market value of assets rather than tax basis.

Under proposed reliance regulations, the amount of ordinary income or loss realized by a member on distribution is equal to the ordinary income or loss that the

---

[111] Reg. § 1.731-1(a)(2).

LLC would allocate to the member if the LLC sold all its hot assets in a taxable transaction immediately prior to the distribution. The ordinary income then reduces the capital gain that a member would otherwise recognize under Code Sec. 731(a)(1).[112] The proposed regulations are discussed at ¶1005.04. The "hot assets" are the unrealized receivables and inventory. These are assets that give rise to ordinary income for the LLC. The various types of hot assets are discussed in Chapter 15.[113] The "cold assets" are the other assets that do not give rise to ordinary income, such as capital assets and Section 1231 assets.

For distributions, inventory is a "hot asset" only if it is substantially appreciated inventory. Substantially appreciated inventory is inventory with a fair market value in excess of 120 percent of its adjusted basis.[114] This rule differs from the rule for transfers of membership interests. After 1997, a member who sells or exchanges a membership interest may recognize ordinary income rather than capital gain if the LLC owns any inventory, whether or not substantially appreciated.[115]

There are two types of disproportionate distributions. The first type is when a member receives more than his share of the hot assets.[116] The second type is when the member receives less than his share of the hot assets.[117] In both cases, the member is treated as first receiving a proportionate share of both types of assets in the distribution and then selling back to the LLC the assets he would have received in a proportionate distribution for the assets actually received in excess of his proportionate share.[118]

.02 Member Receives Less Than Member's Share of Ordinary Income Assets

The most common type of disproportionate distribution is when a member receives less than his proportionate share of hot assets.[119] This type of disproportionate distribution occurs when an LLC owns substantially appreciated inventory, depreciated property, or unrealized receivables (referred to as Section 751 assets), and makes a cash distribution to a member in exchange for the member's interest in LLC property. The member is treated as receiving a proportionate share of all assets, and then using his or her share of hot assets to purchase the disproportionate share of

---

[112] *See* ¶1005.04 *infra*. Prop. Reg. § 1.751-1(b)(2), (g), Examples 2, 3, 4, 5.

[113] *See* ¶1507.01 *infra*.

[114] Code Sec. 751(b)(1)(A), (b)(3); Prop. Reg. § 1.751-1(d)(1). Since the determination is based on total inventory, an LLC could circumvent the rule by purchasing additional unappreciated inventory. Inventory is excluded from the calculation of inventory fair market value if it is purchased with the principal purpose of avoiding Section 751. *See* Code Sec. 751(b)(3)(B).

[115] *See* Code Sec. 751(a), as amended by the Taxpayer Relief Act of 1997, Pub. L. No. 105-34, § 1062, 105th Cong., 1st Sess. (Aug. 5, 1997).

[116] Code Sec. 751(b)(1)(A).

[117] Code Sec. 751(b)(1)(B).

[118] Reg. § 1.732-1(e).

[119] Reg. § 1.751-1(b)(3)(iii).

cold assets actually received. The tax consequences to the distributee member and the LLC are as follows:[120]

Member Tax Consequences

1. The member recognizes gain or loss equal to the difference between the tax basis in the hot assets surrendered and the fair market value of the cold assets received in the deemed exchange.
2. The member's tax basis in the hot assets surrendered is the basis that the property would have had in a current distribution under the regular distribution rules.
3. The fair market value of the cold assets received is the fair market value of member's interest in the hot assets surrendered.
4. The character of the member's gain or loss is always ordinary income.

LLC Tax Consequences

1. The LLC recognizes gain or loss equal to the difference between the LLC's tax basis in the cold assets surrendered by the LLC and the fair market value of the hot assets purchased by the LLC in the deemed exchange.
2. The fair market value of the hot assets purchased by the LLC is the fair market value of the member's interest in the cold assets surrendered to the LLC.
3. The character of the gain or loss to the LLC is determined by reference to the cold assets given up by the LLC. Generally, the gain is capital gain. The gain must be reported as a separately stated item to all members other than the distributee member.

.03 Member Receives More Than Member's Share of Ordinary Income Assets

The second type of disproportionate distribution is when a member receives more than his share of ordinary income assets. The member is treated as receiving a proportionate share of all assets, and then using his or her share of cold assets to purchase the disproportionate share of hot assets actually received. The tax consequences to the distributee member and the LLC are as follows:[121]

Member Tax Consequences

1. The member recognizes gain or loss equal to the difference between the tax basis in the cold assets surrendered and the fair market value of the hot assets received in the deemed exchange.

---

[120] Reg. § 1.751-1(b)(3).
[121] Reg. § 1.751-1(b)(2).

2. The member's tax basis in the cold assets surrendered is the basis that the property would have had in a current distribution under the regular distribution rules.

3. The fair market value of the cold assets received is the fair market value of member's interest in the hot assets surrendered.

4. The character of the member's gain or loss is determined by reference to the cold assets given up. This is normally capital gain or loss.

LLC Tax Consequences

1. The LLC recognizes gain or loss equal to the difference between the LLC's tax basis in the hot assets surrendered by the LLC and the fair market value of the cold assets purchased by the LLC in the deemed exchange.

2. The fair market value of the cold assets purchased by the LLC is the fair market value of the member's interest in the hot assets surrendered to the LLC.

3. The character of gain or loss to the LLC is always ordinary. The ordinary income must be reported as a separately stated item to all members other than the distributee member.[122]

The purpose of this rule is to make sure that the remaining members in the LLC pay their share of tax on the ordinary income property. The rule prevents the LLC from shifting ordinary income to the distributee member. The effect of the rule is that all members recognize approximately the same amount of ordinary income that they would have recognized if there had been no disproportionate distribution.

.04 Proposed Reliance Regulations

Proposed reliance regulations adopt in part the hot asset sale approach to determining the ordinary income or loss recognized by the member on a distribution of assets.[123] Taxpayers may rely on Section 1.751-1(b)(2) of the proposed regulations in determining a member's share of ordinary income assets for distributions on or after December 3, 2014 if they apply the related proposed regulations consistently for all LLC distributions.[124]

Under the proposed regulations, the LLC must first determine each member's interest in Section 751(b) property before and after the distribution using the hypothetical sale approach. Specifically, the LLC must determine:

---

[122] Code Sec. 702(a)(7).

[123] Prop. Reg. §1.751-1(b)(1), which treats distributions as sales or exchanges of property under Prop. Reg. §1.751-1(a)(2), and not as distributions under Code Secs. 731-736, to the extent that the LLC has hot assets.

[124] REG-151416-06 (Nov. 3, 2014).

- the amount of ordinary income or ordinary loss that each member would recognize if the LLC sold its property for fair market value in a fully taxable transaction immediately **prior** to the distribution;[125] and

- the amount of ordinary income or loss that each member would recognize if the distributee member sold the distributed property and the LLC sold its remaining property for fair market value in a fully taxable transaction immediately **after** the distribution.[126]

Each member (including the remaining members of the LLC) will then recognize ordinary income to the extent that the member's share of Section 751 unrealized gain is greater immediately before the distribution than after the distribution. Each member must recognize ordinary loss to the extent that the member's share of Section 751 unrealized loss is greater immediately after the distribution than before the distribution.[127]

EXAMPLE 10-14

ABC LLC has three equal members. It has cash of $210, a zero basis receivable of $90 and no liabilities. The LLC makes a $100 liquidating distribution to Member B. B's share of ordinary income property prior to the distribution is $30 ($1/3 \times 90 receivable). B's share of ordinary income property after the distribution is $0 since B is no longer a member in the LLC and did not receive any of the receivables in the distribution. Thus, B recognizes $30 of ordinary income.[128] If the LLC had instead distributed all of the receivables to B, then A and C would have recognized $30 of ordinary income.

After the Section 751(b) gain or loss is determined, the distributee member must determine the capital gain or loss under Section 731. In a cash-out distribution, this is the difference between the cash received and the member's tax basis in the membership interest. The ordinary income recognized under Code Sec. 751(b) reduces the capital gain or increases the capital loss under Code Sec. 731.[129]

---

[125] Prop. Reg. § 1.751-1(b)(2)(ii).

[126] Prop. Reg. § 1.751-1(b)(2)(iii).

[127] *See* Prop. Reg. § 1.751-1(g), Example 2(v).

[128] Prop. Reg. § 1.751-1(g), Example 2.

[129] *See* Prop. Reg. § 1.751-1(b)(1)(ii), which states that the tax consequences under Section 751(b) first apply, and then the rules under Sections 731 through 736 apply. The difference between the amount of capital gain or loss that a member realizes in the absence of Section 751(b)) and the amount of ordinary income or loss that a member realizes under Section 751(b) is the member's capital gain or loss under Section 731.

EXAMPLE 10-15

ABC LLC has three equal members and no liabilities. Member C's one-third share of the LLC's zero basis accounts receivable is $14,000. The LLC makes a $10,000 liquidating cash distribution to Member C. C's basis in the membership interest is $2,000. C recognizes $14,000 of ordinary income since his share of ordinary income assets was reduced by $14,000. In the absence of Section 751(a), C would recognize $8,000 of capital gain ($10,000 amount realized less $2,000 tax basis). The $14,000 of ordinary income reduces the capital gain. Therefore, C recognizes a $6,000 capital loss ($8,000 gain on distribution less the $14,000 of ordinary income).[130]

EXAMPLE 10-16

An LLC makes a liquidating distribution of $150 to a $^1/_3$ Member B who has a tax basis of $120 in the membership interest. The LLC has a $90 zero basis receivable. Member B recognizes $30 of ordinary income under Code Sec. 751(b) because his share of the receivables prior to the distribution ($30) is greater than his share of the receivables after the distribution ($0). Member B must then determine the capital gain under Code Sec. 731. B recognizes $30 of capital gain under Section 731(a)(1) since B received a distribution of $150 of cash in excess of his $120 tax basis immediately prior to the distribution. However, the $30 of ordinary income under Section 751(b) reduces the capital gain under Section 731 from $30 to $0.[131]

After the LLC determines the amount of Section 751(b) ordinary income, it must determine the other tax consequences of the distribution. The proposed regulations do not require an LLC to use any particular method to determine the tax consequences of a distribution. An LLC must choose a reasonable approach consistent with the purposes of Section 751(b). The LLC must continue to use the same approach once adopted. The proposed regulations provide examples of reasonable approaches. The deemed gain approach and the hot asset approach produce appropriate results in most situations.[132]

Under the deemed gain approach, the LLC may treat the distributee member as recognizing ordinary income immediately prior to the distribution rather than after the distribution. To reflect this deemed gain, the distributee member must increase the basis in its membership interest by the amount of the gain, and the LLC must increase its basis in its Section 731 property by the income recognized by the distributee member.[133]

---

[130] Prop. Reg. § 1.751-1(g), Example 1(ii).

[131] *See* Prop. Reg. § 1.751-1(g), Example 3(ii).

[132] Prop. Reg. § 1.751-1(b)(3).

[133] Prop. Reg. § 1.751-1(g), Example 3(v).

Under the hot asset sale approach, the LLC may recharacterize the transaction as (i) a distribution to the member of his or her proportionate share of ordinary income assets, (ii) the sale of those assets back to the LLC for fair market value, resulting in ordinary income recognition to the distributee member, (iii) the contribution of the sales proceeds by the member back to the LLC, and (iv) the distribution of cash or other property to the member in liquidation of the member's membership interest.[134]

Under both methods, the distributee member recognizes the same amount of ordinary income. However, the LLC's tax basis in its properties, share of Section 704(c) built-in gain or loss, capital accounts, and certain other tax attributes may differ depending on the method used.

If the LLC maintains capital accounts in accordance with the safe-harbor regulations, and if the LLC owns any Section 751(b) property after the distribution, then the LLC must revalue all of its assets for capital account purposes. The capital accounts are revalued so that any built-in gain or loss in LLC property immediately after the distribution is allocated among the remaining members in the same manner as if the LLC made a taxable sale of the property for fair market value. The LLC must account for the book-up or book-down in capital accounts under one of three methods: the traditional method, the traditional method with curative allocations or the remedial allocation method. These methods are discussed at ¶805.07. If the LLC does not keep capital accounts in accordance with the safe-harbor regulations, it must determine each member's share of built-in gain or loss as if the LLC sold all of its assets for cash in a fully taxable transaction. The LLC must then make future allocations of LLC items in a manner that takes into account the built-in gain or loss.[135]

There is an anti-abuse rules that allows the IRS to recharacterize abusive transactions, and requires taxpayers to apply the rules consistently with the purposes of Section 751.[136]

¶1006 SECTION 754 ELECTION

.01 Overview

An LLC may make an election under Code Sec. 754 to adjust the basis of its assets upon distributions to members. This is similar to the basis adjustment when members in an LLC sell their membership interests or transfer their interests upon death. If the LLC makes a Section 754 election, then it must adjust the basis of its assets upon transfers of membership interests under Code Sec. 743 and distributions to members under Code Sec. 734.

The purposes of the basis adjustment are to prevent double taxation and to keep the members' adjusted bases in their membership interests (the outside bases) in line with the LLC's adjusted bases for its assets (the inside bases).

---

[134] Prop. Reg. § 1.751-1(g), Example 3(v).

[135] Prop. Reg. § 1.751-1(b)(2)(iv).

[136] Prop. Reg. § 1.751-1(b)(4).

An LLC that makes an election under Code Sec. 754 must make the following basis adjustments on distributions to members:

- *Money distributions in excess of basis.* A member recognizes gain on distribution of money in excess of the member's basis in the membership interest. The LLC must increase the basis of its assets by the amount of gain recognized by the member.[137] All of the increase must be allocated to capital assets (including Section 1231 property) because the member recognizes capital gain on the distribution.[138]

- *Money distributions that are less than basis.* A member recognizes loss on a distribution if (a) the distribution is in complete liquidation of the membership interest, (b) the member receives only cash and/or receivables and inventory items, and (c) the cash and the LLC's basis of any receivables and inventory items distributed to the member are less than the member's basis in the membership interest. The LLC must decrease the basis of its assets by the amount of loss recognized by the member.[139] All of the decrease must be allocated to capital assets (including Section 1231 property) because the member recognizes capital loss on the distribution.[140]

- *Substituted basis decrease.* A member may in certain cases receive a basis in distributed assets that is less than the LLC's basis in the assets immediately prior to the distribution. The LLC must increase the basis of its assets by the amount of basis decrease to the member.[141]

- *Substituted basis increase.* A member may receive a basis in distributed assets that is greater than the LLC's basis in the assets immediately prior to the distribution. This will occur only on a complete liquidation of the member's interest in the LLC. The LLC must decrease the basis of its assets by the amount of basis increase to the member.[142] If the LLC does not make a Section 754 election, the LLC must still decrease the basis of its assets if the member receives a basis increase of more than $250,000.[143]

- *Depreciation and bifurcated basis.* If the basis of property is increased as a result of the Section 754 election, then the increased portion of the basis must be taken into account as if it were newly purchased recovery property placed in service when the distribution occurs. Consequently, any applicable recovery period and method may be used to determine the depreciation for the increased portion of the basis. The LLC must separately list the Section 754 asset on its schedule of depreciable assets, and show the depreciation for the Section 754 asset. However, there is no change in determining the depreciation periods for the portion of the basis for which there is no increase. If the

---

[137] *See* ¶ 1006.02 *infra.*
[138] Reg. § 1.755-1(c)(1)(ii).
[139] *See* ¶ 1006.03 *infra.*
[140] Reg. § 1.755-1(c)(1)(ii).
[141] *See* ¶ 1006.04 *infra.*
[142] *See* ¶ 1006.05 *infra.*
[143] *See* ¶ 1009 *infra.*

basis of the property is decreased as a result of a Section 754 election, then the decrease in basis must be accounted for over the remaining depreciation period of the property beginning with the depreciation period in which the basis is decreased.[144]

.02 Money Distributions in Excess of Member's Adjusted Basis

A member recognizes gain if the member receives a distribution of money (cash plus debt relief) in excess of the member's adjusted basis in his membership interest.[145] The gain equals the amount by which the money distribution exceeds the adjusted basis.[146] The gain is normally capital gain. An LLC that makes a Section 754 election must increase the adjusted basis of its remaining assets by the amount of gain recognized to the distributee member.[147] The basis increase is allocated only to the capital gain property,[148] and Section 1231(b) assets.[149] The basis increase must be allocated first to capital gain properties with unrealized appreciation (up to the total amount of unrealized appreciation) in proportion to their respective amounts of unrealized appreciation. Any remaining basis increase must be allocated among the capital gain properties in proportion to their fair market values.[150]

EXAMPLE 10-17

An LLC makes an election under Section 754 to adjust the basis of its assets upon transfers of membership interests and distributions to members. The financial statements of the LLC show the following:

Asset	Adjusted Basis to LLC	Fair Market Value
Cash	$ 100,000	$ 100,000
Beach land	80,000	200,000
Desert land	120,000	100,000
	$300,000	$ 400,000
Liabilities		(100,000)
Net equity of LLC		$ 300,000

---

[144] Reg. § 1.7341(e).

[145] Code Sec. 731(a)(1).

[146] Code Sec. 731(a)(1).

[147] Code Sec. 734(b)(1)(A).

[148] Reg. § 1.755-1(c)(1)(ii), referring to distributions under Code Sec. 734(b)(1)(A), referring to gain recognized on money distributions in excess of outside basis under Code Sec. 731(a)(1).

[149] Reg. § 1.755-1(a) defines capital gain property to include Section 1231(b) property for purposes of these rules.

[150] Reg. § 1.755-1(c)(2)(i).

Member A has a one-tenth interest in the LLC. The adjusted basis of her membership interest is $30,000. The LLC makes a liquidating cash distribution to the member of $30,000. Member A recognizes capital gain of $10,000. The money distributed to the member is $40,000, consisting of the $30,000 cash and the $10,000 of debt relief. The money distribution exceeds the member's adjusted basis of $30,000 by $10,000 and is thus taxed as capital gain under Section 731(a)(1). The LLC must increase the basis of its remaining assets by the $10,000 of gain to the member upon distribution. All of this gain must be allocated to its remaining capital gain assets, which are the beach land and desert land. The basis adjustment must first be allocated to the capital gain property with unrealized appreciation. The beach land is the only capital gain assets that has a value in excess of its adjusted basis. The amount of the unrealized appreciation is more than the basis adjustment. Therefore, the entire $10,000 of basis adjustment must be added to the basis of the beach land. The LLC thus has an adjusted basis in the beach land of $90,000 and retains an adjusted basis in the desert land of $120,000.

.03 Money Distributions That Are Less Than Member's Adjusted Basis

A member recognizes loss in a distribution if all of the following occur:[151]

- there is a liquidating distribution;
- the member receives solely money, unrealized receivables, and/or inventory in the complete liquidation; and
- the cash and adjusted bases of such properties received in the liquidation are less than the member's adjusted basis in his membership interest.[152]

In this case, the LLC must decrease the basis of its remaining assets by the amount of the loss recognized by the member.[153] The basis decrease is allocated only to capital gain assets,[154] including Section 1231(b) assets.[155] The basis decrease must first be allocated to capital gain properties with unrealized depreciation (up to the total amount of unrealized depreciation) in proportion to their respective amounts of unrealized depreciation. Any remaining basis decrease must be allocated among the capital gain properties in proportion to their adjusted bases (after making the prior basis adjustment).[156]

---

[151] Code Sec. 731(a)(2).

[152] Code Sec. 731(a)(2).

[153] Code Sec. 734(b)(2)(A).

[154] Reg. § 1.755-1(c)(1)(ii), referring to distributions under Code Sec. 734(b)(2)(A) which referred to gain recognized on money distributions that are less than the member's outside basis under Code Sec. 731(a)(2).

[155] Reg. § 1.755-1(a) defines capital gain property to include Section 1231(b) property for purposes of these rules.

[156] Reg. § 1.755-1(c)(2)(ii).

EXAMPLE 10-18

An LLC makes an election under Section 754 to adjust the basis of its assets upon transfers of membership interests and distributions to members. The financial statements of the LLC show the following:

Asset	Adjusted Basis to LLC	Fair Market Value
Cash	$100,000	$ 100,000
Beach land	80,000	200,000
Desert land	120,000	100,000
	$300,000	$ 400,000
Liabilities		(100,000)
Net equity of LLC		$ 300,000

Member A has a one-tenth interest in the LLC. The adjusted basis of his membership interest is $30,000. The LLC makes a liquidating cash distribution to Member A of $10,000 in complete liquidation of the member's interest in the LLC. The amount of money distributed to the member is $20,000, consisting of the $10,000 cash distribution and the $10,000 of debt relief. The member recognizes a $10,000 capital loss, since the member received a money distribution in complete liquidation that was $10,000 less than the $30,000 adjusted basis in her membership interest immediately prior to the distribution. The basis adjustment must first be allocated to the capital gain property with unrealized depreciation. The desert land is the only capital gain asset that has a value below its adjusted basis. The amount of the unrealized depreciation is more than the basis adjustment. Therefore, the entire $10,000 of basis decrease must be allocated to the desert land. Thus, the LLC has an adjusted basis of $110,000 in the desert land, and retains an $80,000 basis in the beach land.

.04 Substituted Basis Decrease

An LLC must make a third basis adjustment when a member receives a distribution of property with an adjusted basis to the LLC that is greater than the member's basis in his membership interest. In this case, the member receives a substituted basis for the property equal to his lower basis in the membership interest rather than a carryover of the LLC's higher basis for the property. The LLC increases the basis of its remaining assets by the amount of the decrease in basis for the member.[157] The following two types of distributions result in a substituted basis decrease:

---

[157] Code Sec. 734(b)(1)(B).

1. *Nonliquidating distribution.* Normally, a member who receives property from an LLC in a nonliquidating distribution receives a carryover basis for the property equal to the LLC's adjusted basis for the property immediately prior to the distribution. However, the carryover basis cannot exceed the member's adjusted basis in his membership interest, reduced by any money received in the distribution. If the LLC's adjusted basis for the distributed assets exceeds the member's basis in his membership interest, then the basis for the assets is reduced to the member's basis in his membership interest.[158] The member then has a zero basis in his membership interest after the distribution.

2. *Liquidating distribution.* A member receives a substituted basis for property in a liquidating distribution. The cash and money part of the distribution first reduces the member's basis in his membership interest. The member's remaining basis is next allocated to inventory and unrealized receivables and then to capital gain property. If the LLC's adjusted basis for the distributed assets exceeds the member's basis in his membership interest, then the basis for the distributed assets is reduced to the member's basis in his membership interest.[159]

The LLC must allocate the basis increase to property of the same class that caused the basis decrease to the member upon distribution.[160] This is a two-step process. First, the LLC allocates the basis increase either to capital gain property or ordinary income property, depending on the class of property received by the member whose basis was adjusted. Thus, when the LLC's adjusted basis of distributed capital gain property immediately prior to the distribution exceeds the basis of such property to the distributee member, the basis of undistributed capital gain property remaining in the LLC is increased by an amount equal to the excess. Similarly, when the LLC's adjusted basis of distributed ordinary income property (inventory and unrealized receivables) immediately prior to the distribution exceeds the basis of such property to the distributee member, the basis of undistributed ordinary income property in the LLC is increased by an amount equal to the excess.[161]

Second, the LLC must allocate the basis increase within each class first to properties with unrealized appreciation (up to the total amount of unrealized appreciation) in proportion to their respective amounts of unrealized appreciation. Any remaining basis increase must be allocated among the LLC properties within the class in proportion to their fair market values.[162]

---

[158] Code Sec. 732(a)(2).

[159] Code Sec. 732(b).

[160] Reg. § 1.755-1(c)(1)(i).

[161] *Id.*

[162] Reg. § 1.755-1(c)(2)(i).

EXAMPLE 10-19

An LLC has four equal members. The financial statements of the LLC show the following:

Asset	Adjusted Basis to LLC	Fair Market Value
Cash	$ 60,000	$ 60,000
Beach land	40,000	30,000
Desert land	20,000	30,000
	$120,000	$120,000
Liabilities		$ 0
Member A's adjusted basis in LLC		$ 30,000

The LLC distributes the beach land to Member A in complete liquidation of the member's interest in the LLC. Although the beach land has an adjusted basis of $40,000 to the LLC, Member A takes a substituted basis in the property of $30,000. The basis of distributed property in a liquidating or nonliquidating distribution cannot exceed the member's remaining basis in her membership interest. Since no cash was received in the liquidation, Member A's basis in the distributed property is equal to her basis in the membership interest immediately prior to the distribution. If the LLC makes an election under Section 754 to adjust the basis of its assets, it must increase the basis of its remaining property by the amount of basis decrease to Member A. The $10,000 basis increase must be allocated to property that is similar to the distributed property. In this case, the desert land retained by the LLC is a Section 1221 capital asset, which is the same class of asset as the beach land. The fair market value of the desert land is $10,000 above the adjusted basis of the desert land. Therefore, the entire $10,000 basis increase must be allocated to the desert land. The LLC has a $30,000 adjusted basis in the desert land as a result of the Section 754 election.

EXAMPLE 10-20

An LLC makes an election under Section 754. The financial statements of the LLC are as follows:[163]

---

[163] This example is from Reg. § 1.755-1(c)(5).

Asset	Adjusted Basis	Fair Market Value
Capital Gain Property:		
Asset 1	$ 25,000	$ 75,000
Asset 2	100,000	117,500
Asset 3	50,000	60,000
Ordinary Income Property:		
Asset 4	$ 40,000	$ 45,000
Asset 5	50,000	60,000
Asset 6	10,000	2,500
Total	$275,000	$360,000

The LLC distributes Assets 3 and 5 to Member A in complete liquidation of Member A's membership interest. Member A had a basis in the membership interest of $75,000. The basis adjustment to the LLC is determined as follows:

Step 1: Determine the amount of basis increase to the LLC. Member A receives a basis for the property on liquidation equal to his $75,000 basis in the membership interest. Since the LLC had a $100,000 basis in the property prior to distribution, there is a $25,000 decrease in basis for the member. The LLC must therefore increase the basis of its assets by $25,000.

Step 2: Determine the class of asset that caused the basis decrease to the member on distribution. Member A's basis in the membership interest is first reduced by cash distributions. There are no cash distributions. Member A's basis in the membership interest is next allocated to ordinary income property (inventory and unrealized receivables) up to the LLC's adjusted basis in the assets under Code Sec. 732(c)(1)(A). Thus, Member A receives a $50,000 basis in Asset 5. Finally, Member A's remaining basis in the membership interest of $25,000 is allocated to the capital gain property under Code Sec. 732(c)(1)(B). Thus, Member A receives a $25,000 basis in Asset 3. The LLC had a $50,000 basis in the asset immediately prior to distribution. Therefore, the class of asset that caused the $25,000 basis decrease to the member on distribution was a capital gain asset.

Step 3: Allocate the basis increase between classes of LLC assets. Since the class of asset that caused the basis decrease to the member on distribution was a capital gain asset, the entire $25,000 basis increase for the LLC must be allocated to its remaining capital gain assets (Assets 1 and 2).

Step 4: Allocate the basis increase within the class of assets. The basis increase is first allocated among the LLC's remaining capital gain assets with unrealized appreciation (up to the total amount of unrealized appreciation) in proportion to their respective amounts of unrealized appreciation. Asset 1 has appreciated by $50,000. Asset 2 has appreciated by $17,500. The proportion of increase attributable to Asset 1 is approximately 74 percent ($50,000/$67,500). The proportion of increase attributable to Asset 2 is approximately 26 percent ($17,500/67,500). Therefore, the LLC must increase the basis of Asset 1 by $18,519 ($25,000 basis increase × 74%) and increase the basis of Asset 2 by $6,481 ($25,000 basis increase × 26%).

.05 Substituted Basis Increase

There are two potential basis adjustments if member receives a basis in distributed property that is higher than the LLC's basis in the property:

- An LLC must make a downward basis adjustment to its remaining properties if the LLC makes a Section 754 election, and if the member receives a substituted basis in distributed property that is greater than the LLC's basis in the property prior to the distribution.[164] These rules are discussed in this section.
- An LLC must make a mandatory downward basis adjustment to its remaining property if the member receives a substituted basis in distributed property that is $250,000 more than the LLC's basis in the property prior to the distribution.[165] This adjustment applies if the LLC has not made a Section 754 election. These rules are discussed at ¶ 1009.

A member receives a substituted basis increase for distributed property if the member's outside basis in the membership interest is higher than the LLC's basis in the distributed property. The substituted basis increase can occur only upon a complete liquidation of a member's interest in the LLC. It cannot occur in a partial liquidation.

In a complete liquidation, a member must first reduce the basis in his membership interest by the amount of money received in the liquidation. The member must then allocate outside basis to the inventory and unrealized receivables received in the distribution in an amount equal to the LLC's basis in such property, or the member's remaining outside basis if less.[166] The remaining part of the member's adjusted basis is allocated to the other property distributed in the complete liquidation. The member receives a higher basis in the distributed property if the member's remaining adjusted basis in his membership interest exceeds the LLC's adjusted basis in the distributed property immediately prior to the distribution.[167] In this event, the LLC must reduce the basis of its remaining assets by the amount of basis increase for the member.[168]

The LLC must allocate the basis decrease to property of the same class that caused the basis increase to the member on distribution. This is a two-step process. First, the LLC allocates the basis decrease either to capital gain property or ordinary income property, depending on the class of property received by the member whose

---

[164] Code Sec. 734(b)(2)(B).

[165] Code Sec. 734(a), (b), (d).

[166] *See* ¶ 1003.02 *supra.*

[167] Code Sec. 732(b).

[168] Code Sec. 734(b)(2)(B).

basis was adjusted. Thus, when the LLC's adjusted basis of distributed capital gain property immediately prior to the distribution is less than the basis of such property to the distributee member, the basis of undistributed capital gain property remaining in the LLC is reduced by the decrease in basis. Similarly, when the LLC's adjusted basis of distributed ordinary income property immediately prior to the distribution is less than the basis of such property to the distributee member, the basis of undistributed ordinary income property in the LLC is reduced by the decrease in basis.[169]

Second, the LLC must allocate the basis decrease within each class first to properties with unrealized depreciation (up to the total amount of unrealized depreciation) in proportion to their respective amounts of unrealized depreciation. Any remaining basis decrease must be allocated among the LLC properties within the class in proportion to their adjusted bases (after making the basis adjustment above).[170]

EXAMPLE 10-21

An LLC has four equal members. The financial statements of the LLC show the following:

Asset	Adjusted Basis to LLC	Fair Market Value
Cash	$ 60,000	$ 60,000
Beach land	40,000	30,000
Desert land	20,000	30,000
	$ 120,000	$120,000
Liabilities		$ 0
Member A's adjusted basis in LLC		$ 30,000

The LLC distributes the desert land to Member A in complete liquidation of the member's interest in the LLC. Since there is a complete liquidation and no cash distribution, Member A receives a basis in the desert land equal to her $30,000 adjusted basis in her membership interest rather than the LLC's $20,000 adjusted basis in the property immediately prior to the distribution. Since there is a $10,000 basis increase to the member, the LLC must decrease the remaining basis of its assets. The basis decrease must be allocated to its assets that are similar in character to the distributed asset. Since the fair market value of the beach property is $10,000 less than the LLC's adjusted basis in the property, the entire $10,000 downward adjustment must be allocated to the beach land. The LLC therefore has a $30,000 adjusted basis in the beach land, with a fair market value of $30,000.

---

[169] Reg. § 1.755-1(c)(1)(i).
[170] Reg. § 1.755-1(c)(2)(ii).

EXAMPLE 10-22

An LLC makes an election under Section 754. The financial statements of the LLC are as follows:[171]

Asset	Adjusted Basis to LLC	Fair Market Value
Capital Gain Property:		
Asset 1	$ 25,000	$ 75,000
Asset 2	100,000	90,000
Asset 3	50,000	60,000
Ordinary Income Property:		
Asset 4	$ 40,000	$ 45,000
Asset 5	50,000	60,000
Asset 6	10,000	2,500
Total	$275,000	$332,500

The LLC distributes Assets 3 and 5 to Member A in complete liquidation of Member A's membership interest. Member A had a basis in the membership interest of $215,000. The basis adjustment to the LLC is determined as follows:

Step 1: Determine the amount of basis increase to the LLC. Member A receives a basis for the property on liquidation equal to his $215,000 basis in the membership interest. Since the LLC had a $100,000 basis in the property prior to distribution, there is an $115,000 increase in basis for the member. The LLC must therefore decrease the basis of its assets by $115,000.

Step 2: Determine the class of asset that caused the basis increase to the member on distribution. Member A's basis in the membership interest is first reduced by cash distributions. There are no cash distributions. Member A's basis in the membership interest is next allocated to ordinary income property (inventory and unrealized receivables) up to the LLC's adjusted basis in the assets under Code Sec. 732(c)(1)(A). Thus, Member A receives a $50,000 basis in Asset 5. Finally, Member A's remaining basis in the membership interest of $165,000 is allocated to the capital gain property under Code Sec. 732(c)(1)(B). Thus, Member A receives a $165,000 basis in Asset 3. The LLC had a $50,000 basis in the asset immediately prior to distribution. Therefore, the class of asset that caused the $115,000 basis increase to the Member A on distribution was a capital gain asset.

Step 3: Allocate the basis decrease between classes of LLC assets. Since the class of asset that caused the basis increase to the member on distribution was a capital gain asset, the entire $115,000 basis decrease for the LLC must be allocated to its remaining capital gain assets (Assets 1 and 2).

---

[171] This example is from Reg. § 1.755-1(c)(5).

Step 4: Allocate the basis decrease within the class of assets. The $115,000 basis decrease is first allocated among the LLC's remaining capital gain assets with unrealized depreciation (up to the total amount of unrealized depreciation) in proportion to their respective amounts of unrealized depreciation. Asset 1 has appreciated by $50,000. Asset 2 has depreciated by $10,000. Thus, the first $10,000 of basis decrease is allocated to Asset 2 since it is the only capital gain asset that has unrealized appreciation. The basis of Asset 2 is reduced to $90,000 after this reduction. The remaining $105,000 of basis decrease is allocated to the capital gain assets in proportion to their adjusted bases, after taking into account the prior basis adjustment. The percentage of total basis attributable to Asset 1 is approximately 22 percent ($25,000/$115,000). The percentage of total basis attributable to Asset 2 is approximately 78 percent ($90,000/115,000). Therefore, the LLC must decrease the basis of Asset 1 by $23,100 ($105,000 basis decrease × 22%) and decrease the basis of Asset 2 by an additional $81,900 ($105,000 basis decrease × 78%). Asset 1 ends up with a basis of $1,900 ($25,000 − $23,100). Assets 2 ends up with the basis of $8,100 ($100,000 − $10,000 − $81,900).

.06 Tiered LLCs

A distribution from an upper-tier LLC results in a basis adjustment for property in a lower-tier partnership or LLC in which the upper-tier LLC has an interest only if both the upper-tier LLC and lower-tier LLC have made an election under Code Sec. 754.[172]

¶ 1007 SECTION 732(d) OPTIONAL BASIS ADJUSTMENT

Under Code Sec. 732(d), a member who purchased a membership interest without the benefit of a Section 754 election in effect, and within two years after the purchase receives a distribution of property from the LLC, may elect to treat the LLC tax basis of the distributed property as the tax basis that the property would have had if the LLC had made a Section 754 election.

A member may adjust the basis of distributed assets to the basis that the assets would have received if the LLC had made an election under Code Sec. 754 if:[173]

- The member acquires a membership interest by transfer from another member in a sale or exchange, or on the death of a member.
- The LLC did not have an election in effect under Code Sec. 754 at the time of the transfer.

---

[172] Rev. Rul. 92-15, 1992-1 CB 215.
[173] Code Sec. 732(d); Reg. § 1.732-1(d)(1).

- The member receives a liquidating or nonliquidating distribution of property within two years after acquiring the membership interest.
- The member files an appropriate election. The member must make the election with the return for the year of the distribution if the distributed property includes any depreciation, depletion, or amortization.[174] Otherwise, the member must make the election with the return for any taxable year no later than the first year in which the basis of any of the distributed property is relevant in determining taxable income.[175] The member must submit various items of information with the election. The member must state that he is electing to adjust the basis of property received in a distribution pursuant to Code Sec. 732(d). The member must also show the computation of the basis adjustment and the properties to which the adjustment has been allocated.[176]

Any property distributed to an estate of a deceased member within two years after the date of death receives a basis equal to its estate tax value.

The assigned basis is not reduced by any depreciation or depletion that would have been allowed or allowable if the LLC had previously chosen the optional adjustment.[177]

A member should make this election only if the election results in an increase in basis for the distributed assets.

EXAMPLE 10-23

Mary purchased a 25 percent interest in an LLC for $17,000 cash. At the time of the purchase, the LLC owned inventory with the basis of $14,000 and fair market value of $16,000. Thus, $4,000 of the purchase price (25% × $16,000 fair market value of inventory) was attributable to Mary's share of inventory with the basis to the LLC of $3,500. The LLC did not make a Code Sec. 754 election to step up the basis of its property. Within two years after acquiring her interest, Mary withdrew from the LLC and received cash of $1,500, inventory with a basis to the LLC of $3,500, and other property with a basis of $6,000. The value of the inventory received was 25 percent of the value of all LLC inventory. This inventory was not on hand when she acquired her interest. Since Mary withdrew from the LLC within two years, her share of LLC basis for the inventory is increased by $500 (25 percent of the $2,000 difference between the $16,000 fair market value of the inventory and its $14,000 basis to the LLC at the time she acquired her interest). The total outside basis allocated among the distributive properties is $15,500 ($17,000 outside basis less $1,500 cash received). Her basis in the inventory items is $4,000 ($3,500 LLC basis

---

[174] Reg. § 1.732-1(d)(2)(i).

[175] Reg. § 1.732-1(d)(2)(ii).

[176] Reg. § 1.732-1(d)(3)(i).

[177] IRS Publication 541, Partnerships, under the subheading, "Special adjustment to basis."

plus $500 special adjustment under Code Sec. 732(d)). The remaining outside basis of $11,500 is allocated to the other distributed property.[178]

¶ 1008 SECTION 732(d) REQUIRED BASIS ADJUSTMENT

A member must adjust the basis of distributed property if all of the following apply:[179]

- The member acquires the membership interest by transfer at a time when the LLC has not made an election to adjust the basis of its assets under Code Sec. 754.

- The fair market value of all LLC property, other than money, exceeds 110 percent of the LLC's adjusted basis of its assets at the time that the membership interest was acquired.

- If the LLC had made a liquidating distribution to the member immediately after the member's acquisition of the interest, there would have been a decrease in the basis of the property that could not be depreciated, amortized or depleted, and an increase in the basis of the properties that could be.[180]

- The Section 754 election, if it had been made by the LLC, would have changed the member's basis for the distributed property.

When the mandatory basis adjustment applies, the LLC must adjust the basis of its assets immediately before the distribution to reflect the basis that the distributed property would have received if the LLC had made a Section 754 election at the time that the member acquired the membership interest. As a result, the basis of the distributed property in the hands of the LLC immediately before the distribution more closely approximates its fair market value.

The purpose of this rule is to prevent distortions that might inflate the basis of depreciable, depletable, or amortizable property above its fair market value. Changes in the tax laws in 1997 make such distortions less likely to occur. As a result, the IRS has requested comments on the proper scope of Code Sec. 732(d) and under what circumstances, if any, the IRS should exercise its authority to mandate application of Code Sec. 732(d) to transferees.

---

[178] IRS Publication 541, Partnerships, Example under the subheading, "Special adjustment to basis."

[179] Code Sec. 732(d); Reg. § 1.732-1(d)(4).

[180] This determination of basis allocation is made under the general rules discussed in ¶ 1003.03 *supra*.

¶1009 MANDATORY BASIS ADJUSTMENT FOR BUILT-IN LOSS PROPERTY

.01 Distribution of Built-In Loss Property

An LLC must make a mandatory downward basis adjustment to its property if the member receives a substituted basis in distributed property that is at least $250,000 more than the LLC's basis in the property.[181] The $250,000 limitation applies to each member distributee separately, and to all properties distributed to the member as part of the same distribution.[182] The amount of the basis adjustment is equal to the difference between the basis of the property to the member after the distribution and the basis to the LLC immediately prior to the distribution.[183] The purpose of the rule is to prevent double deductions and double losses.

This rule applies only if the LLC makes a liquidating distribution to a member. A member receives a substituted basis in distributed property in a liquidating distribution. The member's basis in the distributed property is the same as the member's basis in the membership interest immediately prior to the distribution, reduced by any money received.[184] This differs from the basis rules for a nonliquidating distribution in which the member receives a carryover basis, rather than a substituted basis.

EXAMPLE 10-24

An LLC purchases a building for $1 million. It takes $1 million of depreciation on the building, resulting in an adjusted basis of $0 for the building. The LLC distributes the building to John in a liquidating distribution. The LLC does not make an election under Section 754. John had a basis in his membership interest of $1 million immediately prior to the distribution. John receives a basis in the distributed property of $1 million, which is equal to his outside basis in the membership interest immediately prior to the distribution. John can then take another $1 million of depreciation deductions on the building after the distribution.

Since John receives a substituted basis in distributed property that is $250,000 more than the LLC's basis in the property, the LLC must make a Section 734(b) downward basis adjustment to its remaining property. The amount of the downward basis adjustment is $1 million, which is the amount by which John's substituted basis exceeds the LLC's basis in the property immediately prior to the distribution.

---

[181] Code Secs. 734(a), (b)(2)(B) and (d); Prop. Reg. § 1.734-2(c).

[182] Prop. Reg. § 1.734-1(a)(2)(i).

[183] Code Sec. 734(b)(2)(B).

[184] Code Sec. 732(d).

.02 Contribution of Built-In Loss Property

An LLC must make a mandatory basis adjustment under Code Sec. 704(c)(1)(C) if a member contributes property to an LLC with built-in losses. The LLC's tax basis in the property with respect to the noncontributing members may not exceed the fair market value of the property on the date of contribution. The LLC's tax basis in the property with respect to the contributing member is increased by the amount of built-in loss associated with the contributed property. This is called a "Code Section 704(c)(1)(C) basis adjustment" under proposed regulations. When the LLC distributes the property to a noncontributing member, the Section 704(c)(1)(C) basis adjustment for that property disappears. However, the contributing member keeps the Section 704(c)(1)(C) basis adjustment by reallocating it to other LLC property.[185] This rule prevents an LLC from shifting pre-contribution losses to noncontributing members by distributing the built-in loss property to the noncontributing members. The basis adjustment under Code Sec. 704(c)(1)(C) is discussed at ¶ 806.

¶ 1010 DISTRIBUTIONS TO RETIRING AND DECEASED MEMBERS

.01 Generally

Code Sec. 736 governs the classification of payments to retiring members and successors in interest of deceased members. Section 736 deals only with the classification of those payments. Once the payments are classified, other LLC tax rules govern the income recognition, basis, timing, and other tax aspects of the distribution.

Section 736 governs liquidating payments to a member if all the following apply:[186]

- The payment is to a retiring member or to the successor in interest of a deceased member. Section 736 does not apply if the member is retiring, but continues to work on part-time basis.[187]

- The payment is made in complete liquidation of the member's interest in the LLC. Section 736 does not apply if the member sells his membership interest to another member.[188] A liquidating distribution includes a series of distributions made in one or more years as long as the member's entire interest is ultimately terminated.[189] A member who retires from an LLC for state law purposes is still considered a member for income tax purposes if he or she is entitled to receive any distributions from the LLC after the date of retire-

---

[185] The Section 704(c)(1)(C) basis adjustment is reallocated to other LLC property in accordance with the rules set forth in Reg. § 1.755-1(c).

[186] Reg. § 1.736-1(a).

[187] Reg. § 1.736-1(a).

[188] Reg. § 1.736-1(a)(1)(i).

[189] Reg. § 1.761-1(d).

ment.[190] However, a series of payments that will ultimately result in the liquidation of a member's entire interest in the LLC will be treated as payment in retirement of the member's interest and will be characterized under Code Sec. 736, rather than under other sections of the Internal Revenue Code.[191]

- The LLC continues to exist after the liquidating payment. Section 736 does not apply if the LLC completely liquidates.[192] However, Section 736 may apply if the LLC liquidates the interest of one member in a two-member LLC.[193] The LLC continues for federal tax purposes as long as the Section 736 payments are made to the withdrawing member.

If Section 736 applies, then liquidating distributions are taxed under either Section 736(a) or 736(b), depending on the character of the payment.

.02 Types of Section 736 Payments

The first step in determining the taxation of distributions to a retiring or deceased member is to classify the payment. There are several different types of payments that a retiring or deceased member may receive from an LLC.

The first type of payment is a distributive share of income for the year and any guaranteed payments under the operating agreement. These payments are taxed as Section 736(a) payments. The payment is taxed as a distributive share of LLC income if the amount is based on LLC income.[194] The payment is taxed as a guaranteed payment if the amount is not based on LLC income.[195] Distributive shares of income are normally ordinary income to the retiring member and reductions in taxable income to the remaining members.[196] Guaranteed payments for services are ordinary income to the retiring member and deductible payments by the LLC.[197]

The second type of payment that a retiring member may receive from an LLC is a payment in exchange for his or her interest in property of the LLC, including capital account, inventory, goodwill, and unrealized receivables. These payments are taxed as income payments under Section 736(a) or property distributions under Section 736(b) depending on the classification of the member and the type of LLC.

---

[190] Reg. § 1.736-1(a)(1)(ii).

[191] Reg. § § 1.731-1(c)(1)(i), 1.761-1(d).

[192] Reg. § 1.736-1(a)(1)(i).

[193] Reg. § 1.736-1(a)(6).

[194] Reg. § 1.736-1(a)(4).

[195] Reg. § 1.736-1(a)(3). IRS Publication 541, Partnerships, under the heading and subheading, "Liquidation at Partner's Retirement or Death/Other payments."

[196] The payment retains the same character when reported by the member that it would have had if reported by the LLC. *See* IRS Publication 541, Partnerships, under the heading and subheading, "Liquidation at Partner's Retirement or Death/Other payments." This is normally ordinary income since Section 736 only applies when the LLC is a service LLC, and the retiring or deceased member is a "general partner" of the LLC.

[197] Reg. § 1.736-1(a)(4).

If the member is classified as a general partner in a service LLC in which capital is not a material income producing factor,[198] then the LLC (i) must classify payments for the member's interest in cash-method accounts receivable as Section 736(a) income payments, (ii) may elect to classify payments for the member's interest in goodwill as Section 736(a) income payments or Section 736(b) property distributions, and (iii) must classify the member's interest in all other property as Section 736(b) property distributions.[199] These distribution rules are discussed at ¶ 1010.05.

If the member is classified as a limited partner in the LLC, or if capital is a material income producing factor, then distributions to a retiring or deceased member are taxed as Section 736(b) property distributions.[200] The LLC does not receive a deduction for the distribution to the member. The member recognizes gain to the extent that a money distribution exceeds the member's basis in the membership interest. These distribution rules are discussed at ¶ 1010.03 (for LLCs in which capital is a material income producing factor) and at ¶ 1010.04 (for service LLCs in which the member is treated as a limited partner).

The valuation placed by the members on the member's interest in LLC property in an arm's length agreement will normally be regarded as correct.[201]

.03 LLCs in Which Capital Is Material Income-Producing Factor

The first type of LLC is an LLC in which capital is a material income-producing factor. All of the payments to the retiring or deceased member in exchange for the member's interest in accounts receivable, inventory, capital account, and other property of the LLC are treated as Section 736(b) property distributions,[202] and taxed under the regular Code provisions governing liquidating distributions. The main Code provisions are as follows:

- *Code Sec. 731(b)*—The LLC does not receive a deduction for the payment to the member.[203]
- *Code Sec. 731(a)(1)*—The member recognizes gain to the extent that a money distribution exceeds the basis of the member's interest in the LLC. The member is taxed in the year the payments are made.[204] The member recovers his or her entire basis before incurring any capital gain. However, if the total distribution amount is fixed and paid in installments, the retiring member may elect to recover basis and recognize capital gain on a *pro rata* basis. The

---

[198] Code Sec. 736(b)(3).

[199] Code Sec. 736(b)(2).

[200] Code Sec. 736(b)(1).

[201] Reg. § 1.736-1(b)(1); Elwood R. Milliken, 72 TC 256 (1979), *aff'd unpub. opinion* (1st Cir. 1980).

[202] Code Secs. 736(b)(1), 736(b)(3)(A). Under the Revenue Reconciliation Act of 1993, Code Sec. 736(a), (b)(2) and (3) do not apply to liquidating payments made to members of an LLC who are classified as limited partners, or who are general partners in an LLC in which capital is a material income-producing factor, effective for liquidating distributions to retiring and deceased members after January 15, 1993.

[203] Reg. § 1.736-1(a)(2).

[204] Reg. § 1.736-1(a)(5).

member must attach a statement of the election to his or her return for the first year in which the payment is received.[205] There is no gain recognition as a result of a property distribution.

- *Code Sec. 731(a)(2)*—The member recognizes loss if three conditions are met. First, the member must receive only cash, unrealized receivables, or inventory. Second, the member must receive a liquidating distribution of his entire membership interest. Third, the adjusted basis of LLC assets distributed to the member must be less than the member's basis in his membership interest. The loss recognized is the amount by which the basis in the membership interest exceeds the money and the LLC's basis in unrealized receivables and inventory items distributed to the member. This differs from the rule for nonliquidating distributions in which no loss is recognized.

- *Code Secs. 741 and 731(a)*—The gain or loss recognized is capital gain or loss,[206] except as provided under Code Sec. 751(b).[207]

- *Code Sec. 751(b)*—A portion of the member's gain is recharacterized as ordinary income to the extent of the member's share of unrealized receivables, depreciation recapture, and substantially appreciated inventory items[208] retained by the LLC (hot assets).[209] A member does not recognize ordinary income if the member receives a distribution of hot assets that is exactly equal to the member's share of unrealized receivables and substantially appreciated inventory items.[210] The LLC may step up the basis of its assets by the amount of ordinary income realized by the member.[211]

---

[205] Reg. § 1.736-1(b)(6). If the election is made, the member recognizes capital loss if he or she does not recover the full amount of basis in the membership interest (e.g., because the expected payments were not received in full).

[206] Code Secs. 731(a) (last sentence), 741.

[207] *See* ¶ 1005 *supra*.

[208] Reg. § 1.736-1(b)(4). Inventory is substantially appreciated if its fair market value exceeds the adjusted basis by more than 120 percent. Code Sec. 751(b)(3)(A).

[209] Under Code Sec. 751(b), a member will recognize ordinary income or loss, or capital gain or loss, if the member does not receive his proportionate share of unrealized receivables, substantially appreciated inventory items, and other property in a distribution. In that case, the member is treated as having received a proportionate distribution of all assets, and as selling back to the LLC the excess assets retained by the LLC in exchange for the excess assets retained by the member. Reg. § 1.732-1(e). Gain on the deemed sale back to the LLC will be ordinary income if the member retains a disproportionate share of capital assets, and the LLC retains a disproportionate share of unrealized receivables and substantially appreciated inventory items. In that case, the member will be treated as having received his proportionate share of the unrealized receivables and inventory items, and as having sold them back to the LLC. Ordinary income is the difference between the fair market value of the capital assets being purchased from the LLC less the adjusted basis of unrealized receivables and inventory items deemed distributed to the member in excess of his proportionate share sold back to the LLC. Gain on the deemed sale back to the LLC will be treated as capital gain if a member receives a disproportionately large share of unrealized receivables and inventory items. In that case, the member will be treated as having received his proportionate share of capital assets and as having sold back to the LLC such capital assets in exchange for the unrealized receivables and inventory items retained by him in excess of his proportionate share.

[210] Reg. §§ 1.751-1(b)(2)(ii)-(iii), (3)(ii)-(iii).

[211] *See* ¶ 1005.02 *supra*.

- *Code Sec. 732(b)*—The member receives a basis in the distributed property equal to his or her basis in the membership interest, reduced by any money distributed. The basis is first allocated to the unrealized receivables and inventory items in an amount equal to the LLC's basis in those assets. Any remaining basis in the membership interest is allocated to the other properties received in the distribution.[212] This is a substituted basis.

- *Code Sec. 735(b)*—The member's holding period for the distributed property includes the LLC's holding period for the property,[213] except for the amount attributable to unrealized receivables and substantially appreciated inventory items.

- *Code Secs. 1245, 1250*—There is no depreciation recapture with respect to the assets distributed to the member.[214]

- *Code Sec. 754*—If the LLC makes an election under Code Sec. 754, it must adjust the basis of its assets under Code Sec. 734. It must increase the basis of its assets by the amount of gain recognized by the member on distribution, and by the amount of any basis decrease in assets to the member as a result of the substituted basis rules for distributed property. It must decrease the basis of its assets by any loss recognized by the member, and by the amount of any basis increase in assets to the member as a result of the substituted basis rules for distributed property.

EXAMPLE 10-25

Harry, Ralph, and Jill are partners in Everett LLC. The LLC's assets consist of stock and land held for investment. Additionally, the LLC has a liability that is secured by the land. The LLC agrees to retire Harry's interest by means of equal cash payments over a period of five years. Harry will remain liable for his share of the LLC's liability until the he receives his last payment. Since this is a capital intensive partnership, the LLC will treat the payments under the general distribution rules. Harry will take these 736(b) payments into account in each tax year in which the payments are made. Under Code Sec. 731(a)(1), he will report any gain as capital gain only after he has recovered his basis.[215]

---

[212] Code Sec. 732(c)(1).

[213] Ltr. Rul. 200204005.

[214] Code Sec. 1245(b)(3) provides that if the basis in the hands of the transferee is determined by the basis in the hands of the transferor, then there is no depreciation recapture. The distributee member receives a substituted basis, rather than a carryover basis, for Section 1245 property. However, Code Sec. 1245(b)(6)(A) provides that the basis of Section 1245 property distributed by an LLC is deemed to have a basis determined by reference to the basis of assets in hands of the LLC. Thus, there is no depreciation recapture. Similar rules apply to Section 1250 real property. Code Sec. 1250(b)(3), (b)(6)(A).

[215] Partnership—Audit Technique Guide—Chapter 7, Dispositions of Partnership Interest (Rev. 3/2008), Example 7-1.

EXAMPLE 10-26

Harry, Ralph, and Jill are partners in Adelphi Plumbing Supply LLC, which is a capital intensive partnership. The assets of the LLC consist entirely of cash, unrealized receivables, and non-appreciated inventory. The LLC agrees to retire Harry's interest in LLC property by means of equal cash payments over a period of ten years. Harry will take these Code Sec. 736(b) payments into account in his taxable year in which the payments are made. Because the unrealized receivables are "hot assets" for purposes of Code Sec. 751, Harry and the LLC will first treat payments for such assets as distributions under Code Sec. 751(b). Harry will treat the remainder of the payments under the regular distribution rules of Code Sec. 731(a)(1) and, thus, will report any gain as capital gain only after he has recovered his basis.[216]

.04 Service LLC in Which Member Treated as Limited Partner

The second type of LLC is a service LLC in which the retiring or deceased member is classified as a limited partner. All of the payments to the retiring or deceased member in exchange for the member's interest in accounts receivable, inventory, capital account, and other property of the LLC are treated as Section 736(b) property distributions,[217] and are taxed under the regular Code provisions governing liquidating distributions. These are the same Code provisions that apply to LLCs in which capital is a material income-producing factor, and are discussed above.[218] Generally, the LLC does not receive a deduction for the payments. The member is not taxed on distributions except to the extent that money distributions exceed the member's basis in the membership interest.

A service LLC is an LLC in which capital is not a material income-producing factor. Substantially all of the income of the LLC must consist of fees, commissions, or other compensation for personal services by individuals. The practice of a profession by a doctor, dentist, lawyer, architect, or accountant is treated as a service LLC, even though the service provider may have a substantial capital investment in professional equipment or in the premises.[219]

The IRS has not yet issued regulations addressing when a member in an LLC is a general or limited partner for Section 736 purposes. Members who do not actively

---

[216] Partnership—Audit Technique Guide—Chapter 7, Dispositions of Partnership Interest (Rev. 3/2008), Example 7-2.

[217] Code Secs. 736(b)(1), 736(b)(3)(B).

[218] See ¶ 1010.03 *supra.*

[219] H. Rept. No. 103-111, Pub. L. No. 103-66, pp. 782-783.

participate in a service LLC are limited partners. Regulations under other sections of the Code indicate that all members of an LLC are limited partners.[220]

.05 Service LLC in Which Member Treated as General Partner

The third type of LLC is a service LLC in which the retiring or deceased member is treated as a general partner. In this case, the LLC must classify the payments for the member's interest in accounts receivable as Section 736(a) income payments. It may elect to classify payments for the member's interest in goodwill as either Section 736(a) income payments or Section 736(b) property distributions. It must classify payments for the member's interest in all other property as Section 736(b) property distributions.

The parties may determine the order and timing of taxable and nontaxable distributions,[221] although distributions are often made in the following order:

Accounts Receivable

The retiring member first reports the distribution as a distribution of the member's share of unrealized receivables of the LLC. After the Tax Reconciliation Act of 1993, unrealized receivables are generally limited to cash basis accounts receivable and unbilled work in process.[222] Payments for unrealized receivables in excess of the LLC's basis in the receivables[223] must be characterized under Section 736(a) as a distributive share of income or a guaranteed payment deductible by the LLC.[224] The member reports taxable income on this amount. The taxable income is based on the fair market value of the member's share of the unrealized receivables. This may be only 30 to 40 percent of the face amount of the receivables, since that is usually the maximum amount that an outside third party would pay for unsecured receivables.

In practice, retiring members often do not report their share of unrealized receivables because it is difficult to determine the member's share of receivables and to value those receivables on a fair market value basis. When an LLC does assign receivables to a retiring member, the LLC usually issues a Schedule K-1 to the member as it collects and distributes the receivables to the member.

---

[220] See, e.g., ¶ 1304.03 infra regarding LLC members as limited partners under the passive loss rules.

[221] See discussion of this issue in BNA Daily Tax Reporter, No. 208, Partnership Redemption Timing Flexible if IRS Still Gets Paid, p. G-5 (Oct. 27, 2016).

[222] Code Secs. 736(b)(2)(A), 751(c) (last paragraph). Depreciation recapture and other ordinary income items defined in Code Sec. 751(c) are not treated as unrealized receivables for purposes of Section 736 but are instead treated as Section 736(b) payments. However, a liquidating cash distribution to the member attributable to depreciation recapture and the other ordinary income items may trigger ordinary income to the member and a step-up in basis to the LLC under Code Sec. 751(b).

[223] Reg. § 1.736-1(b)(2).

[224] Reg. § 1.736-1(a)(3), (4). A fixed payment for the member's share of unrealized receivables is a guaranteed payment. A payment that is contingent on future income of the LLC is a distributive share of income.

Capital Account, Inventory, and Other Assets

The member next reports the payments as a distribution of the member's interest in other LLC property. This property includes cash, inventory, capital assets, tangible property, and all other assets except for goodwill. The payments often correspond to the member's capital account balance.[225] These payments are classified as Section 736(b) payments.

Payments that are characterized as distributions in exchange for a member's interest in LLC property are treated as payments in complete liquidation of the member's interest in the LLC.[226] The member recognizes gain to the extent that the amount received exceeds his adjusted basis in the LLC property.[227] Gain recognized is normally considered gain from the sale or exchange of a capital asset.[228] Therefore, if the member held the membership interest for more than one year, the gain would be a long-term capital gain.[229] The remaining members would not receive a deduction.[230]

If the LLC has substantially appreciated inventory, and makes a cash-out distribution to a retiring member, then part of the member's gain on distribution will be recharacterized as ordinary income. The amount of ordinary income is generally equal to the member's percentage interest in the LLC multiplied by the potential income from sale of the substantially appreciated inventory.[231]

Goodwill

The member must report any remaining distribution as a payment in exchange for the member's interest in goodwill. The LLC may classify the goodwill payments as either Section 736(a) income payments or Section 736(b) property distributions. The rules are as follows:

- If there is no provision in the operating agreement providing for the payment of goodwill, payments by a service LLC to the retiring or deceased member in exchange for the member's interest in goodwill in excess of the LLC's basis in the goodwill are Section 736(a) income payments.[232] The LLC may deduct the payment.[233] An LLC that wants to classify goodwill payments under Section

---

[225] *Wallis v. Comm'r*, TC Memo 2009-243 (2009).

[226] *Wallis v. Comm'r*, 2010-2 USTC ¶50,766, 106 AFTR 2d 2010-5755 (11th Cir. 2010), *citing* Code Secs. 731, 732 and 751; Reg. § 1.736-1(a)(2).

[227] *Wallis v. Comm'r*, 2010-2 USTC ¶50,766, 106 AFTR 2d 2010-5755 (11th Cir. 2010), *citing* Code Sec. 731(a)(1).

[228] *Wallis v. Comm'r*, 2010-2 USTC ¶50,766, 106 AFTR 2d 2010-5755 (11th Cir. 2010), *citing* Code Secs. 731(a), 741.

[229] *Wallis v. Comm'r*, 2010-2 USTC ¶50,766, 106 AFTR 2d 2010-5755 (11th Cir. 2010), *citing* Code Sec. 1222(3).

[230] *Wallis v. Comm'r*, 2010-2 USTC ¶50,766, 106 AFTR 2d 2010-5755 (11th Cir. 2010), *citing* Reg. § 1.736-1(a)(2).

[231] Reg. § 1.751-1(b)(4)(ii).

[232] Code Sec. 736(b)(2)(B); Reg. § 1.736-1(b)(3).

[233] Reg. § 1.736-1(a)(4).

736(a) should have no collateral agreements among the members referring to goodwill. The agreements should provide that the payments will be taxed under Section 736(a). If the LLC has a basis in the goodwill as a result of an acquisition or Section 736(b) basis adjustment, the payment is a Section 736(b) property distribution to the extent of basis.[234]

- The parties may instead classify all goodwill payments as Section 736(b) property distributions. The parties may make this "election" simply by including a provision in the operating agreement that provides for a payment to the retiring or deceased member for goodwill.[235] The parties may amend the operating agreement to provide for goodwill payments at any time prior to the due date for the tax return, not including extensions, for the year in which the member dies or withdraws from the LLC.[236] A collateral agreement among the members specifying that a payment is for goodwill is also effective to qualify the payment as a Section 736(b) payment.[237] The amount allocated to goodwill must be reasonable.[238]

- The LLC may make a Section 754 election. If the LLC makes this election, the LLC may step up the basis of its assets under Section 734(b) by the amount of goodwill payments received by the member in excess of the member's basis in the LLC. The basis step-up is equal to the capital gain recognized by the member. The LLC can amortize the step-up in basis over a period of 15 years.[239] The Section 754 election applies only to goodwill payments that are classified as Section 734(b) property distributions.

---

[234] Reg. § 1.736-1(b)(3).

[235] Code Sec. 736(b)(2)(B); Reg. § 1.736-1(b)(3).

[236] Code Sec. 761(c).

[237] *Jackson Inv. Co. v. Comm'r*, 346 F.2d 187 (9th Cir. 1965), *nonacq.*, 1967-2 CB 4.

[238] Reg. § 1.736-1(b)(3). An arm's-length agreement between the parties regarding the value of goodwill will generally be respected. *See also Smith v. Comm'r*, 37 TC 1033, *aff'd*, 313 F.2d 16 (10th Cir. 1962) which determined that an agreement between the liquidating partner and partnership was controlling with respect to whether a payment was for goodwill.

[239] Code Sec. 197(b)(9)(E); Reg. §§ 1.197-2(c)(1), (g)(3). The complex provisions of the Code and regulations are summarized by the Committee Report on Pub. L. No. 103-66, Omnibus Budget Reconciliation Act of 1993, as follows:

> As discussed more fully below, the bill also changes the treatment of payments made on liquidation of the interest of a deceased or retired partner in exchange for goodwill. Except in the case of payments made on retirement or death of a general partner of a partnership for which capital is not a material income-producing factor, such payments will not be treated as a distribution of partnership income. Under the bill, however, if the partnership makes an election under section 754, section 734 will generally provide the partnership the benefit of a stepped-up basis for the retiring or deceased partner's share of partnership goodwill and an amortization deduction for the increase in basis under section 197.

The Committee Report also makes clear that the anti-churning rules will not disallow the step-up in basis and amortization of goodwill, stating, "In addition, in determining whether the anti-churning rules apply with respect to any increase in the basis of partnership property under section 732, 734, or 743 of the Code, the determinations are to be made at the partner level and each partner is to be treated as having owned or used the partner's proportionate share of partnership property. Thus, for example, the anti-churning rules do not apply to any increase in the basis of partnership property that

EXAMPLE 10-27

Bill is a member of the Aurora LLC, which is an accounting firm (a service partnership). The LLC agrees to retire Bill by paying him one-third of the LLC's income for three years. Bill stops working in the LLC, but for purposes of Code Sec. 736, he is still considered to be a partner until his interest is completely liquidated. The LLC's assets consist solely of unrealized receivables and goodwill. The operating agreement does not state that any of the payments are for the goodwill. Because the payments are determined with regard to LLC income, they must be treated under Code Sec. 736(a)(1) as Bill's distributive share of income. In effect, this provides a deduction for the remaining members of the LLC. Bill will include the income in his taxable year with or within which ends the LLC tax year for which the payment is a distributive share.[240]

.06 Timing of Income Recognition

If a retiring member receives a series of payments over more than one tax year, the parties must make a determination as to whether and to what extent each payment is a Section 736(a) or a Section 736(b) payment. The parties may provide for a reasonable manner of apportioning the payments in the operating agreement. If the operating agreement does not so provide, then the apportionment is calculated based on a ratio set forth in the regulations.[241]

The Section 736(a) portion of each payment is taxed on receipt.[242] The timing of gain or loss recognition for Section 736(b) payments is determined under Code Sec. 731,[243] which generally defers the reporting of gain until the member's entire basis has been recovered,[244] and defers the recognition of loss at least until all distributions have been made.[245]

If the Section 736 payments are not fixed, all payments received are treated as Section 736(b) payments to the extent of the fair market value of the retiring member's interest in LLC property. The remainder is treated as a Section 736(a) payment.[246] A retired member may instead elect to apportion a part of the total gain or loss among the installment payments by allocating a portion of the basis to the

---

(Footnote Continued)

occurs upon the acquisition of an interest in the partnership that has made a section 754 election if the person acquiring the partnership interest is not related to the person selling the partnership interest."

[240] Partnership—Audit Technique Guide—Chapter 7, Dispositions of Partnership Interest (Rev. 3/2008), Example 7-3.

[241] Reg. § 1.736-1(b)(5)(i).

[242] Reg. § 1.736-1(a)(5).

[243] Reg. § 1.736-1(b)(6).

[244] Reg. § § 1.736-1(b)(6), 1.731-1(a)(1).

[245] Code Sec. 731(a)(2).

[246] See Reg. § 1.736-1(b)(5)(ii).

total amount payable under Code Sec.736(b). The election must be made on the retiring member's tax return for the first taxable year in which the member receives a Section 736(b) payment.[247]

If any portion of the Section 736 payments is attributable to Section 751(b) property (unrealized receivables and inventory), then the retired member's interest in the Section 751 property is treated as distributed to him and sold back to the LLC. Therefore, the gain or loss attributable to these payments is reported as a gain or loss on the sale or exchange of property.[248]

Thus, the general rule is that Section 736(b) payments are reported according to a cash-basis, cost-recovery method of accounting, regardless of the method of accounting of the LLC or of the member receiving the payments.

EXAMPLE 10-28

A retired member is scheduled to receive $500 in five annual installments of $100 each in liquidation of his interest in Section 736(b) property, none of which is Section 751 property. The member's basis in his membership interest is $200. Under the general cost-recovery rule, the retired member would recover his entire basis after the second $100 installment, and the remaining three installments would constitute taxable gain in their entirety. If, on the other hand, he elected to apportion the gain among the installments, $40 of each liquidating installment would be treated as basis recovery, computed as follows: $200 (the adjusted basis in the membership interest) divided by the five payments. The $60 balance of each installment would be taxable gain, computed as follows: $100 (the amount of each installment) less $40 portion allocable to basis.[249]

If a Section 754 election has been made, the LLC must step-up the basis of its remaining assets under Section 734(b) to the extent that the Section 736(b) payments to the retiring member exceed his or her outside basis. The LLC must decrease the basis in its remaining assets to the extent that the member's outside basis exceeds the Section 736(b) payments, or if there is a substantial basis reduction,[250] whether or not a Section 754 election has been made.[251]

---

[247] *See* Reg. § 1.736-1(b)(7) for examples.

[248] Reg. § 1.736-1(b)(6).

[249] Example from California Franchise Tax Board, Partnership Technical Manual ¶ 6630 (interpreting federal law).

[250] *See* ¶ 1009 *supra.*

[251] IRS Audit Technique Guide—Partnerships, Chapter 7, under the heading, "Treatment of Cash Liquidating Payments Made Over Several Years."

.07 Death of a Member

There is a termination of an LLC whenever there is a sale or exchange of 50 percent or more of the membership interests in the LLC during any 12-month period.[252] The death of a member does not ordinarily result in a termination of the LLC. The reason is that a disposition by gift, bequest or inheritance is not a sale or exchange.[253] Thus, if a member dies, the tax year of the LLC closes only with respect to the deceased member's interest.[254] The deceased member's share of income, losses, deductions and credits from the beginning of the LLC tax year to the date of the member's death are included in the member's final income tax return.

The person named in the operating agreement as the successor member in the event of death is recognized as the successor for federal income tax purposes.[255] The amount includible in the gross income of a successor in interest of a deceased member under Section 736(a) is income in respect of a decedent under Section 691.[256]

LLC sometimes have a buy-sell agreement that specifies the buyout price on the death of the member. Ordinarily, the sale of an LLC interest by a successor-in interest owning 50 percent or more of the capital and profits of the LLC within a 12-month period will cause the LLC to terminate.[257] The LLC will close with respect to the deceased member. The estate of the deceased member and the new member must each include in income their proportionate shares of LLC income, loss, deductions and credits.[258]

Suspended passive activity losses are deductible on the decedent's final return. However, the amount of the deductible suspended loss is reduced by the amount by which the basis of the membership interest to the successor (stepped-up basis) exceeds the adjusted basis of the membership interest to the deceased member immediately before death.[259] If as a result of this provision, any part of the suspended passive activity loss is not allowed on the decedent's final return, it is extinguished and will not be allowed to anyone.[260]

The basis of the LLC interest to the successor is the fair market value as of the date of death or alternate valuation date.[261] The basis is reduced by LLC items constituting income in respect of a decedent and increased by the successor's share of liabilities as of the date of death or alternate valuation date.[262] The LLC must step-up or step-down the basis of its assets if it has made a Section 754 election and

---

[252] Code Sec. 708(b).

[253] Reg. § 1.708-1(b)(2).

[254] Code Sec. 706(c)(2)(A).

[255] Reg. § 1.706-1(c)(3)(ii).

[256] Code Sec. 753.

[257] Code Sec. 708(b).

[258] Reg. § 1.706-1(c)(3)(iv), (vi), Example (2).

[259] Code Sec. 469(g)(2).

[260] Code Sec. 469(g)(2)(B).

[261] Code Secs. 742, 1014(a).

[262] Reg. § 1.742-1.

distributes property other than cash.[263] There is normally no basis adjustment if the LLC distributes cash in payment of the member's interest in property and capital account since the member receives a step-up or step-down in basis to fair market value as of the date of death.

.08 Allocations Among Categories

An LLC and a withdrawing member should make an allocation among the three categories of property (accounts receivable, goodwill and other property). The IRS will ordinarily respect the valuation that the parties place on a member's interest in the LLC that was negotiated in an arm's-length agreement.[264] The courts may value a withdrawing member's interest in the LLC if the parties do not value the withdrawing member's interest.[265]

.09 Redemption or Sale of Interest

There are different tax consequences if a terminated member sells his membership interest to one or more remaining members, or to the LLC in a redemption. The differences include the following:

1. *Gain on sale.* The gain on the sale of the membership interest in each case is the difference between the amount realized and the departing member's tax basis in the membership interest. However, in an LLC redemption, the LLC and the member have more flexibility in characterizing some of the payments as Section 736(a) income payments rather than Section 736(b) property distributions. The Section 736(a) payments in a redemption are taxed to the member as a guaranteed payment or distributive share of income and reduce the taxable income of the remaining members in the LLC.

2. *Ordinary income portion of the gain.* The gain on sale or redemption of a membership interest is taxed as capital gain under Section 741. A portion of the gain is recharacterized as ordinary income to the extent of the member's share of hot assets. The major items of hot assets include depreciation recapture, inventory items, and cash basis receivables. However, inventory is a hot asset in a redemption only if it is substantially appreciated. Inventory is substantially appreciated if the fair market value is more than 120% of its tax basis. Inventory is a hot asset in a sale whether or not it is substantially appreciated.

3. *Unrecaptured Section 1250 gain.* If a terminating member sells his or her membership interest to one or more remaining partners, then a portion of the gain on sale is taxed at a maximum 25% tax rate to the extent of the member's share of unrecaptured Section 1250 gain. Unrecaptured Section

---

[263] See ¶ 1006 *supra.*

[264] Reg. § 1.736-1(b)(1).

[265] *A.O. Champlin v. Comm'r,* 36 TCM 802 (1977).

1250 gain is the gain that the LLC would recognize on the sale of depreciable real property up to the amount of straight-line depreciation on the property.[266] There is no unrecaptured Section 1250 gain in a redemption. This shifts the burden of tax on unrecaptured Section 1250 gain to the remaining members in the LLC when the property is sold.

4. *Timing of gain recognition.* In a redemption, the departing member may recover his or her full basis before recognizing any gain. Alternatively, the member may elect to recognize the gain on a pro rata basis,[267] although this election is seldom made. In a sale of a membership interest, the terminated partner may elect to use the installment method of reporting. The terminated member then recognizes gain each year equal to the payments received multiplied by the gross profit percentage. The remaining payments are a nontaxable return of basis. The member may not use the installment method of reporting for any portion of the gain attributable to ordinary income items, such as cash basis receivables, depreciation recapture and inventory. This gain must be recognized in the year of sale even if the member receives no payments in the year of sale. The member must increase his or her tax basis by the amount of ordinary income in order to avoid double counting when computing the gross profit percentage. The gain that is taxed at a 25% tax rate on unrecaptured Section 1250 gain does not have to be accelerated to the year of sale, but the first dollars of gain recognized on the installment method are taxed at a 25% rate until all 25% gain has been recognized.

5. *Termination of partnership status.* When a member sells a membership interest, the member's status as a partner in the LLC terminates immediately. The member will then receive a final Schedule K-1 in the year of sale. In a redemption, the member is treated as a partner until receipt of the final payment. The member will receive a Schedule K-1 for each year until the redemption is complete.

6. *Tax basis.* In a redemption, the LLC does not receive a tax basis in the acquired interest since the interest disappears. In a sale, the purchasing members receive a tax basis in the acquired interest equal to the purchase price plus any additional share of LLC liabilities allocated to the purchasing members.

7. *Section 754 election.* In a sale of a membership interest, the LLC may make a Section 754 election to step up the inside basis of assets under Section 743 for the benefit of the purchasing members. In a redemption, the LLC may also make a Section 754 election to step up the inside basis of assets, but the adjustment is computed under Section 734 rather than Section 743. The basis increase benefits all members of the LLC in a redemption, rather than just the purchasing member. The basis step-up is immediate in a sale of a membership interest even though the selling member recognizes gain on the installment basis. In a redemption, an LLC may only step up the basis of

---

[266] Code Sec. 1(h)(6).
[267] Treas. Reg. § 1.736-1.

assets as the departing member recognizes gain. In both cases, the adjustment is allocated under Section 755 based on the appreciation inherent in the assets at the time of termination of the departing member.

¶1011 LOSS RECOGNITION TO MEMBER

A member does not recognize loss upon a distribution unless the following three requirements are met:[268]

1. The adjusted basis of the member's interest in the LLC exceeds the distribution.
2. The member's interest in the LLC is liquidated.
3. The distribution is in money, unrealized receivables, or inventory items.

Any loss recognized is a capital loss.[269]

¶1012 TAX CONSEQUENCES TO LLC

An LLC does not recognize gain or loss upon the distribution of property or money to a member.[270] This differs from the tax treatment applicable to corporations, which recognize gain upon the distribution of appreciated property to shareholders.

There is an exception to the nonrecognition provisions if an LLC makes a disproportionate distribution of "hot assets" and "cold assets" to members. The LLC is treated as having made a proportionate distribution of assets to the member and selling the excess assets actually received by the member in exchange for the proportionate share of assets that the member did not receive. The LLC may recognize gain or loss on the deemed distribution and sale.

There is no effect on the basis of the LLC's remaining assets unless the LLC has made an election under Code Sec. 754 or has made a disproportionate distribution of "hot assets" and "cold assets."[271]

¶1013 DRAWS, ADVANCES, AND LOANS

An LLC does not have profits or income until the last day of its tax year. Therefore, "draws" against profits during the year are treated as advances during the year and as distributions on the last day of the year.[272] The LLC enters the amount of the draw or advance on its books and records, but not as a reduction of capital accounts.

A member cannot avoid taxable income by classifying a payment as a draw or advance, since the entire amount is taxable at the end of the year. However, a

---

[268] Code Sec. 731(a); Reg. §1.731-1(a)(2).

[269] *Id.* (last sentence).

[270] Code Sec. 731(b).

[271] Code Sec. 734(a).

[272] Reg. §1.731-1(a)(1)(ii).

member is not currently taxed on distributions that are bona fide loans. A loan from an LLC is treated as a disguised distribution unless there is an unconditional and legally enforceable obligation to repay the loan at a determinable date.[273] The loan is considered a distribution at the time that the LLC cancels the loan rather than cancellation of indebtedness income.[274]

A member may increase his or her basis in a membership interest by the distributive share of LLC income before taking the advance or draw into account, therefore decreasing the chance that the distribution of money would be a taxable event.[275]

¶1014 REPORTING REQUIREMENTS

An LLC and its members must comply with the following reporting requirements for distributions:

- The LLC must report the amount of withdrawals and distributions during the tax year on each member's Schedule K-1.
- An LLC that makes a disproportionate distribution[276] of hot assets or cold assets must attach Form 8308 to its return for the year of the distribution showing the computation of any income, gain or loss to the LLC under Code Sec. 751.[277] The member receiving the disproportionate distribution must attach a copy of the same form to his or her tax return showing the computation of any income, gain or loss to such member under Code Sec. 751.[278]
- The members, or the LLC on behalf of all members, must disclose potential disguised sales distributions on Form 8275 or on a statement attached to the return.[279] The LLC must file the form if (i) the LLC makes distributions to a member within two years after a member transfers property to the LLC;[280] (ii) the member incurs a liability within two years prior to transferring property to an LLC, and the LLC assumes or takes the property subject to the liability;[281] (iii) the LLC makes distributions to a member within two years before the member transfers property to the LLC;[282] or (iv) the LLC incurs a liability on LLC property, and then transfers the property subject to the debt or has the member assume the liability within two years thereafter.[283]

---

[273] Rev. Rul. 73-301, 1973-2 CB 216.

[274] Ltr. Rul. 201314004; Reg. § 1.731-1(c)(2).

[275] Reg. § 1.731-1(a)(1)(ii).

[276] Reg. § 1.751-1(b)(1)(ii).

[277] Reg. § 1.751-1(b)(5); Prop. Reg. § 1.751-1(b)(6)(i).

[278] Reg. § 1.751-1(b)(5); Prop. Reg. § 1.751-1(b)(6)(ii).

[279] Reg. § 1.707-8.

[280] Reg. § 1.707-3(c)(2).

[281] Reg. § 1.707-5(a)(7)(ii).

[282] Reg. § 1.707-6(c)(1).

[283] Reg. § 1.707-6(c)(2).

- An LLC that has made an election under Code Sec. 754 must adjust the basis of its assets. However, the LLC is not required to file a separate statement or report for distributions, unlike the rules for transfers of membership interests under Code Sec. 754.[284]
- An LLC must attach a statement to its return for the year of distribution[285] if (i) the LLC has not made an election under Section 754, and (ii) there is a substantial basis reduction in LLC assets as a result of the distribution.[286]

---

[284] *See* Reg. § 1.743-1(k) regarding the reporting requirements under Section 754 for transfers of membership interests.

[285] IRS Notice 2005-32, 2005-1 CB 895, Section 8, Example B.

[286] *See* ¶ 1007 *supra*.

11

Reorganizations

¶ 1101 CONVERSION FROM GENERAL PARTNERSHIP TO LLC

.01 Methods of Converting to LLC

There are five principal methods of converting from a general partnership to an LLC:

- *Direct contribution of assets.* The partnership may transfer its assets and liabilities to an LLC in exchange for all of the LLC membership interests. The partnership then dissolves and distributes the membership interests to the partners in liquidation of the partnership.[1] The partnership may also transfer its assets and liabilities to an LLC that is already owned by the partners.

- *Contribution of ownership interests.* The partners may contribute their partnership interests to an LLC in exchange for capital accounts and membership interests, followed by the dissolution of the partnership, the transfer of partnership assets to the LLC, and the assumption of all partnership liabilities by the LLC.[2]

---

[1] Ltr. Ruls. 199916010, 9633021, 9538022, 9525065, 9434027, 9421025, 9321047.

[2] Ltr. Ruls. 9623016, 9538022, 9535036, 9511033, 9452024, 9432018, 9422034, 9407030, 9226035. *See also* Ltr. Ruls. 9416028029, 9119029 (contribution of limited partnership interests to LLC).

- *Liquidation followed by contribution of assets.* The partnership may dissolve and distribute all of its assets to the partners in complete liquidation. The partners then contribute some or all of those assets to the LLC as a capital contribution in exchange for membership interests.

- *Statutory merger.* The partnership may merge into an LLC under the laws of most states.[3] As part of the merger, the LLC assumes all of the assets and liabilities of the partnership. New membership interests are issued to the partners in the old partnership. Normally, the parties must file a certificate of merger with the secretary of state.

- *Statutory conversion.* Several states permit a partnership to convert to an LLC by entering into a conversion agreement and filing a certificate of conversion with the secretary of state.[4] California permits a partnership or other business entity[5] to convert into an LLC.

---

[3] Ltr. Ruls. 9452024, 9412030, 9210019; Ala. Code § 10-12-54 et seq.; Alaska Stat. § § 10.50.500 to 590; Ariz. Rev. Stat. Ann. § § 29-751 to 757; Cal. Corp. Code § § 17710.10 to 17710.19; Colo. Rev. Stat. Ann. § § 7-80-1003 to 7-80-1005; Conn. Gen. Stat. Ann. § § 34-193 to 34-198; Del. Code Ann. tit 6, § 18-209; D.C. Code Ann. § § 29-1039 to 29-1042; Fla. Stat. Ann. § 608.438; Ga. Code Ann. § § 14-11-901 to 14-11-901; Haw. Rev. Stat. Ann. § § 428-904 to 428-907; Idaho Code § § 30-6-1001, 30-6-1002; 805 ILCS § § 180/37-20 to 180/37-35; Ind. Code Ann. § § 23-18-7-1 to 23-18-7-8; Iowa Code § § 490A.1201 to 490A.1206, 490A.1515; Kan. Stat. Ann. § § 17-7701 to 17-7706; Ky. Rev. Stat. § § 275.355 to 275.365; Me. Rev. Stat. Ann. tit. 31, § § 741-745; Md. Corps. & Ass'ns Code Ann. § § 4A-701, 4A-702; M.G.L.A. ch. 156C, § § 59 to 62; Mich. Comp. Laws Ann. § § 450.4701 to 4707a, 450.4910; 507; Minn. Stat. § § 322B.70 to 322B76; Miss. Code Ann. § § 79-29-209 to 79-29-219, 79-29-921; Mo. Rev. Stat. § § 347.127 to 347.135; Mont. Code Ann. § § 35-8-1201 to 35-8-1205; Neb. Rev. Stat. § § 21-2647 to 21-2652; Nev. Rev. Stat. Ann. § § 92A.030, 92A.150; N.H. Rev. Stat. Ann. § § 304-C:18, 304-C:19; N.J. Stat. Ann. § 42:2B-20; N.M. Stat. Ann. § § 53-19-59 to 53-19-62.2; N.Y. LLC § § 1001-1005; N.C. Gen. Stat. § § 57C-9A-20 to 57C-9A-29; N.D. Cent. Code § § 10-32-100 to 10-32-107; Ohio Rev. Code Ann. § § 1705.36 to 1705.42; Okla. Stat. Ann. tit. 18, § 2054; 15 Pa. Cons. Stat. § § 8956-8959; R.I. Gen. Laws § § 7-16-59 to 7-16-64; S.C. Code Ann. § § 33-44-904 to 33-44-906; S.D. Codified Laws Ann. § § 47-34A-904 to 47-34A-906; Tenn. Code Ann. § 48-249-702; Tex. Rev. Civ. Stat. Ann. art 1528n, 10.01-10.07; Utah Code Ann. § § 48-2c-14.01 to 14.10; Va. Code Ann. § § 13.1-1070-1073; Vt. Stat. Ann. tit. 11, § 3124-6; Wash. Rev. Code § § 25.15.395 to 25.15.415; W. Va. Code § § 31B-9-904 to 31B-9-906; Wis. Stat. § § 183.1201 to 183.1206; Wyo. Stat. § 17-15-142.

[4] Ltr. Rul. 200252055; Ala. Code § 10-12-54 et seq.; Alaska Stat. § 10.50.570; Colo. Rev. Stat. Ann. § 7-80-1001.5; Conn. Gen. Stat. Ann. § § 34-198, 34-199; Del. Code Ann. tit. 6, § 18-214; D.C. Code Ann. § 29-1013; Fla. Stat. Ann. § 608.439; Haw. Rev. Stat. Ann. § § 428-902.5 to 428-903; 805 ILCS § § 180/37-10 to 180/37-15; Iowa Code § 490A.304; Kan. Stat. Ann. § § 17-7684 to 17-7685; Ky. Rev. Stat. § § 275.370 to 275.375; La. Rev. Stat. Ann. § § 12:1357 to 12:1362; Md. Corps. & Ass'ns Code Ann. § § 4A-211 to 4A-213; Me. Rev. Stat. Ann. tit. 31, § § 746, 747; Mich. Comp. Laws Ann. § 450.4707; Mo. Ann. Stat. § 347.125; Mont. Code Ann. § § 35-8-1210 to 35-8-1211; Nev. Rev. Stat. Ann. § § 92A.030, 92A.150; N.H. Rev. Stat. Ann. § § 304-C:17-a, 304-C:17-b; N.M. Stat. Ann. § § 53-19-59 to 53-19-62.2; N.Y. LLC Law § § 1006-1007; N.C. Gen. Stat. § § 57C-9A-01 to 57C-9A-19; Okla. Stat. Ann. tit. 18, § § 2054.1, 2054.2; R.I. Gen. Laws § 7-16-5.3; S.C. Code Ann. § § 33-44-902 to 33-44-903; S.D. Codified Laws Ann. § § 47-34A-902 to 47-34A-903; Tenn. Code Ann. § 48-249-703; Tex. Rev. Civ. Stat. Ann. art 1528n, 10.08-10.11; Utah Code Ann. § § 48-2c-14.01 to 14.06; Va. Code Ann. § 13.1-1010.1; Vt. Stat. Ann. tit. 11, § 3122-3; W. Va. Code § § 31B-9-901, 31B-9-902; Wis. Stat. § 183.1207.

[5] Cal. Corp. Code § § 17704.01 to 17701.09.

.02 Tax Consequences

For federal tax purposes, the conversion from a general partnership to an LLC is taxed as follows:

- No gain or loss is recognized to the partnership, LLC, partners, or members as a result of the transfer of assets from the partnership to the LLC, the assumption of liabilities by the LLC, or other steps in the conversion unless there is a change in the partners' share of liabilities.[6] No gain or loss is recognized to the partnership, LLC, partners, or members upon the transfer of partnership interests to the LLC in exchange for LLC membership interests, followed by the liquidation of the general partnership,[7] except as provided under the Internal Revenue Code sections governing recognition of gain or loss upon distributions[8] or the treatment of liabilities.[9] No gain or loss is recognized to the partners under the rules governing unrealized receivables and inventory,[10] since those rules are superseded by the provisions on nonrecognition of gain or loss upon the contribution of property to a partnership.[11]

- There is no termination of the partnership under the IRC provisions governing continuation of a partnership[12] if the LLC continues the business of the partnership.[13] The LLC is treated as the continuation of the general partnership.[14]

---

[6] Rev. Rul. 95-37, 1995-1 CB 130; Ltr. Ruls. 200414013, 200022016, 9637030, 9525065, 9525058, 9421025, 9407030, 9321047, 9226035 (*citing* Rev. Rul. 84-52, 1984-1 CB 157, and Code Sec. 721). The conversion is treated as a nontaxable exchange under Code Sec. 721 (contribution of property to a partnership in exchange for an interest in the partnership). The tax consequences if there is a change in the partners' share of liabilities are discussed below.

[7] Rev. Rul. 95-37, 1995-1 CB 130; Ltr. Ruls. 9841030, 9834040, 9834039, 9809003, 9741021, 9741018, 9623016, 9602018, 9538022, 9511033, 9432018, 9226035.

[8] *See* Code Sec. 731; Ltr. Ruls. 9511033, 9452024 (gain is recognized under Code Sec. 731 to the extent provided under Code Sec. 752).

[9] *See* Code Sec. 752; Ltr. Ruls. 200414013, 9834040, 9834039, 9623016, 9618021-023, 9602018, 9538022, 9525065, 9525058, 9511033, 9452024, 9434027, 9432018, 9422034, 9421025, 9407030, 9350013. Under Code Sec. 752(b), the reduction in liabilities for a partner is treated as a distribution of money. The distribution first reduces basis. Distributions of money in excess of basis are taxable. Ordinarily, Code Sec. 752 will not apply unless there is a refinancing of the debt in connection with the conversion. Recourse debt prior to a conversion remains recourse after the conversion.

[10] Code Sec. 751.

[11] Ltr. Rul. 9421025; *see* Code Sec. 721.

[12] Code Sec. 708.

[13] Rev. Rul. 95-55, 1995-2 CB 313; Rev. Rul. 95-37, 1995-1 CB 130; Ltr. Ruls. 200022016, 9841030, 9834040, 9834039, 9809003, 9637030, 9623016, 9618021023, 9602018, 9538022, 9525065, 9525058, 9511033, 9501033, 9452024, 9417009, 9407030, 9343027, 9432018, 9426037, 9432040, 9432037, 9422034, 9421025, 9420028, 9407030, 9350013, 9321047, 9226035, 9029019, 9010027 (*citing* Rev. Rul. 84-52, 1984-1 CB 157; Code Sec. 708(b); and Reg. § 1.708-1(b)(1)(ii) (transaction under Code Sec. 721 is not treated as sale or exchange under Code Sec. 708)).

[14] Rev. Rul. 95-55, 1995-2 CB 313; Rev. Rul. 95-37, 1995-1 CB 130; Ltr. Ruls. 9841030, 9834040, 9834039, 9637030, 9623016, 9618021023, 9602018, 9538022, 9525065, 9525058, 9511033, 9501033, 9452023, 9432018, 9426037, 9432040, 9432037, 9422034, 9421025, 9420028, 9407030, 9350013, 9321047, 9226035, 9029019, 9010027 (*citing* Rev. Rul. 84-52, 1984-1 CB 157; Code Sec. 708(b); and Reg.

- The tax year does not close with respect to any partner[15] or for the partnership/LLC.[16] The LLC must continue to use the same tax year as the partnership.[17] A change in the tax year requires the consent of the Service.[18]

- A member's basis in the LLC membership interest is equal to the member's adjusted basis in the general partnership interest[19] if the member's share of liabilities does not change after the conversion.[20]

- The holding period for the LLC membership interests includes the holding period for the partnership interests.[21]

- The LLC's basis in the assets is the same as the basis of those assets in the partnership immediately prior to the conversion.[22]

- If there is an increase in a partner's share of liabilities as a result of the conversion, the increase is treated as a contribution of money by the member to the LLC. The basis of the member's interest in the LLC is increased by the amount of the deemed contribution.[23] No gain or loss is recognized.[24]

- If there is a decrease in a partner's share of liabilities as a result of the conversion, the decrease is treated as a distribution of money by the LLC to the member.[25] The basis of the member's interest in the LLC is reduced (but not below zero) by the amount of the deemed distribution.[26] Gain is recognized to the extent the deemed distribution exceeds the adjusted basis of the member's interest in the partnership.[27]

- The LLC must continue to use the same method of accounting as the general partnership until it receives permission to change its accounting method or

---

(Footnote Continued)

§ 1.708-1(b)(1)(ii) (transaction under Code Sec. 721 is not treated as sale or exchange under Code Sec. 708)).

[15] Rev. Rul. 95-37, 1995-1 CB 130; Ltr. Ruls. 9841030, 9834040, 9834039, 9637030, 9501033.

[16] Ltr. Rul. 9501033.

[17] Ltr. Rul. 9525065.

[18] Ltr. Rul. 9525065 (*citing* Temp. Reg. § 1.441-1T(b)(4)).

[19] Rev. Rul. 95-37, 1995-1 CB 130; Ltr. Rul. 9602018 (*citing* Rev. Rul. 95-37, 1995-1 CB 130); Ltr. Ruls. 9841030, 9538022, 9525065, 9452024, 9417009, 9321047 (*citing* Rev. Rul. 84-52, 1984-1 CB 157).

[20] Rev. Rul. 95-37, 1995-1 CB 130; Ltr. Ruls. 9618021-023, 9452024. The tax consequences if there is a change in the partners' share of liabilities are discussed below.

[21] Rev. Rul. 95-37, 1995-1 CB 130; Ltr. Ruls. 200022016, 9841030, 9417009, 9321047 (*citing* Rev. Rul. 84-52, 1984-1 CB 157, and Code Sec. 1223(1)).

[22] Ltr. Ruls. 200022016, 9538022, 9417009 (*citing* Code Sec. 723).

[23] Rev. Rul. 95-37, 1995-1 CB 130.

[24] Ltr. Ruls. 9421025, 9321047 (*citing* Rev. Rul. 84-52, 1984-1 CB 157, and Code Secs. 731, 752(a)). *See also* Reg. § 1.752-1(e). The basis is increased under Code Sec. 722.

[25] Code Sec. 752(b).

[26] Rev. Rul. 95-37, 1995-1 CB 130.

[27] *Id.*; Ltr. Rul. 9321047 (*citing* Rev. Rul. 84-52, 1984-1 CB 157, and Code Secs. 731, 752(b)). Under Code Sec. 733, the basis is first reduced by the amount of money distributed (including the deemed distribution under Code Sec. 752(b)). Under Code Sec. 731, gain is recognized to the extent the distribution of money (including the deemed distribution under Code Sec. 752(b)) exceeds the partner's basis in the partnership units.

until the IRS challenges the method upon examination.[28] The rule applies whether or not the general partnership used the proper method of accounting prior to the conversion.[29] For example, an LLC must continue to use the cash method of accounting if the general partnership used the cash method of accounting.[30] However, the cash method of accounting may not be used if the LLC is classified as a tax shelter after the conversion.[31]

- The LLC is not required to obtain a new employer identification number.[32]
- The members of the LLC are treated as partners for self-employment tax purposes. The members' distributive shares are not excepted from net earnings from self-employment under Code Sec. 1402(a)(13).[33]
- The LLC remains the same employer for withholding tax purposes. The LLC is not required to withhold FICA and FUTA taxes with a new contribution base after the conversion. The same rule applies even if the LLC obtains a new employer identification number after the conversion.
- Because the LLC is a continuation of the partnership, the LLC will not be part of a tiered partnership with the general partnership as the lower-tier partnership.[34]
- There is no depreciation recapture under Code Sec. 1245.[35]
- If two or more general partnerships with identical ownership interests convert or merge into an LLC, the LLC is treated as the continuation of the largest partnership.[36] The LLC retains the employer identification number of the largest partnership.[37] None of the partners, partnerships, or LLC recognizes gain or loss on the exchanges of their partnership interests for interests in the LLC or upon the transfer of assets from the partnership to the LLC.[38]
- The transfer of appreciated assets to the LLC will not result in a contribution or distribution of partnership property under the disguised sales rules with respect to the partnership or the LLC.[39]

---

[28] Rev. Rul. 95-55, 1995-2 CB 313; Ltr. Ruls. 9637030, 9525065, 9501033, 9423040.

[29] Ltr. Ruls. 9501033, 9426030.

[30] Ltr. Ruls. 9623016, 9538022, 9525065.

[31] See ¶1701.05 *infra*.

[32] Rev. Rul. 95-37, 1995-1 CB 130; Ltr. Ruls. 200022016, 9841030, 9834040, 9834039, 9809003, 9618021-023, 9525065.

[33] Ltr. Rul. 9525065. *See* Chapter 16 *infra* for a complete discussion of the rules applicable to self-employment taxes.

[34] Ltr. Ruls. 9834040, 9834039, 9809003, 9618021-023. *See* ¶1505 *infra* for a discussion of tiered partnerships and LLCs.

[35] Ltr. Rul. 9421025 (*citing* Code Sec. 1245(b)(3), which provides that there is no depreciation recapture if the transferee receives a carryover basis and if no gain or loss is recognized upon the transfer).

[36] Ltr. Ruls. 9741021, 9741018.

[37] *Id.*

[38] *Id.*

[39] Ltr. Ruls. 9834040, 9834039, 9809003. The reason is that the conversion is not treated as a sale or exchange under Code Sec. 708(b)(1)(B). *See* ¶605 *supra* for a discussion of Code Secs. 704(c)(1)(B) and 737.

- The members' capital accounts in the LLC are the same as their capital accounts in the partnership prior to conversion.[40]

The federal income tax consequences are the same whether the resulting LLC is formed in the same state or in a different state than the converting partnership.[41] The tax consequences are the same regardless of the manner of conversion under state law.[42] The conversion of an interest in a partnership into an interest in an LLC is treated the same as a partnership-to-LLC conversion.[43]

¶ 1102 CONVERSION FROM LIMITED PARTNERSHIP TO LLC

.01 Direct Conversion

A limited partnership may convert to an LLC. The conversion may take place in one of the five ways that a general partnership converts to an LLC.[44] The tax consequences of converting from a limited partnership to an LLC are basically the same as those of converting from a general partnership to an LLC.[45] These tax consequences include the following:

- No gain or loss is recognized to the LLC, the partnership, the members, or the partners upon the transfer of assets or partnership interests to the LLC in exchange for membership interests or upon the liquidation of the limited partnership[46] except as provided under the rules providing for treatment of liabilities.[47]

- There is no termination of the partnership under the continuation of partnership rules[48] if the LLC continues the business of the partnership. The LLC is treated as the continuation of the limited partnership.[49]

- The tax year does not close with respect to the partnership[50] or any partner.[51]

---

[40] Ltr. Ruls. 200414013, 200022016.

[41] Rev. Rul. 95-37, 1995-1 CB 313.

[42] *Id.*

[43] *Id.*

[44] *See* ¶ 602 *supra.*

[45] Ltr. Ruls. 94156028-029, 9210019, 9119029, 9010027. *See also* Rev. Rul. 84-52, 1984-1 CB 157 (last sentence).

[46] Ltr. Ruls. 9741021, 9741018, 9738013, 9633021.

[47] Code Sec. 752; Ltr. Ruls. 9607006, 9443024, 9417009, 9416028-029.

[48] Code Sec. 708.

[49] Rev. Rul. 95-37, 1995-1 CB 130; Ltr. Ruls. 9633012, 9607006, 9443024, 9417009, 9416028-029 (*citing* Code Sec. 708).

[50] Ltr. Rul. 9633021.

[51] Rev. Rul. 95-37, 1995-1 CB 130.

- A member's basis in the LLC membership interest is equal to the member's adjusted basis in the limited partnership,[52] assuming the member's share of liabilities does not change after the conversion.[53]
- The holding period for the LLC membership interests includes the holding period for the partnership interests.[54]
- The basis of the LLC assets is the same as the basis of those assets in the partnership immediately prior to the conversion.[55]
- If there is an increase in a partner's share of liabilities as a result of the conversion, the increase is treated as a contribution of money by the member to the LLC. The basis of the member's interest in the LLC is increased by the amount of the deemed contribution.[56] No gain or loss is recognized.[57]
- If there is a decrease in a partner's share of liabilities as a result of the conversion, the decrease is treated as a distribution of money by the LLC to the member.[58] The basis of the member's interest in the LLC is reduced (but not below zero) by the amount of the deemed distribution.[59] Gain is recognized to the extent the deemed distribution exceeds the adjusted basis of the member's interest in the partnership.[60]
- There may be adverse tax consequences if recourse debt is changed to nonrecourse debt during the conversion. A member's basis in a partnership or LLC is increased by an allocable share of recourse and nonrecourse debt. Recourse debt is allocated to the partners or members who bear the risk of loss. Nonrecourse debt is allocated to all the LLC members. If the limited partnership has recourse debt prior to the conversion, the debt is allocated entirely to the general partners who are personally liable. After the conversion to an LLC, the LLC rather than the general partner may be liable for the recourse debt. If only the LLC is liable, then the debt is recharacterized as nonrecourse debt and allocated to all the members for basis purposes. The general partners are treated as receiving a distribution of money to the extent of debt relief (i.e., the amount by which their share of recourse and nonrecourse debt in the partnership prior to the conversion exceeds their share of debt in the LLC

---

[52] *Id.*; Ltr. Rul. 9607006 (*citing* Rev. Rul. 95-37, 1995-1 CB 130); Ltr. Ruls. 9417009, 9416029, 9416028 (*citing* Rev. Rul. 84-52, 1984-1 CB 157).

[53] Rev. Rul. 95-37, 1995-1 CB 130; Ltr. Rul. 9607006.

[54] *Id.*; Ltr. Ruls. 9417009, 9416029, 9416028.

[55] Ltr. Ruls. 9417009, 9416029, 9416028.

[56] Rev. Rul. 95-37, 1995-1 CB 130.

[57] Rev. Rul. 95-37, 1995-1 CB 130 (*citing* Rev. Rul. 84-52, 1984-1 CB 157, and Code Secs. 731, 752(a)). *See also* Reg. § 1.752-1(e). The basis is increased under Code Sec. 722.

[58] Rev. Rul. 95-37, 1995-1 CB 130; Code Sec. 752(b).

[59] Rev. Rul. 95-37, 1995-1 CB 130.

[60] Rev. Rul. 95-37, 1995-1 CB 130 (*citing* Rev. Rul. 84-52, 1984-1 CB 157, and Code Secs. 731, 752(b)). Under Code Sec. 733, the basis is first reduced by the amount of the money distributed (including the deemed distribution under Code Sec. 752(b)). Under Code Sec. 731, gain is recognized to the extent the distribution of money (including the deemed distribution under Code Sec. 752(b)) exceeds the partner's basis in the partnership units.

¶1102.01

after the conversion).[61] The deemed distribution first reduces the general partner's basis in the LLC. Gain or loss is recognized to the extent the deemed distribution exceeds the general partner's basis.

- The LLC must continue to use the same method of accounting as the limited partnership until it receives permission to change its accounting method or until the IRS challenges the method upon examination.[62]

- The LLC is not required to obtain a new employer identification number.[63]

- If two limited partnerships with identical ownership interests convert or merge into an LLC, the LLC is treated as the continuation of the largest limited partnership.[64] The LLC retains the employer identification number of the largest limited partnership.[65] None of the limited partners, limited partnerships, or LLC recognizes gain or loss upon the exchanges of their partnership interests for interests in the LLC or upon the transfer of assets from the limited partnerships to the LLC.[66]

The federal income tax consequences are the same whether the resulting LLC is formed in the same state or in a different state than the converting partnership.[67] The tax consequences are the same regardless of the manner of conversion under state law.[68] The conversion of an interest in a limited partnership to an interest in an LLC is treated the same as a general partnership-to-LLC conversion.[69]

.02 Distribution of LLC Membership Interests by Limited Partnership

A limited partnership's distribution of membership interests in an LLC is treated as the distribution of the LLC's assets and liabilities to the partners, immediately followed by a deemed contribution of those assets and liabilities to the LLC that is classified as a partnership. The partners of the limited partnership do not recognize gain on the distribution of LLC assets, except to extent that any money distributed exceeds a partner's basis in the partnership interest.[70]

---

[61] Code Sec. 752(b).

[62] Ltr. Rul. 9423040.

[63] Ltr. Rul. 9633021.

[64] Ltr. Ruls. 9741021, 9741018, 9738013.

[65] Id.

[66] Id.

[67] Rev. Rul. 95-37, 1995-1 CB 130.

[68] Id.

[69] Id.

[70] Ltr. Rul. 200825008, *citing* Code Sec. 731(a).

¶1103 CONVERSION OF GENERAL PARTNERS OF LIMITED PARTNERSHIP TO LLC

The general partners of a limited partnership may convert to an LLC.[71] The purpose of the conversion is normally to reduce liability for the individual general partners.

The conversion may take place by having the general partners contribute their general partnership interests to the LLC in exchange for proportional membership interests in the LLC. After the conversion, the LLC is the sole general partner of the limited partnership.[72]

The tax consequences of the conversion are the same as for conversions of general partnerships to LLCs.[73] The limited partnership may continue to use the cash method of accounting after the conversion if it is not a tax shelter.[74]

¶1104 TRANSFER OF SELECTED PARTNERSHIP ASSETS TO LLC

In some cases, a partnership may transfer only some of its assets to an LLC. The partnership continues in business after the transfer. The transfer is treated as a distribution by the partnership to its partners and a contribution of those assets to the LLC.[75]

A partnership may transfer some of its lines of business to an LLC in order to limit the liability of the partners with respect to that business. Generally, no gain or loss is recognized to the LLC or the members upon the transfer of business or contribution of assets to the LLC.[76]

¶1105 CONVERSION FROM LLP TO LLC

The tax consequences of converting a registered limited liability partnership (LLP) to an LLC are basically the same as those of converting from a general partnership to an LLC.[77] The conversion may take place by merging the LLP[78] or by contributing partnership interests to the LLC in exchange for LLC interests. For federal tax purposes, the transactions are characterized as follows:

- No gain or loss is recognized to the LLP, LLC, or members of the LLP and LLC as a result of the conversion.[79]

---

[71] Ltr. Rul. 9535036.

[72] *Id.*

[73] *Id.*

[74] *Id.*

[75] Ltr. Rul. 9321070.

[76] Ltr. Rul. 9713007 (*citing* Code Sec. 721).

[77] Ltr. Rul. 9412030.

[78] *Id.*

[79] Ltr. Ruls. 9407030, 9321047, 9226035 (*citing* Rev. Rul. 84-52, 1984-1 CB 157, and Code Sec. 721). The conversion is treated as a nontaxable exchange under Code Sec. 721 (contribution of property to a

- There is no termination of the LLP. The LLC is treated as the continuation of the LLP.[80]
- The LLC must continue to use the same tax year as the LLP.[81]

¶ 1106 CONVERSION FROM LLC TO CORPORATION (INCORPORATION OF LLC)

.01 LLC Classified as Partnership

The principal methods of incorporating an LLC that is classified as a partnership are as follows:

- *Method 1.* The LLC transfers its assets and liabilities to a newly formed corporation in exchange for stock. The LLC then distributes the stock to the members of the LLC.
- *Method 2.* The LLC distributes all of its assets and liabilities to its members. The members then transfer the assets and liabilities to the new corporation in exchange for stock.
- *Method 3.* The members transfer their membership interests in the LLC to the new corporation in exchange for stock. The new corporation then liquidates the LLC and becomes the owner of all assets and liabilities of the LLC.
- *Method 4.* The members transfer their membership interests in the LLC to the new corporation in exchange for stock. This method is similar to Method 3. However, the LLC continues in existence. It does not transfer the assets and liabilities to the corporation. The LLC is classified as a disregarded entity wholly owned by the corporation.[82]
- *Method 5.* The LLC elects to be classified as a corporation by filing IRS Form 8832.
- *Method 6.* The members of the LLC form a corporation, and then merge the LLC into the corporation.
- *Method 7.* The members of the LLC form a corporation, and then merge the LLC into the corporation, or convert the LLC into a corporation.

Prior to 1984, the IRS took the position that the tax consequences of incorporating an LLC were the same regardless of the method of incorporation.[83] In 1984, the IRS determined that there were different tax consequences depending on the method of incorporation.[84] The basis and holding periods of assets received by the corpora-

---

(Footnote Continued)

partnership in exchange for an interest in the partnership). The tax consequences if there is a change in the partners' share of liabilities are discussed below.

[80] Ltr. Rul. 9412030.

[81] *Id.*

[82] Ltr. Rul. 200139002.

[83] Rev. Rul. 70-239, 1970-1 CB 74.

[84] Rev. Rul. 84-111, 1984-2 CB 88.

tion, and the basis and holding periods of the stock received by the members of the LLC, will now vary depending on the method of incorporation.

.02 Method 1—Transfer of Assets to Corporation

Under the first method, the LLC transfers its assets and liabilities to a newly formed corporation in return for stock. The LLC then distributes the stock to the members of the LLC in proportion to their membership interests. The LLC terminates after the distribution.[85]

There are the following tax consequences of incorporating an LLC under the first method:

- The LLC does not recognize gain or loss on the transfer of its assets to the corporation in exchange for stock.[86]
- The corporation receives a basis in the assets equal to the LLC's basis in the assets immediately prior to the transfer.[87]
- The LLC receives a basis in the stock equal to the corporation's basis in the transferred assets.[88] There is a special rule when an LLC transfers Section 704(c) property[89] to a corporation.[90] The change in classification from a partnership to corporation is treated as two separate nontaxable exchanges under Section 351. In the first exchange, the LLC is treated as contributing each item of the Section 704(c) property to a corporation in exchange for substituted basis stock that is treated as a Section 704(c) property with the same amount of built-in gain or loss as the Section 704(c) property. This exchange preserves the built-in gain or loss attributable to each member of the LLC. In the second exchange, the LLC is treated as transferring property other than Section 704(c) property to the corporation in exchange for stock. After these exchanges, the LLC will be treated as distributing the stock in the corporation to the members of the LLC in liquidation of their LLC membership interest. Each member in the LLC should receive stock with a basis equal to their outside basis in the LLC prior to the conversion of the LLC into corporation.[91]
- The corporation's assumption of the LLC's liabilities decreases each member's outside basis in the membership interest. The relief of debt is treated as a money distribution to the members.[92]

---

[85] Reg. § 301.7701-3(g)(1)(i). The Treasury Department stated in the preamble to the proposed regulations that the regulations would not affect Rev. Rul. 84-111, 1984-2 CB 88, in which the IRS ruled that it would respect the particular form undertaken by the taxpayer when a partnership converts to a corporation.

[86] Rev. Rul. 84-111, 1984-2 CB 88 (*citing* Code Sec. 351).

[87] Rev. Rul. 84-111, 1984-2 CB 88 (*citing* Code Sec. 362(a)).

[88] Rev. Rul. 84-111, 1984-2 CB 88 (*citing* Code Sec. 358(a)).

[89] Section 704(c) property is discussed at ¶ 805 *supra*.

[90] Reg. § 1.704-3(a)(8)(i); Ltr. Rul. 201505001.

[91] Ltr. Rul. 201505001.

[92] Rev. Rul. 84-111, 1984-2 CB 88 (*citing* Code Secs. 752, 733).

- The LLC's distribution of the corporate stock to the members of the LLC results in a termination of the LLC.[93]
- The members of the LLC receive a basis in the stock of the corporation equal to their basis in the membership interests in the LLC, reduced by any cash received in the liquidation.[94]
- The LLC's holding period for the stock received in the exchange includes the corporation's holding period in capital assets and Section 1231 assets (to the extent that the stock was received in exchange for such assets).[95] The LLC's holding period for stock received in exchange for other assets begins on the date following the date of the exchange.[96] The members' holding periods for the stock received on liquidation of the LLC include the LLC's holding period for the stock.[97]
- The corporation's holding period for the assets received in the exchange includes the LLC's holding period.

.03 Method 2—Distribution of Assets to Members

Under the second method, the LLC distributes all of its assets and liabilities to the members. The members then transfer the assets and liabilities to the new corporation in exchange for stock.

There are the following tax consequences of incorporating an LLC under the second method:

- The LLC terminates on transfer of its assets to its members.[98]
- The basis of assets distributed to each member on liquidation of the membership interest is equal to the member's outside basis in the membership interest, reduced by any money received in the distribution.[99]
- The transfer of liabilities to the members has no effect on the members' basis in the assets. The decrease in their share of LLC liabilities is exactly equal to their corresponding assumption of the liabilities.[100]
- The members do not recognize gain or loss on the transfer to the corporation of assets and liabilities in exchange for stock.[101]
- The members of the LLC receive a basis in the stock that is equal to the basis of the assets distributed to them on the liquidation of the LLC, reduced by

---

[93] Rev. Rul. 84-111, 1984-2 CB 88 (*citing* Code Sec. 708(b)(1)(A)).

[94] Rev. Rul. 84-111, 1984-2 CB 88 (*citing* Code Sec. 732(b)).

[95] Rev. Rul. 84-111, 1984-2 CB 88 (*citing* Code Sec. 1223(1)).

[96] Rev. Rul. 84-111, 1984-2 CB 88 (*citing* Rev. Rul. 70-59, 1970-2 CB 168).

[97] Rev. Rul. 84-111, 1984-2 CB 88 (*citing* Code Secs. 735(b) and 1223).

[98] Rev. Rul. 84-111, 1984-2 CB 88 (*citing* Code Sec. 708(b)(1)(A)).

[99] Rev. Rul. 84-111, 1984-2 CB 88 (*citing* Code Sec. 732(b)).

[100] Rev. Rul. 84-111, 1984-2 CB 88 (*citing* Code Sec. 752).

[101] Rev. Rul. 84-111, 1984-2 CB 88 (*citing* Code Sec. 351).

liabilities assumed by the corporation.[102] The corporation's assumption of liabilities is treated as a payment of money to the members.[103]

- The corporation's basis in the assets received from the members of the LLC is the same as the members' basis in such assets immediately prior to the transfer.[104]
- The members' holding period for the assets distributed to them includes the LLC's holding period for such assets.[105]
- The members' holding period for stock received includes their holding periods in the capital assets and Section 1231 assets transferred to the corporation (to the extent stock was received in exchange for such assets).[106] The members' holding period for stock received in exchange for other assets begins on the date following the date of the exchange.
- The corporation's holding period for the assets received includes the members' holding periods for such assets.[107]

The distribution of assets to the members (at the start of the incorporation process) may result in immediate taxation under the disguised sales rules. For example, if an LLC distributes built-in gain or loss property to a member within seven years from the date of contribution to the LLC, the contributing member recognizes gain or loss equal to the gain or loss that would have been allocated to the contributing member if the LLC had sold the property to the distributing member for its fair market value.[108] This is the principal disadvantage of incorporating an LLC using Method 2. The disguised sales rules do not apply if (i) the LLC is incorporated, (ii) the incorporation occurs by any method other than the method involving an actual distribution of LLC property to the members followed by a contribution of the property to a corporation, and (iii) the LLC is immediately liquidated as part of the incorporation process.[109]

.04 Method 3—Transfer of Membership Interests to Corporation; LLC Terminates

Under the third method, the members transfer their membership interests in the LLC to the new corporation in exchange for stock. The LLC then terminates. The corporation becomes the owner of all assets and liabilities of the LLC.

There are the following tax consequences of incorporating an LLC under the third method:

---

[102] Rev. Rul. 84-111, 1984-2 CB 88 (*citing* Code Sec. 358(a)).

[103] Rev. Rul. 84-111, 1984-2 CB 88 (*citing* Code Sec. 358(d)).

[104] Rev. Rul. 84-111, 1984-2 CB 88 (*citing* Code Sec. 362(a)).

[105] Rev. Rul. 84-111, 1984-2 CB 88 (*citing* Code Sec. 735(b)).

[106] Rev. Rul. 84-111, 1984-2 CB 88 (*citing* Code Sec. 1223(1)).

[107] Rev. Rul. 84-111, 1984-2 CB 88 (*citing* Code Sec. 1223(2)).

[108] Code Sec. 704(c)(1)(B)(i), (ii); Reg. § 1.704-4(a)(1).

[109] Reg. §§ 1.704-4(c)(5), 1.737-2(c).

- The members of the LLC do not recognize gain or loss on the transfer of the membership interests to the new corporation in exchange for stock.[110]
- The corporation does not recognize gain or loss on receipt of the membership interests in the LLC.[111]
- The LLC terminates immediately after the transfer of the membership interests to the new corporation.[112]
- The members of the LLC receive a basis in the stock equal to their basis in the membership interests,[113] reduced by each member's share of liabilities assumed by the corporation plus any liabilities to which the transferred assets are subject.[114]
- The corporation's assumption of the LLC's liabilities is treated as a payment of money to the members.[115]
- The corporation receives a basis in the assets equal to the members' outside basis in their membership interests. The corporation must allocate this outside basis to the assets under Code Sec. 732(c).[116]
- The corporation's holding period for the assets received includes the LLC's holding period in the assets.[117]
- Each member's holding period for the stock received includes his or her holding period for the membership interest transferred. However, the holding period of the stock received by the members in exchange for Section 751 assets (hot assets) that are neither capital assets nor Section 1231 assets begins on the date following the date of the exchange.[118]

.05 Method 4—Transfer of Membership Interests to Corporation; LLC Continues

Under the fourth method, the members transfer their membership interests in the LLC to the new corporation in exchange for stock. However, the LLC continues in existence. It does not transfer the assets and liabilities to the corporation as under Method 3. The LLC is classified as a disregarded entity wholly owned by the corporation,[119] unless it elects to be classified as a corporation.

---

[110] Rev. Rul. 84-111, 1984-2 CB 88 (*citing* Code Sec. 351); Ltr. Ruls. 200820020, 200139002, Ruling No. (3).

[111] Ltr. Rul. 200820020.

[112] Rev. Rul. 84-111, 1984-2 CB 88 (*citing* Code Sec. 708(b)(1)(A)).

[113] Rev. Rul. 84-111, 1984-2 CB 88 (*citing* Code Sec. 358(a)); Ltr. Ruls. 200820020, 200139002, Ruling No. (2).

[114] Ltr. Ruls. 200820020, 200139002, Ruling No. (3) (*citing* Code Secs. 752(d), 358(d)).

[115] Rev. Rul. 84-111, 1984-2 CB 88 (*citing* Code Secs. 752(d), 358(d)).

[116] Rev. Rul. 84-111, 1984-2 CB 88 (*citing* Code Sec. 362(a)).

[117] Rev. Rul. 84-111, 1984-2 CB 88.

[118] Rev. Rul. 84-111, 1984-2 CB 88 (*citing* Code Sec. 1223(1)); Ltr. Rul. 200820020.

[119] Ltr. Rul. 200139002.

The tax consequences under Method 4 are similar to the tax consequences under Method 3, with slight differences in basis and in holding period computations. The tax consequences under Method 4 are as follows:

- The LLC (which was previously classified as a partnership) is treated as liquidating into the new corporation since it will become a disregarded entity wholly owned by the corporation.[120]
- The members of the LLC do not recognize gain or loss on the transfer of the membership interests to the new corporation in exchange for stock.[121]
- The members of the LLC receive a basis in the stock equal to their basis in the membership interests,[122] reduced by each member's share of liabilities assumed by the corporation plus any liabilities to which the transferred assets are subject.[123]
- The corporation's assumption of the LLC's liabilities is treated as a payment of money to the members.[124]
- Each member's holding period for the stock received includes his or her holding period for the membership interest transferred. However, the holding period of the stock received by the members in exchange for Section 751 assets (hot assets) that are neither capital assets nor Section 1231 assets begins on the date following the date of the exchange.[125]
- The corporation does not recognize gain or loss on receipt of the membership interests in exchange for stock.[126]
- The corporation's basis in the membership interest transferred equals the members' basis in such interests immediately before the transfer, increased by the amount of any gain recognized by a corporate member on the transfer.[127]
- The corporation's holding period for each membership interest includes the member's holding period immediately before the transfer.[128]
- The corporation does not recognize gain or loss on the deemed liquidation of the LLC into the corporation when the LLC becomes a wholly owned disregarded entity. However, the LLC recognizes gain to the extent that the deemed distribution of money from the LLC to the corporation exceeds the corporation's basis in the membership interest in the LLC immediately before the distribution.[129]

---

[120] Ltr. Rul. 200139002 (under Summary of Facts).

[121] Ltr. Rul. 200139002, Ruling No. (3).

[122] Ltr. Rul. 200139002, Ruling No. (2).

[123] Ltr. Rul. 200139002, Ruling No. (3) (*citing* Code Secs. 752(d), 358(d)).

[124] Rev. Rul. 84-111, 1984-2 CB 88 (*citing* Code Secs. 752(d), 358(d)).

[125] Ltr. Ruls. 20122201, 201222016, 201222015, 201222014, 200139002, Ruling No. (4) (*citing* Code Sec. 1223(1)); Rev. Rul. 84-111, 1984-2 CB 88.

[126] Ltr. Rul. 200139002, Ruling No. (6) (*citing* Code Sec. 1032(a)).

[127] Ltr. Rul. 200139002, Ruling No. (7) (*citing* Code Sec. 362(a)).

[128] Ltr. Rul. 200139002, Ruling No. (8) (*citing* Code Sec. 1223(2)).

[129] Ltr. Rul. 200139002, Ruling No. (9) (*citing* Code Sec. 731(a)).

- The LLC does not recognize gain or loss on its deemed liquidation into the corporation.[130]
- The corporation's basis in the assets that it holds in the LLC as a disregarded entity is equal to the corporation's basis in the membership interest, reduced by any deemed distribution of money.[131]
- The LLC's holding period for the assets received in the deemed liquidation includes the period that such assets were held by the LLC.[132]

.06 Method 5—Filing Election Classification

Under the fifth method, the LLC elects to be classified as a corporation by filing IRS Form 8832. The election is treated as effective immediately before the close of the day on which the election is made. The LLC's initial taxable year as a corporation begins at the start of the day on which the LLC elects to be classified as a corporation.[133]

The tax consequences of electing to be classified as a corporation are the same as under Method 1. The LLC is treated as having contributed all of its assets and liabilities to the corporation in exchange for stock in the corporation. The LLC is then treated as having liquidated by distributing the stock in the corporation to its members.[134]

The basis of property in a deemed contribution by a partnership electing to be taxed as a corporation includes the special basis adjustment under Code Sec. 743. However, the amount of gain, if any, recognized upon the deemed contribution is determined without reference to the special basis adjustment.[135]

EXAMPLE 11-1

An LLC owns property with a common basis of $1,000. The LLC makes an election to step up the basis of the property under Section 754. A member has a special basis adjustment of $5 under Section 743(b). The LLC elects to be classified as a corporation. The LLC is deemed to contribute all of its assets and liabilities to the corporation in exchange for stock in the corporation. The LLC is then deemed to have distributed the stock to its members. If the transfer qualifies under Code Sec. 351 as a transfer to a corporation controlled by the transferor, then the LLC's basis in the property includes the member's special $5 basis adjustment. The LLC,

---

[130] Ltr. Rul. 200139002, Ruling No. (10) (*citing* Code Sec. 731(b)).

[131] Ltr. Rul. 200139002, Ruling No. (11) (*citing* Code Sec. 732(b)).

[132] Ltr. Rul. 200139002, Ruling No. (12) (*citing* Code Secs. 735(b), 1223(2)).

[133] Ltr. Rul. 201314008.

[134] Ltr. Rul. 201314008; Reg. § 301.7701-3(g)(1)(i).

[135] Reg. § 1.743-2.

which is now classified as a corporation, has a basis in the property of $1,005. The member's basis in the membership units of the LLC, which is now classified as a corporation, will be increased by the $5 special basis adjustment.

.07 Method 6—Merger

Under the sixth method, the members of the LLC form a corporation, and then merge the LLC into the corporation. Some states permit an LLC to merge into a corporation by filing a certificate of merger with the Secretary of State.[136]

.08 Method 7—Formless Conversion (Certificate of Conversion)

Some states permit an LLC to convert into a corporation by filing a certificate of conversion with the Secretary of State.[137] These conversions are sometimes called "formless conversions." A formless conversion is a conversion of an LLC from classification as a partnership to classification as a corporation under state law. There is no actual transfer of the LLC's assets or membership interests.[138]

A conversion from an LLC classified as a partnership to a corporation has the following tax consequences:[139]

- Neither the members of the LLC nor the LLC recognize gain or loss on the conversion.
- The LLC is treated as contributing all of its assets and liabilities to the corporation in exchange for stock in the corporation. The transfer of assets and liabilities to the corporation is nontaxable under Code Sec. 351.
- The aggregate basis of the stock in the corporation deemed received by the LLC will be the same as the aggregate basis of the LLC's assets deemed contributed in exchange for the stock.
- Immediately thereafter, the LLC is treated as liquidating and distributing the stock of the corporation to the members. The LLC's distribution of stock is nontaxable to the members and the LLC under Code Sec. 731.

---

[136] For example, California permits a merger of an LLC into a corporation by filing with the California Secretary of State (a) Form LLC-9, Limited Liability Company Certificate Merger, (b) an Agreement of Merger signed by all managers of the LLC (or by the members in a members-managed LLC), by the Chairman of the Board, President, or Vice President, and by the Secretary or Assisting Secretary of the corporation, and (c) an Officers' Certificate for the corporation. Cal. Corp. Code §§ 1113(g)(1), 17550-17556, 17001(e), (ac).

[137] Ltr. Rul. 201437007. *See, e.g.,* Wyo. Stat. § 17-15-146.

[138] Rev. Rul. 2004-59, 2004 IRB 1050.

[139] Rev. Rul. 2004-59, 2004 IRB 1050; Ltr. Rul. 201437007.

- Rev. Rul. 84-111,[140] which describes the tax consequences of incorporating an LLC through an actual transfer of assets or membership interests to the corporation, does not apply. Instead, a formless conversion is treated in the same manner as an election by a partnership under the federal tax laws to be classified as a corporation.

.09 Which Method to Choose

Methods 2 and 3 are preferable to Method 1 if the members of the LLC have an aggregate basis in their membership interests that is higher than the LLC's basis in its assets. In such case, the LLC will receive the higher carryover basis for the assets under Methods 2 and 3. Under Method 1, the corporation receives a basis in the assets equal to the members' lower basis in their membership interests.

Method 3 may be preferable to Method 2 if the LLC transfers a substantial amount of cash to the new corporation. Under Method 2, the members' holding period for stock received in exchange for cash begins on the day after the incorporation. Under Method 3, the holding period for stock includes the holding period for the membership interests even if LLC assets include cash.

The LLC may be required to recapture investment tax credits under Methods 2 and 3. The corporation's basis in the assets received from the LLC is determined by reference to the members' bases in their membership interests rather than by reference to the LLC's basis in the assets transferred to the corporation.

The corporation may apparently not elect the benefits under Code Sec. 1244 (ordinary loss stock) under Method 1 for the same reason. Section 1244 is not available if stock is originally issued to non-individual shareholders except in limited circumstances. This problem does not arise under Methods 2 and 3 if the members of the LLC are individuals since the stock in the corporation is issued directly to the members of the LLC.

Method 2 should not be used if the members contribute appreciated or depreciated property to the LLC with a capital account value that is different from the adjusted tax basis. A member does not recognize gain or loss under the disguised sales and mixing bowl rules on the incorporation of an LLC under any method of incorporation other than a method involving the actual distribution of LLC property to the members followed by a contribution of that property to the corporation.[141]

.10 LLC Classified as Corporation

An LLC that is classified as a corporation for federal tax purposes may convert to a regular corporation. The following tax consequences apply if the conversion is made by an amendment to or a restatement of the LLC's charter documents:[142]

---

[140] 1984-2 CB 88.

[141] Reg. §§ 1.704-4(c)(5), 1.737-2(c).

[142] Ltr. Ruls. 8908035, 7741040, 7729058. *See also* Ltr. Rul. 8809073, which treated the conversion as a nontaxable exchange of shares in the LLC for shares in the unlimited liability company, with a carryover in basis and holding period for the acquired shares.

- The change in form is an F reorganization. The LLC and the corporation are each treated as a party to the reorganization.[143]
- The conversion is first treated as a constructive transfer of LLC assets and liabilities to the corporation in exchange for stock. No gain or loss is recognized by the LLC upon the constructive exchange of assets for the stock in the corporation and the assumption by the corporation of the LLC's liabilities.[144]
- No gain or loss is recognized by the corporation upon the constructive receipt of assets from the LLC in exchange for stock.[145]
- The LLC is then treated as having transferred the stock to its members in exchange for membership interests. No gain or loss is recognized to the members upon the exchange of membership interests solely for shares in the corporation.[146] Gain (but not loss) may be recognized to the extent boot is received.[147]
- The basis in the stock held by the members is the same basis that the members had in their membership interests prior to the conversion.[148]
- The holding period of the stock is the same as the holding period for the membership interests surrendered.[149]
- The LLC's basis and holding period in the transferred assets carry over to the corporation.[150]
- The corporation succeeds to the LLC's tax attributes.[151] The tax year of the LLC does not end on the date of the conversion. The corporation may carry back a net operating loss or a net capital loss to a pre-conversion tax year of the LLC.[152]

.11 LLC Classified as Disregarded Entity

Methods of Converting

An LLC that is classified as a disregarded entity may convert to a corporation on a tax-free basis. The owner of the LLC may make the conversion by:

---

[143] Ltr. Ruls. 8908035, 7741040 (*citing* Code Secs. 368(a)(1)(F), 368(b)).

[144] Ltr. Ruls. 8908035, 7741040 (*citing* Code Secs. 361(a), 357(a)).

[145] Ltr. Ruls. 8908035, 7741040 (*citing* Code Sec. 1032(a)).

[146] Ltr. Ruls. 8908035, 7741040 (*citing* Code Sec. 354(a)(1)).

[147] Ltr. Rul. 8908035 (*citing* Code Sec. 356(a)(1)).

[148] Ltr. Ruls. 8908035, 7741040 (*citing* Code Sec. 358(a)).

[149] Ltr. Ruls. 8908035, 7741040 (*citing* Code Sec. 1223(1)).

[150] Ltr. Ruls. 8908035, 7741040 (*citing* Code Secs. 362(b), 1223(2)).

[151] Ltr. Rul. 8908035 (*citing* Code Sec. 381(a)(2) and Reg. § 1.381(b)-1(a)(2)). These tax attributes are listed in Code Sec. 381(c).

[152] Ltr. Rul. 8908035 (*citing* Code Sec. 381(b)(3)).

- merging the LLC into a corporation;
- contributing all the assets and liabilities of the LLC to a corporation;[153]
- contributing the membership interest in the LLC to a newly formed corporation in exchange for stock;[154] or
- filing IRS Form 8832 and electing to be classified as a corporation.[155]

Tax Consequences

The conversion of a single-member disregarded LLC to a corporation has the following tax consequences:

- The owner is deemed to have contributed all the assets and liabilities of the LLC to the corporation in exchange for stock.[156]
- The owner does not recognize gain or loss on the transfer of the assets and liabilities from the LLC to the corporation.[157]
- The corporation does not recognize gain or loss on receipt of the assets or membership interests in the LLC.[158]
- The owner's basis in the stock in the corporation is the same as the basis in the assets or the membership interest in the LLC transferred to the corporation.[159]
- The corporation's basis in the assets received is the same as the owner's basis in the assets or the membership interest in the LLC transferred to the corporation, provided that such assets were capital assets in the hands of the owner prior to the transfer.[160]
- The owner's holding period in the shares received in the corporation includes the owner's holding period in the assets or LLC membership interest prior to the transfer.[161]
- The corporation's holding period in the assets received includes the owner's holding period in the assets or LLC membership interest prior to the transfer.[162]

---

[153] Ltr. Rul. 200204005.

[154] Ltr. Rul. 200843024 (Second Reincorporation).

[155] Reg. § 301.7701-3(g); Ltr. Rul. 200843024 (First Reincorporation).

[156] Reg. § 301.7701-3(g); Ltr. Ruls. 200843024, 200830003 (*citing* Reg. § 301.7701-3(g)(1)(iv) with respect to an election to be classified as a corporation).

[157] Ltr. Rul. 200204005 (LLC 2 merged into a newly formed corporation); Ltr. Ruls. 200843024, 200830003, *citing* Code Secs. 351(a), 357(a).

[158] Ltr. Rul. 200843024, 200830003, *citing* Code Sec. 1032(a) and Rev. Rul. 77-449, 1977-2 CB 110.

[159] Ltr. Rul. 200843024, 200830003, *citing* Code Sec. 362(e)(2)(C).

[160] Ltr. Rul. 200843024, 200830003, *citing* Code Sec. 362(a).

[161] Ltr. Rul. 200843024, 200830003, *citing* Code Sec. 1223(1).

[162] Ltr. Rul. 200843024, *citing* Code Sec. 1223(2).

Conversion of Subsidiary LLC into Corporation

A parent corporation may convert a single-member disregarded subsidiary LLC into a subsidiary corporation. The conversion has the following tax consequences:

- The conversion is treated as a contribution by the parent corporation of all the assets of the disregarded LLC to the subsidiary corporation in exchange for all of the stock in the subsidiary corporation and the assumption by the subsidiary corporation of all the liabilities of the disregarded LLC.[163]

- Neither the parent corporation, subsidiary LLC, nor subsidiary corporation recognizes gain or loss on the conversion.[164]

- The subsidiary corporation's basis in the assets received from the LLC equals the basis of those asset prior to the conversion.[165]

- The subsidiary corporation's holding period for each asset received from the LLC in the conversion includes the holding period during which the parent corporation held the asset through the disregarded LLC prior to the conversion.[166]

.12 Conversion of LLC into S Corporation

The election by an LLC to be classified as an S corporation is discussed at ¶406.

.13 Conversion to Corporation Immediately Prior to Reorganization

An LLC that is classified as a partnership or disregarded entity may not participate in a tax-free reorganization under Code Sec. 368.[167] The courts and rulings are divided on whether an LLC that is classified as a partnership may participate in a tax-free reorganization by incorporating immediately prior to the reorganization.[168] For example, one ruling determined that an entity classified as a partnership or other unincorporated entity may not participate in the tax-free corporate reorganization simply by incorporating, followed by reorganization involving a newly created controlled corporation. Under the step transaction doctrine, the transaction would be treated as a taxable exchange of assets by the partnership for stock in the acquiring corporation.[169] However, the weight of authority is that an LLC may participate in a

---

[163] Ltr. Rul. 201033019.

[164] Ltr. Ruls. 201033019, 200830003.

[165] Ltr. Rul. 201033019, *citing* Code Sec. 362(b).

[166] Ltr. Rul. 201033019, *citing* Code Sec. 1223(2).

[167] Reg. §§301.7701-2(b), 301.7701-3(a); Ltr. Rul. 201138015.

[168] *See BNA Daily Tax Report* No. 155, pp. J-1 to J-3 (Aug. 11, 2011).

[169] Rev. Rul. 54-96, 1954-1 CB 111, which determined that the creation of a new subsidiary followed by the immediate exchange of stock of the new subsidiary for stock of the acquiring corporation did not qualify as a stock-for-stock reorganization.

tax-free reorganization by changing its classification from a partnership to a corporation immediately prior to a reorganization.[170]

¶1107 CONVERSION FROM C CORPORATION TO LLC

.01 LLC Classified as Partnership

A corporation may convert to an LLC that is classified as a partnership for federal tax purposes.[171] The corporation is treated as liquidating and distributing its assets to the shareholders, followed by the shareholders' contribution of assets to the new LLC in exchange for interests in the LLC.[172] This type of reorganization is rare because of the adverse tax consequences.

If the corporation is a C corporation, there is potential double taxation. The first tax is on the corporation for the deemed sale of assets to shareholders.[173] The amount of gain or loss is the difference between the fair market value and adjusted basis in the assets. The shareholders recognize gain or loss to the extent that the fair market value of the assets distributed exceeds their basis in the stock.[174] The gain increases the basis of the shareholders' stock in the new corporation. No gain or loss is recognized upon the deemed contribution of property to the LLC.

Some states permit a statutory merger of a corporation into an LLC. The tax consequences are similar. The merger of a corporation into an LLC is treated as a nontaxable contribution of assets by the corporation to the LLC in exchange for membership interests, followed by a taxable distribution of the membership interests to the shareholders of the corporation in redemption of their stock. The corporation recognizes gain to the same extent as if it sold the membership interests to the shareholders for fair market value. The shareholders of the corporation also recognize capital gain or loss on distribution of the membership interests. The gain is equal to the difference between the fair market value of the membership interests less the members' basis in the stock. There is a technical termination of the LLC as a result of the merger. However, no gain or loss is recognized as a result of the deemed termination.[175] The tax consequences of a merger of a C corporation into an LLC that is classified as a partnership are discussed in detail at ¶1120.01.

Because of the adverse tax consequences of converting a corporation to an LLC, LLCs are used mainly for new businesses rather than for conversions of existing

---

[170] *See, e.g., Weikel v. Comm'r*, 51 TCM 432 (1986), which determined that an incorporation followed by a reorganization was valid even though pending negotiations for the sale had occurred within six months of the incorporation. The incorporation had a business purpose if the sale did not take place, and the negotiations were still in progress and tentative.

[171] *See, e.g.,* Del. Code Ann. tit. 8, §266; Wyo. Stat. §17-16-1115.

[172] Reg. §301.7701-3(g)(1)(ii). Ltr. Ruls. 9401014, 9252033.

[173] Code Sec. 336(a). The corporation is subject to taxation on the appreciated assets under Code Sec. 311(b) if there is a distribution of corporate assets to the LLC other than in complete liquidation of the corporation.

[174] Code Sec. 331(a).

[175] Ltr. Rul. 200214016.

corporations. However, a corporation may be able to convert to an LLC without adverse tax consequences in the following cases:

- A parent corporation converts a subsidiary corporation into an LLC.[176]
- The corporation has little or no built-in gain or appreciated assets.
- The shareholders of an S corporation have a tax basis in their stock that exceeds the value of the assets distributed. The capital loss on distribution may be sufficient to offset any gain from the deemed distribution of the assets.[177] An S corporation may convert to an LLC, and retain its status as an S corporation, even though the LLC is not a corporation under local law.[178]
- A C corporation has sufficient net operating losses to offset corporate gain recognized on the deemed distribution of appreciated assets. However, the shareholders will recognize gain on the deemed distribution unless the fair market value of the assets does not exceed the shareholders' tax bases in the shares, or the shareholders have sufficient capital losses to offset the gain on the deemed distribution.

.02 LLC Classified as Corporation

A corporation may convert to an LLC that is classified as a corporation for federal tax purposes.[179] The reorganization normally takes place through a merger, certificate of conversion,[180] exchange of shares for membership interests, transfer of assets, or election classification change.[181]

A corporation may want to convert to an LLC that is classified as a corporation in order to obtain the non-tax benefits available to an LLC under state law.[182] The corporation may also make the conversion in connection with a divisive D reorganization.[183]

The conversion has the following tax consequences:

- The conversion is a tax-free Section 368(a)(1)(F) reorganization assuming that (i) the membership interests have substantially similar rights, preferences and restrictions as the corporate stocks surrendered in the exchange, and (ii) the

---

[176] Ltr. Rul. 9409016. *See* ¶1109 *infra*. The merger of the subsidiary into the LLC must comply with the requirements of Code Sec. 332(b).

[177] Under Code Sec. 1371, the distribution of appreciated property by an S corporation in liquidation results in taxable gain to the corporation equal to the difference between the fair market value of the corporate assets over the corporation's tax basis in the property. The gain is not subject to tax at the corporate level assuming that the corporation has been an S corporation since the date of its incorporation. The gain is passed through to the shareholders. Thus, there is a single tax at the shareholder level.

[178] Ltr. Rul. 9636007.

[179] Ltr. Ruls. 200802011, 200528021, 200515013, 200510012, 200205005, 200109011.

[180] Ltr. Ruls. 200709013, 200708015.

[181] Ltr. Rul. 200515013.

[182] Ltr. Rul. 200119016.

[183] Ltr. Ruls. 200926024, 200802011, 200708015, 200514005, 200450015, 200447031.

exchanging members hold substantially the same interests before and after the transaction.[184]

- The corporation is treated as having transferred all its assets and liabilities to the LLC in exchange for LLC membership interests. This is followed by a deemed distribution of the LLC membership interests to the corporation's shareholders in exchange for their shares.

- No gain or loss is recognized to the corporation upon the transfer of its assets to the LLC in exchange for membership interests in the LLC and the assumption of the corporation's liabilities by the LLC.[185]

- The basis of the corporation's assets in the LLC's hands is the same as the basis of the assets in the corporation's hands immediately before the transfer.[186]

- The holding period of the corporation's assets in the LLC's hands includes the period during which those assets were held by the corporation.[187]

- No gain or loss is recognized to the LLC upon receipt of the corporation's assets in exchange for membership interests in the LLC.[188]

- No gain or loss is recognized by the shareholders upon receipt of membership interests in the LLC in exchange for stock in the corporation.[189]

- The basis of the LLC membership interests received by the shareholders of the corporation in exchange for stock in the corporation is the same as the basis of the stock in the corporation.[190]

- The holding period of the LLC membership interests received by the corporation's shareholders in exchange for stock in the corporation includes the holding period of the stock in the corporation.[191]

- The new LLC is treated as if there had been no reincorporation for purposes of the Internal Revenue Code provision governing carryovers in corporate acquisitions.[192] The tax year does not end on the date of the reincorporation. The other tax attributes of the old LLC carry over to the new LLC.[193]

---

[184] Ltr. Ruls. 200802015, 200802011, 200839017, 200827018, 200719007, 200510012, 199947034.

[185] Ltr. Ruls. 200839017, 200802011, 200719007, 200719006, 200719005, 200718014, 200510012, 7729058; Code Secs. 361(a), 357(a).

[186] Ltr. Rul. 200839017, 200802011, 200719007, 200719006, 200719005, 200718014, 200510012, 7810072 (*citing* Code Sec. 362(b)).

[187] Ltr. Rul. 200839017, 200802011, 200719007, 200719006, 200719005, 200718014, 7810072 (*citing* Code Sec. 1223(2)).

[188] Ltr. Rul. 200839017, 200802011, 200719007, 200719006, 200719005, 200718014, 200510012, 7810072 (*citing* Code Sec. 1032(a)).

[189] Ltr. Ruls. 200839017, 200802011, 200719007, 200719006, 200719005, 200718014, 200510012, 7810072, 7729058, 7111100730A (*citing* Code Sec. 354(a)(1)).

[190] Ltr. Ruls. 200839017, 200802011, 200719007, 200719006, 200719005, 200718014, 200510012, 7810072, 7729058, 7111100730A (*citing* Code Sec. 358(a)).

[191] Ltr. Ruls. 200839017, 200802011, 200719007, 200719006, 200719005, 200718014, 200510012, 7810072, 7729058 (*citing* Code Sec. 1223(1)).

[192] Code Sec. 381.

[193] Ltr. Rul. 8002076 (*citing* Reg. § 1.381(b)-1(a)(2)). These tax attributes are listed in Code Sec. 381(c).

- The tax attributes of the assets in the hands of the corporation carry over to the LLC.[194]
- An S corporation may merge into an LLC. The conversion is treated as an F reorganization. The S election will not terminate as a result of the reorganization if the LLC meets the requirements under Section 1361.[195]
- The LLC may keep the same employer identification number as the corporation.[196]

The tax consequences of the conversion of a subsidiary corporation into an LLC are discussed at ¶1109.

.03 LLC Classified as Disregarded Entity

A corporation may convert to an LLC that is classified as a disregarded entity. The conversion is treated as a distribution by the corporation of its assets and liabilities to the single owner of the LLC in liquidation of the corporation.[197] The regular taxes that apply to a corporate liquidation apply to the conversion.

A parent corporation may convert a subsidiary corporation into an LLC that is classified as a disregarded entity. The conversion is treated as a tax-free liquidation of the subsidiary into the parent.[198]

A corporation may merge into a disregarded LLC that is wholly owned by a new parent holding corporation. The conversion is treated as a nontaxable F reorganization.[199] The subsequent transfer of assets by the LLC to the parent holding corporation is also an F reorganization.[200]

Similar tax consequences apply if a parent corporation merges into a single-member disregarded LLC owned by a subsidiary corporation.[201]

The tax consequences of a merger of a C corporation into an LLC that is classified as a disregarded entity are discussed in detail at ¶1120.03.

¶1108 CONVERSION FROM S CORPORATION TO LLC

.01 Generally

There is typically one level of tax when an S corporation converts to an LLC. This differs from the conversion of a C corporation, where there are typically two levels of tax.

---

[194] Ltr. Rul. 200839017.

[195] See ¶1108.05 infra.

[196] Ltr. Ruls. 200839017, 200719007.

[197] Reg. § 301.7701-3(g)(1).

[198] See ¶1109 infra.

[199] Ltr. Ruls. 200633008, 200630002.

[200] Ltr. Rul. 200633008.

[201] Ltr. Rul. 200802015.

The S corporation is treated as liquidating and distributing its assets to the shareholders, followed by the shareholders' contribution of assets to the new LLC in exchange for LLC membership interests. If the S corporation has appreciated assets, the S corporation is treated as having sold the assets to the shareholders for fair market value.[202] The corporation recognizes gain equal to the difference between the assets' fair market value and their adjusted bases. The gain passes through and is taxable to the shareholders.[203]

An S corporation may convert into an LLC in a nontaxable F reorganization, and then issue membership interest to persons who do not qualify as S corporation shareholders. The various types of F reorganization transactions are discussed at ¶ 408.

.02 LLC Classified as Partnership

Merger into LLC

An S corporation may convert into an LLC that is classified as a partnership by forming an LLC, and then merging into the LLC. The merger has the following tax consequences:

- The merger is treated as a transfer by the S corporation to the LLC in exchange for the assumption of liabilities by the LLC and the S corporation's receipt of LLC membership interests (interests in the items of income, gain, deduction, or loss of the LLC), followed by the distribution of the membership interests in the LLC to the shareholders of the corporation in a complete liquidation of the corporation under Section 331.[204]
- The S corporation's basis in the membership interests upon the initial contribution to the LLC is the adjusted basis of the S corporation's assets,[205] increased by gain recognized to the S corporation upon the transfer of assets to the LLC.[206]
- The S corporation and the LLC do not recognize gain or loss upon the contribution of assets by the S corporation to the LLC in exchange for membership interests[207] unless the S corporation realizes a net decrease in liabilities exceeding its basis in the assets transferred to the LLC,[208] and provided the LLC is not treated as an investment company.[209]
- The merger results in the liquidation of the S corporation. The S corporation recognizes gain or loss upon the distribution of the membership interests and

---

[202] Code Secs. 336(a), 1371(a)(1).

[203] Code Sec. 1366.

[204] Ltr. Rul. 9543017 (*citing* Rev. Rul. 69-6, 1969-1 CB 104).

[205] Ltr. Rul. 9543017 (*citing* Code Sec. 722).

[206] Ltr. Rul. 9543017 (*citing* Code Sec. 721(b)).

[207] Ltr. Rul. 9543017 (*citing* Code Sec. 721).

[208] Ltr. Rul. 9543017 (*citing* Reg. § 1.752-1(f)).

[209] Ltr. Rul. 9543017. *See* Chapter 20 *infra* regarding investment LLCs.

other property (but not cash) to its shareholders in a complete liquidation of the S corporation.[210] Gain or loss is computed as if the corporation had sold the property to its shareholders for fair market value at the time of the distribution. The amount and character of the gain or loss are determined under Sections 741 and 751.[211] Under Section 741, the S corporation recognizes gain upon the transfer of an LLC membership interest. The gain or loss is capital gain or loss except as provided in Section 751, which deals with unrealized receivables and inventory items. The S corporation is not subject to tax under Section 1374, provided the S corporation did not acquire appreciated assets upon conversion from a C corporation.[212]

- Any gain or loss recognized by the S corporation as a result of its liquidation is passed through to its shareholders.[213] The shareholders then increase or decrease the basis in their stock by the amount of the gain or loss.[214]

- The shareholders recognize gain or loss upon the deemed distribution of assets from the S corporation in the liquidation. The distribution is treated as full payment in exchange for the shares in the S corporation.[215] The amount of gain or loss is equal to the difference between the fair market value of the membership interests received by the shareholders in exchange for the shares and the shareholders' adjusted basis in the shares.[216] Gain or loss is capital gain or loss, subject to the limitations of subchapter P of the Code,[217] if the corporation is not a collapsible corporation and the shares are capital assets.[218]

- The basis of the LLC membership interests received by the shareholders upon the complete liquidation of the S corporation is the fair market value of the membership interests at the time of the distribution.[219]

- If the LLC makes a Section 754 election, the LLC may adjust the basis of its assets under Sections 743 and 755.[220]

- The distribution of LLC membership interests by the S corporation to its shareholders constitutes an exchange that results in a termination of the LLC.[221] Under prior regulations, the termination resulted in a deemed distribution of the LLC's assets to the members of the LLC and a deemed immediate recontribution by the members to a new LLC.[222] Under proposed

---

[210] Ltr. Rul. 9543017 (*citing* Code Sec. 708(b)(1)(B)).

[211] Ltr. Rul. 9543017.

[212] Ltr. Rul. 9543017 (*citing* Code Sec. 1374(d)(8)).

[213] Ltr. Rul. 9543017 (*citing* Code Sec. 1366(a)).

[214] Ltr. Rul. 9543017 (*citing* Code Sec. 1367).

[215] Ltr. Rul. 9543017 (*citing* Code Sec. 331(a)).

[216] Ltr. Rul. 9543017.

[217] Code Secs. 1201-1298.

[218] Ltr. Rul. 9543017 (*citing* Code Secs. 341, 1221).

[219] Ltr. Rul. 9543017 (*citing* Code Sec. 334(a)).

[220] Ltr. Rul. 9543017.

[221] Ltr. Rul. 9543017 (*citing* Code Sec. 708(b)(1)(B)).

[222] Ltr. Rul. 9543017 (*citing* Reg. § 1.708-1(b)(1)(iv)).

regulations, the termination is treated as a transfer by a terminated LLC of all of its assets to a new LLC in exchange for an interest in the new LLC, followed immediately thereafter by the old LLC's distribution of the new LLC membership interests to the members in liquidation of the old LLC. This results in the following tax consequences:[223]

— There is no gain to the members under the Code provision governing gain or loss upon distribution.[224]

— The basis in the assets of the LLC remains the same.

— The tax year of the terminated LLC closes.

— The elections of the terminated LLC are invalidated. New elections must be made.

— The new LLC must depreciate any property as if it were newly acquired property under the same depreciation system used by the terminated LLC.

Distribution of Assets and Recontribution to LLC

An S corporation may convert to an LLC by distributing its assets and liabilities to the shareholders who contribute the assets and liabilities to a new entity, either a single-member disregarded LLC or an LLC classified as a partnership. The LLC continues the business of the S corporation.

The major reason for this type of conversion is to allow the S corporation to recognize any built-in loss associated with the assets. The IRS field offices see these conversions in cases where the S corporation's primary business is property development or homebuilding, and where the current fair market value of the property is lower than the outstanding liabilities associated the property. The owners of the S corporation believe that the corporation can recognize the built-in loss (liabilities in excess of fair market value) on liquidation, which loss is then passed on to the shareholders. The shareholders then attempt to increase their stock basis by the amount of liabilities assumed, which would allow the deduction of losses that were otherwise suspended because of the basis limitation.[225]

Liabilities associated with distributed assets are accounted for in calculating an S corporation's gain or loss. However, the S corporation does not recognize any built-in loss because the fair market value of encumbered property distributed in liquidation is deemed to be at least equal to the amount of the liabilities. The shareholder's basis in the distributed assets is not affected by the assumption of a liability or receipt of property subject to liability. To the extent liabilities exceed the fair market value of distributed assets, the shareholders may recognize either a short-term or long-term capital loss on complete liquidation of the corporation.[226]

---

[223] *See* ¶ 1203 *infra* for a complete discussion of the tax consequences.

[224] Code Sec. 731(a).

[225] CCA 201237017.

[226] CCA 201237017.

.03 LLC Classified as Corporation

An S corporation may convert to an LLC that is classified as a C corporation[227] or as an S corporation.[228] The conversion has the following tax consequences:

- The conversion is a tax-free F reorganization.[229] The conversion by an S corporation to an LLC that is classified as a partnership, followed by the LLC's check-the-box election to be classified as a corporation, also constitutes a tax-free F reorganization.[230] The IRS will not rule on whether a conversion constitutes a tax-free F reorganization, unless the transaction involves a significant tax issue that is not addressed by published authorities.[231]
- Neither the corporation nor it shareholders recognize gain or loss on the exchange of stock in the corporation for membership interests in the LLC.[232]
- The basis and holding period of the corporation's assets remain the same after the conversion.[233]
- The conversion does not terminate the corporation's election as an S corporation if the LLC continues to meet the requirements for an S corporation.[234] The LLC's operating agreement will not result in the LLC having a second class of stock if (i) all items of income and loss are allocated among the members pro rata in accordance with their percentage membership interests, and (ii) all distributions (both liquidating and nonliquidating) are made in accordance with their percentage membership interests.[235]
- The LLC may retain the same taxpayer identification number as the corporation.[236]

.04 LLC Classified as Disregarded Entity

An S corporation may convert into an LLC in a nontaxable F reorganization, and then issue membership interests to persons who do not qualify as S corporation shareholders. The shareholders of the S corporation first form a holding company (also an S corporation), and contribute their stock in the S corporation to the holding company. The S corporation then converts to a single-member disregarded LLC. The

---

[227] Ltr. Rul. 200718014.

[228] Ltr. Ruls. 200839017, 200802011, 200719007, 200719006, 200719005, 200718014, 200622025, 200528021, 200248023, 9636007.

[229] Ltr. Ruls. 200839017, 200802011, 200719007, 200719006, 200719005, 200718014, 200622025, 200528021, 200248023, 9636007

[230] Ltr. Ruls. 200528021, 9636007.

[231] Rev. Proc. 2009-3, 2009-1 CB 107, Sec. 3.01(38); Ltr. Ruls. 200528021, 9636007.

[232] Ltr. Ruls. 200839017, 200718014, 200622025, 200528021.

[233] Ltr. Ruls. 200839017, 200718014, 200622025, 200528021.

[234] Ltr. Rul. 200839017, 200622025, 200528021, 9636007.

[235] Ltr. Ruls. 200802011, 200719007, 200548021, 200505010.

[236] Ltr. Ruls. 200839017, 200622025, 200528021.

contribution of stock to the holding company and the conversion of the S corporation to an LLC constitute a nontaxable F reorganization. After the F reorganization, the shareholders own an S corporation holding company which owns a single-member disregarded LLC. The LLC may then convert to a partnership by one of the following methods:

- The holding company sells membership interests in the LLC to third-party investors.
- The disregarded LLC issues membership interests to the third-party investors.
- The disregarded LLC merges into another LLC.

These various types of F reorganization transactions are discussed at ¶ 408.

Alternatively, an S corporation that owns a QSub (wholly owned subchapter S subsidiary) may merge the QSub into a single-member disregarded LLC owned by the S corporation. The S corporation may then sell membership interests in the LLC to unrelated third parties. The merger of the QSub into the LLC and the sale of membership interests in the LLC to an unrelated party have the following tax consequences:[237]

1. The formation of the LLC and the transfer of assets to the LLC pursuant to the merger are disregarded.
2. The sale of the interest to the unrelated third party is treated as a sale of an undivided percent interest in each of the LLC's assets.
3. Immediately thereafter, the S corporation parent company and the unrelated party are treated as contributing their respective interests in those assets to a partnership in exchange for ownership interests in the partnership.
4. The S corporation recognizes gain or loss from the deemed sale of the percentage interest in each asset of the LLC.
5. No gain or loss is recognized by the S corporation or the unrelated party as a result of the deemed contribution of their respective interests in the assets to the LLC in exchange for ownership interests in the LLC.

.05 Contribution of Assets to LLC Classified as Partnership

An S corporation may convert to an LLC by forming an LLC that is classified as a partnership and contributing its assets to the LLC in exchange for membership interests.[238] One or more unrelated parties may also contribute assets to the LLC in exchange for membership interests. There are the following tax consequences:

- Neither the corporation nor the LLC will recognize gain or loss on the contribution of assets to the LLC in exchange for membership interests.[239] The S corporation must remain a member of the LLC after the contribution of assets. The members will recognize gain if the LLC distributes the member-

---

[237] Reg. § 1.1361-5(b)(3), Example 2.

[238] Ltr. Rul. 200123035.

[239] Ltr. Rul. 200123035, *citing* Code Sec. 721(a).

ship interests to the shareholders in liquidation of the S corporation. The members may also recognize gain under the disguised sales rules if another member contributes assets to the LLC that are distributed to the S corporation within two years after the S corporation's contribution to the LLC.[240]

- The contribution of LIFO inventory property to the LLC will not result in the recapture of the LIFO reserve.[241] However, in order to adopt the dollar-value LIFO inventory method, the transferee LLC must file IRS Form 970 and otherwise comply with the requirements of Code Sec. 472 and regulations thereunder.[242]
- If any of the property contributed to the LLC has a fair market value that is different from its basis, the LLC must comply with the general requirements applicable to contributions of appreciated and depreciated property.[243]

.06 Contribution of Membership Interests to LLC

An S corporation may convert to an LLC by forming an LLC, and having the members contribute their stock in the corporation to the LLC. After the transfer, the LLC is the sole owner of the stock in the S corporation.

An LLC is not ordinarily an eligible shareholder in an S corporation. However, the S corporation may retain its status as an S corporation after the transfer of shares from the shareholders to the LLC if the LLC (a) elects to be classified as a corporation for federal tax purposes, (b) elects to be classified as an S corporation, and (c) elects to treat the subsidiary S corporation as a qualified subchapter S subsidiary under Code Sec. 1361(b)(3), effective on the date of the contribution.[244]

¶1109 CONVERSION OF SUBSIDIARY CORPORATION TO LLC

.01 General

A parent corporation may convert a subsidiary corporation into an LLC that is classified as a disregarded entity. The conversion is treated as a liquidation of the subsidiary into the parent under Code Sec. 332(a).[245] There is no tax provided that the liabilities of the subsidiary do not exceed the basis of its assets.

---

[240] See ¶ 605.01 *supra.*

[241] *Id.*

[242] Ltr. Rul. 200123035.

[243] Ltr. Rul. 200123035. These rules are discussed at ¶¶ 606 and 805 *supra.*

[244] Ltr. Rul. 200326025.

[245] Code Sec. 332(a); Ltr. Ruls. 201633014, 201528007, 201404004, 201213018, 201145012, 201107003, 201041029, 201033018, 200716012 (proposed transaction 1), 201017031, 201010018, 200709013, 200701018, 200645012 (regarding Subs 6, 7 and 8 conversions), 200609004, 200608016, 200505009, 200310005, 200214014. *See also* Ltr. Rul. 200305017 in which the IRS determined that the merger of a wholly owned subsidiary corporation of a foreign parent corporation into a disregarded LLC owned

The parent corporation may convert the subsidiary into an LLC through (a) a merger of a subsidiary into an LLC, (b) a transfer of assets from the subsidiary to the LLC, (c) a liquidation of the subsidiary into the parent, and deemed transfer of the assets from the parent to the LLC, (d) an election by the subsidiary to be classified as a disregarded entity, or (e) a conversion of the subsidiary corporation into an LLC pursuant to state law. These forms of conversion are discussed below.

.02 Merger

A parent corporation may convert a subsidiary corporation into an LLC by (i) forming an LLC and merging the subsidiary corporation into the LLC,[246] (ii) merging the subsidiary corporation into a disregarded LLC owned by the subsidiary,[247] or (iii) using any other method permitted by state law.[248] The merger has the following tax consequences:

- The merger of the subsidiary into the disregarded LLC is treated as a transfer of assets by the subsidiary corporation to the LLC in exchange for the assumption of the subsidiary corporation's liabilities by the LLC and the subsidiary corporation's receipt of an LLC membership interest (an increased interest in the LLC's items of income, gain, deduction, or loss).[249]

- The transfer of assets is treated as followed by the subsidiary corporation's distribution of the LLC membership interest to the parent corporation in complete liquidation of the subsidiary corporation.[250] The parent corporation is treated as acquiring and directly holding the assets and assuming the liabilities of the subsidiary for tax purposes.[251]

- Neither the parent nor the subsidiary corporation recognizes gain or loss upon the subsidiary's transfer of assets to the LLC in exchange for the membership interest.[252]

- The parent corporation does not recognize gain or loss upon its receipt of the membership interest distributed in the liquidation of the subsidiary corporation pursuant to the plan of merger if the requirements of Section 332(b) are

---

(Footnote Continued)

by the foreign parent corporation was a liquidation of the subsidiary corporation into the foreign parent corporation, subject to Code Secs. 331 and 336.

[246] Ltr. Ruls. 201111003, 200608016, 200944011, 200536008, 200310005, 200305017, 200129024.

[247] Ltr. Rul. 200701018.

[248] Ltr. Ruls. 201033018, 200830003, 200609004, 200550021, 200129029.

[249] Ltr. Ruls. 201017031, 200645012, 200536008, 200129029, 9409016, 9409014, 9404021.

[250] Code Sec. 332; Ltr. Ruls. 201017031, 200944011, 200645012, 200536008, 200129029, 9409016, 9409014, 9404021 (*citing* Reg. § 1.332-2(d) and Rev. Rul. 69-6, 1969-1 CB 104).

[251] Ltr. Ruls. 201017031, 200944011, 200830003, 200645012, 200536008, 200310005.

[252] Ltr. Ruls. 201111003, 201033018, 200701018, 201017031, 200944011, 200645012, 200609004, 200536008, 200608016 (merger of Sub 2 into Sub 2 LLC), 200129024, 9409016, 9409014, 9404021 (*citing* Code Sec. 721).

met.[253] The merger or conversion constitutes a tax-free liquidation under Code Sec. 332.[254]

- The parent corporation's basis in each of the assets is equal to the basis of the assets in the hands of the subsidiary immediately prior to the conversion to an LLC.[255]

- The parent corporation's basis in the membership interest is the same basis that the subsidiary corporation had in the membership interest immediately prior to its liquidation.[256]

- The subsidiary corporation does not recognize gain or loss upon distribution of the membership interest to the parent corporation in complete liquidation of the subsidiary.[257]

- The parent corporation's holding period for the assets of the subsidiary and the membership interest includes the subsidiary corporation's holding period.[258]

- The parent corporation succeeds to and takes into account the items of the subsidiary corporation set forth in Code Sec. 381(c). These items are subject to certain limitations.[259]

- The parent corporation succeeds to and takes into account the subsidiary corporation's earnings and profits, or deficit in earnings and profits, as of the date of the merger except to the extent that the subsidiary's earnings and profits are reflected in the parent corporation's earnings and profits.[260] Any deficit in earnings and profits of the parent or subsidiary may be used to offset earnings and profits accumulated only after the date of transfer.[261]

---

[253] Ltr. Ruls. 201033018, 201017031, 200944011, 200830003, 200645012, 200536008, 9409016, 9409014, 9404021 (*citing* Code Sec. 332(a)). *See also* Ltr. Ruls. 9822043 and 9822037, which determined that the merger of a subsidiary into an LLC owned by the parent corporation constituted a complete liquidation under Code Sec. 332 and Reg. § 1.331-2(d).

[254] Ltr. Ruls. 201107003, 201033018, 201017031, 200944011, 200645012, 200608016, 200550021, 200536008, 200505009, 200310005, 200137011, 200129029, 200129024.

[255] Ltr. Rul. 201111003, 201033018, 201107003 *citing* Code Sec. 334(b)(1).

[256] Ltr. Ruls. 201017031, 200944011, 200830003, 200645012, 200536008, 200608016 (merger of Sub 2 into Sub 2 LLC), 200129029, 9409016, 9409014, 9404021 (*citing* Code Sec. 334(b)(1)).

[257] Ltr. Ruls. 201107003, 201033018, 201017031, 200830003, 200645012, 200536008, 200608016 (merger of Sub 2 into Sub 2 LLC), 9409016, 9409014, 9404021 (*citing* Code Secs. 337(a), 336(d)(3)).

[258] Ltr. Ruls. 201111003, 201107003, 201033018, 201017031, 200830003, 200645012, 200536008, 200701018, 200608016 (merger of Sub 2 into Sub 2 LLC), 200129029, 9409016, 9409014, 9404021 (*citing* Code Sec. 1223(2)).

[259] *See* Code Secs. 381-384, 1502, and the regulations thereunder; Ltr. Ruls. 201111003, 201107003, 201033018, 200645012, 200608016 (merger of Sub 2 into Sub 2 LLC), 200129029, 9409016, 9409014, 9404021 (*citing* Code Sec. 381(a) and Reg. § 1.381(c)(2)-1).

[260] Ltr. Ruls. 201107003, 201033018, 200645012, 200608038 (merger of Sub 2 into Sub 2 LLC), *citing* Code Sec. 381(c)(2)(A) and Reg. § § 1.381(c)(2)-1, 1.1502-33(a)(2).

[261] Ltr. Ruls. 200608038 (merger of Sub 2 into Sub 2 LLC), *citing* Code Secs. 381, 381(c)(2)(B), 200129029, 9409016, 9409014, 9404021 (*citing* Code Sec. 381(c)(2) and Reg. § 1.381(c)(2)-1).

- If the parent corporation first merges a second-tier subsidiary into a first-tier subsidiary, and then converts the first-tier subsidiary into an LLC, the transaction is treated as a D reorganization with similar tax consequences.[262]

The tax consequences of a merger of a disregarded LLC owned by a subsidiary corporation into a disregarded LLC owned by a parent corporation are discussed at ¶ 1119.07.

.03 Transfer of Assets by Subsidiary

A parent corporation may convert a subsidiary corporation into an LLC by forming an LLC. The subsidiary corporation transfers its assets to the LLC in exchange for membership units. The subsidiary corporation is then liquidated. The membership units in the LLC owned by the subsidiary are transferred to the parent corporation in the liquidation.[263] The tax consequences of the conversion are as follows:

- Neither the subsidiary nor the LLC recognizes gain or loss as a result of the transfer of assets to the LLC.[264]
- The liquidation of the subsidiary corporation and the transfer of the LLC membership units to the parent corporation qualify as a nontaxable liquidation under Section 332.[265]
- Alternatively, the transfer of assets by the subsidiary corporation to the LLC in exchange for interests in the LLC and the assumption of the transferred liabilities by the LLC are disregarded for federal income tax purposes.[266]

The transfer by a spun-off subsidiary of some or all of the assets of its active trade or business to an LLC in exchange for membership interests in the LLC will not prevent the spun-off subsidiary from being treated as engaged in a trade or business for purposes of Code Sec. 355.[267]

.04 Liquidation and Transfer of Assets by Parent

A parent corporation may convert a subsidiary corporation into an LLC by liquidating the subsidiary and contributing the assets received upon liquidation to a newly formed LLC.[268] The tax consequences of the transaction are as follows:

---

[262] Ltr. Rul. 200252055.

[263] *See* Ltr. Rul. 9640010.

[264] Ltr. Rul. 9640010 (*citing* Code Sec. 721).

[265] Ltr. Ruls. 201236014, 200720010, 200709013, 9640010 (*citing* Code Sec. 332(a) and Reg. § 1.332-2(c)). *See also* Ltr. Rul. 200137011.

[266] Ltr. Rul. 200832001.

[267] Ltr. Rul. 200227016.

[268] Ltr. Rul. 9701032.

- The liquidation of the subsidiary corporation qualifies as a nontaxable liquidation under Code Sec. 332. If the subsidiary merges into the parent, the merger is treated as a distribution of assets in complete liquidation of the subsidiary.[269]
- The contribution to the LLC by the parent corporation of assets received from the subsidiary in exchange for membership units is nontaxable under Code Sec. 721. Neither the parent corporation nor the subsidiary corporation nor the LLC recognizes gain as a result of the contribution of assets to the LLC.[270]
- The distribution of membership interests by the subsidiary corporation to the parent corporation is a distribution under Code Sec. 301. If the parent and subsidiary file consolidated returns, the distribution constitutes an intercompany transaction.[271] Any gain or loss recognized under Code Sec. 311(b) on the Section 301 distribution of the membership interests is not taken into account at the time of the distribution.[272]

.05 Conversion of Subsidiary into LLC Owned by Another Subsidiary

A parent corporation may merge a subsidiary corporation into a disregarded LLC owned by the same subsidiary,[273] or by another subsidiary of the parent corporation.[274] The tax consequences are as follows:[275]

- The merger constitutes a reorganization.[276] The subsidiary corporations (including the subsidiary corporation that owns the LLC into which the other subsidiary is merged) will be "parties to the reorganization."[277]
- No gain or loss is recognized by the merging subsidiary on the transfer of its assets to the disregarded LLC in constructive exchange for the stock of the subsidiary corporation that owns the LLC.[278]
- No gain or loss is recognized by the corporation that owns the disregarded LLC.[279]

---

[269] Ltr. Rul. 9701032 (*citing* Reg. § 1.332-2(d)).

[270] Ltr. Rul. 9701032 (*citing* Code Sec. 721).

[271] Ltr. Rul. 9701032 (*citing* Reg. § 1.1502-13(b)).

[272] Ltr. Rul. 9701032 (*citing* Reg. § 1.1502-13(c), (d)).

[273] Ltr. Rul. 200701018.

[274] Ltr. Rul. 200608038.

[275] Ltr. Ruls. 200701018, 200645015, 200608038 (merger of Sub 1 into Sub 1 LLC owned by Controlled, a subsidiary of Distributing).

[276] Ltr. Ruls. 200701018, 200645015, 200608038 (merger of Sub 1 into Sub 1 LLC), *citing* Code Sec. 368(a)(1)(A).

[277] Ltr. Ruls. 200701018, 200645015, 200608038 (merger of Sub 1 into Sub 1 LLC), *citing* Code Sec. 368(b).

[278] Ltr. Ruls. 200701018, 200645015, 200608038 (merger of Sub 1 into Sub 1 LLC), *citing* Code Secs. 361, 357.

[279] Ltr. Ruls. 200701018, 200645015, 200608038 (merger of Sub 1 into Sub 1 LLC), *citing* Code Sec. 1032(a).

- The basis of the assets acquired by the LLC is the same as the basis of such assets to the merging corporation immediately prior to the merger.[280]

- The holding period of assets received by the LLC includes the period during which the assets were held by the merging corporation.[281]

- The corporation that owns the LLC succeeds to and must take into account the merging subsidiary corporation's earnings and profits, or deficit in earnings and profits, as of the date of the date of the merger, subject to the conditions and limitations specified in Code Secs. 381, 382, 383, and 384.[282] Any deficit in earnings and profits of subsidiary may be used only to offset earnings and profits accumulated after the date of the merger.[283]

- The parent corporation does not recognize any gain or loss in the merger.[284]

Alternatively, a parent corporation may contribute the membership interests in a subsidiary LLC classified as a corporation to a newly formed corporation, and then make an election to treat the subsidiary LLC as a disregarded entity of the newly formed corporation. The tax consequences are the same.[285]

.06 Election by Subsidiary to Be Classified as Disregarded LLC

A subsidiary corporation may file an election to be classified as a disregarded LLC. The election has the following tax consequences:

- The election is treated as a Section 332 liquidation of the subsidiary corporation into the parent corporation.[286]

- Neither the parent corporation nor the subsidiary recognize gain as result of the change in classification.[287] However, items of income, gain, loss, and deduction with respect to any intercompany indebtedness between the parent corporation and the subsidiary must be taken into account on the consolidated return as required by the applicable intercompany transaction regulations.[288]

---

[280] Ltr. Ruls. 200701018, 200645015, 200608038 (merger of Sub 1 into Sub 1 LLC), *citing* Code Sec. 362(b).

[281] Ltr. Ruls. 200701018, 200645015, 200608038 (merger of Sub 1 into Sub 1 LLC), *citing* Code Sec. 1223(2).

[282] Ltr. Ruls. 200701018, 200645015, 200608038 (merger of Sub 1 into Sub 1 LLC), *citing* Code Secs. 381(c)(2)(A) and Reg. § 1.381(c)(2)-1.

[283] Ltr. Ruls. 200701018, 200645015, 200608038 (merger of Sub 1 into Sub 1 LLC), *citing* Code Sec. 381(c)(2)(B).

[284] Ltr. Ruls. 200701018, 200645015, 200608038 (merger of Sub 1 into Sub 1 LLC), *citing* Code Sec. 354.

[285] Ltr. Rul. 201411002.

[286] Ltr. Ruls. 201452016, 200709013, 200708015.

[287] Ltr. Ruls. 201452016, 200709013, 200708015, *citing* Code Secs. 332(a), 336(d)(3), 337(a) and 337(b).

[288] Ltr. Ruls. 200709013, 200708015.

- The parent corporation's basis in each asset received from the subsidiary as result of the classification change is the same as the subsidiary's basis in those assets prior to the classification change.[289]

- The parent corporation's holding period in each asset received from the subsidiary as a result of the classification change includes the period during which those assets were held by the subsidiary.[290]

- The parent corporation succeeds to and takes into account the carryover items specified in Code Sec. 381(c).[291]

- The parent corporation succeeds to and takes into account the earnings and profits, or deficit in earnings and profits, of the subsidiary corporation as of the classification change.[292] Any deficit in the earnings and profits of the parent or subsidiary corporation may be used only to offset the earnings and profits accumulated after the date of the classification change.[293]

A foreign subsidiary corporation that is not eligible to elect classification as a disregarded entity may convert to an eligible entity and then elect to be classified as a disregarded entity for U.S. federal income tax purposes.[294]

.07 Conversion of Subsidiary Corporation under State Law

A parent corporation,[295] or parent LLC,[296] may convert a subsidiary corporation into a disregarded LLC under state conversion laws, such as through the filing of a certificate of conversion with the Secretary of State.[297] The conversion has the following tax consequences:

- The conversion will be treated as if the subsidiary distributed all of its assets and liabilities to the parent corporation in complete liquidation of the subsidiary.[298]

- The parent corporation will not recognize gain or loss on the deemed receipt of assets and liabilities of the subsidiary.[299]

---

[289] Ltr. Ruls. 201452016, 200709013, 200708015, *citing* Code Sec. 334(b)(1).

[290] Ltr. Ruls. 201452016, 200709013, 200708015, *citing* Code Sec. 1223(2).

[291] Ltr. Ruls. 201452016, 200709013, 200708015, *citing* Code Sec. 381(c), subject to the conditions and limitations specified in Code Secs. 381, 382, 383, and 384 and the regulations thereunder.

[292] Ltr. Ruls. 200709013, 200708015, *citing* Code Sec. 381(c)(2)(A); Reg. § 1.381(c)(2)-1).

[293] Ltr. Ruls. 200709013, 200708015, *citing* Code Sec. 381(c)(2)(B).

[294] Ltr. Rul. 201452016.

[295] Ltr. Ruls. 201633014, 201411007, 201404004, 201213018, 201228030.

[296] Ltr. Rul. 201252014.

[297] Ltr. Ruls. 201236014, 201213018, 200608016, 200252055.

[298] Ltr. Ruls. 201633014, 201415001, 201404004, 201252014, 201236014, 201213018, 201228030, *citing* Code Sec. 332(a) and Reg. § 1.332-2(d).

[299] Ltr. Ruls. 201415001, 201404004, 201252014, 201236014, 201213018, 201228030, *citing* Code Sec. 332(a).

- The subsidiary corporation will not recognize gain or loss on the deemed distribution of its assets and liabilities to the parent corporation.[300]
- The basis of the assets received by the parent corporation will be the same as the basis of those assets in the hands of the subsidiary immediately prior to the conversion.[301]
- The holding period of each asset received by the parent corporation includes the holding period during which the subsidiary held the asset.[302]
- The parent corporation will succeed to and take into account the tax items described in Code Sec. 381(c), subject to the conditions and limitations specified in Code Secs. 381, 382, 383, 384 and the regulations thereunder.[303]
- Except to the extent that the subsidiary's earnings and profits are already reflected in the parent corporation's earnings and profits, the parent corporation will succeed to and take into account the earnings and profits, or deficits in earnings and profits, of the subsidiary as of the date of the conversion.[304] Any deficit in the subsidiary's earnings and profits may be used only to offset the earnings and profits accumulated by the parent corporation after the date of the conversion.[305]
- The parent corporation will not recognize cancellation of indebtedness income on the extinguishment of the subsidiary's debt in the conversion.[306]

.08 Conversion of U.S. Subsidiary by Foreign Parent Corporation

A foreign parent corporation may convert a subsidiary corporation into a single-member disregarded LLC. The conversion has the following tax consequences:

- The conversion is treated as a liquidation of the subsidiary corporation into the parent corporation.[307]
- The subsidiary corporation recognizes gain on the conversion under Section 367 unless an exception applies. Under one exception, the conversion of the U.S. subsidiary corporation into a disregarded LLC is not taxable if:[308] (i) the foreign parent corporation uses the property transferred to the LLC in the active conduct of a U.S. trade or business for ten years after the conversion;

---

[300] Ltr. Ruls. 201415001, 201404004, 201252014, 201236014, 201213018, 201228030, *citing* Code Secs. 337(a) and 336(d)(3).

[301] Ltr. Ruls. 201415001, 201404004, 201252014, 201236014, 201228030, 201213018, *citing* Code Sec. 334(b)(1).

[302] Ltr. Ruls. 201415001, 201404004, 201236014, 201228030, 201213018, *citing* Code Sec. 1223(2).

[303] Ltr. Ruls. 201415001, 201404004, 201236014, 201228030, 201228030, 201213018, *citing* Code Sec. 381(a)(1) and Reg. § 1.381(a)-1.

[304] Ltr. Ruls. 201415001, 201404004, 201236014, 201228030, 201213018, *citing* Reg. §§ 1.381(c)(2)-1 and 1.1502-33(a)(2).

[305] Ltr. Ruls. 201415001, 201236014, *citing* Code Sec. 381(c)(2)(B).

[306] Ltr. Ruls. 201415001, 201252014, *citing* Code Sec. 61(a)(12), Reg. § 1.301-1(m), Rev. Rul. 74-54, 1974-1 CB 76.

[307] Ltr. Rul. 200720010.

[308] Ltr. Rul. 200720010, *citing* Code Sec. 367(e)(2) and Reg. § 1.367(e)-2(b)(2)(i).

(ii) the liquidating U.S. subsidiary attaches a statement described in Reg. § 1.367(e)-2(b)(2)(i)(C) to its U.S. income tax returns for the tax year of the conversion; and (iii) the foreign parent corporations attaches a description of the property under Reg. § 1.367(e)-2(b)(2)(i)(C)(2) to its U.S. income tax return for the tax year of the conversion.

- The subsidiary corporation recognizes gain on the appreciation in intangible assets transferred to the LLC in the conversion.[309]
- The LLC is treated as a branch of the foreign parent corporation. The income of the LLC is included in the taxable income of the foreign parent corporation and is subject to the branch profits tax.[310]
- Net operating losses of the subsidiary corporation carry over to the parent corporation, and may be deducted against the parent corporation's U.S. income to the extent permitted by Code Sec. 381.[311]

¶ 1110 CONVERSION OF LLC INTO LIMITED PARTNERSHIP

The tax consequences of a conversion from an LLC into a limited partnership are similar to the tax consequences of a conversion from a limited partnership into an LLC.[312] The limited partnership is treated as the continuation of the LLC. The liquidation does not result in the termination of the LLC.[313] Neither the LLC nor its members recognize taxable gain.[314]

The limited partnership may complete a like-kind exchange entered into by the LLC prior to its liquidation. The limited partnership is treated as both the transferor of the relinquished property previously transferred to a qualified intermediary by the LLC before its liquidation, and as the transferee of the replacement property received from the qualified intermediary.[315]

An LLC may merge into a limited partnership in which the members of the limited partnership are different than the members of the LLC. In such case, the merger is treated as an assets-over form of merger or an assets-up form of merger. The tax consequences of the merger are discussed in ¶ 1122.

The conversion of an LLC to a limited partnership may result in taxable gain if the transfer of liabilities from the LLC to the partnership results in a net decrease in an LLC member's share of liabilities.[316] The transfer of nonrecourse liabilities from the LLC to the partnership may result in a net decrease in a member's share of liabilities, if the liabilities are converted to recourse liabilities after the conversion.

---

[309] Ltr. Rul. 200720010.

[310] Ltr. Rul. 200720010. *See* ¶ 1902.06 *infra* regarding the branch profits tax.

[311] Ltr. Rul. 200720010.

[312] *See* ¶ 1102 *infra*.

[313] Ltr. Ruls. 201745005, 199935065.

[314] Ltr. Rul. 201745005.

[315] Ltr. Rul. 199935065.

[316] Ltr. Ruls. 9720008-013, 9719015, 9719019-029 (*citing* Code Sec. 752 and Reg. § 1.752-1(a)(2), (f)).

A liability is nonrecourse as to the members of an LLC if no member currently bears the economic risk of loss for the liability. These liabilities are allocated to all the members in the LLC based on their shares of profits.[317] Thus, a member's basis is increased by the amount of nonrecourse liabilities multiplied by the member's percentage interest in profits.

The nonrecourse liabilities normally become recourse liabilities when they are transferred to a limited partnership in a conversion because a general partner is personally liable for all partnership liabilities.

Recourse liabilities are allocated to the partners who are personally liable. All of the recourse liabilities are allocated to the general partner if no limited partner is currently liable for those debts after the merger.

A member/limited partner is treated as receiving a distribution of money from the limited partnership to the extent of the decrease in his allocable share of liabilities.[318] The deemed distribution of money reduces the limited partner's basis in the partnership interest. The limited partner recognizes gain to the extent the deemed distribution of money exceeds the limited partner's basis in the partnership.[319]

The transfer of recourse liabilities from the LLC to the limited partnership does not result in a deemed distribution of money or taxation to members if the members who were personally responsible for the liabilities prior to the merger continue to be personally liable after the merger.[320]

¶1111 TRANSFERS OF LLC INTERESTS BETWEEN RELATED COMPANIES

A parent corporation may change the ownership of an LLC from one subsidiary corporation to another without adverse tax consequences. The parent company may simply transfer the membership interests of one subsidiary LLC to another subsidiary LLC. The transfer is a nontaxable exchange under Code Sec. 351 if both LLCs are classified as corporations.[321]

A parent corporation may also transfer the membership interests in a subsidiary LLC to another subsidiary corporation in exchange for additional stock. This is treated as a nontaxable exchange under Section 351.[322] No gain or loss is recognized to the subsidiary corporation upon receipt of the LLC membership interests.[323] The subsidiary corporation's basis in the LLC membership interests is the same basis that the parent corporation had immediately prior to the transfer.[324]

---

[317] Reg. § 1.752-1(e).

[318] Ltr. Ruls. 9720008-013, 9719015, 9719019-029 (*citing* Code Sec. 752 and Reg. § 1.752-1(a)(2), (f)).

[319] Ltr. Ruls. 9720008-013, 9719015, 9719019-029 (*citing* Code Secs. 731(a), 752(b)).

[320] Ltr. Ruls. 9720008-013, 9719015, 9719019-029 (*citing* Code Sec. 752 and Reg. § 1.752-1(a)(2), (f)).

[321] Ltr. Rul. 7821084.

[322] Ltr. Rul. 7716015.

[323] Ltr. Rul. 7716015 (*citing* Code Sec. 1032(a)).

[324] Ltr. Rul. 7716015 (*citing* Code Sec. 362(a)).

¶1112 REINCORPORATION

The reincorporation of an LLC is treated as an F reorganization if the LLC is classified as a corporation for federal tax purposes.[325] The following tax consequences apply if one LLC transfers all of its assets and liabilities to a new LLC in order to effect the reincorporation:[326]

- No gain or loss is recognized to the old LLC upon the transfer of its assets to the new LLC in exchange for membership interests in the new LLC and the assumption of the liabilities of the old LLC by the new LLC.[327]

- The basis of the assets of the old LLC in the hands of the new LLC is the same as the basis of the assets in the hands of the old LLC immediately prior to the transfer.[328]

- The holding period of the assets of the old LLC in the hands of the new LLC includes the period during which those assets were held by the old LLC.[329]

- No gain or loss is recognized to the new LLC upon the receipt of the assets of the old LLC in exchange for membership interests in the new LLC.[330]

- No gain or loss is recognized by the members (same members for both LLCs) upon receipt of the membership interests in the new LLC in exchange for the membership interests in the old LLC.[331]

- The basis of the membership interests received by the members of the new LLC in exchange for the membership interests in the old LLC is the same as the members' basis in the membership interests of the old LLC.[332]

- The holding period of the membership interests received by the members of the new LLC in exchange for the membership interests in the old LLC includes the holding period of the membership interests in the old LLC.[333]

- The new LLC is treated as if there had been no reincorporation for purposes of Section 381. The tax year does not end on the date of the reincorporation. The other tax attributes of the old LLC carry over to the new LLC.[334]

---

[325] Ltr. Rul. 8002076.

[326] *Id.*

[327] Ltr. Rul. 8002076 (*citing* Code Secs. 361(a), 357(a)).

[328] Ltr. Rul. 8002076 (*citing* Code Sec. 362(b)).

[329] Ltr. Rul. 8002076 (*citing* Code Sec. 1223).

[330] Ltr. Rul. 8002076 (*citing* Code Sec. 1032(a)).

[331] Ltr. Rul. 8002076 (*citing* Code Sec. 354(a)(1)).

[332] Ltr. Rul. 8002076 (*citing* Code Sec. 358(a)(1)).

[333] Ltr. Rul. 8002076 (*citing* Code Sec. 1223(1)).

[334] Ltr. Rul. 8002076 (*citing* Reg. § 1.381(b)-1(a)(2)). These tax attributes are listed in Code Sec. 381(c).

¶ 1113 DROP-DOWN OF ASSETS INTO SUBSIDIARY LLC

.01 *LLC Classified as Partnership*

The drop-down of assets and liabilities by a corporation into an LLC that is classified as a partnership is a nontaxable transfer under Code Sec. 721.[335] If the corporation then transfers the membership units to its parent corporation in liquidation, the transfer of membership units and the liquidation of the subsidiary qualify as a nontaxable liquidation under Code Sec. 332.[336]

.02 *LLC Classified as Corporation*

The drop-down of assets and liabilities by a parent company into a subsidiary LLC that is classified as a corporation is a nontaxable exchange under Code Sec. 351.[337] However, the transaction is treated as a nondivisive D reorganization if the parent company thereafter transfers the LLC membership units that it receives to its parent corporation.[338]

.03 *LLC Classified as Disregarded Entity*

The drop-down of assets and liabilities by a parent company into a subsidiary LLC that is classified as a disregarded entity is nontaxable to the parent company, its shareholders, and the LLC.[339] The transaction is disregarded for federal tax purposes.[340] The parent company must continue to use the income deferral method of accounting for prepaid subscriptions after the transfer.[341]

¶ 1114 CONVERSION FROM TRUST TO LLC

A trust may convert to an LLC by contributing its assets to an LLC in exchange for membership interests and then distributing the membership interests to the trust beneficiaries. No gain or loss is recognized to the trust, the beneficiaries of the trust, or the LLC upon the contribution of assets to the LLC.[342] No gain or loss is recognized

---

[335] Ltr. Rul. 9640010.

[336] Ltr. Rul. 9640010 (*citing* Code Sec. 332(a) and Reg. § 1.332-2(c)).

[337] Ltr. Rul. 7203140670A.

[338] *See, e.g.,* Ltr. Rul. 7908027. An LLC dropped down assets and liabilities of one of its branches into a newly formed subsidiary LLC in exchange for all of the stock in the new LLC. The parent LLC then transferred the stock in the subsidiary LLC to its parent corporation. *See also* Ltr. Rul. 6612276340A.

[339] Ltr. Rul. 200423016. *See also* ¶ 1108.04 *supra* regarding the drop-down of assets by S corporation into an LLC owned by the S corporation.

[340] Ltr. Rul. 201512001.

[341] Ltr. Rul. 200423016.

[342] Ltr. Ruls. 200734003, 9604014.

to the trust or its beneficiaries upon the distribution of membership interests to the beneficiaries, provided the trust does not elect to recognize gain or loss upon the distribution under Code Sec. 643(e)(3)(B).

¶1115 DIVISION OF LLC

.01 General Rules

An LLC that is classified as a partnership may be divided into two or more LLCs. Any resulting LLC is treated as a continuation of the prior LLC if the members of the LLC had an interest of more than 50 percent in the capital and profits of the prior LLC. Any resulting LLC in which members did not have more than 50 percent of the capital and profits interest in the prior LLC is not considered a continuation of the prior LLC. If the members of none of the new LLCs owned more than 50 percent of the capital and profits interests of the prior LLC, none of the new LLCs will be a continuation of the prior LLC, and the prior LLC will be terminated.[343] If a member is not a member of one of the resulting LLCs after the division, the member's interest will be considered liquidated as of the date of division.[344]

The IRS regulations use four terms to describe an LLC division. The prior LLC is the LLC that existed prior to the division.[345] The resulting LLCs are the LLCs that exist after the merger.[346] The divided LLC is the LLC that transfers its assets to the new LLC.[347] The recipient LLC is the new LLC that receives the assets.[348]

The tax consequences of a division depend on the form of division. There are two forms of division: the assets-over form[349] and the assets-up form.[350]

.02 Assets-Over Form

In an assets-over form of division, the old LLC transfers some of its assets to a new LLC in exchange for membership interests in the new LLC. The old LLC then immediately distributes the new membership interests to some or all of the members in the old LLC in partial or complete liquidation of their membership interests. The LLC that is the continuing LLC for tax purposes is treated as contributing assets to the new LLC in exchange for membership interests.[351] If none of the LLCs are continuing LLCs for tax purposes after the division, the old LLC will be treated as

---

[343] Code Sec. 708(b)(2)(B); Reg. § 1.708-1(d)(1).

[344] Reg. § 1.708-1(d)(1).

[345] Reg. § 1.708-1(d)(4)(ii).

[346] Reg. § 1.708-1(d)(4)(iv).

[347] Reg. § 1.708-1(d)(4)(i).

[348] Reg. § 1.708-1(d)(4)(iii).

[349] *See* ¶1115.02 *infra.*

[350] *See* ¶1115.03 *infra.*

[351] Reg. § 1.708-1(d)(3)(i)(A).

contributing all of its assets and liabilities to each of the LLCs existing after the division in exchange for membership interests in those LLCs, and then immediately liquidating by distributing the membership interests to the members of the old LLC.[352]

This is the default form of division if no form of division is specified, or if the division does not qualify as an assets-up form.[353]

The final regulations on divisions do not discuss the tax consequences of the assets-over form of division in any significant detail. The tax consequences are based on other applicable provisions of the Code, regulations, and rulings.

The tax consequences and mechanics of an assets-over division are as follows:[354]

- The prior LLC transfers certain assets to a resulting LLC in exchange for membership interests in the resulting LLC. The prior LLC then immediately distributes the membership interest in the resulting LLC to designated members. The prior LLC's momentary ownership of all the interests in a resulting LLC will not prevent the resulting LLC from being classified as a partnership on formation.[355]
- A resulting LLC is an LLC resulting from the division that exists after the division and that has at least two members who were members in the prior LLC. For example, where a prior LLC divides into two LLCs, both LLCs existing after the division are resulting LLCs.[356]
- A resulting LLC is treated as a continuation of the prior LLC if the members of the resulting LLC had an interest of more than 50 percent of the capital and profits of the prior LLC. A resulting LLC is treated as a new partnership if the members of the resulting LLC had an interest of 50 percent or less of the capital and profits of the prior LLC. If the members of none of the resulting LLCs owned an interest of more than 50 percent in the capital and profits of the prior LLC, then there is no continuing LLC and the prior LLC is terminated.[357]
- A resulting LLC that is not a continuation of the prior LLC is treated as a new partnership.[358]
- For tax purposes, the divided LLC (rather than the prior LLC) is treated as transferring assets and liabilities to a recipient LLC in exchange for membership interests in the recipient LLC. The divided LLC is then treated as distributing the interests in the recipient LLCs to some or all of its members in partial or complete liquidation of their interests in the divided LLC.[359] The divided LLC is the resulting LLC that is a continuation of the prior LLC if

---

[352] Reg. § 1.708-1(d)(3)(i)(B).

[353] Reg. § 1.708-1(d)(3)(i), (4)(i).

[354] Ltr. Ruls. 201643019, 201643018, 201643017, 201643016.

[355] REG-111119-99, 2000-5 IRB 455.

[356] Reg. § 1.708-1(d).

[357] Code Sec. 708(b)(2)(B); Reg. § 1.708-1(d)(1).

[358] Reg. § 1.708-1(d)(1); Ltr. Ruls. 201643019, 201643018, 201643017, 201643016, 201619001.

[359] Reg. § 1.708-1(d)(3)(i)(A).

there is only one continuing LLC.[360] The divided LLC is the continuing LLC that transferred assets to the resulting LLCs if there is more than one continuing LLC.[361] The divided LLC is the LLC with the greatest fair market value (net of liabilities) if (i) there is more than one continuing LLC, and (ii) the LLC that transferred assets to the resulting LLCs is not a continuing LLC.[362] All LLCs other than the divided LLC are recipient LLCs. For example, if an LLC divides into two LLCs and both LLCs are continuing LLCs (because the members of both LLCs owned more than 50 percent of the capital and profits in the prior LLC), then the LLC that transfers the assets and liabilities is the divided LLC and the transferee LLC is the recipient LLC.[363]

- For tax purposes, if there is no divided LLC (*i.e.,* because there is no continuing LLC owned by more than 50 percent of the members prior to the division), the prior LLC will be treated as contributing all of its assets and liabilities to new resulting LLCs in exchange for membership interests. Thereafter, the prior LLC will be treated as a liquidating by distributing the membership interests in the new resulting LLCs to the members of the prior LLC.[364]

- For state law purposes, the divided LLC is not necessarily the LLC that transfers assets to the resulting LLCs. For example, if the prior LLC transfers its assets to a resulting LLC whose members owned more than 50 percent of the prior LLC, and if such transferee LLC was the only continuing LLC, then the transferee LLC would be the divided LLC.[365]

- The divided LLC must file a return for the tax year of the LLC that has been divided and retain the EIN of the prior LLC. The return must include the names, addresses and EINs of all resulting LLCs that are treated as continuing LLCs. The return must also state that the LLC is a continuation of the prior LLC and set forth separately the respective distributive shares of the members for the period prior to and including the date of the division and subsequent to the date of the division.[366]

- All resulting LLCs other than the divided LLC must file separate returns for the tax year beginning on the day after the date of the division with new EINs for each LLC. The return of any continuing LLC that is not the divided LLC must include the name, address and EIN of the prior LLC.[367]

- If the prior LLC transfers assets to multiple LLCs, the transfer to each resulting LLC is viewed separately. The transfer to one resulting LLC may be

---

[360] Reg. § 1.708-1(d)(3)(i)(A).

[361] Ltr. Rul. 200223036; Reg. § 1.708-1(d)(3)(i)(A).

[362] Reg. § 1.708-1(d)(4)(i).

[363] Ltr. Rul. 200223036.

[364] Reg. § 1.708-1(d)(4)(i).

[365] REG-111119-99, 2000-5 IRB 455.

[366] Reg. § 1.708-1(d)(2)(i).

[367] Reg. § 1.708-1(d)(2)(i).

characterized under the assets-over form while a transfer to another resulting LLC may be characterized under the assets-up form.[368]

- Gain recognition under Code Sec. 704(c)(1)(B) may be triggered by the division if a member contributed appreciated property to the prior LLC. Code Sec. 704(c)(1)(B) provides that if the LLC distributes built-in gain or loss property to a member other than the contributing member within seven years after the date of contribution, the distribution is taxed as a sale on the date of distribution. This forces the contributing member to recognize the built-in gain or loss when the LLC distributes the property to a non-contributing member.[369] The divided LLC's distribution of a membership interest in the recipient LLC will trigger Section 704(c)(1)(B) gain where the interest in the recipient LLC is received by a member of the divided LLC other than the member who contributed the appreciated property to the divided LLC.[370]

- Gain recognition under Section 737 may be triggered if a member who contributed appreciated property to the divided LLC receives an interest in the recipient LLC that is not attributable to such appreciated property.[371] Code Sec. 737 provides that a member who contributes appreciated property to an LLC recognizes a pre-contribution gain if the LLC distributes within seven years other property to the member with a value exceeding the member's basis in the membership interest.[372]

- An LLC division does not create new built-in-gain property under Code Secs. 704(c)(1)(B) and 737 when there is a pro rata division as to all members in the prior LLC. However, the IRS believes that a different result may apply in non-pro rata divisions. It is continuing to study this matter.[373]

- All resulting LLCs that are continuing LLCs are subject to preexisting elections that were made by the prior LLC. A post-division election that is made by a resulting LLC will not bind any other resulting LLC.[374]

- An LLC division cannot occur when there is only a single member in a resulting LLC. To have a division, at least two members of the prior LLC must be members of each resulting LLC that exists after the transaction. The transfer by a prior LLC to a single-member LLC is treated as a distribution of assets rather than a partnership division.

- The partnership tax rules apply to the formation of the recipient LLC and the distribution of membership interests in the recipient LLC because the recipient LLC is treated as a partnership (even though the recipient LLC is a single-

---

[368] Reg. § 1.708-1(d)(5); T.D. 8925 (Jan. 4, 2001).

[369] *See* ¶ 605.03 *supra.*

[370] REG-111119-99, 2000-5 IRB 455.

[371] REG-111119-99, 2000-5 IRB 455.

[372] *See* ¶ 605.04.

[373] T.D. 8925 (Jan. 4, 2001).

[374] Reg. § 1.708-1(d)(2)(ii).

member LLC owned by the divided LLC prior to the distribution of membership interests in the recipient LLC).[375]

- Under the partnership tax rules, the divided LLC receives a basis in the membership interests in the recipient LLC equal to the money and basis of the assets transferred to the recipient LLC.[376]

- The recipient LLC receives a carryover basis in the assets transferred from the divided LLC.[377]

- The members of the divided LLC (and any other continuing LLC) keep the same tax basis in their membership interests as they had in the prior LLC since the divided LLC is treated as the continuation of the prior LLC. The basis of the membership interest is adjusted by money contributions[378] and distributions.[379] A net increase in liabilities allocable to a member is treated as a money contribution.[380] A net decrease in liabilities is treated as a money distribution.[381]

- The members of the recipient LLC who have no continuing interest in the divided LLC keep the same tax basis in their membership interests as they had in the prior LLC,[382] adjusted for any net increase or decrease in liabilities.[383] This is called a substituted basis.

- The members of the recipient LLC who have a continuing interest in the divided LLC receive a basis in their membership interests in the recipient LLC equal to the divided LLC's basis in such membership interests immediately prior to the distribution,[384] adjusted for any net increase or decrease in liabilities.[385] This is called a carryover basis. The carryover basis in the recipient LLC reduces the member's basis in the divided LLC.[386]

- A member will not recognize gain under Code Sec. 752 as a result of the transfer of liabilities from the divided LLC to the recipient LLC unless there is a net decrease in the member's share of liabilities. In such case, gain is recognized to the extent that the net decrease in liabilities exceeds the mem-

---

[375] REG-111119-99, 2000-5 IRB 455.

[376] Code Sec. 722.

[377] Code Sec. 723.

[378] Code Sec. 722.

[379] Code Sec. 733(1).

[380] Code Sec. 752(a); Reg. § 1.752-1(f).

[381] Code Sec. 752(b); Reg. § 1.752-1(f).

[382] Code Sec. 732(b).

[383] *See* Rev. Rul. 87-120 regarding net increases and decreases in liabilities in liquidating distributions. No gain or loss would be recognized by any member on the liquidating distribution of the membership interest in the recipient LLC, and no income would be recognized as a result of any net increase or decrease in liabilities. Rev. Rul. 87-120, 1987-2 CB 161.

[384] Code Sec. 732(a)(1).

[385] *See* Rev. Rul. 79-205, 1979-2 CB 255 regarding net increases and decreases in liabilities in nonliquidating distributions. No gain or loss would be recognized by any member on the distribution of the membership interest in the recipient LLC, and no income would be recognized as a result of any net increase or decrease in liabilities. Rev. Rul. 87-120, 1987-2 CB 161.

[386] Code Sec. 733(2).

ber's basis in the membership interest after the division.[387] A member's debt relief in one LLC after the division may be netted against the member's assumption of liabilities in the other LLC.[388]

- Each LLC must continue to use the same period and method of depreciation and amortization after the division that was used prior to the division.[389]

.03 Assets-Up Form

In an assets-up form of division, the existing LLC distributes assets to some or all of its members who then contribute the assets to a new LLC in exchange for membership interests.[390]

The assets-up form of division requires that the existing LLC actually transfer ownership of its assets to the members under state law. A mere assignment of the right to receive title to the assets is not sufficient. If the split-off group does not become owners, then the division will be treated as an assets-over form of division.[391] The members are not required to assume the liabilities of the terminated LLC. The terminated LLC may transfer the liabilities directly to the new LLC.[392]

In the normal form of division, the divided LLC distributes assets to some of its members, who contribute assets to the recipient LLC.[393] The divided LLC is the LLC that is a continuation of the prior LLC. An LLC is a continuation of the prior LLC if the members of the LLC had an interest of more than 50 percent in the capital and profits of the prior LLC. If more than one LLC is a continuation of the prior LLC, then the LLC with assets having the greatest fair market value, net of liabilities, is the continuing LLC.[394]

In some divisions, there is no continuing LLC after the division. This may occur when an LLC is divided into three or more LLCs, each with a minority group of members from the existing LLC. The division is treated partly as an asset-over form of division and partly as an assets-up form of division. In such case, the existing LLC is treated as (a) transferring the assets that it retains to a recipient LLC under the assets-over form of division, and (b) transferring the assets that it does not retain to the distributee members who then contribute those assets to a second recipient LLC under the assets-up form of division.[395]

---

[387] REG-111119-99, 2000-5 IRB 455.

[388] FSA 200131013.

[389] Code Sec. 168(i)(7); Rev. Rul. 90-17, 1990-1 CB 119; Reg. § 1.197-2(g)(2)(iv)(C), (g)(2)(ii)(B), (g)(3). *See also* Sloan, E.B., Lipton, R., Harrington, D., and Frediani, M., "New Prop. Regs. Provide Expanding Guidance on Partnership Mergers and Divisions—Part 2," 93 J. *Tax'n* 261, 263-264, under the heading, "Recovery Periods—Depreciation and Amortization" (Nov. 2000).

[390] Reg. § 1.708-1(d)(3)(ii), (5), Example 2.

[391] Reg. § 1.708-1(d)(3)(ii)(A).

[392] Reg. § 1.708-1(c)(3)(ii). *See also* T.D. 8925, IRS Final Regulations on Partnership Mergers and Divisions, Explanation of Revisions and Summary of Contents (Jan. 4, 2001).

[393] Reg. § 1.708-1(d)(3)(ii)(A).

[394] Code Sec. 708(b)(2)(B); Reg. § 1.708-1(d)(1).

[395] Reg. § 1.708-1(d)(3)(ii)(B).

The final regulations on divisions do not discuss the tax consequences of the assets-up form of division in any significant detail. The tax consequences are based on other applicable provisions of the Code, regulations, and rulings. The tax consequences are as follows:

- The basis of assets distributed to each member of the split-off group on liquidation of their membership interests is equal to each member's outside basis in the membership interest, reduced by any money received in the distribution.[396]
- The members of the split-off group do not recognize gain or loss on the transfer of assets and liabilities to the recipient LLC in exchange for membership interests in the recipient LLC.[397]
- The members receive a basis in the membership interests in the recipient LLC equal to their basis in the assets distributed on liquidation of the LLC.[398]
- The recipient LLC's basis in the assets received from its members is the same as the members' basis in such assets immediately prior to the transfer.[399]
- The members' holding periods for non-cash assets distributed to them includes the divided LLC's holding periods for such assets.[400]
- The members' holding periods for membership interests in the recipient LLC include their holding periods in the capital assets and Section 1231 assets transferred to the recipient LLC (to the extent membership interests are received in exchange for such assets).[401] The members' holding period for membership interests received in exchange for other assets begins on the date following the date of the exchange.
- The recipient LLC's holding period for the assets includes the members' holding periods for such assets.[402]
- Members of the divided LLC and recipient LLC do not recognize gain under Code Sec. 752 as a result of the transfer of liabilities from the divided LLC to the members or from the divided LLC to the recipient LLC unless there is a net decrease in the member's share of liabilities.[403] In such case, gain is recognized to the extent that the net decrease in liabilities exceeds the member's basis in the membership interest.[404]
- The divided LLC that distributes assets to some of the members may make an election under Section 754. In such case, the divided LLC must (a) increase the basis of its assets by the amount of gain recognized by the members; (b) decrease the basis of its assets by the amount of loss recognized by the

---

[396] Code Sec. 732(b).
[397] Code Sec. 721(a).
[398] Code Sec. 722.
[399] Code Sec. 723.
[400] Code Sec. 735(b).
[401] Code Sec. 1223(1).
[402] Code Sec. 1223(2).
[403] Code Sec. 752; Reg. § 1.752-1(f).
[404] REG-111119-99, 2000-5 IRB 455.

members; (c) increase the basis of its assets by the amount of basis decrease to the member; and (d) decrease the basis of its assets by the amount of basis increase to the members. These rules are discussed in detail in ¶ 1006.01. Normally, the divided LLC should make a Section 754 election only if it distributes assets that have a higher inside basis than the distributee members' outside basis in their membership interests. In such case, the divided LLC may increase the inside basis of its assets by the difference between inside and outside basis.

- Each LLC must continue to use the same period and method of depreciation and amortization after the division that was used prior to the division. However, the recipient LLC must treat the property as newly acquired property for depreciation purposes with respect to that portion of the basis of property that exceeds the basis of the property in the hands of the divided LLC prior to the division.[405]

- The members may recognize gain under the disguised sales and anti-mixing bowl rules.[406] The IRS has not yet decided whether a division will create new Section 704(c) property or Section 737 net precontribution gain. A division will not create new Section 704(c) property or Section 737 net precontribution gain if the division merely affects a restructuring of the form in which the members hold property, and if each member's overall interest in each LLC property does not change. However, the result may be different if the division is non-pro rata as to the members, if some property is extracted from or added to the LLCs as a result of the division, or if new members are added after the division. The IRS is continuing to study the matter.[407]

- The divided LLC may recognize state and local transfer taxes on the distribution.[408]

- The divided LLC, and any recipient LLC that is treated as a continuation of the prior LLC, are subject to the same elections made by the prior LLC. Subsequent elections made by the divided LLC or recipient LLC do not affect the other LLC.[409]

---

[405] Code Sec. 168(i)(7); Rev. Rul. 90-17, 1990-1 CB 119; Reg. § 1.197-2(g)(2)(iv)(C), (ii)(B), (3). *See also* Sloan, E.B., Lipton, R., Harrington, D., and Frediani, M., "New Prop. Regs. Provide Expanding Guidance on Partnership Mergers and Divisions—Part 2," pp. 263, 264, under the heading, "Recovery Periods—Depreciation and Amortization" (JTAX Nov. 2000).

[406] T.D. 8925 (Jan. 4, 2001); REG-111119-99, 2000-5 IRB 455. *See also* Sloan, E.B., Lipton, R., Harrington, D., and Frediani, M., "New Prop. Regs. Provide Expanding Guidance on Partnership Mergers and Divisions—Part 2," pp. 268-272 (JTAX Nov. 2000).

[407] T.D. 8925 (Jan. 4, 2001).

[408] REG-111119-99, 2000-5 IRB 455.

[409] Reg. § 1.708-1(d)(2)(ii).

EXAMPLE 11-2

Four family groups inherit an LLC containing numerous parcels of real estate. Family Group A decides that it wants to have a separate LLC to own its share of LLC property. The parties agree that the split-off LLC will receive property with a tax basis of $1 million and a fair market value of $5 million in exchange for the family group's entire interest in the family LLC. Family Group A has an aggregate basis of $1.5 mil-lion in its membership interests in the family LLC.

Alternative 1—Asset Over Division. The first alternative is an asset over form of division. This is the normal form of characterization. The family LLC would transfer the property directly to the split-off LLC. This split-off LLC would receive the same $1 million tax basis in the property that family LLC had in the property prior to the transfer.

Alternative 2—Asset Up Form. The second alternative is an asset up form of division. This form of division may only be used if the family LLC first transfers the real property into the names of the individual members of Family Group A, who then transfer the property to the split-off LLC. There must be an actual transfer of ownership to the family group members, rather than a mere assignment of the right to receive title. In this case, Family Group A would receive a $1.5 million basis in the distributed properties equal to their outside basis in the family LLC. This is called a substituted basis. The split-off LLC would receive the same $1.5 million basis in the property when Family Group A contributed the property to the split-off LLC. Under this second alternative, the split-off LLC would have a $500,000 greater basis in the transferred property than under the first alternative.

Basis adjustment issues in asset over division. If the family LLC transfers low basis property to the split-off LLC in an asset over division, then the split-off LLC will have more gain to recognize when the property is sold (and the remaining members of the family LLC will have less gain to recognize when their property is sold). If the family LLC transfers high basis property to the split-off LLC, then the split-off LLC will have less gain to recognize when the property is sold (and the remaining members of the family LLC will have more gain to recognize when their property is sold). In an asset over division, the split-off LLC may make an election under Code Sec. 754 to increase the basis of its assets from the $1 million carryover basis to the $1.5 million substituted basis, but only if the family LLC makes a corresponding $500,000 decrease in the basis of its remain-ing assets.[410]

Basis adjustment issues in asset up division. There are similar basis adjustment problems and issues for the family members in an asset up division. If the family LLC had at any time in the past made a Section 754

---

[410] Code Sec. 734(b) (flush language).

election, the family LLC would have to reduce the basis of its properties by the $500,000 basis increase in the properties for the split-off family members.[411] The family LLC would also have to make a mandatory downward basis adjustment to its property, even if it does not make a Section 754 election, since the split-off group would be receiving a substituted basis in the distributed property that was $250,000 more than the family LLC's basis in the property.[412]

.04 Tax Returns

The divided LLC (the continuing LLC with assets having the greatest fair market value of assets net of liabilities) must file a tax return for the tax year in which the division occurred. It must also retain the same employer identification number of the prior LLC. The return must include the names, addresses, and employer identification numbers of all resulting LLCs that are not considered continuations of the prior LLC. The return must state that the LLC is a continuation of the prior LLC. It must set forth separately the respective distributive shares of the members for the periods prior to and including the date of the division and subsequent to the date of the division.[413]

The recipient LLC must file separate returns for the tax year beginning on the day after the division. It must apply for and use a separate employer identification number.[414]

EXAMPLE 11-3

ABCD LLC is in the real estate and insurance business. Member A owns a 40 percent interest in the capital and profits of the LLC. Each of the other members owns a 20 percent interest in the LLC. The LLC and its members report their income on a calendar year basis. They agree to separate the real estate and insurance business on November 1, 2004. The LLC transfers title to the real estate to the AB LLC owned by Members A and B. The LLC transfers the insurance business to CD LLC owned by Members C and D. AB LLC is the divided LLC and continuing LLC since its members owned more than 50 percent of the capital and profits interest of ABCD LLC prior to the division. The division is an assets-over form of division since the assets were transferred directly to the new LLCs. AB LLC must file a return for the entire calendar year 2004. It must indicate on the return that it was the ABCD LLC until November 1, 2004. CD LLC is

---

[411] Code Sec. 734(b)(2)(B).

[412] *See* ¶ 1009 *supra.*

[413] *Id.*

[414] *Id.*

considered a new LLC formed at the beginning of the day on November 2, 2004. It is required to file a return for the tax year that it adopts in compliance with the applicable regulations. Assuming that it adopts a calendar year, it must file a short return for the period from November 2, 2004 until December 31, 2004.[415]

¶1116 CONVERSION AS A RESULT OF CHANGE IN CLASSIFICATION ELECTION

An LLC may convert from one type of entity to another (i.e., corporation, partnership, or disregarded entity) by filing an elective change in classification. The regulations deal with the following four elective changes in classification that are permitted under the final check-the-box regulations:[416]

1. Partnership elects to be taxed as a corporation.
2. Corporation elects to be taxed as a partnership.
3. Corporation with a single member elects to be disregarded as an entity for tax purposes.
4. Disregarded entity elects to be taxed as a corporation.

An entity that is designated as a corporation in its articles of incorporation cannot elect classification as a partnership or disregarded entity. The entity is automatically classified as a corporation under the *per se* rules.[417]

¶1117 CONVERSION FROM SINGLE-MEMBER LLC TO LLC CLASSIFIED AS A PARTNERSHIP

The status of a single-member LLC that is classified as a disregarded LLC changes when the LLC acquires more than one member. The LLC is classified as a partnership for federal tax purposes unless an election is made to classify the LLC as a corporation.[418]

A single-member disregarded LLC may convert to a partnership LLC in several ways, including (a) conversion to a partnership when a new member purchases an interest in the LLC from an existing member, (b) conversion when a new member contributes cash or property to the LLC in exchange for a membership interest, and (c) distribution of membership interests by a trust or corporation that is the sole owner of the LLC to the beneficiaries of the trust or the shareholders of the corporation.

---

[415] Reg. § 1.708-1(d)(5), Example 1.

[416] Reg. § 301.7701-3(g). *See* ¶508.06 *supra* for discussion of the tax consequences of these conversions. Ltr. Rul. 200701032.

[417] *See* ¶503.01 *supra*.

[418] Reg. § 301.7701-3(f).

.01 Conversion by Purchase

A single-member disregarded LLC may convert to a partnership if the member sells part of his or her membership interest to a third party. In this case, the purchasing member pays the purchase price to the selling member and does not contribute any money to the LLC. The purchase of an interest in the LLC that causes the LLC to have more than one owner is treated as the purchase of a percentage interest in each of the LLC's assets equal to the percentage of the membership interests purchased.[419] These assets are treated as held directly by the purchasing member for federal tax purposes. Immediately thereafter, the new member and the old member are treated as contributing their respective interests in those assets to an LLC in exchange for a membership interest in the LLC. The tax consequences are as follows:[420]

- The old member recognizes gain or loss on the deemed sale of the interest in each asset of the LLC to the new member if the old member receives the cash proceeds of sale.[421]

- No gain or loss is recognized by either member as a result of the deemed contribution of assets by both parties to a partnership.[422]

- The new member's basis in the membership interest is equal to the amount paid by the new member to the old member for the assets that the new member is deemed to have contributed to the newly created LLC. The old member's basis in the membership interest is equal to the old member's basis in his share of the assets of the LLC.[423]

- The basis of property treated as contributed to the LLC by both members is the adjusted basis of that property in the members' hands immediately after the deemed sale.[424]

- The old member's holding period for the membership interest received includes the member's holding period in the capital assets and property held by the LLC when it converted from a single-member LLC to a partnership.[425] The new member's holding period for the membership interest begins on the day following the day of purchase of the LLC interest from the old member.[426] The holding period of each purchased asset is computed by excluding the date on which the asset is acquired. The LLC's holding period for the assets deemed

---

[419] *See* Reg. § 1.1361-5(b)(3), Example 2, involving the sale by an S corporation of LLC membership interests in a single-member disregarded LLC to an unrelated third party.

[420] Rev. Rul. 99-5, 1999-5 IRB 8, Situation 1; Reg. § 1.1361-5(b)(3), Example 2.

[421] Rev. Rul. 99-5, 1999-5 IRB 8 (*citing* Code Sec. 1001).

[422] Rev. Rul. 99-5, 1999-5 IRB 8 (*citing* Code Sec. 721(a)).

[423] Rev. Rul. 99-5, 1999-5 IRB 8 (*citing* Code Sec. 722).

[424] Rev. Rul. 99-5, 1999-5 IRB 8 (*citing* Code Sec. 723).

[425] Rev. Rul. 99-5, 1999-5 IRB 8 (*citing* Code Sec. 1223(1)).

[426] Rev. Rul. 99-5, 1999-5 IRB 8 (*citing* Rev. Rul. 66-7, 1966-1 CB 188).

transferred to it includes each member's holding period for such assets.[427] This means that the LLC will have a split holding period for each asset.

- The assets that the original owner is deemed to have contributed to the new LLC are Section 704(c) assets. The LLC must allocate the built-in gain or loss to the original owner for tax purposes.[428] The assets that the purchasing member is deemed to have contributed to the new LLC are not Section 704(c) assets since the purchasing member receives a capital account value equal to the purchase price of those assets. The LLC may allocate depreciation, amortization and gain or loss with respect to such assets to the members in accordance with the operating agreement. Under prior law, the purchasing member would receive all tax allocations with respect to the assets deemed contributed by that member to the LLC.[429]

.02 Conversion by Cash Contribution

A single-member LLC may also convert to a partnership when a new member contributes cash to the LLC in exchange for a membership interest. A new member's contribution is treated as a contribution to a partnership in exchange for an ownership interest in the LLC. The old member is treated as contributing all of the assets of the LLC to the partnership in exchange for a membership interest. The tax consequences are as follows:[430]

- No gain or loss is recognized by either member as a result of the conversion of the disregarded entity to a partnership.[431]
- The new member's basis in the membership interest is equal to the amount of cash contributed to the LLC plus the basis of any property contributed.[432] The old member's basis in the membership interest is equal to its basis in the assets of the LLC, which assets the old member is treated as contributing to a newly created partnership.
- The basis of property that the old member is deemed to have contributed to the LLC is the adjusted basis of that property in the old member's hands prior to the conversion. The basis of property contributed to the LLC by the new member is the amount of cash and the adjusted basis of property contributed to the LLC.[433]
- The old member's holding period for a membership interest received includes the old member's holding period in the capital and assets deemed contributed

---

[427] Rev. Rul. 99-5, 1999-5 IRB 8 (*citing* Code Sec. 1223(2)).

[428] *See* ¶ 805 *supra.*

[429] Prop. Reg. § 1.704-1(c)(4), Example (1) before amendment by TD 8500, 12/21/1993. This was the default rule for property in which the members had an undivided interest prior to the contribution or deemed contribution.

[430] Rev. Rul. 99-5, 1999-5 IRB 8, Situation 2.

[431] Rev. Rul. 99-5, 1999-5 IRB 8 (*citing* Code Sec. 721(a)).

[432] Rev. Rul. 99-5, 1999-5 IRB 8 (*citing* Code Sec. 722).

[433] Rev. Rul. 99-5, 1999-5 IRB 8 (*citing* Code Sec. 723).

upon the conversion from a single-member LLC to a partnership.[434] The new member's holding period for the membership interest begins on the day following the date of the new member's contribution of money and property to the LLC.[435] The LLC's holding period for the assets transferred to it includes the old member's holding period for those assets.[436]

There would be a potential disguised sale taxable to the original member of the LLC if the LLC distributed cash or property to the original member immediately following the contribution of assets by the new member to the LLC.[437]

.03 Distribution by Trust or Corporation

A trust or corporation that is the sole owner of a disregarded LLC may distribute the membership interests in the LLC to the beneficiaries of the trust or the shareholders of the corporation. The distribution has the following tax consequences:[438]

- The distribution of membership interests is first treated as a nontaxable distribution of LLC assets and related liabilities to the beneficiaries or shareholders in accordance with their interests in the trust or the corporation.
- The beneficiaries and shareholders are treated as contributing their respective interests in those assets to the LLC in exchange for membership interests in the LLC.
- The LLC will be classified as a partnership after the conversion unless the LLC makes an election to be classified as a corporation.
- The beneficiaries and shareholders do not recognize gain or loss as a result of the conversion of the disregarded entity to a partnership.[439]

If the LLC distributes marketable securities to the beneficiaries, there is no tax under Section 721(b) because each beneficiary is treated as receiving and then contributing a diversified portfolio of securities to the LLC. The trust beneficiaries are treated as "eligible partners" provided they do not contribute additional property to the LLC. In-kind distributions to the eligible partners of an LLC that is classified as an investment partnership will not result in gain or loss to the members.[440]

.04 Employer Identification Member

An LLC that is classified as a disregarded entity must report, calculate, and pay its employment tax obligation under its own name and employer identification number. When the LLC is reclassified as a partnership after expanding to more than

---

[434] Rev. Rul. 99-5, 1999-5 IRB 8 (*citing* Code Sec. 1223(1)).

[435] Rev. Rul. 99-5, 1999-5 IRB 8 (*citing* Rev. Rul. 66-7, 1966-1 CB 188).

[436] Rev. Rul. 99-5, 1999-5 IRB 8 (*citing* Code Sec. 1223(2)).

[437] *See* ¶ 605.02.

[438] Ltr. Ruls. 200636092, 200633019, *citing* Rev. Rul. 99-5.

[439] Ltr. Rul. 200633019, *citing* the first situation of Rev. Rul. 99-5.

[440] Ltr. Rul. 200633019, *citing* Code Secs. 731(a), 731(c)(3)(C).

one member, the LLC must retain the same employer identification number that it used as a disregarded entity for employment tax and reporting purposes.[441] However, if the LLC did not have a separate employer identification number apart from the Social Security number or tax identification number of the single member, then it must obtain a new employer identification number.[442]

¶1118 CONVERSION FROM AN LLC CLASSIFIED AS A PARTNERSHIP TO A DISREGARDED LLC

An LLC that is classified as a partnership for federal tax purposes may convert to a disregarded entity if one person purchases all of the membership interests in the LLC. The LLC may also convert from a partnership to a disregarded entity as a result of a reorganization. The LLC may elect to be classified as a corporation for federal tax purposes. If no election is made, the LLC will be classified as a disregarded entity.[443] The purchase may be made in one of two ways. First, one member of an LLC may purchase all of the membership interests from the other members in the LLC. Second, a third party may purchase all of the membership interests from the members in the LLC.

.01 Purchase by One Member from Another

The partnership status of the LLC will terminate if one member of an LLC purchases all of the membership interests from the other members. The selling member is treated as selling a partnership interest, and the buying member is treated as acquiring partnership assets. After the purchase, the business may be continued by the LLC, assuming that the state permits a single-member LLC. The tax consequences are as follows:

- The partnership status of the LLC terminates when the member purchases all of the membership interests from the other members.[444] The old members must treat the transaction as a sale of a partnership interest.[445] The old members must report gain or loss, if any, resulting from the sale of the membership interests.[446]

- The LLC is deemed to have made a liquidating distribution of all its assets to its members. Following this deemed distribution, the sole remaining member

---

[441] Rev. Rul. 2001-61, 2001-50 IRB 573.

[442] Reg. § 301.6109-1(h)(2)(ii).

[443] Prop. Reg. § 301.7701-3(f); Rev. Rul. 2002-49, 2002-32 IRB 288.

[444] Rev. Rul. 99-6, 1999-1 CB 432 (*citing* Code Sec. 708(b)(1)(A)); Ltr. Ruls. 201723009, 200603021. The same rule applies if one of the members buys all of the membership interests of the other members through a wholly owned disregarded LLC. Ltr. Rul. 200334037.

[445] Rev. Rul. 99-6, 1999-1 CB 432 (*citing* Reg. § 1.741-1(b)); Ltr. Rul. 201723009.

[446] Rev. Rul. 99-6, 1999-1 CB 432 (*citing* Code Sec. 741).

is treated as acquiring the assets that are deemed to have been distributed to the old members in liquidation of the old members' membership interests.[447]

- The remaining member's basis in the assets attributable to the old members' interests in the LLC is the purchase price for the membership interests.[448] The remaining member's holding period for those assets begins on the day immediately following the date of sale.[449]

- Upon termination of the partnership, the remaining member is considered to have received a distribution of assets attributable to the remaining member's former interest in the LLC. The remaining member must recognize gain or loss, if any, on the deemed distribution of those assets.[450] The remaining member would recognize gain only if the amount of money distributed exceeds his basis in his membership interest.[451] The remaining member would recognize loss only if the only property distributed is money and/or inventory and his basis in the membership interest is more than the sum of the money and his basis in the inventory. The remaining member's basis in the assets received in the deemed liquidation of the membership interest is determined under Code Sec. 732(b). Under that section, the basis in the distributed assets equals the remaining member's basis in his membership interest, less any money received. The remaining member's holding period for those assets attributable to the remaining member's interest in the LLC includes the LLC's holding period for such assets.[452]

- Any debt that the LLC owes to the remaining member is treated as canceled when the LLC becomes a disregarded entity. However, there is no cancellation of indebtedness income.[453]

- The rules are similar if one member of a consolidated group of corporations purchases the membership interests in an LLC from another member of a consolidated group, resulting in a change in classification of the LLC from a partnership to a disregarded entity. The sale of the membership interests is treated as an intercompany transaction. The gain or loss from the sale is an intercompany item.[454] Gain realized on an intercompany transaction is deferred in determining the federal income tax consequences to the selling member until the gain is included in income under either the matching rule of Treas. Reg. § 1.1502-13(c) or the acceleration rule of Treas. Reg. § 1.1502-13(d).

---

[447] Rev. Rul. 99-6, 1999-1 CB 432 (*citing Edwin E. McCauslen v. Comm'r*, 45 TC 588 (1966), and Rev. Rul. 67-65, 1967-1 CB 168); Ltr. Ruls. 201723009, 200603021. *See also* Ltr. Ruls. 200222026, in which the IRS determined that 100 percent of the LLC assets were deemed distributed to the remaining member when that member, as owner of 99 percent of the membership units, purchased the membership units from a one percent member.

[448] Rev. Rul. 99-6, 1999-1 CB 432 (*citing* Code Sec. 1012); Ltr. Ruls. 201723009, 200603021.

[449] Rev. Rul. 99-6, 1999-1 CB 432 (*citing* Rev. Rul. 66-7, 1966-1 CB 188).

[450] Rev. Rul. 99-6, 1999-1 CB 432 (*citing* Code Sec. 731(a)).

[451] Code Sec. 731(a).

[452] Rev. Rul. 99-6, 1999-1 CB 432 (*citing* Code Sec. 735(b)).

[453] Ltr. Rul. 200222026.

[454] Ltr. Rul. 201723009.

.02 Purchase of Membership Interests by Third Party

The partnership status of an LLC will also terminate if a third party who is not a member purchases all of the membership interests in the LLC.[455] The tax consequences are as follows:

- The old members must report gain or loss, if any, resulting from the sale of their membership interests.[456]
- For purposes of classifying the acquisition of membership interests by a new member, the LLC is deemed to have made a liquidating distribution of those assets to its members. Immediately following the distribution, the new member is deemed to have acquired by purchase all of the former LLC's assets.[457]
- The new member's basis in the assets is equal to the cash purchase price for the membership interest.[458] This is equal to the fair market value the assets.[459] The basis is allocated among the assets in accordance with Code Sec. 732(c).[460]
- The new member's holding period for the assets begins on the day immediately following the date of sale.[461]
- The purchaser must file IRS Form 8594, Asset Acquisition Statement Under Section 1060.[462]

.03 Reorganization

An LLC that is classified as a partnership may also convert to a disregarded entity as a result of a reorganization after which a single member becomes the sole owner of the LLC. For example, the conversion of membership interests in an LLC into shares of stock in a corporation that is the sole owner of the LLC results in a change in classification of the LLC from a partnership to a disregarded entity. The tax consequences of such reorganizations are discussed above.[463]

.04 Employer Identification Number and Employment Taxes

When an LLC that is classified as a partnership becomes a single-member LLC, the IRS will accept reporting and payment of employment taxes for the disregarded LLC in one of two ways: (i) calculation, reporting, and payment of all employment tax obligations with respect to employees of a disregarded entity by its owner (as

---

[455] Ltr. Rul. 200603021.

[456] Rev. Rul. 99-6, 1999-1 CB 432 (*citing* Code Sec. 741).

[457] Rev. Rul. 99-6, 1999-1 CB 432; Ltr. Rul. 200603021.

[458] Rev. Rul. 99-6, 1999-1 CB 432 (*citing* Code Sec. 1012).

[459] Ltr. Rul. 200603021.

[460] Rev. Rul. 99-6, 1999-1 CB 432 (*citing Edwin E. McCauslen v. Comm'r,* 45 TC 588 (1966)).

[461] Rev. Rul. 99-6, 1999-1 CB 432.

[462] *See* Instructions to Form 8594, under the heading, "Who Must File."

[463] *See* ¶ 703.09 *supra.*

though the employees of the disregarded entity are employed directly by the owner) and under the owner's name and employer identification number; or (ii) separate calculation, reporting, and payment of all employment tax obligations by the LLC under its own name and employer identification number.[464] For example, if an LLC's tax classification changes from a partnership to a disregarded entity, the LLC must retain the same employer identification number of the partnership for employment tax returns if it chooses to calculate, report, and pay employment tax obligations under its own name.[465]

For all federal tax purposes other than employment tax obligations and reporting, or except as otherwise provided in applicable regulations and IRS notices, the LLC must use the taxpayer identification number of its owner (assuming that it is classified as a disregarded entity).[466]

¶ 1119 MERGER BETWEEN TWO LLCS

.01 LLCs Classified as Partnerships

An LLC may merge into another LLC where both LLCs are classified as partnerships for federal tax purposes. The regulations refer to the surviving LLC as the resulting LLC. The resulting LLC is a continuation of any merging or consolidating LLC whose members own an interest of more than 50 percent in the capital and profits of the resulting LLC.[467] If the resulting LLC is a continuation of more than one of the merging LLCs, the resulting LLC is a continuation of the merging LLC that is credited with the contribution of assets having the greatest fair market value, net of liabilities.[468] Any other merging LLC is considered terminated and is called a terminated LLC. If the members of none of the merging LLCs own more than a 50 percent interest in the capital and profits of the resulting LLC, all of the merging LLCs are treated as terminated, and a new LLC results.[469]

The tax consequences of a merger between LLCs depend on the form of merger. There are two forms of merger: the assets-over form[470] and the assets-up form.[471]

.02 Assets-Over Form

In an assets-over form of merger, the terminated LLC transfers its assets and liabilities to the surviving LLC (the resulting LLC) in exchange for membership

---

[464] Rev. Rul. 2001-61, 2001-50 IRB 573.

[465] CCA 201351018.

[466] Rev. Rul. 2001-61, 2001-50 IRB 573, *citing* Reg. § 301.6109-1(h)(2)(ii); CCA 201351018.

[467] Code Sec. 708(b)(2)(A).

[468] Ltr. Ruls. 200339031-039, 9741021, 9741018, 9738013.

[469] Code Sec. 708(b)(1)(A); Reg. § 1.708-1(c)(1); Ltr. Ruls. 200339039, 200339031-032.

[470] *See* ¶ 1119.02 *infra.*

[471] *See* ¶ 1119.03 *infra.*

interests in the surviving LLC. Immediately thereafter, the terminated LLC distributes the membership interests in the surviving LLC to the members of the terminated LLC.[472] This is the default form of merger if no form of merger is specified, or if the merger does not qualify as an assets-up form.[473]

The final regulations on mergers do not discuss the tax consequences of the assets-over form of merger in any significant detail. The tax consequences are based on other applicable provisions of the Code, regulations, and rulings. The Preamble to the proposed regulations on partnership and LLC mergers also summarizes in detail the laws applicable to assets-over form mergers.[474] The tax consequences are as follows:

- The transfer from a terminated partnership or LLC to the surviving LLC is disregarded for tax purposes if the members of the terminated partnership or LLC own an interest of more than 50 percent in the capital and profits of the surviving LLC. If there is a consolidation of more than two partnerships or LLCs into a surviving LLC, then the transfer from the terminated partnership or LLC to the surviving LLC is disregarded if the surviving LLC is the continuation of the merging LLC that is credited with the contribution of assets having the greatest fair market value, net of liabilities.[475] The surviving LLC will be considered as the historical owner of the assets owned by such terminated LLC.[476]

- The terminated LLC and its members do not recognize gain or loss on the transfer of assets and liabilities to the surviving LLC in exchange for membership interests in the surviving LLC.[477]

- The surviving LLC does not recognize gain or loss as a result of the merger.[478]

- The surviving LLC's basis in assets received from the terminated LLC equals the terminated LLC's basis in the assets at the time of the merger.[479]

- The terminated LLC receives a basis in the membership interests in the surviving LLC equal to the amount of money and the adjusted basis of property contributed to the surviving LLC on the date of the merger.[480]

- Immediately after the merger, the terminated LLC is deemed to have distributed the membership interests in the surviving LLC to the members of the terminated LLC in liquidation of their interest in the terminated LLC.[481]

---

[472] Reg. §1.708-1(c)(3)(i), (5), Example 2; Ltr. Ruls. 201710007, 201710008, 201643019, 201643018, 201643017, 201643016, 200339039, 200339031-032 (involving the consolidation of six partnerships into an LLC).

[473] Reg. §1.708-1(c)(3)(i).

[474] REG-111119-99, 2000-5 IRB 455.

[475] Ltr. Ruls. 200339031-039, 9741021, 9741018, 9738013.

[476] Ltr. Ruls. 200339031-039, 200339039, 200339031-032.

[477] Ltr. Ruls. 9741021, 9741018, 9738013, 9720008-013, 9719015, 9719019-029 (*citing* Code Sec. 721).

[478] Ltr. Ruls. 9741021, 9741018, 9738013.

[479] REG-111119-99, 2000-5 IRB 455 (*citing* Code Sec. 723); Ltr. Ruls. 200339039, 200339031-032, 9741021, 9741018, 9738013, 9720008-013, 9719015, 9719019-029 (*citing* Code Sec. 723).

[480] Ltr. Ruls. 9720008-013, 9719015, 9719019-029 (*citing* Code Sec. 722).

[481] Ltr. Ruls. 9720008-013, 9719015, 9719019-029.

- The members of the terminated LLC receive a basis in the membership interests in the surviving LLC equal to the basis of their membership interests in the terminated LLC, reduced by any money distributed in the same transaction.[482] The basis in the membership interest is increased to the extent that the member's share of LLC debt increases as a result of the merger.[483] The basis in the membership interest is decreased to the extent that the member's share of LLC debt decreases as a result of the merger. Thus, any disparity between the members' outside basis in the membership interests and the surviving LLC's inside basis in the contributed assets will continue after the merger. However, if the surviving LLC makes an election under Section 754, the members of the terminated LLC will receive a special basis adjustment under Section 743 of the Code. The amount of the basis adjustment is the difference between the members' outside basis in their membership interests and their share of inside basis.[484]

- A member will not recognize gain under Code Sec. 752 as a result of the transfer of liabilities from the terminated LLC to the surviving LLC unless there is a net decrease in the member's share of liabilities.[485] In such case, gain is recognized to the extent that the net decrease in liabilities exceeds the member's basis in the membership interest of the surviving LLC.[486]

- The members of the LLC may recognize gain under the disguised sales rules, Sections 704(c)(1)(B)[487] and 737,[488] if the surviving LLC distributes property with built-in gain or loss[489] within seven years after the contribution.[490] The

---

[482] Ltr. Ruls. 9741021, 9741018, 9738013, 9720008-013, 9719015, 9719019-029 (*citing* Code Sec. 732(b)).

[483] Ltr. Ruls. 9741021, 9741018, 9738013.

[484] *See* Sloan, E.B., Lipton, R., Harrington, D., and Frediani, M., "New Prop. Regs. Provide Expanding Guidance on Partnership Mergers and Divisions—Part 2," pp. 261, 262 (JTAX Nov. 2000). The article also discusses the allocation of the basis adjustment to the LLC assets after a merger.

[485] Reg. § 1.752-1(f) (last sentence), (g), Example 2.

[486] REG-111119-99, 2000-5 IRB 455 (*citing* Code Sec. 752); Ltr. Ruls. 9720008-013, 9719015, 9719019-029 (*citing* Code Sec. 752 and Reg. § 1.752-1(a)(2), (f)).

[487] Section 704(c)(1)(B) provides that a partner that contributes Section 704(c) property to a partnership must recognize gain or loss on the distribution of such property to another partner within seven years of its contribution to the partnership in an amount equal to the gain or loss that would have been allocated to such partner under Section 704(c) if the distributed property had been sold by the partnership to the distributee partner for its fair market value at the time of the distribution.

[488] Section 737(a) provides that a partner who contributes Section 704(c) property to the partnership and then receives a distribution of property (other than money) within seven years of its contribution must recognize gain. The gain is equal to the lesser of (1) the excess of the fair market value of property (other than money) received in the distribution over the adjusted basis of the partner's interest in the partnership immediately before the distribution, reduced (but not below zero) by the amount of money received in the distribution, or (2) the net precontribution gain of the partner. Net precontribution gain means the net gain that would have been recognized by the distributee partner under Section 704(c)(1)(B) if all property which (1) had been contributed to the partnership by the distributee partner within seven years of the distribution, and (2) is held by the partnership immediately before the distribution, had been distributed by the partnership to another partner

[489] Built-in gain or loss is the difference between fair market value and basis of assets on the date of contribution.

[490] The disguised sales rules are discussed at § 605 *supra*.

seven-year period for recognizing gain starts on the date of the original contribution to the LLCs with respect to built-in gain or loss on such date. The seven-year period for recognizing gain or loss starts on the date of the merger with respect to additional built-in gain or loss for property transferred by the terminated LLC to the surviving LLC in the merger.[491] Thus, there are two layers of potential gain in an assets-over merger.

- The surviving LLC must continue to use the same period and method of depreciation and amortization after the merger as each merging LLC used prior to the merger.[492]
- The tax year of the terminated LLC closes.[493]
- A sale of all or part of a member's interest in the terminated LLC to the resulting LLC that occurs as part of a merger or consolidation will be respected as a sale of a partnership interest if (i) the merger agreement specifies that the resulting LLC is purchasing interests from a particular member in the merging or consolidating LLC and the consideration that is transferred for each interest sold, and (ii) the selling member in the terminated LLC, either prior to or contemporaneously with the transaction, consents to treat the transaction as a sale of the membership interest.[494]

.03 Assets-Up Form

In an assets-up form of merger, the LLC distributes its assets and liabilities to the members. The members then contribute the assets and liabilities to the surviving LLC in exchange for membership interests in the surviving LLC. This form of merger is less common than the assets-over form.[495]

The assets-up form of merger requires that the terminated LLC actually transfer ownership of its assets to the members under state law. A mere assignment of the right to receive title to the assets is not sufficient. If the members of the LLC do not become owners, then the merger will be treated as an assets-over form of merger.[496]

---

[491] Prop. Reg. §§ 1.704-3(a)(9), 1.704-4(c)(4), 1.737-2(b).

[492] Code Sec. 168(i)(7); Rev. Rul. 90-17, 1990-1 CB 119; Reg. § 1.197-2(g)(2)(iv)(C), (ii)(B), (3). Ltr. Ruls. 200339031-039 involved the consolidation of six partnerships into an LLC. The LLC was treated as the continuation of Partnership 3 since Partnership 3 was credited with the contribution of assets having the greatest fair market value, net of liabilities. The surviving LLC was considered as the historical owner of the assets owned by Partnership 3, and was therefore required to use the same method and period of depreciation used by such partnership. The IRS also ruled that the surviving LLC was required to use the same method and period of depreciation used by the other merging partnerships that acquired their depreciable assets prior to 1981 pursuant to Code Secs. 723, 168(e)(4)(C) (prior to amendment by the Tax Reform Act of 1986), § 168(f)(5), and § 381(c)(6). *See also* Sloan, E.B., Lipton, R., Harrington, D., and Frediani, M., "New Prop. Regs. Provide Expanding Guidance on Partnership Mergers and Divisions—Part 2," pp. 263, 264, under the heading, "Recovery Periods—Depreciation and Amortization" (JTAX Nov. 2000).

[493] Reg. § 1.708-1(c)(2), (5), Example 1.

[494] Reg. § 1.708-1(c)(4); Ltr. Ruls. 201643019, 201643018, 201643017, 201643016.

[495] Reg. § 1.708-1(c)(3)(ii).

[496] *Id.*

The members are not required to assume the liabilities of the terminated LLC. The terminated LLC may transfer the liabilities directly to the surviving LLC.[497]

The final regulations on mergers do not discuss the tax consequences of the assets-up form of merger in any significant detail. The tax consequences are based on other applicable provisions of the Code, regulations, and rulings. The Preamble to the proposed regulations on partnership and LLC mergers also summarizes in detail the laws applicable to assets-up forms of mergers.[498] The tax consequences are as follows:[499]

- The LLC that distributed assets to members terminates on the date of distribution.[500]
- The basis of assets distributed to each member on liquidation of the membership interest is equal to the member's outside basis in the membership interest, reduced by any money received in the distribution.[501]
- The transfer of liabilities to the members has no effect on the members' basis in the assets. The decrease in their share of LLC liabilities is normally equal to their corresponding individual assumption of liabilities.[502]
- The members of the terminated LLC may recognize gain under the disguised sales and anti-mixing bowl rules if the members previously contributed appreciated assets to the LLC.[503] The disguised sales and anti-mixing bowl rules are discussed in Chapter 6.[504]
- The members do not recognize gain or loss on the transfer to the surviving LLC of assets and liabilities in exchange for membership interests in the surviving LLC.[505]
- The members of the LLC receive a basis in the membership interests in the surviving LLC equal to their basis in the assets distributed on liquidation of the LLC.[506]
- The surviving LLC's basis in the assets received from the members of the LLC is the same as the members' basis in such assets immediately prior to the transfer.[507]

---

[497] *Id. See also* T.D. 8925, IRS Final Regulations on Partnership Mergers and Divisions, Explanation of Revisions and Summary of Contents (Jan. 4, 2001).

[498] REG-111119-99, 2000-5 IRB 455.

[499] This form of merger is similar to Rev. Rul. 84-111, 1984-2 CB 88, Scenario (2), in which an LLC converted into a corporation by first distributing its assets and liabilities to the members, who then contributed the assets to the corporation.

[500] Rev. Rul. 84-111, 1984-2 CB 88 (*citing* Code Sec. 708(b)(1)(A)).

[501] REG-111119-99, 2000-5 IRB 455 (*citing* Code Sec. 732); Rev. Rul. 84-111, 1984-2 CB 88 (*citing* Code Sec. 732(b)).

[502] Rev. Rul. 84-111, 1984-2 CB 88 (*citing* Code Sec. 752).

[503] REG-111119-99, 2000-5 IRB 455 (*citing* Code Secs. 704(c)(1)(B), 737).

[504] *See* ¶¶ 605.02, 605.03 *supra*, which discuss the disguised sales rules under Code Secs. 704(c)(1)(B), 737, cited by the IRS in the preamble to the proposed regulations on partnership and LLC mergers.

[505] Code Sec. 721(a).

[506] Code Sec. 722.

[507] REG-111119-99, 2000-5 IRB 455 (*citing* Code Sec. 723).

- The members' holding period for non-cash assets distributed to them includes the LLC's holding period for such assets.[508]

- The members' holding period for membership interest in the surviving LLC includes their holding periods in the capital assets and Section 1231 assets transferred to the surviving LLC (to the extent membership interests were received in exchange for such assets).[509] The members' holding period for membership interests received in exchange for other assets begins on the date following the date of the exchange.

- The surviving LLC's holding periods for the assets include the members' holding periods for such assets.[510]

- The surviving LLC must continue to use the same period and method of depreciation and amortization after the merger as each merging LLC used prior to the merger. However, it must treat the property as newly acquired property for depreciation purposes to the extent that the basis of the assets exceeds its basis prior to the merger as a result of the distribution to the members.[511]

- The members of the terminated LLC may recognize state and local transfer taxes on the distribution.[512]

- The tax year of the terminated LLC closes.[513]

.04 Which Method to Choose

The assets-up form is preferable if the members of the LLC have an aggregate basis in their membership interests that is higher than the LLC's basis in its assets. In an assets-up form, the surviving LLC receives a basis in the assets determined by reference to the members' basis in the terminated LLC. In an asset-over form, the LLC receives a carryover basis for the assets determined by reference to the basis of the assets in the hands of the terminated LLC.[514]

The assets-over form may be preferable if the LLC transfers a substantial amount of cash to the new corporation. Under the assets-up form, the members' holding period for membership interests received in exchange for cash begins on the day after the merger. Under the assets-over form, the holding period for membership interests

---

[508] Rev. Rul. 84-111, 1984-2 CB 88 (*citing* Code Sec. 735(b)).

[509] Rev. Rul. 84-111, 1984-2 CB 88 (*citing* Code Sec. 1223(1)).

[510] Rev. Rul. 84-111, 1984-2 CB 88 (*citing* Code Sec. 1223(2)).

[511] Code Sec. 168(i)(7); Rev. Rul. 90-17, 1990-1 CB 119; Reg. § 1.197-2(g)(2)(iv)(C), (ii)(B), (3). *See also* Sloan, E.B., Lipton, R., Harrington, D., and Frediani, M., "New Prop. Regs. Provide Expanding Guidance on Partnership Mergers and Divisions—Part 2," pp. 263, 264, under the heading, "Recovery Periods—Depreciation and Amortization" (*JTAX* Nov. 2000).

[512] REG-111119-99, 2000-5 IRB 455.

[513] Reg. § 1.708-1(c)(2), (5), Example 1.

[514] REG-111119-99, 2000-5 IRB 455.

in the surviving LLC includes the holding period for the membership interests in the terminated LLC.[515]

The LLC may be required to recapture investment tax credits under the assets-up form. Recapture is required since the surviving LLC receives a substituted rather than a carryover basis for the assets.

The IRS determined that the assets-over form is generally preferable for both the IRS and taxpayers.[516] The reason is that the members of an LLC do not recognize gain under the disguised sales rules in an assets-over form but may recognize gain in an assets-up form. The IRS also noted that the surviving LLC in a merger receives a carryover basis for the assets, rather than a new basis determined by reference to the members' aggregate basis in the terminated LLC.

The LLC should not use Method 2 if a member contributed appreciated property to the LLC within seven years prior to the incorporation. The contributing member may recognize immediate tax under the disguised sales rules.[517]

.05 Tax Returns

The terminated LLC must file a tax return for the tax year ending on the date of the merger.

The surviving LLC must file a tax return for the entire tax year. The return must state that the surviving LLC is a continuation of the merged LLCs. The return must include the names, addresses, and employer identification numbers of the terminated LLCs. It must show as part of the return the distributive shares of the members for the periods prior to and including the date of the merger and subsequent to the date of the merger. The surviving LLC must continue to use the same employer identification number[518] and the same tax year.[519]

EXAMPLE 11-4

Member A and B are members in AB LLC. Each owns a 50 percent interest in the LLC. Members C and D are members in CD LLC. Each owns a 50 percent interest in the LLC. The LLCs merge on September 30, 2001, and form ABCD LLC. All the members have a calendar year. The LLCs also have a calendar year. After the merger, the members have a capital and profits interest in the LLC as follows: A-30 percent; B-30 percent; C-20 percent; D-20 percent. Since Members A and B together own more than 50 percent of the capital and profits of ABCD LLC, that LLC is considered a

---

[515] The holding period for membership interests received in exchange for all other assets would be the same regardless of the former merger. Under Code Sec. 735(b), a member's holding period or property received in a distribution includes the LLC's holding period for such assets.

[516] REG-111119-99, 2000-5 IRB 455.

[517] Reg. §§ 1.704-4(c)(5), 1.737-2(c).

[518] Reg. § 1.708-1(c)(2).

[519] Reg. § 1.708-1(c)(5), Example 1.

continuation of AB LLC. It must continue to file a tax return to the calendar year basis. Since Members C and D own less than 50 percent in the capital and profits of ABCD LLC, the tax year of CD LLC closes as of September 30, 2001, the date of the merger. CD LLC is terminated as of that date. ABCD LLC must file a return for the tax year from January 1, 2001, to December 31, 2001. It must indicate on the return that it was AB LLC until September 30, 2001. CD LLC must file a return for its final tax year from January 1, 2001, until September 30, 2001.[520]

.06 LLCs Classified as Corporations

An LLC may merge into another LLC where both LLCs are classified as corporations for federal tax purposes. The tax consequences are the same as for a reorganization between two regular corporations.[521] For example, the merger of a parent corporation into a subsidiary LLC is a tax-free A reorganization.[522]

A corporation may also use an LLC to effect a divisive or non-divisive D reorganization.[523]

.07 Merger of Disregarded Subsidiary LLCs

A parent corporation may merge a disregarded subsidiary LLCs into each other. There are no adverse tax consequences since the parent corporation is treated as owning all of the assets of both corporations.

If the parent corporation merges an LLC owned by one subsidiary corporation into a disregarded LLC owned by the parent corporation, then there are the following tax consequences:[524]

- The subsidiary corporation will be treated as distributing to the parent corporation all of the assets of the disregarded LLCs owned by the subsidiary corporation.
- Neither the parent corporation nor the subsidiary corporation will recognize gain or loss in the merger.
- The parent corporation's tax basis in the stock of the subsidiary corporation and in each of the assets of the LLCs received by the parent corporation in the merger will be the same as its tax basis in the stock of the subsidiary corporation immediately prior to the merger. The aggregate tax basis must be allocated among the stock of the subsidiary corporation and the assets of the

---

[520] Prop. Reg. § 1.708-1(c)(5), Example 1.

[521] Ltr. Ruls. 201314008, 201016052, 201016051.

[522] Ltr. Ruls. 201016052, 201016051.

[523] See ¶ 1125 *infra*.

[524] Ltr. Rul. 200703030.

disregarded LLCs owned by the subsidiary corporation received by it in the merger.

- The parent corporation's holding period for the assets of the LLC received in the merger will include its holding period for the stock in the subsidiary corporation.

.08 Merger of Disregarded Subsidiary into Parent Corporation

The upstream merger of a disregarded subsidiary LLC into a parent corporation is disregarded for federal tax purposes.[525]

¶1120 MERGER OF CORPORATION INTO LLC

.01 LLC Classified as Partnership

A C corporation may merge into an LLC that is classified as a partnership for federal tax purposes. The merger has the following tax consequences:

- The merger is treated as a transfer of assets by the corporation to the LLC in exchange for the assumption of liabilities by the LLC and the corporation's receipt of LLC membership interests, followed by the corporation's distribution of the LLC membership interests to the corporation's shareholders in a complete liquidation.[526]
- The corporation and the LLC do not recognize gain or loss upon the transfer of assets to the LLC in exchange for the membership interests.[527]
- The corporation recognizes gain or loss upon the corporation's distribution of the ownership interests in the LLC to the LLC members in the complete liquidation of the corporation.[528] Gain or loss is recognized to the same extent as if the corporation sold the distributed membership interests for their fair market value to the members.[529]
- The shareholders of the corporation recognize capital gain or loss upon the deemed distribution of the LLC membership interests from the corporation to its shareholders. The distribution is treated as full payment in exchange for their stock in the corporation.[530] The amount of gain is the difference between the fair market value of the LLC membership interests and the shareholders' basis in their stock. However, if the shareholder is the parent corporation of the corporation that merges into the LLC, no gain or loss is recognized upon

---

[525] Ltr. Rul. 200832001.

[526] Ltr. Ruls. 200606009, 200214016, 9701029, 9543023, 9409021, 9409016, 9404014.

[527] Ltr. Ruls. 200606009, 200214016, 9701029, 9409014, 9409016, 9404024 (*citing* Code Sec. 721(a)).

[528] Ltr. Ruls. 200606009, 9701029.

[529] Ltr. Ruls. 200606009, 200214016, 9701029 (*citing* Code Sec. 336).

[530] Ltr. Ruls. 200606009, 200214016, 9701029 (*citing* Code Sec. 331(a)).

the distribution of the LLC membership interests from the subsidiary to the parent.[531]

- If the LLC makes a Section 754 election to adjust the basis of LLC property before the merger, the distribution of the membership interests to the shareholders constitutes a transfer under Section 743. The LLC must then adjust the basis of its assets under Section 743 and 755.[532]

- The corporation's distribution of membership interests to the shareholders constitutes an exchange that causes the LLC to terminate.[533] The termination results in a deemed distribution of the LLC's assets to the shareholders and a deemed immediate recontribution of those assets to a new LLC by the members.[534] However, the old and new LLCs, the members and the corporation will not recognize gain or loss as a result of the deemed termination.[535]

- The merger of a corporation into an LLC classified as a partnership, or into an LLC classified as a disregarded entity that is owned by a partnership, does not qualify as a tax-free reorganization under Code Sec. 368(a)(1)(A).[536]

- The consolidation by a parent corporation of two wholly owned subsidiaries through a disregarded LLC is treated as a D reorganization.[537]

.02 LLC Classified as Corporation

A corporation may merge into an LLC that is classified as a corporation for federal tax purposes. There are the following types of mergers:

- Merger with unrelated party. A corporation may merge into an unrelated LLC that is classified as a corporation. The merger is a tax-free Section 368(a)(1)(A) reorganization.[538]

- Merger between related subsidiaries. A corporation may merge a subsidiary corporation into a subsidiary LLC or related LLC that is classified as a corporation. The merger is a non-divisive D reorganization. The tax consequences of the merger are discussed at ¶ 1109.05.

- Reincorporation. A corporation may reincorporate into another state by forming an LLC in another state, electing to classify the LLC as a corporation, and then merging the corporation into the LLC. The merger is a tax-free Section 368(a)(1)(F) reorganization.[539]

---

[531] Ltr. Ruls. 9543023, 9409021, 9409016, 9404014 (*citing* Code Secs. 332(a), 337). The subsidiary is treated as having liquidated into its parent as a result of the merger into the LLC.

[532] Ltr. Rul. 9701029.

[533] Ltr. Rul. 200214016; Code Sec. 708(b)(1)(B).

[534] Ltr. Rul. 9701029 (*citing* Reg. § 1.708(b)(1)(iv)).

[535] Ltr. Rul. 200214016.

[536] Prop. Reg. § 1.368-2(b)(1)(iii), Example 4.

[537] Ltr. Rul. 200102038.

[538] Ltr. Ruls. 200204004, 200119016.

[539] Ltr. Rul. 200119016.

- Parent-subsidiary merger. A subsidiary corporation may merge into a parent LLC that is classified as a corporation. The merger is a tax-free Section 332 liquidation.[540]
- Conversion of corporation to LLC. A corporation may want to convert to an LLC that is classified as a corporation in order to obtain the non-tax benefits available to an LLC under state law.[541] The corporation may convert to an LLC through a merger, statutory conversion under state law, transfer of assets, or by other method permitted under state law. The merger is a tax-free Section 368(a)(1)(F) reorganization. The tax consequences of a conversion of a C corporation to an LLC are discussed at ¶ 1108.03.

.03 LLC Classified as Disregarded Entity

Merger of S Corporation into LLC

The merger of an S corporation into a single-member disregarded LLC is taxed as follows:[542]

- The merger is treated as a deemed sale of assets by the corporation, followed by the complete liquidation of the corporation.
- The LLC will have an aggregate basis in the acquired assets equal to the sum of the cash paid by the LLC to the shareholders, and the liabilities of the corporation assumed by the LLC in the merger.
- The S corporation will recognize gain or loss equal to the difference between the consideration received and the adjusted basis of the assets transferred to the LLC. That gain or loss will pass through to the shareholders.[543]
- The corporation will recognize gain or loss on the distribution of any additional non-cash property to the shareholders.
- The proceeds of sale by the corporation will be treated as distributed in complete liquidation. The shareholders will be treated as receiving full payment in exchange for their shares.
- The shareholder will recognize capital gain or loss measured by the difference between the amount of cash received and their adjusted basis in the stock surrendered, after taking into account any adjustment to the stock basis resulting from the gain or loss recognized by the corporation on the deemed sale of assets.

The merger of an S corporation into a single-member disregarded LLC owned by another corporation qualifies as a tax-free reorganization under Code Sec. 368(a)(1)(A) if the requirements for a statutory merger are met.[544]

---

[540] Ltr. Ruls. 200709013, 200204004.

[541] Ltr. Rul. 200119016.

[542] Ltr. Rul. 200628008.

[543] Ltr. Rul. 200628008, *citing* Code Sec. 1366(a), (d).

[544] Ltr. Rul. 200729002.

Merger of C Corporation into LLC

The merger of a C corporation into a single-member disregarded LLC qualifies as a tax-free reorganization under Code Sec. 368(a)(1)(A) if the following requirements are met:[545]

- The LLC is owned by a corporation.[546]

- The merger is made pursuant to state or federal law.[547] The transferor corporation, the transferee LLC, and the corporate owner of the transferee LLC may be organized under the laws of the United States, a state, or the District of Columbia.[548]

- All the assets and liabilities of the transferor corporation become the assets and liabilities of the LLC.[549] The corporation may distribute assets to its shareholders before transferring its remaining assets to the LLC in the merger, even though a distribution prior to a merger would not be allowed in other types of reorganizations. The "all assets" test is met if a disregarded entity owned by the corporate transferor becomes a disregarded entity owned by the transferee LLC, or merges into the transferee LLC or another entity owned by the corporate owner of the transferee LLC.[550]

- The separate legal existence of the transferor corporation ceases after the merger.[551] The transferor or its agent may continue to act after the merger in limited circumstances, such as lawsuits related to its assets or liabilities that arose prior to the merger.

- The shareholders of the corporation that merges into the LLC receive stock in the corporation that owns the LLC,[552] or stock in a corporation that owns the corporate owner of the LLC in a triangular merger.[553] The shareholders of the transferee corporation cannot receive membership interests in the LLC[554] since that would result in a division of the transferee entity into two separate entities (the transferee corporation owned by its shareholders and the LLC owned by the shareholders of the transferor corporation).

---

[545] Reg. § 1.368-2(b)(1); Ltr. Rul. 200236005.

[546] Reg. § 1.368-2(b)(1)(i)(B); Ltr. Rul. 200236005.

[547] Reg. § 1.368-2(b)(1)(ii).

[548] Reg. §§ 1.368-2(b)(1)(iii), 1.368-2T(b)(1)(iv), Example 2(ii).

[549] Reg. § 1.368-2(b)(1)(ii)(A).

[550] Reg. § 1.368-2(b)(1)(iii), Example 8.

[551] Reg. § 1.368-2(b)(1)(ii)(B).

[552] Reg. § 1.368-2(b)(1)(iii), Example 2; Ltr. Rul. 200236005.

[553] Reg. § 1.368-2(b)(1)(iii), Example 4.

[554] Reg. § 1.368-2(b)(1)(iii), Example 7.

- The corporation merges into the LLC. The merger of an LLC that is classified as a disregarded entity into a corporation does not qualify as a tax-free reorganization under Code Sec. 368(a)(1)(A).[555]

The tax consequences of a triangular merger of a target corporation into a disregarded LLC owned by the acquiring corporation are discussed at ¶1123.

Merger of Subsidiary Corporation into LLC Owned by Parent

The merger or conversion of a subsidiary corporation into a disregarded LLC owned by the parent corporation qualifies as a tax-free liquidation under Code Sec. 332.[556] The merger has the following tax consequences:

- The parent corporation, the subsidiary, and the LLC do not recognize gain or loss on the merger.[557]
- The parent corporation's basis in each asset received through the LLC equals the basis of the assets in the hands of the subsidiary prior to the merger.[558]
- The parent corporation's holding period in each asset received through the LLC includes the holding period for such assets by the subsidiary.[559]
- The parent corporation succeeds to and must take into account the tax attributes of the subsidiary.[560]

The merger or conversion of a lower-tier subsidiary corporation into a disregarded LLC owned by the parent corporation qualifies as a tax-free merger under Code Sec. 368(a)(1).[561]

Liability of LLC for Taxes after Merger

After the merger of the corporation into the LLC, the LLC is liable for any taxes owed by the corporation prior to the merger. The IRS may assess a deficiency judgment against the LLC for unpaid corporate taxes. If the LLC fails to pay the

---

[555] Reg. § 1.368-2(b)(1)(iii), Example 6. *See also* IRS Proposed Rules (REG-126485-01) and Hearing Notice on Definition of Statutory Merger or Consolidation, under the heading, "B. Mergers Involving Disregarded Entities" (Nov. 15, 2001).

[556] Ltr. Ruls. 200310005, 200139009, 200129024; Ltr. Rul. 2003108005 (rulings with respect to the "Sub 2 Merger" and the "Sub 5 Conversion"); Ltr. Rul. 200305017 (in which the IRS treated the merger of a wholly owned subsidiary corporation of a foreign parent corporation into a disregarded LLC owned by the foreign parent corporation as a liquidation of the subsidiary corporation into the foreign parent corporation, subject to Code Secs. 331 and 336). *See* ¶1109 *supra*.

[557] Ltr. Rul. 200843011.

[558] Ltr. Rul. 200843011.

[559] Ltr. Rul. 200843011.

[560] Ltr. Rul. 200843011, *citing* Code Secs. 381(c), 381(a) and Reg. § 1.381(a)-1.

[561] Ltr. Ruls. 200310005, 200139009, 200129024; Ltr. Rul. 2003108005 (rulings with respect to the "Sub 2 Merger" and the "Sub 5 Conversion"); Ltr. Rul. 200305017 (in which the IRS treated the merger of a wholly owned subsidiary corporation of a foreign parent corporation into a disregarded LLC owned by the foreign parent corporation as a liquidation of the subsidiary corporation into the foreign parent corporation, subject to Code Secs. 331 and 336). *See* ¶1109 *supra*.

liability after notice and demand, a general lien will arise on all the LLC's property and rights to property.

¶1121 MERGER OF LLC INTO C CORPORATION

The merger of an LLC that is classified as a disregarded entity into a corporation does not qualify as a tax-free reorganization under Code Sec. 368(a)(1)(A),[562] unless the corporate owner of the LLC also merges into the transferee corporation. However, the transfer of assets and liabilities from the disregarded LLC to the corporation may qualify as a tax-free exchange under Code Sec. 351.[563]

The merger of an LLC that is classified as a corporation into a corporation may qualify as a tax-free reorganization under the regular reorganization provisions of the Code.[564]

The merger of an LLC that is classified as a partnership into a corporation is taxable to the members of the LLC, unless the merger qualifies as a tax-free reorganization under Code Sec. 351.[565] The courts and rulings are divided on whether an LLC that is classified as a partnership or disregarded entity may participate in a tax-free reorganization by incorporating immediately prior to the reorganization.[566]

¶1122 MERGER OF LLC INTO LIMITED PARTNERSHIP

An LLC may merge into a limited partnership, after which the members of the LLC are treated as limited partners.[567] The merger of an LLC into a limited partnership is treated in the same manner as a merger between LLCs that are classified as partnerships. The merger is either an assets-over form or an assets-up form of merger. The tax consequences of each of these forms of merger are discussed in ¶1119.

Generally, the members do not recognize gain or loss as a result of the merger. There is one important exception. A member may recognize gain if there is a net decrease in liabilities allocated to the member as a result of the merger.[568]

The members of the terminated LLC are relieved of liabilities when those liabilities are transferred to the limited partnership in a merger. The members of the terminated LLC are then allocated a share of liabilities in the surviving LLC. The IRS permits the members to net the relief of liabilities in the LLC and the assumption of

---

[562] Reg. § 1.368-2(b)(1)(iii), Example 6. *See also* IRS Proposed Rules (REG-126485-01) and Hearing Notice on Definition of Statutory Merger or Consolidation, under the heading, "B. Mergers Involving Disregarded Entities" (Nov. 15, 2001).

[563] *See* ¶1106.01 *supra.*

[564] Ltr. Rul. 200005016. *See also* ¶1106.02 *supra.*

[565] *See* ¶1106.01 *supra.*

[566] *See* ¶1106.02 *supra.*

[567] Ltr. Ruls. 200129018, 200125037, 9720008-013, 9719019-029, 9719015.

[568] REG-111119-99, 2000-5 IRB 455 (*citing* Code Sec. 752); Ltr. Ruls. 9720008-013, 9719019-029, 9719015.

liabilities in the limited partnership in determining taxable gain.[569] The net increase in the member's share of liabilities is treated as a contribution of money to the member. There is no taxable gain in such case. The net decrease in the member's share of liabilities is treated as a distribution of money to the member. The member recognizes gain to the extent that the net decrease in liabilities exceeds the member's outside basis.

The problem arises in a limited partnership merger because the nonrecourse liabilities of the LLC often become recourse liabilities after the transfer to a limited partnership. There must be one general partner in a limited partnership. Under state law, a general partner is personally liable for the debts of the limited partnership (with certain exceptions).[570] Therefore, the nonrecourse liabilities of the LLC prior to the merger (which are normally allocated to all of the members based on their profit sharing percentage in the LLC) are converted into recourse liabilities of the limited partnership after the merger. Recourse liabilities must be allocated to the general partner, or to any limited partner who is personally liable for such debts. The result is that a member of an LLC who becomes a limited partner after the merger often has a net decrease in the liabilities allocated to the member.

The transfer of recourse liabilities from the LLC to a limited partnership does not result in a deemed distribution of money or taxation to the members if the members who were personally responsible for liabilities prior to the merger continue to be personally liable after the merger.[571]

The merger of an LLC into a limited partnership should be contrasted with a merger of an LLC into another LLC. Generally, the members do not have a net decrease in liabilities as a result of merger between LLCs because nonrecourse liabilities prior to the merger continue to be nonrecourse liabilities after the merger. Each member is allocated a share of nonrecourse liabilities before and after the merger based on his or her profit sharing percentage.

¶1123 TRIANGULAR CORPORATE MERGER USING DISREGARDED LLC

.01 Overview

Prior to 2006, there were five principal types of tax-free corporate acquisitions: statutory merger or consolidation, forward triangular merger, reverse triangular merger, B reorganization, and C reorganization. Each of these forms of acquisition had significant tax or non-tax problems.

Under the 2006 regulations, a corporation may use an LLC that is classified as a partnership or disregarded entity to facilitate a tax-free corporate merger. A statutory

---

[569] Reg. §§ 1.752-1(f) (last sentence), 1.752-1(g), Example 2.

[570] For example, a loan secured by a deed of trust or mortgage on real property may be nonrecourse if the loan documents or state law provides that the lender has no recourse except against the property in the event of a default.

[571] Ltr. Ruls. 9720008-013, 9719019-029, 9719015 (*citing* Code Sec. 752 and Reg. § 1.752-1(a)(2), (f)).

merger now includes (a) a merger of a target corporation into a disregarded LLC formed by the acquiring corporation, (b) a triangular merger of a target corporation into a disregarded LLC owned by a subsidiary of the acquiring corporation, and (c) a merger of a corporate partner into a disregarded LLC owned by the other corporate partner.[572]

As a result, an acquiring corporation now has one more method of acquiring a target corporation in a tax-free reorganization without many of the problems associated with the five other types of tax-free acquisitions.

.02 Types of Tax-Free Acquisitions

Prior to 2006, the five major types of tax-free acquisitions, and the tax and non-tax problems associated with each form of acquisition, were as follows:

- *Statutory merger or consolidation.* In a statutory merger or consolidation, the acquiring corporation merges with the target corporation pursuant to state law.[573] The acquiring corporation is normally the surviving corporation. The statutory merger or consolidation is the most flexible type of tax-free reorganization. The parties must comply with the continuity of business enterprise rules[574] and the continuity of proprietary interest rules,[575] which are not difficult to meet. Up to 50 percent or more of the consideration paid to the shareholders of the target corporation may be cash. There are two major non-tax problems with a statutory merger. The first is that the acquiring corporation must obtain the consent of its shareholders, since the acquiring corporation is a party to the reorganization under state law. This is often impractical for a large publicly traded corporation. The second problem is that the acquiring corporation must assume all the liabilities of the target corporation, including contingent and unknown liabilities, since both the target and the acquiring corporation merge together into a single corporation.

- *Forward triangular merger.* In a forward triangular merger, the acquiring corporation forms a subsidiary. The target corporation merges into the subsidiary. The shareholders of the target corporation receive stock in the parent corporation. They may also receive up to 50 percent or more of the aggregate consideration in cash in exchange for their shares in the target corporation.[576] This type of merger is often preferable to the statutory merger. The parent corporation is not subject to any of the liabilities of the target corporation (except under the piercing the corporate veil doctrine). Only the newly formed subsidiary assumes the liabilities of the target corporation. The acquiring corporation is not required to obtain approval from its shareholders.

---

[572] Reg. § 1.368-2(b)(1); Ltr. Ruls. 201105019, 200910028, 200835014, 200835013 (merger of Newco into LLC 3), 200832001, 200729002, 200727001, 200236005.

[573] Code Sec. 368(a)(1)(A).

[574] Reg. § 1.368-1(d).

[575] Reg. § 1.368-1(e).

[576] Code Sec. 368(a)(1)(A), (2)(D).

However, there are several non-tax problems with a forward triangular merger. The target corporation is often required to obtain the consent of its lenders, landlords, and other persons with which it has contracts in order to assign or transfer the contracts to the new subsidiary corporation. The subsidiary corporation must apply for new licenses and permits in its own name from state and local agencies. Title insurance policies in the name of the old target corporation may no longer be valid.

- *Reverse triangular merger.* In a reverse triangular merger, the acquiring corporation forms a subsidiary. The subsidiary corporation merges into the target corporation (rather than vice versa as under a forward triangular merger).[577] The reverse triangular merger is similar to a forward triangular merger in several respects. The shareholders of the target corporation receive stock in the parent corporation in exchange for their shares in the target corporation. Again, the parent corporation is not subject to any of the liabilities of the target corporation. The parent corporation is not required to obtain the consent of the shareholders. The reverse triangular merger is often preferable to the forward triangular merger in several ways. Since the target corporation is the surviving corporation, it is not required to obtain new licenses and permits from state and local agencies. It does not ordinarily need to obtain the consent of lenders, landlords, and other persons with which it has contracts (although a change in ownership of the target corporation may trigger due-on-sale clauses in the loan documents and deeds of trust, or otherwise require the consent of the other party under the terms the contract). There is one major tax problem with a reverse triangular merger. At least 80 percent of the consideration received by the target shareholders must be stock of the acquiring parent corporation.[578] This differs from a statutory merger or consolidation and a forward triangular merger in which 50 percent or more of the consideration may be cash rather than stock in the acquiring parent corporation.

- *B reorganization.* In a B reorganization, the acquiring corporation acquires stock in the target corporation solely in exchange for its voting stock (with one extremely limited exception).[579] The problem with this type of reorganization is that the shareholders of the target corporation may not receive any cash in exchange for their shares.

- *C reorganization.* In a C reorganization, the acquiring corporation acquires substantially all the assets of the target corporation solely in exchange for its voting stock.[580] Again, the major problem is that the shareholders of the target corporation may not receive any cash in exchange for their shares.

---

[577] Code Sec. 368(a)(1)(A), (2)(E).

[578] Code Sec. 368(a)(1)(E).

[579] Code Sec. 368(a)(1)(B).

[580] Code Sec. 368(a)(1)(C).

.03 Requirements for Merger Using LLC

Companies often use a single-member disregarded LLC to effect a tax-free reorganization because of the restrictions on regular corporate reorganizations. The use of an LLC allows the acquiring company to acquire selected assets and liabilities of the target company, and to hold those assets in a wholly owned LLC with separate liability protection.

A regular statutory merger is not normally advisable because the acquiring company may not want to assume all of the liabilities of the target corporation other than through a wholly owned subsidiary. A target corporation that distributes unwanted assets to its shareholders or sells unwanted assets to unrelated third parties prior to a reorganization cannot use a forward triangular merger, reverse triangular, or C reorganization. Those reorganizations require the target corporation to transfer "substantially all" of its assets to the acquiring corporation.

The 2006 regulations now permit the parties to enter into a statutory merger using a disregarded LLC owned by the acquiring or target corporation. After the statutory merger, the acquiring corporation owns selected assets and liabilities of the target corporation through a wholly owned subsidiary LLC. The statutory merger accomplishes the same objectives as a forward triangular merger, reverse triangular merger, and C reorganization.

Under the regulations, a corporation may merge into an LLC that is classified as a partnership or disregarded entity in a tax-free reorganization in one of the following ways:[581]

- *Merger of a target corporation into a disregarded LLC formed by acquiring corporation.* The target corporation merges into a disregarded LLC formed by the acquiring corporation. The target corporation is treated as if it merged into the acquiring corporation.[582] The shareholders of the target corporation receive stock in the acquiring corporation in exchange for stock in the target corporation.[583] This is the preferred form of merger if the target corporation wants to distribute substantial assets to its shareholders prior to the merger. In such case, the target corporation may merge into a disregarded LLC owned by the acquiring corporation, but may not merge into a corporate subsidiary owned by the acquiring corporation.[584]

---

[581] Reg. § 1.368-2(b)(1).

[582] Ltr. Ruls. 201314028, 201105019, 200910028, 200832001, 200729002, 200727001, 200236005.

[583] Reg. § 1.368-2(b)(1)(iii), Example 2; Ltr. Ruls. 201314028, 201105019, 200910028, 200835014, 200835013 (merger of Newco into LLC 3), 200832001.

[584] In a forward triangular merger in which the target corporation merges into a subsidiary corporation of the acquiring corporation, the acquiring corporation must acquire substantially all of the assets of the target corporation. Code Sec. 368(a)(2)(D). "Substantially all" has the same meaning as in a C reorganization. Reg. § 1.368-2(b)(2). For ruling purposes, this means that the subsidiary must acquire 90 percent of the fair market value of the target's net assets and at least 70 percent of the target's gross assets. The forward triangular merger may be disqualified if the target corporation distributes substantial assets to its shareholders prior to the merger. The "substantially all" requirement does not apply to a merger of a target corporation into a disregarded LLC that is owned by the

- *Triangular merger of a target corporation into a disregarded LLC owned by a subsidiary of the acquiring corporation.* All of the assets and liabilities of the target corporation are transferred to the LLC. The shareholders of the target corporation receive stock in the acquiring corporation in exchange for stock in the target corporation. After the merger, the subsidiary of the acquiring corporation owns all of the membership interests in the disregarded LLC.[585]

- *Merger of a corporate partner into a disregarded LLC owned by the other corporate partner.* Two corporations own an LLC that is classified as a partnership. The corporation that owns a minority interest in the LLC merges into the LLC. The shareholders of the merging corporation exchange their stock in the corporation for stock in the other corporate partner of the LLC.[586]

In each case, the merger must be pursuant to state law.[587] The legal existence of the target corporation must cease immediately after the merger.[588] All of the assets and liabilities of the merging corporation must be transferred to the LLC owned by the acquiring corporation.[589]

.04 Tax Consequences

The merger of a target corporation into a disregarded LLC owned by the acquiring corporation has the following tax consequences:

- The merger is treated as a statutory merger under Section 368(a)(1)(A).[590] The acquiring and target corporations are each "a party to the reorganization" within the meaning of Section 368(b).[591]

- The target corporation does not recognize gain or loss on the transfer of the assets to the LLC in the merger if the transfer is made solely in exchange for the common stock of the acquiring corporation and the assumption of liabilities by the acquiring corporation.[592]

(Footnote Continued)

acquiring corporation since the merger is treated as a regular merger rather than a forward triangular merger. *See* Reg. § 1.368-2(b)(1)(iii), Example 8.

[585] Reg. § 1.368-2(b)(1)(iii), Example 4.

[586] Reg. § 1.368-2(b)(1)(iii), Example 11.

[587] Reg. § 1.368-2(b)(1)(ii).

[588] Reg. § 1.368-2(b)(1)(ii)(B). However, the target corporation or its agents may continue to act after the merger in limited circumstances, such as defending lawsuits related to its assets and liabilities that arose prior to the merger.

[589] Reg. § 1.368-2(b)(1)(ii)(A). However, the target corporation may distribute assets and liabilities to its shareholders prior to the merger.

[590] Ltr. Ruls. 201314028, 201109002, 201109001, 201105019, 200910028, 200835014, 200835013 (merger of Newco into LLC 3), 200832001, 200729002, 200727001.

[591] Ltr. Ruls. 201314028, 201109002, 201109001, 201105019, 200910028, 200835014, 200835013 (merger of Newco into LLC 3), 200832001, 200729002, 200727001.

[592] Ltr. Ruls. 201314028, 201109002, 201109001, 201105019, 200910028, 200835014, 200835013 (merger of Newco into LLC 3), 200832001, 200729002, 200727001, *citing* Code Secs. 361(a) and 357(a).

- The acquiring corporation does not recognize gain or loss on the acquiring corporation's receipt of the target corporation's assets in exchange for shares of the acquiring corporation common stock.[593]
- The basis of the target corporation's assets in the hands of the acquiring corporation is the same as the basis of such assets in the hands of the target corporation immediately before the merger.[594]
- The holding period of the target corporation's assets in the hands of the acquiring corporation includes the period during which the target corporation held such assets.[595]
- No gain or loss is recognized by the shareholders who receive only the common stock of the acquiring corporation in exchange for the common stock in the target corporation.[596]
- The basis of the acquiring corporation common stock received by the shareholders is the same as the basis of the target corporation common stock surrendered in the exchange.[597]
- The holding period of the acquiring corporation common stock received by the shareholders includes the period during which the target corporation common stock surrendered in the exchange was held if the target corporation common stock was held as a capital asset on the date of the exchange.[598]
- The acquiring corporation succeeds to and takes into account the items of the target corporation described in Code Sec. 381(c) as of the close of the effective date of the merger.[599]

.05 Advantages and Disadvantages of Using LLC to Facilitate a Merger

Advantages

There are a number of advantages in using an LLC to facilitate a tax-free acquisition, including the following:

---

[593] Ltr. Ruls. 201314028, 201109002, 201109001, 201105019, 200910028, 200835014, 200835013 (merger of Newco into LLC 3), 200832001, 200729002, 200727001, *citing* Code Sec. 1032(a).

[594] Ltr. Ruls. 201314028, 201109002, 201109001, 201105019, 200910028, 200835014, 200835013 (merger of Newco into LLC 3), 200832001, 200729002, 200727001, *citing* Code Sec. 362(b).

[595] Ltr. Ruls. 201314028, 201109002, 201109001, 201105019, 200910028, 200835014, 200835013 (merger of Newco into LLC 3), 200832001, 200729002, 200727001, *citing* Code Sec. 1223(2).

[596] Ltr. Ruls. 201314028, 201109002, 201109001, 201105019, 200910028, 200835014, 200835013 (merger of Newco into LLC 3), 200832001, 200729002, 200727001, *citing* Code Sec. 354(a)(1).

[597] Ltr. Ruls. 201314028, 201109002, 201109001, 201105019, 200910028, 200835014, 200835013 (merger of Newco into LLC 3), 200832001, 200729002, 200727001, *citing* Code Sec. 358(a)(1).

[598] Ltr. Ruls. 201314028, 201109002, 201109001, 201105019, 200910028, 200835014, 200835013 (merger of Newco into LLC 3), 200832001, 200729002, 200727001, *citing* Code Sec. 1223(1).

[599] Ltr. Ruls. 201314028, 201109002, 201109001, 201105019, 200910028, 200835014, 200835013 (merger of Newco into LLC 3), 200832001, 200729002, 200727001, *citing* Reg. § 1.381(a)-1.

- The shareholders of the target corporation may receive up to 50 percent of the consideration in cash in a merger using an LLC. In a reverse triangular merger, the shareholders may only receive 20 percent of the consideration in cash. In a B reorganization or a C reorganization, the shareholders may not receive any cash.
- The acquiring corporation does not have to assume any other liabilities of the target corporation in a merger using an LLC. All the liabilities are assumed by the LLC that is owned by the acquiring corporation.
- The target corporation may distribute assets to its shareholders before transferring its remaining assets to the LLC in a merger using an LLC. A distribution of substantial assets by the target corporation prior to an acquisition is not allowed in other types of reorganizations. The acquiring corporation must acquire substantially all the assets of the target corporation in a forward triangular merger, reverse triangular merger, or C reorganization.[600]

As a result of the 2006 regulations, it is now possible for an acquiring corporation to acquire a target corporation using a wholly owned LLC rather than a corporation as the surviving entity. This achieves the results of a forward triangular merger, with the reorganization status tested under less stringent standards of a direct statutory merger.

EXAMPLE 11-5

An acquiring corporation wants to acquire a target corporation in a tax-free reorganization. The shareholders of the target corporation want 50 percent of the consideration in cash and the balance in stock of the acquiring corporation. The shareholders also want to receive a distribution of certain valuable assets of the target corporation before the merger. Prior to 2003, the only available type of tax-free reorganization was a direct statutory merger or consolidation. A forward triangular merger could not be used since the acquiring corporation was not acquiring substantially all the assets of the target corporate. A reverse triangular merger could not be used since the acquiring corporation was paying more than 20 percent of the consideration in cash and was not acquiring substantially all the assets of the target corporation. A B reorganization and a C reorganization were not available since no cash may be paid to the shareholders of the target corporation and the acquiring corporation must acquire substantially all the assets of the target corporation in such reorganizations.

Even though a direct statutory merger is permissible in this case, there are two major non-tax problems. The acquiring corporation is subject to all the contingent and unknown liabilities of the target corporation after the merger. The acquiring corporation must also obtain the consent

---

[600] Code Sec. 368(a)(1)(C), (2)(D), (E); Reg. § 1.368-2(b)(2), (d)(1).

of shareholders to the merger, which is often impractical in a large publicly traded corporation.

After 2005, the acquiring corporation may avoid these problems by forming a disregarded LLC. The target corporation then merges into the LLC. The shareholders of the target corporation receive stock in the acquiring corporation and/or cash up to 50 percent of the aggregate consideration paid by the acquiring corporation. The shareholders of the target corporation may receive a distribution of certain assets from the target corporation prior to the merger. The acquiring corporation is not required to obtain the consent of shareholders. The acquiring corporation is not subject to the unknown and contingent liabilities of the target corporation. The shareholders of the target corporation are not taxed on receipt of stock in the acquiring corporation. They are taxed only on the cash received.

Disadvantages

There are several problems with using an LLC to facilitate a tax-free acquisition, including the following:

- The target corporation must merge into the LLC owned by the acquiring corporation. The LLC may not merge into the target corporation. The merger of an LLC that is classified as a disregarded entity into a corporation does not qualify as a tax-free reorganization under Code Sec. 368(a)(1)(A).[601] As a result, the LLC may be required to obtain new state licenses and permits for its business after the acquisition and consents of lenders, landlords, and other persons with which it has contracts. In order to avoid this problem, the parties normally use a reverse triangular merger, a B reorganization, or a C reorganization.
- Some states do not permit a corporation to merge into an LLC.

¶1124 CHANGES IN RIGHTS, PREFERENCES AND PRIVILEGES

An LLC may recapitalize by creating new classes of membership units with different rights, preferences, privileges, and restrictions. The LLC may then allow members to convert their membership units into different classes of membership units on a tax-free basis. The recapitalization has the following tax consequences:[602]

- The members do not recognize gain or loss as result of the creation of new classes of membership units, or the conversion of one type of membership units into another type of membership units.

---

[601] Reg. § 1.368-2(b)(1)(iii), Example 6.
[602] Ltr. Ruls. 201722019, 200345007.

- There is no termination of the LLC even if more than 50 percent of the membership units are converted into the newly created membership units.

- The adjusted basis of each member's membership units remains the same after the conversion, assuming that there is no change in each member's share of LLC liabilities.

- There is no change in the holding period of any membership units.

- The creation and conversion of the membership units in the recapitalization does not constitute an issuance of additional units for purposes of determining whether the LLC is a nonpublicly traded partnership under Code Sec. 7704.

- The recapitalization may constitute a transfer subject to gift taxes.[603]

¶1125   D REORGANIZATIONS

.01   Types of Divisive D Reorganizations

A divisive D reorganization involves the separation of different businesses conducted by a single corporation. There must be a qualifying distribution under Code Sec. 355. The most common divisive D reorganizations are the spinoff, the split-up and the split-off. The purpose of many divisive D reorganizations is to transfer a separate line of business to minority shareholders in order to resolve disputes among shareholders. After the reorganization, each group of shareholders manages a separate line of business without interference by the other shareholders.

In a typical D reorganization, a parent corporation transfers a separate line of business to a controlled corporation in exchange for the stock in the controlled corporation. The parent corporation then distributes the stock in the controlled corporation to a minority group of shareholders in exchange for all of their shares in the parent corporation. The transaction is nontaxable to the parent and controlled corporation under Code Sec. 368(a)(1)(D). The transaction is nontaxable to the minority shareholders receiving stock in the controlled corporation under Code Sec. 355.[604] The parties must meet the many requirements under those Code sections in order to avoid recognition of gain.

A corporation may use an LLC to facilitate a nontaxable divisive D reorganization in several ways,[605] including the following:

- The parent corporation may transfer selected assets and liabilities to a subsidiary LLC that is classified as a corporation, and then transfer membership interests in the LLC directly to the minority shareholders in exchange for all their stock in the parent corporation.[606]

---

[603] CCA 201442053. See ¶2102.10 infra.

[604] See, e.g., Ltr. Rul. 201219003.

[605] Ltr. Ruls. 200905018, 200802011, 200832001, 200826022.

[606] Ltr. Rul. 200802011.

- The parent corporation may transfer its membership interests in an LLC classified as a partnership to a controlled corporation. The parent corporation then transfers its stock in the controlled corporation directly to the minority shareholders in exchange for all their stock in the parent corporation.[607]

- The parent corporation may transfer assets and liabilities of a separate business to a newly formed disregarded LLC. The parent corporation transfers the membership interests in the LLC to a newly formed controlled corporation. The parent corporation then transfers the stock in the controlled corporation to the minority shareholders in exchange for all their stock in the parent corporation.[608]

- The parent corporation may transfer selected assets, contracts and liabilities to a disregarded subsidiary LLC, followed by a transfer of membership interests in the disregarded LLC to a newly formed controlled corporation in exchange for stock. The parent corporation then distributes the stock in the controlled corporation to one or more shareholders in exchange for all of their shares in the parent corporation.[609]

- The members of an LLC that is classified as an S corporation transfer their membership interests to a newly formed LLC in exchange for an equity interest. The original LLC then elects to be a disregarded entity or qualified Subchapter S subsidiary, and continues the original Selection. The original LLC then distributes assets from one line of business to the new LLC that is disregarded for tax purposes. The new LLC contributes all the equity in the original LLC to a second newly formed LLC, with equity interests in the second LLC distributed pro rata to the members in a transaction that qualifies under Section 355. The distributed LLC elects S corporation treatment in its own right, so that the members of the original LLC ultimately own membership interests in two new S corporations, each holding a separate line of business.[610]

.02 Tax Consequences of Divisive D Reorganizations

The tax consequences of a divisive D reorganization using an LLC are as follows:

- The transfer by the parent corporation of its membership interests in an LLC to a controlled corporation, followed by the distribution of stock in the controlled corporation to the minority shareholders in exchange for their stock in the parent corporation, constitutes a nontaxable reorganization under Code Sec. 368(a)(1)(D).[611]

---

[607] Ltr. Rul. 201213002.
[608] Ltr. Rul. 201230007.
[609] Ltr. Ruls. 201230007, 200905018.
[610] Ltr. Rul. 201638004.
[611] Ltr. Ruls. 201230007, 201213002.

- The transfer by the parent corporation of selected assets and liabilities to a disregarded LLC classified as a corporation, followed by the distribution of membership interests in the LLC to the minority shareholders in exchange for their stock in the parent corporation, constitutes a nontaxable reorganization under Code Sec. 368(a)(1)(D).[612]
- The parent corporation and the controlled corporation (or disregarded LLC) are each "a party to a reorganization" within the meaning of Code Sec. 368(b).[613]
- No gain or loss is recognized by the parent corporation or the controlled corporation (or disregarded LLC), except that gain is recognized to the extent that liabilities of the parent corporation assumed by the controlled corporation (or disregarded LLC) exceed the parent corporation's basis in the property transferred.[614]
- No gain or loss is recognized by the controlled corporation on the contribution by the parent corporation of selected assets or membership interests.[615]
- The basis of each asset or membership interest received by the controlled corporation equals the basis of that asset in the hands of the parent corporation immediately prior to the contribution.[616]
- The holding period for each asset or membership interest received by the controlled corporation from the parent corporation includes the period during which the parent corporation held the asset.[617]
- No gain or loss is recognized by the parent corporation on the distribution of stock in the controlled corporation or membership interests in the disregarded LLC to the minority shareholders in exchange for their stock in the parent corporation.[618]
- No gain or loss is recognized by, and no amount is otherwise included in income of, minority shareholders on receipt of stock in the controlled corporation or membership interests in the disregarded LLC.[619]
- The minority shareholders' basis in the stock in the controlled corporation or membership interests in the disregarded LLC received in exchange for their stock in the parent corporation is equal to the basis of their stock in the parent corporation surrendered in the exchange.[620]
- The holding period of the stock in the controlled corporation or membership interests in the disregarded LLC received by the minority shareholders includes the holding period of their stock in the parent corporation surrendered

---

[612] Ltr. Rul. 200802011.

[613] Ltr. Ruls. 201230007, 201213002.

[614] Ltr. Rul. 201213002, *citing* Code Secs. 361(a), 357(a), (c); Rev. Rul. 80-323, 1980-2 CB 124.

[615] Ltr. Ruls. 201230007, 201213002, *citing* Code Sec. 1032(a).

[616] Ltr. Ruls. 201230007, 201213002, *citing* Code Sec. 362(b).

[617] Ltr. Ruls. 201230007, 201213002, *citing* Code Sec. 1223(2).

[618] Ltr. Ruls. 201230007, 201213002, *citing* Code Sec. 361(c).

[619] Ltr. Ruls. 201230007, 201213002, *citing* Code Sec. 355(a).

[620] Ltr. Ruls. 201230007, 201213002, *citing* Code Sec. 358(a)(1).

in the exchange, provided that the stock in the parent corporation was held as a capital asset on the date of the exchange.[621]

- There must be an allocation of the parent corporation's earnings and profits between the parent corporation and the controlled corporation or disregarded LLC.[622]

.03 Active Trade or Business Requirement in Section 355 Split-Up

One of the requirements for a Section 355 split-up is that the distributing corporation and the controlled corporation must each be engaged in the active conduct of a trade or business immediately after the distribution that has been carried on for the previous five years. The parties to the reorganization may use an LLC to satisfy the active trade or business requirement. The distributing corporation (which distributes stock in the controlled corporation to the split-off group of shareholders) will be treated as engaged in the active conduct of a trade or business, separate and apart from the trade or business of the controlled corporation, if:

- the distributing corporation owns at least 33 percent of an LLC, and the LLC is engaged in a trade or business;[623] or
- the distributing corporation owns at least a 20 percent interest in an LLC, and the distributing corporation performs active and substantial management functions for the LLC.[624]

.04 Acquisitive D Reorganizations

In an acquisitive or nondivisive D reorganization, the acquiring corporation acquires substantially all of the assets of the target corporation. The target corporation receives at least 50 percent control of the acquiring corporation. The target corporation then liquidates by distributing the stock or ownership interests in the acquiring company to the target corporation shareholders. There must be a qualifying distribution by the target corporation under Code Sec. 354.

A merger between related LLCs and similar reorganizations and consolidations of related LLCs may be treated as nondivisive D reorganizations. For example, if a parent merges two subsidiary LLCs that are classified as corporations for federal tax purposes, the transfer of assets of the first subsidiary to the second subsidiary in exchange for the membership interests of the second subsidiary constitutes a D reorganization. The distribution by the first subsidiary to the parent corporation of the membership interests in the second subsidiary constitutes a Section 354(b)(1)(B) distribution.

---

[621] Ltr. Ruls. 201230007, 201213002, *citing* Code Sec. 1223(1).

[622] Ltr. Ruls. 201230007, 201213002, *citing* Code Sec. 312(h) and Reg. § 1.312-10(a).

[623] Rev. Rul. 2007-42, 2007-2 CB 44.

[624] Rev. Rul. 2002-49, 2002-2 CB 288; Prop. Reg. § 1.355-3(b)(2)(v).

The IRS determined that there was a nondivisive D reorganization in the following cases:

1. A corporation merged into an LLC. The LLC did not issue shares in the merger. Both the corporation and the LLC were owned equally by two unrelated corporations (or their affiliates).[625]
2. An LLC merged into a corporation. The LLC and the corporation were both owned by the same corporation.[626]
3. A parent corporation owned a German LLC (GmbH). The parent also owned a Swiss corporation that owned another German LLC. There was a series of transfers of assets, liabilities, and stock, after which the parent owned a single GmbH, which in turn owned the other GmbH (with the Swiss corporation liquidated into the parent).[627]

Generally, a D reorganization has the same tax consequences as an A reorganization with one exception. Gain is recognized if liabilities exceed the tax basis of assets transferred in a D reorganization even if the transaction also meets the requirements for an A reorganization.[628] This problem can be avoided by having a reverse merger in which the corporation with liabilities in excess of basis is the surviving corporation.[629]

---

[625] Ltr. Rul. 7948066. *See also* Ltr. Rul. 7852111 (corporation merged into LLC; corporation and LLC appeared to have common shareholders).

[626] Ltr. Rul. 7947048.

[627] Ltr. Rul. 7950044.

[628] Code Sec. 357(c).

[629] *See* Rev. Rul. 75-161, 1975-1 CB 114.

12

Terminations

¶ 1201 EVENTS CAUSING TERMINATION

An LLC that is classified as a partnership for federal tax purposes terminates on one of the following events:[1]

- the members completely discontinue the business of the LLC;

- there is a merger or consolidation of two or more LLCs unless the resulting LLC is considered the continuation of the merging or consolidated LLCs;

- there is a division of an LLC, unless one or more of the resulting LLCs is considered as a continuing LLC;

- the LLC files an election to be classified as a corporation; or

- an existing member or a third party acquires all of the membership interests in the LLC. The partnership status of the LLC will terminate on the date that the number of members is reduced to a single member.

---

[1] Code Sec. 708(b).

¶ 1202 CESSATION OF BUSINESS

.01 General Rules

The first event causing termination of an LLC as a partnership is a complete cessation of business. The LLC will terminate if no part of the business or financial operation of the LLC continues to be carried on by any of the members in the LLC.[2]

There is no termination until the end of the winding up period of the liquidating LLC.[3] Thus, a member who withdraws from a liquidating LLC remains a member until receipt of final distribution to the member.[4]

There is no termination if the LLC changes its primary purpose and continues to carry on an active trade or business.[5]

.02 Tax Consequences

The tax consequences of distributions to members on termination of an LLC classified as a partnership are discussed in Chapter 10. The basic Code provisions that apply to liquidating distributions after a cessation of business are as follows:

- *Code Sec. 731(b)*—The LLC does not receive a deduction for the payment to the member.[6]
- *Code Sec. 731(a)(1)*—The member recognizes capital gain to the extent that a money distribution exceeds the basis of the member's interest in the LLC. The member is taxed in the year the payments are made.[7] The member recovers his or her entire basis before incurring any capital gain. However, if the total distribution amount is fixed and paid over more than one tax year, the retiring member may elect to recover basis and recognize capital gain on a pro rata basis. The member must attach a statement of the election to his or her return for the first year in which the payment is received.[8] There is no gain recognition as a result of a property distribution.
- *Code Sec. 731(a)(2)*—The member recognizes loss if three conditions are met. First, the member must receive only cash, unrealized receivables, or inventory. Second, the member must receive a liquidating distribution of his entire membership interest. Third, the adjusted basis of LLC assets distributed to the member must be less than the member's basis in his membership interest. The

---

[2] Code Sec. 708(b)(1)(A).

[3] Reg. § 1.708-1(b). Thus, a member who withdraws from a liquidating LLC remains a member until receipt of the final distribution to the member.

[4] *Brennan v. Comm'r*, TC Memo 2012-209 (2012).

[5] *Ginsburg v. United States*, 396 F.2d 983, 988 (Ct. Cl. 1968).

[6] Reg. § 1.736-1(a)(2).

[7] Reg. § 1.736-1(a)(5).

[8] Reg. § 1.736-1(b)(6). If the election is made, the member recognizes capital loss if the member does not recover the full amount of basis in membership interest (e.g., because the expected payments were not received in full).

loss recognized is the amount by which the basis in the membership interest exceeds the money and the LLC's basis in unrealized receivables and inventory items distributed to the member. This differs from the rule for nonliquidating distributions in which no loss is recognized.

- *Code Secs. 741 and 731(a)*—The gain or loss recognized is capital gain or loss,[9] except as provided under Code Sec. 751(b).[10]
- *Code Sec. 751(b)*—A portion of the member's gain is recharacterized as ordinary income to the extent of the member's share of unrealized receivables, depreciation recapture, and substantially appreciated inventory items[11] retained by the LLC.[12] A member does not recognize ordinary income if the member receives a distribution that is exactly equal to the member's share of unrealized receivables and substantially appreciated inventory items.[13]
- *Code Sec. 732(b)*—The member receives a basis in the distributed property equal to his or her basis in the membership interest, reduced by any money distributed. The basis is first allocated to the unrealized receivables and inventory items in an amount equal to the LLC's basis in those assets. Any remaining basis in the membership interest is allocated to the other properties received in the distribution.[14] This is a substituted basis.
- *Code Sec. 735(b)*—The member's holding period for the distributed property includes the LLC's holding period for the property,[15] except for the amount attributable to unrealized receivables and substantially appreciated inventory items.
- *Code Sec. 736*—Code Sec. 736 normally governs distributions to retiring or deceased members in exchange for their interest in LLC property (e.g., capital

---

[9] Code Secs. 731(a) (last sentence), 741.

[10] *See* ¶ 1005 *supra.*

[11] Reg. § 1.736-1(b)(4). Inventory is substantially appreciated if its fair market value exceeds the adjusted basis by more than 120 percent. Code Sec. 751(b)(3)(A).

[12] Under Code Sec. 751(b), a member will recognize ordinary income or loss, or capital gain or loss, if the member does not receive his proportionate share of unrealized receivables, substantially appreciated inventory items, and other property in a distribution. In that case, the member is treated as having received a proportionate distribution of all assets, and as selling back to the LLC the excess assets retained by the LLC in exchange for the excess assets retained by the member. Reg. § 1.732-1(e). Gain on the deemed sale back to the LLC will be ordinary income if the member retains a disproportionate share of capital assets, and the LLC retains a disproportionate share of unrealized receivables and substantially appreciated inventory items. In that case, the member will be treated as having received his proportionate share of the unrealized receivables and inventory items, and as having sold them back to the LLC. Ordinary income is the difference between the fair market value of the capital assets being purchased from the LLC less the adjusted basis of unrealized receivables and inventory items deemed distributed to the member in excess of his proportionate share sold back to the LLC. Gain on the deemed sale back to the LLC will be treated as capital gain if a member receives a disproportionately large share of unrealized receivables and inventory items. In that case, the member will be treated as having received his proportionate share of capital assets and as having sold back to the LLC such capital assets in exchange for the unrealized receivables and inventory items retained by him in excess of his proportionate share.

[13] Reg. §§ 1.751-1(b)(2)(ii)-(iii), (3)(ii)-(iii).

[14] Code Sec. 732(c)(1).

[15] Ltr. Rul. 200204005.

account, goodwill, accounts receivable, and other property). However, Code Sec. 736 does not apply on termination of an LLC.[16]

- *Code Sec. 1245*—There is no depreciation recapture with respect to the distributed assets.[17]

- *Code Sec. 754*—If the LLC has made an election under Code Sec. 754, the LLC must (a) increase the basis of its assets by the amount of gain recognized by the member on the distribution; (b) decrease the basis of its assets by the amount of loss recognized by the member on the distribution; (c) increase the basis of its assets by the amount of basis decrease to the member; and (d) decrease the basis of its assets by the amount of basis increase to the member.

¶ 1203 TRANSFER OF 50 PERCENT OF LLC

Prior to 2018, an LLC that was classified as a partnership terminated if there was a sale or exchange of 50 percent or more of the capital and profits of the LLC during a 12-month period. The rule was repealed for tax years after 2017.[18]

¶ 1204 MERGERS AND CONSOLIDATIONS

The third event causing a termination of an LLC as a partnership is a merger or consolidation, unless the resulting LLC is considered the continuation of the merging or consolidated LLCs.[19] The surviving LLC is treated as continuing, and the other LLC is treated as terminated. The surviving LLC is the LLC whose members own more than 50 percent of the capital and profits interest in the LLC.[20] If the resulting LLC could be considered a continuation of more than one of the merging LLCs, the LLC that is credited with the greatest dollar contribution value of assets to the resulting LLC is treated as the survivor for tax purposes.[21] If the members of none of the merging or consolidating LLCs own more than a 50-percent interest in the capital and profits of the resulting LLC, all of the merged LLCs are treated as terminated, and a new LLC results.[22]

---

[16] Reg. § 1.736-1(a).

[17] Code Sec. 1245(b)(3) provides that if the basis in the hands of the transferee is determined by the basis in the hands of the transferor, then there is no depreciation recapture. The distributee member receives a substituted basis, rather than a carryover basis, for Section 1245 property. However, Code Sec. 1245(b)(6)(A) provides that the basis of Section 1245 property distributed by an LLC is deemed to have a basis determined by reference to the basis of assets in hands of the LLC. Thus, there is no depreciation recapture.

[18] Code Sec. 708(b)(1), as amended by 2017 Tax Cuts and Jobs Act § 13504(a).

[19] *See* ¶¶ 1119, 1120, 1121, and 1122 *supra*.

[20] Code Sec. 708(b)(1)(A).

[21] Reg. § 1.708-1(b)(2).

[22] Prop. Reg. § 1.708-1(c)(1).

The types of mergers and consolidations, tax consequences, elections, and filing requirements are discussed in Chapter 11.[23]

¶ 1205 DIVISIONS

The fourth event causing a termination of an LLC as a partnership is a division, unless one or more of the resulting LLCs is treated as a continuing LLC. On the division of an LLC into two or more LLCs, any resulting LLC or LLCs are considered a continuation of the prior LLC if the members of the new LLC or LLCs had an interest of more than 50 percent in capital and profits of the prior LLC. Any other resulting LLC in which the members owned less than 50 percent of the prior LLC is considered a new LLC rather than a continuation of the prior LLC. If the members of none of the new LLCs owned more than 50 percent of the prior LLC, then the resulting LLCs are considered new LLCs rather than a continuation of the prior LLC. In such case, the prior LLC will be treated as terminated. The members' interests in the new LLCs that are not continuations of the prior LLC are treated as liquidated as of the date of the division.[24]

The types of divisions, tax consequences, elections, and filing requirements are discussed in Chapter 11.[25]

¶ 1206 CHANGE IN CLASSIFICATION ELECTION

The fifth event causing the termination of an LLC as a partnership is an election to be classified as a corporation. The tax consequences of an election change are discussed in Chapters 5 and 11.[26]

¶ 1207 TRANSACTIONS RESULTING IN SINGLE-MEMBER LLC

The sixth event causing the termination of an LLC as a partnership is a reduction in the number of members in the LLC to one. A single-member LLC cannot be classified as a partnership. The classification of the LLC will change from a partnership to a disregarded entity on such date unless the LLC elects to be classified as a corporation.[27]

The transactions causing termination include the following:

- *Acquisitions*—The acquisition of all membership interests by an existing member or a third party will cause the termination of an LLC as a partnership. The tax consequences of a purchase by an existing member of all membership

---

[23] *See* ¶ 1115 *supra.*
[24] Reg. § 1.708-1(d)(1).
[25] *See* ¶ 1115 *supra.*
[26] *See* ¶¶ 504.06, 1106.01 *supra.*
[27] Reg. § 301.7701-3(f)(2); Ltr. Ruls. 200603021, 200518039.

interests,[28] and the purchase by a third party of all membership interests,[29] are discussed above.

- *Death of member*—The death of a member in a two-member LLC results in the termination of the LLC as a partnership. There is an exception if the estate or other successor in interest of the deceased member continues to share in the profits or losses of the LLC.[30] A two-member LLC that is in the process of being liquidated after the death of a member is not considered terminated as long as the LLC continues to make payments to the estate or successor in interest.[31]

---

[28] *See* ¶ 1118.01 *supra.*
[29] *See* ¶ 1118.02 *supra.*
[30] Reg. § 1.708-1(b)(1)(i).
[31] Reg. § 1.736-1(a)(6).

13

Loss Limitations

¶1310   Related Party Transactions
¶1311   Reporting Requirements

¶1301 GENERALLY

One of the major advantages of an LLC is that the LLC may pass through losses to investors. The losses may offset other taxable income earned by the members. Conversely, shareholders in a C corporation may not deduct corporate losses or excess deductions on their personal income tax returns. The losses may be used only to offset corporate profits, if any.

There are nine main limitations on the pass-through of LLC losses to members:

1. Basis
2. At-risk limitations
3. Passive loss rules
4. Excess business losses
5. Anti-abuse rules
6. Built-in losses
7. Class of liabilities rules
8. Special allocation rules
9. Related party transactions

The loss limitations apply in the following order: (i) Code Sec. 704(d) basis limitation, (ii) Code Sec. 465 at-risk limitation of Sec. 465, and (iii) Code Sec. 469 passive loss.[1] For example, if a member has insufficient basis, losses are suspended and should not be reflected on Form 6198 for the at-risk limitation or on Form 8582 for the passive loss limitation.[2]

¶1302 BASIS

.01 General Rules

The first limitation on losses is basis. A member may deduct his distributive share of LLC losses, including capital losses, only to the extent of the member's basis in his membership interest in the LLC at the end of the LLC's tax year in which the losses occurred.[3] The three methods of determining basis are discussed in Chapters 9 and 15.[4]

Distributions are taken into account before losses in determining a member's adjusted basis in the membership interest.[5]

---

[1] Temp. Reg. § 1.469-2T(d)(6)(i); Instructions to Schedule K-1, under the heading, "Limitations on Losses, Deductions, and Credits."

[2] IRS Audit Technique Guide—Partnerships, Chapter 5, under the heading, "Basis Limitations."

[3] Code Sec. 704(d).

[4] *See* ¶902 *supra*, ¶1503 *infra*.

[5] Rev. Rul. 66-94, 1966-1 CB 166.

.02 *Carryforward of Disallowed Losses*

Losses in excess of basis are not deductible for that year. The disallowed losses may be carried forward and deducted in subsequent years to the extent the member has positive basis in his membership interest at the end of the year.[6] A member may increase his or her basis in the membership interest by (i) contributing additional property or money to the LLC, (ii) receiving an additional allocation of LLC income that is not distributed during the year, or (iii) increasing his or her share of LLC liabilities. A proportionate share of each disallowed loss is carried forward if the total loss is comprised of different types of deductions (such as capital, ordinary income, and other losses).[7]

The disallowed losses may be carried forward indefinitely.[8] The member may absorb the loss during the first subsequent year in which there is sufficient basis. The basis in subsequent years is first determined after an annual adjustment is made for the current year's income, distributions, and contributions.

EXAMPLE 13-1

A member has a basis in her membership interest of $6,000. Her distributive share of LLC losses for 1999 is $10,000. The member may deduct only $6,000 of the losses in 1999. The $6,000 loss reduces the basis in her membership interest to zero. The $4,000 disallowed loss may be carried forward to the year 2000.

EXAMPLE 13-2

Same facts as in above Example. The member's distributive share of LLC income during the year 2000 is $3,000. No part of the income is distributed to the member. Therefore, the member's basis at the end of the year, after making adjustments for the current year's allocations, contributions, and distributions, is increased from zero to $3,000. The member may in the year 2000 deduct $3,000 of the disallowed losses carried over from 1999. The loss deduction in the year 2000 reduces her basis in the membership interest to zero. The remaining $1,000 of disallowed losses may be carried over to 2001 or subsequent years when the member has a positive basis after adjustments for that year's allocations, contributions, and distributions.[9]

---

[6] Code Sec. 704(d); Reg. § 1.704-1(d)(1).

[7] Reg. § 1.704-1(d)(2) and (4), Example (3).

[8] Code Sec. 704(d).

[9] Reg. § 1.704-1(d)(4), Example (1).

The losses carried forward are personal to the member. A member loses the disallowed losses if the member terminates his interest in the LLC upon death, upon withdrawal from the LLC, or otherwise. A purchasing member may not claim disallowed losses incurred by the selling member.

.03 Sale of Membership Interest

A member loses suspended carryover deductions on sale of a membership interest.[10] The reason is that a member may not deduct losses in excess of basis.[11] Gain on sale of a membership interest does not increase basis. However, a member may make a capital contribution in the year of sale and deduct the excess losses. That will increase the value of the membership interest and result in additional capital gain on sale.[12]

A member may offset disallowed losses against gain on sale if the losses are disallowed solely because of the at-risk or passive loss limitations discussed below.

A member does not lose the suspended losses as a result of a partial sale or disposition of the membership interest.[13]

EXAMPLE 13-3

A member has a basis of $10,000 in her membership interest in an LLC. The LLC allocates $6,000 of losses to the member during the current year. Even though the member has sufficient basis to absorb the loss, the member may not deduct the losses in the current year because of the passive loss rules. The $6,000 of disallowed losses under the passive loss rules must still reduce the member's basis in her membership interest from $10,000 to $4,000. If the member sells her membership interest for $10,000, the member will have $6,000 of gain (amount realized of $10,000, less basis of $4,000). The member may offset the $6,000 of gain by the $6,000 of losses that were disallowed under the passive loss rules.

.04 Character of Loss Disallowance

An LLC may have several types of income, gain, loss or deduction. If there are losses in more than one category, such as capital losses and ordinary losses, and if the

---

[10] *Sennett v. Comm'r*, 80 TC 825 (1983), *aff'd per curiam*, 752 F.2d 428 (9th Cir. 1985).

[11] Code Sec. 704(d).

[12] The member will not receive an increase in basis for the capital contribution since the capital contribution will be reduced by the excess loss carryover.

[13] Reg. §1.704-1(d)(1); *Sennett v. Comm'r*, 80 TC 825 (1983), *aff'd per curiam*, 752 F.2d 428 (9th Cir.1985).

basis limitation applies, then each category of loss is limited in proportion to total losses, including disallowed losses from prior years.[14]

¶ 1303 AT-RISK RULES

.01 *In General*

Members in an LLC who are individuals or closely held C corporations[15] are subject to the same at-risk rules[16] as limited partners in a partnership. A member may not deduct losses in excess of the amount "at risk." The at-risk rules apply at the member level in an LLC.[17]

A member is at risk with respect to each separate activity of the LLC. When Congress enacted the at-risk rules in 1976, the at-risk rules applied on an activity-by-activity basis to five activities: farming; exploring for or exploiting oil and gas resources; holding, producing or distributing motion picture films or videotapes; equipment leasing; and exploring for or exploiting geothermal deposits.[18] These were the areas in which there were the most abusive tax shelters.

The at-risk rules now apply to all other activities on an activity-by-activity basis.[19] However, such other activities (including equipment leasing) are grouped together in applying the at-risk rules if (a) the taxpayer actively participates in the management of the trade or business, or (b) the LLC is classified as a partnership or S corporation and 65 percent or more of the losses for the tax year are allocable to members who actively participating in the management of the trade or business.[20]

The at-risk amounts, which are discussed separately below, include the following:

1. The amount of money that member contributes to the LLC.[21]
2. The adjusted basis of property that the member contributes to the LLC.[22]
3. Amounts borrowed or owed by the LLC to the extent that the member is personally liable for repayment, or has pledged property as security for the repayment.[23]
4. Amounts loaned by the member to the LLC.[24]

---

[14] Reg. § 1.704-1(d)(4), Example 2.

[15] A closely held corporation is one in which five or fewer shareholders own more than 50 percent of the corporation's stock during the last half of the tax year. Code Sec. 465(a)(1)(B).

[16] Code Sec. 465.

[17] Ltr. Ruls. 200340024, 9741021.

[18] Code Sec. 465(c)(1).

[19] Code Sec. 465(c)(3).

[20] Code Sec. 465(c)(3)(B).

[21] *See* ¶ 1303.02 *infra.*

[22] *See* ¶ 1303.03 *infra.*

[23] Code Sec. 465(b)(2). *See* ¶ 1303.04 *infra.*

[24] Prop. Reg. § 1.465-7(a). *See* ¶ 1303.05 *infra.*

5. The member's share of "qualified nonrecourse financing" if the LLC obtains financing for real estate that it acquires or holds.[25]

6. Gain on the sale of a membership interest.

The amount at risk is increased by the member's share of income and decreased by the member's share of losses and distributions.[26] Losses that are disallowed under the at-risk rules are suspended and may be carried forward to subsequent years in which the member's at-risk amount is sufficient to absorb the losses.[27] The suspended losses may be carried forward indefinitely. Unlike the basis rules under Code Sec. 704(d), the suspended losses may be used to offset gain on sale of a membership interest.[28] The losses disallowed under the at-risk rules reduce a member's basis in the LLC.[29]

The at-risk rules do not limit the deductibility of expenses arising from an activity. They limit the deductibility of losses. Thus, the member may deduct pass-through expenses up to the amount of income from the same activity. The rule applies even if the member receives a distribution from the LLC in the same year that causes the at-risk amount to become negative.[30] For example, if a member has a negative at-risk amount of $20,000 at the end of the year, a member may deduct $10,000 of pass-through expenses if the LLC allocates to the member at least $10,000 of income from the activity.[31]

A member who has insufficient at-risk basis must deduct losses in the following order during the current year: (i) capital losses; (ii) Section 1231 losses; (iii) all losses and deductions other than Section 57 tax preferences; and (iv) Section 57 tax preference items. The losses retain their character when they are carried over to subsequent years, and must follow the same ordering rule in such years.

Unlike the rules applicable to basis, the amount at risk can be negative.[32] It may become negative as a result of a distribution or conversion of a recourse loan to a nonrecourse loan,[33] but not as a result of loss recognition.[34] A member recognizes taxable income to the extent that the at-risk amount is reduced below zero. The recaptured income is limited to the sum of the loss deductions previously allowed to the member, less any amount previously recaptured.[35] The recaptured income increases the member's amount at risk. A member may deduct the recaptured amounts included in taxable income if and when the member increases the amount at risk.

---

[25] *See* ¶ 1303.06 *infra.*

[26] Code Sec. 465(b)(5).

[27] Code Sec. 465(a)(2).

[28] Prop. Reg. § 1.465-66.

[29] Prop. Reg. § 1.465-1(e).

[30] Prop. Reg. § 1.465-2.

[31] Prop. Reg. § 1.465-11(c)(2).

[32] Prop. Reg. § 1.465-3(b).

[33] Prop. Reg. § 1.465-3(b).

[34] Prop. Reg. § 1.465-3(a).

[35] Code Sec. 465(e).

When activities are grouped together, it is more likely that the amounts at-risk will not fall below zero. For example, if there is grouping, all contributions and recourse loans are accounted for in one activity regardless of the particular activity to which they are attributable.

Members who have losses from at-risk activities must file IRS Form 6198.

.02 Money Contributed to LLC

A member is at risk for the amount of money that the member contributes to an LLC. The member may first borrow the money and then contribute that to the LLC. However, a member is not at risk if the member borrows from a lender who has an interest in the LLC other than as a creditor.[36]

.03 Property Contributed to LLC

A member is at risk for the adjusted basis of property contributed to an LLC, subject to the following rules:

- When a member contributes unencumbered property to an LLC, the amount at risk is increased by the adjusted basis of the contributed property.[37]
- When a member contributes property that is subject only to liabilities for which the member is liable, the amount at risk is increased by the adjusted basis of the contributed property.[38]
- When a member contributes property that is subject to liabilities for which the member is not personally liable, the amount at risk is increased by the adjusted basis in the property, and decreased by the amount of encumbrances to which the property is subject that would not have increased the taxpayer's amount at risk if incurred for use in the activity.[39]

.04 LLC Loans and Debt

Amounts At-Risk

A member is at risk for amounts borrowed by the LLC to the extent that:

- the member is personally liable for repayment;[40]

---

[36] Code Sec. 465(b)(1)(A); NSAR 010421, Vaughn #10421.

[37] NSAR 010421, Vaughn #10421, *citing* Reg. § 1.465-23(a)(1).

[38] NSAR 010421, Vaughn #10421, *citing* Reg. § 1.465-23(a)(2)(ii).

[39] NSAR 010421, Vaughn #10421.

[40] Code Sec. 465(b)(2)(A).

- the member pledges property, other than property used in the activity, as security for the borrowed amount (but only to the extent of the net fair market value of the member's interest in such property);[41] or

- the member personally guarantees the debt,[42] and has no right of reimbursement against any other member for the obligation.[43] There are exceptions to this rule discussed below.

Amounts Not At-Risk

A member is not at-risk with respect to the following amounts, even though the member is personally liable:

- Amounts protected against loss through nonrecourse financing, guarantees, stop loss arrangements, or similar agreements,[44] subject to the exceptions noted below.

- Amounts borrowed from a lender who has a membership interest in the LLC, or from a person related to another member of the LLC.[45]

- Amounts borrowed by an LLC in excess of the fair market value of the assets pledged by the member as security for a loan. Pledged property that is used in the business of the LLC does not count as security or cause the member to be at-risk.

- Liabilities that are nonrecourse liabilities, even though the liabilities are recourse against the LLC.

- Liabilities of the member to the LLC. The amount at-risk is not increased by the amount that the member is required to contribute to the LLC under the operating agreement until such time as the contribution is actually made.[46]

- Deficit restoration obligation amounts. These are amounts that the member is required to contribute to an LLC on liquidation to the extent of the member's negative capital account.[47]

Repayments of Loans

Repayments of LLC loans for which a member is at risk decreases the member's at risk amount.

---

[41] Code Sec. 465(b)(2)(B).

[42] FSA 200025018.

[43] FSA 200025018; NSAR 010426, Vaughn #10426; *Brand v. Comm'r*, 81 TC 821 (1983).

[44] Code Sec. 465(b)(4); Prop. Reg. § 1.465-24(a)(2).

[45] Code Sec. 465(b)(3)(A).

[46] Reg. § 1.465-22(a).

[47] *Hubert Enterprises, Inc. v. Comm'r*, TC Memo 2008-46 (2008); *Hubert v. Comm'r*, 125 TC 72 (2005).

Guarantee of LLC Debt

There is conflicting authority regarding whether the guarantee of LLC debt creates at-risk basis. The proposed regulations, certain courts, and some rulings provide that a member is not at risk for LLC liabilities guaranteed by the member if (a) the member has a right of subrogation against the LLC as the primary obligor under state law or under the terms of the operating agreement,[48] (b) the member has a right of reimbursement against the other members,[49] (c) the member who guarantees the debt is undercapitalized or has insufficient assets to cover the debt in the event of a default,[50] (d) the member guarantees amounts borrowed by another member and contributed to the LLC.[51] or (e) the member signs a bad-boy guarantee that applies only if the company or its officers perform certain bad acts such as filing a voluntary petition in bankruptcy.[52]

The IRS and some courts take the position that guarantees do not increase the at-risk basis until the member actually pays the guaranteed debt and has no right to reimbursement from the LLC or other members.[53]

Other courts permit an increase in basis for guarantees if the member bears ultimate economic responsibility for the entire debt or a portion of the debt on default by the LLC in a worst-case scenario.[54] For example, if the individual owner of an LLC guarantees an LLC loan, and has a right of contribution from a related company for 50 percent of the loan, then the LLC member is at risk for 50 percent of the loan to the LLC.[55]

In 2013, the IRS noted the conflicting rulings and regulations. It determined that a guarantor of debt of an LLC that is classified as a partnership or disregarded entity may be at risk even if the member does not waive rights of subrogation and reimbursement from the LLC. The IRS informally ruled as follows:[56]

- The guarantor will be treated at risk if (i) there is a bona fide guarantee of LLC debt, (ii) the guarantee is enforceable by creditors of the LLC under local law, and (iii) the guarantor member's only recourse with respect to repayment is against the assets of the LLC. The guarantor is not required to waive his or her right of subrogation and reimbursement against the borrowing LLC as the primary obligor. The IRS determined that the proposed regulations should not be followed.

---

[48] Prop. Reg. § 1.465-24; NSAR 010859, Vaughn #10859.

[49] FSA 200025018; NSAR 010426, Vaughn #10426; *Brand v. Comm'r*, 81 TC 821 (1983).

[50] CCA 200246014.

[51] NSAR 010426, Vaughn #10426.

[52] AM 2016-001 (Apr. 15, 2016).

[53] Prop. Reg. § 1.465-6(d); IRS Audit Technique Guide—Partnerships, Chapter 5, under the heading, "Guarantees"; *Brand v. Comm'r*, 81 TC 821 (1983).

[54] *Melvin v. Comm'r*, 894 F.2d 1072 (9th Cir. 1990), *aff'g* 88 TC 63 (1987).

[55] *Moreno v. United States*, 2014-1 USTC ¶ 50,293 (W.D. La. 2014).

[56] CCA 201308028.

- If other persons have co-guaranteed LLC debt, the guarantor member will not be at risk except to the extent that the guarantor has no right of contribution or reimbursement against the other guarantors under local law, or until such time as such rights are exhausted or extinguished.

In 2014, the IRS rejected prior Field Office advice on guarantees of debt for at-risk purposes, and made the following determinations for LLC members:[57]

- When a member of an LLC classified as a partnership or disregarded entity for federal tax purposes guarantees the LLC's debt, the member is at risk for the amount of the guaranteed debt, whether or not the member waives any right to subrogation, reimbursement, or indemnification from the LLC, if (i) the member has no right of contribution or reimbursement from persons other than the LLC, (ii) the member is not otherwise protected against loss within the meaning of Code Sec. 465(b)(4), and (iii) the guarantee is bona fide and enforceable by creditors of the LLC under local law.
- When a member of an LLC classified as a partnership for federal tax purposes guarantees qualified nonrecourse financing of the LLC, the member's amount at risk is increased by the amount guaranteed, but only to the extent such debt was not previously taken into account by that member, the guaranteeing member has no right of contribution or reimbursement from persons other than the LLC, the guaranteeing member is not otherwise protected against loss within the meaning of Code Sec. 465(b)(4), and the guarantee is bona fide and enforceable by creditors of the LLC under local law.
- When a member of an LLC guarantees qualified nonrecourse financing of the LLC, the amount of the guaranteed debt is no longer qualified nonrecourse financing if the guarantee is bona fide and enforceable by creditors of the LLC under local law. The amount of the guaranteed debt will no longer be includible in the at-risk amount of the other non-guarantor members of the LLC. Any reduction that causes an LLC member's at-risk amount to fall below zero will trigger recapture of losses as ordinary income under Code Sec. 465(e).

The IRS argued in one case that a member of an LLC is not at-risk if the member does not have sufficient liquidity to satisfy a guaranteed LLC debt in the event of a default. The IRS stated "that a guarantor must have unencumbered cash or marketable resources to satisfy a claim under a guaranty to be at risk." The court rejected this position.[58]

---

[57] AM 2014-003 (Apr. 4, 2014).

[58] *Moreno v. United States,* 2014-1 USTC ¶ 50,293 (W.D. La. 2014).

¶ 1303.04

.05 Member Loans to LLC

A member is at risk for amounts that the member loans to the LLC.[59] The loan amount also gives the member basis in the LLC since the loan is treated as a recourse loan.[60]

.06 Qualified Nonrecourse Financing

A member is at risk for the member's share of qualified nonrecourse financing on real property owned by the LLC, even though the member is not personally liable for repayment of the debt.[61] Qualified nonrecourse financing is any financing that meets the following requirements:

1. The LLC borrows the money with respect to the activity of holding real property. The fact that a loan is used to purchase or improve real property and/or is secured by real property does not automatically mean that it is used with respect to the activity of holding real property.
2. The LLC borrows the money from a qualified person or from any federal, state, or local government or instrumentality thereof, or that is guaranteed by any federal, state or local government.[62] A qualified person is a person who (i) is actively and regularly engaged in the business of lending money, (ii) is not the seller of the property or person related to the seller, (iii) does not receive a fee with respect to the member's investment in the property, and (iv) is not related to the taxpayer unless the financing is commercially reasonable and on substantially the same terms as loans involving unrelated person.
3. No person is personally liable for repayment of the funds. The debt can be bifurcated and considered part qualified and part nonqualified nonrecourse financing.
4. The loan is not convertible into a membership interest.

EXAMPLE 13-4

An LLC owns and actively manages an equipment rental business. In order to have a place to store and service equipment, it purchases a commercial garage. It uses funds obtained by a nonrecourse loan from a state government agency, secured by the garage. The loan is with respect to the activity of equipment rental, rather than with respect to the activity of holding real property, and the loan therefore cannot be qualified

---

[59] Prop. Reg. § 1.465-7(a).

[60] Reg. § 1.752-2(c)(1).

[61] Ltr. Ruls. 9741021, 9741018, 9738013; Code Sec. 465(b)(6).

[62] Code Sec. 465(b)(6)(B).

nonrecourse financing. If the equipment rental business and the garage could be treated as separate activities, the result would be different.[63]

The requirement that no person be personally liable for repayment previously caused a problem because an LLC is a person for tax purposes. Therefore, any financing for which an LLC was liable was not qualified nonrecourse financing even if no member was personally liable for the financing.[64] The IRS determined that this result was inappropriate if the only activity of the LLC was the real property activity. It provided in the regulations that the personal liability of an LLC is disregarded in determining whether a financing is qualified nonrecourse financing if the LLC's only assets are real property used in the activity of holding real property. No other person may be liable for the financing.[65]

If a member guarantees the LLC's qualified nonrecourse financing, the member may increase his or her amount at risk by the amount guaranteed to the extent not previously taken into account. The guaranteed debt no longer meets the definition of qualified nonrecourse financing, and the amount of the guaranteed debt is no longer includible in the at-risk amount of the other non-guaranteeing members, if the guarantee is bona fide and enforceable by creditors of the LLC under local law.[66]

A right granted to the guaranteeing member to make capital contribution calls to the non-guarantor members, to treat portions of the guaranteed payment as loans to those members, to adjust their fractional interests, or to enter into subsequent allocation agreements to share the risk of the guarantee, are not sufficient to make the non-guarantors personally liable for the debt for Code Sec. 465 purposes.[67]

Financing may also be qualified nonrecourse financing if, in addition to the real property used in the activity of holding real property, the financing is secured by (a) property that is incidental to the activity of holding real property, or (b) property that is neither real property used in the activity of holding real property nor incidental property if the total fair market value of such property is less than ten percent of the total gross fair market value of all the property securing the financing.[68]

LLC debt that is secured by real estate ceases to be qualified nonrecourse financing when a member guarantees the debt.[69]

Reductions in an LLC's qualified nonrecourse liabilities are treated as a cash distribution from the LLC to the members. A member recognizes recapture income if the deemed distributions exceed the member's basis in the membership interest.[70] The recapture income is characterized as ordinary income, capital gain, or Section 1231 gain depending on the type of loss deducted in prior years, although most tax-

---

[63] Example from California Franchise Tax Board, Partnership Technical Manual ¶ 5330 (interpreting federal law).

[64] T.D. 8777 (1998).

[65] Reg. § 1.465-27(b)(4).

[66] CCA 201606027, *citing* Code Sec. 465(b)(6)(B)(iii); AM 2014-003 (Apr. 4, 2014).

[67] CCA 201606027.

[68] Reg. § 1.465-27(b)(2)(i).

[69] AM 2014-003 (Apr. 4, 2014).

[70] AM 2014-003 (Apr. 4, 2014).

preparation software characterizes the recapture income as ordinary income in the absence of a preparer override.[71]

If a member's amount at-risk is reduced to zero, the member may not immediately deduct loss allocations. Any reduction that causes the member's at-risk amount to fall below zero will trigger recapture of losses as ordinary income under Code Sec. 465(e).[72]

.07 Gain on Sale of Membership Interest

Gain on Sale

Gain recognized on sale of a membership interest increases the amount at risk.[73] Therefore, a member may deduct losses disallowed under the at-risk rules on sale of a membership interest to the extent of gain recognized.

This rule is different from the basis rules. Gain on the sale of a membership interest does not increase the member's tax basis. As a result, suspended losses under the basis rules may not offset the gain on disposition.

EXAMPLE 13-5

An LLC is classified as a partnership. It is engaged only in the activity of holding real property. It borrows $5,000 to use in the activity. The LLC is liable on the debt. No members are personally liable. The debt constitutes qualified nonrecourse financing. All of the members may include their shares of the financing as at-risk amounts.[74] If the requirements for qualified nonrecourse financing are met, the at-risk limitations will not apply to the losses generated by the properties held by the LLC.[75]

Nonrecognition Transactions

If an LLC member with suspended at-risk losses transfers a membership interest in a nonrecognition transaction in which the transferee's basis is determined in whole or in part by reference to the member's basis, then the transferee may increase its basis in the membership interest by the amount of the member's suspended at-risk losses.[76]

---

[71] *See* CCH Standard Federal Tax Reports ¶ 21,893.055.

[72] AM 2014-003 (Apr. 4, 2014).

[73] Prop. Reg. §§ 1.465-12, 1.465-66(a).

[74] Reg. § 1.465-27(b)(4), Example (1).

[75] Ltr. Rul. 9738013.

[76] Prop. Reg. § 1.465-67.

¶1304 PASSIVE LOSSES

.01 In General

Members of an LLC who are individuals, trusts, estates, and personal service corporations, may deduct passive activity losses only against passive activity income.[77] The passive losses may not be deducted against other types of income, such as wages, interest, or dividends. Tax credits from passive activities are also limited to the member's regular tax liability allocable to passive activities.

A passive activity is a trade or business in which the taxpayer does not materially participate and any rental activity.[78] A member is treated as materially participating in an activity only if the member is involved in the operations of the activity on a regular, continuous and substantial basis.[79] A passive activity loss is the amount by which the total deductions from the passive activity exceed the total income from the activity for the tax year.

Passive activity losses cannot offset nonpassive activity income, such as interest, dividends, salary, wages and profits from a trade or business in which the member materially participates. A member may deduct passive activity losses only against passive activity income from all sources. Excess passive losses are suspended and carried forward as a deduction to succeeding years when the taxpayer has passive income or when the taxpayer disposes of his entire interest in the activity that generated the excess passive losses.[80]

An LLC or member of an LLC that is classified as a closely held C corporation (other than a personal service corporation) may deduct passive activity losses against both passive and net active income, but not against portfolio income.[81] Portfolio income includes income from interest, dividends, and royalties not derived in the ordinary course of the trade or business. Income that is neither passive income nor portfolio income is "net active income."[82]

---

[77] Code Sec. 469(a)(1). Passive activity income does not include income from interest, dividends, annuities, royalties (except for royalties derived in the ordinary course of the trade or business), or certain capital gains. The passive income must be from a passive activity as defined in the Code.

[78] Code Sec. 469(c); Temp. Reg. § 1.469-1T(e)(1).

[79] Code Sec. 469(h)(1).

[80] Code Sec. 469(g)(1).

[81] Code Secs. 469(a)(2)(B), (e)(2).

[82] Code Sec. 469(b).

.02 *Rental Property*

General Rules

Rental real estate is a passive activity,[83] whether or not the taxpayer materially participates.[84] There are exceptions for (i) certain rentals of tangible property, (ii) rental loss deductions up to $25,000 if the member actively participates in the LLC during the year, (iii) rental loss deductions by real estate professionals who materially participate in the LLC's real estate rental business, (iv) short-term rentals, (v) self-rental property, in which case passive income is recharacterized as nonpassive income, and (vi) ground leases, in which passive income is recharacterized as nonpassive income. These exceptions are discussed below.

Tangible Property

Rentals of tangible property (real and personal) are not treated as rental activities in the following cases:

- the average customer use is seven days or less;[85]
- the average period of customer use is 30 days or less, and the LLC provides significant personal services in connection with making the property available for use by customers;[86]
- the LLC provides extraordinary personal services in making the tangible property available to customers;[87]
- the rental of tangible property is incidental to non-rental services provided by the LLC;[88]
- the taxpayer customarily makes the tangible property available during defined business hours for nonexclusive use by various customers;[89] or
- the taxpayer contributes tangible property to an LLC if (i) the taxpayer contributes the property for use in an activity conducted by the LLC, (ii) the taxpayer owns an interest in the LLC, and (iii) the business conducted by the LLC is not a rental activity.[90] Thus, if a member contributes tangible property to an LLC, the member's distributive share of LLC income is not passive rental income unless the LLC is engaged in a rental activity.[91] Similarly, if the member receives guaranteed payments for use of the property under Code Sec. 707(c), or lease payments, the payments are not income from a rental activity unless the LLC is engaged in a rental activity.

---

[83] Code Sec. 469(c)(2).
[84] Code Sec. 469(c)(4).
[85] Temp. Reg. § 1.469-1T(e)(3)(ii)(A).
[86] Temp. Reg. § 1.469-1T(e)(3)(ii)(B).
[87] Temp. Reg. § 1.469-1T(e)(3)(ii)(C).
[88] Temp. Reg. § 1.469-1T(e)(3)(ii)(D).
[89] Temp. Reg. § 1.469-1T(e)(3)(ii)(E).
[90] Temp. Reg. § § 1.469-1T(e)(3)(ii)(F), (vii).
[91] Temp. Reg. § 1.469-1T(e)(3)(vii).

If the rental of tangible property is not a "rental activity" under the above rules, then the activity is not a "per se" passive activity. Instead, the activity will be a passive activity subject to the passive loss rules if it is a trade or business in which the taxpayer does not materially participate.[92] It will not be a passive activity subject to the passive loss rules if it is a trade or business in which the taxpayer materially participates.[93]

$25,000 Deduction

An individual member of an LLC may deduct up to $25,000[94] of rental real estate losses against non-passive income if the individual "actively participates" in the LLC during the year.[95] An individual member actively participates if the individual owns at least ten percent of the membership interests in the LLC,[96] and materially participates in the business of the LLC.[97] The $25,000 offset is phased out at the rate of $.50 for every dollar of modified adjusted gross income in excess of $100,000. There is no deduction if modified adjusted gross income exceeds $150,000.

Real Estate Professionals

An individual member of an LLC may deduct rental real estate losses against non-passive income if two separate material participation tests are met:

- *Qualifying taxpayer.* The taxpayer must be a qualifying taxpayer under Code Sec. 469(c)(7)(B). A taxpayer is a qualifying taxpayer if (i) more than one-half of the personal services performed in trades or businesses by the taxpayer during such taxable year are performed in real property trades or businesses in which the taxpayer materially participates, and (ii) the taxpayer performs more than 750 hours of services during the taxable year in real property trades or businesses in which the taxpayer materially participates. Only the time that the taxpayer spends in real property trades or businesses (rental and non-rental) in which the taxpayer materially participates counts towards the requirement of being a qualifying taxpayer. In the case of individuals, there are seven tests for material participation. For example, one test provides that an individual will be treated as materially participating in an activity for tax year if the individual participates in the activity for more than 500 hours during such year. The taxpayer is not required to make the election to

---

[92] *Bailey v. Comm'r*, TC Summary Opinion 2011-22 (2011).

[93] *Bailey v. Comm'r*, TC Memo 2001-296 (2001).

[94] The amount is $12,500 for married person filing a separate return. Code Sec. 469(i)(5).

[95] Code Sec. 469(i)(1).

[96] Code Sec. 469(i)(6)(A).

[97] Reg. § 1.469-9(j)(1). The material participation requirements are discussed at ¶ 1304.03.

aggregate rental real estate activities under Reg. § 1.469-9(g). That election is not relevant under this first test. Code Sec. 469(c)(2) (which generally provides that all rental real estate activities are passive activities) does not apply if the taxpayer is a qualified individual.[98] A person who meets his first material participation test is called a real estate professional.

- *Material participation in a separate activity.* If the taxpayer is a qualifying individual, then the taxpayer must pass a second material participation test to avoid passive activity characterization. The taxpayer must materially participate in each rental real estate activity. Each interest that the taxpayer has in a rental real estate property is a separate activity.[99] The taxpayer must meet one of the material participation tests in Reg. § 1.469-5T(a) for each rental property. The taxpayer may make an election to aggregate rental real estate properties to meet one of those tests.[100] The election is relevant only under the second test. The taxpayer may not aggregate participation in real property development trades or businesses with other non-rental property businesses.[101]

The taxpayer may be treated as materially participating in all real estate trades or businesses for purposes of the first test, but not materially participating in one or more separate real estate rental activities under the second test. The rental real estate activity will be treated as a passive activity unless the taxpayer meets both material participation tests.[102]

The written election to group rentals may be made with any original return and binds all future years. It is not retroactive.[103] Very few grouping elections have been filed with the IRS. A separate grouping election may be made by the LLC, depending on whether the member owns more or less than a 50 percent interest in the LLC.

If the member owns less than 50 percent of the membership interests in the LLC, then the member's interest in rental real estate held by the LLC is treated as (i) a single interest if the LLC elects to group all real estate activities as a single rental activity, or (ii) a separate activity for each rental property if the LLC does not make the election. The member may elect to treat all interests in rental real estate, including rental real estate interests held through an LLC and other pass-through entities, as a single rental real estate activity.[104]

If the member owns 50 percent or more of the LLC,[105] each rental property in an LLC is treated as a separate activity, regardless of the LLC's election to group or treat as separate each rental real estate activity.[106] Thus, the member must meet the

---

[98] CCA 201427016.

[99] IRS Publication 925, under the heading, "Real Estate Professional."

[100] Code Sec. 469(c)(7)(A); Reg. § § 1.469-9(g), 1.469-9(h)(1).

[101] CCA 201427016.

[102] Code Sec. 469(c)(7).

[103] Reg. § 1.469-9(e)(3), (g).

[104] Reg. § 1.469-9(h)(1).

[105] Reg. § 1.469-9(h)(2).

[106] Code Sec. 469(c)(7)(A)(ii); Reg. § 1.469-9(e)(3).

material participation standard (work more than 500 hours during the year, perform most of the work, or meet one of the other tests in the regulations) for each rental activity in the LLC. However, the member may make a timely election in such case to group rentals as a single activity, making it easier to meet the material participation test.[107]

Short-term Rentals (Airbnb)

Short-term rentals of real property are not rental activities for purposes of the passive loss rules. Short-term rentals include rentals of real estate if average customer use is seven days or less, or if the average period of customer use is 30 days or less and the LLC provides significant personal services in connection with making the property available for use by renters.[108]

Although a short-term rental is not a "per se passive activity," the short-term rental activity may be a passive activity under the general rule for trades or businesses in which the taxpayer does not materially participate. A taxpayer may not deduct losses from a short-term rental activity against non-passive income unless the taxpayer materially participates in the trade or business or meets one of the exceptions to the passive loss rules.[109]

The first exception from the passive loss rules for short-term rental activities is Section 469(i)(2) which allows a deduction of up to $25,000 for rental real estate activities.[110] However, that exception does not apply if the taxpayer has adjusted gross income in excess of $150,000.[111]

The second exception from the passive loss rules for short-term rental activities is Section 469(c)(7) for real estate professionals. A taxpayer is a real estate professional if (i) more than one-half of the taxpayer's personal services are performed in the real property trades or businesses in which the taxpayer materially participates, and (ii) the taxpayer performs more than 750 hours of services during the tax year in real property trades or businesses in which the taxpayer materially participates. A taxpayer's hours of service in connection with short-term rentals do not qualify as hours of service in real property trades or businesses since a short-term real estate rental activity is not a real estate trade or business.[112]

Self-Rental Income

Many taxpayers hold their buildings, and sometimes equipment, in an LLC. The property is then leased back to a C corporation or S corporation in which the member

---

[107] Reg. § 1.469-9(g).

[108] *Bailey v. Comm'r*, TC Summary Opinion 2011-22 (2011).

[109] *Bailey v. Comm'r*, TC Summary Opinion 2011-22 (2011); *Bailey v. Comm'r*, TC Memo 2001-296 (2001).

[110] *Bailey v. Comm'r*, TC Summary Opinion 2011-22 (2011).

[111] *Id.*

[112] *Id.*

works. The rental income received by the member from the LLC is called self-rental income. The rental income is normally passive income.[113] However, the rental income is recharacterized as nonpassive income if the member materially participates in the business entity leasing the property.[114] The recharacterization means that a taxpayer may not offset passive losses against the rental income received from the LLC. The purpose of the self-rental rule is to prevent a taxpayer with passive activity losses in one activity from artificially generating passive activity income in another activity in order to absorb the losses.

EXAMPLE 13-6

The taxpayer owned an LLC and an S corporation. Both companies leased property to a C corporation owned by the taxpayer in which the taxpayer materially participated. The LLC had net income and the S corporation had net losses from the rental of property to the C corporation. The court determined that the losses incurred by the S corporation were passive losses since the activity was a rental activity. The court determined the rental income earned by the LLC was nonpassive income since the taxpayer materially participated in the C corporation that rented the property. Thus, the taxpayer could not offset the rental losses from the S corporation against the rental income from the LLC.[115]

Similar rules apply if the member leases property to an LLC in which the member materially participates.[116]

The lease of property by an LLC to the corporation will be disregarded if the lease is made for tax avoidance purposes and has no economic substance.[117]

Ground Leases

A member's allocable share of an LLC's net passive income from the rental of ground lease property (and other non-depreciable property) is recharacterized as nonpassive income. The recharacterized income includes gain from the sale of the property, including gain allocable to improvements on the property. The ground lease rules apply if less than 30 percent of the adjusted basis of the leased property is depreciable property.[118]

---

[113] Code Sec. § 469(c)(2).

[114] Reg. § 1.469-2(f)(6); *Dirico v. Comm'r*, 139 TC 396 (2012).

[115] *Veriha v. Comm'r*, 139 TC 45 (2012).

[116] See ¶ 403.02 *infra*.

[117] *Sundrup v. Comm'r*, TC Memo 2010-249 (2010).

[118] Reg. § 1.469-2T(f)(3).

EXAMPLE 13-7

C is a member in an LLC. The LLC acquires vacant land for $300,000, constructs improvements at a cost of $100,000, and leases the land and improvements to a tenant. The LLC then sells the land for $600,000. The unadjusted basis of improvements ($100,000) equals 25 percent of the unadjusted basis of all property ($400,000) used in the rental activity. Therefore, C's allocable share of net passive income from the activity, computed by taking into account the gain from the sale of the property (including gain allocable to depreciable improvements), is treated as nonpassive income.[119]

Suspended Losses on Disposition of Interest

Disallowed passive activity losses for any year may be carried forward indefinitely until they are used (e.g., when the taxpayer has passive activity income).[120] Suspended passive losses are generally allowed when the taxpayer "disposes" of his entire interest in any passive activity.[121] The excess losses from the activity for the year of disposition (including suspended passive losses from earlier tax years), over any net income or gain for such tax year from all other passive activities are recharacterized as nonpassive income. The suspended losses normally offset the member's income for the loss year. Any remaining losses are carried back to the two preceding years and then carried forward to the 20 years following the loss.[122]

Members of an LLC may not deduct suspended passive activity losses when a lender forecloses on rental properties owned by an LLC if the foreclosure does not constitute a complete disposition of the members' entire interest in the activity.[123]

.03 Trade or Business Income

Passive Loss Rules

A member's allocable share of income and losses from an LLC's trade or business is passive activity income and losses if the member does not materially participate in the LLC's business. A member may not deduct passive activity losses activity losses against nonpassive activity income. Excess passive losses are suspended and carried forward as a deduction to succeeding years when the member

---

[119] Reg. § 1.469-2T(f)(3), Example.

[120] Code Sec. 469(b).

[121] Code Sec. 469(g).

[122] *Herwig v. Comm'r*, TC Memo 2014-95 (2014).

[123] *Herwig v. Comm'r*, TC Memo 2014-95 (2014).

has passive activity income or when the member disposes of his entire interest in the LLC that generated the passive activity losses.[124]

Normally, a member wants to materially participate in an LLC for tax purposes in order to deduct the member's allocable share of passive activity losses against ordinary income and portfolio income from other sources.

Material participation is determined at the member level.[125] A member materially participates in an activity only if the member is involved in activity's operations on a regular, continuous, and substantial basis.[126] The determination of whether a member materially participates in an LLC depends on whether the member is classified as a general partner or limited partner.

Members Classified as General Partners

Several courts have determined that a member of an LLC should be classified as a general partner for purposes of the passive loss rules, and that the limited partnership rule under Code Sec. 469(h) does not apply to an LLC.[127]

Under proposed regulations, a member of an LLC cannot be classified as a general partner unless the member has the right to manage the LLC at all times during the tax year.[128]

A member of an LLC who is classified as a general partner is treated as materially participating in the LLC for the tax year if the member meets one of the following tests:[129]

- The member participates in the activity for more than 500 hours during the year.
- The member's participation in the activity for the tax year constitutes substantially all of the participation in such activity for all individuals, including individuals who are not members or owners of the LLC.
- The member participates in the activity for more than 100 hours during the tax year, and the member's participation in the activity for the tax year is not less than the participation in the activity for any other individual, including individuals who are not members of the LLC.
- The activity is a significant participation activity for the tax year, and the member's aggregate participation in all significant participation activities in which the member works 100-500 hours during the tax year exceeds 500

---

[124] Code Sec. 469(g)(1).

[125] Temp. Reg. § 1.469-2T(e)(1).

[126] Code Sec. 469(h)(1).

[127] *Montgomery v. Comm'r*, TC Memo 2013-151 (2013); *Newell v. Comm'r*, TC Memo 2010-23 (2010); *Hegarty v. Comm'r*, TC Summary Opinion 2009-153 (2009); *Thompson v. United States*, 87 Fed. Cl. 728 (2009), *acq.* in result only, AOD 2010-02, 2010-14 IRB 515 (Apr. 5, 2010); *Garnett v. Comm'r*, 132 TC 368 (2009); *Gregg v. United States*, 186 F. Supp. 2d 1123 (D. Or. 2000).

[128] *See* Prop. Reg. § 1.469-5(e)(3)(i)(B) which provides that an interest in an entity will be treated as a limited partnership interest if the member does not have the right to manage the LLC at all times during the tax year.

[129] Temp. Reg. § 1.469-5T(a).

hours.[130] An activity is a significant participation activity if (i) the activity is a trade or business, (ii) the member participates in the activity for more than 100 hours during the year, and (iii) the member cannot establish material participation under any of the other material participation tests in the regulations.[131] The activity must be a passive activity. Thus, if the member does most of the work in the LLC, it cannot be a significant participation since the regulations provide that performing substantially all the work qualifies for material participation.[132]

- The member materially participated in the activity for any five tax years during the ten tax years immediately preceding the current tax year.
- The activity is a personal service activity, and the member materially participated in the activity for any three tax years preceding the current tax year.
- Based on all the facts and circumstances, the individual member participated in the activity on a regular, continuous and substantial basis during the year.

In determining whether any of the seven tests are satisfied, the participation of the individual's nonmember spouse is taken into account.[133]

An LLC member is not required to keep contemporaneous daily time records, logs or other similar documents to establish that the member met the 500-hour test, the substantial participation test, or the other seven tests for material participation. Instead, the member may establish material participation by oral testimony and other reasonable means.[134]

Members Classified as Limited Partners

Under temporary regulations, a membership interest is treated as a limited partnership interest if the member's liability is limited under State law.[135] A member in an LLC that is classified as a partnership has limited liability under the laws of all States. Therefore, the IRS treats LLC members as limited partners.[136]

Under proposed regulations, a member of an LLC is classified as a limited partner if (i) the LLC is classified as a partnership for federal tax purposes, and (ii) the member does not have the right to manage the LLC at all times during the tax year in which the LLC is organized.[137]

If the membership interest is classified as a limited partnership interest, the losses allocated to the member will presumptively be treated as passive losses. The

---

[130] Temp. Reg. § 1.469-5T(a)(4).

[131] Temp. Reg. § 1.469-5T(c).

[132] IRS Audit Technique Guide, Passive Activity Loss—Chapter 4, Material Participation, under the heading, "Significant Participation Activities (SPA)," *citing* Temp. Reg. § 1.469-5T(a)(2).

[133] Code Sec. 469(h)(5); Temp. Reg. § 1.469-5T(f)(3).

[134] *Montgomery v. Comm'r*, TC Memo 2013-151 (2013), *citing* Temp. Reg. § 1.469-5T(f)(4).

[135] Temp. Reg. § 1.469-5T(e)(3)(i)(B).

[136] IRS Audit Technique Guide, Passive Activity Losses, p. 6-11, under the heading, "Material Participation for LLCs."

[137] Prop. Reg. § 1.469-5(e)(3)(i).

¶ 1304.03

member will not be treated as materially participating in the business of the LLC except to the extent provided in regulations.[138]

Under current regulations, a member who is classified as a limited partner will be treated as materially participating in the business of the LLC if the member meets one of the following three tests (instead of one of the seven tests that apply to a member who is classified as a general partner):[139]

- The member participated in the activity for more than 500 hours during the year.
- The member materially participated in the activity for any five tax years during the ten tax years immediately preceding the current tax year.
- The activity is a personal service activity and the member materially participated in the activity for any three tax years preceding the current tax year.[140]

Single-member LLCs are disregarded entities. Since they are not recognized by federal tax law for most purposes, the taxpayer may meet any of the seven tests available to general partners, rather than the three tests available to limited partners. The member will not be subject to the limited partner taint.[141]

.04 Sale of Membership Interest

The gain or loss recognized by a member on the sale of membership interest is classified as passive gain or loss if the LLC was engaged in a passive activity. If the LLC was engaged in a passive activity and one or more nonpassive activities, the gain or loss must be allocated between the different activities and classified on that basis. The allocation is based on the relative amounts of gain or loss that the member would have recognized if the LLC had sold its entire interest in such activities for fair market value and allocated the gain or loss to the member.[142]

.05 Interest Income and Expense

Exclusion as Passive Income

Absent regulations, a person could convert interest income into passive income by forming an LLC, transferring promissory notes and interest income producing investments into the LLC, and then claiming that the person was a passive investor in the LLC. The member could then offset passive losses from other activities against the passive interest income from the LLC. IRS regulations now prevent the sheltering of

---

[138] Code Sec. 469(h)(2).

[139] Temp. Reg. § 1.469-5T(a).

[140] Temp. Reg. § 1.469-5T(e)(2).

[141] IRS Audit Technique Guide, Passive Activity Losses, fn. 26.

[142] Temp. Reg. § 1.469-2T(e)(3).

interest income with losses from passive activities. Passive activity gross income does not include the following interest earned by an LLC:

- Portfolio interest. Portfolio interest includes all interest other than interest earned by an LLC on loans and investments made in the ordinary course of a trade or business of lending money.[143]
- Interest from equity-financed loans.[144] Equity-financed loans are generally loans made with equity funds contributed by the members to an LLC. The loan must be made in the ordinary course of the LLC's trade or business of lending money.[145] The interest income is recharacterized as active income in such case to the extent of the lesser of (a) the member's equity-financed interest income from the LLC, or (b) the member's net passive income from the LLC.[146]

Self-Charged Interest

The LLC must separately report any "self-charged interest" income or expense that results from loans between a member and the LLC (or between the LLC and another partnership or S corporation if both entities have the same owners with the same proportional ownership interest in each entity).

Under prior regulations, the interest income received by a member on a loan to an LLC was portfolio income. The member's allocable share of interest expense on that loan was a passive deduction if the member did not materially participate in the LLC, or if the business of the LLC was a rental business. As a result, the passive interest expense could not offset the portfolio income.

Under current regulations, the member may recharacterize part of the interest income as passive income[147] in an amount equal to the member's "applicable percentage."[148] The applicable percentage is equal to the member's ownership interest in the LLC.

EXAMPLE 13-8

A member loans $10,000 to an LLC in which the member does not materially participate. The member owns a 90 percent interest in the LLC. The LLC pays $700 in interest to the member during the year. The member's allocable share of the interest expense deduction is $630 (90% × $700). The member may include $630 of the interest income as passive income that may be offset by passive losses. The member must include

---

[143] Temp. Reg. § 1.469-2T(c)(3)(i)(A), (ii)(A).

[144] Temp. Reg. § 1.469-2T(f)(4)(i).

[145] Temp. Reg. § 1.469-2T(f)(4)(ii).

[146] Temp. Reg. § 1.469-2T(f)(4)(i).

[147] Reg. § 1.469-7(c).

[148] Reg. § 1.469-7(c)(3).

the remaining $70 as portfolio income that may not be offset by passive losses.[149]

The self-charged interest rules do not apply if the LLC makes an election to avoid the application of these rules.[150]

¶1305 EXCESS BUSINESS LOSSES

For tax years between 2018 and 2025, a non-corporate taxpayer may not deduct "excess business losses" for the current year.[151] Instead, the excess business losses are treated as a net operating loss carryforward that are deductible against any income in subsequent years up to a maximum 80 percent of taxable income.

An excess business loss for the tax year is the excess of the taxpayer's aggregate deductions attributable to the taxpayer's trades and businesses, over the sum of (i) the aggregate gross income or gain of the taxpayer attributable to the trade or business, and (ii) a threshold amount. The threshold amount is $500,000 for married individuals filing jointly and $250,000 for other individuals for 2018, indexed for inflation.[152] The losses do not include losses from a passive activity under Code Sec. 469.[153]

For an LLC, the excess loss limitation applies at the member level.[154]

EXAMPLE 13-9

John and Jane each invest $500,000 in an LLC. The LLC reports $750,000 in losses in 2018 which is allocated equally to John and Jane. John files a single return and Jane files a joint return. The excess business loss for John is $100,000 ($350,000 in losses less the $250,000 threshold amount for single returns). The $100,000 is treated as an NOL deductible in future years. Jane does not have an excess business loss in 2018 ($350,000 in losses which is less than the threshold amount of $500,000 on a joint return). Jane may deduct up to the full amount of losses in 2018 against other nonbusiness income on her 2018 tax return (assuming that the losses are also deductible under the basis, at-risk and passive loss rules).

---

[149] *See* IRS Audit Technique Guide, Passive Activity Losses, pp. 6-11 to 6-12, under the heading, "Self-Charged Interest in a Nutshell."

[150] Reg. § 1.469-7(g).

[151] Code Sec. 461(l).

[152] Code Sec. 461(l)(3).

[153] Code Sec. 461(l)(6).

[154] Code Sec. 461(l)(4).

¶1306 ANTI-ABUSE RULES

.01 Section 701 Regulations

The partnership anti-abuse regulations under Code Sec. 701 permit the IRS to challenge the tax treatment of abusive LLC transactions.[155] There are two anti-abuse tests under the regulations. The IRS must show that (i) a principal purpose of the transaction is to substantially reduce the members' federal tax liability, and (ii) the results of the transaction are inconsistent with Subchapter K of the Code dealing with partnership taxation.[156] The abusive transactions include:

- Claiming double deductions or losses as a result of failure to make a Section 754 election.[157] Congress codified the regulations in this connection in the American Jobs Creation Act of 2004, since it did not believe that the anti-abuse regulations were sufficient to deter abusive transactions.[158]

- Shifting losses from one member to another through contributions, distributions, and transfers of membership interests.[159]

- Use of a temporary member with a nominal interest to generate artificial losses.[160]

- Use of tiered LLCs to create artificial tax losses.[161]

- Entering into transactions for the primary purpose of generating for tax credits.[162]

In such case, the IRS may disregard the LLC and treat the transaction as conducted by one or more of the members,[163] determine that one or more of the members should not be treated as members for tax purposes,[164] adjust the method of accounting,[165] reallocate items of income, gain, loss, and deduction,[166] disallow losses, or otherwise adjust the claimed tax treatment of the transaction.[167]

---

[155] Reg. § 1.701-2; CCA 200613031; FSA 200242004; *Pritired 1, LLC, v. United States,* 108 AFTR 2d 2011-6605, 2011-2 USTC ¶ 50,654 (S.D. Iowa 2011).

[156] Reg. § 1.701-2(b).

[157] Reg. § 1.701-2(d), Examples 8, 9.

[158] *See* ¶ 1307 *infra.*

[159] FSA 200242004. *See also Santa Monica Pictures, LLC v. Comm'r,* TC Memo 2005-104 (2005).

[160] Reg. § 1.701-2(d), Example 7.

[161] *Nevada Partners Fund, LLC v. United States,* 105 AFTR 2d 2010-2133, 2010-1 USTC ¶ 50,379 (SD Miss 2010), 714 F. Supp. 2d 598, *aff'd & vacated,* 720 F.3d 594 (5th Cir. 2013), *vacated & remanded,* 113 AFTR 2d 2014-521 (S. Ct. 2014).

[162] *Pritired 1, LLC, Principal Life Insurance Company v. United States,* 2011-2 USTC ¶ 50,654 (S.D. Iowa 2011).

[163] Reg. § 1.701-2(b)(1).

[164] Reg. § 1.701-2(b)(2).

[165] Reg. § 1.701-2(b)(3).

[166] Reg. § 1.701-2(b)(4).

[167] Reg. § 1.701-2(b)(5).

Any application of the regulation must be coordinated with the Compliance and Office of Chief Counsel to provide fair and consistent treatment of taxpayers when applying the regulations. An IRS agent may not raise the issue with the taxpayer until the agent obtains clearance from the Technical Advisor or Issue Specialist.[168]

For example, leases and other transactions between an LLC and related corporations and individuals will be disregarded under the economic substance doctrine if the transactions are made for tax avoidance purposes and have no economics subject.[169]

.02 Section 704(c) Regulations

In 2010, the IRS issued final anti-abuse regulations under Section 704(c) for LLCs classified as partnerships.[170] The regulations provide that an LLC may not use a Section 704(c) allocation method to achieve tax results inconsistent with the intent of Subchapter K. The principal Section 704(c) allocation methods are the traditional method, the traditional method with curative allocations, and the remedial allocation method.[171]

The IRS may recast a transaction for federal tax purposes in a way that will achieve tax results consistent with Subchapter K if a principal purpose of forming or using the LLC is to substantially reduce federal tax liability for related LLCs and members.

.03 Section 7701(o) Economic Substance Doctrine

The IRS may disallow losses under Code Sec. 7701(o). That section codifies the economic substance doctrine. The economic substance doctrine is a common law doctrine under which tax benefits for a transaction are disallowed if the transaction does not have economic substance or lacks business purpose.[172] A transaction has economic substance only if:[173]

---

[168] IRS Ann. 94-87, 1994-27 IRB 124; Preamble to T.D. 8588.

[169] *Sundrup v. Comm'r*, TC Memo 2010-249 (2010).

[170] Reg. § 1.704-3(a)(1), (10).

[171] *See* ¶ 805 *supra*.

[172] *Princeton Strategic Investment Fund, LLC v. United States*, 2012-1 USTC ¶ 50,122, 108 AFTR 2d 2011-7519 (N.D. Cal 2011); *K-2 Trading Ventures LLC v. United States*, Fed. Cl. No. 04-1419T (2011); *Candyce Martin 1999 Irrevocable Trust v. United States*, 2011-2 USTC ¶ 50,670 (N.D. Cal. 2011); *Pritired 1, LLC, Principal Life Insurance Company v. United States*, 2011-2 USTC ¶ 50,654 (S.D. Iowa 2011); *Southgate Master Fund, LLC v. United States*, 2011-2 USTC ¶ 50,648, 108 AFTR 2d 2011-6488 (5th Cir. 2011); *Jade Trading LLC v. United States*, 80 Fed. Cl. 11 (2007), *aff'd in part and rev'd on other grounds*, 598 F.3d 1372 (Fed. Cir. 2010); *Stobie Creek Investments LLC v. United States*, 608 F.3d 1366 (Fed. Cir. 2010).

[173] Code Sec. 7701(o)(1).

- the transaction changes in a meaningful non-tax way the LLC's or members' economic position;[174] and
- the LLC or members have a substantial non-tax purpose for entering into the transaction.[175]

.04 Judicial Doctrines

The courts have disallowed losses for members of an LLC under the common law economic substance doctrine,[176] the tax avoidance purpose rule,[177] the sham transaction doctrine,[178] the step transaction doctrine, the substance over form doctrine, and the rule that worthless property contributed to an LLC does not give the LLC or the member any basis in the property after the transfer (even though the property has a high basis prior to the transfer).[179]

An LLC that is formed solely for tax avoidance purposes, and that lacks economic substance and business purpose, is not recognized as an entity for federal tax purposes, and thus cannot elect to be taxed as a partnership.[180]

The IRS issued an industry specialization program issue paper in 2008 regarding the partnership and LLC anti-abuse rules.[181] The issue paper discusses the elements necessary for the Commissioner to recast a transaction when the anti-abuse rules apply, and the factors that should be considered in determining whether the IRS may recast a transaction under the partnership anti-abuse rules.

EXAMPLE 13-10

A bank made loans of $1 million that are now worthless. The bank forms an LLC and contributes its worthless loans to the LLC. The bank sells its membership interest to Buyer for $50,000 since the loans have value as a tax write-off. The bank takes a deduction of $950,000. The LLC does not make an election under Section 754. Therefore, the LLC retains a carry-

---

[174] Code Sec. 7701(o)(1)(A).

[175] Code Sec. 7701(o)(1)(B).

[176] *See also* LB&I Directive, LB&I-4-0711-015 (July 12, 2012), in which the IRS issued guidelines to audit agents addressing when the codified economic substance doctrine applies. *Princeton Strategic Investment Fund, LLC v. United States*, 2012-1 USTC ¶ 50,122, 108 AFTR 2d 2011-7519 (N.D. Cal 2011); *Southgate Master Fund, LLC v. United States*, 2011-2 USTC ¶ 50,648, 108 AFTR 2d 2011-6488 (5th Cir. 2011); *Candyce Martin 1999 Irrevocable Trust v. United States*, 2011-2 USTC ¶ 50,670 (N.D. Cal. 2011); *Pritired 1, LLC, Principal Life Insurance Company v. United States*, 2011-2 USTC ¶ 50,654 (S.D. Iowa 2011).

[177] *Curtis Investment Company, LLC v. Comm'r*, TC Memo 2017-150 (2017).

[178] *BCP Trading and Investments, LLC v. Comm'r*, TC Memo 2017-151 (2017).

[179] *Santa Monica Pictures, LLC v. Comm'r*, TC Memo 2005-104 (2005); *Southgate Master Fund, LLC v. United States*, 2011-2 USTC ¶ 50,648, 108 AFTR 2d 2011-6488 (5th Cir. 2011).

[180] *Ad Investment 2000 Fund LLC v. Comm'r*, TC Memo 2015-223 (2015); *Ad Investment 2000 Fund LLC v. Comm'r*, TC Memo 2016-226 (2016).

[181] IRS Appeals Coordinated Issue Settlement Paper on Partnership Audits, Settlement Guideline, Subchapter K Anti-Abuse Rule, Reg. § 1.701-2 (2008).

over basis of $1 million in the loans. The LLC immediately sells the loans for $1. The LLC incurs a loss of $999,999. It allocates all of the loss to the Buyer. Since the Buyer cannot take losses in excess of its $50,000 basis, the Buyer contributes land to the LLC with a basis of $950,000, thereby increasing its basis in the LLC to $1 million. The loss allocation reduces the Buyer's basis from $1 million to $1. Seven years later, the LLC distributes the land back to the Buyer. The Buyer receives a basis in the land of $1 under Code Sec. 732(b) equal to its outside basis in the membership interest. The Buyer can defer the recognition of gain indefinitely by holding on to the land. This scheme is now prohibited under the partnership anti-abuse rules.[182]

.05 Section 165(c)(2)

The IRS may disallow a deduction for an LLC under Code Sec. 165(c)(2) unless the primary motivation for entering into a transaction is economic profit. Transactions that are designed to generate losses for an LLC may be disallowed even if such transactions are part of an overall profit-motivated investment strategy. The Section 165(c)(2) test is separate and independent from the question of economic substance.[183]

.06 General IRS Regulations

The IRS issued general anti-abuse regulations under Code Sec. 704. The regulations provide that:[184]

"an allocation of loss or deduction to a partner that is respected under section 704(b) and this paragraph may not be deductible by such partner if the partner lacks the requisite motive for economic gain (see, e.g., Goldstein v. Commissioner, 364 F.2d 734 (2d Cir. 1966)), or may be disallowed for that taxable year (and held in suspense) if the limitations of section 465 or 704(d) are applicable. Similarly, an allocation that is respected under section 704(b) and this paragraph nevertheless may be reallocated under other provisions, such as section 482, section 704(e)(2), section 706(d) (and related assignment of income principles), and paragraph (b)(2)(ii) of Reg. § 1.751-1. If a partnership has a section 754 election in effect, a partner's distributive share of partnership income, gain, loss, or deduction may be affected as provided in Reg. § 1.743-1 (see paragraph (b)(2)(iv)(m)(2) of this section). A deduction that appears to be a nonrecourse deduction deemed to be in accordance with the partners' interests

---

[182] FSA 200242004 (*citing* Reg. § 1.702-2).

[183] *Candyce Martin 1999 Irrevocable Trust v. United States*, 2011-2 USTC ¶ 50,670 (N.D. Cal. 2011).

[184] Reg. § 1.704-1(b)(1)(iii).

in the partnership may not be such because purported nonrecourse liabilities of the partnership in fact constitute equity rather than debt. The examples in paragraph (b)(5) of this section concern the validity of allocations under section 704(b) and this paragraph and, except as noted, do not address the effect of other sections or limitations on such allocations."

¶ 1307 BUILT-IN LOSSES

The American Jobs Creation Act of 2004 limited the ability of an LLC and its members to shift tax losses from one member to another, or to take duplicate losses and deductions on the same property. The principal anti-abuse provisions include the following:

- *Allocations of built-in loss items.* If a member contributes property to an LLC with a tax basis in excess of fair market value, the LLC must allocate built-in loss items only to the contributing member. It may not allocate built-in loss items to transferees, or to the remaining members after liquidation of the contributing member's interest.[185] The LLC must allocate items to the non-contributing members by assuming that the basis of built-in loss property is equal to the fair market value the property at the time of contribution.[186] This rule denies loss allocations to a transferee member after sale of the contributing member's interest, and to the remaining members after liquidation of the contributing member's interest. This rule is discussed in Chapter 8.[187] It supplements the rule that built-in gains and losses for contributed property must be allocated to the contributing member.[188]
- *Mandatory basis adjustment following transfer of membership interest.* The LLC must make a downward basis adjustment to its property following the transfer of a membership interest if (i) the LLC's adjusted basis in LLC property exceeds the fair market value of such property by more than $250,000, or (ii) the transferee member would receive a loss allocation of more than $250,000 if the LLC sold its assets for cash at fair market value immediately after the transfer.[189] The basis adjustment is made only with respect to the transferee member. The LLC must make the adjustment even though it has not made a Section 754 election. This rule is discussed at ¶ 1509.01.
- *Mandatory basis adjustment following distribution of built-in loss property.* The LLC must make a Section 734(b) downward basis adjustment to its property if a member receives a substituted basis in distributed property that is $250,000 more than the LLC's basis in the property. This rule is discussed in Chapter 10.[190]

---

[185] Code Sec. 704(c)(1)(C)(i).
[186] Code Sec. 704(c)(1)(C)(ii).
[187] *See* ¶ 806 *supra.*
[188] Code Sec. 704(c).
[189] Code Sec. 704(d).
[190] *See* ¶ 1007 *supra.*

¶1308 CLASS OF LIABILITIES RULES

.01 *General*

In 2005, the IRS issued final regulations on LLC and partnership liabilities. The regulations are designed to prevent taxpayers from manipulating the liability rules to accelerate deductions or create duplicate losses. There are now two types of liabilities: § 1.752-1 liabilities and § 1.752-7 liabilities.

.02 *Section 1.752-1 Liabilities*

The first type of liability is a § 1.752-1 liability. A § 1.752-1 liability is a liability that (i) creates or increases the basis of the LLC's assets, including cash, (ii) gives rise to an immediate deduction by the LLC, or (iii) gives rise to nondeductible expense to the LLC that is not chargeable to capital.[191] Most member liabilities assumed by an LLC are § 1.752-1 liabilities. These liabilities include contract obligations, debt obligations, tort obligations, and other fixed and determinable liabilities.[192]

The assumption of § 1.752-1 liabilities by the LLC is treated as a cash distribution to the contributing member and reduces the member's basis in the LLC.[193] If the LLC allocates a share of those liabilities to the member,[194] then there is a netting process. The liabilities assumed by the LLC, less the member's share of those liabilities, are treated as a cash distribution to the member and reduce the member's basis in the LLC.[195] These basis reduction rules prevent the member from claiming an artificial loss on the sale of the membership interest at a later date.

.03 *Section 1.752-7 Liabilities*

Definition

The second type of liability is a § 1.752-7 liability. A § 1.752-1 liability is a fixed or contingent obligation (other than a § 1.752-1 liability) to make payment without regard to whether the obligation is otherwise taken into account for tax purposes. Obligations include debt obligations, environmental obligations, tort obligations, contract obligations, pension obligations, obligations under short sales, and obligations under derivative financial instruments such as options, forward contracts, future contracts, and swaps.[196]

---

[191] Reg. § 1.752-1(a)(4)(i).

[192] Reg. § 1.752-1(a)(4)(ii).

[193] Code Sec. 752(b); Reg. § 1.752-1(c).

[194] *See* ¶ 903 *supra* for rules regarding allocation of recourse and nonrecourse liabilities to members.

[195] Reg. § 1.752-1(f).

[196] Reg. § 1.752-7(b)(3), *referring* to Reg. § 1.752-1(a)(4)(ii).

Under a *de minimis* exception, § 1.752-7 liabilities do not include liabilities that are less than $1 million or ten percent of the gross value of LLC assets immediately before a triggering event.[197] There is also an exception for liabilities transferred to an LLC as part of a trade or business.[198]

Abuse Correction

Prior to enactment of Section 358(h) of the Code and the final regulations under Section 752, there was potential for loss shifting, loss duplication, and loss acceleration through manipulation of the partnership liability rules. The contributing member would take the position that contingent obligations were not liabilities under Section 752(b), and thus did not reduce the member's outside basis in a membership interest. The contingent obligations did, however, reduce the value of the membership interest. The member would then sell the membership interest at a loss that reflected the reduced value for the contingent obligations. When the fixed obligations became fixed and determinable, the LLC would pay the obligation, and take a second deduction for the same amount. The LLC would allocate the loss or deduction to the remaining members of the LLC.

The regulations now prohibit loss shifting, loss duplication, and loss acceleration in connection with § 1.752-7 liabilities.[199] The LLC must treat the contingent liability at a built-loss under Code Sec. 704(c). When the LLC satisfies all or part of the contingent liability, it must allocate any resulting tax deduction or loss to the contributing member to the extent of the built-in-loss at the date of contribution. The rules work as follows:

- There is no initial reduction in tax basis in a membership interest when a member transfers a contingent liability (or other § 1.752-7 liability) to an LLC.

- However, the member's capital account is reduced by the value of the contingent liability. This is the amount of cash that a willing assignor would pay to a willing assignee in an arm's-length transaction to assume the liability.[200] As a result of the capital account reduction, there is a book-tax difference. This is equal to the difference between the assigned capital account value of the asset and the LLC's tax basis in the asset. For example, if a member contributed an asset with a tax basis and fair market value of $400,000, subject to a contingent liability valued at $100,000, the member would receive an initial capital account of $300,000. The LLC's tax basis in the asset would be $400,000. There would be a $100,000 book-tax disparity. The member's outside basis in the membership interest would also be equal to $400,000 since there is no initial reduction in basis for contingent liabilities.[201]

---

[197] Reg. § 1.752-7(d)(2)(i)(B).
[198] Reg. § 1.752-7(d)(2)(i)(A).
[199] Reg. § 1.752-7.
[200] Reg. § 1.752-7(b)(3)(ii).
[201] Reg. § 1.752-7(c)(2), Example.

- The difference between the member's capital account and the LLC's tax basis in the asset is a "built-in loss." The LLC must account for the built-in loss under the traditional method, the traditional method with curative allocations, or the remedial allocation method.[202] The most common method is the traditional method. Under that method, the LLC must allocate all of the tax loss attributable to the contingent liability to the contributing member up to the amount of the built-in loss. There is no book loss allocation for such amounts since the value of the contingent liability reduces the contributing member's capital account on the date of contribution. If the LLC pays additional amounts to satisfy the contingent liability, then it must allocate both the book and tax deductions attributable to such amounts to all of the members in accordance with their membership interests in the LLC. For example, if an LLC paid $150,000 to satisfy a contingent liability initially valued for capital account purposes at $100,000, then it would allocate the first $100,000 of tax deductions to the contributing member and make no book allocations. It would allocate the remaining $50,000 of book and tax deductions to all of the members in accordance with the allocation formula under the operating agreement.

- A member may cease to be a member of the LLC prior to the date that the LLC satisfies a contingent liability. The regulations prevent a member from taking a tax loss at this time attributable to the value of the contingent liability. The regulations accomplish this result by requiring a member to reduce the basis of his or her membership interest whenever there is a "triggering event" that separates the member from the liability. These triggering events include (i) a disposition or partial disposition of the membership interest,[203] (ii) a liquidation of the member's interest in the LLC,[204] or (iii) the assumption of the liability by another member.[205] The basis reduction is generally equal to the value of the § 1.752-7 liability on the date that the contributing member transfers the liability to the LLC, subject to adjustment.[206]

- After the basis reduction, the member may not take a pass-through loss or deduction attributable to the contingent obligation until there is "economic performance" with respect to the obligation.[207] The obligation must become fixed and determinable, and the LLC must satisfy the obligation. The LLC must notify the member of the economic performance of the contingent liability.[208] The member may then take a pass-through loss or deduction up to the amount of the prior basis reduction.

---

[202] *See* ¶ 805 *supra.*
[203] Reg. § 1.752-7(e).
[204] Reg. § 1.752-7(f).
[205] Reg. § 1.752-7(g).
[206] Reg. § 1.752-7(b)(7).
[207] Reg. § 1.752-7(a).
[208] Reg. § 1.752-7(h).

- Neither the LLC nor any member other than the member from whom the obligation was assumed may claim a deduction, loss, or capital expense to the extent of the built-in loss[209] associated with the obligation. The LLC must allocate any tax deduction up to the built-in loss to the contributing member when the LLC satisfies the obligation,[210] or when economic performance otherwise occurs.

¶ 1309 SPECIAL ALLOCATION RULES

The special allocation rules under Section 704 limit the ability of LLC to pass through losses and deductions to certain members. The IRS issued detailed regulations under Section 704(b) limiting pass-through of losses and deductions for book purposes, not tax purposes. However, the regulations indirectly affect tax allocations. The general rule is that tax allocations must follow book allocations, and book allocations must have substantial economic effect.[211] The IRS may disallow tax deductions and credits if the corresponding book allocations do not have substantial economic effect.[212]

The major limitations under the Section 704(b) regulations on the pass-through of book losses and deductions include the following:

- *Safe-harbor allocation test.* If the LLC complies with the safe-harbor test for book allocations, then the LLC must allocate book losses and deductions in accordance with the safe-harbor regulations.[213]
- *Alternate economic effect equivalence test.* If the LLC complies with the alternate economic effect equivalence test for book allocations, then the LLC must allocate losses, deductions and other items so that the member receives book allocations equivalent to what the member would receive on withdrawal of the member or liquidation of the LLC.[214]
- *Failure to comply with safe-harbor regulations.* If the LLC fails to comply with the safe-harbor regulations for book allocations, or the alternate economic effect equivalence test, then the LLC may not allocate tax losses to a member in excess of the member's positive capital account.[215]
- *Member minimum gain.* If a member loans money to an LLC or guarantees debt secured by LLC property, then the "member nonrecourse debt minimum gain" rules apply. Under the safe-harbor regulations, the LLC must allocate member nonrecourse deductions to the member who bears the economic risk of loss for the liability. Member nonrecourse deductions are deductions that

---

[209] Reg. § 1.752-7(b)(6).

[210] Reg. § 1.752-7(b)(8), (c)(2).

[211] *See* ¶ 804.10 *supra.*

[212] *Pritired 1, LLC, Principal Life Insurance Company v. United States,* 2011-2 USTC ¶ 50,654 (S.D. Iowa 2011).

[213] *See* ¶ 804.

[214] *See* ¶ 803.02.

[215] CCA 201741018.

cause the book value of the property to decline below the outstanding loan balance.[216]

- *Contributed property.* Section 704(c) restricts the allocation of losses and deductions for tax purposes if a member contributes property to an LLC with a difference between book value and tax basis. The LLC must allocate losses and deduction with respect to the contributed property for tax purposes in a manner that takes account of the variation between the book value and the tax basis of the property at the time of the contribution (or at the time of revaluation).[217] On sale of the property, the LLC must allocate any built-in loss to the member who contributed the property to the LLC.[218]

¶ 1310 RELATED PARTY TRANSACTIONS

Losses are not allowed on transactions between an LLC and a member who owns, directly or indirectly, more than 50 percent of the capital interest or profits interest in the LLC.[219]

Losses are not allowed on transactions between two LLCs in which the same member owns, directly or indirectly, more than 50 percent of the capital interest or profits interest in the LLC.[220]

The loss disallowance rules on transactions between related parties are discussed in detail in Chapter 14.[221]

¶ 1311 REPORTING REQUIREMENTS

An LLC that is classified as a partnership must disclose reportable loss transactions on Form 8886, Reportable Transaction Disclosure Statement. A transaction is a reportable loss transaction if the LLC claims a loss on its return equal to or greater than:[222]

- $10 million in a single year, or $20 million in any combination of tax years, for LLCs that have only corporations as members;
- $2 million in a single year, or $4 million in any combination of tax years, for all other LLCs classified as a partnership; or
- $10 million in a single year, or $20 million in any combination of tax years, for LLCs classified as a corporation.

A member who has a loss or other deduction from a trade or business activity of an LLC must complete Form 6198, At-Risk Limitations, if there are amounts in the activity for which the member is not at risk. The form is used to determine allowable losses.

---

[216] *See* ¶ 804.06 *supra,* under the heading, "Member Minimum Gain Chargeback."

[217] Code Sec. 704(c).

[218] *See* ¶ 805.02 *supra.*

[219] Code Sec. 707(b)(1)(A); Reg. § 1.707-1(b)(1).

[220] Code Sec. 707(b)(1)(B).

[221] *See* ¶ 1403.03 *infra.*

[222] Rev. Proc. 2004-66, 2004-2 CB 966; CCA 201045022.

14

Payments and Benefits to Members

¶1401 GENERAL RULES

An LLC may make payments to members for salaries, wages, commissions, rents, royalties, interest on loans, and other amounts. The payments are characterized in one of the following nine ways:

1. A guaranteed payment.
2. A payment to the member other than in his capacity as a member of the LLC.
3. A distributive share of LLC income.
4. A fringe benefit.
5. Deferred compensation.
6. A Section 736 payment (a payment to a retired member or the estate of a deceased member in a service LLC if the member is classified as a "general partner").
7. A disguised sale payment.
8. A disguised payment for services.
9. Liquidating and nonliquidating distributions of money and property other than income distributions.

These distributions are discussed in Chapter 10.

¶1402 GUARANTEED PAYMENTS

Guaranteed payments are payments to a member for services or capital that are determined without regard to the income of the LLC.[1] Payments are guaranteed payments if there is a fixed amount payable to the member unrelated to the income of the LLC. Payments are also guaranteed payments if determined by reference to an item of gross income, such as five percent of rental income, if the payments are designed to measure the value of the services or capital provided.[2]

Guaranteed payments are ordinary income to the member.[3] Guaranteed payments for services are subject to self-employment taxes.[4] Guaranteed payments for capital are not subject to self-employment taxes. An LLC may deduct guaranteed payments as a business expense,[5] unless the payment is a capital expenditure under Section 263. Guaranteed payments made to members for organizing the LLC or syndicating interests in the LLC are capital expenses.[6] The payment is taxable income to the member for the year that includes the last day of the tax year of the LLC in

---

[1] Code Sec. 707(c).

[2] Rev. Rul. 81-301, 1981-2 CB 143.

[3] Code Secs. 61(a), 707(c); Reg. §1.707-1(c); Reg. §1.736-1(a)(4) (for guaranteed payments to a retiring or deceased member); *Seismic Support Services v. Comm'r*, TC Memo 2015-151 (2015).

[4] *Seismic Support Services v. Comm'r*, TC Memo 2014-78 (2014).

[5] Code Sec. 707(c); IRS Publication 541, Partnerships, under the heading, "Guaranteed Payments." The expense is deductible under Code Sec. 162(a).

[6] *See* IRS Publication 541, Partnerships, under the heading, "Guaranteed Payments."

which the LLC deducted the guaranteed payments.[7] Thus, if an LLC accrues a guaranteed salary payment to a member, but does not pay the member until the following year, the member must report the income in the year accrued by the LLC, rather than in the following year when received by the member.

Regardless of whether a payment is properly classified as a "guaranteed payment," an LLC may only deduct payments to a member for services if it represents deductible expenses of the LLC.[8]

EXAMPLE 14-1

An LLC uses the cash method of accounting. It has a fiscal year ending May 31. All of its members are individuals who report on a calendar year basis. During the year ended May 31, 2004, the LLC makes guaranteed payments of $120,000 to Member A. Of this amount, $70,000 was paid to Member A between June 1 and December 31, 2003, and the remaining $50,000 was paid to Member A between January 1 and May 31, 2004. The entire $120,000 is includable in Member A's taxable income for the calendar year 2004, even though $70,000 of the guaranteed payments was paid to Member A in 2003.[9]

EXAMPLE 14-2

An LLC has a tax year ending December 31. The LLC promises to pay Member A $60,000 per year for services regardless of the income earned by the LLC. In 1998, the LLC accrues a $60,000 expense on its income tax return. However, it does not pay the member the guaranteed payment until February 1, 1999. Member A must report the guaranteed payment as compensation income on her 1998 tax return even though she does not receive the compensation until the following year.[10]

If a member is entitled to a distributive share of income, with a minimum guaranteed payment, the guaranteed payment is the amount by which the minimum guarantee exceeds the distributive share of income.[11]

---

[7] Reg. §§ 1.706-1(a)(1), 1.707-1(c).

[8] *Cagle v. Comm'r*, 63 TC 86 (1974), *aff'd on other issue*, 539 F.2d 409 (5th Cir. 1976).

[9] Reg. § 1.706-1(a)(2).

[10] Code Sec. 706(a); Reg. § 1.707-1(c).

[11] Reg. § 1.707-1(c), Example (2).

EXAMPLE 14-3

Member C in the CD LLC received 30 percent of LLC income, but not less than $10,000. The LLC's income is $60,000, and C is entitled to $18,000 (30 percent of $60,000). Of this amount, $10,000 is a guaranteed payment to C. The $10,000 guaranteed payment reduces the LLC's net income to $50,000 of which C receives $8,000 as C's distributive share.[12]

An LLC may deduct the guaranteed payment only against the bottom-line income and loss of the LLC.[13]

If guaranteed payments to a member result in an LLC loss in which the member shares, the member must report the full amount of the guaranteed payments as ordinary income. The member must separately take into account his or her distributive share of the LLC loss, to the extent of the adjusted basis of the member's membership interest.

Guaranteed payments to a member do not reduce the member's basis in the LLC except to the extent of the member's distributive share of LLC deduction, loss or other downward capital account adjustment resulting from the guaranteed payment.[14]

Guaranteed payments do not change the recipient member's capital account except to the extent such payments affect the LLC's taxable income resulting from deductions for such payments.[15]

An LLC's use of appreciated property to make a guaranteed payment to a member is a taxable event. The LLC realizes taxable gain equal to the amount of the appreciation.[16]

Between 2018 and 2025, the 20 percent deduction under Section 199A for qualified business income (QBI) passed through to the members does not apply to guaranteed payments for services by the member.[17] A member may take the 20 percent QBI deduction only for the member's distributive share of LLC trade or business income.[18] As a result, some LLCs are converting guaranteed payments into a distributive share of income to qualify for the deduction.

---

[12] Prop. Reg. § 1.707-1(c), Example 2.

[13] Reg. § 1.707-1(c), Example (4).

[14] Reg. § 1.704-1(b)(2)(iv)(o).

[15] Reg. § 1.704-1(b)(2)(iv)(o).

[16] Rev. Rul. 2007-40, 2007-1 CB 1426.

[17] Code Sec. 199A(c)(4)(B).

[18] *See* ¶ 702.

¶ 1403 PAYMENTS TO A MEMBER OTHER THAN IN CAPACITY AS A MEMBER

.01 *General Principles*

A member may engage in transactions with the LLC other than in his capacity as a member. The LLC may deduct the payments to the same extent that it could have deducted the payments to a nonmember. The member must include the payments in taxable income to the same extent that the member would have included the rent, interest, compensation, or other amounts in income received from another entity.[19]

The legislative history describes the following factors that must be considered in determining whether an allocation or distribution is made to a member acting other than in his or her capacity as a member.[20]

- whether the payment is subject to the risk of the LLC's business. To the extent an allocation and distribution to a member is reasonably certain, the member is acting in an individual capacity and should be treated as an independent contractor.

- the duration of the payee's partnership status and the timing of the payment in relation to the provision of services. If a member's status is transitory, an allocation and distribution resemble a fee rather than a return on investment. If an allocation and distribution are close in time to the performance of services or transfer of property, the transactions are likely related. The reason is that the risk of nonpayment increases with time.

- the recipient member's motivation in becoming a member, i.e., whether based on the facts and circumstances, the tax considerations caused the association. This factor is not weighed significantly in the legislative history.

- whether the allocation in question is disproportionately large in relation to the recipient member's interest in the LLC's profits. A short-term allocation that is greater than the recipient's profits interest may suggest that the allocation is a disguised fee.

.02 *Lease of Property to LLC*

If a member leases property to an LLC, the lease is treated as a transaction between an LLC and a member who is not acting in his capacity as a member.[21] The rental payments are deductible by the LLC and taxable to the member receiving the rental income.[22]

---

[19] Code Sec. 707(a)(i); Reg. § 1.721-1(a).

[20] S. Rep. No. 169, 98th Cong., 2d Sess. 228-230 (1984).

[21] Ltr. Rul. 9538036, *citing* Code Sec. 707(a) and Reg. § 1.707-1(a).

[22] Code Sec. 707(a).

A member's lease of property to an LLC in which a member materially participates is subject to the self-rental rules for passive loss deductions. If the lease of property generates net losses, then the losses are passive losses that may be deducted only against passive income. If the lease of property generates net income, then the rental income is nonpassive income (in which case the member cannot offset rental losses from other passive activities against the rental income received from the LLC).[23] The self-rental rules are discussed at ¶ 1304.02.

.03 Sale of Property to LLC or Member

If a member sells property to an LLC, the payments made by the LLC to the member are nondeductible sales proceeds. The member recognizes capital gain or loss, subject to the following rules:

Sale of Property at Loss between LLC and Member

Loss is disallowed on the sale or exchange of property between a member and an LLC if the member owns, directly or indirectly, more than 50 percent of the membership interests in the LLC.[24] The constructive ownership rules under Code Sec. 267(c)(1), (2), (4) and (5) apply in determining direct or indirect ownership.[25] Thus, a member is treated as owning any capital or profits interest owned, directly or indirectly, by or for members of his or her family.

EXAMPLE 14-4

A mother sells property at a loss to an LLC. The mother does not own any interest in the LLC. However, her son owns a 65 percent interest in the profits of the LLC. Losses on the sale are disallowed.[26]

In one ruling, the IRS determined that losses were disallowed on the sale by an LLC of assets to several trusts because the same parties were in effect buying and selling the property under the related party rules of Code Secs. 267 and 707.[27]

Loss is disallowed on the sale or exchange of property between two LLCs if the member owns, directly or indirectly, more than 50 percent of the membership interests in both LLCs.[28]

---

[23] Code Sec. 469(c)(2), (4); Reg. § 1.469-2(f)(6); *Krukowski v. Comm'r*, 279 F.3d 547 (7th Cir. 2002).

[24] Code Sec. 707(b)(1)(A).

[25] Reg. § 1.707-1(b)(3).

[26] IRS Audit Technique Guide—Partnerships, Chapter 5, Example 5-3.

[27] CCA 201343021.

[28] Code Sec. 707(b)(1)(B).

The basis of a member's interest in the LLC is decreased (but not below zero) by the member's share of the disallowed losses.[29] The disallowed loss reduces the gain realized in a subsequent transaction.[30] If the purchasing member or LLC sells the property, only the gain realized that is greater than the disallowed loss is taxable. If any gain from the sale of the property is not recognized because of this rule, the basis of each member's interest in the LLC is increased by the member's share of that gain.[31]

The constructive ownership rules under Section 267(c) apply in determining whether a member owns more than 50 percent of the membership interests in an LLC.[32] However, if a person is not a member, the constructive ownership rules cannot apply to make that person a member.

Sale of Property at Loss between Nonmember and LLC

Losses on sales and exchanges between an LLC and related nonmembers are disallowed if any one of the relationships under Section 267(b) exists.[33] The rule applies regardless of the percentage of capital or profits interest owned by the member.[34]

The sale of property by a related nonmember to an LLC is treated as a sale to each of the members separately. Losses are disallowed to the extent of the percentage interest in the LLC held by persons related to the selling nonmember.[35]

EXAMPLE 14-5

Chuck owns a five percent interest in an LLC. He sells property to the LLC at a loss. The loss is deductible because Chuck owns less than 50 percent of the membership interests in the LLC. Chuck's wife sells property to the LLC during the following year. There is a partial loss disallowance because the wife is related to a member of the LLC.

---

[29] Code Sec. 705(a)(2)(B); Rev. Rul. 96-10, 1996-1 CB 27.

[30] Code Secs. 267(d), 707(d)(1); Reg. § 1.707-1(b)(1).

[31] IRS Publication 541, Partnerships, under the heading, "Sale or Exchange of Property."

[32] Code Sec. 707(b)(3); Reg. § 1.707-1(b)(3).

[33] Reg. § 1.267(b)-1(b)(1). Sales and exchange transactions between an LLC and persons related to a member are governed by Section 267 rather than Section 707(b).

[34] IRS Market Segment Specialization Program, Partnerships, Audit Technique Guide, Chapter 5, under the heading, "Related Non-partners."

[35] Reg. § 1.267(b)-1(b)(1)(ii).

Sale of Property at Gain between Member and LLC

Gain on the sale or exchange of property between a member and an LLC is ordinary if (i) the member owns, directly or indirectly, more than 50 percent of the membership interests in the LLC, and (ii) the property is depreciable in the hands of the transferee[36] or the property is not a capital asset in the hands of the transferee immediately after the transfer.[37] Property that is not a capital asset includes accounts receivable, inventory, stock-in-trade, depreciable real property, and real property used in a trade or business.[38] Therefore, if a 51 percent member sells land (a capital asset) to an LLC for subdivision and resale, the gain is ordinary.

Gain on the sale or exchange of property between a member and an LLC is also ordinary if (i) the member owns, directly or indirectly, more than 50 percent of the membership interests in the LLC, and (ii) the property is depreciable property in the hands of the transferee.[39]

Gain on the sale or exchange of property between two LLCs is ordinary if (i) the member owns, directly or indirectly, more than 50 percent of the membership interests in both LLCs, and (ii) the property is not a capital asset in the hands of the transferee.[40]

Sale of Property at Gain between Nonmember and LLC

Gain on sales of property between a nonmember and an LLC are not covered by Section 707(b) or Section 1239. If a person is not a member, the constructive ownership rules will not apply to make that person a member. Therefore, if a spouse of a five percent member sells depreciable real estate to an LLC at a gain, the gain will be capital gain instead of ordinary income.[41]

.04 Services

Services by the member to the LLC may be treated as nonmember services if the services are unrelated to the LLC's main function. The LLC may deduct the payments if the payments are ordinary and necessary business expenses.[42] The LLC must

---

[36] Code Sec. 1239.

[37] Code Sec. 707(b)(2)(A).

[38] IRS Publication 541, Partnerships, under the heading, "Sale or Exchange of Property."

[39] Code Sec. 707(b)(2)(B).

[40] Code Sec. 1239.

[41] IRS Market Segment Specialization Program, Partnerships, Audit Technique Guide, Chapter 5, under the heading, "Related Non-partners." However, gain to the extent of depreciation taken on the property will be taxed at the higher 25 percent rate.

[42] Rev. Rul. 81-301, 1981-2 CB 144.

capitalize the expenses if the services are capital in nature. The payments are taxable to the member as ordinary income and subject to self-employment taxes.[43]

It is sometimes difficult to distinguish between guaranteed payments and payments to members in a nonmember capacity. Services involving a member's particular technical expertise are nonmember services.[44] Generally, if a member performs services for the LLC that he or she also performs for others (such as an attorney, architect or stockbroker), the payments are for nonmember services.[45] However, if the member works exclusively or primarily for the LLC, the payments are normally a guaranteed payment or distributive share of income.[46]

EXAMPLE 14-6

An LLC pays a member for investment advisory services. The member provides similar services to others as part of his or her regular trade or business. The member in the performance of such services is subject to the supervision of the managers of the LLC. The member pays his own expenses in performing the services. The member is not personally liable to the other members for losses incurred on investments. The LLC may terminate the services and compensation of the member at any time. The investment advisory services are treated as a transaction by a member with an LLC other than in his or her capacity as a member. The LLC may deduct the payments to the member as an ordinary and necessary business expense.[47]

When a member provides management services to an LLC pursuant to an operating agreement (as opposed to a separate management agreement) and based on the gross income of the LLC, there is some confusion as to how the payments should be characterized. The Tax Court held that such payments should be classified as a distributive share of partnership income.[48] The Tax Court's opinion was not consistent with congressional purpose. The IRS consequently ruled that the payments in such situations should be governed by Code Sec.707(c).[49] However, the legislative

---

[43] *Wegener v. Comm'r*, 41 B.T.A. 857 (1940), *aff'd*, 119 F.2d 49 (5th Cir.), *cert. denied*, 314 U.S. 643 (1941); GCM 34001 (Dec. 23, 1969).

[44] IRS Market Segment Specialization Program, Partnerships, Audit Technique Guide, Chapter 1, under the heading, "Payments To A Partner: IRC section 707(A)–Partner Or Non-Partner."

[45] Rev. Rul. 81-301, 1981-2 CB 144.

[46] IRS Market Segment Specialization Program, Partnerships, Audit Technique Guide, Chapter 1, under the heading, "Guaranteed Payments—IRC section 707(c)."

[47] Rev. Rul. 81-301, 1981-2 CB 144.

[48] *Pratt v. Comm'r*, 64 TC 203 (1975).

[49] Rev. Rul. 81-300, 1981-2 CB 143.

history of the Deficit Reduction Act of 1984 states that the payments in such situations should be governed under Code Sec. 707(a), and not Code Sec. 707(c).[50]

The most important reason for distinguishing between guaranteed payments for services and payments for nonmembers services concerns the timing of income recognition. Guaranteed payments are always includable member's taxable income at the end of the tax year in which the LLC deducts or capitalizes the payment. Payments for nonmember services retain their character and timing based on the nature of the payment and the accounting method of the member.[51]

Payments for nonmember services are sometimes recharacterized as guaranteed payments or a distributive share of income so that the LLC can convert nondeductible capital expenditures into deductible business expenses. However, the disguised sales rules now prevent such recharacterization.[52] A distributive share of income or guaranteed payment for a capital item cannot be expensed.[53]

Payments to members for services may be treated as a disguised payment for services if the performance of such services and the allocation and distribution, when viewed together, are properly characterized as a transaction occurring between the LLC and a person acting other than in that person's capacity as a partner. Disguised payments for services are discussed at ¶ 1410.

.05 *Loan by Member to the LLC*

Interest payments by an LLC on a loan from a member are deductible by the LLC and taxable to the member.

If the loan becomes worthless, the member is entitled to a loss deduction. The member must establish worthlessness in the year of the claimed loss. There must be some overt act indicating that the member abandoned his or her right to the amount due under the promissory note from the LLC.[54] The loss deduction is normally a nonbusiness bad debt deductible as a short-term capital loss. The member may not take a business bad debt deduction unless (i) the member was in the lending business, or (ii) the principal purpose of the loan was directly connected with an LLC trade or business in which the member actively participated.[55]

The basis rules that apply to loans by a member to an LLC are discussed at ¶ 902.01 and ¶ 903.02. The at-risk rules that apply to loans by a member to an LLC are discussed at ¶ 1303.05.

---

[50] Senate Comm. on Finance, 98th Cong., 2d Sess., Deficit Reduction Act of 1984, S. Prt. No. 169, at 229, 230.

[51] IRS Market Segment Specialization Program, Partnerships, Audit Technique Guide, Chapter 1, under the heading, "Guaranteed Payments—IRC section 707(c)."

[52] *See* ¶ 605.01*supra*, under the heading, "Services."

[53] IRS Market Segment Specialization Program, Partnerships, Audit Technique Guide, Chapter 1, under the heading, "Guaranteed Payments—IRC section 707(c)."

[54] LAFA 20064601F.

[55] *See Whipple v. Comm'r*, 373 U.S. 193 (1963); *T.V. Post v. Comm'r*, 39 TCM 311 (1979); *Butler v. Comm'r*, 36 TC 1097 (1961).

The LLC must separately report any self-charged interest income or expense that results from loans between the member and the LLC (or between the LLC and another partnership or S corporation if both entities have the same owners with the same proportional ownership interest in each entity). The self-charged interest rules that apply to loans by a member to an LLC for purposes of the net investment income tax (NII tax) are discussed at ¶708.05. The self-charged interest rules that apply to loans by a member to an LLC for purposes of the passive loss rules are discussed at ¶1304.05.

Loans from a member to an LLC may be recharacterized as capital contributions if the facts and circumstances show that the substance of the transaction is actually a capital contribution.[56] This recharacterization is commonly referred to as the "Thin Partnership" doctrine that parallels the "Thin Incorporation" doctrine of corporate tax law. The Thin Partnership doctrine was first applied in *Joseph W. Hambuechen* in 1964.[57] In that case, the taxpayer made substantial advances to a financially faltering partnership under an agreement providing that the advances were to be placed in a special account on the partnership books, not bearing interest, unsecured and subordinated. The taxpayer claimed a business bad debt deduction when the special account was liquidated. The Service denied the deduction on the theory that no debt existed. The Tax Court agreed with the Service that the loan was actually a capital contribution because (i) under the same circumstances, no creditor would have made a similar unsecured, subordinated loan to the partnership, (ii) the advances were unsecured, subordinated to other claims of past, present, and future creditors, and did not bear interest or have a fixed maturity date, and (iii) there was no reasonable expectation of repayment regardless of the success of the partnership. The significance of the Thin Partnership doctrine has been reduced by the enactment of the at-risk limitations under Code Sec. 465, the passive loss rules under Code Sec. 469, and the regulations under Code Sec. 752.

.06 Loan from LLC to Member

A loan is a distribution of money or property to a member who is under an obligation to repay or return the distributed amount to the LLC. A loan is not taxed as a current distribution and will not result in gain recognition to the member. Instead, a loan is treated as a transaction between the LLC and a member not acting in the capacity of a partner.[58]

A payment to a member is not considered a loan unless the member is under an unconditional and legally enforceable obligation to repay a specific sum at a determinable date.[59] The obligation to repay must be created at the time the funds are disbursed. Bookkeeping entries alone are insufficient to establish the existence of a loan. The fact that the payment creates a deficit in the member's account which the

---

[56] Reg. § 1.707-1(a).

[57] *Hambuechen v. Comm'r*, 43 TC 90 (1964).

[58] Code Sec. 707(a); Reg. § 1.731-1(c)(2).

[59] Rev. Rul. 73-301, 1973-2 CB 215.

member is under an obligation to restore upon liquidation is also not enough to create an obligation to repay a loan.

¶ 1404 DISTRIBUTIVE SHARE OF INCOME

A member must report on his tax return his distributive share of LLC income, gain, loss, and deductions.[60] The distributive share includes the member's share of separately stated items, and the member's share of LLC taxable income or loss. The member must include in taxable income the distributive share of income, whether or not the income is actually distributed.[61]

Actual distributions from the LLC do not ordinarily result in taxation. Distributions decrease a member's basis in the LLC.[62] Undistributed income increases the member's basis in the LLC. No gain or loss is recognized on distributions except to the extent that a money distribution exceeds the member's basis in the membership interest.[63]

The amount of income earned by the LLC, and the share of income that must be reported by each member, is determined on the last day of the LLC's fiscal year.[64] The member recognizes income for the year that includes the last day of the LLC's tax year in which the LLC reported the distributive share of income.[65]

EXAMPLE 14-7

An LLC has two equal members. It earns $1 million in income during 2005. It uses all of the income for expansion of the business and makes no distributions. It sends a Schedule K-1 to each member for 2005 showing the member's allocable share of income. Each member must pay taxes on $500,000 of income for 2005 even though no distributions were made.

EXAMPLE 14-8

An LLC uses the cash method of accounting. It has a fiscal year ending May 31. All of its members are individuals who report on a calendar year basis. For the year ended May 31, 2004, the LLC sends Member B a Schedule K-1 showing the member's share of income, gain, loss, and

---

[60] Code Sec. 702.

[61] Code Sec. 702(a).

[62] Code Sec. 733.

[63] Code Sec. 731. *See* Chapter 10 for various exceptions.

[64] Code Sec. 706.

[65] Reg. § 1.706-1(a)(2).

deductions. The member must report the items on his income tax return for the calendar year ending December 31, 2004.[66]

The LLC may not deduct the payment. However, the distribution of income is ultimately the same as a deduction, since it decreases the distributive share of income taxable to the other members of the LLC. The other members' shares of LLC income are reduced by this amount in the same year.

¶ 1405 DIFFERENCES BETWEEN GUARANTEED PAYMENT, DISTRIBUTIVE SHARE OF INCOME, AND OTHER PAYMENTS

In most cases, the tax results are similar whether the payment is characterized as a guaranteed payment, distributive share of income, or distribution to a member other than in his capacity as a member. The LLC reduces its income or receives a tax deduction for the payment, and the member reports taxable income. However, there are the following differences:

- *Character of income to member.* A guaranteed payment is always ordinary income.[67] For example, a member receives ordinary income from a guaranteed payment for the use of capital under Code Sec. 707(c).[68] A distributive share of income retains the same character as reported by the LLC on Form 1065.[69] For example, a distributive share of income may be partially trade or business income, capital gains, Section 1231 gain, or other type of income. A payment to a member acting in a nonmember capacity depends on the type of payment. For example, the payment may be a nontaxable return of principal on a loan, capital gain on the sale of property, or rental income on the lease of property.

- *Deduction by LLC.* An LLC may deduct a guaranteed payment unless the payment is made in connection with a capital expenditure.[70] Payments that are capital expenditures must be capitalized. An LLC may deduct guaranteed payments for the use of capital under Code Sec. 162 (guaranteed payments in exchange for a capital contribution) if the member recognizes ordinary income for the guaranteed payments.[71] An LLC may not deduct a distributive share of income. However, a distributive share income to one member reduces the taxable income that must be reported by the other members. Thus, the effect of a distributive share of income is in most cases the same as a guaranteed

---

[66] *Id.*

[67] Code Secs. 61(a), 707(c); Reg. § 1.707-1(c).

[68] CCA 201741018.

[69] *See* Code Sec. 704.

[70] Code Sec. 707(c); Reg. § 1.707-1(c).

[71] CCA 201741018.

payment. A payment to a member acting in a nonmember capacity may or may not be deductible depending on the nature of the payment.

- *Timing difference.* There are timing differences in income recognition and deduction depending on the character of the payments. A guaranteed payment is included in the member's income in the year in which the guaranteed payment is deducted by the LLC.[72] Thus, if an LLC accrues a guaranteed salary expense in one year, but does not pay that amount to the member until the following year, the member must report the guaranteed payment in the year accrued by the LLC rather than in the following year when received by the member. A distributive share of income is included in the member's income for the tax year that includes the last day of the LLC's fiscal year.[73] Thus, the member must include LLC items in income at the end of the tax year of the LLC, rather than when distributed. A payment by the LLC to a member acting in a nonmember capacity is included in the member's income in the year of receipt, assuming that the member uses the cash method of accounting. The LLC may deduct such payment only in the year that the member recognizes income. Thus, an accrual method LLC may not deduct accrued rents, interest, compensation, or other payments to a member until it actually pays such amounts.[74]

- *Withholding taxes and self-employment income.* There are different withholding and self-employment tax rules depending on the type of payment.[75] For example, a guaranteed payment for services to a member who is classified as a limited partner is subject to self-employment taxes. A distributive share of income to a member who is classified as a limited partner is not subject to self-employment taxes.[76]

  - *Basis of membership interest.* A guaranteed payment does not affect a member's basis in the LLC.[77] A distribution reduces a member's tax basis in the membership interest.

  - *Capital account.* A guaranteed payment does not affect a member's capital account in the LLC.[78] Guaranteed payments cause the capital account of the recipient member to be adjusted only to the extent of the member's distributive share of any LLC deduction, loss or other downward capital account adjustment resulting from such payment.[79] A distribution reduces a member's capital account.

- *Foreign members.* Guaranteed payments to foreign members for services qualify for the foreign earned income exclusion and foreign tax credits. Distribu-

---

[72] Reg. § § 1.706-1(a)(1), 1.707-1(c).

[73] Reg. § 1.706-1(a)(1).

[74] Code Sec. 267(a)(2), (e).

[75] *See* Chapter 27.

[76] *Id.*

[77] CCA 201741018.

[78] CCA 201741018.

[79] Reg. § 1.704-1(b)(2)(iv)(o).

tive shares of income to foreign members may not qualify for the foreign earned income exclusion or foreign tax credits.[80]

- *QBI deduction.* Between 2018 and 2025, a member may deduct 20 percent of the member's allocable share of qualified business income under Code Sec. 199A, Distributive shares of income qualify for the deduction, guaranteed payments do not.[81]

¶1406 FRINGE BENEFITS

Certain fringe benefits qualify for favorable tax treatment. Other fringe benefits are not available to members in an LLC.

.01 Health Plans

Tax Treatment

An LLC may pay health insurance premiums on behalf of its members, spouses, and dependents. It must treat the payment in one of the following ways:

- *Guaranteed payment.* The LLC may treat the payment as a guaranteed payment.[82] The LLC may deduct the guaranteed payment. The LLC must report the payment to the member as a guaranteed payment on Schedule K-1.[83] The member must include the guaranteed payment in gross income on Form 1040.[84] The member must also include the guaranteed payment in self-employment income on Schedule SE.[85] The member may then deduct up to the full amount on his or her tax return.[86]
- *Distribution to member.* The LLC may account for the payment of medical insurance premiums for a member as a distribution to the member.[87] The LLC

---

[80] IRS, LB&I International Practice Service Process Unit - Audit, JTO/P/09_06_05-19 (last updated 08/11/16).

[81] Code Sec. 199A(c)(4)(B). *See* ¶702.

[82] Rev. Rul. 91-26, 1991-1 CB 184, Situation 1; CCA 201228037.

[83] IRS Notice 2005-8, 2005-1 CB 368, Q&A-2. Using the 2005 tax forms as an example, the LLC would include the health insurance premium payments for members as a guaranteed payment in Item 10 of Form 1065. It would include the same amount as both an income item and as a deduction item on Schedule K (Item 4 Guaranteed payments, and Item 13d Other deductions with the notation "Amounts paid for medical insurance" The LLC would also include the same amount as both an income item and as a deduction item on Schedule K-1 for each member (Item 4 Guaranteed payments, and Item 13 Other deductions with Code M for medical insurance payments). The total of the ordinary business income from Item 1 and the guaranteed payments in Item 4 would be included as self-employment earnings in Item 14 of Schedule K-1. *See* Instructions to IRS Form 1065, Line 19.

[84] CCA 201228037.

[85] IRS Notice 2005-8, 2005-1 CB 368, Q&A-2.

[86] Code Sec. 162(l)(1)(B).

[87] Rev. Rul. 91-26, 1991-1 CB 184, Situation 1 (last paragraph).

must report the payment as a distribution of money on Schedule K-1.[88] The LLC may not deduct the premiums in such case and must compute each member's distributive share of income without regard to the health insurance premiums. The member must include in gross income the distributive share of LLC income (determined without reduction for health insurance premium payments).[89] The member may then deduct up to the full amount of premium payments on his or her tax return.[90]

The deduction by the member is in lieu of the medical expense deduction.[91] The deduction is an above-the-line deduction.[92] Thus, a member may deduct medical expenses even though the member does not itemize deductions, and even though the member's aggregate medical expenses are less than 7.5 percent of adjusted gross income.

Limitations on Health Plan Deductions

There are limits on deductibility of health insurance premiums by a member of an LLC that is classified as a partnership or S corporation.[93] The deduction is subject to the following rules and limitations:

- The member may deduct on his or her tax return the amount paid for health insurance for the taxpayer, the spouse, dependents, and any child of the taxpayer who has not attained age 27 as of the end of the tax year, whether or not a dependent.[94]

- The member may not take an above-the-line deduction for payments during any calendar month in which the taxpayer is eligible to participate in a subsidized health plan maintained by the employer of the member, spouse, dependents, or children under age 27.[95]

- The deduction is in lieu of the medical expense deduction.[96] The deduction is an above-the-line deduction. Thus, a member may deduct medical expenses even though the taxpayer does not itemize deductions, and even though the

---

[88] IRS Notice 2005-8, 2005-1 CB 368, Q&A-1.

[89] The actual distributions are not included in the member's net earnings from self-employment under Code Sec. 1402(a) because distributions do not change a member's distributive share of LLC income or loss, which are computed in such case without regard to health insurance premium payments. IRS Notice 2005-8, 2005-1 CB 368, Q&A-1.

[90] Code Sec. 162(l)(1)(B).

[91] Code Sec. 162(l)(5).

[92] IRS Notice 2005-8, 2005-1 CB 368, Q&A-2, Example.

[93] The limitation for S corporations applies to members or shareholders who own more than two percent of the membership interests in the LLC or corporation.

[94] Code Sec. 162(l)(1)(B).

[95] Code Sec. 162(l)(2)(B).

[96] Code Sec. 162(l)(5).

taxpayer's aggregate medical expenses are less than 7.5 percent of adjusted gross income (ten percent beginning in 2019).[97]

- The deduction is limited to the member's earned income from the LLC with respect to which the medical plan is established.[98] The member may not aggregate the net profits and losses of two or more businesses to establish the net income ceiling up to which he or she may claim insurance costs deductions.[99] The member's net earnings for such purposes is the earned income from the LLC, reduced by the deduction for 50 percent of the self-employment taxes and any contributions to a pension or profit sharing plan, SEP or SIMPLE IRA.

- The member may deduct health insurance costs in excess of the deductible amount as an itemized medical expense deduction, subject to the 7.5 percent floor on deductibility (ten percent beginning in 2019).[100]

- Members may not deduct health insurance costs in calculating self-employment taxes, except for 2010.[101]

Large Employer Mandate

The LLC is liable for any assessment payment under Code Sec. 4980H if the LLC has more than 50 employees, and fails to provide health plan coverage, or offers health plan coverage that is unaffordable or does not provide minimum value. In the case of a disregarded LLC, the assessment payment and reporting requirements are imposed on the LLC, and not on the owner of the LLC.[102]

Self-Funded Plans

A self-funded health plan is a plan that is funded in part by premiums from employees and partners. An LLC normally purchases stop-loss insurance for catastrophic claims. An LLC's self-funded plan has the following tax consequences:[103]

---

[97] Code Secs. 56(b)(1)(B), 213(f)(2).

[98] Code Sec. 162(l)(2)(A).

[99] CCA 200524001. This means that the taxpayer must designate the business to which the insurance relates.

[100] JTC Overview of Health Care Tax Provisions and Proposals to Aid Uninsured Individuals, Part I.A.4 (JCX-4-02) (Feb. 13, 2002).

[101] Code Sec. 162(l)(4), as amended by 2010 Small Business Act § 2042(a). For income tax purposes, the member may deduct as an above-the-line deduction one-half of the self-employment taxes. The income tax deduction is computed by disregarding the additional 0.9 percent SECA tax assessed for tax years after 2012. Code Sec. 164(f).

[102] Preamble to IRS Proposed Regulations on Shared Responsibility for Employer Health Coverage, REG-138006-12, Explanation of Provisions, Part VI (Jan. 2, 2013); Reg. § 301.7701-2(c)(2)(v)(A)(5).

[103] Ltr. Rul. 200007025.

- The plan is a health insurance plan under Code Sec. 104(a)(3) if the plan has adequate risk-shifting and is not merely a reimbursement arrangement.
- A partner or other self-employed person may deduct payments to the plan if there is adequate risk shifting.
- Payments from the plan for the benefit of employees and dependents are excludable from income. Payments from the plan for the benefit of partners and other self-employed person are also excludable from income if there is adequate risk-shifting.

.02 Life Insurance

An LLC may not deduct premiums paid on life insurance covering the life of a member. Premiums paid by a member on the life of a co-member are not deductible, regardless of who is named the beneficiary of the proceeds or whether the policy is assigned to the LLC.[104]

An LLC that acquires an insurance policy on the life of a member frequently transfers the policy to the member on retirement or withdrawal by the member from the LLC. The exclusion from income for life insurance proceeds is lost if the LLC transfers the policy for valuable consideration. However, the exclusion is not lost if the LLC transfers the policy to the insured member or any other member of the LLC.[105]

The sale or exchange of membership interests in an LLC that is classified as a partnership will not result in a transfer for "valuable consideration" under Code Sec. 101(a)(2), provided there is no termination of the LLC as a partnership under Code Sec. 708(b)(1)(B).[106]

The transfer of an insurance policy to an LLC in exchange for a membership interest is not a transfer for valuable consideration.[107]

.03 Pension and Profit-Sharing Plans

Code Sec. 401(c)(1) treats members in an LLC, partners in a partnership, and sole proprietors as employees for pension and profit sharing plan purposes. An LLC that is classified as a partnership is treated as the employer of each of the members. Thus, an individual member is not an employer and may not establish a qualified plan with respect to his or her services to the LLC.[108]

An LLC may adopt qualified pension and profit-sharing plans.[109] An LLC that is classified as a partnership may not adopt an ESOP.[110] An LLC may establish a

---

[104] Code Sec. 264(a)(1); Reg. § 1.264-1(b); Rev. Rul. 73, 1953-1 CB 63, 1953 WL 79473; *Ernest J. Keefe v. Comm'r*, 15 TC 947 (1950).

[105] Ltr. Ruls. 9625023, 9625022, 9625013-9625018.

[106] Ltr. Rul. 200826009.

[107] TAM 200432015.

[108] Reg. § 1.401-10(e).

[109] *See* Ltr. Ruls. 200116051, 9343036.

[110] *K.H. Company LLC Stock Ownership Plan v. Comm'r*, TC Memo 2014-31 (2014).

qualified stock bonus plan for distribution of stock of a corporate partner and its parent corporation.[111]

Members of an LLC may make elective contributions to a Section 401(k) plan during the year based on draws or the estimated income that the member will receive at the end of the year.[112]

An LLC may not deduct pension contributions unless the LLC is engaged in a trade or business. This determination is based on all the facts and circumstances. An LLC that is merely the recipient of passive income is not engaged in a trade or business and may not deduct pension contributions.[113]

The LLC may not make pension or profit-sharing contributions for members who are treated as limited partners. The LLC may make contributions only for employees and self-employed persons.[114] The contributions are based on the amount of compensation earned by an employee and the amount of earned income received by a self-employed person.[115] "Earned income" means net earnings from self-employment.[116] A limited partner is not a self-employed person and does not have net earnings from self-employment.

Employees of a disregarded LLC that is owned by a member of a controlled group of corporations may participate in a qualified pension or profit sharing plan, Section 401(k) plan, Section 403(b)annuity plan,[117] Section 457(b) plan,[118] employee stock ownership plan,[119] or other qualified retirement plan of the corporate owner of the LLC or other member of the control group. If the corporate owner maintains an employee stock ownership plan, the stock in the corporate owner or other member of the control group constitutes qualifying employer securities for the employee stock ownership plan adopted by the LLC.[120] The employees of the LLC are treated as employed by the member of the controlled group that owns the membership interests in the LLC.[121]

The transfer of stock from the corporate plan to an LLC stock bonus plan will not change the tax basis of the securities for purposes of computing net unrealized appreciation in the securities.[122] The exclusion of net unrealized appreciation[123] will

---

[111] *Id.*

[112] Reg. § 1.401(k)-1(a)(6).

[113] *Peterson v. Comm'r*, TC Memo 2013-271 (2013).

[114] If a member is classified as a limited partner, the member may fail to meet the definition of an "employee" under Code Sec. 401(c)(1).

[115] Code Secs. 401(c)(1)(A), 404(a)(8).

[116] Code Secs. 1126, 1402(a).

[117] Ltr. Ruls. 200341023, 200334040; CCA 201634021.

[118] CCA 201634021.

[119] Ltr. Ruls. 201124030, 200116051. The same rule applies if an S corporation contributes stock to employees of an LLC that is owned by the S corporation. Ltr. Rul. 201124030.

[120] Ltr. Rul. 200116051.

[121] Ltr. Rul. 200111053.

[122] Ltr. Rul. 9343036.

[123] *See* Code Sec. 402(a), (e)(4).

apply after the transfer.[124] The transferred securities will continue to constitute "employer securities" until distributed by the LLC plan.[125]

A pension or profit-sharing plan may invest in LLCs.[126]

Contributions to a pension or profit-sharing plan are often based on a percentage of each employee's compensation. For an LLC that is classified as a partnership, the total compensation of the member for pension and profit sharing plan purposes includes the member's distributive share of LLC income, whether or not distributed, and guaranteed payments to the extent that such income constitutes earned income under Code Sec. 401(c)(2).[127]

Pension contributions on behalf of partners and other self-employed persons are subject to self-employment taxes even though they are fully deductible for income tax purposes.[128] Therefore, the LLC must separately state the pension contributions rather than deducting the contributions from the net income items that are subject to self-employment taxes. If the LLC is classified as a partnership, then the LLC must report the pension and deferred compensation contributions as follows:[129]

- The LLC may not deduct payments for members to qualified retirement plans or deferred compensation plans as a guaranteed payment on Line 4 or as an expense on Line 18 of Schedule K. Instead, the LLC must report such contributions on Schedule K, Box 13(d), using Code R. The LLC must also report the contributions on Schedule K-1, using Code R. The member may deduct the contribution on his or her own tax return.
- Contributions for common law employees under a qualified pension or profit sharing plan, annuity, SEP or SIMPLE IRAs or other deferred compensation plan are deductible on Line 18 of Schedule K.
- Certain indirect costs relating to inventory, including pension costs, must be capitalized and are not deductible by the LLC in accordance with Reg. § 1.263A-1(e)(3).

For plan years after 2007, a qualified plan that covers only members and their spouses is not required to file an annual report for the plan on Form 5500 if the plan has assets of $250,000 or less as of the close of the plan year.[130]

.04 Working Condition Fringe Benefits

Employees are not taxed on the value of working condition fringe benefits. A working condition fringe benefit is a fringe benefit that the employee would be

---

[124] Ltr. Rul. 9343036.

[125] *Id.*

[126] *See* L. McCarthy, "LLCs: A Flexible Alternative for Pension Plan Investments," Pension World, Aug. 1992.

[127] Reg. § 1.401-11(d)(2)(ii); Ltr. Rul. 200247052.

[128] *LaFlamme v. Comm'r,* TC Memo 2012-36 (2012); *Gale v. United States,* 768 F. Supp. 1305 (N.D. Ill. 2012); Instructions to Line 13 on Form 1065.

[129] *See* instructions to Form 1065, Lines 13(d) and 18.

[130] Pension Protection Act of 2006, Pub. L. No. 109-280, § 1103, 120 Stat. 780.

entitled to deduct as a business expense if the employee paid the expense himself.[131] Members who perform services for an LLC are treated as employees for such purposes.[132] Thus, members are not taxed on the value of the following working condition fringe benefits:

- Business-related use of an automobile owned by the LLC if the member substantiates business use.[133]
- Job-related education expenses that the LLC pays for the member.[134]
- The business-use portion of dues paid to a country club.[135] The LLC may not deduct the country club dues.
- Job placement assistance.[136]
- Cell phones provided to employees primarily for noncompensatory business purposes.[137]

.05 Other Permissible Fringe Benefits

A member of an LLC may exclude from income the value of the following additional fringe benefits:

- *De minimis fringe benefits.* An employee may exclude from income *de minimis* fringe benefits received from the employer. Employees include any recipient of a fringe benefit for purposes of the rule.[138] Thus, members of an LLC may exclude from income (i) supper money and local transportation fare that the LLC provides members on an occasional basis in connection with overtime work,[139] (ii) traditional birthday or holiday gifts of non-cash property with a low fair market value,[140] (iii) traditional awards such as a watch upon retirement after lengthy service,[141] and (iv) personal use of a cell phone provided primarily for business purposes.[142]
- *Dependent care assistance.* Members of an LLC may exclude from income dependent care assistance under Code Sec. 129.[143] The dependent care assistance plan must meet various requirements. The LLC may not pay more than

---

[131] Code Sec. 132(a)(3), (d).

[132] Reg. § 1.132-1(b)(2)(ii).

[133] Reg. § 1.132-5(a)(1).

[134] Reg. § 1.132-1(f).

[135] Reg. § 1.132-5(s).

[136] Rev. Rul. 92-69, 1992-2 CB 51.

[137] IRS Notice 2011-72, 2011-38 IRB 407.

[138] Reg. § 1.132-1(b)(4).

[139] Reg. § 1.132-6(d)(2)(i).

[140] Reg. § 1.132-6(e).

[141] H. Rept. No. 99-436 (Pub. L. No. 99-514), p. 105.

[142] IRS Notice 2011-72, 2011-38 IRB 407.

[143] Code Sec. 129(e)(3).

25 percent of amounts under the plan to members who own more than five percent of the membership interests in the LLC.[144]

- *Qualified employee discounts and no-additional cost services.* An employer may provide qualified employee discounts and no-additional cost services to employees on a tax-free basis. Members of an LLC who performs services are treated as employees for such purposes.[145]

- *Athletic facilities.* An LLC may provide on-premise athletic facilities, such as a gym or swimming pool, to members, their spouses and dependents.[146]

- *Educational assistance program.* An employer may establish an educational assistance program for employees under Code Sec. 127. Members of an LLC who have earned income from the LLC are treated as employees for such purposes.[147] However, the LLC may not pay more than five percent of the annual benefits to members who own more than five percent of the membership interests in the LLC.[148]

- *Health savings account.* An LLC may contribute to a health savings account for the benefit of members under Code Sec. 223. The LLC may account for the contribution as a guaranteed payment or a distributive share of income. The tax consequences are the same as for health insurance premium payments for members.[149]

- *Travel expenses.* Members of an LLC that is classified as a partnership may use the per diem rates to substantiate travel expenses, including lodging, meals and incidental expenses.[150]

.06 Taxable Fringe Benefits

The following types of fringe benefits are normally taxable to members of an LLC:

- *Meals and lodging.* Members may not exclude from income the value of meals and lodging furnished for the convenience of the employer, except in limited cases.[151]

---

[144] Code Sec. 129(d)(4).

[145] Reg. § 1.132-1(b)(1).

[146] Reg. § 1.132-1(b)(3).

[147] Code Secs. 127(c)(2), (c)(3), 401(c)(1).

[148] Code Sec. 127(b)(1).

[149] Reg. § 54.4980G-3, Q&A-3. The contribution to the HSA for members is normally treated as a Section 731 distribution. Contributions for members with guaranteed distributions are treated as guaranteed payments. Contributions for members are not subject to the comparability rules applicable to HSAs.

[150] Rev. Proc. 2011-47, 2011-42 IRB 520, § 3.04.

[151] One court determined that a partner is not considered an employee for purposes of the meals and lodging exclusion. *Robinson v. United States*, 273 F.2d 503 (3d Cir. 1959). However, other courts have determined that a partner may be an employee for purposes of the meals and lodging exclusion if the partner is acting in a capacity other than as a partner. *Papineau, George*, 16 TC 130 (1951), *nonacq*, *Armstrong v. Phinney*, 394 F.2d 661 (5th Cir. 1968).

- *Cafeteria plan.* Members may not participate in a cafeteria plan,[152] although an LLC may sponsor a cafeteria plan for nonmember employees.[153]
- *VEBA.* As a practical matter, only corporations may adopt a VEBA. At least 90 percent of all participants in a VEBA must be employees.[154]
- *Incentive stock options.* Incentive stock options may be granted only to corporate employees.[155] An LLC may not grant incentive stock options to employees unless the LLC is classified as a corporation.[156]
- *Medical expense reimbursement plan.* Members may not participate in a medical expense reimbursement plan.[157] Other employees of an LLC are not taxed on medical expense reimbursements received under a nondiscriminatory plan.
- *Qualified transportation fringe benefits.* Qualified transportation fringe benefits (such as transit passes and free parking) are available only to employees.[158] They are not available to members in an LLC, except as a *de minimis* fringe benefit or working condition fringe benefit.[159] Members and partners may qualify for up to $21 worth of tokens or fare cards in any month under the *de minimis* fringe benefit rules.[160] The token or fare card must enable the recipient to commute on a public transit system (not including privately-owned vanpools). If the value of the pass exceeds $21 per month, the full value of the benefit is includable.[161]
- *Group term life insurance and other insurance.* Members may not deduct premiums for group term life insurance.[162] Employees are not taxed on group term coverage up to $50,000.[163]
- *Section 423 stock purchase plan.* Employees may purchase stock at a discount under a Section 423 employee stock purchase plan.[164] Options under the plan may be granted only to corporate employees.[165] Employees of an LLC may not participate in a Section 423 plan unless the LLC is classified as a corpora-

---

[152] Prop. Reg. § 1.125-1(g)(2)(i), (a)(1), Code Sec. 1372.

[153] Prop. Reg. § 1.125-1(g)(2)(i).

[154] Reg. § 1.501(c)(9)-2(a)(1).

[155] Reg. § 1.422-2(a)(2); Ltr. Rul. 9321049.

[156] Reg. § 1.421-1(i)(1).

[157] *See* Code Sec. 105(g), (h).

[158] Code Sec. 132(a)(5), (f)(5)(E). IRS Notice 93-4, 1993-1 CB 295, Q&A-5, states that qualified transportation fringe benefits may not be provided to partners, two-percent shareholders of S corporations, sole proprietors, and independent contractors.

[159] Reg. § 1.132-9(b), Q&A-5, 24.

[160] Reg. § 1.132-6(d)(1).

[161] Reg. § 1.132-9(b), Q&A-24(b).

[162] This benefit is available only to corporate employees. Prop. Reg. § 1.269A-1(b)(6). Congress indicated that this benefit is not available to partners or two-percent shareholders in S corporations in H.R. Rep. No. 826, 97th Cong., 2d Sess. (1982), n.2, at 21, reprinted in 1982-2 CB 730, 739; S. Rep. No. 640, 97th Cong., 2d Sess. (1982), n. 2 at 22, reprinted in 1982-2 CB 718, 728.

[163] *See* Code Sec. 79; Reg. §§ 1.79-1(a), 1.79-0.

[164] Code Sec. 423.

[165] Code Sec. 423(b)(1).

tion,[166] or is owned by a corporation and classified as a disregarded entity for federal tax purposes.[167]

- *Health reimbursement arrangement.* A self-employed person may not receive medical expense reimbursements under a health reimbursement arrangement.[168]

¶1407 DEFERRED COMPENSATION

.01 General Rules

The determination of when amounts deferred under a nonqualified deferred compensation arrangement are includable in gross income depends on numerous tax principles and Code provisions. These principles and Code provisions include the doctrine of constructive receipt, the economic benefit doctrine, Code Sec. 83 relating to transfers of property in connection with the performance of services, Code Sec. 402(b) relating to nonexempt employee trusts, and Code Sec. 409A.

In general, the time for income inclusion of nonqualified deferred compensation depends on whether the arrangement is unfunded or funded. If the arrangement is unfunded, then the compensation is generally includable in income by a cash basis taxpayer when it is actually or constructively received. If the arrangement is funded, then the income is includable in income for the year in which the individual's rights are transferable or not subject to a substantial risk of forfeiture.[169]

.02 Section 409A Requirements

Under Code Sec. 409A, all amounts deferred by a service provider under a nonqualified deferred compensation plan for all tax years are currently includable in gross income to the extent such amounts are not subject to a substantial risk of forfeiture and not previously included in gross income, unless certain requirements are met. If the requirements of Section 409A are not met, then the service provider is subject to (i) current income inclusion, (ii) interest at the rate applicable to underpayment of tax plus one percentage point on the underpayments that would have occurred had the compensation been includable in income when first deferred, or if later when not subject to substantial risk of forfeiture, and (iii) a 20 percent additional tax on the amount included in income.

Section 409A and regulations do not specifically address arrangements between LLCs and members providing services to the LLC. However, Section 409A may apply to arrangements between an LLC classified as a partnership and its members if the

---

[166] Reg. § 1.421-1(h)(1).

[167] Ltr. Rul. 200046013.

[168] IRS Notice 2002-45, 2002-28 IRB 93, Part III.

[169] *See* H.R. Rep. No. 108-548, pt. 1. (2004).

arrangement provides for the deferral of compensation under a nonqualified deferred compensation plan.[170]

Until further guidance is issued, an LLC may treat the issuance of a membership interest (including a profits interest), or an option to buy a membership interest that is granted in connection with the performance of services, under the same principles that govern the issuance of stock. Generally, this means that the issuance of a profits interest will not result in the deferral of compensation.[171] LLCs may apply the principles applicable to stock options or stock appreciation rights under the final regulations to equivalent rights with respect to LLC interests.[172] LLCs may treat the issuance of a capital interest in connection with the performance of services in the same manner as the issuance of stock.[173] The rules under Code Sec. 409A governing other stock-based compensation may be applied by analogy to grants of equity-based compensation or other compensation that is determined by reference to equity in the LLC.[174]

Until further guidance issued, LLCs may also treat arrangements providing for payments under Code Sec. 736 to retired and deceased partners as not subject to Section 409A. However, arrangements to a member under Code Sec. 1402(a)(10) (applicable to retirement payments that aren't self-employment income) are subject to Code Sec. 409A.[175]

.03 Section 457A Requirements

Deferred compensation paid by domestic or foreign partnerships to an employee or other service provider is includable in gross income when there is no substantial risk of forfeiture if the LLC allocates all or any part of its income to (a) foreign persons with respect to whom such income is not subject to a comprehensive foreign income tax, or (b) a tax-exempt organizations.[176] Compensation is subject to a substantial risk of forfeiture if the right to the compensation is conditioned upon the future performance of substantial services.[177]

.04 Self-Employment Taxes

The self-employment taxes on deferred compensation are discussed at ¶ 2702.05.

---

[170] IRS Notice 2005-1, Q&A-7, 2005-1 CB 274.

[171] IRS Notice 2005-1, Q&A-7, 2005-1 CB 274.

[172] Preamble to TD 9321 (Apr. 10, 2007).

[173] IRS Notice 2005-1, Q&A-7, 2005-1 CB 274.

[174] IRS Notice 2005-1, Q&A-7, 2005-1 CB 274.

[175] IRS Notice 2005-1, Q&A-7, 2005-1 CB 274.

[176] Code Sec. 457A(a); IRS Notice 2009-8, 2009-1 CB 347, Q&A-1.

[177] Code Sec. 457A(d)(1)(A); IRS Notice 2009-8, 2009-1 CB 347, Q&A-3.

.05 State Income Taxes of Nonresident Members

Deferred compensation payments and retirement income payable to members of an LLC classified as a partnership are not subject to income taxes in the state in which the member earned the retirement pay if:[178]

- the member is a resident of another state at the time that the member receives the retirement income;
- the member is a retired member. A retired member is an individual who is described as a partner in Code Sec. 7701(a)(2) and who is retired under the LLC's operating agreement;[179]
- the member receives the payments under any written plan, program, or arrangement in effect at the time of retirement that provides for payments to a retired partner in recognition of prior service;
- the payments are made in substantially equal periodic payments (not less frequently than annually); and
- the payments are made over ten or more years, or over the life or life expectancy of the member (or the joint lives or joint life expectancies of the member and designated beneficiary).

¶ 1408 SECTION 736 PAYMENT

A Section 736 payment is a payment to a retired member or the estate of a deceased member in a service LLC if the member is a "general partner." The payments are classified either as Section 736(a) payments or Section 736(b) payments. These rules are discussed at ¶ 1010.

¶ 1409 DISGUISED SALE PAYMENTS

Payments to a member that are related to a contribution of property or services to the LLC may be reclassified as a payment in exchange for property or services, rather than a nontaxable distribution.

The three principal types of disguised sales are (a) a contribution of money, property or services to an LLC followed by a related distribution of money or property to the contributing member within two years after the contribution, (b) a contribution of appreciated property to an LLC by one member followed by a distribution of that property to another member within seven years after the contribution, and (c) a contribution of appreciated property to an LLC followed by a distribution of other property to the contributing member within seven years after the contribution.

Disguised sale payments are discussed at ¶ 605.

---

[178] 4 USC § 114(b)(1)(I); HR 109-542.
[179] 4 USC § 114(b)(4).

¶1410 DISGUISED PAYMENT FOR SERVICES

Certain LLC arrangements are treated as disguised payment for services rather than a distributive share of income when the member's performance of services is related to the LLC's distribution of income. The advantage of receiving an income allocation is that service provider fees are taxed as ordinary income, whereas income allocations are sometimes taxed at the lower capital gains tax rate. For example, private equity fund managers and hedge fund operators shift earnings from service payments taxed as ordinary income to carried interest taxed at the capital gains rate by fee waiver agreements that exchange fee income for a distributive share of profits. Mitt Romney's firm used this strategy to reduce the partners' taxes by more than $200 million.[180]

Under proposed regulations, arrangements pursuant to which a purported partner performs services for an LLC and receives a related direct or indirect allocation and distribution from the LLC are treated as disguised payments for services and taxed as ordinary income.[181] An arrangement is a disguised payment for services if:[182]

- a service provider, either in a partner capacity or in anticipation of becoming a partner, performs services (directly or through its delegate) to or for the benefit of an LLC;

- there is a related direct or indirect allocation and distribution to such service provider; and

- the performance of such services and the allocation and distribution, when viewed together, are properly characterized as a transaction occurring between the LLC and a person acting other than in that person's capacity as a partner. Whether an arrangement constitutes a payment for services depends on all the facts and circumstances. IRS regulations provide a non-exclusive list of six factors that may indicate that an arrangement constitutes in whole or in part a payment for services.[183] The most important factor is whether the arrangement constitutes a significant entrepreneurial risk. An arrangement under which allocations and distributions to the service provider are subject to significant entrepreneurial risks will generally be recognized as a distributive share. An arrangement that lacks entrepreneurial risk will normally constitute a disguised payment for services taxable as ordinary income.[184]

---

[180] BNA Daily Tax Report, No. 143, at G-5 (July 27, 2015).

[181] Code Sec. 707(a)(2)(A); Reg. § 1.707-1.

[182] Code Sec. 707(a)(2)(A); Prop. Reg. § 1.707-2(b)(1).

[183] Prop. Reg. § 1.707-2(c).

[184] Prop. Reg. § 1.707-2(c)(1).

15

Transfer of Membership Interests

¶ 1501 OVERVIEW

If an LLC is a disregarded entity for federal tax purposes (branch, division, or sole proprietorship), the sale of a membership interest in the LLC is treated as a sale of the underlying assets.[1] The member recognizes gain or loss to the same extent as if the LLC had sold the underlying assets. The member may also be liable for sales taxes under state law if the assets are tangible personal property or other assets subject to sales taxes.

If the LLC is classified as a corporation for federal tax purposes, then the member recognizes capital gain or loss upon the sale of the membership interest. The amount of gain or loss is equal to the difference between the sale price and the member's basis in the membership interest. A portion of the gain may be ordinary income if the LLC is a collapsible corporation.

Most LLCs are classified as partnerships for federal tax purposes. The tax consequences of selling or transferring a membership interest in an LLC that is classified as a partnership are discussed below.

¶ 1502 GAIN OR LOSS RECOGNIZED

A member recognizes gain or loss upon the sale or other disposition of a membership interest. The amount of gain or loss is the difference between the amount realized and the member's adjusted basis in the membership interest.[2]

The amount realized is the amount of cash and the fair market value of property received by the member, plus the amount of debt relief.[3] The debt relief includes the member's decreased share of LLC liabilities allocated to the new member.[4]

There are three methods for determining a member's adjusted basis in the membership interest for purposes of computing gain or loss. These methods are discussed at ¶ 1503.02.

Gain or loss is capital gain or loss, subject to exceptions for U.S. members[5] and foreign members.[6]

---

[1] Rev. Rul. 99-5, 1999-1 CB 434. *See* ¶ 1117.01 *supra.*

[2] Code Sec. 741; Reg. § 1.741-1(a).

[3] Reg. § 1.1001-2(a)(1).

[4] Reg. § § 1.752-1 to 1.752-4.

[5] Code Sec. 741. *See* ¶ 1507 *infra.*

[6] *See* ¶ 1907 *infra.*

EXAMPLE 15-1

An LLC has two equal members. Each member contributed $10,000 to the LLC. The LLC borrowed $20,000. The LLC then purchased property for $40,000. Each member has a basis of $20,000 in the LLC membership units, consisting of the $10,000 cash contribution plus the $1/2$ share of LLC liabilities allocated to each member for basis purposes.

Member A sells her membership units to Member C for $15,000 cash plus assumption of debt. The amount realized on the sale is $25,000. This includes the $15,000 of cash received plus the $10,000 of debt relief. The amount of gain recognized is $5,000 ($25,000 amount realized less $20,000 basis).

¶ 1503 BASIS

.01 Inside Basis of LLC Assets

The inside bases of LLC assets do not change as a result of a sale or exchange of membership interests in the LLC except in the following cases:

- The LLC has a substantial built-loss of more than $250,000 immediately after the transfer. The LLC must make a downward adjustment in the basis of its assets by a portion of the transferee member's share of built-in losses. The inside basis is adjusted only with respect to the transferee member. The basis adjustment for built-in losses is discussed at ¶ 1509.

- The LLC has in effect a Code Sec. 754 election. The inside basis of LLC assets is adjusted to reflect the purchase price, but only for the transferee member. The Section 754 election is discussed at ¶ 1508.

.02 Outside Basis of Membership Interest

A member must determine the adjusted basis in the membership interest in order to determine the amount of gain realized upon the sale or transfer of the membership interest. There are three ways of determining basis:

- *General method.* Under the general method, a member's initial basis in a membership interest is the amount of cash and the adjusted basis of property contributed to the LLC. The initial basis for a member who purchased a membership interest is the purchase price. The initial basis is increased by additional contributions, the member's distributive share of taxable income and tax-exempt income, and the member's share of LLC liabilities. The initial basis is decreased by distributions, the member's distributive share of tax losses and nondeductible LLC expenses, and any decreases in the member's share of LLC liabilities.[7]

- *Asset method.* Under the first alternative method, the member's basis is the member's share of the LLC's basis in its assets.[8] This is the basis of LLC property that would be distributed to the member on termination of the LLC. Generally, it is equal to the LLC's inside basis in its assets multiplied by the member's percentage interest in the LLC. Liabilities are ignored since they are taken into account in determining basis when an asset is purchased. A member may use this method of determining basis only if it is impractical or impossible to determine basis under the general rule.

- *Capital account and liabilities method.* Under the second alternative method (which is more commonly used), a member's basis is equal to the member's capital account plus share of LLC liabilities.[9] The LLC must maintain its books and records on a tax basis rather than an accounting basis. This method is normally easier to apply than the first alternative method. The member does not need access to the LLC books and records. The member can obtain the necessary information from Schedule K-1 that the member receives from the LLC each year. The member's capital account is set forth in Item L. The member's share of debt is set forth in Item F. A member may use this method of determining basis only if it is impractical or impossible to determine basis under the general method.

These methods of determining basis are discussed in detail in Chapter 9. In practice, taxpayers frequently use a modified version of the capital account method. The taxpayer ignores liabilities and computes gain as the difference between the cash received and the capital account. If the member abandons the LLC when the member has a negative capital account, the gain recognized is equal to the negative capital account.[10]

EXAMPLE 15-2

Member A and Member B each own 500 units in an LLC and share equally in profits and losses. The LLC has assets with a fair market value of $1,800, and liabilities of $800. The tax basis of the assets is $1,000. The LLC keeps capital accounts on a tax basis. Member A has a capital account of $175, and Member B has a capital account of $25.

Member B sells her membership interest in the LLC to Member C for $500, representing her one-half share of the value of LLC assets (1/2 × $1,800 fair market value, less $800 debt). Under the short-cut method of

---

[7] Code Sec. 705; Reg. § 1.705-1(a). *See* ¶¶ 901, 902, 903 *supra* regarding detailed rules on the computation of basis in a membership interest.

[8] Code Sec. 705(b); Reg. § 1.705-1(b).

[9] Code Sec. 705(b); Reg. § 1.705-1(b), Example (3).

[10] IRS Market Segment Specialization Program, Partnerships, Audit Technique Guide, under the heading, "Overview, Liquidation/Termination."

¶ 1503.02

determining gain, Member A computes her gain as the cash received upon the sale of $500, less her tax basis capital account of $25, or a total gain of $475. Under the capital account method authorized by the regulations, the amount of gain is the same, computed as follows:

Amount realized:		
Cash	$ 500	
Liabilities assumed by purchaser	400	
Total amount realized		$ 900
Less adjusted basis in membership units:		
Tax basis capital account	$ 25	
Plus $1/2$ share of LLC liabilities	400	
Total adjusted basis		(425)
Gain recognized		$ 475

Normally, the member's share of income and loss is determined on the last day of the LLC's fiscal year. However, a selling member may add to his or her basis the allocable share of income for the fiscal year up to the date of sale.[11]

¶ 1504 ALLOCATION OF INCOME AND LOSS BETWEEN BUYER AND SELLER

The LLC must allocate profit or loss between members who buy and sell membership interests during the tax year of the LLC. The tax year of the LLC does not close upon the sale or exchange of a membership interest.[12] However, the LLC's tax year closes with respect to a member who sells all of his membership interest in the LLC.[13]

Under the varying interest rule, an LLC must take into account the varying ownership interests of the members in the LLC during the tax year in making allocations of income, gain, loss, and deduction between the buyer and the seller.[14] An LLC must normally use one of the following methods to account for the members' varying interests in the LLC:

- interim closing of the books method (discussed at ¶ 807.04);
- proration method (discussed at ¶ 807.05);
- cash method for allocable cash-basis items (discussed at ¶ 807.06);
- proration method for tiered partnerships and LLCs (discussed at ¶ 807.07); or
- time-of-day method for extraordinary items (discussed at ¶ 807.08).

---

[11] Reg. § 1.706-1(c)(2).
[12] Code Sec. 706(c)(1).
[13] Code Sec. 706(c)(2)(A).
[14] Code Sec. 706(d)(1); Reg. § 1.706-1(c)(4).

¶ 1505 LIKE-KIND EXCHANGES

In order to qualify under Section 1031, a taxpayer must exchange property for other property of like kind.[15] Partnership interests do not qualify as property. The taxpayer may not exchange real estate for a membership interest, a membership interest for real estate, or a membership interest for another partnership or LLC interest, even if both entities own real estate.[16]

Like-kind exchanges are discussed at ¶1603.

¶ 1506 INVOLUNTARY CONVERSIONS AND CONDEMNATIONS

An LLC may avoid gain on an involuntary conversion by purchasing replacement property that is similar or related in service or use.[17] The LLC, rather than the members, must reinvest in similar or related property.[18]

A taxpayer may use a single-member LLC to acquire the replacement property. The acquisition of the replacement property by the LLC is treated as the acquisition of the property by the taxpayer if the LLC is classified as a disregarded entity for federal tax purposes.[19]

¶ 1507 CHARACTER OF GAIN AND LOSS

Most members report all of the gain or loss on the sale of a membership interest as capital gain or loss.[20] However, a member must divide the gain or loss into the following five categories:[21]

- Ordinary income or loss under Code Sec. 751(b) if the LLC owns hot assets (unrealized receivables and inventory items);
- 28 percent collectibles gain (but not loss) if the LLC owns collectibles held for more than one year;
- 25 percent unrecaptured Section 1250 capital gain (but not loss) if the LLC owns depreciable real estate held for more than one year;
- Residual short-term capital gain or loss if the member held the membership interest for less than one year; and
- Residual long-term capital gain or loss if the member held the membership interest for more than one year. A member also recognizes long-term capital gain on the sale of a membership interest held for less than one year to the

---

[15] Code Sec. 1031(a)(1).

[16] Code Sec. 1031(a)(2)(D).

[17] Code Sec. 1033; Ltr. Rul. 200518066.

[18] *T.K. McManus v. Comm'r*, 65 TC 197 (1975), *aff'd*, 575 F.2d 1177 (6th Cir. 1978); *M. Demirjian v. Comm'r*, 457 F.2d 1 (3d Cir. 1972); Ltr. Rul. 199935065.

[19] Ltr. Ruls. 199945038, 199909054.

[20] Code Sec. 741; Reg. § 1.741-1(a).

[21] Reg. § 1.1-1(h)-1.

extent that the member contributed capital assets to the LLC that have a combined member/LLC holding period of more than one year.[22]

The LLC must first compute the ordinary income or loss under Code Sec. 751(b).[23] The difference between the amount of capital gain or loss that a member realizes in the absence of Section 751(b) and the amount of ordinary income or loss that a member realizes under Section 751(b) is the member's capital gain or loss. Thus, the ordinary income recognized under Code Sec. 751(b) reduces the member's capital gain or increases the capital loss.[24]

.01 Category 1: Section 751 Ordinary Income or Loss—Hot Assets

The first category of gain or loss is Section 751(b) ordinary income or loss. A member recognizes ordinary income or loss if the LLC has unrealized receivables or inventory items (referred to as "hot assets").[25] These terms are defined to include many items other than unrealized receivables and inventory items.

Unrealized receivables include the following items:[26]

- Accounts receivable for goods delivered. These are unrealized receivables only to the extent that income was not previously included in income of the LLC.[27] An LLC will ordinarily not have any such receivables since an LLC that sells inventory must ordinarily use the accrual method of accounting or a hybrid method that accounts for inventory.[28]
- Unbilled fees for services.[29]
- Accounts receivable for goods to be delivered in the future.[30] These are included as unrealized receivables, even if title has not yet passed, the goods have not yet been segregated for sale to a particular customer, or the goods have not yet been made. There must be an actual contract that locks in the gain. The fair market value of the right to receive this ordinary income item may be discounted based on present value. This Section 751 item is widely ignored by taxpayers.

---

[22] Reg. § 1.1(h)-1(f), Example 5(ii).

[23] *See* Prop. Reg. § 1.751-1(b)(1)(iii).

[24] *See* Prop. Reg. § 1.751-1(g), Example 1(ii).

[25] Code Sec. 741, referring to Code Sec. 751; Reg. § 1.751-1(a)(1).

[26] Code Sec. 751(c).

[27] Reg. § 1.751-1(c)(1).

[28] *See* ¶ 1701.02 *infra.*

[29] *Logan v. Comm'r*, 51 TC 482 (1968). In that case, the court determined that a law firm's work in progress fell within the definition of Section 751(c).

[30] In *Roth v. Comm'r*, 321 F.2d 607 (9th Cir. 1963), *aff'g* 38 TC 171 (1962), a partnership that produced a movie gave Paramount Pictures distribution rights in exchange for a percentage of gross receipts. The court determined that the payment rights under the contract constituted an unrealized receivable. In *Hale v. Comm'r*, T.C. Memo. 1965-274 (1965), the court determined that a partner's right to share in future profits of a real estate development company, conditioned on the partnership's promise to perform future services, was an unrealized receivable

- Accounts receivable for services rendered or to be rendered to the extent not previously included in income of the LLC. There must be a definite right to receive the payments, rather than a mere expectancy or contract that may be terminated by the customer.
- Potential depreciation recapture under Code Secs. 1245 and 1250.[31]
- Mining property for which exploration expenses were deducted.
- Stock in a Domestic International Sales Corporation (DISC).
- Certain farm land for which soil and water conservation or land clearing expenses were deducted.
- Franchises, trademarks, or trade names.
- Oil, gas, or geothermal property for which intangible drilling and development costs were deducted.
- Stock of certain controlled foreign corporations.
- Market discount bonds and short-term obligations.

Inventory items include the following four main categories of assets:[32]

- Inventory and dealer property held primarily for sales to customers in the ordinary course of business.
- Any other property of an LLC that is not a capital asset or Section 1231 property. This includes accounts receivable for services or from the sale of inventory. However, an asset will not be treated as a Section 1231 asset to the extent there would be depreciation recapture on sale of the asset.[33]
- Foreign investment company stock subject to Code Sec. 1246(a).
- Any other property held by an LLC that would fall within one of the first three categories if held by the selling or distributee member.

Under proposed reliance regulations, the amount of ordinary income or loss realized by a member on the sale or exchange of a membership interest is equal to the ordinary income or loss that the LLC would allocate to the member if the LLC sold all its hot assets in a taxable transaction immediately prior to the transfer.[34] The ordinary income then reduces the capital gain that a member would otherwise recognize on the sale.[35]

Taxpayers may rely on Section 1.751-1(b)(2) of the proposed regulations in determining a member's share of ordinary income assets for transfers on or after December 3, 2014 if they apply the related proposed regulations consistently for all LLC sales and exchanges.[36]

---

[31] Reg. § 1.751-1(c)(4).

[32] Code Sec. 751(d).

[33] Code Sec. 64.

[34] Prop. Reg. § 1.751-1(b)(2), (g), Example 1(ii).

[35] Prop. Reg. § 1.751-1(b)(2), (g), Example 1(ii).

[36] REG-151416-06 (Nov. 3, 2014).

¶1507.01

EXAMPLE 15-3

Member B has a $1/3$ membership interest with a tax basis of $120. The LLC has a $90 zero-basis receivable. Member B sells his membership interest for $150. If the LLC had sold all of its assets in a fully taxable transaction immediately prior to the transfer of the membership interest, B would have been allocated $30 of ordinary income. Thus, Member B must recognize $30 of ordinary income under Section 751(b). Member B must then determine the capital gain. B recognizes $30 of capital gain since B received $150 of cash in excess of his $120 tax basis. However, the $30 of ordinary income under Section 751(b) reduces the capital gain from $30 to zero.[37]

.02 Category 2: 28 Percent Collectibles Gain

The second category of gain is 28 percent collectibles gain. The maximum individual tax rate on capital gains from the sale of collectibles held for more than one year is 28 percent.[38] A member recognizes gain (but not loss)[39] in this category on the sale of a membership interest to the extent that:[40]

- The LLC owns collectibles;
- The member would be allocated net gain from the sale of the collectibles if the LLC sold all of its collectibles immediately prior to the member's transfer of the membership units; and
- The member held the membership interest for more than one year. A member is treated as owning a membership interest for more than one year to the extent that a member contributes assets to the LLC that have a holding period of more than one year.[41] Thus, if a member contributed long-term capital gain assets to an LLC in exchange for 50 percent of his membership interests, and sold all his membership interests less than one year thereafter, then 50 percent of the collectibles gain attributable to the member would be classified as 28 percent collectibles gain.[42] The collectibles gain attributable the selling mem-

---

[37] Prop. Reg. § 1.751-1(g), Example 1(ii).

[38] Code Sec. 1(h)(4) and (5).

[39] Reg. § 1.1(h)-1(f), Example 3.

[40] Code Sec. 1(h)(5)(B); Reg. § 1.1(h)-1(b)(2), (f), Examples 1(iv), 2, 3, 5(iv).

[41] Under Code Sec. 1223(1), a member's holding period for the membership interest includes the holding period of capital assets and § 1231 assets that the member contributed to the LLC in exchange for a membership interest.

[42] Reg. § 1.1(h)-1(f), Example 5(iv). In such case, the 28 percent collectibles gain is determined by (a) computing the total gain that the LLC would realize if it sold all its collectibles in a taxable transaction for cash equal to the fair market value of collectibles immediately prior to the transfer of the membership interest, (b) allocating a portion of that gain to the selling member based on the member's percentage interest in the LLC (or based on a special allocation provision under the

ber is treated as collectible gain even though the LLC owned the collectibles for less than one year.[43]

EXAMPLE 15-4

There are two equal members in an LLC, Members A and B. Member B's basis in her membership interest is $10,000. Member B sells her membership interest to Member C for $50,000, more than one year after her acquisition of the membership interest. The LLC's balance sheet on the date of sale is as follows:

Asset	Tax Basis to LLC	Fair Market Value
Cash	$ 1,000	$ 1,000
Collectible 1	0	6,000
Collectible 2	1,000	0
Land held for investment	13,000	94,000
Total Assets	$15,000	$101,000

Member B first computes her net gain in the regular manner. This is $40,000 (sales price of $50,000 less basis of $10,000). Member B then determines the amount of gain that is 28 percent collectibles gain. The LLC has two collectibles that have been held for more than one year, Collectible 1 and Collectible 2. There is $5,000 of potential gain for those collectibles ($6,000 fair market value, less $1,000 basis). Member B's share of that gain is $2,500 (1/2 × $5,000). Therefore, Member B recognizes $2,500 of collectibles capital gain that is taxed at the maximum 28 percent tax rate. The balance of the gain, $37,500, is taxed at the maximum 20 percent long-term capital gain rate. There is no ordinary income since the LLC does not have unrealized receivables or inventory items.

EXAMPLE 15-5

Same facts as in the previous example, except that Member B held her membership interest for less than one year. All of the gain is taxed as short-term capital gain. No part of the gain is taxed at the maximum 28

(Footnote Continued)

operating agreement), and (c) multiplying such amount by the percentage of long-term capital assets that the member contributed to the LLC in exchange for the membership interest.

[43] Reg. § 1.1(h)-1(f), Example 5(iv). All the collectibles gain attributable to the selling member's interest in the LLC is treated as gain from the sale or exchange of a capital asset held for more than one year, whether or not the collectibles have actually been held by the LLC for more than one year. Reg. § 1.1-1(b).

¶ 1507.02

percent collectibles capital gain rate even though the LLC owned collectibles for more than one year.

.03 Category 3: 25 Percent Unrecaptured Section 1250 Gain

The third category of gain is 25 percent unrecaptured Section 1250 gain.

There are two types of Section 1250 gain. The first type of gain is ordinary income recapture. Depreciable real estate placed in service prior to 1987 could be depreciated using accelerated depreciation. If such property is held more than one year, then part of the gain on the sale is subject to recapture as ordinary income. The amount of ordinary income recapture is the excess of total depreciation deductions over the amount that would have been available under straight-line depreciation (but not in excess of the total gain).[44] This first type of Section 1250 gain is taxed in category 1 as a hot asset. It is not taxed in the third category as 25 percent gain.

The second type of Section 1250 gain is unrecaptured Section 1250 gain. This is the gain that the LLC would recognize on sale of the property up to the amount of straight-line depreciation on the property.[45] The gain is called "unrecaptured Section 1250 gain" because the gain is not subject to ordinary income recapture on sale of the property. This second type of Section 1250 gain is taxed in the third category at a 25 percent tax rate.

After 1986, depreciable real estate can only be depreciated under the straight-line method. Therefore, if the property is sold at a profit, none of the gain is recaptured as ordinary income under Code Sec. 1250. All of the gain up to the amount of the depreciation deductions is "unrecaptured Section 1250 gain" that is taxed at a maximum 25 percent capital gains rate. The balance of the gain, if any, is taxed at the maximum 20 percent capital gains rate.[46]

A member recognizes gain (but not loss) in this third category on the sale of a membership interest to the extent that:[47]

- The LLC owns depreciable real property.
- The LLC held the property for over one year.
- The gain is attributable to straight-line depreciation (including the straight-line component of depreciation on property placed in service prior to 1987 for which accelerated depreciation has been taken).
- The depreciation is less than the total potential gain. If the depreciation is more than the total potential gain, then only the depreciation equal to the potential gain is unrecaptured Section 1250 gain.

---

[44] Code Sec. 1250(b)(1). There is no Section 1250 depreciation recapture if the depreciable real property on which accelerated appreciation has been taken is held for the useful life of the property. In such case, the amount of depreciation taken under the accelerated method is equal to the amount that could have been taken using straight-line depreciation, thus eliminating any excess recapture.

[45] Code Sec. 1(h)(6).

[46] Code Sec. 1(h)(1)(D).

[47] Reg. § 1.1(h)-1(b)(3)(ii).

- The member would be allocated depreciation gain from the sale of the property if the LLC sold the property immediately prior to the transfer of the membership interest.
- The member held the membership interest for more than one year.

EXAMPLE 15-6

There are two equal members in an LLC, Members A and B. However, all of the depreciation is allocated to Member B. Member B's basis in her membership interest is $10,000. Member B sells her membership interest to Member C for $50,000, more than one year after her acquisition of the membership interest. LLC's balance sheet on the date of sale is as follows:

Asset	Tax Basis to LLC	Fair Market Value
Cash	$ 1,000	$ 1,000
Building (held more than one year; $1,000 depreciation previously taken)	3,000	11,000
Land held for investment	10,000	88,000
Total Assets	$14,000	$100,000

Member B first computes her net gain in the regular manner. This is $40,000 (sales price of $50,000 less her basis of $10,000). Member B then determines the amount of gain that is unrecaptured Section 1250 gain. The building is the only Section 1250 depreciable asset. There is $8,000 of potential gain, which exceeds the $1,000 of depreciation previously taken on the building. Therefore, gain equal to the depreciation is unrecaptured Section 1250 gain. Member B recognizes $1,000 of capital gain taxed at the maximum 25 percent rate. The balance of the gain, $39,000, is taxed at the maximum 20 percent long-term capital gain rate. There is no ordinary income since the LLC does not have unrealized receivables or inventory items.

.04 Category 4: Residual Short-Term Capital Gain and Loss

If the member sells a membership interest held for less than one year, then the gain or loss is determined as follows:[48]

---

[48] *See, e.g.,* Reg. § 1.1(h)-1(e), Example 4. In that example, the partner had a net gain of $2,500 on the sale of a partnership interest. The partner first recognized $1,500 of ordinary income equal to the partner's share of accounts receivable of the partnership. The remaining $1,000 of gain on the sale was capital gain. In the example, the partner held the partnership interests for less than one year prior to sale, but had received half of the partnership interests in exchange for long-term gain property held

- The member recognizes ordinary income or loss to the extent of the member's share of potential gain or loss on unrealized receivables and inventory items held by the LLC.
- The balance of the gain or loss is short-term capital gain or loss.
- There is no gain or loss in the 28 percent, 25 percent, or 20 percent categories even if the LLC owns collectibles, depreciable real estate or capital assets that it has held for more than one year.

EXAMPLE 15-7

There are two equal members in an LLC, Members A and B. Member B's basis in her membership interest is $10,000. Member B sells her membership interest to Member C for $50,000, less than one year after her acquisition of the membership interest. The LLC's balance sheet on the date of sale is as follows:

Asset	Tax Basis to LLC	Fair Market Value
Cash	$ 1,000	$ 1,000
Accounts Receivable	3,000	11,000
Land held for investment (held more than one year)	10,000	88,000
Total Assets	$14,000	$100,000

Member B first computes her net gain in the regular manner. This is $40,000 (sales price of $50,000 less basis of $10,000). Member B then determines the amount of gain that is Section 751 ordinary income. The amount of Section 751 ordinary income potential is $8,000 ($11,000 fair market value of receivables less LLC's basis of $3,000) Member B's share of that ordinary income potential is 50 percent of $8,000, or $4,000. Therefore, Member B recognizes $4,000 of ordinary income. The balance of the gain, $36,000, is short-term capital gain.

.05 Category 5: Residual Long-Term Capital Gain and Loss

The balance of gain or loss on the sale of a membership interest is long-term capital gain or loss.[49] This gain is normally taxed as follows:

(Footnote Continued)

by the partner for over one year. Therefore, $1/2$ of the residual capital gain on sale ($500) was short-term capital gain, and $1/2$ of the residual capital gain was long-term capital gain.

[49] Reg. § 1.1(h)-1(a), (c).

Effective date	Maximum long-term capital gains rate for individuals, trusts, and estates for regular and alternative minimum tax purposes
After May 5, 2003 and prior to 2013	15 percent for individuals in the 25 percent rate bracket and above
2013 tax year and subsequent years	20 percent for individuals in the 39.6 percent rate bracket* plus 3.8 percent NII tax on income above the Additional Medicare Tax threshold amounts ($250,000 for surviving spouses and married couples filing joint returns, $125,000 for married couples filing separate returns, and $200,000 for single persons and all other persons)

* Code Sec. 1(h)(1)(D).

The total gain and loss in all five categories must equal the net gain or loss from the sale of the membership interest. The ordinary income recognized by a member under Code Sec. 751(b) on the sale of a membership interest reduces the capital gain that a member recognizes on the sale.[50]

¶ 1508 SECTION 754 ELECTION

.01 Overview

An LLC may make an election under Code Sec. 754 to adjust the basis of the LLC's assets when a member sells or exchanges a membership interest or transfers a membership interest upon death. If the election is made, the LLC will then compute depreciation and gain or loss upon the disposition of the assets with reference to the adjusted basis.

The basis adjustment may be upward or downward depending on the sale price. The amount of basis adjustment is the difference between the member's share of the LLC's inside basis in its assets and the member's outside basis in his membership interest. The basis adjustment for the buyer is roughly equal to the gain recognized by the selling member upon the sale, exchange, or other transfer.

The adjustment applies only for tax purposes, and has no effect on the book income of the LLC.

.02 Making the Election

An LLC may adjust the basis of its assets upon the sale or transfer of a membership interest only if it makes an election under Code Sec. 754. The adjustment

---

[50] Prop. Reg. § 1.751-1(b)(2), (g), Example 1(ii).

is made under Section 743(b).[51] The election is made at the LLC level rather than by the members.

The LLC must make the election in the following manner:

- The LLC must file an election statement with its return for the year in which the election is first made. The statement must include (i) the name and address of the LLC, (ii) a declaration that the LLC elects under Section 754 to apply the provisions of Sections 734(b) and 743(b), and (iii) the signature of a member authorized to sign the LLC return.[52]

- The LLC must check Box 12a of Form 1065, Schedule B.

- The LLC must check Box 12b of Form 1065, Schedule B, and attach a statement showing the computation of allocation of the basis adjustment.

- The LLC must report the basis adjustments on Schedule K and the transferee member's Schedule K-1. The LLC must report the adjustments on a Statement to Schedule K-1 using the codes for Other Income or Other Deductions. The LLC must identify the item being adjusted and the amount of the adjustment. The adjustments do not affect the transferee's member's capital account.[53]

The election must be made with a timely return for the tax year of the LLC[54] or an amended return.[55] The LLC may receive an automatic 12-month extension to make the election if it takes corrective action[56] within 12 months of the original deadline for making the election.[57] The LLC may also request a letter ruling from the IRS for a late election or non-automatic extension of time to make the election.[58] The IRS will not grant an extension if the LLC did not act reasonably, or if any tax years that would have been affected by a timely Section 754 election are closed by the statute of limitations.[59]

Once the election is made, it applies to all sales, exchanges, and distributions until the election is terminated.[60] The district director of the Internal Revenue Service

---

[51] Reg. § 1.754-1.

[52] *See* Instructions to Form 1065 under the heading, "Elections Made by the Partnership."

[53] *See* Instructions to Form 1065 under the heading, "Effect of Section 743(b) Basis Adjustment on Partnership Items."

[54] Reg. § 1.754-1(b).

[55] Reg. § 301.9100-2.

[56] Corrective action means that the LLC must file the return or election in accordance with the regulations under which the election or return must be filed. The return must state at the top of the form, "FILED PURSUANT TO SECTION 301.9100-2." The returns of all members affected by the regulation must be filed in a manner consistent with the election having been made. Reg. § 301.9100-2(c)(a)(2)(vi).

[57] Reg. § 301.9100-2.

[58] Reg. § 1.754-1(b)(1); Ltr. Ruls. 201719006, 201626007, 201505026, 201505024, 201410024, 201410023, 201129030, 201129024, 201122015, 201122011, 201013025, 201012032, 201012031, 200922007, 200921006, 200908018, 200838006, 200835007, 200827031, 200826027, 200817026, 200815008, 200806001, 200802001, 200721005, 200550003, 200548002, 200348016; Rev. Proc. 92-85, 1992-2 CB 69 (automatic extensions).

[59] Ltr. Rul. 200917018.

[60] Reg. § 1.754-1(a).

must approve any revocations of the election.[61] The district director may grant a revocation based on a change in the nature of the LLC's trade or business, a substantial increase in assets, a change in the nature of its assets, increasing administrative burden, or other valid business reasons.[62]

.03 Tax Consequences

The Section 743 basis adjustment is an adjustment for the transferee only.[63] The adjustment has the following tax consequences:

- The increased portion of the basis for depreciable property is treated as newly purchased depreciable property placed in service when the transfer occurs. Consequently, any applicable recovery period and method may be used to determine the depreciation for the increased portion of the basis.[64] The LLC must separately list the Section 754 asset on its schedule of depreciable assets, and show the depreciation for the Section 754 asset.[65] It must make a special allocation of this depreciation only to the transferee member for tax purposes, and not for capital account purposes. There is no change in the depreciation method or recovery period for the portion of the basis that has not been increased.[66] During the years following the transfer, the transferee receives a tax allocation of the member's share of common basis depreciation, and all of the tax depreciation on the increased basis.[67]

- A negative basement adjustment to depreciable property decreases the transferee's distributive share of LLC tax depreciation deductions.[68] The decrease in basis must be accounted for over the remaining depreciation period of the property beginning with the depreciation period in which the basis is decreased.[69]

- The LLC must compute book income and loss without regard to the basis adjustment. It must allocate all book items to the members' capital accounts in accordance with the operating agreement.

---

[61] Reg. § 1.754-1(c).

[62] Reg. § 1.754-1(c).

[63] Reg. § 1.743-1(b).

[64] Reg. § 1.743-1(j)(4)(i).

[65] Reg. § 1.743-1(b)(1).

[66] Reg. § 1.743-1(j)(4(i)(B)(1). There are special rules if the LLC uses the remedial allocation method with respect to depreciable property. Reg. § 1.743-1(j)(4(i)(B)(2).

[67] Reg. § 1.743-1(j)(4(i)(C), Example 1.

[68] Reg. § 1.743-1(j)(4)(ii)(A).

[69] Reg. § 1.743-1(j)(4)(ii)(B). The portion of the decrease that is recovered in each year during the recovery period is the product of (i) the amount of decrease to the property's adjusted basis determined on the date of the transfer, (ii) multiplied by a fraction. The numerator of the fraction is the portion of the adjusted basis of the item recovered by the LLC in that year, and the denominator is the adjusted basis of the property on the date of transfer determined before any basis adjustments.

- The basis adjustment does not change the members' capital accounts.[70] The basis adjustment may not be reflected in the transferee member's capital account or on the books of the LLC under the safe-harbor rules. The basis adjustment must also be disregarded in determining adjustments to the members' capital accounts to reflect depreciation, gain and loss for property with an adjusted basis.[71]

- When the LLC sells the property, it must compute its book gain and loss on the sale without regard to the basis adjustment. It must allocate tax gain or loss attributable to the basis adjustment in excess of the book gain or loss to the transferee member.

- A member who receives a nonliquidating distribution from an LLC receives a carryover basis for the distributed property equal to the LLC's basis immediately prior to the distribution. The member may include the Section 754 basis adjustment in the basis of the distributed assets. If the LLC adjusts the basis of its assets for one member, and then distributes those assets to another member, the LLC must take the adjustment off of the distributed assets, and reallocate the basis adjustment to remaining LLC property of like kind[72] in proportion to the relative appreciation in those assets. This reallocated basis adjustment benefits only the member with respect to whom the initial basis adjustment was made.

.04 Determining Basis Adjustment

The LLC must increase the basis of its assets if the purchasing member's basis for the membership interest exceeds the member's share of the adjusted basis of LLC assets.[73] The LLC must decrease the basis of its assets if the purchasing member's basis for the membership interest is less than the member's share of the adjusted basis of LLC assets.[74] The basis adjustment is the difference between the inside and outside basis.

A member's share of the adjusted basis of LLC assets is determined by reference to a hypothetical sale of LLC's assets. The LLC is treated as having sold all of its

---

[70] *See* Instructions to Form 1065 under the heading, "Effect of Section 743(b) Basis Adjustment on Partnership Items."

[71] Reg. § 1.704-1(b)(2)(iv)(m)(2), (3).

[72] The determination of like-kind assets for such purposes is much narrower than a Class 1 or Class 2 determination. Like-kind assets are broken down into groups such as inventory, accounts receivable, capital assets and depreciable assets. Thus, if there had been an optional adjustment to basis for depreciable real property which was distributed to another member, then the optional adjustment that is taken off of the property may not be reallocated to other nondepreciable real property. If there is no like-kind property to which the optional adjustment to basis can be allocated, then the adjustment will be applied to subsequently acquired property of a like character when the LLC acquires additional property. Code Sec. 755(b).

[73] Code Sec. 743(b)(1); Reg. § 1.743-1(b)(1).

[74] Code Sec. 743(b)(2); Reg. § 1.743-1(b)(2).

assets for fair market value for cash in a fully taxable transaction.[75] The purchasing member's share of the adjusted basis of LLC assets is (a) the cash that the purchasing member would receive if the LLC were liquidated after the hypothetical sale, (b) plus the purchasing member's share of LLC liabilities, (c) plus the amount of any tax losses that would be allocated to the purchasing member in the hypothetical sale, (d) less the amount of any tax gain that would be allocated to the purchasing member in the hypothetical sale.

EXAMPLE 15-8

An LLC has three equal members, Members A, B, and C. Member C sells her membership interest to Member T for $22,000 cash. The balance sheet of the LLC shows the following:[76]

Asset	Tax Basis to LLC	Fair Market Value
Cash	$ 5,000	$ 5,000
Accounts receivable	10,000	10,000
Inventory	20,000	21,000
Depreciable asset	20,000	40,000
Total assets	$55,000	$76,000

Liabilities and Capital Accounts		
Liabilities	$10,000	$10,000
Capital accounts		
A	15,000	22,000
B	15,000	22,000
C	15,000	22,000
	$55,000	$76,000

There is a short-cut method of determining the Section 743(b) basis adjustment if the LLC determines the capital accounts of its members on a tax basis. The basis adjustment is the difference between the purchase price (ignoring liabilities and debt relief) and the selling member's tax basis capital account. In this case, the basis adjustment is the $22,000 cash purchase price, less Member B's tax basis capital account of $15,000, or $7,000. Therefore, the LLC must increase the tax basis of its assets by $7,000.

---

[75] Reg. § 1.743-1(d)(2).
[76] Reg. § 1.743-1(d)(3), Example 1.

Under the regulations, the basis adjustment would be determined as follows:[77]

1. Determine the purchasing member's basis in her membership interest.

Cash	$22,000
Liabilities assumed ($1/3$ share of $10,000 liabilities of LLC)	3,333
Member T's adjusted basis	$25,333

2. Determine the purchasing member's share of the adjusted basis of LLC assets.
   (a) Determine the cash the LLC would receive after the transfer if it sold all of its assets at fair market value of $76,000 for cash, less $10,000 of liabilities. — $66,000
   (b) Determine the purchasing member's share of cash that would be received by her in liquidation after the hypothetical sale ($1/3$ of $66,000). — $22,000
   (c) Determine the gain or loss that the LLC would realize in the hypothetical sale of assets. This is equal to the $76,000 sale price/fair market value of the assets, less the LLC's $55,000 adjusted basis in its assets. — $21,000
   (d) Determine the gain or loss that would be allocated to the purchasing member after the hypothetical sale ($1/3$ of $21,000 gain). — $ 7,000
   (e) Decrease the purchasing member's $22,000 share of cash proceeds from the hypothetical sale by the purchasing member's $7,000 share of the gain from the hypothetical sale (or increase the cash share by the member's share of loss). — $15,000
   (f) Add the purchasing member's share of LLC liabilities ($1/3$ of $10,000). — $ 3,333
   (h) The purchasing member's share of adjusted basis of LLC assets. — $18,333

---

[77] This example is set forth in Reg. § 1.743-1(d)(3), Example 1.

3. Determine the Section 743 basis adjustment.

> This is equal to the difference between the purchasing member's $25,333 adjusted basis in her membership interest, determined under step 1, and her $18,333 share of the adjusted basis of LLC assets, determined under step 2. $ 7,000

Therefore, the LLC must increase the basis of its assets by $7,000.

.05 Allocation of Basis Adjustment to LLC Assets

After the Section 743(b) basis adjustment is determined, the LLC must allocate the basis adjustment to its assets. This is a three-step process. First, the LLC must determine the fair market value of each asset. Second, the LLC must allocate the basis adjustment between two classes of assets, capital gain property and ordinary income property. Third, the LLC must allocate the basis adjustment for each class to each item of property within that class.[78]

Valuation of Assets

The first step is to determine the fair market value of each LLC asset. The LLC must value the assets on the basis of all the facts and circumstances. The fair market value of each asset cannot be less than the amount of any nonrecourse debt encumbering the asset.[79] The residual method of valuing assets no longer applies. The fair market value of each asset is determined independently of the purchase price of the membership interest.

EXAMPLE 15-9

An LLC has two assets: inventory valued at $1 million and a building valued at $2 million. John purchases a 1/3 interest in the LLC for $800,000. There is a $200,000 discount in the purchase price because John is acquiring a minority interest. The fair market value of the assets for Section 754 purposes is $1 million for the inventory and $2 million for the building.

There is a special rule if the LLC has Section 197 intangibles.[80] In such case, the LLC must determine the gross value of LLC assets. The gross value is the net proceeds that the LLC would have to receive from the sale of its assets so that the LLC could pay its liabilities in full and distribute to the purchasing member the

---

[78] Reg. § 1.755-1(a)(1).
[79] Reg. § 1.755-1(a)(3).
[80] Reg. § 1.755-1(a)(2), (5).

amount that the member paid for the membership interest (ignoring the purchase price attributable to the purchasing member's assumption of LLC liabilities).[81] If the gross value of LLC assets is less than the fair market value of LLC assets other than the Section 197 intangibles, then the Section 197 intangibles are valued at zero. If the gross value of LLC assets is higher than the fair market value of LLC assets other than the Section 197 intangibles, then the Section 197 intangibles are valued at the excess amount.[82]

EXAMPLE 15-10

An LLC has three assets: inventory valued at $1 million, a building valued at $2 million, and a Section 197 intangible (customer list purchased from another company for $500,000). John purchases a $1/3$ interest in the LLC for $800,000. The fair market value of the Section 197 intangible is zero for Section purposes because the gross value of LLC assets is less than the fair market value of LLC assets other than the Section 197 intangibles. The gross value of LLC assets is $2.4 million. This is the net amount that the LLC would have to receive from the sale of its assets so that the LLC could distribute $800,000 to John ($1/3$ of $2.4 million). Thus, the fair market value of the assets for Section 754 purposes is $1 million for the inventory and $2 million for the building.

EXAMPLE 15-11

Same facts as in prior example except that John purchases a $1/3$ interest in the LLC for $1,100,000. The gross value of LLC assets is $3.3 million. This is the net amount that the LLC would have to receive from the sale of its assets so that the LLC could distribute $1.1 million to John ($1/3$ of $3.3 million sales price). Since the gross value of LLC assets exceeds the fair market value of LLC assets other than the Section 197 intangibles by $300,000, the LLC must value the Section 197 intangible at $300,000 for Section 754 purposes. Thus, the fair market value of the assets for Section 754 purposes is $1 million for the inventory, $2 million for the building, and $300,000 for the Section 197 intangible.

---

[81] Reg. § 1.755-1(a)(4).
[82] Reg. § 1.755-1(a)(5).

Allocation between Classes

The second step is to allocate the basis adjustment between two classes of assets, capital gain property, and ordinary income property.

The amount of basis adjustment allocated to the ordinary income property is the total amount of income, gain, or loss that would be allocated to the transferee if the LLC disposed of all of its assets in a fully taxable transaction at fair market value immediately after the transfer. The amount of basis adjustment allocated to the capital gain property is the remainder of the Section 743 basis adjustment.[83]

The amount of basis adjustment allocated to one class may be an increase even if the amount of basis adjustment allocated to the other class is a decrease. However, any decrease in basis allocated to the capital gain property class may not exceed the LLC's basis in the capital gain property class. If there is a decrease in basis in excess of the LLC's basis in the capital gain property, the excess amount is applied to reduce the basis of ordinary income property.[84]

EXAMPLE 15-12

An LLC has two equal members.[85] Member A contributes $50,000 and Asset 1 to the LLC. Asset 1 is a capital gain asset with an initial fair market value of $50,000 and a tax basis of $25,000. Member B contributes $100,000 to the LLC. The LLC uses cash to purchase Assets 2, 3, and 4. After one year, Member A sells her membership interest to Member T for $120,000. The LLC determines that Member T should receive an upward $45,000 basis adjustment under Section 743(b). Immediately after the sale, the adjusted bases and fair market values of the LLC's assets are as follows:

Asset	Adjusted Basis	Fair Market Value
Capital Gain Property:		
Asset 1	$ 25,000	$ 75,000
Asset 2	100,000	117,500
Ordinary Income Property:		
Asset 3	40,000	45,000
Asset 4	10,000	2,500
Total	$175,000	$240,000

The $45,000 upward basis adjustment for Member T is allocated between the classes of assets as follows:

---

[83] Reg. § 1.755-1(b)(1)(ii).

[84] Reg. § 1.755-1(b)(2).

[85] This example is from Reg. § 1.755-1(b)(2)(ii), Example 1.

Step 1: Divide the assets between capital gain property and ordinary income property.

Step 2: Determine the amount of gain that the LLC would recognize if it sold all of its assets in a fully taxable transaction at fair market value immediately after the transfer of the membership interest from Member A to Member T. The total gain would be $65,000, equal to the difference between the $240,000 fair market value of the assets and the $175,000 adjusted basis of the assets.

Step 3: Divide the gain between the capital gain property and the ordinary income property. There would be $67,000 of capital gain for the capital gain property and $2,500 of ordinary loss for the ordinary income property. This is based on the difference between the fair market value and the adjusted basis of assets for each class.

Step 4: Determine the amount of capital gain that would be allocated to Member T from the sale of the capital gain property. This is $46,250. This amount is equal to $25,000 of the built-in gain from Asset 1, plus 50 percent of the remaining $42,500 of appreciation in the capital gain property. Since Member A contributed appreciated property to the LLC, the member or her successor in interest is taxed on the $25,000 of built-in gain when the LLC sells the property. The remaining gain is divided equally.

Step 5: Determine the amount of ordinary income or loss that would be allocated to Member T upon the sale of the ordinary income property. This is $1,250, representing 50 percent of the $2,500 ordinary loss from the sale of ordinary income property.

Step 6: Allocate the basis adjustment to each class based on the gain or loss that the purchasing member would recognize if the LLC sold the assets. The basis increase for the capital gain property is $46,250. The basis decrease for the ordinary income property is $1,250. The net amount of increase and decrease for both classes, $45,000, is equal to the $45,000 basis increase adjustment.

Allocation within Classes

After the basis adjustment is allocated between the two classes, the LLC must allocate the basis adjustment within each class to each asset within that class. The basis adjustment is allocated to the assets within each class based on the amount of gain or loss that the transferee member would recognize on a hypothetical sale. The basis adjustment allocated to some assets within a class may be an increase, and the basis adjustment allocated to other assets within the same class may be a decrease.[86]

---

[86] Reg. § 1.755-1(b)(3).

The basis decrease to any item of capital gain property may not exceed the LLC's basis in that item. Any excess amount must be applied to reduce the remaining basis of other capital gain assets pro rata in proportion to the LLC's adjusted basis in such assets.[87]

EXAMPLE 15-13

Same facts as in the prior example. Of the $45,000 basis adjustment, $46,250 of gain was allocated as a basis increase to the capital gain property and $1,250 of loss was allocated as a basis decrease to the ordinary income property. The amount of basis increase or decrease is then allocated to the assets within each class based on the amount of gain or loss that the transferee member would recognize in a hypothetical sale even though the gain or loss exceeds the total amount of gain or loss allocable to that particular class. Therefore, the basis adjustment for Member T for the LLC's assets is allocated as follows:

- There is a $37,500 basis increase for Asset 1, since Member T would be allocated $37,500 of gain from the sale of that asset.

- There is an $8,750 basis increase for Asset 2, since Member T would be allocated $8,750 of capital gain from the sale of that asset. The total basis increase for class I assets (Asset 1 and Asset 2) is $46,250.

- There is a $2,500 basis increase for Asset 3 (ordinary income property), since Member T would receive an allocation of $2,500 of ordinary income from the sale of Asset 3. This is equal to 50 percent of the $5,000 of appreciation for Asset 3. There is a positive basis increase even though there is a net basis decrease of $1,250 for all of the ordinary income property.

- There is a basis decrease of $3,750 for Asset 4, since Member T would receive an allocation of $3,750 of loss from the sale of Asset 4 in the hypothetical transaction. This is equal to 50 percent of the $7,500 of ordinary loss from the hypothetical sale of Asset 4. The total basis adjustment for the ordinary income property is a net decrease of $1,250 ($2,500 increase for Asset 3 and $3,750 decrease for Asset 4).

In certain limited cases, the amount of gain or loss that would be allocated to a member on a hypothetical sale of assets at fair market value within a class is not exactly equal to the basis adjustment that must be made for the member within that

---

[87] Reg. § 1.755-1(b)(3)(iii)(B).

class.[88] In such case, a proportionate adjustment must be made based on the fair market value of the assets within each class.[89]

Special Allocations

If there are special allocations within an LLC, then the step-up in basis is allocated only to the assets in which the transferor or deceased partner had an interest.[90]

.06 Distribution of Section 743(b) Assets

An LLC may distribute a Section 743(b) asset to the member for whom the basis adjustment was made or to another member. In a nonliquidating distribution, each member receives a carryover basis, which cannot exceed the member's basis in his membership interest.[91] If the LLC distributes the Section 743(b) asset to the member for whom the special basis adjustment was made, the member's basis includes the Section 743(b) special basis adjustment. If the LLC distributes the Section 743(b) asset to another member, the special basis adjustment is transferred to property of like kind that is still owned by the LLC and continues to benefit only the same member.[92] The Section 743(b) basis adjustment may benefit only the member who acquires a membership interest that results in the basis adjustment.

The LLC may also distribute Section 743(b) property to a member in a liquidating distribution. The member receives a substituted basis when the LLC makes a liquidating distribution of property. The basis of LLC assets distributed to the member is the same as the member's adjusted basis in his membership interest in the LLC, reduced by any money received in the distribution. Therefore, the Section 743(b) basis adjustment has no effect on the total basis of property received by the member. The Section 743(b) basis adjustment will affect only how the basis is allocated among the distributed properties. The regulations require that the allocation be made in proportion to the relative bases of the assets to the LLC. This includes a special basis adjustment under Section 743(b).

---

[88] This may occur when the LLC is initially allocating the basis adjustment between the two classes of assets (rather than within each class of assets). Any decrease in basis allocated to the capital gain property class may not exceed the LLC's basis in the capital gain property class. If there is a decrease in basis in excess of the LLC's basis in the capital gain property, the excess is applied to reduce the basis of ordinary income property. The resulting decreased amount of basis adjustment for the capital gain property class are increased amount of basis adjustment for the ordinary income property class are then allocated to the assets within each class based on the fair market value of the assets within that class.

[89] Reg. § 1.755-1(b)(3).

[90] Reg. § 1.755-1(b)(3)(iii), (iv).

[91] Code Sec. 732(a).

[92] Reg. § 1.743-1(b)(2)(ii).

The LLC succeeds to the entire Section 743(b) basis adjustment as part of its common basis if it makes a liquidating distribution to the member entirely in cash.[93]

.07 Tiered LLCs

A transfer of a membership interest by a member of an upper-tier LLC results in a basis adjustment for property in a lower-tier partnership or LLC in which the upper-tier LLC has an interest only if both the upper-tier LLC and lower-tier LLC have made an election under Code Sec. 754.[94]

¶ 1509 MANDATORY BASIS ADJUSTMENTS FOR LLC WITH BUILT-IN LOSSES

.01 Sale or Exchange of Membership Interest

An LLC must make a mandatory downward basis adjustment to its property under Code Sec. 743(b) if:[95]

- The member sells or exchanges a membership interest or the member dies.
- The LLC has a substantial built-in loss at such time. An LLC has a substantial built-in loss if (i) the LLC's adjusted basis in LLC property exceeds the fair market value of such property by more than $250,000, or (ii) the transferee member would receive a loss allocation of more than $250,000 if the LLC sold its assets for cash at fair market value immediately after the transfer.[96]
- The LLC has not made an election under Code Sec. 754.

An LLC makes the mandatory basis adjustment by checking Box 12b on Form 1065, Schedule B, and attaching a statement showing the computation and allocation of the basis adjustment.[97]

The LLC must make the basis adjustment only with respect to the transferee member. The amount of the downward basis adjustment is equal to the difference between the transferee member's proportionate share of the adjusted basis of LLC property and the transferee's basis in the membership interest.[98] As a result of the rule, the transferee recognizes no loss if the LLC sells its property for fair market value after the transfer.

---

[93] Reg. § 1.743-2(b)(1).

[94] Rev. Rul. 87-115, 1987-2 CB 163.

[95] Code Sec. 743(a), (b)(2), (d). *See also Santa Monica Pictures, LLC v. Comm'r*, T.C. Memo. 2005-104, fn. 81 (2005) in which the court noted that, prior to the American Jobs Creation Act of 2004, if a contributing member of an LLC transferred his membership interest, built-in gain or loss was allocated to the transferee member to the same extent it would have been allocated to the transferor member pursuant to Reg. § 1.704-3(a)(7).

[96] Code Sec. 704(d).

[97] *See* Instructions to Form 1065.

[98] Code Sec. 743(b)(2).

EXAMPLE 15-14

Jane and John are equal members in an LLC. The LLC has not made an election under Section 754 to adjust the basis of its assets on the sale of a membership interest. The LLC has assets with a basis of $1 million and a fair market value of $200,000. It has no liabilities. John sells his 50-percent membership interest in the LLC to Ben for $100,000.

The LLC must make a downward adjustment in the basis of its assets because the basis of LLC assets exceeds the fair market value of its assets by more than $250,000 immediately prior to the transfer.

The amount of the downward basis adjustment is $400,000. This is equal to the difference between Ben's 50 percent share of the adjusted basis of LLC assets after the transfer ($500,000) and Ben's basis in his membership interest ($100,000 purchase price).

The downward basis adjustment applies only to Ben as the transferee member. If the LLC sells its assets for $200,000 immediately after the transfer, Jane will recognize a $400,000 loss. Ben will recognize no loss as a result of the downward basis adjustment in the LLC assets.

The transferee member must provide written notice to the LLC within 30 days after the sale.[99] The LLC must attach a statement to its return for the year of the transfer.[100]

.02 Contribution of Built-In Loss Property

An LLC must also make a mandatory basis adjustment under Code Sec. 704(c)(1)(C) if a member contributes property to an LLC with built-in losses. The LLC's tax basis in the property with respect to the noncontributing members may not exceed the fair market value of the property on the date of contribution. The contributing member recognizes the built-in losses on sale or other disposition of the membership interest. If the contributing member transfers the membership interest, the LLC's special basis adjustment for the contributed property is eliminated.[101] The basis adjustment under Code Sec. 704(c)(1)(C) is discussed at ¶ 806.

¶ 1510 CAPITAL ACCOUNTS

The capital account of a transferee of a membership interest is determined as follows:

- *General rule.* The general rule is that the transferee succeeds to the capital account of the transferor.[102]

---

[99] IRS Notice 2005-32, 2005-1 CB 895, Sec. 8, Example 1, referring to the written notice described in Reg. § 1.743-1(k)(2); IRS Notice 2005-32, Sec. 8, Example A.

[100] IRS Notice 2005-32, 2005-1 CB 895, Sec. 8, Example 1, referring to the written statement described in Reg. § 1.743-1(k)(1); IRS Notice 2005-32, Sec. 8, Example A.

[101] Prop. Reg. § 1.704-3(f)(3)(iii)(A).

[102] Reg. § 1.704-1(b)(2)(iv)(1).

- *Built-in gain or loss.* If a contributing member transfers a membership interest, built-in gain or loss must be allocated to the transferee member as it would have been allocated to the transferor member. If the contributing member transfers a portion of the membership interest, the share of built-in gain or loss proportionate to the interest transferred must be allocated to the transferee member.[103]

- *Technical termination.* If the transfer causes a technical termination of the LLC under Code Sec. 708(b)(1)(B), the transferee's capital account must be adjusted in accordance with Treas. Reg. §1.704-1(b)(2)(iv)(e) and the constructive liquidation rules under Treas. Reg. §1.708-1(b)(1)(iv). The basic capital accounting rule is that the capital accounts of all members must be adjusted to reflect the manner in which the unrealized income, gain, loss, and deduction inherent in LLC property would be allocated to the members had there been a taxable disposition of the property for fair market value.[104]

- *IRC §743.* There is no adjustment to a member's capital account as a result of a basis adjustment under Code Secs. 743 and 754.[105] Any adjustments previously made to the transferor's tax basis of LLC property are not reflected in the capital account of the transferee member or on the books of the LLC. In addition, the subsequent adjustments for depreciation, depletion, amortization, and gain or loss with regard to those basis adjustments are disregarded.[106]

- *IRC §732.* If the LLC has not made a Section 754 election, the LLC may still be required to adjust the basis of LLC property under Code Sec. 732(d). There is no adjustment to a transferee member's capital account as a result of a basis adjustment under Code Sec. 732.[107]

- *IRC §734 liquidating distribution.* If the LLC has a Section 754 election in effect in the case of a liquidating distribution of property, the member whose interest is liquidated will have a corresponding adjustment to his or her capital account. However, if the property to which the adjustment relates has already been booked up, and if the members' capital accounts have already been adjusted to reflect the book-up, no further adjustment is permitted on a subsequent transfer.[108]

- *IRC §734 non-liquidating distribution.* If the LLC has a Section 754 election in effect in the case of a non-liquidating distribution of property, the capital accounts of all members are adjusted to reflect the manner in which the gain

---

[103] Reg. §1.704-3(a)(7).
[104] Reg. §1.704-1(b)(2)(iv)(l).
[105] *See* ¶1508.03.
[106] Reg. §1.704-1(b)(2)(iv)(m)(2).
[107] Reg. §1.704-1(b)(2)(iv)(m)(3).
[108] Reg. §1.704-1(b)(2)(iv)(m)(4).

or loss would have been allocated had the property been sold by the LLC for its re-computed adjusted basis.[109]

¶ 1511 ABANDONMENT, FORFEITURE, AND WORTHLESSNESS

There are three ways that a member can surrender his or her interest in an LLC: worthlessness; abandonment; and forfeiture.

.01 Worthlessness

A member recognizes ordinary loss when the membership interest becomes worthless if (i) the transaction is not a sale or exchange, and (ii) the member does not receive an actual or deemed distribution from the LLC.[110] The determination of worthlessness has both objective and subjective elements.[111]

A member recognizes capital loss on worthlessness of a membership interest if the member receives a deemed distribution, debt relief, or any other assets in connection with the worthlessness.[112]

.02 Abandonment

Abandonment occurs when the member abandons the membership interest completely and receives nothing in return. There must be some overt act on the part of the member to abandon the membership interest.[113]

A member recognizes ordinary loss when a member abandons a membership interest if (i) the transaction is not a sale or exchange, and (ii) the member does not receive an actual or deemed distribution from the LLC.[114]

A member recognizes capital loss if the member receives even a de minimis actual or deemed distribution. For example, a member recognizes capital loss if the membership interest includes an allocation of debt for which the member does not remain liable after the abandonment. The member will have received a deemed distribution under Section 752(b) on surrender of the membership interest. The abandonment will in such case be treated as a sale of a capital asset resulting in capital loss.[115] Even a de minimis amount of consideration for the membership

---

[109] Reg. § 1.704-1(b)(2)(iv)(m)(4).

[110] *Echols v. Comm'r*, 935 F.2d 703 (5th Cir. 1991); IRS Publication 541, Partnerships, under the subheading, "Abandoned or worthless partnership interest."

[111] *Echols v. Comm'r*, 935 F.2d 703 (5th Cir. 1991).

[112] *See* Rev. Rul. 93-80, 1993-2 CB 239.

[113] *Citron v. Comm'r*, 97 TC 200 (1991); IRS Market Segment Specialization Program, Partnerships, Audit Technique Guide, Chapter 7, under the heading, "Abandonment of a Partnership Interest."

[114] Rev. Rul. 93-80, 1993-2 CB 239; *Citron v. Comm'r*, 97 TC 200 (1991); *Echols v. Comm'r*, 935 F.2d 703 (5th Cir. 1991); IRS Publication 541, Partnerships, under the subheading, "Abandoned or worthless partnership interest."

[115] *O'Brien v. Comm'r*, 77 TC 113 (1981), *aff'd per curiam* 693 F.2d 124 (11th Cir. 1982).

interest will make the abandonment a sale.[116] The loss recognized on abandonment is the member's unrecovered basis.

A member recognizes gain on abandonment if (i) the member was relieved of liabilities in excess of his or her basis in the membership interest, or (ii) the LLC has hot assets (ordinary income assets) at the time of abandonment.[117]

.03 Forfeiture

A forfeiture of a membership interest may occur if the member fails to pay required amounts for the membership interest or otherwise breaches the terms of the operating agreement. A forfeiture of the membership interest normally has the same tax consequences as an abandonment.[118] A member recognizes an ordinary loss if the member receives no debt relief or any other consideration. A member recognizes a capital loss if the member receives any consideration.

¶1512 REPORTING REQUIREMENTS

.01 Hot Asset Reporting Requirements

The parties must comply with the following notification and reporting require-ments if the selling member recognizes Section 751 ordinary income or loss, 28 percent collectibles gain, or 25 percent unrecaptured Section 1250 gain:

- The selling member must notify the LLC within 30 days after the sale or exchange, or by January 15 of the following year, if earlier.[119] The notification must include the names and addresses of the transferor and transferee, the taxpayer identification numbers of the transferor and the transferee, if known, and the date of the sale or exchange.

- The LLC must file an information return on Form 8308, Report of a Sale or Exchange of Certain Partnership Interests, if the LLC has Section 751 ordinary income property.[120] The LLC must file the form as part of the partnership return on Form 1065. The form must identify the buying and selling members, and provide such other information as required by the IRS. The form does not require the LLC to provide information regarding the amount of ordinary income, 28 percent collectibles gain, or 25 percent unrecaptured Section 1250 gain on the sale of a membership interest. The LLC must disclose this

---

[116] *La Rue v. Comm'r*, 90 TC 465 (1988).

[117] IRS Audit Technique Guide—Partnerships, Chapter 7, under the heading, "Abandonment of a Partnership Interest."

[118] IRS Market Segment Specialization Program, Partnerships, Audit Technique Guide, Chapter 7, under the heading, "Abandonment of a Partnership Interest."

[119] Code Sec. 6050K(c)(1); Reg. §§ 1.1(h)-1(e), 1.751-1(a)(3), 1.6050K-1(d)(1).

[120] Code Sec. 6050K.

information to the buying and selling member before January 31 of the following calendar year.[121]

- The selling member must submit with his or her income tax return a statement setting forth the date of the sale or exchange, the amount of any gain or loss attributable to the Section 751 property, and the amount of any gain or loss attributable to capital gain or loss on the sale of the LLC interest.[122]

There is a $50 penalty if the member fails to furnish the required information to the LLC. If the failure is due to intentional disregard, the penalty is the greater of $100 or ten percent of the aggregate amount to be reported.[123]

.02 Section 754 Reporting Requirements

The parties must comply with the following notification and reporting requirements if the LLC has made an election under Section 754:

- The buyer must notify the LLC within 30 days after the sale or exchange. The written notice must be signed under penalty of perjury. It must include the names and addresses of the buyer and the seller (if ascertainable), the taxpayer identification numbers of the buyer and the seller (if ascertainable), the relationship between the buyer and seller, if any, the date of transfer, the amount of any liabilities assumed or taken subject to by the buyer, the amount of cash and the fair market value of any other property paid for the LLC interest, and any other information necessary for the LLC to compute the buyer's basis.[124]
- The LLC must attach a statement to the LLC return showing the computation of the basis adjustment under Section 743(b), the LLC properties to which the adjustment is allocated, and the name and taxpayer identification number of the buyer.[125]

.03 NII Tax Reporting Requirements

A person who sells or disposes of a membership interest must attach a Statement of Adjustment to his or her return if the member is subject to the 3.8 percent NII tax.[126] The statement must report the gain or loss subject to the NII tax.

An LLC must provide members with their allocable shares of net gain or loss from the deemed sale of the LLC's Section 1411 property subject to the NII tax (3.8 percent Medicare Contribution Tax) if the owners use the primary computation

---

[121] Code Sec. 6050K(b)(2).

[122] Reg. § 1.751-1(a)(3).

[123] Code Sec. 6722.

[124] Reg. § 1.743-1(k)(2).

[125] Reg. § 1.743-1(k)(1).

[126] Prop. Reg. § 1.1411-7(g)(2).

method of reporting net investment income. The LLC is not required to provide the information to members who qualify to use the optional simplified method of reporting.[127] The NII Tax is discussed at ¶708.01. The primary computation and optional simplified methods of reporting are discussed at ¶708.03.

.04 Short Period Tax Returns

There is a technical termination of an LLC as a partnership if there is a sale or exchange of 50 percent or more of the total interests in the LLC's capital and profits during a 12-month period.[128] The LLC that terminates must file a short-year final return for the taxable year ending with the date of its termination. The new LLC must file a return for its taxable year beginning after the date of termination of the terminated LLC.[129] Some LLCs inadvertently file a single tax return for the entire year in which there is a termination. The single return will be treated as a valid return that will start the statute of limitations running for the short years of the terminated LLC and the new LLC.[130]

¶1513 INSTALLMENT SALES

A member may defer gain recognition by selling a membership interest on the installment basis if the (i) the member reports the full amount of the sales price of the membership interest on his or her tax return (not just the cash received), and (ii) files IRS Form 6252, Installment Sale Income, with the return.[131] However, installment reporting may not be used to the extent that gain is attributable to the sale of a member's share of:[132]

- LLC inventory.[133]
- unrealized receivables, including unrealized receivables for services rendered;[134]
- Section 1245 and 1250 depreciation recapture income items; or
- other ordinary income items.[135]

The gain attributable to such items must be reported in the year of sale. The amount reported as ordinary income results in a basis adjustment, and a decrease in

---

[127] Prop. Reg. § 1.1411-7(g)(1).

[128] *See* ¶1203 *supra.*

[129] FSA 200139009; IRS Notice 2001-5, 2001-3 IRB 327.

[130] FSA 200139009.

[131] *Barry E. Moore v. Comm'r,* TC Memo 2007-134 (2007).

[132] IRS Publication 541, Partnerships, under the subheading, "Installment reporting for sale of partnership interest."

[133] Rev. Rul. 89-108, 1989-2 CB 100.

[134] CCA 200722027; *Mingo v. Comm'r,* TC Memo 2013-149 (2013), *aff'd,* 773 F.3d 629 (5th Cir. 2014).

[135] Code Sec. 453(i)(2).

the capital gain or increase in the capital loss on the sale of the membership interest.[136]

¶ 1514 NII TAX

Gain on the sale of a membership interest may result in net investment income subject to the 3.8 percent NII tax. The NII tax is discussed at ¶ 708. The reporting requirements for transfers by persons subject to the 3.8 percent NII tax are discussed at ¶ 1512.03.

¶ 1515 INVESTMENT TAX CREDIT RECAPTURE

The members of an LLC may be subject to the investment tax credit recapture if the members sell their membership interests or reduce their share of profits in the LLC. Operating agreements sometimes restrict members from selling their membership interests or cashing out for five years after their initial contribution in order to prevent recapture and reallocation of tax credits.

The investment tax credit consists of the rehabilitation credit, the energy credit, the qualifying advanced coal project credit, the qualifying gasification project credit, the qualifying advanced energy project credit, and the qualifying therapeutic discovery project credit.[137] The investment tax credit under Code Sec. 46 is one of the many general business credits under Code Sec. 38.[138]

The members of an LLC may be subject to the investment tax credit recapture in the following cases:

- *Sale of membership interest.* The investment tax credit is earned at the rate of 20 percent per year.[139] Therefore, a member who sells a membership interest before five full years after an equity investment will be subject to recapture at a 20 percent rate for each year less than five. For example, an equity investor who sold after three years would be subject to a 40 percent recapture.

- *66⅔%–33⅓% membership interest reduction rule.* The reduction of a member's interest in an LLC triggers recapture if the change in the member's proportionate interest in profits (or in the particular item of property) is reduced below 66⅔ percent of the member's investment tax credit interest for the tax year in which the property was placed in service. There is no further recapture under this rule until the member's interest is reduced below 33⅓ percent of the member's interest for the tax year in which the property was placed in service.[140]

---

[136] *Mingo v. Comm'r,* TC Memo 2013-149 (2013), *aff'd,* 773 F.3d 629 (5th Cir. 2014).

[137] Code Sec. 46.

[138] Code Sec. 38(b)(1).

[139] Code Sec. 50(a)(1)(B).

[140] Reg. § 1.47-6(a)(2)(ii).

- *Admission of new members.* The admission of new members into an LLC that causes a reduction in a member's proportionate interest in profits (or in the particular item of investment property) may cause recapture if another member's interest is reduced under the $66^2/_3\%$–$33^1/_3\%$ rule discussed above.

- *Sale of investment credit property by LLC.* The members of an LLC are subject to recapture if the LLC disposes of investment tax credit property before the end of the five-year recapture period.[141]

¶1516 PASSIVE LOSS DEDUCTIONS

A member who disposes of his or her entire membership interest in an LLC in a fully taxable transaction may deduct any suspended passive losses for the current and prior tax years (including losses recognized on the disposition of the membership interest) against non-passive income.[142] The suspended losses first offset passive income for the tax year. The excess suspended losses are treated as nonpassive losses and offset nonpassive income.

If an LLC conducts two or more separate passive activities, and the LLC disposes of all the assets used in one of the activities, the disposition constitutes the disposition of the member's entire interest in the activity. The member may in the same manner deduct any suspended losses from that activity for the current and prior years, including the member's share of losses from the sale of the assets.

¶1517 TRANSFERS TO AND BY FOREIGN MEMBERS

.01 Transfers by Foreign Person

A foreign member recognizes gain on sale of a membership interest if (i) the foreign member is a resident alien, which persons are taxed on their worldwide income, (ii) the foreign member is present in the United States for more than 183 days during the year,[143] (iii) the LLC is engaged in a U.S. trade or business,[144] or (iv) the LLC owns U.S. real estate.[145] A foreign owner's gain or loss from the transfer of membership interest is effectively connected with the LLC's U.S. trade or business to the extent that the foreign owner would have recognized effectively connected gain or loss if the LLC had sold all of its assets at fair market value on the date of the transfer.[146] A member's distributive share of gain or loss on the deemed sale is the

---

[141] Reg. § 1.47-6(a)(1).

[142] Code Sec. 469(g).

[143] Code Sec. 871(a)(2).

[144] Code Sec. 864(c)(8), as amended by 2017 Tax Cuts and Jobs Act § 13501(a).

[145] *See* ¶1902.04 *infra.*

[146] Code Sec. 864(c)(8)(B).

same as the member's distributive share of the non-separately stated taxable income or loss of the LLC.[147]

The purchaser of a membership interest from a foreign owner must withhold ten percent of the amount realized by the transferor.[148] If the transferee fails to withhold the correct amount, the LLC must deduct and withhold from distributions to the transferee member an amount equal to the additional amount that should have been withheld.[149]

.02 Transfers by a U.S. Person to Foreign Corporation

A U.S. person recognizes gain on the transfer of a membership interest to a foreign corporation, subject to exceptions.[150] The transfer is treated as a transfer of a proportionate share of the assets of the LLC in an exchange described in Code Sec. 367(a)(1). If the U.S. person recognizes gain, then the following tax consequences result:[151]

1. The U.S. person's basis in the stock of the transferee foreign corporation is increased by the amount of gain recognized.
2. The transferee foreign corporation's basis in the transferred membership interest is increased by the amount of gain recognized by the U.S. person.
3. The U.S. person is treated as having newly acquired an interest in the LLC for an amount equal to the gain recognized, permitting the LLC to make an optional adjustment to basis pursuant to Code Secs. 743 and 754.

---

[147] Code Sec. 864(c)(8)(B).

[148] Code Sec. 1446(f)(1).

[149] Code Sec. 1446(f)(4).

[150] Reg. § 1.367(a)-1T(3)(ii)(A).

[151] Reg. § 1.367(a)-1T(3)(ii)(B).

16

Sales and Exchanges of Assets

¶ 1601 CAPITAL GAIN AND ORDINARY INCOME

.01 General Rules

Gain or loss recognized by the LLC from the sale of property is treated as (i) ordinary income if the property is inventory or if the LLC is a dealer in the property, (ii) capital gain or loss if the property is investment property and is not held in connection with a trade or business of the LLC, or (iii) Section 1231 gain or loss if the property is held for more than 12 months in connection with a trade or business of the LLC. The net Section 1231 gain is taxed as capital gain. However, if a member reported net Section 1231 losses in any of the five years prior to the sale by the LLC, any net Section 1231 gain would be reported as ordinary income to the extent of such reported losses. Net Section 1231 losses incurred by an LLC pass through to the members as ordinary losses.[1]

The determination of whether gain is capital or ordinary is made at the LLC level.[2] For example, a member's distributive share of gain from the sale of depreciable property used in the LLC's trade or business retains its character as gain from the sale of such depreciable property in the hands of the member.[3] Similarly, an LLC's gain from the sale of investment real estate held by the LLC is capital gain to the members even though all of the members earn their income from, or are involved in, commercial real estate development.[4] However, the character of gain or loss on contributed unrealized receivables, inventory items, and capital loss property is made at the member level, subject to exceptions.[5]

The gain or loss on sale of LLC property is equal to the amount realized less the LLC's basis in the property. The LLC's basis in its property is referred to as the inside basis. The computation of the inside basis of property is discussed at ¶904.

Gain or loss is short-term or long-term depending on the length of time that the LLC held the asset, not the length of time that the member held the membership interest.[6]

Short-term capital gains and losses and long-term capital gains and losses are separately netted and stated as two net amounts.[7] The LLC may not carry over unused capital losses.[8]

When an LLC sells depreciable property, the amount of depreciation recapture that is taxed as ordinary income is determined at the LLC level. The result is the same even though one or more of the members had a Section 743 basis adjustment with respect to such property and had taken depreciation with respect to such basis adjustment.[9]

A member in an LLC that sells stock held for the requisite long-term capital gain holding period treats his or her allocable share of the gain as long-term capital gain even though the member held the LLC interest for less than the requisite holding period. The character of the gain for an LLC that is classified as a partnership is determined at the LLC level.[10]

The reporting requirements for capital gains and losses are discussed at ¶703.01.

---

[1] Rev. Rul. 67-188, 1967-1 CB 216.

[2] Code Sec. 702(b); Reg. § 1.702-1(b).

[3] Reg. § 1.702-1(b).

[4] *Phelan v. Comm'r*, TC Memo 2004-206 (2004).

[5] Code Sec. 724. *See* ¶709 *supra*.

[6] Rev. Rul. 68-79, 1968-1 CB 310.

[7] Code Sec. 702(a)(1), (2).

[8] Reg. § 1.703-1(a)(2)(viii).

[9] Reg. §§ 1.1245-1(e)(1), 1.1250-1(f).

[10] Rev. Rul. 68-79, 1968-1 CB 310.

.02 Sale of Contributed Property at a Loss

Loss recognized by the LLC on a sale or disposition of property for a period of five years after the contribution is treated as a capital loss (up to the amount of built-in loss on the date of contribution) even though the property is inventory in the hands of the LLC. Any loss attributable to post-contribution depreciation may be characterized as ordinary loss by the LLC if the property is inventory in the hands of the LLC or is otherwise ordinary loss property.[11]

.03 Pass-Through of Gain and Loss

Capital gains and losses are passed through to the members and retain their same character on distribution. Capital losses and other losses are deductible only to the extent of a member's basis in the LLC. If the member receives short-term and long-term losses in excess of basis, the member must deduct an allocable share of each type of loss. The member may carry forward the excess unused losses to subsequent tax years.[12]

EXAMPLE 16-1

A member has a basis in the LLC of $1,000 at the end of the tax year. The member receives an allocation of $4,000 in ordinary income for the year, which increases his basis to $5,000. The member also receives an allocation of $4,000 in long-term capital losses and $2,000 in short-term capital losses. The member may deduct $3,333 in long-term capital losses, and $1,667 in short-term capital losses ($5,000/$6,000 of each type of loss). The member may carry forward to succeeding tax years $667 as a long-term capital loss and $333 as a short-term capital loss.[13]

Special allocations of capital gains to members are discussed at ¶ 703.01.

.04 Dealer and Investment Property

An LLC realizes ordinary income or ordinary loss on the sale of dealer property. Dealer property is property held by the LLC primarily for sale to customers in the ordinary course of its trade or business.[14]

---

[11] Code Sec. 724(c).

[12] Reg. § 1.704-1(d)(1), (4), Example (3).

[13] Reg. § 1.704-1(d)(4), Example (3).

[14] *See* Code Sec. 1221(a)(1).

An LLC recognizes capital gain or loss that is passed through to the members if the property is held by the LLC for investment.[15]

The determination of whether property owned by an LLC is dealer property or investment property is based on all the facts and circumstances.[16] The courts have identified the following factors in determining whether LLC property is dealer property or property held for investment:[17]

- *Nature of acquisition.* The nature and purpose of the acquisition of the property and the duration of the ownership are important factors. The purchase of property for development and resale indicates that the LLC is a dealer in the property.

- *Frequency and continuity of sales.* Frequent and substantial sales of property indicate that the property is dealer property. Infrequent sales indicate that the property is investment property.[18] Some courts also consider the substantiality of sales when compared to other sources of the member's income.[19]

- *Nature and extent of business.* An LLC's improvements to property, such as subdividing the property, making water and wastewater improvements, and otherwise developing the property indicate that the property is dealer property. However, an LLC is not engaged in a trade or business if development activities are exploratory or in the formative stage.[20]

- *Activity of seller about the property.* The extent and nature of the taxpayer's efforts to sell the property, including the advertising of the property for sale, is one of the factors in determining whether LLC property is dealer property. If the managers and employees of the LLC spend large amounts of time actively participating in the sales of property, the property is more likely to be dealer property. The character and degree of supervision or control exercised by the LLC over any representative selling the property may be considered in determining whether the property is dealer property.[21] An LLC may recognize ordinary income on the sale of partially developed property even if the LLC sells the property in bulk to a single purchaser.[22]

- *Extended substantiality of transactions.* The sale of property to a related party or newly formed entity at an inflated price without a valid business purpose indicates that the transaction is not a bona fide transaction at arm's-length, and that the property is dealer property.

---

[15] *Conner v. Comm'r*, TC Memo 2018-6 (2018); *Phelan v. Comm'r*, TC Memo 2004-206 (2004).

[16] *Conner v. Comm'r*, TC Memo 2018-6 (2018).

[17] *Pool v. Comm'r*, TC Memo 2014-3 (2014); *Boree v. Comm'r*, TC Memo 2014-85 (2014); *Phelan v. Comm'r*, TC Memo 2004-206 (2004); *Boree v. Comm'r*, 118 AFTR 2d 2016-5742 (11th Cir. 2016); *Conner v. Comm'r*, TC Memo 2018-6 (2018).

[18] *Conner v. Comm'r*, TC Memo. 2018-6 (2018).

[19] *Conner v. Comm'r*, TC Memo 2018-6 (2018).

[20] *Conner v. Comm'r*, TC Memo 2018-6 (2018).

[21] *Boree v. Comm'r*, 118 AFTR 2d 2016-5742 (11th Cir. 2016).

[22] *Boree v. Comm'r*, 118 AFTR 2d 2016-5742 (11th Cir. 2016).

No factor or combination of factors is controlling. However, the frequency and substantiality of sales is the most important factor.[23]

EXAMPLE 16-2

An LLC purchased Lakeside property to develop a residential Lakeside community. The LLC prepared design plans, obtained approval for 94-lot subdivision from the local government, obtained approval of boat docks from the Army Corps of Engineers, secured water availability for sewage treatment system, and hired a firm to help with the drawing of design plans. After a period of inactivity, the LLC sold the property at a loss. The LLC claimed an ordinary loss deduction since it held the property as a developer for resale. However, the IRS and the court determined that the property was investment property, and that the loss should be a capital loss, because there was insufficient development activity on the property and only a single sale of all the property.[24]

EXAMPLE 16-3

An LLC purchased 300 undeveloped acres of land with an intent to develop the property. The LLC installed a water and waste water system on the property. The LLC also sold portions of the property. The court determined that gain from the sale of the real estate should be taxed as ordinary income because the LLC held the property as a developer rather than as an investor.[25]

EXAMPLE 16-4

The owners of an LLC that owned undeveloped land in Florida recognized ordinary income when the LLC sold more than 1,000 acres of undeveloped property because the LLC developed an unpaved road through the property, obtained an exemption from local subdivision requirements, signed a declaration of covenants, conditions and restrictions, sold some lot separately, pursued land use approvals from the

---

[23] *Conner v. Comm'r*, TC Memo 2018-6 (2018); *Boree v. Comm'r*, 118 AFTR 2d 2016-5742 (11th Cir. 2016).

[24] *Conner v. Comm'r*, TC Memo 2018-6 (2018).

[25] *Pool v. Comm'r*, TC Memo 2014-3 (2014).

county, spent time and money on zoning activities, and deducted, rather than capitalized, expenses related to the real estate activities.[26]

Gain from a sale of real estate by LLC is passed through to the members as capital gain if the real estate was held by the LLC as a capital asset, even if all the members of the LLC earn their income from, or are involved in commercial real estate development.[27]

¶1602 SALES TO RELATED PARTIES

The sale of property by an LLC to a member or related party is discussed at ¶1403.03. There are separate rules for sales of property at a gain and sales of property at a loss.

¶1603 LIKE-KIND EXCHANGES

.01 In General

No gain or loss is recognized if an LLC exchanges real property[28] held in a trade or business or for investment for like-kind property held in a trade or business or for investment.[29] The party transferring the property in the like-kind exchange must be the same party that receives the replacement property.

In order to qualify under Section 1031, a taxpayer must exchange real property for other real property of like kind.[30] Partnership interests do not qualify as property. The taxpayer may not exchange real estate for a membership interest, a membership interest for real estate, or a membership interest for another partnership or LLC interest, even if both entities own real estate.[31]

An LLC may engage in a tax-free like-kind exchange in one of the following ways:

- *Simultaneous exchange.* The LLC sells the relinquished property and acquires the replacement property at the same time. There is no tax if the purchase price of the replacement property is higher than the sales price of the relinquished property.
- *Forward like-kind exchange.* The LLC sells the relinquished property and acquires the replacement property through a qualified intermediary. The LLC sells the relinquished property first and then acquires the replacement property at a later date.[32] The LLC has 45 days after the transfer of the relinquished

---

[26] *Boree v. Comm'r*, TC Memo 2014-85 (2014).

[27] *Phelan v. Comm'r*, TC Memo 2004-206 (2004).

[28] Code Sec. 1031(a)(1).

[29] Code Sec. 1031.

[30] Code Sec. 1031(a)(1).

[31] Code Sec. 1031(a)(2)(D).

[32] Ltr. Rul. 201302009.

property to identify potential replacement properties. The LLC must complete the purchase of the replacement property within the earlier of 180 days after the transfer of the relinquished property or the due date (including extensions) of the federal tax return for the year in which the relinquished property was transferred.[33] The qualified intermediary is treated as acquiring and transferring the properties in the exchange even though there is direct deeding of the relinquished property from the LLC to the buyer and direct deeding of the replacement property from the seller to the LLC.[34]

- *Reverse like-kind exchange.* An accommodation or intermediary party for the LLC acquires title to the replacement property until the LLC can sell the relinquished property or assign its rights in a sale contract to the accommodation or intermediary party. The LLC has 45 days after acquiring the replacement property to identify the potential relinquished properties to be sold. The LLC must complete the sale of the relinquished property within the earlier of 180 days after the acquisition of the replacement property or the due date (including extensions) of the federal tax return for the year in which the replacement property was acquired.[35] The problem with the reverse exchange is that the LLC may not own both the relinquished property and the replacement property at the same time. There can be direct deeding of either the relinquished property or the replacement property, but not both. The LLC must transfer title to either the relinquished property or the replacement property to an exchange accommodation titleholder (EAT). This is called a parking arrangement. Within five business days after the transfer of property to the EAT, the LLC and the EAT must enter into a qualified exchange accommodation agreement (QEAA). The QEAA must provide that (i) the EAT is holding the property for the benefit of the LLC to facilitate a like-kind exchange in accordance with Revenue Procedure 2000-37, (ii) the parties will report the transaction, holding and disposition of the property in accordance with the Revenue Procedure, and (iii) the EAT will be treated as the owner of the property for federal income tax purposes.[36] There is often a problem in parking the replacement property with the EAT on the first leg of the transaction since lenders do not want to make loans secured by real estate that is temporarily owned by an EAT. This means that the LLC will have to transfer title to the relinquished property to the EAT prior to acquiring title to the replacement property.[37]

---

[33] Code Sec. 1031(a)(3); Reg. § 1.1031(k)-1(b)(2)(ii).

[34] Reg. § 1.1031(k)-1(g)(4).

[35] Code Sec. 1031(a)(3); Reg. § 1.1031(k)-1(b)(2)(ii). The court in *Estate of Bartell v. Commissioner*, 147 TC 140 (2016), *nonacq*, allowed the accommodation party to hold the replacement property in a reverse exchange for 17 months before the taxpayer acquired the replacement property. However, that transaction took place prior to the safe-harbor rules which specify a 180-day time limit for acquiring the replacement property after sale of the relinquished property.

[36] Rev. Proc. 2000-37, 2000-2 CB 308.

[37] *See* discussion of the reverse like-kind exchange rules applicable to LLCs in Ltr. Rul. 201408019.

- *Build-to-suit (improvement or construction) exchange.* This type of exchange allows an LLC to build on, or make improvements to, the replacement property using the proceeds from the sale of the relinquished property. This is similar to a reverse exchange. The LLC must enter into an exchange agreement with a qualified intermediary for the purchase and sale of the exchange properties. The EAT takes title to the replacement property rather than the relinquished property. The EAT and the LLC must enter into a qualified exchange accommodation agreement (QEAA) under which the EAT temporarily holds title to the replacement property, constructs improvements using funds from the sale of the relinquished property or loans from the LLC,[38] and then transfers the property to the LLC within 180 days after the LLC sells the relinquished property. The qualified intermediary normally enters into a qualified exchange trust agreement and deposits the funds from the sale of the relinquished property into a trust account (Qualified Exchange Trust) with a trustee of which the LLC is the beneficiary.[39] The trustee may not be the LLC or a disqualified person. The exchange is tax-free if (i) the LLC as a seller of the relinquished property provides as much detail "as is practical" regarding the construction of the improvements at the time that the identification of the replacement properties is made within 45 days after sale of the relinquished property,[40] and (ii) the contractor completes the improvements to the replacement property and transfers the property to the LLC within 180 days after the LLC transfers the relinquished property. If the contractor does not complete the planned improvements within the 180-day period, the LLC will recognize gain to the extent of any boot received in the exchange. If the cost of improvements is less than the sales proceeds held by the trustee, the LLC will receive the remaining funds as taxable boot unless the LLC timely identifies and acquires additional like-kind replacement property.[41]

.02 Exchange of Property for LLC Interests

A taxpayer may exchange real estate for membership interests in a single-member disregarded LLC that owns property of like kind.[42] The receipt of the interest in the LLC is treated as the receipt of the property from the owner of the LLC.[43] A taxpayer may exchange real estate for 100 percent of the partnership interests in a partnership (or LLC classified as a partnership) that holds the replacement prop-

---

[38] Rev. Proc. 2000-37, 2000-2 CB 308, Sec. 4.03.

[39] Ltr. Rul. 201408019.

[40] Reg. § 1.1031(k)-1(e)(2).

[41] *See* Ltr. Rul. 201408019 involving the exchange of property by an LLC through a qualified intermediary and exchange accommodation title holder, with improvements made to the replacement property prior to transfer of such property to the LLC on the second leg of the exchange.

[42] Ltr. Ruls. 200118023, 200728008.

[43] Ltr. Ruls. 200118023, 200728008.

erty.[44] The acquisition of the partnership interests is equivalent to the acquisition of the real estate owned by the partnership since a partnership terminates when the taxpayer becomes the single owner. The regulations deny nonrecognition treatment under Section 1031 for exchanges of membership interests in an LLC classified as a partnership.[45] This regulation is contrary to Congressional intent.[46]

.03 Requirements for Relinquished Property

An LLC must hold the relinquished property for investment or in a trade or business prior to an exchange. A taxpayer's belief that property owned by an LLC would appreciate in value and could eventually be sold at profit is not sufficient to classify the property as held primarily for investment prior to a like-kind exchange.[47]

.04 Receipt of Replacement Property by LLC

A taxpayer must ordinarily purchase replacement property from the same party that acquired the taxpayer's property in a like-kind exchange. The same taxpayer who transferred the property in a like-kind exchange must receive the replacement property. However, this requirement is not violated if the taxpayer receives the replacement property through a single-member disregarded LLC. The receipt of the replacement property by the LLC is treated as the receipt of the property by the taxpayer. For example, the taxpayer may acquire the replacement property through a single-member disregarded LLC in the following cases:

- A limited partnership transfers property in an exchange, and receives the replacement property through a disregarded LLC wholly owned by the partnership.[48]
- A trust transfers property in an exchange, and receives the replacement property through a disregarded LLC wholly owned by the trust.[49] The trust may thereafter terminate and distribute the membership interests in the LLC to the trust beneficiaries for reasons unrelated to the exchange.
- An LLC transfers property in an exchange, and receives the replacement property through another LLC owned by the exchanging LLC.[50]
- A corporation transfers property in an exchange, and receives the replacement property through a disregarded LLC owned by the corporation.[51]

---

[44] Ltr. Rul. 200807005. In that case, a limited partnership entered into an exchange with a partnership that owned property of like kind. The limited partnership formed a wholly owned LLC to receive the partnership interests in the exchange.

[45] Reg. § 1.1031(a)-1(a)(1).

[46] H. Rept. No. 98-432 (Pub. L. No. 98-369) p. 1234.

[47] *Barry E. Moore v. Comm'r*, TC Memo 2007-134 (2017).

[48] Ltr. Ruls. 200807005, 9807013.

[49] Ltr. Ruls. 200651030, 200521002, 199911033.

[50] Ltr. Rul. 200732012.

[51] Ltr. Rul. 9751012.

The receipt of the replacement property by a single-member disregarded LLC allows the selling taxpayer to avoid liability from holding the replacement property directly. The taxpayer may also avoid transfer taxes by having the property deeded directly to the LLC, rather than receiving the property and then transferring it into the LLC.

A taxpayer may use multiple disregarded LLCs to make a like-kind exchange, including subsidiary LLCs owned by a disregarded LLC. The 45-day designation and the 180-day deadline for the transfer of replacement property may be met by one or more of such LLCs.[52]

.05 Use of LLC as Intermediary

If a direct, simultaneous exchange of properties is not possible, the taxpayer may use a qualified intermediary to acquire the replacement property and/or exchange property. An LLC may act as a qualified intermediary in a like-kind exchange.[53] The taxpayer may also complete a like-kind exchange by acquiring the single-member LLC that acts as the intermediary and owns the replacement property. The acquisition of the LLC is made to avoid state transfer taxes that would otherwise apply if the taxpayer directly acquired the property from the intermediary. The taxpayer's acquisition of the LLC is treated as the acquisition of the replacement property if the LLC is classified as a disregarded entity for federal tax purposes.[54]

.06 Transfer of Replacement Property to LLC after Exchange

After a like-kind exchange, a taxpayer must hold the replacement property for investment or in a trade or business. The taxpayer may transfer the replacement property to a single-member disregarded LLC after the exchange.[55] The transfer of property to a single-member LLC will not violate the requirement that the replacement property be held for investment or in a trade or business provided that the LLC holds the property for investment or in a trade or business. The transfer of property may violate the requirement that the replacement property be held for investment if the property is transferred to an LLC that is classified as a partnership immediately after a like-kind exchange.[56]

The transfer of replacement property to an LLC classified as a partnership immediately after a like-kind exchange may violate the requirement that the parties

---

[52] Ltr. Rul. 200732012.

[53] Ltr. Rul. 200118023.

[54] Ltr. Rul. 200118023.

[55] Ltr. Ruls. 200528011, 200521002, 200131014; CCA 200836024.

[56] *Magnusson v. Comm'r*, 753 F.2d 1490 (9th Cir. 1985); *True v. United States*, 190 F.3d 1165 (10th Cir. 1999); *Dep't of Revenue v. Marks*, 20 Or. Tax 35 (2009).

hold the exchange property for investment or in a trade or business after the exchange.[57]

In *In re Rago Development Corp.*[58] (a California case interpreting federal law), the taxpayer entered into a like-kind exchange of commercial property. The taxpayer held the properties as tenants-in-common both before and after the exchange. The taxpayers then transferred the properties into an LLC approximately seven months after the exchange in order to limit their liability and to comply with lender financing requirements. The Franchise Tax Board determined that the transfer of the properties to the LLC in such a short period of time after the exchange showed that the taxpayers did not have sufficient investment intent. The State Board of Equalization reversed the decision on appeal. It determined that the transfer of the property to the LLC seven months after the exchange did not disqualify the exchange.

The courts and the *Magnuson*[59] and *Marks*[60] cases reached similar conclusions. A 1999 IRS Field Service Advice stated that the IRS will no longer pursue the position that an immediate transfer of property pursuant to a pre-arranged plan evidences the taxpayer's failure to hold the replacement property for investment purposes.[61]

.07 *Distributions of Property from LLC*

Distribution of Relinquished Property Prior to Exchange

LLCs that are classified as partnerships sometimes distribute the relinquished property to the members immediately prior to making a like-kind exchange. This is called a drop-and-swap transaction. There are several potential problems and issues regarding distributions prior to an exchange:

- The deeding of property to members may create a partnership among the individual owners rather than a tenancy in common. The IRS issued detailed requirements for tenancies in common for ruling purposes.[62] If the distribution does not comply with these requirements, then the parties may be treated as owning the distributed property in partnership, thus disqualifying the like-

---

[57] *Magnusson v. Comm'r*, 753 F.2d 1490 (9th Cir. 1985); True v. United States, 190 F.3d 1165 (10th Cir. 1999); Dep't of Revenue v. Marks, 20 Or. Tax 35 (2009); Letter Decision, Appeal of Diamond, Nos. 441030, 464475, Cal. State Bd. of Equalization (Oct. 22, 2010, released Jan. 2011), interpreting federal law.

[58] *In re Rago Development Corp.*, 2015-SPE-001 (June 23, 2015).

[59] *Magnusson v. Comm'r*, 753 F.2d 1490 (9th Cir. 1985). The court in that case found that there was a legitimate Section 1031 exchange, even though the taxpayers immediately contributed the replacement property to a limited partnership in exchange for partnership interests pursuant to a prearranged plan, because the taxpayers continued to hold the property for investment through the limited partnership.

[60] *Department of Revenue v. Marks*, 20 OTR 35 (Or. T.C. 2009). This was not a case interpreting federal law. The court ruled in favor of the taxpayers even assuming that the taxpayers transferred the replacement property received in a Section 1031 exchange to a partnership after the exchange.

[61] FSA 199951004 (Dec. 23, 1999).

[62] Rev. Proc. 2002-22, 2002-1 CB 733. *See also* Rev. Rul. 75-374, 1975-2 C.B. 261.

kind exchange. In *Vaughn*,[63] for example, a general partnership distributed the exchange property to its general partners as tenants-in-common two weeks before an exchange. The general partners then transferred the property to an unrelated LLC in exchange for like-kind property. The IRS determined that the exchange did not qualify for tax-free treatment since the tenancy in common arrangement fell within the broad definition of a partnership. The exchange of the property by the partners was in substance an exchange of partnership interests, which did not qualify as like-kind property.[64]

- The IRS may assert that the property was really sold by the LLC, and that the LLC (rather than the members) should have acquired the replacement property.[65]
- The property distributed by the LLC to the members must be held by the members for investment or in the active conduct of a trade or business. The IRS may determine that the members are not holding the distributed property for investment or in the active conduct of a trade or business, but are merely holding it momentarily to facilitate a like-kind exchange.[66]

If one member wants to be cashed out, then it may be advisable to distribute a fractional interest in the property to the member prior to the exchange. In that event, the cash-out member's gain from the like-kind exchange will be limited to the difference between the member's fractional share of the sales price and the member's substituted basis in the distributed property.

Distribution of Relinquished Property During Exchange

An LLC that has entered into a like-kind exchange may complete the exchange even though it liquidates and transfers its assets and liabilities to a newly formed limited partnership. The limited partnership is treated as the continuation of the LLC. The liquidation does not result in the termination of the LLC. The limited partnership is treated as both the transferor of the relinquished property previously transferred to

---

[63] *Vaughn* #20044, NSAR 020044 (2002).

[64] The IRS took the same position in IRS Market Segment Specialization Program, Partnerships, Audit Technique Guide, Chapter 7, under the heading, "Exchange of a Partnership Interest," stating, "The exchange of a partnership interest for an undivided interest in partnership property followed by a like kind exchange of the distributive property may, in certain circumstances, essentially amount to the taxable exchange of a partnership interest. Such an exchange was at issue in *Chase v. Comm'r*, 92 TC 874 (1989). The Tax Court determined that the substance over form doctrine applied and the transaction failed to qualify for nonrecognition under IRC section 1031. *See* IRC section 1031(a)(2)(D)."

[65] *Delwin G. Chase*, 92 TC 874 (1989); *Crenshaw v. Comm'r*, 450 F.2d 472, 477 (5th Cir. 1971); TAM 9645005. In the *Delwin* case, a limited partnership distributed an apartment building to the partners immediately prior to a like-kind exchange. The partners then received the replacement property in their individual names. The court determined that the distribution to the partners should be disregarded, and that it was the limited partnership that had actually made the sale. There was no like-kind exchange because the limited partnership, rather than the partners, should have received the replacement property.

[66] TAM 9645005.

a qualified intermediary by the LLC before its liquidation, and as the transferee of the replacement property received from the qualified intermediary.[67]

Distribution of Replacement Property after Exchange

After a like-kind exchange, the LLC must hold the replacement property for investment or in a trade or business. The distribution of replacement property to the members immediately after an exchange may violate this requirement. For example, the redemption of membership interests in an LLC following an exchange, resulting in the conversion of the LLC classified as a partnership to a single-member disregarded entity, constitutes a deemed distribution of the replacement property. The deemed distribution immediately after the exchange may disqualify the Section 1031 exchange. The determination of whether there is a tax-free exchange in such case depends on all the facts and circumstances.[68]

The members of an LLC may want to acquire different replacement properties and to own such property separately in their own name after an exchange. One way of achieving this result is for an LLC to acquire the replacement properties in separate single-member LLCs owned by the parent LLC. After a period of two or more years, the LLC may then distribute the separate LLCs to the individual members corresponding with the replacement properties selected by each member. Some LLCs have special allocations prior to such distributions of LLC membership interests, and designate individual members as managers of the subsidiary LLCs that hold the replacement property selected by the member. The IRS has not yet issued rulings on this method.

Cash-Out of Minority Members

An LLC may need to cash-out minority members who do not want to remain members of the LLC after the LLC acquires the replacement property. The LLC may cash-out the minority members prior to[69] or after[70] the exchange by refinancing the property and distributing the proceeds of the refinancing to the minority members. The IRS may challenge refinancings that take equity out of a property prior to or after completing an exchange under the step transaction doctrine or the lack of economic substance doctrine.[71]

The LLC may not be willing or able to obtain additional debt for the replacement property. To avoid this problem, some LLCs transfer a minority interest in the relinquished property to a second LLC owned by the minority members in exchange for their interests in the first LLC. Both LLCs then sell the relinquished property. The minority members in the second LLC receive cash for the sale and are subject to tax.

---

[67] Ltr. Rul. 199935065.

[68] INFO 2009-0060.

[69] *Fred L. Fredericks v. Comm'r*, TC Memo 1994-27, 67 TCM 2005 (1994).

[70] *Phillip Garcia v. Comm'r*, 80 TC 491 (1983), *aff'd*. 1984-2 CB 1.

[71] Ltr. Ruls. 8248039, 8434015, 200131014; Preamble to TD 8343, 56 Fed. Reg. 14851 (Apr. 12, 1991).

The majority members retain their interest in the first LLC, and use the proceeds from the sale of a majority interest in the relinquished property to buy the replacement property. The IRS has not yet issued rulings on this cash-out method.

.08 At-Risk Rules for Like-Kind Exchanges

Under the at-risk rules, a member recognizes taxable income to the extent that the at-risk amount is reduced below zero. There is recaptured income up to the amount of loss deductions previously taken less any amount previously recaptured.[72] This rule causes serious tax problems for some exchanges that cross over the end of a tax year.

Normally, an LLC finances the purchase of real estate with "qualified nonrecourse financing."[73] The qualified nonrecourse financing is allocated to the members based on their interests in the LLC. The allocations give each member additional at-risk basis, and allow the members to take pass-through deductions in excess of the cash and basis of property contributed to the LLC. When the LLC sells the property on the first leg of the like-kind exchange, the qualified nonrecourse financing used to purchase the real estate is repaid. This results in a reduction in the liabilities allocated to each member, and a corresponding reduction in each member's at-risk basis. The member will then recognize taxable gain to the extent that the at-risk amount is reduced below zero.[74] However, there is no taxable gain to the members if the LLC incurs new qualified nonrecourse financing for the replacement property prior to the end of the tax year.[75] Each member's share of the new qualified nonrecourse financing must be at least equal to the member's negative at-risk amount.

.09 Related Party Exchanges

An LLC recognizes gain if it exchanges property with a related party, and the related party sells the exchange property within two years thereafter.[76] However, there is no gain recognition if (i) the LLC transfers the relinquished property to the related party through an unrelated qualified intermediary, (ii) the LLC receives replacement property that is not owned by the related party, and (iii) the transaction is not structured to avoid the purposes of the related party rules for like-kind exchanges.[77]

---

[72] See ¶ 1303.01 *supra.*

[73] See ¶ 1303.06 *supra.*

[74] Code Sec. 465(e). However, the recaptured income is limited to the sum of the loss deductions previously allocable to the member, less any amount previously recaptured.

[75] See Code Sec. 465(e)(1) which provides that these rules apply to the extent that the at-risk amount is less than zero "at the close of any taxable year."

[76] Ltr. Ruls. 200820017, 200810017, 200810016.

[77] Ltr. Rul. 200709036.

An LLC may also recognize gain if it exchanges property with a related party, and the LLC sells the replacement property within two years thereafter.[78]

¶ 1604 INSTALLMENT SALES

An LLC may sell property on the installment method if (i) the LLC is not an accrual basis taxpayer, (ii) the property is not inventory property, and (iii) the sale is not a dealer disposition.[79] Under the installment method, the LLC will recognize income for any tax year from the sale in an amount equal to the proportion of payments received in that year that the gross profit from the sale bears to the sales price, less certain indebtedness assumed by the buyer, if any. Gain subject to recapture is ordinary income and must be recognized in the year of sale. The following special rules apply to an LLC that is classified as a partnership:

- The LLC, rather than the members, may make an election not to use the installment method of reporting.[80]

- An interest charge is imposed on the portion of the tax that is deferred under the installment method if (i) the sales price of the property exceeds $150,000, (ii) the obligation is outstanding at the end of the tax year, and (iii) the face amount of all such obligations held by the taxpayer which arose during and are outstanding at the end of the tax year exceed $5 million.[81] Under regulations to be promulgated, it is expected that the LLC's installment note receivables will be aggregated with other installment note receivables of the members. The installment note receivables of the LLC will be treated as owned directly by the members in proportion to each member's share in the LLC, so that the $5 million threshold will be tested at the member level.[82] The interest charge is imposed at the partnership level for an electing large partnership (an LLC with more than 100 members that makes an election to be classified as a large partnership).[83]

- If the installment sale contract does not provide for adequate stated interest, part of the stated principal amount of the contract may be recharacterized as interest. If Code Sec. 483 applies to the contract, the interest is called unstated interest. If Code Sec. 1274 applies to the contract, the interest is called original issue discount. The IRS issued guidance regarding when an installment sale contract is subject to Section 483 or 1274, computing the amount of unstated interest and original issue discount, determining the test rate for interest, and the tax consequences if the contract does not provide for adequate stated

---

[78] Ltr. Ruls. 200820017, 200810016.

[79] Code Sec. 453(b). A dealer disposition is defined in Code Sec. 453(l).

[80] Reg. § 15a.453-1(d)(1), (3)(i); Rev. Rul. 79-92, 1979-1 CB 180.

[81] Code Sec. 453A.

[82] Conf. Rept. No. 100-495 (Pub. L. No. 100-203), p. 930.

[83] Code Sec. 774(f).

interest.[84] Generally, if an LLC sells property in exchange for a note with stated interest below the applicable federal rates, the shortfall is recharacterized as ordinary interest income rather than gain on sale, which income is recognized over the life of the outstanding note.

¶ 1605 CAPITAL ACCOUNTS

An LLC must allocate the book gain or loss to the members' capital accounts on the sale or exchange of assets. The allocation method under the safe-harbor regulations is discussed at ¶ 804.02.

If an LLC sells or exchanges Section 704(c) property (property with a tax basis different from book value) in a non-recognition transaction in which no gain or loss is recognized, the substituted basis property is treated as Section 704(c) property with the same amount of built-in gain or loss for capital account purposes as the Section 704(c) property disposed of by the LLC. The allocation method for the substituted basis property must be consistent with the allocation method chosen for the original property.[85] The rules applicable to built-in gain and built-in loss property are discussed at ¶ 805.

---

[84] IRS Publication 537, Installment Sales, pp. 11-13 (2012).
[85] Reg. § 1.704-3(a)(8).

17

Accounting Methods and Procedures

¶1701 CASH AND ACCRUAL METHODS OF ACCOUNTING

.01 Overview

An LLC may use any method of accounting that clearly reflects income and that is regularly used in keeping its books.[1] There are two common methods of accounting, (i) the cash method and (ii) the accrual method. A cash basis LLC must include an amount in income when actually or constructively received. An accrual basis LLC must include an amount in income when all the events have occurred that fix the right to receive that income, and the amount of that income can be determined with reasonable accuracy, unless there is an exception that permits a deferral or exclusion.[2] An LLC may defer the advance payment of certain income to the end of the tax year following the tax year of receipt if the income is also deferred for financial statement purposes.[3] Beginning in 2018, a taxpayer must recognize income no later than the tax year in which the income is taken into account on an applicable financial statement (AFS) or another financial statement under rules specified by the IRS.[4] This is called the AFS conformity rule.

An LLC that sells inventory must ordinarily use the accrual method of accounting for purchases and sales if the LLC is required to account for inventories under Code Sec. 471.[5] An LLC must account for inventories under Code Sec. 471 if the production, purchase or sale of inventory is an income-producing factor in the LLC's business.[6]

An LLC other than a tax shelter may use the cash method of accounting, and is not required to account for inventories under Code Sec. 471, if it meets a $25 million gross receipts test.[7] An LLC meets the $25 million gross receipts test if its average annual gross receipts during the prior three years are $25 million or less.[8] The LLC in such a case may use a method of accounting that either (i) treats inventories as non-incidental materials and supplies, or (ii) conforms to the LLC's financial accounting treatment of inventories as reflected in an "applicable financial statement."[9]

An LLC that does not meet the $25 million gross receipts test may use the cash method of accounting if (i) the cash method clearly reflects income, (ii) the LLC does not sell inventory, (iii) the LLC is not classified as a C corporation or tax shelter, and (iv) the LLC does not have C corporation partners.

---

[1] Code Sec. 446(a).

[2] Code Sec. 451(b)(1)(C).

[3] Code Sec. 451(c), as amended by 2017 Tax Cuts and Jobs Act § 13221(b).

[4] Code Sec. 451(b), as amended by 2017 Tax Cuts and Jobs Act § 13221(a).

[5] Reg. § 1.446-1(c)(2)(i).

[6] Reg. § 1.471-1.

[7] Code Sec. 471(c)(1)(A).

[8] Code Secs. 471(c)(1), 448(c)(1).

[9] Code Sec. 471(c)(1)(B).

An LLC must use the accrual method of accounting if:

- the LLC is classified as a C corporation, unless it is a farming business, a personal service corporation, or meets the $25 million gross receipts test;[10]
- the LLC has a C corporation as a member, unless it is a farming business, a personal service corporation, or meets the $25 million gross receipts test;[11] or
- the LLC is classified as a tax-shelter.[12]

The LLC must use the same method of accounting for tax reporting purposes that it uses in preparing its financial statements.[13]

.02 Inventory—$25 Million Exception

An LLC other than a tax shelter is not required to account for inventories under Code Sec. 471 if it meets the $25 million gross receipts test.[14] An LLC meets the $25 million gross receipts test if its average annual gross receipts are $25 million or less during the three prior tax years.[15]

The gross receipts of all related businesses are aggregated in determining average annual gross receipts.[16] The aggregation rules are determined under Code Sec. 52 (which is based on the aggregation rules in Code Sec. 1563) and Code Sec. 414.[17]

Under prior law, an LLC was required to use the accrual method if it failed to meet the gross receipts test in any prior year. Under the current law, an LLC may use the cash method if it passes the gross receipts test only in the current year, and not for all prior years. That means that an LLC can switch back and forth between the accrual and cash method every time that it satisfies, or fails to satisfy, the $25 million average gross receipts test.

An LLC that meets the $25 million gross receipts test may use a method of accounting that either:

- (i) treats inventories as non-incidental materials and supplies. The LLC in such case may deduct only the cost of inventory actually consumed or sold during the year under the rules that govern a non-incidental materials and supplies, or[18]
- (ii) conforms to the LLC's financial accounting treatment of inventories as reflected in an "applicable financial statement."[19]

---

[10] See ¶ 1701.03 infra.
[11] See ¶ 1701.04 infra.
[12] See ¶ 1701.05 infra.
[13] Code Sec. 446(a).
[14] Code Sec. 471(c)(1)(A).
[15] Code Secs. 471(c)(1), 448(c)(1).
[16] Code Sec. 471(c)(1).
[17] Code Sec. 448(c)(2).
[18] Reg. § 1.162-3.
[19] Code Sec. 471(c)(1)(B).

The Section 263A uniform capitalization rules require that direct costs and certain indirect costs be included in the cost of inventory.[20] LLCs that are producers and resellers of personal property and that meet the $25 million gross receipts test are not subject to the uniform capitalization rules, and are thus not required to include the Section 263A costs in inventory.[21]

.03 Accrual Method Required

An LLC must use the accrual method of accounting, whether or not it maintains inventory, if:[22]

- the LLC is classified as a C corporation, unless it is a farming business, a personal service corporation, or meets the $25 million gross receipts test (2018 amount indexed for inflation);[23]
- the LLC has a C corporation as a member, unless it is a farming business, a personal service corporation, or meets the $25 million gross receipts test; or
- the LLC is classified as a tax-shelter.

An LLC meets the $25 million gross receipts test if its average annual gross receipts are less than $25 million for the three prior tax years.[24]

Thus, LLCs that are classified as C corporations or that have C corporation members, are not disqualified from using the cash method of accounting if they meet the $25 million gross receipts test.

.04 $1 Million and $10 Million Exceptions

Prior to the 2017 Tax Cuts and Jobs Act, the IRS issued Revenue Procedures allowing LLCs and other companies that maintained inventory to use the cash method of accounting and to account for inventory as non-incidental materials and supplies. The principal exceptions included the following:

- *$1 million exception.* Under Revenue Procedure 2001-10, certain accrual-basis taxpayer's could convert to the cash basis if average annual gross receipts for the three prior years was less than $1 million.[25]
- *$10 million exception.* Under Revenue Procedure 2002-28, certain taxpayers with average annual gross receipts of $10 million or less over three years could convert to the cash accounting method if their principal activity did not

---

[20] Code Sec. 263A.

[21] Code Sec. 263A(i)(1), as amended by 2017 Tax Cuts and Jobs Act § 13102(b)(1).

[22] Code Sec. 448(a).

[23] Code Sec. 448(c)(4)(B).

[24] Code Sec. 448(c)(1).

[25] Rev. Proc. 2001-10, 2001-2 IRB 272, as modified by Rev. Proc. 2011-14, 2011-4 IRB 330, § 21.03. *See also* Rev. Proc. 2002-28, 2002-18 IRB 815, § 7.04 (last sentence).

fall into certain North American Industry Classification System Codes and if the taxpayer was not engaged in the trade or business of farming.[26]

Under both exceptions, LLCs that maintain inventory may deduct only the cost of inventory actually consumed or sold during the year under the rules that govern non-incidental materials and supplies.[27]

These Revenue Procedures are expected to be revised as a result of the changes made by the 2017 Tax Act.

.05 LLC Classified as Corporation

An LLC may not use the cash method of accounting if it is classified as a C corporation for federal tax purposes.[28] There is an exception if the LLC:[29]

- is a farming business;

- is a qualified personal service corporation; or

- has average annual gross receipts (averaged over the three prior years) of $25 million or less.[30]

.06 C Corporation Member

An LLC may not use the cash method of accounting if it has a C corporation as a member.[31] There is an exception if:[32]

- the LLC is a farming business;

- the C corporation member is a qualified personal service corporation, in which case the personal service corporation is treated as an individual; or

- the LLC has average annual gross receipts (averaged over the three prior years) of $25 million or less.[33]

---

[26] Rev. Proc. 2002-28, 2002-18 IRB 815, as modified by IRS Ann. 2004-16, 2004-1 CB 668, and as modified by Rev. Proc. 2011-14, 2011-4 IRB 330, to remove Section 7.02(1)(a); IRS Notices 2001-76, 2001-2 CB 613, and 2002-14, 2002-1 CB 548.

[27] Reg. § 1.162-3.

[28] Code Sec. 448(a)(1).

[29] Code Sec. 448(b).

[30] Code Sec. 448(b)(3), (c). *See also* ¶ 1701.03 *supra.*

[31] Code Sec. 448(a)(2).

[32] Code Sec. 448(b).

[33] Code Sec. 448(b)(3), (c).

.07 Classification as Tax Shelter

Types of Tax Shelters

An LLC may not use the cash method of accounting if it is a tax shelter. A tax shelter includes:[34]

- an "enterprise" (other than a C corporation) if there a public offering of securities required to be registered under state or federal law,
- a "syndicate," or
- a "tax shelter" as defined under Code Sec. 6662(d)(2)(C)(ii).

These terms are defined below.

EXAMPLE 17-1

The Service has ruled that LLCs organized for the practice of law,[35] medicine,[36] accounting,[37] management consulting,[38] or other business[39] may continue using the cash method of accounting after conversion from a partnership, LLP, or personal service corporation. The rulings concluded that the LLCs were not tax shelters because they were not "enterprises," "syndicates," or "tax shelters under Code Sec. 6662(d)(2)(C)(ii)."

Enterprise

An organization (other than a C corporation) is an "enterprise" if interests in the organization are offered for sale in an offering required to be registered with any federal or state agency that regulates the offering and sale of securities.[40] An LLC is an enterprise if any of the following apply:

- There is a public offering or sale of membership interests.[41]
- Under applicable state or federal law, failure to register the membership interests would result in a violation of the applicable federal or state securities law (regardless of whether the offering is registered).[42]

---

[34] Code Sec. 448(d)(3), making reference to Code Sec. 461(i)(3).

[35] Ltr. Ruls. 9602018, 9538022, 9525065, 9501033, 9432018, 9426030, 9421025, 9415005, 9407030, 9350013, 9321047.

[36] Ltr. Rul. 9452024.

[37] Ltr. Ruls. 9525065, 9525058, 9422034, 9412030 (conversion from an LLP to an LLC).

[38] Ltr. Rul. 9434027.

[39] Ltr. Rul. 9328005.

[40] Code Sec. 461(i)(3)(A); Ltr. Rul. 9421025.

[41] Ltr. Ruls. 9602018, 9525065, 9525058, 9452024, 9434027, 9426030, 9422034, 9421025, 9415005, 9412030, 9407030, 9350013, 9328005, 9321047.

[42] Ltr. Ruls. 9421025, 9415005 (*citing* Reg. § 1.448-1T(b)(2)).

- Under applicable state or federal law, failure to file a notice of exemption from registration would result in a violation of the applicable federal or state securities law (regardless of whether the notice is filed).[43]

Syndicates

An LLC, partnership or other entity (other than a corporation that is not an S corporation) is a "syndicate" if more than 35 percent of the entity's losses are allocated to limited partners or limited entrepreneurs during the year.[44] An LLC is not a syndicate if any one of the three conditions below is met.

No Losses

An LLC is not a syndicate during any year in which it does not have losses.[45] Most personal service LLCs do not have losses. Companies seeking IRS rulings usually represent that they do not expect to ever incur losses.[46]

Active Participation

An LLC is not a syndicate if none of the members are limited partners or limited entrepreneurs. A limited entrepreneur is a person other than a limited partner who does not actively participate in the management of the LLC.[47] A member of an LLC is not a limited partner or limited entrepreneur if the member is:[48]

- A person who actively participates in the management of the LLC;
- A formerly active member who actively participated in management for at least five years;
- The estate of an active member or a formerly active member;
- The spouse, child, grandchild, or parent of an active member for the period that the active member is actively participating in management of the LLC; or
- The estate of the spouse, child, grandchild, or parent of an active member for the period that the membership interest is held by the estate and the assigning active member is actively participating in the management of the LLC.

A member may be treated as an active member even if the member does not actively participate in management. Management of the LLC may be delegated to a management committee.[49] The fact that many of the management responsibilities are

---

[43] *Id.*

[44] Code Sec. 1256(e)(3)(B).

[45] Ltr. Ruls. 9535036, 9415005, 9343027.

[46] *See, e.g.,* Ltr. Rul. 9350013.

[47] Ltr. Rul. 9343027 (*citing* Code Sec. 464(e)(2)).

[48] Ltr. Ruls. 9535036, 9525065, 9525058, 9452024, 9350013 (*citing* Code Secs. 1256(e)(3)(B), 1256(e)(3)(C), 464(e)(2), and Reg. § 1.448-1T(b)(3)).

[49] Ltr. Ruls. 9535036, 9422034, 9421025, 9412030, 9407030.

delegated to an executive committee does not preclude a determination that the members actively participate in management.[50] The voting rights of active members may be limited or restricted to certain major matters affecting the LLC and its management.[51]

35 Percent Allocation

An LLC is not a syndicate during any year in which not more than 35 percent of losses are allocated to members who are classified as limited partners or limited entrepreneurs.[52] For example, an LLC for attorneys is not a syndicate if less than 35 percent of losses are allocated to the nonequity members who have no vote in LLC management.[53]

Tax Shelter

An LLC is a "tax shelter" if a significant purpose of the LLC is tax avoidance or tax evasion.[54] Before August 5, 1997, an LLC was a tax shelter if the principal purpose of the LLC was tax avoidance or tax evasion.[55]

The Service will not normally determine whether a significant purpose of the LLC is tax avoidance or tax evasion.[56] However, the Service may give a favorable ruling on this issue if the LLC represents that it is not organized for any federal income tax avoidance motive.[57] It will also rule that an LLC is not classified as a tax shelter solely because of its organization structure as an LLC.[58]

.08 Personal Service Corporation

An LLC that is classified as a personal service corporation may use the cash method of accounting, regardless of the size of its gross receipts.[59]

---

[50] Ltr. Rul. 9407030.

[51] Ltr. Ruls. 9412030, 9407030, 9350013, 9328005, 9321047.

[52] Ltr. Ruls. 9535036, 9452023, 9434027, 9432018.

[53] Ltr. Rul. 9426030.

[54] *See* Code Sec. 6662(d)(2)(C)(ii).

[55] Code Sec. 6662(d)(2)(C)(iii), prior to amendment by Pub. L. No. 105-34, § 1028, 105th Cong., 1st Sess. (Aug. 5, 1997).

[56] Ltr. Ruls. 9501033, 9434027, 9432018, 9426030, 9407030; Rev. Proc. 97-3, § 3.02(1), 1997-1 CB 507.

[57] Ltr. Ruls. 9525065, 9525058, 9452024, 9422034, 9412030.

[58] Ltr. Rul. 9415005.

[59] Code Sec. 448(b)(2).

¶1702 LONG-TERM CONTRACTS

.01 General Rules

A construction company or manufacturer must account for a contract as a long-term contract if the contract requires the company to produce a unique item or one normally requiring more than 12 months to produce, and if the contract will not be completed within a single tax period. The company must use one of the following methods of accounting for long-term contracts:[60]

- *Percentage-of-completion method.*[61] The general role is that an LLC must use the percentage-of-completion method for all long-term contracts.[62] However, an LLC is not required to use the percentage-of-completion method for home construction contracts or certain small construction contracts. The small construction contract exception applies if (i) the LLC estimates at the time that the contract is entered into that the contract will be completed within two years of commencement of the contract, and (ii) the LLC's average gross receipts for the three prior years did not exceed $25 million.[63] The amount of revenue reported each year is determined by multiplying the total estimated contract price times the percentage of completion at the end of the tax year (completion factor) less any gross receipts reported in the prior tax years of the contract.[64] There are two methods of determining the degree of contract completion: the "cost-to-cost method" and the "simplified cost-to-cost method."[65]

- *Percentage-of-completion/ten-percent method.*[66] An LLC may elect to defer recognition of revenue until ten percent of the total estimated allocable contract costs are incurred. The costs incurred before the ten percent year are considered pre-contracting year costs and thus are not deductible until the ten percent year. This method of accounting is an election and applies to all long-term contracts entered into during, and in all taxable years after, the electing year.[67]

- *Percentage of completion/capitalized cost method.*[68] An LLC may determine the income from a long-term residential construction contract using either the percentage of completion method or the percentage of completion/capitalized

---

[60] *See* Construction Industry Audit Technique Guide (ATG), available at https://www.irs.gov/pub/irs-utl/constructionindustry_atg.pdf.

[61] Code Sec. 460(f)(2), (a); CCA 201222036.

[62] Code Sec. 460(a).

[63] Code Sec. 460(e)(1)(B)(ii), as amended by 2017 Tax Cuts and Jobs Act § 13102(d)(1)(B).

[64] Reg. § 1.460-4(b)(2).

[65] Code Sec. 460.

[66] Code Sec. 460(b)(5); Reg. § 1.460-4(b)(6).

[67] This election is unavailable if the taxpayer elected to use the simplified method for allocation of costs under Code Sec. 460(b)(3)(A) or is exempt under Code Sec. 460(e).

[68] Reg. § 1.460-4(c)(1).

cost method. The percentage of completion/capitalized cost method allows the residential construction contractor to report 70 percent of the contract under the percentage of completion method (as required by Code Sec. 460) and the remaining 30 percent under an exempt method (e.g., completed contract method discussed below). A residential construction contract differs from a home construction contract in that a home construction contract involves buildings with four or fewer dwelling units, whereas a residential construction contract involves buildings with more than four dwelling units (e.g., apartment buildings or condominiums with five or more units in each building).[69]

- *Completed contract method.* Under this method, an LLC does not take into account the gross contract price or allocable contract costs until the contract is completed, even though progress payments are received in years prior to completion. A contract is completed when 95 percent of the total costs have been incurred. An LLC may use this method only if the contract is an exempt long-term contract.[70] The primary examples of exempt long-term contracts are home construction contracts[71] and contracts of construction companies with average annual gross receipts of less than $10 million that are expected to be completed within two years.[72]

- *Accrual method.* A contract is not a long-term contract if the manufactured item does not require more than 12 months to produce and is not unique (e.g., because one of the safe harbors in Reg. § 1.460-2(b)(2) is met). The manufacturer may then account for the contract under the accrual method of accounting. The manufacturer is not required to use the percentage-of-completion method in such case.[73]

- *Capitalization method for spec buildings.* A developer that builds homes on speculation without a contract with a third-party owner must account for income and expenses under the cost capitalization method. The developer must report income from the sale of the property at the time of settlement or closing. Costs incurred in the construction of homes and other permanent improvements to real property are not currently deductible. Instead the cost of unsold homes and construction in progress is a capital expenditure that becomes part of the basis of the real estate, which in turn is recovered either

---

[69] *See* Code Sec. 460(e)(6).

[70] CCA 201222036; Reg. § 1.460-4(c).

[71] A contract is a home construction contract if 80 percent or more of the estimated total contract costs are reasonably expected to be attributable to buildings with four or fewer dwelling units and to improvements to real property directly related to such dwelling units. Code Sec. 460(e)(6). The Tax Court determined that a home construction contracts qualified for the completed contract method even if the home construction contract included common improvements and amenities of a real estate development in addition to the home and its lot. *Shea Homes, Inc. v. Comm'r*, 142 TC 60, CCH Dec. 59,829 (2014). However, an LLC may not use the completed contract method if the home construction contract consists solely of common improvements. *Howard Hughes Co. LLC v. Comm'r*, 142 TC 355 (2014).

[72] Code Sec. 460(e); CCA 201222036.

[73] CCA 201222036.

¶ 1702.01

through a depreciation allowance if the property is used in a trade or business (rented), or as an offset against the price received in the sale or disposition of such property. Since there is no contract with a third-party owner to build the home, long-term contract accounting methods such as the completed contract method and the percentage of completion method do not apply. Any homes on hand at the end of the year are treated in the industry as inventory of unsold homes or work in process. However, these homes do not meet the definition of inventory under the Code. Speculation homes are instead capital assets under Code Sec. 263.[74]

.02 Special Rules Applicable to LLCs

After an LLC enters into a long-term contract, there may be mid-contract changes in the LLC, such as the issuance of additional membership units, additional contributions to the LLC, transfers of membership interest, distributions of long-term contracts, and adjustments in the basis of LLC assets. These mid-contract changes in the LLC are characterized as either "constructive completion transactions" or "step-in-the-shoes transactions."

In a constructive completion transaction, the old taxpayer is treated as completing the contract, and the new taxpayer is treated as entering into a new contract on the transaction date.[75] In a step-in-the-shoes transaction, the old taxpayer's obligation to account for the contract terminates on the transaction date. The new taxpayer assumes the contract, including the old taxpayer's method of accounting for the contract. The contract price and the allocable contract costs are determined based on amounts taken into account by both parties.[76]

The following rules apply to mid-contract changes in an LLC:[77]

- *Contribution of long-term contract to an LLC.* The contribution of a long-term contract to an LLC is a step-in-the shoes transaction. The LLC must assume the contributing member's obligations to account for the long-term contract. The LLC must reduce the total contract price by the amount of income recognized by the contributing member. The member must increase his or her basis in the membership interest by the amount of gross receipts recognized by the member. The member must reduce his or her basis in the membership interest by the amount of receipts that the member has received or reasonably

---

[74] IRS Publication, Construction Industry ATG—Chapter 7 Homebuilders and Developers, under the heading, Homes Built for Speculation (No Contract). *See also W.C. & A.N. Miller Development Co. v. Comm'r*, 81 TC 619 (1983); *Homes by Ayres v. Comm'r*, TC Memo 1984-475, aff'd, 795 F.2d 832 (9th Cir. 1986); Rev. Rul. 86-149, 1986-2 CB 67; Rev. Rul. 66-247, 1966-2 CB 198.

[75] Reg. § 1.460-4(k)(2).

[76] Reg. § 1.460-4(k)(3).

[77] Reg. § 1.460-4; Preamble to Proposed Regulations on Partnership Transactions Involving Long-Term Contracts, REG-128203-02, Fed. Reg. Vol. 68, No. 151, p. 46516.

expects to receive. The member must recognize income to the extent the reduction exceeds the member's basis in the membership interest.[78]

- *Built-in gain and loss.* The long-term contract is treated as Section 704(c) property. The built-in gain or loss must be allocated to the contributing member. There is a three-step process to determine the built-in gain or loss. First, the contributing member must take into account income or loss attributable to the period prior to the date of contribution. Second, the LLC must determine the amount of income or loss that the contributing member would take into account if the contract were disposed of for fair market value. Third, this amount is reduced by the amount of income that the member must recognize as a result of the contribution.[79]

- *Transfer of membership interest.* The transfer of a membership interest is a step-in-the shoes transaction. A long-term contract is an unrealized receivable under Code Sec. 751. Thus, gain or loss recognized by a member on sale of the membership interest attributable to a long-term contract is ordinary income or loss. The amount of ordinary income or loss attributable to the long-term contract is the amount of income or loss that the LLC would take into account if the LLC disposed of the contract for fair market value in a constructive completion transaction at the time the member sold the membership interest.[80]

- *LLC basis adjustment.* An LLC that has made an election under Code Sec. 754 of the Code must adjust the basis of LLC property when a member transfers a membership interest or dies. Any basis adjustment allocated to the long-term contract must reduce or increase the transferee member's distributive share of income or loss from the contract. If the LLC uses the completed contract method of accounting, the LLC must make the adjustment in the year of completion. Otherwise, the LLC must make the adjustment over the remaining term of the contract.[81]

- *Allocation of income to terminated member.* An LLC may allocate income to a member whose interest terminates during the year by closing its books on the termination date, or by prorating LLC income for the year to the members based on the number of days that each person was a member in the LLC.[82] The step-in-the-shoes rules apply to the LLC on the transfer or liquidation of a membership interest in an LLC holding a long-term contract only if the LLC closes its books with respect to the contract. The LLC will then allocate income to the terminated member based on income from the long-term contract earned prior to the liquidation of the membership interest. If the LLC uses the proration method of accounting for the terminated interest instead of the closing of the books method, then the step-in-the-shoes rules do not apply

---

[78] Prop. Reg. § 1.460-4(k)(3)(iv)(A).

[79] Reg. § 1.460-4(k)(3)(v)(A).

[80] Reg. § 1.460-4(k)(2)(iv)(E).

[81] Reg. § 1.460-4(k)(3)(v)(B).

[82] Reg. § 1.706-1(c)(2)(ii).

to the contract. Instead, the LLC must prorate income or loss from each long-term contract under any reasonable method that complies with Code Sec. 706.[83]

- *Distributions of long-term contract to members.* The distribution of a long-term contract by the LLC to a member is a constructive completion transaction.[84] The LLC must determine each member's distributive share of income or loss from the transaction as if the books were closed on the date of the distribution.[85] The LLC is treated as realizing income equal to the fair market value of the contract.

¶ 1703 FISCAL YEAR

.01 *General*

An LLC that is classified as a partnership may adopt one of the following tax years:[86]

- a required tax year determined by reference to the tax year of the members;
- a natural business year (business purpose year) if the LLC obtains the consent of the Commissioner under Section 442;
- a tax year resulting in a deferral of three months or less if the LLC makes an election under Code Sec. 444;
- a 52-53 week fiscal year; or
- a grandfathered fiscal year.

Code Sec. 706 imposes restrictions on adoption of a fiscal year in order to prevent a deferral of income. An LLC that is classified as a partnership recognizes income, gain, loss and deductions on the last day of its fiscal year.[87] Thus, if an LLC has a fiscal year ending January 31, the members of the LLC will have an 11-month deferral of income recognition.

.02 *Required Tax Year*

An LLC must normally adopt a "required tax year." This is a tax year that is determined by reference to the tax year of the LLC's members.[88] The required tax year must be:

---

[83] Reg. § 1.460-4(k)(3)(v)(D).

[84] Reg. § 1.460-4(k)(2)(iv)(A).

[85] Reg. § 1.460-4(k)(2)(iv)(B).

[86] Code Sec. 706(b); Reg. § 1.706-1(b)(2); Reg. § 1.441-1(b)(2)(ii)(B).

[87] Code Sec. 706(a).

[88] Code Sec. 706(b); Reg. § 1.706-1(b)(2)(i).

- the tax year of a majority of its members who own in the aggregate more than 50 percent of the LLC profits and capital;[89]

- the tax year of all the principal (five percent or more) members if there is no tax year of a majority of the members; and

- if neither of the above tax years applies, the tax year that results in the least aggregate deferral of income to the members.[90]

An LLC may obtain automatic approval from the IRS to adopt or change to a required tax year.[91]

An LLC may be required to change its fiscal year as a result of a change in ownership of membership interests. There is a one-year grace period before an LLC is required to change its tax year as a result of minor ownership changes.[92]

.03 Natural Business Year

General

An LLC may adopt a natural business year other than the required tax year if it shows a proper business purpose and obtains the consent of the Commissioner under Code Sec. 442.[93] An LLC can show a proper business purpose by meeting one of the following tests:

- 25 percent gross receipts test;

- annual business cycle test;

- seasonal business test; or

- facts and circumstances test.

An LLC that adopts a natural business year must continue to meet the natural business year requirements in order to continue using the tax year. The LLC must change back to the required tax year or a permitted tax year if it no longer meets one on the natural business-years tests.[94]

---

[89] Code Sec. 706(b)(1)(B)(i). This determination is made on "testing days," which is generally the first day of the LLC's current tax year. The IRS may specify alternative testing days in order to more accurately reflect the ownership of the LLC.

[90] The tax year that produces the least aggregate deferral of income is determined under Reg. § 1.706-1(b)(3).

[91] Rev. Proc. 2002-38, 2002-2 CB 4, § § 3.01, 4.01(1).

[92] Rev. Proc. 2002-38, 2002-2 CB 4. The grace period applies if there is an ownership change of less than ten percent of the aggregate interests in the LLC, and the LLC reasonably foresees that the ownership change may be reversed within one year. An LLC that is required to change its majority interest tax year is not required to further change its tax year for two years after the change. Reg. § 1.706-1(b)(8)(i).

[93] Code Sec. 706(b)(1)(C); Reg. § § 1.442-1, 1.706-1(b)(8).

[94] Rev. Proc. 2002-39, 2002-2 CB 33, § 5.04(4).

25 Percent Gross Receipts Test

An LLC may adopt a natural business year based on the 25 percent gross receipts test. The LLC must show that 25 percent or more of its gross receipts from sales and services for a 12-month period were recognized in the last two months of the 12-month period, and that this has occurred for three consecutive 12-month periods.[95]

If more than one 12-month period satisfies the gross receipts test, and one of the 12-month periods produces a higher average than the requested year, then the requested year will not qualify as a natural business year.[96]

An LLC that been in existence for fewer than three years may not adopt a fiscal year based on the 25 percent gross receipts test.[97] In order to adopt the fiscal year, the LLC must provide information to the IRS on Form 1128 for the most recent 47 months.[98] These months include the 36 months in the requested three-year period, plus 11 additional months for comparing the requested tax year with other potential tax years.

An LLC that meets this test is granted automatic consent to change to its natural business year even though this results in a greater deferral of income than its current tax year.[99] The LLC must send Form 1128, "Application To Adopt, Change, or Retain a Tax Year" to the IRS by the due date, including extensions, for filing the LLC tax return for the first effective year. The LLC must identify the request as an automatic approval request by labeling the form, "Filed Under Rev. Proc. 2002-38." The LLC must send the form to the IRS service center where the LLC files its return and attach a copy of the form to its tax return for the first effective year.[100]

Annual Business Cycle Test

An LLC may adopt a natural business year based on the annual business cycle test. The gross receipts must show that the LLC has a peak and non-peak period of business. An LLC does not meet this test if it has income that is steady from month-to-month throughout the year.[101]

The natural business year must end soon after annual peak period of business.[102] One month is considered "soon after" the close of the highest-peak period of business.[103]

---

[95] Rev. Proc. 2002-38, 2002-2 CB 4, § 5.05.

[96] Rev. Proc. 2002-38, 2002-2 CB 4, § 5.05(2).

[97] Ann. 2002-53, 2002-1 CB 1063.

[98] Rev. Proc. 2002-38, 2002-2 CB 4, § 7.02(6).

[99] Rev. Proc. 2002-38, 2002-2 CB 4, § § 3.02, 4.01(2).

[100] Rev. Proc. 2002-38, 2002-2 CB 4, § 7.02.

[101] Rev. Proc. 2002-39, 2002-2 CB 33, § 5.03(1)(a).

[102] Rev. Proc. 2002-39, 2002-2 CB 33, § 5.03(1).

[103] Rev. Proc. 2002-39, 2002-2 CB 33, § 5.03(1)(b).

The LLC must obtain IRS approval by filing Form 1128.[104] The LLC must include on Form 1128 gross receipts from sales and services for the short period and the three immediately preceding tax years. An LLC that has not been in existence for three years may provide information other than gross receipts to demonstrate a peak and a non-peak period of business, such as a reasonable description of the business and/or reasonable estimates of future gross receipts.[105]

Seasonal Business Test

An LLC may adopt a natural business year based on the seasonal business test. The gross receipts must show that the LLC's business is operational for only part of the year (e.g., due to weather conditions). The LLC must have insignificant gross receipts during the period of business that it is not operational.[106] An amount equal to less than ten percent of the LLC's total gross receipts for the year is considered insignificant.[107]

The LLC's natural business year must end soon after the operations end for the season.[108] One month is considered "soon after" the close of operations.[109]

The LLC must obtain IRS approval by filing Form 1128.[110] The LLC must include on Form 1128 gross receipts from sales and services for the short period and the three immediately preceding tax years. An LLC that has not been in existence for three years may provide information other than gross receipts to demonstrate that it has a seasonal business, such as a description of its business and/or reasonable estimates of future gross receipts.[111]

Facts and Circumstances Test

An LLC that is not able to establish a natural business year based on the gross receipts test, annual business cycle test, or seasonal business test may establish a business purpose for a tax year based on all the facts and circumstances.[112]

The LLC must obtain IRS approval by filing Form 1128.[113] The IRS will grant approval only in "rare and unusual circumstances."[114] The IRS has not provided

---

[104] Rev. Proc. 2002-39, 2002-2 CB 33, § 6.01(1).

[105] Rev. Proc. 2002-39, 2002-2 CB 33, § 5.03(1)(a).

[106] Rev. Proc. 2002-39, 2002-2 CB 33, § 5.03(2)(a).

[107] Rev. Proc. 2002-39, 2002-2 CB 33, § 5.03(2)(b).

[108] Rev. Proc. 2002-39, 2002-2 CB 33, § 5.03(2)(a).

[109] Rev. Proc. 2002-39, 2002-2 CB 33, § 5.03(2)(b).

[110] Rev. Proc. 2002-39, 2002-2 CB 33, § 6.01(1).

[111] Rev. Proc. 2002-39, 2002-2 CB 33, § 5.03(2)(a).

[112] Reg. § 1.441-1(b)(2)(ii)(B); Rev. Proc. 2002-39, 2002-2 CB 33, § 5.02(1)(b).

[113] Rev. Proc. 2002-39, 2002-2 CB 33, § 6.01(1).

[114] Rev. Proc. 2002-39, 2002-2 CB 33, § 5.02(1)(b).

guidance on what constitutes rare and unusual circumstances. However, the following facts and circumstances are not sufficient to establish a business purpose:[115]

- the deferral of income to the members of the LLC;
- the use of a particular year for regulatory or financial accounting purposes;
- the hiring patterns of the LLC, such as the fact that the LLC typically hires staff during certain times of the year;
- the use of a particular year for administration purposes, such as the admission or retirement of members, promotion of staff, and compensation or retirement arrangements with staff and members of the LLC;
- other administrative and convenience business reasons such as those described in Rev. Rul. 87-57,[116] including the need to take advantage of an accountant's reduced rates, to have recordkeeping consistency, and to issue timely tax information forms to members;
- the fact that a particular business involves the use of price lists, a model year or other items that change on an annual basis;
- the use of a particular year by related entities; and
- the use of a particular year by competitors.

.04 Three-Month Deferral Tax Year

A newly formed LLC may elect a fiscal year having a deferral period of three months or less.[117] Other LLCs may adopt such fiscal year by obtaining the consent of the IRS.[118]

In practice, this means that an LLC may have a fiscal year ending September 30, October 31, or November 30 if the members of the LLC are individuals, or if a majority of the members of an LLC have a calendar year.

An electing LLC must make a "required payment" in the form of a noninterest-bearing loan to the government.[119] This is a special tax that is approximately equal to the amount of tax savings that the members realize from the deferral of income. The required payment is redetermined annually based on the income earned by the LLC. The LLC must make additional payments if income increases. The LLC receives a refund of payments if income decreases.[120] An LLC is not required to make the payment if it establishes a fiscal year under one of the business purpose tests discussed above.

---

[115] Rev. Proc. 2002-39, 2002-2 CB 33, § 5.02(1)(b).

[116] Rev. Rul. 87-57, 1987-2 CB 117; Rev. Proc. 2002-39, 2002-2 CB 33, § 5.02(1)(b).

[117] Code Sec. 444(b)(1); Reg. § 1.706-1(b)(7); Rev. Proc. 2002-38, 2002-2 CB 4, § 2.07; Ltr. Ruls. 200617030, 200617029, 200617028.

[118] Reg. § 1.706-1(b)(10).

[119] Code Sec. 444; Temp. Reg. § § 1.444-1T(b)(2), 1.444-3T(b)(1).

[120] Code Sec. 7519(c).

An LLC must follow the following procedures in adopting the fiscal year:

- The LLC must make the election by filing Form 8716, "Election to Have a Tax Year Other Than a Required Tax Year."[121] The election is a one-time election to use the fiscal year. The IRS approval of the election for an LLC that adopts or changes to a three-month deferral tax year is automatic.[122]
- The LLC must complete and file Form 8752, "Required Payment or Refund Under Section 7519," to compute the required payments when the election is in effect. The due date for Form 8752 is May 15 of the calendar year following the calendar year in which the applicable year begins.[123] The LLC must make a payment if the remaining amount on deposit is less than the required amount. It may obtain a refund if the amount on deposit is more than the required payment. The deposit amount is calculated by multiplying the taxable income of the LLC times the deferral ratio times the highest individual tax rate plus one percent. The deferral ratio is the number of months that elapse before the beginning of the calendar year divided by 12.
- The LLC must file an annual return on Form 720, "Quarterly Federal Excise Tax Return." The return must be filed even if no required payment is due for the year.[124]

EXAMPLE 17-2

A newly formed LLC elects a fiscal year ending September 30. This results in a three-month deferral of income, since the income of the LLC earned between October 1 and December 31 of the first year is taxable to the members of the LLC during the following year. Therefore, the deferral percentage is 25 percent (three months divided by 12 months). However, there is no required payment because this is the first year of the LLC. There is no net income during the prior year.[125]

EXAMPLE 17-3

During the LLC's first tax year ending on September 30, it has taxable income of $1 million that it passes through to its members. Therefore, the LLC must make a required payment for its second tax year ending on September 30. The required payment for the second tax year is $90,000 ($1 million of taxable income for the first tax year times the 25 percent

---

[121] Temp. Reg. § 1.444-3T(b)(1); Rev. Proc. 2002-38, 2002-2 CB 4, § 2.07.
[122] Rev. Proc. 2002-38, 2002-2 CB 4, § 2.07.
[123] Temp. Reg. § 1.7519-2T(a)(4)(ii).
[124] Temp. Reg. § 1.7519-2T(a)(2)(i), (a)(4)(ii).
[125] Temp. Reg. § 1.7519-1T(b)(4).

deferral ratio times 36 percent tax rate). The 36 percent tax rate is the highest individual tax rate plus one percent.

EXAMPLE 17-4

The LLC earns $900,000 of taxable income that it passes through to its members during its second tax year. Therefore, the required payment for the third tax year is $81,000 ($900,000 of taxable income times 25 percent deferral ratio times 36 percent tax rate). The LLC is entitled to a refund of $9,000 when it files Form 8752 (deposit amount of $90,000 for the second tax year less the required payment of $81,000 for the third tax year).

.05 *52- to 53-Week Tax Year*

An LLC may adopt a 52- to 53-week fiscal year if the year ends with reference to the fiscal year that the LLC would otherwise be required to adopt.[126]

Most individual members of an LLC report income on a calendar year basis. If the tax year of an LLC with a 52- to 53-week tax year ends in January, the individual members are taxable on their distributive shares of income for the calendar year ending on the prior December 31. Similarly, if the LLC makes a bonus payment to a member in January prior to the end of its fiscal year, the member must report the bonus as income for the calendar year ending on the prior December 31.[127]

.06 *Grandfathered Tax Year*

An LLC may continue to use a fiscal year under grandfather provisions if the LLC received permission by a letter ruling (not by automatic approval) to use a fiscal year between 1974 and 1987, and the fiscal year resulted in more than a three-month deferral.[128]

.07 *Procedures for Adopting and Changing Tax Year*

Adopting a Tax Year

A newly formed LLC may adopt a required tax year, a three-month deferral tax year, or 52-53 week tax year without obtaining the consent of the IRS.[129] The LLC elects the tax year on Form SS-4, "Application for Employer Identification Number."

---

[126] Reg. §§1.441-1(b)(2)(ii)(B), 1.441-2(e)(1), 1.706-1(b)(3)(ii); Rev. Proc. 2002-38, 2002-2 CB 4, §§3.04, 4.01(4).

[127] Reg. §1.441-2(e)(4), Example (1).

[128] Reg. §1.441-1(b)(6).

[129] Reg. §1.706-1(b)(7); Rev. Proc. 2002-38, 2002-2 CB 4, §2.02.

A newly formed LLC may adopt a business purpose tax year only by obtaining the consent of the IRS under Code Sec. 442.[130]

Changing the Tax Year

An existing LLC may change its tax year in one of the following ways:

- Obtain the consent of the IRS for a natural business year based on the annual business cycle test, the seasonal business test, or the facts and circumstances test.[131] The LLC must file an application with the IRS on Form 1128, "Application to Adopt, Change, or Retain a Tax Year." The LLC must file the form prior to the due date of the LLC's federal income tax return, including extensions, for the first effective year.[132]

- Make an election under Code Sec. 444 for a three-month deferral.[133] The LLC may automatically adopt, change to, or retain a three-month deferral tax year by filing Form 8716, "Election to Have a Tax Year Other Than a Required Tax Year."[134]

- Obtain automatic approval for a change to a required tax year,[135] or a change to a natural business year based on the 25 percent gross receipts test.[136]

- Obtain the consent of the IRS,[137] or obtain automatic approval,[138] to adopt, change to, or change from, a 52-53 week fiscal year.

An LLC that changes its tax year must file a return for a short period.[139] The LLC must close its books on the last day of the first effective year.[140] It may not annualize LLC taxable income on the short period return.[141]

An LLC may not request or otherwise make a retroactive change in its fiscal year.[142]

An LLC may not change its fiscal year if the LLC is under examination, without the consent of the appropriate director, or if its annual accounting period is under examination before a federal court or IRS area office.[143]

---

[130] Reg. § 1.706-1(b)(7).

[131] Reg. § 1.706-1(b)(8)(i)(A); Rev. Proc. 2002-39, 2002-2 CB 33, § 5.01(2).

[132] Rev. Proc. 2002-38, 2002-2 CB 4, § § 3.12, 7.02(2).

[133] Reg. § 1.706-1(b)(8)(i)(A).

[134] Rev. Proc. 2002-38, 2002-2 CB 4, § 2.07.

[135] Rev. Proc. 2002-38, 2002-2 CB 4, § § 3.01, 4.01(1).

[136] Reg. § 1.706-1(b)(8)(i)(A); Rev. Proc. 2002-38, 2002-2 CB 4, § § 3.02, 4.01(2).

[137] Rev. Proc. 2002-38, 2002-2 CB 4, § § 3.03, 4.01(1), (2), (3).

[138] Rev. Proc. 2002-38, 2002-2 CB 4, § § 3.03, 4.01(4).

[139] Rev. Proc. 2002-39, 2002-2 CB 33, § 5.04(1).

[140] Rev. Proc. 2002-39, 2002-2 CB 33, § 5.04(3).

[141] Reg. § 1.706-1(b)(8)(i)(B); Rev. Proc. 2002-38, 2002-2 CB 4, § 2.03(2) (last sentence).

[142] Rev. Proc. 2002-38, 2002-2 CB 4, § 2.03(3).

[143] Rev. Proc. 2002-38, 2002-2 CB 4, § § 3.07, 4.02(1)-(4).

¶ 1704 CLOSING OF THE TAX YEAR

The tax year of an LLC does not ordinarily close on the death of a member, the entry of a new member, the liquidation of a membership interest in an LLC, or the sale or exchange of a member's interest in the LLC.[144] However, the tax year of the LLC will close with respect to the individual member who died, or whose interest was sold or liquidated.[145] The LLC must account for changes in membership interests during the year under the proration method or the interim closing of the books method.[146] The rules for specific types of transfers are discussed below.

.01 Dispositions

The tax year of an LLC closes with respect to a member who disposes of his entire interest in the LLC.[147] The tax year of an LLC does not close before the end of the LLC's tax year for a member who disposes of less than his entire interest in the LLC (whether by reason of sale, partial liquidation, gift, or otherwise).[148]

.02 Death

The LLC tax year closes for a deceased member on the date of death,[149] not on the date that the estate of the deceased member transfers the membership interest to the beneficiaries.[150] The final return for the member must include the member's allocable share of income from the LLC for the period prior to the date of death.[151]

Any suspended passive activity losses are allowed on the decedent's final return. However, the suspended losses are reduced by the amount of the step-up in basis for the membership interest as a result of death.[152]

The estate of the deceased member or the successor in interest is taxed on LLC income attributable to the LLC's tax year after the death of the member. If the decedent member's estate or other successor in interest sells the entire membership interest, or if the entire membership interest is liquidated, the LLC's tax year with respect to the estate or successor in interest closes on such date. The sale or exchange of a membership interest does not, for such purpose, include the transfer of a membership interest as a result of inheritance or a testamentary disposition.[153]

---

[144] Code Sec. 706(c)(1); Reg. § 1.706-1(c)(1).

[145] Reg. § 1.706-1(c)(2)(i).

[146] *See* ¶ ¶ 805, 1504 *supra*.

[147] Code Sec. 706(c)(2)(A); Reg. § 1.706-1(c)(2)(i).

[148] Code Sec. 706(c)(2)(B).

[149] Code Sec. 706(c)(2)(A); Reg. § 1.706-1(c)(2)(i).

[150] Reg. § 1.706-1(c)(2)(ii).

[151] Reg. § 1.706-1(c)(2)(i).

[152] Code Sec. 469(g)(2).

[153] Reg. § 1.706-1(c)(2)(i).

EXAMPLE 17-5

A member dies on March 30, 2010. The estate of the member distributes the membership interest to the surviving spouse on November 30, 2010. The deceased member's final return will include an allocable share of income for the period ending on March 30, 2010. The surviving spouse will include the remaining LLC income on his or her return. The distribution by the probate estate to the surviving spouse is not a termination of the tax year with respect to the estate/surviving spouse.[154]

Current regulations provide that income from the LLC for the entire year of death must be allocated to the deceased member's estate or successor in interest.[155] Those regulations are not valid for tax years after 1997.[156]

.03 50 Percent Change in Ownership

An LLC terminates for tax purposes if there is a sale or exchange of 50 percent or more of the LLC's capital and profits during a 12-month period.[157] The tax year of the terminated LLC closes. The terminated LLC must file a short-year final return for the tax year ending with the date of its termination. The new LLC must file a return for its tax year beginning after the date of termination of the terminated partnership. The rule applies even though the new LLC uses the same employer identification number as the terminated LLC.[158]

The tax consequences of a 50 percent change in ownership are discussed in Chapter 12.[159]

.04 Retiring Members

The tax year of the LLC does not close with respect to a retired member until the LLC makes the last distribution payment to the member. The retired member continues to be treated as a member until the liquidation of the member's interest in the LLC is completed.[160]

The tax consequences of distributions to retired members are discussed in Chapter 10.[161]

---

[154] Reg. § 1.706-1(c)(2)(ii), Example.

[155] Reg. § 1.706-1(c)(3); (vi), Example (3).

[156] *See* Taxpayer Relief Act of 1997, amending Code Sec. 706(c)(2)(A).

[157] Code Sec. 708(b); Reg. § 1.708-1(b)(1).

[158] F.S.A. 200132009; IRS Notice 2001-5, 2001-3 IRB 327. *See* ¶ 1203 *supra*, regarding the tax consequences to the terminated and successor LLC on the sale or exchange of more than 50 percent of the membership units during any 12-month period.

[159] *See* § 1203.02 *supra*.

[160] Code Sec. 706(c)(2)(A); Reg. § § 1.708-1(b)(1)(i), 1.736-1(a)(6), 1.761-1(d).

[161] *See* § 1010 *supra*.

¶ 1705 CONSOLIDATED TAX RETURNS FOR SUBSIDIARIES

A corporation may form a subsidiary LLC and obtain the tax advantages of filing a consolidated tax return. There are planning considerations for both domestic and foreign LLCs.

An affiliated group of corporations may file a consolidated federal tax return instead of a separate return for each corporation.[162] The main advantages of filing a consolidated return are these:

- Operating losses of one corporation may offset the profits of another.
- Capital losses of one corporation may offset the capital gains of another in the affiliated group.
- There is no tax on intercompany dividends.
- Income on intercompany transactions is deferred.
- The consolidated group may use a member corporation's excess foreign tax credits.
- The parent corporation may adjust the basis in the stock in the subsidiary to reflect the subsidiary's taxable income or losses, tax-exempt income, and noncapital, nondeductible expenses. The corporate parent may use the increased stock basis to offset gain that it would otherwise recognize upon the sale of the stock in the subsidiary.

A foreign corporation may not be included in a consolidated return.[163] The parent company may obtain the same tax benefits by forming an LLC in a foreign country that has limited liability for foreign purposes and that is disregarded as an entity for U.S. tax purposes. All income and losses of the foreign subsidiary then pass through to the parent corporation to the same extent as those of a foreign unincorporated branch or division.

A single-member domestic LLC also provides many of the same tax benefits as a corporate subsidiary that is part of a consolidated return. The single-member LLC is disregarded as a separate entity, assuming that no election is made to classify the LLC as a corporation. Profits and losses automatically pass through to the parent corporation. Losses pass through without the limitations on net operating loss carryovers and carrybacks that apply to subsidiaries that are part of a consolidated return. Dividends paid by the LLC and gains and losses on intercompany transactions are also disregarded. The parent corporation is not required to file a consolidated return to include the single member's subsidiary LLC as part of its federal return filing. It can thus avoid the cumbersome and burdensome requirements applicable to corporations that have elected consolidated tax treatment.

One disadvantage is that the corporate parent of the single-member LLC may not increase its basis in the LLC membership units by the income that passes through from the LLC to the parent corporation. Since the LLC is disregarded as an entity, the

---

[162] Code Sec. 1501.
[163] Code Sec. 1504(b)(3).

parent corporation is treated as selling all of the underlying assets upon the sale of the LLC to a third party.

¶1706 RULING REQUESTS

.01 Classification of LLC

The IRS issued the check-the-box regulations on the classification of LLCs[164] so that ruling requests will generally not be necessary. However, it will still issue classification rulings under the check-the-box regulations.[165] The IRS will also issue private letter rulings on late election classifications.[166]

.02 Inadvertent Termination of LLC

The IRS may issue a ruling granting relief from inadvertent termination of an S corporation as a result of an LLC's acquisition of stock in the S corporation. The requirements for a ruling are discussed at ¶403.02.

¶1707 ACCOUNTING METHODS FOR SINGLE-MEMBER LLC

A single-member disregarded LLC may conduct a separate and distinct trade or business and elect its own method of accounting separate from the owner's method of accounting. Accounting methods are chosen at the trade or business level. Determining what constitutes a separate trade or business is a factual determination. Thus, if a corporation is the sole member of a disregarded LLC, the LLC may elect its own method of accounting if it conducts a trade or business that is separate from the corporate member.[167]

---

[164] T.D. 8697 (Dec. 18, 1996).
[165] Ltr. Rul. 200214016.
[166] See ¶508.08 supra.
[167] CCA 201430013.

18

Foreign LLCs

¶ 1801 REASONS FOR ESTABLISHING FOREIGN LLC

.01 Pass-Through of Losses

One reason for forming a foreign LLC is to permit the pass-through of losses from foreign operations to the U.S. parent corporation. This is a common reason for start-up foreign manufacturing operations where losses are expected during the initial years. A U.S. corporation may not include a foreign subsidiary corporation in a

¶ 1801.01

consolidated return.[1] Any losses are locked in the foreign corporation and cannot offset taxable income of the U.S. parent corporation.

The foreign LLC results in the immediate recognition of foreign income. The U.S. parent corporation may not defer income on foreign operations of an LLC that is classified as a partnership or disregarded entity. In contrast, a U.S. parent corporation may defer income recognition by using a foreign subsidiary corporation, subject to anti-abuse provisions such as Subpart F.

.02 Foreign Tax Credits

A member of an LLC that is classified as a partnership may claim a foreign tax credit for the member's proportionate share of foreign taxes paid or accrued during the tax year by the LLC to a foreign country or to any U.S. possession.[2] The IRS issued safe-harbor regulations regarding the allocation of foreign tax credits to members, which are discussed at ¶ 804.08.

.03 Dividends Received Deduction

Under the participation exemption system for tax years beginning in 2018, a U.S. corporation that owns ten percent or more of the stock in a foreign corporation receives a 100 percent dividends-received deduction (DRD) on dividends that the foreign corporation pays out of its foreign-source earnings.[3] The U.S. shareholders no longer receive a foreign tax credit on dividends from the foreign corporation.[4] In addition, there are no deductions for foreign taxes, including withholding taxes, on the distributions.[5] The DRD does not apply to shareholders that are not corporations, including LLCs classified as partnerships, even though such shareholders are subject to immediate taxation on their allocable share of retained earnings of the foreign corporation.

.04 Controlled Foreign Corporations

Many private equity structures use an LLC or other fiscally transparent entity to own stock in a foreign corporation. Beginning in 2018, more types of income and investment earnings of a controlled foreign corporation owned by U.S. shareholders (CFC) are treated as distributed to the U.S. shareholders and currently subject to taxation. The income of a CFC is now divided into the following categories:

1. *Subpart F income.* Subpart F income is income that Congress determined could be easily shifted to low-tax jurisdictions, and should be subject to

---

[1] Code Sec. 1504(b)(3).

[2] Code Sec. 901(b)(5).

[3] Code Sec. 245A(a), as added by 2017 Tax Cuts and Jobs Act § 14101(a).

[4] Code Sec. 902, repealed by the 2017 Tax Cuts and Jobs Act.

[5] Committee Report on 2017 Tax Cuts and Jobs Act § 4101.

current tax at the full U.S. tax rates, whether or not distributed. Subpart F income includes insurance income, foreign base company sales income, foreign-based company service income, and foreign personal holding company income. Foreign personal holding company income includes dividends, interest, rents, royalties, certain foreign currency gains, and certain passive gains.[6] The maximum tax rate on Subpart F income is 21% for corporate shareholders, and 37% for individuals, LLCs and other pass-through entities. Once taxed, this income is included in a PTI account (previously taxed account) for each shareholder. Distributions out of the PTI account are not subject to additional tax. U.S. corporate shareholders are eligible for a foreign tax credit on income taxes paid on Subpart F income.[7] The Subpart F income is grossed up by the amount of the deemed paid taxes. LLCs and other non-corporate shareholders in a CFC are not eligible for the foreign tax credit on Subpart F income, and there is no gross up in their income.

2. *Global low-tax intangible income (GILTA)*.[8] GILTA income is income from global intangibles, such as patents, copyrights and trademarks. It includes all income of a CFC other than (i) income effectively connected with the conduct of U.S. trade or business subject to regular U.S. taxes, (ii) Subpart F income, (ii) high-tax kickout income (discussed below) (iv) dividends from a related party, and (v) foreign oil and gas extraction income.[9] A U.S. domestic corporation may deduct 50% of the GILTI income.[10] The effective tax rate for U.S. corporate shareholders is 10.5% in 2018, increasing to approximately 13.125% after 2025.[11] GILTA income is included in the shareholder's PTI account and not subject to further tax on distribution from the PTI account. The shareholder must own 10% or greater ownership of the voting power of the foreign corporation to receive the reduced tax rate. The reduced tax rate is not available to corporate and non-corporate partners in an LLC unless the LLC elects to be classified as a C corporation for U.S. tax purposes.[12] As a result, it may be more efficient for U.S. investors to own foreign company stock through a U.S. corporate blocker entity that is eligible for the reduced GILTI tax rate. The GILTA tax rate is a maximum 37% for non-corporate owners of a foreign corporation. Corporate shareholders in a CFC may claim a tax credit for 80% of the foreign income taxes associated with the GILTA income, in which case the income is grossed up by the amount of taxes paid, and a deduction is then allowed for 50% of the gross-up amount. LLCs and

---

[6] Code Sec. 952.

[7] Code Sec. 960

[8] Code Sec. 951A.

[9] Code Sec. 951A(b)(1)((A), 951A(c)(2)(A).

[10] Code Sec. 250(a)(1)(B).

[11] Code Sec. 250(a)(3)(B).

[12] 100% of the income is included in the taxable income of LLCs and other non-corporate shareholders.

other non-corporate shareholders in the CFC are not eligible for foreign tax credits on GILTA income.

3. *High-tax kickout income.* High-tax kickout income is income that is taxed at a high foreign tax rate, and is not subject to U.S. taxes. The income must be taxed at a rate higher than 90% of the highest U.S. corporate tax rate. Since the highest corporate tax rate is now 21%, the threshold foreign tax rate that qualifies for the kickout exception is 18.9%. This same rate applies to individual and corporate taxpayers. The income is excluded from both Subpart F income[13] and GILTA income,[14] although the exclusions are slightly different.

4. *Net deemed tangible income return (NDTIR).* This income, like the high-tax kickout income, is generally not subject to U.S. taxes when earned or repatriated to the U.S. as a dividend. The NDTIR is 10% of the qualified business asset investments (tangible asset basis) of the CFC.[15]

If the foreign tax rates are sufficiently high, it may be more tax efficient for the U.S. investors to own foreign LLCs and other entities that are classified as partnerships. The U.S. investors will then be entitled to receive the foreign tax credit on GILTI income.

Distributions from a CFC to a U.S. individual or LLC are nontaxable to the extent previously taxed as Subpart F income and included in the shareholder's PTI account. U.S. corporate shareholders in a CFC also receive a 100% dividends received deduction for the CFC's accumulated corporate earnings not previously taxed as Subpart F income. LLCs and other non-corporate shareholders must include in income 100% of the dividend distributions from a CFC that are not distributed out of previously taxed income. The maximum tax rate is 37% on such income, but may qualify for a reduced income tax rate of 20% under a U.S. income tax treaty.

¶ 1802 FORMATION OF FOREIGN LLCs

The tax consequences of forming a foreign LLC and contributing property to the LLC are generally the same as for domestic LLCs, whether the LLC is classified as a partnership[16] or as a corporation.[17] However, there are several exceptions.

U.S. persons who transfer appreciated property to a domestic or foreign LLC are immediately taxed on the built-in gain if (i) a related foreign person is a direct or indirect member of the LLC, and (ii) the U.S. transferor and one or more related persons own more than 80 percent of the membership interests in the LLC.[18] The

---

[13] Code Sec. 954(b)(4).

[14] Code Sec. 951A(c)(2)(A)(i)(III).

[15] Code Sec. 951A(b)(2).

[16] Ltr. Rul. 8106082.

[17] Ltr. Ruls. 8029031, 8011038, 7935046 (*citing* Code Sec. 367(c)(2) and Rev. Rul. 77-449, 1977-2 CB 110).

[18] Code Sec. 721(c); Temporary (T.D. 9811) and proposed (REG-127203-15) regulations (2017); Reg. § 1.197-1T to § 1.721(c)-6T.

regulations override the rules under Code Sec. 721(a) which provide for nonrecognition of gain on a contribution of property to an LLC in exchange for membership interest in the LLC. To avoid nonrecognition, the LLC must adopt the remedial allocation method and satisfy certain other requirements. The purpose of the regulation is to prevent U.S. taxpayers from contributing appreciated property to a partnership, and then allocating income or gain from the contributed property to related foreign persons who are not subject to U.S. taxes. These rules are discussed at ¶1903.

United States persons who contribute property to a foreign LLC must file a report with the IRS on Form 8865.[19]

¶1803 CLASSIFICATION OF FOREIGN LLCs

The classification of foreign LLCs is discussed at ¶505.

An LLC organized under the laws of the United States is a domestic LLC for classification purposes even if the LLC has foreign members.[20]

¶1804 RULING REQUESTS

The IRS will issue rulings on the classification of foreign LLCs as partnerships or corporations. However, the IRS issued the check-the-box regulations on the classification of LLCs so that ruling requests will generally not be necessary.[21]

¶1805 WITHHOLDING TAXES ON WAGES

An "American employer" is required to withhold FICA taxes on wages paid to citizens or residents of the United States who perform services as employees outside of the United States.[22] A U.S. or foreign LLC that is classified as a partnership is an "American employer" for withholding purposes if two-thirds or more of the partners are residents of the United States.[23]

¶1806 TAX RETURNS AND REPORTING REQUIREMENTS

.01 Partnership Return

A foreign LLC must file a partnership return if it has U.S. source gross income or income that is effectively connected with the conduct of a U.S. trade or business.[24]

---

[19] See ¶1806.02 infra.

[20] Ltr. Rul. 9610006.

[21] See Rev. Proc. 89-12, 1989-1 CB 798, declared obsolete by Rev. Rul. 2003-99, 2003-2 CB 388.

[22] Code Sec. 3402; CCA 200814010; Ltr. Rul. 9335062 (citing Code Sec. 3121(h)(3)).

[23] Ltr. Rul. 9335062.

[24] Code Sec. 6031(e).

The losses, credits and deduction of the LLC are disallowed for tax purposes if the foreign LLC fails to comply with the reporting requirements.[25] The LLC filing requirements are discussed in detail at ¶ 2206.01.

.02 U.S. Members of LLC Classified as Partnership

U.S. members in a foreign LLC must file Form 8865, Information Return of U.S. Persons With Respect to Certain Foreign LLCs, to report the following:[26]

- contributions of cash and other property to a foreign LLC in exchange for a membership interest;[27]
- acquisitions or dispositions of at least a ten percent interest in a foreign LLC;[28] and
- information concerning the income and assets of the LLC, certain transactions with the LLC, the names of the members, and other specified information if the U.S. member owns at least a ten percent interest in a controlled foreign LLC.[29]

The filing requirements on Form 8865 are discussed in detail at ¶ 2206.03.

.03 U.S. Owners of Foreign Disregarded LLC

Persons who own an interest in a foreign disregarded LLC must file Form 8858, Information Return of Persons with Respect to Foreign Disregarded Entities. The reporting requirements apply to U.S. persons who own a foreign LLC directly, indirectly, or constructively through a foreign corporation or foreign partnership.[30] The filing requirements on Form 8865 are discussed in detail at ¶ 2206.02.

.04 Anti-Abuse Provisions

The IRS has regulatory authority to treat LLCs created or organized in the United States as foreign LLCs.[31] This prevents a foreign LLC from avoiding the reporting requirements and penalties by organizing the LLC in the United States.

---

[25] Code Sec. 6231(f).

[26] Reg. § 1.6038B-2(a)(1). The reporting requirements were enacted by Congress in 1997 through amendments to (i) Code Sec. 6046A applicable to U.S. members in a foreign LLC when specified reporting events occur, and (ii) Code Sec. 6038(a)(5) applicable to certain members in a foreign LLC that is controlled by U.S. members.

[27] Code Sec. 6038B; Prop. Reg. § 1.6038B.

[28] Code Sec. 6046A; Prop. Reg. § 1.6046A-1.

[29] Code Sec. 6038; Prop. Reg. § 1.6038-3.

[30] IRS Ann. 2004-4, 2004-4 IRB 357.

[31] Code Sec. 7701(a)(4).

¶ 1807 SECURITIES-TRADING LLCs

Foreign persons who invest in U.S. stocks and securities are not taxed on gain from the sale of the stocks and securities unless:

- The foreign person is a U.S. resident. United States residents are taxed on their worldwide income.

- The foreign person is present in the United States for more than 183 days during the year.[32]

- The gain is from the sale of stock in a U.S. real property holding company.[33] Generally, a U.S. real property holding corporation is a corporation in which more than 50 percent of the fair market value of its assets is U.S. real property interests.[34]

- The foreign person is engaged in a U.S. trade or business. Foreign persons who trade stocks and securities for their own account, including through an LLC, are not treated as engaged in a U.S. trade or business even if the trading activity is conducted directly or indirectly through an agent in the United States.[35]

Capital gains from the sale of securities are not treated as FDAP income (fixed, determinable, and periodic income), and are therefore not subject to the 30 percent withholding tax on FDAP income.[36]

Before 1998, a foreign person who invested in an LLC whose principal business was trading in stocks and securities for the member's account was not treated as engaged in a U.S. trade or business if the LLC's principal office was located outside of the United States. The IRS regulations provided a list of ten activities that, if conducted abroad, would result in the LLC being treated as having its principal office outside of the United States.[37] These were referred to as the "Ten Commandments." In practice, the Ten Commandments were largely a nuisance. Their main effect was to shift certain administrative jobs outside of the United States. In 1997, Congress repealed this requirement. Foreign LLCs that trade in stock and securities are no longer required to maintain their principal office outside the United States.[38]

Most securities-trading LLCs still maintain their principal offices outside of the United States. The reason is that foreign investors prefer to maintain the confidentiality of their records and membership information by keeping that information outside of the United States.

---

[32] Code Sec. 871(b).

[33] Code Sec. 897.

[34] Code Sec. 897(c)(2).

[35] Code Sec. 864(b)(2)(A).

[36] Reg. § 1.1441-2(b)(1)(i), (2)(i).

[37] Reg. § 1.864-2(c)(2)(iii).

[38] *See* Taxpayer Relief Act of 1997, Pub. L. No. 105-34, § 1162, 105th Cong., 1st Sess. (Aug. 5, 1997).

¶ 1808 WITHHOLDING TAXES ON PAYMENTS TO FOREIGN LLCs

.01 Overview

A U.S. payor must withhold 30 percent on payments of FDAP income to a foreign LLC. FDAP income is fixed or determinable annual or periodic income. It includes interest, dividends, rents, royalties, and compensation not subject to the regular wage withholding. The withholding agent is not required to withhold at the 30 percent rate on the following types of payments:

- Payments to an LLC that is a withholding foreign partnership.[39] This is a foreign LLC that has entered into an agreement with the IRS to assume primary responsibility for withholding.
- Payments to a foreign LLC that the withholding agent determines are for the benefit of a U.S. member or a foreign member entitled to a reduced rate of withholding. The withholding agent must obtain a foreign withholding certificate and other documentation from the LLC to substantiate the reduced rate of withholding.
- Payments from U.S. sources that are excludable from gross income without regard to the identity of the recipient, such as interest under Code Sec. 103(a).
- Payments to a foreign LLC that are effectively connected with the conduct of a U.S. trade or business and that are includable in the foreign LLC's income. The foreign LLC receiving the income must withhold on the income allocable to foreign members, whether or not distributed, at the highest graduated income tax rates.

.02 Withholding Foreign Partnership

Payments to a foreign LLC that is a "withholding foreign partnership" are not subject to withholding taxes.[40] A withholding foreign partnership includes a foreign LLC that has entered into a withholding agreement[41] with the Internal Revenue Service to withhold taxes on distributions and guaranteed payments that it makes to its members. In such case, the withholding tax obligation shifts from the U.S. withholding agent (the person in the United States making the payment) to the foreign LLC.

Under the terms of the withholding agreement, the withholding procedures are as follows:[42]

- The foreign LLC must first file an application with the IRS to become the withholding partnership. The application must include the information set

---

[39] Reg. § 1.1441-5(c)(2).

[40] Reg. § 1.1441-5(c)(2).

[41] *See* IRS Notice 2002-41, 2002-24 IRB 1153, regarding the form of agreements for LLCs that want to qualify as withholding for partnerships.

[42] Rev. Proc. 2003-64, 2003-32 IRB 306.

forth in Section 3 of Revenue Procedure 2003-64. The LLC must also enter into a Withholding Foreign Partnership Agreement with the IRS in the form attached as Appendix 1 to Revenue Procedure 2003-64.

- The foreign LLC must provide a withholding certificate on Form W-8IMP to each U.S. payor of amounts subject to withholding. The LLC is not required to attach to the form any documentation regarding its members in this case.
- The foreign LLC may receive payments from the U.S. payor in gross without reduction for withholding taxes.
- The foreign LLC must then withhold taxes, if any, based on the Forms W-8 or W-9 that it receives from its members. The LLC must withhold on the date that it makes a distribution to a foreign member, rather than on the date that it receives the amount from the U.S. payor.
- The LLC must report payments to, and taxes withheld from, its foreign members on Form 1042-S on an individual basis or, by election, on a pooled basis.
- The withholding agreement remains in effect indefinitely unless the LLC elects to withhold and deposit taxes on a pooled basis. In such case, there is a six-year renewable term or a 15-year nonrenewable term.

.03 Nonwithholding Foreign Partnerships

Reporting by Foreign LLC

Payments to LLCs that have not entered into a withholding agreement with the IRS are treated as payments to the members.[43] The foreign LLC must provide a withholding certificate (Form W-8IMY) to the payor that identifies each of the members, whether the member is a U.S. or foreign person, the allocable share of each member, and documentation that the payor needs to provide each member with the required IRS reporting forms.[44]

The foreign LLC must use Form W-8IMP (Part VI) as the withholding certificate. The LLC must attach a statement to the form that provides sufficient information for the withholding agent to determine each member's distributive share of the amounts that the LLC is receiving from the payor. The sum of all members' distributive shares, expressed as a percentage, must equal 100 percent.

The LLC must also transmit to the withholding agent appropriate documentation regarding the status of its members.[45] The foreign members may provide the LLC with Form W-8BEN for such purpose. The LLC must keep the original copy of the forms, and transmit photocopies of the forms to the payor along with Form W-8IMP. Form W-8BEN is used to establish that the member is a foreign person, and to claim a

---

[43] Reg. § 1.1441-5(c)(1).

[44] IRS Notice 2002-41, 2002-23 IRB 1153; Reg. § 1.1441-5T(c)(3)(iii). The withholding certificate is referred to as a "nonwithholding foreign partnership withholding certificate."

[45] Reg. § 1.1441-5T(c)(3)(iii).

reduced rate or exemption from withholding as a resident of a foreign country with which the United States has an income tax treaty. A U.S. citizen or resident who is a member in a foreign LLC must provide the LLC with Form W-9 instead of Form W-8BEN.[46]

The foreign member may also be required to submit Form W-8BEN to claim an exemption from domestic information reporting and backup withholding at a 31 percent rate for certain types of income that are not subject to foreign-person withholding (such as broker proceeds, short-term original issue discount, and a deposit interest).

Reporting and Withholding by U.S. Payor

The U.S. payor must report the payments allocated to U.S. members of the foreign LLC on Form 1099, and payments allocated to foreign members on Form 1042-S. The foreign LLC is not obligated to file Form 1042 and 1042-S when it pays the U.S. source income to its members, assuming that the U.S. withholding agent files the returns and that the foreign members' tax liability with respect to U.S. source income has been fully satisfied by withholding.[47]

The payor must withhold at a 30 percent rate on FDAP income paid to the foreign LLC unless the foreign LLC provides the payor with a withholding certificate and documentation showing that one or more of the members are U.S. persons or foreign persons entitled to a reduced rate of withholding.[48]

.04 Presumptions in the Absence of Documentation

The withholding agent may rely on the withholding certificate and documents transmitted with the certificate to determine the residency of the members of the foreign LLC, and to apply a reduced rate of withholding when applicable.

The LLC may not be able to obtain Form W-8BEN or other appropriate documentation from some of its members. In such case, the LLC must state on the form that it lacks documentation for some of its members. It must separately identify the amounts allocated to members for whom documentation is lacking or unreliable. The LLC is not required to name such members and may aggregate the percentage interest payable to such members as a group. The payor must withhold at a 30 or 31 percent rate on payments allocable to such members.[49]

---

[46] Reg. § 1.1441-5(c)(1)(i)(A), (c)(3)(ii).

[47] Reg. § 1.1461-1(b)(2), (c)(4)(iv).

[48] Temp. Reg. § 1.1441-5T(c)(3)(ii). Temp. Reg. § 1.1441-5T(c)(3)(i) provides that the withholding agent must apply various presumptions if it does not receive a valid withholding certificate from a foreign entity that it knows or believes to be a foreign LLC.

[49] Reg. § 1.1441-5T(c)(3) provides that the withholding agent must apply various presumptions if it cannot reliably associate the payment with valid documentation from the member of the foreign LLC that is attached to the withholding certificate of the foreign LLC, or if the withholding agent otherwise has insufficient information to report the payment on Form 1042-S or 1099 to the extent reporting is required.

If the withholding agent does not receive a withholding certificate or any other documentation from an LLC, it must presume that the LLC is a U.S. LLC unless there are indicia of foreign status. Indicia of foreign status exist if the payee's employer identification number begins with the two digits "98," the withholding agent's communications to the payee are mailed to an address in a foreign country, or the payment is made outside the United States. In such case, the withholding agent may presume that the LLC is a foreign LLC and withhold at the 30 or 31 percent rate for FDAP income.

.05 Trade or Business Income

Income that is effectively connected with the conduct of a U.S. trade or business is taxed at the graduated rates applicable to U.S. citizens and residents. There is no withholding on effectively connected income except for

- Personal service income;
- Income subject to withholding on dispositions of U.S. real property interests by foreign persons; and
- A foreign partner's share of effectively connected income.

Thus, there is generally no withholding on payments to a foreign LLC of effectively connected income. If the payor is planning to withhold on such payments, the foreign LLC may submit Form 8-ECI to the payor to claim that the payment is exempt from withholding as effectively connected income. The foreign LLC is not required to attach Forms W-8BEN or other documentation for the foreign members.[50]

When the foreign LLC receives the income, it will offset the income with its business expenses from conducting the trade or business. The net income from the U.S. trade or business allocable to the foreign members is then subject to withholding under Code Sec. 1446, whether or not the income is actually distributed to the foreign members. The withholding tax rate is the highest U.S. individual marginal tax rate for individual members of the foreign LLC and 35 percent for corporate members of the foreign LLC.[51]

The LLC must use Form 8813, Partnership Withholding Tax Payment (Section 1446), to pay the withholding taxes on effectively connected income allocated to its foreign members. The withholding taxes are paid in four quarterly installments. The LLC must report the effectively connected income and the withholding on such income on Form 8804, Annual Return for Partnership Withholding Tax (Section 1446). The LLC must prepare Form 8805 for each foreign member who receives an allocation of effectively connected income, even if no withholding tax was paid with respect to such amount. The LLC must attach a copy of Form 8805 to Form 8804 for each member and provide each member with another copy of Form 8804. The foreign members must attach Form 8805 to their U.S. income tax returns to claim the credit for their shares of Section 1446 taxes withheld by the foreign LLC.

---

[50] Temp. Reg. § 1.1441-5T(c)(3)(ii) (last sentence), (iii).
[51] Code Sec. 1446(b).

.06 Foreign Disregarded LLC

A foreign LLC that elects to be a disregarded entity separate from its owner may not certify that it is the transferor of real property for withholding tax purposes. Instead, the owner of the disregarded entity is treated as the transferor of the property. A buyer of real property from the disregarded entity must in such case withhold 15 percent of the amount realized on the sale.[52]

---

[52] IRS International Practice Unit, RPW/CU/P_08.4_05 (Aug. 23, 2016).

19

Foreign-Owned Domestic LLCs

¶ 1901 GENERALLY

Foreign persons are subject to U.S. taxes on income from sources within the United States and on income that is effectively connected with the conduct of a U.S. trade or business.[1] If an LLC is engaged in a U.S. trade or business, all foreign members of that LLC are treated as engaged in a U.S. trade or business.[2] If an LLC has a permanent establishment in the United States, each of the LLC's members is treated as having a permanent establishment in the United States.[3] This is important, since

---

[1] Code Secs. 871–885.

[2] Ltr. Rul. 9436019; Code Sec. 875(1).

[3] *Id.*

tax treaties with foreign countries may reduce or eliminate the tax on certain income of foreign persons who do not have a permanent establishment in the United States.

An LLC organized in the United States that is owned by foreign persons is classified as a domestic partnership.[4]

¶1902 TAXATION OF FOREIGN MEMBERS

.01 Tax Rates and Withholding Taxes

U.S. taxes on foreign members of a domestic LLC are collected primarily through withholding taxes

If a domestic LLC is classified as a partnership, there are no withholding taxes on amounts paid to the LLC, even if the LLC has foreign members. The LLC must provide the payor with a Form W-9 certifying that it is a U.S. person.[5] The LLC must then withhold taxes on distributions or allocations of income to the foreign members.[6]

If an LLC is a single-member disregarded entity, and the LLC is owned by a foreign person, then the LLC may not furnish the payor with a Form W-9. Instead, the LLC must furnish the payor with a Form W-8 showing the name, address, and taxpayer identification number of the foreign person who is the single owner.[7] The payor must then withhold as if the LLC were a foreign person.

The amount of withholding taxes depends on the type of income earned by the LLC. The most common withholding taxes are discussed below.

.02 Portfolio Income

A foreign member is subject to U.S. income taxes on the member's allocable share of fixed and determinable income (FDAP income) that is not connected with the U.S. trade or business. FDAP income includes interest, dividends, rents, and royalties. The tax rate is 30 percent on a gross basis, without any deductions or credits.[8]

An LLC must withhold at a 30 percent rate on a foreign member's distributive share of FDAP income.[9] The LLC must withhold at the time that it makes distributions to the foreign member.[10] If the LLC does not distribute the foreign member's allocable share of income, the LLC must withhold on the member's allocable share of

---

[4] Ltr. Rul. 9610006 (*citing* Code Sec. 7701(a)(4)).

[5] Reg. §1.1441-5(b)(1).

[6] Reg. §1.1441-5(b)(2).

[7] Reg. §1.1441-1(b)(2)(iii)(A).

[8] Code Secs. 871(a)(1), 881(a).

[9] Code Sec. 1441; Reg. §1.1441-5(b)(2)(i)(A), (v).

[10] Reg. §1.1441-1(a).

income when it sends the Schedule K-1 to the member (but no later than the due date for sending the form to the member).[11]

A partner may make an election to treat rental income and mineral royalties received from an LLC as trade or business income subject to separate withholding tax rules.[12] The election for rental income is discussed below.[13]

The withholding tax rate may be reduced by treaty. The foreign member must file Form W-8BEN, Certificate of Foreign Status of Beneficiary Owner for United States Tax Withholding, with the LLC in order to claim the reduced withholding tax rate and to establish foreign residency in a treaty country.[14]

The LLC must file Form 1042-S, Foreign Person's U.S. Source Income Subject to Withholding, to report the withholding taxes. The LLC may withhold taxes by electronic deposits. Alternatively, it may deposit the withheld income taxes on FDAP income using Form 8109, Federal Tax Deposit Coupon.[15] Capital gains from the sale of securities are not treated as FDAP income, and are therefore not subject to the 30 percent withholding tax.[16]

.03 Trade or Business Income

An LLC must withhold taxes on a foreign member's allocable share of "effectively connected taxable income," whether or not distributed.[17] Effectively connected taxable income is income that is effectively connected with the conduct of a U.S. trade or business.[18] There are two types of effectively connected income. First, there is the regular trade or business income that is taxed at the ordinary income tax rates. Second, there are capital gains and other types of income that are treated as effectively connected with the conduct of a U.S. trade or business, but that are taxed to noncorporate members at the lower tax rates applicable to that type of income. Corporate members are taxed at the same tax rate on all types of income. The withholding tax procedures are as follows:

- *Determination of foreign members.* The LLC must first determine whether it has foreign members and whether the foreign members are corporate or noncorporate members. It may make this determination by obtaining from the members (i) Form W-8BEN if the member is a nonresident alien individual, foreign estate or non-grantor trust, foreign corporation, or foreign govern-

---

[11] Reg. § 1.1441-5(b)(2)(i)(A).

[12] Reg. § 1.703-1(b)(2)(iii).

[13] *See* ¶ 1902.04 *infra.*

[14] Reg. § 1.1441-1(c)(6)(ii)(A), (e)(2).

[15] The deposits are made according to the instructions to Form 8109 and the instructions in IRS Publication 515. An LLC may obtain the necessary deposit coupons by calling 1-800-829-4933.

[16] Reg. § 1.1441-2(b)(1)(i), (2)(i). A foreign member is not taxed on the member's allocable share of capital gains if certain requirements are met. *See* ¶ 1807 *supra.*

[17] Code Sec. 1446; Reg. § 1.1446-1(a).

[18] Code Sec. 864(c); Reg. § 1.1446-2(a). *See* IRS Publication 519, *U.S. Tax Guide for Aliens*, for a detailed discussion of what constitutes effectively connected income.

ment, (ii) Form W-8IMY if the member is a foreign partnership, (iii) Form W-9 if the member is a U.S. person (other than a grantor trust) or U.S. partnership,[19] (iv) Form W-8IMY if the member is a foreign grantor trust, accompanied by Form W-8BEN, W-8IMY, W-8ECI, W-8EXP, or W-9 for each of its owners,[20] or (v) Form W-8ECI from any of its members.[21] The LLC may also develop its own substitute forms.[22] The LLC must retain the certificates and statements for as long as it is relevant to the determination of the withholding tax.[23]

- *Trade or business income.* The LLC must next determine whether U.S. trade or business income is allocable to foreign members.[24] The allocation is made in accordance with the LLC operating agreement.

- *Withholding tax.* If the LLC allocates effectively connected income to foreign members, it must compute the withholding tax. The tax is referred to as the Section 1446 tax. The amount of the withholding is the "applicable percentage,"[25] which is the highest U.S. tax rate for effectively connected income to which each foreign member is subject, depending on the corporate or noncorporate status of the foreign member.[26] The withholding tax rate for corporate foreign members is 35 percent.[27] The withholding tax rate in 2014 for noncorporate foreign members depends on the type of effectively connected income. Generally, the withholding tax rate in 2014 is 39.6 percent for trade or business income,[28] 28 percent for collectibles gain, 25 percent for unrecaptured Section 1250 gain, 20 percent for qualified dividend income, and 20 percent for long-term capital gains.[29] LLC allocations that are effectively connected with the conduct of a U.S. trade or business are not subject to withholding under the Financial Account Tax Compliance Act (FATCA).[30] An LLC with a fiscal year must withhold taxes at the rate in effect at the beginning of its fiscal year, and the member must pay taxes at the rate in effect in the following year (the year of inclusion in taxable income).

- *Reduction in Withholding Tax.* An LLC may reduce the withholding tax rate if the foreign member has deductions and losses that are reasonably expected to reduce the member's U.S. income tax liability.[31] The member must provide the

---

[19] Reg. § 1.1446-1(c)(1), (2)(ii)(A).

[20] Reg. § 1.1446-1(c)(2)(i), (ii)(E).

[21] Reg. § 1.1446-1(c)(2).

[22] Reg. § 1.1446-1(c)(5).

[23] Reg. § 1.1446-1(c)(2)(vi).

[24] Reg. § 1.1446-2.

[25] Code Sec. 1446(b)(1).

[26] Code Sec. 1446(b)(2).

[27] Reg. § 1.1446-3(a)(2).

[28] Ltr. Rul. 201138020; IRS Ann. 2013-30, 2013-1 CB 1134.

[29] *See* Part III of the IRS Form 8804, *Annual Return for Partnership Withholding Tax (Section 1446),* which provides for the different withholding tax rates on effectively connected income.

[30] Prop. Reg. § 1.1474-6(d).

[31] Reg. § 1.1446-6.

LLC with Form 8804-C, *Certificate of Partner Level Items to Reduce Section 1446 Withholding.*[32] There are limits on the amount and type of deductions that may be used to reduce the withholding tax obligation.[33] No withholding is required if a foreign nonresident alien individual certifies that the annual taxes owed will be less than $1,000.[34] The foreign member must have timely filed, or represent that it will timely file, a U.S. income tax return for each of the preceding three tax years, and for the tax year in which it gives the certificate to the LLC, in order to qualify.[35] Estates and trusts (other than grantor trusts) may not certify deductions and losses to the LLC.

- *Treaty.* The withholding tax rate may also be reduced by treaty. Generally, treaties provide that foreign members are exempt from withholding on their allocable share of U.S. trade or business income, provided that the LLC does not earn that income through a "permanent establishment" in the United States.[36] The member may claim a reduced rate of withholding or exemption from withholding by providing to the LLC a valid withholding certificate on Form W-8BEN or other applicable form.[37]

- *Reporting and payment of withholding tax.* The LLC must pay and report the withholding tax.[38] The LLC must pay the withholding tax in quarterly installments[39] on Form 8813.[40] Additional amounts due after the close of the year are reported on Form 8804.[41] The LLC must send each foreign member an information statement on Form 8805 showing the amount of withheld taxes.[42] It must also notify each member of the withholding tax paid on behalf of the member within ten days after each installment payment. There is no form specified for this notice.[43] The LLC is liable to the IRS for underwithholding unless it can show that the foreign member paid the required amount of taxes.[44]

---

[32] Reg. § 1.1446-6(c)(2).

[33] Reg. § 1.1446-6(c)(1)(i). Members may only certify prior-year items and deductions. Credits and charitable contributions may not be considered. An LLC may consider a member's net operating loss deduction up to 90 percent of the member's share of effectively connected income. An LLC that has withheld state and local taxes on behalf of a member may take 90 percent of that amount into account, and the member is not required to submit a certificate for such amounts.

[34] Reg. § 1.1446-6(c)(1)(ii).

[35] Reg. § 1.1446-6(b)(1)(ii). Only returns that report income effectively connected with a U.S. trade or business or deductions or losses properly allocated to such activities will satisfy the tax return filing requirement. Reg. § 1.1446-6(b)(2)(iii).

[36] Rev. Rul. 85-60, 1985-1 CB 187.

[37] Reg. § 1.1446-2(b)(2)(iii).

[38] Reg. § 1.1446-3.

[39] Reg. § 1.1446-3(b).

[40] Reg. § 1.1446-3(d)(1)(i).

[41] Reg. § 1.1446-3(d)(1)(iii).

[42] Reg. § 1.1446-3(d)(1)(iii).

[43] Reg. § 1.1446-3(d)(1)(i).

[44] Reg. § 1.1446-3(e).

- *Returns by member.* Individual members must file Form 1040-NR and corporations must file Form 1120-F to report their allocable share of the LLC's trade or business income. The foreign member must file a tax return even though the LLC has paid all required withholding taxes.[45] Foreign members must pay taxes at the graduated U.S. tax rates on such income.[46] The members receive a credit against the tax for withholding taxes paid on the income, and a refund if the withholding taxes exceed the actual amount owed.[47] Foreign members claim the credit for previously paid withholding taxes by attaching Form 8805 to Form 1040-NR or 1120-F. No deductions, net operating loss carryforwards, or credits are allowed unless the return is filed.[48] Foreign members are not required to attach Form 8833[49] to their U.S. tax returns if the LLC files Form 1042-S to report the foreign member's U.S. source income subject to withholding.
- *Capital account treatment.* The LLC's payment of the withholding tax is treated as a cash distribution to the member,[50] and as a reduction in the member's capital account. However, the withholding tax payment is treated as an advance or draw against the member's distributive share of U.S. trade or business income if the LLC pays the withholding tax in installments.[51]

.04 Real Estate

Rental Income

There is a 30 percent tax on rental income allocated to foreign members in an LLC. The tax is on gross rental income without any deductions or credits.[52]

A member may instead make an election to treat rental income received from the LLC as effectively connected with the conduct of a U.S. trade or business under Code Sec. 871(d).[53] The election is made so that the member may take a deduction for the member's allocable share of depreciation, taxes, interest and operating expenses related to the rental income. If the member makes this election, then the member must file a U.S. tax return on Form 1040NR. The net rental income is then subject to the regular U.S. tax rates on ordinary income.

An LLC must withhold taxes under Code Sec. 1441 if the nonresident member does not make the election to treat the rental income as effectively connected with the

---

[45] Reg. §§1.1446-3(f), 1.6012-1(b)(1)(i).

[46] Code Sec. 871(b) for individuals; Code Sec. 882 for corporations.

[47] Reg. §1.1446-3(d)(2).

[48] Code Sec. 774(b).

[49] Form 8833, Treaty Based Return Position Disclosure under Section 6114 or 7701(b), discloses a position taken on a return that a treaty reduces or eliminate U.S. taxes.

[50] Code Sec. 1446(d)(2); Reg. §1.1446-3(d)(2)(v).

[51] Reg. §1.1446-3(d)(2)(v).

[52] Code Secs. 871(a)(1)(A), 881(a)(1).

[53] Reg. §1.703-1(b)(2)(iii).

conduct of a U.S. trade or business.[54] The Section 1441 withholding tax also applies if the member claims that the rental income is not attributable to a permanent establishment in the United States and is exempt from U.S. tax under an income tax treaty.[55] The Section 1441 withholding tax rate is 30 percent on gross rental income.[56] The member is not required to file US tax return if the Section 1441 withholding tax applies.

An LLC must withhold taxes under Code Sec. 1446 on a foreign member's share of rental income if the member makes an election to treat the rental income as effectively connected with the conduct of the U.S. trade or business.[57] The withholding tax rate is 35 percent of net rental income after deductions (rather than 30 percent on gross rental income under Code Sec. 1441).[58] The foreign member must give Form W-8ECI to the LLC to make the election under Code Sec. 871(d) (or Code Sec. 882(d) in the case of a foreign corporate member). The LLC may rely on a properly completed Form W-8ECI to treat the rental payments as subject to withholding under Code Sec. 1446. The LLC must give the foreign member Form 8805 showing the amount of the withheld taxes. The foreign member receives a credit for the withheld taxes when the member files a US tax return.[59]

The rental income is subject to the second-level branch profits tax under Code Sec. 884 for corporate members of an LLC, including LLCs classified as disregarded entities.

If the rental property is not actually rented, then operating expenses such as condominium association fees, insurance, property taxes and caring charges are not deductible and may not be capitalized, thus providing no tax benefits against any capital gains realized on sale of the rental property.[60]

The withholding tax under the Financial Account Tax Compliance Act (FATCA) does not apply to rental income if the nonresident member makes the election to treat the rental income as effectively connected with the conduct of U.S. trade or business.[61]

Sale of Real Estate by LLC

A foreign member is taxed under FIRPTA[62] on the member's allocable share of gain from the sale of real estate by LLC in the following cases:

---

[54] Code Secs. 1441(a), 1441(c)(1).

[55] Reg. § 1.1441-4(a)(1).

[56] Reg. § 1.1441-3.

[57] Code Sec. 1446(a); Reg. § 1.1446-1(a).

[58] *See* ¶ 1902.03 *supra*.

[59] Instructions to IRS Form W-8ECI, Certificate of Foreign Person's Claim That Income Is Effectively Connected with the Conduct of a Trade or Business in the United States.

[60] Rev. Rul. 91-7, 1991-1 CB 110.

[61] Prop. Reg. § 1.1474-6(d).

[62] Foreign Investment in Real Property Tax Act, Code Sec. 897.

- *LLC classified as partnership.* A foreign member is taxed on the member's allocable share of gain from the LLC's sale or disposition of U.S. real property interests. U.S. real property interests include a direct interest in real estate, and stock in a corporation if U.S. real estate is at least 50 percent of the fair market value of the corporation's real estate and trade or business assets.[63] The gain is treated as effectively connected with the conduct of a U.S. trade or business.[64] This means that the foreign member is taxed at the same rates that apply to similar income received by U.S. persons.[65] Long-term capital gains from real estate allocable to a noncorporate foreign member are taxed at the maximum 20 percent federal tax rate. The LLC must withhold taxes at a 35 percent rate on the foreign member's allocable share of such gain.[66] The IRS may by regulation reduce the withholding tax rate to 20 percent, but has not yet done so.[67] The foreign member must file a U.S. tax return reporting the gain, and receives a credit for the taxes withheld.[68]

- *LLC classified as disregarded entity.* Buyers of real estate from a single-member disregarded LLC must withhold taxes equal to ten percent of the sales price if the owner of the LLC is a foreign person.[69] The owner of a disregarded LLC is treated as the transferor of the U.S. real property interest. The owner must provide a certificate of non-foreign status to avoid withholding under Section 1445.[70] The disregarded LLC may not provide such a certificate.[71]

Sale of Membership Interest

A member is taxed under FIRPTA[72] on the sale of a membership interest in an LLC in the following cases:

---

[63] Code Sec. 897(c).

[64] Code Sec. 897(g).

[65] House Report 108–755, American Jobs Creation Act of 2004.

[66] Code Sec. 1445(e)(1); Reg. § 1.1445-5(c)(1)(ii). However, if the LLC withholds taxes on the member's allocable share of U.S. trade or business income, then the LLC must withhold taxes on the real estate gain under Section 1446. Reg. § 1.1446-3(c)(2)(i). In such case, the LLC must withhold at the tax rates applicable to income effectively connected with the conduct of a U.S. trade or business, rather than at the 35 percent tax rate under Section 1445. The LLC may credit any amount of the Section 1445 tax that it paid on the real estate gain against the v tax that it is obligated to pay.

[67] Code Sec. 1445(e)(1).

[68] Reg. § 1.1445-1(f).

[69] Code Sec. 1445(a); CCA 200836029.

[70] Reg. § 1.1445-2(b)(2)(iv)(B) provides a model form for a person to use when it owns a disregarded entity that transfers a U.S. real property interest. The form must include a certification that the owner of the disregarded LLC is not a foreign corporation, a foreign partnership, a foreign trust or a foreign estate. The owner must also certify that it is not a disregarded entity as defined in Reg. § 1.1445-2(b)(2)(iii). If the owner cannot or does not certify both its non-foreign status and that it is not a disregarded entity, the transferee must withhold ten percent of the amount realized on the disposition of the U.S. real property interest. CCA 200836029.

[71] CCA 200836029, *citing* Reg. § 1.1445-2(b)(2)(iii).

[72] Foreign Investment in Real Property Tax Act, Code Sec. 897.

- *Sale of membership interest classified as USRPI.* A foreign member is taxed under FIRPTA if the member sells a membership interest in an LLC that is classified as a U.S. real property interest.[73] A membership interest is a U.S. real property interest if the gross assets of the LLC consist of 50 percent of U.S. real property interests, and if 90 percent or more the value of the gross assets of the LLC consist of U.S. real property interests and cash or cash equivalents.[74] The withholding tax rate is ten percent of the sales price.[75] The purchaser is responsible for withholding the tax.[76] A membership interest that is a U.S. real property interest for withholding tax purposes is not a U.S. real property interest for income tax purposes. Thus, the selling foreign member is only liable for taxes to the extent of gain attributable to the selling member's share of U.S. real property interests held by the LLC.[77] The member must file a U.S. tax return paying the taxes owed, and receives a credit for the taxes withheld.

- *Sale of membership interest not classified as USRPI.* A foreign member may be taxed under FIRPTA on sale of a membership interest to the extent attributable to U.S. real property interests held by the LLC.[78] Code Sec. 897(g) provides that gain from the sale of a partnership interest is recognized under FIRPTA "under regulations prescribed by the Secretary." The IRS has not yet issued regulations imposing a tax under FIRPTA on the sale of a membership interest by a foreign member except for sales in which the gross assets of the LLC consist of 50 percent of U.S. real property interests, and 90 percent or more the value of the gross assets of the LLC consists of U.S. real property interests and cash or cash equivalents.[79] Beginning in 2018, if a nonresident alien individual or foreign corporation owns an interest in an LLC that is engaged in a U.S. trade or business, gain or loss on the sale or exchange of the interest is treated as effectively connected with the conduct of such trade or business,[80] and is subject to a ten percent withholding by the transferee[81] (or by the LLC if the transferee fails to withhold).[82] However, if the LLC owns any real property at the time of the sale or exchange, then the gain on the sale of a membership interest (to the extent treated as the sale of a U.S. real property interest) is instead taxed under Code Sec. 897,[83] and is subject to the 15 percent withholding tax under Code Sec. 1445(e)(5) rather than the ten percent withholding tax under Code Sec. 1446(f).

---

[73] Temp. Reg. §§ 1.897-7T, 1.1445-11T(d)(1).

[74] Temp. Reg. §§ 1.897-7T, 1.1445-11T(d).

[75] Code Sec. 1445(e)(5); Reg. § 1.1445-5(g).

[76] Code Sec. 1445(e)(5); Reg. § 1.1445-5(f).

[77] Temp. Reg. § 1.897-7T, *citing* Code Sec. 897(g).

[78] Code Sec. 897(g); IRS Notice 88-72, 1988-2 CB 383.

[79] Temp. Reg. §§ 1.897-7T, 1.1445-11T(d).

[80] Code Secs. 864(c)(8)(A), 864(c)(8)(B).

[81] Code Sec. 1446(f)(1).

[82] Code Sec. 1446(f)(4).

[83] Code Sec. 864(c)(8)(C).

Distributions to Member

There is a ten percent withholding tax on the fair market value of any U.S. real property interest distributed to a foreign member in a transaction that would constitute a taxable distribution under the Section 897 regulations.[84] The IRS has not yet issued regulations on distributions to a member of an LLC under Section 897. Therefore, no withholding tax applies at this time to distributions of U.S. real property interests to foreign members.

Reduction in Withholding Tax

The withholding tax rate may be reduced by applicable treaty. The member may also apply to the IRS for a withholding certificate to reduce or eliminate the withholding tax.[85] The IRS will ordinarily issue a withholding certificate if the member's maximum tax liability is less than the required withholding amount.[86]

Payments subject to withholding under FIRPTA are not subject to withholding under the Financial Account Tax Compliance Act (FATCA).[87]

.05 Capital Gains

A foreign member is not subject to tax on capital gains from an LLC except in the following cases:

- *ECTI income.* A foreign member is taxed on capital gains that are effectively connected with the conduct of U.S. trade or business. Capital gains are effectively connected with the conduct of U.S. trade or business if (i) the gain is derived from assets used in or held for use in the conduct of the LLC's trade or business (asset use test), or (ii) the LLC's trade or business activities in the United States were a material factor in the realization of the gain (business activities test).[88] The LLC may segregate such capital gains from its trade or business income for withholding tax purposes.[89] The withholding tax rate is 35 percent on income allocable to foreign corporate members.[90] The withholding tax rate is 25 percent of the unrecaptured Section 1250 gain,[91] 20 percent of the long-term capital gain, and 35 percent of the short-term capital gain

---

[84] Code Sec. 1445(e)(4).

[85] Reg. § 1.1445-3.

[86] Reg. § 1.1445-3(b)(3)(i).

[87] Prop. Reg. § 1.1474-6(c)(1).

[88] Code Sec. 864(c)(2); Reg. § 1.864-4(c)(1).

[89] Reg. § 1.1446-2(b)(1).

[90] Code Sec. 1446(b)(2)(B); Reg. § 1.1446-3(a)(2).

[91] This is the gain allocable to noncorporate members up to the amount of straight-line depreciation taken by the LLC on the property sold.

allocable to noncorporate foreign members.[92] LLC capital losses allocable to a member are allowed only to the extent of capital gains allocable to the member.[93]

- *FDAP income.* A foreign member is taxed on capital gains that are classified as FDAP income (fixed or determinable annual or periodic income).[94] FDAP income includes the member's allocable share of certain gains from the sale of patents, copyrights, trademarks, and other intangibles. The tax rate is 30 percent on a gross basis, without any deductions or offsets.[95] There is a 30 percent withholding tax.[96] A foreign member's allocable share of capital gains from the sale of investment securities[97] and other nonbusiness assets is generally not subject to U.S. taxes or withholding.[98]
- *U.S. real property.* A foreign member is taxed on capital gains attributable to the sale or disposition of U.S. real property.[99]
- *U.S. resident.* A foreign person is taxed on all capital gains if the member is a United States resident (e.g., green card holder).[100] U.S. residents are taxed on their worldwide income at the regular U.S. tax rates.
- *183-day test.* A foreign individual member is taxed on all capital gains if the foreign member is present in the United States for at least 183 days during the tax year.[101] The nonresident member is subject to a 30 percent tax on a gross basis on capital gains that are not effectively connected with the conduct of a U.S. trade or business.[102] The nonresident member is subject to 20 percent withholding tax on a gross basis on long-term capital gains that are effectively connected with the conduct of U.S. trade or business, regardless of the number of days present in the United States.[103] Almost all persons present in the United States for 183 days during the tax year are U.S. residents under the "substantial presence test," and are thus taxed on their worldwide income at the same rates that apply to similar income received by U.S. persons.[104]

---

[92] *See* Part III of the IRS Form 8804, *Annual Return for Partnership Withholding Tax (Section 1446),* which provides for the different withholding tax rates on the capital gain income.

[93] Reg. § 1.1446-2(b)(3)(v).

[94] Code Secs. 871(a)(1)(B), (D), 871(a)(2), 881(a)(2), (4).

[95] Code Sec. 871(a).

[96] Code Sec. 1441; Reg. § 1.1441-5(b)(2)(i)(A), (v).

[97] *See* ¶ 1807 *supra.*

[98] Reg. § 1.1441-2(b)(2).

[99] *See* ¶ 1902.04 *supra.*

[100] Code Sec. 7701(b).

[101] Code Sec. 871(a)(2).

[102] Code Sec. 871(a)(2).

[103] Reg. §§ 1.1446-2(b)(1), 1.1446-3(a)(2)(ii); T.D. 9200, Preamble to the IRS Final and Temporary Regulations on Partnership Withholding of Foreign Partner's Share of U.S. Business Income (2005) in which the IRS stated that a partnership or LLC classified as a partnership "can generally pay the 1446 tax using the highest capital gains rate (currently 15 percent) to the extent long-term capital gain is allocable to a non-corporate foreign partner."

[104] Code Sec. 7701(b)(3). Under the substantial presence test, a foreign person is a resident alien subject to U.S. tax on worldwide income if (i) the person is present in the United States for at least 31

- *Sale of membership interest.* A foreign member is taxed on capital gains from the sale of a membership interest if (i) the foreign member is a resident alien, which persons are taxed on their worldwide income, (ii) the foreign member is present in the United States for more than 183 days during the year,[105] or (iii) the LLC is engaged in a U.S. trade or business.[106] A foreign owner's gain or loss from the transfer of membership interest is effectively connected with the U.S. trade or business to the extent that the foreign owner would have recognized effectively connected gain or loss if the LLC had sold all of its assets at fair market value on the date of the transfer.[107] The purchaser of a membership interest from a foreign owner must withhold ten percent of the amount realized by the transferor.[108] If the transferee fails to withhold the correct amount, the LLC must deduct and withhold from distributions to the transferee member an amount that should have been withheld.[109] The IRS temporarily suspended the withholding tax on the sale by a foreign person of a membership interest in publicly traded partnerships and LLCs,[110] and issued interim guidance on withholding by non-publicly traded partnerships and LLCs.[111] A transferee of a non-publicly traded partnership or LLC is not required to withhold if (i) the transferor furnishes to the transferee a certification that there is no gain,[112] (ii) the transferor furnishes to the transferee a certification that for each of the last three years the transferor's effectively connected taxable income from the LLC was less than 25% of the transferor's total income from the LLC,[113] (iii) the LLC furnishes to the transferee a certification that the amount of gain effectively connected with the conduct of the U.S. trade or business that would be realized on a sale of assets for fair market value would be less than 25% of the total gain,[114] (iv) there is a

---

(Footnote Continued)

days during the calendar year, and (ii) the number of days present in the United States during the current year, plus one-third of the days present in the United States during the prior calendar year, plus one-sixth of the days present during the second prior calendar year, equals or exceeds 183 days. An individual who would otherwise meet the substantial presence test may avoid being taxed as a U.S. resident if (a) the individual is present in the United States for fewer than 183 days during the current tax year, (b) the individual maintains a home in a foreign country, and (c) the individual files a "closer connection statement" on Form 8840 establishing that he has a closer connection with the foreign country than with the United States. Code Sec. 7701(b)(3)(B); Reg. § 301.7701(b)-8(b)(1)(i).

[105] Code Sec. 871(a)(2).

[106] Code Sec. 864(c)(8), as amended by 2017 Tax Cuts and Jobs Act § 13501(a).

[107] Code Secs. 864(c)(8)(A), 864(c)(8)(B).

[108] Code Sec. 1446(f)(1).

[109] Code Sec. 1446(f)(4).

[110] Notice 2018-08, 2018-7 IRB 352.

[111] Notice 2018-29 2018-16 IRB 495.

[112] Notice 2018-29, 2018-16 IRB 495, Secs. 6.02, 6.05.

[113] Notice 2018-29, 2018-16 IRB 495, Sec. 6.03.

[114] Notice 2018-29, 2018-16 IRB 495, Sec. 6.04.

nonrecognition transaction,[115] or (v) the transferor furnishes to the transferee an affidavit that the transferor is not a foreign person.[116]

.06 Branch Profits Tax

Foreign corporations that are members of a U.S. LLC are subject to the branch profits tax if the LLC is engaged in a U.S. trade or business,[117] or has income that is effectively connected with the conduct of a trade or business in the United States.[118] The rule applies to LLCs that are classified as partnerships or disregarded entities, but not to LLCs classified as corporations.[119]

The branch profits tax is in addition to the tax imposed on U.S. trade or business income allocable to foreign corporate members. The tax is designed to parallel the two levels of tax imposed on foreign corporations that receive dividends from a U.S. subsidiary corporation. The branch profits tax is not imposed on foreign individual members of an LLC. The branch profits tax is 30 percent of a foreign corporate member's allocable share of after-tax U.S. trade or business income that is not reinvested in a U.S. trade or business.[120] A member's share of income is treated as reinvested in the United States if there is an increase in the member's share of "U.S. net equity" (U.S. assets less U.S. liabilities).[121] The increase in net equity is determined by comparing U.S. net equity at the close of the current tax year with U.S. net equity at the close of the prior tax year.[122] The net equity computation is based on the member's share of the LLC's U.S. assets, determined by using either the asset method or the income method.[123] Generally, the foreign corporate member will be subject to the branch profits tax if the member receives a distribution of the member's allocable share of LLC income, and will not be subject to the branch profits tax if the member does not receive a distribution of such income.

The branch profits tax may be reduced or eliminated by treaty.[124] A foreign corporation will not be subject to the branch profits tax if (i) it is a qualified resident

---

[115] Notice 2018-29, 2018-16 IRB 495, Sec. 6.05.

[116] Code Sec. 1446(f)(2).

[117] Code Secs. 875, 884; Reg. § 1.884-0(a); Rev. Rul. 85-60, 1985-1 CB 187; Ltr. Rul. 200720010.

[118] Code Secs. 875, 884; Reg. § 1.884-0(a); Rev. Rul. 85-60, 1985-1 CB 187; Ltr. Rul. 200720010.

[119] An LLC classified as a corporation is treated as a subsidiary of the parent company. Instead of the branch profits tax on distributions, a U.S. subsidiary is subject to a dividend withholding tax on a payment to its foreign parent of at least five percent under a treaty, and 30 percent absent a treaty.

[120] Code Sec. 884(a), (b).

[121] Code Sec. 884(c)(1).

[122] Code Sec. 884(b).

[123] Reg. § 1.884-1(d)(3).

[124] Code Sec. 884(e)(2); Reg. §§ 1.884-1(g), 1.884-5. There is no branch profits tax or a reduced branch profits tax for corporations from certain treaty countries specified in IRS regulations: Aruba, Australia, Austria, Belgium, Cyprus, Denmark, Egypt, Finland, Germany, Greece, Hungary, Iceland, Ireland, Italy, Jamaica, Japan, Korea, Luxembourg, Malta, Morocco, Netherlands, Netherlands Antilles, Norway, Pakistan, People's Republic of China, Philippines, Sweden, Switzerland, and United Kingdom. Reg. § 1.884-1(g)(3). Treaties that are modified or negotiated after January 1, 1987, may also

of a country with which the United States has an income tax treaty which entered into force after December 31, 1986,[125] and (ii) the foreign corporation qualifies for treaty benefits under the treaty, including the limitation on benefits article in the treaty with respect to the dividend equivalent amount.

The branch profits tax will not be imposed if the foreign corporation does not have a permanent establishment in the United States.[126] A foreign corporation has a permanent establishment in the United States if it has a fixed place of business in the United States, a construction site in the United States lasting a certain number of months, or a business carried on in the United States through a dependent agent authorized to enter into contracts in the name of the foreign corporation.

The branch profits tax rate for a foreign corporation that is a resident of a treaty country is the treaty rate on branch profits. If the treaty does not specify the branch profits tax rate, the branch profits tax rate is the treaty rate on dividends paid by a wholly owned U.S. corporation to its corporate parent resident in the treaty country.[127]

A foreign corporation claiming the benefits of a treaty must file Form 8833 as an attachment to Form 1120-F. There is a $10,000 penalty if the foreign corporation fails to file Form 8833.[128]

EXAMPLE 19-1

An Indian corporation and an Indian citizen are equal owners of a Delaware LLC. The LLC is engaged in a U.S. trade or business. All of the earnings during 2006 are distributed to the two members in 2007. The Indian citizen is subject to a 35 percent withholding tax and the Indian corporation is subject to a 35 percent withholding tax in 2006 on the undistributed earnings of the LLC. Both members must file U.S. tax returns and pay taxes at the graduated U.S. tax rates. Both receive credits for the withholding taxes paid. The Indian corporation is subject to the branch profits tax in 2007 when the LLC pays the Indian corporation its allocable share of 2006 earnings and profits from the trade or business. The branch profits tax is reduced from 30 percent to 15 percent under the

---

(Footnote Continued)

reduce or eliminate the branch profits tax. For example, there is no branch profits tax under Article X, Sections 2(a), 8, and 9 of the U.S.-Denmark tax treaty for a Denmark corporation that owns a U.S. LLC unless the LLC has a permanent establishment in the United States, in which case the branch profits tax is reduced to five percent. See also IRS Notice 87-56, 1987-35 IRB 9. Section 1 of the Notice lists 28 countries whose tax treaties with the United States would prohibit the imposition of the branch profits tax. Section 2 of the Notice lists nine countries whose treaties with the United States allow imposition of the branch profits tax. The treaties of five of these countries have provisions that providing for a special computation of the branch profits tax.

[125] Reg. § 1.884-1(g)(1).

[126] Reg. § 1.884-1(g)(4)(ii)(B).

[127] Code Sec. 884(e)(2)(A); Reg. § 1.884-1(g)(4)(i)(A).

[128] Code Sec. 6712.

U.S.-Indian tax treaty if the Indian corporation files Form 8833 as an attachment to Form 1120-F. The Indian individual member is not subject to the branch profits tax.

There is no branch profits tax for the final year of the LLC[129] if the corporate owner of the LLC files a waiver of the period of limitations on Form 8848.[130]

¶1903 CONTRIBUTIONS TO LLC WITH FOREIGN MEMBERS

.01 General Rule

U.S. persons who transfer built-in gain property to a domestic or foreign LLC are immediately taxed on the built-in gain if (i) a related foreign person is a direct or indirect member of the LLC, and (ii) the U.S. transferor and one or more related persons own more than 80 percent of the membership interests in the LLC.[131] Built-in gain is the excess of the book value over the tax basis in the property on the date of contribution.[132]

The regulations override the rules under Code Sec. 721(a) which provide for nonrecognition of gain on a contribution of property to an LLC in exchange for membership interest in the LLC. The purpose of the regulation is to prevent U.S. taxpayers from contributing appreciated property to a partnership, and then allocating income or gain from the contributed property to related foreign persons who are not subject to U.S. taxes.

Under a *de minimis* rule, contributions to an LLC are tax-free if the sum of all built-in gain property contributed to the LLC during the tax year does not exceed $1 million.[133]

.02 Avoiding Gain Recognition

The parties may avoid income recognition by applying the Gain Deferral Method to the built-in gain property. Under the Gain Deferral Method, the transferors must comply with the following requirements:[134]

- The LLC must adopt the remedial allocation method for the built-in gain property.[135] Under the remedial allocation method, the LLC must allocate tax income to the contributing member equal to the book income allocated to the contributing member. If the LLC has insufficient tax income under the ceiling

---

[129] Temp. Reg. § 1.884-2T.

[130] Ltr. Rul. 200923006, *citing* Reg. § 1.884-2(a)(2)(ii).

[131] Code Sec. 721(c); Temp. Reg. § 1.721(c)-2T(b).

[132] Temp. Reg. § 1.721(c)-1T(b)(2).

[133] Temp. Reg. § 1.721(c)-2T(c).

[134] Temp. Reg. § 1.721(c)-3T(b).

[135] Temp. Reg. § § 1.721(c)-3T(b)(1)(i)(A), 1.721(c)-3T(d).

rule, the LLC must allocate phantom tax income to the contributing member and an equal offsetting amount of phantom tax deductions to the noncontributing members. The remedial allocation method is discussed at ¶ 1805.04.

- The LLC must apply the consistent allocation method.[136] Under the consistent allocation method, the LLC must allocate all items of income, gain, loss, and deduction from the built-in gain property in the same proportion between the U.S. transferors and the related foreign persons. For example, if the LLC allocates 60 percent of one item of income from the built-in gain property to the U.S transferor and 40 percent to a related foreign member during the tax year, then the LLC must allocate all items of income, gain, loss, and deduction with respect to that property 60 percent to the U.S. member and 40 percent to the related foreign person. The consistent allocation method is applied on a property-by-property basis.

- The U.S. transferor must recognize gain upon an acceleration event, a partial acceleration event, or certain transfers to foreign corporations described in Code Sec. 367.[137] An acceleration event is (ii) any event that would reduce the remaining built-in gain to be recognized, (ii) when any party fails to comply with the gain deferral method requirements with respect to built-in gain property, or (iii) when a U.S. transferor affirmatively treats an acceleration event as having occurred by recognizing the remaining built-in-in gain with respect to that property and satisfying the reporting requirements under the regulations.[138] There are several categories of exceptions to acceleration events.[139]

- Certain procedural and reporting requirements must be satisfied.[140] The U.S. transferor must file Schedule O of Form 8865[141] and report the income from the contributed property allocated to the U.S. transferor, a calculation of any remaining built-in gain, and information about acceleration, termination, successor and partial termination events. The LLC must use the Gain Deferral Method for all built-in gain property subsequently contributed to the LLC by the U.S. transferors.

  The U.S. transferor must extend the period of limitations on assessment of tax for eight years following the date of contribution.[142]

- The LLC must comply with certain rules for tiered partnerships.[143]

---

[136] Temp. Reg. §§ 1.721(c)-3T(b)(1)(i)(B), 1.721(c)-3T(c).

[137] Temp. Reg. § 1.721(c)-3T(b)(2).

[138] Temp. Reg. § 1.721(c)-4T(b).

[139] Temp. Reg. § 1.721(c)-5T.

[140] Temp. Reg. §§ 1.721(c)-3T(b)(3), 1.721(c)-6T(b).

[141] Temp. Reg. § 1.721(c)-6T(b).

[142] Temp. Reg. §§ 1.721(c)-3T(b)(4), 1.721(c)-6T(b)(5).

[143] Temp. Reg. §§ 1.721(c)-3T(b)(5),1.721(c)-2T(d).

¶ 1904 SINGLE-MEMBER LLC

.01 *Reporting Obligations*

A domestic disregarded LLC that is owned by a foreign entity is classified as a domestic corporation for purposes of reporting, records maintenance, and compliance requirements that apply to a 25 percent foreign-owned domestic corporation under Code Sec. 6038A.[144] As a result, a single-member domestic LLC with a foreign owner must comply with the following requirements:[145]

- *Responsible party disclosure.* The LLC must name and provide a U.S. Social Security Number ("SSN") or Individual Taxpayer Identification Number ("ITIN") of a responsible party. A responsible party is the individual who has a level of control over, or entitlement to, the funds or assets in the LLC that enables the individual, directly or indirectly, to control, manage, or direct the LLC and the disposition of its funds and assets.
- *Change in responsible party.* The LLC must report any subsequent change in the responsible party.
- *Related-party disclosures.* The LLC must file IRS Form 5472, Information Return of a 25 percent Foreign-Owned U.S. Corporation or a Foreign Corporation Engaged in a U.S. Trade or Business.[146] This form reports "reportable transactions" with "related parties," including transactions with any direct or indirect 25 percent foreign owner or person under common control with the reporting entity. The reportable transactions include all transactions with related parties, including any sale, assignment, lease, license, loan, advance, contribution, or other transfer of any interest in or right to use any property or money, as well as the performance of any service for the benefit of or on behalf of another taxpayer.[147] There is a $10,000 penalty for failure to file Form 5472 on a timely basis, additional penalties if the failure continues for more than 90 days after notification by the IRS, and criminal penalties for false or fraudulent information.
- *Employer identification number.* The LLC must obtain an employer identification number because it has an obligation to file IRS Form 5472. The IRS has authority to change tax return forms to require the sole member of a disregarded LLC to provide the LLC's employer identification number on the owner's personal tax return.[148]
- *Record Maintenance.* The LLC must keep permanent books of accounts or records that are sufficient to establish the accuracy of federal income tax returns, including information, documents or records to the extent relevant to

---

[144] Reg. §§ 1.6038A-1(c)(1), 1.6038A-2(b)(3)(xi), 1.6038A-2(b)(9), Examples 1 and 2.

[145] Reg. § 301.7701-2(c)(2)(vi).

[146] Reg. §§ 1.6038A-2(d), 1.6038A-2(b)(9), Example 1.

[147] Reg. §§ 1.6038A-2(b)(3)(xi), 1.6038A-2(b)(9), Example 1, 1.482-1(i)(7).

[148] PMTA 2016-08 (Jun. 16, 2016).

determining the correct U.S. tax treatment of transactions with related parties.[149]

- *Withholding tax.* The buyer of real property from a disregarded LLC owned by a foreign person must withhold 15 percent of the purchase price.[150]

- *Tax year.* The LLC must have the same tax year as the foreign owner if the foreign owner has a U.S. tax return filing obligation. If the foreign owner has no U.S. tax return filing obligation, then the tax year of the U.S. LLC is the calendar year unless otherwise provided in IRS guidance.[151]

.02 Ownership by Foreign Parent Corporation

A single-member disregarded LLC that is owned by a foreign parent corporation is treated as a branch of the foreign parent corporation, and is taxed as follows:[152]

- The foreign company and its U.S. branches are subject to U.S. taxes on income that is effectively connected with the conduct of U.S. trade or business.[153] A foreign company will be treated as engaged in a U.S. trade or business if it owns an LLC that is engaged in a U.S. trade or business.[154] Thus, in the absence of a treaty, the foreign corporation will be taxed on income earned by the LLC from a U.S. trade or business. The foreign parent corporation must file Form 1120-F and pay taxes on the income earned by the LLC.

- Since the LLC is a disregarded entity, the foreign parent company may claim treaty benefits for income earned by the LLC. Under most tax treaties, a foreign corporation will not be subject to U.S. taxes if the LLC does not have a permanent establishment in the United States. Under Article 5 of the U.S. Model Income Tax Convention of November 15, 2006, a permanent establishment is a "fixed place of business through which the business of an enterprise is wholly or partly carried on." A permanent establishment includes offices, factories, workshops, mines, oil and gas wells, quarries and certain construction sites. An LLC will not be treated as having a permanent establishment solely on account of sales through independent contractors working on a nonexclusive basis.[155]

- Once the LLC has sufficient presence in the United States to create a permanent establishment, the LLC may convert to a corporate subsidiary subject to the regular U.S. corporate tax rates. When the foreign parent corporation sells the stock in the U.S. subsidiary, gain on the sale will not be subject to U.S.

---

[149] Reg. §§ 301-7701-2(e)(9), 1.6038A-2(b)(9), Example 1,1.6038A-3.

[150] *See* ¶ 1808.06.

[151] Reg. § 301-7701-2(c)(2)(vi)(C).

[152] *See* discussion of this issue in BNA Insights, *Entering the U.S. Without Entering Its Tax System: Holding Company Structures for U.S. Operations,* BNA Daily Tax Rept. at J-1 (Oct. 2, 2015).

[153] Code Sec. 882(a).

[154] The reason is that the single-member LLC is a disregarded entity. *See* Code Sec. 875(1) if the LLC is classified as a partnership.

[155] *See* Article 5(6) of the Model Treaty.

income taxes if the subsidiary does not hold substantial assets in U.S. real property or mineral resources.[156]
- The LLC is subject to a branch profits tax of 30 percent on any profits from the branch that are distributed to the parent corporation. Most tax treaties reduce the branch profits tax rate below 30 percent.
- If the LLC owns real estate, the foreign parent corporation may be subject to tax under the Foreign Investment in Real Property Tax Act on sale of its interest in the LLC.[157]
- Since a foreign corporation is interposed between the shareholders of the foreign corporation and U.S. situs real property owned by the LLC, there are no U.S. estate taxes.

¶ 1905 FOREIGN TAX CREDIT

Some countries, such as Italy and Korea, do not permit taxpayers to take an indirect foreign tax credit. The taxes paid by U.S.-owned corporations may not be credited against the taxes owed in such countries on dividends and other income from the U.S. corporations. An LLC that is taxed as a partnership solves this problem. The foreign owners are treated as having directly paid the U.S. taxes and are thus entitled to a direct foreign tax credit.[158]

¶ 1906 S CORPORATIONS

Foreign corporations and nonresident aliens may not be shareholders of an S corporation.[159] Foreign persons may obtain the benefits of an S corporation (limited liability and pass-through taxation) by using an LLC. An LLC may have corporate and nonresident alien shareholders.

¶ 1907 SALE OF MEMBERSHIP INTERESTS

Effective November 27, 2017, a nonresident alien individual's or foreign corporation's gain or loss from the sale, exchange, or other disposition of a membership interest in an LLC is treated as effectively connected with the conduct of a trade or business in the United States to the extent that the person would have had effectively connected gain or loss had the LLC sold all of its assets at fair market value.[160]

 If any portion of the gain on the sale or disposition of a membership interest is treated as effectively connected with the conduct of a trade or business in the United States, then the transferee must withhold a tax equal to ten percent of the amount

---

[156] *See* CCH Standard Federal Tax Reporter ¶ 27,484.025; Reg. § 1.871-7(d)(2)(ii).

[157] *See* ¶ 1902.04 *supra.*

[158] *See* ¶ 1801.01 *supra.*

[159] Code Sec. 1361(b).

[160] Code Secs. 864(c)(8)(A), 864(c)(8)(B).

realized on the disposition.[161] The LLC must withhold the tax if the transferee fails to withhold.[162] The IRS temporarily suspended the withholding tax on the sale by a foreign person of a membership interest in publicly traded partnerships and LLCs.[163]

A selling foreign member also recognizes gain on the sale of a membership interest to the extent attributable to the selling member's share of U.S. real property owned by the LLC.[164]

¶1908 HYBRID ENTITIES

The withholding tax rates may be reduced by treaty. A foreign person claiming the benefit of a treaty must use IRS Form W-8BEN (which replaces Forms 1001 and 4224). The treaty benefits are not available to a nontreaty jurisdiction hybrid entity that is classified as a partnership for U.S. tax purposes, but as a corporation in the owner's treaty jurisdiction.

Before 1998, a foreign corporation could substantially reduce taxes by forming a U.S. LLC that was classified as a partnership for U.S. tax purposes and as a corporation for foreign tax purposes. The foreign corporation could repatriate cash at the reduced U.S. withholding tax rate free of tax in its home country.

The particular arrangement that concerned Congress involved Canadian corporations. A Canadian corporation would form a U.S. LLC that was classified as a partnership for U.S. tax purposes. The LLC would be classified as a corporation for Canadian tax purposes. Under that arrangement, the Canadian parent corporation would lend money to the wholly owned U.S. LLC. The U.S. LLC would in turn loan the same funds to a U.S. corporate subsidiary of the Canadian parent. The corporate subsidiary would claim a tax deduction for the interest paid to the LLC. This reduced the corporate subsidiary's taxable income in the United States. The LLC would in turn pay interest to the Canadian parent corporation, withholding at the ten percent withholding tax rate under the U.S.-Canada tax treaty. The LLC would claim a tax deduction for the interest paid, thereby reducing its U.S. taxable income to zero. The interest paid to the Canadian parent corporation would be free of Canadian income taxes under Canada's "participation exemption." The participation exemption exempts from tax the dividends received by a Canadian corporation from a U.S. subsidiary corporation. The LLC would be treated as a U.S. subsidiary corporation, and the interest payment by the LLC to the Canadian parent corporation would be treated as a dividend under Canadian law. As a result, the only tax imposed on the interest payment would be the ten percent U.S. withholding tax.

Congress enacted Code Sec. 894(c) of the Internal Revenue Code to combat this perceived abuse. Section 894(c) denies benefits under any tax treaty between the United States and a foreign country to foreign persons that receive income through

---

[161] Code Sec. 1446(f)(1).

[162] Code Sec. 1446(f)(4).

[163] Notice 2018-08, 2018-7 IRB 352.

[164] Rev. Rul. 91-32, 1991-1 CB 107. *See also* ¶1902.04 under the subheading, *Sale of Membership Interest.*

an entity that is classified as a partnership for federal income tax purposes if the three following conditions are met:

1. The item is not treated as an item of income under the tax laws of the foreign country;

2. The treaty does not contain a provision addressing the application of the treaty in the case of the item derived through a partnership or LLC; and

3. The foreign country does not impose a tax on the distribution of the income.

Final regulations establish rules under which U.S. withholding agents may reduce the withholding tax on payments of U.S. source income to hybrid entities.[165] Foreign persons who invest in an LLC or other hybrid entity may claim the benefits of reduced or exempt rates under a treaty only if the income is treated as "derived" by (and thus taxable to) the recipient under the laws of the foreign treaty country.

¶1909 FOREIGN SOURCE INCOME

An LLC with U.S. and foreign members may claim treaty benefits for income from foreign sources to the extent that the members of the LLC are U.S. residents. The tax treaties normally provide that U.S. persons receive a reduced rate of tax on various types of income received from the foreign country.[166] An LLC qualifies as a "U.S. person" for tax treaty purposes and is eligible for treaty benefits for foreign source income:

(i) to the extent that the members of the LLC are U.S. residents;[167]

(ii) the income received from the foreign treaty country is subject to U.S. taxes; and

(iii) the LLC certifies to the foreign country the percentage interest in the LLC owned by U.S. residents. An LLC that is classified as a disregarded entity or partnership must make the certification by filing Form 8802 and requesting a certificate of residency on Form 6166.[168]

---

[165] Reg. § 1.894-1(d).

[166] *See, e.g.,* Competent Authority Agreement with Mexico (Jan. 1, 2006); U.S.-New Zealand Competent Authority Agreement, IR-2005-15 (Feb. 10, 2005); U.S.-Spain Competent Authority Agreement on Treatment of Limited Liability Companies, S Corporations, Other Businesses Entities, Announcement 2006-21, IRB 2006-14 (Apr. 3, 2006); U.K./U.S. Double Taxation Treaty (Mar. 31, 2003).

[167] *See, e.g.,* Competent Authority Agreement with Mexico (Jan. 1, 2006); U.S.-New Zealand Competent Authority Agreement, IR-2005-15 (Feb. 10, 2005); U.S.-Spain Competent Authority Agreement on Treatment of Limited Liability Companies, S Corporations, Other Businesses Entities, Announcement 2006-21, IRB 2006-14 (Apr. 3, 2006); U.K./U.S. Double Taxation Treaty (Mar. 31, 2003).

[168] Form 8802, Application for United States Residency Certification, is used to request a certificate of residency on Form 6166 from the Philadelphia Accounts Management Center. Use of Form 8802 is mandatory. Form 6166 is a letter printed on U.S. Department of Treasury stationery certifying that the individuals or entities listed are residents of the United States for purposes of the income tax laws of the United States.

EXAMPLE 19-2

A U.S. LLC that is classified as a partnership is owned 50 percent by a Canadian resident and 50 percent by a U.S. resident. The LLC receives royalty income from Spain. The LLC may claim treaty benefits as a U.S. resident for 50 percent of the payments because 50 percent of the payments are subject to U.S. taxes in the hands of the U.S. resident member. The LLC must request a certificate of residency on Form 8802 and re-present to the Spanish withholding authorities that the U.S. resident owns a 50 percent interest in the LLC.[169]

---

[169] U.S. Spain Competent Authority Agreement on Treatment of Limited Liability Companies, S Corporations, Other Businesses Entities, Announcement 2006-21, IRB 2006-14 (Apr. 3, 2006).

20

Investment LLCs and Investment Income and Expenses

¶ 2001 OVERVIEW

If an LLC owns investment assets, then it is subject to the following tax rules:

- The LLC may be treated as an investment company, and the transfer of investment assets to the LLC may be taxed. These rules are discussed at ¶ 2002.

- An LLC must separately state on Schedule K-1 each member's share of net investment income and net investment expense. The reporting requirements for investment income and investment expenses are discussed at ¶ 703.04.

- The LLC must also separately state on Schedule K-1 each member's share of investment interest expense. Members may not deduct investment interest in excess of net investment income. Investment interest expense is discussed at ¶ 703.08.

- The member's share of net investment income from the LLC and all other sources is subject to the 3.8 percent NII tax. The NII tax is discussed at ¶ 708.

- Investment expenses are deductible by the LLC under Code Sec. 212 rather than Code Sec. 162. Investment expense deductions are discussed at ¶ 2003.01.

- Most LLC investment expenses other than interest and taxes are a miscellaneous itemized deduction subject to the two percent floor on deductibility.[1] Between 2018 and 2025, a taxpayer may not deduct miscellaneous itemized deductions.[2] Miscellaneous itemized deductions are discussed at ¶2003.02.
- The passive loss rules apply to pass-through deductions from an investment LLC even if the LLC has no rental property and is not conducting a trade or business. The passive loss rules are discussed at ¶2006.
- If an LLC sells investment property, gain or loss on sale is taxed to the members as a capital gain. If the LLC sells property at a gain, the IRS is more likely to assert that the property is inventory or dealer property held for resale, and that the gain should be taxed as ordinary income. If the LLC sells undeveloped property at a loss, the IRS is more likely to assert that the property is investment property, and that the loss should be taxed as a capital loss.[3] The differences between investment property and dealer property owned by an LLC, and the tax rules applicable to each, are discussed at ¶1601.04.

¶2002 TRANSFER OF INVESTMENT PROPERTY TO LLC

.01 Overview

The general rule is that no gain or loss is recognized on the contribution of property to an LLC.[4] However, gain is recognized if the LLC would be treated as an investment company under Code Sec. 351(e)(1) if the LLC were incorporated.[5] A transfer of property is a taxable transfer to an investment company under Section 351 if (i) more than 80 percent of the LLC's assets consist of investment assets, and (ii) the transfer results in diversification of the contributing member's interest.

The law was initially enacted to prevent owners of large blocks of stock in a single company from diversifying their portfolio on a tax-free basis by contributing the securities to a partnership mini-fund.

.02 Investment Company (80 Percent Rule)

An LLC is an investment company if more than 80 percent of the LLC's assets by value consist of the following assets:[6]

---

[1] Code Sec. 67.

[2] Code Sec. 67(g), as amended by 2017 Tax Cuts and Jobs Act § 11045(a).

[3] *Conner v. Comm'r*, TC Memo 2018-6 (2018).

[4] Code Sec. 721(a).

[5] Code Sec. 721(b).

[6] Code Sec. 351(e)(1); Reg. § 1.351-1(c)(1)(ii)(a). *See also* Taxpayer Relief Act of 1997, Pub. L. No. 105-34, § 1002, 105th Cong., 1st Sess. (Aug. 5, 1997), *amending* Code Sec. 351(e)(1), applicable to partnerships under Code Sec. 721(b).

- money. However, cash held for working capital and other non-investment purposes is not an investment asset;[7]
- stocks or securities (whether or not marketable). All stocks and securities held by an LLC, including nonpublic stocks and securities, are investment assets;
- evidences of indebtedness;
- currency;
- options;
- forward or future contracts;
- notional principal contracts or derivatives;
- foreign currency;
- interests in regulated investment companies (RICs);
- real estate investment trusts (REITs);
- common trust funds and publicly traded partnerships;
- certain interests in precious metals;
- certain interests in entities that hold those items, but only to the extent of their value; and
- other assets specified in Treasury regulations.

The determination of whether the 80 percent threshold is met is made after the transfers to the LLC.[8] The regulations apply an "integrated" plan rule to the term "immediately after." If several investors transfer marketable securities at different times, the transfer may be viewed as part of an integrated plan. In that case, the 80 percent measurement will be applied after the last contribution occurs and will include all earlier contributions.[9]

The transfer of a partnership interest to an LLC in exchange for a membership interest in the LLC is not normally subject to the investment company rules.[10]

The stocks and securities that the LLC owns in a subsidiary are disregarded if the LLC owns 50 percent or more of the voting stock or total value of shares of all classes of stock outstanding.[11] In such case, the LLC must look through to the assets of the subsidiary corporation. The LLC will be treated as owning a ratable share of the subsidiary's securities.[12] This rule permits members to transfer stock in a family business to an LLC without income recognition.

EXAMPLE 20-1

The AB LLC's only asset is a 75 percent interest in CD LLC. CD LLC owns $2 million worth of publicly traded stocks. B, a partner in AB LLC,

---

[7] The regulations exclude cash and other investment type assets from the definition of bad assets if such assets are held for non-investment purposes "pursuant to a plan in existence at the time of the transfer." Reg. § 1.351-1(c)(2).

[8] Reg. § 1.351-1(c)(2).

[9] *Comm'r v. Ashland Oil & Refining Co.*, 99 F.2d 588 (6th Cir. 1938).

[10] Ltr. Rul. 200211017.

[11] Reg. § 1.351-1(c)(4).

[12] Reg. § 1.351-1(c)(4).

transfers $200,000 worth of publicly traded stocks with a basis of $50,000 to AB LLC in exchange for an interest in the LLC. AB LLC is treated as owning $1,500,000 (75% × $2,000,000) of marketable securities owned by CD LLC. Immediately after receiving B's contribution, AB is treated as owning $1,700,000 (1,500,000 + 200,000) of marketable securities. Since these assets held by AB exceed the 80 percent threshold, the LLC is classified as an investment company.[13]

.03 Diversification Rule

The transfer of assets to an investment company is taxable to the contributing member if the transfer results in a diversification of the contributing member's interests.[14] A transfer results in diversification if two or more persons transfer nonidentical assets to an LLC in the exchange.[15]

A transfer also results in diversification if it is part of a plan to achieve diversification without gain recognition, such as a plan that contemplates subsequent transfers, however delayed, to an LLC in a transaction purporting to qualify for nonrecognition treatment.[16]

There is no diversification, and no tax to the contributing members, under any one of the following circumstances:

- *25%/50% tests.* There is no diversification if each transferor contributes a diversified portfolio of stocks and securities to the LLC.[17] A stock portfolio is diversified if it satisfies the 25 percent and the 50 percent tests under Code Sec. 368(a)(2)(F)(ii).[18] The portfolio satisfies the 25 percent test if no more than 25 percent of the portfolio value is in stocks or securities of any one issuer. The portfolio satisfies the 50 percent test if no more than 50 percent of the portfolio value is in stocks or securities of five or fewer issuers. Thus, there is no tax on the transfer of appreciated marketable securities to an LLC if each member transfers a diversified portfolio of marketable securities that satisfies the 25 and 50 percent tests. If any one transferor does not transfer a diversified portfolio, then all other transferors recognize gain on the transfer of property to the LLC.[19]

---

[13] Example 2, California Franchise Tax Board, Partnership Technical Manual ¶4540, (interpreting federal law).

[14] Reg. § 1.351-1(c)(1)(i).

[15] Reg. § 1.351-1(c)(5).

[16] Ltr. Rul. 200931042, *citing* Reg. § 1.351-1(c)(5). The IRS stated in the Ltr. Rul. that it would not issue a ruling regarding whether the transfers of cash and diversified portfolios to an LLC were part of a plan to achieve diversification without gain recognition.

[17] Reg. § 1.351-1(c)(6)(i); Ltr. Ruls. 201710008, 201710007, 200931042, 200633019.

[18] Reg. § 1.351-1(c)(6); Ltr. Ruls. 201710008, 201710007, 200931042, 9617020, 9617018, 9617017.

[19] Reg. § 1.351-1(c)(6)(i).

- *De minimis rule.* There is no income recognition on the transfer of investment assets to an LLC if the member contributes a *de minimis* amount of nonidentical investment assets.[20] The transfers are disregarded in determining whether diversification has occurred. One percent of the total value of assets transferred to an LLC is an insignificant portion,[21] whereas 11 percent[22] or 50 percent[23] is not. Thus, there is no diversification resulting in taxation under the investment company rules unless there are at least two significant contributors to the LLC.[24]

- *Transfer of identical assets.* There is no income recognition on the transfer of investment assets to an LLC if each member contributes identical assets.[25] The income recognition rules apply only if the transfers result in diversification.

EXAMPLE 20-2

A parent corporation transfers appreciated marketable securities to an LLC. Its wholly owned subsidiary also transfers appreciated marketable securities to the LLC representing less than one percent of the total fair market value of the contributed assets. The subsidiary's contribution of the nonidentical assets is disregarded in determining whether the LLC's assets are diversified because the contribution amount is de minimis. Thus, the transfer of the appreciated securities does not result in diversification or income recognition.[26]

EXAMPLE 20-3

A husband and wife and their children form an LLC for the purpose of acquiring marketable securities for investment. The husband and wife own a one percent interest, and the children own a 99 percent interest. The husband and wife contribute appreciated marketable securities to the LLC in exchange for a membership interest. The securities transferred consist of a diversified group of publicly owned securities. No one issue of the portfolio represents more than 25 percent of the value of all securities contributed to the LLC. Not more than 50 percent of the value of all securities contributed consist of securities of five or fewer issuers. The

---

[20] Reg. § 1.351-1(c)(5).

[21] Reg. § 1.351-1(c)(5), Examples (1)-(2).

[22] Rev. Rul. 87-9, 1987-1 CB 134.

[23] Reg. § 1.351-1(c)(5), Examples (1)-(2).

[24] Ltr. Ruls. 9751048, 9608026.

[25] Reg. § 1.351-1(c)(5); Rev. Rul. 88-32, 1988-1 CB 113.

[26] Ltr. Rul. 9751048.

membership interests received by the husband and wife in exchange for the contribution of securities is based on the market value of the contributed securities relative to the value of all securities in the LLC after the contribution. There is no income recognition on the transfer of the appreciated securities to the LLC because the assets transferred constitute a diversified investment portfolio.[27]

EXAMPLE 20-4

A husband and wife contribute appreciated securities to an LLC in exchange for a membership interest. The securities consist of a diversified portfolio of publicly owned securities. No one of the securities transferred represents more than 25 percent of the value of the total securities contributed. Not more than 50 percent of value of the securities contributed consist of securities of five or fewer issuers. The membership interest that the husband and wife receive in exchange for the appreciated securities is based on the fair market value of the contributed securities relative to the value of all securities in the LLC after the contribution. After the contribution, the securities of any one issuer that the LLC holds do not represent more than 25 percent of the value of the total assets of the LLC, and not more than 50 percent of the value of all of the LLC's assets are invested in the securities of five or fewer issuers. The transfer by the husband and wife of the diversified portfolio of appreciated stocks and securities is not a transfer to an investment company. Accordingly, no gain or loss is recognized on the contribution.[28]

EXAMPLE 20-5

A parent corporation transferred investment assets to an LLC. Its wholly owned subsidiary transferred an insignificant amount of nonidentical assets to the LLC, representing less than one percent of the total fair market value of the contributed assets. The subsidiary's contribution of the nonidentical assets was thus disregarded for purposes of determining whether the LLC's assets were diversified.[29] Since a transfer of the contributed assets did not result in diversification, there was no transfer of property to a partnership that would be treated as an investment company if it were incorporated.[30] No gain or loss was recognized on the

---

[27] Ltr. Rul. 200002025.

[28] Ltr. Rul. 200002025 (*citing* Reg. § 1.351-1(c)(6)(i)).

[29] *See* Reg. § 1.351-1(c)(5), (7).

[30] *See* Reg. § 1.351-1(c)(1).

transfer of the investment assets to the LLC, assuming the net reduction in the contributing party's liabilities as a result of their assumption by the LLC did not exceed their adjusted basis in the contributed investment assets.[31] Similarly, Code Sec. 721(b), which imposes taxes on the transfer of property to an investment partnership, did not apply.[32]

.04 Amount of Gain Recognized

If a member contributes property to an LLC that is classified as an investment company, and if diversification of the contributor's investment occurs, then the contributing member must recognize gain on the transfer. The gain recognized is equal to the excess of the value of the membership interest received in the exchange over the adjusted basis of the assets contributed to the LLC.[33] If the value of the membership interest cannot be determined, the value of the assets transferred to the LLC may be used.[34]

EXAMPLE 20-6

John owns 100 shares of common stock in a publicly traded corporation. The shares have a basis of $10,000 and a fair market value of $20,000. John transfers the stock to JB LLC in exchange for a ten percent interest in the LLC. JB is an investment partnership by definition. The LLC interest received by John is presumed to be worth $20,000. John recognizes $10,000 capital gain upon the transfer. The LLC's basis in the stock received is $20,000. John's basis in his membership interest is $20,000.[35]

Once an LLC is classified as an investment partnership, the transfer of any appreciated property to the LLC is subject to gain recognition.

No loss is recognized on the contribution of property to an investment company.[36]

---

[31] Ltr. Rul. 9751048 (*citing* Code Secs. 721(a), (b)).

[32] Ltr. Rul. 9751048.

[33] Code Sec. 1001.

[34] *Philadelphia Park Amusement Co. v. U.S.*, 126 F. Supp. 184 (Ct. Cl. 1954); *Farid-Es-Sultaneh v. Comm'r*, 160 F.2d 812 (2d Cir. 1974).

[35] Example 1 from California Franchise Tax Board, Partnership Technical Manual ¶4530 (interpreting federal law). Code Sec. 722 states that basis includes gain recognized under Code Sec. 721(a).

[36] S. Rep. No. 938, 94th Cong., 2d Sess., pt.2 at 43 (1976).

¶ 2003 INVESTMENT EXPENSES

.01 General Rules

Investment expenses are deductible by members of an LLC under Code Sec. 212 rather than Code Sec. 162. Section 212 provides that an individual taxpayer may deduct ordinary and necessary expenses paid or incurred for the production or collection of income, or for the management, conservation or maintenance of property held for the production of income. Section 212 applies to LLC income-producing activities that are not a trade or business.[37]

The expense deductions under Section 162 are more favorable than the expense deductions under Section 212. The reason is that Section 162 expenses are subtracted from gross income in arriving at adjusted gross income. The Section 212 expenses are subtracted from the member's adjusted gross income in arriving at taxable income.[38] The major tax consequences of Section 212 expenses are as follows:

- The member may not deduct the Section 212 investment expenses unless the member itemizes deductions.

- Investment interest expenses are deductible only to the extent of net investment income.

- Certain itemized deductions on Schedule A are subject to limits on deductibility. For example, the deduction for state and local income, sales and property taxes may not exceed $10,000 ($5,000 for a married person filing separately). The limits on deductibility do not apply to taxes for rental property treated as a trade or business, and which are deductible on Schedule C, E or F.

- Investment expenses other than interest and taxes are a miscellaneous itemized deduction that are nondeductible between 2018 and 2025.[39]

- Investment expenses and other itemized deductions are subject to an overall limit on deductibility for tax years after 2025.[40] The overall limit is suspended for tax years between 2018 and 2025.

- Excess investment expenses and other itemized deductions do not give rise to a net operating loss carry forward.

---

[37] *Conner v. Comm'r*, TC Memo 2018-6 (2018).

[38] The general rule is that investment expenses (and other expenses under Section 212) are deductible above the line if attributable to property held for the production of rents or royalties. Code Sec. 62(a)(4). However, a member is not entitled to an above-the-line deduction if an LLC holds property for the production of rents or royalties. The member must himself hold the property for the production of rents or royalties. Ltr. Rul. 9728002.

[39] *See* ¶ 2003.02.

[40] Code Sec. § 68.

EXAMPLE 20-7

In *Conner v. Commissioner*,[41] the taxpayer owned undeveloped real property through several LLCs. The LLCs claimed that it held the property as a developer for resale, and that all of its expenses were deductible above-the-line under Section 162. The Court determined that the property was held for investment because development never progressed beyond the exploratory or formative stage. Thus, the LLC could not deduct its expenses under Section 162. The expenses were deductible below-the-line under Section 212. The investment interest expenses were deductible only against net investment income under Section 163(d)(1). If the LLC had been engaged in a trade or business, the interest expenses would not have been investment interest subject to the limits on deductibility.

.02 Miscellaneous Itemized Deductions

The Section 212 expenses other than interest and taxes are subject to the two percent floor on deductibility for miscellaneous itemized deductions under Section 67(a).[42] The two percent floor on deductibility applies at the member level, not at the LLC level.[43] Between 2018 and 2025, a taxpayer may not deduct miscellaneous itemized deductions.[44]

The limitations on deductibility for miscellaneous itemized deductions do not apply to the LLC.[45] The LLC may not deduct the investment expenses against bottom-line trade or business income reported in Box 1 of Schedule K, or against investment income reported on line 20a of Schedule K. Instead, it must separately state gross investment income and investment expenses, and report each member's allocable share of such income and expenses on Schedule K-1 so that the member can determine the deductibility of the expenses at the member level.[46]

The member must report the member's allocable share of pass-through investment expenses on Schedule A of Form 1040. The expenses are then deductible after 2025 to the extent that such pass-through expenses and all other miscellaneous itemized deductions exceed two percent of adjusted gross income.[47]

---

[41] *Conner v. Comm'r*, TC Memo 2018-6 (2018).

[42] Code Sec. §67(c)(1); Reg. §§1.67-2T(b)(1), 1.67-2T(b)(2), Example; *Lender Management, LLC v. Comm'r*, TC Memo 2017-246 (2017).

[43] Reg. §1.67-2T(a), (b).

[44] Code Sec. §67(g), as amended by 2017 Tax Cuts and Jobs Act §11045(a).

[45] Reg. §1.67-2T(b)(1).

[46] *See* ¶703.04.

[47] IRS, Taxes, Pub. 550, *Investment Income and Expenses.*

EXAMPLE 20-8

An LLC purchases vacant land for investment. It allocates $1,000 of property taxes, $1,000 of interest expense, and $1,000 of accounting fees and insurance expenses to Mary, a member in the LLC. The tax consequences are as follows:

1. The LLC must separately state the investment expenses on Mary's Schedule K-1. The LLC may not deduct the investment expenses against investment income or any other business income.

2. Since the LLC is not engaged in the business of buying and selling real estate as a dealer, Mary may not deduct the expenses as business expenses on Schedule C. Instead, the investment expenses are reported as below-the-line personal expenses on Schedule A.

3. Mary may deduct the property taxes as an itemized deduction on Schedule A. The property taxes are not a miscellaneous itemized deduction.[48] The itemized deductions are subject to an overall limit on deductibility after 2025.

4. Mary may deduct the interest expense as an itemized deduction on Schedule A. The investment interest is deductible only to the extent of net investment income for the year. The net investment income is computed by subtracting annual investment expenses (other than interest expenses) from Mary's investment income. The excess amount may be carried forward to future years. The interest expense is not a miscellaneous itemized deduction.[49]

5. Mary may not deduct the accounting fees and insurance expenses. These investment expenses are a miscellaneous itemized deduction, which are nondeductible between 2018 and 2025.

6. Mary may not deduct any of the investment expenses, including interest and taxes, unless Mary itemizes deductions since all investment expenses are below-the-line deductions.

7. The LLC may make an annual election to capitalize the carrying costs under Code Sec. 266, in which case it would add the investment expenses to basis. The basis increase reduces gain on the LLC's sale of the property. In such case, the LLC would not allocate the investment expenses to Mary on Schedule K-1, and Mary would receive no current deductions. The LLC should make the election if the members of the LLC do not itemize deductions or are not otherwise entitled to a deduction of investment expenses.

---

[48] Code Sec. § 67(b)(1).
[49] Code Sec. § 67(b)(2).

.03 Investment Management Services

If an LLC is engaged primarily in the business of providing investment management services for the owners and family members of the LLC, then the business expenses are deductible under Section 212(1) as a deduction for ordinary and necessary expenses in connection with an activity engaged in for the production or collection of income. If the LLC's investment management services constitute a trade or business, then the business expenses are allowed under Section 162 as a deduction for ordinary and necessary expenses paid or incurred in carrying on a trade or business. The IRS sometimes takes the position that an LLC providing mainly investment management services through a family office may deduct those expenses only under Section 212, and not under Section 162.[50]

¶ 2004 SECURITIES PARTNERSHIPS

An LLC must allocate income, gain, loss, and deduction with respect to property contributed by a member to the LLC so as to take into account any variation between the adjusted tax basis of the property and its fair market value at the time of the contribution.[51] Under the safe-harbor regulations, the LLC must revalue its property for capital account purposes when a new member is admitted to the LLC. The LLC must then allocate income, gain, loss and deduction with respect to the revalued property in order to take account of any variation between the adjusted tax basis of the property and its fair market value at the time of the contribution. These allocations are called reverse Section 704(c) allocations.[52]

Certain securities partnerships may make reverse Section 704(c) allocations on an aggregate basis by aggregating gains and losses from qualified financial assets.[53] Once an LLC adopts an aggregate approach, the LLC must apply the same aggregate approach to all of its qualified financial assets for all taxable years in which the LLC qualifies as a securities partnership.

A securities partnership is a partnership that is either a management company or an investment partnership, and that makes all of its book allocations in proportion to the partners' relative book capital accounts (except for reasonable special allocations to a partner who provides management services or investment advisory services to the partnership).[54] An LLC is an investment partnership if (i) on the date of each capital account restatement, the LLC holds qualified financial assets that constitute at least 90 percent of the fair market value of the LLC's non-cash assets, and (ii) the LLC reasonably expects, as of the end of the first taxable year in which the partnership

---

[50] *Lender Management, LLC v. Comm'r*, TC Memo 2017-246 (2017).

[51] Code Sec. § 704(c)(1)(A).

[52] Reg. § 1.704-3(a)(6).

[53] Reg. § 1.704-3(e)(3)

[54] Reg. § 1.704-3(e)(3)(iii)(A).

adopts an aggregate approach, to make revaluations at least annually.[55] A qualified financial asset is any personal property, including stock, that is actively traded.[56]

A securities partnership may use any reasonable approach to aggregate gains and losses from qualified financial assets that is consistent with the purpose of Code Sec. 704(c), but once it adopts an approach, it must continue to use it. The following methods are considered reasonable methods for allocating gains and losses:

- *Partial netting approach.* Under the partial netting approach, tax gains and losses are netted separately. Gains (losses) are allocated to the members who have positive (negative) capital accounts in proportion to their positive (negative) balances. The excess amounts, if any, are then allocated on a pro rata basis to all of the members. In order to use the partial netting approach, the LLC must establish appropriate accounts for each member for the purpose of taking into account each member's share of the book gains and losses and determining each member's share of the tax gains and losses. Under the partial netting approach, on the date of each capital account restatement, the LLC: (a) nets its book gains and losses from qualified financial assets since the last capital account restatement and allocates the net amount to its members; (b) separately aggregates all realized tax gains and all realized tax losses from qualified financial assets since the last capital account restatement; and (c) separately allocates the aggregate tax gain and aggregate tax loss to the members in a manner that reduces the disparity between the book capital account balances and the tax capital account balances (book-tax disparities) of the individual partners.[57]

- *Full netting approach.* The full netting approach combines all tax gains and losses and allocates only a single net figure to the members.

¶ 2005 PUBLICLY TRADED LLCs

Generally, an LLC will be taxed as a corporation if it is a publicly traded LLC.[58] A publicly traded LLC is an LLC whose interests are traded on an established securities market or are readily traded on a secondary market or the substantial equivalent of a secondary market.[59]

Publicly traded LLCs are discussed at ¶ 506.

---

[55] Reg. § 1.704-3(e)(3)(iii)(B)(2).

[56] Reg. § 1.704-3(e)(3)(ii).

[57] Ltr. Ruls. 201710008, 201710007.

[58] Code Sec. 7704; Reg. § 1.7704-1.

[59] Reg. § 1.7704-1(a)(1).

¶ 2006 PASSIVE LOSS RULES

Passive losses are deductible only to the extent of passive income.[60] Passive losses include losses from a rental business, or a trade or business in which the taxpayer does not materially participate.[61]

Pass-through deductions from an investment LLC are subject to the passive loss rules even if the LLC does not own rental property or does not engage in a trade or business. The reason is that Section 212 applies to income-producing activities that are not a trade or business. Section 469(c)(6)(B) provides that a trade or business for purposes of the passive loss rules includes any activity for which expenses are allowable as a deduction under Section 212.

EXAMPLE 20-9

In *Conner v. Commissioner*,[62] the taxpayer owned undeveloped real property through several LLCs. The Court determined that the property was held for investment and not as part of a trade or business. Thus, expenses were deductible under Section 212 rather than Section 162, and were subject to the interest limitations under Section 163(d). The owner of the LLCs did not materially participate in the businesses of the LLCs. Therefore, loss deductions that passed through from the LLC were disallowed under the passive loss rules.

Income and losses received by member from an LLC that trades in stocks, bonds, or securities for the accounts of its members is nonpassive.[63] Thus, a taxpayer may not offset losses from passive activities against the trading income received from an investment LLC.

---

[60] Code Sec. 469.

[61] Code Sec. 469(c).

[62] *Conner v. Comm'r*, TC Memo 2018-6 (2018).

[63] Temp. Reg. § 1.469-1T(e)(6).

21

Estate and Gift Tax Planning

¶ 2101 ADVANTAGES OF LLC

LLCs have been used in estate planning since 1993, when the IRS issued a ruling permitting minority discounts for transfers of interests in an entity controlled by a single family.[1] An LLC has the following advantages for estate planning purposes:

- *Transfer of property.* An LLC may facilitate the transfer of property, especially real estate and other property that is not easily divisible. For example, a donor can make annual gifts to his children of units in an LLC that owns real estate. This is less expensive and cumbersome than preparing and recording deeds to an undivided interest in the real estate each year. The operating agreement for the LLC may permit the manager to sell or refinance the property at any time without obtaining the consent of the donees.

- *Basis step-up.* A member's death beneficiaries may step-up the basis of a membership interest on the death of the member.[2] No gain or loss is recognized on the subsequent sale or disposition of the membership interest except to the extent of appreciation or depreciation after the date of death or the six-month alternate valuation date.[3] The LLC may also step up the basis of its assets attributable to the deceased member if the LLC makes an election

---

[1] Rev. Rul. 93-12, 1993-1 CB 202.

[2] Code Sec. 1014.

[3] Code Sec. 1001.

under Code Sec. 754.[4] In contrast, the basis step-up for a corporation applies only to the stock and not to the assets owned by the corporation.

- *Valuation discounts.* A taxpayer may receive significant valuation discounts for property transferred to family members through an LLC. The valuation discounts include the minority discount, marketability discount, liquidity discount, and a number of other discounts.[5] However, since 2002, the IRS has successfully challenged gift and estate transfers in certain cases under Code Secs. 2511,[6] 2036,[7] and 2503.[8]

- *Distributions on death.* An LLC may be used to facilitate the distribution of assets to beneficiaries of a trust on the death of the grantor of the trust. When the grantor of a trust dies, the successor trustee must make distributions to the beneficiaries in accordance with the terms of the trust. The trustee may establish one or more LLCs to hold trust assets. As long as the trust remains the single owner of the LLC, the LLC is a disregarded entity, and all items of income, deduction, credit, gains, and losses must be reported on the trust's federal income tax returns. The trustee may distribute the LLC membership interests to the beneficiaries rather than the underlying assets. The LLC will then be converted into a partnership if the LLC has two or more members. The distributions of interests will be treated as a nontaxable pro rata distribution of the underlying assets to the beneficiaries as though the assets and been distributed outright. The beneficiaries are then treated as having contributed their interests in the assets of the trust to an LLC that is classified as a partnership. The beneficiaries do not recognize gain or loss as a result of the conversion of the LLC from a disregarded entity to a partnership.[9]

¶ 2102 GIFTS

.01 *Annual Gift Tax Exclusion*

The general rule is that a gift of a membership interest in an LLC qualifies for the $15,000 (2018 amount) annual gift tax exclusion.[10] The exclusion is available if the donor relinquishes dominion and control over the membership interest,[11] and if the donee has the right to current distributions or the right to sell the membership interest.[12]

---

[4] Code Sec. 743(b).
[5] *See* ¶ 2105 *infra.*
[6] *See* ¶ 2104.13 *infra.*
[7] *See* ¶ 2104.03 *infra.*
[8] *See* ¶ 2102.01 *infra.*
[9] Ltr. Rul. 201421001.
[10] Code Sec. 2503(b).
[11] Ltr. Rul. 9808010.
[12] TAM 199944003.

The annual gift tax exclusion is not available if the donee" lacks the tangible and immediate economic benefit" of a present interest in the property.[13] The gift of membership units in an LLC that is expected to have losses for several years in the future does not qualify for the gift tax annual exclusion if there are restrictions preventing the donee from realizing any substantial financial or economic benefits from the membership units.[14] For example, the gift of a membership interest is a gift of a future interest that does not qualify for the annual exclusion if the operating agreement (a) gives the manager complete discretion to distribute income, or to retain income in the LLC for any reason, (b) prevents the donee from transferring or assigning the gifted interests without the consent of the manager, and (c) prevents the donee from withdrawing from the LLC and receiving a return of capital contributions until a future date.[15]

The gift of LLC membership interests qualifies for the annual exclusion if the donees have either the right to freely transfer their membership interest, or have a present interest in the income of the LLC. To determine whether rights to income from an LLC satisfy the criteria for a present interest under Code Sec. 2503(b), the estate must prove on the basis of surrounding circumstances that (i) the family limited partnership would generate income, (ii) some portion of the income would flow steadily to the donees, and (iii) that portion of the income could be readily ascertained.[16]

In *Fisher v. Comm'r*,[17] the Fishers transferred all of the membership interests in an LLC to their seven children over the course of three years using annual exclusion gifts. The court determined that the annual exclusion did not apply because the timing and amount of annual distributions from the LLC was within the discretion of the General Manager; the children did not receive a substantial present economic benefit from the LLC; and the LLC had a right of first refusal to match any offer to purchase the children's membership interests, and to pay with a note of up to 15 years, which in the opinion of the Court, "effectively prevents the Fisher Children from transferring their interests in exchange for immediate value." In order for the annual exclusion to apply, the taxpayer must show that it meets at least two of the following three conditions: (a) the donees have an unrestricted right to distributions, (b) the donees have a substantial present economic interest, and (c) the donees have an unrestricted right to transfer the membership interests. The Court determined in the *Fisher* case that the taxpayer failed to satisfy all three conditions.

The problem typically arises for LLCs that own nonincome-producing assets. The donee does not receive an immediate economic benefit in such cases unless the

---

[13] Ltr. Rul. 9751003; *Price v. Comm'r*, TC Memo 2010-2 (2010); *Fisher v. United States*, No. 1:08-cv-0908-LJM-Tab (S.D. Ind. 2010).

[14] *Hackl v. Comm'r*, 118 TC 279 (2002), *aff'd*, 92 AFTR 2d 2003-5254 (7th Cir. 2003); *Price v. Comm'r*, TC Memo 2010-2 (2010); *Fisher v. United States*, No. 1:08-cv-0908-LJM-Tab (S.D. Ind. 2010).

[15] Ltr. Rul. 9751003; *Hackl v. Comm'r*, 118 TC 279 (2002); *Price v. Comm'r*, TC Memo 2010-2 (2010).

[16] *Estate of Purdue v. Comm'r*, TC Memo 2015-249 (2015); *Hackl v. Comm'r*, 118 TC 279 (2002); *Price v. Comm'r*, TC Memo 2010-2 (2010).

[17] *Fisher v. Comm'r*, 105 AFTR 2d 2010-1347 (S.D. Ind. 2010).

donee is free to sell the membership interest, to withdraw the capital account, or to force a dissolution of the LLC.[18]

.02 Gift Tax Returns and Statute of Limitations

General Rule

The taxpayer must file a gift tax return for gifts over the annual exclusion amount. The statute of limitations on assessments for gifts of membership interests in an LLC is:[19]

Three years after the return is filed if the donor adequately discloses the gift on the return.[20]

Six years after the return is filed if the taxpayer omits from the total amount of gifts made during the period for which the gift tax return is filed an amount exceeding 25 percent of the total gifts stated on the return. However, in determining which items are omitted as gifts, no item is taken into account for which there is adequate disclosure on the return.[21]

Indefinitely, if the donor fails to make adequate disclosure of the gift on the return.[22]

Adequate Disclosure

In order to start the running of the statute of limitations on gifts of membership interests in an LLC, the donor must make adequate disclosure of the gift on the gift tax return. The donor must provide the following information in order to meet the adequate disclosure requirement:[23]

- A description of the membership units transferred, the number of membership units, the percentage ownership interest represented by the units, and the nature of any class of membership units transferred.
- Any consideration received by the donor.
- The identity of, and relationship between, the donor and each donee.

---

[18] *Hackl v. Comm'r*, 118 TC 279 (2002); *Price v. Comm'r*, TC Memo 2010-2 (2010); *Fisher v. United States*, No. 1:08-cv-0908-LJM-Tab (S.D. Ind. 2010).

[19] IRS Legal Memorandum 200221010.

[20] Code Sec. 6501(a).

[21] Code Sec. 6501(e)(2).

[22] Code Sec. 6501(c)(9); Reg. §301.6501(c)-1(f)(2).

[23] IRS Legal Memorandum 200221010; Reg. §301.6501(c)-1(f)(2). *See also* FAA 20152201F which states that a gift will be treated as adequately disclosed if the return or statement attached to the return provides, among other things, a description of the transferred property, any consideration received by the transferor, the identity of and relationship between the transferor and each transferee, and the method used to determine the fair market value of the gifted interest.

- If the membership units are transferred in trust, the trust's tax identification number and a brief description of the terms of the trust. Alternatively, the donor may provide a copy of the trust.

- An appraisal meeting the requirements of Reg. § 301.6501(c)-1(f)(3). Alternatively, the donor may provide a description of the method used to determine the fair market value of the membership interests. This should include any financial data, such as balance sheet and income statements, used in determining the value the membership interests, any restrictions on the membership interests that were considered in determining the fair market value, and a description of any discounts (such as blockage, minority, marketability, or fractional interests) claimed in valuing the property. The donor must also describe any discount claimed in valuing any property owned by the LLC. If the value of the LLC is determined based on the net value of the assets held by the LLC, the donor must provide a statement regarding the fair market value of 100 percent of the LLC without regard to any discounts, the pro rata portion of the LLC subject to the transfer, and the fair market value of the transferred membership interest as reported on the return. • A statement describing any position that is contrary to any proposed, temporary, or final regulations or revenue rulings published at the time of the gift.

EXAMPLE 21-1

The following description of a gift of membership units on a gift tax return is not sufficient to start the running of the statute of limitations:[24]

Class B units in ABC LLC. Units acquired on April 4, 1997 for $200,000 cash. Gifts made on April 7, 1997 with value on that date of $200,000 and an adjusted basis of $200,000.

.03 Contribution to LLC

The contribution of property to an LLC is treated as a taxable gift to the other members of the LLC in proportion to their ownership interests in the LLC, unless the contribution is credited at fair market value to the capital account of the contributing member.[25]

---

[24] IRS Legal Memorandum 200221010.

[25] *Estate of Theodore R. Thompson v. Comm'r*, 84 TCM 374 (2002); *Harper v. Comm'r*, TC Memo 2001-121 (2002); *Estate of W.W. Jones v. Comm'r*, 116 TC 121 (2001). *See* ¶ 2104.11 *infra* regarding the "gift on creation theory."

.04 Gift of Membership Interest Not Encumbered by Debt

There are no income tax consequences to the donor who gives a membership interest free of liabilities. A membership interest is free of liabilities if the LLC has no liabilities, or if the donor has no share of LLC liabilities under Code Sec. 752.[26] However, a donor realizes taxable income if the donee pays the gift taxes.[27]

.05 Gift of Membership Interest Encumbered by Debt

There may be taxable gain if a donor transfers a membership interest encumbered by debt. A membership interest is encumbered by debt if the LLC allocates recourse or nonrecourse debt to the donor member (usually reflected on Schedule K-1).[28]

The taxable gain is the amount realized (debt relief) in excess of the member's basis in the membership interest.[29] No loss is realized if the debt relief is less than the adjusted basis.[30]

The gain recognized is capital gain. However, some of the gain must be reclassified as ordinary income if there are Section 751 assets.[31] For example, if the LLC has depreciable assets that are subject to depreciation recapture (a Section 751 asset), the donor member's share of the potential recapture amount would be ordinary income.[32]

.06 Basis for Donee Member

The rules for determining the basis of the membership interest received by the donee are discussed at ¶902.01.

.07 Passive Losses

The gift of a membership interest does not trigger a deduction for suspended passive activity losses. Instead, suspended passive activity losses of the donor are added to the donee's basis in the membership interest.[33]

The donee may not deduct the suspended passive activity losses. The tax benefits to the donee are deferred until the donee disposes of the membership interest

---

[26] IRS Market Segment Specialization Program, Partnerships, Audit Technique Guide, Chapter 7, under the heading, "Gift of Partnership Interest Not Encumbered by Debt."

[27] *Diedrich v. Comm'r*, 457 U.S. 191 (1982).

[28] IRS Market Segment Specialization Program, Partnerships, Audit Technique Guide, Chapter 7, under the heading, "Gift of a Partnership Interest Encumbered by Debt."

[29] Code Sec. 752(b).

[30] Reg. § 1.1001-1(e)(1).

[31] Section 751 assets are discussed at ¶¶1005.01, 1507.01 *supra*.

[32] IRS Market Segment Specialization Program, Partnerships, Audit Technique Guide, Chapter 7, under the heading, "Gift of a Partnership Interest Encumbered by Debt."

[33] Code Sec. 469(j)(6)(A).

in a taxable transaction.[34] If the "bloated basis" exceeds the fair market value of the membership interest at the time of the gift, and the donee subsequently disposes of the interest in a taxable transaction resulting in a loss, no loss is allowed. The passive activity loss carryover can reduce gain, but it cannot create a loss.[35]

.08 Required Allocations after Gift

The required allocations of LLC income after the transfer of a membership interest from one family member to another are discussed at ¶ 808.

.09 Valuation of Fixed Formula Gifts

One court determined that a donor may make gifts of a specified dollar value of membership units in an LLC, expressed as a fixed percentage interest in the LLC, and that the fixed percentage interest may be lowered as a result of an IRS audit increasing the value of the membership units in the LLC.[36]

.10 Recapitalizations Subject to Gift Taxes

A recapitalization or other change in the capital structure of an LLC constitutes a transfer subject to gift taxes if the transferor holding an applicable retained interest before the capital structure transaction surrenders a subordinate interest and receives property other than an applicable retained interest.[37] An applicable retained interest is an interest in a family-controlled entity with respect to which there is a distribution right.[38] A subordinate interest is an interest as to which an applicable retained interest is a senior interest.[39] A senior interest is an interest that carries a right to distributions of income or capital that is preferred as to the rights of the transferred interest.[40]

EXAMPLE 21-2

Donor and her family controlled an LLC. The LLC was recapitalized. Donor surrendered her right to participate in future profit and loss, including future gain or loss attributable to the LLC's assets. Both before and after the recapitalization, Donor held an applicable retained interest (an equity interest in the LLC coupled with a distribution right). Donor's

---

[34] IRS Market Segment Specialization Program, Partnerships, Audit Technique Guide, Chapter 7, under the heading, "Effect on Passive Losses."

[35] *Id.*

[36] *Wandry v. Comm'r*, TC Memo 2012-88 (2012), *nonaacq.* AOD 2012-46 IRB.

[37] CCA 201442053, *citing* Reg. § 25.2701-1(b)(2)(i)(B)(2).

[38] CCA 201442053, *citing* Reg. § 25.2701-2(b)(1)(ii).

[39] CCA 201442053, *citing* Reg. § 25.2701-3(a)(2)(iii).

[40] CCA 201442053, *citing* Reg. § 25.2701-3(a)(2)(ii).

interest, which carried a right to distributions based upon an existing capital account balance, is senior to the transferred interests, which carried only a right to distributions based on future profit and gain. Donor received property in the form of the agreement of Child A and Child B to manage the LLC. Accordingly, the recapitalization constituted a transfer by Donor for purposes of Code Sec. 2701.[41]

If there is a recapitalization, the following four steps are used to determine the value of the property transferred for gift tax purposes:[42]

- Determine the fair market value of all the family-held interests in the LLC immediately after the transfer assuming that one person owned all of the interests.
- Subtract (i) the sum of the fair market value of all family-held senior interests immediately after the transfer assuming that one person owned all interests, and (ii) the value of all applicable retained interests held by the donor or in any applicable family members.
- Allocate the remaining amount among the transferred interests and other non-transferred subordinate equity interests held by the transferor and applicable family members.
- Apply a minority discount and further reduce the amount by any consideration received by the transferor.

.11 Gifts of Membership Interests by Foreign Persons

A foreign person is subject to gift taxes on the gift of tangible personal property and real estate located in the United States, but not on the gift of intangible property.[43] The IRS will no longer issue rulings regarding whether a partnership interest is intangible property for purposes of Code Sec. 2501(a)(2) (dealing with transfers of intangible property by a nonresident not a citizen of the United States).[44] The concern is that if it treats a partnership or LLC interest as an intangible, then every foreign person could avoid gift and estate taxes by transferring their tangible personal property and real estate into a partnership and gifting the partnership or LLC membership interests.

A foreign donor is entitled to the annual gift-tax exclusion ($15,000 per year per beneficiary in 2018), but may not use the lifetime combined estate and gift tax exemption (approximately $11.18 million in 2018) for gifts exceeding the annual exclusion. For non-U.S. domiciliaries, there is a $13,000 unified credit[45] ($60,000 exemption amount) available for transfers made at death only, but not for gifts. There

---

[41] CCA 201442053.

[42] CCA 201442053.

[43] Code Sec. 2501(a)(2); Reg. § 25.2501-1(a)(3); INFO 2013-0015.

[44] Rev. Proc. 2014-7, Sec. 4.01(28), 2014-1 IRB 238.

[45] Code Sec. 2102(b)(1).

is no exemption amount made for lifetime transfers of real estate intangible personal property in the United States other than the $15,000 annual exclusion.

.12 Gifts Within Three Years of Death

Gift taxes on gifts of LLC membership interests made by a decedent within three years prior to death are includable in the decedent's taxable estate,[46] even if the gift taxes are paid by the donees after the death of the decedent.[47] The estate is not allowed a deduction for the unpaid gift taxes as of the death of the decedent.[48]

¶2103 VALUATION DISCOUNTS—GENERAL

Property is valued for estate and gift tax purposes based upon what a willing buyer and willing seller would pay and receive for the property in an arm's-length transaction, with neither party under compulsion to buy or sell, and with both parties having reasonable knowledge of all relevant facts.[49] A taxpayer typically takes a valuation discount for estate and gift tax purposes for property held in an LLC. There are many different types of valuation discounts. The various valuation discounts include the minority discount, the marketability discount, the liquidity discount, the portfolio discount, the lack of control discount, the fractionalization discount, and the built-in gain discount.[50]

For many years, the IRS took the position that there should be no valuation discount if a single family group owned all the membership interests in an LLC.[51] It sometimes required taxpayers to value LLC membership interests using the asset valuation method. Under this method, the value of LLC membership interests is based on the value of each asset owned by the LLC as of the date of death.[52]

The IRS reversed its position in 1993. It determined that a 100 percent shareholder of a corporation could take a minority discount for gifts of 20 percent of the stock to each of his five children.[53] After that ruling, LLCs became widely used for estate and gift tax purposes. Taxpayers would transfer property into an LLC, and claim an immediate 30 to 50 percent discount for the property held through the LLC.

In 1994, the Service issued partnership anti-abuse regulations under Code Sec. 701. The regulations prohibited minority and marketability discounts for gifts and bequests of LLC membership interests if the principal purpose of forming the LLC

---

[46] Code Sec. 2035(b).

[47] *Estate of Sheldon C. Sommers v. Comm'r*, 149 TC No. 8 (2017).

[48] *Estate of Sheldon C. Sommers v. Comm'r*, 149 TC No. 8 (2017).

[49] Reg. §§20.2031-1(b), 20.2031-3, 25.2512-1; *United States v. Cartwright*, 411 U.S. 546 (1973); *Knight v. Comm'r*, 115 TC 506 (2000).

[50] *See* ¶2105 *infra*.

[51] Rev. Rul. 81-253, 1981-2 CB 187.

[52] Rev. Rul. 68-154, 1968-1 CB 395.

[53] Rev. Rul. 93-12, 1993-1 CB 202.

was to reduce estate and gift taxes. The regulations were later revised to delete such provisions.[54]

As LLCs and family limited partnerships became increasingly popular for estate planning purposes, the IRS advanced many arguments to challenge valuation discounts claimed by the taxpayers. The courts rejected most of the arguments except in egregious cases.[55] In 2001 and 2002, the IRS finally found a basis for successfully challenging valuation discounts: Code Sec. 2036(a).[56]

Since April 1999, the IRS has coordinated LLC and family limited partnership valuation discount cases at the Appeals and examination level. The IRS designated a national coordinator for LLC and family limited partnership appeals. The purpose was to reach consistent results. Any Appeals officer must contact the national coordinator before offering a settlement in a valuation discount case.[57]

In 2002, the IRS informally decided to settle LLC and family limited partnership cases by agreeing to the following discounts:[58]

Passive asset (securities, cash) LLCs and family limited partnerships	25 percent discount[a]
	25 to 30 percent discount[b]
Real estate LLCs and family limited partnerships	25 to 40 percent discount[c]
	35 to 40 percent discount[d]
Active business assets LLCs and family limited partnerships	35 to 40 percent discount[e]
Cases arising under Code Sec. 2036(a) regarding transfers with a retained life estate where the taxpayer is using the LLC or family limited partnership as a "pocketbook" (e.g., receiving disproportionate distributions)[f]	0 to 15 percent discount
Death-bed partnerships and LLCs created within six months of death	0 to 15 percent discount[g]
Fractional interest in real property	Reasonable cost of partition. IRS will settle cases at a higher discount based on the hazards of litigation[h]

---

[54] Reg. § 1.701-2.

[55] *See* ¶ 2104 *infra.*

[56] *See* ¶ 2104.03 *infra.*

[57] *BNA Daily Tax Report* No. 8, p. G-1 (Jan. 13, 2003).

[58] *BNA Daily Tax Report* No. 213, p. G-4 (Nov. 4, 2002); *BNA Daily Tax Report* No. 8, p. G-1 (Jan. 13, 2003).

a *BNA Daily Tax Report* No. 213, p. G-4 (Nov. 4, 2002). *See also Peracchio v. Comm'r*, TC Memo 2003-280 (2003), in which the court allowed a 25 percent discount for a limited partnership that held only marketable securities.

b *BNA Daily Tax Report* No. 8, p. G-1 (Jan. 13, 2003).

c *BNA Daily Tax Report* No. 213, p. G-4 (Nov. 4, 2002).

d *BNA Daily Tax Report* No. 8, p. G-1 (Jan. 13, 2003).

e *Id.*

f *See* ¶ 2104.06 *infra.*

g *BNA Daily Tax Report* No. 8, p. G-1 (Jan. 13, 2003).

h *Id.*

In 2006, the IRS issued detailed settlement guidelines on valuation discounts for estate and gift tax purposes.[59] The guidelines provide that cases are fact specific, and that each case should be individually reviewed to determine the appropriate discount. Little or no discount should be given for date of death transfers. The settlement offers are made at the Appeals level. The same offers are not necessarily made at the audit level or after the case has been referred to the IRS District counsel.[60]

In 2016, the IRS issued proposed regulations challenging valuation discounts under Code Sec. 2704.

¶ 2104 IRS CHALLENGES TO VALUATION DISCOUNTS

.01 Overview

The IRS may challenge valuation discounts in one of three ways. First, it may argue that there should be a reduced or no valuation discount based on one or more of the following theories:

- Sham transaction and economic substance doctrines.[61]
- Code Sec. 2036(a). This is now the principal concern for tax practitioners who use LLCs to obtain valuation discounts.[62]
- Code Sec. 2036(b).[63]
- Code Sec. 2038.[64]
- Code Sec. 2701.[65]
- Code Sec. 2703.[66]
- Code Sec. 2704(a).[67]

---

[59] IRS Appeals Settlement Guidelines on Family Limited Partnerships and Family Limited Liability Corporations, UIL 2031.01-00 (Oct. 18, 2006).

[60] *BNA Daily Tax Report* No. 8, p. G-1 (Jan. 13, 2003).

[61] *See* ¶ 2104.02 *infra.*

[62] *See* ¶ 2104.03 *infra.*

[63] *See* ¶ 2104.04 *infra.*

[64] *See* ¶ 2104.05 *infra.*

[65] *See* ¶ 2104.06 *infra.*

[66] *See* ¶ 2104.07 *infra.*

[67] *See* ¶ 2104.08 *infra.*

- Code Sec. 2704(b) applicable restrictions.[68]
- Code Sec. 2704(b)(4) disregarded restrictions.[69]
- Gift on creation theory.[70]
- Cost of dissolution and partition theory.[71]
- Code Sec. 2511 indirect gift and step transaction doctrine.[72]
- Code Sec. 2031 estate freezes and buy-sell agreements.[73]
- Code Sec. 2035.[74]
- Recharacterization as a trust.[75]
- Single-member disregarded LLC theory.[76]

Second, the IRS may argue that the valuation discount claimed by the taxpayer is excessive. There are separate rules for determining the proper amount of minority discount, marketability, liquidity and lack of control discounts, built-in gains discount, assignee interest discount, portfolio discount, and other discounts.[77]

Third, the IRS may challenge the taxpayer's appraisal or the qualifications of the appraiser.[78]

.02 *Sham Transaction and Economic Substance Doctrines*

General

The IRS may challenge valuation discounts based on the sham transaction doctrine,[79] lack of economic substance,[80] lack of business purpose,[81] the form over

---

[68] *See* ¶ 2104.09 *infra.*

[69] *See* ¶ 2104.10 *infra.*

[70] *See* ¶ 2104.11 *infra.*

[71] *See* ¶ 2104.12 *infra.*

[72] *See* ¶ 2104.13 *infra.*

[73] *See* ¶ 2104.14 *infra.*

[74] *See* ¶ 2104.15 *infra.*

[75] *See* ¶ 2104.16 *infra.*

[76] *See* ¶ 2104.17 *infra.*

[77] *See* ¶ 2105 *infra.*

[78] *See* ¶ 2107 *infra. See Estate of Gallagher*, TC Memo 2011-148 (2011) in which the court discussed detailed guidelines for valuing a membership interest in an LLC, and separate guidelines for determining minority and marketability discounts.

[79] TAM 9736004.

[80] FSA 200049003, *citing Gregory v. Helvering*, 293 U.S. 465 (1935). The IRS determined that the economic substance doctrine could be used to deny valuation discounts for a membership interest in an LLC if (i) the transfers of property to the LLC and the gifts and transfers of membership interests appreciably changed the taxpayer's economic position, and (ii) the taxpayer did not have a valid business purpose or profit motive for establishing the LLC and making the gifts and transfers. *See also Knight v. Comm'r*, 115 TC 506 (2000).

[81] FSA 200049003; *Estate of Strangi v. Comm'r*, 115 TC 478, 484 (2000).

substance doctrine, and similar doctrines.[82] The theory is that the LLC should be disregarded because the formation of the LLC, the contribution of property to the LLC, the transfer of membership units in the LLC by gift or bequest, and the distribution of the property by the LLC to the transferees, constitute a single testamentary disposition. In these cases, the IRS includes the value of LLC assets in the decedent's gross estate rather than the membership interests owned by the decedent as of the date of death.

Most courts will not disregard an LLC under the sham transaction and similar doctrines, absent unusual circumstances.[83] These courts have determined that a willing buyer would take into account the form of entity in determining whether to buy the underlying assets.[84]

Circumstances Indicating Sham Transaction

The IRS is more likely to challenge minority and marketability discounts based on the sham transaction doctrine if one or more the following circumstances exist:[85]

- The taxpayer forms the LLC shortly before death.[86]
- The taxpayer is gravely ill at the time the LLC is formed.
- The heirs of the decedent orchestrate the formation of the LLC, and transfer the parent's property into the LLC, using a power of attorney.
- The taxpayer makes gifts of membership units in the LLC on the same day that the taxpayer forms the LLC, or shortly thereafter.[87]
- The principal purpose of forming the LLC is to reduce estate taxes.[88]
- The LLC owns the same assets on the date of the decedent's death that the decedent transferred to the LLC. The IRS refers to the LLC in such cases as a mere "wrapper" around the assets.

---

[82] *See Church v. United States*, 85 AFTR 2d 2000-804 (W.D. Tex. 2000); *Estate of Murphy v. Comm'r*, 60 TCM 645 (1990); *Estate of Schauerhamer v. Comm'r*, 73 TCM 2855, TC Memo 1997-242 (1997); *Griffin v. United States*, 89 AFTR 2d 2002-954, 42 F. Supp. 2d 700 (W.D. Tex. 1998); TAMs 9842003, 9736004, 9735003, 9730004, 9725002, 9723009, 9719006.

[83] *Knight v. Comm'r*, 115 TC 506, 513-514 (2000); *Church v. United States*, 85 AFTR 2d 2000-804, ¶19 (W.D. Tex. 2000).

[84] *Knight v. Comm'r*, 115 TC 506, 514 (2000).

[85] TAM 9736004, in which the IRS disallowed minority and marketability discounts for membership interests in an LLC. *See also Estate of Schauerhamer v. Comm'r*, 73 TCM 2855, TC Memo 1997-242 (1997) ; *Griffin v. United States*, 89 AFTR 2d 2002-954, 42 F. Supp. 2d 700 (W.D. Tex. 1998); TAMs 9842003, 9736004, 9735003, 9730004, 9725002, 9723009, 9719006.

[86] *But see Church v. United States*, 85 AFTR 2d 2000-804, Jurisdiction and Venue ¶19 (W.D. Tex. 2000), which allowed a valuation discount even though Mrs. Church died two days after the partnership was formed, and before the certificate limited partnership was filed with the Secretary of State.

[87] *See LeFrak v. Comm'r*, 66 TCM 1297 (1993), in which the court ruled that the gifts were gifts of undivided interests in property and not partnership interest gifts, since the gifts were made the day before the partnership agreements were signed.

[88] TAM 9736004, FSA 200049003; *Estate of Murphy v. Comm'r*, 60 TCM 645 (1990). The IRS lost on this issue in *Church v. United States*, 85 AFTR 2d 2000-804, ¶19 (W.D. Tex. 2000). *But see Keller v. United States*, No. V-02-62 (S.D. Tex. 2009).

- There is no legitimate business purpose for the LLC. The LLC does not transact any business other than holding property. The only purpose for organizing the LLC is to depress the value of the assets that are transferred to the LLC. Nothing of substance changes as a result of the transactions.
- The death beneficiaries receive from the LLC the same assets they would have received from the decedent if the assets had not been contributed to the LLC.
- The death beneficiaries retain control over the assets of the LLC, and their management rights do not change as a result of the transactions.
- The taxpayer fails to transfer legal title to the property to the LLC.[89]
- The taxpayer transfers to the LLC liquid assets, or assets that are not used in a trade or business, prior to the gift or testamentary transfer.[90] These assets include cash, marketable securities, undeveloped real estate, and other passive assets. However, the transfer of marketable securities and other passive assets to an LLC may be permissible if there are legitimate and significant nontax motives to further a buy and hold investment strategy.[91]
- The members fail to comply with the formalities of an LLC. For example, the LLC may be disregarded if the majority owner deposits all income from the LLC in his personal bank account.[92]

Business Purposes Claimed by Taxpayers

Taxpayers must show a proper business purpose in order to avoid application of the sham transaction doctrine. Taxpayers have used the following business purposes to justify the formation of LLC:[93]

- Use of the LLC to facilitate gifts of membership interests.[94]
- Consolidate family interests into a single entity.
- Provide centralized management.
- Avoid fragmentation of interests.
- Preserve the business as an ongoing enterprise for future generations.
- Protect assets from judgment creditors of the members.

---

[89] *See Church v. United States*, 85 AFTR 2d 2000-804, Conclusions of Law ¶4 (W.D. Tex. 2000).

[90] *Estate of Strangi v. Comm'r*, 115 TC 478, 486 (2000). *But see Estate of Davis v. Comm'r*, 110 TC 530 (1998) , in which a discount was allowed for partnership that owned stock; and *Estate of Winkler v. Comm'r*, 57 TCM 373 (1989), in which the court respected a partnership that held the proceeds of a lottery winning.

[91] *Estate of Purdue v. Comm'r*, TC Memo 2015-249 (2015); *Estate of Schutt v. Comm'r*, TC Memo 2005-126 (2005).

[92] *Estate of Schauerhamer v. Comm'r*, 73 TCM 2855, TC Memo 1997-242 (1997). The invalidation of an LLC for failure to comply with the formalities is a separate argument from the sham transaction doctrine.

[93] *Church v. United States*, 85 AFTR 2d 2000-804, ¶¶4, 16 (W.D. Tex. 2000); *Knight v. Comm'r*, 115 TC 506, fn. 10 (2000); *Estate of Strangi v. Comm'r*, 115 TC 478, 485 (2000).

[94] *See Estate of Bigelow v. Comm'r*, TC Memo 2005-65 (2005), *aff'd*, 503 F.3d 955 (9th Cir. 2007), in which the court stated that "a transfer made solely to reduce taxes and to facilitate gift giving is not considered in this context to be made in good faith for a bona fide purpose."

- Protect assets from the family members' spouses in the event of divorce.
- Obtain better rates of return.
- Reduce administrative costs.
- Provide for competent management in case of death or disability.
- Avoid cumbersome and expensive guardianships.
- Avoid or minimize probate delays and expenses.
- Minimize tax liability. This includes avoiding adverse tax consequences that may occur on dissolution of a corporation.
- Provide business flexibility, because the operating agreement may be amended.
- Eliminate ancillary probate proceedings.
- Provide a convenient mechanism for making annual gifts.
- Provide a vehicle to educate family members about assets to increase their value.
- Provide a mechanism to resolve family disputes.
- Provide more flexibility in making investments than a trust because of the fiduciary standards for a trust.

.03 Code Section 2036(a) Retained Enjoyment of Property

General

The IRS may assert that property transferred to an LLC should be brought back into the decedent's estate under Code Sec. 2036(a).[95] Under Code Sec. 2036(a), a decedent's gross estate includes property in an LLC if:[96]

- The decedent transferred property to the LLC or the donee members during his or her lifetime;
- At the time of death, the decedent retained (a) possession or enjoyment of the property, or the right to its income, or (b) the right to determine the persons who would possess or enjoy the property or receive its income; and
- The transfer was not a bona fide sale for adequate and full consideration.

---

[95] *Estate of Nancy H. Powell v. Comm'r*, 148 TC No. 18 (2017); *Estate of Hilda E. Erickson*, TC Memo 2007-207 (2007); *Estate of Harper v. Comm'r*, TC Memo 2002-121 (2002); *Estate of Thompson v. Comm'r*, 84 TCM 374 (2002), *aff'd*, 382 F.3d 367 (3d Cir. 2004); *Estate of Bigelow v. Comm'r*, TC Memo 2005-65 (2005), *aff'd*, 503 F.3d 955 (9th Cir. 2007); *Estate of Strangi*, TC Memo 2003-145 (2003), *on second appeal*, *Strangi v. Comm'r*, 417 F.3d 468 (5th Cir. 2005); *Gulig v. Comm'r*, 89 AFTR 2d 2002-2977 (5th Cir. 2002); *Estate of Reichardt*, 114 TC 144 (2000); *Estate of Stone v. Comm'r*, 86 TCM 551 (2003); *Church v. United States*, 85 AFTR 2d 2000-804, Conclusions of Law ¶7 (W.D. Tex. 2000), *aff'd without published opinion*, 268 F.3d 1063 (*per curiam*) (table), unpublished opinion available at 88 AFTR 2d 2001-5352 (5th Cir. 2001); *Kimbell v. United States*, 93 AFTR 2d 2004-2400 (5th Cir. 2004); *BNA Daily Tax Report* No. 213, p. G-4 (Nov. 4, 2002); *BNA Daily Tax Report* No. 8, p. G-1 (Jan. 13, 2003).

[96] *Estate of Purdue v. Comm'r*, TC Memo 2015-249 (2015); *Estate of Anna Mirowski v. Comm'r*, TC Memo 2008-74 (2008); *Estate of Hilda E. Erickson*, TC Memo 2007-207 (2007).

If Code Sec. 2036(a) applies, the IRS may disregard the LLC and include the transferred assets in the taxpayer's estate at fair market value as of the date of death.[97] In such cases, the IRS does not need to contest the appropriate valuation discount for the LLC membership units since there is no valuation discount.

Since the seminal decision in the *Harper* case in 2002, the IRS has successfully challenged taxpayer discounts under Code Sec. 2036 in 18 cases,[98] and has lost in nine cases.[99]

Transfer Requirement

In order for the IRS to prevail under Section 2036(a), the IRS must first show that the decedent made a transfer of property during his or her lifetime.[100] Frequently, there are two transfers in Section 2036(a) cases. The first transfer is the contribution of property by the decedent to the LLC in exchange for membership interests. The contribution is treated as an inter vivos transfer property under Section 2036.[101] The second transfer is the gift of membership interests by the decedent to family members. Each of these transfers must be separately considered.[102]

The IRS takes the position that the transfer of property to an LLC and the subsequent gifts of membership interests to family members should be treated as part of a single transaction if the decedent formed the LLC in contemplation of making

---

[97] *Estate of Turner v. Comm'r*, TC Memo 2011-209 (2011); *Hurford v. Comm'r*, TC Memo 2008-278 (2008); *Estate of Bigelow v. Comm'r*, TC Memo 2005-65 (2005), *aff'd*, 2007-2 USTC ¶ 60548 (9th Cir. 2007).

[98] *Estate of Holiday v. Comm'r*, TC Memo 2016-51 (2016); *Estate of Paul H. Liljestrand v. Comm'r*, TC Memo 2011-259 (2011); *Estate of Turner v. Comm'r*, TC Memo 2011-209 (2011); *Estate of Gallagher*, TC Memo 2011-148 (2011) (which approved a 23 percent minority discount and a 31 percent marketability discount for membership interests in an LLC); *Estate of Harper v. Comm'r*, TC Memo 2002-121 (2002); *Estate of Thompson v. Comm'r*, 84 TCM 374 (2002), *aff'd*, 382 F.3d 367 (3d Cir. 2004); *Estate of Bongard*, 124 TC 95 (2005); *Estate of Bigelow v. Comm'r*, TC Memo 2005-65 (2005), *aff'd*, 503 F.3d 955 (9th Cir. 2007); *Estate of Korby v. Comm'r*, TC Memo 2005-103 (2005), *aff'd*, 2006 WL 3524501 (8th Cir. 2006); *Estate of Hilda E. Erickson*, TC Memo 2007-207 (2007); *Estate of L.K. Hillgren v. Comm'r*, TC Memo 2004-46 (2004); *Estate of Strangi*, TC Memo 2003-145 (2003), *aff'd*, 417 F.3d 468 (5th Cir. 2005); *Estate of Abraham v. Comm'r*, TC Memo 2004-39 (2004), *aff'd*, 95 AFTR 2d ¶2005-1018 (1st Cir. 2005), *cert. denied*, 547 U.S. 1178 (2006); *Estate of Disbrow v. Comm'r*, TC Memo 2006-34 (2006). *See also Smith v. United States*, Case No. 02-264 Erie (W.D. Pa. 2005); *Estate of Rosen v. Comm'r*, TC Memo 2006-115 (2006); *Estate of Rector*, TC Memo 2007-367 (2007); *Hurford v. Comm'r*, TC Memo 2008-278 (2008); *Estate of Jorgensen*, TC Memo 2009-66 (2009), *aff'd*, 107 AFTR 2d 2011-2069 (9th Cir. 2011).

[99] *Estate of Purdue v. Comm'r*, TC Memo 2015-249 (2015); *Estate of Beatrice Kelly v. Comm'r*, TC Memo 2012-73 (2012); *Stone v. Comm'r*, TC Memo 2012-48 (2012); *Estate of Charlene B. Shurtz v. Comm'r*, TC Memo 2010-21 (2010); *Estate of Black v. Comm'r*, 133 TC 340 (2009); *Estate of Anna Mirowski v. Comm'r*, TC Memo 2008-74 (2008); *Estate of Stone v. Comm'r*, 86 TCM 551 (2003); *Kimbell v. United States*, 93 AFTR 2d 2004-2400 (5th Cir. 2004); *Estate of Shutt*, TC Memo 2005-126 (2005). *See also Kelley v. Comm'r*, TC Memo 2005-236 (2005); *Gallagher v. Comm'r*, TC Memo 2011-148 (2011); and *Anderson v. United States*, Civ. No. 02-2168-S (W.D. La. 2005) in which an estate was allowed a minority discount for ownership interests in four LLCs holding oil, gas, and mineral interests using a weighted combination of market value and net asset approaches.

[100] *Estate of Jorgensen*, TC Memo 2009-66 (2009), *aff'd*, 107 AFTR 2d 2011-2069 (9th Cir. 2011).

[101] *Estate of Turner v. Comm'r*, TC Memo 2011-209 (2011).

[102] *Estate of Anna Mirowski v. Comm'r*, TC Memo 2008-74 (2008).

gifts.[103] Under this theory, the transfer of property to the LLC in exchange for 100 percent of the membership interests would never constitute a bona fide sale for adequate and full consideration. The decedent would be transferring property to the LLC and receiving back less than 100 percent of the membership interests after making the gifts.

Retained Interest under Section 2036(a)(1)

If there is a transfer of property, the IRS must next show that the decedent retained (a) possession or enjoyment of the property transferred to the LLC, or the right to its income, or (b) the right, either alone or in conjunction with any other person, to designate the persons who will possess or enjoy the property or receive its income. There will be a retained interest if the taxpayer retained either one of these rights.

Under Section 2036(a)(1), property is included in the decedent's estate if the decedent retained, by express or implied agreement, possession, enjoyment, or the right to income from the transfer property.[104] This determination is based on all the facts and circumstances.[105] Some of the factors indicating that the decedent retained possession or enjoyment under Section 2036(a) include the following:[106]

- The decedent or family members form the LLC within six months of the decedent's death.[107] However, this is not an adverse factor if the decedent's death was unexpected.[108]
- The taxpayer commingles LLC funds and personal funds after the transfer.[109] The court may find commingling if there are delays in establishing a bank account for the LLC, completing LLC paperwork, or retitling ownership to stocks, bonds and other assets transferred to the LLC.[110]

---

[103] *Estate of Anna Mirowski v. Comm'r*, TC Memo 2008-74 (2008).

[104] *Estate of Turner v. Comm'r*, TC Memo 2011-209 (2011).

[105] *Estate of Turner v. Comm'r*, TC Memo 2011-209 (2011).

[106] *Estate of Harper v. Comm'r*, TC Memo 2002-121 (2002); *Estate of Theodore R. Thompson v. Comm'r*, 84 TCM 374 (2002); *Estate of Strangi*, TC Memo 2003-145 (2003), *aff'd*, 417 F.3d 468 (5th Cir. 2005); *Estate of Abraham v. Comm'r*, TC Memo 2004-39 (2004), *aff'd*, 95 AFTR 2d ¶ 2005-1018 (1st Cir. 2005), *cert. denied*, 547 U.S. 1178 (2006).

[107] *Estate of Hilda E. Erickson*, TC Memo 2007-207 (2007); *Estate of L.K. Hillgren v. Comm'r*, TC Memo 2004-46 (2004); *Estate of Strangi*, TC Memo 2003-145 (2003), *on second appeal, Strangi v. Comm'r*, 417 F.3d 468 (5th Cir. 2005). *Estate of Stone v. Comm'r*, 86 TCM 551 (2003); *BNA Daily Tax Report* No. 8, p. G-1 (Jan. 13, 2003).

[108] *Estate of Anna Mirowski v. Comm'r*, TC Memo 2008-74 (2008).

[109] *Estate of Turner v. Comm'r*, TC Memo 2011-209 (2011); *Estate of Paul H. Liljestrand v. Comm'r*, TC Memo 2011-259 (2011); *Estate of L.K. Hillgren v. Comm'r*, TC Memo 2004-46 (2004) (the partnership did not have its own bank account, and the family partnership bookkeeping did not take place until after the decedent's death); *Estate of Harper v. Comm'r*, TC Memo 2002-121 (2002); *Estate of Reichardt*, 114 TC 144 (2000).

[110] *Estate of L.K. Hillgren v. Comm'r*, TC Memo 2004-46 (2004); *Estate of Harper v. Comm'r*, TC Memo 2002-121 (2002). *But see Estate of Charlene B. Shurtz v. Comm'r*, TC Memo 2010-21 (2010), where the court allowed a discount in a Section 2036(a) case even though there was a four-month delay in establishing the bank account, and the decedent paid partnership expenses with personal funds.

¶ 2104.03

- The taxpayer transfers a home to the LLC, and lives at the home after the transfer without paying fair rent to the LLC.[111]
- The taxpayer transfers other personal-use assets to the LLC, such as an automobile.[112]
- The parties do not respect the formalities of the LLC,[113] and the LLC does not comply with all technical formalities in its creation and operation.[114]
- There is an express agreement that the taxpayer may continue to enjoy LLC property for life after transferring it to the LLC.[115] There is an express agreement if the decedent retains the right to remove or replace the managers or general partners, and appoints himself as the manager or general partner.[116] There is also an express agreement if the decedent owned sufficient membership units to replace the managers of the LLC. The IRS focus in this case is on the legal aspects of the LLC operating agreement under Code Sec. 2036(a)(2).[117] This should be contrasted with the IRS arguments under Code Sec. 2036(a)(1) that the operational aspects of the LLC cause the LLC assets to be brought back into the decedent's estate. The payment of reasonable management fees is not an express agreement that causes inclusion in the gross estate.[118]
- There is an implied agreement among the family members that LLC assets would be readily available to meet the decedent's expenses,[119] or that the decedent may continue to enjoy LLC property for life after transferring it to the LLC.[120] The determination of whether there is an implied agreement

---

[111] *Estate of Disbrow v. Comm'r*, TC Memo 2006-34 (2006); *Estate of L.K. Hillgren v. Comm'r*, TC Memo 2004-46 (2004); *Estate of Reichardt*, 114 TC 144 (2000); *BNA Daily Tax Report* No. 8, p. G-1 (Jan. 13, 2003).

[112] *BNA Daily Tax Report* No. 8, p. G-1 (Jan. 13, 2003).

[113] *Estate of Paul H. Liljestrand v. Comm'r*, TC Memo 2011-259 (2011); *Estate of Harper v. Comm'r*, TC Memo 2002-121 (2002); *Estate of Thompson v. Comm'r*, 84 TCM 374 (2002), *aff'd*, 382 F.3d 367 (3d Cir. 2004).

[114] *Estate of Hilda E. Erickson*, TC Memo 2007-207 (2007); *Estate of L.K. Hillgren v. Comm'r*, TC Memo 2004-46 (2004) (the certificate of limited partnership was filed after the decedent's death, and the decedent never actually transferred the assets to the partnership); *Estate of Rosen v. Comm'r*, TC Memo 2006-115 (2006); and *BNA Daily Tax Report* No. 8, p. G-1 (Jan. 13, 2003). *But see Keller v. United States*, No. V-02-62 (S.D. Tex. 2009).

[115] *Estate of Abraham v. Comm'r*, TC Memo 2004-39 (2004), *aff'd*, 95 AFTR 2d ¶2005-1018 (1st Cir. 2005), *cert. denied*, 547 U.S. 1178 (2006); *Estate of Reichardt*, 114 TC 144 (2000); *Estate of Schauerhamer v. Comm'r*, 73 TCM 2855, TC Memo 1997-242 (1997). *But see Church v. United States*, 85 AFTR 2d 2000-804, 125 (W.D. Tex. 2000), *aff'd without published opinion*, 268 F.3d 1063 (per *curiam*) (table), unpublished opinion available at 88 AFTR 2d 2001-5352 (5th Cir. 2001) in which the court found no implied agreement.

[116] *See Kimbell v. United States*, 93 AFTR 2d 2004-2400 (5th Cir. 2004).

[117] The decedent has retained powers under Code Sec. 2036(a)(2) if the decedent has a legal right under the operating agreement to control LLC assets.

[118] *Estate of Beatrice Kelly v. Comm'r*, TC Memo 2012-73 (2012).

[119] *Estate of Holiday v. Comm'r*, TC Memo 2016-51 (2016); *Estate of Rector*, TC Memo 2007-367 (2007); *Hurford v. Comm'r*, TC Memo 2008-278 (2008).

[120] *Estate of Reichardt*, 114 TC 144 (2000); *Estate of Schauerhamer v. Comm'r*, 73 TCM 2855, TC Memo 1997-242 (1997); *Hurford v. Comm'r*, TC Memo 2008-278 (2008); *Estate of Strangi*, TC Memo 2003-145 (2003), *on second appeal*, *Strangi v. Comm'r*, 417 F.3d 468 (5th Cir. 2005). *Estate of Bongard v. Comm'r*, 124

depends on all the facts and circumstances.[121] There is an implied agreement if the only source of funds for payment of the decedent's living expenses is from the LLC, and the LLC makes preferential distributions to the decedent to cover those living expenses.[122] There may also be an implied agreement if the decedent received a guaranteed payment from the LLC sufficient to cover living expenses.[123] There is no implied agreement if the decedent paid living expenses from income other than the LLC or partnership.[124] The parents must retain sufficient liquid assets outside of the LLC to maintain their standard of living,[125] and to pay estate taxes.[126]

- The parties do not form a business enterprise or conduct a trade or business other than the management of investment assets.[127]

- The LLC does not engage in transactions with persons other than family members.[128]

- There is a history of disproportionate distributions to the decedent or a trust for the benefit of the decedent.[129]

(Footnote Continued)

TC 95 (2005); *Estate of Abraham v. Comm'r*, TC Memo 2004-39 (2004), *aff'd*, 95 AFTR 2d ¶ 2005-1018 (1st Cir. 2005), *cert. denied*, 547 U.S. 1178 (2006); *but see Church v. United States*, 85 AFTR 2d 2000-804, ¶ 25 (W.D. Tex. 2000), *aff'd without published opinion*, 268 F.3d 1063 (per curiam) (table), unpublished opinion available at 88 AFTR 2d 2001-5352 (5th Cir. 2001) in which the court found no implied agreement.

[121] *Estate of Holiday v. Comm'r*, TC Memo 2016-51 (2016); *Estate of Turner v. Comm'r*, TC Memo 2011-209 (2011).

[122] *Estate of Turner v. Comm'r*, TC Memo 2011-209 (2011); *Estate of Paul H. Liljestrand v. Comm'r*, TC Memo 2011-259 (2011); *Estate of Rosen v. Comm'r*, TC Memo 2006-115 (2006); *Estate of L.K. Hillgren v. Comm'r*, TC Memo 2004-46 (2004); *Estate of Theodore R. Thompson v. Comm'r*, 84 TCM 374 (2002), *aff'd*, 382 F.3d 367 (3d Cir. 2004); *Hurford v. Comm'r*, TC Memo 2008-278 (2008); *Estate of Bigelow v. Comm'r*, TC Memo 2005-65 (2005), *aff'd*, 503 F.3d 955 (9th Cir. 2007); *Estate of Abraham v. Comm'r*, TC Memo 2004-39 (2004), *aff'd*, 95 AFTR 2d ¶ 2005-1018 (1st Cir. 2005), *cert. denied*, 547 U.S. 1178 (2006). *See also Estate of Stone v. Comm'r*, 86 TCM 551 (2003), and *Estate of Shutt*, TC Memo 2005-126 (2005), where the decedent retained sufficient assets to maintain his standard of living.

[123] *Estate of Paul H. Liljestrand v. Comm'r*, TC Memo 2011-259 (2011).

[124] *Estate of Beatrice Kelly v. Comm'r*, TC Memo 2012-73 (2012).

[125] *Estate of Stone v. Comm'r*, 86 TCM 551 (2003); *Hurford v. Comm'r*, TC Memo 2008-278 (2008); *Estate of Rector*, TC Memo 2007-367 (2007).

[126] *Estate of Hilda E. Erickson*, TC Memo 2007-207 (2007); *Estate of L.K. Hillgren v. Comm'r*, TC Memo 2004-46 (2004).

[127] *Estate of Hilda E. Erickson*, TC Memo 2007-207 (2007); *Estate of Rosen v. Comm'r*, TC Memo 2006-115 (2006); *Estate of Thompson v. Comm'r*, 84 TCM 374 (2002), *aff'd*, 382 F.3d 367 (3d Cir. 2004).

[128] *Estate of Thompson v. Comm'r*, 84 TCM 374 (2002), *aff'd*, 382 F.3d 367 (3d Cir. 2004). *See also Kimbell v. United States*, 93 AFTR 2d 2004-2400 (5th Cir. 2004).

[129] *Estate of Turner v. Comm'r*, TC Memo 2011-209 (2011); *Estate of Paul H. Liljestrand v. Comm'r*, TC Memo 2011-259 (2011); *Estate of L.K. Hillgren v. Comm'r*, TC Memo 2004-46 (2004); *Estate of Harper v. Comm'r*, TC Memo 2002-121 (2002); *Estate of Thompson v. Comm'r*, 84 TCM 374 (2002), *aff'd*, 382 F.3d 367 (3d Cir. 2004); *Estate of Bigelow v. Comm'r*, TC Memo 2005-65 (2005), *aff'd*, 503 F.3d 955 (9th Cir. 2007); *Estate of Abraham v. Comm'r*, TC Memo 2004-39 (2004), *aff'd*, 95 AFTR 2d ¶ 2005-1018 (1st Cir. 2005), *cert. denied*, 547 U.S. 1178 (2006); *Estate of Strangi*, TC Memo 2003-145 (2003), *on second appeal*, *Strangi v. Comm'r*, 417 F.3d 468 (5th Cir. 2005); *Estate of Rosen v. Comm'r*, TC Memo 2006-115 (2006). *But see Estate of Charlene B. Shurtz v. Comm'r*, TC Memo 2010-21 (2010), where the court allowed a

- The decedent retained, either directly as manager of the LLC or through a person acting under a power of attorney, sole discretion to determine the amount and timing of distributions.[130] However, the right to determine the timing of distributions will not constitute a retained interest if the operating agreement requires annual distributions of cash flow, current distributions of proceeds from capital transactions, and mandatory distributions on liquidation.[131]

- The members of the LLC other than the decedent do not obtain a meaningful economic interest in the property during their lifetimes.[132]

- The decedent made all decisions regarding the creation and structure of the LLC.[133] There should be meaningful negotiations among the parties regarding the formation of the LLC.[134]

- The contributed property consists mainly of marketable securities or other liquid and passive investment assets,[135] unless the LLC reinvests those assets in a valid functioning business enterprise.[136] However, the use of an LLC to perpetuate a buy and hold investment philosophy for marketable securities for a closely held business is a legitimate and significant nontax purpose for the formation of an LLC.[137]

- Persons other than the decedent contribute property to the LLC, and receive a special allocation of all income from such contributed property.[138] There must be a genuine pooling of property and services.[139]

(Footnote Continued)

discount in a Section 2036(a) case even though the partnership had a history of making disproportionate distributions.

[130] *Estate of Strangi*, TC Memo 2003-145 (2003), *on second appeal*, *Strangi v. Comm'r*, 417 F.3d 468 (5th Cir. 2005).

[131] *Estate of Anna Mirowski v. Comm'r*, TC Memo 2008-74 (2008).

[132] *Estate of Strangi*, TC Memo 2003-145 (2003), *on second appeal*, *Strangi v. Comm'r*, 417 F.3d 468 (5th Cir. 2005).

[133] *Estate of Paul H. Liljestrand v. Comm'r*, TC Memo 2011-259 (2011); *Estate of L.K. Hillgren v. Comm'r*, TC Memo 2004-46 (2004); *Estate of Harper v. Comm'r*, TC Memo 2002-121 (2002); *Estate of Strangi*, TC Memo 2003-145 (2003).

[134] *Estate of Paul H. Liljestrand v. Comm'r*, TC Memo 2011-259 (2011). *See also Estate of Shutt*, TC Memo 2005-126 (2005), in which the court ruled for the taxpayer after noting that there were meaningful negotiations concerning the formation of the family limited partnership.

[135] *Estate of Jorgensen v. Comm'r*, TC Memo 2009-66 (2009), *aff'd*, 107 AFTR 2d 2011-2069 (9th Cir. 2011); *Estate of Rector*, TC Memo 2007-367 (2007); *Estate of Thompson v. Comm'r*, 84 TCM 374 (2002), *aff'd*, 382 F.3d 367 (3d Cir. 2004); *Estate of Harper v. Comm'r*, TC Memo 2002-121 (2002); *Estate of Rosen v. Comm'r*, TC Memo 2006-115 (2006); *Estate of Hilda E. Erickson*, TC Memo 2007-207 (2007); *Estate of Holiday v. Comm'r*, TC Memo 2016-51 (2016). *But see Kelley v. Comm'r*, TC Memo 2005-236 (2005) *and Estate of Anna Mirowski v. Comm'r*, TC Memo 2008-74 (2008), which allowed a substantial marketability and minority discount where the LLC and limited partnership owned substantial liquid assets.

[136] *Estate of Thompson v. Comm'r*, 84 TCM 374 (2002), *aff'd*, 382 F.3d 367 (3d Cir. 2004); *Estate of Harrison v. Comm'r*, TC Memo 1987-8 (1987); *Estate of Michelson v. Comm'r*, TC Memo 1978-371 (1978).

[137] *Estate of Black v. Comm'r*, 133 TC 340 (2009); *Estate of Shutt*, TC Memo 2005-126 (2005); *Estate of Purdue v. Comm'r*, TC Memo 2015-249 (2015).

[138] *Estate of Thompson v. Comm'r*, 84 TCM 374 (2002), *aff'd*, 382 F.3d 367 (3d Cir. 2004).

[139] *Estate of Stone v. Comm'r*, 86 TCM 551 (2003).

- There is no substantial change in investment strategy or business activity after the date that the decedent contributed his assets to the LLC.[140]
- The taxpayer transfers property to the LLC, but the LLC does not assume the secured loan on the property. This is treated as an implied agreement that the taxpayer will retain a present economic benefit in the property (the property as collateral), and thus the right to enjoyment from the contributed property.[141]
- Management of the property does not change subsequent to the transfer to the LLC.[142]
- There is no pooling of assets contributed by different members to the LLC.[143]
- The assets of the LLC are used to secure the debts of the taxpayer after the taxpayer transfers the assets to the LLC.[144]
- The decedent retained a majority interest in the LLC.[145]

One case that is very favorable to the taxpayer is *Estate of Anna Mirowski*.[146] The decedent transferred marketable securities and other investment assets to an LLC three days prior to death. She then gifted a 16 percent interest in the LLC to each of her three daughters. The IRS argued that the decedent retained possession and enjoyment of the gifted membership interests because the decedent retained a 52 percent managing member interest in the LLC. As the majority managing member, she retained the right to decide the distribution policy of the LLC and other rights that constituted use, enjoyment, and income. The IRS also argued that there was an express or implied agreement that the decedent would retain possession and enjoyment of LLC property because the LLC made large non-pro rata distributions to her estate after her death to pay estate and gift taxes. However, the court determined that there was no express or implied agreement prior to the date of death that the decedent would have access to the LLC assets or the right to retain possession and enjoyment of those assets. Although the decedent retained significant powers as a managing member, there were significant restrictions on her powers as managing member.[147] The decedent did not have the absolute right to determine the amount of distributions. The operating agreement provided the distributions could be made

---

[140] *Estate of Hilda E. Erickson*, TC Memo 2007-207 (2007); *Estate of L.K. Hillgren v. Comm'r*, TC Memo 2004-46 (2004); *Estate of Thompson v. Comm'r*, 84 TCM 374 (2002), aff'd, 382 F.3d 367 (3d Cir. 2004); *Estate of Strangi*, TC Memo 2003-145 (2003), *on second appeal, Strangi v. Comm'r*, 417 F.3d 468 (5th Cir. 2005); *Estate of Rosen v. Comm'r*, TC Memo 2006-115 (2006); *Estate of Rector*, TC Memo 2007-367 (2007).

[141] *Estate of Bigelow v. Comm'r*, TC Memo 2005-65 (2005), aff'd, 503 F.3d 955 (9th Cir. 2007).

[142] *Estate of Hilda E. Erickson*, TC Memo 2007-207 (2007); *Estate of Bigelow v. Comm'r*, TC Memo 2005-65 (2005), aff'd, 2007-2 USTC ¶ 60548 (9th Cir. 2007); *Estate of Rosen v. Comm'r*, TC Memo 2006-115 (2006).

[143] *Estate of Bigelow v. Comm'r*, TC Memo 2005-65 (2005), aff'd, 503 F.3d 955 (9th Cir. 2007).

[144] *Estate of Bigelow v. Comm'r*, 2007-2 USTC ¶ 60548 (9th Cir. 2007).

[145] *Estate of Rector*, TC Memo 2007-367 (2007).

[146] *Estate of Anna Mirowski v. Comm'r*, TC Memo 2008-74 (2008).

[147] Under the operating agreement, the decedent could not sell or otherwise dispose of LLC assets other than in the ordinary course of operations without the approval of all members. She could not liquidate and dissolve the LLC without the approval of all members. She could not admit additional members without the approval of all members.

only after an accounting for required reserves. Capital accounts were kept, and the value of the decedent's capital contributions were properly credited to her capital account. No member had a right to the return of the member's capital contribution except in the event of liquidation and dissolution. The decedent retained more than enough personal assets outside of the LLC to meet her personal expenses.

There is no retained interest under Code Sec. 2036(a)(1) merely because the decedent retained an income interest in the decedent's own membership interests. The IRS must show that the decedent retained an interest in the transferred or gifted membership interests.[148]

There is no retained interest under Code Sec. 2036(a)(1) merely because the decedent received a reasonable management fee.[149]

Retained Interest under Section 2036(a)(2)

Under Code Sec. 2036(a)(2), property is also included in the decedent's estate if the decedent retained the right, either alone or in conjunction with any other person, to designate the persons who will possess or enjoy the property or the income therefrom.

The right to manage property does not necessarily require inclusion under Section 2036(a)(2).[150] However, the combination of one or more the following factors may indicate that LLC property should be included in the decedent's estate under Section 2036(a)(2):[151]

- retention of broad management powers, including the right to act as the sole manager of the LLC;
- authority to amend the operating agreement at any time without the consent of the other members;
- right to make discretionary pro rata distributions of LLC income;
- right to make distributions in cash or in kind;
- retention of more than 50 percent of the membership interests in the LLC, which would allow the decedent to make any decision requiring a majority vote of the members.

In *Estate of Powell*, the decedent transferred property to a partnership in exchange for a 99 percent partnership interest. Her son, as general partner, had the sole discretion to determine the amount and timing of partnership distributions. The consent of all partners was required to dissolve the partnership. The court determined that the decedent's ability to dissolve the partnership with the consent of the general partner was a right in conjunction with another to designate the persons who would possess or enjoy the transferred property under Code Sec. 2036(a)(2). The

---

[148] *Estate of Beatrice Kelly v. Comm'r*, TC Memo 2012-73 (2012).

[149] *Estate of Beatrice Kelly v. Comm'r*, TC Memo 2012-73 (2012).

[150] *United States v. Byrum*, 408 U.S. 125, 132-134 (1972).

[151] *Estate of Turner v. Comm'r*, TC Memo 2011-209 (2011).

court also determined that the decedent retained the right to determine the amount and timing of distributions through her son who was her attorney-in-fact.[152]

Bona Fide Sale for Adequate Consideration

Finally, in order for the IRS to prevail under Section 2036(a), the IRS must show that the bona fide sale exception does not apply. Section 2036(a) does not apply if the decedent's transfer of property to an LLC and the subsequent gifts of membership interests to family members were "a bona fide sale for an adequate and full consideration in money or money's worth."[153]

Some courts have determined that a transfer to an LLC or partnership is for adequate and full consideration.[154] Other courts have determined that the transfer is not a bona fide sale for adequate and full consideration.[155]

There are two parts to this test: the bona fide sale test; and the adequate and full consideration test.[156]

Bona fide sale requirement

The first part of the exception to Section 2036(a) is the bona fide sale requirement. Generally, there is a bona fide sale if there are legitimate and significant nontax reasons for creating the LLC.[157]

---

[152] *Estate of Nancy H. Powell v. Comm'r*, 148 TC No. 18 (2017).

[153] Code Sec. 2036(a).

[154] *Estate of Purdue v. Comm'r*, TC Memo 2015-249 (2015); *Estate of Beatrice Kelly v. Comm'r*, TC Memo 2012-73 (2012); *Estate of Charlene B. Shurtz v. Comm'r*, TC Memo 2010-21 (2010); *Estate of Black v. Comm'r*, 133 TC 340 (2009); *Estate of Anna Mirowski v. Comm'r*, TC Memo 2008-74 (2008); *Kimbell v. United States*, 93 AFTR 2d 2004-2400 (5th Cir. 2004); *Stone v. Comm'r*, 86 TCM 551 (2003); *Church v. United States*, 85 AFTR 2d 2000-804, Conclusions of Law ¶7 (W.D. Tex. 2000), *aff'd without published opinion*, 268 F.3d 1063 (per curiam) (table), unpublished opinion available at 88 AFTR 2d 2001-5352 (5th Cir. 2001).

[155] *Estate of Holiday v. Comm'r*, TC Memo 2016-51 (2016); *Estate of Turner v. Comm'r*, TC Memo 2011-209 (2011); *Estate of Paul H. Liljestrand v. Comm'r*, TC Memo 2011-259 (2011); *Estate of Harper v. Comm'r*, TC Memo 2002-121 (2002); *Estate of Theodore R. Thompson v. Comm'r*, 84 TCM 374 (2002), *aff'd*, 382 F.3d 367 (3d Cir. 2004); *Estate of Bongard*, 124 TC 95 (2005); *Estate of Bigelow*, 503 F.3d 955 (9th Cir. 2007); *Estate of Korby v. Comm'r*, TC Memo 2005-103 (2005), *aff'd*, 2006 WL 3524501 (8th Cir. 2006); *Estate of Hilda E. Erickson*, TC Memo 2007-207 (2007); *Estate of Rosen v. Comm'r*, TC Memo 2006-115 (2006).

[156] *Estate of Bongard*, 124 TC 95, 119, 122-125 (2005); *Estate of Bigelow v. Comm'r*, 503 F.3d 955, 969 (9th Cir. 2007); *Estate of Purdue v. Comm'r*, TC Memo 2015-249 (2015); *Estate of Turner v. Comm'r*, TC Memo 2011-209 (2011).

[157] *Estate of Holiday v. Comm'r*, TC Memo 2016-51 (2016); *Estate of Beatrice Kelly v. Comm'r*, TC Memo 2012-73 (2012); *Stone v. Comm'r*, TC Memo 2012-48 (2012); *Estate of Turner v. Comm'r*, TC Memo 2011-209 (2011); *Estate of Paul H. Liljestrand v. Comm'r*, TC Memo 2011-259 (2011); *Estate of Charlene B. Shurtz v. Comm'r*, TC Memo 2010-21 (2010); *Estate of Black v. Comm'r*, 133 TC 340 (2009); *Estate of Anna Mirowski v. Comm'r*, TC Memo 2008-74 (2008) ; *Estate of Jorgensen*, TC Memo 2009-66 (2009), *aff'd*, 107 AFTR 2d 2011-2069 (9th Cir. 2011); *Estate of Hilda E. Erickson*, TC Memo 2007-207 (2007); *Estate of Rector*, TC Memo 2007-367 (2007); *Estate of Bigelow v. Comm'r*, 503 F.3d 955 (9th Cir. 2007); *Estate of Bongard*, 124 TC 95 (2005); *Strangi v. Comm'r*, 417 F.3d 468 (5th Cir. 2005).

Significant nontax business purposes include: (i) management expertise through a common investment vehicle;[158] and consolidating investments into a family asset managed by a single advisor;[159] (ii) promoting family cohesiveness through joint management of the family's assets by the children and grandchildren;[160] (iii) maintaining family assets in the single pool of assets in order to allow for investment opportunities that would not be available if separate gifts to each of the children were made;[161] (iv) providing for each child and grandchild on an equal basis;[162] (v) security and preservation of assets and avoidance of personal liability;[163] (vi) capital appreciation;[164] (vii) reduction in administrative costs and accounting costs;[165] (viii) reduction in cost of recording transfers as property is passed from generation to generation; (ix) preservation of the property as separate property rather than community property;[166] (x) providing a mechanism for the resolution of disputes through arbitration;[167] (xi) protecting children from loss of assets in the event of a divorce;[168] (xii) preservation of the family business;[169] (xiii) management efficiency if the business requires active management;[170] (xiv) implementing a buy-and-hold plan for family assets that would restrict family members from selling family assets after the death of the parents;[171] and (xv) holding real estate for future family development.[172]

Significant nontax business purposes do not include: (i) gift-giving;[173] (ii) the estate's goal of efficiently managing assets without evidence that the LLC requires special active management;[174] (iii) protecting assets against creditors unless the record

---

[158] *Estate of Black v. Comm'r*, 133 TC 340 (2009); *Kimbell v. United States*, 93 AFTR 2d 2004-2400 (5th Cir. 2004). *But see Hurford v. Comm'r*, TC Memo 2008-278 (2008), where the court determined that consolidated asset management is not a significant nontax purpose unless the parties can show specific benefits of consolidation from a transfer to a family limited partnership.

[159] *Estate of Bigelow v. Comm'r*, 503 F.3d 955 (9th Cir. 2007).

[160] *Estate of Turner v. Comm'r*, TC Memo 2011-209 (2011); *Estate of Black v. Comm'r*, 133 TC 340 (2009); *Estate of Anna Mirowski v. Comm'r*, TC Memo 2008-74 (2008).

[161] *Estate of Anna Mirowski v. Comm'r*, TC Memo 2008-74 (2008); *Estate of Shutt*, TC Memo 2005-126 (2005).

[162] *Estate of Turner v. Comm'r*, TC Memo 2011-209 (2011); *Estate of Anna Mirowski v. Comm'r*, TC Memo 2008-74 (2008).

[163] *Estate of Charlene B. Shurtz v. Comm'r*, TC Memo 2010-21 (2010); *Kimbell v. United States*, 93 AFTR 2d 2004-2400 (5th Cir. 2004).

[164] *Kimbell v. United States*, 93 AFTR 2d 2004-2400 (5th Cir. 2004).

[165] *Kimbell v. United States*, 93 AFTR 2d 2004-2400 (5th Cir. 2004).

[166] *Kimbell v. United States*, 93 AFTR 2d 2004-2400 (5th Cir. 2004).

[167] *Kimbell v. United States*, 93 AFTR 2d 2004-2400 (5th Cir. 2004).

[168] *Estate of Black v. Comm'r*, 133 TC 340 (2009); *Estate of Anna Mirowski v. Comm'r*, TC Memo 2008-74 (2008).

[169] *Estate of Charlene B. Shurtz v. Comm'r*, TC Memo 2010-21 (2010).

[170] *Estate of Charlene B. Shurtz v. Comm'r*, TC Memo 2010-21 (2010).

[171] *Estate of Black v. Comm'r*, 133 TC 340 (2009).

[172] *Stone v. Comm'r*, TC Memo 2012-48 (2012).

[173] *Estate of Rector*, TC Memo 2007-367 (2007); *Estate of Jorgensen*, TC Memo 2009-66 (2009), *aff'd*, 107 AFTR 2d 2011-2069 (9th Cir. 2011).

[174] *Estate of Rector*, TC Memo 2007-367 (2007).

establishes legitimate concerns about liabilities to creditors;[175] (iv) intent to make a testamentary disposition;[176] or (v) avoiding estate taxes.[177] A good faith transfer must provide the transferor with some potential for benefits other than the estate tax advantages that result from holding assets in LLC or partnership form.[178]

Consolidated asset management may be a legitimate and significant nontax purpose if there is active management, protection against creditors, preventing family members from disposing of stock imprudently, allowing stock representing a potential swing vote to be voted as a bloc, or perpetuation of the decedent's buy-and-hold investment philosophy.[179] However, consolidated asset management is not a legitimate and significant nontax purpose if the LLC is just the vehicle for changing the form of the investment, or a "mere asset container."[180] The courts will closely scrutinize transactions involving transfers of marketable securities or other passive investments to an LLC rather than a business requiring active management.[181]

The courts frequently consider the same factors in applying the bona fide sale test that they use for the retained rights test.[182] For example, the courts have noted the following reasons that there was no bona fide sale or legitimate nontax business purpose: (i) the decedent stood on both sides of the transaction and created the LLC without engaging in any bargaining negotiations with the other anticipated members;[183] (ii) the decedent made all contributions to the LLC which constituted most of his or her of her wealth;[184] (iii) the decedent did not actually transfer the property to the LLC,[185] or contributed the property to the LLC several months after it was formed;[186] (iv) the LLC had no investment strategy or business plan, and only engaged in business transactions with family members;[187] (v) there was commingling of personal and LLC assets;[188] (vi) the decedent's age and poor health indicated that

---

[175] *Estate of Holiday v. Comm'r*, TC Memo 2016-51 (2016); *Estate of Rector*, TC Memo 2007-367 (2007); *Hurford v. Comm'r*, TC Memo 2008-278 (2008).

[176] *Estate of Paul H. Liljestrand v. Comm'r*, TC Memo 2011-259 (2011).

[177] *Estate of Thompson v. Comm'r*, 84 TCM 374 (2002), aff'd, 382 F.3d 367 (3d Cir. 2004); *Estate of Bongard*, 124 TC 95 (2005); *Estate of Rosen v. Comm'r*, TC Memo 2006-115 (2006).

[178] *Estate of Thompson v. Comm'r*, 84 TCM 374 (2002), aff'd, 382 F.3d 367 (3d Cir. 2004).

[179] *Estate of Purdue v. Comm'r*, TC Memo 2015-249 (2015); *Estate of Turner v. Comm'r*, TC Memo 2011-209 (2011); *Estate of Schutt v. Comm'r*, TC Memo 2005-126 (2005).

[180] *Estate of Turner v. Comm'r*, TC Memo 2011-209 (2011); *Estate of Erikson v. Comm'r*, TC Memo 2007-107 (2007); *Estate of Schutt v. Comm'r*, TC Memo 2005-126 (2005).

[181] *Estate of Holiday v. Comm'r*, TC Memo 2016-51 (2016); *Estate of Turner v. Comm'r*, TC Memo 2011-209 (2011).

[182] *Estate of Paul H. Liljestrand v. Comm'r*, TC Memo 2011-259 (2011); *Estate of Jorgensen*, TC Memo 2009-66 (2009), aff'd, 107 AFTR 2d 2011-2069 (9th Cir. 2011).

[183] *Estate of Holiday v. Comm'r*, TC Memo 2016-51 (2016); *Estate of Purdue v. Comm'r*, TC Memo 2015-249 (2015); *Estate of Turner v. Comm'r*, TC Memo 2011-209 (2011).

[184] *Estate of Rector*, TC Memo 2007-367 (2007).

[185] *Estate of Purdue v. Comm'r*, TC Memo 2015-249 (2015).

[186] *Estate of Rector*, TC Memo 2007-367 (2007).

[187] *Estate of Rector*, TC Memo 2007-367 (2007); *Estate of Turner v. Comm'r*, TC Memo 2011-209 (2011).

[188] *Estate of Purdue v. Comm'r*, TC Memo 2015-249 (2015); *Estate of Turner v. Comm'r*, TC Memo 2011-209 (2011).

the transfer was merely a testamentary disposition;[189] (vii) the taxpayer was financially dependent on distributions from the LLC; (viii) the LLC fails to maintain books and records;[190] (ix) the members did not hold formal meetings or keep formal minutes;[191] or (x) the LLC did not make regular distributions.[192]

The lack of apparent nontax reasons for forming an LLC is not by itself enough to disregard the formation of an LLC.[193] There must normally be other factors indicating that the transfer of the property to the LLC is not bona fide. These factors include the taxpayer's financial dependence on distributions from the LLC, commingling of personal funds with LLC funds, the delay or failure to transfer property to the LLC, the taxpayer's old age or poor health when the LLC is formed, and whether the LLC functions as a business enterprise or is otherwise engaged in meaningful economic activity.[194]

Some courts have determined that the transfer of property to the LLC in exchange for a membership interest is not a bona fide sale if the formation of the LLC does not result in a change in the underlying pool of assets or the likelihood of profits.[195] A transfer of property that only changes the form in which the decedent held property (a mere recycling of value) is a paper transaction without substance.[196]

Several courts have determined that a bona fide sale also requires an arm's-length bargain,[197] and that a transfer is not arm's length if the decedent "stood on both sides of the transaction" as the transferor and a member of the LLC.[198] Some courts have rejected this position.[199] Other courts have determined that a transfer to a partnership or LLC may be bona fide even though it is not at arm's-length.[200] Generally, the arm's length requirement does not apply if the decedent fully funded the LLC and then made gifts to family members. There is no arm's-length bargaining if the donees do not contribute property to the LLC in exchange for membership interests.[201]

---

[189] *Estate of Rector*, TC Memo 2007-367 (2007); *Estate of Purdue v. Comm'r*, TC Memo 2015-249 (2015).

[190] *Estate of Holiday v. Comm'r*, TC Memo. 2016-51 (2016).

[191] *Estate of Holiday v. Comm'r*, TC Memo. 2016-51 (2016).

[192] *Estate of Purdue v. Comm'r*, TC Memo 2015-249 (2015).

[193] *Hurford v. Comm'r*, TC Memo 2008-278 (2008).

[194] *Hurford v. Comm'r*, TC Memo 2008-278 (2008).

[195] *Estate of Rector*, TC Memo 2007-367 (2007).

[196] *Estate of Theodore R. Thompson v. Comm'r*, 84 TCM 374, 388 (2002); *Estate of Harper v. Comm'r*, TC Memo 2001-121 (2002); *Strangi v. Comm'r*, 85 TCM 1331, 1344 (2003), *on second appeal*, 417 F.3d 468 (5th Cir. 2005); *Estate of Rosen v. Comm'r*, TC Memo 2006-115 (2006).

[197] *Estate of Bigelow v. Comm'r*, TC Memo 2005-65 (2005), *aff'd*, 503 F.3d 955, 969 (9th Cir. 2007); *Estate of Bongard*, 124 TC 95, 122 (2005); *Estate of Charlene B. Shurtz v. Comm'r*, TC Memo 2010-21 (2010); *Estate of Jorgensen*, TC Memo 2009-66 (2009), *aff'd*, 107 AFTR 2d 2011-2069 (9th Cir. 2011).

[198] *Estate of Harper v. Comm'r*, 83 TCM 1641, 1653 (2002); *Strangi v. Comm'r*, 85 TCM 1331, 1344 (2003), *on second appeal*, 417 F.3d 468 (5th Cir. 2005); *Estate of Korby v. Comm'r*, TC Memo 2005-103 (2005), *aff'd*, 2006 WL 3524501 (8th Cir. 2006); *Estate of Hilda E. Erickson*, TC Memo 2007-207 (2007).

[199] *Estate of Anna Mirowski v. Comm'r*, TC Memo 2008-74 (2008).

[200] *Estate of Thompson v. Comm'r*, 84 TCM 374 (2002), *aff'd*, 382 F.3d 367 (3d Cir. 2004).

[201] *Estate of Anna Mirowski v. Comm'r*, TC Memo 2008-74 (2008).

Intra-family transactions are subject to heightened scrutiny.[202] However, transactions between family members must be judged in the same manner as transactions that do not involve family members (even though such transactions are subject to heightened scrutiny).[203]

The Fifth Circuit in the *Kimbell* case[204] considered a transfer to a partnership in which an LLC was the general partner. It determined that a bona fide sale is one made in good faith, honestly, openly and sincerely, without fraud or deceit. The court noted that tax planning motives do not prevent a sale from being bona fide if the transaction is otherwise real, actual or genuine. The court held that the transfer to the family partnership was a bona fide sale based on the following factors:

- The taxpayer retained sufficient assets outside the partnership for his own support.[205]
- There was no commingling of partnership assets and personal assets.
- LLC and partnership formalities were satisfied. The assets contributed to the partnership were actually assigned to the partnership.
- There were credible non-tax business reasons for the formation of an LLC and partnership that could not be accomplished by a trust.

One court indicated that there may be a difference between transfers to LLCs, and transfers to limited partnerships and general partnerships. A taxpayer's transfer of property to an LLC indicates that there is a bona fide nontax reason for the transfer because no member is personally liable after the transfer. A taxpayer's transfer of property to a general partnership, or a limited partnership in which the decedent or his trust is the general partner, indicates that there is not a bona fide nontax reason for the transfer because the taxpayer retains unlimited liability after the transfer.[206]

Full and adequate consideration requirement

The second part of the exception to Section 2036(a) is the full and adequate consideration requirement.

Some courts have determined that a transfer to an LLC is for full and adequate consideration if (a) the contributing members receive membership interests in proportion to the values of their contributions, (b) a contribution by one member does not confer a financial benefit on or increase the wealth of any other member, (c) the value of contributions is credited to the capital accounts of the contributing members, (d) capital account balances are reduced by the value of distributions received by each member, and (e) a member has a right to a distribution of property based on

---

[202] *Estate of Thompson v. Comm'r*, 84 TCM 374 (2002), *aff'd*, 382 F.3d 367, 383 (3d Cir. 2004); *Estate of Bongard*, 124 TC 95 (2005).

[203] *Kimbell v. United States*, 93 AFTR 2d 2004-2400 (5th Cir. 2004).

[204] *Kimbell v. United States*, 93 AFTR 2d 2004-2400 (5th Cir. 2004).

[205] *See also Estate of Shutt*, TC Memo 2005-126 (2005).

[206] *Estate of Bigelow v. Comm'r*, 503 F.3d 955 (9th Cir. 2007).

capital account values on liquidation of the LLC.[207] There is no requirement that assets contributed to an LLC be equal to the value the membership units received in exchange.[208]

There is also adequate and full consideration if the decedent transferred property to an LLC in exchange for 100 percent of the membership interests, and then subsequently made gifts of membership interests.[209] The subsequent gifts would not be for adequate and full consideration. However, there would be no inclusion in the gross estate under Section 2036(a) as a result of the subsequent gifts unless the decedent retained an interest in the gifted membership interests.[210] The IRS takes the position that the bona fide sale exception should not apply to either transfer, and that both transfers should be treated as part of the same transaction. A taxpayer who forms an LLC in contemplation of making gifts in substance receives less than 100 percent of the membership interests in exchange for the property transferred to the LLC.[211]

A taxpayer's receipt of a membership interest is not a bona fide sale for full and adequate consideration where an intra-family transaction merely changes the form in which the decedent holds property.[212] These are called recycling transactions. Some courts reject the recycling theory if there are legitimate and actual nontax purposes in transferring property to a family LLC.[213]

The transfer to an LLC is not for adequate and full consideration if the LLC legal formalities are not respected,[214] and if all the members in the LLC do not receive interests proportionate to the value of assets transferred to the LLC.[215]

The IRS takes the position that a taxpayer cannot claim a substantial valuation discount as a result of the transfer, and at the same time assert that the transfer is for

---

[207] *Estate of Charlene B. Shurtz v. Comm'r*, TC Memo 2010-21 (2010); *Estate of Black v. Comm'r*, 133 TC 340 (2009); *Estate of Bongard*, 124 TC 95 (2005); *Estate of Shutt*, TC Memo 2005-126 (2005); *Stone v. Comm'r*, 86 TCM 551 (2003); *Church v. United States*, 85 AFTR 2d 2000-804, Conclusions of Law ¶7 (W.D. Tex. 2000), *aff'd without published opinion*, 268 F.3d 1063 (*per curiam*) (table), unpublished opinion available at 88 AFTR 2d 2001-5352 (5th Cir. 2001). *But see Hurford v. Comm'r*, TC Memo 2008-278 (2008), where the court determined that consolidated asset management is not a significant nontax purpose unless the parties can show specific benefits of consolidation from a transfer to a family limited partnership.

[208] *Kimbell v. United States*, 93 AFTR 2d 2004-2400 (5th Cir. 2004).

[209] *Estate of Anna Mirowski v. Comm'r*, TC Memo 2008-74 (2008).

[210] *Estate of Anna Mirowski v. Comm'r*, TC Memo 2008-74 (2008).

[211] *Estate of Anna Mirowski v. Comm'r*, TC Memo 2008-74 (2008).

[212] *Estate of Purdue v. Comm'r*, TC Memo 2015-249 (2015); *Harper v. Comm'r*, TC Memo 2001-121 (2002).

[213] *Estate of Purdue v. Comm'r*, TC Memo 2015-249 (2015).

[214] *Hurford v. Comm'r*, TC Memo 2008-278 (2008). *But see Estate of Charlene B. Shurtz v. Comm'r*, TC Memo 2010-21 (2010), where the court determined that there was adequate and full consideration even though the LLC legal formalities were not respected (LLC did not maintain books of account, the LLC was four months late in establishing a bank account, some of the partners paid expenses of the partnership from their personal bank accounts, and distributions from the partnership were not always proportional).

[215] *Estate of Paul H. Liljestrand v. Comm'r*, TC Memo 2011-259 (2011); *Hurford v. Comm'r*, TC Memo 2008-278 (2008); *Estate of Bongard v. Comm'r*, 124 TC 95 (2005).

adequate and full consideration.[216] Some courts have agreed with this position.[217] Other courts have rejected this position.[218]

The Section 2036(a) exception will not apply unless the taxpayer meets both the adequate and full consideration requirement and the bona fide transfer requirement. For example, several courts have determined that the transfer of property to a partnership in exchange for a proportional interest was for adequate and full consideration, but was not a bona fide sale since the transfer lacked a substantial non-tax purpose.[219] As a result, the Section 2036(a) exception did not apply.

.04 Code Section 2036(b) Retained Voting Rights

The IRS may use Code Sec. 2036(b) to challenge valuation discounts if a member transfers stock in a closely held corporation to an LLC. The value of closely held stock transferred by a taxpayer to an LLC may be includable in his gross estate if the taxpayer retained the right to vote the stock as a manager or member of the LLC until the date of death.[220] The IRS believes that the rule applies even though (a) the decedent was only one of the managers of the LLC, and could vote the stock only in conjunction with another unrelated manager, or (b) the decedent transferred the stock to the LLC in exchange for membership interests one or more years prior to the date of death.[221]

Code Sec. 2036(b) only applies to stock in a controlled corporation. A corporation is a controlled corporation if, at any time after the transfer and during the three-year period before the date of death, the decedent owned or had the right to vote stock processing at least 20 percent of the total combined voting power of all classes of stock.[222]

Code Sec. 2036(b) does not apply if the transfer is a bona fide sale for adequate and full consideration in money or money's worth.[223]

---

[216] *Kimbell v. United States*, 93 AFTR 2d 2004-2400 (5th Cir. 2004).

[217] For example, one court noted that "claiming an estate tax discount on assets received in exchange for an inter vivos transfer should defeat the Section 2036(a) exception outright. If assets are transferred inter vivos in exchange for other assets of lesser value, it seems reasonable to conclude that there is no transfer for adequate and full consideration because the decedent has not replenished the estate with other assets of equal value." *Estate of Thompson v. Comm'r*, 84 TCM 374 (2002), *aff'd*, 382 F.3d 367 (3d Cir. 2004).

[218] This position was rejected by the courts in *Stone v. Comm'r*, 86 TCM 551, 578 (2003) and *Kimbell v. United States*, 93 AFTR 2d 2004-2400 (5th Cir. 2004).

[219] *Strangi v. Comm'r*, 417 F.3d 468 (5th Cir. 2005); *Estate of Turner v. Comm'r*, TC Memo 2011-209 (2011).

[220] Ltr. Rul. 199938005 (*citing* Code Sec. 2036(b)).

[221] Ltr. Rul. 199938005.

[222] Code Sec. 2036(b)(2).

[223] Code Sec. 2036(a).

.05 Code Section 2038 Retained Right to Alter, Amend, or Revoke

The IRS sometimes asserts that property transferred by a taxpayer to an LLC should be brought back into the taxpayer's estate under Code Sec. 2038.[224] That section provides that a decedent's gross estate includes property in an LLC if:

- The decedent transferred property to the LLC during his or her lifetime;
- At the time of death, the decedent retained the power, alone or in conjunction with any other person, to alter, amend, revoke or terminate the transfer, or relinquished such power during the three-year period ending on the date of the decedent's death; and
- The transfer was not a bona fide sale for adequate and full consideration.

If Section 2038 applies, the IRS may disregard the LLC and include the transferred assets in the decedent's estate at fair market value. In such cases, the IRS does not need to contest the appropriate valuation discount for the LLC membership units since there is no valuation discount.

There are normally two transfers for Section 2038 purposes. The first transfer is the contribution of property by the decedent to the LLC in exchange for membership interests. The second transfer is the gift of membership interests by the decedent to family members. Each of these transfers must be separately considered.[225]

A decedent has retained the right to alter, amend, revoke or terminate if the decedent could have revoked the gift and received back the membership interests. A decedent has not retained the right to alter, amend, revoke or terminate merely because the decedent owned a majority interest in the LLC, was the manager, and had the right to make distributions. The right to determine the timing of distributions does not constitute a retained interest if the operating agreement requires annual distributions of cash flow, current distributions of proceeds from capital transactions, and mandatory distributions on liquidation.[226]

The IRS takes the position that a decedent has retained an interest to alter, amend, revoke or terminate "in conjunction with any other person" if the decedent could, with the consent of the donees, amend the operating agreement, dispose of LLC assets other than in the ordinary course of business, and determine the amount of distributions. The courts have rejected this position.[227] Powers that can be exercised only with the consent of parties having an adverse vested or contingent interest in the gifted property are not retained powers for Section 2038 purposes.[228] For example, Section 2038 does not apply if the family members in the LLC own sufficient membership interests to block a proposed amendment to the operating agreement or

---

[224] *Estate of Anna Mirowski v. Comm'r*, TC Memo 2008-74 (2008); *Estate of Reichardt*, 114 TC 144 (2000); *Estate of Schauerhamer v. Comm'r*, 73 TCM 2855, TC Memo 1997-242 (1997).

[225] *Estate of Anna Mirowski v. Comm'r*, TC Memo 2008-74 (2008).

[226] *Estate of Anna Mirowski v. Comm'r*, TC Memo 2008-74 (2008).

[227] *Estate of Anna Mirowski v. Comm'r*, TC Memo 2008-74 (2008); *Church v. United States*, 85 AFTR 2d 2000-804, ¶¶ 4, 16 (W.D. Tex. 2000).

[228] Reg. § 20.2038-1(a)(2).

other action by the donor manager that would otherwise constitute a power to alter, amend, revoke or terminate.[229]

The bona fide sale for adequate and full consideration exception applies when the taxpayer transfers property to an LLC in exchange for all of the membership interests.[230] The subsequent gifts would not be for adequate and full consideration. However, there would be no inclusion in the gross estate under Section 2038 as a result of the subsequent gifts unless the decedent retained the power to alter, amend, revoke, or terminate the donated membership interests.[231]

.06 Code Section 2701 Estate Freezes

The IRS may use Code Sec. 2701 to challenge valuation discounts if there are two or more classes of membership interests. Code Sec. 2701 is designed to discourage "estate freezes." In a typical estate freeze prior to the enactment of Code Sec. 2701, the parent would transfer an interest in an LLC or other business entity while retaining a different type of interest in the same business. The interest that was given away was structured so that it had a very low value at the time of the gift, thereby incurring little or no gift taxes. However, the interest was expected to increase in value as the business grew. The interest retained by the donor was structured so that its value would not increase. For example, the retained membership interest was often entitled to a fixed liquidation amount and a fixed annual rate of return. The size of the donor's estate was frozen for estate tax purposes.

Code Sec. 2701 now contains several rules designed to prevent the member from artificially decreasing the gift tax on the member's initial gift of a partial interest in the LLC to the family member. The rules use the "subtraction method" of valuing a gift.[232] The valuation method ignores the value of certain preferential interests retained by the donor. This has the effect of increasing the value of the gift and the amount of gift taxes payable on the date of transfer.

A donor's retained interest in an LLC is ignored for gift tax valuation purposes if it is an equity interest that has a preference in the form of either of the following:[233]

- an extraordinary payment right, such as a put, call or conversion right, the right to compel liquidation, or a similar right, the exercise or non-exercise of which affects the value of the donated membership interest; or
- a distribution right if, immediately before the gift, the donor and family members control the LLC. A distribution right is a right to receive distributions from an LLC.

The special valuation rules do not apply if (i) the member donates membership interests in the LLC that are of the same class as the preferential retained membership

---

[229] *Church v. United States,* 85 AFTR 2d 2000-804, ¶¶ 4, 16 (W.D. Tex. 2000).

[230] *Estate of Anna Mirowski v. Comm'r,* TC Memo 2008-74 (2008).

[231] *Estate of Anna Mirowski v. Comm'r,* TC Memo 2008-74 (2008).

[232] Reg. § 25.2701-3.

[233] Ltr. Rul. 9802004 (*citing* Code Sec. 2701(b)(1)).

interests, or (ii) the member transfers membership interests that are proportionately of the same type as the retained interests (except for any nonterminating differences with respect to management and limitations on liability).

Normally, a member's gifts of membership interests in an LLC to family members are not subject to the special valuation rules, since the member owns the same type of membership interest after the gift. The parent or other donor may retain management control of the LLC, but retained management rights do not subject the gift to the special valuation rules.[234] However, the special valuation rules may apply if the member indirectly owns a preferential payment or distribution right in a business owned by the LLC.[235]

.07 Code Section 2703

General Rules

The IRS may use Code Sec. 2703 to challenge discounts for membership units in an LLC.[236]

Code Sec. 2703(a)(2) states the general rule that property must be valued for estate and gift tax purposes without regard to any option, agreement, or other right to acquire or use the property at less than fair market value, or any restriction on the right to sell or use such property. Such restrictions may be contained in the operating agreement, or may be implicit in the capital structure of the LLC.[237] The restrictions include restrictions on (i) the right to withdraw from the LLC, (ii) the right to a return of capital, (iii) buy-sell restrictions, (iv) limitations on management and voting rights, and (v) any other restrictions on the right to sell or use the LLC property, however created.[238]

Code Sec. 2703(b) provides an exception to the general rule. It states that a restriction may be considered in valuing membership units if it meets each of the following requirements:[239]

- it is a bona fide business arrangement;[240]
- it is not a device to transfer the property to members of the decedent's family for less than full and adequate consideration in money or money's worth; and
- the terms are comparable to similar arrangements entered into by persons in an arm's-length transaction.

---

[234] Ltr. Rul. 9802004.

[235] *Id.*

[236] *Smith v. United States*, Case No. 02-264 Erie (W.D. Pa. 2005); FSA 200049003; TAM 9736004.

[237] TAM 9736004, *citing* Reg. § 25.2703-1(a).

[238] TAM 9736004, *citing* Reg. § 25.2703-1(a)(2).

[239] Code Sec. 2703(b).

[240] In *Fisher v. United States*, No. 1:08-cv-0908-LJM-TAB (S.D. Ind. 2010), the court denied a claim for a gift tax refund by taxpayers who transferred membership interests in an LLC to each of their seven children. The court determined that the taxpayer failed to show that there was a bona fide business under Section 2703(b).

The IRS believes that Code Sec. 2703 applies to an LLC in two different ways. First, it applies to the entity itself. The LLC should be disregarded for valuation purposes unless all the requirements of Code Sec. 2703(b) are met.[241] The formation of the LLC, the transfer of property to the LLC, and the transfer of membership interests to the beneficiaries at death are treated as a single integrated transaction unless such requirements are met.

Second, if Code Sec. 2703 does not apply to the entity, then it applies to the restrictions in the operating agreement.[242] The restrictions in the operating agreement should be ignored for valuation purposes unless all the requirements of Code Sec. 2703(b) are met. Generally, transfer restrictions contained in an operating agreement are disregarded in valuing membership interests for estate and gift tax purposes if the members of the LLC are family members.[243]

Application of Code Section 2703 to Entity

The IRS first argues that Code Sec. 2703 applies to the LLC itself. Its argument is as follows:

- The LLC should be disregarded if the LLC is not a bona fide business arrangement. The determination of whether a transfer to family members through an LLC is a bona fide transaction is based on all the facts and circumstances.[244] Intra-family transactions involving LLCs are subject to special scrutiny.[245]

- A transfer to an LLC is not a bona fide business arrangement if a member transfers property to the LLC shortly before the member's death, and the beneficiaries receive essentially the same assets that they would have received from the decedent if the assets had not been transferred to the LLC.[246] If the decedent transfers all of his property to the LLC immediately prior to death, there is merely an exchange of liquid assets for an illiquid asset.

- The LLC should be disregarded if the decedent transferred property to the LLC for less than full and adequate consideration in money or money's worth. The transfer of property to an LLC is not for adequate consideration in money or money's worth if the property has a significantly lower value immediately after the transfer as a result of minority or marketability discounts. This is especially true for members who, because of their advanced age or health, are unlikely to ever recoup their immediate loss as a result of the transfer of property to the LLC.[247] The short life expectancy of the

---

[241] *Smith v. United States*, Case No. 02-264 Erie (W.D. Pa. 2005); FSA 200049003; TAM 9736004.

[242] *Id.*

[243] *Holman v. Comm'r*, 105 AFTR 2d ¶ 2010-721 (8th Cir. 2010).

[244] FSA 200049003.

[245] TAM 9736004.

[246] *Id.*

[247] *Id.*

decedent after the transfer of property to the LLC means that there is little opportunity to recoup the diminution in value prior to death.

The courts usually reject this theory because the estate tax is only imposed on property that the decedent owned as of the date of death. If the decedent owned a membership interest in an LLC, then the estate tax applies to the membership interest rather than the property owned by the LLC.[248]

Application to Restrictions in Operating Agreement

The IRS next argues that, if Code Sec. 2703 does not apply to the LLC, then it should apply to the restrictions in the operating agreement.[249] In such case, the IRS believes that any restrictions on the right to transfer an interest in the LLC, to withdraw property from the LLC, or to liquidate an interest in the LLC, should be disregarded under Code Sec. 2703 because the restrictions are a device to transfer the membership interests to the objects of the decedent's bounty for less than full and adequate consideration.

The IRS will challenge valuation discounts for membership interests in an LLC under Code Sec. 2703 if (i) there is an absence of arm's-length bargaining in connection with the formation of the LLC, (ii) the member transfers personal use assets to the LLC, (iii) the member agrees to significant restrictions under the operating agreement, or (iv) the member transfers virtually all of his assets to the LLC in exchange for an interest that severely restricts his control over those assets and his right to income from the assets.[250]

Some courts reject the IRS position because Code Sec. 2703 does not apply to term restrictions, or to restrictions on sale or assignment of a membership interest that preclude membership status for a buyer.[251]

Other courts agree with the IRS that restrictions on transfer and assignment in the operating agreement should be disregarded in valuing a membership interest under Code Sec. 2703.[252] However, the donor is still entitled to a minority and marketability discount. A willing buyer would pay less for stock or other property in an LLC, even after disregarding all the restrictions on transfer and assignment in the operating agreement.[253]

---

[248] *See Church v. United States*, 85 AFTR 2d 2000-804, Conclusions of Law ¶ 8 (W.D. Tex. 2000); *Estate of Strangi v. Comm'r*, 115 TC 478, 487-488 (2000); *Holman v. Comm'r*, 130 TC 170 (2008).

[249] *Estate of Smith, Jr. v. United States*, 96 AFTR 2d 2005-6549 (WD Pa 2005); *Griffin v. United States*, 89 AFTR 2d 2002-954, 42 F. Supp. 2d 700 (W.D. Tex. 1998).

[250] TAM 9736004.

[251] *See Church v. United States*, 85 AFTR 2d 2000-804, Conclusions of Law ¶ 9 (W.D. Tex. 2000); *Knight v. Comm'r*, 115 TC 506, 519-520 (2000).

[252] *Holman v. Comm'r*, 130 TC 170 (2008).

[253] *Holman v. Comm'r*, 130 TC 170 (2008).

Application to Option and Buy-Sell Agreements

Code Sec. 2703 applies to option and buy-sell agreements that establish a purchase price on the death of the owner that is less than the fair market value of the membership interest. The value of the membership interest for estate and gift tax purposes must be determined without regard to such agreements unless:

- the agreement is a bona fide business arrangement;

- the agreement is not a device to transfer property to members of the decedent's family for less than full and adequate consideration in money or money's worth; and

- the terms of the agreement are comparable to similar arrangements entered into by persons in an arm's-length transaction.

Code Sec. 2703 only applies to option and buy-sell agreements entered into or substantially modified after October 9, 1990. However, the courts apply the same analysis to option and buy-sell agreements entered into prior to that date.[254] The requirements under Reg. §20.2031-2(h) that were in effect prior to the enactment of Section 2703 must be met for agreements entered into before and after the enactment of that regulation.

The buy-sell restrictions will be disregarded if the restrictions are not binding on the parties during the life of the decedent and after death. For example, buy-sell restrictions that require the consent of a majority of members to a transfer of membership interests will be disregarded in valuing the membership interest of a majority owner.[255] The agreements will also be disregarded if they represent a testamentary device to transfer the decedent's interest in the LLC to family members for less than full and adequate consideration.[256]

.08 Code Section 2704(a)

The IRS may use Code Sec. 2704(a) to challenge valuation discounts for LLCs.[257] Section 2704(a) provides that the lapse of a voting or liquidation right in an LLC is a gift or testamentary transfer if the individual holding such right immediately before the lapse and members of the individual's family control the entity before and after the lapse. In 2017, the IRS formally withdrew proposed regulations under Section 2704(a).

---

[254] *Estate of Fred O. Godley*, 80 TCM 158 (2000), *aff'd in part*, 89 AFTR 2d 2002-2001(e) (4th Cir. 2002).

[255] *Estate of Smith, Jr. v. United States*, 96 AFTR 2d 2005-6549 (W.D. Pa. 2005).

[256] *Estate of Fred O. Godley*, 80 TCM 158, 164 (2000), *aff'd in part*, 89 AFTR 2d 2002-2001(e) (4th Cir. 2002).

[257] *Estate of W.W. Jones v. Comm'r*, 116 TC 121 (2001); Ltr. Rul. 9802004, *citing* Reg. §25.2704-1(a)(2); TAM 9736004.

.09 Code Section 2704(b) Applicable Restrictions

The IRS may use Code Sec. 2704(b) to challenge valuation discounts for LLCs.[258] Section 2704(b)(1) provides that if a person transfers an interest in a corporation or partnership to a family member, and the transferor and family members control the entity immediately before the transfer, any applicable restrictions are disregarded in valuing the interest. The fair market value of the gifted property or property included in the taxable estate must be determined under generally applicable valuation principles as if the restriction did not exist.[259] In 2017, the IRS formally withdrew proposed regulations under Section 2704(b).

.10 Code Section 2704(b)(4) Disregarded Restrictions

The IRS may use Code Sec. 2704(b)(4) to challenge valuation discounts for LLCs.[260] Section 2704(b)(4) provides that IRS may issue regulations disregarding other restrictions in determining the value of a gifted membership interest. In 2016, the IRS issued proposed regulations stating that "disregarded restrictions" would not be considered in determining the value of a gifted membership interest to a family member[261] if the transferor and family members[262] controlled the LLC immediately before the transfer. In 2017, the IRS formally withdrew proposed regulations under Section 2704(b)(4).

.11 Gift on Creation Theory

The IRS may use the gift on creation theory to challenge valuation discounts. Under this theory, the IRS argues that a gift takes place when property is transferred to the LLC on organization of the LLC. The amount of the gift is the amount of the valuation discount for the property as a result of the transfer. Thus, if the taxpayer transfers property to an LLC, and receives back membership interests in the LLC with a lower value, the disappearing value is the amount of the gift.[263]

---

[258] *Estate of W.W. Jones v. Comm'r*, 116 TC 121 (2001); Ltr. Rul. 9802004, *citing* Reg. § 25.2704-1(a)(2); TAM 9736004.

[259] Prop. Reg. § 25.2704-2(e).

[260] *Estate of W.W. Jones v. Comm'r*, 116 TC 121 (2001); Ltr. Rul. 9802004, *citing* Reg. § 25.2704-1(a)(2); TAM 9736004.

[261] Section 2704(b) applies only to intra-family transfers. Preamble to proposed regulations under Code Sec. 2704, REG-163113-02 (2016).

[262] Family members include the member, spouse, any ancestors or legal descendants of the member or the member's spouse, brothers and sisters, and any spouse of the foregoing. Prop. Reg. § 25.2702-2(a)(1).

[263] *Estate of Jones v. Comm'r*, 116 TC 121, 123-127 (2001); *Kincaid v. United States*, 682 F.2d 1220 (5th Cir. 1982); *Trenchard v. Comm'r*, 69 TCM 2164 (1995); *Estate of Strangi v. Comm'r*, 115 TC 478, 489-491 (2000); *Estate of Mario E. Bosca*, TC Memo 1998-251 (1998); FSA 19995014.

The problem with this theory is that there may be no donee.[264] If the transferor owns 99 percent of the membership interests after the transfer, then the transferor has presumably made a gift of 99 percent of the disappearing value back to himself.[265] The courts have rejected the IRS position where all members of the LLC receive membership interests in proportion to their contributions, each member's contribution is properly reflected in his or her capital account, and each member's contribution does not confer a financial benefit on or increase the wealth of any other member.[266]

The gift on creation theory may apply if other members have a significant interest in the LLC at the time of the gift, and their interests are enhanced as a result of the gift. For example, the gift on creation theory may apply if the contributions by the donor are allocated to the capital accounts of other members.[267] The gift on creation theory may not be used if the contributions by the donor are allocated to the donor's own capital account.[268]

The IRS also uses a closely related theory that a gift occurs when the donor loses control of the LLC.[269]

.12 Cost of Dissolution and Partition

The IRS sometimes argues that the only permissible discount for a majority owner should be the cost of dissolving the LLC. The theory is that a willing buyer would ignore the restrictions in the operating agreement for the LLC if the buyer of the majority interest could vote to dissolve the LLC. This argument has been used mainly for general partnerships. Several courts have rejected the argument.[270]

If the LLC is disregarded, the IRS may still allow valuation discounts for the underlying property held by the LLC, such as a fractionalization discount for real property.[271] The IRS's official position is that the discount should be limited to the cost of partition, although it is willing to settle the cases at a higher discount based on the hazards of litigation.[272]

---

[264] *Church v. United States*, 85 AFTR 2d 2000-804, Conclusions of Law ¶ 6 (W.D. Tex. 2000).

[265] *See also* Reg. § 25.2511-2(a), which states that there is no need for an identifiable donee in order for the gift tax to apply.

[266] *Estate of Jones v. Comm'r*, 116 TC 121, 123-127 (2001); *Church v. United States*, 85 AFTR 2d 2000-804, Jurisdiction and Venue ¶ 26, Conclusions of Law ¶ 5 (W.D. Tex. 2000); *Estate of Strangi v. Comm'r*, 115 TC 478, 489-490 (2000).

[267] *Shepherd v. Comm'r*, 115 TC 376 (2000), *aff'd*, 283 F.3d 1258 (11th Cir. 2002).

[268] *Estate of Strangi v. Comm'r*, 115 TC 478, 488-490 (2000); *Estate of W.W. Jones v. Comm'r*, 116 TC 121 (2001).

[269] *See Estate of Joseph Vac*, 62 TCM 942 (1991).

[270] *LeFrak v. Comm'r*, 66 TCM 1297 (1993); *Estate of Cervin v. Comm'r*, 68 TCM 1115 (1994); *McCormick v. Comm'r*, 70 TCM 318 (1995).

[271] *Shepherd v. Comm'r*, 115 TC 376 (2000), *aff'd*, 283 F.3d 1258 (11th Cir. 2002).

[272] *BNA Daily Tax Report* No. 8, p. G-1 (Jan. 13, 2003). *See Estate of Baird v. Comm'r*, TC Memo 2001-258 (2001), which allowed a substantially higher discount for fractional interest in real estate.

One court determined that a majority owner of an LLC was entitled to a 60 percent discount because the owner would receive only a fractional interest in the property on liquidation of the LLC.[273]

.13 Code Section 2511 Indirect Gifts

The IRS may use the indirect gift theory to challenge valuation discounts. The IRS believes that there is both an indirect gift under the gift tax regulations and under the step transaction doctrine.

Indirect Gift under the Regulations

The IRS asserts that the transfer of property to an LLC, coupled with the donor's transfer of membership interests to family members or a trust for family members, constitutes an indirect gift of the property under Code Sec. 2511 and the regulations thereunder.[274] Gifts to LLCs, like gifts to corporations, are treated as indirect gifts to the members to the extent of their proportionate interests in the LLC.[275]

If the indirect gift theory applies, there is no valuation discount. The value of the gift is determined by reference to the property transferred to the LLC rather than the value of the membership interests.[276] The donor may not receive a minority discount even if the donee is a minority owner.[277]

There are two important factors in determining the applicability of the indirect gift theory. The first concerns the timing of the gift. The taxpayer should transfer the property to the LLC first, and then transfer the membership interests to the family members at least several days later. The courts have made the following rulings:

Time of gift	Applicability of indirect gift theory
Taxpayer transfers membership interests to family members first and subsequently makes a gift of property to the LLC	Indirect gift theory always applies[278]

---

[273] *Estate of Temple v. United States*, No. 9:03-CV-165 (E.D. Tex. Mar. 10, 2006). The LLC owned a winery. Under California law, there would be a distribution of the property in-kind on dissolution, since sale of LLC property is not required on liquidation of an LLC under California law.

[274] *Linton v. United States*, 104 AFTR 2d 2009-5176 (2009); *Holman v. Comm'r*, 130 TC 170 (2008). The regulations cited by the IRS include Reg. § 25.2511-1(a) and (h)(1).

[275] *Shepherd v. Comm'r*, 115 TC 376, 389 (2000), *aff'd*, 283 F.3d 1258, 1261 (11th Cir. 2002).

[276] IRS Appeals Settlement Guidelines on Family Limited Partnerships and Family Limited Liability Corporations (Issue 3), UIL 2031.01-00 (Oct. 18, 2006); *Senda v. Comm'r*, TC Memo 2004-160 (2004), *aff'd*, 433 F.3d 1044 (8th Cir. 2006).

[277] *Shepherd v. Comm'r*, 115 TC 376 (2000), *aff'd*, 283 F.3d 1258 (11th Cir. 2002); *Senda v. Comm'r*, TC Memo 2004-160 (2004), *aff'd*, 433 F.3d 1044 (8th Cir. 2006).

[278] *Shepherd v. Comm'r*, 115 TC 376 (2000), *aff'd*, 283 F.3d 1258 (11th Cir. 2002).

Taxpayer transfers property to an LLC simultaneously with the transfer of membership interests to family members	Indirect gift theory applies in some cases;[279] does not apply in other cases.[280]
Taxpayer makes gifts of membership interests after the transfer of property to the LLC	Indirect gift theory normally does not apply[281]

The second important factor in determining the applicability of the indirect gift theory concerns capital accounts. The taxpayer's contribution to the LLC must be fully reflected in the taxpayer's capital account prior to the gift.[282] A transfer of property to an LLC will be an indirect gift if the taxpayer's contribution is partially reflected in the capital accounts of the noncontributing members.[283]

There is no indirect gift if the taxpayer transfers membership interests in a single-member LLC to family members, even though the LLC is disregarded for tax purposes.[284] The gift is treated as a gift of membership interests rather than the gift of the underlying asset. The donor is entitled to the applicable minority, marketability and lack control discounts.[285]

Indirect Gift under the Step Transaction Doctrine

Alternatively, the IRS believes that there is an indirect gift under the step transaction doctrine.[286] The IRS explained this doctrine in its legal briefs as follows:[287]

> If none of the individual events occurring between the contribution of the property to the partnership and the gifts of partnership interests had any significance independent of its status as an intermediate step in the donors' plan to transfer their assets to the donees in partnership form, then the formation, funding, and transfer partnership units pursuant to an integrated plan is treated as a gift of the assets to a partnership of which the donees are the other partners.

---

[279] *Linton v. United States*, 104 AFTR 2d 2009-5176 (2009), *rev. on appeal*, 630 F.3d 1211 (9th Cir. 2011); *Senda v. Comm'r*, TC Memo 2004-160 (2004), *aff'd*, 433 F.3d 1044 (8th Cir. 2006); *LeFrak v. Comm'r*, 66 TCM 1297 (1993).

[280] *Estate of W.W. Jones v. Comm'r*; 116 TC 121 (2001) (gifts made on same day as partnership was formed).

[281] *Linton v. United States*, 630 F.3d 1211 (9th Cir. 2011); *Holman v. Comm'r*, 130 TC No. 170 (2008) (gift five days after the transfer); *Gross v. Comm'r*, 96 TCM 187 (2008) (gift 11 days after the transfer).

[282] There was no indirect gift in the following cases where the taxpayer's contribution was fully reflected in the taxpayer's capital account prior to the gift: *Estate of W.W. Jones v. Comm'r*, 116 TC 121 (2001); *Gross v. Comm'r*, TC Memo 2008-221 (2008).

[283] *Shepherd v. Comm'r*, 115 TC 376, 389 (2000), *aff'd*, 283 F.3d 1258 (11th Cir. 2002).

[284] *Suzanne J. Pierre v. Comm'r*, TC Memo 2010-106, fn. 3 (2010).

[285] *Suzanne J. Pierre v. Comm'r*, 133 TC 24 (2009); *Suzanne J. Pierre v. Comm'r*, TC Memo 2010-106 (2010).

[286] *Linton v. United States*, 630 F.3d 1211 (9th Cir. 2011); *Holman v. Comm'r*, 130 TC 170 (2008); *Gross v. Comm'r*, 96 TCM 187 (2008).

[287] *Holman v. Comm'r*, 130 TC 170 (2008); *Gross v. Comm'r*, TC Memo 2008-221 (2008), under the heading, "3. Indirect Gifts under the Step Transaction Doctrine."

The step transaction doctrine generally will not apply if the donor first funds the LLC, and then makes the gifts of membership interests at least one week later.[288]

Some courts have determined that the step transaction doctrine applies in the context of gifts of LLC membership interests if all of the elements of at least one of three tests are satisfied:[289]

- *End result test.* The end result test asks whether a series of steps was undertaken to reach a particular result, and, if so, treats the steps as one. Under this test, a taxpayer's subjective intent is "especially relevant," and the court asks "whether the taxpayer intended to reach a particular result by structuring a series of transactions in a certain way."[290] The end result test does not apply if the result sought and achieved was the gifting of LLC interests rather than the gifting of assets owned outside of an LLC.[291]

- *Interdependence test.* The interdependence test asks "whether on a reasonable interpretation of objective facts the steps were so interdependent that the legal relations created by one transaction would have been fruitless without a completion of the steps." Under this test, it may be "useful to compare the transactions in question with those we might usually expect to occur in otherwise bona fide business settings." The step transaction doctrine does not ordinarily apply under this test since the placing of assets into an LLC is an ordinary and objectively reasonable business activity that makes sense with or without any subsequent gift.[292]

- *Binding commitment test.* The binding commitment test asks whether, at the time the first step of a transaction was entered into, there was a binding commitment to take the later steps. The test only applies to transactions spanning several years. The step transaction doctrine does not ordinarily apply under this test, where the transfer of property to an LLC and the gift take place over the course of no more than a few months.[293]

.14 Code Section 2031 Estate Freezes and Buy-Sell Agreements

The IRS may use the regulations under Code Sec. 2031 to challenge buy-sell agreements that establish a fixed price for a membership interest on the death of a member.[294]

Prior to enactment of Code Sec. 2703 in 1990, restrictive agreements and buy-sell arrangements were not considered in valuing a membership interest unless the agreements met certain requirements under Estate Tax Reg. § 20.2031-2(h) and Rev.

---

[288] *Gross v. Comm'r*, 96 TCM 187 (2008); *Holman v. Comm'r*, 130 TC 170 (2008).

[289] *Linton v. United States*, 630 F.3d 1211 (9th Cir. 2011).

[290] *Linton v. United States*, 630 F.3d 1211 (9th Cir. 2011).

[291] *Linton v. United States*, 630 F.3d 1211 (9th Cir. 2011).

[292] *Linton v. United States*, 630 F.3d 1211 (9th Cir. 2011).

[293] *Linton v. United States*, 630 F.3d 1211 (9th Cir. 2011).

[294] Reg. § 20.2031-2(h).

Rul. 59-60. The courts still consider the Estate Tax Regulations independently of Code Sec. 2703 since Code Sec. 2703 merely expanded upon and incorporated certain provisions of pre-existing law.[295]

The stated price in a buy-sell agreement for transfer of a membership interest on the death of the member will control for estate tax purposes if:[296]

- The price is determinable from the agreement.
- The terms of the agreement are binding throughout life and death.
- The agreement is legally binding and enforceable.
- The agreement was entered into for bona fide business reasons and is not a testamentary substitute intended to pass on the decedent's interests for less than full and adequate consideration.

A fixed price for a membership interest under a buy-sell agreement may be disregarded in determining the value of the membership interest unless (a) the fixed price represents the fair market value of the membership interest at the time that the parties enter into the buy-sell agreement, (b) there is an outside valuation of the membership interests, (c) there is negotiation between the parties regarding the terms of the agreement, and (d) there is a bona fide business reason for entering into the agreement.[297]

The buy-sell restrictions will be disregarded under the regulations if the restrictions are not binding on the parties during the life of the decedent and after death. For example, buy-sell restrictions that require the consent of a majority of members to a transfer of membership interests will be disregarded in valuing the membership interests of a majority owner.[298]

.15 Code Section 2035

The IRS may use Code Sec. 2035 to challenge valuation discounts.[299] Code Sec. 2035 provides that a decedent's gross estate includes the value of any property transferred or relinquished by the decedent within three years prior to death that would have been included in the decedent's estate under Code Sec. 2036(a) or 2038 if the transfer had not been made.

For example, the decedent's gross estate includes the value of an insurance policy that the decedent transferred to an LLC within three years prior to death. The transfer of the policy to the LLC in exchange for a membership interest is not a bona fide sale or exchange for adequate consideration under the Section 2035 exception. The marital deduction does not apply unless the surviving spouse is the sole owner of a single-member LLC.[300]

---

[295] *See Estate of Smith, Jr. v. United States,* 96 AFTR 2d 2005-6549 (W.D. Pa. 2005).

[296] Reg. § 20.2031-2(h); *True v. Comm'r,* 390 F.3d 1210 (10th Cir. 2004).

[297] *True v. Comm'r,* 390 F.3d 1210 (10th Cir. 2004).

[298] *Estate of Smith, Jr. v. United States,* 96 AFTR 2d 2005-6549 (W.D. Pa. 2005).

[299] *Estate of Anna Mirowski v. Comm'r,* TC Memo 2008-74 (2008); *Estate of Bongard v. Comm'r,* 124 TC 95 (2005).

[300] TAM 200432015.

Code Sec. 2035 does not apply if the court determines that the decedent did not retain any powers under Code Sec. 2036(a) or 2038 at any time within three years prior to death.[301]

In *Estate of Powell*,[302] the decedent transferred cash and securities to a family limited partnership approximately one week prior to death. The court determined that the assets transferred to the partnership were includable in the estate under either (i) Section 2036(a)(2) because there was an implied agreement that the decedent retained possession or enjoyment of the transferred property or the right to income from that property until death, or (ii) Section 2035(a) because the decedent relinquished the right to those assets within three years prior to death. The exception for a bona fide sale for adequate and full consideration did not apply to the transfer in exchange for partnership interests because the partnership served no valid business purpose. In either case, the amount includable in the decedent's estate would be limited under Section 2043(a) to the amount by which the transfer depleted the decedent's estate (fair market value at the time of death of the cash and securities transferred to the partnership over the value of the limited partnership interest received in exchange for those assets). Thus, the decedent's estate included the amount of any discounts applicable in valuing the 99 percent limited partner interest issued in exchange for the cash and securities.

.16 Recharacterization as Trust

The IRS sometimes attempts to recharacterize an LLC or partnership as a trust if the taxpayer contributes stocks, bonds and other nonoperating assets to an LLC. Under this argument, an interest in an LLC or partnership is more analogous to an interest in a trust than to an interest in an operating business, and should be valued as such for federal estate and gift tax purposes. This means that there should be little or no minority and marketability discounts. The IRS initially raised this argument at the audit level in the *Holeman* case,[303] but then withdrew the argument at the hearing.

.17 Single-Member Disregarded LLC Theory

The IRS sometimes argues that there should be no lack of control or lack of marketability discounts for a single-member disregarded LLC. Since the LLC is disregarded under the check-the-box regulations, the transfers of interests in the LLC should instead be treated as transfers of a proportionate share of LLC assets. One court rejected this argument, and determined that the transfers of an interest in a

---

[301] *Estate of Anna Mirowski v. Comm'r*, TC Memo 2008-74 (2008); *Estate of Bongard v. Comm'r*, 124 TC 95 (2005).

[302] *Estate of Nancy H. Powell v. Comm'r*, 148 TC No. 18 (2017).

[303] *Holman v. Comm'r*, 130 TC 170 (2008).

single-member disregarded LLC should be valued as a transfer of an interest in the LLC with the appropriate discounts.[304]

¶2105 TYPES OF VALUATION DISCOUNTS

If the court respects the LLC, then the court will value the membership interests rather than the underlying value of the LLC assets. The courts usually start with the value of the underlying assets, and then discount that value based on the nature of the LLC, restrictions in the operating agreement,[305] and various other factors. The major valuation discounts are as follows:

.01 Minority Discount

The most common type of valuation discount is the minority discount. There are different rules for estate and gift tax purposes.

Gift Taxes

A donor may take a minority discount for the gift of a membership interest if (a) the donor is a minority owner in the LLC, or (b) the donee is a minority owner in the LLC after receipt of the gift. For example, a majority owner is entitled to a minority discount for gifts of minority interests to family members and other persons. The rule applies even if the donor owned a majority interest in the LLC before and after the transfer.[306] The gift tax is imposed on the value of the property received by the donee rather than the value of the property owned by the donor prior to the gift.

Estate Taxes

The estate of a minority owner in an LLC may take a valuation discount for the membership interests owned by the deceased member.[307] The estate may not take a minority discount if the deceased member owned a majority interest in the LLC, even if all of the beneficiaries receive a minority interest. All of the membership units owned by the decedent are aggregated for estate tax purposes.[308]

A 50 percent ownership interest in an LLC may or may not be entitled to a minority discount, based on all facts and circumstances.[309]

---

[304] *Suzanne J. Pierre v. Comm'r*, 133 TC 24 (2009).

[305] *Estate of Fred O. Godley*, 80 TCM 158 (2000), *aff'd in part*, 89 AFTR 2d 2002-2001(e) (4th Cir. 2002).

[306] Rev. Rul. 93-12, 1993-1 CB 202; TAM 9449001; TAM 9436005; *Estate of Bright v. United States*, 658 F.2d 999 (5th Cir. 1981); *Estate of Andrews v. Comm'r*, 79 TC 938 (1982).

[307] *See Estate of Gallagher*, TC Memo 2011-148 (2011), which approved a 23 percent minority discount for membership interests in an LLC.

[308] *Ahmanson Foundation v. United States*, 674 F.2d 761 (9th Cir. 1981).

[309] *Estate of Fred O. Godley*, 80 TCM 158 (2000), *aff'd in part*, 89 AFTR 2d 2002-2001(e) (4th Cir. 2002).

A decedent's estate is entitled to a minority discount for a minority interest in an LLC whose sole asset is a one percent general partnership interest in a family limited partnership.[310]

.02 Marketability, Liquidity, and Lack of Control Discounts

The second major type of valuation discount is the marketability,[311] liquidity, and lack of control discount. These discounts are based on the assumption that the indirect ownership of property through an LLC is worth less than the direct ownership of property outside an LLC. The court may allow a combined discount for lack of marketability, lack of liquidity, and lack of control without specifying the exact amount of each discount.[312] Other courts will specify the amount of each discount.[313]

For example, the courts may allow discounts in the following cases:

- A member may receive a lack of control discount if the member is not allowed to participate in management of the LLC.[314]
- A minority member may receive a marketability and liquidity discount because it is much more difficult for a member to sell a minority membership interest in an LLC. A minority member usually does not have the right to force a liquidation of the LLC or to receive back the member's capital contribution on withdrawal from the LLC. The IRS often challenges a marketability discount for a majority owner who has a right to liquidate an LLC.[315] Several courts have allowed marketability discounts even where the majority owner has the right to liquidate the entity.[316]
- A member may receive a small discount for an onerous right of first refusal provision in the operating agreement.[317]
- One court allowed a 20 percent marketability discount because (a) there was no ready market for the partnership interests, (b) a purchaser would be subject to the requirements of the operating agreement that made one of the family members the managing partner, and (c) there was a 60-day right of first refusal provision that forced a period of illiquidity on every selling partner.[318]

---

[310] *See also Kelley v. Comm'r*, TC Memo 2005-236 (2005).

[311] *See Estate of Gallagher*, TC Memo 2011-148 (2011), which approved a 31 percent marketability discount for membership interests in an LLC.

[312] *Estate of Barudin*, TC Memo 1996-395 (1996).

[313] *Adams v. United States*, 2001-2 USTC ¶ 60,379 (D.C. Tex. 2000); *Kelley v. Comm'r*, TC Memo 2005-236 (2005).

[314] *McCormick v. Comm'r*, 70 TCM 318 (1995).

[315] *See Ltr. Rul. 7953001; Estate of Jephson v. Comm'r*, 87 TC 297 (1986).

[316] *Estate of Curry v. United States*, 706 F.2d ¶424 (7th Cir. 1983); *Von Hagke v. United States*, 79-1 USTC ¶ 13,290 (E.D. Wis. 1979); *Estate of Bennett v. Comm'r*, 65 TCM 1816 (1993); *Estate of Ford v. Comm'r*, 66 TCM 1507 (1993); *Estate of Folks v. Comm'r*, 43 TCM 427 (1982).

[317] *Estate of W.W. Jones v. Comm'r*, 116 TC 121 (2001).

[318] *Estate of Fred O. Godley*, 80 TCM 158 (2000), *aff'd in part*, 89 AFTR 2d 2002-2001(e) (4th Cir. 2002).

.03 Built-In Gains Discount

A number of courts have allowed a valuation discount for estate[319] and gift tax[320] purposes for the built-in capital gains of a corporation. The theory is that a willing buyer would pay less for the company if the buyer would have to pay a capital gains tax on sale of the appreciated assets in the corporation.

The courts have not allowed a built-in capital gains discount for an LLC.[321] The reason is that a buyer can avoid the tax on the built-in gains if the LLC makes an election to adjust the basis of its assets under Code Sec. 754. If this election is in effect at the time of the purchase, then the inside basis of the LLC's assets is increased to match the buyer's cost basis in the purchased membership units. The basis adjustment benefits only the purchasing member. Thus, a hypothetical willing buyer and seller would not reduce the purchase price based on a reduction for built-in capital gains because both parties could influence the manager of the LLC to make a Code Sec. 754 election, thereby eliminating any capital gains for the buyer and obtaining the highest sales price for the seller.[322]

.04 Assignee Interest Discount

A taxpayer may claim an assignee discount for the membership interest if the donee is not admitted as a full member of the LLC. The theory is that an assignee does not have the same rights to force a liquidation of the LLC.[323] The uncertainties regarding the legal rights of the assignee under state law may further depress the price that the willing buyer would pay for the assignee interest.[324] Some courts have rejected the assignee discount.[325] No assignee discount is permitted if the donee or beneficiary automatically becomes a full member of the LLC.[326]

.05 Portfolio Discount

The taxpayer is entitled to a portfolio discount if the LLC owns two or more business operations or types of assets, the combination of which would be unattractive to a buyer. However, the taxpayer must clearly demonstrate that the LLC's mix

---

[319] *Estate of Welch v. Comm'r*, 85 AFTR 2d ¶ 2000-534 (8th Cir. 2000).

[320] *Eisenberg, Irene v. Comm'r*, 155 F.3d 50 (2d Cir. 1998), *acq.* 1999-4 IRB 4; *Estate of Davis v. Comm'r*, 110 TC 530 (1998).

[321] *Estate of W.W. Jones v. Comm'r*, 116 TC 121 (2001); *BNA Daily Tax Report* No. 8, p. G-1 (Jan. 13, 2003).

[322] *Estate of W.W. Jones v. Comm'r*, 116 TC 121 (2001).

[323] *Estate of Ethel S. Nowell*, 77 TCM 1239 (Issue 2) (1999); *Adams v. United States*, 283 F.3d 383 (5th Cir. 2000).

[324] *Adams v. United States*, 283 F.3d 383 (5th Cir. 2000). However, on remand, the lower court refused to apply an additional assignee interest discount because the discount already been considered as part of the other valuation discounts.

[325] *Kerr v. Comm'r*, 113 TC 499 (1999), *aff'd*, 292 F.3d 490 (5th Cir. 2002).

[326] *Estate of Ethel S. Nowell*, 77 TCM 1239 (Issue 2) (1999).

of assets would be unattractive to a buyer. Otherwise, the court will not allow a portfolio discount.[327]

.06 LLC as General Partner of Limited Partnership

A general partner of a limited partnership is liable for the debts and other obligations of the limited partnership under state law. An LLC or corporation is frequently used as the general partner of a limited partnership so that the individuals who own the partnership will not be personally liable.

A taxpayer is entitled to the applicable minority and marketability discounts for an interest in an LLC that is the sole general partner in a family limited partnership.[328] The valuation discounts are applied to the assets owned by the limited partnership.

¶ 2106 SWING VOTE PREMIUM

In 1994, the IRS determined that a swing-vote premium was applicable to the valuation of a block of stock transferred to a family member if the block of stock enabled the donee to join with another family member to form a majority interest.[329] In that ruling, the 100 percent shareholder of a corporation transferred a 30 percent block of stock to each of his three children. The taxpayer claimed a 25 percent discount for each gift. The IRS reduced this discount to reflect the fact that each donee had the ability to combine with another donee to obtain majority control.

The court rejected the IRS position in *Estate of Davis*.[330] In that case, the taxpayer transferred a 25.77 percent block of stock to two of his family members. The IRS attempted to reduce the valuation discount claimed by the taxpayer because the two donees could combine to obtain majority control. The court determined that the IRS gave undue weight to this argument.

¶ 2107 APPRAISALS

The appraisal of the membership interest and the assets held by the LLC is one of the most important factors in determining the appropriate estate or gift tax value.[331] The IRS often attempts to discredit the taxpayer's appraisals,[332] even without initially

---

[327] *Knight v. Comm'r*, 115 TC 506, 516-517 (2000). *See also Adams v. United States*, 2001-2 USTC ¶ 60,379 (D.C. Tex. 2000), in which the court stated that the estate was entitled to determination regarding the appropriate discount for ownership by the partnership of an undesirable mix of assets.

[328] *Kelley v. Comm'r*, TC Memo 2005-236 (2005).

[329] TAM 9436005.

[330] *Estate of Davis v. Comm'r*, 110 TC 530 (1998).

[331] *BNA Daily Tax Report* No. 8, p. G-1 (Jan. 13, 2003). *See also Estate of Gallagher*, TC Memo 2011-148 (2011) in which the court discussed detailed guidelines for valuing a membership interest in an LLC.

[332] *Kelly v. Comm'r*, TC Memo 2005-236 (2005); *Estate of Helen A. Deputy v. Comm'r*, TC Memo 2003-176 (2003); *Holman v. Comm'r*, 130 TC 170 (2008).

obtaining its own independent appraisal.[333] The IRS frequently claims that the taxpayer's appraisal understates the actual value of the membership interest. The IRS may also challenge the appraiser's valuation of the underlying LLC assets.[334]

The courts will first consider the qualifications of the appraiser and the completeness of the appraisal.[335] For gift tax purposes, the taxpayer should obtain a qualified appraisal[336] by a qualified appraiser.[337] Alternatively, the donor may disclose the information required under the gift tax regulations.[338]

The appraiser should base the appraisal on companies that are comparable to the LLC.[339] For LLCs and limited partnerships, the IRS prefers comparisons to closed-end mutual funds, particularly to funds that hold securities comparable to those held in the LLC or family limited partnership.[340] The appraiser must show how the various discount factors apply to the LLC. For example, if the appraiser makes a list of factors that affect the discount, the appraiser must explain how those factors account for the discount claimed for the LLC.[341]

With respect to the valuation of real estate, the IRS prefers the use of an appraiser located in the same geographic area as the property, clear maps showing comparable properties, and rental rates comparable for income producing properties. For businesses, the IRS recommends five years of income statements and balance sheets, including footnotes.[342]

¶2108 HOME OWNERSHIP

.01 Exclusion of Gain on Sale of Property

A taxpayer who owns a home through a single-member disregarded LLC may exclude up to $250,000 of gain on sale of the home if the taxpayer meets the requirements under Code Sec. 121.[343]

The regulations do not specifically address home ownership through an LLC owned by spouses or that is otherwise classified as a partnership. The IRS at one time ruled that a taxpayer who owned a home through an LLC would be treated as the owner of the home under Code Sec. 121.[344] The taxpayer and his spouse could

---

[333] *Estate of Fred O. Godley*, 80 TCM 158, 165 (2000), *aff'd in part*, 89 AFTR 2d 2002-2001(e) (4th Cir. 2002).

[334] *Estate of F. Wallace hanger v. Comm'r*, TC Memo 2006-232 (2006).

[335] *Estate of Fred O. Godley*, 80 TCM 158 (2000), *aff'd in part*, 89 AFTR 2d 2002-2001(e) (4th Cir. 2002).

[336] Reg. § 301.6501(c)-1(f)(3)(ii).

[337] Reg. § 301.6501(c)-1(f)(3)(i).

[338] Reg. § 301.6501(c)-1(f)(2)(iv).

[339] *Knight v. Comm'r*, 115 TC 506 (2000).

[340] *BNA Daily Tax Report* No. 8, p. G-1 (Jan. 13, 2003); *Holman v. Comm'r*, 130 TC 170 (2008).

[341] *Knight v. Comm'r*, 115 TC 506 (2000); *Holman v. Comm'r*, 130 TC 170 (2008).

[342] *BNA Daily Tax Report* No. 8, p. G-1 (Jan. 13, 2003).

[343] Reg. § 1.121-1(c)(3)(ii).

[344] Ltr. Rul. 200004022.

exclude up to $500,000 of gain on sale of the house if the house was not used in a trade or business and the taxpayer used the home as a principal residence (or met the ownership test for at least two out of five years ending on the date of sale). The IRS later revoked the ruling.[345]

Home ownership through an LLC is not widespread because lenders are reluctant to make loans or refinance loans on homes owned by an LLC. The lenders must carry the loans in their own portfolio. They are not able to sell loans in the after-market.[346]

.02 Estate Taxes

The value of the house may be included in the taxpayer's gross estate if the taxpayer continues to live in the house after the transfer to the LLC without paying fair rent to the LLC.[347] The reason is that the gross estate includes all property that the taxpayer transfers during his or her lifetime if the taxpayer retains possession or enjoyment of the property for life, and if the transfer is not a bona fide sale for adequate and full consideration.[348]

¶ 2109 CODE SECTION 704(e) FAMILY PARTNERSHIPS

A taxpayer who makes a gift of a membership interest to a family member may be taxed on the donee's distributive share of income under Code Sec. 704(e). Code Sec. 704(e) is designed to prevent a taxpayer from assigning income attributable to personal services to a family member in a lower income tax bracket.

The requirements under Code Sec. 704(e) are discussed in Chapter 8.[349]

¶ 2110 SECTION 6166 DEFERRAL OF ESTATE TAX PAYMENTS

An estate may defer the payment of estate taxes if at least 35 percent of the estate consists of an interest in a closely held business. An LLC is one of the types of entities for which an estate may make a Section 6166 deferral.[350] If the LLC is classified as a partnership, the estate must satisfy the partnership interest tests of Code Sec. 6166(b)(1)(B) and, if more than one business is involved in the Section 6166 election, the 20 percent value test of Code Sec. 6166(c).

The sale or disposition of 50 percent or more of the ownership interests in a closely held business will terminate the extension to pay and accelerate the payment of taxes. The owners' transfer of their interest in a closely held business to an LLC in

---

[345] Ltr. Rul. 200119014; CCA 200029046.

[346] *Estate of Helen A. Deputy v. Comm'r*, TC Memo 2003-176 (2003).

[347] *Wuebker*, 85 AFTR 2d ¶ 2000-496 (6th Cir. 2000); *Estate of Reichardt*, 114 TC 144 (2000).

[348] Code Sec. 2036(a).

[349] *See* ¶ 806 *supra*.

[350] Rev. Rul. 2006-34, 2006-1 CB 1172; Ltr. Rul. 200321006.

exchange for membership interests does not constitute a disposition or result in termination of the estate tax deferral.[351]

¶2111 DISCLAIMERS

A beneficiary of an estate may disclaim an interest in an LLC even though the person holds an interest in the LLC and is a manager of the LLC.[352] If the beneficiary makes a qualified disclaimer, the interest in the LLC will be treated as passing to the person who receives the membership interest rather than the named beneficiary for estate tax purposes.

¶2112 DOLLAR GIFT FORMULA AND REALLOCATION CLAUSES

A taxpayer may make gifts and bequests of LLC membership interests using a dollar formula clause for the membership interests assigned to non-charitable beneficiaries with the remainder to charitable beneficiaries. The purpose of such clauses is to avoid federal estate and gift taxes if the IRS at a later date determines that the LLC membership interests were under-valued for estate or gift tax purposes.[353] The dollar formula and reallocation clauses typically work as follows:

- The taxpayer makes a gift or bequest of LLC membership interests equal to a dollar amount as finally determined for federal estate or gift tax purposes. This dollar amount is normally under the unified credit amount, so that no estate or gift taxes will be due as a result of the gift or bequest.
- An appraiser determines the value of the membership interests. Based on the appraisal, membership interests equal to the dollar formula amount are allocated to the noncharitable beneficiaries. The remaining membership interests are transferred to charitable beneficiaries.
- If the IRS determines that the membership interests were under-valued by the appraiser, then more membership interests are reallocated to the charitable beneficiaries and taken away from the noncharitable beneficiaries, so that no estate and gift taxes will be due.

¶2113 SECTION 754 ELECTION

.01 Elective Basis Adjustment

An LLC may make an election under Code Sec. 754 to adjust the basis of its assets under Code Sec. 743(b) on the death of a member.[354] The basis of LLC assets is

---

[351] Ltr. Ruls. 201129020, 200129019, 201129018, 201129016.

[352] Ltr. Rul. 200406038.

[353] *Estate of Anne Y. Petter v. Comm'r*, 108 AFTR 2d 2011 (9th Cir. 2011).

[354] Code Sec. 743(a).

adjusted by the amount of basis adjustment to the LLC membership interest as a result of death. The basis adjustment may be upward or downward depending on the fair market value of the membership interest on the date of death. The basis adjustment benefits only the estate and transferees of a deceased member.

If there is a positive basis adjustment as a result of a step-up in basis of the membership interest, the basis adjustment is shown as a separate asset on the books of the LLC, and is separately depreciated for the benefit of the transferee member.

If an LLC makes a Section 754 election, a transferee that acquires the membership interest on death must notify the LLC in writing within one year of the death of the deceased member. The written notice to the LLC must be signed under penalty of perjury and must include the names and addresses of the deceased member and the transferee, the taxpayer identification numbers of the deceased member and the transferee, the relationship (if any) between the transferee and the transferor, the deceased member's date of death, the date on which the transferee became the owner of the membership interest, the fair market value of the membership interest on the applicable valuation date as set forth in Code Sec. 1014, and the manner in which the fair market value of the membership interest was determined.[355]

Normally, it is advisable for an LLC to make a Section 754 election if the LLC assets have appreciated in value. However, this is not always the case because the tax preparers for the estate of a deceased member often take valuation discounts for the membership interest in order to reduce the taxable estate. If the fair market value of the membership interest as so determined is less than the estate's share of the LLC's inside basis in its assets, then the LLC must step-down the basis of such assets to the lower fair market value of the membership interest.

.02 Mandatory Basis Adjustment

An LLC must make a mandatory basis adjustment to its assets after a transfer of a membership interest (including transfers at death), if the LLC has "substantial built-in-loss" after the death or transfer.[356] An LLC has a substantial built-in-loss if, immediately after the transfer or death, the LLC's adjusted basis in his property exceeds the fair market value of LLC property by more than $250,000.[357]

The LLC must make the downward basis adjustment only with respect to the interest of the deceased member. The amount of the downward basis adjustment is equal to the difference between the transferee member's proportionate share of the adjusted basis of LLC property and the transferee's basis in the membership interest. Thus, the estate of the deceased member or transferees of the membership interest would recognize no loss if the LLC sold the asset for fair market value immediately after the death of the member.

---

[355] Reg. § 1.743-1(k)(2)(ii).
[356] Code Sec. 743(b).
[357] Code Sec. 743(d).

EXAMPLE 21-3

An LLC has assets with an adjusted basis of $1 million. The fair market value of the assets declined to $700,000. Member A, who owns a ten percent interest in the LLC, dies. The LLC must make a mandatory downward basis adjustment because the basis of its assets exceeds the fair market value of its assets by more than $250,000. The downward basis adjustment is $30,000 equal to Member A's share of the LLC's basis in its assets. The downward basis adjustment applies only to the transferees of the deceased member. The downward basis adjustment will increase their gain or reduce their losses by $30,000 on their future sale of the property.

22

Federal and State Filing Requirements

¶ 2201 FEDERAL FORMS

.01 *Form 1065 Partnership Return*

An LLC that is classified as a partnership for federal tax purposes must file a partnership return on IRS Form 1065.[1] The form must be filed even if the LLC's principal place of business is located outside of the United States or if all of its members are nonresident aliens. However, an LLC is not required to file a return in the following cases:

- The LLC has no income, deductions, or credits for federal income tax purposes.[2]
- The LLC is a foreign LLC that does not engage in a U.S. trade or business or have income from sources within the United States.[3]
- The LLC is a foreign LLC that has income from sources within the United States, but is exempt from the filing requirements under IRS regulations.[4]

Form 1065 is an information return. It is used to report information about the LLC and each member's distributive share of income, deductions, gains, losses, and credits from the operation of the LLC. The LLC does not pay tax on this income.[5] Instead, all of the income, losses, and deductions pass through to the members.

Effective for tax years after 2015, a domestic LLC must file IRS Form 1065 by the 15th day of the third month following the close of its tax year.[6] An LLC whose members are all nonresident aliens must file the return by the 15th day of the sixth month following the close of the tax year.[7]

One member of the LLC must sign the return.[8] The member need not be a manager or officer.

The statute of limitations for the IRS to assess additional taxes with respect to an LLC return is discussed at ¶ 2811.

---

[1] Code Sec. 6031(a); Reg. § 1.6031(a)-1(a)(1).

[2] Reg. § 1.6031(a)-1(a)(3).

[3] Code Sec. 6031(e); Reg. § 1.6031(a)-1(b).

[4] *See* ¶ 1806 *supra,* for a discussion of the exceptions.

[5] Code Sec. 701.

[6] Code Sec. 6072(b); Reg. § 1.6031(a)-1(e)(2).

[7] Code Sec. 6072(c).

[8] *See* Instructions to Form 1065.

.02 Schedules K and K-1

An LLC uses Schedule K-1 to report each member's share of income, credits, deductions, and losses.[9] The members then report these items on their income tax returns. The LLC must separately state for each member on Schedule K-1 the members' distributive shares of the following items, whether or not they are actually distributed:[10]

- Ordinary income or loss from trade or business activities.
- Net income or loss from rental real estate activities.
- Net income or loss from other rental activities.
- Gains and losses from sales or exchanges of capital assets.
- Gains and losses from sales or exchanges of property described in Section 1231 of the Internal Revenue Code.
- Charitable contributions.
- Dividends passed through to corporate members that qualify for the dividends received deduction.
- Taxes paid to foreign countries and to possessions of the United States.[11]
- Other items of income, gain, loss, deduction, or credit to the extent provided in IRS regulations. The IRS requires separate itemization of such items as nonbusiness expenses, intangible drilling and development costs, and soil and water conservation expenditures.

Schedule K of Form 1065 is a summary schedule of all the members' shares of LLC income, credits, and deductions. Schedule K-1 shows each member's separate share. The LLC must attach a copy of each Schedule K-1 to the Form 1065 that is filed with the IRS. A copy of Schedule K-1 must be furnished to each member. If a membership interest is held by a nominee on behalf of another person, the LLC may be required to furnish Schedule K-1 to the nominee.[12]

The LLC must give a Schedule K-1 to each member who was a member in the LLC at any time during the year. It must provide the form to each member on or before the date on which the LLC must file its return, determined with regard to extensions.[13]

The LLC must prepare a separate Schedule K-1 for a husband and a wife if the husband and the wife each have an interest in the LLC. If the husband and the wife hold the membership interest together, one Schedule K-1 may be prepared if the two are considered to be one member.

A member which holds different types of interests in the LLC (e.g., managing member/general partner interest and investor member/limited partner interest) is

---

[9] The rules governing LLC statements to members and nominees are set forth in Code Sec. 6031(b) and Reg. § 301.7701-3(c)(2).

[10] Code Secs. 702(a), 703(a)(1).

[11] *See* Code Sec. 901.

[12] Temp. Reg. §§ 1.6031(b)-1T, 1.6031(c)-1T.

[13] Temp. Reg. § 1.6031(b)-1T(b).

provided only one Schedule K-1 which contains the member's combined tax attributes for the tax year. The details of tax attributes allocated to each type of interest should be provided in supplemental schedules to the member.

Generally, the members must report LLC items shown on Schedule K-1 and any attached schedules in the same way that the LLC treated the items on its return.

An LLC may provide an electronic Schedule K-1 to members of an LLC that is classified as a partnership if the member affirmatively consents in advance.[14] The LLC must inform the members that they have the option of receiving the Schedule K-1 in paper and that they have the option to withdraw their consent. The Schedules K-1 must include all of the information that would be included if sent in paper format.

LLCs that are classified as partnerships that have foreign member partners may also be required to attach certain forms and supplemental information in certain circumstances. See Chapter 19 for a detailed discussion.

.03 Separate Statement for Each Activity

An LLC must provide each member with a separate statement of income, expenses, deductions and credits for each activity engaged in by the LLC. The member must use the separate statement to compute at-risk and passive loss deduction limits.[15]

If the member is subject to the at-risk rules for any activity, the member must check the box on the appropriate line in Schedule E, Part II, column (e), and use Form 6198 to compute the amount of any deductible loss. If the activity is nonpassive, the member must enter any deductible loss from Form 6198 on the appropriate line of Schedule E, Part II, column (h).[16]

If the member has passive activity losses, the member must in most cases complete Form 8582 to compute the amount of allowable loss to enter in Schedule E, Part II, column (f). If the member has passive activity income, the member must complete Schedule E, Part II, column (g) for that activity. If the member has nonpassive income or losses, the member must complete Schedule E, Part II, columns (h) through (j) as appropriate.[17]

.04 Extension Requests

For tax years after 2015, an LLC may obtain an automatic six-month extension by filing Form 7004, Application for Automatic Extension of Time to File Certain Business Income Tax, Information, and Other Returns.[18] The extended due date is

---

[14] Rev. Proc. 2012-17, 2012-1 CB 453.

[15] *See* Instructions to Form 1040, under the heading, "Part II, Income or Loss from Partnerships and S Corporations."

[16] *Id.*

[17] *Id.*

[18] Highway Trust Fund Extension Law, § 2006(b); Reg. § 1.6081-2(a)(1), (b)(1).

September 15 for a calendar year LLC classified as a partnership.[19] An LLC does not need to sign the extension request or provide an explanation for requesting the extension. The IRS will not issue a confirmation of receipt of the request. It will issue a response only if the extension request is denied.

An LLC may not obtain an additional extension of time to file a partnership return.[20]

The automatic extension of time for filing a partnership return does not extend the time for filing a member's income tax return or the time for payment of any tax due on the member's income tax return.[21]

.05 Form 8832 Classification Election

The default classification rules are designed to provide most LLCs with the classification that they would likely choose without requiring them to file an election. For example, most domestic LLCs that have two or more members are automatically classified as partnerships for federal tax purposes, while most domestic LLCs that have only one member are classified as disregarded entities. Partnership classification is normally the desired tax classification. It permits a single tax at the member level. All items of income, gain, loss, credit, and deduction of the LLC pass through to and are taxed at the member level. Partnership (for multi-member LLCs) or disregarded entity (for single-member LLCs) classification is automatic without the need for a filing for alternate classification.

In certain exceptional cases, an LLC may not want to be classified under the default rules. In that event, the LLC may file Form 8832 to elect a different classification permitted by the IRS regulations.

An LLC should file the election on Form 8832 only in the following three cases:[22]

1. The LLC wants initially to be classified differently than under the default rules.

2. The LLC wants to change its previous classification.

3. There is doubt about the proper classification.

Some states require an LLC to attach a copy of Form 8832 to the state information return. In Hawaii, for example, an LLC formed after January 1, 1997, must attach a copy of that form to the LLC's first Hawaii income tax return or information return.[23]

---

[19] IR-2017-148 (Sept. 8, 2017).

[20] Reg. § 1.6081-2(a)(1).

[21] Reg. § 1.6081-2(e).

[22] *See* ¶ 504 *supra* for discussion of the procedures for making the election.

[23] Tax Information Release No. 97-4, Hawaii Department of Taxation (Aug. 4, 1997).

.06 Domestic Single-Member LLCs

Domestic single-member LLCs that are classified as disregarded entities and that are owned by individuals must file federal tax returns as sole proprietors.[24] The owner of the LLC must report income and expenses of the LLC on the appropriate schedule or form with their individual income tax return. For example, if the LLC's business activity is an ordinary trade or business, the individual would report the LLC's income and deductions on Form 1040, Schedule C; if the LLC's business is rental real estate, a Form 1040, Schedule E should be prepared.

Domestic single-member LLCs which are wholly owned by a C corporation, S corporation or partnership must report the LLC's income and deductions on its income tax return (Form 1120, Form 1120S, or Form 1065, respectively) as if the LLC were simply a division of the corporation or partnership.

Domestic single-member LLCs that are classified as corporations must file corporate tax returns.

.07 Magnetic Media Filings

An LLC must file a partnership return and Schedules K-1 on magnetic media if it has 200 or more members in 2018, 150 or more members in 2019, 100 or more members in 2020, 50 or more members in 2021, and 20 or more members thereafter.[25] The number of members is determined by counting the number of members over the LLC tax year. It does not matter that there were fewer than the threshold number of members on any particular day during the tax year or that the members were not members for the full tax year.

.08 Section 6041 Reporting Requirements

All persons engaged in a trade or business who make payments of $600 or more to an LLC are required to report the payments to the IRS. There is an exception if the LLC is classified as a corporation, or is a partnership all of whose members are corporations.[26]

---

[24] IRS Publication 334, Tax Guide for Small Businesses; Reg. § 301.7701-2(a).

[25] Code Sec. 6025(e)(5); Reg. § 301.6011-3(a). The IRS may waive the electronic filing requirement in the case of hardship. Reg. § 301.6011-3(b). IRS Publication 1524 explains how LLCs must file returns electronically.

[26] CCA 201447025.

.09 Penalties for Failure to File

An LLC that fails to file a complete return on a timely basis is subject to a penalty unless the failure is due to reasonable cause.[27] In 2018,[28] the penalty is $200 per month[29] per member for up to 12 months[30] for each person who was a member at any time during the tax year. The period of assessment for taxes attributable to LLC items remains open indefinitely if the LLC fails to file a return.[31] The failure to file may result in a disallowance of deductions, losses and credits flowing through to the members.[32]

The LLC is subject to penalties for failure to furnish Schedule K-1 to the members, failure to include all of the required information, or inclusion of incorrect information.[33] The penalty is $100 for each statement with respect to which a failure occurs. The maximum penalty is $1.5 million for all such failures during the calendar year. If the LLC intentionally disregards the requirement to report the information on Schedule K-1, each $100 penalty is increased to $250, or if greater, ten percent of the aggregate amount of items required to be reported, and the $1.5 million maximum penalty does not apply.

There may be additional penalties for failure to file specific forms related to the LLC, including:

- Form 8865, Return of U.S. Person with Respect to Certain Foreign Partnerships.
- Form 8938, Statement of Specified Foreign Financial Assets.
- Form 8804, Annual Return for Partnership Withholding Tax (Section 1446).

¶ 2202 STATE FORMS

There are four types of state filings: (1) the tax return for the LLC; (2) the tax returns for the resident and nonresident members; (3) the composite return for the nonresident members; and (4) the annual report for the LLC.

.01 State Tax Returns for LLC

The state tax return is often similar to the federal tax return. If the LLC is classified as a partnership, the state return is normally an information return. Some states do not require a state return if all members of the LLC are residents of the state.

---

[27] Code Sec. 6698; Reg. § 1.6031(a)-1(a)(4).
[28] Rev. Proc. 2017-58, 2017-45 IRB 489.
[29] Code Sec. 6698(b)(1).
[30] Code Sec. 6698(a)(2).
[31] Code Sec. 6229(a).
[32] Code Sec. 6231(f).
[33] Code Sec. 6722.

In that event, members report on a state tax return their allocable shares of income as set forth on the federal Schedule K-1.

The LLC state tax return is used to take account of state adjustments. It is also used to apportion income of the LLC that has business or sources of income within and outside the state. Nonresident members are taxed only on income from sources within the state and from a trade or business carried on within the state. The tax filings and returns for each state are discussed in detail in Chapter 23. The following table shows the tax filings that are required in each state and the District of Columbia for LLCs that are classified as partnerships as well as the agency from which to obtain the forms.[34]

The following tables assume that the federal classification of the LLC is partnership. If the LLC is classified as an entity type other than partnership for federal income tax purposes, use the state tables for the federal entity classification type of the LLC.

State	State Forms Required	Due Date of Return/ E-File Option	Revenue Departments
Alabama	•Form 65, Partnership/ Limited Liability Company Return of Income A copy of the federal partnership return on Form 1065 must be attached to the state return •Form BPT-IN, Initial Business Privilege Tax Return Form PPT, Alabama Business Privilege Tax Return and Annual Report •PPT, Alabama Business Privilege Tax Return and Annual Report	Form 65 must be filed on or before the 15th day of the third month following the close of the fiscal year (March 15 for calendar year LLCs). Form PPT must be filed no later than three and a half months after the beginning of the LLC's tax year (April 15 for calendar year LLCs). The return for a single-member disregarded LLCs is due no later than the time that its member is required to file.	Alabama Department of Revenue Individual and Corporate Tax Division Pass Through Entity Unit P.O. Box 327441 Montgomery, AL 36132-7441 Alabama Department of Revenue Business Privilege Tax Section PO Box 327431 Montgomery, AL 36132-7431

---

[34] *See* Chapter 23 *infra* for discussion of the tax filings and returns required for each state.

State	State Forms Required	Due Date of Return/ E-File Option	Revenue Departments
Alaska	An LLC that is classified as a partnership and has only individual members is not required to file a return An LLC that has corporate members must submit a copy of the signed IRS Form 1065, pages 1-4, with "Alaska" marked on the top of page 1, and a copy of Schedule K-1 for each corporate member	30th day after federal return E-File option available	Department of Revenue Tax Division P.O. Box 110420 Juneau, AK 99811-0420 Phone: (907) 465-2320 www.revenue.state.ak.us
Arizona	• Form 165 Partnership Income Tax Return • A single-member LLC must report its income to Arizona as a corporation on Form 120 • Form 120 for LLC classified as a corporation	15th day of third month following close of tax year No E-File option	Department of Revenue P.O. Box 52153 Phoenix, AZ 85072-2153 (602) 255-3381 Forms: (602) 542-4260 https:// www.azdor.gov
Arkansas	Form AR1050, Partnership Return of Income LLC Franchise Tax Report	• 15th day of 4th month after close of tax year • May 1 after close of tax year for Franchise Tax Report No E-File option	State Income Tax P.O. Box 8026 Little Rock, AR 72203-8026 (501) 682-1100 or (800) 882-9275 www.dfa.arkansas.gov

State	State Forms Required	Due Date of Return/ E-File Option	Revenue Departments
California	• Form 568, Limited Liability Company Return of Income • Schedule D (568), Capital Gain or Loss • Schedule K-1 (568), Member's Share of Income, Deductions, Credits, Etc. • Schedule K-1 NR (568), Member's Share of Income, Deductions, Credits, Etc. • FTB 3522, Limited Liability Company Tax Voucher • FTB 3537, Payment Voucher for Automatic Extension for Limited Liability Companies • FTB 3885L, Depreciation and Amortization • FTB 3832, Limited Liability Company's List of Members and Consents	15th day of 3rd month following close of tax year E-File option available	California Franchise Tax Board P.O. Box 942857 Sacramento, CA 94257-0631 (800) 852-5711 Forms: (800) 338-0505 www.ftb.ca.gov
Colorado	• Form 106 (Part II), Colorado State Partnership or S Corporation Return of Income and Composite Nonresident Income Tax Return • Form 106 CR, Colorado Partnership—S Corporation Credit Form	15th day of 4th month following close of tax year (with automatic six-month extension) E-File option available	Department of Revenue 1375 Sherman Street Denver, CO 80261 (303) 866-3091 Forms: (303) 232-2414 www.colorado.gov/revenue

State	State Forms Required	Due Date of Return/ E-File Option	Revenue Departments
Connecticut	Form CT-1065, Connecticut Partnership Income Tax Return A copy of the federal partnership return on Form 1065 must be attached to the state return	15th day of 4th month following close of tax year E-File option available	Department of Revenue Accounts Receivable Unit P.O. Box 5019 Hartford, CT 06102-5019 (860) 297-5962 Forms: (860) 297-4753 www.ct.gov/drs
Delaware	Form 300, Delaware Partnership Return	15th day of 4th month following close of tax year E-File option available	Delaware Division of Revenue P.O. Box 8703 Wilmington, DE 19899-8703 (302) 577-8200 Forms: (302) 577-8201 www.revenue.delaware.gov
District of Columbia	• Form D-30, Delaware Partnership Return • Form D-65, Partnership Return of Income • Form D-2030 Must attach a copy of federal Form 1065	15th day of 4th month following close of tax year No E-File option	Government of District of Columbia Office of Tax & Revenue 1101 4th Street, SW, 4th Floor Washington, DC 20024 (202) 442-6300 or (202) 727-4TAX otr.cfo.dc.gov/
Florida	Form F-1065, Florida Partnership Information Return; Only if at least one member is subject to Florida Corporate income tax	First day of the 5th month following the close of the tax year No E-File option	Department of Revenue 5050 W Tennessee St. Tallahassee, FL 32399-0135 (850) 488-6800 Forms: (850) 922-9645 dor.myflorida.com/ Pages/default.aspx

State	State Forms Required	Due Date of Return/ E-File Option	Revenue Departments
Georgia	Form 700, State of Georgia Partnership Income Tax Return	15th day of 3rd month following close of tax year E-File option available	Department of Revenue P.O. Box 740315 Atlanta, GA 30374-0315 (404) 656-4188 Forms: (404) 656-4293 www.dor.georgia.gov
Hawaii	Form N-20, Partnership Return of Income An LLC that files IRS Form 8832 must attach a copy of that form to its first state return	20th day of 4th month following close of tax year No E-File option	Department of Taxation P.O. Box 3559 Honolulu, HI 96811-3559 (800) 222-3229 Forms: (808) 587-7572 or (800) 222-7572 http:// tax.hawaii.gov
Idaho	Form 65, Partnership Return of Income; Attach Federal Form 1065	15th day of 4th month following close of tax year E-File option available	State Tax Commission P.O. Box 56 Boise, ID 83756-0056 (208) 334-7660 or (800) 972-7660 www.tax.idaho.gov
Illinois	• Form IL-1065 • Form IL-2569 • Form NUC-1, Illinois Business Registration	15th day of 4th month following close of tax year No E-File option	Department of Revenue P.O. Box 19031 Springfield, IL 62794-9031 (217) 782-3336 or (800) 732-8866 http:// www.revenue.state.il.us

State	State Forms Required	Due Date of Return/ E-File Option	Revenue Departments
Indiana	• Form IT-65 • Form IN K-1 • Form WH-18, Indiana Miscellaneous Withholding Tax Statement for Nonresidents. The first four pages of the federal partnership return on Form 1065 must be attached to the state return	15th day of 4th month following close of tax year No E-File option	Department of Revenue 100 N. Senate Avenue, Room N105 Indianapolis, IN 46204 (317) 232-2240 Forms: (317) 486-5103 www.in.gov/dor/
Iowa	Form IA 1065, Partnership Return of Income; Attach Federal Form 1065	Last day of the 4th month following close of tax year No E-File option	Department of Revenue Hoover State Office Building Des Moines, IA 50319 (515) 281-3114 Forms: (515) 281-7239 www.iowa.gov/tax
Kansas	•Form K-120S, Kansas Partnership or S Corporation Income. The first four pages of the federal partnership return on Form 1065 must be attached to the state return •Form K-150, Franchise Tax Return	15th day of the 4th month following close of tax year E-File option available	Department of Revenue 915 S.W. Harrison St. Topeka, KS 66699-4000 (785) 368-8222 Forms: (785) 296-4937 http://www.ksrevenue.org
Kentucky	•Form 765, Kentucky Partnership Income and LLET Return; Attach Federal Form 1065 •Form 740NP-WH, Nonresident Income Tax Withholding	15th day of 4th month following close of tax year No E-File option	Department of Revenue Cabinet 200 Fair Oaks Lane Frankfort, KY 40620 (502) 564-4581 Forms by fax: (502) 564-4459 revenue.ky.gov/

State	State Forms Required	Due Date of Return/E-File Option	Revenue Departments
Louisiana	Form IT-565 if any member is a nonresident of Louisiana or is not a natural person	15th day of 4th month following close of tax year No E-File option	Department of Revenue P.O. Box 3440 Baton Rouge, LA 70821-3440 (225) 925-7537 Forms: (225) 925-7532 http:// revenue.louisiana.gov/
Maine	Form 941P-ME, Maine Income Tax Withholding for Pass-through Entities (if LLC has non-resident members).	15th day of 3rd month following close of tax year E-File option available	Maine Revenue Services P.O. Box 1064 Augusta, ME 04332-1064 (207) 287-2076 www.maine.gov/ revenue
Maryland	Form 510, Pass-Through Entity Income Tax Return	15th day of 4th month following close of tax year E-File option available	Comptroller of the Treasury Revenue Administration Division Annapolis, MD 21411-0001 (410) 260-7980 or (800) MD TAXES www.comp.state.md.us
Massachusetts	Form 3, Partnership Return of Income A copy of the federal partnership return on Form 1065 and all schedules must be attached to the state return	15th day of 3rd month following close of tax year E-File option available (Note: E-Filing is required if income or loss threshold is met, or partnership has 25 or more partners)	Department of Revenue P.O. Box 7017 Boston, MA 02204 (617) 887-6367 or in MA only: (800) 392-6089 www.mass.gov/ dor/

State	State Forms Required	Due Date of Return/ E-File Option	Revenue Departments
Michigan	Form 807, Composite Return, if non-resident members	15th day of 4th month following close of tax year E-File mandated	Department of Treasury Revenue Administrative Services Treasury Building 430 W. Allegan Street Lansing, MI 48922 (517) 373-3200 Forms: (800) 367-6263 www.michigan.gov/
Minnesota	• Form M-3, Partnership Return Schedule • Form M-KPI, Partner's Share of Income, Credits and Modifications Form M-KPC, Partner's Share of Income, Credits and Modifications (for corporate and partnership members) • Form MW-3NR, Withholding on Nonresidents	15th day of 3rd month following close of tax year E-File option available	Minnesota Partnership Tax, Mail Station 1760 St. Paul, MN 5514t5-1760 (651) 296-3781 or (800) 652-9094 www.taxes.state.mn.us
Mississippi	• Form 84-105, Mississippi Pass-Through Entity Tax Return • Form 84-387, Partnership Income Tax Withholding Voucher	15th day of 3rd month following close of tax year E-File option available	Office of Tax Administration P.O. Box 23050 Jackson, MS 39225-3050 (601) 923-7000 Forms: (601) 923-7815 www.dor.ms.gov
Missouri	• Form MO-1065, Partnership Return of Income • Form MO-NRP, Nonresident Partnership Form	15th day of 4th month following close of tax year No E-File option	Department of Revenue P.O. Box 3000 Jefferson City, MO 65105-3000 (573) 751-5337 Forms: (800) 877-6881 www.dor.mo.gov

State	State Forms Required	Due Date of Return/E-File Option	Revenue Departments
Montana	• Form PR-1, Partnership Return of Income • Form DER-1, Montana Disregarded Entity Information Return	• 15th day of 3rd month following close of tax year E-File option available	Department of Revenue P.O. Box 8021 Helena, MT 59604-8021 (406) 444-6900 https://revenue.mt.gov
Nebraska	Form 1065N, Nebraska Partnership Return of Income	15th day of 3rd month following close of tax year E-File option available	Department of Revenue Box 94818 Lincoln, NE 68509-4818 (402) 471-2971 or (800) 742-7474 www.revenue.ne.gov
Nevada	None	No income tax. Commerce tax payable online, due 45 days after fiscal year end. LLC must also make an annual business license tax filing.	Department of Taxation 1550 E. College Parkway, Suite 100 Carson City, NV 89706 (775) 687-4892 www.tax.state.nv.us

State	State Forms Required	Due Date of Return/ E-File Option	Revenue Departments
New Hampshire	• Form BET, Business Enterprise Tax Return for Corporations, Combined Groups, Partnerships, Fiduciaries and Nonprofit Organizations • Form NH-1065, Partnership Business Profits Tax Return • Form DP-80, Apportionment of Income • Form BTSUMMARY, Business Tax Summary • Form NH-1065-ES, Estimated Partnership Business Tax Quarterly Payment Voucher • DP-10 - Interest and Dividends Tax Return •NH-1065, Partnership Business Profits Tax Return •BPT-ES, Estimated Business Profits Tax	• 15th day of 3d month following close of tax year; • 15th day of 4th month following close of tax year for Form NH-1065 No E-File option available	Department of Revenue Administration 45 Chenell Drive P.O. Box 457 Concord, NH 03302-0457 (603) 271-2191 Forms: (603) 271-2192 www.nh.gov/ revenue
New Jersey	• Form NJ-1065, State of New Jersey Partnership Return • PART-100, Partnership Return Voucher for LLCs with two or more members. (Mail separately from Form NJ-1065)	15th day of 4th month following close of tax year E-File option available (Note: a partnership with ten or more partners is required to E-File)	Division of Taxation – Revenue Processing Center P.O. Box 194 Trenton, NJ 08646-0194 (609) 292-6400 Forms: (800) 323-4400 www.state.nj.us/ treasury/taxation

State	State Forms Required	Due Date of Return/ E-File Option	Revenue Departments
New Mexico	PTE New Mexico Income and Information Return for Pass-Through Entities	15th day of the 3rd month following the close of tax year; March 31 if filing online;	Taxation and Revenue Department P.O. Box 25122 Santa Fe, NM 87504-5122 (505) 827-0700 www.tax.newmexico.gov
New York	• Form IT-204, Partnership Return • Form IT-204-LL, Limited Liability Company/ Partnership Filing Fee Payment Form • Form IT-204-ATT, Partners' Identifying Information (corporate partners) •IT-2658, Report of Estimated Tax for Nonresident Individual Partner	• 15th day of the 3rd month following the close of the tax year for IT-204 • 30 days after close of tax year for Form IT-204-LL E-File option available	Department of Finance P.O. Box 5040 Kingston, NY 12402-5040 (518) 485-6800 or (800) 225-5829 Forms: (800) 462-8100 www.tax.ny.gov
New York City	• Form IT-204 NYC, City of New York Nonresident Partner Allocation • Form IT-204-ATT, Partners' Identifying Information (corporate partners)	15th day of the 3rd month following the close of the tax year E-File option available	NYC Tax Processing Center 101 Enterprise Center Kingston, NY 12401-7401 (212) 639-9675 www.nyc.gov/dof
North Carolina	Form D-403, Partnership Income Tax Return The LLC must attach a copy of the federal partnership return on Form 1065 and all schedules to the state return	15th day of 4th month following close of tax year No E-File option	Department of Revenue P.O. Box 25000 Raleigh, NC 27640-0640 (919) 733-3991 Forms: (919) 715-0397 www.dornc.com

State	State Forms Required	Due Date of Return/E-File Option	Revenue Departments
North Dakota	Form 58, North Dakota Partnership Return of Income	15th day of 4th month following close of tax year E-File option available	Office of State Tax Commissioner 600 East Boulevard Avenue, Dept. 127 Bismark, ND 58505-0599 (701) 328-2770 Forms: (701) 328-3017 www.nd.gov/tax/
Ohio	• Form IT 1140, Pass-Through Entity and Trust Withholding Tax Return • Form IT-4708, Nonresident Partners' Income Tax Return	15th day of 4th month following close of tax year No E-File option	Department of Taxation P.O. Box 182382 Columbus, OH 43218-2382 (614) 466-2166 www.tax.ohio.gov
Oklahoma	•Form 514, Partnership Return of Income •BT-190, Annual Business Activity Tax Return	15th day of 4th month following close of tax year No E-File option	Oklahoma Tax Commission P.O. Box 26800 Oklahoma City, OK 73126-0800 (405) 521-3212 Forms: (405) 521-3108 www.tax.ok.gov
Oregon	Form 65, Oregon Partnership Return of Income	15th day of 3rd month following close of tax year No E-File option	Department of Revenue P.O. Box 14790 Salem, OR 97309 (503) 378-4988 www.oregon.gov/dor

State	State Forms Required	Due Date of Return/ E-File Option	Revenue Departments
Pennsylvania	• PA-20S/PA-65, PA S Corporation/ Partnership Information Return • RCT-101, PA Corporate Tax Report (to report and pay the Pennsylvania capital stock and franchise taxes)	15th day of the 4th month following close of the tax year E-File option available	Department of Revenue Bureau of Individual Taxes P.O. Box 280502 Harrisburg, PA 17128-0502 (717) 783-1405 or (888) PA-TAXES Forms by fax: (800) 362-2050 www.revenue.state.pa.us
Rhode Island	Form RI-1065, Rhode Island Partnership Income Return	For all filers except for calendar year and non-June 30 fiscal year end single-member LLC filers, Form RI-1065 is due on or before the 15th day of the 3rd month following the close of the taxable year. For calendar year and non-June 30 fiscal year end single-member LLC filers, Form RI-1065 is due on or before the 15th day of the 4th month following the close of the taxable year E-File option available	Division of Taxation One Capitol Hill, Suite 9 Providence, RI 02908-5811 (401) 222-3934 Forms: (401) 222-1111 www.dor.ri.gov/
South Carolina	Form SC1065, Partnership Return of Income The LLC must attach a copy of the federal partnership return on Form 1065 and all schedules to the state return.	15th day of 3rd month following close of tax year No E-File option	SC Department of Revenue Partnership Return Columbia, SC 29214-0008 (803) 898-5000 Forms: (803) 898-5320 or (800) 768-3676 www.sctax.org

State	State Forms Required	Due Date of Return/ E-File Option	Revenue Departments
South Dakota	None	No income tax	Department of Revenue 445 E. Capitol Avenue Pierre, SD 57501 (605) 773-5141 or (800) 829-9188 dor.sd.gov/
Tennessee	• Form FAE 170, Tennessee Department of Revenue Franchise, Excise Tax Return • Form INC 250, Individual Income Tax Return (check Box 10 for limited liability company status)	15th day of 4th month following close of tax year No E-File option	Department of Revenue Andrew Jackson State Office Building 500 Deaderick Street Nashville, TN 37242 (615) 741-2594 Forms: (615) 741-8239 www.tn.gov/ revenue
Texas	05-158 Franchise Tax Report • 05-163 No tax due information report (if tax is less than $1,000 AND total revenue is less than the no-tax-due threshold) • 05-169 E-Z Computation (at taxpayer election, if total revenue is less than $10 million) • 05-102 Public Information Report	May 15 No E-File option	Comptroller of Public Accounts P.O. Box 13528, Capitol Station Austin, TX 78711-3528 (512) 463-4600 www.window.state.tx.us/ taxes

State	State Forms Required	Due Date of Return/ E-File Option	Revenue Departments
Utah	Form TC-65, Utah Partnership/ Limited Liability Partnership/ Limited Liability Company Return of Income (no return required unless LLC has income from Utah sources and nonresident members)	15th day of 4th month following close of tax year E-File option available	State Tax Commission 210 N. 1950 West Salt Lake City, UT 84134 (801) 297-2200 or (800) 662-4335 www.tax.utah.gov
Vermont	• B1-471, Vermont Business Income Tax Return • Form B1-473, Partnership/ Limited Liability Company Schedule (if LLC has nonresident members)	15th day of 3rd month following close of tax year No E-File option	Department of Taxes 133 State Street Montpelier, VT 05633-1401 (802) 828-2868 Forms: (802) 828-2515 www.state.vt.us/ taxredirect/
Virginia	Form 502, Pass-Through Entity Return of Income	15th day of 4th month following close of tax year No E-File option	Department of Taxation P.O. Box 1500 Richmond, VA 23218-1500 (804) 367-8031 Forms: (804) 236-2760 or (804) 236-2761 www.tax.virginia.gov
Washington	Business & Occupations Activities Return, or the Combined Excise Tax Return	15th day of 4th month following close of tax year E-File option available	Department of Revenue P.O. Box 34051 Seattle, WA 98124-1051 (360) 753-3181 Forms by fax: (800) 647-7706 www.dor.wa.gov

State	State Forms Required	Due Date of Return/ E-File Option	Revenue Departments
West Virginia	• Form WV/SPF-100, Income/Business Franchise Tax Return for S Corporation and Partnership • Form WV/NRW-2, Statement of WV Income Tax Withheld for Nonresident Individual or Organization • WV/NRW-4, West Virginia Nonresident Income Tax Agreement	15th day of third month following close of tax year. No E-File option	State Tax Department, Tax Account Administration Division P.O. Box 11751 Charleston, WV 25339-1751 (304) 558-3333 or (304) 558-3632 Forms: (304) 344-2068 or (800) 422-2075 www.revenue.wv.gov
Wisconsin	• Form 3, Wisconsin Partnership Return • Form 3S, Wisconsin Partnership Recycling Surcharge	15th day of 4th month following close of tax year E-File option available	Department of Revenue P.O. Box 8908 Madison, WI 53708-8908 (608) 266-1607 Forms by fax: (608) 261-6229 www.revenue.wi.gov
Wyoming	None	No income tax	Department of Revenue Herschler Bldg., 2nd Floor West 122 West 25th Street Cheyenne, WY 82002-0110 (307) 777-7961 revenue.wyo.gov/

.02 State Tax Returns for Resident and Nonresident Members

In most states, resident members are taxed on their allocable share of LLC income, gain, loss, credits, and deductions. Corporate members are taxed on their share, subject to either allocation or apportionment.

Nonresident members are generally taxed on their share of income attributed to the state. Corporate members are taxed on their entire share of income, subject to either allocation or apportionment.

The following table shows the tax forms the resident and nonresident members must file in each state.

State	Resident Members	Nonresident Members
Alabama	Form 40 for residents and part-year residents Form 20 (corporate members)	Form 40NR and Form 40NC (credits for both nonresidents and part-year residents Form 20C (corporate members) and Form 20S (S corporation members)
Alaska	N/A for individuals Form 04-611 (corporate members)	N/A for individuals Form 04-611 (corporate members)
Arizona	Form 140 Form 120 (corporate members)	Form 140NR for nonresidents Form 140PY for part-year residents Form 120 (corporate members)
Arkansas	Form AR 1000 Form AR 1100 (corporate members)	Form AR 1000 NR for nonresidents and part-year residents Form AR 1100 (corporate members)
California	Form 540 Form 100 (corporate members)	Form 540NR for nonresidents and part-year residents Form 100 (corporate members)
Colorado	Form 104 Form DR 112 (corporate members)	Form 104 PN for nonresidents and part-year residents Form DR 112 (corporate members)
Connecticut	Form CT-1040 Form CT-1120 (corporate members	Form CT-1040 NRPY for nonresidents and part-year residents Form CT-1120 (corporate members)
Delaware	Form 200-01 Form 1100 (corporate members)	Form 200-02 for nonresidents and part-year residents Form 1100 (corporate members)
District of Columbia	Individual income tax return Corporate income tax return	Individual income tax return Corporate income tax return
Florida	N/A for individuals Form 1120 (corporate members)	N/A for individuals Form 1120 (corporate members)
Georgia	Form 500 Form 600 (corporate members)	Form 500 and Schedule 3 for nonresidents and part-year residents Form 600 (corporate members)

State	Resident Members	Nonresident Members
Hawaii	Form N-11 Form 1100 (corporate members)	Form N-15 for nonresidents and part-year residents Form 1100 (corporate members)
Idaho	Form 40 Form 41 (corporate members)	Form 43 for nonresidents and part-year residents Form 41 (corporate members)
Illinois	Form IL 1040 Form 1120 (corporate members)	Form 43 for nonresidents and part-year residents Form 1120 (corporate members)
Indiana	Form IT-40 Form IT-20 (corporate members)	Form IT-40PNR for nonresidents and part-year residents Form IT-20 (corporate members)
Iowa	Form IA 1040 Form IA 1120 (corporate members)	Forms IA 1040 and IA 126 (NR and PY credits) for nonresidents and part-year residents Form IA 130 (Iowa out-of-state credit calculation) for part-year residents only Form IA 1120 (corporate members)
Kansas	Form K-40 Form 120 (corporate members)	Form K-40 and Schedule 3 for nonresidents and part-year residents Form 120 (corporate members)
Kentucky	Form 740 Form 720 (corporate members)	Form 740-NP for nonresidents and part-year residents Form 720 (corporate members)
Louisiana	Form IT-540 Form 120 (corporate members)	Form IT-540B Form 120 (corporate members)
Maine	Form ME 1040 Form ME 1120 (corporate members)	Form ME 1040NR for nonresidents and part-year residents Form ME 1120 (corporate members)
Maryland	Form 502 Form 500 (corporate members)	Form 505 for nonresidents and part-year residents Form 500 (corporate members)
Massachusetts	Form 1 Form 355A/B (corporate members)	Form 1-NR/PY for nonresidents and part-year residents Form 355A/B (corporate members)

State	Resident Members	Nonresident Members
Michigan	Form MI 1040 Form C 8000 (corporate members)	Form MI 1040 and Schedule NR for nonresidents and part-year residents Form C 8000 (corporate members)
Minnesota	Form M-1 Form M-4 (corporate members)	Forms M-1NR and M-1 for nonresidents and part-year residents Form M-4 (corporate members)
Mississippi	Form 80-200 Form 83-105 (corporate members)	Form 80-205 for nonresidents and part-year residents Form 83-105 (corporate members)
Missouri	Form MO 1040 Form 1120 (corporate members)	Form MO 1040 for nonresidents and part-year residents Form 1120 (corporate members)
Montana	Montana Individual Income Tax Return, Form 2 Form CLT-4 (corporate members)	Montana Individual Income Tax Return, Form 2 for nonresidents and part-year residents
Nebraska	Form 1040N Form 1120N (corporate members)	Form 1040N and Schedule III for nonresidents and part-year residents Form 1120N (corporate members)
Nevada	No income tax	
New Hampshire	No tax due from owners when the entity files a return	
New Jersey	Form NJ 1040 Form CBT100 (corporate members)	Form NJ 1040NR for nonresidents and part-year residents Form PART-100, Partnership Return Voucher Form CBT100 (corporate members)
New Mexico	Form PIT-1 Form CIT-1 (corporate members)	Forms PIT-110 and PIT-1 for nonresidents and part-year residents CIT-1 (corporate members)
New York	Form IT-200 Form CT3 (corporate members)	Form IT-203 for nonresidents and part-year residents Form CT3 (corporate members)

¶ 2202.02

State	Resident Members	Nonresident Members
New York City	Form NYS IT-200 Form 4 (corporate members)	Form IT-203 Form 4 (corporate members)
North Carolina	Form D 400 Form CD 405 (corporate members)	Form D 400 for nonresidents and part-year residents Form CD 405 (corporate members)
North Dakota	Form 37 and Schedule 2 Form 40 (corporate members)	Form 32 and Schedule 3 for nonresidents and part-year residents
Ohio	Form IT-1040 and OH-10 Form FT 1120 (corporate members)	Forms IT-1040 and OH-10 for nonresidents and part-year residents Form FT1120 (corporate members)
Oklahoma	Form 511 Form 512 (corporate members)	Form 511NR for nonresidents and part-year residents Form 512 (corporate members)
Oregon	Form 40 Form 20 (corporate members)	Form 40N for nonresidents Form 40P for part-year residents Form 20 (corporate members)
Pennsylvania	Form PA 40 and Schedule G, credit for taxes paid by Pennsylvania residents to other states Form PA 20 (corporate members)	Form PA 40 for nonresidents and part-year residents Form PA 20 (corporate members)
Rhode Island	Form RI 1040 Form RI 1120 (corporate members)	Form RI 1040 NR for nonresidents and part-year residents Form RI 1120 (corporate members)
South Carolina	Form SC 1040 Form SC 1120 (corporate members)	Form SC 1040 for nonresidents and part-year residents Form SC 1120 (corporate members)
South Dakota	No income tax	
Tennessee	Form INC 250 (tax only on dividends and interest)	Not taxed
Texas	No individual income tax Form 05000 (corporate members)	No tax

State	Resident Members	Nonresident Members
Utah	Forms TC-40 and TC-40A Form 20 (corporate members)	Forms TC-40 and TC-40A for nonresidents and part-year residents Form 20 (corporate members)
Vermont	Form IN-111 Form CO 411 (corporate members)	Forms IN-111 and IN-113 (income adjustment schedule) for nonresidents and part-year residents Form CO 411 (corporate members)
Virginia	Form 760, Schedule 1, contributions and authorized deductions	Form 763 NR for nonresidents Form 760 PY for part-year residents Form 500 (corporate members)
Washington	No tax	
West Virginia	Form IT-140 Form WV/CNF 120 (corporate members)	Form IT-140N/PY for nonresidents and part-year residents Form IT-140NRS for residents of Kentucky, Virginia, Pennsylvania, Maryland, and Ohio Form WC/CNT 112 (corporate members)
Wisconsin	Form 1 Form 4 (corporate members)	Form 1 for nonresidents and part-year residents Form 4 (corporate members)
Wyoming	No income tax	No income tax

.03 Composite Return for Nonresident Members

Many states permit an LLC to file a composite return for nonresident members. A composite return is sometimes referred to as a group or block return.

The composite return is an informational return that reports the nonresident members' respective share of income, gain, losses, credits, and deductions. The return includes other information required by the state, such as the computation of the withholding or other taxes that the LLC must pay to the state with respect to the nonresident members' share of income. The composite return is similar to a Schedule K-1.

The composite return may be filed only for eligible members of the LLC. Normally, an eligible member is a person who resided outside of the state for the entire tax year and had no income from the state other than from the LLC. Some states require the member to consent to the election to file a composite return. Other states require the LLC to obtain consent from the state taxing authority before filing a composite return. An LLC may file the composite return on behalf of some or all of the eligible nonresident members.

The following table shows the states that permit a composite return.

State	Composite Return Allowed	Statutory Provisions
Alabama	Yes. Form PTE-C, Alabama Nonresident Composite Payment and Schedule PTE-CK1	Ala. Code §§ 40-18-24.1, 10-8A-1108, Ala. Admin. Code 810-3-24-.01
Alaska	N/A	
Arizona	Yes. Form 140NR	Ariz. Dept. of Rev. ITR 16-2, Composite Individual Income Tax Returns
Arkansas	Yes. Forms AR1000CR, AR99NRM	Ark. Code Ann. § 26-51-918(d); Reg. § 1.26-51-405, issued by the Ark. Director of the Dept. of Fin. & Admin.
California	Yes. Form 540NR; FTB Publication 1067, Guidelines for Filing a Group Form 540NR	Cal. Rev. & Tax Code § 18535(d)
Colorado	Yes. Form 106—Colorado State Partnership or S Corporation Return of Income and Composite Nonresident Income Tax Return	Col. Rev. Stat. Ann § 39-22-601(5)(d); *but see* Col. Rev. Stat. Ann § 39-22-601(4.5), which permitted composite filings by LLCs, was repealed by HB 95-1061
Connecticut	Yes. Form CT-1065/CT-1120SI, Composite Income Tax Return	Conn. Gen. Stat. Ann. § 12-719(b); IP 2005(13.1), Connecticut Income Tax Changes Affecting Pass-Through Entities, Connecticut Department of Revenue Services
Delaware	Yes. Form 200-C, Delaware Composite Personal Income Tax Return	
District of Columbia	N/A	
Florida	N/A	
Georgia	Yes. Form IT-CR, Georgia Nonresident Composite Tax Return for Partners and Shareholders; Form CR ES, Composite Return Estimated Tax	Ga. Code Ann. § 48-7-129(b); Ga. Dept. of Rev. Rule 560-7-8.34(3)

State	Composite Return Allowed	Statutory Provisions
Hawaii	Yes. Form N-15	Instructions to Form N-20
Idaho	Yes. Form 65, Idaho Partnership Return of Income (and checking the box in Item 1 that the return is a composite return); Schedule PTE-12, Idaho Schedule for Pass-Through Owners	Idaho Code § 63-3022L
Illinois	No. On August 16, 2013, Illinois enacted H.B. 3157 which, effective for tax years after December 31, 2014, (i) eliminated composite returns, and (ii) required LLCs classified as partnerships to withhold tax on nonbusiness income distributable to nonresident members.	35 Ill. Comp. Stat § 5/502(f); Ill. Admin. Code § 100.5100(a)
Indiana	Schedule Composite-COR for corporate members not domiciled in Indiana and Schedule Composite for nonresident individual members. There is no provision for a member to opt out of a composite filing.	IT-65 Partnership Return Booklet (2018)
Iowa	Yes. Form IA 1040C, Composite Individual Income Tax Return	Iowa Code § 422.13(5); Iowa Department of Revenue in Finance Reg. § 701-48.1(422)
Kansas	Yes. Schedule K-40C, Form K-40	Kan. Reg. § 92-12-106
Kentucky	Form 740NP-WH, Kentucky Nonresident Income Tax Withholding on Net Distributive Share Income Transmittal Report and Composite Income Tax Return	KRS § 141.206(13)
Louisiana	Yes. Form R-6922, Louisiana Composite Partnership Return	La. Rev. Stat. Ann. § 47:201.1; LAC 61:I:1401
Maine	Form 941CF-ME, Agreement to Participate in a Composite Filing of Maine Income Tax; Form 941E-ME, Withholding Exemption; 1040ME; Schedule 1040C-ME (instructions for the composite filing included on Schedule 1040C-ME)	36 M.R.S.A. § 5192 (5); Me. Reg. Rule No. 805

State	Composite Return Allowed	Statutory Provisions
Maryland	Yes. Form 510C, Maryland Composite Pass-Through Entity Income Tax Return	Md. Reg. §§ 03.04.02.04, 03.04.07.05, 03.04.02.01B(5); Md. Admin. Release No. 6 (Rev. Sept. 2011)
Massachusetts	Yes. Form NRCR and Form M-8453 CR (electronic filing only)	830 CMR 62.5A.1(12)(f)
Michigan	Yes. Form 807, Michigan Composite Individual Income Tax Return	Mich. Comp. Law Ann. § 206.315; Michigan Department of Treasury Bulletin RAB 2004-1
Minnesota	Yes. Form M3 and Schedule KP1	Minn. Stat. Ann. § 289A.08, Subd. 7
Mississippi	Yes. Form 86-106, Composite Partnership Income Tax Return	Miss. State Tax Comm. Reg. § 901(E)
Missouri	Yes. Form MO-1040, with the words "Composite Return" typed at the top. The LLC must pay tax at a 6% tax rate on the income of nonresident members reported on the composite return; alternatively, the LLC may file an individual tax return on behalf of the nonresident member and pay tax at the 6 percent tax rate or the lesser exact amount	12 Mo. Code Regs. tit. 10-2.190(1)(A); Mo. Stat. Ann. § 143.411(4)
Montana	Yes. Form PR-1, Partnership Information and Composite Tax Return; Schedule IV, Montana Composite Income Tax Schedule	Mont. Code Ann. §§ 15-30-1112, 1113; Mont. Admin. Reg. §§ 42.9.201-204, 42.15.702
Nebraska	No	
Nevada	No state income tax	
New Hampshire	N/A	
New Jersey		
New Mexico	No	3NMAC 3.12.14
New York	Yes. Form IT-203-GR, Group Return for Nonresident Partners	N.Y. St. Dept. of Taxn. & Fin. Reg. § 158.13
New York City	No	
North Carolina	Yes. Form D-403	N.C. Admin. Code § 17:06B.3513

State	Composite Return Allowed	Statutory Provisions
North Dakota	Yes. Form 58 and Schedule KP (col. 8) to Form 58	N.D. Cent. Code § 57-38-31.1
Ohio	Yes. Form IT-4708, Annual Composite Income Tax Return for Investors in Pass-Through Entities. Composite tax return is not allowed for the Commercial Activity Tax (CAT)	Ohio Tax Comm'r. R. 5703-7-03
Oklahoma	Yes. Form 514-PT, Partnership Composite Income Tax Supplement, and Form 514, Part 1, Tax Computation for Nonresident Composite Filers Only	Okla. Stat. Ann. § 18-2049; Rule 710:50-19-1
Oregon	Yes. Form OR-OC, Oregon Composite Return	Or. Admin. R. 150-314 and instructions to Schedule MNR
Pennsylvania	Yes. Form PA-40 NRC, Nonresident Consolidated Income Tax Return	Instruction to Form PA-40NCR, Nonresident Consolidated Income Tax Return, and PA-65, Commonwealth of Pennsylvania Information Booklet for Partnerships
Rhode Island	Yes. Form RI-1040C, Rhode Island Composite Income Tax Return, Form RI 1040C-NE, Rhode Island Nonresident Income Tax Agreement/Election to be Included in a Composite Return	
South Carolina	Yes. Schedule NR attached to Form SC1040 (one individual tax return); Form I-338, SC1040 Composite Filing For S Corporations, Partnerships, and Limited Liability Companies	S.C. Code § 12-6-5030
South Dakota	No state income tax	
Tennessee	N/A	
Texas	N/A	

State	Composite Return Allowed	Statutory Provisions
Utah	Yes. For professional athletes only on Form TC-65A, Utah Composite Return for Nonresident Professional Athletes.	Utah Admin. Rule R865-9I-13
Vermont	Yes. BI-471, Vermont Business Income Tax Return (check Composite Return box and obtain approval to file a composite return); Form BI-473 Composite Schedule	Vt. Stat. Ann. tit. 32, § 5920(b); Vt. Dept. of Taxes Technical Bulletin TB-05 (rev. 9-26-08)
Virginia	Yes. Form 765, Unified Nonresident Individual Income Tax Return (Composite Return)	Guidelines for Pass-Through Entity Withholding, Virginia Department of Taxation (Sept. 21, 2007)
Washington	No state income tax	
West Virginia	Yes. Form IT-140NCR, West Virginia Nonresident Composite Income Tax Return	W. Va. Code § 11-21-51a
	Form WV/NRN-4, West Virginia Nonresident Income Tax Agreement	
Wisconsin	Yes. Form 1CNP	Tax Bulletin No. 53, Department of Revenue, October 1997; Instructions to Form ICNP, Combined Wisconsin Partnership Form 3
Wyoming	No state income tax	

.04 Annual Report

The third type of state filing is the annual report. Many states require an annual report. The annual report sets forth basic information, such as the address of the LLC, the registered agent for service of process, and the names of managers. Most states require a nominal fee. Some states use the annual report to report payment of the state franchise tax or annual registration fee.

The following table shows the annual reports that are required in each state and the District of Columbia:

State	Required	Comments	To Obtain and to File Forms
Alabama	Not required	Alabama Form DLL-2, Report of Domestic Limited Liability Company, must be filed; this is not an annual report, but an initial filing report	Secretary of State Business Div. P.O. Box 5616 Montgomery, AL 36103 Phone: (334) 242-7205 Fax: (334) 242-4993
Alaska	Required	Biennial registration	Department of Commerce & Economic Development Div. of Banking Securities & Corporations Corporations Section P.O. Box 110808 Juneau, AK 99811-0808 Phone: (907) 465-3520 Fax: (907) 465-5400
Arizona	Not required		Arizona Corporation Comm. 1300 West Washington Phoenix, AZ 85007-2929 Phone: (602) 542-3135
Arkansas	Corporation and Limited Liability Company Franchise Tax Report		Secretary of State State Capitol, Rm. 256 Little Rock, AR 72201-1094 Phone: (501) 682-1010 Fax: (501) 682-3510
California	Form LLC-E012R, Statement of Information Renewal	Biennial registration	Secretary of State Limited Liability Company Div. 1500 11th St. P.O. Box 944228 Sacramento, CA 94244-2280 Phone: (916) 653-7244 Fax: (916) 653-4620

State	Required	Comments	To Obtain and to File Forms
Colorado	Required	Preprinted form generated by secretary of state for each LLC at due date of filing	Secretary of State 1560 Broadway, Ste. 200 Denver, CO 80202 Phone: (303) 894-2200 Fax: (303) 894-7732
Connecticut	Required		Secretary of State 30 Trinity St. P.O. Box 150470 Hartford, CT 06115-0470 Phone: (860) 566-2739 Fax: (860) 566-6318
Delaware	Not required		Secretary of State Townsend Bldg. P.O. Box 898 Dover, DE 19903 Phone: (302) 739-4111 Fax: (302) 739-3811 E-mail: efreel@state.de.us
D.C.	Biennial Report for Foreign and Domestic Limited Liability Companies (LLC)		Department of Consumer & Regulatory Affairs Business Regulation Admin. Corporations Div. P.O. Box 37200 Washington, DC 20013-7200 Phone: (202) 727-7283 Fax: (202) 727-3582
Florida	Form 202, L.L.C. A/ R, Limited Liability Company Annual Report		Division of Corporations Florida Dept. of State P.O. Box 6327 Tallahassee, FL 32314 Phone: (850) 487-6051 Fax: (850) 487-2214 E-mail: smortham@mafl.dos.state.fl.us

State	Required	Comments	To Obtain and to File Forms
Georgia	Required		Secretary of State Corporations Div. Suite 315, West Tower #2 Martin Luther King, Jr., Dr., SE Atlanta, GA 30334-1530 Phone: (404) 656-2817 Fax: (404) 657-5804
Hawaii	Required		Department of Commerce & Consumer Affairs Business Registration Div. P.O. Box 40 Honolulu, HI 96810 Phone: (808) 586-2727 (documents processing); (808) 586-2744 (administration) Fax: (808) 586-0231
Idaho	Not required		Secretary of State State Capitol, Rm. 203 700 W. Jefferson P.O. Box 83720 Boise, ID 83720-0080 Phone: (208) 334-2300 Fax: (208) 334-2282
Illinois	• Form LLC-50.1(D), Domestic Limited Liability Company Annual Report • Form LLC-50.1(F), Foreign Limited Liability Company Annual Report		Secretary of State 213 State House Springfield, IL 62756 Phone: (217) 782-2201 Fax: (217) 785-0358

State	Required	Comments	To Obtain and to File Forms
Indiana	Not required		Secretary of State State House, Rm. 201 200 W. Washington St. Indianapolis, IN 46204 Phone: (317) 232-6576 Fax: (800) 726-8000
Iowa	Not required		Secretary of State State Capitol 1007 E. Grand Ave. Des Moines, IA 50319 Phone: (515) 281-5204 Fax: (515) 242-5952
Kansas	Form LC, State of Kansas/Domestic And Foreign Limited Liability Company Annual Report	Secretary of State Corporations Div. State Capitol Bldg., 2d Fl. 300 S.W. 10th Ave. Topeka, KS 66612-1594 Phone: (913) 296-4575 Fax: (913) 296-4570	
Kentucky	Required		Secretary of State P.O. Box 718 Frankfort, KY 40602-0718 Phone: (502) 564-3490 Fax: (502) 564-5687
Louisiana	Required		Secretary of State P.O. Box 94125 Baton Rouge, LA 70804-9125 Phone: (225) 925-4704 Fax: (225) 925-4726

State	Required	Comments	To Obtain and to File Forms
Maine	Required		Bureau of Corporations, Elections & Commissions Dept. of the Secretary of State 101 State House Station Augusta, ME 04333-0101 Phone: (207) 626-8400 Fax: (207) 287-8598
Maryland	Not required		Department of Assessments & Taxation Business Services & Finance Div., Rm. 809 301 W. Preston St. Baltimore, MD 21201 Phone: (410) 767-1350; (410) 767-1330 (corporate charter information) Fax: (410) 333-7097
Massachusetts	Required		Secretary of the Commonwealth Corporations Div. One Ashburton Pl., 17th Fl. Boston, MA 02108-1512 Phone: (617) 727-2850 Fax: (617) 742-4722
Michigan	Form C&S 2700, Annual Statement-Limited Liability Company	Preprinted form generated by Department of Consumer & Industry Services for each LLC at due date of filing	Department of Consumer & Industry Services Corporation, Securities and Land Development Bureau P.O. Box 30222 Lansing, MI 48909 Phone: (517) 373-2510 Fax: (517) 373-0727

State	Required	Comments	To Obtain and to File Forms
Minnesota	Minnesota Form #68, Biennial Registration for Minnesota or Foreign Limited Liability Companies, Minnesota Statutes Chapter 322B	Biennial registration	Secretary of State 180 State Office Bldg. 100 Constitution Ave. St. Paul, MN 55155-1299 Phone: (612) 296-2079 Fax: (612) 297-5844 E-mail: secretarystate@state.mn.us
Mississippi	Not required		Secretary of State 401 Mississippi St. P.O. Box 136 Jackson, MS 39205-0136 Phone: (601) 359-1633 Fax: (601) 354-6243
Missouri	Not required		Secretary of State 208 State Capitol P.O. Box 778 Jefferson City, MO 65102 Phone: (573) 751-3318 Fax: (573) 526-4903
Montana	Annual Limited Liability Company Report		Secretary of State State Capitol Bldg., Rm. 225 P.O. Box 202801 Helena, MT 59620-2801 Phone: (406) 444-3665 Fax: (406) 444-3976
Nebraska	Not required		Secretary of State State Capitol, Ste. 2300 P.O. Box 94608 Lincoln, NE 68509-4608 Phone: (402) 471-2554 Fax: (402) 471-3237
Nevada	Annual List of Managers or Members		Secretary of State 101 N. Carson St., No. 3 Carson City, NV 89701-4786 Phone: (702) 687-5203 Fax: (702) 687-3471

State	Required	Comments	To Obtain and to File Forms
New Hampshire	Form LLC-8, Annual Report		Secretary of State State House, Rm. 204 107 N. Main St. Concord, NH 03301-4989 Phone: (603) 271-3242 Fax: (603) 271-6316
New Jersey	Not required		State of New Jersey Dept. of State P.O. Box 450 Trenton, NJ 08625 Phone: (609) 984-1900 Fax: (609) 292-9897
New Mexico	Not required		State Corporations Commission Corporation Dept. P.O. Box 1269 Santa Fe, NM 87504-1269 Phone: (505) 827-3600 Fax: (505) 827-3634
New York	Required	Biennial statement	State of New York Dept. of State Bur. of Corporations 41 State St. Albany, NY 12231-0001 Phone: (518) 473-2492 Fax: (518) 474-4765
North Carolina	Required		Secretary of State P.O. Box 29622 Raleigh, NC 27626-0622 Phone: (919) 807-2225 Fax: (919) 807-2039
North Dakota	Required	Preprinted form generated by secretary of state for each LLC at due date of filing	Secretary of State State Capitol, 1st Fl. 600 E. Blvd. Ave., Dept. 108 Bismarck, ND 58505-0500 Phone: (701) 328-2900 Fax: (701) 328-2992 E-mail: sos@pioneer.state.nd.us

State	Required	Comments	To Obtain and to File Forms
Ohio	Not required		Secretary of State 30 East Broad St., 14th Fl. Columbus, OH 43266-0418 Phone: (614) 466-2655 Fax: (614) 644-0649
Oklahoma	Required		Secretary of State State Capitol Bldg., Rm. 101 2300 N. Lincoln Blvd. Oklahoma City, OK 73105-4897 Phone: (405) 521-3911 Fax: (405) 521-3771
Oregon	Required		Secretary of State Corporation Div. 255 Capitol St. NE, Ste. 151 Salem, OR 97310-1327 Phone: (503) 986-1523 Fax: (503) 986-1616
Pennsylvania	Required		Secretary of the Commonwealth Dept. of State 302 N. Capitol Bldg. Harrisburg, PA 17120-0029 Phone: (717) 787-7630 Fax: (717) 787-1734
Rhode Island	Form LLC-19, Limited Liability Company Annual Report		Secretary of State Corporations Div. 100 North Main St. Providence, RI 02903-1335 Phone: (401) 222-3040 Fax: (401) 277-1356
South Carolina	State of South Carolina Annual Report, Limited Liability Company		Secretary of State Wade Hampton Bldg. P.O. Box 11350 Columbia, SC 29211 Phone: (803) 734-2170 Fax: (803) 734-2164

State	Required	Comments	To Obtain and to File Forms
South Dakota	Required		Secretary of State State Capitol 500 E. Capitol Ave., Ste. 204 Pierre, SD 57501-5070 Phone: (605) 773-4845 Fax: (605) 773-6580
Tennessee	Required		Department of State Division of Business Services 312 Eighth Avenue North 6th Floor, William R. Snodgrass Tower Nashville, TN 37243 Phone: (615) 741-0537 and (615) 741-2286
Texas	Form 05-102, Texas Franchise Tax Public Information Report		Secretary of State Statutory Filings Div. Corporations Section P.O. Box 13697 Austin, TX 78711-3697 Phone: (512) 463-5701 Fax: (512) 475-2761
Utah	Required		Department of Commerce Division of Corporations and Commercial Code Heber M. Wells Building 160 East 300 South, Second Floor P.O. Box 146705 Salt Lake City, UT 84114-6705 Phone: (801) 530-4849 Fax: (801) 538-1557 E-mail: owalker@state.ut.us

State	Required	Comments	To Obtain and to File Forms
Vermont	Required		Secretary of State Corporations Division Heritage 1 Building 81 River Street, Drawer 09 Montpelier, VT 05609-1104 Phone: (802) 828-2386 Fax: (802) 828-2496 E-mail: jmilne@sec.state.vt.us
Virginia	Not required		Commonwealth of Virginia State Corporation Commission P.O. Box 1197 Richmond, VA 23218-1197 Phone: (804) 786-2441 Fax: (804) 371-0017
Washington	Required		Secretary of State Corporations Div. 2nd Fl., Republic Bldg. 505 E. Union Ave. P.O. Box 40234 Olympia, WA 98504-0234 Phone: (360) 753-7121 Fax: (360) 586-5629
West Virginia	Required		Secretary of State Bldg. 1, Ste. 157K 1900 Kanawha Blvd. E. Charleston, WV 25305-0770 Phone: (304) 558-6000 Fax: (304) 558-0900
Wisconsin	Not required	Foreign LLCs must file an annual report on Form 518, Annual Report; domestic LLCs are not required to file	Department of Financial Institutions Div. of Corporate & Consumer Affairs P.O. Box 7846 Madison, WI 53707-7846 Phone: (608) 261-9555

State	Required	Comments	To Obtain and to File Forms
Wyoming	Required		Secretary of State State Capitol Bldg. Cheyenne, WY 82002-0020 Phone: (307) 777-5333 Fax: (307) 777-6217

¶ 2203 AMENDED RETURNS AND ADMINISTRATIVE ADJUSTMENT REQUESTS (AAR)

.01 *Overview*

For tax years after 2017,[35] the Bipartisan Budget Act of 2015 provided that all LLCs classified as partnerships may amend a partnership return by filing a request for an administrative adjustment.[36] Any additional taxes as a result of the administrative adjustment are paid at the entity level rather than by the members. An LLC may elect to pass through the taxes to the persons who were members during the audit year. Qualified small LLCs may elect out of these rules, in which case each member of the LLC must file amended individual returns.

Prior to the Tax Equity and Fiscal Responsibility Act of 1982 (TEFRA), each member of an LLC was generally required to file an amended return to correct a partnership item on the LLC's tax return.

For partnership tax years after 1982 and prior to 2018, Code Sec. 6227 established a procedure for TEFRA partnerships to amend a partnership return for all members. An LLC was a TEFRA partnership if the LLC had (i) 11 or more members, (ii) any member that was a pass-through entity or nonresident alien, or (iii) any other member who was not an individual, C corporation, or estate of a deceased member.[37] Non-TEFRA LLCs could not file amended returns. Instead, each member was required to file an amended return. A TEFRA partnership amended its tax return by filing an Administrative Adjustment Request (AAR). The tax matters partner (TMP) could file the AAR for the LLC. Additionally, any member could file an AAR on his or her own behalf. The AAR was the primary (though not exclusive) TEFRA procedure for refunds or credits of overpayments attributable to partnership items. Code Sec. 6228 provided rules for judicial review where an AAR was not allowed in full.

---

[35] Bipartisan Budget Act of 2015, § 1101(g).
[36] Code Sec. 6227; Prop. Reg. § 301.6227-1.
[37] Code Sec. 6231(a)(1).

.02 Filing of AAR

An LLC may file an Administrative Adjustment Request on Form 8082, Notice of Inconsistent Treatment or Administrative Adjustment Request (AAR), with respect to one or more items of income, gain, loss, deduction, or credit in any member's distributive share.[38]

An LLC must file an AAR within three years after the later of the date that the partnership return for the LLC tax year was filed or the last day for filing the LLC's return without extensions. An LLC may not file an AAR for a tax year after the IRS issues a notice of administrative proceeding to the LLC with respect to the tax year.[39] A member of an LLC may not file an AAR unless the member is doing so on behalf of the LLC as a partnership representative.[40]

.03 Adjustment Items and Payment of Taxes

If an LLC files an amended return (AAR), the LLC and its members must take into account the adjustments that result in an imputed underpayment "under rules similar to the rules in Section 6226."[41] Generally, the LLC may account for the adjustment in one of two ways.[42]

First, the LLC may pay the taxes.[43] The tax rate on the imputed underpayments is the highest corporate or individual tax rate in effect in the reviewed year.[44] The LLC must pay any imputed underpayment resulting from the adjustments requested in an AAR on the date the LLC files the AAR.[45] The IRS may assess the amount of the imputed underpayment reflected on the AAR on the date that the AAR is filed.[46]

Alternatively, the LLC may make a pushout election to pass through the taxes to the persons who were members of the LLC during the tax year of the amended return.[47] The LLC is relieved of all tax liability in such case. The LLC must furnish an information statement to the members setting forth each member's share of the adjustment items on the amended return.[48] The information statement is binding on the member. A member may not treat items on his or her return inconsistently with the items on the information statement.[49]

---

[38] Code Secs. 6227(a), 6227(b)(2); Prop. Reg. § 301.6227-1(a).

[39] Code Sec. 6227(c); Prop. Reg. § 301.6227-1(b).

[40] Code Sec. 6227(c); Prop. Reg. § 301.6227-1(a).

[41] Code Sec. 6227(b)(2).

[42] Code Sec. 6227(b).

[43] Prop. Reg. § 301.6227-2(b)(1).

[44] Prop. Reg. § 301.6225-1(c)(2).

[45] Prop. Reg. §§ 301.6227-2(b)(1), 301.6232-1(b).

[46] Prop. Reg. § 301.6232-1(b).

[47] Code Sec. 6227(b)(2); Prop. Reg. §§ 301.6227-1(a), 301.6227-2(c).

[48] Prop. Reg. §§ 301.6227-1(c), 301.6227-2(c), 301.6227-1(e).

[49] Prop. Reg. § 301.6227-1(f).

There are several important differences between payment of additional taxes (referred to as imputed underpayments) on the amended return and payment of the additional taxes if the imputed underpayments result from an IRS audit. These differences include the following:[50]

1. *Modifications.* An LLC may not request a reduction or modification of adjustments on the amended return under the rules applicable to modifications resulting from an IRS audit. For example, if the imputed underpayments result from an IRS audit, the LLC may request a reduction in the amount payable by the LLC if one or more reviewed-year members file an amended individual return and pay the applicable taxes. An LLC that files an AAR may not request a modification of amounts shown on the amended return based on amended individual returns filed by the members.

2. *Increases and decreases.* If an LLC files an amended return, the reviewed-year members may take into account both increases and decreases in taxes resulting from adjustments on the amended return. If the adjustment items result from an IRS audit, the reviewed-year members may not take into account decreases in taxes.

3. *Interest.* If an LLC files an amended return, and makes a pushout election, the reviewed-year members must pay interest at the federal short-term rate plus three percent. If there is an IRS audit, and the LLC makes a pushout election, the reviewed-year members must pay interest at the federal short-term rate plus five percent.

The IRS may initiate an administrative proceeding with respect to the LLC for any tax year regardless of whether the LLC filed an AAR for the tax year. The IRS may then adjust any item subject to adjustment under the Internal Revenue Code.[51]

¶ 2204 NOTICE OF INCONSISTENT TREATMENT

Members must report on their individual tax returns all LLC items in the same way that the LLC reported them on IRS Form 1065 and Schedule K-1.[52] The consistency requirements apply to the LLC return in all respects, including the amount, timing and characterization of the item.[53]

If a member files a return that is not consistent, the member must notify the IRS of the inconsistency on Form 8082.[54] Form 8082 must be attached to the member's tax return for the tax year in which the member treated a partnership item inconsistently. There is an underpayment penalty if the member files a return that is inconsistent with the LLC's K-1 without also filing Form 8082, Notice of Inconsistent Treatment.[55]

---

[50] Prop. Reg. § 301.6227-3(b)(1).

[51] Prop. Reg. § 301.6227-1(g).

[52] Code Sec. 6222(a); Reg. § 301.6222(a)-1(a).

[53] Code Sec. 6222(a); Reg. § 301.6222(a)-1(a).

[54] Code Sec. 6222(b).

[55] Code Sec. 6222(b).

¶ 2205 TAX SHELTERS AND REPORTABLE TRANSACTIONS

.01 Reportable Transactions

An LLC must file Form 8886, Reportable Transaction Disclosure Statement, with its tax return, and send a copy the form to the Office of Tax Shelter Analysis, if the LLC engages in a reportable transaction. A reportable transaction includes the following:[56]

- *Listed transaction.* A listed transaction is a transaction that is the same or substantially similar to one of the types of transactions that the IRS has determined to be a tax avoidance transaction.[57] These transactions are identified by notice, regulation or other form of published guidance as a listed transaction.[58] A member of an LLC is not required to report listed transactions that are the same or substantially similar to the transactions described in Notice 2002-35 if the member participated in the transaction solely as a result of his or her direct or indirect interest in an LLC.[59]

- *Confidential transactions.* A confidential transaction is a transaction that is offered under conditions of confidentiality and for which the LLC or related party paid an advisor a minimum fee.[60] The minimum fee for an LLC in which all of the owners are corporations (excluding S corporations) is $250,000. The minimum fee is $50,000 for all other LLCs. A transaction is considered offered under conditions of confidentiality if the advisor placed a limitation on disclosure of the tax treatment or tax structure of the transaction, and the limitation on disclosure protects the confidentiality of the advisor's tax strategies.

- *Transactions with contractual protection.* A transaction with contractual protection is a transaction in which the LLC a related party has a right to a full or partial refund of fees if all or part of the intended tax consequences from the transaction are disallowed. It also includes a transaction for which fees are contingent on realization of tax benefits from the transaction.[61]

- *Loss transactions.* A loss transaction is a transaction that results in claiming a loss under Code Sec. 165 in excess of a threshold amount.[62] For an LLC with only corporations as members (excluding S corporations), the amount of the loss must be at least $10 million in any single tax year or $20 million in any combination of tax years, whether or not any losses flow through to one or more of the members. For all other LLCs that are classified as partnerships,

---

[56] Reg. § 1.6011-4(b).
[57] Reg. § 1.6011-4(b)(2).
[58] IRS Notice 2009-59, 2009-31 IRB 170.
[59] IRS Notice 2002-35, 2002-21 IRB 992.
[60] Reg. § 1.6011-4(b)(3).
[61] Reg. § 1.6011-4(b)(4).
[62] Reg. § 1.6011-4(b)(5).

the amount of the loss must be at least $2 million in any single tax year or $4 million in any combination of tax years, whether or not the losses flow through to one or more members. In determining whether a transaction results in an LLC claiming a loss that meets the threshold amounts, the losses claimed by the LLC during the year in which the transaction is entered into and the five succeeding tax years are combined. A member of an LLC must separately report a loss transaction if the tax return reflects a Section 165 loss allocable from the LLC that equals or exceeds the applicable threshold amount even if the LLC is under the threshold level and is not required to report the loss.[63]

- *Transaction of interest.* A transaction of interest is a transaction that is substantially the same or similar to one of the transactions that the IRS has identified by notice, regulation or other form of published guidance as a transaction of interest.[64] It is a transaction that the IRS and the Treasury Department believe has the potential for tax avoidance or evasion, but for which there is not enough information to determine if the transaction should be identified as a tax avoidance transaction.[65]

.02 Registered Tax Shelters

After October 22, 2004, the IRS no longer issues tax shelter registration numbers. The American Jobs Creation Act of 2004 amended Code Sec. 6111 to replace the tax shelter registration requirement with a new disclosure requirement for material advisors who provide material aid, assistance, or advice with respect to any reportable transaction.[66] Material advisors must now disclose reportable transactions on Form 8918. Reportable transactions are defined by reference to the regulations under Code Sec. 6111. Reg. § 1.6011-4 imposes disclosure rules on LLCs and members with respect to reportable transactions. Thus, there is a uniform definition of reportable transaction that applies in determining which transactions must be disclosed by an LLC, its members, and material advisors.

.03 List Maintenance Requirements

A material advisor of a reportable transaction must keep the list of advisees, which includes all LLCs and partnerships entering into a reportable transaction.[67]

A material advisor is a person who provides material aid, assistance or advice with respect organizing, managing, promoting, selling, implementing, ensuring or

---

[63] IRS website, Requirements for Filing Form 8886, Q&A 15, http://www.irs.gov/Businesses/Corporations/Requirements-for-Filing-Form-8886-Questions-and-Answers.

[64] Reg. § 1.6011-4(b)(6).

[65] IRS Notice 2009-55, 2009-31 IRB 170.

[66] *See* IRS Notice 2004-80, 2004-50 IRB 963.

[67] Code Sec. 6011.

carry out a reportable transaction. The material advisor must also derive gross income in excess of the threshold amount for the aid, advice and assistance.

.04 Schedule M and Book-Tax Differences

For returns timely filed on or after January 6, 2006, an LLC is not required to file Form 8886 in order to report significant book-tax differences. The IRS determined that this category of reportable transaction was no longer necessary since an LLC must now report certain book-tax differences on Schedule M-3.[68]

¶ 2206 FOREIGN LLCs AND MEMBERS

.01 Tax Filing Requirements for Foreign LLCs

Partnership Return

A foreign LLC must file a partnership return if it has U.S. source gross income, or income that is effectively connected with the conduct of a U.S. trade or business.[69] The losses, credits and deduction of the LLC are disallowed for tax purposes if the LLC fails to comply with the reporting requirements.[70]

The LLC must obtain an identifying number from its foreign members (such as a NRA Social Security number) for purposes of filing returns and other documents.[71]

The LLC must file the partnership return with the Service Center for the area in which the LLC has its principal place of business in the United States. The LLC must file the return with the Internal Revenue Service, Philadelphia, PA 19255-0011 if the LLC has no office or place of business in the United States.[72] The foreign LLC must file the return on or before the fifteenth day of the fourth month following the close of the LLC's tax year.[73]

Exception for Foreign LLCs with U.S. Members

A foreign LLC with U.S. members is not required to file a return if all of the following apply:[74]

- The LLC had no income effectively connected with the conduct of U.S. trade or business during the tax year.
- The LLC had U.S. source income of $20,000 or less during its tax year.

---

[68] *See* IRS Notice 2006-6, 2006-1 CB 385.

[69] Code Sec. 6031(e).

[70] Code Sec. 6231(f).

[71] Reg. § 301.6109-1(b)(2)(i); Rev. Rul. 84-158, 1984-2 CB 262.

[72] Reg. § 1.6031(a)-1(e)(1).

[73] Reg. § 1.6031(a)-1(e)(2).

[74] Reg. § 1.6031(a)-1(b); Instructions to Form 1065.

- Less than one percent of any partnership item of income, gain, loss, deduction, or credit was allocable in the aggregate to direct U.S. members at any time during its tax year.
- The LLC is not a withholding foreign partnership as defined in Reg. § 1.1441-5(c)(2)(i).

Exception for Foreign LLCs with No U.S. Members

A foreign LLC with no U.S. members is not required to file a return if all of the following apply:[75]

- The LLC had no income effectively connected with the conduct of U.S. trade or business during the tax year.
- The LLC or another withholding agent filed all required Forms 1042 and 1042-S.
- The tax liability of each member for amounts reportable under Reg. § 1.1441-5(c)(2)(i) was fully satisfied by the withholding of tax at the source.
- The LLC is not a withholding foreign partnership.

Failure to File Return

A foreign LLC that fails to file a tax return on a timely basis is not allowed deductions, losses, and credits if (i) the tax matters partner for the LLC resides outside the United States, or (ii) the LLC maintains its books outside of the United States.[76]

.02 Members of Foreign LLC Classified as Disregarded Entity

Persons who own an interest in a foreign disregarded LLC must file Form 8858, Information Return of Persons with Respect to Foreign Disregarded Entities. The reporting requirements apply to (a) a U.S. person who is a direct owner of the membership interests in a foreign disregarded LLC, (b) certain U.S. persons required to file form 5471 with respect to a controlled foreign corporation (CFC) that is a tax owner of the membership interests in a foreign disregarded LLC, and (c) certain U.S. persons required to file Form 8865 with respect to a controlled foreign partnership (CFP) that is an owner of a foreign disregarded LLC at any time during the CFP's annual accounting period.[77]

A U.S. corporation that owns a foreign disregarded LLC must also attach Schedule N to its tax return. If the foreign disregarded LLC has net operating losses,

---

[75] Reg. § 1.6031(a)-1(b); Instructions to Form 1065.
[76] Code Sec. 6231(f).
[77] IRS Ann. 2004-4, 2004-4 IRB 357.

the U.S. owner must attach to its return a domestic use election[78] and an annual certification election.[79] The purpose of the election and the annual certification is to prevent the U.S. owner from using the net operating losses of the foreign LLC to offset both the income of the U.S. company and the income of a foreign consolidated group.

If a foreign LLC's single owner is a U.S. person, payments by U.S. payors are treated as payments to a U.S. person. Therefore, based on the savings clause in U.S. income tax treaties, the foreign LLC may not claim benefits under an income tax treaty even if the LLC is organized in a country with which the United States has an income taxed treaty in effect.[80]

.03 Members of Foreign LLC Classified as Partnership

A United States person that contributes property to a foreign partnership must report the contribution on Form 8865 Information Return of U.S. Persons with Respect to Certain Foreign Partnerships, if:[81]

- immediately after the transfer, the United States person owns, directly, indirectly, or by attribution, at least a ten percent interest in the LLC; or
- the value of the property transferred to the LLC, when added to the value of any other property transferred in a Code Sec. 721 contribution by such person (or any related person) during the 12-month period ending on the date of the transfer, exceeds $100,000.

The U.S. member must report the following on Form 8865:

- transfers of cash and other property to a foreign LLC in exchange for a membership interest;[82]
- the acquisition or disposition of at least a ten percent interest in a foreign LLC;[83] and
- information concerning the income and assets of the LLC, certain transactions with the LLC, the names of the members, and other specified information if the U.S. member owns at least a ten percent interest in a controlled foreign LLC.[84]

The form must be filed with the member's tax return for the year of the transfer.[85] A member who fails to file or report all of the information on Form 8865 is subject to a penalty of $10,000 for each failure for each reportable transaction. There is

---

[78] Reg. § 1.1503(d)-6(d).

[79] Reg. § 1.1503(d)-6(d).

[80] Reg. § 1.1441-1(b)(2)(iii)(B).

[81] Reg. § 1.6038B-2(a)(1).

[82] Code Sec. 6038B; Reg. § 1.6038B.

[83] Code Sec. 6046A; Reg. § 1.6046A-1, 6038B-2(a)(4).

[84] Code Sec. 6038; Reg. § 1.6038-3.

[85] Reg. § 1.6038B-2(a)(6).

an additional penalty of up to $50,000 if the failure continues for more than 90 days after notice of failure by the IRS. There is also a loss or reduction of the U.S. member's foreign tax credits, and criminal penalties for fraudulent returns.[86]

.04 Members of Foreign LLC Classified as Corporation

U.S. members in a foreign LLC that is classified as a corporation must file several forms with the IRS. The main reporting forms include the following:

- Form 926, Return by a U.S. Transferor of Property to a Foreign Corporation;

- Form 5471, Information Return of U.S. Persons With Respect to Certain Foreign Corporations. If U.S. members directly or indirectly own in the aggregate more than 50 percent of a foreign company, the company qualifies as a controlled foreign corporation (CFC). Each shareholder with at least ten percent interest in a CFC must file Form 5471 along with his or her personal annual tax return. If the LLC has any Subpart F income, a ten percent shareholder must include the part of this income attributable to his or her share, even if the LLC has not yet distributed this income.

- Form 5472, Information Return of a 25 percent Foreign-Owned U.S. Corporation or a Foreign Corporation Engaged in a U.S. Trade or Business.

.05 Classification Election for Foreign LLCs

The classification of a foreign LLC as a partnership, corporation, disregarded entity or hybrid entity is discussed at ¶505. The automatic classification of certain types of foreign LLCs as corporations is discussed at ¶503.01. The LLC may change the default classification by filing Form 8832, Election Classification. The procedures for making this election are discussed at ¶508.

.06 Withholding Taxes

The withholding tax requirements and reporting forms for payments to foreign LLCs are discussed at ¶1808.

The withholding tax requirements and reporting forms for payments to foreign members of a domestic LLC are discussed at ¶1902. A member may claim a reduced rate of withholding by filing Form W-8BEB or similar form. An LLC must withhold taxes on income allocated to foreign members, whether or not distributed.

---

[86] Reg. § 1.6038-3(k).

.07 Tax Identification Number

Beginning with the 2012 tax year, U.S. taxpayers must provide a unique reference identification number (URI) or employer identification number for all foreign entities reported on the following forms:

- Form 8858, Information Return of U.S. Persons with Respect to Foreign Disregarded Entities;
- Form 8865, Information Return of U.S. Persons with Respect to Foreign Partnerships; and
- Form 5471, Information Return of U.S. Persons with Respect to Foreign Corporations.

¶ 2207 FOREIGN ASSETS OF DOMESTIC LLC

.01 FATCA—Foreign Financial Accounts

A U.S. person must file a report under the Foreign Account Tax Compliance Act (FATCA) on Form 8865, Return of U.S. Persons with Respect to Certain Foreign Partnerships, if the person owns an interest in a foreign LLC.[87]

A domestic LLC must report specified foreign financial assets on Form 8938, Statement of Specified Foreign Financial Assets, if the LLC is formed or availed of for the purpose of holding, directly or indirectly, specified foreign financial assets.[88] A domestic LLC is formed or availed of for the purpose of holding specified foreign financial assets if:

- The LLC is closely held by a specified individual.[89] A specified individual includes (i) a U.S. citizen; (ii) a resident alien of the United States for any portion of the taxable year; (iii) a nonresident alien for whom an election to be taxed as a U.S. resident is in effect; or (iv) a nonresident alien who is a bona fide resident of Puerto Rico or a Section 931 possession.[90] An LLC classified as a partnership is closely held by a specified individual if at least 80 percent of the capital or profits interest in the LLC is held, directly, indirectly or constructively by a specified individual on the last day of the LLC's tax year.[91] An LLC classified as a corporation is closely held if at least 80 percent of the total

---

[87] Reg. § 1.6038D-7(a)(1).

[88] Code Sec. 6038D; Reg. § 1.6038D-6(a).

[89] Reg. § 1.6038D-6(b)(1)(i).

[90] Reg. § 1.6038D-1(a)(2).

[91] Reg. § 1.6038D-6(b)(2)(ii). The passive asset percentage is based on a weighted average approach similar to the rule in Reg. § 1.1472-1(c)(1)(iv). An LLC may use either the fair market value or book value (as reflected on the LLC's balance sheet and as determined under either a U.S. or international financial accounting standards) to determine the value of the LLC's assets.

combined voting power or value of the stock in the corporation is owned by a specified individual on the last day of the corporation's tax year.[92]
- At least 50 percent of the LLC's gross income for the tax year is passive income, or at least 50 percent of the LLC's assets produce or are held for the production of passive income.[93]

An LLC meeting these requirements must file a report on Form 8939 if it has an interest in specified foreign financial assets with an aggregate value exceeding $50,000 on the last day of the tax year or $75,000 at any time during the year.[94] Specified foreign financial assets include (i) financial accounts with foreign financial institutions, (ii) stocks or securities in foreign entities, (iii) financial instruments or contracts that have a non-U.S. issuer or counterparty, (iv) an interest in a foreign partnership or other non-U.S. entity, (v) a hedge fund or an equity fund, and (vi) an interest in a foreign trust, estate, pension plan, or deferred compensation plan.[95]

.02 FBAR

United States persons must electronically file FinCEN Report 114, Report of Foreign Bank and Financial Accounts (FBAR) if (i) the United States person had a financial interest in or signature authority over at least one financial account located outside of the United States; and (ii) the aggregate value of all foreign financial accounts exceeded $10,000 at any time during the calendar year. United States persons include U.S. limited liability companies classified as partnerships or corporations.[96]

¶2208 NEXUS AND APPORTIONMENT RULES

An LLC that is organized in one state may be required to file a tax return and pay taxes in another state as a result of the nexus and apportionment rules. All states except for six have taken the position that nexus and tax filing requirements may arise if a nonresident member owns a management or non-management interest in an LLC organized in the state.[97] For example, the following states have adopted rules regarding the taxation of members in an LLC and other pass-through entities doing business in the state:

---

[92] Reg. § 1.6038D-6(b)(2)(i).

[93] Reg. § 1.6038D-6(b)(1)(ii).

[94] Code Sec. 6038D(a); Reg. § 1.6038D-2(a)(1).

[95] Code Sec. 6038D(b); Reg. § 1.6038D-3.

[96] IRS, Report of Foreign Bank and Financial Accounts (FBAR), *available at* https://www.irs.gov/Businesses/Small-Businesses-&-Self-Employed/Report-of-Foreign-Bank-and-Financial-Accounts-FBAR.

[97] Bloomberg BNA 2013 Survey of State Tax Departments, 20 Multistate Tax Report 4 (Apr. 26, 2013); Patrick Smith *et al.*, "Recent State Tax Developments for Passthrough Entities: Nexus Over Nonresident Owners and Apportionment of Income," *BNA Daily Tax Report* No. 174, p. J-1 (Sept. 9, 2013); B. Ely and W.T. Thistle II, "Surveying the Battlefield, States' Continued Assertion of Nexus Over Nonresident Owners of Pass Entities," *BNA Daily Tax J.* No. 66, p. J-1 (Apr. 7, 2014).

Alabama	Alabama may impose a composite return filing requirement for an Alabama LLC with respect to nonresident members having no contact with Alabama. *Tsitalia LLC v. Ala. Dep't of Rev.*, Administrative Law Judge Rulings Doc. No. BIT. 12-492 (Feb. 1, 2013). Although Alabama has authority to collect an income tax from an Alabama-based LLC, Alabama may not tax nonresident owners directly. Alabama could not personally assess income taxes against an individual who resided and worked in Minnesota and received income from an Alabama-based LLC because the taxpayer had no contacts in or connections with Alabama. Alabama may assess the tax against the LLC through composite tax filing requirements, but not against the nonresident member personally. *Vogt v. Ala. Dep't of Rev.*, Administrative Law Judge Rulings, Doc. No. INC. 11-660 (Jan. 3, 2013). The mere ownership of the limited partnership interest does not provide sufficient minimum contacts with the state for the state to exercise taxing jurisdiction. *Lanzi v. Ala. Dept. of Rev*, 968 So. 2d 18 (Ala. Civ. App. 2006), *cert. denied,* Ala. Doc. No. 1051475 (Apr. 13, 2007).
Arizona	A corporation that owns an LLC in Arizona that is classified as a disregarded entity may be treated as doing business in and subject to corporate taxes in Arizona, with an exception for a foreign state insurance company that does business in Arizona through a disregarded LLC. Taxpayer Information Ruling LR11-01, Arizona Dep't of Rev. (Feb. 8, 2011).

California	FTB Legal Ruling 2014-01 (Jul. 22, 2014) sets forth detailed guidelines regarding when business entities that are members of an LLC must file a California return and pay franchise taxes, in addition to the gross receipts tax and minimum tax payable by the LLC.
	California enacted new laws effective in 2011 for determining California source income, whether a foreign LLC must qualify to do business in California, and whether a foreign LLC is subject to the California franchise tax, minimum tax, and income tax. Cal. Rev. & Tax Code § 23101(b). *See* ¶ 2306.08. For tax years beginning on or after January 1, 2013, business income of an LLC or other trade or business is apportioned to the state by multiplying the business income by the sales factor. Proposition 39, Cal. Rev. & Tax. Code § 25128.7. There is an exception for businesses described in Cal. Rev. & Tax. Code § 25128(b) that derive more than 50% of gross receipts from agricultural, extractive, savings and loan, and/or banking or financial activities.
	The Franchise Tax Board does not have legal authority to assess the $800 minimum franchise tax on a passive out-of-state investor in an LLC in which the LLC investment funds are based and managed in California. The Superior Court ruling determined that a passive member of an LLC is not doing business in California merely because the LLC does business in California. *Swart Enters., Inc. v. Cal. Franchise Tax Board,* No. 13CECG2171 (Nov. 14, 2014).
	The California cases and rules applicable to nonresident members are discussed at ¶ 2306.09.
Florida	Owning and controlling a subsidiary LLC organized in or transacting business within Florida does not constitute doing business in Florida. Florida Limited Liability Company Act § 608.501(2)(k).
Idaho	Idaho limits to $250,000 in any calendar year the amount of guaranteed payments that an LLC doing business in Idaho may attribute to the state in which the member performs the services. Amounts paid in excess of $250,000 per year are sourced to Idaho based on the Idaho apportionment factor. The $250,000 is adjusted annually for inflation. All guaranteed payments made to retired members are sourced to the recipient state of domicile. H.B. 139, Laws 2013, Idaho Code § 63-3026A.

Illinois	An out-of-state individual taxpayer who had no connections with Illinois except for the receipt of guaranteed payments and business income apportionable to Illinois from a partnership operating in Illinois had sufficient nexus within the state to be subject to the Illinois income tax. Ill. Dept. of Rev., General Information Letter No. IT 12-0028-GIL (Sept. 27, 2012). Nonresident members of an Illinois LLC were not subject to the Illinois income tax and gain from the sale of the LLC's interest in a foreign partnership. The LLC's only business activity was investing in other companies, Company1 income for the year was from the sale of the interest in the form partnership. Ill. Dept. of Rev., Private Letter Ruling ITR-12-0001-PLR (Oct. 25, 2012).
Indiana	The income allocated by an Indiana LLC to an out-of-state corporate member was not subject to withholding because the foreign corporation was not domiciled in Indiana, and derived its income from the membership interest which was tangible personal property. *Riverboat Development, Inc. v. Dep't of Rev.*, Ind. Tax Ct. No. 49T10-0506-TA-52 (Feb. 22, 2008).
Kentucky	An ownership interest in an LLC that conducts business in Kentucky does not by itself establish personal jurisdiction over the individual owners of the LLC under the Due Process Clause. *United States v. Bacara Partners, LLC*, 2012-1 USTC ¶ 50,404, 109 A.F.T.R. 2d 2357 (E.D. Ky. 2012). A Delaware corporation that owned a 99% limited partnership interest in a Delaware limited partnership, which had its principal place of business in Tennessee, and also conducted business in Kentucky, was taxed on its receipt of a distributive share of partnership income received from profits of the limited partnership doing business in Kentucky. *Revenue Cabinet v. Ashworth Corp*, Nos. 2007-CA-002549-MR, 2008-CA-000023-MR (Ky. Ct. App. Nov. 20, 2009).

Louisiana	The Louisiana Department of Revenue takes the position that the corporate owner of a single-member LLC doing business in Louisiana is subject to Louisiana tax laws, and if either the corporation or the single-member LLC owned by the corporation has a nexus in Louisiana, both would have nexus for Louisiana tax purposes. La. Dep't of Rev., Revenue Information Bulletin Nos. 04-003 (2004), and 02-018 (2002). The Louisiana Administrative Code also provides that mere ownership of property in Louisiana "whether owned directly or through a partnership or joint venture or otherwise, renders a corporation subject to franchise tax in Louisiana." La. Admin. Code tit. 61, § 1.301(D). The Louisiana courts have invalidated this regulation, and have determined that the mere ownership of an interest in an LLC, a limited partnership or other pass-through entity doing business in Louisiana will not by itself subject an out-of-state corporation to Louisiana franchise taxes. *Bridges v. Polychim USA, Inc.,* No. 2014 CA 0307, 2015 BL 117716 (La. Ct. App. Apr. 24, 2015); *UTELCOM Inc. v. Bridges,* 77 So. 3d 39 (2011), *writ denied,* No. 2011-C-2632 (La. 2012).
Massachusetts	A corporation that owns an LLC in Massachusetts that is classified as a partnership may be treated as doing business in and subject to corporate taxes in Massachusetts. *Sahi USA Inc. v. Massachusetts Comm'r of Rev,* No. C262668, Mass. Appellate Tax Bd. (2006). A Georgia corporation was subject to Massachusetts taxation when it acquired a Massachusetts LLC that was classified as a disregard entity; the Georgia corporation was treated as doing business in Massachusetts based on its ownership of the membership units in the LLC; and the Georgia corporation was entitled to apportion its income in accordance with the provisions of Georgia law in determining the taxable income allocable to Massachusetts. Mass. Dep't of Rev. Let. Rul. LR 00-9 (June 9, 2000).

Michigan	Mich. Comp. Laws § 206.661, effective January 1, 2012, provides that a corporate taxpayer with a direct or indirect ownership interest or beneficial interest in a flow-through entity in a foreign state must apportion its business income directly attributable to the business activity of the flow-through entity, even if the flow-through entity has no business activity in the state of incorporation of the corporate owner.

The Michigan Department of Treasury issued a detailed guidance regarding when the ownership by a foreign entity of a membership interest in an LLC or other flow-through entity creates nexus with Michigan. Michigan Department of Treasury, Revenue Administrative Bulletin 2014-5 (Jan. 29, 2014). For example, a New York corporation (Corporation S) is subject to the Michigan corporate income tax as a result of its ownership interests in flow-through entities under the following circumstances: "Corporation S, located in New York and with no physical presence in Michigan, has a 5% ownership interest in Partnership A, also located in New York and with no presence in Michigan. Partnership A is a member with three other entities in Acme, LLC, located in Ohio with no physical presence in Michigan, and that is treated as a partnership for federal income tax purposes. Acme, LLC is a partner with a 25% ownership interest in Partnership B, which is located and conducts business activities in Michigan. Corporation S has an indirect ownership interest in Partnership B through two flow-through entities, Partnership A and Acme, LLC (treated as a partnership for federal income tax purposes and a flow-through entity for CIT purposes). Corporation S has nexus with Michigan." RAB 2014-5, Example 12. The Michigan Department of Revenue also determined that the distributive share of income "of a corporation that has nexus with Michigan that is attributable to (or derived from) its ownership in a flow-through entity whose activities are otherwise protected by PL 86-272 is not itself protected by PL 86-272 and is not excluded from the corporation's corporate income tax base." RAB 2014-5, at 8. *See also* Gandhi, Lynn, "Michigan's Treatment of Flow-Through Entities Under Its New Corporate Income Tax Nexus Standards," *BNA Daily Tax Report* No. 64, p. J-1 (Apr. 3, 2014).

A Michigan taxpayer may report gain on the sale of an interest in an LLC as business income, which is apportioned to Michigan based on the entity's factors. Thus, a Michigan resident who sells a membership interest in an LLC with business assets outside of Michigan may treat the gain as non-Michigan source income to the extent the LLC's business assets are located outside of Michigan. *Aikens v. Dep't of Treasury*, No. 310528, 2014 BL 24505 (Mich. Ct. App 2014).

A single-member disregarded LLC owned by a corporation may file a separate tax return under the state's single business tax act, and does not have to file as part of a combined return with the parent corporation. *Kmart Michigan Property Services LLC v. Michigan Treasury Dep't*, No. 282058 (Mich. Ct. App. 2009). Under 2010 legislation, a subsidiary disregarded LLC is

	not required to file a separate return in Michigan. Mich. Comp. Laws § 205.27a.
Minnesota	An out-of-state corporation was not required to file a unitary tax return or apportion its income to Minnesota as a result of its membership interest in a Minnesota LLC. *Express Scripts, Inc. v. Comm'r of Rev.*, No. 8272R (Minn. Tax Ct. Aug. 20, 2012).
New Jersey	A limited partnership interest in a New Jersey limited partnership did not subject the out-of-state limited partner to New Jersey taxes because the foreign company (i) was not a general partner, (ii) did not have control of the business of the limited partnership, (iii) did not have a place of business in New Jersey, (iv) did not have employees, agents or representatives in New Jersey, (v) did not have property in New Jersey, even though it received 100% of its income from the limited partnership interest, and (vi) did not have a unitary relationship with the New Jersey limited partnership because the two companies were not integrally related. *BIS LP, Inc. v. Dir., Div. of Tax'n*, 25 N.J. Tax 88 (N.J. Tax Ct. 2000), *aff'd*, 26 N.J. Tax 489, 2001 BL 338365 (N.J. Super. Ct. App Div. 2011). However, a foreign corporation's ownership of a limited partnership interest in a New Jersey limited partnership subjected to the corporation to New Jersey taxes where the corporation was operating a unitary business with the partnership. *Village Super Market PA, Inc. v. New Division of Tax'n*, 27 N.J. Tax 394 (2013). The ruling was in accordance with a New Jersey regulation covering the issue of when a corporation's interest in a limited partnership is unitary. N.J.A.C. 18:7–7.6(c).
New Mexico	An out-of-state Internet retailer was subject to the New Mexico gross receipts tax on sales to New Mexico residents because it had a substantial nexus with New Mexico based on the in-state sales activity of a related corporation. *Tax'n & Rev. Dep't v. Barnesandnoble.com LLC*, No. 33,627 (N.M. June 3, 2013).
New York	An online retailer is presumed to have nexus with New York if it posts a link to its website on the website of a New York resident who receives compensation on a commission basis. The New York statute that subjects online retailers to New York sales and use taxes even though they do not have a presence in New York is constitutional. *Overstock.com, LLC v. Dep't of Tax'n & Fin.*, 965 N.Y.S. 2d 61 (2013). Two Delaware holding companies that were members of an LLC that held a general partnership interest in a company doing business in New York were subject to the New York franchise tax. The court determined that New York had the right to tax income derived from sources within New York. *Matter of Shell Gas Gathering Corp. No. 2*, Nos. 821569 and 821570 (N.Y. Tax App. Trib. June 11, 2009).

North Carolina	An out-of-state corporation that owned a membership interest in a North Carolina LLC classified as a partnership was treated as doing business in North Carolina for corporate income tax purposes, and its income from the LLC was apportionable business income for purposes of determining its North Carolina corporate income tax liability. Secretary of Rev. Decision No. 2007-28, N.C. Dep't of Rev. (Sept. 14, 2007). Income from a unitary business of a partnership is apportionable, and income from an activity of a partnership that is not part of unitary business activities is allocated according to the business side is of the activity. PD-14-02, N.C. Department of Revenue.
Pennsylvania	The Ohio corporate owners of an Ohio LLC that was doing business in LLC were subject to the Pennsylvania corporate net income tax because the income and activity of the LLC doing business in Pennsylvania flowed through to the corporate members, but the corporate members were not subject to the Pennsylvania capital stock and franchise tax. Corporation Tax Opinion, Penn. S Corp. Filing Responsibilities, Penn. Dep't of Rev. (Feb. 2, 2000).
	A Texas individual who owned the limited partnership interest in a Connecticut-based limited partnership had sufficient nexus with Pennsylvania and was subject to Pennsylvania taxes, even though the Texas individual was a passive investor and never participated in the management of the partnership or its property. *Marshall v. Commw.*, 41 A.3d 67, 2012 BL 360 (Pa. Commw. Ct. 2012) (on appeal).
Tennessee	A British company that owned a 45% general partnership interest had nexus with and was doing business in Tennessee. The British company was subject to the Tennessee franchise/ excise tax, even though there were management and voting limitations placed on it by the partnership agreement. *Vodafone Ams. Holdings Inc. v. Roberts*, No. 07-1860-IV (Tenn. Ch. Ct. Mar. 19, 2013) (on appeal).
Texas	A foreign corporation is not subject to the Texas franchise tax as a result of its ownership of a disregarded LLC doing business in Texas. Letter No. 200606695L, Tex. Comptroller of Public Accts (June 1, 2006); Letter No. 200606694L, Tex. Comptroller of Public Accts (June 1, 2006).
Virginia	An out-of-state LLC that provided engineering services to clients in Virginia was not required to file a Virginia corporate or personal income tax return because (i) the LLC had no property or payroll in Virginia, (ii) the LLC had no sales attributable to Virginia because more than 50% of the cost of providing services to Virginia customers were incurred outside of the state, and (iii) the LLC did not have other sources of income in Virginia. Ruling of the Commissioner, P.D. 14-48, Virginia Department of Taxation (Apr. 2, 2014).

Washington	An out-of-state LLC did not have sufficient nexus for purposes of the Washington's business and occupations tax where the LLC's use of leased railcars to deliver its products in Washington was not significantly associated with its ability to establish and maintain a market in Washington. *Sage v. Foods, LLC v. Dep't of Rev.*, No. 11-704 (Wash. Bd. Tax App. 2012), appeal docketed, No. 12-2-01893-3 (Wash. Super. Ct. 2012).

¶2209 DESIGNATION OF RESPONSIBLE PARTY

Beginning January 1, 2014, an LLC must file Form 8822-B to report changes in the name of its responsible party, business mailing address, or business location. Form 8822-B must be filed within 60 days of the change.

A "responsible party" is the person who has a level of control over, or entitlement to, the funds or assets in the LLC that enables the individual, directly or indirectly, to control, manage or direct the LLC and the disposition of its funds and assets. The ability to fund the LLC or the entitlement to the property of the LLC alone, however, without any corresponding authority to control, manage, or direct the LLC, does not cause the individual to be a responsible party.[98]

---

[98] Instructions to Form 8822-B.

23

State Tax Laws

¶ 2301 OVERVIEW

All 50 states and the District of Columbia have enacted laws authorizing the formation of LLCs.

In most states, the LLC is a pass-through entity for tax purposes. However, several of the states impose a franchise or entity-level tax. Other states impose a withholding tax, usually on the distributive shares of income of nonresident members. The following chart shows the states that impose an entity-level tax on LLCs classified as partnerships.

State Franchise of Entity-Level Tax

State	No franchise tax	Franchise or entity-level tax
Alabama	x	Business Privilege Tax from $100 to $15,000; 5% tax on nonresident members included in composite return
Alaska		$100 biennial fee on domestic LLCs and $200 on foreign LLCs.
Arizona	x	
Arkansas		Annual $150 franchise tax. An LLC must withhold taxes at the highest rate attributable to corporate or individual taxpayers on income that is derived from or attributable to sources within Arkansas and distributed to nonresident members not included in a composite return. Alternatively, the LLC may report on a composite return and pay on behalf of each electing nonresident member Arkansas income taxes at the highest income tax rate for corporate or individual taxpayers for income derived from or attributable to Arkansas sources. The withholding and composite tax rate is 6.9% in 2017.
California		• LLCs that are classified as disregarded entities or partnerships must pay an $800 annual franchise tax. The LLC must also pay a gross receipts tax based on "total income." The tax ranges from $900 for total income between $250,000 and $500,000 to $11,790 for total income over $5 million. The LLC must pay all taxes attributable to income of nonresident members unless it obtains agreements from the nonresident members to file returns and pay all taxes, which agreements must be filed with the LLC return. • LLCs that are classified as corporations must pay the California franchise tax. The tax is 8.84% for LLCs other than banks and financial LLCs. There is a minimum $800 annual franchise tax on LLCs classified as corporations.
Colorado	x	$10 annual filing fee. An LLC with nonresident members must either file a nonresident partners agreement for each nonresident member or pay a 4.63% tax on the nonresident member's distributive share of income.*

State	No franchise tax	Franchise or entity-level tax
Connecticut	x	$10 annual report fee. An LLC must pay the business entity tax of $250. The business entity tax is payable every two years. An LLC that is classified as a partnership must withhold 5% of the income allocable to nonresident members, or include the members on a nonresident composite return.
Delaware		$300 annual tax on domestic and foreign LLCs.
D.C.		Biennial report fee of $300; 8.25% tax in 2018 on D.C. source income earned by unincorporated businesses; $250 minimum tax if the LLC engages in a D.C. trade or business and has gross receipts over $12,000.
Florida	x	Annual report and supplemental fees of $138.75.
Georgia	x	$30 annual fee; 4% withholding tax on distributions to nonresident members, or graduated composite tax rate up to 6%.
Hawaii	x	$15 annual filing fee.
Idaho	x	An Idaho LLC is subject to the Idaho income tax if its income is not fully distributed to the members. LLCs are taxed at the corporate rate of 7.4% on undistributed income. The LLC is also taxed on nonresident member income if the LLC derives income from Idaho sources and the nonresident members do not file the required returns. The tax rate is the corporate tax rate of 7.4% on the nonresident members' income. The permanent building excise tax also applies to such income.
Illinois		$250 annual report filing fee; 1.5% replacement tax, unless paid by the members.
Indiana	x	$22.44 annual fee. An LLC must withhold 3.23% of the distributive share of Indiana source income in 2017 for nonresident individuals and 6.25% for nonresident corporations.
Iowa	x	$45 biennial report fee. An LLC must withhold tax on the payment of income to nonresidents.
Kansas		$55 annual report fee. An LLC must pay an annual franchise fee of $55 to the Kansas Secretary of State.

State	No franchise tax	Franchise or entity-level tax
Kentucky		$15 annual report fee. An LLC must pay an annual limited liability entity tax (LLET) beginning January 1, 2007, on Kentucky gross receipts or Kentucky gross profits. The LLET is the lesser of $0.095 per $100 of the LLC's Kentucky gross receipts or $0.75 per $100 of the LLC's Kentucky gross profits. There is a small business exclusion if the LLC's gross receipts or gross profits from all sources are $3 million or less, and a partial exclusion if gross receipts or gross profits are between $3 million and $6 million. There is a minimum tax of $175.
Louisiana	x	$25 annual fee. The LLC must make a composite tax payment of 6% on the distributive shares of resident members and nonresident members included on the composite return.
Maine	x	$85 annual fee. An LLC must pay a 10.15% composite tax or withhold 10.15% of Maine-source income of nonresident members in 2017. LLC financial institutions are taxed at the entity level at a rate of 1% of Maine net income and $0.08 per $1,000 of Maine assets at the end of the tax year.
Maryland	x	$300 annual fee. The withholding tax rate in 2017 is 7.5% on nonresident individual members (including nonresident fiduciary members) and 8.25% on nonresident entity members.
Massachusetts	x	$500 annual fee.
Michigan		$25 annual fee. The MBT tax on LLCs classified as partnerships or disregarded entities was repealed effective January 1, 2013.
Minnesota		• Minimum fee from $100 to $5,000 if amount specified on Schedule A of return is over $500,000. • 9.85% withholding tax on nonresident members' distributive shares of income.
Mississippi	x	$25 annual fee. 5% withholding tax on net income allocated to all members. If the LLC does not withhold, the LLC and managers are personally liable for personal income taxes that the members should have paid on their distributive shares of income.
Missouri	x	6% withholding tax or composite tax required on distributive shares of income of nonresident members.

State	No franchise tax	Franchise or entity-level tax
Montana	x	$15 annual fee. The LLC must withhold taxes at a 6.9% rate on income allocable to non-resident members, or pay a composite tax on behalf of such members ranging from 1% to 6.9%.
Nebraska	x	$10 biennial report fee. 6.84% withholding tax in 2017 on share of income from Nebraska sources of each nonresident member if the member does not file Form 12N with the LLC.
Nevada		$150 annual list fee, $200 annual business license fee, and 0.63% tax (0.0063) on taxable wages of Nevada employees. There is an annual commerce tax on each business entity engaged in business in Nevada if gross revenue in a fiscal year exceeds $4 million.
New Hampshire		$100 annual fees; 8.2% tax to LLC on business profits; .72% tax to LLC on taxable enterprise tax base if tax base is greater than $50,000 or gross business receipts exceed $100,000; $100 annual report filing fee. Distributions from the LLC are subject to the dividends and interest tax. Distributions from an LLC are subject to the interest and dividends tax.
New Jersey	x	An LLC that has three or more members and New Jersey source income or loss must pay an annual filing fee of $150 per owner, up to a maximum of $250,000. An LLC must pay the corporate business (income) taxes at the highest marginal tax rate on a foreign member's allocable share of New Jersey income if it fails to obtain the consent of the member to New Jersey taxation of that income. An LLC must also pay a 6.37% tax (8.97% for members with New Jersey source income of $250,000 or more) on income from nonresident members who are included in a composite return.
New Mexico	x	4.9% withholding tax (2017 tax rate) on nonresident members' New Mexico source income.
New York		Annual filing fee ranges from $25 (LLC's New York source gross income is $100,000 or less) to $4,500 (if LLC's New York gross income exceeds $25 million); annual filing fee for single-member disregarded LLC is $25. New York City may impose similar filing fees.
North Carolina	x	$200 annual fee. Manager must pay taxes owed by individual nonresident members on such members' shares of LLC income. The tax rate is 5.499% in 2017.

State	No franchise tax	Franchise or entity-level tax
North Dakota	x	$50 annual fee. An LLC must withhold taxes on income distributed to nonresident members at the highest individual tax rate or pay such taxes on income allocable to nonresident members as part of a composite return. The withholding and composite tax rates are 2.9% in 2017.
Ohio	x	An LLC must pay the Commercial Activity Tax, with a $150 minimum tax for gross receipts under $1 million. An LLC must withhold tax at a 4.997% rate in 2017 on the distributive share of income for nonresident members unless the LLC files a composite return for resident nonresident members and makes composite tax payments.
Oklahoma	x	An LLC must pay a Business Activities Tax of $25 and 1% of net revenue if it does business in Oklahoma. An LLC must withhold tax at a 5% rate on distributions to nonresident members attributable to Oklahoma source income, or the Oklahoma net distributed income if determinable at the time of distribution. The composite tax rates for nonresident members are graduated tax rates up to 6.5%.
Oregon	x	$150 annual minimum tax; $100 annual report fee. An LLC must withhold taxes at a 9.9% tax rate on the distributive share of income of nonresident members attributable to Oregon source income unless the member elects to be included on a composite return.
Pennsylvania		Capital stock and franchise tax previously imposed on all LLCs eliminated in 2016; 3.07% withholding tax in 2018 on income allocable to nonresident members.
Rhode Island		$400 annual fee; an LLC must withhold tax on distributions to nonresident members at 5.99% for individual members, or 7% for C corporate members, if the member's distributive share of income is $1,000 or more in the member is not included in a composite return.
South Carolina	x	5% withholding tax on nonresident members' distributive shares of income.
South Dakota		$50 annual fee.

State	No franchise tax	Franchise or entity-level tax
Tennessee		Franchise tax of .25% of net worth and excise tax of 6.5% on Tennessee net earnings; "Hall Income Tax" of 5% in 2017 on dividends, bond interest, and similar instruments. $50 annual fee per member; minimum fee of $300; maximum fee of $3,000.
Texas		Margin tax of 0.75% per year on taxable margin, or 0.375% on taxable margin if LLC is engaged primarily in retail or wholesale trade.
Utah	x	$12 annual fee; 7% tax rate on Utah income attributable to nonresident members included in composite filing.
Vermont		$250 minimum tax; $25 annual fee. An LLC must also withhold estimated taxes for each nonresident member. The estimated tax rate is 7.8% for 2012 on income allocated or distributed to the nonresident member as reported on the federal Schedule K-1. The composite tax rate for nonresident members is 7.8% for 2017.
Virginia		Annual registration fee of $50.
Washington		Annual fee of $59. Business and occupation tax from 0.138% to 1.6% of gross income, less specified deductions and exemptions.
West Virginia		$25 annual fee; franchise tax equal to the greater of $50 or a percentage of capital accounts (capital accounts are the balances of members' capital accounts as set forth on IRS Form 1065). LLC must also withhold at 6.5% rate on each nonresident member's distributive share of income unless the member provides the LLC with Form WV/NRW-4, West Virginia Nonresident Income Tax Agreement. Alternatively, the LLC may pay a composite tax rate of 6.5% on income allocable to nonresident members.
Wisconsin		An LLC must withhold taxes at a 7.65% rate in 2018 on a nonresident member's allocable share of income.
Wyoming		An LLC must pay an annual report license tax of $50 or two-tenths of one mill on the dollar ($.0002), whichever is greater, based on the LLC's assets located and employed in the state of Wyoming.**

* Colo. Rev. Stat. Ann. § 39-22-601(5)(e).
** Wyo. Stat. § § 17-15-132(a)(vi), 17-16-1630(a).

Most states have two types of LLC laws: the enabling legislation for the formation, operation, and dissolution of the LLC and the tax laws.[1] The following chart sets forth the citations to the applicable tax laws in each state.

State LLC Tax Laws

State	LLC Tax Laws
Alabama	Ala. Code §§10A-5A-1.07(b); Ala. Admin. Code §§810-2-8-01(1)(c), 810-3-24-.01 to 810-3-24-.05, 810-3-28-.01
Alaska	Alaska Stat. §§43.20.012, 43.20.030, 43.20.051
Arizona	Ariz. Rev. Stat. Ann. §§4-32-1313, 29-857, 43-141 to 43-1413; CTR 97-2
Arkansas	Ark. Code Ann. §§26-51-918, 26-51-102(4), 26-51-802; Ark. Director of the Dept. of Fin. & Admin. Reg. §§6.26-51-102
California	Cal. Rev. & Tax. Code §§17087.6, 17220(b)(3), 17941, 17942, 17943, 18535(d), 18633.5(e), 18662, 18666, 23091, 23092, 23093
Colorado	Colo. Rev. Stat. Ann. §§39-22-103, -201, -303
Connecticut	Conn. Gen. Stat. Ann. §§12-701, 34-113
Delaware	Del. Code Ann. tit. 6, §§18-1105, -1107; tit. 30, §§1601-1624
D.C.	D.C. Code Ann. §§10-215, 29-1074, 47-1808.6
Florida	Fla. Stat. Ann. §§608.471, 220.02, 220.03(e), 608.405
Georgia	Ga. Code Ann. §§14-11-203, -212, -1104; Ga. Dept. of Rev. Reg. §560-7-3.08
Hawaii	Tax Information Release No. 97-4
Idaho	Idaho Code §§63-3006A, 63-3022L(1), (2), 63-3030(a)(9); Idaho State Tax Comm. R. 35.01.01.107
Illinois	35 Ill. Comp. Stat. 180/5-1, 5/201, 5/501, 5/1501
Indiana	Ind. Code Ann. §§6-3-4-10, 6-3-4-11, 6-3-4-12, 23-18-6-0.5
Iowa	Iowa Code Ann. §§422.16.4, 422.32.4; Iowa Dept. of Rev. & Fin. R. 701-45.1(422) to 701-45.4(422)
Kansas	Kan. Stat. Ann. §§17-76, 138, 17-76, 139(c), 79-32,130, 79-32,131, 79-32,133

---

[1] *See* Chapter 2 *supra* for discussion of, and citations to, the enabling legislation in each state.

State	LLC Tax Laws
Kentucky	Ky. Rev. Stat. Ann. §§ 141.0401, 141.010(24), 141.120(8), 141.200, 141.208(2).
Louisiana	La. Rev. Stat. Ann. §§ 12:1368, 47:201 to 47:220
Maine	Me. Rev. Stat. Ann. tit. 31, § 761; tit. 36, § 5180
Maryland	Md. Code Ann., Tax-Gen. §§ 10-102, -104, -210, -207
Massachusetts	Mass. Gen. Laws Ann. ch. 62 § 17
Michigan	Mich. Comp. Laws Ann. § 208.3(2)
Minnesota	Minn. Stat. Ann. §§ 289A.08(7), 289A.12(3), 290.01(3b), 290.06(22h), 290.92(4b), 322B.11; Minn. Dept. of Rev. Rs. 8038.3000, 8031.0100
Mississippi	Miss. Code Ann. §§ 79-29-112, 27-7-25; Miss. State Tax Comm. Reg. § 901
Missouri	Mo. Ann. Stat. §§ 347.187.2, 143.411.5, 143.581, 143.401; Mo. Dept. of Rev. R. 10-2.1901
Montana	Mont. Admin. R. 42.23.701 to .703; Mont. Stat. Ann. § 15-30-3301 *et seq.*
Nebraska	Neb. Rev. Stat. §§ 21-2633, 77-2734.01, 21-2612, 77-2727 to 2729; Neb. Admin. R. & Reg. §§ 25.001 to 25-07
Nevada	(no taxes)
New Hampshire	N.H. Rev. Stat. Ann. §§ 77:3.I(b), 77:3-a, 77:4, 77:15, 77:16, 77-A:6, 77-E; N.H. Dept. of Rev. Admin. Reg. § 902.06
New Jersey	N.J. Stat. Ann. §§ 42:B-69, 54A:2-2, 54A:5-4, 54A:8-6; N.J. Dept. of Treas. Reg. § 18:35-1
New Mexico	N.M. Admin. Code §§ 15.100.8, 3.11.12
New York	N.Y. Tax Law §§ 2.5, 2.6, 503, 601(f), 617, 632, 658(c)
North Carolina	N.C. Gen. Stat. §§ 57C-10-06, 105-114(b)(2), 105-134.1(7a), (10a), 105-163; N.C. Admin. Code Rule § 17.06B.3501 to .3529
North Dakota	N.D. Cent. Code §§ 57-38-07, 57-38-08
Ohio	Ohio Rev. Code Ann. §§ 5733.01(E), 5733.04(H)
Oklahoma	Okla. Stat. Ann. tit. 68, §§ 202(j), 2368.D, 2363; Okla. Admin. R. 710:50-19-1
Oregon	Or. Rev. Stat. §§ 63.810, 63.787, 314.710 to 314.727; Or. Admin. R. 150–314.
Pennsylvania	72 Pa. Cons. Stat. Ann. §§ 7301(n.0), 7306, 7401(1); Dept. of Rev. Reg. §§ 107.1 to 107.6

State	LLC Tax Laws
Rhode Island	R.I. Gen. Laws §§ 7-16-67, 7-16-73
South Carolina	S.C. Code Ann. §§ 12-6-600, 33-44-201, 12-2-25(A), 12-6-630
South Dakota	S.D. Codified Laws Ann. §§ 47-34-5, 47-34-54, 10-43-1(1)
Tennessee	Tenn. Code Ann. §§ 67-4-2004(16), 67-4-2106, 67-4-2019, 48-249-1003, 48-249-1007
Texas	Tex. Tax Code Ann. § 171.101(B), 171.002
Utah	Utah Code Ann. §§ 48-2c-117, 59-10-507, 59-10-801, 59-10-301 to 59-10-303
Vermont	Vt. Stat. Ann. tit. 32, §§ 5820, 5914, 5920, 5921
Virginia	Va. Code Ann. §§ 13.1-1005, 13.1-1069, 58.1-301; 23 Va. Admin. Code 10-130-10 to 10-130-265
Washington	Wash. Rev. Code Ann. § 31B-2-201
West Virginia	W. Va. Code §§ 11-13A-2(b)(8), 11-23-3(b)(2)(C), 11-23-6(b)(3), 11-21-3(b), 11-21-71a; W. Va. State Tax Dept. Reg. §§ 3.2, 58.2
Wisconsin	Dept. of Rev. Pub. No. 119
Wyoming	Wyo. Stat. §§ 17-15-132(a)(vi), 71.04(3)

¶ 2302 ALABAMA

Alabama adopted the Alabama Limited Liability Company Law of 2014.[2] The law is effective January 1, 2015, and applies to all LLCs formed on or after that date. It also applies to LLCs formed before January 1, 2015 that elect to be governed by the new law. The law becomes applicable to all LLCs on January 1, 2017 regardless of the date of formation.[3]

.01 State Tax Classification

The Alabama tax classification of an LLC follows the federal classification.[4] An LLC is classified as a "subchapter K entity" taxable as a partnership if the LLC is

---

[2] H.B. 2, 2014 Ala. Acts; Ala. Code § 10A-5-1.01 *et seq.*

[3] Ala. Code § 10A-5-12.01.

[4] Ala. Code § 10A-5-1.07(b).

classified as a partnership under federal law.[5] The LLC may elect to be classified as a corporation instead of a partnership.

Effective January 1, 1997, a single-member LLC is classified for Alabama corporate and personal tax purposes in the same manner that the LLC is classified for federal tax purposes under the check-the-box regulations.[6] Prior to 1997, a single-member LLC was classified as a partnership or corporation.[7]

.02 Taxation of LLC

An LLC, including a single member disregarded LLC, must pay the Alabama Business Privilege Tax.[8] The tax is imposed on domestic LLCs and foreign LLCs qualified to do business in Alabama.

The tax is imposed on net worth at graduated rates from .00025 to .00175 ($0.25 to $1.75 per $1,000).[9] The minimum tax is $100.[10] The maximum tax is $500 for an electing family limited liability entity[11] and $15,000 for other LLCs.[12]

The Alabama Department of Revenue issued detailed guidelines on the four steps that LLCs must follow in computing net worth subject to the Business Privilege Tax.[13]

An LLC must also pay the county business license taxes. A single-member disregarded LLC that conducts business in Alabama must pay the state and county

---

[5] Ala. Code §§ 10A-5-1.07(b), 40-18-1(H).

[6] Rev. Proc. No. 98-001, Ala. Dept. of Rev. (Mar. 16, 1998); Rev. Ruls. Nos. 01-003 and 01-009 (regarding an out-of-state single-member LLC that did business in Alabama). *See also* Rev. Rul. No. 01-007, in which the Alabama Department Revenue determined that it would follow the federal procedures regarding withholding by a single-member LLC. The LLC may separately calculate, report, and pay to the Department its withholding obligations under its own name and taxpayer identification number or under the owner's name and taxpayer identification number. The owner remains ultimately responsible to the Department for payment of the withholding taxes.

[7] *See also* Rev. Proc. No. 97-001, Ala. Dept. of Rev., Ala. St. Tax Rep. (CCH) ¶ 200-674 (Feb. 21, 1997), which states that a domestic or foreign LLC of two or more members is classified as a partnership unless the LLC elects classification as a corporation under the federal check-the-box regulations and that the Alabama Department of Revenue will not follow the federal classification of single-member LLCs.

[8] Ala. Code § 40-14A-22(a); Ala. Admin. Code § 810-2-8-.01(1)(c).

[9] Ala. Code § 40-14A-22(b).

[10] Ala. Code § 40-14A-22(c).

[11] An Electing Family Limited Liability Entity is defined in Ala. Code § 40-14A-1. The LLC must be more than 80 percent owned, directly or indirectly, by an individual and family members. The LLC must have more than 90 percent of its gross receipts from interest, dividends, rents and certain other passive assets. The LLC must make an election on Form BPT-E.

[12] Ala. Code § 40-14A-22(d).

[13] Ala. Dept. of Rev., Computation of Taxable Income for Alabama BPT Purposes (June 17, 2009), prepared by Ed Cutter, Individual and Corporate Tax Division. *See also* Alabama Business Privilege Tax TY2011 Forms and Schedules Preparation Instructions, which discusses how the net worth computation should be made for LLCs classified as partnerships and disregarded entities.

business license tax. The Department of Revenue may disregard the LLC and assess the tax against the owner of the LLC.[14]

Members of an LLC are not personally liable for the sales taxes and other non-income taxes owed by the LLC.[15]

.03 Taxation of Members

Members of an LLC that is classified as a partnership are taxed on their distributive share of income.[16] Each member must include in gross income the distributive share of income or loss of the LLC from all sources.[17]

Alabama resident members of an LLC are allowed a tax credit for income taxes paid or accrued to other states or territories on behalf of the members. The credit applies to the member's proportionate share of income tax actually paid by the LLC to the foreign state or territory on account of business transacted, or property held, outside of Alabama.[18] The credit may not exceed the amount of tax that would be due on the same taxable income computed using the applicable Alabama income tax rates.[19] The tax credit does not apply to taxes based on net worth, capital or asset value, and does not apply to any tax for which a deduction or exclusion is claimed in the calculation of taxable income reported on an Alabama income tax return.

An Alabama resident member is also allowed a credit equal to 50 percent of the LLC's proportionate share of income taxes paid or accrued to a foreign country for tax years beginning after 2011.[20]

.04 Nonresident Members

Nonresident members are taxed on their distributive shares of income attributable to Alabama.[21]

The LLC must file a composite return and make composite payments on behalf of nonresident members if it has one or more nonresident members at any time during the tax year.[22] Composite returns and composite payments are due on the 15th day of the fourth month following the close of the tax year.[23] The return is filed on Form PTE-C, Alabama Nonresident Composite Payment Return, and Schedule PTE-

---

[14] *First American Holding, LLC v. Alabama Department of Revenue*, Administrative Law Decision, No. Misc 07-773 (Dec. 20, 2007).

[15] *Capitol Machine and Equipment Company LLC v. Alabama Department of Revenue*, No. S-08-619 (Administrative Law Division, Apr. 20, 2009).

[16] Ala. Admin. Code § 810-3-24-.01(1)(a).

[17] Ala. Admin. Code § 810-3-24-.01(3)(a).

[18] Ala Code § 40-18-21(a).

[19] Ala Code § 40-18-21(a)(3).

[20] Ala Code § 40-18-21(c)(1).

[21] Ala. Code § 14-18-24; Ala. Admin. Code §§ 810-3-24-.01(3)(b), 810-3-24.2-.01(2)(c).

[22] Ala. Code §§ 40-18-24.1, 10-8A-1108; Ala. Admin. Code §§ 810-3-24.2-.01(2)(a).

[23] Ala. Admin. Code § 810-3-24.2-.01(2)(h).

CK1. The composite return must contain information regarding each member's share of income, deductions, and losses.

The composite tax rate is the maximum individual income tax rate applied to each nonresident member's distributive share of income.[24] For 2012, the composite tax rate is five percent of the nonresident member's distributive shares of non-separately stated income, portfolio income and guaranteed payments allocated and apportioned to Alabama, but excluding the member's distributive share of separately stated expenses, deductions and losses.

Since an LLC is required to file a composite return on behalf of nonresident members, the Alabama the Department of Revenue may not personally assess a nonresident member for the taxes due on the member's share of Alabama source income.[25] An Alabama LLC that fails to report and pay Alabama income taxes on its nonresident member's distributive share of Alabama source income may be assessed for the taxes and interest due. Penalties may be waived for reasonable cause.[26]

All of the income or loss of an Alabama LLC that does business solely outside of the state will be allocated back to Alabama if the LLC's activities are not taxable outside of Alabama.[27]

An LLC doing business in Alabama and at least one other state must allocate and apportion its income pursuant to the Alabama apportionment tax laws.[28] The allocation and apportionment provisions do not apply if the LLC is not subject to income tax in any state other than Alabama or if it has income or loss from only one state. In those circumstances, assuming Alabama has nexus, the income or loss from the foreign state income is thrown back into Alabama.

.05 Tax Returns

A newly organized LLC that is classified as a partnership, corporation or disregarded entity must file Form BPT-IN, Initial Business Privilege Tax Return.[29]

An LLC must file Form PPT, Alabama Business Privilege Tax Return and Annual Report, if the LLC is classified as a partnership or disregarded entity. An LLC that qualifies as a Family Limited Liability Entity may pay a reduced rate of tax by filing Form BPT-E, Family Limited Liability Entity Election Form. An LLC that is classified as a corporation must file Form CPT, Alabama Business Privilege Tax Return and Annual Report for C-corporations and Other Specified Tax Entities.

If the owner of the disregarded LLC is subject to the Alabama business privilege tax, both the LLC and the owner are required to file an Alabama business privilege

---

[24] Ala. Admin. Code § 810-3-24.2-.01(2)(c).

[25] *Vogt v. Alabama Department of Revenue, Administrative Law Division*, No. INC. 11-660 (Jan. 3, 2013).

[26] *Tsitalia LLC v. Alabama Department of Revenue, Administrative Law Division*, No. BIT. 12-492 (Feb. 1, 2013).

[27] Letter from Alabama Department of Revenue and Michael E. Mason to Bruce P. Ely, *BNA Daily Tax Report*, H-1 (Jan. 25, 1999).

[28] Ala. Admin. Code § 810-3-24.2-.01(2)(b).

[29] Ala. Code § 40-14A-29.

tax return. If the owner of the disregarded LLC is not subject to the Alabama business privilege tax, the owner is not required to file a business privilege tax return. However, the LLC must disclose the owner's name and tax identification number. The LLC must also attach a statement to the return explaining why the owner is not subject to the Alabama business privilege tax.[30]

Form PPT is due no later than three and a half months after the beginning of the LLC's tax year (April 15 for calendar year LLCs). The return for single-member disregarded LLCs is due no later than the time that its member is required to file.

An Alabama LLC that is classified as a partnership or single-member LLC must file an annual tax return on Form 65, Partnership/Limited Liability Company Return of Income.[31] The form must be filed on or before the 15th day of the fourth month following the close of the LLC's fiscal year.[32] It must be mailed to the Alabama Department of Revenue, Individual and Corporate Tax Division, Pass Through Entity Unit, P.O. Box 327441, Montgomery, AL 36132-7441. Commencing in 2006, an LLC may file the return electronically using Form AL8453-C, Corporate/Partnership Income Declaration for Electronic Filing.[33]

The LLC must attach IRS Form 1065 to the state return. Form 65 is designed as a cover sheet to the federal Form 1065.[34]

Form 65 must include the names, addresses, and Social Security numbers of the members who are entitled to shares of net income, and the distributive share for each member, whether or not distributed. The names and addresses of the individual members, including nonresidents of Alabama, and each member's share of adjusted gross income must be entered on Schedule K to Form 1065.

If the LLC's books and accounts are kept on the accrual basis, the LLC must report all income accrued even though it has not actually been received or entered on the books. All income received or constructively received, such as bank interest, and all expenses actually paid must also be reported.

An Alabama LLC is not allowed a deduction for net operating losses.

One member of the LLC must sign the return. A paid preparer must also sign the return and complete the required return information.[35]

.06 Foreign LLCs

A foreign LLC that qualifies to do business in Alabama must file an Initial Business Privilege Tax Return and pay the business privilege tax within two and one-half months after the date of qualification.[36]

---

[30] Ala. Admin. Code § 810-2-8-.09.

[31] Ala. Admin. Code § 810-3-28-.01(1)(a).

[32] Ala. Admin. Code § 810-3-28-.01(3).

[33] Ala. Admin. Code § § 810-3-28-.02 through 810-3-28-.06.

[34] Ala. Admin. Code § 810-3-28-.01(1)(d).

[35] Ala. Admin. Code § 810-3-28-.01(1)(e).

[36] Form BPT-IN Instructions.

A foreign LLC maintaining a home office outside of Alabama and doing business within and without the state of Alabama must file Form 1065 and attach a rider showing the income, deductions, and net income attributable to Alabama. The allocation must be made using either the direct accounting method or the proration method corresponding to the books and accounting system maintained by the LLC. If the direct accounting method is used, the LLC must first obtain approval from the Alabama Department of Revenue. If the proration method is used, Alabama net income must be determined in the manner provided for multistate corporations.[37]

.07 Allocations

Income, deductions, losses, and credits must be allocated among members in the manner provided in the operating agreement. If there is no provision in the operating agreement, income, deductions, losses, and credits must be allocated to members on the basis of the pro rata value of contributions made by each member to the LLC (less any contributions returned).[38] The computations of distributed income for single-member LLCs and LLCs classified as partnerships are subject to various state adjustments.[39]

.08 Sales Taxes

The withdrawal of inventory is subject to Alabama sales taxes. A corporation cannot avoid the sales tax by setting up a wholly owned LLC and selling the inventory to the LLC for resale. The sale for resale exception does not apply, since a wholly owned subsidiary LLC is a disregarded entity that is treated as a separate branch or division of the parent corporation.[40]

.09 Filing Fees

The filing fees in Alabama are as follows:[41]

Articles of organization	$100 (plus $50 minimum judge probate fee)
Foreign LLC registration application	$150

---

[37] *See* Ala. Code § 40-18-31.

[38] Ala. Code § 10-12-28.

[39] Ala. Admin. Code § § 810-3-28-.01(2), 810-3-24-.01 *et seq.*

[40] Rev. Rul. No. 98-05, Ala. Dept. of Rev. (June 18, 1998).

[41] Ala. Code § 10-12-60.

¶2303 ALASKA

Alaska adopted the Alaska Revised Limited Liability Act originally effective July 1, 1995.[42]

.01 State Tax Classification

Alaska classifies an LLC in the same manner that the LLC is classified for federal tax purposes.

.02 Taxation of LLC and Members

Alaska does not tax LLCs that are classified as partnerships for federal tax purposes. Corporate members of an LLC must pay the regular corporate tax on their distributive shares of income from the LLC. There is no Alaska income tax on individual members or on their distributive shares of income from an LLC.[43]

.03 Tax Returns

Alaska LLCs and foreign LLCs doing business in Alaska must file Alaska returns consistent with their federal tax status.

An LLC that is classified as a partnership, but that has no corporate members, is not required to file a return or report.[44]

An LLC with one or more corporate members must follow the instructions applicable to partnerships with corporate partners. The LLC must submit the following portions of the LLC's federal tax return on Form 1065:[45]

- A copy of the signed Form 1065, pages 1-4, with "Alaska" marked on the top of page 1
- A copy of Schedule K-1 for each corporate partner only

An LLC that is classified as a corporation for federal income tax purposes must file an Alaska corporate tax return on Form 0405-611, Corporation Net Income Tax Return. Form 0405-611 is the standard Alaska corporate tax return designed to accommodate any taxpayer, including the most complex filings under the water's edge method. The standard form must be used whenever the LLC has a taxable nexus or business activity outside of Alaska or is a member of an affiliated group. The short form, Form 0405-611SF, is designed for taxpayers with less complex filing requirements. The short form is available to LLCs that conduct business only in Alaska and that are not members of an affiliated group.

---

[42] H.B. 420, ch. 99, 1994 Alaska Sess. Laws, Alaska Stat. §§ 10.50.010 to 10.50.995.

[43] Alaska Stat. § 43.20.012.

[44] Instructions to 2006 Alaska Corporation Net Income Tax Return Form 0405-611, p. 3.

[45] Alaska Stat. §§ 43.20.030, 43.20.051.

.04 Biennial Report

An Alaska LLC must file a biennial report on or before January 2 of the filing year.[46]

.05 Filing Fees

The filing fees in Alaska are as follows:[47]

Articles of organization	$250
Foreign LLC registration application	$350
Biennial registration	$100

¶ 2304 ARIZONA

Arizona adopted the Arizona Limited Liability Company Act effective September 30, 1992.[48] Professional LLCs are generally treated the same as other LLCs.[49]

.01 State Tax Classification

Arizona classifies an LLC in the same manner that the LLC is classified for federal tax purposes. Arizona LLCs and foreign LLCs doing business in Arizona are classified as partnerships for Arizona income tax purposes unless classified as corporations or sole proprietorships for federal tax purposes.[50]

The Arizona Department of Revenue issued the following rulings regarding state tax classifications:

- The federal tax classification of an LLC or other entity under the federal check-the-box regulations determines the LLC's classification for Arizona tax purposes.[51]
- The state classification of a single-member LLC follows the federal classification. If the single-member LLC is classified as a corporation for federal income tax purposes, the LLC must report its income to Arizona as a corporation. If a single-member LLC is classified as a corporation for federal income tax purposes and makes a valid federal election to be taxed as an S corporation, the LLC must report its income to Arizona as an S corporation. If a single-

---

[46] Alaska Stat. §§ 10.50.750 to 10.50.765.

[47] Alaska Stat. § 10.50.850; 03 AAC 16.065 Fees and Charges for Limited Liability Companies.

[48] Ch. 113, § 2, 1992 Ariz. Sess. Laws; Ariz. Rev. Stat. Ann. §§ 29-601 to 29-857.

[49] Ariz. Rev. Stat. Ann. §§ 29-841, 29-846.

[50] Ariz. Rev. Stat. Ann. § 29-857.

[51] Ariz. Corp. Tax Rul., CTR 97-1, Ariz. Dept. of Rev., Ariz. St. Tax Rep. (CCH) ¶ 300-240 (July 22, 1997); Ariz. Partnership Tax Rul., PTR 97-1, Ariz. Dept. of Rev., Ariz. St. Tax Rep. (CCH) ¶ 300-242 (July 22, 1997).

member LLC is disregarded as an entity separate from its owner for federal income tax purposes, the LLC's income will be included in the Arizona tax return of its owner.[52]

- The classification of an LLC for Arizona income tax purposes applies retroactively from December 31, 1996. It also applies retroactively to LLCs that determined their federal tax classifications under the check-the-box regulations before the effective date of the Arizona Limited Liability Company Act.[53]

.02 Taxation of LLC and Members

There is no tax on an LLC that is classified as a partnership for federal tax purposes. The LLC is treated as a pass-through entity.[54] Members of the LLC are taxed on their distributive shares of income, whether or not distributed.[55]

Members of an LLC may not deduct expenses paid by the members and behalf of the LLC unless they are required to pay those expenses under the operating agreement.[56]

.03 Taxation of Nonresident Members

Nonresident members of an LLC that is classified as a partnership are taxed on their allocable share of income from Arizona sources.[57] There is no withholding tax on the distributive share of income payable to nonresident members.

An LLC may file a composite return on behalf of nonresident members.[58] The LLC must check the composite return box in the Residency Status section of Form 140NR. The top of the front page of Form 140NR must be labeled "COMPOSITE RETURN." Each member included in the composite return must file an affidavit with the LLC stating that the member qualifies for inclusion in the composite return. The nonresident member must also sign a power of attorney authorizing the LLC to file a composite return on behalf of the member. Each member's deductions, exemptions and liability must be computed separately on the return.[59]

---

[52] Ariz. Corp. Tax Rul., CTR 97-2, Ariz. Dept. of Rev., Ariz. St. Tax Rep. (CCH) ¶ 300-244 (Aug. 8, 1997); Ariz. Partnership Tax Rul., PTR 97-2, Ariz. Dept. of Rev., Ariz. St. Tax Rep. (CCH) ¶ 300-247 (Aug. 8, 1997).

[53] Ariz. Corp. Tax Rul., CTR 97-2, Ariz. Dept. of Rev., Ariz. St. Tax Rep. (CCH) ¶ 300-244 (Aug. 8, 1997); Ariz. Partnership Tax Rul., PTR 97-2, Ariz. Dept. of Rev., Ariz. St. Tax Rep. (CCH) ¶ 300-247 (Aug. 8, 1997).

[54] Ariz. Rev. Stat. Ann. § 29-857.

[55] Ariz. Rev. Stat. Ann. § 43-1412.

[56] Case No. 201200088-I, Arizona Department of Revenue, Decision of Officer (Sept. 28, 2012).

[57] Ariz. Admin. Code R15-2C-601.

[58] Ariz. Dept. of Rev. ITR 16-2, Composite Individual Income Tax Returns.

[59] Ariz. Individual Income Tax Rul., ITR 13-2. Ariz. Dep't of Rev. (May 6, 2013).

The member must pay the tax liability by direct remittance to the state, remittance by the member to the LLC, or by a charge against the member's loan account. The LLC may not incur the tax liability itself.[60]

The LLC may file a composite return if all of the following requirements are met:[61]

- the member is a nonresident individual of the state for the full tax year;
- the member and spouse has no income from sources within the state other than the distributive share of LLC income;
- the member is not the estate of a deceased member;
- all members included in the composite return have the same tax year;
- the composite return has a least ten participating members;
- the member is not required to make payments of Arizona estimated taxes; and
- the LLC complies with the other requirements for composite returns in Arizona Individual Income Tax Ruling ITR 13-2.

.04 Tax Returns

An Arizona LLC that is classified as a partnership for federal tax purposes must file Arizona Form 165. The LLC's income is included in the Arizona tax returns of its members.[62]

An Arizona LLC that is classified as a corporation must report its income to Arizona as a corporation on Arizona Form 120. An Arizona LLC that is classified as a corporation for federal income tax purposes and that makes a valid federal election to be taxed as an S corporation must report its income to Arizona on Arizona Form 120S.

The income of a single-member LLC that is disregarded as an entity for federal tax purposes is included in the Arizona return of its owner.[63]

The returns for LLCs that are classified as partnerships are due by the 15th day of the third month following the close of the tax year. This is April 15 in the case of a calendar year return. If an LLC has filed an extension, the LLC must attach a copy of the completed federal Form 1065 and supporting schedules to the Arizona return. The return must be filed with the Arizona Department of Revenue, P.O. Box 52153, Phoenix, AZ 85072-2153.

The members' shares of income from the LLC are reported on Schedule K-1NR to Arizona Form 165. The LLC is required to adjust its federal income to an Arizona basis. Line 3 of Arizona Form 165 Schedule K-1NR is the member's distributive share of that adjustment. This amount is reported on the member's Arizona tax return.

---

[60] *Id.*

[61] *Id.*

[62] Ariz. Corp. Tax Rul., CTR 97-2, Ariz. Dept. of Rev., Ariz. St. Tax Rep. (CCH) ¶300-244 (Aug. 8, 1997); Ariz. Partnership Tax Rul., PTR 97-2, Ariz. Dept. of Rev., Ariz. St. Tax Rep. (CCH) ¶300-247 (Aug. 8, 1997).

[63] Arizona Partnership Tax Ruling PTR 97-2; Instructions to Arizona Form 165.

One of the members of the LLC must sign the return. When someone other than a member or employee of the LLC prepares a return, the preparer must also sign the return.

The LLC may apply for an Arizona extension by filing a completed Form 120EXT by the original due date of the return. The LLC can substitute a valid federal extension for an Arizona extension. Composite return filers must use Arizona Form 204 to obtain an extension.

The LLC must maintain books and records substantiating the information reported on the return and keep these documents for inspection. There are special procedures for maintaining books and records through computer, electronic, and imaging processes and systems.[64]

.05 Allocations

The profits and losses of an LLC are allocated among the members as provided in the operating agreement. If the operating agreement does not provide for allocations, profits are allocated among the members according to the manner in which they share distributions that exceed the repayment of their capital contributions. Losses are allocated among the members according to the relative capital contributions that they make or promise to make in the future.[65]

.06 Filing Fees

The filing fees in Arizona are as follows:[66]

Articles of organization	$ 50
Foreign LLC registration application	$150
Notice of winding up	$ 25
Articles of merger and certificate of merger	$ 50
Furnishing written information on any LLC	$ 10
Name reservation	$ 10

¶ 2305 ARKANSAS

Arkansas enacted the Small Business Entity Tax Pass Through Act and the Arkansas Limited Liability Company Act, which authorize LLCs, effective April 12, 1993.[67]

---

[64] Ariz. Gen. Tax Rul., GTR 96-1, Ariz. Dept. of Rev., Ariz. St. Tax Rep. (CCH) ¶ 300-223 (Mar. 6, 1996).

[65] Ariz. Rev. Stat. Ann. § 29-709.

[66] Ariz. Rev. Stat. Ann. § 29-851.

[67] Act 100 (H.B. 1419), 1993 Ark. Acts; Ark. Code Ann. §§ 4-32-101 to 4-32-1401.

.01 State Tax Classification

Arkansas classifies an LLC in the same manner in which the LLC is classified for federal tax purposes, effective January 1, 2003.[68]

.02 Taxation of LLC and Members

Arkansas imposes an annual franchise tax of $150 on LLCs.[69] Members of an LLC are taxed for Arkansas income tax purposes in the same manner that the members are taxed for federal income tax purposes.[70] Members of an LLC that is classified as a partnership must pay tax on their distributive shares of income from the LLC.[71]

.03 Tax Returns

An LLC that is classified as a partnership must file a return on Form AR1050, Partnership Return of Income. Every domestic or foreign LLC that is doing business in Arkansas or that receives income from sources within Arkansas, regardless of the amount, must file Form AR1050.

Fiscal year returns must be filed on or before the 15th day of the fourth month following the close of the fiscal year. Calendar year returns are filed on or before April 15.

Each member's share of income must be reported on the same form. All income must be reported, whether or not distributed. An explanatory statement must be attached to the return if distributed income is determined on a basis other than a percentage basis.

An LLC may request an extension of time for filing a return by filing Form AR1055, Request for Extension of Time for Filing Income Tax Returns. Federal extension requests are honored as valid state extension requests.[72]

The income and expenses of an LLC having only one member must be reported on the member's individual income tax return.[73]

An Arkansas LLC, regardless of its classification, must also file LLC Franchise Tax Report on or before May 1 following the close of the tax year. The LLC must initially file Limited Liability Company Franchise Tax with the Arkansas Secretary of State at the time that it files its Articles of Organization in order to receive the annual franchise tax reporting form. The LLC must pay the annual $150 franchise tax with the report, plus a $5 online transaction fee.

---

[68] Ark. Code Ann. § 4-32-1313.

[69] *See* Arkansas Form LLC Franchise Tax Report.

[70] *Id.*

[71] Ark. Code Ann. § 4-32-1313; Reg. § 6.26-51-102, issued by the Ark. Director of the Dept. of Fin. & Admin.

[72] *Id.*

[73] Ark. Code Ann. § 4-32-1313.

.04 Nonresident Members

Nonresident members must pay tax on their distributive shares of income from the LLC.[74]

The LLC must withhold taxes at the highest rate attributable to corporate or individual taxpayers on income that is derived from or attributable to sources within Arkansas and distributed to nonresident members.[75] The withholding tax rate is 6.9 percent in 2018.[76]

The LLC must file an annual withholding return on Form AR941PT on or before the 15th day of the fourth month after the close of the tax year setting forth the amount of income distributed to nonresident members and the amount of taxes withheld.[77] The annual return must be in electronic format.[78] The LLC must pay the withholding taxes to the director of the Department of Finance and Administration. It must inform the nonresident members on Form AR1099PT by the 15th day of the fourth month after the end of the tax year of the amount of taxes withheld.[79] The LLC must file Form AR1099PT for each nonresident member subject to withholding with the Arkansas Department of Finance along with Form AR1096. Nonresident members must attach a copy of Form AR1099PT with their Arkansas personal income tax return.[80] An LLC must also file Form AR941PT with the Arkansas Department of Finance by April 15 after the close of each tax year.[81]

An LLC may file a composite tax return on Form AR1000CR on behalf of electing full-year nonresident members.[82] The LLC must report on the composite return and pay on behalf of each electing nonresident member Arkansas income taxes at the highest income tax rate for corporate or individual taxpayers for income derived from or attributable to Arkansas sources.[83] The composite tax rate is 6.9 percent in 2018. No deductions or credits are allowed. A nonresident may elect to be included in the composite return if the member's only source income or losses within Arkansas is from one or more pass-through entities.[84] The nonresident member may then file an individual income tax return in Arkansas and receive a credit for income taxes paid

---

[74] Reg. § 6.26-51-102.

[75] Ark. Code Ann. § 26-51-919(a)(2), (b)(1)(A); Rule 2006-3, Arkansas Department of Finance and Administration, effective December 1, 2006.

[76] Arkansas 2017 Composite Estimated Tax Worksheet.

[77] Ark. Code Ann. § 26-51-919(b)(2)(A); Rule 2006-3, Arkansas Department of Finance and Administration, effective Jan. 1, 2008.

[78] Ark. Code Ann. § 26-51-919(b)(2)(B).

[79] Ark. Code Ann. § 26-51-919(b)(2)(A); Rule 2006-3, Arkansas Department of Finance and Administration, effective Jan. 1, 2008.

[80] Rule 2006-3, Arkansas Department of Finance and Administration, effective October 4, 2007.

[81] Rule 2006-3, Arkansas Department of Finance and Administration, effective October 4, 2007.

[82] Ark. Code Ann. § 26-51-919(d); Reg. § 2.26-51-405, issued by the director of the Arkansas Department of Finance and Administration.

[83] Ark. Code Ann. § 26-51-919(d)(1).

[84] Ark. Code Ann. § 26-51-919(d)(2).

as part of the composite return.[85] The LLC must file a composite return on or before the 15th day of the fourth month following the close of the tax year.[86] The LLC must make the filing by magnetic media if there are more than ten participants. An LLC that files a composite return for nonresident members must also file Form AR1099PT. The amount of composite payment reported on Form AR1000CR must equal the amount reported on Form AR1099PT.

An LLC is not required to withhold taxes if:[87]

- The nonresident member's distributive share of income from the LLC attributable to Arkansas sources is less than $1,000.
- The nonresident member elects to be included as part of the composite return.
- The member submits an affidavit to the LLC on Form AR4PT, Nonresident Member Withholding Exemption Affidavit. The LLC must transmit the form to the Arkansas Department of Finance and Administration on Form AR4PT-A.
- The LLC is a publicly traded LLC that is classified as a partnership for federal income tax purposes and has agreed to file an information return.
- The LLC has filed an agreement by the nonresident member to file a tax return in Arkansas, pay any Arkansas income tax due, and be subject to Arkansas jurisdiction for any income tax due.
- The income is exempt from tax under the applicable Arkansas tax laws.
- The director of the Department of Finance and Administration determines that no withholding is required.

An LLC must register with the Arkansas Department of Finance using Form AR4ER. The LLC must check the pass-through entity box. It must add the processing number 70 at the end of its federal employer identification number for all personal income tax withholding forms and payments to nonresidents.[88]

Effective January 1, 2018, Arkansas changed its withholding tax laws so that nonresident C corporation owners of LLCs are subject to withholding. Prior to that time, C corporations were exempt from withholding. A C corporation may avoid withholding by participating in a composite return or by filing a form agreeing to be subject to Arkansas income tax.[89]

.05 Allocations

Allocations and distributions of income, loss, cash, and other assets must be shared among members in accordance with the operating agreement.[90] If the operat-

---

[85] Ark. Code Ann. § 26-51-919(d)(3).

[86] Ark. Code Ann. § 26-51-919(d)(4).

[87] Ark. Code Ann. § 26-51-919(c); Rule 2006-3, Arkansas Department of Finance and Administration, effective Jan. 1, 2008.

[88] Rule 2006-3, Arkansas Department of Finance and Administration, effective October 4, 2007.

[89] Act 760, 91st General Assembly, 2017 Regular Session.

[90] Ark. Code Ann. § 4-32-601.

ing agreement is silent, each member shares equally in the profits and assets remaining after all liabilities have been satisfied.[91]

.06 Filing Fees

The filing fees in the state of Arkansas are as follows:[92]

Articles of organization	$ 50
Articles of merger and certificate of merger	$ 50
Articles of dissolution	$ 50
Application for certificate of authority by foreign LLC	$300
Annual registration*	$150

* Ark. Code Ann. § 4-32-202.

¶ 2306 CALIFORNIA

California enacted the Revised Uniform Limited Liability Company Act effective January 1, 2014.[93]

.01 State Tax Classification

California follows the federal check-the-box regulations in determining the state tax classification of an LLC for income and franchise tax purposes for tax years beginning after 1996.[94] Effective in 2010, California follows the federal tax classification of an LLC for state unemployment tax law purposes.[95] An LLC is classified for state tax purposes in the same manner that it is classified for federal tax purposes. However, an LLC will continue to be taxed as a corporation until it elects otherwise if the LLC was properly classified and taxed as a corporation for California tax purposes during any income year beginning within the 60-month period before January 1, 1997.[96]

---

[91] Ark. Code Ann. § 4-32-503.

[92] Ark. Code Ann. § 4-32-1301.

[93] Cal. Corp. Code §§ 17701.01-17713.13. The California Revised Uniform Limited Liability Company Act is popularly known as RULLCA. It was signed into law by Governor Jerry Brown as 2012 Stats, ch 419. It will apply to all existing California limited liability companies and foreign LLCs previously registered with the Secretary of State on January 1, 2014. It replaces the Beverly-Killea Limited Liability Company Act, Cal. Corp. Code §§ 17000-17656.

[94] Cal. Rev. & Tax. Code § 23038(b)(2); 18 Cal. Code Reg. § 23038(b)-1(b); FTB Legal Ruling 2014-01 (July 22, 2014).

[95] S.B. 1244 (Aug. 13, 2010), amending Sections 621, 623, 928.7 and 13009 of the California Unemployment Insurance Code.

[96] Cal. Rev. & Tax. Code § 23038(b)(2)(C).

.02 Franchise Tax

LLCs must pay an annual $800 franchise tax.[97] The tax applies whether the LLC is classified as a disregarded entity,[98] corporation or a partnership. The tax is payable on the 15th day of the fourth month of the taxable year.[99] If the LLC is classified as a corporation, the LLC must pay an additional $800 deposit at the time of organization. A foreign LLC registered in the state must pay the minimum tax even if it does no business in California.[100]

.03 Gross Receipts Tax

LLCs that are classified as disregarded entities[101] or partnerships must also pay an entity-level tax based on "total income" from all sources derived from or attributable to California.[102] "Total income" means gross income, plus the cost of goods sold, paid or incurred in connection with the LLC's business.[103] Total income includes income from rents, interest, dividends, and trade or business activities.[104] Total income is computed using the LLC Income Worksheet in the instructions to FTB Form 568.

The gross receipts taxes for tax years beginning on or after 2001 are as follows for 2001:[105]

Income from all sources	Fee
Over $250,000, but less than $500,000	$ 900
$500,000 or more, but less than $1,000,000	$ 2,500
$1,000,000 or more, but less than $5,000,000	$ 6,000
$5,000,000 or more	$11,790

The Franchise Tax Board (FTB) may aggregate the income of all commonly controlled LLCs. This determination may be made for only one LLC in a controlled group. The FTB may aggregate income only if it first determines that multiple LLCs were formed to reduce the fees payable by members of the same group. Commonly controlled LLCs include all other partnerships doing business in California in which the same persons own, directly or indirectly, more than 50 percent of the capital or

---

[97] Cal. Rev. & Tax. Code § 17941.

[98] Cal. Rev. & Tax. Code § 23038(b)(2)(B)(iii).

[99] Cal. Rev. & Tax. Code § 17941(c).

[100] R.E.A., LLC, California State Board of Equalization (July 17, 2007).

[101] Cal. Rev. & Tax. Code § 23038(b)(2)(B)(iii).

[102] Cal. Rev. & Tax. Code § 17942(b)(1). LLCs determine total income from California sources by using the rules for sales assignment under Sections 25135 and 25136 and the related regulations, as modified by regulations under Section 25137, other than those provisions that exclude receipts from the sales factor (R&TC Section 17942(b)(1)(B)). FTB Publication 3556, Limited Liability Company Filing Information.

[103] Cal. Rev. & Tax. Code § 24271.

[104] California Franchise Tax Board, *Tax News* (July 2010).

[105] Cal. Franchise Tax Bd. Notice 2001-7 (Nov. 9, 2001), effective for tax years beginning in 2001.

profits interests.[106] The result is that if a foreign LLC with separate series does business in California,[107] each series is treated as a separate entity for purposes of the $800 minimum tax, but all series are aggregated for purposes of determining the gross receipts tax.

Once the total income of the group is aggregated, each group member is jointly and severally liable for the LLC fee. A commonly controlled LLC for aggregation purposes includes the LLC and any other partnership or LLC that does business in California and that is required to file a partnership return if the same persons own more than 50 percent of the capital or profits interests in the LLC.[108]

An LLC that owns an interest in a pass-through entity must report its distributive share of the pass-through entities' total income from all sources derived from or attributable to California. The distributive share must include the associated cost of goods sold and any deductions subtracted from gross ordinary income to obtain ordinary income.[109]

However, an LLC that owns an interest in another LLC is not subject to the gross receipts tax attributable to income received from the other LLC.[110] For example, an LLC that is a member of a disregarded LLC does not separately report any amounts attributable to its membership interest in the disregarded entity in computing gross income.[111]

The gross receipts tax is based only on the income from California sources.[112] In 2014, the California Franchise Tax Board issued proposed regulations clarifying the calculation of the annual LLC fee and the total income from all sources derived from or attributable to California on which the fee is based. Under the regulations, the following rules apply:[113]

- An LLC's distributive share of income from another LLC will not be included in total income from all sources attributable to California if (i) the income of the other LLC was subject to the LLC fee, or (ii) such other LLC's income from all sources attributable to California was below $250,000.

- An LLC's distributive share of income from other pass-through entities is treated as if the LLC derived the income and distributions directly.

- The LLC's distributive share of income from another pass-through entity must be adjusted to include the cost of goods sold by the pass-through entity allocable to California in order to determine the total income subject to the California tax.

---

[106] Cal. Rev. & Tax. Code § 17942(b)(2).

[107] *See* Instructions to Form 568.

[108] *Id.*

[109] FTB Publication 3556, Limited Liability Company Filing Information.

[110] *See* instructions to Form 568 which states, "The definition of 'Total Income' excludes allocations, distributions, or gains to an LLC from another LLC, if that allocation, distribution, or gain was already subject to the LLC fee. Use line 1b to exclude these amounts."

[111] FTB Publication 3556, Limited Liability Company Filing Information.

[112] Cal. Rev. & Tax. Code § 17942(a), (b).

[113] https://www.ftb.ca.gov/law/regs/17942/07012014_Regulation_Final.pdf.

- Income derived from or attributable to sources outside California is not subject to the LLC fee. The determination of the source of income is based on assignment rules. Income derived from the passive holding of intangible property must be assigned to the location where the intangible property is managed. For example, if an Indiana LLC doing business in California holds bonds through a portfolio manager located in Nevada, the interest income from the bonds must be assigned to Nevada for LLC fee purposes. Income received from a pass-through entity (other than an LLC already subject to the LLC tax) must be assigned to the state where the pass-through entity assigned the income on Schedule K-1 provided to the LLC.

- The regulations provide simplified methods of calculating the LLC fee and determining the sales factor that must be used in the calculation.

Beginning in 2009, the LLC must pay the fee by the 15th day of the six-month of the tax year.[114] There is a ten percent penalty for failure to pay the tax on a timely basis. There is no penalty if the LLC pays a fee by the deadline that is at least equal to the total amount of the fee for the preceding tax year.[115]

.04 Property Taxes

An LLC that is classified as a partnership is subject to property taxes in the same manner as a partnership except where a specific property tax provision otherwise provides.[116]

There is no documentary transfer tax on the transfer of property to an LLC if the owners of the property retain the same proportional interests in the property after the transfer. The transfer is treated as a mere change in the form of ownership.[117]

There is no reassessment of property under Proposition 13 upon transfer of the property to an LLC if the owners of the property retain the same proportional interests in the property after the transfer.[118]

There is no reassessment of property under Proposition 13 as a result of a statutory conversion or merger of a partnership into an LLC if the owners of the converting or disappearing entity maintain the same ownership interest in the surviving LLC as held in the disappearing entity.[119]

The transfer of membership interests in an LLC may constitute a change in ownership resulting in reassessment in the following cases:

- If the LLC acquired the property by purchase or in another transaction that resulted in reassessment of the property, then there would be a change in ownership when any person acquires more than 50 percent of the member-

---

[114] 18 CCR § 17942(d)(1).

[115] 18 CCR § 17942(d)(2).

[116] Cal. Rev. & Tax. Code § 28.5.

[117] Cal. Rev. & Tax. Code § 11923(a)(4).

[118] Cal. Rev. & Tax. Code § 62(a)(2); 18 Cal. Code Regs. tit. 462, § 180(b)(2).

[119] Rule § 462.180(d)(4), Example 10.

ship interests.[120] All the property owned by the LLC would be reassessed when a member or any third party acquired direct or indirect ownership or control of the LLC. The property would be reassessed even though the person acquired control through an acquisition of less than 50 percent of the membership interests. Thus, there would be a reassessment if a 49 percent owner acquired an additional two percent interest in the LLC. There would be no reassessment if the members sold all of the membership interests to third parties, none of whom acquired more than a 50 percent interest in the LLC.[121]

- If the LLC acquired property in a transaction that was exempt from reassessment, then there would be a change in ownership resulting in reassessment if the "original co-owners" (the owners of the LLC at the time of the exempt transaction) cumulatively transferred, in one or more transactions, more than 50 percent of the membership interests. There would be a reassessment even if no one person acquired more than a 50 percent interest in the LLC from the original co-owners.[122] For example, the contribution of property to an LLC would be exempt from reassessment if each of the parties retained the same proportional interest in the LLC that they had in the property prior to the contribution. Each of the members in the LLC who contributed property to the LLC in the exempt transaction would be an "original co-owner." There would be a reassessment of the property when these original co-owners cumulatively transferred, in one or more transactions, more than 50 percent of the membership interests.

.05 Tax Reporting Requirements for LLCs Classified as Corporations

An LLC that is classified as a corporation must file a franchise tax return and pay the $800 minimum franchise tax.[123] The LLC pays the $800 by using Form 3522, Limited Liability Company Tax Voucher. The LLC must file Form 100, Corporation Franchise or Income Tax Return. The LLC is subject to the applicable provisions of the bank and corporation tax laws. These laws include the requirement that a corporation prepay the minimum franchise tax when it is formed or qualifies to do business in California.

.06 Tax Reporting Requirements for LLCs Classified as Partnerships

An LLC that is classified as a partnership must file Form 568, Limited Liability Company Return of Income.[124] The return is due by the 15th day of the fourth month

---

[120] Rule 462.180(d)(1).

[121] Rule 462.180(d)(1) (last paragraph).

[122] Rule 462.180(d)(2).

[123] Cal. Rev. & Tax. Code § 18633.5(h).

[124] Cal. Rev. & Tax. Code § 18633.5(a), (i)(1).

following the close of the tax year. The LLC may obtain an automatic six-month extension by filing Form 3537.[125]

Every LLC doing business in California, organized in California, or organized in another state or foreign country and registered with the California Secretary of State must pay an annual tax of $800 with Form 3522, Limited Liability Company Tax Voucher. Payment is due on or before the 15th day of the fourth month after the beginning of the LLC's tax year.[126]

The LLC must use Form 568 to report and pay the gross receipts tax and any nonconsenting member taxes (taxes of nonresident members who do not consent to the jurisdiction of the California taxing authorities).[127] If the LLC obtains an extension of time to file return, it must pay the tax by the regular filing date by using Form 3537, Payment Voucher. The minimum $800 annual tax should not be remitted with Form 568.

The members of an LLC are subject to California taxes in the same manner as partners in a partnership.[128] However, members are not entitled to deduct the entity-level taxes paid by the LLC.[129]

The resident and nonresident members must file California tax returns with respect to their shares of California source income.[130]

An LLC that fails to respond to a Demand for Past Due Return will have its powers, rights and privileges suspended (domestic LLC) or forfeited (foreign LLC). The LLC will be subject to a $2,000 penalty for failure to file a return within 60 days after receiving the demand. The penalty will be in addition to the delinquent filing penalties and the filing enforcement fee. The penalties may be waived for reasonable cause.[131]

The special forms applicable to California LLCs classified as partnerships are as follows:

Form	Name
568	Limited Liability Company Return of Income
Schedule D (568)	Capital Gain or Loss
Schedule K-1 (568)	Member's Share of Income, Deductions, Credits, Etc.
Schedule K-1 NR (568)	Member's Share of Income, Deductions, Credits, Etc.
FTB 3522	Limited Liability Company Tax Voucher (for payment of annual $800 tax)
FTB 3537	Payment Voucher for Automatic Extension for Limited Liability Companies
FTB 3885L	Depreciation and Amortization

---

[125] Cal. Rev. & Tax. Code § 18567.

[126] Cal. Rev. & Tax. Code § 17941(c).

[127] Cal. Rev. & Tax. Code § 17942.

[128] Cal. Rev. & Tax. Code § 17087.6.

[129] Cal. Rev. & Tax. Code § 17220(c).

[130] Cal. Franchise Tax Bd. Notice 92-5 (Aug. 21, 1992).

[131] California Franchise Tax Board, *Tax News* (Dec. 2012).

Form	*Name*
FTB 3832	Limited Liability Company Nonresident Members' Consent
FTB 3555L	Request for Tax Clearance Certificate

The LLC must provide each member with the following tax reporting information:[132]

- A copy of the information shown on FTB Form 568;
- FTB Schedule K-1 of FTB Form 568 for resident members showing the member's distributive share of LLC income, gain, loss, deduction, credit, and other tax items; and
- FTB Schedule K-1 NR for nonresident members showing the same information.

.07 Single-Member LLCs

A single-member LLC may be formed in California effective January 1, 2000.[133] A single-member LLC that is classified as a disregarded entity for federal purposes will also be classified as a disregarded entity for California purposes.[134]

A husband and wife who each have a separate interest in LLC will be treated as separate members. The LLC must file a partnership return and issue them a separate Schedule K-1 (FTB Form 568). A husband and wife who hold a membership interest together are treated as a single member. The LLC must file a return as a disregarded entity if they are the sole owners, and issue them a single K-1 (FTB Form 568).[135]

A single-member LLC whose entity is disregarded for federal and California tax purposes is subject to the following three tax provisions in California:[136]

1. *LLC taxes.* The LLC must pay the annual $800 California franchise tax if the LLC is doing business in California, filed articles of organization with the California Secretary of State, or received a certificate of registration by the California Secretary of State.[137]

   The single-member LLC must pay the California annual gross receipts tax imposed on LLCs. This tax ranges from $900 to $11,790 depending on the "total income" of the LLC.[138]

   The LLC is required to pay tax to California on any amount due on behalf of the owner at the highest marginal tax rate. The LLC is subject to penalties

---

[132] Cal. Rev. & Tax. Code § 18633.5.

[133] 1999 Cal. Stat. ch. 490, amending Cal. Corp. Code § § 17001, 17050, and 17101.

[134] Cal. Rev. & Tax. Code § 23038(b)(2).

[135] Instructions to 1999 Limited Liability Company Tax Booklet, published by the California Franchise Tax Board.

[136] Cal. Rev. & Tax. Code § 23038(b)(2)(B)(iii); 18 Cal. Code Reg. § 23038(b)-1(a)(4).

[137] Cal. Rev. & Tax. Code § 23038(b)(2)(B)(iii); Cal. Rev. & Tax. Code § 17941.

[138] Cal. Rev. & Tax. Code § 23038(b)(2)(B)(iii); Cal. Rev. & Tax. Code § 17942.

and interest for failure to timely pay the tax unless the owner timely files and pays the amount due.

2. *LLC information returns.*[139] A single-member LLC is only required to complete Side 1 of FTB Form 568. This form is used to determine the gross receipts fee and to pay the annual LLC franchise tax and fee. The single-member LLC must also file an information return with the California Secretary of State on Form LLC-EO12R, Statement of Information Renewal.

3. *Tax credit limitations.* A taxpayer that directly or indirectly owns an interest in a single-member LLC that is disregarded for tax purposes may only claim credits or credit carryforwards from the LLC to the extent the member's tax liability is attributable to the LLC. Disallowed credits may be carried forward to future years.[140]

There are additional limits on the amount of credits that the LLC may claim for purposes of computing the member's alternative minimum tax. The amount of credit attributable to the LLC that is classified as a disregarded entity, including credit carryovers, that may be applied against the member's net tax is limited to the excess of the member's regular tax. This is determined by including income attributable to the LLC, less the member's regular taxes, determined by excluding the income attributable to the LLC. The LLC may carry forward to a subsequent income or tax year any excess credit that may not be claimed against the net tax during the current income or tax year.[141]

The Franchise Tax Board determined that the following tax filing requirements apply to a single-member LLC.[142]

- The LLC will be treated as a disregarded entity and all income and expenses of the LLC will be reported on the member's tax return as a sole proprietorship (Schedule C business).
- If the LLC is owned by a corporation or other business entity, it will be treated as a disregarded entity and all income and expenses of the LLC will be reported on the member's tax return as a division of the company.
- The LLC must file Form 568, Side 1, Side 2, Side 6 (Schedule IW), and pay the annual tax and LLC fee if applicable.
- If the member is a nonresident and has not signed the Single Member LLC Information and Consent on bottom of Form 568 Side 1, consenting to California's jurisdiction, then the LLC must complete Schedule T and pay the tax on behalf of its single owner.
- The LLC must file Schedule B and Schedule K if either (i) the income or loss amount reported on Schedule B, line 1 or line 3 through line 11, is $3 million or more, or (ii) the total distributive income/payment items on Schedule K, line 21a, is greater than or equal to $3 million.

---

[139] Cal. Rev. & Tax. Code § 23038(b)(2)(B)(iii); Cal. Rev. & Tax. Code § 18633.5.

[140] Cal. Rev. & Tax. Code §§ 17039, 17941, 23036. The Franchise Tax Board gives numerous examples of how to make the calculations in Tax News, Franchise Tax Board (June 2009).

[141] Cal. Rev. & Tax. Code §§ 18633.5(i)(1), 23038.

[142] https://www.ftb.ca.gov/businesses/Structures/Limited-Liability-Company.shtml.

¶ 2306.07

- California Form 568 or 565 must be filed by the 15th day of the fourth month after the close of the LLC's taxable year.
- The LLC must pay a fee if the California total income is equal to or greater than $250,000. The LLC must estimate the fee it will owe for the year and make an estimated fee payment.
- The annual tax is due by the 15th day of the fourth month of the taxable year, and is paid using Form 3522, Limited Liability Company Tax Voucher.
- The LLC must complete Schedule EO, Pass-Through Entity Ownership (568), to report any ownership interest in other partnerships or limited liability companies regardless of whether these entities are required to file a tax return in California, or are subject to California annual tax or LLC fee.

.08 Nonresident Members

Personal Income Taxes

A nonresident member is taxed on the member's allocable share of California source income. For example, the nonresident member of an LLC that provided management services to an equity fund located in California was subject California personal income taxes on the member's allocable share of income.[143]

Withholding Taxes by LLC

An LLC that does business in California must withhold California taxes if it distributes California source income to domestic nonresident members,[144] or if it allocates California source income to foreign (non-U.S.) members.[145]

The 2018 withholding tax rate for domestic nonresident members is seven percent unless a waiver or reduction is granted by the Franchise Tax Board.[146] The withholding tax applies to the following: (i) gross payments made to nonresident independent contractors for services performed in California, (ii) gross payments made to nonresident recipients of California rents or royalties, (iii) distributions of California source income made to nonresident beneficiaries of estates or trusts, and (iv) distributions of California source income to domestic nonresident S corporation shareholders and partners.[147] The withholding tax rates reflect California case law that California may not tax nonresidents on non-California source income.

---

[143] Chief Counsel Ruling 2013-04, Cal. Franchise Tax Board (Dec. 30, 2013).

[144] Cal. Rev. & Tax. Code §§ 18662, 18666; FTB Publication 1017, Resident and Nonresident Withholding Guidelines, California Franchise Tax Board (revised December 2012), Q&A-13, 105.

[145] Cal. Rev. & Tax. Code § 18666; FTB Publication 1017, Resident and Nonresident Withholding Guidelines, California Franchise Tax Board (revised December 2012), Q&A-113.

[146] Instructions to FTB Form 588.

[147] Instructions to FTB Form 592-B, Resident and Nonresident Withholding Tax Statement; FTB Publication 1017, Resident and Nonresident Withholding Guidelines, California Franchise Tax Board (revised December 2012), Q&A-13.

The withholding tax rate is the highest marginal tax rate for allocations of income to foreign (non-U.S.) members and for domestic nonresident members who do not sign the consent form on Form FTB 3832. The withholding tax rates in 2018 are 12.3 percent for individual members, 8.84 percent for corporate members, and 10.84 percent for foreign banking financial institution members.[148]

In order to determine the amount subject to withholding, the LLC must make a good faith estimate of the total amount of California source income for the current year. If it is impractical or impossible to estimate, the LLC must use the amount of California source income recognized as of the date of each distribution.[149]

Guaranteed payments to nonresident members are subject to withholding if the guaranteed payments represent income from California sources.[150]

There is no withholding if the total payments or distributions of California source income to a nonresident member are $1,500 or less for the calendar year.[151] There is no minimum threshold amount for foreign (non-U.S.) members. The LLC must withhold on all allocable California source income to foreign members.[152]

An LLC must use the following forms to report and remit the withholding taxes:[153]

- FTB Form 588, Nonresident Withholding Waiver Request. The Franchise Tax Board may authorize a waiver of withholding if the member filed California tax returns for the two most recent taxable years in which the member had a filing requirement and has paid all outstanding tax obligations. If the member does not have a current filing history, but is making estimated tax payments for the current tax year and is current on any outstanding FTB tax obligations, the Franchise Tax Board may issue a waiver that is good for a one-year period ending on December 31 of the same calendar year. Waivers of the withholding requirements are available to domestic nonresident payees only.[154] The FTB issues a Waiver Determination Notice for each waiver request. Withholding waivers are effective for a maximum term of 24 months and end on December 31 of the succeeding calendar year granted.[155]

---

[148] Instructions to FTB Form 592-B, Resident and Nonresident Withholding Tax Statement; FTB Publication 1017, Resident and Nonresident Withholding Guidelines, California Franchise Tax Board (revised December 2015), Q&A-14. *See also* Instructions to FTB Form 592-F, under the heading, "Amount of Tax Withheld."

[149] FTB Publication 1017, Resident and Nonresident Withholding Guidelines, California Franchise Tax Board (revised December 2015), Q&A-104.

[150] FTB Publication 1017, Resident and Nonresident Withholding Guidelines, California Franchise Tax Board (revised December 2015), Q&A-105.

[151] FTB Publication 1017, Resident and Nonresident Withholding Guidelines, California Franchise Tax Board (revised December 2015), Q&A-15.

[152] Cal. Rev. & Tax. Code § 18666; FTB Publication 1017, Resident and Nonresident Withholding Guidelines, California Franchise Tax Board (revised December 2012), Q&A-113.

[153] Cal. Rev. & Tax. Code § 18666; FTB Publication 1017, Resident and Nonresident Withholding Guidelines, California Franchise Tax Board (revised December 2015), Q&A-120.

[154] FTB Publication 1017, Resident and Nonresident Withholding Guidelines, California Franchise Tax Board (revised December 2015), Q&A-61.

[155] Instructions to FTB Form 588.

¶ 2306.08

- FTB Form 589, Nonresident Reduced Withholding Request.
- FTB Form 592, Resident and Nonresident Withholding Statement, to report the income and withholding amount for each nonresident member.
- FTB Form 592-V, Payment Voucher for Resident and Nonresident Withholding, to remit the withholding amount reported on Form 592.
- FTB Form 592-A, Payment Voucher for Foreign Partner or Member Withholding, to remit withholding payments to the FTB made during the year, or to remit the balance due on partnership or LLC income or gain allocable under Code Sec. 704 to foreign (non-U.S.) partners or members.
- FTB Form 592-F, Foreign Partner or Member Annual Return, to report the total withholding for the taxable year and to allocate the income or gain and related withholding to the foreign partners or members.
- FTB Form 592-B, Resident and Nonresident Withholding Tax Statement, to show the amount of income subject to withholding and tax withheld.
- FTB Form 590, Withholding Exemption Certificate, for a California LLC subject to California taxes. Some nonresident member distributions are exempt from withholding, including: (i) corporations with a permanent place of business in California; (ii) corporations qualified through SOS to do business in California; (iii) partnerships and LLCs with a permanent place of business in California; (iv) tax-exempt organizations, under either California or federal law; (v) insurance companies, IRAs, or qualified pension/profit sharing plans; (vi) California nongrantor trusts; and (vii) estates where the deceased was a California resident at the time of death. Nonresident members claiming one of the exemptions must file FTB Form 590 to certify their status.
- FTB Form 590-P, Nonresident Withholding Exemption Certificate for Previously Reported Income of Partners and Members.

Consent Forms

The LLC must obtain a signed Form FTB 3822, Limited Liability Company Nonresident Members' Consent, from each nonresident member. This form must be filed with Form 568. The nonresident members must agree to pay California taxes on California source income from the LLC. If the nonresident member fails to sign the form, the LLC must pay taxes on the member's distributive share of California source income at the highest marginal tax rate, reduced by the nonresident withholding tax paid on behalf of the nonconsenting member.[156] The LLC must use Schedule T, Nonconsenting Nonresident Members' Tax Liability, to calculate and report the taxes that the LLC must pay for the nonresident members.

An LLC must also withhold taxes on nonresident members who have failed to file Form FTB 3832 at the highest marginal tax rates, even if the LLC has paid the nonconsenting nonresident member's tax for the tax year.[157] However, an LLC that

---

[156] FTB Publication 3556, Limited Liability Company Filing Information.

[157] FTB Publication 1017, Resident and Nonresident Withholding Guidelines, California Franchise Tax Board (revised December 2015), Q&A-30.

pays the nonconsenting nonresident member tax on all nonconsenting members may request a waiver from the California Franchise Tax Board for withholding on the nonconsenting members.[158]

An LLC must withhold taxes on nonresident members who have signed Form FTB 3832.[159] However, the withholding tax rate is lower for members who have signed the consent form (e.g., seven percent for individual members).

A nonresident member may also request a waiver from withholding (using FTB Form 588), a reduced rate of withholding (using FTB Form 589), or an exemption from withholding (using FTB Form 590).[160] There is no reduced rate or exemption allowed for foreign (non-U.S.) members.[161]

EXAMPLE 23-1

A California LLC has four individual nonresident members. Member A signed the consent form on Form FTB 3832. Member B did not sign the consent form. Member C filed California tax returns for the two most recent tax years and paid all outstanding FTB tax obligations. Member D is a foreign citizen and resident. The withholding tax rate is as follows:

The withholding tax rate for Member A is seven percent since Member A signed the consent form.

The withholding tax for Member B is 12.3 percent (the highest marginal tax rate) since Member B failed to sign the consent form. The LLC must withhold from the distribution payment even if it pays the tax on behalf of the nonconsenting member, unless it obtains a waiver from the FTB prior to the payment. The FTB will grant a waiver from withholding only if the LLC pays the tax at the highest marginal tax rate for all nonconsenting members.[162]

The LLC may request a waiver from withholding for Member C on Form 588 since the member filed California tax returns for the two most recent taxable years and is current in his California tax payments. The LLC must withhold taxes unless it receives the waiver from the Franchise Tax Board prior to making payments to Member C.[163]

The withholding tax for Member D is 12.3 percent (the highest marginal tax rate) since Member D is a foreign person.

---

[158] FTB Publication 1017, Resident and Nonresident Withholding Guidelines, California Franchise Tax Board (revised December 2015), Q&A-30.

[159] FTB Publication 1017, Resident and Nonresident Withholding Guidelines, California Franchise Tax Board (revised December 2015), Q&A-29.

[160] FTB Publication 1017, Resident and Nonresident Withholding Guidelines, California Franchise Tax Board (revised December 2015), Q&A-54.

[161] FTB Publication 1017, Resident and Nonresident Withholding Guidelines, California Franchise Tax Board (revised December 2015), Q&A-53.

[162] FTB Publication 1017, Resident and Nonresident Withholding Guidelines, California Franchise Tax Board (revised December 2015), Q&A-30

[163] Instructions to FTB Form 588.

Withholding Taxes on Payments to LLC

Payments to an LLC are subject to withholding taxes if the LLC does not have a permanent place of business in California and is not registered through the Secretary of State.[164]

An LLC on which withholding has been made receives a credit for the withholding taxes. The LLC may allocate the entire withholding credit to its members or use a portion of the credit to offset any LLC tax (including nonconsenting nonresident member tax) or fees still due with FTB Form 568. The LLC must allocate any excess to its members.[165] The LLC may not receive a refund of withholding on FTB Form 568.[166] The LLC must allocate the withholding credit to all members, whether they are resident or nonresident members, in proportion to their ownership or beneficial interest.[167]

An LLC that is withheld upon receives a withholding document (FTB Form 592-B or similar form) from the withholding agent showing how much was withheld. An LLC allocates the withholding credit to its members by completing FTB Form 592 showing each member's share of the withholding.[168]

Group Return

An LLC may file a group return on behalf of nonresident members.[169] The group return is commonly referred to as a composite return.[170] The filing is made on Long Form 540NR, California Nonresident or Part-Year Resident Income Tax Return, and on Nonresident Group Return Schedule 1067A. The LLC must pay the tax on behalf of the electing nonresident members. The income is taxed at the highest personal income tax marginal rate on income up to $1 million. The composite tax rate is 12.3 percent in 2018 (13.3 percent on the entire taxable income if the member has taxable income over $1 million).[171] The LLC must make estimated group nonresident payments on Form 540-ES, Estimated Tax for Individuals, if the group nonresident return's net tax after allowable tax credits is $200 or more.

---

[164] FTB Publication 1017, Resident and Nonresident Withholding Guidelines, California Franchise Tax Board (revised December 2015), Q&A-22.

[165] FTB Publication 1017, Resident and Nonresident Withholding Guidelines, California Franchise Tax Board (revised December 2015), Q&A-95.

[166] FTB Publication 1017, Resident and Nonresident Withholding Guidelines, California Franchise Tax Board (revised December 2015), Q&A-95.

[167] FTB Publication 1017, Resident and Nonresident Withholding Guidelines, California Franchise Tax Board (revised December 2015), Q&A-96.

[168] FTB Publication 1017, Resident and Nonresident Withholding Guidelines, California Franchise Tax Board (revised December 2015), Q&A-98.

[169] Franchise Tax Board Publication 1067, Guidelines for Filing a Group Form 540NR.

[170] Franchise Tax Board Publication 1067, Guidelines for Filing a Group Form 540NR.

[171] Franchise Tax Board Publication 1067, Guidelines for Filing a Group Form 540NR.

A member may be included in a group nonresident return if:[172]

- The member is an individual.
- The member is a full-year resident of California.
- The member's only California source income is from distributions reported on a group nonresident return. The nonresident member may be included in more than one group returned.
- The member elects on an annual basis to be included in the group return. The election is irrevocable.

The LLC must file the group return on a calendar year basis. It may not claim individual deductions and credits on the return except for a deduction for deferred compensation contributions for members with no other earned income, and credits directly attributable to the LLC's activity.

Once the return is filed, it cannot be amended to include or exclude a nonresident member. Any member included in the nonresident return may not subsequently file an individual nonresident return, unless the member later discovers that he or she has other income from California sources and was therefore not qualified to participate in a group nonresident return. The LLC must inform nonresident members of the conditions for filing a group return on Form FTB 3864, Group Nonresident Return Election.

.09 Foreign LLC

Not Doing Business in California

An LLC that has California source income, but that is not doing business in California, is not subject to the $800 minimum tax and is not required to qualify to do business in California. The LLC in such case must file California Form 565, Partnership Return of Income, instead of California Form 568, Limited Liability Company Return of Income.[173]

Doing Business in California

An LLC that is organized in a foreign state is subject to California taxes if it does business in California. For tax years beginning on or after January 1, 2011, a foreign LLC is treated as doing business in California if:[174]

---

[172] Franchise Tax Board Publication 1067, Guidelines for Filing a Group Form 540NR.

[173] Franchise Tax Board, https://www.ftb.ca.gov/businesses/structures/llc-filing-requirements.shtml.

[174] Cal. Rev. & Tax. Code § 23101; FTB Notice 2011-06; FTB Legal Ruling 2014-01 (July 22, 2014); FTB Publication 3556, Limited Liability Company Filing Information.

- It is a nonregistered foreign LLC that is a member of an LLC that does business in California.

- It is a general partner in a partnership or limited partnership that does business in California.

- Any of the LLC's members, managers, or other agents conducts business in California on behalf of the LLC.

- The LLC is organized or commercially domiciled in California.

- The LLC's sales, as defined in Revenue and Taxation Code § 25120(e) or (f) in California, including sales by the LLC's agents and independent contractors, exceed the lesser of $ 561,951 in 2017[175] or 25 percent of the LLC's total sales.

- The LLC's real and tangible personal property in California exceed the lesser of $56,195 in 2017[176] or 25 percent of the LLC's total real and tangible personal property.

- The amount paid in California by the LLC for compensation, as defined in Revenue and Taxation Code § 25120(e), exceeds the lesser of $56,195 in 2017[177] or 25 percent of the total compensation paid by the LLC.

In determining the property, payroll and sales in California, a foreign LLC must also include its pro rata share of amounts from other partnerships, LLCs classified as partnerships, and S corporations doing business in California. A partnership or LLC is doing business in California if it has general partners or members in California. Likewise, partners and members are considered doing business in California if the partnership or LLC is doing business in California.

A foreign LLC that has less than the threshold amounts of property, payroll and sales in California may still be considered doing business in this state if the LLC actively engages in any transaction for the purpose of financial or pecuniary gain or profit in California. California cases have broadly interpreted what constitutes active engagement in a business transaction. For example, some rulings have determined that a foreign LLC is subject to California taxes in the following cases:

- A member, manager or agent conducts business in California on behalf of the LLC.[178]

- The LLC purchases interests in other LLCs and partnerships that invest in California real estate.[179]

- A person residing in California is a manager of the LLC. The LLC is subject to California tax if a California resident has a right to hire, fire, and oversee an out-of-state property management company that manages out-of-state property. For example, a Nevada LLC owning rental property in Nevada must pay

---

[175] FTB Notice (Aug. 29, 2017).

[176] FTB Notice (Aug. 29, 2017).

[177] FTB Notice (Aug. 29, 2017).

[178] FTB Publication 3556, Tax Information for Limited Liability Companies (Feb. 5, 2007).

[179] In re International Health Institute LLC, No. 305199, California State Board of Equalization (2006) (single-member Nevada LLC).

¶ 2306.09

the annual $800 minimum tax if one of the managers is a California resident.[180]

- A California resident member conducts, or has the right to conduct, any activity on behalf of the LLC.[181] For example, a foreign LLC with no property or business in California is treated as doing business in California if (i) a California member participates in negotiations on behalf of the LLC preparatory to the execution of a formal agreement, (ii) the LLC enters into a loan transaction with one of its California members, (iii) the operating agreement provides that a California member is responsible for general and financial administration, or (iv) the LLC gives a California member signing privileges on a California bank account.[182] In one case, a California resident formed a Delaware LLC to purchase property in Texas. The State Board of Equalization determined that the Delaware LLC was required to file a tax return in California because the California resident was a manager of the LLC, and failed to establish that he left the State of California whenever he conducted management activities on behalf of the LLC. The State Board of Equalization also noted that the accountant prepared the tax return for the LLC in California.[183]
- A California resident member pays LLC bills and does the bookkeeping for the LLC.[184]
- California members receive rental checks, receive mail, or authorize repairs on property, even if the LLC has no property or business in California and is not registered in California.[185]
- The LLC uses a California accountant to prepare the tax returns and uses a California address on its tax returns.[186]

The corporate owner of a single-member disregarded LLC is treated as doing business in California, and subject to the state franchise tax, if the LLC does business in California. The rule applies even though the corporate owner has no activity or business in California.[187]

EXAMPLE 23-2

An out-of-state LLC has employees who work out of their homes in California. The employees sell and provide warranty work to California customers. The LLC's property, payroll and sales in California fall below

---

[180] Appeal of Destino Properties LLC, No. 339961, State Board of Equalization (2007).

[181] Appeal of Destino Properties LLC, No. 339961, State Board of Equalization (2007).

[182] Appeal of Destino Properties LLC, No. 339961, State Board of Equalization (2007).

[183] Legend Plus Enterprise, LLC, No. 486026, State Board of Equalization (Feb. 22, 2011).

[184] FTB Publication 3556, Tax Information for Limited Liability Companies (Feb. 5, 2007).

[185] FTB Publication 3556, Tax Information for Limited Liability Companies (Feb. 5, 2007).

[186] FTB Publication 3556, Tax Information for Limited Liability Companies (Feb. 5, 2007).

[187] Legal Ruling 2011-01, Franchise Tax Board (Jan. 11, 2011).

the threshold amounts. The LLC is considered doing business in California even if the property, payroll and sales in California fall below the threshold amounts. The LLC is doing business in California through its employees because those employees are actively engaged in transactions for profit on behalf of the LLC.[188]

EXAMPLE 23-3

Paul is a California resident and a member of a Nevada LLC. The Nevada LLC owns property in Nevada. The LLC hires a Nevada management company to collect rents and provide maintenance. Paul has the right to hire and fire the management company. He occasionally has telephone discussions with the management company regarding the property. He is ultimately responsible for the property and oversees the management company. Paul conducts business in California on behalf of the LLC. The LLC must file Form 568.[189]

EXAMPLE 23-4

Rachel is a California resident and member of an Oregon LLC. The Oregon LLC has a retail store in Oregon. Rachel uses a California address for the LLC's tax filings and a California accountant to prepare the LLC's tax returns. Rachel conducts business in California on behalf of the LLC. The LLC must file Form 568.[190]

EXAMPLE 23-5

Sara is a California resident and a member of a Texas LLC. The Texas LLC receives royalties from Texas oil wells. Sara maintains a California business bank account and secures financing in California for the LLC's Texas investments. Sara conducts business in California on behalf of the LLC. The LLC must file Form 568.[191]

---

[188] *Id.*

[189] Example from FTB Publication 3556, Limited Liability Company Filing Information.

[190] Example from FTB Publication 3556, Limited Liability Company Filing Information.

[191] Example from FTB Publication 3556, Limited Liability Company Filing Information.

Gross Receipts Tax

A foreign LLC must pay the California gross receipts tax if it has income and gross receipts apportioned to California.[192] Limited liability companies that do business in California and other states must apportion their income using Form 568, Schedule R, Apportionment and Allocation of Income.[193]

Prior to 2008, California taxed an LLC on gross receipts from all sources, within and outside the state. The courts determined that this assessment was unconstitutional and violated the federal Commerce Clause.[194] As a result, the gross receipts tax may now be assessed only on gross receipts apportioned to California.

An LLC that does business in California is not required to pay the gross receipts tax if it sales are protected from tax under Public Law 86-272. California issued Publication FTB 1050, Application and Interpretation of Public Law 86-272, discussing what activities by a foreign LLC are protected and unprotected activities. Generally, a foreign LLC whose only connection with California is solicitation of sales of tangible personal property in California will not be subject to the California gross receipts tax, but will be subject to the $800 California minimum tax if sales exceed the threshold levels.

An LLC that owns an interest in a pass-through entity in California is treated as doing business in California. The LLC will not be subject to the gross receipts tax based solely on the ownership of the pass-through entity, but will be subject to the California minimum tax.[195]

Minimum Tax

An LLC that does business in California must pay the $800 minimum tax even if it has no intrastate sales and is not subject to California income taxes under Public Law 86-272. The $800 minimum tax is a tax on the privilege of doing business, and is not an income tax.

Thus, a foreign LLC must pay the minimum tax if it sales exceed the minimum threshold of $500,000 or 25 percent of total sales, even though the LLC makes only interstate sales of tangible personal property and is exempt from state income tax under Public Law 86-272. Similarly, an LLC whose only connection with California is the performance of services and sales of intangibles to California customers is subject to the minimum tax if the sales and services exceeds the threshold levels, even if the LLC has no California source income. Sales of services and intangibles are sourced under Section 25136(b) for purposes of applying the doing business test and assessing the minimum tax. Sales of services and intangibles are sourced under other provi-

---

[192] Cal. Rev. & Tax. Code § 17942.

[193] California Franchise Tax Board, Doing Business in California and In Other States, http://www.taxes.ca.gov/Income_Tax/limliacobus.shtml.

[194] *Ventas Finance I, LLC v. California Franchise Tax Board,* 81 Cal. Rptr. 3d 823 (App. 1 Dist. 2008), *rev. denied, cert. denied,* 556 U.S. 1176, 129 S. Ct. 1917 (2009).

[195] *See* California Franchise Tax Board, "What Constitutes a Valid Filing?," *Tax News* (Apr. 2013).

sions of the Revenue and Taxation Code for income apportionment purposes if the LLC has California source income.[196]

California issued guidelines on how a foreign LLC may designate a California return filing as only a minimum tax due return and protected by Public Law 86-272 without it being considered an incomplete return.[197]

The minimum $800 tax is due by the 15th day of the fourth month of the tax year. Existing foreign LLCs that register or commence business in California after that date must pay the $800 minimum tax by the earlier of (i) immediately when they commence to do business in California, or (ii) when they register to do business with the California Secretary of State.[198]

Registration with California Secretary of State

LLCs organized under the laws of another state or foreign country must register with the California Secretary of State before entering into intrastate business in California. Nonregistered foreign LLCs that are members of an LLC doing business in California are considered doing business in California. Regardless of where the trade or business of the LLC is primarily conducted, an LLC is treated as doing business in California if any of its members, managers, or other agents are conducting business in California on behalf of the LLC.[199]

Apportionment

For tax years beginning on or after January 1, 2013, business income of an LLC or other trade or business is apportioned to the state by multiplying the business income by the sales factor.[200]

.10 Franchise Taxes on Corporate and LLC Members

The California Franchise Tax Board takes the position that if an LLC that is classified as a partnership is doing business in California, then the members of the LLC are treated as doing business in California. In such case, the members must file a California tax return and pay all applicable fees and taxes on the members' allocable share of California source income, even if the members otherwise have no contacts with and are not doing business in California.[201] The taxes and fees on each member's

---

[196] *See* General Information on New Rules for Doing Business in California, California Franchise Tax Board, http://www.ftb.ca.gov/businesses/New_Rules_for_Doing_Business_in_California.shtml.

[197] California Franchise Tax Board, "What Constitutes a Valid Filing?," *Tax News* (Apr. 2013).

[198] FTB Publication 3556, Limited Liability Company Filing Information.

[199] Instructions to California Form 568.

[200] Prop. 39, Cal. Rev. & Tax. Code § 25128.7. There is an exception for businesses described in Cal. Rev. & Tax. Code § 25128(b) that derives more than 50 percent of gross receipts from agricultural, extracted, savings and loan, and/or banking or financial activities.

[201] FTB Legal Ruling 2014-01 (July 22, 2014).

allocable share of income are in addition to the gross receipts tax and minimum tax on such income payable by the LLC.

For example, a foreign LLC that is a member of an LLC doing business in California is treated as doing business in California and must file a California tax return if (i) it is a nonregistered foreign LLC that is a member of an LLC that does business in California, or (ii) it is a general partner in a partnership or limited partnership that does business in California.[202]

In *Swart Enters, Inc. v. California Franchise Tax Board*,[203] the California Attorney General argued that an Iowa corporation was required to file a California corporate franchise tax return and pay the minimum franchise tax because it owned an interest in a California LLC that was classified as a partnership and was doing business in California. The Franchise Tax Board cited California Revenue and Taxation Code Sec. 23101, which provided that "A foreign business entity . . . is considered doing business in California if it is a member of an LLC that is doing business in California." The court rejected that position and determined that Swart was not doing business in California merely because it was a passive minority investor in the California LLC. The Franchise Tax Board stated that it will follow this decision in cases where the facts are similar.[204]

FTB Legal Ruling 2014-01[205] gives the following examples of tax filing requirements and corporate franchise taxes payable by business entities that are members of an LLC classified as a partnership:

1. *LLC registered to do business in California.* An LLC that is registered to do business in California, but is not doing any business in California, must file a California tax return and pay the LLC taxes and fees. A corporate member of the LLC is not required to file a California return or pay corporate franchise taxes and fees because the LLC is not doing business in California.

2. *LLC organized in California.* An LLC that is organized in California, but is not doing business in California, must file tax return and pay the LLC taxes and fees. A corporate member of the LLC is not required to file a California return or corporate franchise pay taxes and fees because the LLC is not doing business in California.

3. *LLC domiciled in California.* An LLC that is domiciled in California must file a California tax return and pay the LLC taxes and fees. A corporate member of the LLC that has no contact with California is required to file a California return and pay corporate franchise taxes and fees on the member's allocable share of California source income because an LLC that is domiciled in California is treated as doing business in California.

4. *Foreign LLC doing business in California.* A foreign LLC that is doing business in California must file a California tax return and pay the LLC taxes and fees. A corporate member of the LLC that has no contacts with California is

---

[202] FTB Publication 3556, Limited Liability Company Filing Information.

[203] 7 Cal. App. 5th 497, 212 Cal. Rptr. 3d 670 (2017).

[204] FTB Notice 2017-01 (Feb. 28, 2017).

[205] FTB Legal Ruling 2014-01 (July 22, 2014).

¶ 2306.10

required to file a California return and pay corporate franchise taxes and fees on the member's allocable share of California source income because an LLC that is domiciled in California is treated as doing business in California.

5. *Manager-managed LLC doing business in California.* A manager-managed LLC that is doing business in California must file a California tax return and pay the LLC taxes and fees. A corporate member of the LLC that has no contacts with California is required to file a California return and pay corporate franchise taxes and fees on the member's allocable share of California source income because the LLC is doing business in California.

6. *Sales by foreign LLC in California exceed amount specified in Section 23101(b)(2).* A foreign LLC is treated as doing business in California if its sales in California, including sales by its agents and independents contractors, exceed the lesser of $500,000 or 25 percent of the LLC's total sales.[206] The LLC must file a California tax return and pay the LLC taxes and fees. A corporate member of the LLC that has no contacts with California is required to file a California return and pay corporate franchise taxes and fees on the member's allocable share of California source sales income because the LLC is doing business in California.

.11 Commencing and Dissolving LLCs

Commencing and dissolving LLCs are exempt from tax during the year of organization or dissolution if the tax year is 15 days or less and the LLC does no business in California during the tax year. For example, a calendar year LLC that is formed between December 17 and December 31 is exempt from tax during the first tax year if it does no business in California during that period.[207]

A dissolving LLC is not liable for the minimum tax for the year after termination of business if (i) the LLC files a certificate of dissolution within 15 days after the end of the tax year, and does no business in California during the 15-day period,[208] or (ii) the LLC files a timely tax return for the preceding tax year, does no business in the state after the end of the tax year, and (iii) the LLC files a certificate of cancellation with the California Secretary of State before the end of the 12-month period beginning with the date the final annual tax return was filed.[209]

Many terminating LLC's liquidate without filing a final California tax return or paying taxes for the final year of doing business. The LLC is liable for the taxes for the final year, even though it is inactive and has never done business.[210] However, the

---

[206] Cal. Rev. & Tax. Code § 23101(b)(2).

[207] Cal. Rev. & Tax. Code § 17946; FTB Publication 3556, Limited Liability Company Filing Information.

[208] Cal. Rev. & Tax. Code § 17946.

[209] Cal. Rev. & Tax. Code § 17947; FTB Publication 3556, Limited Liability Company Filing Information.

[210] Margate Properties LLC, California State Board of Equalization, No. 592006 (Dec. 17, 2013).

members of the LLC are not personally liable for the unpaid taxes absent transferee liability issues.

.12 Biennial Report

The LLC must file a biennial report on Form LLC-12R, Statement of Information Renewal. The LLC must file the report within 90 days after it is formed.[211] The secretary of state sends the form to the LLC with the filed articles of organization. In subsequent years, the LLC must file the report during the calendar month in which the original articles of organization were filed or during any of the immediately preceding five calendar months. Foreign LLCs must file biennially in the month during which the application for qualification was filed or during any of the preceding five months.[212]

.13 Estimated Taxes

An LLC must pay estimated taxes by the 15th day of the sixth month of each tax year. This is June 15 for a calendar year LLC. The estimated fees are 100 percent of the current year's fees. The LLC must use Form 3536, Estimated Fees, to pay the taxes. Alternatively, the LLC may make the payment online using the Franchise Tax Board's Web Pay feature.[213]

There is a ten percent penalty if the LLC makes a late payment or pays less than the amount owed. The LLC may avoid the penalty if the estimated taxes are equal to or greater than the prior year's LLC taxes. There is no requirement that the prior year tax be a full 12 months. The Franchise Tax Board cannot waive the penalty for reasonable cause.[214]

.14 Filing Fees

There are the following filing fees in California:[215]

Articles of organization	$ 70
Articles of organization if the LLC is classified as a corporation	$880
Registration of foreign LLC	$ 70
Biennial report	$ 20

---

[211] Cal. Corp. Code § 17060(a).

[212] Cal. Corp. Code § 17060(c).

[213] California Franchise Tax Board, *Tax News* (May 2011). The Web Pay feature is at http://ftb.ca.gov, and then click on Payment Options.

[214] California Franchise Tax Board, *Tax News* (May 2011).

[215] Cal. Gov. Code § 12190.

.15 Series LLCs

Although California law does not allow a series LLC to be formed in California, it does recognize LLC's that are formed outside California if the LLC has the following features:[216]

- Each unit (series in the master LLC) has its own members and is not managed separately from the master LLC and other units.

- Each unit maintains separate books and records.

- As with a regularly formed LLC, the owners/members of each unit are not financially responsible for the unit's debts and obligations.

- The unit does not conduct part of the business of the master LLC, or conduct a wholly different business.

- Each unit has its own assets and liabilities. The members of each unit are treated under the laws of the state where the master LLC is formed as owning an interest in only that unit, and have no rights as members of one unit in the assets or income of any other unit.

- Each unit is liable only for its own debts and obligations. In general, creditors of one unit may only make claims against the assets of that unit.

If each unit has the features listed above under the laws of the state where the series LLC was formed, then each unit will be treated as a separate entity for filing and tax purposes. In that case, the same filing guidelines and estimated taxes that apply to a regular LLC will apply to each unit of a series LLC. If the LLC elects to be taxed as a corporation, it must follow California corporation filing guidelines and estimated tax requirements, and will be subject to the minimum franchise tax.[217]

Each series that does business in California is treated as a separate entity that must pay the minimum $800 California tax.[218] However, all series within an LLC are treated as a single entity for purposes of the gross receipts tax.[219]

If the series LLC registers in California, the first LLC in the series uses the Secretary of State number as the identification number on its initial payment voucher. All other LLCs in the series must leave the identification numbers blank on their first payment vouchers. The LLC must write "Series LLC #_____" in red ink on the top of all payment vouchers, tax returns, and correspondence. The Franchise Tax Board will then assign an identification number to the rest of the LLCs in the series. The Franchise Tax Board will notify each series of its assigned number after the FTB receive its initial payment voucher.[220]

---

[216] California Franchise Tax Board, *Tax News* (Oct. 2011).

[217] California Franchise Tax Board, *Tax News* (Oct. 2011).

[218] *See* instructions to Form 568.

[219] Cal. Rev. & Tax. Code § 17942(b)(2).

[220] FTB Publication 3556, Limited Liability Company Filing Information.

.16 Penalties

There is a $2,000 penalty imposed on foreign LLCs that fail to qualify to do business in California or whose rights and privileges to do business in California have been forfeited. The penalty also applies to California LLCs whose charter has been suspended. The Franchise Tax Board must impose a penalty if the LLC fails to file the required return within 60 days after the Franchise Tax Board sends a notice and demand to file the return.[221]

.17 Sale of Membership Interest

Gain or loss on the sale of a membership interest in an LLC that is classified as a partnership is allocable to California in the ratio of the original cost of LLC tangible property in the state to the original cost of LLC tangible property everywhere, determined at the time of the sale. If more than 50 percent of the value of LLC's assets consists of intangibles, gain or loss from the sale of the LLC interest is allocated to California in accordance with the sales factor of the LLC for its first full tax period immediately preceding the tax period of the LLC during which the LLC interest was sold.[222]

.18 Foreign State Tax Credits

A California resident or nonresident member of an LLC that is classified as a partnership may receive a credit for the pro rata share of the net income taxes paid to another state by the LLC as if those taxes had been paid directly by the taxpayer member.[223] A member may thus receive the credit under the following circumstances:

Credit for a California resident: A California resident is allowed a credit for taxes paid by the LLC to another state if:

1. the taxes are net income taxes imposed by and paid to another state;
2. the income is also taxed by California;
3. the income is derived from sources within the other taxing state; and
4. the other state does not allow California residents a credit against the taxes imposed by that state for taxes paid to California.

Credit for a California nonresident: A California nonresident is allowed a credit for the net income taxes imposed by and paid to the taxpayer's state of residence on income that is also taxed by California, if the state of residence either: (a) does not tax the income of California residents derived from sources within that state; or (b) allows California residents a tax credit against the taxes imposed by that state on income derived from sources within that state. However, a tax credit is not allowed for taxes paid by the LLC to a state that allows its residents a tax credit for net tax

---

[221] Cal. Rev. & Tax. Code § 19135.
[222] Cal. Rev. & Tax. Code § 25125(d).
[223] FTB Legal Ruling 2017-01 (Feb. 1, 2017).

paid to California irrespective of whether its residents are allowed a California tax credit.

The California Franchise Tax Board gave the following example of a credit claimed by a California resident on the resident's pro rata share of taxes paid by the LLC to a foreign state:

> **Situation 5**: B is a California resident and a member of Y, an LLC. Y does business in Kentucky and paid a Limited Liability Entity Tax (LLET) to Kentucky. The LLET is computed as the lesser of $0.095/$100 of Kentucky gross receipts or $0.75/$100 of Kentucky gross profits. Kentucky gross profits are defined as Kentucky gross receipts reduced by returns and allowances attributable to Kentucky gross receipts, less the cost of goods sold attributable to Kentucky gross receipts. Under Kentucky law, an individual who is a member, shareholder, or partner of a limited liability pass through entity shall be allowed a nonrefundable LLET credit equal to the individual's proportionate share of the entity's LLET after it is reduced by the minimum tax due of $175 and any other nonrefundable credits. B reported an income tax liability (before credits) to Kentucky based on his distributive share of Y's income, and used, as provided under Kentucky law, his proportionate share of the Kentucky LLET credit to fully satisfy his personal income tax liability owed to Kentucky.
> B is not entitled to a California Other State Tax Credit ("OSTC") based on the LLET credit used to satisfy his Kentucky tax liability, since the LLET credit is not an amount "paid" to the other state. The LLET credit is a nonrefundable tax credit. It is not a payment of tax. Nonrefundable tax credits are part of the overall calculation to arrive at the amount of net tax shown on a return, and not part of the satisfaction or payment of the net tax after it is calculated. Additionally, B is not entitled to compute the OSTC using his pro rata share of taxes paid to Kentucky by Y, as if those taxes had been paid by the member of the LLC taxed as a partnership, because the other state tax is the LLET, which is not a net income tax. The LLET is a single, indivisible tax, in which the taxpayer only pays one tax rate on one base. However, various taxpayers subject to the Kentucky LLET could be paying the LLET on amounts that, for some, are not based on income (i.e. gross receipts), and therefore the LLET is a tax not on, or according to, or measured by income. Further, B cannot deduct on his California income tax return his proportionate share of the Kentucky LLET credit used to fully satisfy his personal income tax liability owed to Kentucky, since it was not an income tax paid to the other state.

The California Franchise Tax Board gave the following example of a credit claimed by a nonresident on the nonresident's pro rata share of taxes paid by the LLC to a foreign state:

> **Situation 1**: A is an Arizona resident and is a 25 percent partner in Z, a partnership that does business only in California. Z files a California partnership return of income reporting $100,000 of California-source income. A files an Arizona resident income tax return and reports her $25,000 pro rata share of Z's income, and pays tax to Arizona on this

income totaling \$2,500. A also files a California nonresident personal income tax return reporting her pro rata share of Z's income. A claims a \$2,500 OSTC against her California income tax liability based on the tax that she paid to Arizona on her pro rata share of Z's income.

A is entitled to the OSTC in determining her California income tax liability based on the \$2,500 of tax that she paid to Arizona on her pro rata share of Z's income. Pursuant to RTC § 18002, a nonresident of California may claim a California OSTC if his or her state of residence either does not tax income of California residents derived from sources within that state or allows California residents a credit against the taxes imposed by that state on income derived from sources within that state for net tax paid to California. Arizona provides a credit to California residents for tax paid to California on income sourced to Arizona, so it is a "reverse credit state," and an Arizona resident taxpayer is entitled to claim a California OSTC in determining taxes payable to California on California-source income. The payment of the Arizona tax meets the requirement under RTC § 18002 that the tax imposed by and paid to the other state be a net income tax because, as determined by California law, the tax was paid on A's pro rata share of Z's ordinary income from its trade or business, which was computed by deducting all allowable ordinary and necessary business expenses from total gross income. Because Arizona is a reverse credit state and the tax paid to Arizona on A's pro rata share of Z's income is a net income tax, the California OSTC is allowed.

¶ 2307 COLORADO

Colorado enacted the Colorado Limited Liability Company Act on April 12, 1990.[224]

.01 State Tax Classification

Colorado classifies an LLC in the same manner that an LLC is classified for federal tax purposes. An LLC that is classified as a partnership under federal law is classified as a partnership for state tax purposes.[225] An LLC that is classified as a corporation for federal tax purposes is classified as a corporation for state tax purposes.[226] A single-member LLC that is classified as a disregarded entity for federal purposes is classified as a disregarded entity for state purposes.[227]

---

[224] S.B. 90-74, 1990 Colo. Sess. Laws; Colo. Rev. Stat. Ann. §§ 7-80-101 to 7-80-1101.

[225] Colo. Rev. Stat. Ann. §§ 39-22-103(5.6), 39-22-201.5. A partnership includes limited liability companies filing as partnership for federal income tax purposes. A partner includes members of the LLC for state tax purposes.

[226] Colo. Rev. Stat. Ann. § 39-22-103(2.5), (10.5).

[227] 1 CCR 201-2(c) INCOME TAX.

.02 Taxation of LLC and Members

An LLC that is classified as a partnership is not subject to the regular taxes. Persons carrying on business as members are liable for the tax and the alternative minimum tax only in their individual capacities.[228]

.03 Tax Returns

An LLC that is classified as a partnership must file Form DR 106, Colorado Pass-Through Entity Return of Income and Composite Nonresident Income Tax Return. The return is due 3 1/2 months after the close of the tax year.

.04 Nonresident Members

An LLC with nonresident members must comply with the nonresident member filing requirements in one of the following three ways:[229]

1. *Composite return.* The LLC may file a composite return for nonresident members by completing Part II of Form DR 106 and paying the applicable tax on Colorado source income.[230] Nonresident members must elect to be included on the composite return. The election is an agreement between the LLC and the member. The agreement may be made in any manner agreed to by the parties. A written signed agreement is not required. The election is communicated to the Department of Revenue in column 4 of Form 106, Part III.[231] The members do not have to file a Colorado individual return. The tax due on the composite filing in 2017 is 4.63 percent of the Colorado-source income of the nonresident members included in the composite return. A net operating loss cannot be carried forward or back on a composite return.[232] The LLC must make estimated tax payments on Form 106EP.[233] The LLC may not include on the composite return nonresident corporate members or members who have other Colorado income that requires the filing of a separate return.[234]

2. *Agreement by nonresident member.* A nonresident member may provide a completed Form DR 0107 to the LLC each year certifying that he/she will

---

[228] Colo. Rev. Stat. Ann. § 39-22-201.

[229] Colo. Rev. Stat. § 39-22-601(5). FYI Income 54, Colorado Department of Revenue (Nov. 2007). *See also* Instructions to Form 106.

[230] Colo. Rev. Stat. § 39-22-601(5)(d).

[231] FYI Income 54, Colorado Department of Revenue (Nov. 2007).

[232] Col. Rev. Stat. Ann. § 39-22-504.

[233] FYI Income 54, Colorado Department of Revenue (Nov. 2007).

[234] FYI Income 54, Colorado Department of Revenue (Nov. 2007).

file a Colorado income tax return.[235] The LLC must file the form with the Colorado Department of Revenue along with Form DR 108.

3. *Withholding.* The LLC may withhold 4.63 percent of each nonresident member's Colorado source income and submit the payment with Form DR 0108.[236] The LLC must withhold for any nonresident member who fails to complete, sign and return Form 0107 to the LLC, and who is not included in a composite return. The LLC must send the withheld amount to the Department of Revenue with Form 0108, Statement of Colorado Tax Remittance for Nonresident Partner or Shareholder. The amount withheld is credited to the member's account and is claimed on the member's return as an estimated tax payment.[237]

The LLC must indicate in Part III, Column 4 of Form DR 106 which of these three filing requirements each nonresident member has selected.

The LLC must elect on behalf of nonresident members whether to determine Colorado-source income in one of the following three ways:

1. by use of Colo. Rev. Stat. § 39-22-109, relating to Colorado-source income of nonresident individuals;

2. by use of Colo. Rev. Stat. § 39-22-303, relating to the Colorado Income Tax Act corporation two-factor apportionment formula (part IV, Form 106); or

3. by use of the Multistate Tax Compact UDITPA three-factor apportionment formula (part V, Form 106).

The LLC may make a new election each year, but may not change the election after the due date or the filing date of the return, whichever is later.[238]

.05 Annual Report

A Colorado LLC must file an annual report with the Colorado Secretary of State. The secretary of state issues a preprinted report form to the LLC each year.[239]

.06 Filing Fees

The filing fees in Colorado are as follows:[240]

---

[235] Col. Rev. Stat. Ann. § 39-22-601(5)(f). The forms are completed and signed by the nonresident member and returned to the LLC. The LLC must attach completed and signed forms to the LLC's return on Form 106. The LLC must submit Form 0107 to the Department of Revenue each year. FYI Income 54, Colorado Department of Revenue (Mar. 2010).

[236] Col. Rev. Stat. Ann. § 39-22-601(5)(h).

[237] FYI Income 54, Colorado Department of Revenue (Nov. 2007).

[238] *See* Instructions to Form 0106.

[239] Colo. Rev. Stat. Ann. § 7-80-303.

[240] Colo. Rev. Stat. Ann. § 7-80-307.

Articles of organization	$125
Registration as foreign LLC	$125
Annual registration	$10 for e-filing; $100 for paper filing

¶ 2308 CONNECTICUT

Connecticut enacted the Connecticut Limited Liability Company Act effective October 1, 1993.[241]

.01 State Tax Classification

A Connecticut LLC is classified for state tax purposes in the same manner that it is classified for federal tax purposes.[242] Foreign LLCs transacting business in Connecticut are also classified for state tax purposes in accordance with their federal classifications.

.02 Taxation of LLC and Members

A Connecticut LLC is a pass-through entity. Profits and losses pass through and are taxable to the members. Nonresident members are taxed on their distributive shares of LLC income derived from or connected with Connecticut sources.[243]

An LLC that is classified as a partnership or disregarded entity for federal tax purposes must pay the business entity tax.[244] The business entity tax is $250. It is payable every two years (rather than every year) commencing in 2013.

.03 Real Estate Taxes

There is a tax imposed on the transfer of a controlling interest in an LLC if the LLC owns, directly or indirectly, an interest in Connecticut real property. This tax is reported on Form AU-330, Controlling Interest Transfer Taxes.[245]

If an LLC transfers real estate in Connecticut, it must complete and file Form OP-236, Real Estate Conveyance Tax Return, in the town in which the real estate is situated.[246]

The transfer of real property by an individual to a single-member LLC owned by the individual is not subject to the Connecticut real estate conveyance tax. There is no

---

[241] Pub. Act No. 93-267, 1992 Conn. Acts (Reg. Sess.); Conn. Gen. Stat. Ann. §§ 34-100 to 34-299.

[242] Conn. Gen. Stat. Ann. § 34-113; Special Notice 98(3), Conn. Dept. of Rev. Servs. (Jan. 22, 1998).

[243] Department of Revenue Services Policy Statement 98 (1.1) (1998).

[244] Conn. Gen. Stat. § 12-284b.

[245] See Special Notice 2003(11), Legislation Affecting the Controlling Interest Transfer Tax.

[246] See instructions to Form OP-424, Business Entity Tax Return.

change in ownership for tax purposes if the LLC is classified as a disregarded entity.[247]

.04 Sales Taxes

A contribution of property or services by an individual to a single-member LLC is subject to sales and use taxes unless expressly exempt. Services by an owner to the LLC are subject to tax if the owner is compensated other than through a distribution of LLC profits.[248]

.05 Tax Returns

An LLC must file Form OP-424 (DRS/N), Business Entity Tax Return, if the LLC is classified as a partnership or disregarded entity.[249] The biennial business entity tax is $250. The return is due on or before April 15, 2017 for the biennial period beginning January 1, 2015 and ending December 31, 2016.[250]

An LLC that does business in Connecticut, or that has income derived from or connected with sources within Connecticut, must file Form CT-1065/CT-1120SI, regardless of the amount of its income or loss. The LLC must first complete the federal Form 1065, U.S. Partnership Return of Income. Information on the federal return is needed to complete Form CT-1065/CT-1120SI.

The LLC must furnish Schedule CT K-1, Member's Share of Certain Connecticut Items, to each resident and nonresident noncorporate member and each member that is a pass-through entity on or before the 15th day of the fourth month following the close of the tax year (April 15 for calendar year filers). The members must then report taxable income from the LLC as follows:[251]

- *Resident individuals.* If the member is a resident individual, his or her share of LLC income or loss is included in his or her federal adjusted gross income, and therefore is includable in the federal adjusted gross income reported on the member's Form CT-1040, Connecticut Resident Income Tax Return. The LLC must provide the member with Schedule CT K-1 reporting Connecticut modifications that the member must include on Form CT-1040, Schedule 1.

- *Resident trust or estate.* If the member is a resident trust or estate, its share of LLC income or loss is included in its federal taxable income, and therefore is includable in the federal taxable income reported on the member's Form CT-1041, Connecticut Income Tax Return for Trusts and Estates. The LLC must provide the member with a Schedule CT K-1 reporting Connecticut modifications that the member must include on Form CT-1041, Schedule A.

---

[247] *Mandell,* Connecticut Superior Court, No. SC 16672 (Mar. 18, 2003).

[248] Special Notice 98(3), Conn. Dept. of Rev. Servs. (Jan. 22, 1998).

[249] *See* instructions to Form OP-424, Business Entity Tax Return.

[250] *See* http://www.ct.gov/drs/cwp/view.asp?a=3750&q=441426.

[251] *See* Instructions to Form CT-1065/CT-1120SI.

- *Nonresident individual.* If the member is a nonresident individual, his or her share of LLC income or loss is included in federal adjusted gross income, and therefore is includable in the federal adjusted gross income reported on the member's Form CT-1040NR/PY, Connecticut Nonresident or Part-Year Resident Income Tax Return. The LLC must provide the member with a Schedule CT K-1 reporting Connecticut modifications that the member must include on Form CT-1040NR/PY, Schedule 1, and amounts of LLC income or loss derived from or connected with Connecticut sources the member must include on Form CT-1040NR/PY, Schedule CT-SI.

- *Nonresident trust or estate.* If the member is a nonresident trust or estate, its share of LLC income or loss is included in federal taxable income, and therefore is includable in the federal taxable income reported on the member's Form CT-1041. The LLC must provide the member with a Schedule CT K-1 reporting Connecticut modifications that the member must include on Form CT-1041, Schedule A, and amounts of LLC income or loss derived from or connected with Connecticut sources that the member must include on Form CT-1041, Schedule CT-1041FA.

.06 Annual Report

A Connecticut LLC must file an annual report on the anniversary date of the filing of the articles of organization.[252] The annual report must set forth the name of the LLC and the LLC's current principal office address. The secretary of state mails the appropriate form to each LLC at its principal office.

A foreign LLC qualified to do business in Connecticut must also file an annual report on the anniversary date of its registration or its qualification to do business in the state of Connecticut.[253]

.07 Nonresident Members

Nonresident members of an LLC must pay taxes on their Connecticut source income. Income from an LLC doing business in Connecticut is treated as Connecticut source income.[254] Nonresident members must include their distributive shares of LLC Connecticut source income on Form CT-1040 NR/PY, Connecticut Nonresident or Part-Year Resident Income Tax Return.

An LLC may not file a group return on behalf of nonresident members. Instead, the LLC must file a composite return and pay income taxes at the highest marginal tax rate (6.99 percent for 2017) on each noncorporate nonresident member's share of

---

[252] Conn. Gen. Stat. Ann. § 34-106.

[253] Conn. Gen. Stat. Ann. § 34-229.

[254] Form CT-1040 NR/PY Instructions.

income from Connecticut sources[255] if income is at least $1,000.[256] The composite return is filed on Form CT-1065/CT-1120SI, Composite Income Tax Return. Estimated tax payments are no longer required.[257]

If the member receives Connecticut income only from the LLC and other pass-through entities, then the member is not required to file a separate nonresident return.[258] If the member earns other Connecticut source income, then the member must file a nonresident return, and receives a credit for the taxes paid by the LLC on the member's behalf.[259] The LLC must report to the member the amount that the LLC paid on the member's behalf by the 15th day of the fourth month following the close of the LLC's tax year.

.08 Filing Fees

Connecticut imposes the following filing fees on LLCs:[260]

Articles of organization	$120
Certificate of registration for foreign LLC	$120
Annual report	$20

¶ 2309 DELAWARE

Delaware enacted the Delaware Limited Liability Company Act effective October 1, 1992.[261]

.01 State Tax Classification

Delaware classifies an LLC in the same manner that the LLC is classified for federal tax purposes.[262] The same rule applies to a foreign LLC qualified to do business in Delaware.

A member or an assignee of a member of an LLC formed in Delaware or qualified to do business in Delaware is treated as either a resident or a nonresident partner if the LLC is classified as a partnership for federal tax purposes. If the LLC is not classified as a partnership, the member or assignee has the same status as the member or assignee has for federal income tax purposes.[263] This rule applies for

---

[255] Conn. Gen. Stat. Ann. § 12-719(b)(1). *See* Instructions to FORM CT-1065/CT-1120SI.

[256] Conn. Gen. Stat. Ann. § 12-719(b)(2)(C).

[257] *Press Release*, Connecticut Department of Revenue Services (June 14, 2006).

[258] Conn. Gen. Stat. Ann. § 12-719(b)(2)(B)(i), (E).

[259] Conn. Gen. Stat. Ann. § 12-719(b)(2)(B)(ii), (E).

[260] Conn. Gen. Stat. Ann. § 34-112.

[261] H.B. 608, 1992 Del. Laws; Del. Code Ann. tit. 6, §§ 18-101 to 18-1109.

[262] Del. Code Ann. tit. 6, § 18-1107(a); Tech. Information Mem. 98-1, Del. Div. of Rev. (Apr. 24, 1998).

[263] *Id.*

purposes of any tax imposed by the state of Delaware or by any instrumentality, agency, or political subdivision of the state of Delaware.

.02 Taxation of LLC and Members

There is a $300 annual tax on domestic and registered foreign LLCs.[264] The tax is payable to the secretary of state on or before June 1 following the close of the calendar year or upon cancellation of a certificate of formation. LLCs that fail to pay the fee on a timely basis are subject to interest at the rate of $1^1/_2$ percent per month.

The LLC is otherwise a pass-through entity for state tax purposes.[265] Resident members must file Form 200-01, Delaware Resident Income Tax Return, to report their share of LLC income or loss. Members are liable for taxes only in their individual capacities.[266] Each item of income, gain, loss, or deduction of the LLC received by the member has the same character for the member as it has for federal income tax purposes. The applicable federal tax laws apply in determining a member's distributive share and the validity of any special allocations.[267]

.03 Nonresident Members

Distributive Share of Income

Nonresident members are taxed on their distributive shares of LLC income derived from or connected with Delaware sources.[268] Nonresident members must file Form 200-02 NR, Non-Resident Delaware Income Tax Return, to report their share of Delaware source income or loss. The following four items of income, gain, loss, and deduction are treated as derived from or connected with Delaware sources:[269]

- Compensation for personal services rendered in Delaware or attributable to employment in Delaware.
- Income attributable to the ownership or disposition of any interest in real or tangible personal property in the state of Delaware.
- Income from a business, trade, commerce, profession, or vocation carried on in Delaware.
- Winnings for pari-mutuel wagering in Delaware.

Income from intangible personal property does not constitute income derived from Delaware sources unless the LLC uses the property in a business, trade, commerce, profession, or vocation carried on in Delaware. Stocks, bonds, investment

---

[264] Del. Code Ann. tit. 6, § 18-1107(b).

[265] Del. Code Ann. tit. 30, § 1621.

[266] Del. Code Ann. tit. 30, § 1621(a).

[267] Del. Code Ann. tit. 30, § 1622.

[268] Del. Code Ann. tit. 30, § 1623.

[269] Del. Code Ann. tit. 30, §§ 1623, 1124(b).

assets, and other intangible assets that are held for investment by a Delaware entity are not treated as property used by the LLC in a Delaware business, trade, commerce, profession, or vocation.[270]

Composite Return

Nonresident members are not required to file a Non-Resident Delaware Income Tax Return if the LLC files a composite tax return and pays a composite tax on the distributive share of income of nonresident members. The composite tax return is filed on Form 200-C, Delaware Composite Personal Income Tax Return. The composite tax rate is 6.6 percent for tax years beginning after 2014.

Nonresident members may be included in the composite return if:

- The members are individual full-year nonresident members.
- The member elects to be included on the composite return.
- The nonresident members have no income (including spouse's) from sources within Delaware other than his or her distributive share of LLC income whose source is within Delaware.
- All individuals included in the composite return have the same tax year for income tax purposes.

Members who are included in the composite filing are not allowed tax credits, other than non-refundable credits from Form 700. Net operating losses are not allowed on the composite return. Any refund or overpayment of income taxes made on a composite basis must be remitted to the LLC for distribution to the members. A composite return may not be changed or corrected except by an amended composite return filed by the LLC. LLCs must file estimated taxes with Form 200-ES coupons. Composite returns are due on the 15th day of the fourth month following the close of the tax year of the members included in the composite return. Federal Extensions of Time to File are accepted as a valid extension to file the Delaware Form 200-C. The LLC must file Schedule K-1 for all non-resident members filing the composite return. The composite return must be signed by an authorized member of the LLC.[271]

.04 Tax Returns

A Delaware LLC that is classified as a partnership must file a partnership tax return on Delaware Form 300, Delaware Partnership Return. This is an information return. The LLC must file the return if it has one or more members who are Delaware residents or has any income or loss, regardless of the amount, derived from or connected with a Delaware source.[272]

---

[270] Del. Code Ann. tit. 30, § § 1623, 1124(c).

[271] Instructions to Form 200-C, Delaware Composite Personal Income Tax Return.

[272] Del. Code Ann. tit. 30, § 1605.

The return must be filed by the 15th day of the fourth month following the close of the taxable year. It must be mailed to the Delaware Division of Revenue, P.O. Box 8703, Wilmington, DE 19899-8703.

An LLC may request an extension to file the return by submitting a copy of the federal extension request on or before the due date of the return. A photocopy of the approved federal extension must be attached to the final return when filed. The approved federal extension extends the due date of the Delaware return to the same date as the federal extended due date.

An LLC that elects to be classified as a corporation for federal tax purposes must attach a copy of IRS Form 8832, Entity Classification Election, to its Delaware corporate income tax return.[273]

Members of an LLC, which has not elected to be classified as a corporation and that does business in Delaware, are subject to the tax filing requirements in Delaware for all years that the LLC does business in Delaware.[274]

A nonresident member of an LLC with income from Delaware sources must file Form Individual PY/NR Income Tax Return, and report his share of Delaware source LLC income or loss. A resident member must file Form 200, Delaware Resident Income Tax Return, and report his share of LLC income or loss.

An LLC must pay the annual $250 tax online.[275] Taxes are due on or before June 1 of each year. There is no annual report.

.05 Single-Member LLCs

There are special rules for single-member LLCs doing business in Delaware, which are classified as disregarded entities for federal tax purposes. An individual who is the only member of an LLC is subject to the tax filing requirements under Title 30 of the Delaware Code for each year in which the LLC conducts business in the state.[276] A corporation that is the sole member of an LLC must file a corporate income tax return and business license and gross receipts tax return for each year in which the LLC conducts business in the state.[277]

.06 Filing Fees

Delaware imposes the following filing fees on LLCs:[278]

Certificate of formation	$ 90
Foreign LLC registration application	$200
Annual tax	$300

---

[273] Tech. Info. Mem. 98-1, Del. Div. of Rev. (Apr. 24, 1998).

[274] *Id.*

[275] http://www.corp.delaware.gov/paytaxes.shtml.

[276] *Id.*

[277] *Id.*

[278] Del. Code Ann. tit. 6, §§ 18-1105, 18-1107.

There is also a $20 courthouse municipality fee imposed on LLC documents filed with the Secretary of State.[279]

¶ 2310 DISTRICT OF COLUMBIA

The District of Columbia enacted the District of Columbia Limited Liability Company Act of 1994 effective July 23, 1994,[280] and the Uniform Limited Liability Act of 2010.[281]

.01 Tax Classification

The District of Columbia classifies LLCs in the same manner in which they are classified for federal tax purposes.[282] Foreign LLCs qualified to do business in the District of Columbia are classified as partnerships unless classified as corporations or proprietorships for federal tax purposes.[283]

A member or an assignee of a member of an LLC formed in the District of Columbia or qualified to do business in the District as a foreign LLC is treated as either a resident or a nonresident partner unless classified otherwise for federal income tax purposes. In that case, the member or assignee of a member has the same status that the member or assignee of a member has for federal income tax purposes.[284]

.02 Taxation of LLCs and Members

The District of Columbia imposes a 8.25 percent tax in 2018 on D.C. source income earned by unincorporated businesses.[285] The minimum tax is $250 if D.C. gross receipts are $1 million or less. The minimum tax is $1,000 if D.C. gross receipts are more than $1 million, even if the LLC has a loss. An LLC is subject to the tax if it engages in an unincorporated business.[286] LLC income that is subject to the unincorporated business franchise tax is not taxed again by the District on the LLC members' individual District of Colombia income tax returns. Thus, an LLC will avoid double taxation of income, except in cases where the LLC has elected to be taxed as a corporation for federal income tax purposes. The individual members are taxed on

---

[279] Del. Code Ann. tit. 6, § 18-206(e).

[280] Act 10-243, 1994 D.C. Stat. (approved by the mayor on May 18, 1994; effective after a 30-day period of congressional review); D.C. Code Ann. § § 29-801.01 to 29-810.01.

[281] D.C. Code Ann. § § 29.801.01 to 29-810.01.

[282] D.C. Code Ann. § 47-1808.06a. Members are also classified as partners or shareholders for D.C. tax purposes based on their federal classification.

[283] D.C. Code Ann. § 47-1808.06a.

[284] Id.

[285] D.C. Code Ann. § 47-1808.03. See Instructions to Form D-30 District of Columbia (DC) Unincorporated Business Franchise Tax Forms and Instructions.

[286] D.C. Code Ann. § 47-1808.06a.

their distributive shares of income if the unincorporated business tax does not apply.[287]

An unincorporated business is any trade or business conducted or engaged in by an individual, whether resident or nonresident, other than a trade or business conducted or engaged in by a corporation. It includes any trade or business that would be taxable if conducted by a corporation. An unincorporated business does not include the following:

- A trade or business that by law, customs, or ethics cannot be incorporated;
- A trade or business in which more than 80 percent of the gross income is derived from personal services by the individuals or members of the LLC; or
- An entity conducting or carrying on a trade or business in which capital is not a material income-producing factor.

.03 Real Estate Taxation

There is an exemption from the deed recordation tax and the real estate transfer tax for a partnership that converts to an LLC and that signs a deed transferring partnership real estate in connection with the conversion.[288]

.04 Tax Returns

An LLC with gross income over $12,000 from a trade or business plus other income from D.C. sources must file Form D-30, Unincorporated Business Franchise Tax Return (whether or not it has net income). Gross income includes income from all DC sources before deducting the cost of goods sold, expenses and other deductions in calculating net income.

An LLC with gross income of $12,000 or less must file Form D-65, Partnership Return of Income.

.05 Annual and Biennial Reports

An LLC must file Form BRA-25, Two-Year Report for Foreign and Domestic Limited Liability Companies (LLC) and pay a biennial report fee of $300. That report is also due on June 15.

.06 Filing Fees

The filing fees in the District of Columbia are as follows:[289]

---

[287] D.C. Code Ann. § 47-1808.06a.

[288] D.C. Code Ann. § 47-902(16)(B).

[289] D.C. Code Ann. § 29-102.12.

Articles of organization	$220
Foreign LLC registration application	$220
Biennial report	$300

¶ 2311 FLORIDA

Florida enacted the Florida Limited Liability Company Act in April 1982. Florida adopted the Revised Limited Liability Company Act in 2013 which became effective for all Florida limited liability companies on January 1, 2015 (whether organized before or after that date).[290]

.01 State Tax Classification

Florida classifies an LLC in the same manner that the LLC is classified for federal tax purposes.[291] An LLC that is classified as a partnership under federal law is classified as a partnership for state tax purposes. Prior to July 1, 1998, a Florida LLC or a foreign LLC qualified to do business in Florida was classified as a corporation regardless of its federal classification.[292]

Effective July 1, 1998, Florida permits the formation of a single-member LLC.[293] Effective January 1, 2003, single-member LLCs are treated as separate legal entities for all non-income-tax purposes.[294] Such LLCs are subject to the sales and use taxes, property taxes, excise taxes, and other miscellaneous taxes.

There is no documentary transfer tax on the conversion of a partnership to an LLC.[295]

.02 Taxation of LLC and Members

There is no franchise or corporate income tax on an LLC that is classified as a partnership or single-member disregarded entity for federal income tax purposes. An LLC that is classified as a partnership or single-member disregarded entity is not a corporation subject to the corporate income tax.[296]

Effective January 1, 2003, a single-member LLC that is classified as a disregarded entity is treated as a separate legal entity for all non-income tax purposes. The single-

---

[290] Fla. Stat. Ann. §§ 605.0101 to 605.1108, 608.401 to 608.703.

[291] Tax Information Publication No. 0460BB-01, Florida Department of Revenue (Jan. 16, 2004).

[292] Fla. Stat. Ann. §§ 220.03(1)(e), 608.471.

[293] Fla. Stat. Ann. § 605.0201(4).

[294] Fla. Stat. Ann. § 605.0201(4).

[295] Technical Assistant Advisement, No. 11B4-007, Florida Department of Revenue (May 23, 2011).

[296] Fla. Stat. Ann. § 220.03(1)(e).

member LLC may report and account for income, employment, and other taxes under the owner's taxpayer identification number.[297]

There is no tax on any individual who engages in business in Florida as a member or manager of an LLC that is classified as a partnership.[298] A foreign LLC that is qualified to do business in the state is not subject to the corporate income tax either.[299] However, a corporation that becomes a member of an LLC cannot avoid the corporate income tax merely by becoming a member of an LLC.

A corporation is not subject to the Florida corporate income tax merely because the corporation has an ownership interest in a foreign LLC that does business in Florida.[300]

.03 Documentary Transfer Tax

There is a documentary transfer tax on the transfer of real property to an LLC. The following transfers are subject only to the minimum Florida documentary transfer tax:[301]

- Transfer for no consideration of unencumbered real property from an individual to the individual's wholly owned LLC. The property cannot be transferred to the LLC in exchange for a membership interest. If the property is encumbered, the documentary transfer tax will be due based on the amount of the outstanding balance on any mortgages encumbering the property.

- Transfer of unencumbered real property between two related LLCs.

- Transfer of real property by an LLC or other entity.

- Transfer of unencumbered real property to an LLC that is owned by a revocable trust for estate planning purposes.[302] This is not a taxable transfer work for Florida documentary stamp tax purposes because there is no change in beneficial ownership.

.04 Unemployment Taxes

Effective January 1, 2004, LLCs are added to the definition of "Employing Unit." For unemployment tax purposes, an LLC has the same status as its classification for federal income tax purposes. Members of an LLC who perform services for an LLC

---

[297] Fla. Stat. Ann. § 605.0201(4).

[298] Fla. Stat. Ann. § 220.02.

[299] Id.

[300] Technical Assistance Investment No. 98(C)1-004, Fla. Dept. of Rev. (May 4, 1998).

[301] Technical Assistance Advisement, No. 05B4-003, Florida Department of Revenue (June 21, 2005); Technical Assistance Advisement, No. 05B4-004, Florida Department of Revenue (June 23, 2005). *See also* Florida Form DR-219, Return Transfers of Interest in Real Property.

[302] Technical Assistance Advisement, No. 07B4-001, Florida Department of Revenue (Jan. 18, 2007).

that is classified as a corporation for federal income tax purposes are considered employees.[303]

For reporting purposes, Florida treats LLCs in the same way as other reporting entities. For example, members of an LLC that is classified as a partnership or as a sole proprietor are not reportable, while members who perform services for an LLC classified as a corporation are reportable.[304]

.05 Apportionment of Income

LLCs doing business within and outside the state of Florida must apportion their business income to Florida based on a three-factor formula. The three factors are the value of property, payroll, and sales factors. Taxpayers may request permission from the Department of Revenue to apportion their income using a different method.

.06 Tax Filing Requirements

An LLC may be required to file a tax return in Florida depending on its classification as follows:

- An LLC that is classified as a corporation for Florida and federal tax purposes is subject to the Florida Income Tax Code and must file Form F-1120, Corporate Income/Franchise and Emergency Excise Tax Return.
- An LLC that is classified as a partnership for Florida and federal tax purposes must file Form F-1065, Florida Partnership Information Return, if one or more of its members is a corporation.[305] In addition, the corporate member of an LLC that is classified as a partnership for Florida and federal tax purposes must file a Florida corporate income tax return
- A single-member LLC that is disregarded for Florida and federal tax purposes is not required to file a separate Florida corporate income tax return. However, the income of the LLC is not exempt from tax if it is owned by a corporation, whether directly or indirectly. In this case, the corporation must file Form F-1120 reporting its own income, together with the income of the single-member LLC.

.07 Annual Report

Florida LLCs and foreign LLCs qualified to do business in Florida must file annual reports with the Department of State between January 1 and May 1 of each year.

---

[303] Fla. Stat. Ann. § 443.036(20); Tax Information Publication No. 0460BB-01, Florida Department of Revenue (Jan. 16, 2004).

[304] Tax Information Publication No. 0460BB-01, Florida Department of Revenue (Jan. 16, 2004).

[305] *See* Instructions to Form F-1065, under the heading, "Who Must File Form F-1065?"

.08 Filing Fees

The Department of State charges the following filing fees for LLCs:[306]

Articles of organization	$125
Annual report and supplemental fees	$138.75

¶ 2312 GEORGIA

Georgia enacted the Georgia Limited Liability Company Act effective March 1, 1994.[307]

.01 State Tax Classification

A Georgia LLC is classified for state tax purposes in the same manner that it is classified for federal tax purposes.[308] A member or assignee of a member of an LLC or a foreign LLC that is classified as a partnership is treated for Georgia tax purposes as either a resident or a nonresident partner. If the LLC is not classified as a partnership, the member or assignee of the member has the same status for Georgia tax purposes that the member or assignee of the member has for federal income tax purposes.[309]

A single-member LLC may be formed in Georgia.[310]

.02 Taxation of LLC and Members

A Georgia LLC is not subject to tax. Members of the LLC are taxed on their distributive shares of income, whether or not distributed.[311] The members of the LLC must include their distributive shares of income on their individual returns.[312]

A Georgia LLC is not subject to the net worth tax.[313]

.03 Real Estate Transfer Taxes

No real estate transfer taxes are due as a result of the recordation of the election to form an LLC.[314] The election is filed with the office of the clerk of the superior court

---

[306] Fla. Stat. Ann. § 605.0213.

[307] H.B. 264, ch. 174, 1993 Ga. Laws; Ga. Code Ann. §§ 14-11-100 to 14-11-1109.

[308] Ga. Code Ann. § 14-11-1104.

[309] Id.

[310] Ga. Code Ann. § 14-11-203.

[311] Ga. Dept. of Rev. Rule § 560-7-3-.08.

[312] Ga. Dept. of Rev. Rule § 560-7-3-.08(5).

[313] Form IT-711, under the heading, "Net Worth Tax."

[314] Ga. Code Ann. § 14-11-212.

in the county in which any of the LLC's real property is located. The certified copy of the election is then recorded in the clerk's books. The LLC is indexed as the grantee.

A buyer of real property must withhold taxes if the seller is a nonresident. A single-member LLC whose status is disregarded for federal income tax purposes is not considered the seller. Thus, the buyer must determine if the owner of the LLC is a nonresident for withholding tax purposes.[315]

.04 Conversion to LLC

A corporation, limited partnership, or general partnership may elect to become an LLC by filing an election.[316] An LLC formed by election may file a copy of the election, certified by the secretary of state, in the office of the clerk of the superior court of the county where any real property owned by the LLC is located and may record the certified copy of the election in the books kept by such clerk for recordation of deeds in the county. The entity electing to become the LLC is indexed as the grantor. The LLC is indexed as a grantee. No real estate taxes are due with respect to the recordation of the election.[317]

.05 Tax Returns

An LLC organized or qualified to do business in Georgia or deriving income from property located in Georgia must file a Georgia return on Form 700, State of Georgia Partnership Income Tax Return.[318] The return must be filed on or before the 15th day of the third month following the close of the tax year. It must be filed with the Georgia Income Tax Division, Department of Revenue, P.O. Box 740315, Atlanta, GA 30359-0315.

The Georgia return is similar to the federal return on Form 1065 in most respects. The accounting period and accounting methods for the Georgia return must be the same as those for the federal return. A copy of the federal return and all supporting schedules must be attached to the Georgia return.

If the Internal Revenue Service adjusts the net income of the LLC or has adjusted the net income of the LLC during the previous five years, the LLC must submit a detailed statement of the adjustment under separate cover to the Georgia Income Tax Division.

---

[315] Policy Statement No. IT2005-08-02-1, Georgia Department of Revenue (Aug. 2, 2005).

[316] *Id.*

[317] Ga. Code Ann. § 48-6-1.

[318] Ga. Dept. of Rev. Reg. § 560-7-3-.08(5).

.06 Nonresident Members

Nonresident members are taxed on their allocable share of LLC income, whether or not distributed.[319] The nonresident member must also file a Georgia income tax return.[320]

An LLC may file a composite return on Form IT CR, Georgia Nonresident Composite Tax Return, for its nonresident members.[321] The LLC must also check the "Composite Return Filed" box on Page 1 of Form 700. Nonresident members may only be included on the composite return if they have no other Georgia source income.[322] The composite tax rate is a graduated rate up to six percent of Georgia net taxable income.[323] The LLC may elect to pay the flat composite rate of six percent on all Georgia source income attributable to nonresident members (Option 3).[324] The composite tax is determined without exemptions or deductions, or on a pro rata basis with exemptions and deductions using the LLC's income. The LLC must pay composite estimated taxes on Form CR ES, Composite Return Estimated Tax.

The LLC must withhold taxes on the nonresident member's share of Georgia-sourced taxable income, whether or not distributed. The withholding applies to the nonresident member's share of Georgia separately income, guaranteed payments, loss, deduction or expense, and the nonresident member's share of the non-separately stated income, loss, deduction or expense.[325] The LLC and its members are jointly and severally liable for the withholding tax. There is a 25 percent penalty for failure to withhold.[326] No withholding is required for a nonresident member who is included on a composite return.[327] The withholding tax rate is four percent.[328] The LLC must report and pay the taxes using Form G-7-NRW, subject to certain exemptions if the nonresident member completes Form NRW-Exemption and Form GA-V, Payment Voucher.[329] Withholding is not required if the aggregate annual distributions paid or credited to the nonresident members are less than $1,000.[330]

---

[319] Ga. Code Ann. § 48-7-24.

[320] Ga. Dept. of Rev. Rule 560-7-8.34(3)(d).

[321] Ga. Code Ann. § 48-7-129(b); Ga. Dept. of Rev. Rule 560-7-8.34(3).

[322] *See* Instructions to Form IT-CR.

[323] Ga. Dept. of Rev. Reg. § 560-7-8-.34(3).

[324] *See* Instructions to Form IT-CR.

[325] Ga. Dept. of Rev. Reg. § 560-7-8-.34. *See also* Form NRW-Exemption.

[326] Ga. Code Ann. § 48-7-129(a).

[327] Ga. Dept. of Rev. Rule 560-7-8.34(3)(d); Ga. Code Ann. § 48-7-129(b). The procedures for withholding are set forth in Ga. Dept. of Rev. Rule 560-7-8.34(5).

[328] Ga. Dept. of Rev. Reg. § 560-7-8-.34(2)(a).

[329] Ga. Code Ann. § 48-7-129(e)(1)(B).

[330] Ga. Code Ann. § 48-7-129(d)(1).

.07 Apportionment of Income

If an LLC does business within and outside the state of Georgia, there is an apportionment and allocation formula that must be used to compute Georgia net income.[331] If business income from the LLC is derived from property owned or business done within the state and outside the state, the tax is imposed only on that portion of the business income that is reasonably attributable to the property owned and business done within the state. Where income is derived principally from the manufacture, production, or sale of tangible personal property, the portion of the net income attributable to property owned or business done within Georgia is based on the three-factor formula. The three factors are the property, payroll, and gross receipts factors.

.08 Annual Report

An LLC must file an annual report in Georgia.[332] Foreign LLCs qualified to do business in Georgia are also required to file annual reports. The annual report is filed with the secretary of state. It must set forth the name of the LLC, the jurisdiction under whose laws it is organized in the case of a foreign LLC, the street address and county of its registered office, the name of its registered agent at that office, the mailing address of its principal place of business, and any additional information required by the secretary of state. The annual report must be filed between January 1 and April 1 or such later date required by the secretary of state.

.09 Filing Fees

Georgia imposes the following filing fees on LLCs:[333]

Articles of organization	$100
Certificate of authority to do business in Georgia	$225
Annual registration (foreign or domestic)	$ 50

¶ 2313 HAWAII

Hawaii adopted the Uniform Limited Liability Company Act effective April 1, 1997.[334]

---

[331] Ga. Code Ann. § 48-7-31; Ga. Dept. of Rev. Rule 560-7-8-.34(2)(b).
[332] Ga. Code Ann. § 14-11-1103.
[333] Ga. Code Ann. § 14-11-1101.
[334] Haw. Rev. Stat. § § 428-101 to 428-1302.

.01 State Tax Classification and Applicability of General Tax Laws

The Hawaii Department of Taxation issued a tax information release regarding the classification of LLCs under the federal check-the-box regulations pending adoption by the department of its own rules on the subject.[335] The release also discusses the applicability of the Hawaii general tax laws to LLCs. The following interim rules apply:

- The department will follow the federal check-the-box regulations for purposes of the Hawaii income tax law. Each entity, owner, or other appropriate person specified under the check-the-box regulations that is responsible for filing a return must file a Hawaii return consistent with the federal classification. The effective date of the rules is January 1, 1997. If an LLC is classified as either a partnership or a corporation for federal income tax purposes, the same classification applies for Hawaii income tax purposes regardless of whether the classification is by default or election. If a single-member LLC is disregarded as an entity separate from its owner for federal income tax purposes, the entity is also disregarded for Hawaii income tax purposes.

- An LLC that elects its classification by filing Form 8832 with the IRS must attach a copy of that form to the LLC's Hawaii income tax or information return. The form must be attached to the return covering the first tax year in which the LLC carries on business in Hawaii, derives income from sources in Hawaii, or makes distributions that are received by a pass-through entity owner who either is a resident of Hawaii or carries on a business in Hawaii.[336] If an LLC elects this classification, but is not required to file a Hawaii return for the tax year, the appropriate person specified under the check-the-box regulations must attach a copy of Form 8832 to that person's Hawaii income tax or information return for the tax year that includes the date on which the election was effective.

- The check-the-box regulations are applicable to the general excise tax law under chapter 237 of the Hawaii Revised Statutes and to other gross receipts and transaction-type Hawaii taxes. There are modifications for single-member LLCs. The entity classification under federal law controls the classification of the entity for purposes of the general excise tax,[337] transient accommodations tax,[338] public service company tax,[339] fuel tax,[340] liquor tax,[341] cigarette and tobacco tax,[342] conveyance tax,[343] rental motor vehicle and tour vehicle

---

[335] Tax Information Release No. 97-4, Haw. Dept. of Taxn. (Aug. 4, 1997).

[336] See Haw. Admin. Rules § 18-235-95.

[337] See Haw. Rev. Stat. ch. 237.

[338] See Haw. Rev. Stat. ch. 237D.

[339] See Haw. Rev. Stat. ch. 239M.

[340] See Haw. Rev. Stat. ch. 243.

[341] See Haw. Rev. Stat. ch. 244D.

[342] See Haw. Rev. Stat. ch. 245.

[343] See Haw. Rev. Stat. ch. 247.

surcharge tax, and nursing facility tax laws.[344] All LLCs, including single-member LLCs, are taxable at the entity level for purposes of the general excise tax and the other gross receipts and transaction-type Hawaii taxes.[345] For example, if an LLC is classified as a partnership for income tax purposes, the general excise tax and the other gross receipts and transaction-type taxes are imposed at the entity level. Similarly, a single-member LLC is treated as a taxable entity for purposes of these taxes even though the LLC is disregarded under the federal check-the-box regulations.

- An LLC is taxable on its business with its members, and they are taxable on their business with the LLC. A single-member LLC is taxable on its business with its member, and the member is taxable on its business with the LLC unless specifically exempted under applicable law.[346]

- Members are not subject to the general excise tax on distributive shares of income or distributions from an LLC that is classified as a partnership, provided those shares or distributions represent a return on the members' investment in and not from their business with the LLC. The same treatment applies to distributive shares of income or distributions from an LLC to its members.

- License and registration requirements are applicable at the entity level of the LLC. All LLCs, including single-member LLCs, must have a general excise tax license. They must also have, if appropriate, licenses and certificates of registration required by the transient accommodations tax, field tax, liquor tax, cigarette and tobacco tax, rental motor vehicle and tour vehicle surcharge tax, and nursing facility tax laws. A single-member LLC that is disregarded as an entity separate from the owner for income tax purposes must be licensed and registered in the LLC's name.

- The Department of Taxation will follow the IRS regulations and rulings relating to the need for a new federal employer identification number in determining whether a new general excise tax license and other new licenses or registrations are necessary. Thus, if a new federal employer identification number is required, as is the case when the business of a sole proprietorship is transferred to a partnership or to a corporation, then a new general excise tax license and other new licenses and applicable registrations are also required. However, a new federal employer identification number, a new general excise tax license, and other applicable new licenses and registrations are not required when the LLC elects, under the federal check-the-box regulations, to change its federal and Hawaii income tax classification or when a domestic partnership converts into an LLC classified as a partnership (or vice versa). When a change in name occurs, but a new license is not required, taxpayers must provide the Department of Taxation with the name change information on Form GEW-TA-RB-5.

---

[344] *See* Haw. Rev. Stat. ch. 346E.

[345] *See In re Island Holidays, Ltd.*, 59 Haw. 307 (1978).

[346] *See, e.g.*, Haw. Rev. Stat. § 237-23.5.

¶ 2313.01

.02 Allocations

Income, gain, loss, deductions, and credits must be allocated among the members according to the LLC operating agreement for sharing income or loss generally. If the members agree, specific items may be allocated among them in a ratio different from the ratio for sharing income or loss generally.

.03 Tax Filing Requirements

When an LLC commences doing business in Hawaii, it must file a business tax license application and obtain a general excise tax license number. The State of Hawaii Basic Business Application, BB-1 Packet, must be completed and submitted to the Department of Taxation with a one-time $20 license fee. The Department of Taxation recommends that the LLC mail the application to the Department. An LLC may also apply for the license number at any of the district offices. The application form is available on the Department's website. The Department no longer automatically mails tax booklets. Instead, it recommends that LLCs view and manage their tax records online, file returns online, and pay taxes online at hitax.hawaii.gov.

Hawaii LLCs and LLCs qualified to do business in Hawaii must file Form N-20, Partnership Return of Income.[347] The form is an information return. It is used to report the income, deductions, credits, gains, and losses from the operation of the LLC.

The LLC must list all items of gross income and allowable deductions, as well as various additional items of information. The return must include the income, deductions, and credits attributable everywhere, together with the income, deductions, and credits attributable only to Hawaii. Hawaii follows the provisions of federal law, Subchapter K, in determining Hawaii taxable income.[348]

The return must be filed on or before the twentieth day of the fourth month following the close of the tax year of the LLC. It must be filed with the taxation district office in which the LLC has its principal place of business. If the LLC does not have a place of business in Hawaii, the return must be filed with the Department of Taxation, P.O. Box 3559, Honolulu, HI 96811-3559.

An Application for Automatic Extension of Time to File Hawaii Return for Partnership may be filed on Form N-100. There is an automatic three-month extension. The form must be filed by the due date of the LLC return.

An LLC must file an information return if it makes payments of rents, commissions, or other fixed or determinable income totaling $600 or more to any one person in the course of its trade or business during the calendar year. It must report interest payments totaling $10 or more. For example, if an LLC pays a person $600 or more in a calendar year to perform services under a subcontract-type arrangement in which

---

[347] Haw. Rev. Stat. § 235-95; Haw. Admin. Rules § 18-235-4-07(e).
[348] Haw. Rev. Stat. §§ 235-2.2, 235-2.3.

no employment taxes are withheld, the LLC must file federal Form 1099-MISC, Miscellaneous Income.

LLCs must use Form N-196, Annual Summary Transmittal of Hawaii Information Returns, to summarize and send information returns to the respective taxation district office.

Although a Hawaii LLC is not subject to income tax, the members are liable for income tax on their distributive shares of LLC income, whether or not distributed. These items are included on their individual tax returns. The total amount of distributive share items is reported on Schedule K to Form N-20.

There are no separate tax returns for a single-member disregarded LLC. A single-member disregarded LLC is also disregarded for Hawaii income tax purposes.[349] The owners of the LLC must file the appropriate tax return.

.04 Apportionment of Income

Each LLC must state specifically the income attributable to the state and the income attributable outside the state with respect to each member. Ordinary income or loss from a trade or business is attributable to the state of Hawaii by use of the apportionment of business income allocation provisions of the Uniform Division of Income for Tax Purposes Act.[350] Business income is apportioned to Hawaii by multiplying the income by a fraction, the numerator of which is a property factor, payroll factor, and sales factor, and the denominator of which is three. If the apportionment does not fairly represent the extent of the LLC's business activities in the state, the LLC may request the use of separate accounting, the exclusion of one or more of the factors, the inclusion of one or more additional factors, or the use of any other method to accurately reflect the LLC's business activities in the state. Schedules O and P of Form N-20 are used to show this computation. Income or loss of an LLC is allocated to a member only for the part of the year in which that member is a member of the LLC. The LLC must either allocate on a daily basis or divide the partnership year into segments and allocate income, loss, or special items in each segment among the persons who are members during that segment.

.05 Nonresident Members

An LLC that is classified as a single-member disregarded LLC[351] or as a partnership[352] must withhold five percent of the amount realized that is allocable to nonresident members on the sale of Hawaii property. The LLC must file Form N-288A, Statement of Withholding on Dispositions by Nonresident Persons of Hawaii Real Property Interests.

---

[349] Hawaii Department of Taxation, Tax Information Release No. 97-4, II.A (Aug. 4, 1997).

[350] Haw. Rev. Stat. § 235-29.

[351] Hawaii Act 23 (S.B. No. 842, S.D. 1).

[352] See instructions for Form N-20.

There are no statutory provisions that permit an LLC to file composite return on behalf of nonresident members. However, the Hawaii Department of Taxation administratively allows LLCs to elect to file a composite nonresident income tax return on behalf of participating nonresident members. The LLC may make composite payments for the participating member's distributive share of Hawaii source income based on their own individual tax rate, with no standard deduction or personal exemption. The LLC must file Form N-15, Individual Income Tax Return, Nonresident and Part-year Resident.[353] The nonresident member may be included on the composite return if the following conditions are met:[354]

- The member is an individual.
- The member's income from the LLC is the member's only income from Hawaii sources. If a member has other income from Hawaii sources such as multiple partnerships, even though the LLCs are related, the member must file a separate net income tax return.
- The LLC obtains a power of attorney from each of its members to file an income tax return on the members' behalf. A copy of each power of attorney must be attached to the initial composite tax return filed by the LLC.
- The LLC, as an agent for the participating members, must pay tax, additions to tax, interest, and penalties owed by the members.

.06 Annual Report

An LLC must file an annual report in Hawaii.[355] The annual report must set forth the following information:

- The name of the LLC and the country of organization
- The address of its designated office and the name of its agent at that office
- The name of each manager
- The name of each member if the LLC is managed by members

.07 Filing Fees

Hawaii imposes the following filing fees on LLCs:[356]

Articles of organization	$ 50
Certificate of authority of foreign LLC	$ 50
Annual report	$ 15

---

[353] The instructions for completing the form as a composite return are set forth in the Instructions to Form N-20, Partnership Return of Income.

[354] Instructions to Form N-20, Partnership Return of Income.

[355] Haw. Rev. Stat. § 428-210.

[356] Haw. Rev. Stat. § 428-1301.

¶ 2314 IDAHO

Idaho enacted the Idaho Uniform Limited Liability Company Act effective July 1, 2008.[357] It was the first state to adopt the Revised Uniform Limited Liability Company Act ("RULLCA"), drafted by the Uniform Law Commission.

.01 State Tax Classification

Limited liability companies are classified in Idaho in the same manner as under the federal income tax laws.[358] Effective January 1, 1998, Idaho adopted the federal check-the-box regulations for determining whether an LLC is classified as a partnership, corporation or sole proprietorship for Idaho personal income and corporate franchise tax purposes.[359]

.02 Taxation of LLC

An LLC is taxed at the 7.4 percent corporate income tax rate in 2017 on taxable income allocated to nonresident members. Taxable income is the sum of (i) income allocated to Idaho, (ii) net business income apportioned to Idaho, (iii) compensation paid to the members not reported to Idaho, (iv) less LLC income reported to Idaho on the members' individual income tax returns.[360] There is normally no income tax if an LLC allocates all of its income to Idaho members or arranges for the payment of the nonresident tax through withholding or a composite return.

An LLC must pay other miscellaneous taxes, including the permanent building fund tax, recapture income tax credits, fuels tax, sales/use taxes due on mail order, Internet and other nontax purchases, and tax from the recapture of qualified investment exemption.[361]

.03 Taxation of Members

Members of an LLC are taxed on their distributive shares of income.

The sale of a membership interest does not qualify for capital gain treatment under Idaho law.[362]

---

[357] Idaho Code § § 30-6-101 to 30-6-1104.

[358] Idaho Code § 63-3006A.

[359] Ch. 55, H.D. 485, Laws 1998.

[360] *See* Form 65, Idaho Partnership Return of Income.

[361] *See* Form 65, Idaho Partnership Return of Income.

[362] Decision No. 19824 (Mar. 13, 2007).

.04 Taxation of Nonresidents

An LLC must pay taxes on income allocable to nonresident members in one of the following ways:

- *Withholding.* An LLC must withhold taxes at the highest marginal tax rate[363] on Idaho source income allocable to nonresident members. The withholding tax rate is 7.4 percent in 2017. The LLC must file Form PTE-01, Idaho Income Tax Withheld for an Individual Nonresident Owner of a Pass-Through Entity. Withholding is not required for nonresident members (i) with income of less than $1,000 for the tax year, (ii) who are included in a composite return,[364] (iii) who file an Idaho Nonresident Owner Agreement, or (iv) who are not natural persons (including corporations, partnerships, trusts, and estates that are members of the LLC). The withholding is a prepayment of Idaho income tax for the nonresident owner. The LLC must send a statement to the each nonresident member setting for the tax withheld.[365]

- *Direct payment to Commission.* In lieu of withholding, an LLC may make a direct payment to the Commission on behalf of an officer, director or individual member of the LLC.[366]

- *Agreement to file tax return.* A member may file Form PTE-NROA, Idaho Nonresident Owner Agreement. The member must consent to the jurisdiction of Idaho for purposes of the collection of unpaid income tax, together with related penalties and interest. No withholding is required for members filing this agreement.

- *Composite return.* The LLC may file a composite return on behalf of electing members in the LLC.[367] The composite tax rate is 7.4 percent in 2017. The composite return is filed on Form 65, Idaho Partnership Return of Income, and includes the composite income reported on Schedule PTE-12, Idaho Schedule for Pass-Through Owners. The LLC must check the box in Item 1 that the return is a composite return. The nonresident members are taxed on wages, salaries, guaranteed payments, distributive share of income and other Idaho source income from the LLC.[368] A nonresident member may make a new election each year.[369] The LLC must withhold taxes if no election is made.[370] A member may make the election to have the LLC report and pay taxes on the member's share of income and compensation from the LLC attributable to Idaho sources by filing with the LLC Form PTE-WX, Withhold-

---

[363] The highest marginal tax rate is set forth in Idaho Code § 63-3024.

[364] Instructions to Form PTE-01.

[365] Idaho Code § 63-3036B(2)-(6).

[366] Idaho Code § 63-3036B(6).

[367] Idaho Code § 63-3022L(1).

[368] Idaho Code § 63-3022L(2).

[369] Idaho Code § 63-3022L(3).

[370] Idaho Code § 63-3022L(4).

ing Exemption Certificate for Individual Owners/Officers/Directors/Beneficiaries of Pass-through Entities.

The LLC must complete Form PTE-12 as the reconciliation schedule to be included with Form 65. The form must include each nonresident member's information with respect to withholding and composite taxes.

Effective in 2011, an LLC is not liable for the tax owed by a member on income from the LLC. However, the LLC must withhold income taxes if the nonresident member does not elect to have taxes paid on the LLC's return.

.05 Tax Returns

An Idaho LLC that is classified as a partnership for federal income tax purposes must file an Idaho partnership tax return on Form 65, Idaho Partnership Return of Income. The return must be filed if the LLC has one or more members residing in Idaho or if the LLC transacts business in Idaho.[371] Transacting business in Idaho is indicated by, but not limited to, the following activities:

- Owning or leasing, as lessor or lessee, any property in Idaho
- Soliciting business in Idaho
- Being a member of a partnership with business in Idaho
- Engaging in any Idaho activity from which income is received, realized, or derived
- Having an agent, such as a collector, repair person, delivery person, or other person acting on behalf of the LLC in Idaho

A complete copy of the federal income tax return must be attached to the Idaho partnership income tax return. All Schedules K-1 must be attached to the return or submitted with the return on microfiche. The return must be signed by an authorized individual on behalf of the LLC.

The return and payment must be sent to Idaho State Tax Commission, P.O. Box 56, Boise, ID 83756-0201. The LLC must also pay the 7.6 percent corporate tax rate on LLC income reported on the return, less LLC income reported to Idaho on the members' individual tax returns.

The due date of the return is the 15th day of the fourth month following the close of the tax year. For calendar year LLCs, the due date is April 15. LLCs that are classified as corporations for federal income tax purposes must file Idaho corporation income tax returns on Form 41.

.06 Accounting Periods and Methods

The LLC must use the same accounting period as used for federal tax purposes. A change in the accounting period must have prior approval from the Internal

---

[371] Idaho Code § 63-3030(a)(9).

Revenue Service. A copy of the federal approval on Form 1128, Application to Adopt, Change, or Retain a Tax Year, must be attached to the return.

An Idaho LLC must also use the same accounting methods as used for federal tax purposes. A change of accounting methods must have prior approval from the Internal Revenue Service. The LLC must attach a copy of the federal approval on Form 3115, Application for Change in Accounting Method.

.07 Amended Returns

Amended returns must be filed on Form 41X, Amended Business Income Tax Return.

If the LLC is subject to a federal audit and if the federal taxable income or tax credit is changed because of the federal audit, the LLC must send written notice to the Idaho State Tax Commission within 60 days of the final federal determination. The LLC must include copies of all schedules supplied by the Internal Revenue Service. If additional taxes are owed, the LLC is subject to a five percent negligence penalty if it fails to send timely notice. If the final federal determination results in an Idaho refund and the statute of limitations is closed, the LLC has one year from the date of final determination to file for a refund.

Nonresident members of an LLC may elect to pay individual income taxes on the LLC's tax return.[372] The LLC must pay taxes at the 7.6 percent corporate tax rate on such members' distributive shares of income.

An LLC is taxed on a nonresident member's distributive share of income if the LLC derives income from Idaho sources and the nonresident member does not file the required Idaho returns or pay the Idaho taxes.[373] The LLC must pay tax at the 7.6 percent corporate tax rate on such member's distributive share of income. The permanent building excise tax also applies to such income.

For tax years beginning in 2011, the LLC must withhold taxes on the distributive share of income for nonresident members who do not elect to have the LLC file a return and pay the taxes due.[374]

.08 Apportionment of Income

There are special rules that apply to LLCs that operate in Idaho and in another state or country or that have at least one member that is a member of a unitary group. Business income must be apportioned. The apportionment formula consists of three factors: property, payroll, and sales. The three percentages are averaged to arrive at the Idaho apportionment factor. For most taxpayers, the sales factor is double-weighted.

---

[372] Idaho Code § 63-3022L(1), (2).

[373] Idaho Code § 63-3022L(3); State Tax Commission Rule 35.01.01.107.

[374] Idaho Code §§ 63-3022L(3), 63-3036B; IDAPA 35.01.01.290; Form 65 Instructions, Partnership Return of Income.

Business income subject to apportionment includes income from transactions or activities in the regular course of the LLC's trade or business. Business income also includes income from tangible or intangible property if the acquisition, management, or disposition of the property is an integral part of the LLC's regular trade or business.

If the allocation and apportionment provisions do not fairly represent the LLC's business activities in Idaho, the LLC may take advantage of one of the exceptions. The exceptions include separate accounting, exclusion of a factor, and modified factors for certain industries.

An Idaho LLC is treated as part of a unitary multistate business when the operations conducted in Idaho are integrated with, depend on, or contribute to the business outside Idaho. There are two tests to determine whether the LLC is part of a unitary business. The first test is the three unities test. The three elements of a unitary business include (1) unity of ownership; (2) unity of operation as evidenced by central divisions for such functions as purchasing, advertising, accounting, and management; and (3) unity of use in the LLC's centralized executive force and centralized system of operation.

An alternative test is a contribution or dependency test. The operation of the LLC meets a contribution or dependency test if the operation of the portion of the business done in Idaho depends on or contributes to the operation of the overall business.

If unity of ownership exists, the presence of any of the following factors creates a strong presumption that the activities of the LLC constitute a unitary business:

1. All activities of the group are in the same general line or type of business.
2. The activities of the group constitute different steps in a vertically integrated enterprise.
3. The group is characterized by centralized management.

The LLC must complete Schedule 42, Supplemental Schedule for Multistate/ Multinational Business, to compute the apportionment factor. Schedule 42 is also used by LLCs that have income from business activities that is taxable in Idaho or another state or country.

.09 Filing Fees

There are the following filing fees in Idaho:[375]

Articles of organization	$100
Foreign LLC registration application	$100
Annual fee	$ 0

---

[375] Idaho Code § 30-6-210.

¶ 2315 ILLINOIS

Illinois enacted the Illinois Limited Liability Company Act in 1992, effective January 1, 1994.[376]

.01 State Tax Classification

Illinois LLCs and foreign LLCs doing business in Illinois are classified for state tax purposes in the same manner as LLCs are classified for federal tax purposes.[377] A foreign or domestic LLC that is classified under federal law as a corporation is classified as a corporation for state tax purposes.[378] A foreign or domestic LLC that is classified as a partnership for federal income tax purposes is classified as a partnership for Illinois tax purposes.[379] A foreign or domestic LLC that is classified as a disregarded entity for federal tax purposes is a disregarded entity for state income tax purposes.[380] Effective January 1, 1998, an LLC may have one or more members.[381]

.02 Taxation of LLC and Members

Illinois LLCs that are classified as partnerships must pay a personal property replacement tax at a rate of 1.5 percent of net income.[382] There is a deduction for personal service income of an LLC.[383]

The state imposes the personal property replacement tax on all corporations subject to the regular income tax. A corporation includes an LLC that is classified as a corporation for federal tax purposes.[384]

If an LLC is classified as a partnership, income and losses of the LLC are passed through to members and taxed to them individually. Illinois adopted the federal base as a starting point in determining income.[385]

.03 Tax Returns

An LLC that is classified as a partnership must file the following replacement tax forms:

---

[376] Pub. Act No. 87-1062 (S.B. 2163), 1992 Ill. Laws; 805 Ill. Comp. Stat. 180/1-1 to 180/60-1.

[377] 35 Ill. Comp. Stat. 5/1501.

[378] 35 Ill. Comp. Stat. 5/1501(a)(4).

[379] 35 Ill. Comp. Stat. 5/1501(a)(16).

[380] Ill. Dept. of Revenue No. IT 01-0004-PLR (Feb. 13, 2001).

[381] 805 Ill. Comp. Stat. 180/5-1.

[382] 35 Ill. Comp. Stat. 5/201(c).

[383] 35 ILCS 5/203(d)(2)(H).

[384] 35 Ill. Comp. Stat. 5/1501(a)(4).

[385] 35 Ill. Comp. Stat. 5/203(e).

IL-1065	Partnership Replacement Tax Return
IL-1065-X	Amended Partnership Replacement Tax Return
IL-477	Replacement Tax Investment Credits
IL-505-B	Automatic Extension Payment

The LLC reports the 1.5 percent replacement tax on Form IL-1065. The LLC must pay the replacement tax on Illinois income, excluding income distributed to members who are subject to the replacement tax. All LLCs doing business in LLC must file Form IL-1065 except for LLCs formed for the sole purpose of playing the Illinois state lottery.

Illinois LLCs that are required to file Form IL-1065 must register in Illinois by filing Form NUC-1, Illinois Business Registration. Form NUC-1 may be obtained from the Illinois Department of Revenue, P.O. Box 19010, Springfield, IL 62794-9010. The LLC must register with the Illinois Department of Revenue before filing its return.

An LLC must pay the Illinois replacement tax in full on or before the 15th day of the fourth month following the close of the tax year. The payment date applies even though the LLC has obtained an automatic extension of time for filing the return. LLCs are not required to pay estimated taxes.

The LLC must apportion its income if any part of the income is derived outside of Illinois. The apportionment is based on a three-factor formula: the property, payroll, and sales factors.

Illinois LLCs, managers, and members are subject to the following taxes effective January 1, 1994: the Illinois retailers' occupation (sales) tax; hotel operators' occupational, service occupation, use, and service use taxes; motor fuel and cigarette taxes; real estate transfer, automobile renting, and utility taxes; and the personal liability provisions of the Uniform Penalty and Interest Act.[386]

.04 Nonresident Members

An LLC with nonresident members must comply with one of the following requirements:

- *Withholding Tax.* An LLC must report and pay tax on behalf of nonresident individual members.[387] The pass-through withholding payment amount is calculated on Schedule K-1-P(3) which must be completed for each nonresident member. The aggregate amounts from Schedule K-1-P(3) must also be reported to the Illinois Department of Revenue on Form IL-1065, Schedule B. The withholding tax rate for 2018 is 4.95 percent of taxable income from Illinois sources plus 1.5 percent of the member's share of income for the replacement tax, subject to credits and other adjustments.[388] The payments

---

[386] Pub. Act No. 88-480 (S.B. 553), 1993 Ill. Laws.

[387] Schedule K-1-P(1); Illinois Department of Revenue Informational Bulletin FY 2018-14, Blended Income Tax Rates for Use with Your 2017 Illinois Income Tax Returns (Nov. 2017).

[388] *See* Schedule K-1-P(3) and instructions.

must be made by the original due date, without regard to extensions, for filing the Illinois income tax return. The LLC must notify the nonresident member on Schedule K-1-P(1) or Schedule K-1-T of the amount of payments made on the member's behalf. If the LLC's payment covers the nonresident member's Illinois individual income tax obligation, the member is not required to file Form IL-1040, Individual Income Tax Return.[389] If the member does file an Illinois income tax return, the member will receive a credit for the payment made by the LLC by attaching Schedule K-1-P(1) or Schedule K-1-T to his or her return.

- *Composite Return.* An LLC may not file a composite return or pass-through entity payment return for any nonresident members in the LLC. The composite tax return on Form IL-1023-C and Form IL-1000 were eliminated for tax years ending on or after December 31, 2014.[390]
- *Certificate of Exemption.* Prior to 2015, an LLC was not required to make a pass-through payment or file a composite return if the member certified to the LLC on Form IL-1000-E, Certificate of Exemption for Pass-through Entity Payments, that the member would file an Illinois tax return and pay the income tax. Form IL-1000-E was eliminated for tax years ending on or after December 31, 2014.[391]

.05 Annual Report

Illinois LLCs must file an annual report on Form LLC-50.1 with the Illinois Secretary of State.[392] The filing fee is $250. Foreign LLCs qualified to transact business in Illinois must also file annual reports. The report must set forth the following information:

- The name of the LLC
- The address, including street number, of its registered office in the state and the name of its registered agent at that address
- The address, including street number, of its principal place of business; the name and address of its managers or, if none, its members
- Any additional information required by the secretary of state

.06 Filing Fees

Illinois imposes the following filing fees on LLCs effective January 1, 1998:[393]

---

[389] Illinois Department of Revenue Informational Bulletin FY 2009-02, *Pass-through Entity Payments* (Oct. 2008).

[390] H.B. 3157 (2013).

[391] H.B. 3157 (2013).

[392] 805 Ill. Comp. Stat. 180/50-1.

[393] 805 Ill. Comp. Stat. 180/50-10.

Articles of organization
Regular LLC	$500
Series LLC	$750
Additional online filing fee	$100
Annual report	$250

¶2316 INDIANA

Indiana enacted the Indiana Business Flexibility Act effective July 1, 1993.[394] The act was added to the Indiana Code to provide for the formation of LLCs. It also amended the adjusted gross income tax definition of "partnership" to include LLCs that are treated as partnerships for federal tax purposes.

.01 State Tax Classification

Indiana LLCs are classified for state income tax purposes in the same manner that they are classified for federal tax purposes.[395]

A tax directive issued before the IRS issued the federal check-the-box regulations determined that an Indiana LLC would be classified as a partnership or corporation for tax purposes depending on whether the LLC possessed or lacked the four corporate characteristics of centralization of management, continuity of life, free transferability of interest, and limited liability.[396]

Indiana permits single-member LLCs.[397] These LLCs are classified as corporations or proprietorships depending on their classification for federal tax purposes.

.02 Taxation of LLC and Members

LLCs are not subject to an Indiana income or franchise tax.[398] However, publicly traded partnerships that are treated as LLCs under section 7704 of the Internal Revenue Code are classified for Indiana tax purposes in the same manner that they are classified for federal tax purposes.[399]

Members of the LLC are taxed on their distributive shares of income, gain, loss, credit, and deductions.[400] A member's share of profit or loss from the Indiana LLC is included in the member's calculation of federal adjusted gross income and is generally subject to the same rules for arriving at Indiana adjusted gross income. Therefore,

---

[394] S.B. 485, 1993 Ind. Acts; Ind. Code Ann. §§ 23-18-1-1 to 23-18-12-11.

[395] Ind. Code Ann. § 6-3-1-19.

[396] Tax Policy Directive No. 2, Ind. Dept. of Rev. (May 1992).

[397] Ind. Code Ann. § 23-18-6-0.5.

[398] Ind. Code Ann. § 6-3-4-11(a).

[399] 45 IAC 1.1-3-12.

[400] Id.

a member's distributive share, before any modifications required by Indiana statutes, is the same ratio and amount as determined under section 704 of the Internal Revenue Code and regulations thereunder. The members must include their shares of all LLC income, whether or not distributed, on their separate or individual Indiana income or franchise tax returns. Each member's distributive share of income is adjusted by modifications provided in the Indiana statutes.[401]

.03 Tax Returns

LLCs that are classified as partnerships must file an annual return on Form IT-65, Indiana Partnership Return and an information return on Schedule IN K-1. These forms must disclose each member's share of distributed and undistributed income. The return must be filed with the Indiana Department of Revenue.[402]

The first four pages of the LLC's partnership return on Form 1065 must be attached to the state return. The federal Schedules K-1 may not be attached to the return, but must be available for inspection upon request by the Indiana Department of Revenue.[403]

Any LLC doing business in Indiana or deriving gross income from sources within Indiana is required to file the return.[404] The following activities constitute doing business in Indiana or deriving income from Indiana sources:[405]

- Maintaining an office, warehouse, construction site, or other place of business
- Maintaining an inventory of merchandise or material for sale, distribution, or manufacture or of consigned goods
- Selling or distributing merchandise to customers directly from company-owned or-operated vehicles when the title to the merchandise is transferred from the seller or distributor to the customer at the time of sale or distribution
- Providing services to customers in Indiana or used in Indiana
- Owning, renting, or operating a business or income-producing real or personal property in Indiana
- Accepting orders in Indiana with no right of approval or rejection in another state
- Transporting interstate

The accounting period for which Form IT-65 is filed and the method of accounting adopted must be the same as used for federal tax purposes. If the LLC changes its tax year or method of accounting, it must give notice to the Department of Revenue.

The initial due date for the return is the 15th day of the fourth month following the close of the LLC's tax year. The Department of Revenue recognizes the Internal Revenue Service's Application for Automatic Extension of Time on Form 8736 or

---

[401] *See* Ind. Code Ann. § 6-3-1-3.5(A), (B); 45 IAC 1.1-3-12.

[402] 45 IAC 1.1-5-4.

[403] Ind. Code Ann. § 6-3-4-10(b).

[404] Ind. Code Ann. § 6-3-4-10.

[405] Instructions to Form IT-65, p. 1.

Form 8800. It is not necessary to file a separate copy of the form with the department to request an Indiana extension. Instead, the federal extension form must be attached to the Indiana return of the LLC.

An LLC that files an amended federal return that affects the Indiana income or taxable income reportable by the members must file an amended Indiana return. The amended return must be filed within 120 days after the filing of the amended federal return.

The LLC must complete Schedule IN K-1, Partners' Share of Income, Deductions, Modifications, and Credits, for each member. Schedule IN K-1 shows the member's share of income, credits, and modifications. The LLC must show the federal Schedule K-1 amounts for full-year Indiana resident members. For all corporate members and nonresident individual members, the federal Schedule K-1 amounts are multiplied by the apportionment percentage calculated on the worksheet.

An LLC that is classified as a corporation for federal tax purposes must file Form IT-20.

.04 Nonresident Members

Effective January 1, 2015, an LLC must include all nonresident members in a composite return schedule, and the LLC must withhold Indiana adjusted gross income tax for all nonresident members.[406] There is no provision for a member to opt out of the composite filing.[407] The composite filing is made using Schedule Composite-COR for corporate members not domiciled in Indiana and Schedule Composite for nonresident individual members.[408]

An LLC that files a composite return must withhold Indiana state and/or county income taxes from all nonresident members into the corporate account using Form IT-6WTH and reflect a credit for the withholding/composite tax on Form IN K-1 for each member. The state withholding tax rate is 3.23 percent in 2018. The county tax withholding rate is one percent in 2018.[409] Form IT-6WTH is available by calling the Corporate Tax section at (317) 232-0129. Payment is due the 15th day of the fourth month following the close of the LLC's tax period. Each nonresident member's composite tax is calculated at the relevant tax rate.[410]

An LLC must withhold AGI tax at the corporate tax rate on the amount it pays or credits for the distributive share derived from Indiana sources to all nonresident corporate partners. The withholding must be an amount reflecting the ultimate

---

[406] Ind. Code Ann. § 6-3-4-12.

[407] Information Bulletin #72, S Corporation, Trust, and Partnership Mandate to File a Composite Return on Behalf of Nonresident Shareholders and Partners, Effective Date: Jan. 1, 2015.

[408] IT-65, Partnership Return Booklet.

[409] Indiana Department of Revenue Departmental Notice #1, effective Jan. 1, 2018.

[410] Ind. Code Ann. § 6-3-4-12.

Indiana tax liability due by respective corporate members because of the LLC's activities.[411]

.05 Use Tax

LLCs are subject to the use tax. The use tax is due upon the storage, use, or consumption of tangible personal property purchased in a transaction in Indiana or elsewhere unless the transaction is exempted from the sales and use tax by law or the sales tax due and paid on the transaction equals the use tax due.[412]

.06 Apportionment and Allocation

An Indiana LLC must file an apportionment worksheet with its return if the LLC is doing business both within and outside of Indiana and has any members who are not domiciled in Indiana.

An LLC may file a composite adjusted gross income tax return on behalf of non-Indiana-resident individual members electing to participate in the composite return.

A full-year resident member of an Indiana LLC reports the entire distributive share of LLC income or loss, as adjusted, no matter where the LLC's business is located or in which state it does business. The individual member of the LLC must complete Form IT-40, Indiana Individual Income Tax Return.

Part and full-year nonresident members must report their shares of income or loss, as adjusted, from the LLC that is derived from or attributed to sources within Indiana. Indiana source income is determined by use of the apportionment formula described in the Indiana statutes.[413] When an LLC both has nonresident members and conducts business within and outside of Indiana, the LLC must include the apportionment worksheet with Form IT-65. The nonresident members must complete Form IT-40PNR, Indiana Part-Year or Nonresident Individual Income Tax Return. The members may claim credit on their returns for amounts withheld by the LLC from the members' income. Copy C of Form WH-18 must be attached to the return to verify any such credit.

An LLC may file a composite return on behalf of nonresident members.[414] Nonresident members are exempt from the filing an Indiana individual income tax return only if they are included as members of a composite return.

A part-year nonresident member is required to file Form IT-40PNR, reporting the total amount of income or loss received while residing in Indiana and that part of Indiana's source income received while a nonresident. The member also reports apportioned Indiana income or loss, as adjusted, on Form IT-40PNR.

---

[411] The withholding tax is computed under Ind. Code Ann. §6-5.5-4 for corporate partners; IT-65, Partnership Return Booklet.

[412] IT-65, Partnership Return Booklet.

[413] *See* Ind. Code Ann. §6-3-2-2(B).

[414] Ind. Code Ann. §6-3-4-12(g). The composite return is filed on Schedule IT-65 COMP, Partner's Composite Adjusted Growth Income Tax Return.

.07 Corporate Members

Corporate members of the LLC must report their distributive shares of the LLC's income or loss on Form IT-20, IT-20S, IT-20NP, IT-65, or IT-41. The distributions are fully taxable for gross, adjusted gross, and supplemental net income tax purposes.

Corporate partners doing business within and outside of Indiana must determine their taxable income from Indiana sources using the allocation and apportionment provisions set forth in the Indiana statutes.[415] These allocation and apportionment provisions generally follow the Uniform Division of Income for Tax Purposes Act. A multistate corporation that is a member of an LLC must first determine what part of its adjusted gross income (which includes all LLC income) constitutes business income and what part is nonbusiness income according to the regulations. If the corporate member's activities and the LLC's activities constitute a unitary business, the business income of the unitary business attributable to Indiana is determined by a three-factor formula. The formula consists of the property, payroll, and sales of the corporate member and its actual share of the LLC's factors for any LLC tax year ending within or with the corporate member's income year.

A corporation that is the sole owner of an LLC classified as a corporation may file a consolidated tax return with that corporation.[416]

.08 Filing Fees

Indiana imposes the following filing fees on LLCs:[417]

Articles of organization	$90
Certificate of authority for foreign LLC to do business in the state	$90
Biennial report on Form 48725 (in writing)	$30
Biennial report (filed electronically)	$20

¶2317 IOWA

Iowa enacted the Iowa Limited Liability Company Act effective July 1, 1992.[418]

.01 State Tax Classification

Iowa follows federal law in its classification of LLCs.[419] An LLC that is classified as a partnership for federal tax purposes is classified as a partnership for Iowa tax

---

[415] *See* Ind. Code Ann. § 6-3-2-2(B) to (H).

[416] Rev. Rul. No. 2001-12 IT, Indiana Department of Revenue (2002).

[417] Ind. Code Ann. § 23-18-12-3.

[418] H.F. 327, 1992 Iowa Acts; Iowa Code Ann. §§ 489.101 to 489.1304.

[419] Iowa Code Ann. § 422.15.2; Iowa Dept. of Rev. & Fin. R. 701-45.1(422).

purposes.[420] An LLC that is classified as a corporation under federal law is treated as a corporation for state income tax purposes.[421] Iowa follows the federal tax classification for single-member LLCs.[422]

.02 Taxation of LLC and Members

Iowa LLCs that are classified as partnerships are not taxpayers under Iowa law. All items of income, gain, loss, credit, and deduction pass through to the members. The members are taxable on their distributive shares, computed on the same basis as under federal law.[423]

Nonresident members are taxed on their distributive shares of income allocable to Indiana.[424]

The Iowa corporate income tax applies to each corporation organized under Iowa law and to foreign corporations qualified to do business in Iowa. A corporation includes an LLC that is classified as a corporation under federal law.

.03 Tax Returns

Every LLC deriving income from property owned in Iowa or from a trade, business, profession, or occupation carried on within Iowa and every Iowa LLC having a place of business in the state must file a partnership return on Form IA 1065, Partnership Return of Income.[425] A complete copy of IRS Form 1065, including Schedule K-1 for each member and all other supporting documents, must be attached to the Iowa return. The return must be filed regardless of the amount of income or loss and regardless of the residence of the members.

The return must be filed on the same period basis as for federal tax purposes. This rule applies even though the members may be reporting their incomes on different tax year bases.

Residents of Iowa who are members in an LLC must report on Form IA 1040 all items of income or loss shown on the federal Schedule K-1 for the LLC. These items are reported in a similar manner as on IRS Form 1040. Net modifications of the Iowa partnership return are reported on each member's IA 1040 either as "other income" if the modifications are a positive amount or as "other adjustments" if the modifications are a negative amount.

---

[420] *Tax News*, Vol. 20, No. 1, Dept. of Rev. & Fin. (Aug. 1994); Rule 701-45.1(422), issued by Iowa Dept. of Rev. & Fin.

[421] Iowa Code Ann. § 422.32.1.d; *Tax News*, Vol. 20, No. 1, Dept. of Rev. & Fin. (Aug. 1994); Iowa Dept. of Rev. & Fin. R. 701-45.1(422); Iowa Dept. of Rev. & Fin. R. 701-45.1(422).

[422] Iowa Dept. of Rev. & Fin. R. 701-45.1(422).

[423] Iowa Dept. of Rev. & Fin. R. 701-45.4(422).

[424] Iowa Dept. of Rev. & Fin. R. 701-46.4(422).

[425] Iowa Dept. of Rev. & Fin. Rs. 701-45.1(422) to 701-45.3(422).

.04 Nonresident Members

Every nonresident member who has $1,000 or more in net income from property located in Iowa, or from any business, trade, profession, or occupation carried on within Iowa, and who along with his or her spouse has Iowa source income of $13,500 or more ($9,000 or more for single individuals) must file an Iowa income tax return. Nonresidents compute their tax on all source net income, less federal tax and standard or itemized deductions. Members then compute their tax on a pro rata basis based on Iowa source net income compared to all source net income.

An LLC must withhold taxes at a five percent rate[426] on the income allocable to nonresident members attributable to Iowa source income.[427]

An LLC may file a composite return on behalf of nonresident members. The return is filed on Form IA 1040C Composite Individual Income Tax Return, Partnerships, Subchapter S Corporations, Trusts and Limited Liability Companies for Filing on Behalf of Nonresident Partners, Shareholders, Beneficiaries or Members. There is a graduated composite tax rate. The maximum tax rate is 8.98 percent in 2017.[428] A nonresident member may not be included on the composite return if the member has income from Iowa sources other than from another LLC or other entity. There is an exception if income does not exceed the amount of one standard deduction for single taxpayers plus income necessary to create tax liability at the effective tax rate on the composite return to offset one personal exemption.

An LLC must file Iowa Schedule K-1 as an attachment to Form IA 1065 for nonresident members only.

.05 Apportionment of Income

If an LLC is doing business wholly within Iowa, then all LLC income is taxable to Iowa. If the LLC is doing business both within and outside of Iowa, then the LLC can apportion the income received by nonresidents. Iowa taxes only the apportioned income. Iowa has its own Schedule K-1 for nonresident members. The state schedule shows how much of the federal Schedule K-1 income is taxable to Iowa. If the LLC is doing business wholly within Iowa, then 100 percent of the Schedule K-1 income will be taxed by Iowa. If the LLC is doing business within and outside of Iowa, then the Schedule K-1 income will be apportioned to Iowa using a single-factor business activity ratio.

.06 Annual Report

An LLC must file a biennial report in Iowa.[429]

---

[426] Instructions to Form IA 1065, Partnership Return of Income.

[427] Iowa Code § 422.16.12; Iowa Administrative Code r.701.46.4(422).

[428] *See* Tax Rate Schedule, Form IA 1040C.

[429] Iowa Code Ann. § 489.209.

.07 Filing Fees

The filing fees in the state of Iowa are as follows:[430]

Articles of organization	$ 50
Certificate of authority for foreign corporation	$100
Biennial report	$ 45 ($30 if filed online)

¶ 2318 KANSAS

Kansas enacted the Kansas Revised Limited Liability Company Act effective January 1, 2000.[431]

.01 State Tax Classification

A Kansas LLC is classified for state tax purposes in the same manner that it is classified for federal tax purposes.[432] Thus, a Kansas LLC and a foreign LLC qualified to do business in Kansas are taxed as partnerships unless classified as corporations for federal tax purposes.[433]

.02 Taxation of LLC and Members

A Kansas LLC must pay a franchise fee and franchise tax.[434]

The annual franchise fee is $55 payable to the Kansas Secretary of State along with the LLC's annual report. An LLC that is classified as a partnership for federal tax purposes is not otherwise subject to tax.[435]

In 2017, Kansas repealed legislation enacted in 2012 which eliminated the tax on income received from pass-through entities.[436] Under the prior law effective in 2013 through 2016, members of an LLC were not taxed on non-wage business income passed through from an LLC.[437]

.03 Tax Returns

A Kansas LLC must file a partnership return on Form K-120S, Kansas Partnership or S Corporation Income. A copy of pages 1 through 4 of the federal Form 1065

---

[430] Iowa Code Ann. § 490A.124.

[431] H.B. 3064, 1990 Kan. Sess. Laws; Kan. Stat. Ann. §§ 17-7663 to 17-76,142.

[432] Kan. Stat. Ann. § 17-76,138.

[433] Kan. Admin. Regs. 92-12-8.

[434] Kan. Stat. Ann. § 79-5401(a)(2).

[435] Kan. Stat. Ann. § 79-32,129(a).

[436] Kan. Senate Bill 30 (S.B. 30) (2017).

[437] Kan. Stat. Ann. 2011 Supp. § 79-32,117; H.B. 2117, Laws 2012.

must be attached to the Kansas return. Schedules K-1 to the federal return are not attached to the state return. The Department of Revenue has the right to request additional information as necessary. The return must be mailed to Kansas Income Tax, Kansas Department of Revenue, 915 S.W. Harrison Street, Topeka, KS 66699-4000.

The Kansas partnership return is an information return. It must be filed by every LLC that has income or loss derived from Kansas sources regardless of the amount of income or loss. Income or loss derived from Kansas sources includes the following:[438]

- Income or loss attributable to any ownership interest in real property or tangible personal property located in Kansas and in intangible property to the extent it is used in a trade, business, profession, or occupation carried on in Kansas
- Income or loss attributable to a trade, business, profession, or occupation carried on in Kansas

The Kansas partnership return must cover the same period as the corresponding federal partnership return. If the LLC files a return for the tax year that begins before January 1, the LLC must use the form for the calendar year in which the tax period begins.

The return must also be filed using the same accounting methods used for federal purposes. If the LLC changes its accounting methods for federal purposes, the change automatically applies to the Kansas partnership return.

The return is due by the 15th day of the fourth month following the close of the tax year. The return is due on or before April 15 for LLCs operating on a calendar year basis.

The director of taxation may grant a reasonable extension of time for an LLC to file a partnership return. LLCs that file Form 8736 with the IRS seeking an automatic extension of time automatically receive a three-month extension of time to file the Kansas partnership return. If an additional federal extension is requested, the Department of Taxation will honor that extension as well. A copy of the federal extension must be attached to the Kansas return when filed.

LLCs that receive business income within and outside the state of Kansas must apportion the income. There are two different methods for apportionment based on a property factor, payroll factor, and sales factor.

.04 Nonresident Members

In 2014, Kansas enacted legislation repealing the requirement that an LLC withhold income taxes from LLC income allocable to nonresident members.

An LLC may elect to file a composite income tax return for nonresident members which derive income from the LLC. A nonresident member may be included in a composite return unless the member has income from a Kansas source other than the LLC or an S corporation. An LLC files a composite return by completing Schedule

---

[438] Kan. Stat. Ann. § 79-3220(d); Kan. Admin. Reg. § 92-12-55(e).

K-40C to Form K-120S, Partnership or S Corporation Income Tax Return. The LLC must then complete Form K-40, Kansas Individual Income Tax, in the LLC's name. The totals from Schedule K-40C are then transferred to Form K-40. The LLC must attach a copy of the Schedule K-40C to Form K-40. The composite return must then be filed and any applicable tax must be paid by the 15th day of the fourth month following the close of the LLC's tax year.[439] Members included in a composite return are not required to file a separate Kansas income tax return.

The composite tax rate is based on the Kansas Tax Computation Schedules in the instructions to Form K-40ES, Kansas Individual Estimated Income Tax Voucher.[440] The maximum composite tax rate is 5.7 percent in 2018. The composite return does not recognize itemized deductions or modifications, either additions or subtractions.[441]

.05 Annual Report

An LLC must file an annual report in Kansas on Form LC, Limited Liability Company Annual Report. The annual fee is $55. The report must be filed at the time prescribed for filing the state's income tax return.[442] If the LLC's tax year is other than the calendar year, it must give notice of the different tax year in writing to the secretary of state before December 31 of the year that it commences the different tax year. If the LLC applies for an extension of time for filing its annual income tax return under the Internal Revenue Code, the LLC must also apply to the secretary of state for an extension of time for filing its annual report. The extension request must be filed not more than 90 days after the due date of its annual report.

The annual report must set forth the name of the LLC, a reconciliation of the capital accounts for the preceding tax year as required to be reported on the federal partnership return, and a list of the members owning at least five percent of the capital of the company.

The secretary of state has authority to maintain the confidentiality of an annual report of an LLC containing the financial information required by the report. The confidentiality will be maintained upon application to the secretary of state verifying that the LLC meets the following requirements:

- Has a net worth of at least $5,000 that is equal to at least five percent of its total assets, determined in accordance with generally accepted accounting principles;

- Has never been the subject of a proceeding under chapter 7, 11, or 13 of the federal bankruptcy laws or any similar provisions of any state law, any amendments to the federal bankruptcy laws, or any predecessor;

---

[439] Instructions to Schedule K-40C, Kansas Composite Income Tax Schedule.

[440] Instructions for Schedule K-40C, Column 10.

[441] Kansas Administrative Regulation (K.A.R.) 9212106; Kansas Department of Revenue, Notice 1317, Kansas Composite Returns (Sept. 12, 2013).

[442] Kan. Stat. Ann. § 17-76,139.

- Is not subject to the reporting requirements under the Securities Exchange Act of 1934;
- Is not an applicant for or a holder of a license under the Kansas Parimutuel Racing Act; and
- Is not a vendor under the Kansas Lottery Act.

.06 Filing Fees

Kansas imposes the following filing fees on LLCs:[443]

Articles of organization	$150
Certificate of registration for foreign LLC	$150
Annual report	$55

¶ 2319 KENTUCKY

Kentucky enacted laws authorizing LLCs in 1994.[444]

.01 State Tax Classification

For tax years beginning on or after January 1, 2007, LLCs will no longer be classified as corporations subject to corporation income tax.[445]

.02 Taxation of LLC and Members

An LLC must pay an annual limited liability entity tax (LLET) on Kentucky gross receipts or Kentucky gross profits.[446] For LLCs with gross receipts less than $3 million, the LLET is $175. For LLCs with $3 million or more in gross receipts, the LLET is the lesser of 9.5¢ per $100 of gross receipts or 75¢ per $100 of gross profits.

Kentucky gross profits are Kentucky gross receipts reduced by returns and allowances attributable to Kentucky gross receipts, less the cost of goods sold attributable to Kentucky gross receipts.

A corporation or LLC that is a partner, member, or shareholder of an LLC is allowed a credit against its LLET equal to its proportionate share of the LLC's LLET, after the LLET is reduced by the minimum tax due of $175 and any other nonrefundable credits. An individual that is a partner, member, or shareholder of an LLC is allowed a nonrefundable credit against the tax equal to the individual's proportionate

---

[443] Kan. Stat. Ann. §§ 17-76,136, 17-76,139(c).

[444] S.B. 184, 1994 Ky. Acts; Ky. Rev. Stat. Ann. §§ 275.001 to 275.455.

[445] Notice, Kentucky Department of Revenue, June 6, 2007.

[446] KRS §§ 141.020, 141.0401; Notice, Kentucky Department of Revenue, June 6, 2007.

share of the LLC's LLET, after the LLET is reduced by the minimum tax due of $175 and any other nonrefundable credits.[447]

After 2006, a Kentucky LLC is not required to pay the corporate franchise tax.[448]

.03 Tax Returns

An LLC must file one of the following forms for 2017:

720	Disregarded LLC whose single member is a C corporation; nexus consolidated group of affiliated corporations if LLC common parent elects to be taxed as a corporation for federal income tax purposes; nexus consolidated group of affiliated corporations with a C corporation common parent and LLC affiliates; nexus consolidated group of affiliated corporations if single-member LLC common parent is owned by a C corporation
720S	Disregarded LLC whose single member is an S corporation
725	Disregarded LLC whose single member is an individual; nexus consolidated group of affiliated corporations if single-member LLC common parent is owned by and with a single-member LLC common parent and individual LLC affiliates
765	LLC classified as a partnership or corporation for federal tax purposes; disregarded LLC whose single member is a partnership; nexus consolidated group of affiliated corporations if common parent is taxed as a partnership for federal tax with a multi-member LLC common parent and LLC affiliates

An LLC must register for the LLET using Form 10A100, Kentucky Tax Registration Application. The Kentucky Department of Revenue provided instructions for completing the form for LLCs.[449]

LLCs subject to the LLET must make estimated tax payments on Form 720-ES, Limited Liability LLC/Corporation Income Tax, vouchers.[450]

.04 Foreign LLC and Nonresident Members

LLCs that are classified as partnerships must pay income taxes on behalf of nonresident members in one of the following ways:

---

[447] Notice, Kentucky Department of Revenue, June 6, 2007.

[448] KRS § 141.010(24).

[449] Notice, Kentucky Department of Revenue, June 6, 2007.

[450] Notice, Kentucky Department of Revenue, June 6, 2007.

- *Withholding.* The LLC must withhold income tax at the maximum state rate under KRS § 141.020 or KRS § 141.040 on the net distributive share of income of each nonresident member, whether or not distributed.[451] The withholding tax rate is six percent for 2017. Withholding must be reported on Form 740NP-WH with Forms PTE-WH attached for each nonresident individual or C corporation member that is doing business in Kentucky only through its ownership interest in the LLC. The LLC must give a copy of Form PTE-WH to each nonresident member.[452] Withholding is due on the 15th day of the fourth month following the close of the tax year. Withholding is not required if the nonresident member elects to be included in the LLC's composite income tax return.[453] A member may be exempt from withholding if Forms KY 720740NP-WH for the prior year were filed. The LLC must file Form 740NP-WH to substantiate eligibility for the exemption.[454]
- *Statement from member.* A member may file with the LLC, before the due date of the LLC's annual return, a signed notarized statement of intent to pay the member's proportionate share of tax due.[455] The member must agree to pay any additional taxes that may be due as a result of audit adjustments or amended returns. The LLC must file as part of its return a statement identifying the name, address and social security number of each electing member. It must provide to each member a statement showing the amount of taxes due by the member.[456] The LLC must then collect the tax on from the member and pay the tax with its return. It must also collect from the member any taxes owed as a result of audit adjustments or amended returns.[457] The LLC is liable for the entire tax if not paid.[458]
- *Composite return.* An LLC may file a composite income tax return on behalf of electing nonresident individual members.[459] The tax is computed at the maximum individual tax rate[460] on the net distributive share income, whether or not distributed, of each nonresident individual member included in the composite return. The composite tax rate is six percent for 2017. The members who may be included on the composite return include (i) nonresident individual members whose net distributive share income was not subject to withholding; (ii) nonresident individual members whose only source of income within Kentucky is the net distributive share income from one or more pass-through entities; (iii) nonresident individual members who have elected to be

---

[451] KRS § 141.206(5); 103 Ky. Admin. Regs. 18:160; Letter to Kentucky Society of CPAs, Kentucky Department Revenue (Aug. 22, 2006).

[452] Kentucky Department of Revenue website, http://revenue.ky.gov/Business/Pass-Through-Entities/Pages/default.aspx.

[453] 103 KAR 18:160E, Sec. 2. The composite return is not applicable for periods after 2005.

[454] Ky. Pass-Through Entities Tax, http://revenue.ky.gov/Business/Pass-Through-Entities/Pages/default.aspx.

[455] 103 KAR 16:020E, Sec. 2.

[456] 103 KAR 16:210E, Sec. 3.

[457] 103 KAR 16:210E, Sec. 5.

[458] 103 KAR 16:210E, Sec. 4.

[459] Ky. Rev. Stat. § 141.206(16).

[460] *See* Ky. Rev. Stat. § 141.020 for maximum tax rates.

¶ 2319.04

included in a composite income tax return by submitting a written statement to the LLC within 30 days after the close of the LLC's tax year. The composite income tax return must be filed with the Department of Revenue on Form 740NP-WH (by checking composite income tax return box) on or before the 15th day of the fourth month after the close of the LLC's tax year. The LLC must file Form PTE-WH (and check the composite box) for each nonresident member included in the composite return and provide a copy of the form to the member. The LLC must make estimated taxes if required under the Kentucky estimated tax provisions.[461] The LLC must make the estimated tax payments on Form 740NP-WH.

- *Estimated tax return.* An LLC must make a declaration and payments of estimated tax if (i) a nonresident individual member's estimated tax liability can reasonably be expected to exceed $500, or (ii) a corporate member's estimated tax liability can reasonably be expected to exceed $5,000. The LLC must report and pay the estimated taxes using Form 740NP-WH-ES, Kentucky Estimated Tax Vouchers.[462]

- *Individual return.* Members included in a composite return may file an individual tax return to take advantage of the graduated tax rates and any credits, and receive credit for any tax paid by the LLC on the member's behalf.[463]

A single-member LLC may file a composite return on Form 725, Schedule CP, Kentucky Single Member LLC Composite Return Schedule A single-member disregarded LLC is treated as one corporation in determining taxable income and the applicable apportionment factor.[464] A corporation that owns a single-member disregarded LLC doing business in Kentucky is also treated as doing business in Kentucky. Similarly, if the corporation is doing business in Kentucky, any single-member disregarded LLC that it owns is also treated as doing business in Kentucky.[465] The corporate owner and any single-member LLCs must be treated as one corporation in determining taxable income and the applicable apportionment factor.[466]

A foreign LLC must apportion its income to Kentucky by multiplying the income by a fraction. The numerator of the fraction is the property factor, representing 25 percent of the fraction, plus the payroll factor, representing 25 percent of the fraction, plus the sales factor, representing 50 percent of the fraction. The denominator of the fraction is four, reduced by the number of factors, if any, having no denominator. If the sales factor does not have a denominator, then the denominator must be reduced by two.[467]

---

[461] *See* Ky. Rev. Stat. § 141.300.

[462] Ky. Rev. Stat. § 141.207(3).

[463] Kentucky Department of Revenue website, http://revenue.ky.gov/Business/Pass-Through-Entities/Pages/default.aspx.

[464] 103 KAR 16:300E, Sec. 3.

[465] 103 KAR 16:300E, Sec. 2.

[466] 103 KAR 16:300E, Sec. 3.

[467] Ky. Rev. Stat. § 141.120(8).

.05 Annual Report

A Kentucky LLC must file an annual report. The report must be filed between January 1 and June 30 of each year.[468] The annual report must set forth the name and address of the LLC, the state or country under whose laws it is organized, the address of its registered office, the name of its registered agent, the address of its principal office, and the names and business addresses of its managers. The first annual report is due between January 1 and June 30 of the year following the year of organization or qualification to do business in the state of Kentucky. Subsequent annual reports must be filed between January 1 and June 30 following each calendar year.

.06 Filing Fees

Kentucky imposes the following filing fees on LLCs:[469]

Articles of organization	$40
Certificate of authority for foreign LLCs	$90
Annual report	$15

¶ 2320 LOUISIANA

Louisiana enacted the Louisiana Limited Liability Company Act on July 7, 1992.[470]

.01 State Tax Classification

A Louisiana LLC or foreign LLC qualified to do business in Louisiana is classified for state income and franchise tax purposes in the same manner that it is classified for federal income tax purposes.[471] A Louisiana LLC is classified as a limited partnership for all other state tax purposes.

.02 Taxation of LLC and Members

The LLC is taxed for state income and franchise tax purposes in the same manner as for federal income tax purposes.[472] For all other taxes, the LLC is taxed as a limited partnership.[473] There is no franchise or entity-level tax on Louisiana LLCs that

---

[468] Ky. Rev. Stat. § 275.190.

[469] Ky. Rev. Stat. Ann. § 275.055.

[470] La. Rev. Stat. Ann. § § 12:1301 to 12:1369.

[471] La. Rev. Stat. Ann. § 12:1368; Revenue Information Bulletin No. 03-015, Louisiana Department of Revenue (Aug. 25, 2003).

[472] La. Rev. Stat. Ann. § 12:1368; Louisiana Act 12, HB 19, Laws 2016; Louisiana Department of Revenue, Rev. Rul. No. 02-018 (2002) (*citing* Louisiana Revenue Statutes Annotated § 12:1368).

[473] Louisiana Department of Revenue, Rev. Rul. No. 02-018 (2002).

are classified as partnerships. A Louisiana LLC is a pass-through entity. Members are taxed on their distributive shares of income from the LLC, whether or not distributed.[474] An LLC that is classified as a corporation for federal tax purposes is subject to the corporate income tax.

A corporation that is a single-member of a Louisiana LLC is subject to the Louisiana corporate franchise tax because the corporation is considered doing business in Louisiana.[475] A single-member LLC is treated as a division of the corporate owner. All items of income and expense are treated as items of the corporate owner for Louisiana income tax purposes.[476] The single-member LLC is treated as a partnership for Louisiana franchise tax purposes, and is thus disregarded for income tax purposes and not subject to the Louisiana franchise tax.[477] A foreign corporation that is the sole member of the Louisiana LLC must apportion its income between Louisiana and any other state in which it does business.[478]

An LLC that is classified as an S corporation for federal tax purposes is not subject to the Louisiana franchise taxes.[479]

.03 Tax Returns

An LLC doing business in Louisiana or deriving any income from sources in Louisiana must file an information return on Form IT-565, Partnership Return of Income, if any member is a nonresident of Louisiana or if any member is not an individual member. The LLC must file the return on or prior to the 15th day of the fifth month following the close of the tax year. An LLC is not required to file return if all members are individual persons who are residents of Louisiana.[480]

If the LLC has income that is derived from sources partly within and partly outside Louisiana, the LLC must file Form IT-565B with Form IT-565.

An LLC that is classified as a partnership or sole proprietorship for federal tax purposes is not required to file a Louisiana corporate income tax return. Only LLCs that have elected to file federally as C corporations or S corporations are required to file a Louisiana corporation income tax return. In no case is an LLC required to file and pay franchise tax. If an LLC has received a non-filing assessment for a corporation income tax return and no such return is due, the LLC may return the assessment to the Louisiana Department of Revenue with a letter clarifying its federal filing status.[481]

---

[474] La. Rev. Stat. Ann. §§ 47:201, 47:202.

[475] Louisiana Department of Revenue, Rev. Rul. No. 02-018 (2002).

[476] Revenue Information Bulletin No. 04-003, Louisiana Department of Revenue (Jan. 8, 2004).

[477] Revenue Information Bulletin No. 04-003, Louisiana Department of Revenue (Jan. 8, 2004).

[478] *See* Louisiana Department of Revenue, Rev. Rul. No. 02-018 (2002), which discusses the apportionment formula.

[479] La. Rev. Stat. Ann. § 47:601(C)(1)(c).

[480] La. Rev. Stat. Ann. § 47:201.

[481] Louisiana Department of Revenue News Release, "Filing Requirements for Partnerships and Sold Proprietorships" (Sept. 29, 2010).

Each member of the LLC that is a natural person must include on Form IT-540 the distributive share of the net income of the LLC during the LLC's accounting period (whether fiscal or calendar) that ended during this taxable year. Individual members must use the information on the federal partnership return for the LLC.[482]

.04 Nonresident Members

Nonresident members are taxed on their distributive share of LLC income attributable to Louisiana sources, whether or not distributed. The nonresident members must report such income on Form IT-540 and include on Form IT-540B the distributive share of income derived from Louisiana sources.[483]

An LLC that is classified as a partnership for federal tax purposes must file a composite return on Form R-6922, Louisiana Composite Partnership Return, and make a composite payment on behalf of nonresident members using Form R-6922ES unless:[484]

- All nonresident members are corporations or tax exempt trusts; or
- All nonresident members, other than corporations and tax exempt trusts, have a valid agreement on file with the Department of Revenue in which the member agreed to file an individual return and pay income tax on all income derived from or attributable to sources in Louisiana. No composite return is required on behalf of any member who has a valid agreement on file.[485] Nonresident members who have a valid agreement on file or who have other income derived from Louisiana sources must include all income derived from Louisiana sources on Form IT-540B.[486]

The composite return must be filed by May 15, or the 15th day of the fifth month following the close of the tax year for a fiscal year LLC. The return must be filed for all nonresident members who are individuals, estates and trusts that have not agreed to file individual returns. The LLC may include on the composite return resident owners, other than tax-exempt trust, corporations and pass-through entities.

The composite tax rate in 2018 is six percent on the distributive shares of LLC income attributable to Louisiana, as reflected on the LLC's return for the year.

The composite tax return must be filed electronically.[487]

Corporate members, and members who are themselves partnerships, cannot be included in a composite return. These members must file all applicable Louisiana tax returns, and must report all Louisiana source income on those returns.[488] Corporate

---

[482] *See* Instructions to Form IT-565.

[483] Corporate members of the LLC should refer to La. Rev. Stat. §47:287.93.A(5).

[484] La. Rev. Stat. Ann. §47:201.1; La. Admin. Code §61:I.1401.B.

[485] La. Admin. Code §61:I.1401.E.1.

[486] Partnership Return of Income with Instructions and Form IT-565B Apportionment of Income Schedule.

[487] La. Rev. Stat. Ann. §47:201.1.F(4).

[488] La. Admin. Code §61:I.1401.B.2.

members must file Form CIFT-620 to report their distributive share of Louisiana source income.

Nonresident members may claim their respective shares of credits earned by the LLC when the LLC files a composite return. If the LLC claims credits on the composite return, then all nonresident members must be included on the composite return.[489] Nonresident members are no longer required to file an additional tax return to claim a share of the LLC credits.

.05 Annual Report

An LLC must file an annual report in Louisiana.[490] A foreign LLC qualified to do business in Louisiana must also file an annual report.[491]

.06 Filing Fees

Louisiana imposes the following filing fees on LLCs:[492]

Articles of organization	$ 60
Certificate of authority for foreign LLCs	$100
Annual fee	$ 25

¶ 2321 MAINE

Maine enacted laws authorizing LLCs effective January 1, 1995.[493]

.01 State Tax Classification

Maine classifies an LLC for state tax purposes in the same manner that the LLC is classified for federal tax purposes.[494] Thus, an LLC that is classified as a partnership for federal purposes is classified as a partnership for state purposes. Effective June 30, 1998, the Maine statutes were amended to clarify that a single-member LLC could be formed in Maine.[495]

---

[489] La. Rev. Stat. Ann. § 47:201.1.F; La. Admin. Code § 61:I.1401.B.3.

[490] La. Rev. Stat. Ann. § 12:1308.1.

[491] La. Rev. Stat. Ann. § 12:1350.1.

[492] La. Rev. Stat. Ann. § 12:1364.

[493] H.B. 1123, ch. 718, 1994 Me. Laws; Me. Rev. Stat. Ann. tit. 31, §§ 1501 to 1693.

[494] Me. Rev. Stat. Ann. tit. 36, § 5180.

[495] Ch. 633, H.P. 1498, Laws 1998.

.02 Taxation of LLC and Members

Maine does not impose a franchise or entity-level tax on LLCs. An LLC that is classified as a partnership is a pass-through entity. All items of income, gain, loss, deduction, and credit are passed through to and taxable to the members.[496]

.03 Real Estate Taxes

There is an exemption from the Maine real estate transfer tax for deeds between an LLC and its members for the purpose of organization, dissolution, or liquidation of the LLC. No consideration may be given in connection with the transfer other than shares, interests, or debt securities of the LLC. There is also an exemption for deeds to an LLC from a corporation, partnership, or other LLC if the grantor or grantee owns an interest in the LLC in the same proportion as in the real estate being transferred.[497]

.04 Tax Returns

For tax years beginning on or after January 1, 2012, an LLC is not required to file an income tax information return.[498] LLCs that have nonresident members must file Form 941P-ME to report certain entity-level information, pass-through entity withholding for nonresident members and nonresident members exempt from pass-through entity withholding.[499]

.05 Nonresident Members

General Rules

Nonresident members are taxed on their distributive shares of income allocable to Maine.[500] All income derived from or effectively connected with a trade or business within Maine is Maine-source income. That income is subject to Maine tax if the business is either domiciled in Maine or has a nexus with Maine. The nonresident member is subject to income taxes on that portion of his or her distributive share apportioned to Maine based on property, payroll, and sales of the LLC.[501]

---

[496] Me. Rev. Stat. Ann. tit. 36, § 5190.

[497] H.B. 1123, ch. 718, 1994 Me. Laws.

[498] Ch. 655 (H.P. 1405), Laws 2012, Part QQ (*see* Summary of Part QQ H.P. 1405).

[499] *See* Instructions to Form 941P-ME.

[500] Me. Rev. Stat. Ann. tit. 36, § 5192; Information Release from Bur. of Taxn. (June 1, 1987).

[501] The minimum taxability thresholds are set forth in 36 M.R.S.A. § 5142(8)(B).

Withholding Tax

An LLC must withhold income taxes on the income apportioned nonresident members attributable to Maine sources.[502] The withholding tax rate in 2017 is 10.15 percent of Maine-source distributable income for each individual nonresident member.[503] The withholding tax rate is 8.93 percent if the nonresident member is a corporation.[504]

The withholding taxes are reported on Form 941P-ME, LLC Return of Maine Income Tax Withheld from Members. The LLC must withhold taxes on a quarterly basis based on the Maine-source income of the nonresident members for each quarter. Quarterly installments must be at least the amount calculated by multiplying the tax rate by the lesser of (a) 90 percent of the current year Maine-source income for the nonresident member, or (b) the prior year's Maine-source income of the nonresident member if the prior tax year consisted of 12 months.[505] Beginning in calendar year 2012, Form 941P-ME (previously required to be filed quarterly) was replaced with an annual Form 941P-ME and quarterly estimated pass-through entity withholding payments for nonresident members. Form 941P-ME is due January 31 following the calendar year for which it is filed.[506]

Each quarterly estimated payment must, in order to avoid interest and penalty charges, equal the nonresident member's annual share of Maine-source LLC income for the prior year (or 90 percent of the estimated annual Maine-source income of the LLC for the current year) multiplied by 10.15 percent and the result divided by 4. The due dates for the quarterly payments are the last day of the month following the end of the quarter. For example, the 2018 first quarter payment is due April 30, 2018. The estimated payments must be made electronically or by using Form 900ME payment vouchers.[507]

For calendar years 2012 and after, Form 941E-ME (Pass-through Entity Withholding Exemption Form) and Form 941LM-ME (List of Participating Members in the Compliant Taxpayer Exemption Request) are discontinued.[508]

There is no withholding on the distributive share of income allocated to nonresident members if:[509]

- Maine-source income allocated to a single member for an entire calendar year is less than $1,000;[510]
- the member files an agreement to pay taxes;
- the member is included in a composite return;

---

[502] 18-125 CMR 806.10(B); 36 MRSA § 5250-B.

[503] Me. Rev. Stat. Ann. tit. 36, § 5250-B; Code Me. R. § 18-125-803; Instructions to Form 941P-ME.

[504] Instructions to Form 941P-ME, Maine Income Tax Withholding for Pass-through Entities.

[505] Rule 803, 18-25 CMR 803, § 3.3(B)(2).

[506] Tax Alert, Maine Revenue Services, Vol. 21, Issue 8 (Nov. 2011).

[507] Tax Alert, Maine Revenue Services, Vol. 21, Issue 8 (Nov. 2011).

[508] Tax Alert, Maine Revenue Services, Vol. 21, Issue 8 (Nov. 2011).

[509] Instructions for 941P-ME; Tax Alert, Maine Revenue Services, Vol. 21, Issue 8 (Nov. 2011).

[510] Me. Rev. Stat. Ann. tit. 36, § 5250-B; Reg. § § 803.01, 803.02.

- the nonresident member is a tax-exempt entity; or
- the nonresident member is a pass-through entity that realizes income from another pass-through entity upon which an amount has already been withheld.

The LLC must send each member by January 31 following each calendar year a copy of Form 1099ME showing the total amount withheld for the year for the member. The member must attach this form to his or her income tax return.

If an LLC believes that it should be exempt from the withholding for other reasons, or would like to propose an alternate application of the withholding requirement, the LLC may apply for an exemption. In order to apply, the LLC must file with the Maine Revenue Services Form 941E-ME and a letter of explanation. The LLC must reapply for the exemption annually.[511]

Agreement to Pay Taxes

No withholding is required for a nonresident member who agrees to comply with all Maine income tax laws. The member must provide the LLC with an Affidavit and Agreement to Comply with Maine Income Tax on Form 941AF-ME, Nonresident Member Affidavit and Agreement for Compliance with Maine Income Tax. The LLC must keep the document on record for at least three years.[512]

Composite Filing

No withholding is required for a nonresident member included in a composite return. A composite filing is a simplified group return for two or more nonresident individual members of an LLC. Only natural persons and certain trusts may participate in the composite filing.[513] Resident members may not participate in the composite filing.[514] The composite tax rate is 10.15 percent in 2017.

The advantages to the LLC of composite filing are that participating individual nonresident members need not be listed separately on the quarterly return (as is required by the LLC withholding requirement), and Form 1099ME need not be issued to the participating member. The advantage to the individual nonresident member is that the LLC files the member's Maine income tax return (Form 1040ME) and pays the tax due.

The procedures for filing a composite return include the following:[515]

- Each participating member must provide the LLC with an Agreement to Participate in a Composite Filing of Maine Income Tax on Form 941CF-ME. This statement must be obtained prior to the mailing of the LLC Withholding

---

[511] Tax Alert, Maine Revenue Services, Vol. 21, Issue 8 (Nov. 2011).

[512] Instructions for Form 941P-ME.

[513] For a full description of the composite filing return and process, *see* Schedule 1040C-ME at www.maine.gov/revenue/forms.

[514] Rule 805, 18-125 CMR 805.01.C.

[515] Instructions for 941P-ME.

¶ 2321.05

Exemption on Form 941E-ME. The LLC must keep this for on file for at least three years.[516]

- The LLC must file with the Maine Revenue Services an LLC Withholding Exemption on Form 941E-ME. A list of participating members is not required.

- The LLC must make estimated payments on Form 1040ES-ME on behalf of the composite filing group if the aggregate Maine income tax liability is greater than $1,000. All members of the composite return are grouped together and treated as one filer for estimated tax purposes. If the tax liability of the composite group is anticipated to exceed $1,000, the LLC must make four equal estimated payments in order to avoid the penalty for the underpayment of estimated tax. Estimated payments for the composite group are due based on 10.15 percent of Maine-source LLC income in 2017. The estimated taxes may be based either on 90 percent of the current year's Maine source member income or 100 percent of the previous year's Maine source member income.[517]

- The LLC must then file the composite return on Form 1040ME. The worksheet and instructions for the composite filing are included on Schedule 1040C-ME. The LLC must complete and include Schedule 1040C-ME.

.06 Annual Report

An LLC must file an annual report in Maine. The annual report must set forth the name of the LLC, the name of its registered agent, the address of its registered office in Maine, a brief statement of the character of the business in which the LLC is actually engaged in the state, and the name and business or residence address of each manager (or each member if there are no managers).

.07 Filing Fees

Maine imposes the following filing fees on LLCs:[518]

Articles of organization	$175
Certificate of authority for foreign LLC	$250
Annual report on Form MLLC-13	$ 85

¶2322 MARYLAND

Maryland enacted the Maryland Limited Liability Company Act effective October 1, 1992.[519]

---

[516] Tax Alert, Maine Revenue Services, Vol. 21, Issue 8 (Nov. 2011).

[517] *See* Instructions and worksheets for Forms 1040ES-ME and 2210ME.

[518] Me. Rev. Stat. Ann. tit. 31, § 1680.

[519] Md. Code Ann., Corps. & Assns. § § 4A-101 to 4A-1303.

.01 State Tax Classification

A Maryland LLC is classified in the same manner as the LLC is classified for federal purposes. Domestic and foreign LLCs are classified as partnerships for Maryland income tax purposes unless classified as corporations or disregarded as entities for federal tax purposes.

.02 Taxation of LLC and Members

The Maryland income tax does not apply to an LLC that is classified as a partnership for federal tax purposes.[520]

.03 Tax Returns

LLC Classified as Partnership

An LLC that is classified as a partnership must file a return on Form 510, Pass-Through Entity Income Tax Return.[521] This is an information tax return. Every Maryland LLC must file the form even if it has no income or the LLC is inactive. Every foreign LLC that is subject to Maryland income tax laws must also file Form 510.

A multistate pass-through LLC that operates in Maryland, but that is not subject to the Maryland income tax law, is not required to file. However, a return reflecting no income allocable Maryland may be filed for record purposes. Letters in lieu of filing are not accepted.

Form 510 must be filed by the 15th day of the fourth month following the close of the tax year. The return must be filed with the Comptroller of the Treasury, Revenue Administration Division, Annapolis, Maryland 21411-0001. A manager or other duly authorized official of the LLC must sign Form 510.

An LLC must report all items that are reported for federal purposes in the same manner as reported for federal purposes. The character of an item cannot be changed from that required or elected for federal purposes. The tax year period used for the federal return must be used on the Maryland return.

All items of income, loss, credit and deduction on Form 510 are passed through to the individual members and taxed at that level. Each member must file an individual income tax return on Form 502. Nonresident individual members of the LLC must file Form 505.

---

[520] Md. Tax General Art. § 10-104(8).
[521] Md. Tax General Art. § 10-819(b)(1).

Single-Member LLCs

An LLC that is classified as a single-member disregarded entity must report the income of the LLC on the member's income tax return.[522] The LLC has the filing status of its member and must file an appropriate return for that member.

LLCs Classified as Corporations

An LLC that is classified as a corporation is subject to the Maryland corporate income tax.[523] Effective October 1, 1992, an LLC that is taxable as a corporation must file a return on Form 500, Maryland Corporation Income Tax Return.[524] The corporate income tax rate is 8.25 percent of Maryland taxable income.[525] An LLC that is classified as a corporation must file a return on or before the 15th day of the third month after the end of the tax year.

.04 Nonresident Members

Taxation of Members

A nonresident member is taxed on his or her share of LLC income attributable to Maryland sources.[526]

The Maryland income tax is based on the federal adjusted gross income. Various amounts are subtracted from federal adjusted gross income of residents to determine Maryland adjusted gross income.[527] Nonresidents may make the same subtractions from federal adjusted gross income as residents. However, nonresidents may not subtract income derived from business that is wholly carried on in the State and in which the individual is a member of an LLC taxable as a partnership or proprietorship for federal tax purposes.[528]

LLC Tax on Behalf of Nonresident Members

An LLC must pay a tax on behalf of nonresident individual or fiduciary members of 7.5 percent in 2017 equal to the sum of:[529]

---

[522] Md. Tax General Art. § 10-819(c).

[523] Md. Tax General Art. § 10-104.

[524] Md. Tax General Art. § 10-819(b)(2).

[525] Md. Tax General Art. § 10-105(b).

[526] Md. Tax General Art. §§ 10-401; Comptroller of Maryland Administrative Release No. 6 (Rev. Sept. 2012) Subject: Taxation of Pass-Through Entities Having Nonresident Members.

[527] Md. Tax General Art. § 10-207(a). The percentage of LLC income allocated to Maryland is determined under Md. Tax General Art. § 10-401.

[528] Md. Tax General Art. § 10-210.

[529] Md. Tax General Art. § 10-102.1; Md. Regs. §§ 03.01.02.02 and 03.04.01.01 to 07.02 (nonconsecutive); Administrative Release No. 6; Form 510, Pass-Through Entity Tax Return; http://

- The nonresident individual members' taxable income from Maryland sources multiplied by the top-marginal state tax rate (5.75 percent in 2017).
- The nonresident individual members' taxable income multiplied by the special nonresident income tax.[530] This is equal to the lowest county income tax rate (1.75 percent in 2017) on each item of net income includible in the nonresident individual member's distributive or pro rata share of LLC income from business carried on in Maryland.

An LLC must pay an 8.25 percent tax on the taxable income of nonresident entity members that are not registered with the Department of Assessments and Taxation to do business in Maryland.[531] The tax is on each item of net income includible in the nonresident entity member's distributive or pro rata share of LLC income attributable to business carried on in Maryland. The tax does not apply to nonresident entities that are qualified to do business in Maryland.

Any tax paid by the nonresident members individually may not be deducted from the tax imposed on the LLC.[532]

The tax liability of an LLC is limited to the sum of all the nonresident members' shares of the LLC's distributable cash flow.[533] Distributable cash flow means taxable income reportable by the LLC on its federal income tax return for the year, subject to the adjustments. The cash flow is computed on Form 510. However, the cash flow limitation does not affect the tax liability of any single nonresident member. The limitation operates solely for the relief of an LLC that has taxable income attributable to the nonresident members, but does not have sufficient distributable cash flow to pay the total nonresident tax.

If an LLC calculates its tax based on the applicable tax rate applied to the total distributive or pro rata shares of its nonresident members attributable to income from Maryland sources, then it is not required to calculate the cash-flow limitation. The tax against the LLC does not change the filing requirements or the tax liability of nonresident members with income from Maryland sources.[534]

An LLC must make estimated tax payments during the year. The LLC must file Form 510D, Pass-Through Entity Declaration of Estimated Income Tax, based on the total distributive or pro rata share of income of all the nonresident members, if the total tax is expected to exceed $1,000.

A nonresident member is allowed a credit against the income tax for the tax year for income tax withheld and estimated tax payments made for the year. The member may also claim a credit against the state income tax year for taxes paid by the LLC

(Footnote Continued)

taxes.marylandtaxes.com/Business_Taxes/Business_Tax_Types/Income_Tax/Employer_Withholding/Withholding_Information/Nonresident_Income_Tax_Rate.shtml.

[530] *See* Md. Tax General Art. § 10-106.1.

[531] Md. Tax General Art. § 10-106.1.

[532] Comptroller of Maryland Administrative Release No. 6 (Rev. Sept. 2012) Subject: Taxation of Pass-Through Entities Having Nonresident Members.

[533] Md. Tax General Art. § 10-102.1(d)(2); Md. Reg. § 03.04.07.02.

[534] Comptroller of Maryland Administrative Release No. 6 (Rev. Sept. 2012) Subject: Taxation of Pass-Through Entities Having Nonresident Members.

attributable to the individual's share of LLC nonresident taxable income.[535] The number may claim the credit on the member's tax return, or on a composite return filed by the LLC on behalf of the electing nonresident member.[536]

Composite Return

An LLC may elect to file a composite return on behalf of qualified nonresident members.[537] The composite tax rate is 7.5 percent in 2017.[538] The return must be filed on Form 510C, Maryland Composite Pass-Through Entity Income Tax Return, and include various schedules.[539] All members who qualify and elect to be included on the composite return must agree that the LLC is their agent for the receipt of any refund or for the payment of any tax due. The composite return is considered the return of each nonresident individual member participating in the composite return filing for all purposes, including the date on which the statute of limitations on assessment begins to run. The LLC may not claim credit on the return, except for estimated tax payments. Amendments to composite returns must be made by the LLC. Participating nonresident individuals may not amend the composite return or file separate returns.

An LLC that files a composite return must meet the following requirements:[540]

1. Only nonresident individual members may be included on a composite return. Nonresident fiduciary members and nonresident entity members cannot be included on a composite return.

2. A nonresident individual member must elect to join in the filing of a composite return. A statement to this effect must be attached to the return and signed by an authorized official of the LLC. A composite return may be filed even though not all nonresident individual members elect to be included in the return.

3. An electing nonresident individual member must be subject to Maryland income tax solely because of the income from the LLC. Any nonresident individual member having taxable income derived from other Maryland sources may not make the election and must file an individual nonresident return.

---

[535] Md. Tax General Art. § 10-701.1; Md. Reg. § 03.04.07.03.

[536] Md. Reg. § 03.04.07.03.

[537] Comptroller of Maryland Administrative Release No. 6 (Rev. Sept. 2012) Subject: Taxation of Pass-Through Entities Having Nonresident Members; Md. Reg. § § 03.04.07.05, 03.04.02.01(B)(5), 03.04.02.04.

[538] This is equal to the highest Maryland individual income tax rate of 5.75 percent in 2012 plus the 1.25 percent special nonresident tax. *See* Maryland 2012 Nonresident Tax Forms & Instructions booklet.

[539] The required schedules are set forth in Comptroller of Maryland Administrative Release No. 6 (Rev. Sept. 2012).

[540] Comptroller of Maryland Administrative Release No. 6 (Rev. Sept. 2012).

.05 Real Estate Taxes

Effective October 1, 1997, a deed or other instrument transferring real estate from a predecessor entity or trustee of that entity to an LLC is not subject to the Maryland document recording tax.[541] The members of the LLC must be identical to the partners or individuals who owned the predecessor entity. Each member's allocation of profits and losses must remain the same. Qualifying predecessor entities include limited partnerships, limited liability partnerships, limited liability limited partnerships, joint ventures, and proprietorships with one or more persons who are principally involved in buying, selling, leasing, or managing real property.

.06 Annual Report

An LLC must file an annual report and pay an annual fee of $300.

.07 Filing Fees

Maryland imposes the following filing fees on LLCs:

Articles of organization	$100
Foreign LLC registration application	$100
Annual report fee	$300

¶2323 MASSACHUSETTS

Massachusetts enacted the Massachusetts Limited Liability Company Act effective January 1, 1996.[542]

.01 State Tax Classification

Massachusetts classifies an LLC in the same manner that the LLC is classified for federal purposes under the IRS check-the-box regulations.[543] Single-member LLCs may be formed in Massachusetts for tax years after 2002.[544]

Massachusetts follows the federal tax classification of a non-U.S. business entity if the entity is a foreign LLC.[545] There are nine non-U.S. business entities that

---

[541] H.B. 671, ch. 683, 1997 Md. Laws.

[542] H.B. 4045, 1995 Mass. Acts; Mass. Gen. Laws Ann. ch. 156C, §§1-72.

[543] Mass. Gen. Laws Ann. ch. 62, §17; Massachusetts Department of Revenue Ltr. Rul. No. 08-1 (2008); Massachusetts Department of Revenue Letter Ruling LR 00-8 (June 9, 2000); Tech. Info. Rel. No. 08-11 (Aug. 15, 2008); 830 CMR 63.30.3.

[544] S.B. 1949, Laws, 2003; Mass. Gen. Laws Ann. ch. 156C, §2; Massachusetts Department of Revenue Letter Ruling LR 00-8 (June 9, 2000).

[545] Massachusetts Department of Revenue Ltr. Rul. No. 08-1 (2008); Massachusetts Department of Revenue Directive 01-8 (2001).

Massachusetts classifies as foreign LLCs. A foreign LLC may request a letter ruling from the Massachusetts Department of Revenue to determine the LLC's tax treatment for Massachusetts purposes.[546]

.02 Taxation of LLC and Members

Massachusetts LLCs are not subject to the Massachusetts income tax. Instead, individuals carrying on business as members of the LLC are liable for the taxes in their individual capacities.[547]

A member of an LLC who is a resident of Massachusetts, whether or not the LLC has a usual place of business in Massachusetts, is subject to the Massachusetts income taxes on his distributive share of the income received or earned by the LLC from sources taxable under the Massachusetts income tax law. The member must separately include in his return his distributive share of the LLC income or loss from sources taxable in Massachusetts and any item of deduction or credit.[548]

A single-member LLC that is a disregarded entity for federal purposes is not taxed as a corporation under Massachusetts law for purposes of the corporate excise tax, the minimum excise tax, or the income or property measures of corporate excise tax laws. A single-member LLC is treated as a branch or division of its owner if the owner is a C corporation, or as a sole proprietorship if the owner is an individual. Therefore, all tax attributes of the single-member LLC, its properties, and activities are attributed to the single member.[549]

The character of any item of income, loss, deduction, or credit included in the member's distributive share is determined as if that item were realized directly by the member from the source realized by the LLC or incurred in the same manner as incurred by the LLC. The amount of each item to be taken into account by the LLC in determining the total of its income, loss, deductions, or credits to be reported on the returns of the members must be computed in the same manner in the case of an individual.[550] However, adjustments must be made. The LLC is not allowed certain offsets, exemptions, and credits.[551]

Each nonresident member is taxable on the member's distributive share of income from any of the following categories:

---

[546] Directive No. 01-8, Massachusetts Department of Revenue (Nov. 13, 2001).

[547] Mass. Gen. Laws Ann. ch. 62, § 17. *See* Mass. Gen. Laws Ann. ch. 62, § 17 (last sentence of first paragraph), which states that an LLC formed under chapter 156C or a foreign LLC as defined in chapter 156C, § 2, will be deemed to be a partnership if it is classified for the tax year as a partnership for federal income tax purposes.

[548] Mass. Gen. Laws Ann. ch. 62, § 17(a).

[549] S.B. 1946, Laws, 2003; Massachusetts Department of Revenue Ltr. Rul. LR 00-8 (June 9, 2000); TIR No. 04-4 (Feb. 25, 2004).

[550] Mass. Gen. Laws Ann. ch. 62, § 17(c).

[551] *Id.*

- Income derived from or connected with the LLC's business carried on in Massachusetts
- Income from the ownership of any interest in real or tangible personal property located in Massachusetts
- Interest, dividends, annuities, and capital gains from property employed in the LLC's business carried on in Massachusetts

A foreign corporation that owns a single-member LLC doing business in Massachusetts is treated as doing business in and subject to tax in Massachusetts if the LLC is a disregarded entity.[552]

A disregarded LLC that is owned by a C corporation is treated as a division of the corporate owner. All the LLC's income, losses, and other tax attributes flow through to the corporate owner. All transactions between the LLC and the corporate owner must be eliminated for apportionment purposes if the LLC is organized in the foreign jurisdiction. All the LLC's property, sales, and payroll are treated as those of the corporate owner for apportionment purposes.[553]

A disregarded LLC that is owned by an S corporation is taxed as an S corporation in Massachusetts. The LLC and the parent corporation must compute the income and non-income measures of the excise (income) tax as S corporations. The parent corporation's items of income, loss, deduction and credit are combined with those of the subsidiary LLC. Thus, in determining whether and at what rate a disregarded LLC that is owned by an S corporation is subject to Massachusetts tax, the LLC must determine its total receipts by combining its receipts with the parent corporation and any other related entity that is engaged in a unitary business.[554]

Beginning 2003, a manufacturing corporation includes an LLC. Therefore, an LLC is eligible for the benefits available to manufacturing corporations. These benefits include (a) an investment tax credit against the corporate tax, (b) a property tax exemption for machinery, and (c) a sales and use tax exemption on certain items purchased and used in research and development.[555]

.03 Allocations

The member's distributive share of any item of income, loss, deduction, or credit is determined by the operating agreement. If the operating agreement contains no provision with respect to a member's distributive share of a particular item of income, loss, deduction, or credit, the item must be apportioned in accordance with

---

[552] *See, e.g.,* Mass. Dept. of Revenue Ltr. Rul. LR 00-9 (June 9, 2000), which determined that a Georgia corporation was subject to Massachusetts taxation when it acquired a Massachusetts LLC that was classified as a disregarded entity. The Georgia corporation was treated as doing business in the state based on its ownership of the membership units in the LLC. The Georgia corporation was entitled to apportion its income in accordance with the provisions of Georgia law in determining the income allocable to Massachusetts for tax purposes.

[553] Mass. Dept. of Revenue Ltr. Rul. LR 00-11 (Aug. 29, 2000).

[554] Mass. Dept. of Revenue, TIR No. 04-4 (Feb. 25, 2004).

[555] S.B. 1949, Laws, 2003. The exemption for personal property owned by manufacturing corporations was not available prior to 2003 for a taxpayer organized and doing business as an LLC. *See* RCN Beco-Com, LLC, Massachusetts Appellate Tax Board, Nos. F253495, F257397 (Aug. 19, 2003), which determined that an LLC's tangible personal property was subject to property taxes.

the member's ratio of sharing income or loss of the LLC. The member's distributive share of the various classes of income, loss, deductions, and credits must be included by the member in her return for the tax year during which or with which the taxable year of the LLC ends.[556]

.04 Tax Returns

An LLC that is classified as a partnership for federal tax purposes must file Form 3, Partnership Return of Income.[557] A copy of IRS Form 1065 and all schedules, including Schedules K-1, must be attached to the return.

An LLC must file the return if the LLC has a usual place of business in Massachusetts or receives federal gross income of more than $100 during the tax year.

The LLC reports each member's distributive share of income, gain, loss, credit, and deduction on Schedule 3K-1, Partner's Massachusetts Information. Form 3 and Schedule 3K-1 are designed to isolate income and deduction items in order to produce a correct Massachusetts LLC total, as well as each member's correct Massachusetts distributive share.

There are a number of differences between the Massachusetts and U.S. personal income tax laws that are reflected on these returns. For example, for Massachusetts tax purposes, an LLC is allowed only those expense deductions that an individually owned business is allowed. Deductions that are itemized by an individual on Schedule A of Form 1040 are not allowed. The deduction for charitable contributions or for net operating loss carryover or carryback is not allowed to the LLC or the individual under Massachusetts income tax law. Massachusetts also has a net long-term capital gain deduction of 50 percent.

Each member must report his distributive share of each item of income on a tax return under state law. The type of tax return depends on the type of member of an LLC. The following table shows which returns should be filed by each member of an LLC:

Type of Member	Form to File
Resident individual	1
Nonresident/part-year resident individual	1-NR/PY
Trust or estate	2
Domestic corporation	355A
Foreign corporation	355B
Domestic corporation (part of a Massachusetts combined group)	355C-A
Foreign corporation (part of a Massachusetts combined group)	355C-B
Corporate trust	3F
Domestic S corporation	355S-A
Foreign S corporation	355S-B

---

[556] Mass. Gen. Laws Ann. ch. 62, § 17(d).
[557] Mass. Gen. Laws Ann. ch. 62C, § 17; 830 CMR 62.5A.1(11)(b).

The LLC must file the partnership return on or before the 15th day of the third month after the close of the LLC's tax year. If the LLC was dissolved or reorganized during the year, it must file Form 3 to reflect LLC business activity as of the date of dissolution or reorganization. The form must be signed by one of the general partners. A manager is treated as a general partner.

LLCs may obtain an extension of time to file the state tax return by filing Form M-4868, Application for Automatic Six-Month Extension. The form must be filed on or before April 15 in the case of calendar year LLCs or on or before the original due date of the return for fiscal year filers. The return may be filed by telephone if the LLC meets certain requirements.

.05 Nonresident Members

Taxation of Nonresident Members

A nonresident member is subject to tax on his distributive share of LLC income to the same extent as if received by a resident.[558] The member must include in his return his distributive share of such income or loss and any item of deduction or credit.[559]

A nonresident member is taxed only on LLC income attributable to sources or business conducted within Massachusetts. An LLC that does business both within and outside of Massachusetts must apportion its income under the Massachusetts regulations.[560]

Withholding Taxes

An LLC with Massachusetts source income must withhold tax on income allocated to nonresident members.[561] The withholding tax rate depends on whether the income is capital gains, dividends, interest or other income.[562] No withholding is required if the member participates in a composite return,[563] or agrees to file a Massachusetts return, make quarterly estimated tax payments, and accept personal jurisdiction in the Massachusetts state courts on tax matters.[564] A member who claims an exemption from withholding must submit certification to the LLC on Form PTE-EX. The Commissioner may require withholding or nonresident members with a history of failing to file returns and pay taxes on a timely basis.[565]

---

[558] 830 CMR 62.5A.1(1)(a); M.G.L.A. ch. 62, §5A.

[559] M.G.L.A. ch. 62, §17(b).

[560] 830 CMR 62.5A.1(6).

[561] 830 CMR 62B.2.2. Mass. Gen. Laws ch. 62B, §2; Guide for Pass-Through Entities.

[562] 830 CMR 62B.2.2(3)(c), referring to M.G.L.A. ch. 62, §4.

[563] 830 CMR 62B.2.2(3)(c).4.a.

[564] 830 CMR 62B.2.2(3)(c).4.b.

[565] 830 CMR 62B.2.2(3)(d).

Composite Return

An LLC may file a composite return on behalf of two or more qualified nonresident members.[566] The LLC must pay income taxes on such nonresident members' distributive shares of Massachusetts source income.[567] The composite tax rate in 2017 is 5.1 percent on regular income and 12 percent on short-term capital gain and collectibles gain.[568] A nonresident member may be included in a composite return if:[569]

- The nonresident is an individual, or an entity that is taxed as an individual, such as an electing small business trust (ESBT), or the estate or trust of a deceased nonresident member.

- The member is a nonresident for the entire tax year.

- The member elects to be included in the composite return by signing a statement.

- The member waives the right to claim deductions, exemptions and credits under Massachusetts law.

- The member signs a statement under penalty of perjury stating the member's qualifications and election to file composite return.[570]

- All persons included in the composite return must have the same tax year.[571]

An LLC must file a composite return electronically on Form NRCR along with Schedules B, D, and E as needed. The total Massachusetts gross income reported on the composite Form MA NRCR must be the sum of all qualified electing nonresident members' Massachusetts source income from the filing LLC and any other upper-tier entities that are included in the return. The filing LLC must file an electronic 2K-1, 3K-1, or SK-1 on behalf of each nonresident member electing to participate in the composite return. Each member must file Form M-8453 CR, Nonresident Composite Return Tax Declaration for Electronic Filing. Professional athletes must file a composite return on Form 1-NR/PY.[572]

Members may be included on one or more composite returns if they have other Massachusetts-source income. Members for whom a composite return has been filed have a separate filing obligation for Massachusetts source income not included on the composite return. Items included on the composite return must not be included on the separate return, or used to calculate any items on the separate return.[573]

---

[566] 830 CMR 62.5A.1(12)(f).

[567] 830 CMR 62.5A.1(12)(f).1.

[568] Instructions to Form MA 2017, Nonresident Composite Return.

[569] 830 CMR 62.5A.1(12)(f).1.b.

[570] 830 CMR 62.5A.1(12)(f).2.

[571] 830 CMR 62.5A.1(12)(f).3.

[572] Instructions to Form 1-NR/PY.

[573] Instructions to Form 1-NR/PY.

Estimated Taxes

The LLC must make estimated tax payments for nonresident members on Form 1-ES, Estimated Income Tax Vouchers. The LLC must note on the form that it is a "Composite estimated tax payment."[574] Estimated tax payments made by individuals cannot be credited against the tax due with the composite return. Individual members who have made such payments with respect to a tax year and desire to participate in a composite return filing for that year may request a refund of their individual estimated tax payments.[575]

The estimated tax rate in 2017 is 5.1 percent (12 percent on short-term capital gains and collectibles gain).[576]

Agreement to Pay Taxes

No withholding is required for an individual nonresident member if the member agrees on Form PTE-EX to file a Massachusetts return.[577] An individual nonresident who has filed a Composite Return Filing Statement need not also file a Form PTE-EX since the individual must acknowledge on Form CRFS that he or she will (i) file a Massachusetts tax return, (ii) make estimated tax payments if required, (iii) pay his or her pro rata share of any penalty and interest due for any underpayment of estimated taxes, and, further, and (iv) be subject to jurisdiction in Massachusetts. A Form CRFS filed with the LLC in lieu of the Form PTE-EX must be filed according to the Form PTE-EX filing dates. An individual that elects not to participate in a composite return must file with the LLC a Form PTE-EX within 30 days after his or her exemption status changes.[578]

A Massachusetts return is required to be filed if income is below the personal exemption amount multiplied by the ratio of Massachusetts income to total income. An individual may check box 3 on the Form PTE-EX, agreeing to file tax returns in Massachusetts, whether or not a return is required in a particular year.

If a member has filed an exemption certificate with the LLC indicating an intention to self-file, the LLC may withhold on the member if the member and the LLC agree.[579]

---

[574] 830 CMR 62.5A.1(12)(f).5.

[575] 830 CMR 62.5A.1(12)(f).5.

[576] Instructions to Form 1-ES, Massachusetts Estimated Income Tax.

[577] 830 CMR 62B.2.2(3)(c).4.b.

[578] Guide for Pass-Through Entities—Including Registration Information, Massachusetts Department of Revenue (2010).

[579] Guide for Pass-Through Entities—Including Registration Information, Massachusetts Department of Revenue (2010).

¶2323.05

.06 Annual Report

Massachusetts LLCs are required to file annual reports. The annual report is due on the anniversary of the filing of the certificate of organization.[580] Foreign LLCs that are qualified to do business in Massachusetts must also file annual reports. The report is due on the anniversary of their registration.[581]

.07 Filing Fees

Massachusetts imposes the following filing fees on LLCs:

Certificate of organization*	$500
Annual report for domestic LLCs**	$500
Foreign LLC registration application***	$500
Annual report for foreign LLC****	$500

* Mass. Gen. Laws Ann. ch. 156C, § 12.
** Mass. Gen. Laws Ann. ch. 156C, § 12.
*** Mass. Gen. Laws Ann. ch. 156C, § 48.
**** Id.

¶ 2324 MICHIGAN

Michigan adopted the Michigan Limited Liability Company Act effective June 1, 1993.[582]

.01 State Tax Classification

Michigan follows the federal check-the-box regulations in classifying an LLC. The federal entity classification applies to all components of the tax that are related to the federal income tax.[583]

A single-member LLC that is a disregarded entity for federal purposes is treated as a branch, division, or sole proprietor. A member of an LLC that is classified as a partnership is treated as a partner for purposes of the statutory exemption and the small-business credit. A single-member disregarded LLC owned by a corporation may file a separate tax return under the state's single business tax act, and does not have to file as part of a combined return with the parent corporation.[584]

---

[580] Mass. Gen. Laws Ann. ch. 156C, § 12.

[581] Mass. Gen. Laws Ann. ch. 156C, § 48.

[582] Pub. Act No. 23 (H.B. 4023), 1993 Mich. Pub. Acts; Mich. Comp. Laws Ann., § § 450.4101 to 450.5200.

[583] Revenue Administration Bulletin 1999-9, Michigan Department of Treasury (Nov. 29, 1999).

[584] *Kmart Michigan Property Services LLC v. Michigan Treasury Department*, 283 Mich. App. 647 (2009).

A member of an LLC that is classified as a corporation is treated as a shareholder for purposes of the statutory exemption, but not a shareholder's for purposes of the small-business credit (because they do not meet the statutory definition of a "shareholder" for purposes of the credit).[585]

An LLC is not required to make an entity classification election at the state level because Michigan follows the federal election.[586]

The federal entity classification determination is also effective for purposes of the Michigan personal income tax return for members of the LLC. The Michigan personal income taxes based on federal adjusted gross income. The Michigan income tax return must conform to the entity elections reported on the federal return.[587]

.02 Taxation of LLC and Members

Laws Effective in 2012

Michigan repealed the Michigan Business Tax (MBT) for tax years beginning on or after January 1, 2012 unless the taxpayer elects to continue to file under the MBT provisions. The MBT is replaced by the six percent Corporate Income Tax (CIT). The CIT is imposed only on corporations and on LLCs that are classified as C corporations under federal law.

The income of an LLC may also be included in the CIT base of a unitary business group.

LLCs that are classified as partnerships or disregarded entities are not required to file a CIT return or pay the CIT taxes.[588] Members of an LLC that is classified as a partnership are taxed on their allocable share of income.

LLCs that are classified as disregarded entities for federal income tax purposes are also classified as disregarded entities for purposes of the CIT.[589]

Laws Effective from 2008-2011

Effective January 1, 2008, Michigan repealed the Single Business Tax (SBT), and replaced it with the Michigan Business Tax (MBT).[590] The MBT is imposed on all

---

[585] *Id.*

[586] Revenue Administration Bulletin 1999-9, Michigan Department of Treasury (Nov. 29, 1999).

[587] *Id.*

[588] H4361, Laws 2011 (P.A. 38) and H4362, Laws 2011 (P.A. 39).

[589] Mich. Comp. Laws § 206.699, enacted on December 27, 2011, provides that an LLC classified as a disregarded entity for federal income tax purposes will be classified as a disregarded entity for purposes of the CIT under Mich. Comp. Laws §§ 206.601 to 206.699 and the miscellaneous reporting provisions under Mich. Comp. Laws §§ 206.701 to 206.713.

[590] Mich. Comp. Laws §§ 208.1101 to 208.1601.

persons doing business in Michigan,[591] including LLCs.[592] The MBT includes the following taxes:

- *Business income tax.* The tax rate is 4.95 percent on business income.[593] The tax base starts with federal taxable income, subject to adjustment.
- *Modified gross receipts tax.* The tax rate is 0.8 percent of gross receipts less purchases from other firms.[594]
- *Annual surcharge* equal to a 21.99 percentage of an LLC's MBT liability[595] after allocation or apportionment to Michigan, but before the calculation of credits available under the MBT Act. The maximum annual surcharge is $6 million.

LLCs with gross receipts under $350,000 are not subject to tax.[596] The tax is phased in for LLCs with gross receipts between $350,000 and $700,000.[597]

The apportionment formula is based on the LLCs percentage of Michigan sales.[598]

.03 Tax Returns

Beginning in 2012, an LLC that is classified as a partnership or disregarded entity is not required to file an MBT or CIT tax return, or pay income taxes at the entity level.

For 2011, an LLC must file the following forms to pay the Michigan Business Tax:

- Form 4567, Michigan Business Tax Annual Return;
- Form 4583, Michigan Business Tax Simplified Return; and
- Form 4548, Michigan Business Tax (MBT) Quarterly Return

A taxpayer with estimated tax liability exceeding $800 must make estimated tax payments on a quarterly basis.[599] The taxpayer must also file an annual return by the last day of the fourth month after the end of the tax year.[600] An LLC that is classified as a partnership must file an information return.[601]

LLCs with fiscal years must file an MBT return through December 31, 2011.

---

[591] The tax is imposed on any taxpayer that meets one of two nexus tests. Under the first test, nexus is established if the taxpayer has a physical presence in Michigan for at least two days during the tax year. Under the second test, nexus is established if the taxpayer actively solicits sales in Michigan and has at least $350,000 of gross receipts.

[592] Mich. Comp. Laws § 208.1113(3).

[593] Mich. Comp. Laws § 208.1201(1).

[594] Mich. Comp. Laws § 208.1203(1).

[595] The surcharge rate is 21.99 percent for 2010.

[596] Mich. Comp. Laws § 208.1200(1).

[597] Mich. Comp. Laws § 208.1411.

[598] Mich. Comp. Laws § 208.1301 to § 208.1309.

[599] Mich. Comp. Laws § 208.1501.

[600] Mich. Comp. Laws § 208.1505.

[601] Mich. Comp. Laws § 208.1505.

Single-member disregarded LLC's are required to file an MBT return, but with a different due date.[602]

.04 Nonresident Members

Withholding

Withholding on income allocable to nonresident members is no longer required or permitted for tax years beginning after June 30, 2016.[603]

Composite Returns

An LLC may file a composite return on Form 807 if it has two or more nonresident members who elect to participate in the composite filing.[604] A member may elect to be included on the composite return if (i) the member does not have income from other state sources, (ii) the member does not claim certain credits or more than one Michigan personal exemption, and (iii) the member is not a part-year or full-year resident of Michigan.

The return is filed on Form 807, Composite Individual Income Tax Return. The composite tax rate is 4.25 percent in 2017 of the income allocable to the nonresident members included on the return.

An LLC filing Form 807 must report to each nonresident member that participates in the composite filing the member's distributive share of business income and other taxable income of the LLC that has been allocated or apportioned to Michigan. The Michigan Treasury recommends that the LLC provide the information to its members as a supplemental attachment to the federal Schedule K-1, which will provide the participant with the information necessary to file a MI-1040 if the participant has other Michigan-sourced income.

An LLC with one electing nonresident member may file an individual or fiduciary income tax return on behalf of the member if the member executes a power of attorney authorized in the LLC to make the filing.[605]

A nonresident member who participates in a composite filing and who has no other Michigan source income is not required to file a Michigan income tax return.[606]

---

[602] Notice to Taxpayers Regarding Federally Disregarded Entities and the Michigan Business Tax (revised Jan. 26, 2012).

[603] Michigan Public Act 158 of 2016.

[604] Mich. Comp. Laws § 206.315; Michigan Department of Treasury Bulletin RAB 2004-1.

[605] Michigan Department of Treasury Bulletin RAB 2004-1.

[606] Michigan Department of Treasury Bulletin RAB 2004-1.

Estimated Taxes

LLCs may have to file estimated tax vouchers and pay estimated tax on behalf of each member. Estimated vouchers and payments are required if the annual income tax liability for each member is expected to exceed $500 after exemptions and credits.[607] The estimated payments must be remitted with a Fiduciary Voucher for Estimated Income Tax (Form MI-1041ES) with the name of the LLC and the LLC's federal tax identification number. The LLC must write "Composite return" on the top of the voucher. Estimated payments should only be remitted for those members who will participate on the Composite Return (Form 807).

LLCs using a calendar tax year must file vouchers and pay quarterly estimated tax by April 15, July 15, October 15, and January 15. LLCs that are not using a calendar year must file vouchers and pay quarterly estimated tax on the appropriate due dates that, in the LLC's fiscal year, correspond to the calendar year. Fiscal year filer due dates apply regardless of the tax years of the participants.

Disregarded LLCs

A single-member LLC that is a disregarded entity for federal purposes is subject to the apportionment factors for MBT and personal income tax based on the combined property, payroll, and sales of the combined entities. Sales between the single-member LLC and its owner are disregarded in computing the sales factor.[608]

An owner of an LLC that is classified as a disregarded entity for federal tax purposes has nexus with Michigan based on the LLC's property and activities. The owner of the LLC must file an MBT return. If the owner of a single-member LLC is a flow-through entity, its partners, members, or shareholders who are individuals must file personal income tax returns.[609]

.05 Personal Income Tax Withholding

An LLC that is an employer under federal law is also an employer for state personal income tax withholding purposes. The LLC must register for income tax withholding. The Michigan withholding taxpayer may be different from the taxpayer for federal tax purposes. An LLC that is classified as a disregarded entity is not required to have a federal employer identification number. Such LLCs will be issued a Michigan Department of Treasury number for Michigan withholding tax purposes.[610]

---

[607] Instructions to 2017 MI-1041ES, Michigan Estimated Income Tax for Fiduciaries.

[608] Revenue Administration Bulletin 1999-9, Michigan Department of Treasury (Nov. 29, 1999).

[609] *Id.*

[610] *Id.*

The Michigan Department of Treasury may enter into an agreement allowing a disregarded single-member LLC to file a combined withholding tax return with its owner.[611]

.06 Sales and Use Tax

An LLC is subject to the Michigan sales and use tax regardless of his classification for federal income tax purposes. A single-member LLC that is classified as a disregarded entity for federal purposes is still a legal entity for Michigan purposes, and must register for sales tax if it makes retail sales in Michigan.[612]

An LLC that purchases for use, storage, or consumption in Michigan must register for the Michigan use tax. An out-of-state LLC that is a disregarded entity and that is liable for the use tax must register as a seller.[613]

.07 Annual Report

A Michigan LLC must file an annual report. The annual report must contain the name of the registered agent and the address of the registered office. It must be filed on or before February 15 of each year.[614]

.08 Filing Fees

Michigan imposes the following filing fees on LLCs:[615]

Articles of organization	$50
Application for certificate of authority of foreign LLC	$50
Annual report (reduced to 15 after September 30, 2015)*	$25

* Act 310 (H.B. 5820, Laws 2012).

¶ 2325 MINNESOTA

Minnesota enacted the Minnesota Limited Liability Company Act effective January 1, 1992.[616]

---

[611] *Id.*

[612] *Id.*

[613] *Id.*

[614] Mich. Comp. Laws § 450.4207.

[615] Mich. Comp. Laws § 450.5101.

[616] H.F. 1910, 1991 Minn. Laws; Minn. Stat. Ann. § § 322B.01 to 322B.960.

.01 State Tax Classification

Minnesota classifies an LLC in the same manner that the LLC is classified for federal tax purposes.[617] An LLC formed in Minnesota or in a foreign state is classified as a partnership for state tax purposes if it is classified as a partnership for federal tax purposes.[618] Effective August 1, 1997, one member may form an LLC.[619]

.02 Taxation of LLC and Members

There is no income tax imposed on LLCs in Minnesota. The LLC is treated as a pass-through entity. All items of income, gain, credit, loss, and deduction pass through to and are taxed to the members.[620] Profits and losses of the LLC are allocated among members in the same manner that applies to partnerships.

However, the LLC is subject to a minimum fee if the sum of its Minnesota source property, payroll, and sales or receipts is at least $970,000 in 2017. The minimum fee ranges from $200 to $9,770 depending on payroll, sales and property in Minnesota.[621] An LLC is exempt from the minimum fee if 80 percent or more of its income is from farming.

Minnesota treats an LLC, including a single-member LLC classified as a disregarded entity, as a separate legal entity for sales and use tax purposes. Thus, transfers of tangible personal property between a person and a single-member LLC or any other LLC are subject to the sales and use tax, subject to various exemptions.[622]

A resident member of an LLC that is classified as a partnership is entitled to a credit for taxes paid by the LLC to a foreign state. The member is treated as having paid a tax in an amount equal to the member's pro rata share of any net income tax paid by the LLC to another state. The net income tax means any tax imposed on or measured by the LLC's net income.[623]

Nonresident members are taxed on their distributive shares of income allocable to Minnesota,[624] whether or not distributed.[625]

An LLC must pay quarterly estimated taxes if the sum of its estimated minimum fee, nonresident withholding and composite income tax for all nonresident members electing to participate in composite income tax, less any credits, is $500 or more.

---

[617] Notice #13-08, Minn. Dep't of Rev. (Dec. 23, 2013).

[618] Minn. Stat. Ann. § 290.01(3b).

[619] Minn. Stat. Ann. § 322B.11.

[620] Minn. Stat. Ann. § 290.311.

[621] Minn. Stat. Ann. § 290.0922(1)(b). *See also* Minimum Fee Table on the instructions to Form M-3, Partnership Return.

[622] Revenue Notice No. 02-10, Minn. Dept. of Rev. (July 8, 2002).

[623] Minn. Stat. Ann. § 290.07.

[624] Minn. Stat. Ann. § 290.92(4b).

[625] Minn. Dept. of Rev. R. 8031.0100.

.03 Tax Returns

Every LLC that has gross income from Minnesota sources must file a partnership return on Form M3, Partnership Return.[626] Each member of the LLC is required to include his share of income on an individual tax return. The entire share of LLC income is taxed to the member, whether or not actually distributed. However, the LLC must pay the minimum fee.

LLCs that are classified as partnerships for federal income tax purposes must check the box on the top of Form M3 specifying that the entity is an LLC.

LLCs must file the return by March 15 for calendar year LLCs and by the 15th day of the third month after the end of the fiscal year for other LLCs.

Form M3 must be filed with Minnesota Partnership Tax, Mail Station 1760, St. Paul, MN 55145-1760. The LLC must attach all federal forms and schedules. LLCs with more than 200 members must submit the federal K-1 schedules and the Minnesota KPI and KPC schedules (if applicable) on diskette or microfiche.

If the IRS makes changes to the federal return, the LLC must file an amended Minnesota partnership return with the Department of Revenue or explain why no amended return is needed. The filing must be made within 180 days after notification of the change by the IRS. A copy of the IRS report must be attached to the Minnesota return.

The LLC must provide the members with enough information for them to complete their Minnesota income tax returns and determine the correct Minnesota tax. The LLC must complete a separate Schedule M-KPI for each individual, estate, or trust member, showing the specific share of LLC income, credit, and modifications for each.

The LLC must use Schedule KPC to show each corporate and partnership member's share of LLC income, credit, and modifications. The form must be attached to the LLC's Form M3. The LLC must also attach copies of the federal Schedules K and K-1 to its state partnership return.

.04 Estimated Taxes

The LLC must file estimated tax deposit forms and make quarterly payments if it has estimated minimum fees of $1,000 or more or if any nonresident individual member's share of composite income tax is $500 or more. Quarterly estimated payments must be paid on Form M71, Partnership Estimated Tax, before the 15th day of the fourth, sixth, and ninth months of the tax year and of the first month following the end of the tax year. Both the minimum fee and the composite income tax may be included on the same quarterly tax payment.

---

[626] Minn. Stat. Ann. § 289A.12(3); Minn. Dept. of Rev. R. 8038.3000.

.05 Nonresident Members

Taxation of Nonresident Members

Nonresident individual members must pay Minnesota taxes if their Minnesota gross income is more than the minimum filing requirement for the year.

Composite Return

An LLC may file a composite Minnesota income tax return on behalf of nonresident members who elect to be included.[627] The LLC must pay a composite tax on behalf of electing members at the highest individual tax rate, which is 9.85 percent for 2017.[628] The LLC files a composite return by checking the box for composite income tax on the first page of Form M3 and by attaching Schedule KPI to the form.

The electing individual members may not have any Minnesota source income other than the income from the LLC or other entities electing composite filings. The individuals who have other Minnesota income may not be included on the composite schedule and must file Form M1, Minnesota Income Tax Return.

Nonresident individual members of an LLC who are included in the composite income tax return are not subject to the nonresident partner withholding requirements.

Withholding Taxes

LLCs are required to withhold Minnesota income tax for nonresident members if all of the following requirements are met:[629]

- The member is not included in the composite income tax return;
- The member has Minnesota distributive income of $1,000 or more; and
- The income was not generated by a transaction related to the termination or liquidation of the LLC in which no cash or property was distributed in the current or prior taxable year.

The withholding tax rate is 9.85 percent in 2017 on the nonresident member's distributive share of income. However, the Department of Revenue will permit a reduced withholding tax rate if it more accurately reflects the Minnesota tax the member. The member must file Form AWC, Alternative Withholding Certificate, to request the reduced rate.

No withholding is required for nonresident members included in a composite return.

---

[627] Minn. Stat. Ann. § 289A.08(7).

[628] Minn. Stat. Ann. § 290.06; Instructions to Form AWC, Alternative Withholding Certificate.

[629] Minn. Stat. Ann. § 290.92(4b).

Estimated Taxes

An LLC must pay estimated tax if the sum of its estimated minimum fee, nonresident withholding and composite income tax for all nonresident partners electing to participate in composite income tax, less any credits, is $500 or more: The LLC must pay quarterly installments based on its required annual payment. If the minimum fee/nonresident withholding and composite income tax are subject to the estimated tax requirements, the LLC must include all in the same quarterly payments. An LLC is not required to pay estimated taxes the first year it is subject to tax in Minnesota.

Required Annual Payment

The required annual payment is the lesser of (i) 90 percent of the current year's tax liability; or (ii) 100 percent of the prior year's tax liability. The required annual payment must be paid in four equal installments unless certain exceptions apply.[630]

.06 Annual Report

A Minnesota LLC must file an annual report with the secretary of state.[631] The annual report must be filed by December 31 of each year.

.07 Filing Fees

Minnesota imposes the following filing fees on LLCs:

Articles of organization	$155
Certificate of registration for foreign LLC	$205
Annual report	$ 0 (unless changes made from prior year)

¶ 2326 MISSISSIPPI

Mississippi enacted the Mississippi Limited Liability Company Act effective July 1, 1994.[632]

---

[630] Instructions to Form M3.

[631] Minn. Stat. Ann. § 322B.960.

[632] S.B. 2395, ch. 402, 1994 Miss. Laws; Miss. Code Ann. §§ 79-29-101 to 79-29-1201.

.01 State Tax Classification

Mississippi classifies an LLC in the same manner that the LLC is classified for federal tax purposes.[633] The same rule applies to foreign LLCs qualified to do business in Mississippi.[634]

A single member limited liability company (SMLLC) that is disregarded for federal reporting purposes will likewise be disregarded for state reporting purposes. The SMLLC's activity in Mississippi is reported by the owner of the SMLLC when making its return filings. A corporate owner of an SMLLC must make income and franchise tax return filings based on its activities and the activities of any disregarded entities. If the owner of the SMLLC is itself an SMLLC or other type of disregarded entity, then such amounts will be reported by the ultimate owners which are not disregarded entities.[635]

.02 Taxation of LLC and Members

There is no franchise or other entity-level tax on LLCs that are classified as partnerships. The LLC is a pass-through entity. All items of income, gain, deduction, credit, and loss pass through to and are taxed to the members.[636]

However, if the individual members fail to report and pay the tax, then the LLC and any member treated as a general partner are jointly and severally liable for the tax liability and subject to assessment.[637] The LLC and managers are not liable if the LLC withholds and remits five percent of the net gain or profit of the LLC for the tax year. The amounts are treated as payment of the estimated tax of the members. They are allocated pro rata to the members' taxpayer accounts.

LLC net income is computed under Mississippi law in the same manner and on the same basis as for individuals. No personal exemptions are allowed for an LLC. LLC income distributed to members is subject to passive activity limitations in the same manner as under federal law. Each member must be provided with a schedule of passive activity and rental real estate activity income or loss.

A single-member LLC that is disregarded for federal reporting purposes is disregarded for state reporting purposes. The LLC's activities in Mississippi are reported by the owner of the LLC when filing its returns. A corporate owner of a single-member LLC must file an income and franchise tax return based on its activities and the activities of any disregarded entities. If the owner of the single-member LLC is itself a single-member LLC or other type of disregarded entity, then such amounts must be reported by the ultimate owners who are not disregarded entities.

---

[633] Miss. Code Ann. § 79-29-112.

[634] *Id.*

[635] *See* Instructions to Form 84-105, Mississippi Pass-Through Entity Tax Return.

[636] Miss. Code Ann. § 27-7-25.

[637] Miss. Code Ann. § 27-7-25; Miss. State Tax Commn. Reg. § 35.III.9.01.

.03 Tax Returns

Each Mississippi LLC and foreign LLC with income from Mississippi must file Form 84-105, Mississippi Pass-Through Entity Tax Return, if the LLC is classified as a partnership for federal income tax purposes.[638] The return must be filed if the LLC has income derived from a business, trade or occupation in Mississippi and/or property located within the state of Mississippi.

The LLC must attach a copy of its federal return and use federal net income as a beginning point for computing its net taxable income for Mississippi tax purposes.

The return must be filed by March 15 for calendar year LLCs and by the 15th day of the third month following the end of the fiscal year for other LLCs. The return must be mailed to the Bureau of Revenue, P.O. Box 960, Jackson, Mississippi 39205. An LLC may obtain an extension of time to file a return. An extension of time to file a federal partnership return is automatically recognized in Mississippi. The LLC must attach a copy of the federal extension to the Mississippi return.

An LLC and its members are jointly and severally liable for any tax liability owed by its members who fail to report and pay Mississippi taxes on their allocable share of Mississippi income. However, the LLC and its managers are not liable if the LLC withholds five percent of the net gain or profit of the LLC for the tax year and pays that amount to the Commissioner.[639] An LLC that elects to withhold must file Form 84-387, Partnership Income Tax Withholding Voucher. The LLC must submit a separate voucher for each member in order that payment can be properly credited. An LLC that has income from sources within and without Mississippi should withhold from Mississippi source income only.

A member may claim a share of withheld taxes by the LLC as estimated taxes on the member's individual income tax return. The LLC must provide Form 86-387 to each member to show the correct amount withheld.

A resident member of an LLC must include his entire distributive share of LLC profits in his individual tax return.

The LLC must attach copies of the federal Schedules K and K-1 with the state partnership return. It must also distribute the federal Schedule K-1 to the individual members.

.04 Nonresident Members

Tax Liability

Nonresident members are taxed on their distributive shares of income from Mississippi sources, whether or not distributed.[640] If any member of an LLC is a nonresident member, then the LLC must compute income or loss from sources within

---

[638] *Id.*

[639] *See* Instructions to Form 86-100.

[640] Miss. State Tax Comm. Reg. § 35.III.9.01.

Mississippi separately from the income from other states. The income taxable to nonresident members and the loss deductible by nonresident members are limited to the income or loss from Mississippi sources.

Composite Return

The LLC may file a composite return for nonresident members who have no other income from Mississippi.[641] The return is filed on Form 84-105, Pass-Through Entity Tax Return and Form 84-122, Pass Through Entity Net Taxable Income Schedule. The LLC should identify electing members on Form 84-131 Schedule K by checking the composite box in Column B after each member's name.

The net income for each electing member included in a composite filing is computed in the same manner as in a separate individual filing. However, there is a deduction of $5,000 or ten percent of the composite net income, whichever is less, in lieu of any individual exemption and deduction. The tax liability is computed on the combined income of all electing members. Composite members are allowed tax credits, net operating loss and capital loss deductions, if they are computed and tracked on an individual basis.[642]

The composite tax rates are three percent on the first $5,000 of composite taxable income, four percent on the next $5,000 of taxable income, and five percent on composite taxable income in excess of $10,000.

Estimated Tax Payments

Every taxpayer, filing a composite return, with an annual income tax liability in excess of $200 must make estimated tax payments. At least 90 percent of the current income tax liability of the S Corporation filing a composite return must be paid by submitting quarterly payments. The remaining of the balance is due by the due date of the return. Partnerships filing composite returns must follow the Individual tax rules on estimated tax payments.

Withholding Taxes

Withholding is optional for nonresident members, except for members who fail to pay a report taxes attributable to Mississippi source income. In that case, the LLC is jointly and severally liable for the member's tax liability.[643]

---

[641] Miss. State Tax Comm. Reg. § 35.III.9.01.

[642] Instructions to Mississippi Form 86-100, Partnership, LLP, LLC Income Tax Instructions.

[643] Miss. Code. Ann. § 27-7-25; Miss. Reg. 35.111.9.01.

.05 Filing Fees

Mississippi imposes the following filing fees on LLCs:[644]

Certificate of formation	$ 50
Certificate of registration for foreign LLC	$250
Annual fee	$ 0

¶ 2327 MISSOURI

Missouri enacted laws authorizing LLCs in 1993.[645] Missouri authorized the formation of series LLCs in 2013.[646]

.01 State Tax Classification

A Missouri LLC is classified in the same manner that the LLC is classified for federal tax purposes.[647]

Before May 20, 1997, an LLC that was classified as a corporation for federal income tax purposes was treated as a corporation. The persons authorized to act on behalf of the LLC were treated as officers and directors for state tax purposes. The members of the LLC were treated as shareholders for state tax purposes.[648]

.02 Taxation of LLC and Members

There is no franchise or entity-level tax on a Missouri LLC. The LLC's income passes through to the members, who are subject to personal income tax.[649]

.03 Nonresident Members

Withholding Taxes

An LLC must withhold Missouri income tax on the distributive shares paid or credited to nonresident individual members.[650] The withholding tax rate is six percent of the member's share of Missouri source distributive income. Alternatively, the LLC

---

[644] Miss. Code Ann. § 79-29-1203.

[645] S.B. 66, 1993 Mo. Laws; Mo. Ann. Stat. § § 347.010 to 347.740.

[646] Mo. Ann. Stat. § 347.186.

[647] Mo. Ann. Stat. § 347.187.2.

[648] *Id.*

[649] Mo. Stat. Ann. § 143.401.

[650] Mo. Stat. Ann. § 143.411.5; 12 Mo. Code Regs. § 10-2.190.

may determine the withholding tax based on Missouri withholding tables if the member submits a Form MO W-4, Missouri Withholding Allowance Certificate.[651]

No withholding is required for members of the LLC who are partnerships, corporations, trusts, or estates.[652] The LLC is not required to withhold if any of the following apply:[653]

- The nonresident member, who is not otherwise required to file a return, elects to have the Missouri income tax paid as part of a composite return.
- The nonresident member has Missouri income from the LLC of less than $1,200.[654]
- The LLC is liquidated or terminated and income was generated by a transaction related to termination or liquidation, or no cash or other property was distributed in the current or prior taxable year.[655]
- The member files Form MO-3NR, agreeing to file a return and pay the applicable state taxes.[656]

Withholding taxes are paid to the Department of Revenue on Form MO-1NR, Income Tax Withheld for Nonresident Individual Partners or S Corporation Shareholders. The form and payment must be filed by the due date, or an extension of the due date for filing the LLC's income tax return must be requested. An extension of time for filing the LLC's return automatically extends the time for filing Form MO-1NR. The form and Copy C of Form MO-2NR must be filed with the Department of Revenue either before or at the same time the LLC provides Copy A of Form MO-2NR to the nonresident member. Form MO-2NR, Statement of Income Tax Payments for Nonresident Individual Partners or S Corporation Shareholders, must be completed for each nonresident member to whom payments or credits subject to withholding were made.

Composite Return

The LLC may file a composite return on behalf of nonresident members.[657] A member may be included on the composite return if the member makes an election and has no income from other State sources.

The LLC must file the composite return on Form MO-1040. It must write "Composite Return" at the top of the form and fill in the name and federal identification number of the LLC rather than the individual members. It must also attach a schedule listing all members, their Social Security numbers, and Missouri source income. The LLC must pay tax at a six percent tax rate on the income of nonresident

---

[651] Mo. Stat. Ann. § 143.411.5; 12 Mo. Dept. of Rev. R. 10-2.190(4).

[652] 12 Mo. Code Regs. § 10-2.190(4)(A).

[653] Instructions to Form MO-1065, Partnership Return of Income.

[654] Mo. Dept. of Rev. R. 10-2.1901(4).

[655] Mo. Stat. Ann. § 143.411.7; 12 Mo. Dept. of Rev. R. 10-2.190(4).

[656] *Id.*

[657] Mo. Dept. of Rev. R. 12 CSR 10-2.190.

members reported on the composite return.[658] A corporate partner of an LLC must file a separate corporate income tax return and must be excluded from the composite return.[659]

An LLC that files a composite return must also check the composite box at the top of Form MO-1065.[660]

.04 Tax Returns

A Missouri LLC must file Form MO-1065, Partnership Return of Income. The LLC must check the box on the top of the form that it is an LLC that is classified as a partnership.[661] The return must cover the same period as the corresponding federal Form 1065. The form must be filed if IRS Form 1065 is required to be filed and the LLC has a member who is a Missouri resident or has any income derived from Missouri sources.[662] An LLC is treated as having income derived from Missouri sources if the items are attributable to the ownership or disposition of any interest in real or tangible property in Missouri or to a trade, business, profession, or occupation carried on in Missouri. Income from intangible personal property also constitutes income derived from sources within Missouri.

The LLC must file the partnership return by the 15th day of the fourth month following the close of the tax year. The LLC must file the return on or before April 15 if the LLC operates on a calendar year basis. Any member of the LLC may sign the return. The return must be mailed to the Department of Revenue, P.O. Box 2200, Jefferson City, MO 65105-2200.

The LLC must file Form MO-NRP, Nonresident Partnership Form, if it has any nonresident members.

.05 Filing Fees

Missouri imposes the following filing fees on LLCs:[663]

Articles of organization	$105 ($50 online fee)
Foreign LLC registration application	$105
Annual fee (no annual report)	$ 0

---

[658] Mo. Dept. of Rev. R. 12 CSR 10-2.190.

[659] Ltr. Rul. No. LR4110, Missouri Department of Revenue (Oct. 1, 2007).

[660] Complete instructions for filing the composite return can be found at the Department of Revenue's website, http://dor.mo.gov/forms/Composite_Return_2014.pdf.

[661] Mo. Dept. of Rev. R. 10-2.1901(2); Mont. Code Ann. § § 35-8-101 to 35-8-1307.

[662] Mo. Stat. Ann. § 143.581.

[663] Mo. Stat. Ann. § § 347.039, 347.179.

¶ 2328 MONTANA

Montana enacted the Montana Limited Liability Company Act effective October 1, 1993.[664]

.01 State Tax Classification

Montana classifies an LLC in the same manner that the LLC is classified for federal tax purposes.[665] An LLC may be formed in Montana with one member. However, to be taxed as a partnership for Montana and federal tax purposes, the LLC must have at least two members.[666] An LLC with one member is classified as a corporation.[667]

.02 Taxation of LLC and Members

Montana does not impose a franchise or entity-level tax on an LLC.[668] Each of the members of the LLC is taxed on the distributive share of income, gain, loss, credit, and deductions.[669] All owners of LLCs that have Montana source income are subject to the Montana personal income tax. This includes nonresident individuals, foreign corporations not engaged in doing business in Montana, and the owners of pass-through entities that own an interest in the LLC.[670]

.03 Allocations

Profits, losses, and surpluses of the LLC are shared equally among members unless otherwise provided in the articles of organization or operating agreement.[671]

.04 Tax Returns

An LLC that is classified as a partnership for federal tax purposes must file a partnership return reflecting each member's share of the income and loss of the LLC.[672] The return is filed on Form PR-1, Partnership Information and Composite Tax Return. The return must be filed by the 15th day of the third month following the close of the tax year. The LLC must file the return with the Income Tax Division,

---

[664] S.B. 146, ch. 120, 1993 Mont. Laws.

[665] Mont. Admin. Rs. 42.23.702(1), 42.23.701-.702.

[666] Mont. Admin. R. 42.23.702.

[667] Mont. Admin. R. 42.23.701-.702.

[668] Mont. Code Ann. §§ 15-30-3302(1)(a), (c), 15-30-101(23).

[669] Mont. Code Ann. § 15-30-3311(1).

[670] Mont. Code Ann. §§ 15-30-3302(2), 15-30-3311(1).

[671] Mont. Code Ann. § 35-8-503.

[672] Mont. Code Ann. §§ 15-30-3302(4)a; Mont. Admin. R. 42.23.702.

Montana Department of Revenue, P.O. Box 8021, Helena, MT 59604-8021. The LLC must attach the federal return to Form PR-1.[673]

The members must file Montana individual income tax returns reflecting their shares of the income and loss of the LLC.

An LLC that is classified as a C corporation for federal tax purposes must file a Montana corporation license return (income tax return), Form CLT-4, with the Natural Resource and Corporation Tax Division of the Montana Department of Revenue.[674] An LLC that is classified as an S corporation must file Form CLT-S.

An LLC that is classified as disregarded entity must file Form DER-1, Montana Disregarded Entity Information Return. However, no filing is required for a single-member LLC whose sole member is a full-year resident individual, estate, or trust, in which case the LLC activity is reported on the resident owner's personal income tax return.[675]

.05 Nonresident Members

An LLC with nonresident members must either (i) obtain an agreement from the member to file a Montana return, (ii) file a composite tax return and pay a composite tax on behalf of consenting nonresident members at graduated rates up to 6.9 percent, or (iii) withhold taxes at a 6.9 percent rate on Montana source income allocable to foreign members who do not sign the agreement to file a Montana return, and who do not give the LLC permission to pay the composite tax on such income.[676] An LLC must file the following forms in connection with nonresident members:

- Form PT-AGR (Montana Pass-Through Entity Owner Tax Agreement) signed by the member agreeing to be subject to personal jurisdiction of Montana. The LLC must file this form separately with the Department rather than attaching it to the partnership return.[677] Form PT-AGR may be filed electronically on TAP (Taxpayer Access Point). The LLC must also retain these agreements along with its tax records.
- Form PR-1, Montana Partnership Information and Composite Tax Return. The LLC must use this form to report the composite tax paid on behalf of nonresident members electing to be included in composite return. A nonresident member may be included on the composite return if the member makes an election and has no income from Montana sources other than the LLC and other composite returns. The member must submit a power of attorney to the LLC. The LLC may not use credits to reduce the composite tax. A member may not file a separate personal income tax return or information returns apart from the composite return.[678] The LLC must make estimated tax pay-

---

[673] Mont. Code Ann. § 15-30-3302(5).

[674] Mont. Admin. R. 42.23.702(1).

[675] *Tax News You Can Use*, Montana Department of Revenue (Mar. 13, 2014).

[676] Mont. Code Ann. § 15-30-3313; Mont. Admin. R. 42.9.104, 42.9.105, 42.9.106.

[677] Mont. Admin. R. 42.9.104.

[678] Mont. Admin. R. 42.9.106.

¶ 2328.05

ments throughout the year if it expects to owe a composite income tax liability of at least $500.

- Schedule IV (Montana Composite Income Tax Schedule) of Form PR-1 for eligible members who elect to participate in a composite filing. The composite tax rate ranges from 1 percent to 6.9 percent of Montana source income, depending on the amount of income.[679] The LLC must pay through estimated installments the lesser of (i) 90 percent of the member's current year's total composite tax liability, after payments, or (ii) an amount equal to 100 percent of the member's total composite tax liability. Payments made with extensions are not considered estimated payments.

- Schedule V (Pass-through Entity Backup Withholding Schedule) of Form PR-1 for a member who is not participating in the LLC's composite return or who has not provided the LLC with a signed Form PT-AGR. The withholding tax rate is 6.9 percent for individual members and 6.75 for corporate members.

- Form PT-STM (Montana Second-Tier Pass-Through Entity Owner Statement) if the LLC has a member which is a pass-through entity (partnership, S corporation, or disregarded entity) that itself has a nonresident individual, foreign C corporation or another pass-through entity as a member at any time during the tax year. Beginning in 2012, the LLC must file this form separately with the Department rather than attaching it to the partnership return. Form PT-STM may be filed electronically on TAP (Taxpayer Access Point).

- Form PT-WH, Montana Income Tax Withheld for a Nonresident Individual, Foreign C Corporation, or Second Tier Pass-Through Entity. This form was discontinued in 2012. The LLC will now report a member's share of pass-through income only on Schedule K-1.

- Montana Pass-through Entity Tax Payment Form.

Beginning in 2016, LLCs are required to withhold on behalf of their owners that are also pass-through entities, also known as a second-tier pass-through entity. An owner that qualifies as a domestic second-tier pass-through entity may file Form PT-AGR to request a waiver from the withholding requirement. A domestic second-tier pass-through entity is a pass-through entity whose interest is entirely held, either directly or indirectly, by one or more resident individuals.

.06 Annual Report

An LLC must file an annual report in Montana between January 1 and April 15 of the year following the calendar year in which the LLC is organized. A foreign LLC must file the annual report between January 1 and April 15 in each year after it qualifies to do business in Montana.[680]

---

[679] Mont. Admin. R. 42.9.203.
[680] Mont. Code Ann. § 35-8-208.

.07 Filing Fees

Montana imposes the following filing fees on LLCs:[681]

Articles of organization	$70
Foreign LLC registration application	$70
Annual registration	$15

¶ 2329 NEBRASKA

Nebraska enacted laws authorizing LLCs effective September 9, 1993.[682] In 1994, Nebraska law was amended to make reference to LLCs in the tax laws applicable to motor and special fuel licensing requirements, personal property tax lists, personal income tax credits for taxes paid to another state, and sales and use tax credits for investment in qualified business or employment expansion.[683]

.01 State Tax Classification

Nebraska classifies an LLC in the same manner that the LLC is classified for federal tax purposes.[684] State regulations dealing with partnership taxation specify that a partnership includes an LLC that is classified as a partnership for federal tax purposes.[685] The federal classification of an LLC as a partnership is conclusive for Nebraska purposes.[686]

.02 Taxation of LLC and Members

Nebraska does not impose a franchise or entity-level tax on an LLC.[687] Each of the members of the LLC is taxed on her distributive share of income, gain, loss, credit and deductions.[688] Residents of Nebraska who are members of an LLC must include in their Nebraska taxable income, to the extent includible in federal gross income, their proportionate shares of the LLC's federal income adjusted pursuant to the Nebraska tax laws.[689] A member of an LLC who is a Nebraska resident must include in taxable income the member's proportionate share of the net income or loss from the conduct of such business within Nebraska. The income of the LLC that is derived

---

[681] Mont. Code Ann. §§ 35-8-211, 35-8-212.

[682] H.B. 121, 1993 Neb. Laws; Neb. Rev. Stat. §§ 21-2601 to 21-2653.

[683] L.B. 884, 1994 Neb. Laws (eff. Apr. 4, 1994).

[684] Neb. Rev. Stat. § 21-2633.

[685] Neb. Admin. R. & Regs. 25.001.

[686] Id.

[687] Neb. Rev. Stat. § 77-2727(1); Neb. Admin. R. & Regs. 25.002.01.

[688] Neb. Rev. Stat. § 77-2727(2).

[689] Neb. Rev. Stat. § 77-2727(1).

from or connected with Nebraska sources is determined in the normal manner, subject to adjustments.

Resident members of a Nebraska LLC are allowed a credit against Nebraska income tax for the amount of any income tax imposed by or paid to another state on income derived from sources in other jurisdictions that is also subject to the Nebraska income tax laws.[690]

.03 Member Liability for Unpaid Taxes

The members are liable for unpaid taxes of the LLC in the same manner as corporate officers are liable for unpaid taxes of a corporation if the LLC's management is reserved to the members. The managers of the LLC are liable for the unpaid taxes in the same manner as corporate officers if management of the LLC is not reserved to members.[691]

.04 Allocations

An LLC allocates profits and losses in the manner stipulated in the operating agreement. However, the aggregate fair market value of the LLC assets must exceed liabilities after any distribution is made.[692]

.05 Nonresident Members

Taxation of Nonresidents

Nonresident members are taxed on their distributive shares of Nebraska source income.[693] The apportionment of Nebraska source income is determined in the same manner as for resident members.[694]

Withholding Taxes

The LLC must withhold Nebraska income taxes from allocable share of income of nonresident individual members who do not complete Form 12N.[695] The withholding tax rate is the highest personal income tax rate on the nonresident member's

---

[690] Neb. Rev. Stat. §§ 77-2730, 2715.07; Neb. Admin. R. & Regs. 22-011.

[691] Neb. Rev. Stat. § 21-2612.

[692] Neb. Rev. Stat. § 21-2618.

[693] Neb. Rev. Stat. § 77-2727(2); Neb. Admin. R. & Regs. 25.003.

[694] Neb. Rev. Stat. § 77-2727(3).

[695] Neb. Rev. Stat. § 77-2727(4)(a); Instructions to Form 12N, Nebraska Nonresident Income Tax Agreement.

share of Nebraska's source income.[696] That rate is 6.84 percent in 2017.[697] The LLC must report the amount withheld from each nonresident member on the Schedule K-1N, Nebraska Partner's Share of Nebraska Income, Deductions, Modifications, and Credits. The LLC must attach the forms to the partnership return. A nonresident individual member may claim the amount withheld and remitted by the LLC as a credit against his or her Nebraska income tax liability by attaching a copy of the Nebraska Schedule K-1N to the Form 1040N.[698]

A member is not required to file a Nebraska income tax return if the member's only source of Nebraska income is the member's share of LLC income, the member did not sign an agreement to file a Nebraska income tax return, and the LLC paid the required withholding taxes on behalf of member. The withholding taxes are treated as full satisfaction of the Nebraska income tax liability of nonresident member.[699]

Agreement to Pay Taxes

An LLC is not required to withhold taxes on the income allocable to nonresident members if the nonresident provides the LLC with an agreement to file a Nebraska return and pay the applicable taxes. The agreement is made using Form 12N, Nebraska Nonresident Income Tax Agreement. The LLC must attach the agreement to its Nebraska tax return.[700]

Composite Filing

Nebraska does not allow the filing of a composite income tax return for nonresident members. The LLC must either obtain a Form 12N from the nonresident individual member, or withhold and remit Nebraska income taxes on the nonresident member's share of Nebraska income with Form 1065N.[701]

.06 Tax Returns

A Nebraska LLC that is classified as a partnership for federal tax purposes must file Form 1065N, Nebraska Partnership Return of Income, unless all members are residents of Nebraska and all income is derived from Nebraska sources. The LLC must attach a copy of the federal return and all supporting schedules to the Nebraska return. A foreign LLC having either a resident member or income derived from sources within Nebraska must also file a return.[702] The return must be filed on or

---

[696] Neb. Rev. Stat. § 77-2727(4); Neb. Admin. R. & Regs. 25.003.03.

[697] *See* Instructions to Form 12N.

[698] Instructions to Form 1065N.

[699] Neb. Rev. Stat. § 77-2727(4).

[700] Neb. Rev. Stat. § 77-2727(3).

[701] Instructions to Form 1065N.

[702] Neb. Admin. R. & Regs. 25.002.

before the 15th day of the third month following the close of the tax year.[703] The return must be filed with the Nebraska Department of Revenue, P.O. Box 94818, Lincoln, NE 68509-4818.

An LLC may obtain an extension of time to file the return by filing Form 2688N.[704] The form is not used if the LLC has obtained a federal extension on or before the due date of the federal return. The Nebraska Department of Revenue accepts an approved federal extension if the copy of the approval is attached to the Nebraska return.

A nonresident member must forward the completed Form 12N, Nebraska Nonresident Income Tax Agreement, to the LLC before the original filing of the Nebraska Partnership Return of Income. The LLC must attach this agreement to its return. The nonresident member may claim the amount withheld as a credit against the member's Nebraska income tax return by attaching a copy of Form 14N to the Nebraska individual tax return that is filed on Form 1040N.

The LLC must provide all members with a schedule similar to federal Schedule K-1. The schedule must list the amounts and types of income or deductions that are included in each member's Nebraska tax return. The LLC may use federal Schedule K-1 for resident members when the amounts of income from U.S. government obligations and non-Nebraska state and local obligations are also listed. The LLC may also use federal Schedule K-1 for nonresident or corporate members when the amounts of state, local, and government obligations are also listed and all income is attributable to Nebraska.

The LLC must use the same fiscal year that the LLC uses for federal tax purposes. If the LLC changes its tax year, it must change its Nebraska tax year. A copy of an approval from the IRS to change accounting periods must accompany the first return that reflects the change.

The LLC must use the same methods of accounting for Nebraska income tax purposes that it uses for federal income tax purposes. It may not change the methods of accounting unless the change is approved by the Internal Revenue Service. A copy of the approval must accompany the first return that reflects the change in the methods of accounting.

An LLC that has reported income or deductions that are changed by the Internal Revenue Service must report the change or correction to the Nebraska Department of Revenue. The LLC must report the change within 90 days of the determination by filing a Nebraska Partnership Return of Income, Form 1065N, and checking the box "Amended Return" at the top of the return. An LLC that has reported income or allowed credits in another state that are changed or corrected by that state in a way that materially affects the tax liability in Nebraska must also report the change to Nebraska within 90 days. An LLC that files an amended return with the Internal Revenue Service or with another state that materially changes the Nebraska tax liability must file an amended return with the Nebraska Department of Revenue within 90 days of filing of the amended federal or state return. The LLC must furnish

---

[703] Neb. Admin. R. & Regs. 25.002.05.
[704] Neb. Admin. R. & Regs. 25.002.0513.

the Department with complete information regarding the amount of income and deductions reported to the Internal Revenue Service after the change or correction.[705]

An LLC filing an amended return must revise the amount of Nebraska personal income tax to be withheld from any nonresident member and must issue a revised statement of income tax withheld to the nonresident member for use in filing the member's amended Nebraska personal income tax return. The Department may assess taxes at any time if the nonresident member fails to file an amended return. The assessment period is limited to two years if a member properly reports the change in his federal tax liability.[706]

.07 Apportionment of Income

An LLC that has income from sources within and outside of Nebraska must determine the portion of taxable income subject to Nebraska taxes for nonresident or corporate members.[707] Each LLC must determine the portion of income subject to tax by either the apportionment formula or an approved alternative method. Corporate members must comply with Corporate Income Tax Regulation 24-056 in calculating their apportionment factors. An LLC with one or more corporate members must also provide each corporate member with a copy of Nebraska Schedule I of Form 1065N.

Any LLC that derives income from sources within and outside of Nebraska must complete Schedule I to Form 1065N if the LLC has at least one nonresident or corporate partner. The LLC must complete Schedule I without regard to the residence of its members. An LLC using an alternative method of apportionment must attach a copy of the approval of the alternative method and a computation of the apportionment factor.

Nebraska uses a single sales-factor-only formula to apportion income. The sales factor is a fraction. The numerator of the fraction is the total sales of the LLC in Nebraska during the tax year. The denominator is the total sales of the LLC everywhere during the tax year. Total sales include gross sales of real and tangible personal property, less returns and allowances, and all other items of gross receipts. An LLC must include the following sales in the sales factor:

- Sales of property derived or shipped to a purchaser, other than the U.S. government, within Nebraska regardless of the f.o.b. point or other conditions of sale;

- Sales to the U.S. government of property shipped from an office, store, warehouse, factory, or other place of storage in Nebraska; and

- One-third of the sales of property shipped from an office, store, warehouse, factory, or other place of storage in the state if the taxpayer is not subject to tax in Nebraska when the property is delivered.

---

[705] 316 Neb. Admin. Code § 25.007.

[706] Id.

[707] Neb. Rev. Stat. § 77-2727(3).

¶ 2329.07

An LLC must complete Schedule III when the LLC has income derived from or attributable to sources within Nebraska and has nonresident or corporate partners.

.08 Health Care Provider

A health care provider operated as an LLC may distribute the health care provider credits to the members in the same manner as income is distributed for use against their income tax. Health care providers were formerly entitled to a nonrefundable income tax credit equal to the amount of taxes paid under the Health Care Provider Income Tax Act.[708]

.09 Community Betterment Programs

Each member of an LLC is entitled to report the member's share of LLC credit for contributions to certified community betterment programs as provided in the Community Development Assistance Act. The member must report the member's share of this credit in the same manner and in the same proportion as reported by the LLC.[709]

.10 Annual Report

A Nebraska LLC must file a biennial report with the Nebraska Secretary of State. The report is filed online.

.11 Filing Fees

Nebraska imposes the following filing fees on LLCs:[710]

Articles of organization	$100 plus $5 per page recording fees
Foreign LLC registration application	$100 plus $5 per page recording fees
Biennial report fee	$ 10

¶ 2330 NEVADA

Nevada enacted the Nevada Limited-Liability Companies Act effective October 1, 1991.[711]

---

[708] Neb. Rev. Stat. § 77-2715.07(4) (repealed).

[709] Neb. Rev. Stat. § 77-2715.07.

[710] Neb. Rev. Stat. § 21-2634.

[711] Nev. Rev. Stat. Ann. § § 86.011 to 86.590.

.01 Taxation of LLC and Members

Nevada does not impose an income tax on LLCs or their members. There is no partnership income tax return. However, the LLC must pay a $150 annual list fee, a $200 annual business license tax,[712] and various payroll taxes on wages of Nevada employees.

Effective July 1, 2015, there is an annual commerce tax on each business entity engaged in business in Nevada if gross revenue in a fiscal year exceeds $4 million.[713] The tax rate is based on the industry in which the business entity is primarily engaged. All businesses are required to file the Commerce Tax Return Form annually regardless of whether they have a tax liability. Businesses are preregistered for the Nevada commerce tax based on the Nevada Business License Information received by the Nevada Secretary of State. The tax is due 45 days after the end of the fiscal year. LLCs may file and pay the tax online through the Nevada tax system.

.02 Allocations

An LLC may allocate and distribute the profits to members as provided in the operating agreement. However, the assets of the LLC must be in excess of all liabilities of the LLC after the distribution is made except for liabilities to members on account of their contributions.[714]

.03 Tax Returns

An LLC must file an Initial/Annual List of Managers or Managing Members and State Business License Application.[715] The initial and annual list filing fee is $150. The initial and annual business license fee is $200.

An LLC doing business in Nevada must file Modified Business Tax Return— General Business, and pay various payroll tax wages of employees in Nevada. The modified business tax replaced the $25 per employee tax in 2003.

.04 Annual Report

The annual report must list the post office box or street address, either residence or business, of each manager or member.[716] The secretary of state may refuse to file the list if the LLC does not list all the addresses.

---

[712] Nev. Rev. Stat. Ann. § 360.780.

[713] Nev. Rev. Stat. Ann. § 363C.010 *et seq.*

[714] Nev. Rev. Stat. Ann. § 86.341.

[715] The form is available at http://nvsos.gov/sos/home/showdocument?id=2863.

[716] Nev. Rev. Stat. Ann. § 86.269.

.05 *Filing Fees*

Nevada imposes the following filing fees on LLCs:[717]

Articles of organization	$ 75 ($200 for expedited filing)
Registration of a foreign LLC	$ 75 ($200 for expedited filing)
Annual report	$125

¶ 2331 NEW HAMPSHIRE

New Hampshire enacted laws authorizing LLCs effective July 1, 1993.[718]

.01 *State Tax Classification*

New Hampshire classifies an LLC as a separate legal entity regardless of its classification for federal tax purposes.

.02 *Taxation of Members*

Effective January 1, 2010, members of an LLC are no longer subject to the dividends and interest tax.[719]

.03 **Taxation of LLC**

Business Profits Tax

For tax periods ending after 2016 and before 2019, an LLC must pay an 8.2 percent tax on business profits.[720] The business profits tax (BPT) is calculated before distributions are made. Every business organization having gross income from all sources, before expenses, in excess of $50,000 is subject to the business profits tax.[721] LLCs are subject to the business profits tax in the same manner as partnerships.[722]

For tax periods ending on or after December 31, 2018, the BPT rate is reduced to 7.9 percent, contingent upon combined unrestricted general and education trust fund revenues of $4.64 billion being collected during the biennium ending June 30, 2017. For tax periods ending on or after December 31, 2019, the BPT rate is reduced to 7.7

---

[717] Nev. Rev. Stat. Ann. § 86.561.1.

[718] H.B. 690, ch. 313, 1993 N.H. Laws; N.H. Rev. Stat. Ann. § § 304-C:1 to 304-C:85.

[719] The procedures regarding the repeal are discussed in Technical Information Release TIR 2010-006, New Hampshire Department of Revenue Administration (June 28, 2010).

[720] N.H. Rev. Stat. Ann. § 77-A:2.

[721] N.H. Rev. Stat. Ann. § 77-A:6.I.

[722] N.H. Rev. Stat. Ann. § 77-A:1.I.

percent. For taxable periods ending on or after December 31, 2021, the BPT rate is reduced to 7.5 percent.

Partnerships and LLCs having a place of business in the state are subject to the tax if any member of the LLC is a resident of the state. If any member of an LLC is not an inhabitant of New Hampshire, then the LLC is subject to the business profits tax only on so much of the income that is proportionate to the aggregate interest of the members who are inhabitants of the state in the profits of the LLC.[723]

Business Enterprise Tax

An LLC must pay a business enterprise tax (BET). In 2017, the tax is imposed at the rate of .72 percent on the compensation, interest, and dividends paid by an LLC engaged in business activities in New Hampshire for periods after July 1, 1993.[724]

For tax periods ending on or after December 31, 2018, the BET rate is reduced to 0.675 percent, contingent upon combined unrestricted general and education trust fund revenues of $4.64 billion being collected during the biennium ending June 30, 2017. For tax periods ending on or after December 31, 2019, the BET rate is reduced to .6 percent. For taxable periods ending on or after December 31, 2021, the BET rate is reduced to .5 percent.

All LLCs carrying on business in New Hampshire are required to pay the tax if the gross business receipts exceed $207,000 during the year or the enterprise value tax base is greater than $103,000.[725] A business enterprise subject to the tax includes an LLC.[726]

For purposes of the tax, taxable compensation includes all wages, salaries, fees, bonuses, commissions, and other payments to employees, officers, and directors of the LLC. It also includes the amount of deduction allowed under the business profits tax for certain personal service income and net earnings from self-employment income.[727]

Taxable dividends include any distribution of money or property paid to owners of an LLC or other business enterprise from the accumulated revenues and profits of the business.

Interest subject to the business enterprise tax includes interest paid or accrued on business debt.

Property Transfer Taxes

An LLC must pay a tax on the sale or other transfer of real property. The tax is $0.75 per $100 of the sales price or consideration for the transfer. The transfer of real property to an LLC for zero consideration is subject to the New Hampshire real estate

---

[723] *Id.*

[724] N.H. Rev. Stat. Ann. § 77-E:2.

[725] N.H. Rev. Stat. Ann. § 77-E:5.

[726] N.H. Rev. Stat. Ann. § 77-E:1.III.

[727] N.H. Rev. Stat. Ann. § 77-E:1.

transfer tax. The tax is measured by the fair market value the property transferred to the LLC.[728]

Interest and Dividends Tax

An LLC must pay a five percent tax on interest and dividends. The taxable amount is the interest and dividends received by the LLC that would be taxable if received by a resident individual. If some of the members are nonresidents, the taxable amount is proportionate to the aggregate interest of the members who are residents of New Hampshire.[729] Nonresident members are not subject to the tax.[730]

.04 Tax Returns

LLC Classified as Partnership

An LLC must file the following tax returns in New Hampshire:

- Form BET, Business Enterprise Tax Return for Corporations, Combined Groups, Partnerships, Fiduciaries and Non-Profit Organizations. The LLC must file the return only if the gross receipts are greater than $208,000 or the enterprise value tax base is greater than $104,000 in 2017.
- Form NH-1065, Partnership Business Profits Tax Return if the LLC is carrying on business activity in New Hampshire and its gross business income from everywhere exceeds $50,000.
- Form BT-SUMMARY, Business Tax Summary. This form is used to summarize the payments of the business enterprise tax, the business profits tax, estimated taxes, penalties, and additions to tax. The LLC must attach a complete copy of the applicable federal forms and schedules with this return.
- Form NH-1065-ES, Estimated Partnership Business Tax Quarterly Payment Voucher. Every LLC required to file a business profits tax return and/or a business enterprise tax return must also make estimated tax payments unless the annual estimated tax payment is less than $200 for the Business Profits Tax and less than $260 for the Business Enterprise Tax. Estimated tax payments must be sent to Document Processing Division, P.O. Box 637, Concord, NH 03302-0637. Quarterly payments are due on April 15, June 15, September 15, and December 15 of each year for calendar year LLCs.
- Form DP-10, Interest and Dividends Tax Return. The LLC must file the return if (i) the LLC has non-transferable shares, (ii) gross interest and dividend income from all sources exceeds $2,400 during the tax period, (iii) the LLC's

---

[728] Declaratory Ruling No. 7934, New Hampshire Department of Revenue Administration (Sept. 20, 2003).

[729] Instructions to Form DP-10.

[730] N.H. Rev. Stat. Ann. §77:14.

primary or central place of business is in New Hampshire, and (iv) any member is a resident of New Hampshire.[731]

- Form DP-80, Business Profits Tax Apportionment. An LLC must apportion its income if its business activities are conducted both within and outside the state of New Hampshire and the business and the LLC are subject to a net income tax, a franchise tax based on net income, or a capital stock tax in another state, whether or not actually imposed by the other state.

Single-Member LLC

A single-member LLC is recognized as an entity separate from its member for New Hampshire tax purposes. A single-member LLC is required to report and file New Hampshire taxable activities at the entity level. A single-member LLC is required by law to file a New Hampshire tax return even though the single-member LLC does not file a separate federal tax return. A single-member LLC that is not disregarded for federal purposes is classified in the same way as for federal tax purposes. It must file its tax returns using:[732]

- Form NH-1120, Business Profits Tax Return, if the member is a corporation;
- Form NH-1040, Business Profits Tax Return, if the member is an individual;
- Form NH-1065, Business Profits Tax Return, if the member is a partnership; and
- Form NH-1041, Business Profits Tax Return, if the member is a trust or estate.

.05 Annual Report

An LLC must file an annual report between January 1 and April 1 of each year.[733]

.06 Filing Fees

New Hampshire imposes the following filing fees on LLCs:[734]

Certificate of formation	$100
Foreign LLC registration application	$100
Annual report	$100

---

[731] Instructions to Form DP-10.

[732] New Hampshire Department of Revenue Administration General Instructions for Filing Business Enterprise & Business Profits Taxes.

[733] N.H. Rev. Stat. Ann. § 304-C:80.

[734] N.H. Rev. Stat. Ann. § 304-C:81.

¶ 2332 NEW JERSEY

New Jersey enacted the New Jersey Limited Liability Company Act effective January 26, 1994.[735]

.01 State Tax Classification

A New Jersey LLC is classified for state tax purposes in the same manner that it is classified for federal tax purposes. Members of an LLC that is classified as a partnership are liable for the New Jersey gross income tax only in their individual capacities.[736] A member or an assignee of a member of an LLC is treated as a partner in a partnership for all purposes of taxation under New Jersey law unless the LLC is otherwise classified for federal income tax purposes.[737]

A single-member LLC may be formed in New Jersey effective August 14, 1998. A single-member LLC is classified as a sole proprietorship unless the LLC elects to be classified as a corporation under federal law.[738]

.02 Taxation of LLC and Members

Annual Filing Fee

A New Jersey LLC that has three or more members and New Jersey source income or loss must pay an annual filing fee of $150 per owner, up to a maximum of $250,000.[739] The LLC must pay the filing fee by the original due date for the NJ-1065 tax return. It must also pay at that time one-half of the fee amount as a prepayment of the next year's filing fee.[740] The total fee amount due is generally determined by the number of K-1s filed by (or due from) the LLC.[741]

There is no exemption or proration of the fee for members who own an interest for only a portion of the year. Similarly, there is no proration for the fee if the LLC was in existence for only part of the tax year for which the NJ-1065 is due. If an LLC dissolves shortly after the end of a tax year, before filing the return for that tax year, the filing fee is due for that tax year, plus half of that fee as the prepayment towards the next year's filing fee (the next tax year being a partial year.)[742]

---

[735] S.B. 890, ch. 210, 1993 N.J. Laws; N.J. Stat. Ann. §§ 42:2B-1 to 42:2B-70.

[736] N.J. Stat. Ann. §§ 42:2B-69, 54A:2-2.

[737] N.J. Stat. Ann. § 42:2B-69.

[738] S.B. 378, ch. 79, 1998 N.J. Laws; N.J. Stat. Ann. § 42:2B-69.b; N.J. Dept. of Treas. Reg. § 18:35-1.1.

[739] N.J. Stat. Ann. § 54A:8-6(b)(2)(A); N.J. Division of Taxation Technical Bulletin, TB-55(R), Topic: Partnership Filing Fee and Nonresident Partnership Filing Fee Tax (Apr. 3, 2009).

[740] N.J. Stat. Ann. § 54A:8-6(b)(2)(B).

[741] However, the fee is also due for members that do not receive a K-1.

[742] When "Final Return" is checked off on the NJ-1065 return, no prepayment of the next year's fee is required. However, the filing fee for the final return is required.

There is no extension for late payment of the fee, even if the LLC has an extension for the filing of the LLC return. If the LLC does not pay the fee on a timely basis, it will be subject to late payment penalties and interest.[743]

If an LLC has nonresident members, the full $150 filing fee is due for each nonresident member that has physical nexus with New Jersey. If the LLC has income earned outside New Jersey, the filing fee for nonresident members that do not have physical nexus with New Jersey may be apportioned based on New Jersey source income.[744]

There is no filing fee if the LLC has no New Jersey source income and all of its operations and facilities are located outside New Jersey. Generally, the LLC will not qualify for the exception if it has New Jersey source expenses, deductions, or losses. For example, if an LLC owns vacant land in New Jersey, the LLC has New Jersey source income or expense due to expenses such as real property taxes. However, expenses that the LLC pays for, a New Jersey checking account or to hire a New Jersey accounting firm, are not sourced to New Jersey for filing fee purposes. Similarly, fees paid for filing an annual report in New Jersey are not sourced to New Jersey for filing fee purposes.[745]

Other Taxes

There is no other entity-level or franchise tax on New Jersey LLCs that are classified as partnerships.[746] The members of the LLC are liable for the tax only in their individual capacities. Members are taxed on their distributive shares of income, whether or not distributed.[747]

An LLC that is classified as a corporation for federal tax purposes is subject to the New Jersey entity-level corporate income tax.

A foreign corporation that is the sole member of a single-member LLC is subject to the New Jersey corporation business (income) tax unless the LLC is classified as a corporation for federal income tax purposes. In that case, the corporation is not disregarded as an entity for federal tax purposes and is required to pay tax. If the LLC is disregarded as an entity for federal tax purposes, the corporate member is subject to the New Jersey corporation business tax.[748]

---

[743] N.J. Division of Taxation Technical Bulletin, TB-55(R), Topic: Partnership Filing Fee and Nonresident Partnership Filing Fee (Apr. 3, 2009).

[744] *See* NJ-1065 for the New Jersey corporate allocation factor to apply for the nonresident members lacking nexus.

[745] N.J. Division of Taxation Technical Bulletin, TB-55(R), Topic: Partnership Filing Fee and Nonresident Partnership Filing Fee (Apr. 3, 2009).

[746] N.J. Stat. Ann. § 54A:2-2; Dept. of Treas. Reg. § 18:35-1.3.

[747] N.J. Stat. Ann. § 54A:5-4; N.J. Dept. of Treas. Reg. § 18:35-1.3(b), (c).

[748] *State Tax News*, N.J. Dept. of Treas., Winter 1998.

.03 Tax Returns

New Jersey has two partnership tax returns, Forms NJ-1065 and NJ-CBT-1065. The Gross Income Tax Act (GIT) requires LLCs classified as a partnership for federal income tax purposes and having a resident owner or income derived from New Jersey sources to file a Gross Income Tax return, Form NJ-1065.[749] The LLC must file a copy of the federal return with its state return.[750]

LLCs with more than two owners and income or loss from New Jersey sources may also be subject to a filing fee. The fee is computed and reported on Form NJ-1065.

The Corporation Business Tax Act (CBT) imposes a tax on certain partnerships that have nonresident owners.[751] LLCs subject to the CBT tax must file Form NJ-CBT-1065.

The separate forms help distinguish the differences that exist between the Gross Income Tax and Corporation Business Tax Acts. The filing fee is reported directly on Form NJ-1065. The GIT filing fee is remitted with the Partnership Payment Voucher (NJ-1065-V). If the LLC is also required to compute and report Corporation Business Tax, the LLC must complete and file Form NJ-CBT-1065. If the LLC has a CBT balance due, it is remitted with the Corporation Business Tax-Partnership Payment Voucher (NJ-CBT-V).[752]

.04 Nonresident Members

An LLC must pay a tax on behalf of nonresident members that have New Jersey-allocated income at the highest rate for New Jersey Gross Income Tax purposes.[753] The highest tax rates in 2017 are 8.97 percent for an individual, trust, or estate member, and nine percent for a corporate or partnership member.[754] All income is New Jersey source income if the LLC has no place of business outside New Jersey.[755]

The tax must be paid by the original due date for filing the NJ-1065. Quarterly installments are required.[756]

The LLC must also pay the full $150 filing fee for each nonresident member who has physical nexus with New Jersey. If the LLC has income earned outside of New

---

[749] N.J. Stat. Ann. §54A:8-6.

[750] N.J. Dept. of Treas. Reg. §18:35-1.3(f).

[751] N.J. Stat. Ann. §54:10A-15.11.

[752] Instructions to Forms NJ-1065 and NJ-CBT-1065.

[753] N.J. Stat. Ann. §54:10A-12.a.

[754] http://www.tax-brackets.org/newjerseytaxtable.

[755] N.J. Division of Taxation Technical Bulletin, TB-55(R), Topic: Partnership Filing Fee and Nonresident Partnership Filing Fee (Apr. 3, 2009). *See* NJ-1065 for determining the allocation factor.

[756] N.J. Division of Taxation Technical Bulletin, TB-55(R), Topic: Partnership Filing Fee and Nonresident Partnership Filing Fee (Apr. 3, 2009).

Jersey, the filing fee for nonresident members who do not have physical nexus with New Jersey may be apportioned based on New Jersey source income.[757]

Generally, if an LLC files a composite return and makes estimated payments on a timely, quarterly basis for the composite return, the LLC is not required to pay the nonresident member tax for the nonresident members filing compositely.[758]

An LLC is exempt from the nonresident member tax if the LLC:[759]

- Is listed on a U.S. national stock exchange;
- Is a qualified investment LLC;
- Is an investment club; or
- Has no income is allocated to New Jersey. To qualify for this exception, all operations and facilities must be located outside New Jersey.

An LLC is not required to pay the nonresident member tax for the following members:[760]

- A Code Sec. 501(c)(3) entity or a corporate member that is exempt from the Corporation Business Tax, such as a nonprofit corporation.
- A corporate member that has a regular place of business in New Jersey. A regular place of business refers to a bona fide office (other than a statutory office), factory, warehouse, or other space of the corporation that is regularly maintained, occupied, and used by the corporation in carrying on its business and in which one or more regular employees are in attendance. The regular place of business must be owned or rented by the corporation (the cost being born directly by the corporation and not by a related entity or person); or
- An individual, trust, or estate member of an LLC that qualifies for hedge fund status.

.05 Composite Returns

An LLC doing business or conducting activities in New Jersey or having income derived from sources within New Jersey may file a composite return on behalf of qualified nonresident individual members.[761] The composite tax rate is 8.97 percent in 2017. The LLC must check the box "Composite Return is filed for Nonresident Partners" at the top of Form NJ-1065 and attach Form NJ-1080-C.[762] The composite return is treated as a group of separate returns for the members. It also meets the

---

[757] N.J. Division of Taxation Technical Bulletin, TB-55(R), Topic: Partnership Filing Fee and Nonresident Partnership Filing Fee (Apr. 3, 2009).

[758] N.J. Division of Taxation Technical Bulletin, TB-55(R), Topic: Partnership Filing Fee and Nonresident Partnership Filing Fee (Apr. 3, 2009).

[759] N.J. Division of Taxation Technical Bulletin, TB-55(R), Topic: Partnership Filing Fee and Nonresident Partnership Filing Fee (Apr. 3, 2009).

[760] N.J. Division of Taxation Technical Bulletin, TB-55(R), Topic: Partnership Filing Fee and Nonresident Partnership Filing Fee (Apr. 3, 2009).

[761] N.J. Dept. of Treas. Reg. § 18:35-1.30(a).

[762] N.J. Dept. of Treas. Reg. § 18:35-5.2.

individual filing requirements of each qualified individual included on the composite return.[763]

An LLC may include a nonresident member on the composite return if all of the following apply:

1. The member was a nonresident individual for the entire tax year.

2. The member did not maintain a permanent place of abode in New Jersey at any time during the tax year.

3. The member was not a fiscal year filer.

4. The member did not have income derived from or connected with New Jersey sources other than income reported on a composite return.

5. The member waives the right to claim any New Jersey personal exemption, credit, or deduction and agrees to have the tax calculated directly on such income at the highest tax rate in effect for single taxpayers for the tax year.

6. The member elects to be included in a composite return. The election is made by completing and delivering to the LLC Form NJ-1080-E (Election to be Included in a Composite Return) or a form substantially similar to that form. The form must be filed prior to the filing of the composite return by the LLC.[764]

The member must make the composite return election annually. The election is binding on the member and the member's heirs, successors, and assigns. The member must also consent to personal jurisdiction in New Jersey for New Jersey personal income tax purposes.

The nonresident member may not revoke the election to be included in the composite return or make an election to be included in a composite return after April 15 following the close of the tax year.

The LLC must file the composite return on or before the 15th day of the fourth month following the close of the tax year of the qualified electing nonresident members. The LLC may obtain an extension of time to file by filing Form NJ-630.[765]

.06 Filing Fees

New Jersey imposes the following filing fees on LLCs:[766]

Certificate of formation	$100
Registration as foreign LLC	$100
Annual report	$ 50

---

[763] N.J. Dept. of Treas. Reg. § 18:35-1.30(i).

[764] N.J. Dept. of Treas. Reg. § 18:35-1.30(b).

[765] N.J. Dept. of Treas. Reg. § 18:35-1.30(f).

[766] N.J. Stat. Ann. § 42:2B-65.

¶ 2333 NEW MEXICO

New Mexico enacted the New Mexico Limited Liability Company Act effective June 12, 1993.[767]

.01 State Tax Classification

New Mexico classifies an LLC in the same manner that the LLC is classified for federal purposes.[768]

.02 Taxation of LLC and Members

There is no franchise or entity-level tax on New Mexico LLCs that are classified as partnerships for federal tax purposes.

An LLC that is not required to file a return as a corporation for federal income tax purposes is not a corporation and is therefore not subject to the New Mexico franchise tax.[769]

An LLC that is required to file a return as a corporation for federal income tax purposes and that does business in New Mexico is considered a corporation subject to the New Mexico franchise tax.[770]

Members of an LLC that is classified as a partnership for federal income tax purposes are taxed on their distributive shares of income.[771] The members of an LLC must report their distributive shares on their individual tax returns.

.03 Tax Returns

An LLC must file Form PTE, New Mexico Income and Information Return for Pass-Through Entities. The return is due on or before the 15th day of the third month after the end of fiscal year (March 31 if filing online). The filing requirement applies to LLCs registered to do business in the state, transacting business in, into or from the state, or receiving any income from property or employment within the state. Effective January 1, 2012, the filing requirement applies to an LLC that is classified as a corporation or a single-member disregarded entity.[772]

---

[767] H.B. 448, ch. 280, 1993 N.M. Laws; N.M. Stat. Ann. §§ 53-19-1 to 53-19-74.

[768] 3 N.M. Admin. Code § 15.100.8.

[769] 3 N.M. Admin. Code § 15.100.8.1.

[770] 3 N.M. Admin. Code § 15.100.8.2.

[771] 3 N.M. Admin. Code § 3.11.12.1.

[772] Instructions to Form PTE, New Mexico Income and Information Return for Pass-Through Entities (PTE).

.04 Nonresident Members

Each nonresident member of an LLC is taxed on his or her distributive share of LLC income from New Mexico sources. An LLC and the nonresident member may pay the New Mexico taxes in one of the following ways:

1. *Withholding Taxes.* An LLC must report and pay withholding taxes on behalf of nonresident members having New Mexico source income. The withholding tax rate is 4.9 percent in 2017.[773] The LLC must file and pay the tax annually (rather than quarterly under law prior to 2012) using Form RPD-41367, Annual Withholding of Net Income from a Pass-Through Entity Detail Report. Form RPD-41367 is filed separately from the PTE return, and can be filed and paid electronically on the Department's web file services page. If there are more than 50 nonresident members, the report must be filed electronically. Annual statements of withholding are not required to be submitted to the Department, but must be submitted to the member using form RPD-41359, Annual Statement of Pass-Through Entity Withholding, or Form 1099-Misc.[774] Annual withholding is due on or before the due date of the federal tax return required for the LLC. To establish that a member is a New Mexico resident or maintains a principal place of business in New Mexico and that no withholding is required, the LLC may rely on a member's New Mexico address on Form 1099-Misc or RPD-41359, Annual Statement of Pass-Through Entity Withholding. If the 1099-Misc or Form RPD-41359 does not have a New Mexico address for the member, the LLC may instead have the member sign Form RPD-41354, Declaration of Principal Place of Business or Residence in New Mexico.[775]

2. *Agreement to Pay Taxes.* There is no withholding if the member enters into an agreement with the LLC to pay the tax otherwise required to be withheld by the LLC. The agreement may be made by completing Form RPD-41353, Owner's or Remittee's Agreement to Pay Withholding on Behalf of a Pass-Through Entity or Remitter. Form RPD-41353 must be completed and on file with the LLC at the time it files its annual reports for the tax year to which the agreement relates. The member may make the required taxes by making estimated payments, by filing a New Mexico income tax return, and paying the tax due. If the Department notifies the LLC that the member failed to pay the required taxes, the LLC must then withhold taxes. The LLC must provide each owner annual statements of withholding before February 15th

---

[773] N.M. Admin. Code tit. 3, § 3.3.2.10; N.M. Bulletin B-200.25 (rev. March 2014); FYI-104, New Mexico Taxation and Revenue Department (October 2009); Instructions for Income and Information Return for Pass-Through Entities, Form PTE. The withholding tax rate is equal to the maximum bracket rate set by Section 7-2-7 NMSA 1978 of the Personal Income Tax Act.

[774] Instructions to Form PTE, New Mexico Income and Information Return for Pass-Through Entities (PTE).

[775] New Mexico Department of Taxation and Revenue, Bulletin B-200.25 (2012).

of the year following the year for which the statement is made.[776] A nonresident member who receives income from sources within New Mexico other than from the LLC must file a separate New Mexico income tax return.[777]

3. *Composite Return.* Composite returns are not allowed after 2010. Prior to 2011, an LLC could file a composite return using Form PIT-1.

.05 Filing Fees

New Mexico imposes the following filing fees on LLCs:[778]

Articles of organization	$ 50
Registration as foreign LLC	$100
Annual fee (no annual report)	$ 0

¶ 2334 NEW YORK

New York enacted laws authorizing LLCs effective October 24, 1994.[779]

.01 State Tax Classification

New York classifies an LLC in the same manner that the LLC is classified for federal tax purposes.[780] A member of an LLC is classified as a partner for state tax purposes if the LLC is classified as a partnership for federal tax purposes.[781]

An LLC that is classified as a partnership for federal tax purposes is also considered a partnership for New York tax purposes.[782]

An LLC that is owned by a single partnership is treated as a branch of the partnership unless the LLC elects to be classified as a corporation under federal law.[783] The partners of the partnership are not considered members of the LLC. The partnership must include the income, gain, loss, and deduction items of the LLC on its New York partnership return. The LLC is not required to file a separate partner-

---

[776] New Mexico Department of Taxation and Revenue, Bulletin B-200.25 (2012).

[777] Instructions to Form PTE, New Mexico Income and Information Return for Has-Through Entities.

[778] N.M. Stat. Ann. § 53-10-63.

[779] S.B. 7511-A, ch. 576, 1994 N.Y. Laws; N.Y. L.L.C. Law § § 101 to 1403.

[780] N.Y. Tax Law § § 2.5, 2.6, 601(f); Publication 16, New York Tax Status of Limited Liability Companies and Limited Liability Partnerships, New York State Department of Taxation and Finance (Sept. 2009).

[781] N.Y. Tax Law § 2.6; Advisory Opinion TSB-A-02(14)C, New York Commissioner of Taxation and Finance (July 9, 2002).

[782] FGIC CMRC Corp. (Advisory Opinion), N.Y. Comm'r of Taxn. & Fin., TSB-A-96(11)C (Apr. 1, 1996); N.Y. St. Dept. of Taxn. & Fin. Mem. TSB-M-94(6)I, (8)C (Oct. 25, 1994).

[783] Hirth Real Estate Entities (Advisory Opinion), N.Y. Comm'r of Taxn. & Fin., TSB-A-97(7)I (Aug. 6, 1997).

ship return. Neither the partners nor the partnership are liable for the LLC's annual member filing fee.

An LLC that meets the required gross income threshold and that is not a dealer in stocks and securities is considered a portfolio investment partnership. If the LLC meets the portfolio investment partnership criteria, the preferred members of the LLC are treated as limited partners.[784]

A New York corporation that forms a foreign state LLC that is classified as a partnership for federal and New York State tax purposes is itself treated as a corporate member of a partnership for New York State tax purposes. The New York corporation may exclude from the receipts factor of the business allocation percentage a portion of its receipts from the sales to the LLC.[785]

.02 Taxation of LLC and Members

An LLC that is classified as a disregarded entity or that has no New York source gross income must pay an annual $25 filing fee.[786]

An LLC that is classified as a partnership must pay a fee based on New York source gross income. The New York source gross income is calculated for the tax year immediately preceding the tax year for which the fee is due. New York source gross income is the sum of the members' share of federal gross income from the LLC derived from or connected with New York State sources without any allowance or deduction for cost of goods sold. New York source gross income is determined in accordance with the provisions of Section 631 of the New York State Tax Law as if those provisions and any related provisions expressly referred to a computation of federal gross income from New York sources.[787]

If the New York source gross income is:	The fee is:
not more than $100,000	$ 25
more than $100,000 but not over $250,000	$ 50
more than $250,000 but not over $500,000	$175
more than $500,000 but not over $1,000,000	$500
more than $1,000,000 but not over $5,000,000	$1,500
more than $5,000,000 but not over $25,000,000	$3,000
more than $25,000,000	$4,500

---

[784] FGIC CMRC Corp. (Advisory Opinion), N.Y. Comm'r of Taxn. & Fin., TSB-A-96(11)C (Apr. 1, 1996).

[785] New Venture Gear, Inc. (Advisory Opinion), N.Y. Comm'r of Taxn. & Fin., TSB-A-97(13)C (June 26, 1997).

[786] Notice N-08-16, New York State Department of Taxation and Finance, December 2008.

[787] Instructions for Form IT-204-LL, Partnership, Limited Liability Company, and Limited Liability Partnership Filing Fee Payment Form; Notice N-08-16, New York State Department of Taxation and Finance, December 2008.

The fee is on due or before the 30th day following the last day of the tax year using Form IT-204-LL, Partnership, Limited Liability Company, and Limited Liability Partnership Filing Fee Payment Form.

A domestic or foreign LLC that does not have any income, gain, loss, or deduction from New York sources is required to file a New York State Partnership Return if it has a member who is a New York State resident. However, it is not subject to the minimum filing fee.[788] Domestic and foreign LLCs with no New York source income are not subject to the filing fee solely because they were formed under the laws of New York. Dormant LLCs with no income, gain, or loss are also not subject to the fee.

The fee must be paid within 30 days after the last day of the LLC's tax year. In the case of a calendar year LLC, the fee must be paid by January 30.

An LLC that is classified as a partnership for federal tax purposes is not subject to New York income taxes.[789] Members are taxed on their distributive shares of income as determined under federal law, subject to certain modifications under state law.[790] Nonresident members are taxed on their distributive shares of income derived from or connected with New York sources.[791]

An LLC that is classified as a partnership is not subject to the corporate franchise (income) tax, even if the members are corporations. However, the corporate members of an LLC that conducts business in New York are subject to the corporate franchise (income) tax.[792]

An LLC that provides telecommunications services in New York is subject to the excise (telecommunications) tax even if the LLC is classified as a partnership.[793]

The transfer of real estate from a general partnership to an LLC is exempt from the New York real estate transfer tax if there is no change in beneficial ownership of the real property as a result of the transfer.[794]

An LLC is treated as carrying on a business in New York if it maintains or operates an office, shop, store, warehouse, factory, agency, or other place where its affairs are systematically and regularly carried on. It is also treated as carrying on a business in New York if it performs any series of acts or transactions with regularity and continuity for profit, as distinguished from isolated or incidental transactions.

---

[788] N.Y. St. Dept. of Taxn. & Fin. Mem. TSB-M-94(6)I, (6)C, (7)S.

[789] N.Y. Tax Law § 601-A(f). The statute provides that a partnership includes a "subchapter K LLC," which is an LLC that is classified as a partnership for federal tax purposes. *See also* Advisory Opinion TSB-8-02(14), New York Comm'r of Taxation and Finance (July 9, 2002).

[790] N.Y. Tax Law § 617.

[791] N.Y. Tax Law § 632.

[792] Advisory Opinion TSB-8-02(14) to Grant McCarthy Gagnon, New York Comm'r of Taxation and Finance (July 9, 2002).

[793] *Id.*

[794] 149 Realty Associates et al. (Advisory Opinion), New York Comm'r of Taxation and Finance, TBS-A-99(5)R.

.03 Allocations

An LLC allocates profits and losses among members as provided in the operating agreement. If the operating agreement is silent, profits and losses are allocated on the basis of the value of each member's contribution, as provided in the business records of the LLC.[795]

.04 Nonresident Members

Taxation of Nonresidents

A nonresident member must include in New York source income his or her distributive share of LLC income, gain, loss and deduction to the extent derived from or connected with New York sources.[796]

A nonresident member is not subject to New York tax if the LLC's only business in New York is the solicitation of orders for sales of tangible personal property that are sent outside of New York for approval, and the goods are delivered from outside the state.[797]

Nonresidents investing in an LLC are not subject to the New York income tax on passive income earned from the LLC if the LLC limits its in-state activities to trading for its own account. The investment income is passive income if the members are nonmanaging members. The New York tax does not apply to such income, since passive investment income does not fall within the federal definition of net earnings from self-employment.[798]

Estimated Taxes

An LLC must make estimated tax payments for nonresident individual members, and report the estimated taxes on Form IT-2658, Report of Estimated Tax for Nonresident Individual Partners.[799]

Estimated taxes are based on a member's distributive share of LLC income from New York sources for the year, less the member's share of certain LLC deductions allocated to New York, and multiplied by the highest rate of tax under Tax Law Section 601 for the year (8.82 percent for 2018). This amount is reduced by the member's distributive or pro rata share of any allowable credits from the LLC. A fiscal year LLC must base payments on the member's distributive share of income for the fiscal year ending in the year for which the estimated tax payments are made. The payment of estimated tax by the LLC is treated as a payment of estimated tax by the

---

[795] N.Y. L.L.C. Law § 503.

[796] N.Y. Tax Law § 660(a); N.Y. St. Dept. of Taxn. & Fin. TSB-A-08(7)C (2009).

[797] N.Y. St. Dept. of Taxn. & Fin. TSB-A-08(7)C (2009).

[798] N.Y. St. Dept. of Taxn. & Fin., TSB-A-98(8) (1998).

[799] N. Y. Tax Law § 658.

member. The member may take this payment into account in determining how much individual estimated taxes must be paid.[800]

Estimated taxes are not required if (i) the member's required estimated tax payments for the year are $300 or less, (ii) the LLC is authorized to file a group return and the member has elected to be included on the group return, or (iii) the member files an agreement to pay New York taxes and comply with the New York income and estimated tax laws.[801]

Agreement to Pay Taxes

A nonresident member may file with the LLC Form IT-2658-E, Certificate of Exemption from Partnership or New York S Corporation Estimated Tax Paid on Behalf of Nonresident Individual Partners and Shareholders. In such case, the member is not included on the group return, and is not subject to estimated taxes.

Group Return

An LLC may file a group return for nonresident members on Form IT-203-GR, Group Return for Nonresident Partners if the LLC complies with the following requirements:[802]

- Each electing member must be full-year nonresident individuals who have the same accounting period.
- Neither the member nor the member's spouse may have income from New York other than from the LLC.
- Neither the member nor the member's spouse may be subject to the minimum income tax or the separate tax on the ordinary income portion of lump-sum distributions.
- The electing members must waive any claim to the standard or itemized deduction, dependent exemption, personal income tax credits, or net operating loss carry back for carryovers.
- The LLC must request and obtain permission from the New York State Department of Taxation and Finance to file a group return on behalf of electing qualified members. The LLC must request permission by submitting an application on Form TR-99, Application for Permission to File a Group Return. Form TR-99 must be submitted to NYS Tax Department, Taxpayer Contact Center, W A Harriman Campus, Albany NY 12227. The LLC must file Form TR-99 no later than 30 days following the close of the initial tax year for which it is requesting to file a group return. After receipt of a properly

---

[800] Instructions for Form IT-2658, Report of Estimated Tax for Nonresident Individual Partners and Shareholders.

[801] Instructions for Form IT-2658, Report of Estimated Tax for Nonresident Individual Partners and Shareholders.

[802] Instructions to Form IT-203-GR, Group Return for Nonresident Partners; N.Y. St. Dept. of Taxn. & Fin. Regs. § 151.17(a) (2015); Notices N.09-8 and N-09-9, N.Y. St. Dept. of Taxn. & Fin. (May 2009).

¶ 2334.04

completed Form TR-99, the Tax Department will determine whether permission will be granted and will notify the LLC accordingly. If approval is granted, the LLC will receive a special New York State identification number to be used only for filing the group return. The Tax Department's approval to file on a group basis is contingent upon the receipt of the group return for the applicable tax year. The approval is subject to revocation upon audit. An approval to file on a group basis will remain in effect unless it is revoked. Annual approval is not required.

- Unless the LLC is exempt, Form TR-99 must be accompanied by an individual power of attorney for each qualified nonresident member who the group agent knows, at the time of application, will be participating in the group return. The power of attorney must authorize the group agent to represent the participating member in the filing of the group return. If, after the application date, an additional member elects to participate in the group return (or subsequent year's group return), a power of attorney for that member must be attached to the first group return on which the member is included. The filing of Form DTF-350, *Group Affidavit*, in accordance with the instructions of that form, is acceptable evidence that may be submitted instead of individual powers of attorney.

- The LLC must have 11 more qualified nonresident members. The approval to file a group return will not be retroactively revoked after the return has been filed simply because the LLC fails to maintain 11 qualified electing partners. For example, if an LLC filed a group return for 13 qualified electing nonresident members for the current tax year, and it is subsequently determined that three of the members did not qualify to be included on the group return, the approval to file the group return for the current tax year will not be revoked. However, approval to continue filing any further group returns for future years will be revoked unless the LLC has 11 or more qualified electing members for those years.

- The LLC must appoint one of the members as the group agent. The group agent must have legal authority to act as an agent in matters relating to the group return for all members participating in the return. The group agent is required to sign the group return. Any communications from the Tax Department will be sent to the group agent. Any notices required by law, such as a notice of deficiency or a notice and demand, will be sent to the group agent and to the individual member involved. The group agent will be personally liable for only those penalties relating to making or signing an erroneous, false or fraudulent return, but only if the agent was actually responsible for the error.

A group return is considered a group of individual returns that meets the New York State tax return filing requirements. Therefore, if a qualified member elects to participate in the group return, the member is not required to file an individual New York State or Yonkers personal income tax return or nonresident income tax return for the year.

.05 Sales Taxes

The transfer of property between a single-member LLC and its member is a taxable retail sale unless an exemption applies.[803]

.06 Tax Returns

Form IT-204

An LLC that is classified as a partnership must file Form IT-204, Partnership Return,[804] and Form IT-204-ATT, Partners' Identifying Information.

LLCs with only Article 22 partners (individuals, estates, and trusts) may file Forms IT-204 and IT-204-IP and may issue Form IT-204-IP to their members. LLCs with Article 9-A corporate members must file Forms IT-204 and IT-204.1 and attach a copy of Form IT-204-CP for each corporate member subject to tax under Article 9-A.[805]

Form IT-204 is used to report income, deductions, gains, losses, and credits from operations of the LLC during the calendar year or fiscal year. The form is an information return. Every LLC must file the return if the LLC has a partner who is a resident of New York or has any income from New York State sources regardless of the amount of income. A partner that is a corporation or a partnership is not treated as a resident of New York State even though the entity may have been formed under the laws of New York.

Form IT-204-LL

An LLC must file Form IT-204-LL, Limited Liability Company/Limited Liability Partnership Filing Fee Payment Form, and pay a New York State filing fee, if the LLC is:[806]

- a limited liability company (LLC) that is a disregarded entity for federal income tax purposes that has income, gain, loss, or deduction from New York State sources; or

- a domestic or foreign LLC (including limited liability investment company (LLIC), limited liability trust company (LLTC)), or a limited liability partnership (LLP) that is required to file a New York State partnership return and that has income, gain, loss, or deduction from New York State sources.

---

[803] N.Y. St. Dept. of Taxn. & Fin., TBS-A-99(7)S (Jan. 28, 1999).

[804] N.Y. Tax Law § 658(c).

[805] https://www.tax.ny.gov/forms/partner_llc_llp_cur_forms.htm.

[806] Publication 16, New York Tax Status of Limited Liability Companies and Limited Liability Partnerships, New York State Department of Taxation and Finance (Sept. 2009); Notice N-08-16, New York State Department of Taxation and Finance, December 2008.

The determination of whether an LLC has New York source income is based on whether the LLC has a physical presence in the state. It is not based on the amount of receipts that the LLC has from customers in the State.[807] Service receipts are sources to the state where the services are performed.[808]

The LLC must file Form IT-204-LL within 30 days after the last day of the LLC's tax year to remit the filing fee or to indicate why the LLC does not owe the filing fee for the current year.[809]

There is no proration of the filing fee if the LLC has a short taxable year for federal tax purposes.

Accounting Period

The LLC must use the same accounting period and methods for state tax purposes as it uses for federal tax purposes. If the LLC changes its partnership tax year or accounting methods for federal purposes, it must do the same for state tax purposes.

Extension to File

An LLC may obtain an extension of time to file the partnership return by filing Form IT-370-PF, Application for Automatic Extension of Time to File for Partnerships of Fiduciaries. The extension request must be filed by the due date of the partnership return. Federal Form 8736 may be used in lieu of the state form. Federal Forms 2758 and 4868 are not acceptable.

Estimated Payments

An LLC must make estimated tax payments for C corporation members, and report the estimated taxes on Form CT-2658, Report of Estimated Tax for Corporate Partners.[810]

Amended Returns

An LLC must file an amended return if it files an amended federal partnership return or if a federal audit of the partnership return changes any item of income, deduction, or tax preference previously reported to the Internal Revenue Service. The amended return must be filed within 90 days of the date of the federal amended partnership return. In the case of a federal audit, the amended return must be filed

---

[807] N.Y. Comp. Codes R. & Regs. tit. 20, § 132.15.

[808] N.Y. Comp. Codes R. & Regs. tit. 20, § 132.15(f).

[809] Notice N-08-16, New York State Department of Taxation and Finance (Dec. 2008).

[810] N. Y. Tax Law § 658.

within 90 days after the final determination of the change. The LLC must attach a copy of the federal report of examination changes.

.07 Filing Fees

New York imposes the following filing fees on limited liability companies:[811]

Articles of organization	$200
Application for authority of foreign LLC	$250

Every new LLC must announce its formation within 120 days of filing (and before the LLC's first sale) by placing notices in two publications for six weeks, at a cost of up to $2,000. Online services estimate the publication costs between $800 and $1,200 in the five boroughs of New York City. The LLC must then file a certificate of publication from each of the newspapers at a cost of $50 per certificate.

The New York Secretary of State also imposes the following filing fees on professional service LLCs:[812]

Application of authority for professional LLC	$200
Certificate of authority for professional LLC (issued by New York State Department of Education)	$ 50
Biennial Statement	$ 9

¶ 2335 NORTH CAROLINA

North Carolina enacted the North Carolina Limited Liability Company Act effective October 1, 1993.[813]

.01 State Tax Classification

North Carolina classifies an LLC in the same manner that the LLC is classified for federal tax purposes.[814] Accordingly, if the LLC is classified as a corporation, the LLC is subject to the North Carolina corporate tax.[815] If the LLC is classified as a partnership, the LLC and its members are subject to tax in the same manner as partnerships and partners.[816] If the LLC is classified as a disregarded entity (proprietorship, division, or branch), the LLC and its members are subject to tax in a manner consistent with that classification.[817] The classification does not require the foreign or

---

[811] N.Y. L.L.C. Law § 1101.

[812] N.Y. L.L.C. Law § 1306.

[813] N.C. Gen. Stat. §§ 57C-1-01 to 57C-10-7.

[814] N.C. Gen. Stat. § 57C-10-06.

[815] N.C. Gen. Stat. § 105-130.2(5).

[816] N.C. Gen. Stat. § 105-134.1(7a), (10a).

[817] *Id.*

domestic LLC to obtain an administrative ruling from the IRS on its classification under the Internal Revenue Code.[818]

An LLC is defined for North Carolina personal income tax purposes to include domestic LLCs and foreign LLCs that are classified as partnerships for federal income tax purposes.[819]

.02 Taxation of LLC and Members

LLCs are not subject to the North Carolina franchise tax, since the definition of corporation specifically excludes LLCs.[820]

Members of the LLC are taxed on their distributive shares of income.[821] The taxable income of the LLC is determined under federal law, subject to certain adjustments.[822]

There are special rules if an LLC that is classified as a partnership or disregarded entity passes through income to a corporate member. The LLC's income, assets, and activities flow through to the corporate member for purposes of determining the corporate member's income tax and the corporate member's capital stock, surplus, and undivided profits franchise tax base under the North Carolina tax laws. If an LLC is classified as a corporation, the income, assets, and other tax attributes do not flow through to the corporate member for purposes of determining the corporate member's franchise tax base. Instead, the LLC must report the income and franchise tax as a corporate entity.[823]

.03 Investment Credit

LLCs qualify for the North Carolina investment credit.[824] An individual member of an LLC is allowed a credit equal to the allocated share of the tax credit for which the LLC is eligible.[825] The aggregate amount of the credit allowed for individual members for one or more investments in a single tax year may not exceed $5,000. The rule applies whether paid directly to the owner or indirectly as a member of the LLC or other pass-through entity. An LLC must file an application for the credit.

---

[818] *Id.*

[819] N.C. Gen. Stat. § 105-134.1(7a), (10a).

[820] *Id.*

[821] N.C. Gen. Stat. § 105-134.5(d).

[822] N.C. Admin. Code § 17:06B.3501.

[823] Directive CD-02-2, North Carolina Department of Revenue (May 31, 2002).

[824] N.C. Gen. Stat. § § 105-163.011(b1), 105-163.010(7).

[825] N.C. Gen. Stat. § 105-163.011(b1).

.04 Tax Returns

LLCs doing business in North Carolina that are required to file partnership returns must file Form D-403, Partnership Income Tax Return. The LLC must attach a copy of the federal partnership return on Form 1065 and all schedules to the federal return.[826] The return must include the names of the individual members of the LLC and should be signed by a managing member and the person preparing the return. The LLC must attach a copy of the federal return and all schedules, including each federal Schedule K-1.

The return must be filed on or before the 15th day of the fourth month following the close of the fiscal year. The return must be filed by April 15 for calendar year LLCs.

An LLC may obtain an extension of time to file the return. There is an automatic six-month extension. To receive the extension, the LLC must file Form D-410, Application for Automatic Extension of Time to File State Income Tax Return. The LLC must pay the full amount of tax that the partnership expects to owe for its nonresident partners by the original due date of the return. The LLC may use federal Form 8736 in lieu of the state form.

The LLC must furnish to each member a completed Schedule NC K-1, Partner's Share of North Carolina Income, Adjustments, Tax Credit, Etc. The form must be sent to each member on or before the due date for filing the partnership return. The Schedule NC K-1 is used to report each member's share of LLC income, adjustments, credits, and taxes paid by the manager of the LLC.[827] The LLC must provide each member with a list of the amounts and sources of dividends. It must also provide each member with the amounts and types of tax credits that are set forth as the member's distributive share of tax credits.

.05 Nonresident Members

An LLC that has one or more nonresident members must report the distributive share of income of each nonresident member on Form D-403. It must also include with the return the tax due on the nonresident member's share of that income.[828] The managing member is responsible for reporting the share of the income of nonresident members and is required to compute and pay the tax due for each nonresident member.[829] The tax rate in 2017 is 5.499 percent of each nonresident's share of North Carolina taxable income.[830]

The managing member is responsible for making the report and is required to compute and pay the tax due for each nonresident member. If the nonresident member is a corporation, partnership, trust, or estate, the managing member is not

---

[826] N.C. Admin. Code § 17:06B.3503.

[827] *Id.*

[828] N.C. Gen. Stat. § 105-154(d); 1995-1996 Individual Income Tax Bulletin, N.C. Dept. of Rev.

[829] *See* Instructions to Form D-403.

[830] *See* Part 3.C of Form D-403.

required to pay the tax on that member's share of LLC income if the member signs an affirmation on Form NC-NPA, Nonresident Partner Affirmation, that the member will pay the tax with its corporate, partnership, trust, or estate income tax return. In those cases, a copy of the affirmation must be attached to the LLC return when it is filed. The tax rate is the same as the tax rate for single individuals.[831]

The manager of the LLC may withhold taxes from the distributions to nonresident members and use the withheld amounts to pay the taxes due. In such case, the nonresident member is not required to file a return.[832]

A nonresident member, other than a corporation, is not required to file a North Carolina individual income tax return if the only income from North Carolina sources is the nonresident member's share of income from the LLC and the manager of the LLC has reported the income and paid the tax due. A nonresident member may file an individual income tax return and claim credit for the tax paid by the manager of the LLC if the payment is properly identified on the individual income tax return.[833]

In determining the tax owed by nonresident members, an LLC must apportion to North Carolina the income derived from activities carried on within and outside of North Carolina. Income derived by the LLC from activities outside of North Carolina that are segregated from its other business activities are not included in determining the tax due for nonresident members. The allocation does not affect the income of the resident member. The resident member is taxed on his share of the net income of the LLC, whether or not attributable to North Carolina.

.06 Estimated Income Taxes

An LLC is not required to estimate its taxes. Resident individual members who meet certain statutory requirements must pay estimated income taxes on Form NC-40. Nonresident individual members are not required to pay the estimated tax on their distributive shares of LLC income.

.07 Annual Report

An LLC must file an annual report in North Carolina. The report must be filed within 60 days following the last day of the month in which the LLC was organized. Effective January 1, 1998, the due date is the 15th day of the fourth month following the close of the LLC's fiscal year.[834]

---

[831] Instructions to Form D-403A, Partnership Income Tax Return.

[832] N.C. Admin. Code § 17:06B.3513(c); N.C. Gen. Stat. § 105-154(d); Form D-403A, Instructions for Partnership Income Tax Return.

[833] 1995-1996 Individual Income Tax Bulletin, N.C. Dept. of Rev.

[834] N.C. Gen. Stat. § 57C-2-23.

.08 Filing Fees

North Carolina imposes the following filing fees on LLCs:

Articles of organization	$125
Application for certificate of authority of foreign LLC	$250
Annual report	$202

¶ 2336 NORTH DAKOTA

North Dakota enacted the North Dakota Limited Liability Company Act effective July 1, 1993.[835]

.01 State Tax Classification

North Dakota classifies an LLC in the same manner that the LLC is classified for federal tax purposes. An LLC having two or more members that is formed in North Dakota or in another state is classified as a partnership if the LLC is classified as a partnership for federal tax purposes.[836] The members are treated as partners of the partnership.

An LLC that has two or more members that is classified as a corporation for federal tax purposes is also classified as a corporation for state tax purposes.[837] An LLC having a single member that is classified as a corporation for federal tax purposes is classified as a corporation for state tax purposes. An LLC having a single member that is disregarded for federal tax purposes is also disregarded as an entity separate from its owner for state tax purposes.[838]

.02 Taxation of LLC and Members

An LLC is not subject to tax. There is no entity-level or franchise tax on LLCs. Members of the LLC are taxed on their distributive shares of profits of the LLC, whether or not distributed. The members are also entitled to deduct their shares of any net losses of the LLC.[839]

.03 Tax Returns

An LLC doing business in North Dakota or having sources of income in North Dakota must file a North Dakota partnership return if it is required to file a federal

---

[835] S.B. 2222, 1993 N.D. Laws; N.D. Cent. Code §§ 10-32-01 to 10-32-156.

[836] N.D. Cent. Code § 57-38-07.1.

[837] *Id.*

[838] N.D. Cent. Code § 57-38-07.2.

[839] N.D. Cent. Code § 57-38-08.

partnership return. The return is filed on Form 58, North Dakota Partnership Return of Income. A copy of the federal return must be attached to the North Dakota Partnership Return.

The LLC must use the same tax year for state purposes as it uses for federal purposes.

Form 58 must be filed on or before the 15th day of the fourth month following the close of the tax year. The return must be filed with the Office of the State Tax Commissioner, State Capitol, 600 East Boulevard, Bismarck, ND 58505-0599. At least one member of the LLC must sign the return.

An LLC doing business in North Dakota that is required to file federal Form 1099 must also file the form with the Office of the State Tax Commissioner. A Form 1099 reporting interest, dividends, pensions, or annuities does not have to be filed unless the LLC withholds income taxes from the payment.

An LLC may file an application for an extension of time to file the return on Form F-101, Application of Extension of Time for Filing Return.

.04 Apportionment and Allocation

An LLC that carries on its business entirely within North Dakota must report all of its income or loss in North Dakota.

An LLC that carries on its business partly within and partly outside of North Dakota must allocate and apportion its income under North Dakota law, which follows the Uniform Division of Income Tax Act. An LLC must complete Schedule B to apportion the income. However, if a multistate LLC consists entirely of resident members (limited to individuals, states, and trusts), the LLC is not required to complete Schedule B.

.05 Nonresident, Withholding Tax

An LLC must withhold taxes on the year-end allocable share of income of nonresident members. The withholding tax rate is the highest individual income tax rate.[840] The tax rate is 2.90 percent in 2018.[841] The year-end distributive share of income is the income shown on Schedule A of North Dakota Form 58.[842] The nonresident member may claim the withheld tax as a credit on his or her individual income tax return.[843]

---

[840] N.D. Cent. Code § 57-38-31.1; Notice on Pass-Through Withholding Requirement.

[841] N.D. Cent. Code § 57-38-30.3.

[842] N.D. Cent. Code § 57-38-31.1; North Dakota, Office of the Tax Commissioner, Update (Dec. 1, 2005).

[843] Notice, North Dakota Office of State Tax Commissioner (Dec. 4, 2006).

Withholding is not required if:[844]

- The member's distributive share of North Dakota income is less than $1,000 per year;
- The Tax Commissioner determines that no withholding is required for the member;
- The member elects to pay taxes as part of a composite return; or
- The LLC is a publicly traded LLC.

The amount withheld for a member is reported in Column 7, Schedule KP, Form 58. The LLC must submit a payment with Form 58 for the total withholding reported on Schedule KP.

Composite Return

An LLC may file a composite income tax return and report and pay income taxes for nonresident members if there are one or more nonresident members who elect to be included on the composite return.[845] The electing nonresident member must be an individual or a pass-through entity member.[846] The composite tax rate is 2.90 percent in 2017.[847] The LLC must file the composite return on Form 58 and Schedule KP (col. 8) to Form 58.[848] A nonresident member may elect to be included as part of a composite return if the nonresident member's only income from North Dakota is from pass-through entities.[849] A nonresident member who files an individual income tax return receives a credit for state taxes paid on the composite return.[850]

The LLC must report the distributive share of income or loss of nonresident members on Schedule A of Form 58. The income or loss is limited to the income or loss from North Dakota sources. An LLC must use Form 37-S or Form 37 if the member is an individual. The LLC must use Form 38 if the member is an estate or a trust. The LLC must use Form 40 for a Subchapter C corporation and Form 60 for a Subchapter S corporation.

Estimated Taxes

An LLC may, but is not required to, make estimated payments of income taxes expected to be due on Form 58. The estimated payments are made using the payment voucher on Form 58-ES, Partnership Estimated Tax Payment.

---

[844] N.D. Cent. Code § 57-38-31.1.3.c.

[845] N.D. Cent. Code § 57-38-31.1; Notice, "Passthrough entity withholding and composite filing for the 2006 tax year," North Dakota Office of State Tax Commissioner (Dec. 4, 2006).

[846] S.B. 2104, Laws 2013.

[847] Instructions to Form 58.

[848] Instructions to Form 58.

[849] N.D. Cent. Code § 57-38-31.1.2.b.

[850] N.D. Cent. Code § 57-38-31.1.2.c.

.06 Filing Fees

North Dakota imposes the following filing fees on LLCs:[851]

Articles of organization	$135
Certificate of authority for foreign LLC	$135
Annual report	$ 50

¶2337 OHIO

Ohio enacted laws authorizing LLCs effective July 1, 1994.[852]

.01 State Tax Classification

Ohio classifies an LLC in the same manner as the LLC is classified for federal tax purposes. An LLC that is classified as a corporation for federal tax purposes is classified as a corporation for state tax purposes.[853] Single-member LLCs may be formed in Ohio effective November 21, 1997.[854]

Ohio issued an information release in response to the federal check-the-box regulations. For Ohio corporate income tax purposes, an LLC that does business in Ohio and that defaults or makes the federal election to be treated as a partnership will generally not be taxed as a corporation.[855] If an LLC chooses to be taxed as a corporation for federal income tax purposes, the LLC will be subject to the Ohio franchise tax for taxable years ending after September 28, 1997.[856]

.02 Taxation of LLC and Members

Income, gains, losses, deductions, and credits pass through to the members and are taxed to them individually.

An LLC must pay the commercial activity tax (CAT).[857] The CAT is an annual tax imposed on the privilege of doing business in Ohio, measured by gross receipts from business activities in Ohio. LLCs with annual taxable gross receipts of $150,000 or less are not subject to the CAT. LLCs with annual taxable gross receipts of more than $150,000 must pay an amount that corresponds with their overall commercial activ-

---

[851] N.D. Cent. Code § 10-32-150.

[852] H.B. 170, 1994 Ohio Laws; Ohio Rev. Code Ann. §§ 1705.01 to 1705.58.

[853] Ohio Rev. Code Ann. § 5733.01(E).

[854] H.B. 170, 1997 Ohio Laws; Ohio Rev. Code Ann. §§ 1705.01 to 1705.58.

[855] Ohio Information Release, Income Tax Audit Div., Ohio Dept. of Taxn. (Aug. 19, 1997).

[856] Id. (citing Ohio Rev. Code Ann. § 5733.01(E), (F), which states that if a for-profit entity is taxed as a corporation for federal income tax purposes, then the entity is taxed as a corporation for Ohio franchise tax purposes).

[857] Ohio R.C. § 5751.01(A) which, defines a "person" subject to tax to include an LLC.

ity. The minimum tax for the current year is based on the LLC's previous calendar year's taxable gross receipts. The annual minimum tax for 2017 is as follows:[858]

Taxable Gross Receipts	Annual Minimum Tax	CAT
Less than $150,000	$0	
$150,000 to $1 million or less	$150	No Additional Tax
More than $1 million but less than or equal to $2 million	$800	0.26% × (Taxable Gross Receipts − $1 million)
More than $2 million but less than or equal to $4 million	$2,100	0.26% × (Taxable Gross Receipts − $1 million)
More than $4 million	$2,600	0.26% × (Taxable Gross Receipts − $1 million)

For tax periods beginning on January 1, 2013 and thereafter, an LLC that pays tax on a quarterly basis may exclude the first $1 million of taxable gross receipts on its first quarter return and carry forward any unused portion of the exclusion amount to subsequent quarters within the same calendar year.[859]

An LLC must withhold taxes on the "adjusted qualifying amounts" payable to nonresident members.[860] The LLC is not required to withhold if the LLC files a composite tax return for nonresident members and pays estimated taxes on a quarterly basis. The composite tax rate is 4.997 percent for 2017.[861]

.03 Tax Returns

An LLC must register to pay the CAT tax using Form CAT 1, Commercial Activity Registration Form, CAT 12, Annual, and CAT Q, Quarterly.

An LLC must file the following forms to report the taxes payable by a nonresident member:

- Form IT 4708, Pass-Through Entity Composite Income Tax Return, on behalf of all equity investors who are not full-year Ohio resident taxpayers (individuals, estates and trusts).[862] The composite tax rate before certain credits and grants is 4.997 percent in 2017.[863] The LLC must make an annual election to

---

[858] Ohio Department of Taxation, Tables CAT-1 & CAT-2 No. 72 & 73 (Oct. 5, 2017).

[859] Ohio Department of Revenue Information Release CAT 2013-01, Commercial Activity Tax: Change to the Million Dollar Exclusion (Feb. 2013).

[860] Ohio R.C. § 5741.231.

[861] *See* Instructions to Form IT 4708ES.

[862] Ohio R.C. § § 5747.01(I) and (N), 5747.08(D); Ohio Tax Comm'r R. 5703-7-03.

[863] Ohio R.C. § 5747.08; Instructions to Form IT Form 4708.

file a composite return.[864] A nonresident member is not required to file an Ohio income tax return if the member is included on a composite return, and the member's only source of Ohio income is a distributive share of income from one or more LLCs. The nonresident member in such case cannot file an Ohio Form IT-1040 and may not receive a refundable pass-through entity credit for any part of the tax paid on the composite return.[865] A nonresident member having other Ohio source income may be included on the composite return, but must also file an Ohio income tax return to report all other Ohio source income. The nonresident member in such case may receive a refundable pass-through entity credit for the share of the tax paid by the LLC on behalf of the member.[866]

- Form IT 4708ES, Ohio Estimated Income Tax Payment Coupon for Investors in Pass-Through Entities. The LLC must make composite payments for nonresident members on a quarterly basis.

- Form IT 1140, Pass-Through Entity and Trust Withholding Tax Return. An LLC is not required to file this form if it files the composite return on Form IT 4708.[867]

- IT 1140ES, Estimated Ohio Withholding Tax and Entity Tax Payment for Pass-through Entities and Trusts. An LLC may use this form to make estimated payments of the withholding tax. The LLC may elect to use some or all of the estimated withholding tax payments to satisfy the composite tax due on Form IT 1140ES.

- Voluntary disclosure letter. The Ohio Department of Taxation offers a Voluntary Disclosure Program that allows LLCs and other pass-through entities to resolve potential issues regarding the amount of Ohio source income. By voluntarily disclosing potential tax liability, the LLC may avoid the penalties and other tax consequences associated with a nexus investigation. An LLC is eligible for the program if it enters into a pass-through entity tax agreement prior to any contact from the Ohio Department of Taxation. The LLC must send the Ohio Department of Taxation a letter explaining in detail the LLC's activities in Ohio and how long the activities were conducted in Ohio.[868]

Investors included in the annual composite return may not claim personal exemptions or credits, may not claim nonbusiness credits, and must pay the highest tax rate of 4.997 percent in 2017.[869] If a member is included on the composite return, then the investor is not a "qualifying investor," and the LLC is not subject to the withholding tax or the entity tax on the distributive share of income passing through to such investor.[870]

---

[864] Ohio R.C. § 5747.08(D).

[865] Release, Ohio Department of Taxation (Aug. 10, 2011).

[866] Release, Ohio Department of Taxation (Aug. 10, 2011).

[867] *See* instructions to Form IT 1140.

[868] http://www.tax.ohio.gov/pass_through_entities/voluntary_disclosure_guidelines.aspx

[869] Instructions to Form IT 4708ES.

[870] Instructions to Form IT 4708.

The LLC must make estimated composite tax payments on Form IT 4708ES if the annual composite tax liability after nonrefundable credits is more than $500.

An LLC that has only nonresident individuals and nonresident trusts may elect to file either Form IT 1140 or Form IT 4708. An LLC that has other equity investors must generally file Form IT 1140 and may file Form IT 4708.[871]

.04 Filing Fees

Ohio imposes the following filing fees on LLCs:[872]

Articles of organization	$125
Certificate of registration of foreign LLC	$125
Annual fees	$ 0

¶ 2338 OKLAHOMA

Oklahoma enacted the Oklahoma Limited Liability Company Act effective September 1, 1992.[873]

.01 State Tax Classification

Oklahoma classifies an LLC in the same manner that the LLC is classified for federal tax purposes. A domestic LLC and a foreign LLC are taxed for all purposes as domestic partnerships and foreign partnerships under title 68 of the Oklahoma Statutes.[874] Single-member LLCs are disregarded as separate entities under Oklahoma law.

.02 Taxation of LLC

On November 6, 2012, Oklahoma voters approved Question 766, which resulted in the repeal of Oklahoma's Business Activity Tax on LLCs and other entities, and the reinstatement of Oklahoma's franchise tax on corporations for tax years beginning on or after January 1, 2013. There is no franchise tax or other entity tax on LLCs that are classified as partnerships or disregarded entities.

---

[871] Instructions to Form IT 1140.

[872] Ohio Rev. Code Ann. § 111.16(F).

[873] Okla. Stat. Ann. tit. 18, § § 2000-2060.

[874] Okla. Stat. Ann. tit. 68, § 202(j).

.03 Taxation of Members

Members are taxed on their distributive shares of income.[875] A member's distributive share of income is the same as under federal law.[876] Nonresident members are subject to tax if gross income from Oklahoma sources is more than $1,000. Resident and nonresident members are not allowed credits for income taxes paid to other jurisdictions on LLC income.[877]

.04 Tax Returns

LLCs that are classified as partnerships for federal tax purposes must file returns each year on Form 514, Partnership Return of Income.[878] An LLC that has elected not to file a partnership income tax return under Code Sec. 761 is not required to file an Oklahoma return.[879] The partnership return sets forth the taxable income and the adjustments to arrive at Oklahoma income. The return includes a schedule showing the distributions to members of the various items of income as set forth on the federal return and the adjustments required by applicable Oklahoma tax laws. The return must be signed by one of the members.[880]

The Oklahoma distributive share of LLC income is the same portion as that reported for federal income tax purposes. OTC Form 514 is used to report that income.[881]

An LLC must file an amended return if it later becomes aware of any changes made to income, deductions, credits, or loss or if the federal return is corrected due to an Internal Revenue Service audit. In such case, the LLC must file OTC Form 514, labeled "Amended" at the top of page 1. The LLC must attach to the Oklahoma amended return a copy of the federal amended Form 1065 or a copy of the federal audit changes. The LLC must then give a corrected Schedule K-1 to each member, reflecting Oklahoma distributable income as adjusted.[882]

An LLC that registers with the Oklahoma Secretary of State must file an income tax return in the same manner as required under the Internal Revenue Code. All rulings issued by the Internal Revenue Service are binding in regard to the filing of tax returns and the reporting of income.[883] A domestic LLC is treated in the same manner as a domestic partnership, and a foreign LLC is treated and taxed in the same

---

[875] Okla. Stat. Ann. tit. 68, § 2363.

[876] Id.

[877] Okla. Admin. R. 710:50-19-1(3).

[878] Okla. Stat. Ann. tit. 68, § 2368.D.

[879] Id.

[880] Id.

[881] Okla. Admin. R. 710:50-19-1.

[882] Okla. Admin. R. 710:50-19-2.

[883] Okla. Admin. R. 710:50-20-1(a).

manner as a foreign partnership if the LLC is classified as a partnership for federal tax purposes.[884]

The LLC must report the income to Oklahoma on the same form as prescribed under federal regulations and in the manner provided in the Oklahoma Statutes.[885] An LLC's operations carried on within and outside the state of Oklahoma must be the same as for corporations, subchapter S corporations, partnerships, and other organizations that are covered under Public Law 86-272. The activities described in title 18, section 2049 of the Oklahoma Statutes are not considered in determining the transaction of business by an LLC for Oklahoma income tax purposes.[886]

The LLC must attach a copy of federal Form 1065 and all Schedules K-1 to Form 514.

All LLCs having Oklahoma source income must file their returns on Form 514. Each member having Oklahoma source income sufficient to make the return must also make a return reporting the distributive share.

The LLC must file the partnership return with the Oklahoma Tax Commission, P.O. Box 26800, Oklahoma City, OK 73126-0800. The return must be filed on or before the 15th day of the fourth month following the close of the tax year. The LLC may obtain an extension of time to file the return for a period of up to six months. The LLC may use the federal extension of time and attach it to the Oklahoma tax return.

The LLC must use the same taxable year and methods of accounting for state tax purposes as used for federal income tax purposes.

Every LLC making payments of salaries, wages, premiums, annuities, or other periodic gains, profits, or income of $750 or more during the tax year to any taxpayer must complete a report. The report must be made on Forms 500 and 501 on or before February 15 of the following calendar year. The LLC may file Form 504, Application for Extension of Time to File Oklahoma Income Tax Return.

A foreign LLC must file a partnership return in Oklahoma if it has income from sources in Oklahoma or carries on a business in Oklahoma. The Oklahoma statute sets forth the activities of a foreign LLC that do not constitute transacting business within Oklahoma for purposes of the state tax laws.[887]

All resident members must file individual income tax returns in Oklahoma if they are required to file federal individual income tax returns. All nonresident members who have gross income of $1,000 or more must file Oklahoma returns even though their net income may actually be a loss.[888]

.05 Apportionment of Income

The LLC must apportion income to sources within and outside the state of Oklahoma using a three-factor formula unless its income is from real and tangible

---

[884] *Id.*

[885] Okla. Admin. R. 710:50-20-1(b); *see* Okla. Stat. Ann. tit. 68, § 2385.

[886] Okla. Stat. Ann. tit. 68, § 2049(c); Okla. Admin. R. 710:50-20-1(c).

[887] Okla. Stat. Ann. tit. 18, § 2049.

[888] Okla. Admin. R. 710:50-19-1(2).

personal property, such as rents, oil and mining production, and gains or losses from the sale of such property. In that case, the income or loss must be allocated in accordance with the situs of such property. The member's distributive share of Oklahoma income or loss must be in the same proportion as the member's distributive share of income or loss shown on the federal partnership return.[889]

.06 Nonresident Members

Withholding Taxes

An LLC must withhold income taxes at the rate of five percent of the Oklahoma share of income that the LLC distributes to each nonresident member.[890] The withheld amounts are due on or before April 30, July 31, October 31, and January 31 of the succeeding calendar year. The LLC must file a return with each payment to the Oklahoma Tax Commission.[891] The withheld taxes are credited against the taxes payable by the nonresident member on his or her distributive share of Oklahoma income.[892]

An LLC must file Form WTP10003, Oklahoma Nonresident Distributed Income Withholding Tax Annual Return (formerly Form OW-9-C) to report and pay the withholding taxes. The LLC must file the form on or before the due date including extensions, of the LLC's income tax return. The LLC must provide the nonresident members with Form 500-B showing their respective amount of income and tax withheld. Copies of Form 500-Bs, along with the cover Form 501, must be sent to the Oklahoma Tax Commission. Each nonresident member must enclose a copy of the Form 500-B to his or her Oklahoma income tax return as verification for this withholding.

Any nonresident member from whom an amount is withheld is entitled to a credit for the amount withheld and should claim the credit on their Oklahoma income tax return. If the amount withheld is greater than the tax due, the nonresident member will be entitled to a refund of the amount of the overpayment.

A disregarded LLC is not required to withhold taxes.

Agreement to Pay Taxes

An LLC is not required to withhold taxes on distributions to a nonresident member if the LLC files an affidavit with the Tax Commission on behalf of the nonresident member. The member must sign and complete the affidavit on Form OW-15, Nonresident Member Withholding Exemption Affidavit. The member must

---

[889] Id.

[890] Okla. Stat. Ann. tit. 68, §§ 2385.29, 2385.30, 2385.31. Okla. Adm. Code §§ 710:90-3-11, 710:50-3-54; Form 500-B, 4Information Return Record of Nonresident Member.

[891] Okla. Stat. Ann. tit. 68, § 2385.30; Okla. Adm. Code 710:50-3-54, 710:90-3-11, 710:90-7-3, Oklahoma Tax Commission, effective June 25, 2004.

[892] Okla. Stat. Ann. tit. 68, § 2385.30 C; Okla. Admin. R. 710:90-3-11.

agree in the affidavit to be subject to the personal jurisdiction of the Tax Commission in Oklahoma courts for the purpose of determining and collecting any Oklahoma taxes, including estimated tax payments, interest, and penalties.[893] The Tax Commission may revoke an exemption at any time it determines that the nonresident member is not abiding by the terms of the affidavit.[894]

Composite Returns

An LLC is not required to withhold taxes on distributions to a nonresident member included in a composite return. The inclusion of the member's income in the composite return satisfies the requirement contained in the affidavit.[895]

An Oklahoma LLC may elect to file a composite return on behalf of electing nonresident members by completing Form 514-PT, Partnership Composite Income Tax Supplement, and Form 514, Part 1, Tax Computation for Nonresident Composite Filers Only.[896] The LLC computes the tax liability of nonresident members on the composite return, and pays the tax liability with the partnership return. The composite tax rates are graduated rates up to 6.5 percent in 2017.[897]

A nonresident member may be included in the composite return unless the member has income from Oklahoma sources other than the LLC, or the member is an S corporation or partnership. Nonresident members included in a composite return may not have other Oklahoma income and may not file separate Oklahoma income tax returns.[898] Effective for tax years beginning on or after January 1, 2013, an LLC may file a composite return on behalf of nonresident members who are who are individuals, partnerships, trusts, S corporations and C corporations.[899]

The LLC must make estimated tax payments on behalf of the nonresident members included in the composite return under the LLC's name and federal identification of number.

.07 Sales and Use Taxes, Other Taxes

LLCs are subject to sales and use taxes; to gasoline, cigarette, and tobacco products taxes; and to severance, tourism promotion, motor vehicle, aircraft excise, real estate mortgage, and documentary stamp taxes effective September 1, 1993.[900] LLCs are exempt from franchise taxes.

---

[893] Okla. Stat. Ann. tit. 68, § 2385.30 F; Okla. Admin. R. 710:90-3-11.

[894] Okla. Stat. Ann. tit. 68, § 2385.30 F.

[895] Okla. Admin. R. 710:90-3-11.

[896] Okla. Admin. R. 710:50-19-1.

[897] *See* Table in the Instructions to Form 514-PT: Partnership Composite Income Tax Supplement Instructions (Rule 710:50-19-1).

[898] Okla. Admin. R. 710:50-19-1(4).

[899] Okla. Admin. R. 710:50-19-1.

[900] S.B. 527, 1993 Okla. Sess. Laws.

.08 Filing Fees

Oklahoma imposes the following filing fees on LLCs:[901]

Articles of organization	$100
Foreign LLC registration application	$300
Limited Liability Companies Annual Certificate	$ 25

¶ 2339 OREGON

Oregon enacted the Oregon Limited Liability Company Act effective January 1, 1994.[902]

.01 State Tax Classification

Oregon classifies an LLC in the same manner that the LLC is classified for federal tax purposes.[903] The same rule applies to foreign LLCs qualified to do business in Oregon. A member of a foreign or domestic LLC is treated for Oregon tax purposes in the same manner as the member is treated for federal income tax purposes.[904] Single-member LLCs are allowed effective October 4, 1997.[905]

Before 1997, Oregon classified LLCs as partnerships unless otherwise classified under federal law. Single-member LLCs were not permitted.

.02 Taxation of LLC and Members

Oregon law follows federal partnership law effective April 15, 1995. An LLC that is classified as a partnership for federal tax purposes is not subject to tax,[906] except for a $150 annual minimum tax,[907] and a $100 annual report fee.

Members of the LLC are taxed on their distributive shares of income.[908] The income of the LLC is determined under federal law, subject to certain modifications.[909] Each item of income, gain, loss, credit, and deduction has the same character

---

[901] Okla. Stat. Ann. tit. 18, § 2055.

[902] S.B. 285, ch. 173, 1993 Or. Laws; Or. Rev. Stat. §§ 63.001 to 63.990.

[903] Or. Rev. Stat. § 63.810.

[904] *Id.*

[905] Or. Rev. Stat. § 63.001(13).

[906] Or. Rev. Stat. § 314.712.

[907] Oregon Measure 67, Section 3 (2010).

[908] *Id.*

[909] *Id.*

as under federal law.[910] The members' distributive shares are the same as on the federal return.[911]

The Oregon Employment Division treats members of LLCs as employees for unemployment tax purposes. However, members are responsible for their own income taxes and withholdings.

.03 Tax Returns

An LLC must pay the $150 annual minimum tax on Form 65-V, Partnership Payment Voucher.[912] The payment is due by the 15th day of the third month after the end of the tax year.

An LLC that is classified as a partnership for federal tax purposes must file Form 65, Oregon Partnership Return of Income. All LLCs having income from sources in Oregon or having one or more Oregon resident members must file the partnership return.[913]

The LLC must attach the following information to the return in the following order:

- A list of members if the LLC has more than ten members at any time during the year.
- An apportionment schedule if the LLC has business activities both within and outside the state of Oregon or has members who are not Oregon residents during the year.
- An Oregon depreciation schedule on Form 150-101-025 if Oregon depreciation is different from federal depreciation.
- A schedule showing to whom all assets and liabilities were distributed if the return is the final return for the LLC.
- A copy of federal Form 1065, pages 1 through 4, and all supporting schedules.
- The federal Schedules K-1 if the LLC has fewer than 11 members during the year.

The LLC must file the return by the 15th day of the third month after the end of the LLC's tax year. The due date is March 15 for calendar year LLCs. The partnership tax return must be sent to the Oregon Department of Revenue, P.O. Box 14260, Salem, OR 97309-5060.

Members report their shares of modifications to federal LLC income on Form 40, 40N, or 40P. The Oregon individual income tax booklet lists the filing requirements for members' individual income tax returns. There are separate instructions for full-year resident members and part-year nonresident members. Nonresident members of an LLC may file individual nonresident returns or join together to file a multiple nonresident tax return.

---

[910] Or. Rev. Stat. § 314.714(1).

[911] Or. Rev. Stat. § 314.714(2).

[912] Oregon Measure 67, Section 3 (2010).

[913] Or. Rev. Stat. § 314.724.

The Oregon tax forms may be obtained from the Oregon Department of Revenue, P.O. Box 14999, Salem, OR 97309-0990.

.04 Nonresident Members

Composite Returns

An LLC doing business in or deriving income from sources within Oregon must file a composite tax return Form OR-OC, Oregon Composite Return, if requested by one or more electing members.[914] A member may elect to be included on a composite return if the member was not a resident of Oregon at any time during the tax year. The member must also make a separate election for each year.[915]

The composite tax return is due the 15th day of the fourth month after the close of the tax year of the majority of the electing members.[916] The LLC must pay estimated tax payments if the total Oregon tax due for any electing member is expected to be $1,000 or more. The LLC must calculate the tax for each electing member based on the member's filing status. The maximum composite tax rate is 9.9 percent in 2017. The tax is imposed on the difference between the member's share of the LLC's Oregon-source distributive income for the tax year and the member's self-employment tax deduction. The LLC must report on the Oregon composite nonresident return the tax computed for each electing member and total amounts for all electing members.[917]

The LLC may be required to make quarterly estimated tax payments for nonresident members.[918]

Withholding Taxes

An LLC with Oregon-source distributive income, and one or more nonresident members that have no other Oregon-source income, must withhold tax on behalf of the member.[919] The withholding tax rate in 2017 is 9.9 percent of each member's share of Oregon-source distributive income for the tax year.[920] The withholding tax rate for corporate members is 6.6 percent on the first $1 million of allocable income and 7.6 percent on the amount over $1 million of allocable income. These amounts are then multiplied by 25 percent in determining the quarterly withholding amount.[921] The LLC must file, on or before the last day of the second month following the close of the

---

[914] Or. Admin. R. 150-314.775, 150-314.778.

[915] Or. Admin. R. 150-314.775(2).

[916] Or. Rev. Stat. § 314.385; Or. Admin. R. 150-314.778(3)(a).

[917] Or. Admin. R. 150-314.778(1).

[918] Or. Admin. R. 150-778(5).

[919] Or. Admin. R. 150-314.781(1).

[920] Or. Admin. R. 150-314.781(4).

[921] Or. Admin. R. 150-314.778(4)(a)(ii).

tax year, an annual withholding report on Form OR-19 containing the withheld tax and a calculation of the amount of required withholdings.[922] The LLC must pay the withheld amounts on a quarterly basis, using Form TPV-19, Payment of Tax Withheld for Nonresidents.[923] The LLC must report the withholding amounts to members on Form OR-19, Report of Nonresident Owner Tax Withheld.[924]

No withholding is required if:[925]

- the member elects to be included on a composite return;
- the member's share of Oregon-source distributive income from the LLC is less than $1,000;
- the member made estimated tax payments for the prior tax year based on the member's share of Oregon source distributive income from the LLC and continues to make estimated tax payments for the current tax year; or
- the member files a signed affidavit (Form 150-101-175, Oregon Affidavit for a Nonresident Owner in a Pass-through Entity) with the Department stating that the member agrees to file the member's Oregon income or excise tax return and make timely payments of all taxes imposed with respect to the member's share of the Oregon income of the LLC, and that the member is subject to the jurisdiction of the State of Oregon for purposes of collection of unpaid income tax, penalties, and interest; or
- the LLC is a publicly traded partnership that files annual information returns.

Withholding is required for owners of single-member LLCs if the owner is a nonresident individual or C corporation.[926]

.05 Filing Fees

Oregon imposes the following filing fees on LLCs:[927]

Articles of organization	$100
Foreign LLC registration application	$275
Domestic annual report	$100
Foreign LLC annual report	$275

¶ 2340 PENNSYLVANIA

Pennsylvania enacted laws authorizing formation of LLCs effective February 5, 1995.[928]

---

[922] Or. Admin. R. 150-314.784(5).

[923] Or. Admin. R. 150-314.781(4)(a), (b).

[924] *See* Or. Admin. R. 150.314.784(4).

[925] Or. Admin. R. 150-314.784(1).

[926] Instructions to Form OR-19.

[927] Or. Rev. Stat. § 63.007.

[928] Act 106 (S.B. 1059), 1994 Pa. Laws; 15 Pa. Cons. Stat. Ann. § § 8901-8998.

.01 State Tax Classification

Pennsylvania classifies an LLC as follows:[929]

- The LLC is classified in the same manner that the LLC is classified for federal tax purposes for purposes of the corporate net income tax.[930] Therefore, an LLC that is classified as a partnership for federal tax purposes is not subject to the corporate net income tax for tax years after 1997.[931] The same rule applies to single-member disregarded entities.

- An LLC is classified under Pennsylvania law in the same manner that the LLC is classified under federal law for purposes of the Pennsylvania personal income tax.[932] Therefore, an LLC that is classified as a partnership for federal tax purposes is also classified as a partnership for state tax purposes. Each member is taxed on his or her distributed share of income of the LLC.[933]

.02 Taxation of LLC

Income Taxes

An LLC is not subject to Pennsylvania income taxes.[934]

Capital Stock and Foreign Franchise Tax

Pennsylvania imposed a Capital Stock/Foreign Franchise tax on LLCs prior to 2016. The Capital Stock/Foreign Franchise tax was eliminated for tax years beginning on or after January 1, 2016.[935]

Corporate Tax

Pennsylvania exempts LLCs from the state's corporate net income tax. An LLC that is classified as a partnership or disregarded entity for federal tax purposes is not

---

[929] Corp. Tax Opinion: Subjectivity of Limited Liability Companies, Pennsylvania Department of Revenue (Feb. 2, 2000).

[930] 72 Pa. Cons. Stat. Ann. § 7401 (definition of corporation).

[931] Corp. Tax Opinion: Subjectivity of Limited Liability Companies, Pennsylvania Department of Revenue (Feb. 2, 2000).

[932] 72 Pa. Cons. Stat. Ann. § 7301(d.1) and (n.0).

[933] Corp. Tax Opinion: Subjectivity of Limited Liability Companies, Pennsylvania Department of Revenue (Feb. 2, 2000).

[934] 72 Pa. Cons. Stat. Ann. § 7306.

[935] Pa. Dept. of Rev., Capital Stock and Foreign Franchise Taxes, http://www.revenue.pa.gov/GeneralTaxInformation/Tax%20Types%20and%20Information/Corporation%20Taxes/CapitalStock-ForeignFranchise/Pages/default.aspx.

subject to the corporate net income taxes. An LLC is subject to the corporate net income taxes only if it is classified as a corporation for federal tax purposes.[936]

Local Taxes

A political subdivision of Pennsylvania may impose any applicable taxes or license fees on LLCs to the extent authorized pursuant to the Local Tax Enabling Act.[937]

.03 Taxation of Members

Members of an LLC are taxed in their distributive shares of income attributable to Pennsylvania sources,[938] whether or not distributed.[939] The LLC must place all items of LLC income, gains, losses, expenses, costs, and liabilities for the taxable year in one of the following seven classes:

1. Net income or loss from operations of a business, profession, or farm
2. Pennsylvania taxable interest derived from obligations that are not statutorily free from taxation in Pennsylvania
3. Pennsylvania taxable dividends
4. Net gain or loss from the sale, exchange, or disposition of property
5. Net income or loss from rents, royalties, patents, and copyrights
6. Estate and trust income received from an estate or trust
7. Gambling and lottery winnings

.04 Nonresident Members

Withholding Tax

An LLC must withhold Pennsylvania personal income taxes on its income from sources within Pennsylvania that is allocable to nonresident members.[940] The withholding tax rate is 3.07 percent in 2017 on the Pennsylvania income allocable to nonresident members.[941]

---

[936] *See* Act of June 7, 1997, No. 1997-7 (H.B. 134), 1997 Pa. Laws, amending Act of Mar. 4, 1971, Pub. L. 6, No. 2, 1971 Pa. Laws.

[937] Act of Dec. 31, 1965, Pub. L. 1257, 1965 Pa. Laws.

[938] 72 Pa. Cons. Stat. Ann. §7301(d.1) and (n.0); Pa. Dept. of Rev. Reg. 107.2.

[939] 72 Pa. Cons. Stat. Ann. §7306.

[940] 72 P.S. §7324; Form REV-413 P/S, Instructions for Withholding PA Personal Income Tax From Nonresident Members by Partnerships and PA S Corporations; Act 22 of 1991; Corp. Tax Opinion: Subjectivity of Limited Liability Companies, Pennsylvania Department of Revenue (Feb. 2, 2000), *citing* 72 Pa. Cons. Stat. Ann. §7324.

[941] 72 Pa. Cons. Stat. Ann. §7324.1; REV-414(P/S), PA Nonresident Withholding Tax Worksheet for Partnerships and PA S Corporations.

An LLC must withhold using the procedure set forth in Form REV-413 (P/S), Instructions for Withholding PA Personal Income Tax from Nonresident Members by Partnerships and PA S Corporations. These instructions include the following:

- The LLC must use the REV-414 (P/S), PA Nonresident Tax Withholding Worksheet for Partnerships and PA S Corporations, to determine the nonresident quarterly withholding amount.
- The LLC must use the PA-40ES (P/S) pre-printed form from the department or PA-40ESR (F/C), Declaration of Estimated or Estimated Withholding Tax for Fiduciaries & Partnerships, tax forms to pay the 2017 nonresident quarterly withholding.
- The LLC must use Part A and Part B of the REV-414(P/S), PA Nonresident Tax Withholding Worksheet for Partnerships and PA S Corporations, to compute the correct amount of nonresident quarterly withholding to pay.
- The LLC must use Part C to keep a record of nonresident quarterly withholding payments made and the amount of remaining balance of nonresident quarterly withholding due when filing the PA-20S/PA-65 Information Return.
- The LLC must use the PA-40ES (P/S) or PA-40ESR (F/C) forms for properly paying the nonresident quarterly withholding.
- If the LLC does not receive its preprinted Forms PA-40ES (P/S) forms or the forms are damaged, the LLC must use the PA-40ESR (F/C) form. Failure to receive department-provided forms does not relieve a partnership or PA S corporation from filing and paying the tax.

Composite Return

An LLC may file a composite return for nonresident members by filing Form PA-40 NRC, Nonresident Consolidated Income Tax Return. The composite tax rate is 3.07 percent in 2018.[942] A member may be included in a composite filing if (i) the member elects to be included in the composite filing, (ii) the member is an individual, (iii) the member is not a partner, shareholder or owner in another entity, (iv) there is more than one member who elects to be included in the composite filing, and (v) the member does not have income from other State sources.[943]

If the tax of the nonresident members exceeds the nonresident withholding tax payments, the LLC must pay the deficiency by the date prescribed for filing the PA-40 NRC LLC. The LLC must make the final/catch-up payment with the PA-40 NRC or with an extension request.[944]

An LLC that makes a composite filing is still required to file the PA-20S/PA-65 Information Return and issue PA-20S/PA-65 Schedules RK and NRK to its members.[945]

---

[942] PA-40 NRC Nonresident Consolidated Income Tax Return (08-15).

[943] Instructions to Form PA-40 NRC.

[944] Instructions to Form PA-40 NRC.

[945] Instructions to Form PA-40 NRC.

.05 Tax Returns

An LLC that is classified as a partnership or S corporation must file Form PA-20S/PA-65, PA S Corporation/Partnership Information Return, and Form PA-65 Corp, Directory of Corporate Partners.[946] The LLC must submit with the PA-20S/PA-65 (i) a complete copy of its federal income tax return, including all schedules, statements, federal Form 1065 Schedule(s) K-1; (ii) PA-20S/PA-65 Schedule(s) RK-1 and/or NRK-1 received as an owner in other pass-through entities such as a partnership, PA S corporation or LLC; (iii) copies of the PA-20S/PA-65 Schedule RK-1 that it provides to resident partners; and (iv) copies of the PA-20S/PA-65 Schedule NRK-1 that it provides to nonresident partners. If the LLC and has already forwarded a complete copy of its federal return to the Bureau of Corporation Taxes with the RCT-101, PA Corporate Tax Report, it should not attach another copy to Form PA-20S/PA-65.

Members of an LLC must file Form PA-40 to report their allocable shares of income that flows through to them from the LLC, whether the LLC is classified as a partnership or disregarded entity.[947]

The LLC must provide Form PA Schedule RK-1 to each resident partner and Form PA Schedule NRK-1 to each nonresident member. The LLC must apportion allocated income in accordance with the instructions set forth on the forms. Qualifying nonresident members may file a consolidated or group return to apportion and allocate their Pennsylvania taxable income. The LLC must use Form PA-40NRC for the consolidated group return.

.06 Reorganizations

Domestic and foreign LLCs are treated as corporations in applying the reorganization provisions of Pennsylvania law.[948]

.07 Filing Fees

Pennsylvania imposes the following filing fees on domestic and foreign LLCs:[949]

Certificate of organization	$125
Foreign LLC registration application	$250

---

[946] 72 P.S § 7335(c); Pa. Dept. of Rev. Reg. § 107.6.

[947] Corp. Tax Opinion: Subjectivity of Limited Liability Companies, Pennsylvania Department of Revenue (Feb. 2, 2000).

[948] Tax Reform Code of 1971, § 303(a).

[949] 15 Pa. Cons. Stat. Ann. § 153.

¶ 2341 RHODE ISLAND

Rhode Island enacted the Rhode Island Limited Liability Company Act on September 19, 1992.[950]

.01 State Tax Classification

Rhode Island classifies an LLC in the same manner that the LLC is classified for federal tax purposes.[951]

.02 Taxation of LLC and Members

An LLC is not subject to the Rhode Island personal income tax.[952] An LLC that is classified as a partnership or sole proprietorship for federal tax purposes must pay an annual fee of $400.[953] An LLC that is classified as a corporation for federal tax purposes must pay the regular corporate taxes.[954]

Members in a domestic or foreign LLC that is classified as a partnership for federal tax purposes are subject to state income taxes on their distributive shares. The member must file a Rhode Island income tax return. The member must include in gross income that portion of the LLC's Rhode Island income allocable to the member.[955]

.03 Tax Returns

An LLC that is classified as a partnership or disregarded entity must file Form RI-1065, Rhode Island Partnership Income Return, to pay the $450 annual minimum franchise tax and the five percent jobs growth tax on certain performance-based compensation.[956] For all filers except for calendar year and non-June 30 fiscal year end single-member LLC filers, Form RI-1065 is due on or before the 15th day of the third month following the close of the taxable year. For calendar year and non-June 30 fiscal year end single-member LLC filers, Form RI-1065 is due on or before the 15th day of the fourth month following the close of the taxable year.[957]

An LLC that is classified as C corporation must file Form RI-1120C. An LLC that is classified as an S corporation must file Form RI-1120S. An LLC that is classified as

---

[950] S.B. 2413, 1992 R.I. Pub. Laws; R.I. Gen. Laws §§ 7-16-1 to 7-16-75.

[951] R.I. Gen. Laws § 7-16-73(b).

[952] R.I. Gen. Laws § 44-30-1(b).

[953] R.I. Gen. Laws § 7-16-67(b)(2); Reg. § CT 98-14, R.I. Div. of Taxn., effective May 1, 1998.

[954] R.I. Gen. Laws § 7-16-67(b)(1); Reg. § CT 98-14, R.I. Div. of Taxn., effective May 1, 1998.

[955] R.I. Gen. Laws § 7-16-73(c)(1); Reg. § CT 98-14, R.I. Div. of Taxn.

[956] R.I. Gen. Laws § 7-16-67.

[957] Instructions to Form RI-1065.

disregarded entity must obtain a federal employer identification number in order to file a Rhode Island return.[958]

Each member must include on the member's individual tax return the member's distributive share of LLC net income for the tax year, whether or not distributed. The return must be filed on or before the 15th day of the third month following the close of the tax year. The return must be mailed to the Division of Taxation, One Capital Hill, Providence, RI 02908-5801. A copy of the federal return for the fiscal year must be attached to the annual return.[959]

Any member of a domestic or foreign LLC that is classified as a partnership or sole proprietorship must include in Rhode Island gross income that portion of the member's share of the LLC's Rhode Island gross income.[960]

The tax year for the LLC must be the same as the federal tax year.

The LLC must report to the Rhode Island Division of Taxation any changes or corrections in the federal taxable income within 90 days after a final determination is made. An LLC filing an amended federal income tax return must also file an amended Rhode Island return within 90 days thereafter.

An LLC may obtain an extension of time to file the tax return by filing Form RI-8736, Application for Automatic Extension of Time to File R.I. Partnership or R.I. Fiduciary Income Tax Return. The LLC must file Form RI-8800, Application for Additional Extension of Time to File R.I. Partnership or R.I. Fiduciary Income Tax Return, in order to obtain an additional extension of time.

.04 Nonresident Members

Withholding

An LLC that is classified as a partnership must withhold income taxes on the allocable share of Rhode Island income for nonresident members.[961] The withholding tax rate is 5.99 percent for individual members in 2017 and seven percent for C corporation members.[962] The LLC may not take into account any losses that the member may realize from other sources or Rhode Island withholding taxes related to Rhode Island employment.

The LLC must file Form RI-1096PT to report the Rhode Island withholding taxes. The LLC is not required to file this form if it has no nonresident members. The LLC must send to the member Form RI-1096PT informing the member of the withholding taxes paid. The LLC must attach copies of all corresponding Form RI 1099-PTs to Form RI 1096-PT. If all the nonresident members have Rhode Island source income

---

[958] Reg. § CT 13-14, R.I. Div. of Tax'n.

[959] Reg. § CT 98-14, R.I. Div. of Taxn., effective May 1, 1998.

[960] Id.

[961] R.I. Gen. Laws § 44-11-2.2(b)(1); Bulletin on Pass-Through Entities to Nonresident Taxpayers; Form RI 1096-PT, Pass-Through Withholding Return and Transmittal.

[962] 2017 Form RI-1096PT, Pass-through Withholding Return and Transmittal.

less than $1,000, Form RI 1096-PT must be filed as a zero return. All of the corresponding RI 1099-PTs should show the nonresident members' withholding as zero.

The LLC must make estimated withholding tax payments using Form RI 1096PT-ES, Rhode Island Estimated Payment Coupons.

The member must file a Rhode Island income tax return (RI-1040 for individuals) even if the LLC makes withholding tax payments on behalf of that member. The member may claim as a credit any withholding taxes paid by the LLC.[963]

An LLC is not required to make withholding tax payment on behalf of a nonresident member if:

- The member's pro rata or distributive share of Rhode Island income is less than $1,000. In this case, the filing of the Form RI 1096-PT is still required, even though a payment is not required.

- The member elects to be included on a composite return on Form RI 1040C-NE (Rev. 10/04), Rhode Island Nonresident Income Tax Agreement/Election to be Included in a Composite Return.

- The LLC is a publicly traded LLC that has agreed to file an annual information return reporting the name, address, taxpayer identification number and other information requested by the tax administrator of each member with Rhode Island income in excess of $500.

- The LLC is not allowed to distribute funds due to federal or state restrictions.

Composite Return

The LLC is not required to withhold taxes or file the withholding tax returns for any nonresident members who elect to file a composite return. The composite return is filed using Form RI-1040C and 2017 Form RI-2210C, Underpayment of Estimated Tax by Composite Filers. The composite tax rate in 2017 is 5.99 percent.[964]

The LLC may file a composite tax return only for qualified electing members. A member is a qualified electing member if:[965]

- The member was a nonresident individual for the entire tax year;
- The member did not maintain a permanent place of abode in Rhode Island at any time during the tax year;
- The member (or his or her spouse, if a joint federal income tax return is or will be filed) did not have any income derived from or connected with Rhode Island sources other than from one or more pass-through entities;
- The member waives the right to claim any Rhode Island standard or itemized deductions and any Rhode Island personal exemption;

---

[963] Bulletin on Pass-through Entities to Nonresident Taxpayers, Rhode Island Department of Administration, Division of Taxation, http://www.tax.state.ri.us/help/.

[964] *See* Instructions to Form RI 1040C.

[965] Bulletin on Pass-through Entities to Nonresident Taxpayers, Rhode Island Department of Administration, Division of Taxation, Q&A-14, http://www.tax.state.ri.us/help/.

- The member has the same tax year as the other qualified electing nonresident members; and

- The member elects to be included on Form RI-1040C by submitting a completed Form RI 1040C-NE, Rhode Island Nonresident Income Tax Agreement/Election to be Included in a Composite Return, to the pass-through entity prior to the filing of Form RI-1040C by the pass-through entity.

Members who are included on a composite return are not required to file Form RI-1040NR. However, the Division of Taxation retains the right to require the filing of an individual Rhode Island income tax return by any of the members. An election to be included on the composite return will remain in effect unless the member revokes the agreement by providing notice to the LLC. The revocation does not take effect until the tax year following the date written notification was given to the LLC.[966]

Estimated Rhode Island composite income tax payments are required for a member included on Form RI-1040C if the aggregate tax liability derived from or connected with Rhode Island sources from the LLC is expected to be $250 or more for the tax year. For each installment, the LLC must aggregate the estimated Rhode Island composite income tax payments made on behalf of nonresident members and file one Form 1040-C ES, Estimated Payment Coupons.[967]

.05 Filing Fees

Rhode Island imposes the following filing fees on LLCs:[968]

Articles of organization	$150
Foreign LLC registration application	$150
Annual report	$ 50

¶ 2342 SOUTH CAROLINA

South Carolina enacted the Limited Liability Company Act effective June 16, 1994.[969] The law was replaced by the Uniform Limited Liability Company Act effective June 1, 1996.[970] The 1996 law incorporated several pro-taxpayer provisions consistent with IRS pronouncements since original enactment.

---

[966] Bulletin on Pass-through Entities to Nonresident Taxpayers, Rhode Island Department of Administration, Division of Taxation, Q&A-15.

[967] Bulletin on Pass-through Entities to Nonresident Taxpayers, Rhode Island Department of Administration, Division of Taxation, Q&A-16.

[968] R.I. Gen. Laws §7-16-65.

[969] H.B. 4283, 1994 S.C. Acts; S.C. Code Ann. §§33-44-101 to 33-44-1207.

[970] H.B. 4830, Rat. 396, 1996 S.C. Acts.

.01 State Tax Classification

South Carolina classifies an LLC in the same manner that the LLC is classified for federal tax purposes.[971] An LLC is included in the definition of a partnership or corporation for state tax purposes depending on its federal classification.[972]

Effective June 10, 1997, single-member LLCs that are disregarded for federal tax purposes (not classified as corporations) are disregarded for all South Carolina tax purposes.[973] If the LLC is owned by an individual, it will be treated as a sole proprietorship. The income from the LLC is reported on the individual's tax return. If the LLC is owned by a corporation (a 100 percent owned subsidiary), it will be treated as a division of the corporation. The income of the LLC is reported on the parent corporation's income tax return.[974] A single-member LLC that is classified as a corporation for federal tax purposes is classified as a corporation for South Carolina tax purposes.[975]

After the IRS issued the check-the-box regulations, the South Carolina Department of Revenue reaffirmed that it would follow the federal entity classification rules. The effective date of the federal rules for South Carolina was also January 1, 1997.[976]

LLCs are also exempt from classification as distinct legal entities and from choice of law issues, subject to certain exceptions.[977]

.02 Taxation of LLC and Members

An LLC that is classified as a partnership for federal income tax purposes is not subject to South Carolina taxes.[978]

Each member of an LLC must include the member's share of South Carolina LLC income on the member's individual income tax return.[979] All of the provisions of the Internal Revenue Code apply in determining the gross income, adjusted gross income, and taxable income of an LLC and its members, subject to modification provided by South Carolina and to allocation and apportionment for nonresident members.[980] The amount included must be based on the LLC income of the year ending within the member's tax year if the tax year of the LLC and the member are different.

---

[971] S.C. Code Ann. § 12-6-630.

[972] S.C. Code Ann. § 12-2-25(A).

[973] S.C. Code Ann. § 12-2-25(B).

[974] Rev. Rul. No. 98-11, S.C. Dept. of Rev. (May 6, 1998).

[975] *Id.*

[976] Information Letter No. 96-25, S.C. Dept. of Rev. (Dec. 19, 1996).

[977] S.C. Code Ann. §§ 33-44-201, 33-44-1001(a).

[978] S.C. Code Ann. § 12-6-600.

[979] *Id.*

[980] *Id.*

Single-member LLCs that are classified as corporations for federal tax purposes are required to file federal corporate returns and pay corporate license fees.[981] The law changed in 1994 as a result of the change in the definition of "corporation."[982] A corporation was defined to include an LLC that is classified as a corporation. The change was effective June 16, 1994. An LLC formed after June 16, 1994, is required to complete the initial annual report of corporations and pay the initial license fee with the Department of Revenue upon formation if the LLC is classified as a corporation.[983]

The statute exempting a single-member LLC from income tax if the LLC is classified as a disregarded entity does not exempt the LLC from other South Carolina taxes. Thus, a single-member LLC must pay sales taxes. However, contributions of substantially all the assets and liabilities of a corporation into a new single-member LLC that elects to be classified as a division of the corporate owner for federal and South Carolina tax purposes are not subject to South Carolina sales taxes.[984]

.03 Tax Returns

Every foreign and domestic LLC doing business or owning property in South Carolina must file an information return on Form SC1065, Partnership Return of Income.[985] The LLC must file the partnership return with the South Carolina Department of Revenue, Partnership Return, Columbia, SC 29214-0008. The LLC must attach a copy of federal Form 1065 and copies of all schedules to the return. The income or loss of the LLC is computed in the same manner and on the same basis as for individuals.

The LLC must attach a copy of each federal Schedule K-1 to Form SC1065. Members who have income or loss must file tax returns regardless of their tax liability. The LLC must furnish Schedule SC-K to each individual member. This schedule shows the amount of each item apportioned or allocated to South Carolina. The LLC must furnish to South Carolina members information concerning the total amounts of their proportionate shares of South Carolina adjustments and the amounts allocated or apportioned to states other than South Carolina.

An LLC may obtain an extension of time to file the return by filing Form SC4868.

.04 Apportionment of Income

If the LLC carries on a trade or business entirely within the state, all of the net income must be apportioned to South Carolina. Multistate LLCs whose principal profits are derived from manufacturing, producing, collecting, buying, assembling, processing, selling, distributing, or dealing in tangible personal property must com-

---

[981] Information Letter No. 94-23, S.C. Dept. of Rev. (Sept. 12, 1994).

[982] The definition is contained in S.C. Code Ann. § 12-2-25-3.

[983] Information Letter No. 94-23, S.C. Dept. of Rev. (Sept. 12, 1994).

[984] Private Revenue Opinion No. 00-4, S.C. Dept. of Rev. (July 10, 2000).

[985] S.C. Code Ann. § 12-6-4910.

pute the portion of business income attributable to South Carolina by applying a four-factor apportionment formula. LLCs whose principal profits are derived from other sources must compute the income attributable to South Carolina based on a ratio of gross receipts within the state to total gross receipts.

.05 Nonresident Members

Withholding Taxes

LLCs must withhold annually five percent of the South Carolina taxable income of members who are nonresidents of South Carolina.[986] The withholding tax rate is five percent in 2017. The LLC must complete Schedule W-H of Form SC1065 to compute the withholding. Any South Carolina real estate gain subject to buyer withholding is not subject to this withholding. The income tax must be paid to the South Carolina Department of Revenue along with Form 1065. The return must be filed by the 15th day of the fourth month following the end of the tax year of the LLC. The LLC must provide each nonresident member with Form 1099-MISC (with "SC only" written at the top of the form) by that date, showing the respective amounts of income and tax withheld. The nonresident member claiming credit for the withholding must attach a copy of Form 1099-MISC to the member's tax return as verification. The LLC must attach a schedule disclosing the name, address, tax identification number, South Carolina taxable income, and tax withheld for each nonresident member.

LLCs that request an extension of time to file Form SC1065 must estimate the South Carolina taxable income of nonresidents and pay a five percent withholding tax on this amount along with the filing of the extension request. The extension request must be filed by the 15th day of the fourth month following the end of the tax year.

Agreement to Pay Taxes

An LLC is not required to withhold taxes for a nonresident member who submits an affidavit and agrees to pay South Carolina taxes. The member must submit the affidavit on Form I-309, Nonresident Shareholder or Partner Affidavit and Agreement Income Tax Withholding. The LLC must attach the affidavit to Form SC1065. An affidavit does not need to be filed again once it is first submitted. The LLC is not required to withhold income taxes if it has no South Carolina taxable income for the year.

---

[986] S.C. Code Ann. § 12-8-590; Revenue Procedure 92-5.

Composite Return

An LLC may report the income of nonresident members on a composite return.[987] The LLC must follow the instructions on Form I-348, Composite Filing Instructions. A composite return is a single return for two or more members having the same tax year. The return is filed on Schedule NR attached to Form SC1040NR.[988] The LLC must mark the box on the form for filing a composite return. It must also mark "Single" filing status and one exemption on the first page of the form.

Each member included on the composite return must sign and give to the LLC Form I-338, Composite Return Affidavit. Each member's share of the LLC's tax is computed separately and added together to determine the total tax due on the composite return.[989] The LLC must pay taxes at a seven percent tax rate on all income allocable to South Carolina sources if the nonresident member does not sign Form RI-338.[990]

The LLC must file the return on or before April 15 following the members' tax year for an individual member or other member with a calendar year.[991] The LLC must pay any taxes with the filed return.

The LLC may determine each nonresident member's tax due using one of several methods. If the nonresident member provides an affidavit on Form I-338[992] to the Department of Revenue through the LLC stating that he or she has no income other than income from the LLC, the LLC may compute the nonresident member tax in one of the following two ways:[993]

> Option 1: (i) Prorate the standard deduction or itemized deductions and personal exemptions. For an individual, this means multiplying the standard deduction or itemized deductions and personal exemptions by the amount of South Carolina adjusted gross income, and dividing the result by the amount of federal adjusted gross income. (ii) At the member's election, tax active trade or business income at the active trade or business income rate. (iii) Tax all other taxable income using the graduated rate for individuals, estates and trusts.

> Option 2: (i) Do not use the standard deduction, itemized deductions or personal exemptions. (ii) At the member's election, tax active trade or business income at the active trade or business income rate. (iii) Tax all other taxable income using the graduated rate for individuals, estates and trusts.

---

[987] S.C. Code Ann. § 12-6-5030.

[988] Instructions to Form SC1040, Partnership Return.

[989] S.C. Code Ann. § 12-6-5030(B)(1).

[990] Instructions to Form I-338.

[991] Instructions to Form I-338.

[992] Form I-338, Composite Return Affidavit.

[993] S.C. Code Ann. § 12-6-5030(B)(1); Instructions to SC1040 Composite Filing For S Corporations, Partnerships, And Limited Liability Companies.

¶ 2342.05

If the nonresident member does not provide an affidavit to the Department on Form I-338, the LLC must compute each nonresident member's share of South Carolina income tax without regard to deductions or exemptions by using the active trade or business income tax rate on the member's allocable share of active trade or business income,[994] and using the highest marginal rate of seven percent in 2018 for other income.[995]

After 2004, a member may be included in a composite return even if the member has income from South Carolina sources other than the LLC.

.06 LLCs Classified as Corporations

LLCs that are classified as corporations for federal tax purposes may use federal Form 1099 for reporting dividends and other distributions to members.[996]

.07 Conversion to LLC

When a partnership converts to an LLC, the LLC is considered to be the same entity as the partnership. The partnership will not terminate. There will be no change in the adjusted bases of the owners' interests if there is no change in the owners' shares of liabilities. There is a carryover in the owners' holding period for their ownership interests. The tax year of the partnership does not close. The new LLC does not need to obtain a new taxpayer identification number. No documentary transfer tax is due. The LLC is not required to obtain a new retail license for sales tax purposes. However, the LLC should obtain a new retail license for each retail location. If the license is transferred to the name of the LLC, the Department of Revenue will assume that the managing members are personally liable for any sales or use tax that the LLC fails to pay.[997]

.08 Filing Fees

South Carolina imposes the following filing fees on LLCs:[998]

Articles of organization	$110
Certificate of authority for foreign LLC	$110
Annual report	none

---

[994] The computations are made using Form I-335, Active Trade or Business Income Reduced Rate Computation.

[995] S.C. Code Ann. § 12-6-5030(B)(1)(b); Form I-348, Composite Filing Instructions.

[996] Act 101, uncodified § 12,1995 S.C. Acts.

[997] Rev. Rul. 95-9, S.C. Dept. of Rev. (June 27, 1995).

[998] S.C. Code Ann. §§ 33-43-1401, 33-44-1204.

¶ 2343 SOUTH DAKOTA

South Dakota enacted the South Dakota Limited Liability Company Act on July 1, 1993.[999] South Dakota adopted the Uniform Limited Liability Company Act, effective July 1, 1998.[1000]

.01 Taxation of LLC and Members

There is no state income tax in South Dakota. LLCs are not subject to the South Dakota bank franchise (income) tax. Banks and other financial institutions that are organized as LLCs are classified as separate corporations for purposes of the bank franchise (income) tax.[1001] Effective July 1, 2004, financial institutions that are organized as LLCs may subtract imputed federal income taxes in an amount equal to the taxes that the LLC would have paid on net income if the LLC had elected classification as a C corporation.

LLCs must pay an annual reporting fee of $50 and a paper filing fee of $15.[1002] The tax is due and payable on January 2 of each year. The tax is delinquent if not paid by February 1. There is a penalty of $50 for late filings.

Officers, managers, and member-managers of an LLC are personally liable for unpaid sales and use, motor fuel and telecommunications taxes. The dissolution of the LLC or the resignation of the person as an officer or manager will not discharge the person from liability for failure by the LLC to pay the taxes due.[1003]

.02 Tax Returns

An LLC must file an annual report with the Secretary of State. The LLC must file the annual report on or before the first day of the second month following the anniversary month of the filing date.[1004]

.03 Filing Fees

Articles of organization*	$150
Certificate of Authority for foreign LLC	$750
Annual report**	$ 50

* S.D. Codified Laws Ann. § 47-34A-1206.
** S.D. Codified Laws Ann. § 47-34A-212(c).

---

[999] S.B. 139, 1993 S.D. Laws; S.D. Codified Laws Ann. § § 47-34-1 to 47-34-59.

[1000] S.D. Codified Laws Ann. § § 47-34A-101 to 47-34A-1207.

[1001] S.D. Codified Laws Ann. § 10-43-1(1), (10).

[1002] S.D. Codified Laws Ann. § 47-34A-212(c).

[1003] S.D. Codified Laws Ann. § 10-45-55.

[1004] S.D. Codified Laws Ann. § 47-34A-211.

¶2344 TENNESSEE

Tennessee enacted the Tennessee Revised Limited Liability Company Act effective January 1, 2006.[1005]

.01 State Tax Classification

Tennessee classifies an LLC in the same manner that the LLC is classified for federal tax purposes. An LLC that is classified as a partnership for federal tax purposes is classified as a partnership for state tax purposes. An LLC that is classified as a corporation for federal tax purposes is classified as a corporation for purposes of all state and local Tennessee taxes.[1006]

A single-member LLC that is disregarded for federal tax purposes will be treated as a separate entity for Tennessee franchise and excise tax purposes, and must file its own separate franchise and excise tax return, unless its sole member is a corporation.[1007]

The Tennessee laws governing classification of LLCs were enacted before the federal check-the-box regulations were issued by the Treasury Department. The state statute does not specifically address the classification of LLCs in light of the revisions made by the check-the-box provisions. However, the intent of the state statute is to classify LLCs for state and local tax purposes in the same way they are classified for federal tax purposes. Therefore, the Tennessee Department of Revenue follows the federal check-the-box regulations in classifying LLCs for purpose of Tennessee franchise, corporate excise (income), and stocks and bonds income taxes.[1008]

.02 Taxation of LLC and Members

For tax years beginning on or after July 1, 1999,[1009] LLCs are subject to a franchise tax of $.25 per $100 of the greater of (i) total net worth, or (ii) total real and tangible personal property.[1010] The minimum franchise tax is $100.[1011]

An LLC that is classified as a corporation, partnership, or disregarded entity must pay an excise tax of 6.5 percent on Tennessee net earnings.[1012]

Tennessee imposes an annual fee on LLCs equal to $50 per member of the domestic or foreign LLC. The fee is imposed on the date of the initial filing with the

---

[1005] S.B. 421, ch. 286, 2005 Tenn. Pub. Acts; Tenn. Code Ann. §§48-249-101 to 48-249-1133.

[1006] Tenn. Code Ann. §48-249-1003. *See also* Rev. Rul. No. 01-23, Tennessee Department of Revenue (Oct. 29, 2001) regarding the taxation of LLCs that elect to be classified as a corporation.

[1007] Notice 13-16, Tenn. Dep't of Rev. (Nov. 1, 2013).

[1008] Rev. Rul. 97-41, Tenn. Dept. of Rev. (Oct. 14, 1997).

[1009] *See* Important Notice, Tennessee Department of Revenue (June 16, 1999), regarding the application of the franchise tax in the excise tax to LLCs.

[1010] Tenn. Code Ann. §§67-4-2004(16), 67-4-2106.

[1011] Tenn. Code Ann. §§67-4-2019.

[1012] Tenn. Code Ann. §§67-4-2004(16), 67-4-2007.

secretary of state and on the date that the annual report is filed each year thereaf-ter.[1013] There is a minimum fee of $300 and a maximum fee of $3,000.[1014] If the LLC is prohibited by its articles from doing business in Tennessee and represents that it has not and is not doing business in Tennessee, the filing fee is $300 regardless of the number of members.[1015]

There is a Hall Income Tax of three percent in 2018 (two percent in 2019 and one percent in 2020) on dividends and interest over $1,250 per person ($2,500 for married couples filing jointly).[1016] If the LLC is classified as a corporation, any distribution received by, or accrued or credited to, an owner is taxable as a dividend. If an LLC is classified as a partnership, any distribution paid to, or accrued or credited to, a member is taxable as a dividend if the member is equivalent to a limited partner and has a transferable certificate of ownership. A member is equivalent to a limited partner if an LLC is managed by managers, and the member is not one of the managers. A member has a transferable certificate of ownership only if there is a written instrument requiring the LLC to pay interest to the member.[1017]

An LLC organized outside the state of Tennessee that is commercially domiciled in Tennessee and that is classified as a corporation for federal income tax purposes is taxed as a financial institution for Tennessee franchise tax and corporate excise (income) tax purposes if the LLC derives more than 50 percent of its income from making, acquiring, selling, or servicing loans or extensions of credit. If the LLC receives all applications for loans in Tennessee and the LLC is unable to determine where the loan proceeds were applied, then the LLC must source all of the income from the loans in question to Tennessee. The LLC may apportion its net worth and net income for tax purposes if it files a corporate income tax return in at least one other state, even though it maintains an office only in Tennessee. If the LLC maintains two offices, one in Tennessee and one in another state, it has the right to apportion its income.[1018]

The members of a foreign LLC that is classified as a partnership for federal tax purposes are subject to all state and local Tennessee taxes in the same manner and to the same extent as partners in a foreign partnership.[1019]

The members of a domestic LLC that is classified as a partnership for federal tax purposes are subject to all state and local Tennessee taxes in the same manner and to the same extent as partners in a domestic partnership.[1020]

[1013] Tenn. Code Ann. § 48-249-1007(d).

[1014] Tenn. Code Ann. § 48-249-1007(d); Tennessee Department of State, Division of Business Services, Fee Schedules for Corporations, Limited Liability Companies, Limited Partnerships, and Limited Liability Partnerships, http://www.state.tn.us/sos/forms/corpfeeschedules.pdf.

[1015] *Id.*

[1016] Tenn. Code Ann. § 67-2-102.

[1017] Tenn. Department of Revenue, Frequently Asked Questions, Q&A-16, http://www.state.tn.us/revenue/faqs/indincome.shtml.

[1018] Rev. Rul. No. 98-43, Tenn. Dept. of Rev. (Oct. 21, 1998).

[1019] Tenn. Code Ann. § 48-249-1003.

[1020] *Id.*

.03 Sales Taxes

The transfer of inventory and other assets by a parent corporation to a newly formed LLC in exchange for 100 percent of the membership interests in the LLC is not subject to the Tennessee sales and use tax. The transfer of assets is exempt as an occasional sale.[1021]

.04 Real Estate Taxes

An LLC may file various documents with the office of the register of deeds in the county where the LLC has its principal office in Tennessee. In the case of a merger, the documents must be filed in the county in which the newer surviving LLC has its principal office in Tennessee. The register of deeds may charge $5 plus $.50 per page in excess of five pages as the filing fee.[1022]

.05 Tax Returns

An LLC must file Form FAE 170, Tennessee Department of Revenue Franchise, Excise Tax Return, to pay the franchise tax and the excise tax. An LLC must file an annual report with the Tennessee Secretary of State to pay the annual $50 per member fee ($300 minimum and $3,000 maximum).

An LLC must file Form INC 250, Individual Income Tax Return (and check Box 10 for LLC status), if the LLC has taxable interest and dividend income exceeding $1,250. The LLC is liable for the tax, if any.

.06 Filing Fees

Tennessee imposes the following filing fees on LLCs:[1023]

Articles of organization	$50 per member ($300 minimum, $3,000 maximum)
Annual report	$300–$3,000 ($50 per member), plus an additional $20 if there is a change in the registered agent or registered office.
Filing with the office of the register of deeds	$5
Application for certificate of authority of foreign LLC	$300-$3,000 ($50 per member)

[1021] Ltr. Rul. No. 00-47, TN, Tenn. Dept. of Rev. (Nov. 29, 2000).

[1022] Tenn. Code Ann. § 48-249-1007(e).

[1023] Tenn. Code Ann. §§ 48-249-1007, 1017.

¶ 2345 TEXAS

Texas adopted the Texas Limited Liability Company Act effective September 1, 1991.[1024]

.01 State Tax Classification

Texas classifies an LLC as a corporation for franchise tax purposes. The franchise tax is imposed on every LLC doing business in Texas, including (a) a foreign LLC qualified to do business in Texas,[1025] (b) an LLC that is classified as a partnership under federal law or the laws of a foreign state,[1026] and (c) a single-member disregarded LLC.[1027]

.02 Taxation of LLC

Effective January 1, 2008, an LLC that is classified as a corporation, partnership,[1028] or single-member disregarded entity[1029] must pay a franchise tax.[1030] The tax is commonly referred to as a margins tax.[1031]

The franchise tax is assessed on the LLC's tax base (taxable margin), and is computed in one of the following ways: (i) Total Revenue times 70 percent; (ii) Total Revenue minus Cost of Goods Sold (COGS); (iii) Total Revenue minus Compensation; or (iv) Total Revenue minus $1 million. The franchise tax rates for returns due on or after January 1, 2017, are:[1032]

- 0.75 percent (0.0075) of taxable margin for most entities;

- 0.375 percent (0.00375) of taxable margin for qualifying wholesalers and retailers; and

- 0.331 percent (0.00331) of taxable margin for those entities with $20 million or less in annualized total revenue using the EZ computation.

[1024] H.B. 278, 1991 Tex. Gen. Laws; Tex. Rev. Civ. Stat. Ann. art. 1528n, 1.01 to 11.07.

[1025] Tex. Tax Code Ann. § 171.001(A)(2).

[1026] Tex. Tax Code Ann. § 171.0002(a); Texas Admin. Code, Title 34, Rule § 3.581.

[1027] Tex. Tax Code Ann. § 171.0002(d); Texas Comptroller of Public Accounts, Let. Rul. No. 200609761L (Sept. 7, 2006).

[1028] Tex. Tax Code Ann. § 171.0002(a).

[1029] Tex. Tax Code Ann. § 171.0002(d).

[1030] Texas Administrative Code, Title 34, Part 1, Chapter 3, Subchapter V, Sections 3.581 to 3.595.

[1031] *BNA Daily Tax Reporter*, p. H-2 (Feb. 5, 2008).

[1032] Texas Franchise Tax Report Information and Instructions.

There is no tax if the computed tax is less than $1,000, or if the LLC's total annualized revenue is less than $1,130,000 in 2018.[1033]

.03 Foreign LLCs

An LLC qualified to do business in Texas may not withdraw from qualification until it pays all franchise taxes, penalties, and interest owed through the end of the period in which it is dissolved.[1034] A foreign LLC that is dissolved, merged out of existence, or otherwise terminated under the laws of its state of incorporation or organization must also pay all taxes, penalties, and interest through the date of dissolution.[1035]

.04 Single-Member LLCs

The reportable federal taxable income of an LLC that is classified as a sole proprietor for federal tax purposes is the taxable income and deductions reported on the member's individual income tax return. This includes any schedules and attachments to the member's income tax return that relate to the LLC.[1036] Compensation to a member who is treated as the sole proprietor for federal income tax purposes is not deductible in computing income.

The reportable federal taxable income of a single-member LLC that is treated as a division or branch of a corporation for federal income tax purposes is computed as if the LLC were a separate corporation for federal income tax purposes. A single-member LLC may not deduct officer and director compensation from earned surplus.[1037]

.05 LLC Classified as Corporation

The reportable federal taxable income of an LLC that is classified as a corporation for federal income tax purposes is computed as if the LLC were a corporation.[1038]

.06 Corporate Members of an LLC

A corporate member of an LLC must use the cost method of accounting for its investment in the LLC. A corporate member's distributive share of the LLC's income

---

[1033] Tex. Code Ann. § 171.002(d); Texas Franchise Tax Report Information and Instructions.

[1034] Tex. Admin. Code Ann. tit. 34, § 3.568.

[1035] Id.

[1036] Tex. Admin. Code Ann. tit. 34, § 3.562; 23 Tex. Treas. Reg. 4236 (May 1, 1998).

[1037] Tex. Admin. Code tit. 34, § 3.562(g); 23 Tex. Treas. Reg. 4236 (May 1, 1998).

[1038] Tex. Comp. Pub. Accts., Reg. § 3.562, 23 Tex. Reg. 4236 (May 1, 1998).

or loss is not included in the member's earned surplus or gross receipts to the extent the items were reflected on the LLC's report.[1039]

.07 Withdrawals and Distributions

Withdrawals and distributions from the LLC are not included in earned surplus. They are not considered gross receipts for apportionment purposes unless the corporate member recognized a gain for federal income tax purposes. The distributions and withdrawals are allocated based on the LLC's state of incorporation.[1040]

.08 Sales Taxes

The contribution of property to a newly formed LLC in exchange for membership interests is not subject to the Texas sales tax because the transfer is a nontaxable contribution, and not a sale.[1041]

.09 Tax Returns

An LLC must file one of the following forms to pay the margins tax:

- Form 05-163, No Tax Due Information Report. The LLC may file this form if the LLC (a) has zero Texas gross receipts, (b) $1,220,000 or less in total revenue, annualized over 12 months[1042] for reports due on or after January 1, 2016, and before January 1, 2018,[1043] or (c) is a passive entity exempt from the margins tax.

- Form 05-169, E-Z Computation. An LLC is eligible to use this form if it has annual gross receipts of less than $20 million.[1044]

- Forms 05-158-A and 05-158-B, Texas Franchise Tax Report. An LLC that does not elect to file using the E-Z Computation, or that does not qualify to file a No Tax Due Information Report, must file this report.

An LLC must also file Form 05-102, Texas Franchise Tax Public Information Report. The filing is due at the same time that the LLC files the annual franchise tax report.

[1039] *Id.*

[1040] *Id.*

[1041] Decision, Hearing No. 104,123, Texas Comptroller of Public Accounts (Jan. 26, 2012).

[1042] Form 05-394, 2010 Texas Franchise Tax Report Information and Instructions.

[1043] House Bill 4765.

[1044] Form 05-394, 2010 Texas Franchise Tax Report Information and Instructions.

.10 Filing Fees

Texas imposes the following filing fees on LLCs:[1045]

Articles of organization	$300
Application by foreign LLC for certificate of authority	$750
Annual report	none

¶ 2346 UTAH

Utah enacted the Utah Limited Liability Company Act and began accepting filings for LLCs on July 1, 1991.[1046] Utah adopted the Revised Limited Liability Company Act, effective July 1, 2001.[1047] Utah adopted the Unincorporated Business Entity Act and the Utah Revised Uniform Limited Liability Company Act[1048] (i) effective January 1, 2014 for all LLCs formed after January 1, 2014, (ii) effective January 1, 2014 for LLCs formed prior to that date that elect to be governed by the new law, and (iii) effective January 1, 2016 for all LLCs regardless of when formed.[1049] There are transition provisions that apply to LLCs formed on or before December 31, 2013 that elect to be governed Chapter 3a, Utah Revised Uniform Limited Liability Company Act.[1050]

Utah authorized low-profit LLCs (also known as "L3Cs") in 2009.[1051] Low-profit LLCs are discussed in Chapter 26.

.01 State Tax Classification

Utah classifies an LLC in the same manner that the LLC is classified for federal tax purposes.[1052] Before January 1, 1994, the Utah State Tax Commission treated Utah LLCs as partnerships for state tax purposes.

.02 Taxation of LLC and Members

There is no franchise or entity-level tax imposed on Utah LLCs. An LLC is a pass-through entity.[1053]

[1045] Tex. Rev. Civ. Stat. Ann. art. 1528n, 9.01.

[1046] H.B. 221, 1991 Utah Laws; Utah Code Ann. §§ 48-2b-101 to 48-2b-158.

[1047] Utah Code Ann. §§ 48-2c-101 to 48-2c-1902.

[1048] Utah Code Ann. § 48-3a-101 *et seq.*

[1049] Utah Code Ann. § 48-3a-1405.

[1050] Utah Code Ann. § 48-2c-100.

[1051] Utah Code Ann. §§ 48-2c-102(11), 48-2c-106(8), 48-2c-403(1)(c), 48-2c-412; S.B. 148, Utah Laws, 2009.

[1052] Utah Code Ann. §§ 59-10-1401 *et seq.*, 59-10-801.

[1053] Utah Code Ann. §§ 59-10-301, 59-10-1403(1).

The members of the LLC are taxed in Utah on their distributive shares of income.[1054] Each item of LLC income, gain, loss, or deduction has the same character for a member as it has for federal income tax purposes.[1055] When an item is not characterized for federal income tax purposes, it has the same character for a member as if the member realized the income from the same source or incurred the expense in the same manner as did the LLC.

An LLC must withhold taxes on the allocable share of income for resident business entity members, but not for resident individual members.[1056] A single-member disregarded LLC is not required to withhold income taxes.[1057]

.03 Nonresident Members

Taxation of Nonresidents

Nonresident members are taxed on their distributive shares of income derived from or connected with Utah sources.[1058] Nonresident members must file a Utah tax return.[1059]

Withholding Taxes

For tax years beginning on or after January 1, 2009, an LLC must withhold Utah income taxes on income allocable to nonresident members.[1060] The withholding tax rate is five percent of Utah source income in 2017.[1061] The withholding tax applies to Utah business income allocated to nonresident members, and non-business income derived from or connected with Utah sources allocated to nonresident members.[1062]

The LLC must use Form TC-65 Schedule A (if it is taxed as a partnership) to compute the total Utah income. It must then use Form TC-65, Schedule N to allocate the Utah income and calculate the Utah withholding tax for each nonresident member.[1063]

An LLC may request a waiver of the withholding requirement by checking a box on Schedule N. The extension period for partnership returns is five months. Therefore, to qualify for the waiver, the LLC should ensure that all members for whom the

---

[1054] Utah Code Ann. § 59-10-1403.1(2).

[1055] Utah Code Ann. § 59-10-302.

[1056] Utah Code Ann. § 59-10-1403.2.

[1057] Utah Admin. Cod R865-9I-13(7).

[1058] Utah Code Ann. § § 59.10-303, 59-10-1403.1.

[1059] Utah Code Ann. § § 59.10-303, 59-10-1403.1(3).

[1060] Utah Code Ann. § § 59-10-1403.2, 59-10-1402(9), 59-10-1402(10); Utah Admin. Code R865-91-13.

[1061] Publication 68, Pass-through Entity Withholding, Utah State Tax Commission; Instructions to Form TC-65.

[1062] Publication 68, Pass-through Entity Withholding, Utah State Tax Commission, Sept. 2013.

[1063] Publication 68, Pass-through Entity Withholding, Utah State Tax Commission, Sept. 2013.

waiver is claimed file and pay their Utah taxes on or before the expiration of the five-month extension period.[1064]

The LLC is liable for the withholding tax if it fails to withhold and does not qualify for a waiver or any of the exceptions.[1065]

A disregarded LLC owned by an individual Utah resident member is not required to withhold.[1066]

If an LLC withholds taxes for a member, and the member has no other Utah source income or Utah credits, the member is not required to file a Utah return. However, if the member has any other Utah source income or Utah credits, the member must file a return reporting such income and claiming such credits, including the credit for the withholding tax paid on the member's behalf by the LLC.[1067]

For 2010 and future returns, the LLC must complete the Utah Schedule K-1 showing the withholding for each member.

Composite Returns

An LLC may no longer file a composite return for tax years beginning in 2009. The composite return was replaced by the withholding tax.[1068]

.04 Tax Returns

A Utah LLC with nonresident members and income from Utah sources must file a tax return on Form TC-65, Utah Partnership/Limited Liability Partnership/Limited Liability Company Return of Income.[1069] An LLC that is a partner in another partnership or LLC must also file a state tax return.[1070] The return must be filed with the Utah State Tax Commission, 210 North 1950 West, Salt Lake City, UT 84134-0270. The return must be filed on or before the 15th day of the fourth month after the close of the fiscal year or by April 15 for calendar year LLCs.

For tax years after June 6, 2005, an LLC is not required to file Form TC-65, Utah Partnership Return, if all of its members are Utah resident individuals. The LLC must maintain records showing each member's share of income, losses, credits, and other

---

[1064] Publication 68, Pass-through Entity Withholding, Utah State Tax Commission, Sept. 2013.

[1065] Publication 68, Pass-through Entity Withholding, Q&A-12, Utah State Tax Commission, Sept. 2013.

[1066] Publication 68, Pass-through Entity Withholding, Q&A-8, Utah State Tax Commission, Sept. 2013.

[1067] Publication 68, Pass-through Entity Withholding, Utah State Tax Commission, Sept. 2013.

[1068] Publication 68, Pass-through Entity Withholding, Q&A-7, Utah State Tax Commission, Sept. 2013.

[1069] Utah Admin. R. R865-9I-21; Utah Code Ann. §§ 59-10-507, 59-10-1403(3).

[1070] Publication 68, Pass-through Entity Withholding, Q&A-3, Utah State Tax Commission, Sept. 2013.

distributive items. The LLC must make such records available to the Tax Commission on request.[1071]

.05 Filing Fees

Utah imposes the following filing fees on LLCs:[1072]

Articles of organization	$70
Foreign LLC registration application	$70
Annual registration (Annual Report/Renewal Form)	$15

¶ 2347 VERMONT

Vermont enacted laws authorizing the formation of LLCs effective July 1, 1996.[1073]

.01 State Tax Classification

Vermont classifies an LLC in the same manner that the LLC is classified for federal tax purposes.[1074] Single-member LLCs are permitted.

.02 Taxation of LLC and Members

An LLC that is classified as a partnership for federal tax purposes must pay an annual tax of $250 for tax years beginning on or after January 1, 1998.[1075] An LLC that is classified as a single-member disregarded entity is not subject to the tax. An LLC that is classified as a corporation is subject to the corporate income tax and must file a corporate income tax return.[1076]

The members of the LLC are subject to tax on their distributive shares of Vermont LLC income. Vermont conformed its state laws to the Internal Revenue Code.[1077] Therefore, the federal provisions applicable to taxation of LLC members apply for state tax purposes.

[1071] Instructions to Form TC-65.

[1072] Utah Code Ann. § 48-2c-214.

[1073] H.B. 112, ch. 179, 1996 Vt. Laws; Vt. Stat. Ann. tit. 11, § § 3001-3162.

[1074] Vt. Stat. Ann. tit. 32, § 5921.

[1075] *Id.*

[1076] Vt. Rul. of Comm'r, P.D. 98-152 (Oct. 14, 1998); Vt. Stat. Ann. tit. 32, § 5921.

[1077] Vt. Stat. Ann. tit. 32, § 5820(a).

.03 Tax Returns

An LLC must file Form BI-471, Vermont Business Income Tax Return, to pay the annual $250 tax. The return is due by the 15th day of the third month following the close of the tax year.

Beginning 2013, an LLC that is owned entirely by Vermont residents and that has no requirement for nonresident estimated tax payments may file Form VI-471 only. The LLC in such case is no longer required to complete and attach (i) Schedule BA-402, Apportionment and Allocation Schedule, (ii) VI-472/3, as Corporation and Partnership/Limited Liability Company Schedules, or (iii) K-1VT(s), Shareholder's, Partner's, or Member's Information.[1078]

.04 Nonresident Members

Withholding Taxes

A nonresident member is taxed in Vermont on income derived from LLC operations in Vermont. An LLC is liable for all taxes, interest and penalties owed by nonresident members with respect to Vermont source income allocable to the nonresident members.[1079]

The LLC must withhold and pay estimated taxes with respect to nonresident members. The LLC must make quarterly estimated payments using Form WH-435, Estimated Income Tax Payments for Nonresident Shareholders or Partners. The withholding tax rate is 6.8 percent for 2017.[1080] The amount of withholding from each nonresident member is a credit against the member's individual tax liability. The nonresident member is considered to have paid all income taxes based on the withholding.[1081]

The LLC must pay the withholding taxes by making estimated tax payments on a quarterly basis. The payments are made using Form WH-435, Estimated Income Tax Payments For Nonresident Shareholders, Partners, or Members.

An LLC with nonresident members must file Form BI-473, Vermont Partnership/ Limited Liability Company Schedule.[1082] Form BI-473 is used to determine the amount of Vermont-sourced income distributed to nonresident members. The LLC is liable for all income taxes and related interest and penalties imposed by Vermont on Vermont-sourced income of nonresident members. The withholding taxes are due quarterly, and are made with Form WH-435.[1083] The LLC must file Form BI-473 by the due date of IRS Form 1065. The LLC must attach a copy of the completed Form 1065

[1078] VTax Connect Newsletter, Volume 1, Issue 3, Vermont Department of Taxes (Apr. 9, 2014).

[1079] *See* instructions to Form BI-473 Instructions—Partnership/LLC Schedule.

[1080] *See* Form BI-473 Instructions—Partnership/LLC Schedule.

[1081] Vt. Stat. Ann. tit. 31, § 5920(e).

[1082] Vt. Stat. Ann. tit. 32, § 5861a.

[1083] Instructions to Form BI-473, Partnership Schedule.

and Schedule K-1 for each member. The LLC must use Form VT Form BA-402, Vermont Apportionment & Allocation Schedule, if the LLC has income or losses from Vermont and at least one other state.

Composite Returns

An LLC may file a composite return on behalf of nonresident members.[1084] The composite (block) return is filed using Form BI-471, Vermont Business Income Tax Return. The LLC must check the Composite Return box and obtain approval from the Department of Taxes. The election is binding for five years unless the election is revoked for failure to meet the requirements for composite filing. The LLC must make the election before the due date for the first quarterly estimated tax payments.[1085] The composite tax rate is 7.8 percent in 2017 (linked to the middle marginal personal income tax rate).[1086]

An LLC must make a composite filing if the LLC has more than 50 non-Vermont-resident members. An LLC that files a composite return must include all non-Vermont-resident members in the composite filing. "Partial composite" returns are not accepted.[1087]

.05 Filing Fees

There are the following filing fees in Vermont:[1088]

Articles of organization	$100
Application for certificate of authority of foreign LLC	$100
Annual report (domestic LLC)	$ 25
Annual report (foreign LLC)	$125

¶ 2348 VIRGINIA

Virginia enacted the Virginia Limited Liability Company Act effective July 1, 1991.[1089]

[1084] Technical Bulletin TB-05.

[1085] Instructions to Form BI-471, Vermont Business Income Tax Return.

[1086] Instructions to Vermont Schedule BI-473, Composite Schedule.

[1087] H.B. 436, Laws 2011; 32 V.S.A. § 5920(b).

[1088] Vt. Stat. Ann. tit. 11, § 3013.

[1089] Va. Code Ann. §§ 13.1-1000 to 13.1-1123. *See also* S.B. Farmer and L. Mezzullo, *The Virginia Limited Liability Company Act*, 25 U. Rich. L. Rev. 789 (Summer 1991).

.01 State Tax Classification

Virginia classifies an LLC in the same manner as the LLC is classified for federal tax purposes.[1090] An LLC may not elect to be classified as a partnership for federal purposes and as a corporation for state purposes.[1091]

.02 Taxation of LLC

An LLC that is classified as a partnership is not subject to Virginia income taxes.[1092]

An LLC is required to pay a $50 annual registration fee. All domestic and foreign LLCs registered to transact business in Virginia must pay the fee. The payment must be made on or before September 1 of each year after the calendar year in which the LLC was formed or registered to do business in Virginia. There is a $25 late payment penalty fee.[1093] The Tax Commission sends a statement of assessment to the comptroller and to each LLC on or before August 15 of each year. If the LLC fails to pay the tax on or before October 1 of the year assessed, the commission will mail a notice to the LLC of impending cancellation of its certificate of organization or certificate of registration. The certificate is automatically canceled if the annual fee is not paid by December 31 of that year. A domestic LLC is dissolved upon cancellation.

No member, manager, or agent of the LLC has personal obligations for liabilities of the LLC, whether in tort, contract, or otherwise, as a result of the failure of the LLC to pay the annual registration fee or by reason of the cancellation and dissolution of the LLC for failure to pay.

An LLC is subject to the Virginia local business, professional, and occupational license (BPOL) taxes even if the LLC is classified as a disregarded entity under federal law. LLCs that maintain a definite place of business within the taxing jurisdiction are subject to adopt BPOL tax. The tax is based on the gross receipts of the LLC attributable to the definite place of business. If both a parent LLC and an operating LLC have a definite place of business in Virginia, both entities are subject to the BPOL tax.[1094]

.03 Taxation of Members

A Virginia LLC is a pass-through entity. Profits and losses pass through to the members.[1095] The members of an LLC that is classified as a partnership are subject to

---

[1090] Va. Code Ann. § 58.1-301; Rul. of the Comm'r, Va. Dept. of Taxn., P.D. 03-83 (Nov. 3, 2003).

[1091] Rul. of the Comm'r, Va. Dept. of Taxn., P.D. 03-83 (Nov. 3, 2003).

[1092] 23 Va. Admin. Code 10-130-10.

[1093] Va. Code Ann. §§ 13.1-1061 to 13.1-1066.

[1094] Rul. of the Comm'r, Va. Dept. of Taxn., P.D. 99-9 (Jan. 11, 1999).

[1095] 23 Va. Admin. Code 10-130-10.

Virginia income taxes in their individual capacities.[1096] Each item of LLC income, gain, loss, or deduction has the same character for state tax purposes as for federal tax purposes.[1097] Each member's share of LLC income is the same as that reported on the federal return, subject to certain state modifications.[1098]

An LLC that is owned by two other LLCs may not pass through the property, payroll, and sales factors to the members of the member LLC. Instead, the LLC must pass through these factors to the intervening LLC entities.[1099]

.04 Tax Returns

An LLC that does business in Virginia or that has income from Virginia sources must file Form 502, Pass-Through Entity Return of Income. A single-member disregarded LLC is not required to file the return.[1100] The form must be filed on or before the 15th day of the fourth month following the close of the tax year.

An LLC that is established solely to invest in intangible personal property, such as stocks and bonds, and that has no employees, real property, or tangible property, is not considered to be carrying on a trade or business.[1101]

Beginning on January 1, 2015, effective for the 2014 tax returns, an LLC must file its Virginia personal income tax withholding returns and make all withholding tax payments electronically.[1102] Form 502 may be filed through the Federal/State e-File.

.05 Single-Member LLCs

Members of an LLC are liable for Virginia taxes only in their separate or individual capacities on income passed through to them as owners of the LLC. Any taxes imposed on the LLC itself, such as sales and use taxes, withholding taxes for employees and nonresident owners, and minimum taxes in lieu of income taxes, must be paid by the LLC.[1103]

A single-member LLC is required to file a Virginia corporate income tax return only if it makes an election to be classified as a corporation for federal tax purposes. If no election is made, the single-member LLC is taxed as a pass-through entity, and the LLC's income is reported on the member's personal income tax return.[1104] The LLC is not required to file Form 502.

[1096] Va. Code Ann. § 13.1-1069.

[1097] 23 Va. Admin. Code 10-130-20.A.4.

[1098] 23 Va. Admin. Code 10-130-20.A.1.

[1099] Rul. of the Comm'r, Va. Dept. of Taxn., P.D. 97-59 (Feb. 12, 1997).

[1100] Instructions for Preparing Form 502, Virginia Pass-Through Entity Return of Income.

[1101] Tax Bulletin 05-6, Virginia Department of Taxation (May 6, 2005).

[1102] *Electronic Filing Mandate for PTEs Begins Jan. 1, 2015,* Virginia Department of Taxation.

[1103] Va. Code Ann. § 58.1-390.2.

[1104] Rul. of the Comm'r, Va. Dept. of Taxn., P.D. 99-57 (Apr. 20, 1999).

The single member of the LLC is required to file and pay estimated personal income taxes on the income of the LLC.[1105]

The LLC is not subject to the Virginia personal income tax withholding requirements if it has no employees, and if the LLC does not pay wages or salary to its sole member. There are no withholding requirements until the LLC pays wages or salary.[1106]

A single-member LLC is not required to register and collect sales taxes if it provides only nontaxable services. It is required to register and submit to the use tax on any purchases that it makes for which the sales tax was not collected.[1107]

Receipts from business conducted between a single-member LLC and an affiliated group are subject to the Virginia business, professional, and occupational licenses tax. A single-member LLC may not benefit from the exclusion from the tax that is available for transactions between members of an unaffiliated group. An individual owner of an LLC is not an incorporated entity, and therefore cannot be a common parent corporation for purposes of the exclusion.[1108]

If the LLC conducts business within and outside of the State of Virginia, the LLC's income, property, payroll, and sales are included in the member's return to determine the income apportioned to Virginia.[1109]

A taxpayer may deduct items reported on the federal Form 1040, Schedule C, relating to the operation of a single-member disregarded LLC if the LLC business was engaged in for the purpose of making a profit. This determination is based on all the facts and circumstances of each case.[1110]

.06 Nonresident Members

Withholding Taxes

An LLC doing business in Virginia and having taxable income from Virginia sources must withhold a five percent tax on each nonresident member's share of Virginia source income.[1111] An LLC with corporate members must withhold taxes if the LLC has taxable income from Virginia sources and allocate some of that income to the corporate members.[1112] In determining the amount of withholding tax, the LLC may apply any tax credits earned by it and allowable under the Virginia tax laws that pass through to the nonresident member. The credit may not reduce the tax liability of any nonresident member to less than zero, and may not be carried forward on a

---

[1105] *Id.*

[1106] *Id.*

[1107] *Id.*

[1108] Rul. of the Comm'r, Va. Dept. of Taxn., P.D. 99-176 (June 30, 1999).

[1109] Rul. of the Comm'r, Va. Dept. of Taxn., P.D. 97-343 (Aug. 28, 1997).

[1110] Rul. of the Comm'r, Va. Dept. of Taxn., P.D. 10-209 (Sept. 9, 2010).

[1111] Va. Code Ann. §58.1-486.1 *et seq.*; P.D. 07-150, Guidelines for Pass-Through Entity Withholding, Virginia Department of Taxation (Sept. 21, 2007).

[1112] PD 08-147, Virginia Department of Taxation (July 30, 2008).

unified return.[1113] The LLC liability for the tax is determined annually without regard to whether the LLC actually withholds amounts from any member's distributions, allocations, or payments.

A foreign LLC doing business in Virginia must also file Virginia nonresident income tax returns reporting Virginia source income. The nonresident who travel into Virginia to work must file Virginia personal income tax returns. The LLC must apportion Virginia income using a three factor formula based on payroll, property and sales.[1114]

The determination of nonresident member status is based on the member's address of record given to the LLC unless the LLC has other information indicating that the member is a resident. If the member is a nonresident for only a portion of the tax year, the income allocated to the member for withholding tax purposes must be prorated based on the number of days of residence outside of Virginia.[1115]

The LLC must make the withholding using Form 502 and Form 502W, Pass-Through Entity Withholding Tax Payment. The LLC must file the return and pay the withholding tax by the 15th day of the fourth month following the close of the taxable year. The time for filing the Form 502 may be extended, but the time for paying the amount of withholding tax due may not be extended.

LLCs must provide each nonresident member with a statement on a form to be prescribed by the Tax Commissioner that shows:[1116]

- the name, address, federal employer identification number (FEIN), and Virginia account number of the LLC;

- the amount of Virginia taxable income allocable to the member, whether or not distributed for federal income tax purposes by the LLC to the nonresident member;

- the member's share of any credits taken into account by the LLC in computing the withholding tax attributable to the nonresident member; and

- the amount of withholding tax paid on behalf of the nonresident member.

A copy of the statement must also be filed with the withholding tax return filed for the applicable taxable year in a manner prescribed by the Tax Commissioner.

An LLC will not be required to pay the withholding tax if the Tax Commissioner determines that compliance will cause undue hardship. An LLC seeking an undue hardship exemption may petition the Tax Commissioner by letter explaining the facts and circumstances creating the hardship.

[1113] Rul. of the Comm'r, Va. Dept. of Taxn., PD 09-59 (May 1, 2009). An LLC is not required to withhold taxes if credits for taxes paid to another state are sufficient to offset all Virginia income tax attributable to the income distributed from the LLC.

[1114] PD 12-164, Virginia Department of Taxation.

[1115] P.D. 07-150, Guidelines for Pass-Through Entity Withholding, Virginia Department of Taxation (Sept. 21, 2007).

[1116] P.D. 07-150, Guidelines for Pass-Through Entity Withholding, Virginia Department of Taxation (Sept. 21, 2007).

¶ 2348.06

Individual Return

Nonresident members of an LLC that is classified as a partnership must pay state income taxes on Virginia source income.[1117] The payment of the withholding tax does not relieve nonresident members of the obligation to file a Virginia income tax return. Penalties and interest may be imposed on any tax owed by the nonresident member after credit for the withholding tax paid by the LLC.

A nonresident member is allowed a credit for the member's share of the withholding tax paid by the LLC when the member files an individual or corporate income tax return relating to income received from the LLC. The credit may only be taken if the LLC files Form 502, the LLC pays the withholding tax in full, the member receives Form VK-1 and the required withholding statement from the LLC, and the member includes a copy of that statement with his or her income tax return.

An individual nonresident member is not required to file an individual income tax return if the individual consents to be included in the Form 765 filed by each LLC in which he or she owns an interest, and he or she has no other income from Virginia sources.

If an individual nonresident member is included on one or more Form 765, but has other income from Virginia sources, he or she must file Form 763, Nonresident Individual Income Tax Return. The individual may deduct income that was previously reported on Form 765.

Unified Returns

An LLC is not required to pay the withholding tax if it files a composite return on Form 765, Unified Nonresident Individual Income Tax Return (Composite Return). The LLC must obtain the consent of each nonresident member to be included in the return. An LLC may not file a unified return if any qualified member declines to participate. The consent must be on a form to be prescribed by the Tax Commissioner and must indicate that the nonresident member agrees to be taxed under the following conditions:[1118]

- The LLC must provide a schedule showing the total income of the LLC and the amount attributable to Virginia under either the applicable state apportionment formula, as provided in Virginia Code § § 58.1-408 through 58.1-421, or by using an approved alternative method.
- The return must include each nonresident partner's name, address, social security number, and Virginia taxable income attributable to each nonresident member.
- The composite tax amount is computed on the Virginia taxable income by applying the tax rates for individual income tax specified in Va. Code

---

[1117] Rul. of the Comm'r, Va. Dept. of Taxn., P.D. 04-29 (June 24, 2004).

[1118] P.D. 07-150, Guidelines for Pass-Through Entity Withholding, Virginia Department of Taxation (Sept. 21, 2007); Instructions for Preparing Form 502, Virginia Pass-Through Entity Return of Income and Return of Nonresident Withholding Tax.

§ 58.1-320 or by reference to the tax tables published by the Department, without regard to the number of members.[1119]

- A member, officer, or employee of the LLC who is authorized to act on behalf of the LLC in tax matters (authorized representative) must sign the unified return.
- The LLC must make estimated payments on behalf of those included on a unified return on a unified basis.

.07 Filing Fees

Virginia imposes the following filing fees on LLCs:[1120]

Articles of organization	$100
Certificate of registration for foreign LLC	$100
Annual report fee*	$ 50

* Va. Code Ann. § 13.1-1062.

¶ 2349 WASHINGTON

Washington enacted laws authorizing LLCs effective October 1, 1994.[1121]

.01 State Tax Classification

An LLC is a business entity distinct from its members.[1122] The classification of an LLC for state income tax purposes is not applicable, since LLCs are taxed in the same manner as other businesses for purposes of the Washington business and occupations tax.

.02 Taxation of LLC and Members

LLCs that do business in Washington are subject to various taxes, including the state business and occupations tax;[1123] sales and use taxes; local, city, and county sales and use taxes; lodging taxes; convention and trade center taxes; special hotel/motel taxes; state public utility taxes; and other miscellaneous excise taxes. The main tax is the state business and occupations tax, which is imposed on any entity doing business in the state of Washington. The tax rate depends on the business or occupation in which the LLC engages. Different businesses are subject to varying

---

[1119] Instructions for 2017 Virginia Form 765.

[1120] Va. Code Ann. § 13.1-1005.

[1121] H.B. 1235, 1994 Wash. Laws; Wash. Rev. Code Ann. § § 25.15.005 to 25.15.902.

[1122] Wash. Rev. Code Ann. § 25.15.060.

[1123] Wash. Rev. Code Ann. § 82.04.

types of exemptions and deductions. The tax is not an income tax. It is a tax imposed on the privilege of engaging in business activities in Washington.

Washington does not impose state personal income taxes on individuals.

.03 Tax Returns

An LLC doing business in Washington must file monthly, quarterly, and annual tax returns, reporting the state business and occupations tax, the sales tax, and other excise taxes. The return must be filed on Business & Occupations Activities Return, or the Combined Excise Tax Return. The due date is printed on each monthly, quarterly, and annual return mailed to the taxpayer. The monthly returns are due on the 25th day of the month following the close of the month. The quarterly returns are due on the last day of the month following the close of the quarter. The annual return is due by January 31.

.04 Filing Fees

There are the following filing fees in the state of Washington.[1124]

Articles of organization	$180
Foreign LLC registration application	$180
Initial registration fee	$ 10
Annual registration fee after initial registration	$ 69

¶ 2350 WEST VIRGINIA

West Virginia enacted the West Virginia Limited Liability Company Act on March 6, 1992.[1125]

.01 State Tax Classification

An LLC that is classified as a partnership for federal tax purposes is classified as a partnership for West Virginia income tax purposes.[1126] An LLC that is classified as a corporation or disregarded entity or federal tax purposes is classified as a corporation for West Virginia income tax purposes.[1127]

The West Virginia Corporation Net Income Tax Act conforms with federal law, subject to certain exceptions.[1128]

[1124] Wash. Rev. Code Ann. § 25.15.805.

[1125] W. Va. Code §§ 31B-1-101 to 31B-13-1306.

[1126] TSE-391, pt. B.8 (last sentence), W. Va. Dept. of Tax & Rev. (Jan. 19, 1993).

[1127] *See* instructions to Form WV/SPF-100, Income/Business Franchise Tax Return for S Corporation and Partnership.

[1128] W. Va. Code § 11-24-3.

.02 Taxation of LLC and Members

An LLC that is classified as a partnership is not subject to the West Virginia personal income tax.[1129] Members are taxed on their distributive shares of income.[1130]

For tax years beginning on or after January 1, 2015, the Business Franchise tax was eliminated.[1131]

.03 Tax Returns

An LLC must file Form SPF-100, Income/Business Franchise Tax Return for S Corporation and Partnership, to report its annual business franchise tax. The return is due by the 15th day of the third month following the close of the fiscal year.

An LLC must pay the business franchise tax using Form WV 100V, Income/business Franchise Tax for S Corporations and Partnerships. Electronic Payment Voucher, and Form WV/SPF-100ES, West Virginia Estimated Income/Business Franchise Tax Payment for S Corporation and Partnership.

.04 Nonresident Members

Withholding Taxes

An LLC doing business in West Virginia or deriving income from real or tangible property in West Virginia must withhold West Virginia income taxes from distributions for members who are not residents of West Virginia.[1132] An LLC must complete Form WV/NRW-2, Statement of West Virginia Income Tax Withheld for Nonresident Individual or Organization, for each nonresident member who received actual or deemed distributions of West Virginia source income or gain unless the LLC shows the information on a Schedule K-1's for the nonresident member (or as an attachment). A corporate member is a nonresident when its commercial domicile is located outside West Virginia. An LLC must also file Form IT-140W, West Virginia Withholding Tax Schedule, as an attachment to Form WV/NRW-2.

The withholding tax rate in 2017 is 6.5 percent of the nonresident member's share of the LLC's federal taxable income or the portion of that income that is derived from or attributable to West Virginia sources, whether or not distributed.[1133] The entire amount withheld must be remitted with the West Virginia partnership tax return.

[1129] W. Va. Code § 11-21-3(b); W. Va. State Tax Dept. Reg. § 3.2.

[1130] *Id.*

[1131] W. Va. Code pt. Reg.; 2015 West Virginia S Corporation & Partnership Income Tax (Pass-Through Entities) Instructions.

[1132] TSD-391, W. Va. Dept. of Tax & Rev. (Jan. 19, 1993); W. Va. Code § 11-21-71a; Publication TDS-390; Publication TDS-391.

[1133] W. Va. Code § 11-21-71a(b)(1); Instructions to Form SPF-100. The withholding taxes are computed under W. Va. Code § 11-21-71a(b).

The LLC is statutorily liable for payment of the amount of tax required to be withheld.[1134] The tax is treated as a tax on the LLC. No member of the LLC has a right of action against the LLC with respect to any money withheld from members' distributive shares of income that is paid over to the tax commissioner.[1135]

The LLC must furnish each nonresident member with a written information statement setting forth the following information:

- The amount of West Virginia effectively connected taxable income, whether distributed or not, for federal income tax purposes
- The amount deducted and withheld under West Virginia law
- Any other information that the tax commissioner may require

The LLC may satisfy this requirement by setting forth this information on any of the following:

- Form WV/NRW-2, Statement of West Virginia Income Tax Withheld for Nonresident Individual or Organization
- The supplemental information area of the nonresident member's copy of IRS Schedule K-1
- An attachment to the federal Schedule K-1 listing the same information

Each nonresident member files Form IT-140, Personal Income Tax Return, or Form IT-140NRS for certain residents of Kentucky, Maryland, Ohio, Pennsylvania, or Virginia. A nonresident member classified as a corporation must file Form WV/CNF-120, West Virginia Corporation Net Income/Business Franchise Tax Return. The member is allowed a credit for the member's share of the tax withheld by the LLC.[1136] The nonresident member's share of the withholding taxes is treated as distributed by the LLC to the member.[1137] The nonresident member may claim the amount withheld as a credit against the West Virginia income tax liability by attaching a copy of the information statement provided by the LLC.

Agreement to Pay Taxes

An LLC is not required to withhold taxes if the nonresident member provides the LLC with Form NRW-4, WV Nonresident Income Tax Agreement.[1138]

Composite Returns

An LLC is not required to withhold taxes on distributions to nonresidents if it files Form IT-140NRC, West Virginia Nonresident Composite Income Tax Return.[1139]

[1134] W. Va. Code § 11-21-71a(j), (k).

[1135] W. Va. Code § 11-21-71a.

[1136] *Id.*

[1137] *Id.*

[1138] W.V. Code § 11-21-71a(k).

[1139] W. Va. Code § 11-21-51a.

The composite tax rate in 2017 is 6.5 percent of the West Virginia income allocable to nonresident members.[1140] The composite return may be filed for one or more electing nonresident members. A member must file a nonresident return if the member has taxable income from other State sources. A member may file a separate return even if included on the composite return. The nonresident member must include income from the LLC on the separate return, and may claim a credit for taxes remitted with the composite return. The composite return is filed on a group basis as though there was only one taxpayer. The LLC must maintain a list setting forth the name, address, taxpayer identification number, and percentage of ownership of each nonresident member included in the return. This list may not be submitted with the composite return. Instead, it must be available to the department upon request. The return does not have to be signed by each nonresident member if it is signed by a member of the LLC. The LLC is responsible for collecting and remitting all income tax due at the time the return is filed. The return must be filed by the 15th day of the fourth month following the close of the tax year. There is a $50 processing fee that must accompany the composite return.

.05 Real Property Sales

An LLC must withhold income taxes on sales of West Virginia real property if the LLC has nonresident members. The withholding tax rate is 2.5 percent of total payments or 6.5 percent of the estimated capital gain. The LLC must allocate the withholding tax to the nonresident members. The LLC must file a withholding income tax return on Form WV/NRSR with the deed or other document of transfer that is recorded with the County Clerk.[1141]

.06 Filing Fees

There are the following filing fees in West Virginia:

Articles of organization	$100
Registration as foreign LLC	$150
Annual fee*	$ 25

* W. Va. Code § 31B-1-108(c).

¶ 2351 WISCONSIN

Wisconsin enacted the Wisconsin Limited Liability Company Act effective January 1, 1994.[1142]

[1140] Line 2 of IT-140 NRC, West Virginia Nonresident Composite Return.

[1141] Recent Updates, West Virginia State Tax Department (Jan. 2008).

[1142] Act 112 (A.B. 820), 1993 Wis. Laws; Wis. Stat. Ann. § § 183.0102 to 183.1305.

.01 Department of Revenue Publication No. 119

The Wisconsin Department of Revenue issued Publication No. 119, revised in January, 2017, setting forth its interpretation of the Wisconsin laws applicable to LLCs.

.02 State Tax Classification

Wisconsin classifies an LLC in the same manner that the LLC is classified for federal tax purposes. An LLC that is classified as a partnership under federal law is classified as a partnership under Wisconsin law.[1143] An LLC that is classified as a corporation under federal law is classified as a corporation under Wisconsin law.[1144] An LLC that is a disregarded entity under federal law is a disregarded entity for Wisconsin franchise and income tax purposes, and its owner is subject to tax on or measured by its net income.[1145]

.03 Contributions to LLC

Wisconsin follows the Internal Revenue Code with respect to the tax consequences of forming an LLC. To the extent allowed under the Code, contributions to an LLC are tax-free to both the LLC and the member. The member's basis in the LLC is equal to the basis in the property contributed.[1146]

.04 Economic Development Surcharge

For tax years beginning on or after January 1, 2013, LLCs are not subject to the Wisconsin economic development surcharge.[1147]

An LLC classified as a corporation must compute the surcharge on Forms 4, 5 or 5S as appropriate. An LLC classified as a disregarded entity does not compute its own economic development surcharge. Instead, the owner includes information on the owner's return.[1148]

[1143] Wis. Stat. § 71.195.

[1144] Wis. Stat. § 71.22(1k).

[1145] Wis. Stat. §§ 71.02(1), 71.20(1), and 71.22(1).

[1146] Publication 119, Wisconsin Department of Revenue, Part VII.A.3 (Jan. 2013).

[1147] *See* Publication 400, Wisconsin Economic Development Surcharge, Wisconsin Department of Revenue (Feb. 2014).

[1148] Wisconsin Department of Revenue Publication 119, Limited Liability Companies (LLCs), Part VII.B (Jan. 2013).

.05 Employment Withholding Taxes

LLCs with two or more members are treated in the same manner as other business entities for withholding tax purposes. If the LLC is an employer, the LLC must withhold, deposit, and furnish reports of Wisconsin income taxes withheld in the same manner as other employers.[1149]

If a member of an LLC performs services for the LLC and the IRS does not treat the member as an employee, the LLC is not required to withhold income taxes from payments made to the member for services performed.

A member, employee, or other responsible person who has a duty to withhold and deposit taxes for an LLC may be held personally liable for the LLC's Wisconsin income taxes withheld or required to be withheld.[1150]

Effective January 1, 2009, a single-member disregarded LLC is treated as the employer for withholding tax purposes. A disregarded LLC must obtain a Wisconsin employer identification number, collect and pay the withholding taxes.[1151]

.06 Sales and Use Taxes

For sales and use tax purposes, LLCs with two or more members and LLCs that are classified as corporations are treated in the same manner as other business entities. The LLC, as a retailer or consumer, must register, report, and pay Wisconsin sales and use taxes in the same manner as other retailers or consumers.[1152]

A single-member disregarded LLC is also disregarded as a separate entity for purposes of Wisconsin sales and use taxes. The owner of the LLC has the option to (i) include the information from the LLC on the member's individual return, or (ii) file a separate electronic sales and use tax return for the LLC.[1153]

A member, employee, or other responsible person who is under a duty to collect and remit sales and use taxes for an LLC may be personally liable for the LLC's Wisconsin sales and use taxes.[1154]

.07 Excise Taxes (Beverage, Fuel, Cigarette, and Tobacco)

For excise tax purposes, LLCs are treated in the same manner as other business entities. The LLC is required to register, pay, and furnish reports of Wisconsin excise taxes in the same manner as other business entities.[1155]

[1149] Wis. Stat. Ann. §§ 71.63(3), 71.65(1)(a), 71.77.

[1150] Wis. Stat. Ann. § 71.83(1)(b)(2).

[1151] New for Tax Practitioners, Wisconsin Department of Revenue (Feb. 12, 2009).

[1152] Wis. Stat. Ann. §§ 77.52(7), 77.53(9), 77.53(9m).

[1153] Wisconsin Department of Revenue Publication 119, Limited Liability Companies (LLCs), Part VII.D (Jan. 2013).

[1154] Wis. Stat. Ann. § 77.60(9).

[1155] Publication 119, Wisconsin Department of Revenue, Part VII.E (Jan. 2013).

A member, employee, or other responsible person who is under a duty to pay motor vehicle fuel, alternate fuel, or aviation fuel taxes for the LLC may be held personally liable for the LLC's Wisconsin excise taxes that the LLC is required to pay.[1156]

.08 Taxation of LLC Members Who Are Full-Year Wisconsin Resident Individuals, Estates, and Trusts

All LLC income or loss of full-year Wisconsin residents is includible in the computation of Wisconsin taxable income regardless of the situs of the LLC or the nature of income from the LLC. This includes business income, service income, and professional income unless otherwise exempt. Exempt income includes U.S. government interests.[1157]

EXAMPLE 23-6

An LLC is engaged in business in and outside of Wisconsin. Member A is a full-year Wisconsin resident and has a ten percent interest in the LLC. The LLC has ordinary income of $100,000, of which $60,000 is attributable to business conducted in Wisconsin. Member A is subject to Wisconsin income tax on $10,000 of the income.

The gain or loss from the disposition of an LLC interest is includible in Wisconsin net income for a full-year Wisconsin resident.[1158]

.09 Taxation of LLC Members Who Are Nonresident Individuals, Estates, and Trusts

A nonresident member's share of LLC income or loss attributable to a business located in Wisconsin, services performed in Wisconsin, or real or tangible personal property located in Wisconsin is includible in the computation of Wisconsin taxable income. Business income is taxable whether or not the individual member conducts business in Wisconsin. However, LLC income derived from personal services, including professional services, is taxed to nonresident members if those nonresident members personally perform services in Wisconsin. Personal service income attributable to services in Wisconsin is not taxable to nonresidents unless the nonresident performs the personal services.[1159]

[1156] Wis. Stat. Ann. § 78.70(6).

[1157] Wis. Stat. Ann. §§ 71.02(1), 71.04(1)(a).

[1158] Wis. Stat. Ann. § 71.04(1)(a).

[1159] *Murphy v. Wisconsin Department of Revenue*, Wisconsin Tax Appeals Commission, Nos. 09-I-134, 09-I-142 (Dec. 30, 2010); Wis. Stat. §§ 71.02(1), 71.04(1)(a).

EXAMPLE 23-7

A nonresident member of an LLC has a 30 percent interest in the LLC. The LLC is engaged in business within and outside of Wisconsin. The LLC has ordinary income of $150,000, of which $60,000 is attributable to its business activities in Wisconsin. The nonresident member is subject to Wisconsin income taxes on $18,000 of that income.

EXAMPLE 23-8

A nonresident member of an LLC has a five percent interest in an engineering firm that is organized as an LLC and operates within and outside of Wisconsin. The LLC receives income solely from the performance of engineering services. The nonresident member does not personally perform engineering services in Wisconsin. The nonresident's share of LLC income is not taxed in Wisconsin.

An interest in an LLC is intangible personal property. Any gain or loss realized on the disposition of an LLC interest is not includible in Wisconsin taxable interest. Gain or loss from the sale of intangible personal property follows the residence of a nonresident member.[1160]

An LLC with two or more nonresident members whose only Wisconsin taxable income is their shares of LLC income or loss may file a composite Wisconsin individual fiduciary return on behalf of those qualified members. The LLC files its return on Form 1CNP.[1161]

.10 Taxation of LLC Members Who Are Part-Year Wisconsin Resident Individuals

Members of an LLC who are part-year residents must compute income taxes on their shares of LLC income or loss for the part of the year during which they were residents.[1162] The computation is made as follows:[1163]

Step 1. Assign an equal portion of each item of income, loss, or deduction to each day of the LLC's tax year.

Step 2. Multiply each daily portion of those items of income, loss, or deduction by a fraction that represents the member's portion, on that day, of the total LLC interest.

[1160] Wis. Stat. § 71.04(1)(a).

[1161] Publication 119, Wisconsin Department of Revenue, Part VIII.B (Jan. 2013).

[1162] Wis. Stat. Ann. § 71.04(3)(a).

[1163] *Id.*

Step 3. Net the items of income, loss, or deduction against the prior calculation for all of the days during which the member was a resident of the state.

During the time that the member is a nonresident, all LLC income or loss attributable to a business located in Wisconsin, to services the individual personally performs in Wisconsin, or to real and tangible personal property located in Wisconsin is taxable to the nonresident. The disposition of a membership interest in an LLC while a member is a nonresident is treated in the same manner as for nonresident partners. Since a member's interest in an LLC is classified as intangible personal property, any gain or loss realized on the disposition of an LLC interest for a nonresident is not includible in Wisconsin taxable income. Gain or loss from the sale of intangible personal property follows the residence of a nonresident member.[1164]

EXAMPLE 23-9

A member has a 25 percent interest in an LLC that is engaged in business within and outside of Wisconsin. The LLC has ordinary income of $50,000, of which $40,000 is attributable to business activities in Wisconsin. The member is a Wisconsin resident for 90 days during the LLC's tax year. The member is subject to Wisconsin income taxes on $10,616 of LLC income, calculated as follows:

For the period of residence: 25% × 90/365 × $50,000	$ 3,082
For the period of nonresidence: 25% × 275/365 × $40,000	7,534
Total:	$10,616

.11 *Withholding Taxes and Composite Return for Nonresident Members*

An LLC that is classified as a partnership or S corporation must withhold taxes on the income allocable to nonresident members.[1165] The withholding tax payments must normally be made by electronic fund transfers.[1166] The LLC may also use Form PW-1 to make the withholding tax payments.

The amount of withholding tax in 2018 is 7.65 percent of the nonresident member's share of income attributable to Wisconsin.[1167]

[1164] Wis. Stat. Ann. §§ 71.02(1), 71.04(2) and (3).

[1165] Wis. Stat. Ann. § 71.775; Instructions to Form PW-1.

[1166] Wis. Admin. Code Reg. §§ 1.12, 2.04.

[1167] Wisconsin Publication 119, Limited Liability Companies (February 2016).

Alternatively, the LLC may file a composite return on Form 1CNP, Composite Wisconsin Individual Income Tax Return for Nonresident Partners, for nonresident members who derive no taxable income or deductible loss from Wisconsin other than their distributive shares of the Wisconsin LLC income or loss. The composite tax rate is 7.65 percent in 2018. The nonresident member may not claim any tax credits or itemized deductions on the composite return.

A nonresident member's share of income from an LLC is not subject to withholding if any of the following applies:[1168]

- The nonresident member's share of Wisconsin income from the LLC is less than $1,000.

- The nonresident files an affidavit with the Department on Form PW-2, Wisconsin Nonresident Partner, Member, Shareholder, or Beneficiary Withholding Exemption Affidavit. The LLC must maintain a Department-approved copy of the nonresident's Form PW-2 in its records to substantiate the exemption.

- The nonresident is exempt from Wisconsin income and franchise taxation. The LLC may rely on a written statement from the member claiming to be exempt from taxation, if the LLC attaches a copy of the statement to its income or franchise tax return for the taxable year. The statement must specify the nonresident's name, address, federal employer identification number, and reason for claiming an exemption.

Each LLC must pay the withholding tax by the 15th day of the fourth month following the close of the tax year.[1169]

An LLC must notify each nonresident member on or before the due date, including extensions, for filing the LLC's return of the amount of tax withheld by the LLC on the nonresident member's share of income. The LLC must provide a copy of the notice to the Wisconsin Department of Revenue with it state tax return. The nonresident member may claim a credit on his or her Wisconsin income or franchise tax return for the amount of the withheld tax.[1170]

The amount of income allocable to nonresident members is discussed below.

.12 Taxation of Corporate Members in LLC Classified as Partnership

Corporations engaged in business in Wisconsin are subject to the Wisconsin franchise or income tax. A corporation that is a member of an LLC is taxed depending on the location of the corporation's activities and the LLC's activities and on whether or not the LLC is an extension of the corporation's business.[1171]

[1168] Wisconsin Tax Bulletin No. 144, Part H.1 (Sept. 2005).

[1169] Wisconsin Tax Bulletin No. 144, Part H.1 (Sept. 2005).

[1170] Wisconsin Tax Bulletin No. 144, Part H.1 (Sept. 2005).

[1171] Publication 119, Wisconsin Department of Revenue, Part VIII.D (Jan. 2013).

Corporate Member Engaged in Business Wholly Within Wisconsin

A corporation that is engaged in business only in Wisconsin and that is a member of an LLC is taxed on the corporation's share of LLC net income or loss. A corporation engaged in business solely within Wisconsin is subject to tax on all income under the Wisconsin franchise or income tax laws.[1172]

EXAMPLE 23-10

A corporation that is a member of an LLC is engaged in business only in Wisconsin. It owns a 40 percent membership interest in the LLC that is engaged in business only in Wisconsin. The LLC has $250,000 of net income. The corporation must include its $100,000 share of LLC net income in its Wisconsin net income.

EXAMPLE 23-11

A corporation is engaged in business only in Wisconsin. It acquires a two percent interest in an LLC that is engaged in business within and outside of Wisconsin. Its membership interest in the LLC is not an extension of the corporation's business. The corporation is not engaged in business in the states where the LLC is engaged in business. The LLC has $200,000 of net income, of which $80,000 is attributable to the Wisconsin operations. The corporation must report 100 percent of its net income to Wisconsin, including its $4,000 share of LLC net income, since the corporation is engaged in business only in Wisconsin.

Corporate Member Engaged in Business Within and Outside of Wisconsin

A corporation that is engaged in business within and outside of Wisconsin and that is a member of an LLC is taxable on the corporation's share of LLC income or loss based on an apportionment formula.[1173] The apportionment formula and factors depend on whether the LLC membership interest is an extension of the corporation's business. If the LLC is an extension of the corporation's business, the corporation must combine its share of the LLC's apportionment data with its own apportionment data to determine the income allocable to Wisconsin. If the ownership interest is not an extension of the corporation's business, no part of the LLC's property, payroll, or

---

[1172] Wis. Stat. Ann. § 71.25(4).
[1173] Wis. Stat. Ann. § 71.25(5)(a)14.

sales is included in either the numerator or the denominator of the corporation's property, payroll, and sales factors, respectively.[1174]

EXAMPLE 23-12

A corporation is engaged in business within and outside of Wisconsin. It acquires a 60 percent interest in an LLC that is engaged in business in Wisconsin. The LLC is an extension of the corporation's business. The corporation must determine its Wisconsin net income under the apportionment method. The LLC has $300,000 of business income. The corporation must include $180,000, or 60 percent of the $300,000 of business income, in the corporation's apportionable income or loss. Sixty percent of the LLC's Wisconsin property, payroll, and sales are included in the numerator of the corporation's property, payroll, and sales factors, respectively, and 60 percent of the LLC's total property, payroll, and sales are included in the denominator of the corporation's property, payroll, and sales factors, respectively.

EXAMPLE 23-13

A corporation is engaged in business within and outside of Wisconsin. It acquires a five percent interest in an LLC that is engaged in business within and outside of Wisconsin. Its interest in the LLC is not an extension of the corporation's business. The corporation must determine its Wisconsin net income under the apportionment method. The LLC must include five percent of the LLC's business income or loss in the corporation's apportionable income or loss. No part of the LLC's property, payroll, or sales is included in either the numerator or the denominator of the corporation's property, payroll, and sales factors, respectively.

EXAMPLE 23-14

A corporation is engaged in business only in Wisconsin. It acquires a 55 percent interest in an LLC that is engaged in business within and outside of Wisconsin. The LLC is an extension of the corporation's business. Therefore, the corporation is engaged in business in the states where the LLC is engaged in business. The corporation must determine its Wisconsin net income under the apportionment method. It must include 55 percent of the LLC's business income or loss in its apportionable income

---

[1174] Wis. Stat. Ann. § 71.25(9)(e)8; Wis. Admin. Code § Tax 2.39(7).

or loss. Fifty-five percent of the LLC's Wisconsin property, payroll, and sales are included in the numerator of the corporation's property, payroll, and sales factors, respectively. Fifty-five percent of the LLC's total property, payroll, and sales are included in the denominator of the corporation's property, payroll, and sales factors, respectively.

Corporate Member Not Engaged in Business in Wisconsin

A corporation is subject to the Wisconsin franchise or income tax if it is not engaged in business in Wisconsin, but acquires an interest in an LLC that is engaged in business in Wisconsin where the LLC is an extension of the corporation's business. The corporate member is treated as engaged in business in Wisconsin as a result of holding an interest in the LLC. The corporation's share of LLC income or loss is includible in its apportionable income.[1175] The corporation must combine its share of the LLC's apportionable data with its own apportionable data to determine the income allocable to Wisconsin.[1176]

EXAMPLE 23-15

A corporation is not engaged in business in Wisconsin. It acquires a 50 percent interest in an LLC that is engaged in business in Wisconsin. The LLC is an extension of the corporation's business. Therefore, the corporation is engaged in business in Wisconsin and is subject to the Wisconsin franchise or income tax. The corporation must determine its Wisconsin net income under the apportionment method. It must include 50 percent of the LLC's business income or loss in its apportionable income or loss. Fifty percent of the LLC's Wisconsin property, payroll, and sales are included in the numerator of the corporation's property, payroll, and sales factors, respectively. Fifty percent of the LLC's total property, payroll, and sales are included in the denominator of the corporation's property, payroll, and sales factors, respectively. In addition, any Wisconsin destination sales made by the corporation are included in the numerator of its sales factor.

A corporation that is not engaged in business in Wisconsin and that acquires an interest in an LLC that is engaged in business in Wisconsin is not subject to Wisconsin franchise or income taxation if the LLC membership interest is not an extension of the corporation's business. The corporate member is not treated as engaged in business in Wisconsin based on an investment in an LLC.

[1175] Wis. Stat. Ann. § 71.25(5)(a)14.
[1176] Wis. Stat. Ann. § 71.25(9)(e)8; Wis. Admin. Code § Tax 2.39(7).

EXAMPLE 23-16

A Delaware LLC that is a corporation is not engaged in business in Wisconsin. It acquires a three percent interest in an LLC that is engaged in business in Wisconsin. Its interest in the LLC is not an extension of the corporation's business. The corporation is not engaged in business in Wisconsin and is not subject to Wisconsin franchise or income tax on a share of the LLC's Wisconsin income.

.13 Taxation of LLC Members That Are Partnerships

An LLC or a partnership that is a member in another LLC doing business in Wisconsin must file a Wisconsin partnership return. The LLC member is considered to have income from business transacted in Wisconsin.

Partners in a partnership that is a member of an LLC are treated in the same manner as partners in other partnerships doing business in Wisconsin. Therefore, full-year Wisconsin resident individual partners must pay Wisconsin income taxes on their distributive shares of partnership income, including their shares of LLC income earned by the partnership. Nonresident individual partners are subject to Wisconsin income taxes on their distributive shares of partnership income, including their shares of LLC income derived by the LLC from business transacted in Wisconsin.

.14 Taxation of LLCs Classified as Corporations

A membership interest in an LLC that is classified as a corporation is treated in the same manner as stock in a regular corporation. The members in the LLC are taxed as follows.[1177]

Full-Year Wisconsin Resident Members

Full-year resident individuals, estates, and trusts that are members of an LLC are subject to Wisconsin income tax on distributions of income received from an LLC regardless of where it is located. A Wisconsin resident must include any gain or loss in taxable income from the disposition of an LLC membership interest.[1178]

Nonresident Members

Nonresident members are not subject to Wisconsin income tax on distributions of LLC income if the LLC is classified as a corporation. Nonresident members do not

---

[1177] Publication 119, Wisconsin Department of Revenue, Part IX (Jan. 2013).
[1178] Wis. Stat. Ann. §§ 71.02(1), 71.04(1)(a).

include in their taxable income gain or loss realized on the sale or other disposition of a membership interest.[1179]

Part-Year Wisconsin Resident Members

Part-year resident members of an LLC that is classified as a corporation are taxed on distributions of LLC income received while residents of Wisconsin. Part-year residents must include in Wisconsin taxable income gain or loss realized on the disposition of LLC interests while Wisconsin residents.[1180] Part-year residents are not taxed on distributions of LLC income received while nonresidents of Wisconsin. Part-year residents do not include in Wisconsin taxable income gain or loss realized on the disposition of LLC membership interests while nonresidents.

Corporate Members

A corporation that is a member of an LLC that is also classified as a corporation is subject to Wisconsin franchise or income tax on income distributions from the LLC, regardless of where the LLC is located, if the corporation's entire business income is attributable to Wisconsin. The corporation must include in Wisconsin net income gain or loss on the sale or other disposition of a membership interest.[1181]

A multistate corporation that is a member of an LLC classified as a corporation must include income distributions and gain or loss upon disposition of an LLC membership interest in apportionable income if there is a unitary relationship between the corporation and the LLC or if the LLC is not an affiliate or a subsidiary and the LLC membership interest is part of the corporation's unitary investment activity and serves an operational function.[1182]

Members Classified as Partnerships

An LLC that is classified as a corporation may have members who are partnerships or LLCs classified as partnerships. Distributions from the corporate LLC to the partnership LLC are treated in the same manner as dividend income. The partnership LLC member of the corporate LLC must include in Wisconsin taxable income gain or loss from the disposition of the LLC income. Gain or loss from the disposition is treated as income or loss from intangibles.

[1179] Publication 119, Wisconsin Department of Revenue, Part VIII.E (Jan. 2013).

[1180] Wis. Stat. Ann. §§ 71.02, 71.04(2), (3).

[1181] Wis. Stat. Ann. §§ 71.25(4), 71.26(2).

[1182] Wis. Stat. Ann. §§ 71.25(5)(a), 71.26(2).

.15 Taxation of LLC Classified as Disregarded Entity

The activities of a disregarded LLC are treated in the same manner as a sole proprietorship, branch, or division of the owner. The owner is subject to the Wisconsin tax on or measured by the LLC's income.[1183]

Full-year residents must treat LLC income or loss as if it were from a sole proprietorship. They must include it in their Wisconsin adjusted gross income, regardless of where the LLC is located or the nature of its income.[1184]

Nonresidents who are individuals, estates, or trusts must treat the LLC income or loss as if it were from a sole proprietorship. They must include it in their Wisconsin taxable income to the extent attributable to a business located in Wisconsin, services performed in Wisconsin, or real or tangible personal property located in Wisconsin.[1185]

Part-year residents must treat LLC income or loss as if it were from a sole proprietorship. The amount of income that they must include in Wisconsin taxable income depends on the period of time that they were residents or nonresidents, and whether the member is an individual, corporation or partnership.[1186]

.16 Disregarding Provisions in Operating Agreement

The provisions of an LLC operating agreement are disregarded in computing taxes, a member's distributive share of income, and the situs of LLC income if the provisions of the operating agreement do any of the following:[1187]

- Characterize the consideration for payments to the member as services for the use of capital;

- Allocate to the member as income or gain from sources outside the state a greater proportion of the member's distributive share of LLC income or gain than the ratio of LLC income or gain from sources outside the state to LLC income or gain from all sources;

- Allocate to a member a greater proportion of LLC items of loss or deduction from sources in Wisconsin than the member's proportionate share of total LLC loss or deduction; or

- Determine a member's distributive share of an item of LLC income, gain, loss, or deduction for federal income tax purposes if the principal purpose of that determination is to avoid or evade Wisconsin taxes.

[1183] Publication 119, Wisconsin Department of Revenue, Part IX.F (Jan. 2013).

[1184] Wis. Stats. § 71.02(1).

[1185] Wis. Stats. § 71.02(1), 71.04(1)(a).

[1186] *See* Publication 119, Wisconsin Department of Revenue, Part X.C (Jan. 2013).

[1187] Wis. Stat. Ann. § 71.04(3)(c).

.17 Allocations

Profits and losses of a Wisconsin LLC are allocated among members on the basis of their contributions unless otherwise provided in the operating agreement. Distributions of cash or the assets of an LLC are made to members in the same manner that profits are allocated unless a distribution is varied by an operating agreement.[1188]

.18 Credit for Taxes Paid to Another State

Wisconsin residents who are members of an LLC that is classified as a partnership may claim credits for income or franchise taxes paid by the LLC to another state.[1189] The income taxed by the other state is also considered income for Wisconsin tax purposes.

.19 Other Credits

Members of an LLC classified as a partnership may claim the same credits that are available to partners of partnerships. An LLC that is classified as a corporation may claim the same tax credits as a regular C corporation, unless the LLC has elected to be classified as an S corporation. The owner of an LLC classified as a disregarded entity may claim any tax credits based on the LLC's activities for which the owner would otherwise be eligible.[1190]

.20 Tax Returns

Wisconsin requires an LLC that is classified as a partnership to file the following tax returns:

- Form 3, Wisconsin Partnership Return.[1191] A copy of federal Form 1065 and any other required schedules and statements must be attached to the return. A copy of any extension must be attached to the return. This form is used to report the income, deductions, gains, and losses from the operations of the LLC. Every LLC that is classified as a partnership and that has income from Wisconsin sources, regardless of the amount, must file Form 3. The return must be filed with the Wisconsin Department of Revenue, P.O. Box 59, Madison, WI 53785-0001. The return must be filed by the 15th day of the fourth month following the close of the LLC's tax year. The LLC may obtain an extension of time to file the return by obtaining a federal extension request and attaching the copy of the federal extension to the Wisconsin return.

[1188] Wis. Stat. Ann. §§ 183.0503, 183.0602.

[1189] Wis. Stat. Ann. § 71.07(7).

[1190] Publication 119, Wisconsin Department of Revenue, Part VII.A.2 (Jan. 2013).

[1191] Wis. Stat. Ann. § 71.20(1).

- Schedule 3K-1, Partner's Share of Income, Deductions, Etc. This form sets forth each member's distributive share of the LLC's income, gain, loss, deductions, and credit.

An LLC that is classified as a corporation must file Wisconsin Form 4 or 5, Corporation Franchise or Income Tax Return.[1192]

.21 Conversion from Partnership to LLC

If an existing partnership becomes an LLC and the IRS does not treat it as a termination of the existing partnership, the same treatment applies for Wisconsin tax purposes. If the members' interests in the LLC's profits, losses, and capital remain the same after the conversion from a partnership to an LLC, no gain or loss is recognized upon the conversion. If the conversion is not treated as a partnership termination, no existing accounting periods or methods are affected. The partnership and the LLC do not have to file short-period returns for the year of the conversion.

If an existing partnership becomes an LLC and the IRS does not require the LLC to obtain a new federal employer identification number, the LLC is not required to obtain a new Wisconsin employer identification number.

If a partnership becomes an LLC and the IRS does not require the LLC to obtain a new federal employer identification number, the LLC is not required to obtain a new Wisconsin seller's permit or a new use tax or consumer's use tax number. An existing partnership that becomes an LLC is not subject to sales or use tax on the transfer of its assets to the LLC if there is no change in the ownership interest of its members.

.22 Conversion of Corporation to LLC

The conversion of a corporation into an LLC is generally treated as a taxable reorganization. The corporation must dissolve and reorganize as an LLC. An existing corporation that dissolves and becomes an LLC must obtain a new Wisconsin employer identification number. An existing corporation that dissolves and becomes an LLC must obtain a new Wisconsin seller's permit and a new use tax or consumer's use tax number. An existing corporation that becomes an LLC is not subject to sales or use tax on the transfer of its assets to the LLC if there is no change in the ownership interest of its members.

.23 Real Estate Transfer Fees

The conveyance of real estate from a partnership to an LLC pursuant to the reorganization of a partnership as an LLC is subject to the Wisconsin real estate transfer fee.[1193]

[1192] Wis. Stat. Ann. §§ 71.22(1), 71.24(1).

[1193] Wolter, Wis. Tax Appeals Comm'n, No. 96-T-941 (May 6, 1998).

.24 Filing Fees

There are the following filing fees in Wisconsin:[1194]

Articles of organization	$170 ($130 if filed electronically)
Foreign LLC registration certificate	$100
Annual report	$25 ($80 for a foreign LLC)

¶2352 WYOMING

Wyoming was the first state to authorize LLCs. It enacted the Wyoming Limited Liability Company Act in 1977.[1195]

.01 Taxation of LLC and Members

An LLC must pay an annual report license tax of $50 or two-tenths of one mill on the dollar ($.0002), whichever is greater, based on the LLC's assets located and used in the state of Wyoming.[1196]

Wyoming has no other individual or corporate income taxes. Members are not taxed on their distributive shares of LLC income.

.02 Allocations

Unless otherwise provided in the operating agreement, an LLC's profits and losses are allocated on the basis of the value of the contributions made by each member, less the contributions returned by the LLC to the member.[1197]

.03 Filing Fees

Wyoming imposes the following filing fees on LLCs:[1198]

Articles of organization	$100
Registration of foreign LLC	$100

[1194] Wis. Stat. Ann. § 183.0114.

[1195] Wyo. Stat. §§ 17-15-101 to 17-15-147.

[1196] Wyoming Business Division Filing Fee Schedule, Wyoming Secretary of State's Office Business Division (rev. Apr. 6, 2007).

[1197] Wyo. Stat. § 17-15-119.

[1198] Wyo. Stat. § 17-15-132.

24

Asset Protection, Charging Orders, Creditors' Rights

¶ 2401 CREDITORS OF LLC—FORWARD PIERCING

In forward piercing cases, a creditor first obtains a judgment against the LLC, and then seeks to hold the members of the LLC personally liable for the judgment. Under the veil piercing doctrine, the creditors may be allowed to disregard the entity and its liability protections under certain circumstances, and hold the members of the LLC liable for LLC debts. This is sometimes referred to as the alter ego doctrine.

Several states provide that members of an LLC may be personally liable for the debts, judgments, and other liabilities of an LLC to the same extent the shareholders are liable to corporate creditors under the "piercing the corporate veil" doctrine.[1] For example, the members of an LLC may be liable to creditors in those states if the LLC is undercapitalized, fails to obtain sufficient insurance to cover the risks of the business, or is used for fraudulent purposes.[2]

A number of states provide that the failure to hold meetings of members or to comply with other formalities does not result in personal liability of the member.[3]

¶2402 CREDITORS OF MEMBERS—REVERSE PIERCING

In reverse piercing cases, a creditor first obtains a judgment against a member of the LLC, and then seeks to collect on the judgment by proceeding against the member's interest in the assets of the LLC. The reverse veil piercing subjects an LLC's property to the claims of a member's creditors.[4] For example, the court in the *Litchfield*[5] case allowed a judgment creditor of an individual member to attach LLC assets in satisfaction of the judgment.

State laws and court rulings provide that reverse piercing may be available based on one or more of the following theories:

- Charging order (discussed at ¶2404).
- Foreclosure of charging order (discussed at ¶2405).
- Broad charging order, including substitution of the creditor as an LLC member, dissolution of LLC, sale of LLC assets, and other remedies approved by the court (discussed at ¶2406).
- Resulting trust. A resulting trust is an equitable remedy imposed by the court if the transferor intended the transferee to hold the property for the transferor's benefit.
- Constructive trust. A constructive trust is an equitable remedy imposed by the court to avoid unjust enrichment to a defendant. The remedy is imposed on a person "who holds legal right to property, which in equity and good conscience belongs to another."[6] Unlike a resulting trust claim, it is irrelevant whether the transferee intended to have the transferor hold the property in trust.

---

[1] CCA 201116019; Cal. Corp. Code § 17703.04(b); Colo. Rev. Stat. Ann. § 7-80-107(1); Fla. Stat. Ann. § 608.701; Me. Rev. Stat. Ann. tit. 31, § 645.3; Minn. Stat. § 322B.303, subd. 2; N.D. Cent. Code § 10-32-29.3; Wash. Rev. Code § 25.15.060; Wis. Stat. § 183.0304(2).

[2] *See, e.g.*, Cal. Corp. Code § 17703.04(d) regarding insurance.

[3] Cal. Corp. Code § 17703.04(b); Colo. Rev. Stat. Ann. § 7-80-107(2); Fla. Stat. Ann. § § 605.0304(2); Haw. Rev. Stat. Ann. § 428-303(b); Idaho Code § 30-6-304(2); 805 ILCS § 180/10-10(c); Iowa Code § 490A.603.2; Me. Rev. Stat. Ann. tit. 31, § 645.2; Mont. Code Ann. § 35-8-304(2); Or. Rev. Stat. § 63.1165(2); S.C. Code Ann. § 33-44-303(c); S.D. Codified Laws Ann. § 47-34A-303(b); Tenn. Code Ann. § 48-217-101(f); Utah Code Ann. § 48-2c-602(5); Wash. Rev. Code § 25.15.060; W. Va. Code § 31B-3-303(b).

[4] CCA 201116019.

[5] *Litchfield Asset Mgmt. Corp. v. Howell*, 799 A.2d 298, 315-16 (Conn. App. 2002).

[6] *American Diabetes Ass'n v. Diabetes Soc.*, 31 Ohio App.3d 136, 141 (Clinton 1986).

- Creditor's bill. A creditor's bill or creditor's suit is a lawsuit filed by a judgment creditor against the judgment debtors to collect money owed to the judgment debtors in order to satisfy the debts of the judgment creditors. The courts will not normally permit a creditor's bill in jurisdictions which provide that a charging order is the exclusive remedy in legal actions against LLC members.[7]

The following state statutory laws provide that creditors of a member of an LLC may obtain a charging order, foreclosure of a charging order, and/or other remedies against the LLC:

State	Charging Order	Foreclosure	Other Remedies	Statutory Authority
Alabama	x			Ala. Code § 10-12-35
Alaska	x			Alaska Stat. § 10.50.380
Arizona	x			Ariz. Rev. Stat. Ann. § 29-655
Arkansas	x			Ark. Code Ann. § 4-32-705
California	x	x		Cal. Corp. Code § 17705.03; Cal. Code of Civ. Proc. §§ 708.310, 708.320. Cal. Corp. Code § 17705.03(d) permits another member of the LLC to buy a charged member's interest by paying "to the judgment creditor the full amount due under the judgment." This makes LLCs less attractive than California limited partnerships which permit another partner to buy the interest of a charged partner on terms less attractive to the creditor based on the price or terms set forth in the limited partnership agreement. Cal. Corp. Code § 15907.03(c)(2).
Colorado	x	x	x	Colo. Rev. Stat. § 7-80-703
Connecticut	x			Conn. Gen. Stat. Ann. § 34-171
D.C.	x			D.C. Code Ann. § 29-1038
Delaware	x			Del. Code Ann. tit. 6, § 18-703

---

[7] *See, e.g., Matter of Pischke*, 11 B.R. 913, 917 (Bankr. E.D. Va. 1981).

State	Charging Order	Foreclosure	Other Remedies	Statutory Authority
Florida	x			Fla. Stat. Ann. § 608.433(4); Patch Amendment provided that the charging order is the exclusive remedy for LLC creditors except for single-member LLCs, thus overruling *Olmstead v. F.T.C.*, 44 So. 3d 76 (Fla. 2010).
Georgia	x	x	x	Ga. Code Ann. § 14-11-504
Hawaii	x	x		Haw. Rev. Stat. Ann. § 428-504
Idaho	x	x	x	Idaho Code § 30-6-503
Illinois	x	x	x	805 ILCS § 180/30-20
Indiana	x			Ind. Code Ann. § 23-18-6-7
Iowa	x			Iowa Code § 490A.904
Kansas	x			Kan. Stat. Ann. § 17-76,113
Kentucky	x			Ky. Rev. Stat. § 275.260
Louisiana	x			La. Rev. Stat. Ann. § 12:1331
Maine	x			Me. Rev. Stat. Ann. tit. 31, § 686
Maryland	x			Md. Corps. & Ass'ns Code Ann. § 4A-607
Massachusetts	x			M.G.L.A. ch. 156C, § 40
Michigan	x			Mich. Comp. Laws Ann. § 450.4507
Minnesota	x			Minn. Stat. § 322B.32
Mississippi	x			Miss. Code Ann. § 79-29-703
Missouri	x			Mo. Rev. Stat. § 347.119
Montana	x	x	x	Mont. Code Ann. § 35-8-705
Nebraska	x	x	x	Neb. Rev. Stat. § 67-430
Nevada	x			Nev. Rev. Stat. Ann. § 86.401; Nevada statute specifically provides that the charging order is also the exclusive remedy of creditors of a single-member LLC.

State	Charging Order	Foreclosure	Other Remedies	Statutory Authority
New Hampshire	x			N.H. Rev. Stat. Ann. § 304-C:47
New Jersey	x			N.J. Stat. Ann. § 42:2B-45. Effective September 19, 2012, New Jersey deleted the foreclosure provisions for judgment creditors against LLCs. A.B. 4023, Laws 2014.
New Mexico	x			N.M. Stat. Ann. § 53-19-35
New York	x			N.Y. LLC § 607
North Carolina	x			N.C. Gen. Stat. § 57C-5-03
North Dakota	x			N.D. Cent. Code § 10-32-34
Ohio	x			Ohio Rev. Code Ann. § 1705.19
Oklahoma	x			Okla. Stat. Ann. tit. 18, § 2034
Oregon	x			Or. Rev. Stat. § 63.259
Pennsylvania	x	x	x	15 Pa. Cons. Stat. § § 8904(a), 8345
Rhode Island	x			R.I. Gen. Laws § 7-16-37
South Carolina	x	x	x	S.C. Code Ann. § 33-44-504
South Dakota	x	x	x	S.D. Codified Laws Ann. § 47-34A-504
Tennessee	x			Tenn. Code Ann. § 48-249-509
Texas	x		x (case law)	Tex. Rev. Civ. Stat. Ann. art. 1528n, 4.06A
Utah	x	x	x	Utah Code Ann. § 48-2c-1103
Vermont	x	x	x	Vt. Stat. Ann. tit. 11, § 3074
Virginia	x			Va. Code Ann. § 13.1-1041
Washington	x			Wash. Rev. Code § 25.15.255

State	Charging Order	Foreclosure	Other Remedies	Statutory Authority
West Virginia	x	x	x	W. Va. Code § 31B-5-504
Wisconsin	x			Wis. Stat. § 183.0705
Wyoming	x	x		Wyo. Stat. § 17-15-145; Wyoming statute specifically provides that the charging order is also the exclusive remedy of creditors of a single-member LLC.

¶ 2403 ENTERPRISE LIABILITY

Enterprise liability is an alternative legal theory to veil piercing. Under this theory, a plaintiff may argue that several entities are operating as a single enterprise, and therefore all such entities should together be liable.[8] The courts sometimes refer to the enterprise theory as the "single entity theory,"[9] or the "single business enterprise theory."[10] Joint-enterprise liability refers to circumstances in which courts will disregard the legal fiction that business entities owned by a parent corporation retain a distinct existence from one another.[11] Concerted-action is a similar theory, and refers to situations where courts can impute the tortious conduct of one person to other members of a group.[12] Under all of the theories, if entities do not operate as separate entities, but rather integrate their resources to achieve a common business purpose, then each constituent corporation may be held liable for debts incurred in pursuit of that business purpose."[13] The seminal case, *Walkovsky v. Carlton*,[14] involved a New York taxicab company that incorporated each separate taxicab owner to insulate the enterprise from liability.

The courts in some jurisdictions impose enterprise liability on groups of companies involving LLCs.[15]

---

[8] *Miners. Inc. v. Alpine Equipment Corp.*, 722 A.2d 691, 695 (Pa. Super. Ct. 1998).

[9] *Miners. Inc. v. Alpine Equipment Corp.*, 722 A.2d 691, 695 (Pa. Super. Ct. 1998).

[10] *SSP Partners v. Gladstrong Investments (USA) Corp.*, 275 S.W.3d 444, 452 (Tex. 2009).

[11] *Donastorg v. Daily News Publ'g Co.*, No. ST-2002-CV-117, 2015 WL 5399263, at *65 (V.I. Super. Aug. 19, 2015).

[12] *Donastorg v. Daily News Publ'g Co.*, No. ST-2002-CV-117, 2015 WL 5399263, at *65 (V.I. Super. Aug. 19, 2015).

[13] *Paramount Petroleum Corp. v. Taylor Rental Ctr.*, 712 S.W.2d 534, 536 (Tex. App. 1986) (abrogated by *SSP Partners*, 275 S.W.3d at 453). *See also SSP Partners*, 275 S.W.3d at 453 (explaining that the Supreme Court of Texas does not suggest "that unity of enterprise alone would justify disregarding corporate structures").

[14] 223 N.E.2d 6 (N.Y. 1966).

[15] *See, e.g., Litchfield Asset Mgmt. Corp. v. Howell*, 799 A.2d 298, 315-16 (Conn. App. 2002).

¶ 2404 CHARGING ORDER

.01 Definition

All of the states permit a creditor of an LLC member to obtain a charging order against a member's membership interest. A charging order requires that any future distributions from the LLC to a member be made to the creditor who obtained the charging order against the member. It is similar to an assignment of income. This remedy is only available to outside creditors for satisfaction of outside debts.

A judgment creditor must apply to the court of competent jurisdiction for the charging order. The charging order charges the member's interest in the LLC with payment of the judgment, plus interest. To the extent charged, the judgment creditor is treated as an assignee of the member's economic interest.

The major limitation of the charging order for a creditor is that it only gives a creditor a right to receive a pro rata share of distributions if and when distributions are made. The creditor has no voting or management rights. The managers of the LLC may in their discretion decide not to make any distributions to members.

.02 Exclusive Remedy States

Some states provide that the charging order is the exclusive remedy for a judgment creditor of an LLC member.[16] This denies the creditor direct assets to LLC. It is normally advisable to organize an LLC in an exclusive remedy jurisdiction if the LLC is used for asset protection purposes. The LLC may then qualify to do business in other states where it is actually conducting business. The most favorable exclusive remedy jurisdictions are Alaska, Arizona, Delaware, Nevada, New Jersey, Oklahoma, and Wyoming. It is unclear whether a court in a non-exclusive remedy jurisdiction will limit creditor remedies to a charging order if the LLC is organized in an exclusive remedy jurisdiction.[17]

---

[16] *See, e.g.,* Ala. Code § 10-12-35(a); Alaska Stat. § 10.50.380(c); Ariz. Rev. Stat. Ann. § 29-1044.E; Cal. Corp. Code § 17302(e); 805 ILCS § 180/30-20(e); Kan. Stat. Ann. § 17-76,113; Minn. Stat. § 322B.32; Nev. Rev. Stat. Ann. § 86.401.5; N.J. Stat. Ann. § 42:2B-45; N.D. Cent. Code § 10-32-34.3; Okla. Stat. Ann. tit. 18, § 2034; S.C. Code Ann. § 33-44-504(e); S.D. Codified Laws Ann. § 47-34A-504(e); Utah Code Ann. § 48-2c-1103(5), (6); Vt. Stat. Ann. tit. 11, § 3074(e); W. Va. Code § 31B-5-504(e); Wyo. Stat. § 17-15-145.

[17] *See, e.g., Am. Institutional Partners, LLC v. Fairstar Res. Ltd.,* No. CA 10-489-LPS, 2011 WL 1230074, at *1 (D. Del. Mar. 31, 2011).

.03 Tax Consequences

Prior to foreclosure, the charging order is a lien on the member's transferable interest. The tax consequences of income allocations and distributions are as follows:[18]

- Distributions by the LLC to the judgment creditor are treated as distributions in satisfaction of a judgment. The distributions are taxable based on the underlying cause of action under the "origin of the claim" test.[19] For example, the distribution will be taxed as capital gains if the judgment is for damages to a capital asset.[20] The distribution will be nontaxable if the judgment is for personal physical injuries.[21] The distribution will be taxed as ordinary income if the judgment is for lost wages or other compensation.
- The member of the LLC against whom the charging order is made is taxed on the member's allocable share of income regardless of the tax consequences to the judgment creditor. The member is the owner of the economic interest prior to foreclosure. The distribution by the LLC to the judgment creditor is treated as payment of a liability owed by the member. The payment of the member's debts through a charging order does not relieve the member of tax on the member's allocable share of income.
- The member may be able to obtain a deduction for the distributions to the judgment creditor if the judgment relates to the member's separate business, is treated as an ordinary and necessary business expense, or is an investment expense.

¶ 2405 FORECLOSURE OF CHARGING ORDER

.01 State Laws

Many states permit a creditor to foreclose a charging order against an LLC interest.[22] This is a court-ordered process whereby the charged interest in the membership interest is sold in a public sale, at an auction, or is appraised and sold to the creditor at fair market value. Foreclosure normally makes the creditor a permanent owner of the member's economic rights associated with the charged membership interest.

---

[18] *See* Asset Protection in a Troubled Economy, pp. 101-103, Los Angeles County Bar Association (May 18, 2011).

[19] *United States v. Gilmore*, 372 U.S. 39 (1963).

[20] Rev. Rul. 74-251, 1974-1 CB 234.

[21] Code Sec. 104(a).

[22] *See, e.g.*, Ariz. Rev. Stat. Ann. §29-1044.B; Ga. Code Ann. §14-11-504; Mont. Code Ann. §35-8-705; Nev. Rev. Stat. Ann. §86.401.3, 4; 15 Pa. Cons. Stat. §8345; S.C. Code Ann. §33-44-504(c); S.D. Codified Laws Ann. §47-34A-504(b), (c); Utah Code Ann. §48-2c-1103(3); Vt. Stat. Ann. tit. 11, §3074(b), (c); W. Va. Code §31B-5-504(b), (c).

To protect the rights of the judgment debtor and the other members of the LLC, the statutes normally provide that the foreclosed membership interest may be redeemed (a) by the judgment debtor, (b) with property other than LLC property, by one or more of the other members of the LLC, and (c) with LLC property, by one or more of the other members with the consent of all the members whose interests are not so charged.[23]

Some states, such as Texas, permit foreclosure by case law rather than statute. Other states, such as Alaska, Arizona, Delaware, Nevada, New Jersey, Oklahoma, and Wyoming, prohibit foreclosure, and provide that a charging order is the sole remedy for creditor of an LLC member. Some courts have interpreted statutes in exclusive remedy states as allowing foreclosure on the theory that foreclosure is not a separate remedy but is the right of a holder of a charging order. Most jurisdictions have interpreted the exclusive remedy language as disallowing foreclosure.

.02 Tax Consequences

After foreclosure of the charging order, the judgment creditor owns an economic interest in the LLC rather than a lien. There is a split of authority on the tax consequences of the charging order after a foreclosure.

Some commentators believe that the creditor who obtains the charging order is liable for taxes on the debtor's allocable share of LLC income.[24] In such case, the LLC must send the creditor a Schedule K-1 reflecting the taxable income allocated to the charging order. The creditor must pay taxes on the income whether or not distributed. A creditor may be reluctant to seek a charging order since the creditor will be "KO'd by the K-1."

Other commentators believe that the creditor who obtains a charging order is not liable on the undistributed income allocable to the judgment debtor. Instead, the creditor is only liable for actual distributions of income to the creditor.[25]

One commentator suggested that if a judgment creditor is somehow taxable on the charging order proceeds, then the debtor should have cancellation of indebtedness income to the extent that the judgment creditor actually receives distributions (thereby relieving the debtor of the obligation to pay the creditor).[26]

In Revenue Ruling 77-137, the IRS determined that the assignee of a limited partnership interest was the beneficial owner of such interest. As assignee, the creditor was required to "report the distributive share of partnership items of income,

---

[23] *See, e.g.,* Ariz. Rev. Stat. Ann. § 29-1044.C; Cal. Corp. Code § 17302(c); 805 ILCS § 180/30-20(c); Mont. Code Ann. § 35-8-705; Nev. Rev. Stat. Ann. § 86.401.3, 4; N.H. Rev. Stat. Ann. § § 304-A:28.II; 15 Pa. Cons. Stat. § 8345; S.C. Code Ann. § 33-44-504(c); S.D. Codified Laws Ann. § 47-34A-504(b), (c); Utah Code Ann. § 48-2c-1103(3); Vt. Stat. Ann. tit. 11, § 3074(b), (c); W. Va. Code § 31B-5-504(b), (c).

[24] *See, e.g.,* Arthur A. DiPadova & Kevin A. Kilroy, "How Family With the Partnerships Help Protect Assets," 137 N.J. L.J. 11, 44 (1994); Lewis D. Solomon & Lewis J. Saret, Asset Protection Strategies, § 3.06[E] (CCH CPA Client Advisor/Wealth Planning Online Library 2015); Asset Protection in a Troubled Economy, pp. 101-103, Los Angeles County Bar Association (May 18, 2011).

[25] Christopher M. Riser, "Tax Consequences of Charging Orders," Asset Protection J. (Winter 1999).

[26] *Id.*

gain or loss, deduction, and credit attributable to the assignee interest . . . in the same manner and the same amounts that would be required if [the assignee] was a substitute limited partner." The most important factor was that the assignee acquired substantially all dominion and control over the limited partnership interest, even though the general partner did not consent to the transfer. Under the terms of the assignment, the assignee irrevocably assigned profits and losses of the partnership and all distributions, including liquidating distributions, to the assignee. The assigning partner agreed to exercise any residual powers in favor of and in the interests of the assignee partner. The assignor was the nominal limited partner under local law after the assignment.

In *Evans v. Commissioner*,[27] the court concluded that the assignee of a general partner, and not the assigning general partner himself, was the "partner" for purposes of reporting partnership distributive shares.

In GCM 36960, the IRS determined that an assignee of a limited partnership interest is required to report distributive shares of partnership income or loss attributable to the assigned interest, even though he or she does not become a substituted limited partner, when the assignee acquires dominion and control over the partnership interest. However, to the extent that the assignor retains substantial rights with respect to the interest that are not exercisable solely on behalf of the assignees, the assignee does not have the requisite dominion and control.

These rulings deal with a partner who voluntarily assigns his partnership interest to a third party. They do not deal with a judgment creditor and a debtor partner or member of an LLC. A judgment creditor who obtains a charging order arguably does not have the requisite dominion and control. The assignee does not participate in the management and affairs of the LLC without the consent of the manager or members of the LLC. The assignee is not a party to any action affecting the assignor's retained economic rights as a member of the LLC. The managers and members of the LLC do not have any fiduciary obligations to the assignee. The assignee may not become a member of the LLC without compliance with the terms of the LLC operating agreement. The judgment creditor receives only a right to future distributions allocable to the judgment debtor, if and when such distributions are made. The debtor retains all other rights.[28]

¶2406 BROAD CHARGING ORDER AND OTHER REMEDIES

In some states, a creditor may apply for a "broad charging order" if the creditor believes that the managers of the LLC are unreasonably withholding distributions in order to interfere with the judgment creditor's economic rights. The broad charging order may provide for (i) substitution of the creditor as a full voting member of the LLC, (ii) management rights for the creditor, (iii) appointment of a receiver of LLC income, (iv) judicial dissolution of the LLC and liquidation of LLC assets, (v)

---

[27] *Evans v. Comm'r*, 447 F.2d 547 (7th Cir. 1971).

[28] Christopher M. Riser, "Tax Consequences of Charging Orders," Asset Protection J. (Winter 1999).

garnishment served on the LLC,[29] (vi) forcing the manager to make distributions if funds are available, (vii) sale of the membership interest, or (viii) such other remedies determined by the court.[30]

The courts will not ordinarily order the appointment of a receiver or judicial dissolution except in cases of bad faith, breach of fiduciary duty and/or fraud. However, the courts sometimes consider broad remedies, including substitution of the creditor as a member of the LLC[31] and liquidation of LLC assets, for a single-member LLC. The Florida statute provides that a charging order is the exclusive remedy for judgment creditors except for single-member LLCs. The Nevada and Wyoming statutes specifically provide that the charging order is the exclusive remedy of creditors of all LLCs.[32]

In *In re Ashby Albright*,[33] Ashby Albright was the sole member and the manager of a Colorado LLC. Colorado law provided that a charging order was the exclusive remedy for judgment creditor of an LLC member. Ashby Albright filed for bankruptcy. The bankruptcy court determined that the trustee in bankruptcy could substitute himself for the debtor as the sole member and manager of the LLC, and in that capacity cause the LLC to sell the LLC's real property and distribute the proceeds of sale to the bankruptcy estate. The debtor argued that the trustee in bankruptcy was only entitled to a charging order and to receive distributions from the LLC, if and when made in the debtor's discretion. However, the bankruptcy court noted that the debtor's membership interest was personal property under Colorado law, and that the debtor had by law transferred her membership interest to the bankruptcy estate upon the bankruptcy filing. Since the debtor was the sole member of the LLC, the court did not need the consent of other members to the admission of the bankruptcy trustee as the substituted member.

In *Herring v. Keasler*,[34] a multi-member LLC, the court granted charging order against the defendant's membership interest. However, it refused to seize and sell the defendant's membership interest in several LLCs or permit the plaintiff to become the substituted member.

¶ 2407 BANKRUPTCY

Many operating agreements place restrictions on involuntary transfers and assignments of membership interests, including assignments to creditors in bankruptcy

---

[29] *See, e.g.*, Ga. Code Ann. § 14-11-504(b).

[30] *See, e.g.*, Ariz. Rev. Stat. Ann. § 29-1044.A; 805 ILCS § 180/30-20(a); Mont. Code Ann. § 35-8-705; Nev. Rev. Stat. Ann. § 86.401; N.H. Rev. Stat. Ann. § § 304-A:28.I; 15 Pa. Cons. Stat. § 8345; S.C. Code Ann. § 33-44-504(a); S.D. Codified Laws Ann. § 47-34A-504(a); Utah Code Ann. § 48-2c-1103(1); Vt. Stat. Ann. tit. 11, § 3074(a); W. Va. Code § 31B-5-504(a).

[31] *In re A-Z Electronics, LLC*, 350 B.R. 886 (Bankr. D. Idaho 2006); *In re Albright*, 291 B.R. 538 (Bankr. D. Colo. 2003); *Olmstead v. F.T.C.*, 44 So. 3d 76 (Fla. 2010) which was later reversed by the Florida legislature in the Patch Amendment.

[32] *See* ¶ 2402 *supra*.

[33] 291 B.R. 538 (Bankr. D. Colo. 2003).

[34] Case No. COA01 (N.C. Ct. App. 2002).

proceedings. Operating agreement sometimes permit the LLC and other members to buy out the interest of a member in the event of bankruptcy or assignment to creditors.

Some bankruptcy trustees have overcome the restrictions on transfer in the operating agreement by using the provisions of Section 541 of the Bankruptcy Code, thus stepping into the shoes of the bankrupt debtor as a full member of the LLC.[35]

¶ 2408 IRS LEVY AGAINST MEMBER

If a taxpayer is liable to the IRS for unpaid personal taxes, the IRS may serve a notice of levy upon an LLC in which the taxpayer is a member. The levy may be against income and distributions payable by the LLC to the member. The IRS may not levy against other assets owned by the LLC since the LLC is separate and distinct from the member under the laws of most states.[36]

If the taxpayer is the owner of a single-member disregarded LLC, the IRS may levy against the owner's share of net profits held by the LLC for services prior to the notice of levy.[37] The IRS may not levy against other LLC assets to satisfy a judgment for personal tax liabilities.[38]

If the taxpayer is a member of an LLC that is classified as a partnership, distributions from the LLC may be subject to an IRS wage levy against the member even though profit distributions are not technically wages or salaries. The distributions are subject to a wage levy if the member works for the LLC and receives distributions based on services performed for the LLC.[39] The LLC is liable if it fails to honor the wage levy.[40]

The IRS has other collection options against the member, including (a) collecting from the taxpayer's distributive share of income (whether or not connected with services), (b) collecting from the assets of the LLC on the grounds that it is the alter ego of the taxpayer, and (c) attaching the assets of a single-member LLC on the nominee theory if there is a close relationship between the member and the LLC.[41] The availability of these options is determined on a case-by-case basis.[42]

If the IRS makes an assessment against a disregarded LLC, and provides a collection due process notice to the LLC, the IRS must also issue a separate collection

---

[35] *In re Ehmann*, 319 B.R. 200 (Bankr. D. Ariz. 2005); *In re A-Z Electronics, LLC*, 350 B.R. 886 (Bankr. D. Idaho 2006); *In re Albright*, 291 B.R. 538 (Bankr. D. Colo. 2003); *Olmstead v. F.T.C.*, 44 So. 3d 76 (Fla. 2010) which was later reversed by the Florida legislature in the Patch Amendment.

[36] CCA 201117030, 201116019, 200835030, 200235023; Ltr. Rul. 199930013.

[37] CCA 200835030, 200235023; Ltr. Ruls. 200835030, 199930013.

[38] CCA 201117030, 201116019, 200835030, 200235023; Ltr. Rul. 199930013.

[39] *Mission Primary Care Clinic, PLLC v. Director, IRS*, 2010-1 USTC ¶ 50,308, 105 AFTR 2d ¶ 2010-671 (2010); CCA 200836002.

[40] *Mission Primary Care Clinic, PLLC v. Director, IRS*, 2010-1 USTC ¶ 50,308, 105 AFTR 2d ¶ 2010-671 (2010).

[41] *Berkshire Bank v. Town of Ludlow, Massachusetts*, 708 F.3d 249 (1st Cir. 2013).

[42] CCA 200235023; Ltr. Rul. 199930013; *Berkshire Bank v. Town of Ludlow, Massachusetts*, 708 F.3d 249 (1st Cir. 2013).

due process notice to the single-member owner if the IRS adds the owner's name to the assessment.[43]

In limited cases, a disregarded LLC is liable for federal taxes for prior periods during which it was not a disregarded entity, or because it is a successor or transferee of a taxable entity. In such cases, the LLC will be treated as an entity separate from its owner. The assets of LLC may be subject to lien and levy for unpaid taxes. A disregarded LLC may consent to extend the period of limitations on assessments against the LLC.[44]

¶2409 IRS LEVY AGAINST LLC

A levy served upon an LLC will attach to property or rights to property belonging to the owners of the LLC.[45]

The IRS may collect employment taxes against an LLC as if the LLC were a corporation.[46]

The IRS may collect an LLC's federal tax liability for payroll taxes, excise taxes or other taxes from the LLC's successor in interest if the successor in interest is liable under applicable state law.[47]

¶2410 LIABILITY FOR TAXES

.01 Disregarded LLC

A disregarded LLC is not normally liable for the federal tax liabilities of its owner during periods in which it is a disregarded entity.[48] However, a disregarded LLC may be liable for taxes for periods during which it was not a disregarded entity, or because it is a successor or transferee of a taxable entity.

If a disregarded LLC is liable for federal taxes, it will be treated as an entity separate from its owner. The IRS may, in such case, assess taxes against the LLC. The assets of the LLC may be subject to lien and levy. The disregarded LLC may consent to extend the period of limitations on assessments against the LLC.[49]

.02 Successor Liability

An LLC that purchases the assets of a corporation is not liable as a transferee for the unpaid taxes of the corporation unless there is proof that the corporation's stock or assets were fraudulently transferred.[50]

---

[43] CCA 200235023, 200216028.

[44] Reg. § 301.7701-2(c)(2)(iii).

[45] CCA 200836002.

[46] *See* ¶1603 *supra.*

[47] CCA 200840001.

[48] CCA 201117030, 201116019, 200835030, 200235023; Ltr. Rul. 199930013.

[49] Reg. § 301.7701-2(c)(2)(iii).

[50] *LR Development Company LLC v. Comm'r*, TC Memo 2010-203, CCH Dec. 58,334(M) (2010).

25

Series LLCs

¶ 2501 OVERVIEW

A series LLC is a single LLC that is divided into separate divisions for liability purposes.

On July 19, 2017, the Uniform Law Commission approved the Uniform Limited Liability Company Protected Series Act (ULLCPSA) at its annual meeting. The Uniform Act is now being reviewed by states that may amend their LLC laws to permit series LLCs.

The following states either allow the formation of LLCs, recognize the formation of the LLCs in other states, or tax series LLCs:

State	Statutory authority
Alabama	Ala. Code §§ 10A-5A-11.01 *et seq.*, 10A-5A-1.04(d), 10A-5A-4.05(b), 10A-5A-4.05(c), 10A-5A-4.06(b), 10A-5A-4.07(b)(1)(B), 10A-5A-4.07(b)(1)(C).
California	California does not allow a series LLC to be formed in the state. The California Franchise Tax Board recognizes series LLCs formed in other states. California Franchise Tax Board, Tax News (Oct. 1, 2011). Each series that does business in California is treated as a separate entity that must pay the minimum $800 California tax. *See* instructions to Form 568. However, all series within an LLC are treated as a single entity for purposes of the gross receipts tax. Cal. Rev. & Tax. Code § 17942(b)(2). The Franchise Tax Board issued provisional identification numbers so that the separate series do not have to file under the same employer identification number.
Delaware	Delaware allows the formation of a series LLC. 6 Del. Code Ann. § 18-215.
District of Columbia	The District of Columbia allows the formation of a series LLC. DC Code Ann. § 29-802.06.
Florida	Florida will follow the federal income tax treatment of a series LLC, unless that treatment conflicts with Florida law. Florida Technical Assistance Advisement, No. 02(M)-009 (Nov. 27, 2002).
Illinois	Illinois allows the formation of a series LLC. 805 ILCS 180/37-40.
Iowa	Iowa allows the formation of a series LLC. Iowa Code Ann. § 490A.305.
Kansas	Kansas allows the formation of a series LLC. Substitute H.R. 2207 (2012).
Massachusetts	The Massachusetts rules for classifying an LLC extend to a series LLC established under Delaware law. Massachusetts Department of Revenue Ltr. Rul. 08-2 (Feb. 15, 2008). Each series in an LLC is classified as a separate entity for Massachusetts income tax purposes.
Minnesota	Minnesota allows series LLCs, but does not specifically provide for a liability shield between the different series. Minn. Stat. Ann. § 322B.03, Subd. 6, 38, 44.
Missouri	Missouri permits the formation of a series LLC. The articles of organization must separately identify each series, and the name of each series. The name is required to contain the entire name of the LLC and to be distinguishable from the names of the other series set forth in the articles of organization. Mo. Ann. Stat. § 347.186.
Montana	Montana permits the formation of a series LLC. HB0362 (2013), amending numerous sections of the Montana Limited Liability Company Act.
Nevada	Nevada allows the formation of a series LLC. Nev. Rev. Stat. § 86.296.
New York	Series LLCs that are treated as partnerships for federal income tax purposes are also treated as partnerships for state personal income tax purposes. New York Advisory Opinion No. TSB-A-98(8)I, New York Department of Taxation and Finance (Sept. 4, 1998).

North Dakota	North Dakota allows series LLCs, but does not specifically provide for a liability shield between the different series. N.D. Cent. Code §§ 10-32-17.5, 10-32-48, 10-32-56.5.a, 10-32-56.7.
Oklahoma	Oklahoma allows the formation of a series LLC. 18 Okla. St. Ann. §§ 2005(B), 2054.4.
Tennessee	Tennessee allows the formation of a series LLC. T.C.A. § 48-249-309. A Tennessee series LLC must file a separate franchise and excise tax return for each individual series. Tennessee Department of Revenue Ltr. Rul. 11-42 (Sept. 6, 2011). Each series in an LLC is classified as a separate entity for Tennessee franchise and excise tax purposes. A master LLC and each series are each treated as a separate entity for purposes of assessments, refunds and taxpayer remedies unless the LLCs are classified as disregarded entities. A master LLC and each series must separately register and establish separate tax accounts in Tennessee. For state franchise and excise tax purposes, the master LLC and each series LLC will be classified as a corporation, partnership or other business entity based on its classification under federal law. The master LLC and each series must file separate franchise and excise tax returns unless they are classified as disregarded entities.[1]
Texas	Texas allows the formation of a series LLC. Texas Business Organizations Code §§ 101.601 to 101.621, 21.152(A), (C), (D), 21.153(A), 21.361(A)(2). A Texas series LLC is treated as a single entity for purposes of franchise tax reporting. It must pay a single filing fee and register as a single entity with the Texas Secretary of State. It must file one franchise tax report and one public information report as a single entity, and not as a combined group, using its Texas taxpayer identification number. Tex. Comp. Pub. Accts., Reg. § 3.581; Franchise Tax Frequently Asked Questions, Taxable Entities, Comptroller of Public Accounts (Jan. 6, 2014); Texas Policy Ltr. Rul. 201005184L (May 5, 2010).
Utah	Utah allows the formation of a series LLC. Utah Code Ann. §§ 48-3a-1201 to 1209.
Wisconsin	Wisconsin allows series LLCs, but does not specifically provide for a liability shield between the different series. Wis. Stat. Ann. § 183.0504.
Puerto Rico	Puerto Rico allows the formation of a series LLC. Puerto Rico Laws Ann. Title 14, § 3426(p).

Delaware was the first state to permit series LLCs and is the most frequently used jurisdiction for the formation of series LLCs.

The main advantage of a series LLC is that the owners of the LLC can place their assets in separate "series" which are treated as separate businesses for liability purposes. The debts and obligations of each series are enforceable only against that series. The insolvency of one series will not adversely affect any other series.

---

[1] Notice No. 13-15, Tenn. Department of Revenue (Nov. 1, 2013).

Each series may have different members, managers, businesses and ownership percentages. The LLC may make distributions to members in one series without regard to the members in any other series.

The use of a series LLC may save substantial organization costs. The series LLC is typically used by a taxpayer who has numerous parcels of real estate. Instead of incurring the cost of forming multiple LLCs, the taxpayer can form a single LLC and place each parcel of real estate in a separate series.

¶2502 PROCEDURES TO FORM SERIES LLC

The series LLC is established as follows:

- The taxpayer must file a Certificate of Organization for the LLC in one of the states that permits series LLCs. The Certificate of Organization must state that the LLC will have one or more series. It must also state that the debts, liabilities, obligations and expenses incurred by, contracted for or otherwise existing with respect to a particular series of the LLC will be enforceable only against the assets of that series, and not against the assets of any other series or against the LLC generally. Illinois has a separate form, Form LLC-5.5(S), that must be filed to form a series LLC. A series LLC may be formed in Nevada by checking a box on the standard form of articles issued by the Secretary of State. The Delaware form of Certificate of Formation is set forth in the Appendix to this chapter.
- Some states require additional filings with the Secretary of State after the LLC is formed. In Illinois, the master LLC must file a Certificate of Designation with the Illinois Secretary of State designating each series.[2]
- The operating agreement for the LLC must establish the separate series. It must designate the managers and members of each series, the property that is being placed in each series, and the rights, preferences and privileges of the members of each series. The applicable provisions of the operating agreement to establish separate series are set forth in the Appendix to this chapter.
- The LLC must qualify to do business in each state in which it is conducting intra-state business. In the absence of the statute, an LLC is not required to qualify to do business in a state merely as a result of the acquisition, holding and disposing of real property.[3]

---

[2] 805 ILCS 180/37-40(b).

[3] *See* What Constitutes Doing Business, p. 109, under the heading, "Real Property Ownership (CT Corporation 2008)," which cites numerous cases for this position. Section 15.01(b)(9) of the Revised Model Business Corporation Act also provides that "owning, without more, real property" does not require qualification to do business. This provision has been adopted by the States of Arizona, Arkansas, Colorado, Connecticut, Florida, Georgia, Idaho, Illinois, Indiana, Iowa, Kentucky, Michigan, Mississippi, Nebraska, New Hampshire, North Carolina, Oregon, South Carolina, Tennessee, Utah, Vermont, Virginia, Washington, and Wyoming. *But see In re International Health Institute LLC,* No. 305199, California State Board of Equalization (2006), in which the California State Board of Equalization determined that a single-member LLC organized in Nevada was properly deemed to be doing business in California based on the LLC's purchases of interests in other LLCs and partnerships that invested in California real estate.

- The LLC must file a fictitious business name statement for each separate series. For example, if the name of the LLC is "XYZ LLC," and the property being transferred into the LLC is located at 1000 Main Street, then the fictitious business name statement could be filed for the following name: "XYZ LLC Series 1000 Main Street." It is not necessary to file a fictitious business name statement in Illinois for each series because the Master LLC must file a Certificate of Designation with the Secretary of State listing the name of each separate series.[4] Illinois also requires that each series have a name that contains the name of the master LLC, and that is distinguishable from the name of the other series.[5]
- The property must be transferred into the LLC. The LLC is the owner of the assets in each separate series. Under Delaware law, a separate series within the LLC cannot hold title to real or personal property because it is not a separate legal entity. However, the LLC must segregate its assets and liabilities within the separate series. In order to do this, the LLC should transfer legal title to real property into the name of the dba for each separate series. For example, if the name of the Delaware LLC is XYZ LLC, and the name of the separate series into which the property is being placed is XYZ LLC Series 1000 Main Street, then legal title on the deed for real property should be: "XYZ LLC, a Delaware limited liability company, dba XYZ LLC Series 1000 Main Street."
- The LLC should establish separate bank accounts for each series.
- There must be separate accounting for the assets of each separate series.[6] The LLC must keep separate books and records of each series.
- The LLC must file a tax return in each state in which it is doing business. It must also file a separate tax return for each series in the states that require a separate filing for each series.

¶2503 TAX CLASSIFICATION OF SERIES

.01 Overview

Under proposed regulations, there is a two-part test for determining the tax classification of a series within an LLC. The first test is whether each series should be classified as a separate legal entity. Each series is a separate entity if the statute under which it is formed permits the segregation of assets and liabilities.

If a series is classified as a separate entity, then the second test is whether the series should be classified as a partnership, corporation, or disregarded entity. There are special rules for foreign LLCs and insurance companies.[7]

---

[4] 805 ILCS 180/37-40(b).

[5] 805 ILCS 180/37-40(c).

[6] Del. Code Ann. tit. 6, § 18-215.

[7] Prop. Reg. § 301.7701-1(a)(5).

.02 Classification as a Separate Legal Entity

The first classification test is whether each series within the LLC should be classified as a separate legal entity. This determination is made using general tax principles and Reg. § 301.7701-1(b).[8]

A series may be classified as a separate legal entity only if it is established under the laws of a state or foreign jurisdiction which:[9]

- Permit members of the series to have rights, powers or duties with respect to the series.

- Permit a series to have separate rights, powers, or duties with respect to specify property or obligations.

- Permit the segregation of assets and liabilities so that none of the debts and liabilities of the LLC (other than liabilities to the state or foreign jurisdiction related to the organization or operation of the LLC, such as franchise taxes or administrative costs) or of any other series of the LLC are enforceable against the assets of the titular series within the LLC. An election, agreement or other arrangement that permits the debts and liabilities of other series for the LLC to be enforceable against the assets of a particular series does not prevent the series from being classified as a separate legal entity. The series will not cease to be a separate entity simply because it guarantees the debts of another series within the LLC.

A series may be treated as a separate entity even though the series does not possess all the attributes that its enabling statute permits it to possess.[10]

A failure to comply with the recordkeeping requirements for the limitation on liability available under state law does not prevent the series from being classified as a separate legal entity.[11]

A series may be a separate legal entity even though the individual series may not enter into contracts, sue or be sued, or hold property in its own name under local laws.[12]

Federal tax law, and not local law, governs whether a series is a separate entity for federal tax purposes. However, the series is treated as created under local law rather than federal law. A series may be a separate tax entity even though it is not considered a separate entity for local law purposes.[13]

---

[8] Prop. Reg. § 301.7701-1(a)(5)(iii).

[9] Prop. Reg. § 301.7701-1(a)(5)(viii)(B).

[10] REG-119921-09, Notice of Proposed Rulemaking, Series LLCs and Cell Companies, 2010-45 IRB 626, Explanation of Provisions ¶ 1 (Nov. 8, 2010).

[11] REG-119921-09, Notice of Proposed Rulemaking, Series LLCs and Cell Companies, 2010-45 IRB 626, Explanation of Provisions ¶ 1 (Nov. 8, 2010).

[12] REG-119921-09, Notice of Proposed Rulemaking, Series LLCs and Cell Companies, 2010-45 IRB 626, Explanation of Provisions ¶ 1 (Nov. 8, 2010).

[13] REG-119921-09, Notice of Proposed Rulemaking, Series LLCs and Cell Companies, 2010-45 IRB 626, Explanation of Provisions ¶ 1 (Nov. 8, 2010).

.03 Classification as a Partnership, Corporation or Disregarded Entity

If the series is classified as a separate legal entity, then it must be classified as a partnership, corporation, or disregarded entity. This determination is made under Reg. §301.7701-1(b).[14] A series with a single member is by default classified as a disregarded entity unless it elects to be classified as a corporation. A series with two or more members is by default classified as a partnership unless it elects classification as a corporation.[15]

If the series is not classified as a separate legal entity, then it is treated as part of the LLC. All classification elections in such case would be made by the LLC rather than by the series.

If the LLC that owns the series is itself a disregarded entity, then all income, gain, loss, deductions, and credits of each series must be reported on the tax return of the owner of the LLC. For example, the owner of a single-member disregarded LLC may establish two series within the LLC, and transfer marketable securities to each series in exchange for membership interests in the series. Each series will then be treated as a disregarded entity of the LLC, and the LLC will be treated as a disregarded entity of the owner.[16]

.04 Classification of Foreign Series

Until further guidance is issued, the entity status of a foreign series that does not conduct insurance business is determined under applicable law. Foreign series raise novel federal income tax issues that continue to be considered and addressed by the IRS and the Treasury Department.[17]

.05 Insurance Companies

A series that is organized or established under the laws of foreign jurisdiction is treated as a separate entity if the arrangements and other activities of the series, if conducted by domestic company, would result in the series being classified as an insurance company.[18] A foreign series is treated as a separate entity if more than half of the series' business is the issuance or reissuance of insurance contracts.

A foreign series that is a separate entity is then classified as a per se corporation under Code Sec. 7701(a)(3) since an insurance company may not be classified as a partnership or disregarded entity.[19]

---

[14] Prop. Reg. §301.7701-1(a)(5)(x), Example 1(ii).

[15] Prop. Reg. §301.7701-1(a)(5)(x), Example 1(ii).

[16] Ltr. Rul. 201421001.

[17] REG-119921-09, Notice of Proposed Rulemaking, Series LLCs and Cell Companies, 2010-45 IRB 626 (Nov. 8, 2010).

[18] Prop. Reg. §301.7701-1(a)(5)(ii).

[19] Prop. Reg. §301.7701-1(a)(5)(x), Example 2(ii).

¶2504 TAX CLASSIFICATION OF LLC

The proposed regulations do not address the entity status of the LLC that includes separate series. For example, the regulations do not address whether the LLC is classified as a separate entity for federal tax purposes if it has no assets and engages in no activities independent of its series.[20]

¶2505 OWNERSHIP OF INTERESTS IN LLC

The ownership of interests in a series and its associated assets is determined under general tax principles. The LLC itself is not treated as owning a series or its assets for federal income tax purposes solely because legal title to its assets is held by the LLC.[21]

The determination of who owns membership interests in a series generally depends on who bears the economic benefits and burdens of ownership. Common law principles also apply in determining whether a person is a member in a series that is classified as a partnership for federal tax purposes.

¶2506 TAX CONSEQUENCES OF SEPARATE SERIES

.01 Filing Fees and Expenses

The filing fees of a series organization paid by the series or the series organization are treated as expenses of the series and not as expenses of the series organization.[22]

.02 Tax Elections

A series may make any federal tax election that it is otherwise eligible to make independently of other series or the LLC itself, regardless of whether other series or the LLC makes certain elections or makes different elections.[23]

.03 Employment Taxes

The proposed regulations do not provide how a series should be treated for federal employment tax purposes.[24] Application of the employment tax requirements

---

[20] REG-119921-09, 2010-45 IRB 626, Preamble to IRS Proposed Regulations on Classification, Federal Income Tax Treatment of Domestic, Foreign Series LLCs, Explanation of Provisions, ¶3.

[21] Prop. Reg. § 301.7701-1(a)(5)(vi).

[22] REG-119921-09, 2010-45 IRB 626, Preamble to IRS Proposed Regulations on Classification, Federal Income Tax Treatment of Domestic, Foreign Series LLCs, Explanation of Provisions, ¶3.

[23] REG-119921-09, 2010-45 IRB 626, Preamble to IRS Proposed Regulations on Classification, Federal Income Tax Treatment of Domestic, Foreign Series LLCs, Explanation of Provisions, ¶2.

[24] Prop. Reg. § 301.7701-1(a)(5)(ix).

depends principally on whether the workers are employees, and if so, who is considered the employer for federal income and employment tax purposes. In general, an employment relationship exists when the person for whom services are performed has the right to control and direct the individual who performs the services as to the result to be accomplished by the work and as to the details and means by which that result is accomplished.[25]

Treatment of a series as a separate person for federal employment tax purposes may mean that the series is the "employer" for federal employment tax purposes. This would raise substantive and administrative issues which the IRS will address at a later date.[26]

.04 Anti-Abuse Rules

The IRS may disregard a series that has no business purpose or business activity other than tax avoidance. The anti-abuse rules under Code Sec. 701 are applicable to a series or LLC that is classified as a partnership for federal tax purposes.

.05 Employment Benefits

Various issues arise regarding the ability of a series to maintain an employee benefit plan. The proposed regulations do not address these issues. However, to the extent that a series can maintain an employee benefit plan, the aggregation rules under Code Sec. 414(b), (c), (m), (o), and (t), and the leased employee rules under Code Sec. 414(n), would apply. The IRS and Treasury Department expect to issue regulations under Code Sec. 414(o) that would prevent the avoidance of any employee benefit plan requirement through the use of the separate entity status of a series.[27]

.06 Tax Collection

To the extent that federal or local law permits a creditor to collect a liability attributable to a series from the LLC or other series within the LLC, the IRS may also collect a tax assessment against one series from the LLC and any other series. If a creditor is permitted to collect a liability against the LLC from any series within the LLC, the IRS may also collect a tax liability assessed against the LLC from any series within the LLC by any administrative or judicial means.[28]

---

[25] REG-119921-09, 2010-45 IRB 626, Preamble to IRS Proposed Regulations on Classification, Federal Income Tax Treatment of Domestic, Foreign Series LLCs, Explanation of Provisions, ¶7.A, *citing* Reg. §§31.3121(d)-1(c)(2), 31.3306(i)-1(b), 31.3401(c)-1(b).

[26] REG-119921-09, 2010-45 IRB 626, Preamble to IRS Proposed Regulations on Classification, Federal Income Tax Treatment of Domestic, Foreign Series LLCs, Explanation of Provisions, ¶7.B.

[27] REG-119921-09, 2010-45 IRB 626, Preamble to IRS Proposed Regulations on Classification, Federal Income Tax Treatment of Domestic, Foreign Series LLCs, Explanation of Provisions, ¶7.C.

[28] Prop. Reg. §301.7701-1(a)(5)(vii).

.07 Single-Member Disregarded LLC

A taxpayer that owns all the membership interests in a disregarded entity may not split the interest into separate classes of interest, and then allocate income, loss, deduction, credit, and basis among those assets for federal tax purposes.[29] The IRS may disallow any tax benefits attributable to split or series entity interests by asserting arguments that include:

- Revenue Ruling 99-5 which provides that a taxpayer who sells part of an interest in a disregarded entity is treated as selling a pro rata share of each asset owned by the disregarded entity.
- A disregarded LLC may not make distributions to its owner since it is treated as a sole proprietorship, branch or division of the owner.

¶ 2507 RETURNS AND REPORTING REQUIREMENTS

.01 Statement Containing Identifying Information

Under proposed regulations, the LLC and each series must file a statement for each tax year that includes the identifying information with respect to the series or series organization.[30] The statement is a stand-alone statement. It is due by March 15 following the end of the tax year.[31]

.02 Employer Identification Number

The IRS and Treasury Department are considering revising Form SS-4, Application for Employer Identification Number, to include questions regarding series organizations.[32]

.03 Partnership Return

The proposed regulations do not address the filing requirements of an LLC that has separate series.[33] They do not address whether a single partnership return should be filed for the entire series organization, or if one Form 1065 should be filed for the LLC with separate forms filed for each series under the LLC.[34] However, an LLC that

---

[29] IRS Legal Advice Memorandum AM 2012-001.

[30] Prop. Reg. § 301.6071-2.

[31] Prop. Reg. § 301.6071-2(a).

[32] REG-119921-09, 2010-45 IRB 626, Preamble to IRS Proposed Regulations on Classification, Federal Income Tax Treatment of Domestic, Foreign Series LLCs, Explanation of Provisions, ¶ 8.

[33] REG-119921-09, 2010-45 IRB 626, Preamble to IRS Proposed Regulations on Classification, Federal Income Tax Treatment of Domestic, Foreign Series LLCs, Explanation of Provisions, ¶ 3.

[34] *BNA Daily Tax Reports*, No. 217, p. G-2 (Nov. 12, 2010).

is classified as a partnership for federal tax purposes, but which allocates all income, gain, loss, deductions and credits to the separate series within the LLC, need not file a partnership return for the year.[35]

¶ 2508 SERIES LLC FORMS

Form 25-1: Delaware Certificate of Formation for Series LLC

XYZ LLC
CERTIFICATE OF FORMATION

First: The name of the limited liability company is XYZ LLC.

Second: The address of its registered office in the state of Delaware is 1201 N. Orange, Suite 723, Wilmington, DE 19801-1186, County of New Castle. The name of its registered agent at such address is Global Corporate Services, Inc.

Third: Pursuant to Section 18-215(b) of the Delaware Limited Liability Company Act, the debts, liabilities, obligations and expenses incurred by, contracted for or otherwise existing with respect to a particular series of this limited liability company, whether such series is now or hereafter authorized and existing pursuant to the operating agreement of this limited liability company, shall be enforceable against the assets associated with that series only, and not against the assets associated with the assets of the LLC generally, or the assets of any other series.

Fourth: The period of duration for this limited liability company is perpetual from the date of filing of the Certificate of Formation with the State of Delaware, unless sooner dissolved by the members or as provided by Delaware state law.

Fifth: The business of the Company shall be conducted under the exclusive management of one or more managers, including any separate managers for one or more series now or hereafter authorized pursuant to the operating agreement of this limited liability company.

DATED: _____, 2007

_____

John Doe, Organizer

---

[35] REG-119921-09, 2010-45 IRB 626, Preamble to IRS Proposed Regulations on Classification, Federal Income Tax Treatment of Domestic, Foreign Series LLCs, *citing* Reg. § 1.6031(a)-1(a)(3)(i).

Form 25-2: Provisions in Operating Agreement of Series LLC
Article _____

(a) **Establishment and Designation of Series.** The Manager may from time to time authorize the division of Members, Managers and Membership Units into two or more Series.[36] The relative rights, preferences, privileges, restrictions and limitations on the Membership Units of each Series shall be set forth in a Schedule attached to this Operating Agreement.

(b) **Assets and Liabilities Associated with Series.** The Manager shall maintain separate and distinct records for each Series. The assets, debts, liabilities, obligations, expenses, profits and losses of each Series shall be held and accounted for separately from the other assets, debts, liabilities, obligations, expenses, profits and losses of the LLC or any other Series.[37] All amounts received by the LLC for the issuance or sale of Membership Units of a particular Series, and all other assets, income, earnings, profits and proceeds thereof of each separate Series, shall irrevocably belong to that Series for all purposes, subject only to the rights of creditors of such Series and except as otherwise required by applicable tax laws.

(c) **Allocation by Manager.** The Manager shall have authority to allocate assets, liabilities, income, gain, loss, deduction and credit to each of the Series in the Manager's reasonable discretion, subject to the provisions of the Operating Agreement and the rights of the Members of each Series as set forth herein. The Manager shall allocate all liabilities, expenses, costs, charges and reserves of the LLC that are readily associated with a particular Series to that particular Series. The Manager shall allocate any liabilities, expenses, costs, charges and reserves of the LLC that are not readily associated with a particular Series between or among any one or more of the Series, in the Manager's reasonable discretion.

(d) **Creditors of LLC.** The liabilities, debts, expenses and other obligations incurred by, contracted for or otherwise existing with respect to a particular Series shall be enforceable against the assets associated with that Series only, and not against the assets of the LLC generally or any other series. All persons who extend credit to or with respect to a particular Series, or who contract with or have a claim against a particular Series, may look only to the assets associated with that Series for repayment of such credit or to enforce or satisfy any such contract or claim.[38] In no event shall any of the Members of the LLC or of any separate series be personally liable for the debts, expenses, liabilities or other obligations of the LLC or any separate series except to the extent that such Member has personally guaranteed or agreed to be liable for such amount.[39]

(e) **Rights of Members under Operating Agreement.** Unless otherwise provided in the authorization creating the Series as set forth in the Schedule attached to this Operating Agreement, and except as set otherwise forth in this Article, the rights,

---

[36] *See* Del. Code Ann. tit. 6, § 18-215(a).

[37] *See* Del. Code Ann. tit. 6, § 18-215(b).

[38] *See* Del. Code Ann. tit. 6, § 18-215(b).

[39] *See* Del. Code Ann. tit. 6, § 18-215(c).

powers, privileges, limitations, and restrictions of the Members of a particular Series shall be as set forth in the Operating Agreement.

Form 25-3: Schedule to Operating Agreement of a Series LLC (include a separate schedule for each separate series)

SCHEDULE A
XYZ LLC SERIES 1000 MAIN STREET

Pursuant to Article _____ of the Operating Agreement, the Managers hereby designate the following Series LLC with the following rights, preferences and privileges:

1. **Name of Series LLC**

   The name of this Series LLC is XYZ LLC Series 1000 Main Street.

2. **Property Owned by XYZ LLC Series 1000 Main Street**

   The property owned by XYZ LLC Series 1000 Main Street includes the following:

   Address: 1000 Main Street, Los Angeles, California

   Assessor's Parcel Number:

   Tract No.

3. **Purposes of XYZ LLC Series 1000 Main Street**

   The purpose of XYZ LLC Series 1000 Main Street is to purchase, acquire, buy, sell, own, trade in, hold, develop, lease, manage, subdivide and otherwise deal in and with the real property and improvements referred to in Paragraph 2 above, and to do any and all things necessary, convenient, or incidental to that purpose.

4. **Members of XYZ LLC Series 1000 Main Street**

Names and addresses of Members of XYZ LLC Series 1000 Main Street	Property Contributed By Members	Units Issued to Members

5. **Limitation of Liability**

   Pursuant to Section 18-215(b) of the Delaware Limited Liability Company Act, the debts, liabilities, obligations and expenses incurred by, contracted for or otherwise existing with respect to XYZ LLC Series 1000 Main Street shall be enforceable only against the assets associated with XYZ LLC Series 1000 Main Street, and not against the assets associated with any other series (or against the assets of the LLC generally).

   All persons who extend credit to (or with respect to) XYZ LLC Series 1000 Main Street, or who contract with (or with respect to) or have a claim against XYZ LLC Series 1000 Main Street all, may look only to the assets associated with XYZ LLC Series 1000 Main Street for repayment of such credit or to enforce or satisfy any such contract or claim.

6. **Managers of XYZ LLC Series 1000 Main Street**

John Doe

Mary Doe

7. **Assets and Liabilities Associated with XYZ LLC Series 1000 Main Street**

The Managers shall cause the LLC to maintain separate and distinct records for XYZ LLC Series 1000 Main Street, and shall cause the assets, debts, liabilities, obligations, expenses, profits and losses associated with such Series to be held and accounted for separately from the other assets, debts, liabilities, obligations, expenses, profits and losses of the LLC or any other Series.

All consideration received by the LLC for the issue or sale of XYZ LLC Series 1000 Main Street Membership Units, together with all LLC assets in which such consideration is invested or reinvested, all income, earnings, profits, and proceeds thereof, including any capital proceeds received by the LLC from a capital transaction involving such assets, shall irrevocably belong to XYZ LLC Series 1000 Main Street for all purposes, subject only to the rights of creditors of XYZ LLC Series 1000 Main Street and except as may otherwise be required by applicable tax laws.

All liabilities, expenses, costs, charges and reserves of the LLC that are readily associated with XYZ LLC Series 1000 Main Street shall be charged against the assets associated with XYZ LLC Series 1000 Main Street, and any liabilities, expenses, costs, charges and reserves of the LLC that are not readily associated with XYZ LLC Series 1000 Main Street shall be allocated and charged by the Managers to, between or among any one or more of the Series, in such manner and on such basis as the Managers, in their sole discretion, deem fair and equitable. Each such allocation by the Managers shall be conclusive and binding upon the Members of XYZ LLC Series 1000 Main Street for all purposes.

8. **Transferability and Issuance of New XYZ LLC Series 1000 Main Street Membership Units**

The XYZ LLC Series 1000 Main Street Membership Units shall be subject to the transfer restrictions set forth in the Operating Agreement. The Managers may admit new or substitute Members in this Series for such consideration that the Managers deem appropriate or advisable in their sole discretion upon compliance with the provisions of the Operating Agreement.

9. **Dissolution of XYZ LLC Series 1000 Main Street**

XYZ LLC Series 1000 Main Street may be dissolved and its affairs wound up without causing a dissolution of the LLC. Upon the dissolution, the Managers shall provide for claims and obligations of the Series as provided in the Operating Agreement. XYZ LLC Series 1000 Main Street may be dissolved on one of the following two events:

(a) the determination of the Managers of XYZ LLC Series 1000 Main Street to dissolve XYZ LLC Series 1000 Main Street and the approval of such determination by XYZ LLC Series 1000 Main Street Members holding 50 percent of the XYZ LLC Series 1000 Main Street Membership Units; or

(b) judicial determination pursuant to Section 18-215(l) of the Delaware General Corporation Law.

10. **Fictitious Business Name Statement**

The Managers of XYZ LLC Series 1000 Main Street may file a fictitious business name in any county in which the LLC owns real property designating XYZ LLC Series 1000 Main Street as a dba of the LLC.

11. **Rights, Preferences and Privileges of Members of XYZ LLC Series 1000 Main Street**

Except as provided herein, the Members of XYZ LLC Series 1000 Main Street shall be subject to all of the other provisions of the Operating Agreement, except that:

(a) all references to Membership Units in the Operating Agreement shall mean XYZ LLC Series 1000 Main Street Membership Units when applied to this XYZ LLC Series 1000 Main Street;

(b) all references to Members in the Operating Agreement shall mean XYZ LLC Series 1000 Main Street Members when applied to this XYZ LLC Series 1000 Main Street; and

(c) the Members of this Series shall have the right to vote separately with respect to all matters associated with this Series based on the Membership Units owned by each Member associated with this Series compared to the total Membership Units owned by all Members associated with this Series.[40]

12. **Effective Date**

This XYZ LLC Series 1000 Main Street shall be effective on the date set forth below, and shall continue indefinitely thereafter until terminated in accordance with the Operating Agreement.

DATED: _____

XYZ LLC

dba XYZ LLC SERIES 1000 MAIN STREET

By: _____

    John Doe, President

MANAGERS OF

XYZ LLC SERIES 1000 MAIN STREET

_____

Jane Doe, Manager

---

[40] *See* Del. Code Ann. tit. 6, § 18-215(e).

MEMBERS OF

XYZ LLC SERIES 1000 MAIN STREET:

_____

John Doe

_____

Jane Doe

26

Low-Profit and Charitable LLCs

¶ 2601 OVERVIEW

An LLC may be formed for charitable purposes. The main types of charitable LLCs are:

- a low-profit LLC;[1]
- a tax-exempt Section 501(c)(3) LLC;[2]
- an LLC that receives an investment or loan from a Section 501(c)(3) organization to be used for charitable purposes, but which is not a tax-exempt organization or a low-profit LLC;[3]
- a joint venture or partnership between a tax-exempt organization and an LLC in which the tax-exempt organization participates as a member, manager, or joint venturer with the LLC;[4] and
- a subsidiary LLC wholly owned by a tax-exempt organization.[5]

¶ 2602 LOW-PROFIT LLCs

.01 State Laws

A low-profit LLC (also known as an "L3C") is a cross between a nonprofit organization and a for-profit LLC. The LLC is not a Section 501(c)(3) tax-exempt organization, but is organized for social benefit purposes.

The low-profit LLC may engage in a trade or business, but does not try to maximize profits. Instead, its major purpose is to promote social or charitable causes. Under state law, management is not vulnerable to lawsuits by investors if the company reduces profitability in order to increase social causes. The low-profit LLC provides a vehicle for private foundations and other investors who want to support business operations with strong social benefits, such as a daily newspaper.

The states that permit low-profit LLCs or that have pending legislation are:

State	Statutory authority
Illinois	805 ILCS 180/1-26; 805 ILCS 180/1-5 (under definitions of "L3C or low-profit limited liability company"); 805 ILCS 180/1-10(a)(1); P.A. 96-126 creating new Section 1-26 in the Limited Liability Company Act
Kansas	H.B. 2207, § 1
Louisiana	La. Rev. Stat. Ann. § § 12:1302.C, 12:1306.A(1)(b)
Maine	31 MRSA § 1611
Michigan	MCL § § 450.4102, 450.4204(2)

---

[1] See ¶ 2602 infra.

[2] See ¶ 2603 infra.

[3] See ¶ 2604 infra.

[4] See ¶ 2605 infra.

[5] See ¶ 2606 infra.

North Carolina	N. C. Gen. Stat. § 57C-1-03 As of January 1, 2014, North Carolina no longer authorizes L3Cs, but L3Cs formed prior to that date may continue to use the designation. According to the drafters of the legislation, the L3C entity type is no longer necessary as a result of the broad purposes allowed for LLCs under the revised law.
Rhode Island	R.I. Gen. Laws § 7-16-76
Utah	Utah Code Ann. § § 48-3a-1301 to 48-3a-1304.
Vermont	Vt. Stat. Ann. tit. 11, § 3001(27)
Wyoming	Wyo. Stat. § § 17-15-102(a)(ix);17-15-105(a), 17-15-112(e).

State laws typically provide that a low-profit LLC must meet the following requirements:

- The articles of organization must state that the company is a low-profit LLC.[6]
- The name of the LLC must contain "L3C" or "low-profit limited liability company."[7]
- The LLC must significantly further the accomplishment of one or more charitable or educational purposes, and demonstrate that it would not be formed but for the LLC's relationship to the accomplishment of the charitable or educational purpose.[8]
- The LLC may not have as a significant purpose the production of income or the appreciation of property.[9] However, the fact that the LLC produces significant income or appreciation does not conclusively provide evidence that the production of income or the appreciation of property is a significant purpose.[10]
- The LLC may not be formed for political or legislative purposes.[11]

The low-profit LLC is similar to a benefit corporation. As of August 1, 2013, Delaware and 18 other states permit the incorporation of, and merger or conversion into, a benefit corporation. Ten other states introduced legislation permitting benefit corporations. A benefit corporation permits the corporation to have a positive social purpose. The corporation must consider the impact of its business on the shareholders, the promotion of the company's public benefit purpose, and the best interests of

---

[6] La. Rev. Stat. Ann. § 12:1305(B)(3); Utah Code Ann. § 48-2c-403(1)(c).

[7] 805 ILCS 180/1-10(a)(1); La. Rev. Stat. Ann. § 12:1306(A)(1)(b); MCL § 450.4204(2); Utah Code Ann. § 48-2c-106(8); Wyo. Stat. § 17-15-105(a).

[8] La. Rev. Stat. Ann. § 12:1302(C)(1)(a); MCL § 450.4102(m)(i); N.D. Cent. Code § 10-32-02.39.a; Utah Code Ann. § 48-2c-412(1)(b); Vt. Stat. Ann. tit. 11, § 3001(27)(A); Wyo. Stat. § 17-15-102(a)(ix)(A).

[9] 805 ILCS 180/1-5 (under definitions of "L3C" or "low-profit limited liability company"); La. Rev. Stat. Ann. § 12:1302(C)(1)(b); MCL § 450.4102(m)(ii); MCA § 35-8-102(19)(c); N.D. Cent. Code § 10-32-02.39.c; Utah Code Ann. § 48-2c-412(1)(b)(iii); Vt. Stat. Ann. tit. 11, § 3001(27)(B); Wyo. Stat. § 17-15-102(a)(ix)(B).

[10] 805 ILCS 180/1-26(b)(1); La. Rev. Stat. Ann. § 12:1302(C)(1)(b); MCL § 450.4102(m)(ii); N.D. Cent. Code § 10-32-02.39.c; Utah Code Ann. § 48-2c-412(3), Vt. Stat. Ann. tit. 11, § 3001(27)(B).

[11] 805 ILCS 180/1-26(b)(2); La. Rev. Stat. Ann. § 12:1302(C)(1)(c); MCL § 450.4102(m)(iii); N.D. Cent. Code § 10-32-02.39.b; Utah Code Ann. § 48-2c-412(1)(b)(iv); Vt. Stat. Ann. tit. 11, § 3001(27)(C); Wyo. Stat. § 17-15-102(a)(ix)(C).

those materially affected by the companies conduct. The corporation is not required to maximize value for shareholders.

.02 Tax Consequences

Federal law does not yet recognize low-profit LLCs. Private groups are encouraging Congress to amend the code to provide that a private foundation's investment in a low-profit LLC affords a presumption that the investment qualifies as a "program related investment." Private groups are also requesting that the IRS establish a streamlined method to acknowledge particular investments as program related investments.[12]

An IRS senior technical advisor to the Tax Exempt and Government Entities Division warned that a private foundation's investment in a low-profit LLC may result in a jeopardy assessment excise tax. A foundation and its managers are each subject to a ten percent excise tax on investments if the managers do not exercise ordinary business care and prudence in providing for the financial needs of the foundation. The IRS adviser stated that the IRS has not yet made a final determination on this issue, and urged private foundations to exercise caution before investing in low profit LLCs because of the potential jeopardy assessment.[13]

Marc Owens, a former director of the IRS Exempt Organizations, disagreed with this analysis, and stated that a private foundation may invest in an L3C if the investment qualifies as a program related investment (PRI). The IRS has frequently approved investments by foundations in for-profit LLCs and other entities where the investment meets the requirements for a program related investment.[14]

The tax issues regarding contributions and investments in low-profit LLCs are similar to the tax issues regarding contributions and investments in for-profit LLCs discussed at ¶ 2604.

---

[12] *BNA Daily Tax Report* No. 66, P. H-2 (Apr. 9, 2009).

[13] *BNA Daily Tax Report* No. 126, p. G-3 (July 6, 2009).

[14] *BNA Daily Tax Report* No. 131, p. G-3 (July 13, 2009), *citing* Reg. § 53.4944-3(b), Example 5, and numerous IRS rulings, including Rev. Rul. 2004-51, 2004-22 IRB 974.

¶ 2603 TAX-EXEMPT ORGANIZATIONS

.01 Qualification as Tax Exempt Organization

An LLC may qualify as a tax-exempt organization.[15] However, qualification as and participation in an LLC are subject to special scrutiny.[16] An LLC that wants to qualify as a tax-exempt organization must have a compelling reason why it should be organized as an LLC.[17]

.02 Tax Exemption Application

An LLC that files Form 1023 is treated as a corporation rather than a partnership. As a corporation, it may file Form 1023.[18]

An LLC may not file an exemption application if it wants to be treated as a disregarded entity by its tax-exempt parent. The IRS will only recognize an LLC under Section 501(c)(3) if all its members are Section 501(c)(3) organizations.[19]

.03 Benefit for Related Organizations

A nonprofit LLC that benefits related for-profit organizations and entities will not qualify as a tax-exempt organization.[20]

¶ 2604 FOR-PROFIT LLCs PERFORMING CHARITABLE ACTIVITIES

A tax-exempt Section 501(c)(3) organization may make loans to or investments in for-profit LLCs that perform charitable activities if the loan or contribution furthers the tax-exempt purposes of the Section 501(c)(3) organization.

The final regulations issued by the IRS in 2016 gives the following example of a loan to an LLC classified as a partnership:[21]

---

[15] *See, e.g.,* Ltr. Rul. 9736043, in which exempt organizations formed an LLC to provide financing for prepaid group general services to subscribers of the nonprofit organization; Ltr. Rul. 9840054, in which exempt organization used an LLC as an exempt title-holding company under Code Sec. 501(c)(25); Ltr. Ruls. 9839016–017, in which nonprofit organizations formed an LLC to promote a regional network of hospitals and other health care entities that agreed to common supervision and oversight by the LLC; Ltr. Rul. 200118054, in which a nonprofit health system participated in an ambulatory surgery center.

[16] *BNA Daily Tax Report,* G-3, G-4 (May 23, 1995).

[17] *Id.*

[18] IRS Frequently Asked Questions about Form 1023, https://www.irs.gov/charities-non-profits/frequently-asked-questions-about-form-1023.

[19] IRS Frequently Asked Questions about Form 1023, https://www.irs.gov/charities-non-profits/frequently-asked-questions-about-form-1023.

[20] Ltr. Rul. 201701020.

[21] Reg. § 53.4944-3(b), Example 16.

EXAMPLE 26-1

X is a limited liability company treated as a partnership for federal income tax purposes. X purchases coffee from poor farmers residing in a developing country, either directly or through farmer-owned cooperatives. To fund the provision of efficient water management, crop cultivation, pest management, and farm management training to the poor farmers by X, Y, a private foundation, makes a loan to X bearing interest below the market rate for commercial loans of comparable risk. The loan agreement requires X to use the proceeds from the loan to provide the training to the poor farmers. X would not provide such training to the poor farmers absent the loan. Y's primary purpose in making the loan is to educate poor farmers about advanced agricultural methods. No significant purpose of the loan involves the production of income or the appreciation of property. The loan significantly furthers the accomplishment of Y's exempt activities and would not have been made but for such relationship between the loan and Y's exempt activities. Accordingly, the loan is a program-related investment.

A nonprofit organization may also make an equity investment in a for-profit LLC that is classified as a partnership. However, the equity investment raises numerous issues. The preamble to the final regulations in 2016 explained the problem as follows:[22]

One commenter suggested modifying Example 16, which described a loan to a limited liability company (LLC), to describe an equity investment in an LLC. When a private foundation makes an equity investment in an LLC (or other entity) treated as a partnership for federal tax purposes, the activities of the LLC are attributed to the foundation for purposes of determining both whether the foundation operates exclusively for exempt purposes (and therefore continues to qualify for exemption under section 501(c)(3)) and whether the foundation has engaged in an unrelated trade or business described in section 511. See Rev. Rul. 2004-51 (2004-1 CB 974). As a result, investments in partnership interests by section 501(c)(3) organizations raise a host of issues that are not raised by loans or by investments in stock of corporations. These issues necessitate consideration and analysis of a variety of facts and circumstances that are difficult to summarize in examples in regulations, and hence investments by section 501(c)(3) organizations in partnership interests have been addressed primarily through revenue rulings. See Rev. Rul. 2004-51, Rev. Rul. 98-15 (1998-1 CB 718). Accordingly, the Treasury Department and the IRS do not adopt this comment but are considering whether to address

---

[22] T.D. 9762 (May 9, 2016); Preamble to final regulations § 53.4944-3, Examples of Program-Related Investments, 77 FR 23429 (2016).

PRIs [program-related investments] in the form of investments in partnership interests through the issuance of a revenue ruling.

¶ 2605 PARTICIPATION AS MEMBERS, MANAGERS, OR JOINT VENTURERS

A nonprofit organization may participate as a member, manager, or joint venture with an LLC. The LLC may be a tax-exempt charitable organization or a for-profit organization.

.01 Participation with Charitable Organizations

Two or more charities may form an LLC for charitable purposes and contribute assets to the LLC.[23] The charities may place certain charitable activities under the control of the managers of the LLC. The LLC may also share management services with other Section 501(c)(3) organizations.[24]

The activities of the LLC will not jeopardize the tax-exempt status of the owners or the nonprivate foundation status of the owners.[25] There is no unrelated business taxable income as a result of the reorganization. The public charities may retain control of the LLC after the reorganization, with the LLC serving the interests only of the charities.[26]

Managing an LLC in which one of the members is a Section 501(c)(3) tax-exempt organization does not constitute a tax-exempt activity simply because the manager and member are both tax-exempt organizations.[27] An organization will not qualify for tax exemption if its primary activity is management of an LLC rather than an exempt purpose.[28]

---

[23] Ltr. Rul. 200325003.

[24] Ltr. Rul. 200551023.

[25] Ltr. Ruls. 200551023, 200517031, 200411044, 200330042, 200327067, 200327065, 200325004, 200325003.

[26] Ltr. Ruls. 200411044, 200330042, 200327067, 200327065, 200325004, 200325003.

[27] Ltr. Rul. 201149044.

[28] Ltr. Rul. 201149044.

.02 Participation with Noncharitable Organizations

A tax-exempt organization may participate as a member or manager in an LLC with a noncharitable organization.[29] The tax-exempt organization may contribute all[30] or a substantial part of its assets to the LLC if the following requirements are met:[31]

- The charity has the right to select a majority of the managers, and otherwise maintains control over the operations and business of the LLC.[32] Alternatively, the charity may be given the right to select only 50 percent of the members of the board of directors if the LLC is an ancillary operation of the charity, and the charity has substantial involvement in the operations of the LLC.[33] A charity may lose its tax-exempt status if it forms an LLC with a for-profit organization and gives control over the LLC to the for-profit entity.[34]
- The LLC's activities are primarily intended to further the charity's tax-exempt purposes. The business of the LLC should be substantially related to the charity's exempt purposes.[35] The governing instruments of the LLC should require that the LLC give charitable purposes priority over maximizing profits for the owners of the LLC.[36] The activities of an LLC that is classified as a partnership for federal income tax purposes are attributable to the charitable member of the LLC in determining whether the charity is operated exclusively for exempt purposes under Code Sec. 501(c)(3).[37]
- Any benefit to private parties is incidental to the accomplishment of the charity's tax-exempt purposes.[38]
- If the LLC designates a management company to run the operations of the LLC, the terms of the management contract must be reasonable.[39]
- Distributions by the LLC to the charity should be used for charitable purposes.[40]

If a charity cannot meet these requirements, it may still invest in an LLC with noncharitable members. However, the investment in the LLC should not in such case represent a substantial portion of the charity's assets. The charity's allocable share of

---

[29] Ltr. Ruls. 200304042, 200206058.

[30] Rev. Rul. 98-15, 1998-12 IRB 6; Ltr. Ruls. 9739036–039.

[31] Ltr. Ruls. 200528029, 200351033, 200330042, 200327067, 200327065, 200333031–033, 200325004, 200325003, 200304042, 200304041, 200304036, 200303065, 200252096, 200249014, 200044040, 199913051, 199913035, 199909056, 9739036–039, 9736043.

[32] Rev. Rul. 98-15, 1998-12 IRB 6; Ltr. Ruls. 200351033, 200304042, 199909056; NSAR 0854, Vaughn #0854 (Jan. 10, 2003).

[33] Rev. Rul. 2004-51, 2004-22 IRB 974.

[34] *St. David's Health Care System v. United States,* 2003-2 USTC ¶ 50,713 (5th Cir. 2003).

[35] Rev. Rul. 2004-51, 2004-22 IRB 974; Ltr. Ruls. 200304042, 200528029, 200351033.

[36] Rev. Rul. 98-15, 1998-12 IRB 6; Ltr. Rul. 200118054; *BNA Daily Tax Report,* G-3, G-4 (May 23, 1995).

[37] Rev. Rul. 2004-51, 2004-22 IRB 974; Ltr. Ruls. 200304042, 200327067, 200327065, 200325004, 200325003, 200304041, 200303065.

[38] Rev. Rul. 98-15, 1998-12 IRB 6; NSAR 0854, Vaughn #0854 (Jan. 10, 2003); Ltr. Rul. 200304042.

[39] Rev. Rul. 98-15, 1998-12 IRB 6.

[40] Rev. Rul. 98-15, 1998-12 IRB 6; Ltr. Ruls. 9739036-039.

income from the LLC may constitute unrelated business taxable income. The charity's substantial investment in an LLC with noncharitable members may also impair the charity's ability to conduct its other charitable activities and result in loss of tax-exempt status.[41]

The tax-exempt status of the charity will be denied if (i) the charity has a single function, which is to participate in an LLC, (ii) the charity does not control the LLC, and (iii) the LLC provides substantial benefits to private investors in addition to furthering the exempt function activities of the charity.[42]

.03 Examples

A public charity or private foundation may participate as a member or manager in an LLC with for-profits entities in the following cases:

- *Lending to low income populations.* A publicly supported charity may participate in a joint venture through an LLC to finance small businesses for the benefit of low-income populations.[43] The LLC may make loans to businesses (a) located in distressed areas, (b) that use funds for activities that employ individuals who are part of a targeted population or who live in a distressed area, or (c) that use funds to provide necessary services or products that are otherwise unavailable to residents of distressed areas.[44] The charity may provide underwriting, loan servicing, technical assistance to borrowers, and accounting services to the LLC. The charity may lease space to the LLC for its offices for fair rental value.[45] The tax-exempt status of the charity will not been adversely affected even though the charity receives interest and loan fees, and pays a profit participation interest to investors.[46]
- *Hospitals.* A tax-exempt organization may form an LLC with a for-profit corporation and contribute its hospital and other operating assets to the LLC. For example, a hospital may form a single-member disregarded LLC to act as a partner in a limited partnership that provides diagnostic imaging services not currently available in or near the local area.[47] The tax-exempt organization will not be a private foundation, and will not have unrelated business income, even though its only source of revenue is distributions from the LLC.[48] However, the hospital may lose its tax-exempt status if the LLC can deny services to certain segments of the community such as indigents, or if the general requirements discussed above are not met.[49]

---

[41] Ltr. Rul. 200351033. *See also* Rev. Rul. 2004-51, 2004-22 IRB 974.

[42] NSAR 0854, Vaughn #0854 (Jan. 10, 2003).

[43] Ltr. Ruls. 200351033, 199909056.

[44] Ltr. Rul. 200351033.

[45] Ltr. Rul. 200351033.

[46] Ltr. Rul. 199909056.

[47] Ltr. Rul. 200436022.

[48] Rev. Rul. 98-15, 1998-12 IRB 6; Ltr. Ruls. 200436022, 9739036–039.

[49] Rev. Rul. 98-15, 1998-12 IRB 6; Ltr. Ruls. 9739036–039.

- *Trade shows.* One or more trade associations may form an LLC to operate trade shows. Income received by the trade association from the LLC does not constitute unrelated business taxable income.[50]
- *Revitalization of inner cities.* Public charities may form an LLC to acquire, develop, finance and market inner city property for the purpose of fighting community deterioration and promoting urban revitalization.[51] An LLC may construct and operate public recreational facilities for lease to unrelated parties at fair rental value.[52]
- *Education and teacher training.* A university may form an LLC with a for-profit corporation to provide teacher training seminars at off-campus locations using interactive video technology contributed by the for-profit corporation.[53] A private operating foundation may form an LLC to operate an accredited university.[54]

¶ 2606 SUBSIDIARY LLC

.01 *General*

A tax-exempt organization may form a single-member LLC to receive and hold contributions and acquisitions of real estate and other high liability assets.[55] The LLC is used to protect the tax-exempt parent organization from liability.[56] Normally, the LLC should be classified as a disregarded entity since there are limits on the amount of stock that a private foundation may own in an LLC that is classified as a corporation.

The contribution of property to the LLC is deductible as a charitable contribution under Code Sec. 170(a), subject to the same percentage limitations and other restrictions that apply to deductible contributions made directly to the exempt entity.[57] However, the IRS will not rule on the deductibility of a charitable contribution of real property to an LLC.[58]

The assets owned by or transferred to the LLC are treated as owned by or transferred to the charitable organization.[59] The LLC is treated as part of the charitable organization unless it elects classification as a separate corporation.[60] Thus, the

---

[50] Ltr. Ruls. 200510030, 200333031–033.

[51] Ltr. Rul. 200411044.

[52] Ltr. Rul. 200532058.

[53] Rev. Rul. 2004-51, 2004-22 IRB 974.

[54] Ltr. Rul. 200431018.

[55] Ltr. Rul. 201603032 (low income housing).

[56] Ltr. Rul. 200642009.

[57] Ltr. Ruls. 200436022, 200134025.

[58] Ltr. Rul. 200150027, *citing* Rev. Proc. 2000-1, 2000-1 IRB 4, § 5.14(3).

[59] Ltr. Rul. 200150027.

[60] Ltr. Ruls. 200551023, 200642009, 200634015, 200150027, *citing* Ann. 99-102, 1999-43 IRB 545; Info 2006-0031.

charitable organization is not required to file separate returns or make separate public disclosures for the LLC.[61]

A single-member LLC is not required to file an application for exemption on Form 1023.[62] The acceptance of the charitable contribution by the LLC will not adversely affect the tax-exempt status of the charitable organization that owns the LLC.[63] If the LLC acquires property encumbered by debt, it may obtain an exemption from the unrelated business income tax for its debt-financed income.[64]

A disregarded LLC whose sole owner is exempt from federal income tax is not required to pay federal taxes or file a federal tax or information return. That is the responsibility of its sole owner. The disregarded LLC receives the benefit of its owner's tax-exempt status. An exception applies to employment taxes for wages paid to employees of a disregarded entity on or after January 1, 2009. The disregarded LLC must file separate employment tax returns.[65]

A subsidiary LLC may, but is not required to, obtain its own employer identification number separate from the employer identification number of the tax-exempt owner. The subsidiary LLC may not use its own EIN for federal tax purposes, and must normally use the tax-exempt owner's EIN. However, the disregarded LLC subsidiary may use its own name and obtain and use its own EIN (i) for reporting and paying employment taxes, or (ii) if it elects to be classified as a corporation or partnership for federal tax purposes.[66]

A subsidiary LLC may claim its own tax-exempt status if it elects to be classified separately from its sole member or owner for federal tax purposes. It may elect to be classified separately from its sole owner by (i) claiming its own tax-exempt status, in which case it will be classified as a corporation, (ii) having more than one owner or member, or (iii) filing Form 8832 and electing classification as a corporation. A subsidiary LLC that claims its own tax-exempt status must file its own tax-exempt application on Form 1023 or 1024 and its own annual information return on Form 990.[67]

.02 Subsidiary for Charitable Purposes

A tax-exempt charitable organization may form a wholly owned LLC to perform charitable activities that are related to the parent organization's exempt purposes.[68] The subsidiary LLC may also act as a partner with other organizations in charitable

---

[61] Ltr. Rul. 200150027.

[62] Ltr. Ruls. 200150027, 200134025.

[63] Ltr. Rul. 200150027.

[64] Ltr. Rul. 200134025, *citing* Code Sec. 514(c)(9).

[65] INFO 2013-0006 (Mar. 29, 2013).

[66] INFO 2013-0006 (Mar. 29, 2013).

[67] INFO 2013-0006 (Mar. 29, 2013).

[68] Ltr. Ruls. 201603032 (low income housing), 201136004, 200642009, 200551023, 200538027, 200532058, 200431048, 200431018, 200124022, 200249014, 200202077, 200124022.

ventures.[69] If the LLC is a disregarded entity, the charitable activities performed by the LLC will be attributable to the parent organization.[70] The LLC is treated as a component of the parent corporation.[71] The exempt owner of the disregarded LLC generally must treat the operations of the LLC as a branch or division of the owner.[72]

The use of the LLC as a separate charitable entity will not jeopardize the tax-exempt status of the parent organization.[73] The tax-exempt status of the owner of a disregarded LLC will not be jeopardized merely because the organizational documents of the LLC do not contain specific language limiting the LLC's purposes to one or more exempt purposes. However, the exempt status of the owner may be adversely affected if the disregarded LLC's organizational documents provide that the LLC will be operated for purposes that are contrary to the tax-exempt purposes of the owner.[74]

The LLC's ownership and operation of a functionally related business will not constitute a business enterprise or result in the excess business holdings excise tax to the charitable organization that owns the LLC.[75]

Charitable purposes include "lessening the burdens of government."[76] A subsidiary LLC may engage in activities that lessen the burden of government. For example, a subsidiary LLC of a charitable organization may manage the investment funds of governmental organizations. Activities by a subsidiary LLC that lessen the burden of government will not jeopardize the tax-exempt status of the parent organization.[77]

The tax exempt owner of a charitable disregarded LLC must include the LLC's finances and operations as part of its own in filing the annual information return.[78] As a general rule, a disregarded LLC owned by a tax-exempt organization is not required to pay federal taxes or file a federal tax or information return. That is the responsibility of the tax exempt owner.

A subsidiary LLC may enter into shared management agreements with other charitable organizations for charitable purposes.[79]

A subsidiary LLC formed for charitable purposes may engage in substantial activities that are not in furtherance of the parent organization's exempt purposes.

---

[69] Ltr. Rul. 200436022.

[70] INFO 2010-0052; Ltr. Ruls. 200551023, 200551023, 200538027, 200532058, 200249014.

[71] INFO 2010-0052; Ltr. Ruls. 200634015, 200637041, 200538027, *citing* IRS Publication 3402 (Rev. 72000) "Tax Issues for Limited Liability Companies"; IRS Ann. 99-102, 1999-2 CB 545.

[72] INFO 2010-0052.

[73] Ltr. Ruls. 201603032, 200723030, 200642009, 200551023, 200532058, 200436022, 200249014, 200202077, 200124022.

[74] INFO 2010-0052.

[75] Ltr. Ruls. 200532058, 200202077.

[76] Reg. § 1.501(c)(3)-1(d)(2) provides that the term "charitable" is used in Code Sec. 501(c)(3) in its generally accepted legal sense and includes the lessening of the burdens of government.

[77] Ltr. Rul. 200606047.

[78] INFO 2010-0052.

[79] Ltr. Rul. 200551023.

The unrelated businesses will not jeopardize the parent organization's exempt status.[80]

The contribution by a charitable foundation to an LLC is treated as a qualifying distribution.[81]

A private foundation that operates charitable activities through a disregarded LLC may continue to act as a private foundation. Distributions that the private foundation makes through the disregarded LLC for charitable purposes constitute qualifying distributions.[82] The use of assets to operate charitable programs through the LLC may be used to satisfy the endowment test.[83] Revenues derived from the operations of the LLC may be treated as support for purposes of the support test.[84]

The employees of the LLC may participate in a Section 403(b) tax-sheltered annuity plan sponsored by the parent organization if the LLC does not elect to be classified as a corporation.[85]

.03 Subsidiary for Noncharitable Purposes

A tax-exempt organization may also form a subsidiary LLC to perform noncharitable activities unrelated to the parent organization's exempt purposes.[86] The tax-exempt organization will not jeopardize its exempt status merely because the organizational documents of the LLC do not contain specific language limiting the LLC's purposes to one or more exempt purposes.[87] For example, a tax-exempt organization may own an LLC that engages in for-profit activities.[88]

The subsidiary LLC's business activities will not adversely affect the tax-exempt status of the parent organization if the subsidiary LLC has a business purpose, the activities at the LLC are not attributed to the tax-exempt organization, and the LLC is not merely an instrumentality, arm, agent or integral part of the parent organization.[89] The officers and directors of the tax-exempt organization should not control or be involved in the day-to-day operations of the LLC. The tax-exempt organization should maintain separate facilities, addresses, telephone numbers, telephone listings, operational records, bank accounts and other financial records, stationary, tax filings, and insurance. If the tax-exempt organization leases office space or provides administrative services to the LLC, the LLC should reimburse the tax-exempt organization for such space and services based on reasonable compensation.[90]

---

[80] Ltr. Rul. 200532058.

[81] Ltr. Rul. 200532058, *citing* Code Sec. 4942(g)(2).

[82] INFO 2010-0052; Ltr. Rul. 200431018, *citing* Code Secs. 4942(g)(1), (2), 4942(j)(3).

[83] Ltr. Rul. 200431018, *citing* Code Sec. 4942(j)(3)(B)(i).

[84] Ltr. Rul. 200431018, *citing* Code Sec. 4942(j)(3)(B)(iii).

[85] Ltr. Ruls. 200851044, 200341023, 200334040.

[86] Ltr. Rul. 200752042.

[87] INFO 2013-0006 (Mar. 29, 2013).

[88] Ltr. Rul. 200752042.

[89] Ltr. Ruls. 200436022, 200321021.

[90] Ltr. Rul. 200321021.

The tax-exempt status of an organization may be adversely affected if it operates an LLC for purposes that are contrary to the tax-exempt purposes of the owner.[91]

.04 Real Property Holding LLC

The general rule is that rental income received by a tax-exempt organization is not unrelated business taxable income if (i) the rent is from real property, or is an incidental amount from the lease of personal property leased with the real property, (ii) the amount of rent does not depend in whole or in part on the income or profits from the leased property, (iii) the property is not debt-financed, and (iv) the property is not inventory.[92]

A tax-exempt organization may form a single-member disregarded LLC to hold and manage the real estate investments of the tax-exempt organization. The formation and operation of the LLC have the following tax consequences:[93]

- The real property holding LLC will not jeopardize the tax-exempt status of the parent corporation.
- The rental income received by the parent corporation from the LLC or by the LLC from third-party commercial tenants will not constitute unrelated business taxable income.[94]
- Income received from the sale or exchange of property by the LLC will not constitute unrelated business taxable income.
- One or more of the officers and directors of the tax-exempt corporation (who are disqualified persons), may manage the business of the LLC. The management services will not constitute an act of self-dealing.
- The ownership of 100 percent of the LLC will not constitute excess business holdings under Code Sec. 4943.[95]
- The property owned by the LLC that is used for charitable purposes, including property rented to other tax-exempt organizations, will constitute a program-related investment under Code Sec. 4944(c), and will therefore not be subject to tax under Code Sec. 4944 on investments that jeopardize the carrying out of the tax-exempt purposes of the owner of the LLC.[96]
- The amounts expended by the owner of the LLC to acquire and construct improvements to the real property owned by the LLC will not constitute taxable expenditures under Code Sec. 4945.[97]
- The rental activities by the LLC will not cause the LLC or its parent corporation to be classified as a feeder organization under Code Sec. 502.[98]

---

[91] INFO 2010-0052 (June 25, 2010); INFO 2013-0006 (Mar. 29, 2013).
[92] Code Sec. 512(b)(3)–(5). *See* ¶ 2607 *infra.*
[93] Ltr. Ruls. 201444043, 201136004, 200637041.
[94] Ltr. Rul. 201134023, *citing* Code Sec. 512(b)(3)(A)(i).
[95] Ltr. Ruls. 201134023, 200637041.
[96] Ltr. Ruls. 201134023, 200637041.
[97] Ltr. Rul. 201134023.
[98] Ltr. Rul. 201444043.

However, a trust that distributes its income to other charitable organizations will not qualify as a tax exempt organization if it is formed to acquire real estate through investments in LLCs. The trust would be treated as operating for a substantial nonexempt purpose. The holding of real estate or other assets through an LLC until market conditions improve is not an exempt purpose.[99]

.05 Tax Deduction for Contribution to Subsidiary LLC

A contribution to a single-member disregarded LLC owned by a tax-exempt charity is treated as a charitable contribution to a branch or division of the charity. The contribution will be tax-deductible if it meets all other requirements for deduction under Code Sec. 170.

¶ 2607 UNRELATED BUSINESS TAXABLE INCOME

.01 Income Unrelated to Exempt Functions

Income received by a tax-exempt organization from an LLC is unrelated business taxable income if the business of the LLC is unrelated to the organization's tax-exempt purposes.[100] A tax-exempt organization must pay taxes at the highest trust or corporate income tax rate on such income. There are several exceptions. The major exceptions include dividends, interest, royalties, gains from the sale of property, and certain real and personal property rents.[101]

.02 Income Related to Exempt Functions

Income received by a tax-exempt organization from an LLC as a distributive share of income, or for goods, property, services or personnel in connection with the business of the LLC, is not unrelated business taxable income if the income is from a trade or business that is substantially related to the organization's tax-exempt purposes.[102] For example, income received by a tax-exempt organization from a single-member disregarded LLC is not unrelated business taxable income if the business is substantially related to the parent corporation's exempt purposes.[103]

A tax-exempt organization may be a member of a for-profit LLC that engages in a trade or business. The income received by the tax-exempt organization from the

---

[99] Ltr. Rul. 201044021.

[100] Ltr. Rul. 200752042.

[101] Code Sec. 512(b); Ltr. Rul. 201329028.

[102] Rev. Rul. 2004-51, 2004-22 IRB 974; Rev. Rul. 98-15, 1998-2 IRB 6; Ltr. Ruls. 201603032, 200717019, 200551023, 200532058, 200528029, 200436022, 200411044, 200351033, 200330042, 200327067, 200327065, 200325004, 200325003, 200304042, 200304041, 200304036, 200303065, 200252096, 200249014, 200206058, 200118054, 200044040, 199913051, 199913035, 9739036-039, 9736043.

[103] Ltr. Ruls. 200723030, 200605013, 200551023.

LLC will not constitute unrelated business taxable income if the trade or business is substantially related to the exempt organization's purposes. The IRS will "look through" the LLC to determine whether the LLC's trade or business is substantially related.[104] The trade or business is substantially related if it furthers the organization's exempt purposes.[105] However, if the exempt organization's ownership percentage in the LLC exceeds its percentage contribution to the LLC's gross income, then the excess percentage of the exempt organization's distributive share of LLC income constitutes unrelated business taxable income.[106]

Under the fragmentation rule, income derived by an LLC from ancillary activities that are not directly related to the charity's exempt purposes will not constitute unrelated business taxable income if the LLC's activities as a whole are substantially related to the charity's exempt purposes.[107]

.03 Sale of Real Property

Income received by a tax-exempt LLC from the sale of real property investments is not unrelated business taxable income. The income is passive income that is excluded from unrelated business taxable income.[108]

.04 Rental Income

Income received by a tax-exempt LLC,[109] or by a tax-exempt organization from an LLC,[110] from the rental of real property (less the deductions directly connected with carrying on the rental business) may be unrelated business taxable income unless the LLC meets the Code Sec. 512(b)(3) test and the Code Sec. 512(b)(4) test.

Code Sec. 512(b)(3) excludes from unrelated business taxable income all rents from real property unless (i) more than 50 percent of the total rents received is attributable to personal property, or (ii) the amount of rent depends in whole or in part on the income or profits derived from the leased property (other than the amount based on a fixed percentage of receipts or sales).

Code Sec. 512(b)(4) provides that rental income will nevertheless be unrelated business taxable income if the property is debt-financed. Property is debt-financed if the property is held to produce income (e.g., rents) and there is "acquisition indebtedness" at any time during the tax year.[111] Acquisition indebtedness includes:[112]

---

[104] Ltr. Ruls. 200605013, 200536023.

[105] Ltr. Rul. 200605013.

[106] Ltr. Rul. 200605013.

[107] Ltr. Rul. 200532058, *citing* Code Sec. 513(c), Rev. Rul. 74-399, 1974-2 CB 172; Reg. § 1.501(c)(3)-1(d)(2).

[108] Code Sec. 512(b)(5); Ltr. Rul. 200637041.

[109] Ltr. Rul. 200436022.

[110] Ltr. Ruls. 200637041, 200517031.

[111] Code Sec. 514(b)(1).

[112] Code Sec. 514(c)(1).

- indebtedness incurred by the organization in acquiring or improving the property;

- indebtedness incurred before the acquisition or improvement of such property if the indebtedness would not have been incurred but for such acquisition or improvement; and

- indebtedness incurred after the acquisition or improvement of such property if the indebtedness would not have been incurred but for such acquisition or improvement and the incurrence of such indebtedness was reasonably foreseeable at the time of such acquisition or improvement.

EXAMPLE 26-2

A tax-exempt private foundation owns all of the membership interests in an LLC that rents property to unrelated third parties. The rents are not unrelated business taxable income if (i) not more than 50 percent of the total rents received under the lease is attributable to personal property, (ii) the amount of rent does not depend in whole or in part on the income or profits derived by third parties from the leased property, and (iii) the property is not encumbered by debt.[113]

Normally, real property rent received by a tax-exempt LLC (or by a tax-exempt organization as pass-through rental income from a wholly owned LLC) is unrelated business taxable income if the leased property is encumbered by debt,[114] and is not unrelated business taxable income if the leased property is not encumbered by debt.[115]

"Debt-financed property" does not include any property owned by an LLC if substantially all the use of the property is substantially related to the parent corporation's tax-exempt purposes.[116] "Substantially all" means 95 percent.[117]

Rents received by an LLC from third parties is not unrelated business taxable income if the charitable owner of the LLC loans money to the LLC to purchase the property.[118] The rule applies even if the lease payments received by the charity through the LLC are not in furtherance of the charity's exempt purposes.[119]

---

[113] Ltr. Rul. 201435017.

[114] Ltr. Rul. 200351033.

[115] Ltr. Ruls. 201136004, 200637014, 200436022.

[116] Ltr. Ruls. 200717019, 200538027, 200532058, *citing* Code Sec. 514(b)(1)(A).

[117] Ltr. Ruls. 200717019, 200517031, *citing* Code Sec. 514(b)(1)(A).

[118] Ltr. Ruls. 201444043, 200532058, 200411044, *citing* Code Sec. 514(b)(1)(A)(i). The property is not treated as debt-financed property in such case.

[119] Ltr. Rul. 200532058.

There are additional exceptions to the tax for educational organizations, title holding companies owned by tax-exempt organizations, and certain other tax-exempt organizations.[120]

¶2608 EXCESS BUSINESS HOLDINGS

Code Sec. 4943 imposes an excise tax on excess business holdings of a private foundation in a business enterprise. A private foundation has a certain number of years after acquisition of a business to reduce its ownership interest to permissible levels.

There is no excess business holdings tax for any trade or business if at least 95 percent of the gross income of the trade or business is from passive sources. For example, if a private foundation owns an LLC that rents real property, there is no excess business holdings tax if at least 95 percent of the gross income from the LLC is derived from rental income.[121]

¶2609 SELF-DEALING TAX

Code Sec. 4941 imposes a tax on any act of self-dealing between a disqualified person and a private foundation. An act of self-dealing means any direct or indirect sale, exchange or leasing of property between a private foundation and a disqualified person. The transfer of LLC interests by a disqualified person to a private foundation is not an act of self-dealing if the transfer is a gift, bequest or other transfer without consideration paid or liability assumed. There is no prohibition against a disqualified person making a donation or contribution to a private foundation if there is no obligation, lien, debt or other restriction. The gift of LLC membership interests does not constitute a sale, exchange, or leasing of property between a private foundation and a disqualified person.[122]

¶2610 DEDUCTION FOR CHARITABLE CONTRIBUTION OF MEMBERSHIP INTEREST

The IRS will not issue rulings regarding whether a charitable contribution deduction is allowed for the contribution of a membership interest in an LLC that is classified as a partnership.[123]

The transfer of a membership interest in an LLC to a private foundation does not constitute an act of self-dealing or prohibited transaction if the liabilities assumed by

---

[120] Code Sec. 514(c)(9)(C).

[121] Ltr. Ruls. 201435017, 201136004, 200637014.

[122] Ltr. Rul. 201435017.

[123] Rev. Proc. 2013-3, 2013-1 IRB 113, § 3.01(25).

the LLC are nonrecourse and constitute less than two percent of the LLC's fair market value.[124]

¶ 2611 INVESTMENT LLC

A tax-exempt organization may own an interest in an LLC that generates passive income from investments. The ownership of the LLC has the following tax consequences:

- *Unrelated business taxable income.* There is no unrelated business taxable income if the LLC generates dividends, interest, annuities, royalties, rents, and gains and losses from the sale, exchange or other disposition of property other than inventory or property held primarily for sale to customers. Such income is excluded from the definition of unrelated business taxable income.[125]

- *Excess business holdings.* There is no excise tax on excess business holdings of a private foundation if certain conditions are met. The holdings of the private foundation in the LLC do not constitute excess business holdings of a business enterprise if the LLC derives 95 percent of its income from passive sources.[126] However, the proportionate share of the private foundation's holdings in any business enterprises owned by the LLC are imputed to the private foundation in determining whether there is an excise tax on excess business holdings.[127]

- *Jeopardizing investment.* There is a ten percent excise tax on private foundations that invest in a manner that jeopardizes the carrying out of its exempt purpose. However, if a private foundation receives a gratuitous transfer of LLC membership interests or other investments, such investments will not be considered a jeopardizing investment if the private foundation did not pay for the investment.[128]

¶ 2612 DEPRECIATION

If an LLC has tax-exempt and non-tax exempt members, a portion of the property owned by the LLC may be deemed tax-exempt use property. In such case, the LLC must depreciate the property over the greater of 40 years or 125 percent of any long-term lease.[129]

---

[124] Ltr. Rul. 201012050.

[125] Ltr. Ruls. 201333020, 201329028, *citing* Code Sec. 512(b).

[126] Ltr. Ruls. 201333020, 201329028, *citing* Code Sec. 4943 and Reg. § 53.4943-10(c)(1).

[127] Ltr. Ruls. 201333020, 201329028, *citing* Code Sec. 4943(d)(1).

[128] Ltr. Ruls. 201333020, 201329028, *citing* Code Sec. 4944(a)(1) and Reg. § 53.4944-1(a)(2)(ii)(a).

[129] Code Sec. 168(h)(6). *See* ¶ 703.07.

¶ 2613 EMPLOYEE BENEFIT PLANS

Employees of a single-member disregarded LLC established by a tax-exempt organization may participate in a Section 403(b) annuity plan established by the tax-exempt organization.[130]

¶ 2614 CHARITABLE GIFTS OF LLC INTERESTS

The IRS will not issue rulings on whether a charitable contribution deduction under Code Sec. 170 is allowed for a transfer of an interest in a limited liability company taxed as a partnership to an organization described in Code Sec. 170(c).[131]

¶ 2615 FRACTIONS RULE

The fractions rule is a rule designed to prevent real estate LLCs and partnerships from allocating income to tax-exempt investors such as pension funds and losses to taxable members.[132] An LLC must allocate to tax-exempt members their allocable share of income, gain, loss and deduction consistent with the fractions rule under IRS regulations. The IRS proposed regulations in 2016,[133] and is planning to issue final regulations with small changes.[134]

The tax-exempt members must be allocated their share of LLC income, gain, loss, and deduction consistent with the fractions rule under regulations issued by the IRS. The IRS regulations address such issues as preferred returns, member-specific expenditures, unlikely losses, tiered partnerships, and chargebacks of member-specific expenditures and unlikely losses.

LLCs with qualified exempt members that own five percent or less of the LLC's profits interests do not have to comply with the fractions rule.[135]

¶ 2616 CHARITABLE LEAD AND REMAINDER TRUSTS

An LLC may be the grantor of a charitable remainder unitrust. An LLC that is classified as a partnership for federal tax purposes is a permissible recipient of the unitrust amount.[136]

The use of an LLC to manage the assets of a charitable remainder unitrust established by family members to benefit a single tax-exempt charitable foundation

---

[130] Ltr. Rul. 200851044.

[131] Rev. Proc. 2016-3, 2016-1 IRB 126, § 3.01(28).

[132] Code Sec. 514(c)(9)(E).

[133] Prop. Reg. § 1.514(c)-2; REG-136978-12 (2016).

[134] *BNA Daily Tax Report* No. 30, p. 10 (Feb. 13, 2018).

[135] Code Sec. 514(c)(9)(B)(vi).

[136] Ltr. Rul. 199952071 (*citing* Reg. § 1.664-3(a)(3)).

and relatives of one family member will not trigger the various private foundation excise taxes.[137]

A charitable lead annuity trust may form an LLC and sell an interest in the LLC to the remainder beneficiaries in exchange for a promissory note. The sale does not constitute an act of self-dealing under Section 4941 of the Code.[138]

A charitable remainder trust's share of LLC income from investments in a foreign corporation does not constitute unrelated business taxable income.[139]

---

[137] Ltr. Rul. 200423029.

[138] Ltr. Rul. 200124029.

[139] Ltr. Rul. 200623069.

27

Self-Employment and Employment Taxes

¶ 2701 GENERAL RULE

The general rule is that members of an LLC are not subject to employment taxes. The LLC is not required to withhold income, FICA, or FUTA taxes. However, each member of the LLC must pay estimated taxes on his or her distributive share of income. The member is also subject to self-employment taxes (FICA and FUTA) on the member's share of income attributable to a trade or business if the member actively participates in the business of the LLC.

Nonmember employees of the LLC are subject to employment taxes. The LLC must withhold income, FICA, and FUTA taxes for such employees.

¶2702 MEMBERS OF THE LLC

.01 Employment Taxes

The owner of an LLC that is classified as a disregarded entity is not an employee for employment tax purposes. Income and wages received by the member are not subject to income or employment withholding taxes.[1]

A member of an LLC that is classified as a partnership is not an employee for wage-withholding purposes. The income and wages received by a member of the LLC are not subject to income, FICA, or FUTA withholding taxes.[2] Guaranteed payments to a member are not subject to employment taxes.[3] In 1969, the IRS ruled that an individual cannot be a partner and an employee at the same time.[4] The IRS is actively considering repealing that ruling.[5]

.02 Self-Employment Taxes for LLC Classified as Partnership

Distributive Share of Income

Members of an LLC are potentially liable for self-employment taxes on their allocable shares of trade or business income under three theories of liability:

1. *Classification as general partner.* Under the first theory, members are liable for self-employment taxes if they are classified as general partners, and are not subject to self-employment taxes if they are classified as limited partners.[6] The IRS has relied heavily on state law to determine the status of LLC members for such purpose.[7] A member of an LLC with substantial management powers is classified as a general partner for self-employment tax purposes.[8] Under this theory, a member who is classified as a general

---

[1] Reg. § 301.7701-2(c)(2)(iv)(C), Example (iii).

[2] CCA 200117003 (*citing* Rev. Rul. 69-184, 1969-1 CB 256); Reg. § 1.707-1(c); *Riether v. United States,* 919 F. Supp. 2d 1140 (D.N.M. 2012); CCA 201436049 TD 9766 (2016) (stating that partners cannot be treated as employees of a disregarded entity owned by the partnership). TD 9766 (2016) (stating that partners cannot be treated as employees of a disregarded entity owned by the partnership); TD 9766 (2016) (stating that partners cannot be treated as employees of a disregarded entity owned by the partnership).

[3] Reg. § 1.707-1(c).

[4] Rev. Rul. 69-184, 1969-1 CB 256. *See also Riether v. United States,* 919 F. Supp. 2d 1140 (D.N.M. 2012).

[5] "IRS Eying Repeal of Rev. Rul. on Partner-Employees, Official Says," *BNA Daily Tax Report* No. 99, p. G-5 (May 22, 2013).

[6] CCA 201640014 involving a franchisee that operated several restaurant businesses through an LLC classified as a partnership.

[7] Code Secs. 1401-1402; Regs. §§ 1.1402(a)-1(a)(2), 1.1402(a)-2(d), (e), (f), (g); *Castigliola v. Comm'r,* TC Memo 2017-62 (2017); "Upcoming Guidance on Self-Employment Tax for LLCs Could Address Other Entities," *BNA Daily Tax Report* No. 232, G-5 (Dec. 3, 2014).

[8] *Castigliola v. Comm'r,* TC Memo 2017-62 (2017).

partner is subject to self-employment taxes on the member's share of all LLC earnings from a trade or business whether or not the member is an active or passive member with respect to the production of such income.[9] A member of an LLC that is classified as a general partner is not entitled to exempt from self-employment income a reasonable return on invested capital beyond the compensation for services required to operate the business of the LLC.[10]

2. *Active service providers.* Under the second theory of liability, members are liable for self-employment taxes if they are active service providers rather than passive investors in the LLC. These cases and rulings focus on the purposes of the law rather than a member's classification as a general or limited partner.[11] For example, members of an LLC who actively engage in the practice of law are subject to self-employment taxes on their distributive shares of income from a law LLC.[12] Members of an LLC who are passive investors and who are not managers of the LLC are not subject to self-employment taxes on their distributive shares of income except for guaranteed payment for services rendered.[13]

3. *Continuity of services.* Under the third theory of liability, members are liable for self-employment taxes if they provide services to the LLC with sufficient continuity, regularity, and a profit motive such that they are engaged in a trade or business.[14] This test focuses on the amount of services provided, not just whether the services are active or passive.

EXAMPLE 27-1

A surgeon with an active medical practice owned a minority interest in a separate LLC. The LLC owned and operated a surgical center at which the doctor performed approximately ten percent of his surgeries during each year. Income earned from the LLC was passive income against which the surgeon could deduct passive losses because the LLC was a passive activity for the surgeon. The surgeon was not involved in the operation of the LLC on a regular, continuous, and substantial basis. He had no input into management decisions. He treated the surgical facilities as a separate unit from his medical practice. He had no day-to-day responsibilities for the LLC.[15]

---

[9] CCA 201436049.

[10] CCA 201640014.

[11] CCA 201436049; *Riether v. United States*, 919 F. Supp. 2d 1140 (D.N.M. 2012); "Upcoming Guidance on Self-Employment Tax for LLCs Could Address Other Entities," *BNA Daily Tax Report* No. 232, G-5 (Dec. 3, 2014).

[12] Ltr. Ruls. 9525058, 9432018 (both involving members of a law LLC); *Renkemeyer, Campbell, and Weaver LLP v. Comm'r*, 136 TC 137 (2011).

[13] Code Sec. 1402(a)(13).

[14] *Chai v. Comm'r*, TC Memo 2015-42 (2015); *Hardy v. Comm'r*, TC Memo 2017-16 (2017).

[15] *Hardy v. Comm'r*, TC Memo 2017-16 (2017).

If an LLC withholds taxes on "wages" of a member that should have been treated as self-employment income, the IRS will normally overlook the problem since the self-employment taxes on that income are paid through withholding.[16]

A member's share of LLC income is not subject to self-employment taxes if the income is:

- Rental income from real estate and personal property leased with real estate (except for real estate dealers).[17]

- Dividends and interest (except for dealers in stocks and securities).[18]

- Capital gains.[19]

Guaranteed Payments

Guaranteed payments to all members for services rendered are subject to self-employment taxes, regardless of the member's classification as a general or limited partner.[20] For example, guaranteed payments for services rendered to a member classified as a limited partner are subject to self-employment taxes.[21]

Members of an LLC who are classified as limited partners are not subject to self-employment taxes on their distributive shares of income in excess of guaranteed payments for services rendered.[22]

Member Classification Issues

It is unclear how these rules apply to LLCs, since there are no general partners or limited partners. Members of an LLC have some of the characteristics of limited partners (e.g., limited liability) and some of the characteristics of general partners (e.g., management and voting rights).

Members of an LLC who actively engage in the business of the LLC are treated as general partners for self-employment tax purposes.[23] Their distributive shares of trade or business income from the LLC are net earnings from self-employment.

A taxpayer who is actively involved in business may not avoid self-employment taxes by forming two separate corporations, one of which is classified as a limited partner of an LLC and the other of which is classified as a general partner. The

---

[16] *Riether v. United States,* 919 F. Supp. 2d 1140 (D.N.M. 2012); CCA 201436049.

[17] Code Sec. 1402(a)(1).

[18] Code Sec. 1402(a)(2).

[19] Code Sec. 1402(a)(3).

[20] Code Sec. 1402(a)(13); Reg. § 1.1402(a)-1(b); *Support Services, LLC v. Comm'r,* TC Memo 2014-78 (2014).

[21] Code Secs. 1402(a)(13), 707.

[22] *Castigliola v. Comm'r,* TC Memo 2017-62 (2017); Code Sec. 1402(a)(13).

[23] CCA 201436049.

income allocable to both corporations will be subject to self-employment taxes if the ownership of the LLC is structured for tax avoidance purposes.[24]

Payments to an inactive member in an LLC who is the spouse of an active member may be treated as a self-employment income of the active member if the spouse is merely a nominee for the active member.[25] The inactive spouse may also have self-employment income if the spouse provides advice to the active member, signs LLC documents, enters into contracts on behalf of the LLC, and allows the LLC to use his or her credit card and credit rating.[26]

Proposed Regulations

The IRS issued proposed regulations in 1997 on self-employment taxes for members of an LLC classified as a partnership.[27]

Congress prohibited the IRS from issuing temporary or final regulations prior to July 1, 1998, on self-employment taxes for limited partners and members of an LLC classified as limited partners.[28] The Congressional moratorium expired without Congress taking action to clarify the issue. The IRS did not withdraw the proposed regulations. It gave no official indication whether taxpayers may rely on the proposed regulations. However, the IRS informally determined that a taxpayer may rely on the 1997 proposed regulations (but not the 1994 proposed regulations).[29] The IRS also indicated that it was unlikely to re-issue the regulations or issue final regulations until Congress provided a legislative solution.[30]

The proposed regulations are discussed below. Under the regulations, the member is generally subject to self-employment taxes if the member works more than 500 hours for the LLC, has personal liability for LLC debts, or has authority to sign contracts on behalf of the LLC.

Under the proposed regulations, a member will be classified as a general partner (and the trade or business income of the LLC will be subject to self-employment taxes) if the member meets any one of the following tests:

1. *Liability Test.* The member is personally liable for the debts of or claims against the LLC by reason of being a member. For example, a member is classified as a general partner under the proposed regulations if the member personally guarantees LLC debts.
2. *Authority Test.* The member has authority to create binding contracts on behalf of the LLC under the statute or law pursuant to which the LLC is organized. The managers of the LLC who have authority to sign contracts are classified as general partners.

---

[24] *Robucci v. Comm'r*, TC Memo 2011-19 (2011).

[25] *Howell v. Fisher*, TC Memo 2012-303, fn. 12 (2012).

[26] *Howell v. Fisher*, TC Memo 2012-303 (2012).

[27] Prop. Reg. § 1.1402(a)-2(g), (h).

[28] Taxpayer Relief Act of 1997, § 935.

[29] *BNA Daily Tax Report* No. 9, pp. G-2, G-3 (Jan. 15, 2010).

[30] *BNA Daily Tax J.*, p. G-3 (July 7, 1998).

3. *Hours Worked Test.* The member participates in the LLC's trade or business for more than 500 hours during the year.
4. *Personal Services Test.* The member provides more than a de minimis amount of services for the LLC in the areas of health, law, engineering, architecture, accounting, actuarial science, or consulting.[31] All of the income from professional LLCs in such areas is subject to self-employment taxes.

Under the proposed regulations, a member who is not a limited partner may nevertheless exclude from self-employment earnings a portion of his distributive share if he owns more than one class of membership interest. The member will be treated as a limited partner, and will be exempt from self-employment taxes, with respect to one of the classes of membership interests if, immediately after acquiring the interest:[32]

- Other members who are treated as limited partners own a substantial, continuing interest in the same class of membership interest. Ownership of 20 percent or more of the class is substantial;[33] and
- The member's rights and obligations with respect to that class of membership interest are identical to the rights and obligations of the same class held by members who are limited partners.

Under the proposed regulations, a member who is not a limited partner because the member works more than 500 hours for the LLC may also exclude from self-employment earnings a portion of the member's distributive share. The member must own only one class of membership interest.[34] The member must bifurcate the membership interest by excluding from income any guaranteed payment. The member is treated as a limited partner and is exempt from self-employment taxes with respect to the remaining income if, immediately after acquiring the membership interest, both of the following apply:[35]

- Other members who are treated as limited partners own a substantial, continuing interest in the same class of membership interest; and
- The member's rights and obligations with respect to that class of membership interest are identical to the rights and obligations of the same class held by members who are limited partners.

.03 Self-Employment Taxes for LLC Classified as Disregarded Entity

An owner of a disregarded LLC is subject to self-employment taxes on the member's trade or business income from the LLC.[36] The owner is a self-employed

---

[31] Prop. Reg. § 1.1402(a)-2(h)(5).
[32] Prop. Reg. § 1.1402(a)-2(h)(3).
[33] Prop. Reg. § 1.1402(a)-2(h)(6)(iv).
[34] Prop. Reg. § 1.1402(a)-2(h)(4).
[35] Prop. Reg. § 1.1402(a)-2(h)(3).
[36] Reg. § 301.7701-2(c)(2)(iv)(A).

person for self-employment taxes purposes, and is not an employee for employment tax purposes.[37]

.04 Self-Employment Taxes for LLC Classified as Corporation

The owner of an LLC that is classified as a corporation is not subject to self-employment taxes. The member's compensation from the LLC is taxed as wages subject to regular income and employment withholding taxes.

.05 Deferred Compensation and Retirement Plans

Deferred compensation and retirement benefits paid to retiring members are not subject to self-employment taxes if:[38]

- The LLC makes payments on a periodic basis, according to written plan, at least until the retired member's death.
- The retired member does not perform services for the LLC during the LLC's tax year ending within the member's tax year in which the payment was received.
- Other members are not obligated to make payments to the retired member except for retirement payments or other benefits due to medical expenses or death.
- The LLC pays the retired member's share of LLC capital to the retiree before the end of the LLC's tax year.

The retirement payments to the retired member qualify for the exclusion from self-employment taxes even though the payments are front-loaded. For example, the LLC may pay deferred compensation to the retired member in five annual installments, and monthly payments thereafter that never fall below $100 per month until the retiree's death.[39]

.06 Death of Member

For self-employment tax purposes only, a deceased member's self-employment income will include the decedent's distributive share of LLC income or loss through the end of the month in which death occurred. For this purpose, the LLC's income or loss is considered to be earned ratably over the LLC's tax year.[40]

---

[37] Reg. § 301.7701-2(c)(2)(iv)(C), Example (iii).

[38] Code Sec. 1402(a)(10); Reg. § 1.1402(a)-17(c); Ltr. Rul. 200403056.

[39] Ltr. Rul. 200403056.

[40] IRS Publication 559, Survivors, Executors, and Administrators.

¶ 2703 NONMEMBER EMPLOYEES

.01 General Rule

Nonmember employees of an LLC are subject to the regular wage withholding and employment taxes with one exception.

A member of a Section 501(d) religious organization who works under a vow of poverty, in an enterprise conducted and owned by the organization, is not subject to employment taxes if the duties are required by the religious order.[41] The member must have taken a vow of poverty and have no rights to the organization's assets when he leaves the organization. The transfer of a tax-exempt religious organization's unincorporated commercial enterprises to an LLC owned by the organization does not change this result.[42]

The procedures and responsibility for collection and payment of the withholding taxes depend on whether the LLC is classified as a disregarded entity, partnership, or corporation. These rules are discussed below.

.02 LLC Classified as Disregarded Entity

Beginning January 1, 2009, a single-member disregarded LLC is classified as a corporation for employment tax purposes.[43] The LLC is liable for all withholding and employment tax obligations for non-member employees of the LLC.[44] The LLC must file under its own name and employer identification number the employment tax forms on Forms 940 and 941, make withholding tax deposits, and provide Form W-2 wage statements to non-member employees.[45]

The IRS may send a notice of intent to levy on the property of the LLC and file tax liens if the LLC does not pay the taxes in the notice of proposed assessment or contest the assessment notice.[46]

The owner of a single-member of disregarded LLC is not personally liable for the collection and payment of employment taxes as an owner. However, the IRS may collect unpaid employment taxes from the owner under the Section 6672 trust fund penalty tax if the owner is a "responsible person."[47] The IRS must make a separate responsible person penalty assessment under Section 6672 before it imposes liability against the owner.

---

[41] Ltr. Ruls. 9752005, 9752004, 9752003, 9752002 (*citing* Code Sec. 3121(b)(8)(A) and Rev. Rul. 77-290, 1977-2 CB 26).

[42] Ltr. Ruls. 9752005, 9752004, 9752003, 9752002.

[43] Reg. § 301.7701-2(c)(2)(iv).

[44] Reg. § 301.7701-2(c)(2)(iv)(B); CCA 201012046; CCA 200840001.

[45] Reg. § 301.7701-2(c)(2)(iv)(C), Example (ii).

[46] *LG Kendrick, LLC v. Comm'r*, 119 AFTR 2d 2017-1488 (2017).

[47] Rev. Rul. 2004-41, 2004-18 IRB 846; Ltr. Rul. 200235023.

The sole owner of a single-member LLC is not personally liable for the employment taxes incurred by the LLC while it was a multi-member LLC classified as a partnership for federal tax purposes.[48]

A disregarded LLC remains disregarded for backup withholding and related information reporting purposes. Accordingly, the owner of the disregarded LLC is responsible for any backup withholding that is required with respect to reportable payments considered made by the owner rather than the disregarded entity.[49]

The LLC is treated as a sole proprietorship for income tax purposes. Thus, the owner of the disregarded LLC may deduct the employer's share of employment taxes imposed on nonmember employees on Schedule C of Form 1040.[50]

.03 LLC Classified as Corporation

An LLC that is classified as a corporation is responsible for payment of employment taxes.[51] The IRS may file a Notice of Federal Tax Lien against the LLC and file a suit to foreclose the federal tax lien or levy on the LLC assets. The collection due process requirements under Sections 6320 and 6330 must also be met.[52] The members of the LLC are not liable for unpaid employment taxes of the LLC.[53] However, the members may be liable for the trust fund recovery penalty under Code Sec. 6672, depending on the facts and circumstances of each case.[54] In addition, the LLC may proceed against the members of the LLC if there are fraudulent transfers or other special circumstances.[55]

.04 LLC Classified as Partnership

An LLC that is classified as a partnership is responsible for payment of employment taxes. The members of an LLC are not responsible for employment taxes incurred by the LLC,[56] even if the LLC later converts to a single-member disregarded LLC.[57] Unlike the typical partnership situation where the IRS asserts employment tax liability against the partners who are liable for the debts of the partnership under

---

[48] CCA 200946050.

[49] Temp. Reg. § 301.7701-2T(c)(2)(iv)(C)(2); T.D. 9554, preamble to IRS Final, Temporary Regulations (Nov. 1, 2011).

[50] Reg. § 301.7701-2(c)(2)(iv)(C), Example (iii).

[51] CCA 200840001, 200235023.

[52] CCA 200235023.

[53] CCA 200840001.

[54] Rev. Rul. 2004-41, 2004-18 IRB 846; CCA 200840001, 200235023.

[55] CCA 200840001.

[56] Rev. Rul. 2004-41, 2004-18 IRB 846; Ltr. Rul. 199922053; *Miller v. Comm'r*, TC Memo 2006-125 (2006); CCA 200840001

[57] FFA 20093701F.

state law, the IRS will not assert an employment tax liability against members of the LLC if they are not liable for the debts of the LLC under state law.[58]

The members of the LLC may be liable for the trust fund recovery penalty under Code Sec. 6672, depending on the facts and circumstances of each case.[59] The controlling member-manager of an LLC is a "responsible person" under Section 6672, and is personally liable for unpaid employment taxes.[60] A co-owner of a member-managed LLC with check-writing authority who approves financial transactions may be liable for unpaid payroll taxes.[61] A minority member of an LLC may also be a responsible party liable for unpaid payroll taxes.[62]

A chief operating officer and manager of an LLC classified as a partnership may be liable as a responsible person for unpaid payroll taxes if the officer has knowledge of the unpaid trust fund taxes when paying other creditors.[63]

.05 Foreign Employees

An LLC must withhold payroll taxes from the wages of U.S. citizens and U.S. resident alien employees working abroad. The withholding tax does not apply to the portion of wages of U.S. citizens that qualify for the foreign earned income exclusion. The employee must submit to the employer Form 673, *Statement for Claiming Exemption from Withholding on Foreign Earned Income Eligible for the Exclusion Provided by Section 911*. There is no exemption from withholding for U.S. resident aliens working abroad.[64]

.06 Successor Liability

The federal tax liability owed by an LLC for employment taxes may be collected from its successor in interest if the successor LLC is liable under relevant state law.[65]

---

[58] Rev. Rul. 2004-41, 2004-18 IRB 846; CCA 200235023.

[59] Rev. Rul. 2004-41, 2004-18 IRB 846; CCA 200840001.

[60] *O'Brien v. United States*, 2011-1 USTC ¶ 50,279 (D. Nev. 2011).

[61] *United States v. Commander*, 119 AFTR 2d 2017-1365 (2017).

[62] *See Birbari v. United States*, 109 AFTR 2d 2012-2497 (10th Cir. 2012).

[63] *Romano-Murphy v. Comm'r*, TC Memo 2012-330 (2012).

[64] Code Sec. 3402; CCA 200814010; Ltr. Rul. 9335062.

[65] CCA 200840001.

28

Tax Audit Procedures

¶ 2801 AUDIT RULES FOR TAX YEARS PRIOR TO 2018

Prior to 2018, there were three different regimes for auditing LLCs classified as partnerships:[1]

1. *Separate partner audit.* The IRS audited members of an LLC separately with respect to partnership items if the LLC had ten or fewer members, and each member of the LLC was a resident individual, C corporation, or estate of a deceased member.[2]

2. *Tax Equality and Fiscal Responsibility Act of 1982 (TEFRA)[3] audit.* The IRS conducted a single administrative proceeding at the entity level under the TEFRA rules with respect to partnership items that were more appropriately determined at the LLC level.[4] After the audit was completed, the IRS recalculated the tax liability of each member in the LLC for the audit year.

3. *Electing Large Partnership audit.* The IRS conducted an audit at the LLC level for LLCs that had 100 or more members and that elected to be treated as an Electing Large Partnership (ELP). The major difference between an ELP audit and a TEFRA audit was that LLC adjustments in an ELP audit flowed through to the members for the year in which the adjustment took place, rather than the audit year.

¶ 2802 AUDIT RULES FOR TAX YEARS AFTER 2017

.01 *General*

For tax years beginning on or after January 1, 2018,[5] the Bipartisan Budget Act of 2015 created a centralized system for audits of LLCs classified as partnership. Under

---

[1] Bipartisan Budget Act of 2015, § 1101(g).

[2] Code Sec. 6231(a)(1)(B)(i).

[3] Pub. L. No. 97-248.

[4] Code Secs. 6221, 6225; *Petaluma FX Partners LLC v. Comm'r*, 2010-1 USTC ¶ 50,163, 105 AFTR 2d 2010-435 (D.C. Cir. 2010).

[5] Bipartisan Budget Act of 2015, § 1102(g).

the default rules, assessments and adjustments are made at the LLC level,[6] rather than at the member level, absent an election by the LLC to "push out" liability to the members. This is referred to as the "centralized partnership audit regime."[7] The TEFRA and Electing Large Partnership audit regimes were repealed.

The centralized partnership audit regime is the exclusive method by which the IRS may audit an LLC in one unified proceeding. The IRS is no longer required to determine each member's share of adjustments to partnership items followed by a separate computational adjustment for each member.

The partnership audit rules are now streamlined into the following rules for LLCs that are classified as partnerships:

- *Default rules.* Under the default rules applicable to LLCs of any size, the IRS must audit items of income, gain, loss, deduction, credit and distributive shares at the LLC level.[8] The IRS may then assess and collect "imputed underpayments" (net audit adjustments items multiplied by the highest corporate or individual tax rate) at the LLC level rather than at the member level.[9] The LLC must take into account the audit adjustments items for a "reviewed year" (the year of the tax audit) in the "adjustment year" (the year in which the audit or judicial review is completed). The default rules are discussed at ¶ 2803.

- *Request for modification.* The imputed underpayment calculation will normally overstate the amount of tax that should have been paid by the members. To correct the overstatement, the LLC may request a reduced rate of tax for the audit adjustment items within 270 days after the IRS issues a notice of proposed partnership adjustment. Under the modification process, the reviewed-year members may amend their returns to take into account the adjustments. This will result in tax payments that are approximately the same as if the IRS had passed through the adjustments to the reviewed-year members under the prior TEFRA audit procedures. The modification procedures are discussed at ¶ 2806.

- *Pushout election.* The LLC may elect to pass through the audit adjustment items to the persons who were members of the LLC during the reviewed year (rather than the members during the current adjustment year). This is called a pushout election. The pushout election is mandatory if the LLC ceases to exist or does not have the ability to pay the adjustment.[10] The pushout election is discussed at ¶ 2808.

- *Separate member audit for electing small LLCs.* An LLC with 100 or fewer qualifying members may elect out of the default rules, and instead be audited at the member level. The LLC and the members are then audited under the

---

[6] Code Sec. 6221(a); Prop. Reg. § 301.6221(a)-1(a).

[7] REG-136118-15, Preamble to proposed regulations on Centralized Partnership Audit Regime (2017).

[8] Code Sec. 6221(a); Prop. Reg. § 301.6221(a)-1(a).

[9] Code Secs. 6226(a), 6225(b)(1)(A), (B); Prop. Reg. § 301.6225-1(c).

[10] *See* ¶ 2805.03 *infra.*

general rules applicable to individual taxpayers. The election procedures for small LLCs are discussed at ¶ 2810.

.02 Scope of Audit Rules at LLC Level

Under the centralized partnership audit regime, the following matters are determined at the LLC level:[11]

- *Partnership-related items.* The IRS may assess taxes at the LLC level with respect to partnership-related item.[12] Partnership-related items are discussed at ¶ 2802.03. Items that are not partnership-related items are discussed at ¶ 2802.04.
- *Taxes resulting from adjustment items.* Taxes resulting from audit adjustment items are assessed and collected at the LLC level.[13]
- *Interest.* Interest begins on the day after the due date of the partnership return for the reviewed year, without extensions.[14]
- *Penalties.* Penalties, additions to tax, or additional amounts relating to adjustments are determined at the LLC level as if the LLC had been the individual subject to tax.[15]

.03 Partnership-Related Items

The IRS may audit partnership-related items at the LLC level. Partnership-related items include any item or amount with respect to the LLC that is relevant in determining the income tax liability of any person, whether or not the item or amount appears on the LLC's return.[16] Partnership-related items include the following:

(i) an imputed underpayment,
(ii) tax basis of a member's interest in the LLC,
(iii) tax basis of the LLC in LLC property,
(iv) an item or amount related to a determination of LLC liabilities or to the effect on a member of an increase or decrease in the member's share of LLC liabilities, and
(v) a member's distributive share of any item.

A court has jurisdiction to determine all partnership-related items of an LLC for the tax year to which a notice of final partnership adjustment relates, the allocation of

---

[11] Prop. Reg. § 301.6221(a)-1.
[12] Code Sec. 6241(2)A).
[13] Prop. Reg. § 301.6232-1(b).
[14] Prop. Reg. § 301.6223(a)-1(b).
[15] Prop. Reg. § 301.6223(a)-1(c).
[16] Code Sec. 6241(2)(B).

such items among the members, and any penalty, addition to tax, interest or other amount for which the LLC may be liable.[17]

.04 *Non-Partnership-Related Items*

Partnership-related items do not include any of the following:[18]

(i) self-employment income taxes,

(ii) taxes on net investment income, and

(iii) withholding tax on nonresident alien individuals or foreign corporations, or withholding tax for certain foreign accounts.

¶2803 DEFAULT AUDIT PROCEDURES AFTER 2017

Under the default audit rules applicable to LLCs classified as partnerships, the IRS must audit LLCs under the following procedures for tax years after 2017:

- *NAP.* The IRS must commence the audit by issuing a notice of administrative proceedings (NAP) with respect to one or more partnership items.[19] The IRS must send the notice to the LLC and the partnership representative.[20] The tax year audited by the IRS is called the "reviewed year."[21]

- *Imputed underpayment.* If there are adjustments to the LLC return, the IRS must determine the tax underpayment resulting from such adjustments. The tax underpayment is called the "imputed underpayment." The imputed underpayment is determined by netting all adjustments for the reviewed year and multiplying the net amount by the highest corporate or individual tax rate.[22] The computation of imputed underpayments is discussed at ¶2804.

- *NOPPA.* If the IRS proposes adjustments to an LLC return, it must send a notice of proposed partnership adjustment (NOPPA) to the LLC and the partnership representative.[23] The IRS must send the NOPPA no later than three years after the latest of (i) the date on which the LLC return for the year was filed, (ii) the due date for the return, or (ii) the date on which the LLC files an administrative adjustment request.[24] The NOPPA sets forth the amount of imputed underpayment determined by the IRS.[25] The IRS and the partnership representative may then attempt to resolve any issues in dispute.

---

[17] Code Sec. 6234(c).

[18] Code Sec. 6241(9)(A).

[19] Code Sec. 6231(a)(1).

[20] Prop. Reg. § 301.6231-1(a)(1).

[21] Code Sec. 6225(d)(1).

[22] Code Secs. 6226(a), 6225(b)(1)(A); Prop. Reg. § 301.6225-1(c).

[23] Code Sec. 6225(d)(2); Prop. Reg. §§ 301.6231-1(a)(2), 301.6225-1(a)(3).

[24] Code Sec.6231(b)(1).

[25] Code Sec. 6231; Prop. Reg. §§ 301.6225-1(a)(3), 301.6225-1(c)(1).

- *Request for modification.* The LLC may request a reduction in the amount of the proposed assessment and imputed underpayment based on documents and other relevant information provided to the IRS.[26] The LLC must submit the request for modification and relevant information to the IRS on or before 270 days after the date that the NOPPA is mailed (subject to extension).[27] The modification procedures are discussed at ¶ 2806.
- *FPA.* The IRS must send a notice of final partnership adjustment (FPA) to the LLC and the partnership representative if it does not accept the partnership return as filed.[28] The FPA may not be mailed earlier than 270 days after mailing the notice of proposed adjustment.[29] The FPA will reflect any audit adjustment issues resolved by the parties after issuance of the NAP and the NPAA.[30] The IRS may assess taxes within the one-year period commencing 90 days after the date on which the notice of final partnership adjustment is mailed.[31]
- *Contesting the FPA.* An LLC may contest the FPA by seeking judicial review of a partnership adjustment within 90 days after the IRS mails an FPA to the LLC and partnership representative.[32] The LLC may contest the FPA by filing a petition for readjustment for the reviewed year with (i) the Tax Court, (ii) the District Court for the district in which the LLC's principal place of business is located, or (iii) the Court of Federal Claims.[33] The LLC may file the petition for readjustment with the District Court or the Court of Federal Claims only if it deposits the amount of the imputed underpayment with the IRS on or before the date the petition is filed.[34] The IRS may not mail a second FPA to the LLC for the same tax year after the LLC files a petition contesting the FPA for such tax year.[35] Any defense to an IRS assessment of tax, penalty or additional amount must be raised by the LLC in a partnership-level proceeding.[36]
- *Defaulting the FPA.* If the LLC does not contest the FPA during the 90-day period, then the LLC is liable for an amount not exceeding the amount determined in accordance with the FPA.[37]
- *Assessment of tax deficiency.* The IRS must assess the LLC for any tax deficiencies reflected in the FPA prior to collection.[38] The IRS may not assess a tax deficiency before (i) 90 days after the date on which it mails an FPA to the

---

[26] Prop. Reg. § 301.6225-2.

[27] Prop. Reg. § 301.6225-2(c)(3).

[28] Code Sec. 6231(a)(3); Prop. Reg. § 301.6231-1(a)(3).

[29] Code Sec. 6231(6)(2)(A); Prop. Reg. § 301.6231-1(b)(2).

[30] Prop. Reg. § 301.6225-1(a)(1).

[31] Code Secs. 6241(9)(C), 6501(c)(12).

[32] Code Sec. 6234(a); Prop. Reg. § 301.6234-1(a).

[33] Code Sec. 6234; Prop. Reg. § 301.6234-1(a).

[34] Code Sec. 6234(b)(1); Prop. Reg. § 301.6234-1(b).

[35] Code Sec. 6231(d).

[36] Prop. Reg. § 301.6221(a)-1(c).

[37] Code Sec. 6232(e).

[38] Code Sec. 6221(a).

LLC and partnership representative, or (ii) if a Tax Court/Court of Claim petition is filed with respect to such notice, the decision of the court becomes final.[39] The IRS may assess the taxes within (i) one year after the decision of a court becomes final, or (ii) in any other case, within the one-year period commencing 90 days after the date on which the notice of final partnership adjustment is mailed.[40] The LLC may waive this requirement.[41] The IRS may immediately assess and collect taxes that arise on account of mathematical or clerical errors.[42]

- *Tax year of assessment.* The IRS will assess the taxes in the adjustment year rather than the reviewed year.[43] The adjustment year is the year in which the audit or the judicial review is completed.[44] The LLC must reflect any audit adjustment items in the adjustment year. This means that members of the LLC during the adjustment year will (absent a pushout election) bear the burden of tax liabilities that should have been incurred by the members of the LLC during the prior reviewed year.

- *Payment of taxes, tax rates and imputed underpayments.* The LLC must pay taxes equal to the imputed underpayment.[45] The LLC must also pay any applicable interest and penalties.[46] Imputed underpayments are discussed at ¶ 2805.

- *Pushout election.* The LLC is not liable for the taxes if it makes a pushout election to pass through the audit adjustment items to the reviewed-year members.[47] The LLC must make the pushout election within 45 days after the IRS mails the notice of final partnership adjustment (FPA), with no extensions.[48] The pushout election is discussed at ¶ 2808.

PRACTICE NOTE

Purchasers of membership interests in an LLC need to review prior returns and financial records to determine if the LLC previously took aggressive tax positions that could result in a tax assessment against the LLC and members in the LLC in the adjustment year. A purchaser should also review the operating agreement for the LLC to determine if the LLC is required to make a pushout election to pass through any additional

---

[39] Code Sec. 6232(b); Prop. Reg. § 301.6232-1(c).

[40] Code Secs. 6241(9)(C), 6501(c)(12).

[41] Code Sec. 6232(d)(2); Prop. Reg. § 301.6232-1(d)(2).

[42] Code Sec. 6213(b)(1); Prop. Reg. § 301.6232-1(d)(1).

[43] Code Secs. 6225(a)(1), 6232.

[44] Code Sec. 6225(d)(2).

[45] Code Secs. 6225(a), 6332; Prop. Reg. § 301.6225-1(a)(1); Prop. Reg. § 301.6232-1(b).

[46] Code Sec. 6233(a).

[47] Code Sec. 6226.

[48] Code Sec. 6226.

taxes during a current or future audit to the members of the LLC during the prior reviewed year.

¶ 2804 IMPUTED UNDERPAYMENTS

.01 Amount of Imputed Underpayment

If there are LLC audit adjustment items, the LLC must pay taxes equal to the "imputed underpayment."[49] The imputed underpayment is the net amount of all adjustments for any reviewed year multiplied by the highest individual or corporate tax rate, adjusted for any increase or decrease in credits resulting from the adjustments.[50]

The partnership adjustments, and any imputed underpayment resulting from such adjustments, are set forth in the notice of proposed partnership adjustment (NOPPA) mailed to the LLC and the partnership representative.[51] The imputed underpayments are nondeductible.[52]

.02 Groupings and Netting of Adjustments

Types of Groupings

Adjustments are grouped together and netted within each category of items.[53] The groupings provide a framework for the netting of adjustments. Within each grouping, adjusted items may be further divided into subgroups depending on their character or to account for preferences, sources, categories, limitations, or other restrictions. The groupings and subgroupings provide the IRS with the ability to net adjustments according to applicable limitations and restrictions.[54] There are four types of groupings:[55]

1. *Reallocation grouping.* These are adjustments that reallocate items among the members.[56] An adjustment that reallocates an item from one or more members to one or more other members is treated as two adjustments. The first adjustment is a decrease in the amount of the items allocated by the LLC on its return to one or more members. The second adjustment is an increase in the amount of the items allocated by the IRS to the other members. The two

---

[49] Code Secs. 6225(a), 6332; Prop. Reg. § 301.6225-1(a).

[50] Code Sec. 6226(a), 6225(b)(1); Prop. Reg. § 301.6225-1(c).

[51] Prop. Reg. § 301.6225-1(a)(3).

[52] Code Sec. 6241(4); Prop. Reg. § 301.6241-4.

[53] Code Sec. 6225(b)(3).

[54] Prop. Reg. § 301.6225-1(d).

[55] Prop. Reg. § 301.6225-1(d)(2)(i).

[56] Prop. Reg. § 301.6225-1(d)(2)(ii).

adjustments are not netted. Each adjustment is grouped in its own reallocation subgrouping to prevent the two adjustments from netting to zero. After
application of the netting rules, any net non-positive adjustment is disregarded in the calculation of the imputed underpayment.

2. *Credit grouping.* These are adjustments to items that are claimed or could be
claimed by the LLC as a credit on the partnership return.[57]

3. *Creditable expenditure grouping.* These are adjustments to creditable expenditures. The IRS reserved a place in the regulations for future guidance on
creditable expenditure groupings.[58]

4. *Residual grouping.* All remaining adjustments are grouped together according
to the character, preferences, restrictions, and other limitations of the item
adjusted. The adjustments of a particular item may warrant further subgroupings for other items (for instance, long-term capital versus short-term
capital). An adjustment that recharacterizes the character of an item is
treated as two separate adjustments, one adjustment decreasing the amount
of the item as reported by the LLC, and a second adjustment increasing the
amount of the item as recharacterized by the IRS. Each adjustment is
grouped separately with similar items.

Netted Partnership Adjustment

After the IRS makes the appropriate groupings and subgroupings, the IRS must
calculate the imputed underpayment for all groupings. In order to make this computation, the IRS must first determine the "netted partnership adjustment" for the
reallocation grouping and the residual grouping as follows:[59]

- Step 1: Net all adjustments within each group or subgroup. Items within the
same group or subgroup are netted first. For example, all ordinary adjustments are netted against each other, regardless of whether such adjustments
were part of a related transaction or whether they were increases or decreases
to income. Adjustments in the capital subgrouping are netted against each
other within that subgroup. None of the ordinary adjustments are netted
against the adjustments in the capital subgrouping. Adjustments from one tax
year may not be netted against adjustments from another tax year, even if
they would otherwise be part of the same grouping.[60]

- Step 2: Disregard any net non-positive adjustment. Once adjustments within
each subgroup have been netted, each group or subgroup will have either a
net positive adjustment or a net non-positive adjustment. Any netted amount
that is a net non-positive adjustment in the reallocation grouping or the
residual grouping is disregarded in calculating the imputed underpayment.

---

[57] Prop. Reg. § 301.6225-1(d)(2)(iii).
[58] Prop. Reg. § 301.6225-1(d)(2)(iv).
[59] Prop. Reg. § § 301.6225-1(c)(3), 301.6225-1(d)(3).
[60] Prop. Reg. § 301.6225-1(c)(4).

- Step 3: Add the net positive adjustments in the residual grouping and the net positive adjustments in the reallocation grouping to arrive at the total netted partnership adjustment.

Calculating the Imputed Underpayment

After the IRS determines the netted partnership adjustment, it must calculate the imputed underpayment for all groupings as follows:[61]

- Step 1: Multiply the total netted partnership adjustment in the residual grouping and the reallocation grouping by the highest rate of tax in effect for the reviewed year under Code Sec. 1 or 11.

- Step 2. Net the adjustments in the credit grouping, and then increase or decrease the tax determined under Step 1 by any net adjustments to the credits. The IRS requested comments on how credits should be grouped and whether credits should be applied in any particular order.

- Step 3: There is an imputed underpayment if the result under Step 2 is a net positive adjustment. There is no imputed underpayment if the result under Step 2 is a net-non-positive amount. The IRS (or the LLC in the modification process) may allocate "specific imputed underpayments" to one member, or to a group of members with the same characteristics or which participated in the same or similar transactions.[62] There may be multiple specific imputed underpayments during the same tax year. All other imputed underpayments are "general imputed underpayments." General imputed underpayments are calculated based on all adjustments, other than adjustments that do not result in an imputed underpayment and that are not taken into account in determining a specific imputed underpayment.[63]

Penalties

Finally, the IRS must calculate the portion of the imputed underpayment to which the penalty applies. It does this by grouping together all of the partnership adjustments in a manner similar to groupings for purposes of determining the imputed underpayment.[64]

---

[61] Prop. Reg. § 301.6225-1(c)(1).
[62] Prop. Reg. § § 301.6225-1(e)(2)(iii), 301.6225-2(d)(6).
[63] Prop. Reg. § 301.6225-1(e)(2)(i).
[64] Prop. Reg. § 301.6223(a)-1(c)(ii)(B)(1).

¶ 2805 PAYMENT OF IMPUTED UNDERPAYMENTS

.01 Payment by LLC

The general rule is that the LLC is obligated to pay any imputed underpayment resulting from a tax audit at the LLC level.[65] The LLC must pay the imputed underpayment in the adjustment year when the audit is completed.[66] The LLC may instead make a push-out election to pass the tax liabilities to the members in the reviewed year.[67] The tax liability of the LLC is reduced to the extent that the reviewed year members pay the taxes on an amended return, or under an alternative pull-in procedure.[68]

If the audit adjustments do not result in an imputed underpayment, then the LLC must take the adjustments into account in the adjustment year.[69] The proposed regulations reserve a place for discussion of the tax consequences on capital accounts and basis resulting from payments by an LLC.

.02 Failure by LLC to Pay

If the LLC does not pay the imputed underpayments, interest or penalties within ten days after notice and demand for payment by the IRS, then the IRS may assess each member of the LLC as of the close of the adjustment year a tax equal to the member's proportionate share[70] of such amount.[71] The tax liability of the LLC is reduced to the extent payments are made by the adjustment year members after notice and demand by the IRS.[72]

.03 Insolvent or Terminated LLCs

If the LLC has ceased to exist at the time of an assessment, the IRS may assess each of the "former partners" in the LLC a tax equal to such member's share of imputed underpayments, interest and penalties.[73] An LLC ceases to exist if (i) the LLC terminates, or (ii) the LLC does not have the ability to pay, in full, the tax assessment.[74] Only the IRS may determine that an LLC has ceased to exist. The IRS is

---

[65] Code Sec. 6221(a); Prop. Reg. § 301.6221(a)-1(a).

[66] Code Sec. 6225(a)(1).

[67] *See* ¶ 2808.

[68] *See* ¶ 2806.01 *infra*.

[69] Code Sec. 6225(a)(2).

[70] Code Sec. 6232(f)(3).

[71] Code Secs. 6232(f)(1)(B), 6241(7).

[72] Code Sec. 6232(f)(4).

[73] Code Sec. 6232(f)(1)(B).

[74] Prop. Reg. § 301.6241-3(b)(2).

not required to determine that an LLC has ceased to exist for audit purposes even if the LLC technically meets the definition of ceasing to exist.[75]

The "former partners" of the LLC are the adjustment year partners of the LLC, not the reviewed year partners.[76] If there are no adjustment year partners, then the former partners are the members of the LLC during the last tax year for which a partnership return was filed.[77] This situation could arise if the LLC ceased to exist before the adjustment year (the year in which the audit or judicial review was completed).

The result is that the regulations treat an insolvent or terminated LLC as having made a pushout election, but define the "former partners" as adjustment year partners rather than reviewed year partners.

¶ 2806 MODIFICATION OF IMPUTED UNDERPAYMENTS

.01 Types of Modification

The IRS may reduce the imputed underpayment assessment if the LLC can show that a lower amount is appropriate based on certain member-level information.[78] Only the partnership representative may request a modification of the imputed underpayment.

The IRS may approve a modification in one of the following cases:[79]

- *Amended returns.* An LLC may request a reduction in the imputed underpayment if (i) one or more reviewed-year members file an amended return for the reviewed year and all other years with respect to which any tax attribute is affected by reason of the partnership adjustments, (ii) such returns take into account all adjustments made by the IRS that are properly allocable to the members, (iii) the members pay any tax due with the amended returns, (iv) the partnership representative provides affidavits from each member for which a modification is sought that the member did in fact file an amended return and make appropriate payments, and (v) the amended return is filed prior to the expiration of the statute of limitations.[80] A member may file an amended return claiming a refund as part of the modification process after the expiration of the period of limitation on assessments under Section 6511, but may in such case only claim a refund for adjustments that are the direct result of the partnership audit.[81] Once a member files an amended return under the modification procedures, the member may not file a subsequent amended

---

[75] Prop. Reg. § 301.6241-3(b)(1).

[76] Prop. Reg. § 301.6241-3(d)(1)(i).

[77] Prop. Reg. § 301.6241-3(d)(2).

[78] Code Secs. 6225(c)(1), 6225(c)(7); Prop. Reg. § 301.6225-2(c).

[79] Prop. Reg. § 301.6225-2(d).

[80] Code Sec. 6225(c)(2); Prop. Reg. § 301.6225-2(d)(2).

[81] Code Sec. 6225(c)(2)(A)(i); Prop. Reg. § 301.6225-2(d)(2)(v)(B).

return for that tax year without IRS approval.[82] A pass-through member of the LLC may file an amended return and pay the "safe harbor amount" applicable to a pushout election.[83] The applicable tax rate for a pass-through member is based on the total net income of the pass-through member rather than taxable income.[84]

- *Alternative procedure to filing amended return (pull-in procedure).* A member of an LLC is not required to file an amended return for a modification under an alternative procedure referred to as a pull-in procedure.[85] Under this procedure, the IRS determines the LLCs imputed underpayment as reduced by the adjustments to partnership-related items that direct reviewed-year members take into account. The pull-in procedure may be used if (i) the reviewed-year member pays the tax that would be due with an amended return (unless the IRS provides that another member, such as a third party or the LLC, may make the payment on the member's behalf), (ii) the reviewed-year member pays the tax within 270 days after the IRS mails the notice of proposed partnership adjustment (unless the period is extended with the consent of the IRS), (iii) the reviewed-year member makes binding changes to his or her tax attributes for later years, and (iv) the reviewed-year member provides the IRS with information necessary to substantiate that the tax was correctly computed and paid, and such other information requested by the IRS. Under this procedure, the reviewed-year member is not required to file an amended return. The pull-in procedure does not require participation of all reviewed-year members.

- *Tax-exempt members.* The imputed underpayment may be reduced if a member would not owe the tax as a result of its tax-exempt status during the reviewed year.[86]

- *Rate reduction modification.* The imputed underpayment may be reduced if the imputed underpayment is allocable to a member that is a C corporation, or an individual in the case of capital gains and qualified dividends.[87] However, the applicable rate in such case will be the highest rate in effect with respect to the type of income and member for whom the modification is requested.[88] For example, the highest corporate tax rate during the reviewed year will apply to all C corporation adjustments, regardless of the rate that would apply to the C corporation based on the amount of the C corporation's taxable income.[89] The LLC may not request modifications based on the tax attributes or status of current year members. The LLC may request a modification based on rate

---

[82] Prop. Reg. § 301.6225-2(d)(2)(vii)(B).

[83] Prop. Reg. § 301.6225-2(d)(2)(vii)(A).

[84] Prop. Reg. § 301.6225-2(d)(2)(vii)(B).

[85] Code Sec. 6225(c)(2)(B).

[86] Code Sec. 6225(c)(3); Prop. Reg. § 301.6225-2(d)(3).

[87] Code Sec. 6225(c)(4).

[88] Prop. Reg. § 301.6225-2(d)(4).

[89] Prop. Reg. § 301.6225-2(d)(4).

reduction only with respect to adjustments attributable to a reviewed-year member that is a C corporation and adjustments with respect to capital gains are qualified dividends attributable to a reviewed-year member who is an individual.[90]

- *Passive losses of publicly traded LLCs.* A publicly traded LLC may request a modification of an imputed underpayment in the case of a net decrease in passive activity losses for certain members.[91]

- *Modification in the number and composition of imputed underpayments.* The LLC may request a modification in the number and composition of imputed underpayments. For example, the LLC may request different groupings or subgroupings of partnership adjustments, and request that the IRS redetermine the imputed underpayments based on the new groupings and subgroupings.[92]

- *Qualified investment entities.* A qualified investment entity that distributes deficiency dividends after the IRS issues the notice of proposed partnership adjustment (NOPPA) may request a modification in the imputed underpayment.[93]

- *Closing agreements.* The LLC may request modifications based on a closing agreement entered into by the IRS with any member.[94]

- *Other modifications.* The IRS may in its discretion consider alternative types of modifications.[95] An LLC may request the type of modification that is not specifically described in the regulations. The IRS may also issue guidance allowing additional types of modification.

.02 Procedures for Requesting Modification

The LLC must make a request for modification as follows:

- The LLC must submit the request for modification on applicable IRS forms[96] no later than the close of the 270-day period beginning on the date on which the NOPPA is mailed.[97] The LLC may request an extension of time to submit the request,[98] or a waiver of the 270-day period.[99]

---

[90] Prop. Reg. § 301.6225-2(d)(4).
[91] Code Sec. 6225(c)(5); Prop. Reg. § 301.6225-2(d)(5).
[92] Code Sec. 6225(c)(6); Prop. Reg. § 301.6225-2(d)(6).
[93] Prop. Reg. § 301.6225-2(d)(7).
[94] Prop. Reg. § 301.6225-2(d)(8).
[95] Prop. Reg. § 301.6225-2(d)(9).
[96] Prop. Reg. § 301.6225-2(c)(1).
[97] Code Sec. 6225(c)(7); Prop. Reg. § 301.6225-2(c)(3).
[98] Prop. Reg. § 301.6225-2(c)(3)(ii).
[99] Prop. Reg. § 301.6225-2(c)(3)(ii).

- The LLC may request a modification for an adjustment that does not result in an imputed underpayment only if the LLC also has an imputed underpayment that is eligible to be modified.[100]
- The LLC must submit information to the IRS to substantiate the modification of imputed underpayments.[101]
- The LLC and its partnership representative must agree to the audit adjustments proposed by the IRS.
- The LLC must issue an information statement to all affected members.
- The reviewed-year members must file amended returns consistent with the information statements for the years directly or indirectly affected by the information statement (such as for carryback items and similar tax adjustments). There is no requirement that all reviewed-year members file an amended return for the LLC to request a modification. However, the IRS will not approve a modification in the case of a reallocation adjustment unless all members affected by the reallocation adjustment file amended returns that take into account the reallocation adjustment.[102]
- The members must pay any additional taxes with their amended returns.

¶ 2807 ADJUSTMENTS THAT DO NOT RESULT IN IMPUTED UNDERPAYMENTS

.01 Types of Adjustments That Do Not Result in Imputed Underpayments

LLC adjustments do not result in imputed underpayments if:

1. the adjustment relates to a distributive share reallocation that is disregarded;
2. after the grouping and netting of the adjustments, the result is a net non-positive adjustment; or
3. the imputed underpayment calculation results in an amount that is zero or less than zero after application of the highest tax rate and any applicable tax credits.[103]

.02 Tax Consequences

Adjustments that do not result in an imputed underpayment are taken into account by the LLC as a reduction in non-separately stated income or as an increase

---

[100] Prop. Reg. § 301.6225-2(a).
[101] Prop. Reg. § 301.6225-2(c)(2).
[102] Prop. Reg. § 301.6225-2(d)(2)(vi).
[103] Prop. Reg. § 301.6225-1(c)(2).

in non-separately stated loss for the adjustment year, depending on whether the adjustment is an item of income or loss.[104]

The adjustments are taken into account by the LLC in the adjustment year.[105] The adjustment year is the LLC tax year in which:[106]

- the decision of a court in a proceeding brought under Section 6234 becomes final;
- the LLC makes an administrative adjustment request under Section 6227 (AAR); or
- in any other case, the IRS mails an FPA under Section 6231, or the date that a waiver is signed by the IRS if the LLC waives the restrictions under Section 6232(b) related to limitations on assessment.

¶ 2808   PUSHOUT ELECTION

.01   General

An LLC may shift the audit tax payment obligation from the LLC to the persons who were members in the LLC during the reviewed year. This is called a pushout election.[107] An LLC that makes a valid election is not liable for the imputed underpayments.[108] The reviewed-year members who receive a statement from the LLC are liable for any taxes, penalties, additions to tax, and interest.[109]

Members are not subject to joint and several liability for the imputed underpayment if the LLC makes the pushout election.[110]

.02   Procedures for Making Election

The LLC must do the following to make the pushout election:[111]

- The LLC must make the election within 45 days after the date that the IRS mails the FPA to the LLC.[112] The time for making the election may not be extended.[113]
- The LLC is not required to make the pushout election with respect to all reviewed-year members. The LLC may make the election with respect to one

---

[104] Code Sec. 6225(a)(2)(A); Prop. Reg. § 301.6225-3.

[105] Code Sec. 6225(a)(2).

[106] Prop. Reg. § 301.6241-1(a)(2).

[107] Prop. Reg. § 301.6226-1(a).

[108] REG-136118-15, Preamble to proposed regulations on Centralized Partnership Audit Regime (2017).

[109] Prop. Reg. § 301.6226-1.

[110] Code Sec. 6226(b).

[111] Code Sec. 6226(a)(1); Prop. Reg. § 301.6226-1(a).

[112] Code Sec. 6226(a)(1).

[113] Prop. Reg. § 301.6226-1(c)(3).

or more imputed underpayments identified in an FPA (notice of final partnership adjustment). For example, if an FPA includes a general imputed underpayment and one or more specific imputed underpayments, the LLC may make an election with respect to any or all of the imputed underpayments.[114]

- The partnership representative for the LLC must sign the election and file the election in accordance with IRS forms and instructions.[115]
- The LLC must send an information statement to each person who was a member during the reviewed year. The statement must reflect each member's distributive share of LLC adjustments, including adjustments to income, gain, loss, deduction, or credit as determined by the FPA.[116] The statement is in addition to any other information statements that must be sent to members, such as a Schedule K-1.[117] The LLC may not include the partnership adjustments in a Schedule K-1.[118] The LLC must issue the statement within 60 days after the date on which all partnership adjustments to which the statement relates are finally determined.[119] This is the later of (i) the expiration of the time for filing a petition for readjustment with the Tax Court (or the U.S. District Court or Claims Court in certain cases) under Section 6234, or (ii) if a petition is filed under Section 6234, the date when the court's decision becomes final. The petition for readjustment under Section 6234 must be filed within 90 days after the IRS mails the FPA.
- The LLC must electronically file with the IRS the information statements that the LLC furnishes to each reviewed-year member, along with a transmittal form.[120] The LLC must file the statement within 60 days after the date on which all partnership adjustments to which the statement relates are finally determined.[121]
- Each member during the reviewed year is liable for taxes on the member's allocable share of adjustment items.[122]

.03 Amounts Payable by Reviewed-Year Members

If an LLC makes a pushout election, each reviewed-year member must pay the member's share of the following amounts:

- adjustment amounts (¶ 2808.04);
- interest on the tax underpayment (¶ 2808.05);

---

[114] REG-136118-15, Preamble to proposed regulations on Centralized Partnership Audit Regime (2017).

[115] Prop. Reg. § 301.6226-1(c)(4).

[116] Prop. Reg. § § 301.6226-2(a), 301.6226-2(e).

[117] Prop. Reg. § 301.6226-2(a).

[118] Preamble to proposed regulations on Centralized Partnership Audit Regime (2017).

[119] Code Sec. 6226; Prop. Reg. § 301.6226-2(b)(1).

[120] Prop. Reg. § 301.6226-1(c).

[121] Prop. Reg. § 301.6226-2(b).

[122] Code Sec. 6226(c)(1); Prop. Reg. § § 301.6226-1(b)(1), 301.6226-3.

- penalties, additions to tax, and additional amounts as reflected on the pushout statement.[123] A member may not raise a penalty defense, such as reasonable cause. Any defense to a penalty, addition to tax or additional amount must be raised by the LLC in a partnership-level proceeding;[124] and

- interest on any penalties, additions to tax or additional amounts calculated from the due date without extensions of the reviewed-year member's return for the first affected tax year until the amount is paid.[125]

.04 Adjustment Amounts

A reviewed-year member must pay the member's share of adjustment amounts as reflected in an adjustment statement from the LLC.[126] The adjustment amount is the sum of the "correction amounts" for the first affected tax year plus the "correction amounts" for each intervening year. In the case of a tax year of the member that includes the end of the LLC's reviewed year (first affected year), the correction amount is the amount by which the member's tax would increase for that year.[127] In the case of any tax year after the first affected year and before the reporting year (the intervening years), the correction amount is the amount by which the member's tax would increase by reason of the adjustments in each of the intervening years.[128]

.05 Interest

Each reviewed-year member must pay interest on underpayments. Interest is determined at the member level from the due date of the LLC's return for the reviewed year.[129] The interest rate on the underpayment amount is two percent higher than the normal rate for tax underpayments.[130] Interest is calculated from the due date (without extensions) of the reviewed-year member's return for the first affected year until the amount is paid.

.06 Tiered Partnerships

An LLC may push out tax liabilities through one or more upper tiers to the ultimate non-pass-through partners and members who must then take the adjust-

---

[123] Prop. Reg. § 301.6226-3(a).

[124] Prop. Reg. § 301.6221(a)-1(c).

[125] Prop. Reg. § 301.6226-3(d)(3).

[126] Prop. Reg. § 301.6227-3(b)(1)

[127] Code Sec. 6226(b)(2)(A).

[128] Code Sec. 6226(b)(2)(B).

[129] Code Secs. 6226(c)(2)(B), 6226(c)(6).

[130] Prop. Reg. §§ 301.6226-3(d)(1), 301.6226-3(d)(4). The underpayment rate is determined by substituting five percentage points for three percentage points under Code Sec. 6621(a)(2)(B).

ments into account.[131] Pass-through partners include S corporations, certain trusts and estates, and their shareholders and beneficiaries.[132] A pass-through partner who receives a pushout statement must take the adjustment into account in one of the following two ways:[133]

1. The pass-through partner may furnish statements to each person who was a partner in the pass-through entity at any time during the tax year of the pass-through entity to which the adjustment relates.[134] The upper tier partners are called affected partners. The pass-through entity must file a partnership adjustment tracking report with the IRS.[135] The partnership adjusted tracking report must include the statements given to affected partners with the IRS along with a transmittal that includes a summary of the statements.[136] The affected partners who receive the push-out notices must take the adjustments into account as if the affected partners were the reviewed-year partners.[137]

2. The pass-through partner may instead pay the adjustment amount computed as if it were an imputed underpayment, with interest and penalties.[138] If the LLC does not file the partnership adjustment tracking report with the IRS or the push-out statement to the upper tier members, then the pass-through LLC member is required to pay the adjustment amounts.[139]

Thus, each pass-through partner in the ownership chain who receives a pushout notice has the option either to pay the adjustment amount or to push out the adjustment to its partners, shareholders or beneficiaries.

The pushout through the upper tiers must occur before the extended due date for the adjustment year of the lower level LLC under audit. The pass-through partners must file with the IRS detailed information along with statements to its affected partners, shareholders and beneficiaries prior to that date. If the pass-through partner fails to pay the adjustment amount or to push through the liability to its partners, shareholders and beneficiaries on a timely basis, then the pass-through partner must pay the adjustment amount with interest and penalties.[140]

---

[131] Prop. Reg. § 301.6226-3(e)(1).

[132] Prop. Reg. § 301.6226-3(e)(5).

[133] Prop. Reg. § 301.6226-3(e)(1).

[134] Code Sec. 6225(b)(4)(A)(ii)(I).

[135] Code Sec. 6225(b)(4)(A)(i).

[136] Prop. Reg. § 301.6226-3(e)(2),

[137] Prop. Reg. § 301.6226-3(e)(3)(iv).

[138] Code Sec. 6225(b)(4)(A)(ii)(II); Prop. Reg. § 301.6226-3(e)(4).

[139] Code Sec. 6225(b)(4)(A)(ii)(II).

[140] Prop. Reg. § 301.6226-3(e)(3)(i).

.07 Multiple Imputed Underpayments

If an LLC has multiple imputed underpayments, the LLC may push out one or more specific imputed underpayments to one or more of the members who would be responsible for the payment of tax liability. The LLC may pay the remaining imputed underpayments at the LLC level. The LLC is not required to push out all of the imputed underpayments.

.08 Successors to Reviewed-Year Members

An LLC may push out underpayments to persons who were not members of the LLC in a reviewed year if the reviewed-year member to whom the payments should be allocated no longer exists.

¶2809 ADJUSTMENTS ON AMENDED RETURN

If an LLC files an amended return (AAR), then the LLC and the members must take into account the adjustments that result in an imputed underpayment "under rules similar to the rules in Section 6226."[141] However, there are several significant differences. The adjustment procedures for an AAR are discussed at ¶2203.

¶2810 ELECTION OUT OF THE DEFAULT RULES FOR SMALL LLCS

An LLC with 100 or fewer members may elect out of the default rules applicable to audits at the LLC level.[142] The LLC and the members are then audited under the general rules applicable to individual taxpayers. The individual members must file amended returns and pay tax on their allocable share of audit adjustment items. An LLC may elect out of the default rules if:[143]

- The LLC has 100 or fewer members. An LLC has 100 or fewer members if it is required to furnish 100 or fewer Schedule K-1's for the tax year.[144] If an S corporation is a member of the LLC, each shareholder in the S corporation is treated as a member for purposes of determining whether there are 100 or fewer members.[145]
- The LLC must have only eligible members. Eligible members include an individual, a C corporation, a foreign entity that would be treated as a C corporation if it were domestic entity, an S corporation, or an estate of a

---

[141] Code Sec. 6227(b)(2).
[142] Code Sec. 6225(b); Reg. § 301.6221(b)-1.
[143] Code Sec. 6225(b); Reg. § 301.6221(b)-1(b)(1)(i).
[144] Code Sec. 6221(b)(1)(B); Reg. § 301.6221(b)-1(b)(2).
[145] Code Sec. 6221(b)(2); Reg. § 301.6221(b)-1(b)(2)(ii).

deceased member.[146] A trust, including a revocable trust for estate planning purposes, is not an eligible member.

- The LLC must file an election under Code Sec. 6221(b).[147] The election must be filed on an annual basis with a timely filed return for the year.[148]
- The LLC must notify each member of the election within 30 days after making the election.[149]
- The LLC must disclose to the IRS information about each person who was a member at any time during the LLC tax year to which the election applies, including the member's name, taxpayer identification number, federal tax classification, an affirmative statement that the member is an eligible member under the IRS regulations, and any other information required by the IRS in forms, instructions, or guidance.[150]

¶2811 STATUTE OF LIMITATIONS

.01 Statute of Limitations for IRS Adjustments

The statute of limitations for the IRS to adjust taxes for an LLC classified as a partnership is as follows:[151]

- The general rule is that the IRS may not make a partnership adjustment or assess taxes more than three years after the later of (i) the date on which the LLC filed a partnership return for the tax year, (ii) the return due date, or (iii) the date on which the LLC files an administrative adjustment request (amended return).[152] The parties may extend the statute of limitations by agreement.[153]
- If an LLC requests a modification of an imputed underpayment, the IRS may not make a partnership adjustment more than 270 days after the date on which the LLC submits to the IRS all required documents for the modification request (plus the number of days of an extension of the modification period).[154]
- If the LLC fails to include on its return or statement any information with respect to a listed transaction, the statute of limitations for making an adjustment does not expire before the date set forth in Code Section 6501(c)(10).[155]

---

[146] Code Secs. 6221(b)(1)(C), 6225(b); Reg. § 301.6221(b)-1(b)(3).

[147] Code Sec. 6221(b)(1)(A); Reg. § 301.6221(b)-1(c).

[148] Code Sec. 6221(b); Reg. § 301.6221(b)-1(c)(1).

[149] Reg. § 301.6221(b)-1(c)(3).

[150] Reg. § 301.6221(b)-1(c)(2).

[151] Code Sec. 6235.

[152] Code Sec. 6235(a)(1); Prop. Reg. § 301.6235-1(a)(1).

[153] Code Sec. 6235(b); Prop. Reg. §§ 301.6235-1(a)(1).

[154] Prop. Reg. §§ 301.6235-1(a)(2), 301.6235-1(b).

[155] Code Sec. 6235(c)(6).

- If there is a notice of proposed partnership adjustment, the IRS may not assess taxes 330 days or more after the date of such notice (plus the number of days of any extension consented to by the IRS).[156]
- The statute of limitations remains open forever in the event of a false return or fraud.
- The statute of limitations is extended from three years to six years in the event of a substantial omission of income.
- The statute of limitations is suspended if the IRS mails a notice of final partnership adjustment to the LLC and its partnership representative.
- The statute of limitations is suspended during the period that a petition for judicial review is brought, plus one year.[157]
- The statute of limitations is suspended if the IRS is prohibited from making adjustments due to bankruptcy proceedings, plus an additional 60 days for adjustments and assessments, and six months for collection.[158]

.02 Statute of Limitations for Assessments

If there are partnership adjustments, the IRS may assess the taxes within (i) one year after the decision of a court becomes final, or (ii) in any other case, within the one-year period commencing 90 days after the date on which the notice of final partnership adjustment is mailed.[159]

If the LLC does not pay the imputed underpayments, interest or penalties within ten days after notice and demand for payment by the IRS, then the IRS may assess each member of the LLC as of the close of the adjustment year a tax equal to the member's proportionate share of such amount.[160] The IRS must make an assessment or proceed in court within two years after the date on which the IRS sends the notice and demand for payment in such case.[161]

.03 Statute of Limitations for AAR

The statute of limitations for an LLC to file an administrative adjustment request (AAR) (amended tax return) is three years after the later of (i) the date on which the partnership return is filed, or (ii) the last date for filing the partnership return determined without extensions.[162]

An extension of the statute of limitations to assess taxes by agreement among the parties does not simultaneously extend the period to file an AAR.

---

[156] Code Sec. 6235(a)(3); Prop. Reg. §§ 301.6235-1(a)(3), 301.6235-1(c).

[157] Code Sec. 6235(d), effective after 12/31/2017.

[158] Code Sec. 6241(6), effective after 12/31/2017.

[159] Code Secs. 6241(9)(C), 6501(c)(12).

[160] Code Secs. 6232(f)(1)(B), 6241(7).

[161] Code Secs. 6232(f)(6).

[162] Code Sec. 6227(c); Prop. Reg. § 301.6227-1(b).

An LLC may not file an AAR after the IRS issues a notice of administrative proceeding to the LLC.[163]

AARs are discussed at ¶ 2203.

¶ 2812 PARTNERSHIP REPRESENTATIVE

An LLC that is classified as a partnership must designate a member or other person with a substantial presence in the United States[164] as the partnership representative with sole authority to act on behalf of the LLC in any tax audit proceedings.[165] The partnership representative may be an individual or an entity if the entity designates a qualified individual to act on behalf of the entity in tax audit matters.[166] The LLC must designate the partnership representative on the partnership return filed for each tax year.[167]

The partnership representative is similar to the tax matters partner under prior law. However, the partnership representative has significantly more powers. The partnership representative has sole authority to act on behalf of the LLC for all tax audit purposes,[168] including:

1. agreeing to settlements;
2. agreeing to a notice of final partnership adjustment;
3. making a pushout election to pass through the audit adjustments to the members during the reviewed year;[169]
4. filing an amended tax return (AAR) and furnishing statements to members reflecting the adjustments made on the amended return;[170]
5. agreeing to an extension of the period for adjustments; and
6. agreeing to any adjustments to any partnership tax items.[171]

No state law, operating agreement or other document may limit the authority of the partnership representative.[172]

The IRS must provide notifications only to the partnership representative regarding any LLC-level examination or audit adjustment. Members may not participate in or contest the results of an examination or other proceeding involving an LLC without permission of the IRS.[173]

---

[163] Prop. Reg. § 301.6227-1(b).

[164] Prop. Reg. § 1.6223-1(b)(2).

[165] Code Sec. 6223(b).

[166] Prop. Reg. § 301.6223-1(b)(3).

[167] Prop. Reg. § 301.6223-1(c).

[168] Code Sec. 6223(b); Prop. Reg. § 301.6223-2(a), (c).

[169] Prop. Reg. § 301.6223-1(d).

[170] Prop. Reg. § 301.6227-1(f).

[171] Prop. Reg. § 301.6223-2.

[172] Prop. Reg. § 301.6223-2(c).

[173] Prop. Reg. § 301.6223-2(c)(1).

Unlike the prior law requiring a tax matters partner to be a partner, the partnership representative does not need to be a member of the LLC. The only requirement is that the partnership representative must have a substantial presence in the United States.[174]

If there is no partnership designation in effect, the IRS may select the partnership representative.[175] An LLC should normally designate a representative in order to maintain control over the audit. Conflicts of interest may arise if a former member was designated as the partnership representative, and has not been replaced. A former member may be unwilling to make the elections that shift the entity level tax back onto the former members.

An LLC may not change the designation of a partnership representative for a given tax year through resignation, revocation or otherwise unless the IRS issues a notice of administrative proceeding to the LLC or the LLC files a valid AAR. An LLC may not file an AAR only to change the partnership representative.[176]

¶ 2813 CONSISTENCY REQUIREMENT

Members must report on their individual tax returns all LLC items in the same way that the LLC reported them on IRS Form 1065.[177] Any underpayment of tax because a member fails to comply with the consistency requirement is treated as a mathematical or clerical error subject to summary assessment procedures which the IRS may immediately assess and collect.[178] The members may not request an abatement of the assessment.[179] The IRS is not required to issue a notice of deficiency in order to assess or collect the additional taxes.

The consistency requirement does not apply if the member (i) attaches Form 8082, Notice of Inconsistent Treatment, to his or her tax return identifying the inconsistency, (ii) shows that the treatment of the item on the member's return is consistent with the treatment of the item on a statement furnished by the LLC to the member, and (iii) makes an election under Code Sec. 6222(c)(2)(B).[180]

The IRS may conduct proceedings against the LLC and separately against the member when one or more members treat an item inconsistently from the treatment by the LLC.[181]

Under the prior TEFRA audit procedures, the IRS was not required to conduct a partnership-level proceeding before making computational adjustments at the member level or assessing a deficiency attributable to an inconsistent item. Code Sec. 6222 now provides that any underpayment of tax by a member resulting from a failure to

---

[174] Prop. Reg. § 301.6223-1(b)(2).

[175] Code Sec. 6223(a); Prop. Reg. § 301.6223-1(f)(1).

[176] Prop. Reg. § 301.6223-1(a).

[177] Code Sec. 6662(a); Reg. § 301.6222(a)-1(a); Prop. Reg. § § 301.6221(a)-1(d), 301.6222-1(a)(1).

[178] Code Sec. 6662(b); Prop. Reg. § § 301.6222-1(b)(3), 301.6232-1(d)(1)(ii)(B).

[179] Prop. Reg. § 301.6222-1(b)(2).

[180] Code Sec. 6222(c)(2); Prop. Reg. § 301.6222-1(c).

[181] Prop. Reg. § 301.6222-1(c)(4)(i).

treat an item consistently will be assessed and collected as if the underpayment were on account of a mathematical or clerical error appearing on the member's return, permitting the IRS to immediately assess and collect such tax.[182]

The members are bound by adjustments in an AAR or pushout statement. If a member takes a position on return that is inconsistent with an item reflected on an AAR or pushout statement, the IRS may assess and collect resulting underpayments as if the underpayment were due to a mathematical or clerical error, whether or not the member identifies the inconsistency on his or her return.[183]

¶ 2814 PENALTIES

The Revenue Reconciliation Act of 1989 consolidated penalties for negligence, overvaluation, and substantial understatement into Code Sec. 6662. This is now referred to as the "accuracy related" penalty.

Penalties relating to adjustments of partnership items are determined at the LLC level. The penalties are assessed in the same manner as partnership items.[184]

Penalties for failure to file a partnership return on a timely basis are discussed at ¶ 2201.09.

¶ 2815 ADJUSTMENTS TO CAPITAL ACCOUNTS AND TAX BASIS

.01 LLC Pays Tax at Entity Level

The LLC and the members must adjust certain tax attributes when an LLC pays taxes at the entity level as a result of an IRS audit or amended tax return.[185] The LLC makes the adjustments by creating a notional item of income, gain, loss, deduction or credit.[186] The LLC then allocates the notional items to the members in the manner in which the corresponding actual item would have been allocated in the reviewed year.[187]

The LLC must then make appropriate adjustments to the book value and basis of LLC property, and determine the effect of those notional items for the LLC and its reviewed-year members or their successors.[188] The tax attributes that must be adjusted include the following:

---

[182] Code Sec. 6662(b); Prop. Reg. § 301.6222-1(b)(3).

[183] Prop. Reg. § 301.6222-1(b)(2).

[184] Reg. § 301.6221-1(c), (d).

[185] Prop. Reg. § 301.6225-4(a)(1).

[186] Prop. Reg. § § 301.6225-4(b), 301.6225-4(b)(3), 301.6225-4(b)(6).

[187] Prop. Reg. § 1.704-1(b)(4)(xi), (xii), (xiii), (xiv).

[188] Prop. Reg. § 301.6225-4(a)(1). A reviewed year partner's successor is generally defined as either a transferee that succeeds to the transferor partner's capital account under Prop. Reg. § 1.704-1(b)(2)(iv)(l), or, in the case of a complete liquidation of a partner's interest, as the remaining partners to the extent their interests increased as a result of the liquidated partner's departure. *See* Prop. Reg. § § 1.704-1(b)(1)(viii)(b), 301.6225-4(e), Example 3.

(i) *Tax basis and book value of LLC property.* The LLC must make an appropriate adjustment to the book value and tax basis of LLC property to take into account any partnership adjustment. No adjustments are made with respect to property that was held by the LLC in the reviewed year but is no longer held by the LLC in the adjustment year.[189]

(ii) *Contributed Section 704(c) property.* The LLC must make appropriate adjustments to the tax basis contributed property with built-in gain or loss.[190]

(iii) *Basis in membership interest.* A member's basis in the membership interest must be adjusted to reflect any notional item allocated to the member by treating the notional item as an item described in Code Sec. 705(a).[191] For example, an adjustment year member must increase its outside basis in the membership interest for notional income that is allocated to the member.[192]

(iv) *Capital accounts.* The notional items must be reflected in the members' capital accounts.[193] The notional items must be treated as items of income, gain, loss, deduction or credit in determining capital accounts and book values of assets.[194]

(v) *Credits.* If a tax audit results in a net increase or net decrease in credits, the LLC must create one or more notional items of income, gain, loss or deduction that reflect the change in the item giving rise to the credit.[195]

(vi) *Interest and penalties.* LLC payments of interest and penalties must be allocated to the reviewed-year members and their successors in the same manner as the imputed underpayment is allocated.[196] These items are allocated to make sure that the member who should have paid the tax bears the reduction in the capital account.

The adjustment year partners must adjust their tax attributes,[197] even though the notional items are allocated only to the reviewed-year members and their successors. Thus, any adjustment year member who was a member in the reviewed year, or a successor to a reviewed-year member, must adjust tax attributes based on the allocation of notional items.

The adjustments are made in the adjustment year, which is the year in which the audit is completed and the taxes are assessed.[198] The adjustments must be reported on the tax return for the adjustment year.[199]

---

[189] Prop. Reg. § 301.6225-4(b)(2).

[190] Prop. Reg. § 301.6225-4(b)(2).

[191] Prop. Reg. § 301.6225-4(b)(6)(iii).

[192] REG-118067-17, Preamble to Proposed Regulations (2018).

[193] Prop. Reg. § 301.6225-4(a)(2).

[194] Prop. Reg. § 301.6225-4(b)((6)(ii).

[195] Prop. Reg. § 301.6225-4(b)((3)(vi).

[196] Prop. Reg. § 1.704-1(b)(2)(iii)(f)(3).

[197] Prop. Reg. § 301.6225-4(a)(1).

[198] Prop. Reg. § 301.6225-4(a)(2).

[199] Prop. Reg. § 301.6225-4(b)(3).

.02 LLC Makes Pushout Election

If the LLC makes a pushout election, the members must make adjustments to their tax attributes under separate rules for pushout elections. The reviewed-year members or affected partners must take into account their share of income, gain, loss, deduction or credit as reflected on the pushout notice statement. The members must report the adjustments on their tax return for the year in which the LLC furnishes the pushout statement to the member.[200] If a reviewed-year member disposes of a membership interest prior to the reporting year, the member may take into account any outside basis adjustment in an amended return to the extent otherwise permitted under the Code.[201]

The LLC must also adjust tax attributes as a result of pushout items in the adjustment year. The adjustments are calculated with respect to each year beginning with the reviewed year, followed by any subsequent tax years, and concluding with the adjustment year.[202]

.03 No Imputed Underpayment

If an LLC audit adjustment does not result in an imputed underpayment, the allocation of that item to the members cannot have substantial economic effect. However, the payment will be treated as made in accordance with the members' interest in the LLC if it is allocated in a manner in which the item would have been allocated in the reviewed year under the Code Sec. 704 regulations, taking into account the Code Sec. 704 successor rules.[203]

---

[200] Prop. Reg. § 301.6226-4(b).
[201] REG-118067-17, Preamble to Proposed Regulations (2018).
[202] Prop. Reg. § 301.6226-4.
[203] Prop. Reg. § 1.704-1(b)(4).

Appendix A

Forms

FORM 1-1

IRS Form 8832, Election Classification

Form **8832** (Rev. December 2013) Department of the Treasury Internal Revenue Service	**Entity Classification Election** ▶ Information about Form 8832 and its instructions is at *www.irs.gov/form8832*.	OMB No. 1545-1516

	Name of eligible entity making election	Employer identification number
Type or Print	Number, street, and room or suite no. If a P.O. box, see instructions.	
	City or town, state, and ZIP code. If a foreign address, enter city, province or state, postal code and country. Follow the country's practice for entering the postal code.	

▶ Check if: ☐ Address change   ☐ Late classification relief sought under Revenue Procedure 2009-41
                   ☐ Relief for a late change of entity classification election sought under Revenue Procedure 2010-32

Part I	**Election Information**

1   Type of election (see instructions):

a ☐ Initial classification by a newly-formed entity. Skip lines 2a and 2b and go to line 3.
b ☐ Change in current classification. Go to line 2a.

2a Has the eligible entity previously filed an entity election that had an effective date within the last 60 months?

☐ **Yes.** Go to line 2b.
☐ **No.** Skip line 2b and go to line 3.

2b Was the eligible entity's prior election an initial classification election by a newly formed entity that was effective on the date of formation?

☐ **Yes.** Go to line 3.
☐ **No.** Stop here. You generally are not currently eligible to make the election (see instructions).

3 Does the eligible entity have more than one owner?

☐ **Yes.** You can elect to be classified as a partnership or an association taxable as a corporation. Skip line 4 and go to line 5.
☐ **No.** You can elect to be classified as an association taxable as a corporation or to be disregarded as a separate entity. Go to line 4.

4 If the eligible entity has only one owner, provide the following information:

a Name of owner ▶ ....
b Identifying number of owner ▶ ....

5 If the eligible entity is owned by one or more affiliated corporations that file a consolidated return, provide the name and employer identification number of the parent corporation:

a Name of parent corporation ▶ ....
b Employer identification number ▶ ....

For Paperwork Reduction Act Notice, see instructions.	Cat. No. 22598R	Form **8832** (Rev. 12-2013)

Form 8832 (Rev. 12-2013)   Page **2**

Part I	**Election Information** (Continued)

6   Type of entity (see instructions):

   a ☐ A domestic eligible entity electing to be classified as an association taxable as a corporation.
   b ☐ A domestic eligible entity electing to be classified as a partnership.
   c ☐ A domestic eligible entity with a single owner electing to be disregarded as a separate entity.
   d ☐ A foreign eligible entity electing to be classified as an association taxable as a corporation.
   e ☐ A foreign eligible entity electing to be classified as a partnership.
   f   ☐ A foreign eligible entity with a single owner electing to be disregarded as a separate entity.

7   If the eligible entity is created or organized in a foreign jurisdiction, provide the foreign country of
         organization ▶ --

8   Election is to be effective beginning (month, day, year) (see instructions) . . . . ▶ _____

9 Name and title of contact person whom the IRS may call for more information	**10** Contact person's telephone number

Consent Statement and Signature(s) (see instructions)

Under penalties of perjury, I (we) declare that I (we) consent to the election of the above-named entity to be classified as indicated above, and that I (we) have examined this election and consent statement, and to the best of my (our) knowledge and belief, this election and consent statement are true, correct, and complete. If I am an officer, manager, or member signing for the entity, I further declare under penalties of perjury that I am authorized to make the election on its behalf.

Signature(s)	Date	Title

Form **8832** (Rev. 12-2013)

Part II	Late Election Relief

11 Provide the explanation as to why the entity classification election was not filed on time (see instructions).

Under penalties of perjury, I (we) declare that I (we) have examined this election, including accompanying documents, and, to the best of my (our) knowledge and belief, the election contains all the relevant facts relating to the election, and such facts are true, correct, and complete. I (we) further declare that I (we) have personal knowledge of the facts and circumstances related to the election. I (we) further declare that the elements required for relief in Section 4.01 of Revenue Procedure 2009-41 have been satisfied.

Signature(s)	Date	Title

Appendix A

General Instructions

Section references are to the Internal Revenue Code unless otherwise noted.

Future Developments

For the latest information about developments related to Form 8832 and its instructions, such as legislation enacted after they were published, go to *www.irs.gov/form8832*.

What's New

For entities formed on or after July 1, 2013, the Croatian Dionicko Drustvo will always be treated as a corporation. See Notice 2013-44, 2013-29, I.R.B. 62 for more information.

Purpose of Form

An eligible entity uses Form 8832 to elect how it will be classified for federal tax purposes, as a corporation, a partnership, or an entity disregarded as separate from its owner. An eligible entity is classified for federal tax purposes under the default rules described below unless it files Form 8832 or Form 2553, Election by a Small Business Corporation. See *Who Must File* below.

The IRS will use the information entered on this form to establish the entity's filing and reporting requirements for federal tax purposes.

Note. An entity must file Form 2553 if making an election under section 1362(a) to be an S corporation

 A new eligible entity should not file Form 8832 if it will be using its default classification (see Default Rules below).

Eligible entity. An eligible entity is a business entity that is not included in items 1, or 3 through 9, under the definition of **corporation** provided under *Definitions*. Eligible entities include limited liability companies (LLCs) and partnerships.

Generally, corporations are not eligible entities. However, the following types of corporations are treated as eligible entities:

1. An eligible entity that previously elected to be an association taxable as a corporation by filing Form 8832. An entity that elects to be classified as a corporation by filing Form 8832 can make another election to change its classification (see the *60-month limitation rule* discussed below in the instructions for lines 2a and 2b).

2. A foreign eligible entity that became an association taxable as a corporation under the foreign default rule described below.

Default Rules

Existing entity default rule. Certain domestic and foreign entities that were in existence before January 1, 1997, and have an established federal tax classification generally do not need to make an election to continue that classification. If an existing entity decides to change its classification, it may do so subject to the 60-month limitation rule. See the instructions for lines 2a and 2b. See Regulations sections 301.7701-3(b)(3) and 301.7701-3(h)(2) for more details.

Domestic default rule. Unless an election is made on Form 8832, a domestic eligible entity is:

1. A partnership if it has two or more members.

2. Disregarded as an entity separate from its owner if it has a single owner.

A change in the number of members of an eligible entity classified as an **association** (defined below) does not affect the entity's classification. However, an eligible entity classified as a partnership will become a disregarded entity when the entity's membership is reduced to one member and a disregarded entity will be classified as a partnership when the entity has more than one member.

Foreign default rule. Unless an election is made on Form 8832, a foreign eligible entity is:

1. A partnership if it has two or more members and at least one member does not have limited liability.

2. An association taxable as a corporation if all members have limited liability.

3. Disregarded as an entity separate from its owner if it has a single owner that does not have limited liability.

However, if a qualified foreign entity (as defined in section 3.02 of Rev. Proc. 2010-32) files a valid election to be classified as a partnership based on the reasonable assumption that it had two or more owners as of the effective date of the election, and the qualified entity is later determined to have a single owner, the IRS will deem the election to be an election to be classified as a disregarded entity provided:

1. The qualified entity's owner and purported owners file amended returns that are consistent with the treatment of the entity as a disregarded entity;

2. The amended returns are filed before the close of the period of limitations on assessments under section 6501(a) for the relevant tax year; and

3. The corrected Form 8832, with the box checked entitled: Relief for a late change of entity classification election sought under Revenue Procedure 2010-32, is filed and attached to the amended tax return.

Also, if the qualified foreign entity (as defined in section 3.02 of Rev. Proc. 2010-32) files a valid election to be classified as a disregarded entity based on the reasonable assumption that it had a single owner as of the effective date of the election, and the qualified entity is later determined to have two or more owners, the IRS will deem the election to be an election to be classified as a partnership provided:

1. The qualified entity files information returns and the actual owners file original or amended returns consistent with the treatment of the entity as a partnership;

2. The amended returns are filed before the close of the period of limitations on assessments under section 6501(a) for the relevant tax year; and

3. The corrected Form 8832, with the box checked entitled: Relief for a late change of entity classification election sought under Revenue Procedure 2010-32, is filed and attached to the amended tax returns. See Rev. Proc. 2010-32, 2010-36 I.R.B. 320 for details.

Definitions

Association. For purposes of this form, an association is an eligible entity taxable as a corporation by election or, for foreign eligible entities, under the default rules (see Regulations section 301.7701-3).

Business entity. A business entity is any entity recognized for federal tax purposes that is not properly classified as a trust under Regulations section 301.7701-4 or otherwise subject to special treatment under the Code regarding the entity's classification. See Regulations section 301.7701-2(a).

Corporation. For federal tax purposes, a corporation is any of the following:

1. A business entity organized under a federal or state statute, or under a statute of a federally recognized Indian tribe, if the statute describes or refers to the entity as incorporated or as a corporation, body corporate, or body politic.

2. An association (as determined under Regulations section 301.7701-3).

3. A business entity organized under a state statute, if the statute describes or refers to the entity as a joint-stock company or joint-stock association.

4. An insurance company.

5. A state-chartered business entity conducting banking activities, if any of its deposits are insured under the Federal Deposit Insurance Act, as amended, 12 U.S. C. 1811 et seq., or a similar federal statute.

6. A business entity wholly owned by a state or any political subdivision thereof, or a business entity wholly owned by a foreign government or any other entity described in Regulations section 1.892-2T.

7. A business entity that is taxable as a corporation under a provision of the Code other than section 7701(a)(3).

8. A foreign business entity listed on page 7. See Regulations section 301.7701-2(b)(8) for any exceptions and inclusions to items on this list and for any revisions made to this list since these instructions were printed.

9. An entity created or organized under the laws of more than one jurisdiction (business entities with multiple charters) if the entity is treated as a corporation with respect to any one of the jurisdictions. See Regulations section 301.7701-2(b)(9) for examples.

Disregarded entity. A disregarded entity is an eligible entity that is treated as an entity not separate from its single owner for income tax purposes. A "disregarded entity" is treated as separate from its owner for:

• Employment tax purposes, effective for wages paid on or after January 1, 2009; and

• Excise taxes reported on Forms 720, 730, 2290, 11-C, or 8849, effective for excise taxes reported and paid after December 31, 2007.

Form 8832 (Rev. 12-2013)   Page **5**

See the employment tax and excise tax return instructions for more information.

Limited liability. A member of a foreign eligible entity has limited liability if the member has no personal liability for any debts of or claims against the entity by reason of being a member. This determination is based solely on the statute or law under which the entity is organized (and, if relevant, the entity's organizational documents). A member has personal liability if the creditors of the entity may seek satisfaction of all or any part of the debts or claims against the entity from the member as such. A member has personal liability even if the member makes an agreement under which another person (whether or not a member of the entity) assumes that liability or agrees to indemnify that member for that liability.

Partnership. A partnership is a business entity that has at least two members and is not a corporation as defined above under *Corporation.*

Who Must File

File this form for an eligible entity that is one of the following:

• A domestic entity electing to be classified as an association taxable as a corporation.

• A domestic entity electing to change its current classification (even if it is currently classified under the default rule).

• A foreign entity that has more than one owner, all owners having limited liability, electing to be classified as a partnership.

• A foreign entity that has at least one owner that does not have limited liability, electing to be classified as an association taxable as a corporation.

• A foreign entity with a single owner having limited liability, electing to be an entity disregarded as an entity separate from its owner.

• A foreign entity electing to change its current classification (even if it is currently classified under the default rule).

Do not file this form for an eligible entity that is:

• Tax-exempt under section 501(a);

• A real estate investment trust (REIT), as defined in section 856; or

• Electing to be classified as an S corporation. An eligible entity that timely files Form 2553 to elect classification as an S corporation and meets all other requirements to qualify as an S corporation is deemed to have made an election under Regulations section 301.7701-3(c)(v) to be classified as an association taxable as a corporation.

All three of these entities are deemed to have made an election to be classified as an association.

Effect of Election

The federal tax treatment of elective changes in classification as described in Regulations section 301.7701-3(g)(1) is summarized as follows:

• If an eligible entity classified as a partnership elects to be classified as an association, it is deemed that the partnership contributes all of its assets and liabilities to the association in exchange for stock in the association, and immediately thereafter, the partnership liquidates by distributing the stock of the association to its partners.

• If an eligible entity classified as an association elects to be classified as a partnership, it is deemed that the association distributes all of its assets and liabilities to its shareholders in liquidation of the association, and immediately thereafter, the shareholders contribute all of the distributed assets and liabilities to a newly formed partnership.

• If an eligible entity classified as an association elects to be disregarded as an entity separate from its owner, it is deemed that the association distributes all of its assets and liabilities to its single owner in liquidation of the association.

• If an eligible entity that is disregarded as an entity separate from its owner elects to be classified as an association, the owner of the eligible entity is deemed to have contributed all of the assets and liabilities of the entity to the association in exchange for the stock of the association.

Note. For information on the federal tax consequences of elective changes in classification, see Regulations section 301.7701-3(g).

When To File

Generally, an election specifying an eligible entity's classification cannot take effect more than 75 days prior to the date the election is filed, nor can it take effect later than 12 months after the date the election is filed. An eligible entity may be eligible for late election relief in certain circumstances. For more information, see *Late Election Relief,* later.

Where To File

File Form 8832 with the Internal Revenue Service Center for your state listed later.

In addition, attach a copy of Form 8832 to the entity's federal tax or information return for the tax year of the election. If the entity is not required to file a return for that year, a copy of its Form 8832 must be attached to the federal tax returns of all direct or indirect owners of the entity for the tax year of the owner that includes the date on which the election took effect. An indirect owner of the electing entity does not have to attach a copy of the Form 8832 to its tax return if an entity in which it has an interest is already filing a copy of the Form 8832 with its return. Failure to attach a copy of Form 8832 will not invalidate an otherwise valid election, but penalties may be assessed against persons who are required to, but do not, attach Form 8832.

Each member of the entity is required to file the member's return consistent with the entity election. Penalties apply to returns filed inconsistent with the entity's election.

If the entity's principal business, office, or agency is located in:	Use the following Internal Revenue Service Center address:
Connecticut, Delaware, District of Columbia, Florida, Illinois, Indiana, Kentucky, Maine, Maryland, Massachusetts, Michigan, New Hampshire, New Jersey, New York, North Carolina, Ohio, Pennsylvania, Rhode Island, South Carolina, Vermont, Virginia, West Virginia, Wisconsin	Cincinnati, OH 45999

If the entity's principal business, office, or agency is located in:	Use the following Internal Revenue Service Center address:
Alabama, Alaska, Arizona, Arkansas, California, Colorado, Georgia, Hawaii, Idaho, Iowa, Kansas, Louisiana, Minnesota, Mississippi, Missouri, Montana, Nebraska, Nevada, New Mexico, North Dakota, Oklahoma, Oregon, South Dakota, Tennessee, Texas, Utah, Washington, Wyoming	Ogden, UT 84201
A foreign country or U.S. possession	Ogden, UT 84201-0023

Note. Also attach a copy to the entity's federal income tax return for the tax year of the election.

Acceptance or Nonacceptance of Election

The service center will notify the eligible entity at the address listed on Form 8832 if its election is accepted or not accepted. The entity should generally receive a determination on its election within 60 days after it has filed Form 8832.

Care should be exercised to ensure that the IRS receives the election. If the entity is not notified of acceptance or nonacceptance of its election within 60 days of the date of filing, take follow-up action by calling 1-800-829-0115, or by sending a letter to the service center to inquire about its status. Send any such letter by certified or registered mail via the U.S. Postal Service, or equivalent type of delivery by a designated private delivery service (see Notice 2004-83, 2004-52 I.R.B. 1030 (or its successor)).

If the IRS questions whether Form 8832 was filed, an acceptable proof of filing is:

• A certified or registered mail receipt (timely postmarked) from the U.S. Postal Service, or its equivalent from a designated private delivery service;

• Form 8832 with an accepted stamp;

• Form 8832 with a stamped IRS received date; or

• An IRS letter stating that Form 8832 has been accepted.

Form 8832 (Rev. 12-2013)

Page **6**

Specific Instructions

Name. Enter the name of the eligible entity electing to be classified.

Employer identification number (EIN). Show the EIN of the eligible entity electing to be classified.

Do not put "Applied For" on this line.

Note. Any entity that has an EIN will retain that EIN even if its federal tax classification changes under Regulations section 301.7701-3.

If a disregarded entity's classification changes so that it becomes recognized as a partnership or association for federal tax purposes, and that entity had an EIN, then the entity must continue to use that EIN. If the entity did not already have its own EIN, then the entity must apply for an EIN and not use the identifying number of the single owner.

A foreign entity that makes an election under Regulations section 301.7701-3(c) and (d) must also use its own taxpayer identifying number. See sections 6721 through 6724 for penalties that may apply for failure to supply taxpayer identifying numbers.

If the entity electing to be classified using Form 8832 does not have an EIN, it must apply for one on Form SS-4, Application for Employer Identification Number. The entity must have received an EIN by the time Form 8832 is filed in order for the form to be processed. An election will not be accepted if the eligible entity does not provide an EIN.

Do not apply for a new EIN for an existing entity that is changing its classification if the entity already has an EIN.

Address. Enter the address of the entity electing a classification. All correspondence regarding the acceptance or nonacceptance of the election will be sent to this address. Include the suite, room, or other unit number after the street address. If the Post Office does not deliver mail to the street address and the entity has a P.O. box, show the box number instead of the street address. If the electing entity receives its mail in care of a third party (such as an accountant or an attorney), enter on the street address line "C/O" followed by the third party's name and street address or P.O. box.

Address change. If the eligible entity has changed its address since filing Form SS-4 or the entity's most recently-filed return (including a change to an "in care of" address), check the box for an address change.

Late-classification relief sought under Revenue Procedure 2009-41. Check the box if the entity is seeking relief under Rev. Proc. 2009-41, 2009-39 I.R.B. 439, for a late classification election. For more information, see *Late Election Relief,* later.

Relief for a late change of entity classification election sought under Revenue Procedure 2010-32. Check the box if the entity is seeking relief under Rev. Proc.

2010-32, 2010-36 I.R.B. 320. For more information, see *Foreign default rule,* earlier.

Part I. Election Information

Complete Part I whether or not the entity is seeking relief under Rev. Proc. 2009-41 or Rev. Proc. 2010-32.

Line 1. Check box 1a if the entity is choosing a classification for the first time (i.e., the entity does not want to be classified under the applicable default classification). Do not file this form if the entity wants to be classified under the default rules.

Check box 1b if the entity is changing its current classification.

Lines 2a and 2b. 60-month limitation rule. Once an eligible entity makes an election to *change* its classification, the entity generally cannot change its classification again during the 60 months after the effective date of the election. However, the IRS may (by private letter ruling) permit the entity to change its classification by election within the 60-month period if more than 50% of the ownership interests in the entity, as of the effective date of the election, are owned by persons that did not own any interests in the entity on the effective date or the filing date of the entity's prior election.

Note. The 60-month limitation does not apply if the previous election was made by a newly formed eligible entity and was effective on the date of formation.

Line 4. If an eligible entity has only one owner, provide the name of its owner on line 4a and the owner's identifying number (social security number, or individual taxpayer identification number, or EIN) on line 4b. If the electing eligible entity is owned by an entity that is a disregarded entity or by an entity that is a member of a series of tiered disregarded entities, identify the first entity (the entity closest to the electing eligible entity) that is not a disregarded entity. For example, if the electing eligible entity is owned by disregarded entity A, which is owned by another disregarded entity B, and disregarded entity B is owned by partnership C, provide the name and EIN of partnership C as the owner of the electing eligible entity. If the owner is a foreign person or entity and does not have a U.S. identifying number, enter "none" on line 4b.

Line 5. If the eligible entity is owned by one or more members of an affiliated group of corporations that file a consolidated return, provide the name and EIN of the parent corporation.

Line 6. Check the appropriate box if you are changing a current classification (no matter how achieved), or are electing out of a default classification. Do not file this form if you fall within a default classification that is the desired classification for the new entity.

Line 7. If the entity making the election is created or organized in a foreign jurisdiction, enter the name of the foreign country in which it is organized. This information must be provided even if the entity is also organized under domestic law.

Line 8. Generally, the election will take effect on the date you enter on line 8 of this form,

or on the date filed if no date is entered on line 8. An election specifying an entity's classification for federal tax purposes can take effect no more than 75 days prior to the date the election is filed, nor can it take effect later than 12 months after the date on which the election is filed. If line 8 shows a date more than 75 days prior to the date on which the election is filed, the election will default to 75 days before the date it is filed. If line 8 shows an effective date more than 12 months from the filing date, the election will take effect 12 months after the date the election is filed.

Consent statement and signature(s). Form 8832 must be signed by:

1. Each member of the electing entity who is an owner at the time the election is filed; or

2. Any officer, manager, or member of the electing entity who is authorized (under local law or the organizational documents) to make the election. The elector represents to having such authorization under penalties of perjury.

If an election is to be effective for any period prior to the time it is filed, each person who was an owner between the date the election is to be effective and the date the election is filed, and who is not an owner at the time the election is filed, must sign.

If you need a continuation sheet or use a separate consent statement, attach it to Form 8832. The separate consent statement must contain the same information as shown on Form 8832.

Note. Do not sign the copy that is attached to your tax return.

Part II. Late Election Relief

Complete Part II only if the entity is requesting late election relief under Rev. Proc. 2009-41.

An eligible entity may be eligible for late election relief under Rev. Proc. 2009-41, 2009-39 I.R.B. 439, if *each* of the following requirements is met.

1. The entity failed to obtain its requested classification as of the date of its formation (or upon the entity's classification becoming relevant) or failed to obtain its requested change in classification solely because Form 8832 was not filed timely.

2. Either:

a. The entity has not filed a federal tax or information return for the first year in which the election was intended because the due date has not passed for that year's federal tax or information return; or

b. The entity has timely filed all required federal tax returns and information returns (or if not timely, within 6 months after its due date, excluding extensions) consistent with its requested classification for all of the years the entity intended the requested election to be effective and no inconsistent tax or information returns have been filed by or with respect to the entity during any of the tax years. If the eligible entity is not required to file a federal tax return or information return, each affected person who is required to file a federal tax return or information return must have timely filed all such returns (or if not timely, within 6 months after its due date, excluding extensions) consistent with the entity's requested classification for all of the years the entity intended the requested election to be effective and no inconsistent tax or information returns have been filed during any of the tax years.

3. The entity has reasonable cause for its failure to timely make the entity classification election.

4. Three years and 75 days from the requested effective date of the eligible entity's classification election have not passed.

Affected person. An affected person is either:

• with respect to the effective date of the eligible entity's classification election, a person who would have been required to attach a copy of the Form 8832 for the eligible entity to its federal tax or information return for the tax year of the person which includes that date; or

• with respect to any subsequent date after the entity's requested effective date of the classification election, a person who would have been required to attach a copy of the Form 8832 for the eligible entity to its federal tax or information return for the person's tax year that includes that subsequent date had the election first become effective on that subsequent date.

For details on the requirement to attach a copy of Form 8832, see Rev. Proc. 2009-41 and the instructions under *Where To File.*

To obtain relief, file Form 8832 with the applicable IRS service center listed in *Where To File,* earlier, within 3 years and 75 days from the requested effective date of the eligible entity's classification election.

If Rev. Proc. 2009-41 does not apply, an entity may seek relief for a late entity election by requesting a private letter ruling and paying a user fee in accordance with Rev. Proc. 2013-1, 2013-1 I.R.B. 1 (or its successor).

Line 11. Explain the reason for the failure to file a timely entity classification election.

Signatures. Part II of Form 8832 must be signed by an authorized representative of the eligible entity and each affected person. See *Affected Persons,* earlier. The individual or individuals who sign the declaration must have personal knowledge of the facts and circumstances related to the election.

Foreign Entities Classified as Corporations for Federal Tax Purposes:

American Samoa—Corporation

Argentina—Sociedad Anonima

Australia—Public Limited Company

Austria—Aktiengesellschaft

Barbados—Limited Company

Belgium—Societe Anonyme

Belize—Public Limited Company

Bolivia—Sociedad Anonima

Brazil—Sociedade Anonima

Bulgaria—Aktsionerno Druzhestvo

Canada—Corporation and Company

Chile—Sociedad Anonima

People's Republic of China—Gufen Youxian Gongsi

Republic of China (Taiwan) —Ku-fen Yu-hsien Kung-szu

Colombia—Sociedad Anonima

Costa Rica—Sociedad Anonima

Croatia—Dionicko Drustvo

Cyprus—Public Limited Company

Czech Republic—Akciova Spolecnost

Denmark—Aktieselskab

Ecuador—Sociedad Anonima or Compania Anonima

Egypt—Sharikat Al-Mossahamah

El Salvador—Sociedad Anonima

Estonia—Aktsiaselts

European Economic Area/European Union—Societas Europaea

Finland—Julkinen Osakeyhtio/Publikt Aktiebolag

France—Societe Anonyme

Germany—Aktiengesellschaft

Greece—Anonymos Etairia

Guam—Corporation

Guatemala—Sociedad Anonima

Guyana—Public Limited Company

Honduras—Sociedad Anonima

Hong Kong—Public Limited Company

Hungary—Reszvenytarsasag

Iceland—Hlutafelag

India—Public Limited Company

Indonesia—Perseroan Terbuka

Ireland—Public Limited Company

Israel—Public Limited Company

Italy—Societa per Azioni

Jamaica—Public Limited Company

Japan—Kabushiki Kaisha

Kazakstan—Ashyk Aktsionerlik Kogham

Republic of Korea—Chusik Hoesa

Latvia—Akciju Sabiedriba

Liberia—Corporation

Liechtenstein—Aktiengesellschaft

Lithuania—Akcine Bendroves

Luxembourg—Societe Anonyme

Malaysia—Berhad

Malta—Public Limited Company

Mexico—Sociedad Anonima

Morocco—Societe Anonyme

Netherlands—Naamloze Vennootschap

New Zealand—Limited Company

Nicaragua—Compania Anonima

Nigeria—Public Limited Company

Northern Mariana Islands—Corporation

Norway—Allment Aksjeselskap

Pakistan—Public Limited Company

Panama—Sociedad Anonima

Paraguay—Sociedad Anonima

Peru—Sociedad Anonima

Philippines—Stock Corporation

Poland—Spolka Akcyjna

Portugal—Sociedade Anonima

Puerto Rico—Corporation

Romania—Societe pe Actiuni

Russia—Otkrytoye Aktsionernoy Obshchestvo

Saudi Arabia—Sharikat Al-Mossahamah

Singapore—Public Limited Company

Slovak Republic—Akciova Spolocnost

Slovenia—Delniska Druzba

South Africa—Public Limited Company

Spain—Sociedad Anonima

Surinam—Naamloze Vennootschap

Sweden—Publika Aktiebolag

Switzerland—Aktiengesellschaft

Thailand—Borisat Chamkad (Mahachon)

Trinidad and Tobago—Limited Company

Tunisia—Societe Anonyme

Turkey—Anonim Sirket

Ukraine—Aktsionerne Tovaristvo Vidkritogo Tipu

United Kingdom—Public Limited Company

United States Virgin Islands—Corporation

Uruguay—Sociedad Anonima

Venezuela—Sociedad Anonima or Compania Anonima

 CAUTION *See Regulations section 301.7701-2(b)(8) for any exceptions and inclusions to items on this list and for any revisions made to this list since these instructions were printed.*

Paperwork Reduction Act Notice

We ask for the information on this form to carry out the Internal Revenue laws of the United States. You are required to give us the information. We need it to ensure that you are complying with these laws and to allow us to figure and collect the right amount of tax.

You are not required to provide the information requested on a form that is subject to the Paperwork Reduction Act unless the form displays a valid OMB control number. Books or records relating to a form or its instructions must be retained as long as their contents may become material in the administration of any Internal Revenue law. Generally, tax returns and return information are confidential, as required by section 6103.

The time needed to complete and file this form will vary depending on individual circumstances. The estimated average time is:

Recordkeeping . . . . 2 hr., 46 min.

Learning about the law or the form . . . . 3 hr., 48 min.

Preparing and sending the form to the IRS . . . . 36 min.

If you have comments concerning the accuracy of these time estimates or suggestions for making this form simpler, we would be happy to hear from you. You can write to the Internal Revenue Service, Tax Forms and Publications, SE:W:CAR:MP:TFP, 1111 Constitution Ave. NW, IR-6526, Washington, DC 20224. Do not send the form to this address. Instead, see *Where To File* above.

FORM 1-2

_____, LLC

OPERATING AGREEMENT

This Operating Agreement is made by and among _____, a California limited liability company ("LLC") and the persons signing this Agreement as members ("Members") and managers ("Managers") of the LLC. The parties agree as follows:

ARTICLE I. FORMATION

Section 1.01 Organization of LLC

The Members formed the LLC pursuant to the Revised California LLC Act, Title 2.6 (Sections 17701.01-17713.13) of the California Corporations Code. Articles of Organization have been filed with the California Secretary of State.

Section 1.02 Name of LLC

The name of the LLC is _____LLC. The business of the LLC shall be operated under that name or any other name for which the LLC has filed a fictitious business name statement.

Section 1.03 Purpose of LLC

The principal purpose of the LLC shall be to engage in the business of _____ and such other activities that are related or incidental thereto. The LLC may engage in any other lawful activities.

Section 1.04 Principal Place of Business

The principal place of business of the LLC shall be _____. The Managers may change the principal place of business of the LLC by giving notice of the change of address to each Member.

Section 1.05 Term of LLC

The term of the LLC shall be perpetual unless terminated or dissolved as provided in this Agreement.

Section 1.06 Agent for Service of Process

The agent for service of process of this LLC shall be _____. The Managers may designate a new agent for service of process at any time.

ARTICLE II. MEMBERS

Section 2.01 Initial Members

The names and addresses of the initial Members of the LLC are set forth on Exhibit A attached to this Agreement.

Section 2.02 Liability of Members

The liability of the Members is restricted and limited to the amount of capital contributions that each Member makes or agrees to make to the LLC. Except as provided in Section 17701.10(g) of the California Corporations Code, no Member shall be personally liable for the debts, obligations, liabilities or judgments of the

LLC, whether arising in contract, tort or otherwise, solely by reason of being a Member of the LLC.

Pursuant to Section 17701.10(g) of the California Corporations Code, this Agreement does not eliminate or limit a Member's liability to the LLC and other Members for money damages for: (i) breach of the duty of loyalty; (ii) a financial benefit received by the Member or Manager to which the Member or Manager is not entitled; (iii) a Member's liability for excess distributions under Section 17704.06 of the California Corporations Code; (iv) intentional infliction of harm on the LLC or a Member; or (v) an intentional violation of criminal law.

Section 2.03 Voting Rights of Members

(a) **Majority Vote Required**. The following actions shall be taken by a vote of the holders of a majority of Membership Units:

(i) election and removal of Managers under Sections 3.01 and 3.02 of this Agreement;

(ii) determining salaries and other compensation of Managers and Members under Sections 8.01 and 8.02 of this Agreement;

(iii) dissolution of the LLC under Section 17707.01 of the California Corporations Code and Section 16.01(b) of this Agreement;

(iv) continuing the business of the LLC after all of the Managers cease to be Managers for any reason under Section 16.01(c) of this Agreement;

(v) amending the Articles of Association or the Operating Agreement under Sections 17.01 and 17.02 of this Agreement. However, the Managers may amend Exhibit A attached to this Agreement without the consent of the Members to reflect changes in the Members of the LLC, the number of units owned by each Member, and the percentage ownership of each Member as a result of the admission of new Members, withdrawals of Members, or transfers of Membership interests;

(vi) a merger of the LLC under Section 17710.12 of the California Corporations Code.

(b) **Unanimous Vote Required.** The unanimous vote of all Members shall be required before the LLC may enter into agreements, commitments or obligations which increase the personal liability of Members who have not consented to assuming such personal liability.

(c) **Other Actions**. Except as otherwise provided in this Agreement, all other actions may be taken by the Managers by majority vote without approval of the Members, including the issuance of additional Membership Units.

Section 2.04 Signing Documents

No Member, acting solely in his capacity as a Member, may bind the LLC or sign any document on behalf of the LLC.

ARTICLE III. MANAGERS

Section 3.01 Election of Managers

The Members shall by a vote of a majority of Membership Units elect _____ Managers to manage the business and affairs of the LLC. The Managers shall serve until their successors are duly elected and qualified. The Managers need not be

Members. In voting for Managers, each Member shall have a number of votes equal to the number of Membership Units owned by that Member. The initial Managers of the LLC, who have been elected by the holders of a majority of Membership Units, are the following persons:

_____

_____

Section 3.02 Removal and Resignation

The Members may remove a Manager at any time, with or without cause, by vote of the holders of a majority of Membership Units. A Manager may resign at any time by giving written notice to the Members or to the other Managers. The Members may fill a vacancy caused by resignation or removal of a Manager by a vote of the holders of a majority of Membership Units.

Section 3.03 Powers of Managers

The Managers shall have the sole and exclusive right to manage the business and affairs of the LLC except as otherwise provided in this Agreement. The Managers shall have the power and authority to take such action that they deem necessary, appropriate or convenient in connection with the management and conduct of the business and affairs of the LLC, including without limitation the power to:

(a) acquire real or personal property for the LLC;

(b) dispose of property, either in the ordinary course of the business or when the Managers determine that such disposition is in the best interests of the LLC;

(c) finance the LLC's activities by borrowing money from third parties on such terms and conditions that the Managers deem appropriate. When the LLC borrows money, the Managers are authorized to pledge, mortgage, encumber or grant a security interest in LLC properties as security for the repayment of the loan;

(d) employ, retain or otherwise secure the services of professionals or other persons;

(e) admit additional Members and issue additional Membership Units for such consideration determined by the Managers; or

(f) take any and all other action permitted by law and which is customary or reasonably related to the conduct of the business of the LLC, including the powers set forth in Section 17003 of the California Corporations Code.

Section 3.04 Standard of Care of Managers

The Managers shall exercise a duty of care and a duty of loyalty in managing the affairs of the LLC pursuant to Section 17704.09 of the California Corporations Code. The Managers shall not be liable or obligated to the Members for any mistake of fact or judgment made by the Managers in operating the business of the LLC that results in any loss to the LLC or its Members unless fraud, deceit or a wrongful taking is involved. The Managers do not in any way guarantee the return of the Members' capital or a profit from the operations of the LLC. The Managers shall not be responsible to any Member because of a loss of that Member's investment or a loss in operations, unless it is caused by fraud, deceit or a wrongful taking by the Managers.

Section 3.05 Devotion of Time by Managers

The Managers shall devote such care, time and attention to the affairs of the LLC that is reasonably necessary. In this connection, the Members acknowledge that the Managers may be Managers of other LLCs and general partners of other partnerships. The Managers may engage in other business of the type conducted by the LLC, whether or not competitive with the business of the LLC.

Section 3.06 Voting Rights of Managers

When there is more than one Manager, decisions of the Managers shall be made by a majority vote of the Managers at a meeting, or by unanimous written consent. Each Manager has equal rights in the management and conduct of the activities of the LLC. The consent of all Managers is required to do any of the following:

(a) Sell, lease, exchange, or otherwise dispose of all, or substantially all, of the LLC's property, with or without the goodwill, outside the ordinary course of the LLC's business.

(b) Approve a merger or conversion under Article 10 of the California Corporations Code (commencing with Section 17710.01).

(c) Undertake any other act outside the ordinary course of the LLC's activities.

(d) Amend the Operating Agreement.

Section 3.07 Restrictions on Managers

Except as otherwise provided in this Agreement, the Managers shall be subject to all the restrictions imposed on managers by the California LLC Act, and shall have all the rights and powers granted to managers under that Act.

Section 3.08 Liability of Managers

No Manager shall be personally liable for the debts, obligations, liabilities or judgments of the LLC, whether arising in contract, tort or otherwise, solely by reason of being a Manager or officer of the LLC.

Section 3.09 Restrictions on Authority of Managers and Members

Pursuant to Section 17703.01(b) of the California Corporations Code, the following restrictions shall apply to Members and Managers of the LLC:

(a) No Member acting solely in the capacity of a Member is an agent of the LLC nor can any Member bind or execute any instrument on behalf of the LLC.

(b) Every Manager is an agent of the LLC for the purpose of its business or affairs, and the act of any Manager, including, but not limited to, the execution in the name of the LLC of any instrument for apparently carrying on in the usual way the business or affairs of the LLC of which the person is a Manager, binds the LLC, unless the Manager so acting has, in fact, no authority to act for the LLC in the particular matter and the person with whom the Manager is dealing has actual knowledge of the fact that the Manager has no such authority.

(c) No act of a Manager or Member in contravention of a restriction on authority shall bind the LLC to persons having actual knowledge of the restriction.

Appendix A

(d) Notwithstanding Section 17703.01(c) of the California Corporations Code, any note, mortgage, evidence of indebtedness, contract, certificate, statement, conveyance, or other instrument in writing, and any assignment or endorsement thereof, executed or entered into between the LLC and any other person, when signed by at least two Managers, or by one Manager in the case of a LLC whose Articles of Organization state that it is managed by only one Manager, is not invalidated as to the LLC by any lack of authority of the signing Managers or Manager in the absence of actual knowledge on the part of the other person that the signing Managers or Manager had no authority to execute the same.

ARTICLE IV. OFFICERS

Section 4.01 Officers

The Managers may appoint officers for the purpose of signing documents and taking other actions on behalf of the LLC. The officers shall hold office until the Managers remove such persons or elect new officers. The Managers may remove an officer at any time, with or without cause. The officers shall have only the powers delegated to them by the Managers. The officers may resign at any time after notice to the Managers.

Section 4.02 Initial Officers

The following persons shall be the initial officers of the LLC:

_____ President
_____ Secretary
_____ Treasurer

Section 4.03 President

The President shall be the general manager and chief executive officer of the LLC. The President shall have general supervision, direction and control of the business of the LLC, subject to the control of the Managers. The President shall preside at all meetings of Members and Managers. The President shall have the general powers and duties of management usually vested in the president and general manager of an LLC and such other powers and duties prescribed by the Managers from time to time.

Section 4.04 Vice President

In the absence or disability of the President, the Vice President shall perform all the duties of the President. The Vice President shall have such other powers and perform such other duties as from time to time determined by the Managers.

Section 4.05 Secretary

The Secretary shall keep minutes of all meetings of Members and Managers at the principal office of the LLC. The Secretary shall work with the Managers in maintaining the other books and records of the LLC that the Managers are required to maintain under Article 11 of this Agreement.

Section 4.06 Treasurer.

The Treasurer is the chief financial officer of the LLC. The Treasurer shall maintain adequate books and records of the financial transactions of the LLC. The Treasurer shall also send to Members financial statements and other financial reports that the LLC is required to send to Members. The Treasurer shall have such other powers and perform such other duties prescribed by the Managers from time to time.

Section 4.07 Authority of Officers Signing Documents

Any note, mortgage, evidence of indebtedness, contract, certificate, statement, conveyance, or other instrument in writing, and any assignment or endorsement thereof, executed or entered into between the LLC and any other person, when signed by the chairperson of the board, the president, or any vice president and any secretary, any assistant secretary, the chief financial officer, or any assistant treasurer of the LLC, is not invalidated as to the LLC by any lack of authority of the signing officers in the absence of actual knowledge on the part of the other person that the signing officers had no authority to execute the same.

ARTICLE V. CONTRIBUTIONS AND CAPITAL ACCOUNTS

Section 5.01 Initial Capital Contributions

Each Member shall contribute to the capital of the LLC cash and/or property in the amount set forth on Exhibit A attached to this Agreement. A Member's interest in the LLC shall be evidenced by Units. The number of Units owned by each Member is set forth on Exhibit A attached to this Agreement.

Section 5.02 Additional Capital Contributions

The Managers may issue additional Units to existing Members and new Members. The Managers shall determine the consideration to be issued for such Units. The Units need not be issued for the same type or amount of consideration.

The Members shall not be required to make additional capital contributions, but may make additional capital contributions with the consent of the Managers.

Section 5.03 Interest on Contributions

No interest shall be paid on contributions to the capital of the LLC.

Section 5.04 Withdrawal and Return of Capital

A Member may withdraw from the LLC at any time. No Member shall have the right on withdrawal from the LLC for any reason to withdraw any portion of the capital of the LLC or to a return of that Member's capital contribution, except upon dissolution of the LLC under Section 16.03 of this Agreement.

If there is a withdrawal of a Member that does not cause a dissolution of the LLC, the LLC shall not be required to buy back the Membership Units of the withdrawing Member or to return that Member's capital account balance.

Section 5.05 Capital Accounts

(a) The LLC shall establish a capital account for each Member (and for each transferee who has not become a Member) in accordance with the rules set forth in Treas. Reg. § 1.704-1(b)(2)(iv).

(b) The capital account for each Member shall be increased by (a) the cash contributed by the Member to the LLC, (b) the fair market value of property contributed by the Member to the LLC, as determined by the Member and the LLC at the time of contribution, net of liabilities encumbering the property or assumed by the LLC, (c) the amount of income and gain allocated by the LLC to the Member, including income and gain exempt from tax, and (d) the amount of LLC liabilities assumed by the Member or secured by property distributed to the Member (to the extent not already netted out under subparagraph (c) below).

(c) The capital account for each Member shall be decreased by (a) cash distributions from the LLC to the Member, (b) the fair market value of property distributed to the Member, as determined by the LLC and the Member at the time of distribution, net of any liabilities encumbering the property or assumed by the Member, (c) the amount of losses and deductions allocated by the LLC to the Member, and (d) the amount of any liabilities of the Member assumed by the LLC or which are secured by property contributed by Member to the LLC (to the extent not already netted out under subparagraph (b) above).

(d) If a Member transfers Membership Units in accordance with Article 14, the capital account attributable to the transferred Units shall carry over to the new owner of the Units except as otherwise provided in the written agreement between the parties transferring the Membership Units.

ARTICLE VI. ALLOCATIONS

Section 6.01 Allocation of Profits and Losses

After giving effect to the special tax and capital account allocations set forth on Exhibit B attached to this Agreement, the net profits and net losses of the LLC, and other items of income, gain, loss, deductions and credits, shall be allocated to the Members in proportion to the number of Membership Units owned by each Member compared to the number of Membership Units owned by all Members.

Section 6.02 Determination of Profits and Losses

The LLC's net profits and losses, and all other items of income, gain, loss, deductions and credits, shall be determined by the accountant regularly engaged by the LLC to audit the books and records of the LLC. The determination shall be made as soon as practical after the close of the calendar year.

The income and deductions of the LLC for tax purposes shall be determined under Section 703 of the Internal Revenue Code. The tax allocations of income and deductions to each Member shall follow the book allocations to each Member's capital account, subject to (i) the required adjustments under Section 704(c) of the Internal Revenue Code with respect to contributed property where there is a difference between book value and tax basis, and (ii) such other required adjustments under the Internal Revenue Code and regulations thereunder.

ARTICLE VII. DISTRIBUTIONS

Section 7.01 Amount and Time of Distributions

The Managers shall distribute cash available for distribution to the Members at such time that the Managers deem advisable. In determining the amount of cash available for distribution, the Managers shall set aside a reasonable allowance for anticipated expenses, contingencies, capital needs and other reserves and costs incident to the business of the LLC. The Managers shall normally distribute to Members each year an amount that is at least equal to the income taxes that the Members are required to pay on their distributive share of income and gain.

Section 7.02 Allocation of Distributions

Distributions shall be made to Members in proportion to the number of Membership Units owned by each Member compared to the number of Membership Units owned by all Members.

Section 7.03 Distributions Other Than Cash

No Member shall have the right to receive property other than money upon the distribution of profits or cash available for distribution. No Member may be compelled to accept a distribution of any asset in kind in lieu of a proportionate distribution of money made to the other Members. The LLC may distribute an asset in kind if each part of the asset is fungible with each other part and each person receives a percentage of the asset equal in value to the Member's share of distributions. Except on dissolution and winding up of the LLC, no Member may be compelled to accept a distribution of any asset in kind.

Section 7.04 Priorities among Members

No Member shall be entitled to any priority or preference over any other Member as to the distribution of cash available for distribution or as to the return of capital on dissolution of the LLC.

Section 7.05 Restrictions on Distributions

The LLC shall not make a distribution to Members if after the distribution either of the following applies:

(a) The LLC would not be able to pay its debts as they become due in the ordinary course of the LLC's activities.

(b) The LLC's total assets would be less than the sum of its total liabilities plus the amount that would be needed, if the LLC were to be dissolved, wound up, and terminated at the time of the distribution, to satisfy the preferential rights upon dissolution, winding up, and termination of Members whose preferential rights are superior to those of persons receiving the distribution.

The LLC may base a determination that a distribution is not prohibited as provided above on financial statements prepared on the basis of accounting practices and principles that are reasonable in the circumstances or on a fair valuation or other method that is reasonable under the circumstances.

Section 7.06 Withholding Taxes

The LLC shall withhold all such amounts required by law. Any amounts so withheld shall be treated as a distribution to the Member with respect to whom such withholding obligation arose. The LLC shall remit the sums so withheld and file the required forms with the Internal Revenue Service or other applicable government agency. In the event of any claimed over-withholding, the Member shall be limited to an action against such government agency for a refund and hereby waives any claim or right of action against the LLC on account of such withholding.

Appendix A

ARTICLE VIII. COMPENSATION OF MANAGERS AND MEMBERS

Section 8.01 Salaries of Managers

The Managers of the LLC shall be entitled to reasonable salaries, wages or other compensation only if approved in advance by the holders of a majority of Membership Units.

Section 8.02 Salaries of Members

The Members shall be entitled to salaries, wages or other compensation only if approved in advance by the holders of a majority of Membership Units.

ARTICLE IX. MEETINGS OF MEMBERS

Section 9.01 Place of Meetings

No regular annual, special or other means of Members are required to be held. If held, meetings of Members may be held at any place, by electronic video screen communication or by electronic transmission by and to the LLC pursuant to Sections 17701.02(i)(1) and (2) of the California Corporations Code, either within or without the State of California, selected by the person or persons calling the meeting and subject to approval by the Managers. All meetings shall be held at the principal office of the LLC unless otherwise provided by the Managers.

Section 9.02 Call of Meetings

A meeting of the Members may be called by any Manager or by any Member or Members holding more than 10 percent of the Membership Units for the purpose of addressing any matters on which the Members may vote.

Section 9.03 Notice of Meeting

(a) Whenever Members are required or permitted to take any action at a meeting, a written notice of the meeting shall be given not less than 10 days nor more than 60 days before the date of the meeting to each Member entitled to vote at the meeting. The notice shall state the place, date, and hour of the meeting, the means of electronic transmission by and to the LLC or electronic video screen communication, if any, and the general nature of the business to be transacted. No other business may be transacted at that meeting.

(b) Any report or any notice of a Members' meeting shall be given personally, by electronic transmission by the LLC, or by mail or other means of written communication, addressed to the Member at the address of the Member appearing on the books of the LLC or given by the Member to the LLC for the purpose of notice, or, if no address appears or is given, at the place where the principal office of the LLC is located or by publication at least once in a newspaper of general circulation in the county in which the principal office is located. The notice or report shall be deemed to have been given at the time when delivered personally, delivered by electronic transmission by the LLC, deposited in the mail, or sent by other means of written communication. An affidavit of mailing or delivered by electronic transmission by the LLC of any notice or report in accordance with this article, executed by a Manager, shall be prima facie evidence of the giving of the notice or report.

(c) If any notice or report addressed to the Member at the address of the Member appearing on the books of the LLC is returned to the LLC by the United States Postal

Service marked to indicate that the United States Postal Service is unable to deliver the notice or report to the Member at the address, all future notices or reports shall be deemed to have been duly given without further mailing if they are available for the Member at the principal office of the LLC for a period of one year from the date of the giving of the notice or report to all other Members.

(d) Notice given by electronic transmission by the LLC shall be valid only if it complies with Section 17701.02(i)(1) of the California Corporations Code.

(e) Notwithstanding this condition, notice shall not be given by electronic transmission by the LLC after either of the following has occurred: (i) the LLC is unable to deliver two consecutive notices to the Member by that means; or (ii) the inability to so deliver the notices to the Member becomes known to the Secretary, any Assistant Secretary, or any other person responsible for the giving of the notice.

(f) Upon written request to a Manager by any person entitled to call a meeting of Members, the Manager shall immediately cause notice to be given to the Members entitled to vote that a meeting will be held at a time requested by the person calling the meeting, not less than 10 days nor more than 60 days after the receipt of the request. If the notice is not given within 20 days after receipt of the request, the person entitled to call the meeting may give the notice or, upon the application of that person, the superior court of the county in which the principal office of the LLC is located, or if the principal office is not in this state, the county in which the LLC's address in this state is located, shall summarily order the giving of the notice, after notice to the LLC affording it an opportunity to be heard. The procedure provided in Section 305(c) of the California Corporations Code shall apply to the application. The court may issue any order as may be appropriate, including, without limitation, an order designating the time and place of the meeting, the record date for determination of Members entitled to vote, and the form of notice.

Section 9.04 Quorum

(a) A majority of the Members represented in person or by proxies shall constitute a quorum at a meeting of Members.

(b) The Members present at a duly called or held meeting at which a quorum is present may continue to transact business until adjournment, notwithstanding the loss of a quorum, if any action taken after loss of a quorum, other than adjournment, is approved by the requisite percentage of interests of Members specified .in the California Corporations Code, the Articles of Organization or the Operating Agreement.

(c) In the absence of a quorum, any meeting of Members may be adjourned from time to time by the vote of a majority of the interests represented either in person or by proxy, but no other business may be transacted, except as provided in the prior paragraph

Section 9.05 Adjournment of Meetings

When a Members' meeting is adjourned to another time or place, unless the Articles of Organization or Operating Agreement otherwise require and except as provided in this Article IX, notice need not be given of the adjourned meeting if the time and place thereof or the means of electronic transmission by and to the LLC or electronic video screen communication, if any, are announced at the meeting at which the adjournment is taken. At the adjourned meeting, the LLC may transact any business that may have been transacted at the original meeting. If the adjournment is for more than 45 days, or if after the adjournment a new record date is fixed for the adjourned meeting, a notice of the adjourned meeting shall be given to each Member of record entitled to vote at the meeting.

Section 9.06 Meetings Not Duly Called, Noticed or Held

The actions taken at any meeting of Members, however called and noticed, and wherever held, shall have the same validity as if taken at a meeting duly held after regular call and notice, if a quorum is present either in person or by proxy, and if, either before or after the meeting, each of the Members entitled to vote, not present in person or by proxy, provides a waiver of notice or consents to the holding of the meeting or approves the minutes of the meeting in writing. All waivers, consents, and approvals shall be filed with the LLC records or made a part of the minutes of the meeting after conversion to the form in which those records or minutes are kept. Attendance of a person at a meeting shall constitute a waiver of notice of the meeting, except when the person objects, at the beginning of the meeting, to the transaction of any business because the meeting is not lawfully called or convened. Attendance at a meeting is not a waiver of any right to object to the consideration of matters required by this title to be included in the notice but not so included, if the objection is expressly made at the meeting. Neither the business to be transacted nor the purpose of any meeting of Members need be specified in any written waiver of notice.

Section 9.07 Conference Telephone

Members may participate in a meeting of the LLC through the use of conference telephones or electronic video screen communication, as long as all Members participating in the meeting can hear one another, or by electronic transmission by and to the LLC pursuant Section 17701.02(i)(1) and (2) of the California Corporations Code. Participation in a meeting pursuant to this provision constitutes presence in person at that meeting.

Section 9.08 Statement of Proposal

Any action approved at a meeting, other than by unanimous approval, shall be valid only if the general nature of the proposal so approved was stated in the notice of meeting or in any waiver of notice.

Section 9.09 Consent to Action without Meeting

(a) Any action that may be taken at any meeting of the Members may be taken without a meeting if a consent in writing, setting forth the action so taken, is signed and delivered to the LLC within 60 days of the record date for that action by Members having not less than the minimum number of votes that would be necessary to authorize or take that action at a meeting at which all Members entitled to vote thereon were present and voted.

(b) Unless the consents of all Members entitled to vote have been solicited in writing, (i) notice of any Member approval of an amendment to the Articles of Organization or Operating Agreement, a dissolution of the LLC as provided in Section 17707.01 of the California Corporations Code, or a merger of the LLC as provided in Section 17710.10 of the California Corporations Code, without a meeting by less than unanimous written consent shall be given at least 10 days before the consummation of the action authorized by the approval, and (ii) prompt notice shall be given of the taking of any other action approved by Members without a meeting by less than unanimous written consent, to those Members entitled to vote who have not consented in writing.

(c) Any Member giving a written consent, or the Member's proxy holder, may revoke the consent personally or by proxy by a writing received by the LLC prior to the time that written consents of Members having the minimum number of votes that would be required to authorize the proposed action have been filed with the LLC, but may not do so thereafter. This revocation is effective upon its receipt at the office of the LLC required to be maintained pursuant to Section 17701.13 of the California Corporations Code.

Section 9.10 Proxies

The use of proxies in connection with this section shall be governed in the same manner as in the case of corporations formed under the California General Corporation Law, Division 1 of Title 1. Proxies shall be given as follows:

(a) Every Member entitled to vote may authorize another person or persons to act by proxy for that Member.

(b) No proxy shall be valid after the expiration of 11 months from the date of the proxy unless otherwise provided in the proxy.

(c) A Member may revoke a proxy by a writing stating that the proxy is revoked, by a subsequent proxy signed by the Member, or by attendance and voting at a meeting by the Member who signed the proxy.

(d) The Managers may, in advance of any meetings of Members, prescribe additional regulations concerning the manner of signing and filing of proxies and their validation.

Section 9.11 Record Date

In order that the LLC may determine the Members of record entitled to notices of any meeting or to vote, or entitled to receive any distribution or to exercise any rights in respect of any other lawful action, a Manager, or Members owning more than 10 percent of the Membership Units, may fix, in advance, a record date, that is not more than 60 days nor less than 10 days prior to the date of the meeting and not more than 60 days prior to any other action. If no record date is fixed the following shall apply:

(a) The record date for determining Members entitled to notice of or to vote at a meeting of Members shall be at the close of business on the business day next preceding the day on which notice is given or, if notice is waived, at the close of business on the business day next preceding the day on which the meeting is held. The record date for determining Members entitled to give consent to LLC action in writing without a meeting shall be the day on which the first written consent is given.

(b) The record date for determining Members for any other purpose shall be at the close of business on the day on which the Managers adopt the resolution relating thereto, or the 60th day prior to the date of the other action, whichever is later.

(c) The determination of Members of record entitled to notice of or to vote at a meeting of Members shall apply to any adjournment of the meeting unless a Manager or the Members who called the meeting fix a new record date for the adjourned meeting, but the Manager or the Members who called the meeting shall fix a new record date if the meeting is adjourned for more than 45 days from the date set for the original meeting.

Section 9.12 Electronic Meetings

A meeting of the Members may be conducted, in whole or in part, by electronic transmission by and to the LLC or by electronic video screen communication if both of the following requirements are met:

(a) The LLC implements reasonable measures to provide Members, in person or by proxy, a reasonable opportunity to participate in the meeting and to vote on matters submitted to the Members, including an opportunity to read or hear the proceedings of the meeting substantially concurrently with those proceedings.

(b) When any Member votes or takes other action at the meeting by means of electronic transmission to the LLC or electronic video screen communication, a record of that vote or action shall be maintained by the LLC.

ARTICLE X. MEETINGS OF MANAGERS

Section 10.01 General

When there is more than one Manager, the provisions set forth in this Article shall govern meetings of Managers.

Section 10.02 Time of Meetings

Meetings of Managers shall be held when meetings are called pursuant to Section 10.03 of this Agreement.

Section 10.03 Call of Meetings

Meetings may be called pursuant to the written request of one or more Managers. Meeting may be held for consideration of any of the matters as to which Managers are entitled to vote under this Agreement or under the California LLC Act.

Section 10.04 Notice, Time and Place of Meeting

The Manager or Managers calling a meeting shall give notice of the meeting to all Managers at least 48 hours prior to the meeting. The notice shall state the time and place of the meeting. The notice shall be given by facsimile, personal delivery, telephone or mail. If the notice is given by mail, the notice shall be sent at least four days prior to the meeting.

Meetings of the Managers shall be held at the principal office of the LLC or at any place designated by the Managers calling the meeting.

Section 10.05 Quorum

A majority of the Managers present in person or by conference telephone shall constitute a quorum at a meeting of Managers.

Section 10.06 Meetings Not Duly Called, Noticed or Held

The transactions of any meeting of Managers, however called and noticed, shall be as valid as though taken at a meeting duly held after regular call and notice, if (a) all Managers are present at the meeting and sign a written consent to the holding of the meeting, (b) all Managers are present at the meeting and do not protest prior to the meeting that the meeting was not properly called or noticed, or (c) a majority of the Managers are present at the meeting, either in person or by conference telephone, and those not present sign a waiver of notice and consent to the meeting either before or after the meeting.

Section 10.07 Consent to Action without Meeting

Any action that may be taken at any meeting of the Managers may be taken without a meeting if all of the Managers sign a consent in writing, setting forth the action so taken.

ARTICLE XI. BOOKS, RECORDS AND BANK ACCOUNTS

Section 11.01 Accounting Practices

The LLC shall use the cash method of accounting. The fiscal year of the LLC is the year ending December 31.

Section 11.02 Financial Statements

The Managers shall maintain true and proper books, records, reports and accounts in which all transactions of the LLC shall be accurately entered.

Section 11.03 Maintenance of Records

The Managers shall maintain at the principal office of the LLC within California all of the following records:

(a) A current list of the full name and last known business or residence address of each Member and of each holder of a transferable interest in the LLC set forth in alphabetical order, together with the contribution and the share in profits and losses of each Member and holder of a transferable interest.

(b) A current list of the full name and business or residence address of each manager.

(c) A copy of the Articles of Organization and all amendments thereto, together with any powers of attorney pursuant to which the Articles of Organization or any amendments thereto were executed.

(d) Copies of the LLC's federal, state, and local income tax or information returns and reports, if any, for the six most recent fiscal years.

(e) A copy of the LLC's Operating Agreement, and any amendments thereto, together with any powers of attorney pursuant to which the Operating Agreement or any amendments thereto were executed.

(f) Copies of the financial statement of the LLC, if any, for the six most recent fiscal years.

(g) The books and records of the LLC as they relate to the internal affairs of the LLC for at least the current and past four fiscal years.

Upon request of an assessor, the LLC shall make available at the LLC's principal office in this state a true copy of the business records relevant to the amount, cost, and value of all property that the LLC owns, claims, possesses, or controls within the county.

Section 11.04 Access to Records and Inspection Rights

(a) **Request for Documents**. Upon the request of a Member or holder of a transferable interest, for purposes reasonably related to the interest of that person as a Member or a holder of a transferable interest, a Manager or a Member in possession of the requested information, shall promptly deliver, in writing, to the Member or holder of a transferable interest, at the expense of the LLC, a copy of the information required to be maintained under Sections 17701.13(d)(1), (2), and (4) of the California Corporations Code, and the Operating Agreement of the LLC.

(b) **Other Inspection Rights**. Each Member, Manager, and holder of a transferable interest shall have the right, upon reasonable request, for purposes reasonably related to the interest of that person as a Member, Manager, or holder of a transferable interest, to each of the following: (i) to inspect and copy during normal business hours any of the records required to be maintained pursuant to Section 17701.13 of the Corporations Code; and (ii) to obtain in writing from the LLC, promptly after becoming available, a copy of the LLC's federal, state, and local income tax returns for each year.

(c) **Articles of Organization in Operating Agreement**. A Manager shall promptly furnish to a Member a copy of any amendment to the Articles of Organization or Operating Agreement executed by a Manager pursuant to a power of attorney from the Member. The Articles of Organization or Operating Agreement may be sent by electronic transmission by the LLC.

(d) **Time for Sending Information**. The LLC shall send or cause information to be sent in writing to each Member or holder of a transferable interest within 90 days after the end of each tax year the information necessary to complete federal and state income tax or information returns and, in the case of a LLC with 35 or fewer Members, a copy of the LLC's federal, state, and local income tax or information returns for the year.

(e) **Agent**. Any request, inspection, or copying by a Member or holder of a transferable interest may be made by that person or by that person's agent or attorney.

(f) **Over 35 Members**. If the LLC ever has more than 35 Members, the following additional reporting and inspection rights shall apply:

(i) The Managers shall send an annual report to each of the Members not later than 120 days after the end of the fiscal year. The report may be sent by electronic transmission. The annual report shall contain a balance sheet as of the end of the fiscal year and an income statement and statement of cash flows for the fiscal year.

(ii) Members representing at least five percent of the voting interests of Members, or three or more Members, may make a written request to a Manager for an income statement of the LLC for the initial three-month, six-month or nine-month period of the current fiscal year ended more than 30 days prior to the date of the request, and a balance sheet of the LLC as of the end of that period. The statement shall be delivered or mailed to the Members within 30 days thereafter.

(iii) The financial statements referred to in subparagraphs (f)(i) and (ii) shall be accompanied by the report, if any, of the independent accountants engaged by the LLC. If there is no report or independent account, the financial statements shall be accompanied by a certificate of a Manager of the LLC that the financial statements were prepared without audit from the books and records of the LLC.

Section 11.05 Banking

The Managers shall open and maintain one or more bank accounts in the name of the LLC. All of the funds of the LLC shall be deposited in the bank accounts. No other funds shall be deposited in the accounts. The funds in the LLC bank accounts shall be used solely for the business of the LLC. All withdrawals from the bank account shall be made only on checks signed by the Managers or such other persons as the Managers may from time to time designate.

Section 11.06 Statement of Information

The LLC shall file a Statement of Information with the California Secretary of State within 90 days after the filing of its Articles of Organization and biannually thereafter.

ARTICLE XII. LLC CERTIFICATES

Section 12.01 LLC Certificates

The Managers may in their discretion issue certificates evidencing the Units owned by each Member. The certificates shall be signed by one or more Managers or officers, whose signature may be a facsimile.

Section 12.02 Restrictive Legend

Each LLC certificate shall bear the following restrictive legend, in addition to any other legend that may be required by state and federal securities laws:

THE UNITS REPRESENTED BY THIS CERTIFICATE ARE SUBJECT TO CERTAIN RESTRICTIONS ON TRANSFER PURSUANT TO THE TERMS OF AN OPERATING AGREEMENT ENTERED INTO BY THIS LLC AND THE HOLDER HEREOF, A COPY OF WHICH MAY BE OBTAINED AT THE PRINCIPAL OFFICE OF THE LLC.

ARTICLE XIII. TAXES

Section 13.01 Tax Elections

The Managers may make any tax elections under the Internal Revenue Code or the tax laws of any applicable state or local jurisdiction, including the following:

(a) amortization of the organizational and startup expenses of the LLC under Section 195 of the Internal Revenue Code ratably over a period of 60 months as permitted by Section 709(b) of the Code;

(b) election under Section 754 of the Internal Revenue Code to adjust of the basis of LLC property if the LLC distributes property under Section 734 of the Internal Revenue Code or if a Member transfers a Membership Unit under Section 743 of the Code. The Managers may in their sole discretion decide not to make such an election; and

Appendix A

(c) any other election that the Managers deem appropriate and in the best interests of the LLC.

ARTICLE XIV. TRANSFER OF MEMBERSHIP INTERESTS

Section 14.01 Conditions for Transfer

A Member may not sell, assign, transfer, encumber or otherwise dispose of Membership Units except pursuant to the provisions of this Article 14. Transfers without compliance with this Agreement shall be treated as void.

Section 14.02 Transfers to Family Members

A Member may transfer Units by inter vivos gift, testamentary disposition or sale to a Family Member, or to a trust for the benefit of Family Members, if (a) the Managers consent to the transfer, which consent shall not be unreasonably withheld, and (b) the transferee complies with Section 14.07 of this Agreement. A Family Member shall mean a Member's spouse, parents, siblings, in-laws, children or grandchildren.

Section 14.03 Transfers to Existing Members

A Member may sell or transfer Units to another Member if the transferee complies with Section 14.07 of this Agreement.

Section 14.04 Sales to Third Parties

A Member may sell or transfer Units to a person other than a Family Member (as defined in Section 14.02) or existing Member upon compliance with the following conditions:

(a) **Offer to Purchase**. If a Member decides to sell Membership Units and receives a bona fide offer for the purchase of all or a part of such Units, the Member shall give the Managers written notice setting forth full details of the offer. The notice shall specify the name of the offeror, the number of Units covered by the offer, the terms of payment, and all other material terms and conditions of the offer.

(b) **Right of First Refusal**. Upon receipt of the notice of sale, the LLC may within 60 days thereafter elect to purchase the Units at the same price and on the same terms as offered be the third party. If the LLC does not exercise this option, the Managers shall send a copy of the notice to all Members. The Members shall then have the exclusive right and option, exercisable at any time during a period of 30 days from the date of the notice, to purchase the Units covered by the offer at the same price and on the same terms and conditions set forth in the notice. If there is more than one purchasing Member, each purchasing Member shall be entitled to purchase the offered Units based on the number of Units owned by that Member compared to the number of Units owned by all purchasing Members. If the purchasing Members do not purchase all of the offered Units, the selling Member may sell the remaining Units on the terms and conditions set forth in the notice of sale.

(c) **Rights of Transferee**. A transfer to anyone who is not already a Member or a Family Member (as defined in Section 14.02) shall give the transferee an economic interest in the LLC (the right to receive distributions and allocations of income, gains, losses, deductions, credits or similar items to which the Member would have been entitled to receive prior the sale or other transfer). The transferee shall not become a Member after the sale and the transfer shall not give the transferee information rights or voting rights unless a majority of the Managers consent and the transferee complies with Section 14.07 of this Agreement. The transferee shall be liable for the Member's obligations under Sections 17704.03 and 17704.06(c) of the California Corporations Code.

Section 14.05 Death, Bankruptcy or Incompetency

(a) **Option to Purchase.** If a Member dies, or is adjudged incompetent or a bankrupt by a court of competent jurisdiction, the LLC and the remaining Members shall have a right of first refusal to purchase the Membership Units of any successor in interest in accordance with Section 14.04 of this Agreement when such successor in interest sells or transfers the Membership Units.

(b) **Interest of Successor in Interest.** The successor in interest shall receive only an economic interest in the LLC (the right to receive distributions and allocations of income, gains, losses, deductions, credits or similar items to which the Member would have been entitled to receive prior to death, bankruptcy or incompetency). The successor in interest shall not become a Member and shall not have voting rights or information rights unless a majority of the Managers consent to the successor in interest becoming a Member and the successor in interest complies with Section 14.07 of this Agreement.

(c) **Exercise of Rights by Legal Representative.** If a Member who is an individual dies or is adjudged by a court of competent jurisdiction to be incompetent to manage the Member's person or property, the Member's executor, administrator, guardian, conservator or other legal representative may exercise all of the Member's rights for the purpose of settling the Member's estate or administering the Member's property, including any power the Member had under the Articles of Organization or this Agreement.

Section 14.06 Transfer of Economic Interest

(a) **Right to Transfer.** A Member may not transfer an economic interest in a Membership Unit without transferring the entire Membership Unit unless the Member obtains the consent of the Managers.

(b) **Rights of Transferee.** A transfer of an economic interest does not dissolve the LLC, entitle the transferee to vote or participate in the management and affairs of the LLC, to have information rights, to have put rights with respect to the membership interest, or allow the transferee to become or exercise any rights of a Member. A transfer of an economic interest only gives the transferee an economic interest in the LLC (the right to receive, to the extent transferred, the distributions and the allocations of income, gains, losses, deductions, credits or similar items to which the transferor would have been entitled to receive). The transferee may become a Member if a majority of the Managers consent and the transferee complies with Section 14.07 of this Agreement.

(c) **Effect of Transfer.** Upon the transfer of all or part of an economic interest, the transferor shall provide the Managers with the name and address of the transferee and the details of the interest transferred.

Appendix A

(d) Liabilities. Except to the extent assumed by agreement, the transferee shall have no liability to the LLC prior to becoming a Member solely as a result of the transfer.

(e) Encumbrances. The pledge of or granting of a security interest, lien or other encumbrance in or against a Membership Unit shall not cause the Member to cease to be a Member or give to anyone else the power to exercise any rights or powers of a Member.

Section 14.07 Restrictions on All Transfers

No transfer may be made to any person unless all of the following requirements have been met:

(a) The transferee agrees to be bound by all of the restrictions and provisions of this Agreement. Any person who becomes a Member will be deemed to have assented to all of the provisions of the Operating Agreement.

(b) The transfer does not violate any state or federal securities laws. The Managers may require the Member or transferee to obtain an opinion of counsel that the transfer is being made in compliance with the applicable state and federal securities laws.

(c) The transferee pays any reasonable expenses in connection with the transfer.

(d) The transfer, when added to the total of all other Units sold, transferred or transferred during the preceding 12 month period, does not result in a termination of the LLC under Section 708 of the Internal Revenue Code. An LLC is terminated under Section 708 if there is a sale or exchange of 50 percent or more of the Membership Units during any 12-month period. The Managers may waive compliance with this requirement.

Section 14.08 Disassociation.

(a) Disassociation Events. A person is disassociated as a Member from the LLC when any of the following occur:

(i) The LLC has notice of the person's express will to withdraw as a Member, but, if the person specified a withdrawal date later than the date the LLC had notice, on that later date.

(ii) An event stated in the Operating Agreement as causing the person's dissociation to occur.

(iii) The person is expelled as a Member pursuant to the Operating Agreement.

(iv) The person is expelled as a Member by the unanimous consent of the other Members because any of the following applies: (a) It is unlawful to carry on the LLC's activities with the person as a Member; (b) there has been a transfer of all of the person's transferable interest in the LLC, other than a transfer for security purposes, or a charging order in effect under Section 17705.03 of the California Corporations Code that has not been foreclosed; (c) the person is a corporation and, within 90 days after the LLC notifies the person that it will be expelled as a Member because the person has filed a certificate of dissolution or the equivalent, its charter has been revoked, or its right to conduct business has been suspended by the jurisdiction of its incorporation and the certificate of dissolution has not been revoked or its charter or right to conduct business has not been reinstated; or (d) the person is an LLC or partnership that has been dissolved and whose business is being wound up.

(v) On application by the LLC, the person is expelled as a Member by judicial order because the person has done any of the following: (a) engaged, or is engaging, in wrongful conduct that has adversely and materially affected, or will adversely and materially affect, the LLC's activities; (b) willfully or persistently committed, or is willfully and persistently committing, a material breach of the Operating Agreement or the person's duties or obligations under Section 17704.09 of the California Corporations Code; or (c) engaged, or is engaging, in conduct relating to the LLC's activities that makes it not reasonably practicable to carry on the activities with the person as a Member.

(vi) In the case of a person who is an individual, the person dies;

(vii) In the case of a person that is a trust or is acting as a Member by virtue of being a trustee of a trust, the trust's entire transferable interest in the LLC is distributed but not solely by reason of a substitution of a successor trustee.

(viii) In the case of a person that is an estate or is acting as a Member by virtue of being a personal representative of an estate, the estate's entire transferable interest in the LLC is distributed but not solely by reason of a substitution of a successor personal representative.

(ix) In the case of a Member that is not an individual, partnership, LLC, corporation, trust, or estate, the termination of the Member.

(x) The LLC participates in a merger under Article 10 of the California General Corporation Law (commencing with Section 17710.01 of the California Corporations Code), and either of the following applies: (a) the LLC is not the surviving entity; or (b) otherwise as a result of the merger, the person ceases to be a Member.

(xi) The LLC terminates.

(b) Effect of Disassociation. When a person is dissociated as a Member of a LLC, all of the following shall apply:

(i) The person's right to participate as a Member in the management and conduct of the LLC's activities terminates.

(ii) Subject to Section 17705.04 and Article 10 of the California General Corporation Law (commencing with Section 17710.01), any transferable interest owned by the person immediately before dissociation in the person's capacity as a Member is owned by the person solely as a transferee.

(iii) A person's dissociation as a Member of a LLC does not of itself discharge the person from any debt, obligation, or other liability to the LLC or the other Members that the person incurred while a Member.

ARTICLE XV. INDEMNIFICATION

Section 15.01 Indemnification in Actions by Third Parties

The LLC shall have power to indemnify any person who was or is a party or is threatened to be made a party to any proceeding, by reason of the fact that such person is or was a Manager, Member, employee, officer or agent of the LLC, against expenses, judgments, fines, settlements and other amounts actually and reasonably incurred in connection with such proceeding. The indemnification shall be made only if the Managers determine that the Member or Manager complied with the duties set forth in Section 17704.09 of the California Corporations Code, including (i) the duty of loyalty by a Manager, (ii) the duty of care by a Manager, and (iii) the discharge by a Member of the duties to the LLC and the other Members under the California Corporations Code or under the Operating Agreement or exercise of any other rights, consistent with the obligation of good faith and fair dealing.

Section 15.02 Advance of Expenses

The LLC shall have the power to advance expenses incurred in defending any proceeding prior to the final disposition of such proceeding.

Section 15.03 Liability of Members

The amount of indemnification shall be limited to the assets of the LLC. No Member shall be personally liable as a result of an agreement by the LLC to indemnify any person.

ARTICLE XVI. TERMINATION AND DISSOLUTION

Section 16.01 Dissolution Events

The LLC shall be dissolved, and its affairs shall be wound up, upon any of the following events:

(a) the expiration of the term provided for the existence of the LLC in Section 1.05 of this Agreement;

(b) the consent to dissolve by the holders of a majority of Membership Units;

(c) the passage of 90 consecutive days during which the LLC has no Members, except that on the death of a natural person who is the sole Member of an LLC, the status of the Member, including a membership interest, may pass to the heirs, successors, and assigns of the Member by will or applicable law. The heir, successor, or assign of the Member's interest becomes a substituted Member pursuant to Section 17704.01(d) of the Corporations Code, subject to administration as provided by applicable law, without the permission or consent of the heirs, successors, or assigns or, those administering the estate of the deceased Member;

(d) a decree of judicial dissolution under Section 17707.03 of the California Corporations Code;

(e) a dissolution where the LLC is not performing business pursuant to Section 17707.02 of the California Corporations Code.

Section 16.02 Responsibility for Winding Up

(a) Upon dissolution of the LLC, the business of the LLC shall be wound up by the Managers. If there is no remaining Manager, the business of the LLC shall be wound up by the Members. The person's winding up the affairs of the LLC shall give written notice of the commencement of winding up by mail to all known creditors and claimants whose addresses appear on the records of the LLC.

(b) Upon the petition of any Manager or of any Member or Members, or three or more creditors of a LLC, a court of competent jurisdiction may enter a decree ordering the winding up of the LLC, if that appears necessary for the protection of any parties in interest. The decree shall designate the Managers or Members, or if good cause is shown, another person or persons, who are to wind up the affairs of the LLC.

(c) The persons winding up the business of the LLC shall be entitled to reasonable compensation.

Section 16.03 Liquidation and Winding Up

The persons responsible for winding up the affairs of the LLC shall liquidate the assets of the LLC as promptly as possible, consistent with obtaining a reasonable value for the assets. The liquidation proceeds shall be distributed in the following order:

(a) to creditors of the LLC other than Members;

(b) to Members who are creditors for unpaid loans and advances to the LLC;

(c) to any reserve that the Managers deem reasonably necessary for contingent or unforeseen liabilities or obligations of the LLC;

(d) to the Members in accordance with their positive capital account balances;

(e) to the Members in proportion to the Membership Units owned by each Member compared to the Membership Units owned by all Members.

To the extent possible, a Member shall receive as his or her distributive share the same property that the Member contributed to the LLC.

No Member shall have any obligation to restore a negative capital account upon the liquidation of the LLC.

Section 16.04 Filing Dissolution Documents

Upon dissolution of the LLC, the Managers or person winding up the business of the LLC shall sign and file in the office of the California Secretary a Certificate of Cancellation on Form LLC-4/7.

ARTICLE XVII. AMENDMENT

Section 17.01 Amendment of Articles of Organization

The Articles of Organization may be amended by the vote of the holders of a majority of Membership Units.

Section 17.02 Amendment of Operating Agreement

This Operating Agreement may be amended by the vote of the holders of a majority of Membership Units.

ARTICLE XVIII. SECURITIES LAWS

Section 18.01 California Securities Laws

Pursuant to Section 25102(f) of the California Corporations Code, the Members who are acquiring Units by original issuance (rather than by transfer) certify that:

Appendix A

(a) They have (i) a preexisting personal or business relationship with the LLC or one or more of its officers, Managers or control persons, or (ii) the capacity to protect their own interests in connection with the LLC and the acquisition of Units by reason of their business or financial experience or the business or financial experience of their professional advisors who are unaffiliated with and who are not compensated by the LLC or any affiliate or selling agent of the LLC, directly or indirectly,

(b) They are acquiring the Units for their own account (or for a trust account if the Member is a trust) and not with a view to or for sale in connection with any distribution of the Units.

Section 18.02 Other Investment Representations

Each Member also represents, acknowledges or understands that:

(a) The Member is a bona fide resident of the State of California.

(b) The Member is financially able to bear the economic risk of an investment in the LLC, including a total loss of the investment.

(c) The Membership Units are restricted under the Securities Act of 1933 and may not be resold without registration under that Act or pursuant to an exemption from registration.

(d) The LLC is newly organized and has no financial or operating history. The Membership Units are a highly speculative investment and involve a high degree of risk of loss.

(e) The Member has received and reviewed all information that the Member considers necessary or appropriate in deciding whether to acquire the Membership Units. The Member has had an opportunity to ask question and receive answers from the LLC and its officers and Managers regarding the terms and conditions of purchase of the Membership Units and the business, financial affairs and other aspects of the LLC. The Member has also had the opportunity to obtain all information (to the extent the LLC possesses such information or can acquire it without unreasonable effort or expense) which the Member deems necessary or advisable to evaluate the investment and to verify the accuracy of information provided to the Member.

(f) Neither the officers, Managers, employees, agents nor any other person associated with the LLC has made any representations that (i) the Member may freely transfer the Units, (ii) that a specified profit or other amount will be realized as a result of the investment in the LLC, (iii) that past performance by officers, Managers or other persons in any way indicates a predictable investment return or overall business results for the LLC, (iv) that the LLC will be able to make cash distributions from operations or otherwise by a specified date, or that such distributions will be made at all, or (v) that the investment in Units will result in any specific tax benefits.

(g) The Member has been advised to consult with his or her own attorney and accountant regarding all legal and tax matters concerning an investment in the LLC, and the Member has done so to the extent the Member considers necessary. The Member has and will in the future look solely to and rely upon his or her own advisers regarding the tax consequences of this investment.

ARTICLE XIX. RESTRICTIONS ON POWERS

Section 19.01 General Restrictions

Notwithstanding any provision of this Agreement to the contrary, this Agreement shall not do any of the following except as provided in Section 17701.10 of the California Corporations Code:

(a) vary the LLC's capacity under Corporations Code Section 17701.05 to sue and be sued in its own name;

(b) vary the law applicable under Corporations Code Section 17701.06;

(c) vary the power of the California courts under Corporations Code Section 17702.04;

(d) except as provided in Corporations Code Section 17701.10(d)-(g) eliminate the contractual obligation of good faith and fair dealing under Corporations Code Section 17704.09(d);

(e) unreasonably restrict the duties and rights under Corporations Code Section 17704.10 with respect to the disclosure obligations of the LLC and the inspection rights of Members;

(f) vary the power of the court to decree dissolution in the circumstances specified in Corporations Code Section 17707.03 or the provisions for avoidance of dissolution in Corporations Code Section 17707.03(c);

(g) vary the requirements under Corporations Code Sections 17707.04 to 17707.08 regarding the winding up and dissolution of the LLC except as provided therein;

(h) unreasonably restrict the right of a Member to maintain an action under Article 9 regarding class actions and actions against the LLC;

(i) restrict the rights of Members to approve a merger, conversion or domestication under Corporations Code Section 17710.14 with respect to a Member that will have a personal liability to a surviving, converted or domesticated organization;

(j) restrict the rights of a person other than a Member or Manager except as provided in Corporations Code Section 17701.12(b);

(k) vary any provision under Article 10 of the California Corporations Code, Section 17710.01 et seq. regarding mergers and conversions;

(l) vary any provision under Article 12 of the California Corporations Code, Section 17712.01 et seq. regarding different classes of membership interests;

(m) eliminate the duty of loyalty under Corporations Code Section 17704.09(b) except as provided in Corporations Code Section 17701.10(c)(14);

(n) unreasonably reduce the duty of care of Members under Corporations Code Section 17704.09(c);

(o) eliminate the obligation of good faith and fair dealing under Section 17704.09(d) except as provided therein;

(p) vary the definitions in Corporations Code Section 17701.02 except as specifically provided therein;

(q) eliminate or limit the Member's or Manager's liability to the LLC and other Members to the extent provided in Corporations Code Section 17701.10(g).

Appendix A

ARTICLE XX. FEDERAL AUDIT PROCEDURES

Section 20.01 Partnership Representative

The Managers shall designate one of Members or other person with a substantial presence in the United States to be the "partnership representative" pursuant to Section 6223(a) of the Internal Revenue Code. The partnership representative shall have sole authority to act on behalf of the LLC in any tax audit proceedings, to settle or compromise any matter in respect of taxes of the LLC, to waive any period of limitations, and to otherwise bind the LLC in any proceeding or claim in respect of taxes. The initial partnership representative is _____.

Section 20.02 Indemnity and Reimbursement for LLC Tax Liabilities

Each of the Members agrees to indemnify and reimburse the LLC for any tax liabilities incurred by the LLC as a result of a federal or state tax audit pursuant to the following provisions:

(a) If the LLC, pursuant to Section 6225 of the Internal Revenue Code (and/or any successor provisions thereto), the LLC is liable for U.S. federal income taxes, including interest and penalties thereon, with respect any adjustment resulting from a U.S. federal income tax audit of the LLC, the Members and/or former Members of the LLC shall indemnify and hold the LLC harmless from and against any such taxes, interest and penalties based on their respective pro rata shares of such amounts. For purposes of the preceding sentence, each Member's or former Member's "pro rata share" of any such amounts shall be in proportion to his or her respective distributive or allocable shares of the items of net income, gain, profits or other items which give rise to such taxes, interest or penalties, such distributive or allocable shares being determined pursuant to the terms of this Agreement for the year to which such audit relates. If the amount of such taxes, penalties or interest which the LLC is otherwise required to pay has been reduced pursuant to Section 6225(c) of the Internal Revenue Code (and/or any regulations promulgated thereunder) by reason of the status, attributes or actions of a particular Member or former Member (the "Specified Member"), then the Board shall have the authority (in its reasonable discretion) to apply such reduction as reduction solely to such Specified Member's indemnity obligations pursuant to this paragraph. Such allocation by the Managers shall be final, conclusive and binding upon all Members and/or former Members.

(b) Payment by each Member or former Member of any amount that it is obligated to pay to the LLC pursuant to this Section shall be made within five business days following written notice from the LLC. The LLC shall, at its election, be entitled to withhold from and offset any amounts distributable or payable by the LLC to any Member or former Member to the extent of any obligation of such Member or former Member pursuant to this Section, and any amounts that are so withheld shall, for purposes of this Agreement, be treated as though they had been distributed and/or paid to such Member or former Member. Each of the Members hereby acknowledges and agrees that their respective obligations and duties pursuant to this Section shall (unless otherwise expressly provided otherwise in a written agreement by and among such Member and the LLC) continue following such Member's withdrawal or termination as a Member for any reason

(c) Each of the Members covenants and agrees to provide to the LLC (from time to time) such certificates, forms or instruments regarding the identity and/or classification for U.S. federal and applicable state tax purposes of such Member (and/or any direct or indirect beneficial owners of such Member), together with such identifying information relating to such Member (and/or any such direct or indirect beneficial owners of such Member), including but not limited to names, addresses, taxpayer identification numbers and/or similar information, as may be requested from time to time by the LLC in order to comply with and/or make any election pursuant to, any provision of U.S. federal and/or applicable state or local tax laws, rules or regulations from time to time. Each Member hereby further agrees that, after providing the LLC with any information described in the immediately preceding sentence, such Member shall notify the LLC of any change with respect to such information from time to time.

Section 20.03 Separate Member Audit

The Managers may in their discretion elect under Section 6221 of the Internal Revenue Code not to have any partnership item (and any penalty, addition to tax, or additional amount which relates to an adjustment to a partnership item) determined at the LLC level. The election may be made during any year in which the LLC meets the following requirements:

(a) Each Member of the LLC is an individual, C corporation, a foreign entity that would be treated as a C corporation if it were domestic entity, an S corporation, or an estate of a deceased member. A Member may not transfer Membership Units to any person who is not one of such qualified persons without the prior consent of the Managers.

(b) The LLC has 100 or fewer members.

(c) The LLC files an election under Section 6221(b) of the Internal Revenue Code. The election must be filed on an annual basis with a timely filed return for the year. The election must include the name and taxpayer identification number of each Member, including the name and tax identification number of each S corporation shareholder if an S corporation is a member of the LLC.

Section 20.04 Pass-Through to Members During Reviewed Year (Pushout Election)

The Managers may in their discretion elect under Section 6226 of the Internal Revenue Code to issue to each Member during the "reviewed year" an adjusted information return showing each Member's share of adjustments to income, gain, loss, deduction or credit as determined in the notice of final ownership adjustment. The "reviewed year" is the tax year to which a federal tax audit adjustment relates. The LLC must issue the adjusted information return within 45 days after the IRS issues the notice of final partnership adjustment. In such case, each Member during the reviewed year (rather than the LLC) shall be responsible for his or her allocable share of the taxes attributable to the audit adjustment item.

Section 20.05 Adjustment of Tax Assessment Amount

The Managers may in their discretion request that the IRS reduce the amount of any imputed underpayment pursuant to Section 6225(c) of the Internal Revenue Code and regulations thereunder based on certain member-level information provided to the IRS, including a request based on amended tax returns and payments of additional taxes by Members during the audit review year pursuant to Section 6225(c)(2) of the Internal Revenue Code and Prop. Treas. Reg. § 301.6225-2(d)(2). In

Appendix A

such event, the Members agree to take all actions reasonably requested by the Managers to qualify for such modification.

ARTICLE XXI. MISCELLANEOUS PROVISIONS

Section 21.01 Severability

If any provision of this Agreement is declared by a court of competent jurisdiction to be invalid, void or unenforceable, the remaining provisions shall continue in full force and effect.

Section 21.02 Counterparts

This Agreement may be signed in several counterparts, and all counterparts so executed shall constitute one agreement which shall be binding on all of the parties. It shall not be necessary for all Members to sign the same copy of this Agreement.

Section 21.03 Arbitration

If there is a dispute which cannot be resolved by or among the Members and/or Managers arising out of or related to this Agreement or the LLC, or to the interpretation, application, enforceability or validity of this Agreement, the dispute shall be resolved by binding arbitration in Los Angeles, California in accordance with the Rules of the American Arbitration Association. Judgment on the award may be entered in any court having jurisdiction thereof. The arbitration proceedings shall be limited to one day of oral hearings in order to reduce costs and expenses.

Section 21.04 Successors

Subject to the restrictions against transfer of interests contained herein, this Agreement shall inure to the benefit of and shall be binding upon the heirs, successors in interest, assigns, personal representatives, estates and legatees of each of the Members.

Section 21.05 Entire Agreement

This Agreement and the Articles of Organization for the LLC contain the entire understanding among the Members and supersede any prior written or oral agreements respecting the subject matter contained herein. There are no representations, agreements, arrangements or understandings, oral or written, between or among the Members relating to the subject matter of this Agreement that are not set forth herein.

Section 21.06 Third Party Beneficiaries

There are no third party beneficiaries to this Agreement.

Section 21.07 Facsimile and Scanned Signatures

This Agreement may be signed by a party's signature transmitted by facsimile ("fax") or by scanned copy (pdf file), and copies of this Agreement signed and delivered by means of faxed or scanned signatures shall have the same force and effect as copies signed and delivered with original signatures. Each party may rely upon faxed or scanned signatures as if such signatures were originals. Any party signing and delivering this Agreement by fax or pdf file shall promptly thereafter deliver a counterpart signature page of this Agreement containing the party's original signature.

Section 21.08 Waiver of Conflict of Interest

Each of the Members and other parties to this Agreement understand and acknowledge that (a) the LLC has retained the law firm of Barton, Klugman & Oetting LLP to prepare this Agreement and the other organization documents for the LLC, and to represent him and the LLC after its formation; (b) Barton, Klugman & Oetting LLP does not represent any Member and has no duty to advise or consult with any Member in the absence of a written agreement explicitly providing for such representation; (c) each Member has been and is hereby advised to seek and consult with independent legal and investment counsel regarding the legal and investment consequences to him or her arising from or in connection with this Agreement; (d) if there is a dispute between or among the LLC, Members, Managers, officers, employees or other persons, then Barton, Klugman & Oetting LLP may represent the LLC and/or any Member or Manager to the extent permitted by the California Rules of Professional Conduct; (e) there is an inherent conflict of interest among the parties to this Agreement because the LLC, Members, Managers, officers and employees have conflicting rights, interests, responsibilities and liabilities in the formation, operation and dissolution of the LLC; and (f) each Member waives any and all objections to such conflicts of interest.

DATED: _____, 2018

_____, LLC

By _____

MANAGERS:

_____

_____

MEMBERS

_____

_____

EXHIBIT A			
Name and Address of Each Member	Capital Contribution	Membership Units	Percentage

EXHIBIT B
SPECIAL BOOK AND TAX ALLOCATIONS

ARTICLE I. SPECIAL ALLOCATIONS RULES

Section 1.01 Special Book Allocations

The LLC shall make the following special book allocations in the following order:

(a) Partnership Minimum Gain Chargeback. Except as otherwise provided in Treas. Reg. § 1.704-2(f), if there is a net decrease in Partnership Minimum Gain during any tax year of LLC, the LLC shall specially allocate to each Member items of LLC income and gain for such year (and, if necessary, subsequent years) in an amount equal to such Member's share of the net decrease in Partnership Minimum Gain, determined in accordance with Treas. Reg. § 1.704-2(g). Such allocations shall be made in proportion to the respective amounts required to be allocated to each Member pursuant thereto. The items so allocated shall be determined in accordance with Treas. Reg. §§ 1.704-2(f)(6) and 1.704-2(j)(2). Section 1.01(a) of Exhibit B is intended to comply with the partnership minimum gain chargeback requirement in Treas. Reg. § 1.704-2(f) and shall be interpreted consistently therewith.

(b) Partner Minimum Gain Chargeback. Except as otherwise provided in Treas. Reg. § 1.704-2(i)(4), if there is a net decrease in Partner Nonrecourse Debt Minimum Gain attributable to a Partner Nonrecourse Debt during any tax year of LLC, each Member who has a share of the Partner Nonrecourse Debt Minimum Gain attributable to such Partner Nonrecourse Debt, determined in accordance with Treas. Reg. § 1.704-2(i)(5), shall be specially allocated items of LLC income and gain for such year (and, if necessary, subsequent years) in an amount equal to such Member's share of the net decrease in Partner Nonrecourse Debt Minimum Gain, determined in accordance with Treas. Reg. § 1.704-2(i)(4). Such allocations shall be made in proportion to the respective amounts required to be allocated to each Member pursuant thereto. The items so allocated shall be determined in accordance with Treas. Reg. §§ 1.704-2(i)(4) and (5) and 1.704-2(j)(2). Section 1.01(b) of Exhibit B is intended to comply with the partner minimum gain chargeback requirement in Treas. Reg. § 1.704-2(i)(4) and shall be interpreted consistently therewith.

(c) Qualified Income Offset. If a Member unexpectedly receives an adjustment, allocation or distribution described in Treas. Reg. § 1.704-1(b)(2)(ii)(d)(4), 1.704-1(b)(2)(ii)(d)(5) or 1.704-1(b)(2)(ii)(d)(6), the LLC shall specially allocate items of income and gain to such Member in an amount and manner sufficient to eliminate, to the extent required by the Treasury Regulations, the Adjusted Capital Account Deficit of the Member as quickly as possible. An allocation pursuant to this Section 1.01(c) shall be made only if and to the extent that the Member would have an Adjusted Capital Account Deficit after all other allocations provided for in this Exhibit B have tentatively been made. The LLC shall use the alternative safe-harbor test under Section 1.704-1(b)(2)(ii) of the Treasury Regulations (including the qualified income offset provision referred to above) so that Members will not be required to restore deficit capital account balances on dissolution of the LLC.

Section 1.02 Stop Loss Reallocations

The LLC shall not allocate losses or deductions to a Member to the extent that such losses or deductions create a deficit Capital Account balance for that Member in excess of the sum of the amounts that such Member is deemed obligated to restore pursuant to the penultimate sentences of Treas. Reg. §§ 1.704-2(g)(1) and 1.704-2(i)(5), including (i) any deficit amount that the Member is required to pay back to the LLC on liquidation, and (ii) the Member's share of Partnership Minimum Gain. Any loss not allocated to a Member as result of this restriction must be allocated to the other members (to the extent such other Members are not also limited with respect to loss allocations). Partnership Nonrecourse Deductions that create a deficit Capital Account balance shall be disregarded for such purposes since Partnership Nonrecourse Deductions result in Partnership Minimum Gain that is added back to the Member's Adjusted Capital Account.

Section 1.03 Nonrecourse Deductions

(a) Partnership Nonrecourse Deductions. The LLC shall allocate Partnership Nonrecourse Deductions, as defined in Treas. Reg. § 1.704-2(b)(1) and determined in accordance with Treas. Reg. § 1.704-2(c), to the Members pro rata in accordance with the number of Membership Units held by each Member.

(b) Partner Nonrecourse Deductions. The LLC shall specially allocate Partner Nonrecourse Deductions to the Members who bear the economic risk of loss with respect to the liability to which such Partner Nonrecourse Deductions are attributable in accordance with Treas. Reg. § 1.704-2(i)(1).

Section 1.04 Curative Allocations

The allocations set forth in §§ 1.01 through 1.03 of this Exhibit B ("Regulatory Allocations") are intended to comply with certain requirements of the Treasury Regulations. To the extent possible, all Regulatory Allocations shall be offset either with other Regulatory Allocations or with special allocations of other items of LLC income, gain, loss or deduction. Therefore, notwithstanding any other provision of the Operating Agreement or this Exhibit B (other than the Regulatory Allocations), the LLC shall make such offsetting special allocations of LLC income, gain, loss or deduction in whatever manner the Managers determine appropriate so that, after such offsetting allocations are made, each Member's Capital Account balance is, to the extent possible, equal to the Capital Account balance such Member would have had if the Regulatory Allocations were not part of this Agreement and if all LLC items were allocated pursuant to § 6.01 of the Operating Agreement.

Section 1.05 Section 754 Adjustments

If the LLC makes an election under Section 754 of the Internal Revenue Code, the LLC will adjust the tax basis of its assets pursuant to Sections 734(b) or 743(b) of the Internal Revenue Code. If the LLC is required to adjust the Capital Accounts of Members pursuant to Treas. Reg. § 1.704-1(b)(2)(iv)(m)(2) or 1.704-1(b)(2)(iv)(m)(4), any such adjustment shall be treated as an item of gain (if the adjustment increases the basis of the asset) or loss (if the adjustment decreases such basis). The gain or loss shall be specially allocated among the Members in a manner consistent with the manner in which their capital accounts are required to be adjusted. The gain or loss shall also be included in any calculation of the aggregate net profit or net loss allocated to a Member for the purpose of determining the amount of any subsequent allocation that Member is to receive pursuant to this Agreement.

Section 1.06 Guaranteed Payments

To the extent the Internal Revenue Service determines that compensation paid by the LLC to a Member is not a guaranteed payment under Code Section 707(c) or is not paid to the Member other than in its capacity as a Member within the meaning of Code Section 707(a), the LLC shall specially allocate to such Member gross income in an amount equal to that compensation.

Section 1.07 Section 704(c) Tax Allocations

If a Member contributes property to the LLC (or is deemed to have contributed such property on revaluation of LLC assets) that has a tax basis different from its capital account value on the date of contribution, the LLC shall allocate income, gain, loss and deduction with respect to such property among the Members so as to take account of the variation between the tax basis and fair market value of the property at the time of contribution. The allocations shall be made in accordance with Code Section 704(c) and the Regulations thereunder. In making the allocations for contributed property, the LLC shall use the traditional method described in Treas. Reg. § 1.704-3(b). Such allocation shall be made solely for purposes of federal, state and local taxes. The LLC shall not take these allocations into account in computing a Member's share of profits, losses or other capital account items, or share of distributions.

Section 1.08 Revaluation of Assets

The Capital Accounts of the Members shall be adjusted to reflect a revaluation of all of the assets of LLC (including intangible assets) in accordance with Treas. Reg. § 1.704-1(b)(2)(iv)(f) if there is (i) a capital contribution of money or other property (other than a de minimis amount) by a new or existing Member as consideration for a Membership Unit, (ii) the liquidation of LLC or a distribution of money or other property (other than a de minimis amount) by LLC to a Member as consideration for a Membership Unit, or (iii) the grant of a Membership Unit (other than a de minimis Interest) as consideration for the provision of services to or for the benefit of LLC by an existing Member acting in the capacity of a Member or by a new Member acting in the capacity of a Member or in anticipation of being a Member. After the revaluation, the LLC shall determine each Member's share of depreciation, depletion, amortization and gain or loss for tax purposes so as to take account of the variation between the adjusted tax basis and book value of such revalued LLC assets. The revaluation allocations shall be made in the manner required under Section 704(c) of the Internal Revenue Code and regulations thereunder.

Section 1.09 Book Depreciation, Amortization

The amount of book depreciation, depletion or amortization for each tax year shall be based on the tax depreciation, depletion or amortization multiplied by a fraction. The numerator of the fraction shall be the book value of the asset on the date of contribution, and the denominator shall be the tax basis. If such property has a zero adjusted tax basis, the book depreciation, depletion, or amortization may be determined under any reasonable method selected by the Managers.

Section 1.10 Allocations in Respect of Transferred Units and New Units Issued

(a) If Membership Units are transferred, or if a Member's percentage interest in the LLC is increased or decreased as a result of the issuance of additional Membership Units or otherwise, each item of income, gain, loss, deduction and credit of the LLC during such fiscal year shall be assigned pro rata to each day in the year to which such items are attributable (i.e., the day on or during which it is accrued or otherwise incurred). The amount of each such item so assigned shall be allocated to the Members based on the Membership Units owned by each Member at the close of the day.

(b) For the purpose of accounting convenience, the LLC shall treat such transfer of a Unit, or increase or decrease in a Member's percentage interest, which occurs at any time during a semi-monthly period as having taken place on the last day of the semi-monthly period. Sales, dispositions and issuances of Units that take place during the first 15 days of a month shall be treated as having been made on the 15th day of the month. All other sales, dispositions and issuances of Units shall be treated as having been made on the last day of the month.

(c) Notwithstanding the foregoing, gain or loss realized by the LLC on the sale or other disposition of assets of the LLC shall be allocated solely to the Members owning Membership Units as of such date.

(d) The Managers may elect to use any reasonable proration method of accounting instead of the interim closing of the books method of accounting.

ARTICLE II. DEFINITIONS

In this Agreement, including in this <u>Exhibit B</u>, except as otherwise provided or the context otherwise requires, the following terms shall have the following meanings:

"Adjusted Capital Account" means the capital account at the end of a tax year (i) increased by amounts that the Member is obligated to restore under Treas. Reg. § 1.704-1(b)(2)(ii)(c), (ii) increased by the amount that the Member is deemed obligated to restore under Treas. Reg. § § 1.704-2(g) and 1.704-2(i)(5), (iii) decreased by the amount of all losses and deductions that, as of the end of the tax year are reasonably expected to be allocated to such Member in subsequent tax years under Sections 704(e)(2) and 706(d) of the Internal Revenue Code and Treas. Reg. § 1.751-1(b)(2)(ii), and (iv) decreased by the items described in Treas. Reg. § § 1.704-1(b)(2)(ii)(d)(4), (5), and (6), including the amount of distributions that, as of the end of the tax year, are reasonably expected to be made to the Member in subsequent taxable periods in accordance with the terms of this Agreement. The foregoing definition of Adjusted Capital Account is intended to comply with the provisions of Treas. Reg. § 1.704-1(b)(2)(ii)(d) and shall be interpreted consistently therewith.

"Adjusted Capital Account Deficit" means, with respect to any Member, the deficit balance, if any, in the Member's Adjusted Capital Account.

"Capital Account" shall have the meaning specified in Section 5.05 of this Agreement. If any Interests are transferred pursuant to the terms of this Agreement, the transferee shall succeed to the Capital Account of the transferor to the extent the

Capital Account is attributable to the transferred Interests in accordance with Treas. Reg. § 1.704-1(b)(2)(iv)(1). If the book value of property of LLC is revalued pursuant to Section 1.08 of this Exhibit B, the Capital Account of each Member shall be adjusted to reflect the aggregate adjustment in the same manner as if LLC had recognized gain or loss equal to the amount of such aggregate adjustment. The definition of "Profits" and "Losses" of LLC includes any such adjustment as a gain or loss from the disposition of such asset so that the amount of the adjustment to each Member's Capital Account is properly determined. It is intended that the Capital Accounts of all Members shall be maintained in compliance with the provisions of Treas. Reg. § 1.704-1(b), and all provisions of this Agreement relating to the maintenance of Capital Accounts shall be interpreted and applied in a manner consistent with that Regulation.

"Code" means the Internal Revenue Code of 1986, as amended.

"Partner Nonrecourse Debt" has the meaning set forth in Treas. Reg. § 1.704-2(b)(4).

"Partner Nonrecourse Debt Minimum Gain" means an amount, with respect to each Partner Nonrecourse Debt, equal to the Partnership Minimum Gain that would result if such Partner Nonrecourse Debt were treated as a Nonrecourse Liability, determined in accordance with Treas. Reg. § 1.704-2(i)(3).

"Partnership Minimum Gain" has the meaning set forth in Treas. Reg. §§ 1.704-2(b)(2) and 1.704-2(d).

"Partnership Nonrecourse Deductions" is defined in Treas. Reg. §§ 1.704-2(b)(1) and determined in accordance with Treas. Reg. § 1.704-2(c). Partnership Nonrecourse Deductions are deductions that cause the book value of LLC assets to fall below the outstanding nonrecourse loan balance encumbering such assets. Partnership Nonrecourse Deductions create Partnership Minimum Gain that is added to the Adjusted Capital Accounts of Members, thus eliminating any negative Adjusted Capital Account balance caused by such allocation.

"Partner Nonrecourse Deductions" has the meaning set forth in Treas. Reg. §§ 1.704-2(i)(1) and 1.704-2(i)(2).

"Nonrecourse Deductions" has the meaning set forth in Treas. Reg. § 1.704-2(b)(1).

"Nonrecourse Liability" has the meaning set forth in Treas. Reg. § 1.704-2(b)(3).

"Profits" and "Losses" mean, for each tax year of LLC, the LLC's taxable income or loss determined in accordance with Code Section 703(a), with the following adjustments:

(i) All items of income, gain, loss, deduction or credit required to be stated separately pursuant to Code Section 703(a)(1) shall be included in computing taxable income or loss;

(ii) Any income of LLC that is exempt from federal income tax and not otherwise taken into account in computing Profits or Losses pursuant to this definition of "Profits" and "Losses" shall be added to such taxable income or loss;

(iii) Gain or loss resulting from any taxable disposition of property of LLC shall be computed by reference to the book value of the property disposed of as adjusted under Treas. Reg. § 1.704-1(b) ("adjusted book value"), notwithstanding the fact that the adjusted book value differs from the adjusted basis of the property for federal income tax purposes;

(iv) In lieu of the depreciation, amortization or cost recovery deductions allowable in computing taxable income or loss, there shall be taken into account the depreciation computed based upon the adjusted book value of the asset;

(v) Any expenditures of the LLC described in Code Section 705(a)(2)(B) or treated as such pursuant to Treas. Reg. § 1.704-1(b)(2)(iv)(i) and not otherwise taken into account in computing Profits or Losses pursuant to this definition of "Profits" and "Losses" shall be subtracted from taxable income or loss;

(vi) If the book value of property of LLC is revalued pursuant to Section 1.08 of this Exhibit B, then the amount of such adjustment shall be taken into account as gain or loss from the disposition of such asset; and

(vii) Notwithstanding any other provision of this definition, any items which are specifically allocated pursuant to the provisions of Sections 1.01 through 1.04 of this Exhibit B, shall not be taken into account in computing Profit or Loss.

Appendix B

Summary of Revenue Rulings, Revenue Procedures, and Announcements

PART 1.

REVENUE RULINGS

2007-42 Tax-Free Spin-Off

A corporation that owned an interest in an LLC that was classified as a partnership satisfied the active trader business test for a spin-off under Code Sec. 355(b). The business activities of the LLC were attributed to the corporate owner of the LLC even though the owner and its employees were not involved in the management or operation of the LLC.

2004-88 Tax Matters Partner and Unified Audit Procedures

If a single-member disregarded LLC is the general partner of a limited partnership, the owner of the disregarded LLC may not become a tax matters partner for the limited partnership. However, the disregarded LLC may be designated as a tax matters partner.

A limited partnership with fewer than 10 partners cannot be excluded from the TEFRA partnership audit provisions if the general partner is a single-member disregarded LLC.

2004-77 Classification of LLC with Disregarded Member

An LLC cannot be classified as a partnership if it has two members, one of which is a corporation and the other which is a single-member disregarded LLC owned by the corporate member.

2004-47 LLC Owned Jointly by Charity and For-Profit Corporation

A university may form an LLC with a for-profit corporation to provide teacher training seminars at off-campus locations using interactive video technology contributed by the for-profit corporation. The university will not lose its exempt status if it contributes part of its assets to the LLC, if the activities of the LLC are substantially related to the university's tax-exempt purposes. There may be shared control between the university and the for-profit corporation under appropriate circumstances.

There is no unrelated business taxable income on the distributive share of income payable by the LLC to the university if the activities of the LLC are substantially related to the university's exempt purposes.

2004-41 Liability of Members for Employment Taxes

Members of a multi-member LLC are not liable for unpaid federal employment taxes if the members are not liable for the debts of the LLC under state law. However, the members may be liable for the trust fund recovery penalty under Code Sec. 6672, depending on the facts and circumstances.

99-6 Conversion from Partnership Status to Disregarded Entity[1]

An LLC that is classified as a partnership for federal tax purposes may convert to a disregarded entity if one person purchases all of the membership interests in the LLC. The LLC may elect to be classified as a corporation for federal tax purposes. If no election is made, the LLC will be classified as a disregarded entity.

The tax consequences are as follows if one member of an LLC purchases all of the membership interests from the other members:

- The partnership status of the LLC terminates when the member purchases all the membership interests from the other members. The old members must treat the transaction as a sale of a partnership interest. The old members must report gain or loss, if any, resulting from the sale of the membership interests.
- The LLC is deemed to have made a liquidating distribution of all its assets to its members. Following this deemed distribution, the sole remaining member is treated as acquiring the assets that are deemed to have been distributed to the old members in liquidation of the old members' membership interests.
- The remaining member's basis in the assets attributable to the old members' interests in the LLC is the purchase price for the membership interests. The remaining member's holding period for those assets begins on the day immediately following the date of sale.
- Upon termination of the partnership, the remaining member is considered to have received a distribution of assets attributable to the remaining member's former interest in the LLC. The remaining member must recognize gain or loss, if any, on the deemed distribution of those assets. The remaining member's basis in the assets received in the deemed liquidation of the membership interest is determined under Code Sec. 732(b). The remaining member's holding period for those assets attributable to the member's interest in the LLC includes the LLC's holding period for such assets.

The tax consequences are as follows if a third party who is not a member purchases all of the membership interests in the LLC:

- The old members must report gain or loss, if any, resulting from the sale of their membership interests.
- For purposes of classifying the acquisition of membership interests by a new member, the LLC is deemed to have made a liquidating distribution of those assets to its members. Immediately following the distribution, the new member is deemed to have acquired by purchase all of the former LLC's assets.

---

[1] 1999-5 IRB 6.

- The new member's basis in the assets is equal to the basis of the membership interest allocated among the assets in accordance with Code Sec. 732(c).
- The new member's basis in the assets is equal to the cash purchase price for the membership interest.
- The new member's holding period for the assets begins on the day immediately following the date of sale.

99-5 Conversion from Partnership Status to Disregarded Entity[2]

An LLC that is classified as a partnership for federal tax purposes may convert to a disregarded entity if one person purchases all of the membership interests in the LLC. The LLC may elect to be classified as a corporation for federal tax purposes. If no election is made, the LLC will be classified as a disregarded entity.

The tax consequences are as follows if one member of an LLC purchases all of the membership interests from the other members:

- The partnership status of the LLC terminates when the member purchases all the membership interests from the other members. The old members must treat the transaction as a sale of a partnership interest. The old members must report gain or loss, if any, resulting from the sale of the membership interests.
- The LLC is deemed to have made a liquidating distribution of all its assets to its members. Following this deemed distribution, the sole remaining member is treated as acquiring the assets that are deemed to have been distributed to the old member in liquidation of the old members' membership interests.
- The remaining member's basis in the assets attributable to the old members' interests in the LLC is the purchase price for the membership interests. The remaining member's holding period for those assets begins on the day immediately following the date of sale.
- Upon termination of the partnership, the remaining member is considered to have received a distribution of assets attributable to the remaining member's former interest in the LLC. The remaining member must recognize gain or loss, if any, on the deemed distribution of those assets. The remaining member's basis in the assets received in the deemed liquidation of the membership interest is determined under Code Sec. 732(b). The remaining member's holding period for those assets attributable to the member's interest in the LLC includes the LLC's holding period for such assets.

The tax consequences are as follows if a third party who is not a member purchases all of the membership interests in the LLC:

- The old members must report gain or loss, if any, resulting from the sale of their membership interests.
- For purposes of classifying the acquisition of membership interests by a new member, the LLC is deemed to have made a liquidating distribution of

---

[2] 1999-5 IRB 8.

those assets to its members. Immediately following the distribution, the new member is deemed to have acquired by purchase all of the former LLC's assets.

- The new member's basis in the assets is equal to the basis of the membership interest allocated among the assets in accordance with Code Sec. 732(c).
- The new member's basis in the assets is equal to the cash purchase price for the membership interest.
- The new member's holding period for the assets begins on the day immediately following the date of sale.

98-37 Entity Classification[3]

The IRS determined that 37 revenue rulings and one revenue procedure, a majority of which dealt with the entity classification of LLCs, were now obsolete.

98-15 Tax-Exempt Organizations[4]

A tax-exempt hospital may form an LLC with a for-profit corporation and contribute its hospital and other operating assets to the LLC. The tax-exempt organization will continue to maintain its tax-exempt status if (a) the governing instruments of the LLC require that the LLC give charitable purposes priority over maximizing profits for the owners of the LLC, (b) the tax-exempt organization appoints a majority of the board of directors of the LLC, (c) the LLC designates an independent management company to run the hospital, (d) the terms of the management contract are reasonable, and (e) distributions by the LLC to the tax-exempt organization are used for charitable purposes.[5] The tax-exempt organization will not be a private foundation and will not have unrelated business income even though its only source of revenue is distributions from the LLC.[6]

However, the hospital may lose its tax-exempt status if (a) the LLC can deny services to certain segments of the community such as indigents, (b) the for-profit owner of the LLC can appoint one-half or more of the directors of the LLC, (c) the governing documents for the LLC do not require the LLC to give priority to charitable purposes instead of profits, or (d) the for-profit owner controls the management company.

95-55 Conversion of General Partnership to LLC;[7] Classification of New York LLC

There is no termination of a general partnership on conversion of the partnership to an LLC. The LLC must continue to use the same method of accounting after the conversion.

New York LLCs are classified as partnerships or corporations depending upon the provisions of the articles of organization and the operating agreement.

---

[3] 1998-2 CB 133.

[4] 1998-12 IRB 6.

[5] *Id.*

[6] *Id.*

[7] 1995-2 CB 313.

95-37 Conversion of Partnership into an LLC[8]

The conversion of a partnership into an LLC is treated the same as a partnership to partnership conversion. No gain or loss is recognized if the partners' shares of liabilities remain the same. There is no termination of the partnership. The tax year of the partnership does not end. The LLC is not required to obtain a new employer identification number.

95-9 Classification of South Dakota LLC[9]

A South Dakota LLC is classified as a partnership for federal tax purposes.

94-79 Classification of Connecticut LLC[10]

Connecticut LLCs are classified as partnerships or corporations depending upon the provisions of the articles of organization and the operating agreement.

94-51 Classification of New Jersey LLC[11]

New Jersey LLCs are classified as partnerships or corporations depending upon the provisions of the articles of organization and the operating agreement.

94-30 Classification of Kansas LLC[12]

Kansas LLCs are classified as partnerships or corporations depending upon the provisions of the articles of organization and the operating agreement.

94-6 Classification of Alabama LLC[13]

Alabama LLCs are classified as partnerships or corporations depending upon the provisions of the articles of organization and the operating agreement.

94-5 Classification of Louisiana LLC[14]

Louisiana LLCs are classified as partnerships or corporations depending upon the provisions of the articles of organization and the operating agreement.

93-93 Classification of Arizona LLC[15]

Arizona LLCs are classified as partnerships or corporations depending upon the provisions of the articles of organization and the operating agreement.

---

[8] 1995-1 CB 130.
[9] 1995-1 CB 222.
[10] 1994-2 CB 407.
[11] 1994-2 CB 407.
[12] 1994-1 CB 316.
[13] 1994-1 CB 314.
[14] 1994-1 CB 312.
[15] 1993-2 CB 321.

93-92 Classification of Oklahoma LLC[16]

Oklahoma LLCs are classified as partnerships or corporations depending upon the provisions of the articles of organization and the operating agreement.

93-91 Classification of Utah LLC[17]

Utah LLCs are classified as partnerships or corporations depending upon the provisions of the articles of organization and the operating agreement.

93-81 Classification of Rhode Island LLC[18]

Rhode Island LLCs are classified as partnerships or corporations depending upon the provisions of the articles of organization and the operating agreement.

93-53 Classification of Florida LLC[19]

Florida LLCs are classified as partnerships or corporations depending upon the provisions of the articles of organization and the operating agreement.

93-50 Classification of West Virginia LLC[20]

West Virginia LLCs are classified as partnerships.

93-49 Classification of Illinois LLC[21]

Illinois LLCs are classified as partnerships or corporations depending upon the provisions of the articles of organization and the operating agreement.

93-38 Classification of Delaware LLC[22]

Delaware LLCs are classified as partnerships or corporations depending upon the provisions of the articles of organization and the operating agreement.

93-30 Classification of Nevada LLC[23]

Nevada LLCs are classified as partnerships for federal tax purposes.

93-6 Classification of Colorado LLC[24]

Colorado LLCs are classified as partnerships for federal tax purposes.

93-5 Classification of Virginia LLC[25]

Virginia LLCs are classified as partnerships for federal tax purposes.

---

[16] 1993-2 CB 318.
[17] 1993-2 CB 316.
[18] 1993-2 CB 314.
[19] 1993-2 CB 312.
[20] 1993-2 CB 310.
[21] 1993-2 CB 308.
[22] 1993-2 CB 233.
[23] 1993-1 CB 231.
[24] 1993-1 CB 229.
[25] 1993-1 CB 227.

93-4 Classification of German GmbH[26]

A German GmbH is classified as a corporation for U.S. tax purposes.

91-32 Sale of a Membership Interest

A selling foreign member recognizes gain on sale of a membership interest to the extent attributable to the selling member's share of U.S. real property owned by the LLC.

88-76 Classification of Wyoming LLC[27]

Wyoming LLCs are classified as partnerships for federal tax purposes.

88-8 Classification of Foreign LLC[28]

An entity organized under foreign law is classified for federal tax purposes solely on the basis of the characteristics set forth in Reg. § 301.7701-2(b)(1). The IRS determined that this ruling was applicable to determining the classification of foreign LLCs.[29]

84-52 Conversion of General Partnership into LLC[30]

A conversion of a general partnership into a limited partnership is a nontaxable exchange if the partners retain the same percentage interest in the limited partnership. There is no termination of the partnership. The IRS determined that this ruling governs the conversion of a general partnership into an LLC,[31] the conversion of a limited partnership into an LLC,[32] and a merger of a limited partnership into an LLC.[33]

77-214 Classification of German GmbH[34]

A German GmbH that is owned by two domestic subsidiaries of a U.S. parent corporation is classified as a partnership for federal tax purposes.

PART 2.
REVENUE PROCEDURES

2010-32 Mistaken Classification Election by Foreign LLC

The IRS will grant election classification relief to a (a) foreign LLC that made a check-the-box election to be classified as a partnership under a reasonable but mistaken assumption that it had more than one member, or (b) a foreign LLC that

---

[26] 1993-1 CB 255.

[27] 1988-2 CB 360.

[28] 1988-1 CB 403.

[29] Ltr. Ruls. 9216004, 9210039, 9152009.

[30] 1984-1 CB 157.

[31] Rev. Rul. 95-37; Ltr. Rul. 9321047.

[32] Rev. Rul. 95-37; Ltr. Rul. 9119029.

[33] Ltr. Rul. 9210019.

[34] 1977-1 CB 408.

made a check-the-box election to be classified as disregarded entity under a reasonable but mistaken assumption that it had only one member.

2009-41 Late LLC Classification Election

The IRS set forth the procedures for obtaining IRS approval for late classification elections for an LLC. The procedures apply to both initial classification elections and changes in classification elections.

2002-69 Community Property LLCs

An LLC that is owned by a husband and wife may elect to be classified either as a partnership or disregarded entity if (a) the LLC is wholly owned by a husband and wife as community property under the laws of a state, a foreign country, or a U.S. possession, (b) no person other than one or both of the spouses are owners for tax purposes, and (c) the LLC is not classified as a corporation for federal tax purposes.

2002-59 Late Election Classification

An LLC may request relief from the IRS for a late initial classification election. The LLC must apply to the IRS prior to the unextended due date for the first tax return. It must file an application on Form 8832. The form must state at the top of the document that it is "FILED PURSUANT TO REV. PROC. 2002-59." The LLC must attach a statement to the form explaining the reason for failure to file a classification election on a timely basis. The LLC is eligible to apply for relief if (a) the LLC failed to obtain the desired classification solely because of failure to file Form 8832 on a timely basis, (b) the due date for the LLC's tax return for the tax year beginning with the date of formation has not yet passed, and (c) the LLC has reasonable cause for failure to make the classification election on a timely basis.[35] There is no filing fee for requesting the late classification.

2002-15 Late Election Classification

An LLC that fails to file a timely classification election on Form 8832 may request the IRS to approve the late election classification. The LLC may request relief from the IRS for a late initial classification election by complying with Rev. Proc. 2002-15. The LLC must apply to the IRS within six months and 75 days after the formation of the LLC. It must file an application on Form 8832. The form must state at the top of the document that it is "FILED PURSUANT TO REV. PROC. 2002-15." The LLC must attach a statement to the form explaining the reason for failure to file a classification election on a timely basis. The LLC is eligible to apply for relief under this Revenue Procedure if (a) the LLC failed to obtain the desired classification because of failure to file Form 8832 on a timely basis, (b) the due date for the LLC's tax return for the tax year beginning with the date of formation has not yet passed, and (c) the LLC has reasonable cause for failure to make the classification election on a timely basis. Rev. Proc. 2002-59 superseded this Revenue Procedure.

---

[35] Rev. Proc. 2002-15, § 4.

99-49 Audit Examination Procedures[36]

The audit examination under the TEFRA unified audit and litigation provisions for LLCs begins on the date of notice from the IRS of the beginning of an administrative proceeding sent to the Tax Matters Partner. The notice is sometimes referred to as the NBAP.

The audit examination ends on one of the following dates:

- In a case in which the Service accepts the LLC return as filed, on the date of the "no adjustments letter" or the "no change" notice of final administrative adjustment sent to the tax matters partner.
- In a fully agreed case, when all of the members of the LLC sign Form 870-P or 870-L.
- In an unagreed or partially agreed case, on the earliest of the date the tax matters partner or its representative is notified by Appeals that the case has been referred to Appeals from Examination, the date that the tax matters partner or member requests judicial review, or the date on which the period for requesting judicial review expires.

96-1 Rulings on Classification[37]

The IRS will issue rulings on whether a domestic or foreign limited liability company is classified as a partnership for federal tax purposes.

95-10 Ruling Requests on Classification[38]

An LLC must meet certain requirements in order to obtain a ruling that it is classified as a partnership for federal tax purposes.

93-45 Ruling Requests for Foreign LLCs[39]

Rev. Proc. 93-3 was modified with respect to ruling requests for foreign LLCs.

93-44 Ruling Requests for Foreign LLCs[40]

The Service will rule on the classification of foreign LLCs. Section 3.01.04 of Rev. Rul. 93-7 which restricted such rulings in specified cases was deleted.

93-7 Ruling Requests for Foreign LLCs[41]

The Service will not issue rulings on the classification of a foreign LLC if a taxpayer who holds an interest in the LLC (a) is a corporation and independent parties hold less than 20 percent of the interests in the LLC, or (b) is not a corporation

---

[36] 1999-52 IRB 725, Sec. 3.08(2).

[37] 1996-1 CB 385.

[38] 1995-1 CB 501.

[39] 1993-2 CB 545.

[40] 1993-2 CB 545.

[41] 1993-1 CB 465.

and independent parties hold only a nominal interest in the LLC. [Sec. 3.01.04 of Ruling].

89-12 Ruling Requests[42]

In order to obtain an IRS ruling on the classification of an LLC, the LLC or it members must make all of the applicable representations and supply all of the relevant information required by Rev. Proc. 89-12. However, Section 4 of Rev. Proc. 89-12 is not applicable to LLCs,[43] if managers are not members,[44] or if all members continue to share management authority equally.[45] Otherwise, the LLC must continue to comply with Section 4 of Rev. Proc 89-12 at all times after issuance of the ruling, and in particular Sections 4.01 and 4.03 of the ruling.[46] Those sections require the managers to maintain a minimum interest in LLC income, gain, loss, deduction and credit and a minimum capital account balance.

PART 3.

NOTICES

2012-52 Gift to LLC Owned by Charity

A contribution to a single-member disregarded LLC owned by a tax-exempt charity is treated as a charitable contribution to a branch or division of the charity. The contribution will be tax-deductible if it meets all other requirements for deduction under Code Section 170.

2002-15 Late Election Classification

An LLC that fails to file a timely classification election on Form 8832 may request the IRS to approve the late election classification. The LLC may request relief from the IRS for a late initial classification election by complying with Rev. Proc. 2002-15. The LLC must apply to the IRS within six months and 75 days after the formation of the LLC. It must file an application on Form 8832. The form must state at the top of the document that it is "FILED PURSUANT TO REV. PROC. 2002-15." The LLC must attach a statement to the form explaining the reason for failure to file a classification election on a timely basis. The LLC is eligible to apply for relief under this Revenue Procedure if (a) the LLC failed to obtain the desired classification because of failure to file Form 8832 on a timely basis, (b) the due date for the LLC's tax return for the tax year beginning with the date of formation has not yet passed, and (c) the LLC has reasonable cause for failure to make the classification election on a timely basis.

---

[42] 1989-1 CB 798 (declared obsolete by Rev. Proc. 2003-99, 2003-2 CB 38).

[43] Ltr. Rul. 9321070.

[44] Ltr. Rul. 9227033.

[45] Ltr. Rul. 9030013.

[46] Ltr. Rul. 9218078.

Notice 97-1, TD 8697[47]

On December 17, 1996, the IRS issued final regulations on the classification of LLCs and other entities for federal tax purposes. The regulations are referred to as "check the box" rules because they permit most unincorporated entities to select classification as a proprietorship, partnership or corporation by checking the applicable box on an IRS form.

Notice of Proposed Rulemaking PS-34-92 (Oct. 27, 1995) Tax Matters Partner

The Service issued proposed regulations regarding the designation of a tax matters partner (TMP) for an LLC.

Notice 95-14 Classification of LLCs[48]

The IRS stated that it was considering a proposal to treat all domestic unincorporated business organizations as partnerships unless all members elect to be treated as a corporation.

PART 4.
ANNOUNCEMENTS

Announcement 97-5 Entity Election Classification[49]

IRS Form 8832, Entity Classification Election, may be used by entities that elect classification under the Code Sec. 7701 regulations. This form is used by LLCs that do not want the default classification or wish to change their previous classification.

Announcement 95-34 Self-Employment Taxes of Members[50]

The IRS will hold public hearings on the proposed regulations concerning the treatment of members of LLCs.

Announcement 88-118 Classification of Various Entities[51]

The IRS reported that it had completed its six-year investigation on the classification of various entities, with a special emphasis on limited liability. An entity could be classified as a partnership for federal tax purposes even though no person was personally liable.

Announcement 83-4 Classification of LLC

The IRS withdrew proposed regulations on the classification of LLCs. The proposed regulations would have provided that an entity may not be classified as a partnership unless some member is personally liable for the debts and liabilities of the entity.

---

[47] 1997-2 IRB 22.

[48] 1995-1 CB 297.

[49] 1997-3 IRB 15.

[50] 1995-18 IRB 19.

[51] 1988-38 IRB 26.

Announcement 82-140 Classification of LLC

The IRS announced a delay in the effective date of regulations on the classification of LLCs. The proposed regulations provide that an entity may not be classified as a partnership unless some member is personally liable for the debts and liabilities of the entity.

Announcement 82-60 Classification of LLC

The IRS announced a delay in the effective date of regulations on the classification of LLCs. The proposed regulations provide that an entity may not be classified as a partnership unless some member is personally liable for the debts and liabilities of the entity.

Announcement 81-166 Classification of LLC

The IRS announced a delay in the effective date of regulations on the classification of LLCs. The proposed regulations provide that an entity may not be classified as a partnership unless some member is personally liable for the debts and liabilities of the entity.

Appendix C

Summary of Private Letter Rulings and General Counsel Memoranda

PART 1.
PRIVATE LETTER RULINGS

201745005, Conversion of LLC into Limited Partnership

The conversion of an LLC into a limited partnership does not result in a termination of the entity as a partnership. No gain or loss is recognized to the LLC or its members. The conversion does not result in the classification of the LLC as a corporation.

201741018 Failure of Allocations to Have Substantial Economic Effect

An LLC which did not comply with any of the requirements for substantial economic effect can make special allocations of losses in accordance with the operating agreement provided the LLC did not allocate losses to the members in excess of their positive capital accounts.

201722019 Conversion of Preferred to Common Membership Units

No gain or loss will be recognized by a member as a result of the conversion of its membership interest from preferred interests for common interests with the same fair market value.

201044021 Charitable Organization Ownership of Real Property Through LLC

A trust that distributes its income to other charitable organizations will not qualify as a tax exempt organization if it is formed to acquire real estate through investments in LLCs. The trust would be treated as operating for a substantial nonexempt purpose. The holding of real estate or other assets through an LLC until market conditions improve is not an exempt purpose.

201041029 Conversion of Subsidiary into Disregarded LLC

The conversion of a subsidiary corporation into a single member disregarded LLC owned by the parent corporation is treated as a liquidation of the subsidiary into the parent.

201017031 Conversion of Subsidiary into LLC

The conversion of a subsidiary corporation into an LLC is treated as a distribution by the subsidiary to the parent corporation in complete liquidation under IRC

Section 332(a). No gain or loss is to be recognized by either the subsidiary or parent corporation on the deemed distribution and receipt of the subsidiary's assets and liabilities.

201016052 Merger of Parent Corporation into Subsidiary LLC

The merger of a parent corporation into a subsidiary LLC is a tax-free A reorganization.

201012050 Contribution of Membership Interest to Private Foundation

The transfer of a membership interest in an LLC to a private foundation does not constitute an act of self dealing or prohibited transaction if the liabilities assumed by the LLC are nonrecourse and constitute less than two percent of the LLC's fair market value.

200953005 Cancellation of Indebtedness Income

An LLC's debt that is collateralized by the LLC's ownership interest in a disregarded LLC that owns real property is "qualified real property business indebtedness" that qualifies for the exclusion.

200931042 Transfer of Investment Assets to an LLC

There is no tax on the transfers of cash and diversified investment portfolios to an LLC provided that the transfers are not part of a plan to achieve diversification.

200927014 Ownership of Stock in S Corporation by LLCs

Each of the shareholders in an S corporation with multiple shareholders may transfer their shares to a single-member disregarded LLC.

200923006 Branch Profits Tax for Final Year of LLC

There is no branch profits tax for the final year of the LLC, provided that the corporate owner of the LLC files a waiver of the period of limitations on Form 8848.

200922007 Extension of Time for Section 754 Election

An LLC was granted an extension of time to make a Section 754 election.

200917018 Extension of Time for Section 754 Election Denied

The IRS denied a request for an extension to make a Section 754 election because certain tax years that would have been affected by a timely Section 754 election were closed by the statute of limitations.

200910028 Merger of Target Corporation into Subsidiary LLC

A target corporation may form a subsidiary, and merge into the subsidiary as part of a tax-free reorganization pursuant to which the target corporation is acquired by the acquiring corporation. The shareholders of the target corporation exchanged their stock in the target corporation for stock in the acquiring corporation in the merger.

200910030 Distribution by S Corporation of Membership Interests in LLC

The distribution by an S corporation to its shareholders of membership interests in a wholly owned LLC is treated as a sale of the assets of the LLC at fair market value. The corporation recognizes gain under Section 311(b) on the deemed sale of appreciated assets owned by the LLC.

200851044 Section 403(b) Annuity Plan for Subsidiary LLC

Employees of a single-member disregarded LLC established by a tax-exempt organization may participate in a Section 403(b) annuity plan established by the tax-exempt organization.

200845023 Estate Tax on Value of LLC Interest

The value of a decedent's interest in an LLC attributable to real property qualified as an interest in a closely held business under Code Section 6166. Accordingly, provided the other requirements under Code Section 6166 are met, payment of the estate tax attributable to the non-passive assets (real properties) of the LLC may be paid in installments under Code Section 6166. The federal estate tax attributable to the value of other real property that was a passive asset may not be paid in installments.

200843024 Incorporation of Single-Member Disregarded LLC

A single-member disregarded LLC may convert to a corporation on a tax-free basis by filing an election to be classified as a corporation, or by transferring the membership interest in the LLC to the corporation in exchange for stock.

200843011 Subsidiary Merger into LLC

A parent corporation may merge a subsidiary corporation into a single-member disregarded LLC owned by the parent corporation on a tax-free basis.

200839017 Conversion of S Corporation into LLC

An S corporation may merge into an LLC. The conversion is treated as an F reorganization. Neither party recognizes gain or loss on the exchange. The tax attributes of the assets in the hands of the corporation carry over to the LLC. The S election will not terminate as a result of the reorganization if the LLC meets the requirements under Section 1361.

200839003 Late S Corporation Election for LLC

The IRS granted an LLC an extension of time to file an election to be classified as an S corporation.

200835030 Levy Against LLC for Taxes Owed by Member

The IRS may issue a Notice of Levy against a single-member disregarded LLC for income owed to the member for services by the LLC prior to the Notice of Levy.

200835014 Merger of Target Corporation into Disregarded LLC

The merger of a target corporation into a disregarded LLC owned by the acquiring corporation is a tax-free merger under Code Section 368(a)(1)(A).

200832001 Merger of Target Corporation into Disregarded LLC; Conversion of Subsidiary Corporation into Disregarded LLC; Up-stream Merger of Disregarded Subsidiary LLC into Parent Corporation

The merger of a target corporation into a disregarded LLC owned by the acquiring corporation is a tax-free merger under Code Section 368(a)(1)(A). The upstream merger of a disregarded subsidiary LLC into a parent corporation is disregarded for federal tax purposes.

200830010 Late Classification Election Denied

The IRS denied an LLC's application for a late election to be classified as a corporation because the taxpayer did not act in good faith.

200830003 Conversion of Subsidiary to Disregarded LLC; Classification of Disregarded LLC as Corporation

Neither the parent corporation nor its wholly owned subsidiary recognize gain or loss on conversion of the subsidiary to a disregarded LLC. The basis of each asset received by parent through the subsidiary in the conversion is equal to the basis of that asset in hands of the subsidiary immediately prior to the conversion. The holding period of each asset received by the parent corporation includes the period during which the subsidiary held that asset.

A parent corporation does not recognize gain or loss on the classification of a disregarded subsidiary LLC as a corporation.

200826009 Transfer of Insurance Policy for Valuable Consideration

The sale or exchange of membership interests in an LLC that is classified as a partnership will not result in a transfer for "valuable consideration" under Code Section 101(a)(2), provided there is no termination of LLC as a partnership under Code Section 708(b)(1)(B).

200820020 Conversion of LLC to Corporation

No gain or loss is recognized by the members of an LLC or a corporation on the contribution of the membership interests by the members to the corporation in exchange for stock. The basis of common stock in the new corporation received by each member is the same as the basis of the membership interest transferred to the new corporation, reduced by the LLC's liabilities assumed by the new corporation.

200820017 Like-Kind Exchange With Related Party

An LLC may engage in a like-kind exchange with a related party provided that the related party does not dispose of the replacement property within two years after receipt of the replacement property.

200816004, 200816003, 200816002 S Corporation Stock Owned by LLC

The transfer by a sole shareholder of all of the stock in an S corporation to a single member disregarded LLC will not result in termination of the S corporation election.

200812012 Like-Kind Exchange Following LLC Distribution

The deemed termination of an LLC under Code Section 708(b)(1)(B), resulting from the distribution of the membership interests in the LLC by a trust will not disqualify a like-kind exchange or preclude the replacement property acquired by the LLC in a reverse like-kind exchange from being held for investment or for productive use in a trade or business under Code Section 1031(a).

Appendix C

200810016 Like-Kind Exchange With Related Party

An LLC may engage in a like-kind exchange with a related party provided that the LLC does not dispose of the replacement property within two years after receipt of the replacement property, and provided that the related party does not dispose of the exchange property within two years after the exchange.

200803004 Series LLC

Each separate series of an LLC was a separate entity for classification purposes, where each series invested in a different portfolio of shares and had different owners.

200802015 Merger of Parent Corporation into LLC

The merger of a parent corporation into a single-member disregarded LLC owned by a subsidiary corporation is treated as a tax-free F reorganization.

200802011 S Corporation Election

The operating agreement of an LLC that elected to be classified as an S corporation did not constitute a second class of stock since (i) all items of income and loss were allocated among the members pro rata in accordance with their percentage membership interests, and (ii) all distributions (both liquidating and nonliquidating) were made in accordance with their percentage membership interests.

200802011 Divisive D Reorganization

The transfer by a corporation of assets and liabilities of one of its lines of business to a controlled LLC in exchange for membership interests, followed by a transfer of the membership interest to the shareholders of the corporation, is a tax-free D reorganization.

200801038 Cooperative Housing Corporation

Tenant-shareholders may contribute their shares in a cooperative housing corporation to an LLC in exchange for membership interests on a tax-free basis.

200752042 Subsidiary LLC Formed by Charitable Organization

A tax-exempt social welfare organization may form a disregarded subsidiary LLC to operate as a licensed insurance agency selling supplemental insurance. The business of the LLC did not adversely affect the organization's tax exempt status where the income from the LLC constituted less than two percent of the tax exempt organization's total revenues.

200734003 Conversion of Trust into LLC

A trust may contribute its assets to an LLC in exchange for membership interests in the LLC. The trust may then distribute the membership interests to the beneficiaries of the trust, and terminate the trust. No gain or loss is recognized by the trust, the beneficiaries or the LLC as a result of the trust's distribution to the beneficiaries.

200732012 Like-Kind Exchange Using Multiple Disregarded LLCs

A taxpayer may use multiple disregarded LLCs to make a like-kind exchange, including subsidiary LLCs owned by a disregarded LLC. The 45-day designation and the 180-day deadline for the transfer of replacement property may be met by one or more of such LLCs.

200730010 Casualty Losses

An LLC as lessee is entitled to a casualty loss deduction for uninsured and unreimbursed costs of replacing leased property destroyed in a casualty event. The LLC may deduct its basis in the original property, any lease-hold improvements destroyed by the casualty, and any costs incurred to satisfy the uninsured and unreimbursed portion of its replacement obligation.

200729002 Merger of S Corporation into LLC

The merger of an S corporation into a single-member disregarded LLC owned by another corporation qualifies as a tax-free reorganization under Code Sec. 368(a)(1)(A) if the requirements for a statutory merger are met.

200723030 Unrelated Business Taxable Income by Exempt LLC

The sale of prescription drugs by a single-member disregarded LLC will not generate unrelated business taxable income or jeopardize the tax-exempt status of the parent corporation if the business is substantially related to the parent corporation's exempt purposes.

200720010 Conversion by Foreign Parent Corporation of U.S. Subsidiary into LLC

A foreign parent corporation may convert a U.S. subsidiary corporation into a disregarded LLC on a tax-free basis provided that the LLC continues to use the assets in a trade or business for a period of 10 years after the conversion.

200719007 S Corporation Conversion into LLC Classified as S Corporation

An S corporation may convert into an LLC that is classified as an S corporation. The conversion will be treated as a tax-free F reorganization.

200718014 Conversion of S Corporation into LLC Classified as C Corporation

The conversion of an S corporation into an LLC classified as a C corporation is a tax-free F reorganization. The corporation does not recognize any gain or loss in the conversion. The basis and holding period of the assets carry over to the LLC.

200717019 LLC Payments of Income to Tax-Exempt Organization

An LLC's payment of interest and rent to a nonprofit healthcare corporation does not generate unrelated business taxable income where the leasing activity of the medical office building is substantially related to the nonprofit corporation's exempt purposes, and revenues that fund rental and interest payments are derived from such leases.

200709051 Disproportionate Distributions from LLC Classified as S Corporation

Distributions from an LLC classified as an corporation that are not based on each member's percentage interest in the LLC may cause a termination of the S corporation election. However, there is no termination in such case if the shareholders eliminate the capital account disparity resulting from the disproportionate distributions on a current basis.[1]

200709036 Section 1031 Exchange With Related Party

An LLC may enter into a tax-free Section 1031 exchange with a related party if (i) the LLC transfers the relinquished property to the related party through an unrelated qualified intermediary, (ii) the LLC receives replacement property that is not owned by the related party, and (iii) the transaction is not structured to avoid the purposes of the related party rules for like-kind exchanges.[2]

200709013 Election Classification by Subsidiary Corporation as Disregarded LLC

A subsidiary corporation may file an election to be classified as a disregarded LLC. The election is treated as a tax-free Section 332 liquidation of the subsidiary into the parent corporation.

200703030 Merger of Subsidiary LLCs

There is no income recognition if a parent corporation merges an LLC owned by one subsidiary corporation into a disregarded LLC owned by the parent corporation.

200701018 Merger of Subsidiary Corporation into Disregarded LLC

A parent corporation merged a subsidiary corporation into a disregarded LLC owned by the subsidiary corporation. The merger was a tax-free liquidation of the subsidiary corporation into the parent corporation under Code Sec. 332. The tax basis and the holding periods of the assets remained the same after the merger.

200651010 Rental Income Received by S Corporation from LLC

Rental income received by an S corporation from an LLC is not passive investment income under Code Sec. 1362(d)(3)(C).

200650014 Liquidating Distribution of Property

A partnership formed an LLC that it used to acquire a house in which the departing partner intended to live. The partnership then distributed the LLC membership interests to the partner in liquidation of the partner's interest in the partnership. The partner took the position that there was no tax in the liquidating distribution because the partner had not received a money distribution in excess of basis. Instead, the partner received property with a basis equal to the partner's outside basis in the partnership interest immediately prior to the distribution. The IRS disagreed with this position. It ruled that the distribution was really a money distribution under the anti-abuse regulations, the step-transaction doctrine, and a variety of other theories.

---

[1] Ltr. Rul. 200709051.

[2] Ltr. Rul. 200709036.

200645012 Conversion of Subsidiary Corporation into Disregarded LLC

The conversion of a subsidiary corporation into disregarded LLC owned by the parent corporation is treated as a Section 332 liquidation of the subsidiary corporation into the parent corporation.

200642009 Disregarded LLC owned by Charitable Foundation

A Section 501(c)(3) organization may form a disregarded LLC to operate a low-income mobile home park. The activities of the LLC will not jeopardize the tax-exempt status of the parent organization.

200637041 Real Property Holding LLC of Tax-Exempt Corporation

A tax-exempt organization may form a single-member disregarded LLC to hold and manage the real estate investments of the tax-exempt organization. The real property holding LLC will not jeopardize the tax-exempt status of the parent corporation. The rental income received by the parent corporation from the LLC will not constitute unrelated business taxable income. Income received from the sale or exchange of property by the LLC will not constitute unrelated business taxable income. One or more of the officers and directors of the tax-exempt corporation (who are disqualified persons), may manage the business of the LLC. The management services will not constitute an act of self-dealing. The ownership of 100 percent of the LLC will not constitute excess business holdings under Code Section 4943. The holding of real property through the LLC will not jeopardize the charitable purposes of the tax-exempt corporation under Code Section 4944.

200636092 Cooperative's Distribution of LLC Interests

A cooperative's distribution of LLC interests and issuance of cooperative stock relating to nonresidential units does not adversely affect the tax-exempt status of the cooperative.

200633019 Distribution by Trust of Membership Interests to Beneficiaries

The distribution of membership interests by a trust as the sole member of a disregarded LLC to the beneficiaries of the trust changed the classification of the trust to a partnership. No gain or loss was recognized by the beneficiaries. Even though the LLC distributed marketable securities to the trust beneficiaries, there was no tax under Section 721(b) because each beneficiary was treated as receiving and then contributing a diversified portfolio of securities to the LLC.

200633008 Merger of Corporation into Disregarded LLC Owned by New Parent Holding Corporation

A corporation may merge into a disregarded LLC that is wholly owned by a new parent holding corporation. The conversion is treated as a nontaxable F reorganization. The subsequent transfer of assets by the LLC to the parent holding corporation is also an F reorganization.

200630002 Conversion of Publicly Traded Corporation into Disregarded LLC

A publicly traded corporation may convert into a disregarded LLC that is wholly owned by a new parent holding corporation. The conversion is a nontaxable F reorganization.

Appendix C

200623069 Charitable Remainder Trust Income From LLC

A charitable remainder trust's share of LLC income from investments in a foreign corporation does not constitute unrelated business taxable income.

200622025 S Corporation Conversion into LLC Classified as S Corporation

An S corporation may convert into an LLC that is classified as an S corporation. The conversion is treated as a tax-free F reorganization.

200613031 Anti-Abuse Rules

The IRS applied the anti-abuse rules under Reg. § 1.701-2 to recast a portion of a series of transaction involving the establishment of limited liability companies, the contribution of cash and appreciated stock to the LLCs, the transfer of interests in the LLCs to a charitable remainder unitrust using a minority discount, and the redemption of the interests owned by the charitable remainder trust after the sale of the stock at fair market value.

200613027 Rescission of Conversion from LLC to Corporation

An LLC that was classified as a partnership converted into a corporation, and was then allowed to rescind the conversion and keep its classification as a partnership for the entire year of the conversion.

200608038 Merger of Subsidiary Corporation into Subsidiary LLC

The merger of a subsidiary corporation into a disregarded LLC owned by the parent corporation constitutes a tax-free liquidation under Code Sec. 332.

The merger of a subsidiary corporation into a disregarded LLC owned by another subsidiary corporation owned by the same parent corporation constitutes a tax-free reorganization under Code Sec. 368(a)(1)(A).

200606047 Charitable Activities by Subsidiary LLC

Activities by a disregarded LLC owned by a Code Sec. 501(c)(3) organization that lessen the burden of government will not jeopardize the tax-exempt status of the parent organization. The subsidiary LLC managed the investment funds of school districts and governmental organizations.

200603021 Second Change In Classification Election

The IRS approved a change in classification election less than 60 months after the LLC filed an initial classification election. The subsequent election was approved because there was a deemed sale of assets to a purchaser of all of the membership interests in the LLC.

200551023 Formation of LLCs by Charitable Organization

A publicly supported charity formed multiple single-member LLCs for social welfare purposes. Each LLC entered into joint management agreements with other charitable organizations. The formation of the subsidiary LLCs did not change the public charity status of the parent organization. The receipt of income from the subsidiary LLCs did not generate unrelated business taxable income.

200548002 Extension for Code Sec. 754 Election

The IRS granted the LLC an extension of time to make a Code Sec. 754 election following the death of the member.

200538027 LLC Payments of Income to Tax-Exempt Organization

An LLC's payment of rent to a nonprofit healthcare corporation does not generate unrelated business taxable income where the leasing activity is substantially related to the nonprofit corporation's exempt purposes, and revenues that fund rental payments are derived from such leases.

200528029 Investment by Tax-Exempt Organization in LLC

The investment by a tax-exempt organization in an LLC did not jeopardize the tax-exempt status of the LLC, or result in unrelated business taxable income, where the activities of the LLC were substantially related to the exempt functions of the tax-exempt organization.

200528021 F Reorganization

The conversion by an S corporation to an LLC, followed by the LLC's check-the-box election to be classified as a corporation, constitutes a tax-free F reorganization.

200517031 Acquisition and Leasing of Land Through LLC by Charitable Foundations

The formation of an LLC by three charitable foundations to acquire and lease land to another unrelated LLC did not result in loss of tax exempt status for the foundations, cause the foundations to have excess business holdings, or constitute self-dealing.

200513022 Disguised Sale to LLC

A series of transactions resulting in the transfer of property to an LLC followed by a related distribution of cash and membership interests was a disguised sale of the property.

200506019 Contribution of Patents to LLC

Each contributing inventor of a patent to an LLC that is classified as a partnership is treated as a partner of the LLC for purposes of Code Sec. 1235. Thus, each partner retains his or her status as a "holder" under Code Sec. 1235. Each inventor's share of any gain recognized by the LLC on disposition of an interest in the patent qualifies under Code Sec. 1235 as long-term capital gain, provided the other requirements of Code Sec. 1235 are met.

200451032 Exempt Organization LLC

An LLC that was formed to provide administrative services, health care benefits, and pension benefits to its sole member and other trust funds cannot qualify as an exempt VEBA if it provides pension benefits.

200450041 LLC Denied Status as Exempt Organization

An LLC formed to own and operate an aircraft for the members of a social club was denied status as a tax-exempt Code Sec. 501(c)(7) organization since the purposes and operations of the LLC were primarily of a business nature.

Appendix C

200436022 Hospital Ownership of LLC

A hospital formed a single-member disregarded LLC to act as a partner in a limited partnership that provided diagnostic imaging services not currently available in or near the local area. The hospital's distributive share of profits to the partnership did not constitute unrelated business taxable income. The use of the LLC did not adversely affect the tax-exempt status of the hospital.

200432015 Insurance Transferred to LLC

The decedent's gross estate includes the value of an insurance policy that the decedent transferred to an LLC within three years prior to death. The transfer of the policy to the LLC in exchange for a membership interest is not a bona fide sale or exchange for adequate consideration under the Section 2035 exception. The marital deduction does not apply is the surviving spouse is not the sole member of the LLC.

200431018 Private Operating Foundation Ownership of LLC

A private foundation that operates an accredited university through a disregarded LLC may continue to act as a private foundation. Distributions that the private foundation makes through the disregarded LLC for charitable purposes constitute qualifying distributions. The use of assets to operate charitable programs through the LLC may be used to satisfy the endowment test. Revenues derived from the operations of the LLC may be treated as support for purposes of the support test.

200425004 Gain on Sale of Membership Interest by Foreign Members; Election Classification Extension for LLC with Foreign Members

Gain on the sale of a membership interest in an LLC by foreign members is taxed to the foreign members as income that is effectively connected with the conduct of the U.S. trade or business.

An LLC was granted an extension of time to elect classification as a partnership on the condition that the foreign members of the LLC file all applicable U.S. tax returns.

2004243029 LLC Management of Charitable Remainder Unitrust

The use of an LLC to manage the assets of a charitable remainder unitrust established by family members to benefit a single tax-exempt charitable foundation and relatives of one family member will not trigger the various private foundation excise taxes.

200423016 Drop-Down of Assets into Subsidiary LLC

The drop-down of assets and liabilities by a parent company into a subsidiary LLC that is classified as a disregarded entity is nontaxable to the parent company, its shareholders, and the LLC. The parent company must continue to use the income deferral method of accounting for prepaid subscriptions after the transfer.

200414013 Conversion from General Partnership to LLC

There is no tax to the LLC or its members on conversion from a general partnership to an LLC. The capital accounts of the members remain the same after the conversion.

200411044 Unrelated Business Taxable Income

Public charities formed an LLC to acquire, develop, finance and market inner city property for the purpose of fighting community deterioration and promoting urban revitalization. The income received by the public charities from the LLC did not constitute unrelated business taxable income. The LLC did not jeopardize the tax-exam status of its owners. The debt incurred by the LLC to acquire property did not give rise to debt-financed property and unrelated business taxable income since the property was acquired in connection with the tax exempt purposes of the owners of the LLC.

200406038 Disclaimers for Estate Tax Purposes

A beneficiary of an estate may disclaim an interest in an LLC even though the person holds an interest in the LLC and is a manager of the LLC.

200401007 LLC as S Corporation

An LLC was granted an extension of time to elect classification as a corporation and as a S corporation.

200351033 Charitable Organization as Member of an LLC to Provide Loans to Low Income Populations

A publicly supported charity did not lose its tax-exempt status by participating in a joint venture through an LLC to finance small businesses for the benefit of low-income populations. The operating agreement provided that the businesses to which the charity or the LLC made loans are businesses (a) located in distressed areas, (b) that use the funds for activities that employ individuals who are part of a targeted population or who live in a distressed area, or (c) that use the funds to provide necessary services or products that are otherwise unavailable to residents of distressed areas. The tax-exempt status of the charity is not adversely affected even though the charity receives interest and loan fees, and pays a profit participation interest to investors.

200348016 Extension for Code Sec. 754 Election

An LLC was granted an extension of time to make election under Code Sec. 754.

200345007 Recapitalization of LLC

An LLC may recapitalize by creating new classes of membership units with different rights, preferences, privileges and restrictions. The LLC may then allow members to convert their membership units into different classes of membership units on a tax-free basis.

200341023 Tax-Sheltered Annuity of Subsidiary LLC

The employees of a subsidiary LLC or of a charitable organization may participate in a Code Sec. 403(b) tax-sheltered annuity plan sponsored by the parent organization if the LLC does not elect to be classified as a corporation.[3]

---

[3] Ltr. Rul. 200341023.

Appendix C

200339039, 200339031-032 Consolidation of Partnerships into LLC; Method of Depreciation After Merger

Six partnerships consolidated into a single LLC. The LLC was treated as the continuation of Partnership 3 since Partnership 3 was credited with the contribution of assets having the greatest fair market value, net of liabilities. The surviving LLC was considered as the historical owner of the assets owned by Partnership 3, and was therefore required to use the same method and period of depreciation used by such partnership. The IRS also ruled that the surviving LLC was required to use the same method and period of depreciation used by the other merging partnerships that acquired their depreciable assets prior to 1981 pursuant to Code Secs. 723, 168(e)(4)(C) (prior to amendment by the Tax Reform Act of 1986), 168(f)(5), and 381(c)(6).

200339026 LLC Ownership of Stock in S Corporation

An LLC owned by a trust may own stock in an S corporation since the trust is the sole owner of the LLC, the trust is a disregarded entity, and the trust is a revocable grantor trust.

200338012 Payroll Tax Liability

The IRS may not place a lien on the assets of a single-member disregarded LLC for unpaid payroll taxes of the LLC. The owner of the LLC is personally liable for the unpaid payroll taxes.

200334037 Termination of LLC

A partnership terminated when one of the members purchased the partnership interest of the other member through a disregarded LLC owned by the purchasing partner. The selling partner may treat the transaction as a sale.

200333031-033 Unrelated Business Taxable Income from LLC Formed by Trade Associations

Three Code Sec. 501(c)(6) trade associations formed an LLC to operate trade shows. Income received by the trade associations from the LLC does not constitute unrelated business taxable income.

200321021 Formation of LLC by Tax-Exempt Organization

A tax-exempt organization may also form a subsidiary LLC to perform noncharitable activities unrelated to the parent organization's exempt purposes. The subsidiary LLC's business activities will not adversely affect the tax-exempt status of the parent organization if the subsidiary LLC has a business purpose, the activities at the LLC are not attributed to the tax-exempt organization, and the LLC is not merely an instrumentality, arm, agent or integral part of the parent organization. The income earned by the LLC is not attributed to the tax-exempt organization if both entities are separate for federal income tax purposes. Distributions by the LLC to the tax-exempt organization are not subject to the unrelated business income tax in such case.

200321006 Deferred Payment of Estate Taxes

The change in business operations of a farm from a sole proprietorship to cash leases of the farm to disregarded LLCs owned and operated by the beneficiaries of the residuary trust do not materially alter the decedent's closely held business. Thus, the leases of the farmland do not constitute a distribution, sale, exchange, or other disposition of an interest in a closely held business and thus does not result in acceleration of estate taxes that have been deferred on an installment basis.

200318023 Relief from Inadvertent Termination of S Corporation

The IRS granted an S corporation relief from inadvertent termination of its election as an S corporation when the corporation issued stock to an LLC. An LLC that is classified as a partnership is not eligible to be a shareholder in an S corporation.

200318021 Relief from Inadvertent Termination of S Corporation

The IRS granted an S corporation relief from inadvertent termination of its election as an S corporation when the corporation issued stock to an LLC. An LLC that is classified as a partnership is not eligible to be a shareholder in an S corporation.

200317006 LLC Election to be Classified as S Corporation

An LLC that elected to be classified as a corporation was given an additional 60-day extension to elect classification as an S corporation.

200316003 Synthetic Fuel Credit

The indirect owner of a single-member LLC is entitled to the synthetic fuel credit under Code Sec. 29 attributable to the single-member LLC. The two lower-tier LLCs are disregarded entities. The topmost LLC is therefore regarded as owning their assets and is entitled to the credit.

200315010 LLC Election to be Classified as S Corporation

A single-member LLC that elected to be classified as a corporation was given an additional 60-day extension to elect classification as an S corporation.

200315009 Classification of Foreign LLC

A foreign LLC is automatically classified as a corporation if all members have limited liability under the laws of the foreign country in which the LLC was organized.[4] A member has limited liability if the member has no personal liability for the debts of or claims against the LLC by reason of being a member. This determination is based solely on the statute or law pursuant to which the entity is organized.

2003108005 Conversion of Subsidiary and Merger of Subsidiary into Disregarded LLC

The merger of a subsidiary corporation into a disregarded LLC owned by the parent corporation and the conversion of a subsidiary corporation into a disregarded LLC owned by the parent corporation qualified as a tax-free liquidation under Code Sec. 332 (rulings with respect to the "Sub 2 Merger" and the Sub 5 Conversion").

---

[4] Reg. § 301.7701-3(b)(2)(i)(B); Ltr. Rul. 200315009.

Appendix C

200310005 Code Sec. 332 Liquidation of Subsidiary into LLC owned by Parent Corporation

The merger of a parent corporation's subsidiary into an LLC owned by the parent corporation qualifies as a complete liquidation under Code Sec. 332. Since the LLC was a disregarded entity, the parent corporation was treated as acquiring and directly holding assets and assuming liabilities of the subsidiary for tax purposes.

200305017 Merger of Subsidiary into Disregarded LLC

The merger of a wholly owned subsidiary corporation of a foreign parent corporation into a disregarded LLC owned by the foreign parent corporation was treated as a liquidation of the subsidiary corporation into the foreign parent corporation, subject to Code Secs. 331 and 336. The merger did not trigger recognition of gain under gain recognition agreement entered into by the parties under Code Sec. 367.

200304041-042 Formation of LLC by Private Foundation

The tax-exempt status of a private foundation will not be adversely affected by the creation of an LLC, and the private foundation's participation in the LLC. The activities of an LLC that is classified as a partnership for federal income tax purposes are considered to be the activities of a nonprofit organization that is a member of the LLC when evaluating whether the nonprofit organization is operated exclusively for exempt purposes under Code Sec. 501(c)(3). The receipt of income and the distributive share of profits by the foundation from the LLC will not be unrelated business taxable income.

200304036 Tax-Exempt Organization's Ownership of LLC

A tax-exempt organization's creation of a single-member disregarded LLC to own and operate student housing facilities will not adversely affect its exempt status under Code Sec. 501(c)(3). The tax-exempt organization's leasing of the facilities to students through the LLC will not constitute an unrelated trade or business or result in unrelated business taxable income.

200303065 Tax-Exempt Organization's Ownership of LLC

A tax-exempt scientific research organization may form an LLC to carry out business that is substantially related to its exempt purposes. The participation in the LLC will not adversely affect its status as the tax-exempt organization. Income received from the LLC will not result in unrelated business taxable income.

200303032 LLC Ownership of Stock in S Corporation

A trust's contribution of its stock in an S corporation to an LLC in exchange for 100 percent of the membership interest in the LLC will not terminate the corporation's election as an S corporation. The LLC was a disregarded entity, and the trust was a qualified S corporation shareholder.

200301024 Synthetic Fuel Credit

An LLC's facility's process and use of chemical reagents produces "qualified fuel" under Code Sec. 29(c)(1)(C). As a result, the LLC is entitled to the Code Sec. 29 credit for production of qualified fuel sold to unrelated persons.

200257007-008 Ownership by LLC of Stock in S Corporation

An LLC that is classified as a partnership for federal tax purposes may not own stock in an LLC. The IRS granted an S corporation relief from inadvertent termination of its status as an S corporation as a result of the transfer of stock in the corporation to an LLC.

200252096 Distributions by LLC to Corporation Owned by Tax-Exempt Trust

Income distributed by an LLC from a corporation owned by tax-exempt trust will not constitute unrelated business income to the trust.

200252055 Conversion of Subsidiary into LLC

A parent corporation merged a second-tier subsidiary into a first-tier subsidiary, and then converted the first-tier subsidiary into an LLC. The transaction was treated as a D reorganization. No gain or loss was recognized by the parent corporation as a result of the conversion.

20025012 Unified Partnership Audit and Litigation Procedures

LLCs with 10 or fewer members are not subject to the unified partnership audit and litigation procedures if each of the members is an individual, a C corporation, or an estate of a deceased partner. The small LLC exception does not apply if any member of the LLC during the tax year is a pass-through partner. A "pass-through" partner is a partnership, estate, trust, S corporation, nominee, or other similar person through whom other persons hold an interest in the LLC. Thus, if an LLC that is classified as a disregarded entity owns a membership interest in a second LLC that is classified as a partnership, the second LLC does not qualify as a small partnership exempt from unified partnership audit and litigation procedures even if the second LLC has 10 or fewer members.

200249014 Tax-Exempt Organization's Ownership of LLC

A tax-exempt organization's construction, ownership, and leasing of student housing project through an LLC will not affect the organization's tax-exempt status or constitute unrelated trade or business.

200248023 Merger of Corporation into LLC Classified as an S Corporation

The merger of a corporation into an LLC that was classified as an S corporation pursuant to a Code Sec. 368(a)(1)(F) reorganization did not adversely affect the LLC's status as an S corporation.

200243023 LLC Formed by State Agency

A state or other governmental organization may form an investment LLC. Membership must be limited to a state, a political subdivision of a state, or another entity that may exclude its income under Code Sec. 115(1). The gross income from the LLC allocable to the members qualifies for the exclusion under Code Sec. 115(1).

200242004 Anti-Abuse Rules and Shifting of Losses to Third Parties

The anti-abuse rules prevent an LLC from shifting losses in high basis, low value assets to new members. The anti-abuse rules also prohibit the taxpayer from creating duplicate losses by contributing property with built-in losses to an LLC, selling its membership interest in the LLC to a third party at a loss, and then having the LLC

Appendix C

sell the contributed property at a loss that is allocated to the buyer. The taxpayer may not receive any basis in a membership interest issued in exchange for the contribution of worthless property.

200240048 LLC as Subchapter S Corporation

An LLC may elect to be classified as an S corporation by filing Form 2553 and by filing Form 8832. The LLC was granted an extension of time to file Form 8832.

200236005 Merger of Corporation into LLC

The merger of a target corporation into an LLC that is a disregarded entity owned by the acquiring corporation is a tax-free merger under Code Sec. 368(a)(1)(A).

200235023 Employment Tax Liability and IRS Collection Procedures

If a multi-member LLC elects to be taxed as a corporation, then the LLC is liable for the employment tax. The members of the LLC may be liable for the trust fund recovery penalty under Code Sec. 6672, depending on the facts and circumstances of each case. If the LLC is classified as a partnership, the partnership will be liable for the employment tax. The Service will not assert an employment tax liability against the members of the LLC because they are not liable for the debts of the LLC under state law. These members, however, may be liable for the trust fund recovery penalty, depending on the facts and circumstances of each case.

If a single-member LLC elects to be taxed as a corporation, then the LLC is liable for the employment taxes. The single-member owner of the LLC and others may be liable for the trust fund recovery penalty under Code Sec. 6672, depending on the facts and circumstances of each case. If there has been no corporate election, then the LLC is disregarded for federal tax purposes and the single-member owner is the taxpayer. When the single-member owner is the taxpayer, the Service may recover the tax liability from the property and rights to property of the single-member owner, but the single-member owner under state law has no interest in the assets of the LLC. In short, the Service may not look to the LLC's assets to satisfy the tax liability of the single-member owner. The Service, however, may take collection action against the single-member owner's ownership interest in the LLC.

An assessment made against a disregarded LLC is a valid assessment against the single-member owner. Because of the close relationship of the disregarded LLC to the single-member owner, an assessment against the disregarded LLC is tantamount to an assessment against the single-member owner.

A Notice of Federal Tax Lien ("NFTL") identifying the disregarded LLC as the taxpayer may be a valid notice against the single-member owner, depending on the facts of each case. The IRS's position is that a NFTL need not precisely identify the taxpayer. Instead, the NFTL is valid if it substantially complies with the filing requirement so that constructive notice is provided to third parties. To avoid litigating this issue, the IRS recommends that the NFTL be filed in the name of the single-member owner for the tax liabilities generated by the disregarded LLC.

There are a variety of state law theories that the Service could use to collect a single-member owner's tax liability from the disregarded LLC: asserting alter ego liability and asserting nominee or transferee liability.

200227016 Transfer of Assets to LLC Following Code Sec. 355 Spin-Off

The transfer by a spun-off subsidiary off some or all of the assets of its active trade or business to an LLC in exchange for membership interests in the LLC will not prevent the spun-off subsidiary from being treated as engaged in the trade or business for purposes of Code Sec. 355.

200223036-045 Division of an LLC Owning Marketable Securities

If an LLC owns marketable securities, and then divides into two or more LLCs in an asset-over form, then the members of each LLC must compute the amount of gain from a marketable securities distribution based only on the marketable securities held by the divided LLC in which they are a member.[5]

200222026 Conversion from Partnership Classification to Cap Disregarded Entity; Cancellation of Indebtedness Income

All of the assets of an LLC were deemed distributed to the remaining member when that member, as owner of 99 percent of the membership units, purchased the membership units from a related one percent member. The debt from the LLC to the remaining member was treated as canceled. However, there was no cancellation of indebtedness income.

200214016 Merger of Corporation into an LLC

The merger of a corporation into an LLC is treated as a nontaxable contribution of assets by the corporation to the LLC in exchange for membership interests, followed by a taxable distribution of the membership interests to the shareholders of the corporation in redemption of their stock. The corporation recognizes gain to the same extent as if it sold the membership interests to the shareholders for fair market value. The shareholders of the corporation also recognize capital gain or loss on distribution of the membership interests. The gain is equal to the difference between the fair market value of the membership interests less their basis in the stock. There is a technical termination of the LLC as a result of the merger. However, no gain or loss is recognized as result of the deemed termination.

200211015 Transfer to Investment LLC

The transfer of a partnership interest to an LLC in exchange for a membership interest in the LLC does not constitute a transfer of property to an investment company under Code Sec. 721(b).

200209027 Code Sec. 754 Basis Adjustment

An LLC was granted an extension of time to make an election to adjust the basis of its assets under Code Sec. 754.

200205025 Code Sec. 754 Basis Adjustment

An LLC was granted an extension of time to make an election to adjust the basis of its assets under Code Sec. 754.

---

[5] Ltr. Ruls. 200223036-045.

200205005 Extension of Time to Elect Classification

An LLC was granted an extension of time to elect classification as a corporation.

200204005 Capital Call Provisions

The amendment of an LLC's operating agreement that imposed below-market call provisions on capital accounts in order to facilitate a public offering did not constitute a taxable transfer of property under Code Sec. 83 because the member's right to the capital accounts was substantially vested prior to the amendment to the operating agreement.

200204004 Extension of Time to Elect Classification

An LLC was granted an extension of time to elect classification as a corporation.

200202077 Charitable Organization Ownership of LLC

A private foundation formed an LLC to own, build, operate and lease a racetrack and campground that was related to the exempt functions of the private foundation. The LLC's ownership and operation of the functionally related business did not constitute a business enterprise or result in the excess business holdings excise tax to the charitable organization that owned the LLC.

200201024 Multiple Member LLC Classified as Disregarded Entity

An LLC with two members was classified as a single-member disregarded entity since the second member had no interest in the profits or losses of the LLC, and had limited participation in the LLC.

200151046 Unrelated Business Income from Timber Contracts

A charity's share of income from an LLC's disposition of timber contracts is not subject to the tax on unrelated business income.

200151039 Extension of Time to Elect Classification

An LLC was granted an extension of time to elect classification as a corporation.

200150027 Charitable Organization's Ownership of LLC

A tax-exempt organization formed a single-member LLC to receive a charitable contribution of real estate. The LLC was used to protect the charitable organization from liabilities. The IRS would not rule on the deductibility of a charitable contribution of real property to the LLC.

The assets owned or transferred to the LLC are treated as owned or transferred to the charitable organization. The LLC is treated as part of the charitable organization unless it elects classification as a separate corporation. Thus, the charitable organization is not required to file separate returns or make separate public disclosures for the LLC. The single-member LLC is not required to file an application for exemption on Form 1023. The acceptance of the charitable contribution by the LLC will not adversely affect the tax-exempt status of the charitable organization that owns the LLC.

200147018-020 Extension of Time to Elect Classification

A foreign LLC was granted an extension of time to elect classification as a corporation.

200143012 S Corporation Ownership of LLC

An S corporation owned all of the stock in another S corporation that was a qualified Subchapter S subsidiary. The qualified Subchapter S subsidiary was the sole owner of an LLC that was classified as a disregarded entity. The LLC owned a general partnership interest in a limited partnership. The parent S corporation was treated as the general partner in the limited partnership since both the qualified Subchapter S subsidiary and the LLC were disregarded entities.[6]

200139020 Cooperative LLC

An LLC that is formed under the state's cooperative LLC act may elect to be classified as either a corporation or partnership if it has at least two members.

200139016 Extension of Time for Classification Election

The IRS granted a foreign LLC an extension of time to elect classification as a partnership.

200139002 Conversion of LLC into Corporation

An LLC converted to a corporation by forming a new corporation. The conversion was completed by a merger of the corporate member into the new corporation, and by a transfer of membership units in the LLC to the corporation by the other member. After the conversion, the LLC was a wholly owned subsidiary of the new corporation. The transfer of property and/or membership units to the corporation in exchange for shares is treated as a tax-free incorporation under Code Sec. 351. The LLC is treated as liquidating into the corporation because the classification of the LLC changes from a partnership to a disregarded entity when it becomes wholly owned by the new corporation. The LLC does not recognize gain or loss on the deemed distribution of its assets in liquidation.

200137038 Foreign Sales Corporation (FSC)

A U.S. parent corporation is entitled to a 100 percent dividends received exclusion for dividends received from a foreign sales corporation. The foreign sales corporation was owned indirectly through a single-member LLC that was classified as a disregarded entity.

200135015 Transfer of Patent to LLC

The holder of a patent may transfer patent rights to an LLC that is classified as a partnership. The LLC is treated as any other partnership for purposes Code Sec. 1235 and regulations thereunder. After the transfer, the holder of the patent rights retains his status as a "holder" for purposes of Code Sec. 1235. Thus, assuming the other requirements of Code Sec. 1235 are met, the member's share of gain recognized by the LLC on disposition of an interest in the patents qualifies as long-term capital gain.

---

[6] Ltr. Rul. 200143012.

200134025 Charitable Contribution to Single Member LLC Owned by Tax-Exempt Organization

A tax-exempt organization may form single-member LLCs to receive and hold separate contributions of real estate and other high-liability assets. The LLC is used to protect the tax-exempt parent organization from liability. The contribution of property to the LLC is deductible as a charitable contribution under Code Sec. 170(a), subject to the same percentage limitations and other restrictions that apply to deductible contributions made directly to the exempt entity. The single-member LLC is not required to file an application for exemption on Form 1023.

200133038 Extension of Time to Elect Classification

An LLC was granted an extension of time to elect classification as a disregarded entity. The LLC had previously made an election to be classified as a corporation.

200133030 Ordinary Income on Sale of Depreciable Property to Related LLC

The sale by a corporation of assets to an LLC will not result in the recognition of ordinary income if the LLC is not a related party under Code Sec. 1239. The same rule applies whether the LLC is classified as a partnership or as a corporation.

200133018 Extension of Time to Elect Classification

A foreign LLC was granted an extension of time to elect classification as a disregarded entity.

200132014 Prepaid Subscription Income on Transfer to LLC

A publisher will not recognize prepaid subscription income under Code Sec. 455(b) on the transfer of his assets and liabilities to an LLC that is classified as a disregarded entity.

200132009 Tax Returns for Terminated LLC

An LLC terminates if the members sell more than 50 percent of the membership interests to a related party. The LLC that terminates must file a short-year final return for the taxable year ending with the date of its termination. The new LLC must file a return for its taxable year beginning after the date of termination of the terminated partnership. A full-year return starts the running of the statute of limitations for the new and old LLC if the members fail to file the short-year returns.

200131016 Extension of Time to Elect Classification

A foreign LLC was granted an extension of time to elect classification as a disregarded entity.

200131014 Like-Kind Exchange

The taxpayer may complete a like-kind exchange by transferring the replacement property to a single-member LLC that is classified as a disregarded entity.

200130025 Code Sec. 754 Election

The IRS granted an extension of time for an LLC to make an election under Code Sec. 754 to adjust the basis of its assets.

200129029 Conversion of Subsidiary Corporation into LLC

The conversion of a subsidiary corporation into an LLC that is classified as a disregarded entity is treated as the liquidation of the subsidiary corporation into the parent corporation. The conversion constitutes a liquidation under Code Sec. 332. No gain or loss is recognized by the parent corporation on the deemed receipt of assets and liabilities from the subsidiary corporation pursuant to Code Sec. 332(a). Capital gain or loss is recognized by the subsidiary on its deemed distribution of assets to, or the assumption of liabilities by, the parent corporation pursuant to Code Secs. 336(d)(3) and 337(a). The basis of each asset in the hands of the parent corporation is equal to the basis of the assets in the hands of the subsidiary corporation immediately before his conversion into a single-member LLC pursuant to Code Sec. 334(b)(1). The holding period of each asset of the subsidiary corporation in the hands of the parent corporation includes the period during which the assets were held by the subsidiary corporation pursuant to Code Sec. 1223(2). The parent corporation will succeed to and take into account the items of the subsidiary described in Code Sec. 381(c), subject to the conditions and limitations specified in Code Secs. 381–384 and regulations thereunder pursuant to Code Sec. 381(a) and Reg. §1.381(a)-1. Except to the extent that the subsidiary's earnings in profits are already reflected in the parent corporation earnings and profits, the parent corporation must take into account the earnings and profits, or deficit in earnings and profits, of the subsidiary as of the date of the subsidiary's conversion into a single-member LLC pursuant to Code Sec. 381(c)(2)(A), and Reg. §§1.381(c)(2)-1, 1.1502-33(a)(2).

200129024 Merger of Subsidiary Corporation into LLC Owned by Parent

The merger of a subsidiary corporation into an LLC owned by the parent corporation qualifies as a tax-free liquidation under Code Sec. 332 if the LLC is classified as a disregarded entity for federal tax purposes. The merger was tax-free even though the parent corporation, the subsidiary and the LLC made a number of purchases and sales of stock prior to the transaction.

200129019 Deferral of Estate Taxes

The owners' transfer of their interest in a closely held business to an LLC in exchange for membership interests does not constitute a disposition or result in the termination of the estate tax deferral under Code Sec. 6166.

200129018 Extension of Time to Pay Estate Taxes

The transfer of real estate assets from a trust to an LLC does not materially alter the business, and is a mere change in form. Thus, the transfer of real estate from two trusts to an LLC does not constitute disposition of property of a closely held business under Code Sec. 6166(g)(1)(A), or result in the acceleration of estate taxes.

200125037 Transfer of Real Estate to Trust; Generation-Skipping Tax

The transfer of commercial real estate from a trust to an LLC will not affect the trust's generation-skipping transfer tax exemption.

200125013 Cooperative Housing Corporation

A cooperative housing corporation may issue stock allocable to nonresidential space leased to a bank to its tenant stockholders without affecting its status and without the recognition of gain or loss by the co-op or its stockholders. The contribution by the tenant-stockholders of the shares of stock allocated to the commercial space to an LLC in exchange for membership interests is not taxable to the tenant-stockholders or to the LLC pursuant to Code Sec. 721(a). The basis in the membership interests received by each tenant-stockholder is the same as the basis the tenant-stockholder had in the corporation shares allocated to the commercial space contributed to the LLC pursuant to Code Sec. 722. The basis in the corporation shares received by the LLC from the tenant-stockholders is the cumulative bases that the tenant-stockholders had in the shares prior to their contribution to the LLC pursuant to Code Sec. 723.

200124030 Contribution of LIFO Inventory to LLC

The contribution of LIFO inventory by LLC members to an LLC that is classified as a partnership does not trigger recapture of the LIFO reserve. However, the LLC must file IRS Form 970 and comply with Code Sec. 472 in order to adopt the dollar-value LIFO inventory method. Any LIFO inventory contributed to the LLC is Code Sec. 704(c) property. Thus, any built-in gain or loss attributable to the inventory must be allocated to the contributing member for tax purposes when the inventory is sold. On approval by the IRS, the LLC may treat the items included in its opening inventory as having been acquired at the same time, and determine their cost by the average cost method as provided under Code Sec. 472(b)(3).

200124029 Charitable Lead Annuity Trust

A charitable lead annuity trust may form an LLC and sell an interest in the LLC to the remainder beneficiaries in exchange for a promissory note. The sale does not constitute an act of self-dealing under Code Sec. 4941 of the Code.

200124022 Disregarded LLC Owned by Charitable Organization

A tax-exempt charitable organization may form a wholly owned LLC to purchase, renovate, and operate a parking lot. The LLC was a disregarded entity. The operation of the parking lot constituted charitable activities related to be exempt functions of the parent organization. There was no unrelated business income or debt-financed property. The LLC's charitable activities were attributable to the parent organization but did not jeopardize the tax-exempt status of the parent organization.

200123035 Conversion of S Corporation to LLC; Contribution of LIFO Inventory to LLC

An S corporation may convert to an LLC by forming an LLC and contributing its assets to the LLC in exchange for membership interests. Neither the corporation nor the LLC recognize gain or loss on the contribution of assets to the LLC in exchange for membership interests. The contribution of LIFO inventory property to the LLC will not result in the recapture of the LIFO reserve. However, in order to adopt the dollar-value LIFO inventory method, the transferee LLC must file IRS Form 970 and otherwise comply with the requirements of Code Sec. 472 and regulations thereunder. The LIFO inventory contributed to the LLC constitutes Code Sec. 704(c) property, and any built-in gain or loss attributable to the inventory contributed by a member must be allocated back to the member when the LLC recognizes that gain or loss on the sale of the inventory.

200122035 Extension of Time to Elect Partnership Classification

A foreign LLC was granted an extension of time to elect classification as a partnership.

200119016 Conversion of Cooperative from Corporation to LLC

A corporation that was taxed as a cooperative converted from a corporation to an LLC that was classified as a corporation under federal law. After the reorganization, the LLC continued to be treated as a cooperative under subchapter T of the Code.

200118054 Nonprofit Organization Participation in an LLC

A tax-exempt organization may participate in an ambulatory surgery center organized as an LLC. The participation in the LLC will not result in unrelated business income, or jeopardize the tax-exempt status of the LLC.

200118023 LLC as Qualified Intermediary in Like-Kind Exchange

An LLC may act as a qualified intermediary in a like-kind exchange.[7] The taxpayer may also complete a like-kind exchange by acquiring the single-member LLC that acted as the intermediary and owned the replacement property. The acquisition of the LLC is made to avoid state transfer taxes that would otherwise apply if the taxpayer directly acquired the property from the intermediary. The taxpayer's acquisition of the LLC is treated as the acquisition of the replacement property if the LLC is classified as a disregarded entity for federal tax purposes.[8]

200116051 Employee Stock Ownership Plan

The employees of an LLC may participate in a Code Sec. 423 employee stock purchase plan of the corporate owner of the LLC. If the corporate owner of the LLC is a subsidiary of a parent corporation, the employees of the LLC may receive stock of the parent corporation under a Code Sec. 423 stock purchase plan or an incentive stock option plan.

200114017 Extension of Time to Elect Taxation as Corporation

The IRS granted an extension of time for an LLC to file an election on Form 8832 to be classified as a corporation. The extension was requested after the deadline for filing the classification election.

200114006 Employment Tax Assessments

Employment tax assessments erroneously made under the name and employment identification number of a single member LLC still serve as valid assessments against the sole owner of the LLC.

---

[7] Ltr. Rul. 200118023.

[8] Ltr. Rul. 200118023.

Appendix C

200114004 Gift Taxes

An LLC's prepayment of annual distributions on preferred membership interests constitutes a qualified payment under Code Sec. 2701(c)(3) and Reg. § 25.2701-2(b)(6)(i)(B).

200112021 Stock Option Plans for Corporate Owned LLCs

If the corporate owner of the LLC is a subsidiary of a parent corporation, the employees of the LLC may receive stock of the parent corporation under a Code Sec. 423 stock purchase plan or an incentive stock option plan.

200112004 Extension of Time to Elect Classification

A foreign LLC owned by a limited partnership was granted an extension of time to elect classification as a disregarded entity. The deadline for filing an election had already passed.

200111053 Participation in ESOP by Disregarded LLC

Employees of an LLC that is owned by a member of a controlled group of corporations, and that is classified as a disregarded entity, may participate in an employee stock ownership plan or other qualified plan of the controlled group. The employees of the LLC are treated as employed by the member of the controlled group that owns the membership interests in the LLC.

200110016 Extension to File a Classification Election

The IRS granted an extension of time for an LLC to file an election on Form 8832 to be classified as a corporation. The extension was requested after the deadline for filing the classification election.

200109032-033 Extension of Time to Elect Classification

A foreign LLC owned by a qualified S corporation subsidiary was granted an extension of time to elect classification as a disregarded entity. The deadline for filing an election had already passed.

200109019 Conversion of Corporation to LLC Classified as Corporation

A corporation may convert to an LLC that is classified as a corporation without adverse tax consequences by filing an election to be classified as a corporation effective as of the date of the conversion.

200107018 S Corporation Ownership of S Corporation Subsidiary through LLC

An S corporation may own stock in another S corporation only if it owns 100 percent of the stock in the S corporation subsidiary and files an election with the IRS.[9] The parent S corporation may transfer some or all of the stock in the S corporation subsidiary to an LLC if the parent corporation owns the LLC, and if the LLC is classified as a disregarded entity for federal tax purposes. The transfer of the stock to

---

[9] Code Sec. 1361(b)(3).

the subsidiary will not cause the termination of the parent corporation's qualified Subchapter S subsidiary election.

200105045 Employment Tax Assessments

Employment tax assessments erroneously made under the name and employment identification number of a single member LLC still serve as valid assessments against the sole owner of the LLC.

200103023 LLC Owned by Trust

An LLC owned by a trust is a disregarded entity and treated as a branch of the trust.

200102038 D Reorganization

The consolidation by a parent corporation of two wholly owned subsidiaries through a disregarded LLC is treated as a D reorganization.

200102037 Rental Income Received by Disregarded Entity; LLC Owned by Grantor Trust

The owner of the LLC that is a disregarded entity may not deduct rent paid to the LLC to lease real property owned by the LLC, and the LLC is not taxed on the rental income received.

The LLC may be treated as a disregarded entity even though it is owned by an individual and by a grantor trust owned by the individual.

200102024 S Corporation's Receipt of LLC's Gross Receipts Not Passive

An S corporation's distributive share of LLC gross receipts attributable to an active trade or business (commercial contracting) is not passive income under Code Sec. 1375.

200052005 Extension of Time to Elect Classification

A foreign LLC was granted an extension of time to elect classification as a disregarded entity. The deadline for filing an election had already passed.

200049003 Denial of Estate Tax Valuation Discounts

The economic substance doctrine may be used to deny valuation discounts for a membership interest in an LLC if (i) the transfers of property to the LLC and the gifts and transfers of membership interests appreciably changes the taxpayer's economic position, and (ii) the taxpayer does not have a valid business purpose or profit motive for establishing the LLC and making the gifts and transfers.

200046031 Extension to File a Classification Election

The IRS granted an extension of time for an LLC to file an election on Form 8832 to be classified as a corporation. The extension was requested after the deadline for filing the classification election.

200045024 Extension of Time to Elect Partnership Classification

A foreign entity that was acquired by two foreign LLCs was granted an extension of time to elect classification as a partnership.

Appendix C

200045022 Extension of Time to Elect Partnership Classification

A foreign LLC was granted an extension of time to elect classification as a partnership.

200045015 Extension of Time to Elect Partnership Classification

A foreign LLC was granted an extension of time to elect classification as a partnership.

200025018 At-Risk Amounts

A member of an LLC is at risk for amounts that the LLC owes to a supplier if the member signs a stipulation of judgment for delinquent payments on behalf of the LLC in his individual capacity. The member is at risk because the member is liable for payment of the amount owed to the supplier. A member is also at risk for amounts that the LLC owes to the lessor for delinquent rent if the member signed a personal guarantee. Each member of the LLC is at risk for the entire amount of the defaulted rent if the member does not have a right of reimbursement against the other members on payment of the defaulted amount. Each member of the LLC is not at risk to the extent the member has a right to reimbursement against the other members on payment of the defaulted amount.

200024024 Extension to File a Classification Election

The IRS granted an extension of time for an LLC to file an election on Form 8832 to be classified as a corporation. The extension was requested after the deadline for filing the classification election.

200022016 Conversion of General Partnership in the LLC

There is no tax to the general partnership, the LLC or its members get a general partnership converged into an LLC, or the liabilities of the members remain the same. There is no termination of the general partnership. The LLC is not required to obtain a new employer identification number after the conversion. The LLC's basis in the assets is the same as the partnership's basis in its assets immediately prior to conversion. The members' holding period includes their holding period in their general partnership interest. The members retain their same capital accounts.

200019042 Residency of Single Member LLC

The Philadelphia Service Center will not certify that a single-member LLC is a resident of United States for purposes of reduced withholding taxes payable in foreign countries with respect to the income received by the LLC from foreign sources. However, the Service may certify that the single owner of the LLC is a resident of the United States. This should establish that the income derived by the LLC in the treaty country is derived by a U.S. resident and entitled to treaty benefits.

200009025 Corporate Member of LLC; Dividends Received Deduction; Allocation of FSC Income; Multi-Tiered LLC

A corporate member of an LLC is entitled to a dividends received deduction for the member's allocable share of dividends received by the LLC, including a 100 percent deduction for dividends received by the LLC from a foreign sales corporation. The dividends received deduction applies to a corporation that is a shareholder and LLC that in turn owns a membership interest in another LLC that owns the foreign sales corporation.

200008015 Single Member LLC Ownership in an S Corporation

A single member LLC may own stock in an S corporation if the LLC is classified as a disregarded entity for federal tax purposes, and the LLC is owned by an individual.

200005016 C Reorganization

The acquisition of membership units in an LLC that has elected to be classified as a corporation qualifies as a tax-free C reorganization.

200002025 Valuation of Family LLC for Estate and Gift Tax Purposes

The IRS may ignore restrictions in an LLC operating agreement, and deny any minority, marketability, or liquidity discounts for estate and gift tax purposes, if the LLC has no economic substance other than to reduce taxes. The valuation discounts may be denied based on the economic substance doctrine, Code Sec. 2703, or Code Sec. 2704.

200010004 Investment Interest Limitations

Investment interest paid by an LLC may be deducted only to the extent of investment income. Investment income includes interest income earned by the LLC on bank accounts, but does not include interest income earned on deferred payments of accounts receivable.

200001016 Classification Election Extension

The IRS granted a foreign LLC an extension of time to elect classification as a partnership for federal tax purposes. The LLC failed to file a timely election.

199952071 Charitable Remainder Unitrust

An LLC may be the grantor of a charitable remainder unitrust. An LLC that is classified as a partnership for federal tax purposes is a permissible recipient of the unitrust amount.

199952068 Classification Election Extension

The IRS granted a foreign LLC an extension of time to elect classification as a partnership for federal tax purposes. The LLC failed to file a timely election.

199947034 Special Valuation Rules

The reorganization of a C corporation as an LLC that is classified as a corporation does not constitute a transfer of an interest subject to the Code Sec. 2701 special valuation if (a) the membership units have identical rights, preferences, and restrictions as the corporate stocks surrendered in the exchange, or (b) the exchanging family member holds substantially the same interest before and after the transaction.

199945038 Condemnations

A taxpayer whose property has been taken in a condemnation may avoid nonrecognition on the gain by acquiring replacement property. The taxpayer must purchase the replacement property in order to qualify for nonrecognition. The

Appendix C

taxpayer may use a single-member LLC that is classified as a disregarded entity to acquire the replacement property.

199938016 Tax Audit Procedures

The IRS commences audit proceedings for an LLC by filing a notice of beginning of administrative proceeding (NBAP). If there is no settlement as to all of the members, then the IRS will issue a notice of a final partnership administrative adjustment (FPAA) (Code Sec. 6225). The FPAA cannot be issued sooner than 120 days after the NBAP is issued. If the IRS issues the FPAA less than 120 days subsequent to the issuance of the NBAP, then the members may elect to have their membership items treated as nonmembership items. It is not appropriate for the IRS to intentionally fail to issue timely notices so as to allow the LLC and members to elect out of the regular audit procedures for LLCs.

199936011 Disguised Sales

An LLC is treated as having made a disguised sale under Code Sec. 707 if it makes a cash distribution to a member who contributed property to the LLC within two years after the date of the contribution, where the purpose of the cash distribution was to make an adjusting payment to the members in order to change the relative percentage interests in the LLC. The LLC receives a cost basis in the assets that it is treated as having purchased from the member. The antiabuse regulations under Code Sec. 701 do not apply to the transaction because the principal purpose of the transaction was not to reduce the member's aggregate tax liability in a manner inconsistent with Subchapter K.

199935065 Like-Kind Exchanges

A limited partnership is treated as the continuation of an LLC where the LLC liquidates and transfers its assets and liabilities to its members, after which the members immediately retransfer the assets and liabilities to a newly formed limited partnership. The liquidation does not result in the termination of the LLC. The limited partnership may complete a like-kind exchange entered into by the LLC prior to its liquidation. The limited partnership is treated as both the transferor of the relinquished property previously transferred to a qualified intermediary by the LLC before its liquidation, and as the transferee of the replacement property received from the qualified intermediary.

199930013 Levy Against Owner of Single-Member LLC

A single-member disregarded entity is treated as a separate entity for IRS tax collection and tax lien purposes. The IRS may only collect from the property of a taxpayer to satisfy the taxpayer's liability. It may not proceed against the taxpayer's limited liability company even though the LLC is disregarded for federal tax purposes. The IRS has various other collection options, including (1) collecting from the taxpayer's distributive share of income, and (2) collecting from the assets of the LLC on the ground that it is the alter ego of the taxpayer. Whether any of these options is available must be determined on a case-by-case basis.

199922053 Self-Employment Taxes

The members of an LLC with more than one member are not responsible for employment taxes incurred by the LLC. The sole member of a single-member LLC bears personal responsibility for employment taxes incurred by the LLC.

199920023 Extension to File a Classification Election

The IRS granted an extension of time for an LLC to file an election on Form 8832 to be classified as a corporation. The extension was requested after the deadline for filing the classification election.

199917049-051 LLC as an Investment Company

There is no tax on the transfer to an LLC of partnership interests containing a diversified portfolio of investment assets. The LLC is not treated as an investment company. There is no tax on the distribution of membership units in the LLC in exchange for the contribution of partnership interests.

199916010 Withholding Taxes after Conversion from General Partnership to LLC

The LLC remains the same employer for withholding tax purposes after the conversion from a general partnership. The LLC is not required to begin withholding FICA and FUTA taxes with a new contribution base after the conversion. The same rule applies even if the LLC obtains a new employer identification number after the conversion.

199915040 Contribution of Leasehold Interest to LLC

The contribution of a long-term leasehold interest to an LLC in exchange for a membership interest is a nontaxable contribution of property to the LLC.

199914006 Two-Member LLC Treated as Single-Member LLC; Reimbursement by LLC of Capital Expenditures

The reimbursement of capital expenditures by an LLC to a member in excess of 20 percent of the fair market value at the time of the contribution did not cause the contribution of property to the LLC to be treated as a sale under Code Sec. 707. Even though the LLC had two members, it was treated as owned by a single member, since the second member had no interest in profits and losses, did not manage the LLC, and had only limited voting rights. The LLC was not classified as a partnership, since the members did not enter into an agreement to share profits and losses from the operation of a business.

199913051 Reorganization of Group Health Care Organizations

Two groups of health care organizations may combine their operations by forming a limited liability company and contributing their assets to the limited liability company. Placing the charitable activities under the control of the LLC will not change the exempt status of the charities or the nonprivate foundation status of the exempt entities involved in the reorganization. There will be no unrelated business taxable income as a result of the reorganization. The public charities may remain in control of the LLC after the reorganization, with the LLC serving the interests only of the charities.

Appendix C

199913035 Reorganization of Group Health Care Organizations

Two groups of health care organizations may combine their operations by forming a limited liability company and contributing their assets to the limited liability company. Placing the charitable activities under the control of the LLC will not change the exempt status of the charities or the nonprivate foundation status of the exempt entities involved in the reorganization. There will be no unrelated business taxable income as a result of the reorganization. The public charities may remain in control of the LLC after the reorganization, with the LLC serving the interests only of the charities.

199912030 Sale of Membership Units

The sale of membership units by a majority member to a third party does not result in the termination of the LLC, provided that no membership units in the LLC are transferred within a 12-month period before or after the sale to the third party.

199911033 Like-Kind Exchanges

An LLC with two members will be treated as owned by a single member for like-kind exchange purposes if the second member has no interest in profits and losses, does not manage the LLC, and has only limited voting rights. The LLC cannot be classified as a partnership, since the members have not entered into an agreement to share profits and losses from the operation of a business. The LLC will be treated as a disregarded entity if the LLC does not elect to be classified as a corporation for federal tax purposes.

199909056 Formation of LLC by Public Charity; Unrelated Business Income

A public charity formed an LLC to obtain loans and financing for minority and disadvantaged businesses in the community. The tax-exempt status of the public charity was not adversely affected even though the public charity acted as the manager of the LLC, received interest and loan fees, issued membership interests in the LLC to for-profit investors, and paid a profit participation interest to the investors. The public charity must own a controlling interest in the LLC and operate the LLC primarily for charitable purposes. Income earned by the public charity from the LLC is not considered income from an unrelated business under Code Sec. 513.

199909045 Involuntary Conversion

A taxpayer may avoid gain on an involuntary conversion by purchasing replacement property that is similar or related in service or use.[10] The same taxpayer whose property was taken in the involuntary conversion must acquire the replacement property. However, a single-member LLC that is owned by the taxpayer, and that is classified as a disregarded entity for federal tax purposes, may be used to acquire the replacement property. Receipt of the replacement property by the LLC is treated as receipt of the replacement property directly by the owner of the LLC for purposes of the nonrecognition of gain rules.

---

[10] Code Sec. 1033.

199909025 Aggregation of Built-In Gains and Losses

A securities LLC may make Code Sec. 704(c) allocations for built-in gains and losses and reverse Code Sec. 704(c) allocations by aggregating gains and losses from qualified financial assets using any reasonable approach that is consistent with Code Sec. 704(c). Once the LLC adopts the aggregate approach, the LLC must apply the same aggregate approach to all of its qualified financial assets for all taxable years in which the LLC qualifies as a securities LLC.

199908057 Extension to File a Classification Election

The IRS granted an extension of time for an LLC to file an election on Form 8832 to be classified as a corporation. The extension was requested after the deadline for filing the classification election.

199908043 Division of LLC

An LLC classified as a partnership was divided into two LLCs. Each LLC was considered as a continuation of the original LLC where the members of the original LLC were also members of the newly formed LLCs, holding the same proportionate interests.

199906028 Allocation of Tax Credits

The allocation of tax credits and tax credit recapture are not reflected by adjustments to the capital accounts of members of an LLC. Therefore, any allocations of tax credits or tax credit recapture cannot have economic effect under the safe-harbor regulations for special allocations. Accordingly, the tax credits must be allocated in accordance with the members' interest in the LLC at the time the tax credit or tax credit recapture arises. If the expenditure that gives rise to tax credit in a tax year also gives rise to a valid allocation of LLC loss or deduction, or other downward adjustment in capital accounts, for such year, then the members' interest in the LLC for such credit must be in the same proportion as the members' respective distributive shares of such loss or deduction (and adjustments). The same principles apply in determining the members' interest in an LLC for tax credits that arise from receipts by the LLC. The fuel tax credit under Code Sec. 29 is based on receipts from the sale of qualified fuels. Therefore, the LLC may allocate the credit in proportion to the allocation of receipts from the sale of qualified fuel if the allocation of the receipts complies with the safe-harbor regulations on allocations.

199904027 Allocation of Tax Credits under Code Sec. 29

The fuel tax credit under Code Sec. 9 is based on receipts from the sale of qualified fuels. Therefore, the LLC may allocate the credit in proportion to the allocation of receipts from the sale of qualified fuel if the allocation of the receipts complies with the safe-harbor regulations on allocations.

199904020-199904022 Extension to File a Classification Election

The IRS granted an extension of time for an LLC to file an election on Form 8832 to be classified as a corporation.

199904018 Extension to File a Classification Election

The IRS granted an extension of time for an LLC to file an election on Form 8832 to be classified as a corporation.

Appendix C

199904008 Inadvertent Termination of S Corporation

The transfer of stock in an S corporation to an LLC that is classified as a partnership will disqualify the corporation as an S corporation. An LLC that is classified as a partnership is not an eligible shareholder of an S corporation. The IRS may grant relief from inadvertent termination in such cases.

9853045 Extension of Time to Elect Classification as Corporation

The IRS may grant an extension of time for an LLC to elect classification as a corporation. The LLC wanted to be classified as a corporation so that it could elect to be classified as an S corporation.

9850001 Like-Kind Exchange

A taxpayer may use an LLC to acquire replacement property in a like-kind exchange if the LLC is a single-member LLC that is classified as a disregarded entity for federal tax purposes. The taxpayer may also merge an LLC that has acquired the replacement property into another LLC owned by the taxpayer without adversely affecting the like-kind exchange.

9846027 Patronage Dividends of Cooperatives

A cooperative's distributive share of operational income from an LLC that is attributable to sales to persons to whom the cooperative has a preexisting obligation to pay patronage dividends with respect to such income constitutes patronage source income eligible for the patronage dividend deduction. For purposes of Code Sec. 1388(a), it was appropriate to look through the LLC to its cooperative owners. Thus, the patrons were continuing to do business with the cooperative on a cooperative basis. The LLC was treated as a pass-through entity wholly owned by the cooperative, which was in turn wholly owned by its members.

9846022 Patronage Dividends of Cooperatives

A cooperative's distributive share of operational income from an LLC that is attributable to sales to persons to whom the cooperative has a preexisting obligation to pay patronage dividends with respect to such income constitutes patronage source income eligible for the patronage dividend deduction. For purposes of Code Sec. 1388(a), it was appropriate to look through the LLC to its cooperative owners. Thus, the patrons were continuing to do business with the cooperative on a cooperative basis. The LLC was treated as a pass-through entity wholly owned by the cooperative, which was in turn wholly owned by its members.

9845010 Extension of Time to Elect a Tax Year

The IRS granted a limited liability company an extension of time to elect a taxable year other than the required year. The extension of time was granted after the LLC filed Form 8716 electing the change after the due date. The late filing was due to an error or misunderstanding on the part of the tax professional hired by the LLC to file the election. Form 8716 was filed within 90 days after its due date, and the late filing was not due to any lack of due diligence on the part of the LLC. The IRS acted pursuant to its authority under Reg. § 301.9100-3.

9845009 Extension to File Election Classification

The IRS granted an extension for an LLC to file a classification election on Form 8832. The foreign LLC wanted to elect classification as a partnership, but had failed to file the form on a timely basis.

9845008 Extension to File Election Classification

The IRS granted an extension for an LLC to file a classification election on Form 8832. The foreign LLC wanted to elect classification as a disregarded entity, but had failed to file the form on a timely basis.

9841030 Conversion from General Partnership to LLC; Employer Identification Number

There is no tax to the general partnership, the LLC, or the members if a general partnership converts into an LLC, except as provided under Code Sec. 752. There is no termination of the general partnership. The LLC is treated as the continuation of the partnership. The taxable year of the partnership does not close.

A member's basis in the LLC membership interest is equal to the member's adjusted basis in the general partnership interest if the member's share of liabilities does not change after the conversion.

An LLC is not required to obtain a new employer identification number after the conversion from a general partnership.

9841013 Allocation of Tax Credits under Code Sec. 29

The fuel tax credit under Code Sec. 29 is based on receipts from the sale of qualified fuels. Therefore, the LLC may allocate the credit in proportion to the allocation of receipts from the sale of qualified fuel if the allocation of the receipts complies with the safe-harbor regulations on allocations.

9840054 LLC as Title Holding Company

An organization may use an LLC for an exempt title-holding company under Code Sec. 501(c)(25). The merger of the title-holding company into an LLC will not adversely affect the status of the company as a title-holding company or result in the imposition of the unrelated business income tax on either of the merged parties.

9839016-017 LLC as Nonprofit Organization

Nonprofit organizations formed an LLC to coordinate mutually beneficial activities and promote a regional network of hospitals and other health care entities that agreed to common supervision and oversight by the LLC.

9834040 Conversion from General Partnership to LLC; Employer Identification Number; Tiered Partnership Rules

There is no tax to the general partnership, the LLC, or the members if a general partnership converts into an LLC, except as provided under Code Sec. 752. There is no termination of the general partnership. The LLC is treated as the continuation of the partnership. The taxable year of the partnership will not close for any of the partners.

An LLC is not required to obtain a new employer identification number after the conversion from a general partnership. The tiered partnership rules do not apply.

Appendix C

The transfer of appreciated assets to the LLC will not result in a contribution or distribution of partnership property with respect to the partnership or the LLC under Code Secs. 704(c)(1)(B) and 737.

9834039 Conversion from General Partnership to LLC; Employer Identification Number; Tiered Partnership Rules

There is no tax to the general partnership, the LLC, or the members if a general partnership converts into an LLC, except as provided under Code Sec. 752. There is no termination of the general partnership. The LLC is treated as the continuation of the partnership. The taxable year of the partnership will not close for any of the partners.

An LLC is not required to obtain a new employer identification number after the conversion from a general partnership. The tiered partnership rules do not apply.

The transfer of appreciated assets to the LLC will not result in a contribution or distribution of partnership property with respect to the partnership or the LLC under Code Secs. 704(c)(1)(B) and 737.

9822043 Merger of Subsidiary into LLC

The merger of a subsidiary into an LLC owned by the parent corporation constitutes a complete liquidation under Code Sec. 332 and Reg. § 1.331-2(d).

9822037 Merger of Subsidiary into LLC

The merger of a subsidiary into an LLC owned by the parent corporation constitutes a complete liquidation under Code Sec. 332 and Reg. § 1.331-2(d).

9814006 Low-Income Housing Credits

An LLC may be formed to invest in low-income housing buildings eligible for the low-income housing credit under Code Sec. 42.

9811027 Special Valuation Rules

A partnership is not subject to the special valuation rules of Code Sec. 2703 if it was entered into prior to October 9, 1980, provided the partnership agreement was not substantially modified after that date. A general partner's transfer of a partnership interest to an LLC in order to limit liability does not constitute a substantial modification of the partnership agreement for such purposes.

9811026 Special Valuation Rules

A partnership is not subject to the special valuation rules of Code Sec. 2703 if it was entered into prior to October 9, 1980, provided the partnership agreement was not substantially modified after that date. A general partner's transfer of a partnership interest to an LLC in order to limit liability does not constitute a substantial modification of the partnership agreement for such purposes.

9809003 Conversion from General Partnership to LLC; Employer Identification Number; Tiered Partnership Rules

There is no tax to the general partnership, the LLC, or the members if a general partnership converts into an LLC, except as provided under Code Sec. 752. There is no termination of the general partnership. The LLC is treated as the continuation of the partnership. The taxable year of the partnership will not close for any of the partners.

An LLC is not required to obtain a new employer identification number after the conversion from a general partnership. The tiered partnership rules do not apply.

The transfer of appreciated assets to the LLC will not result in a contribution or distribution of partnership property with respect to the partnership or the LLC under Code Secs. 704(c)(1)(B) and 737.

9807013 Like-Kind Exchanges

A taxpayer may transfer replacement property directly to the taxpayer's wholly owned, single-member LLC in a Code Sec. 1031 exchange. The transfer of the property to the LLC will not disqualify the like-kind exchange.

9802047 Cooperative Housing Corporation

Tenant-shareholders may contribute some of their shares in a cooperative housing corporation to an LLC. The income that the cooperative housing corporation receives from the LLC in its capacity as a tenant-shareholder qualifies as income derived from the tenant-shareholders for purposes of the 80 percent rule under Code Sec. 216(b)(1)(D). The LLC must be classified as a partnership for federal income tax purposes. All of the stock in the LLC must be freely transferable and not stapled to any stock in the cooperative housing corporation.

9802004 Estate Freezes and Special Valuation Rules

Code Sec. 2704 applies to the transfer of general partnership interests in a partnership to an LLC if the LLC does not become the new general partner of the partnership. There is a termination of the member's voting and liquidation rights in the partnership if the member cannot exercise those same rights through the LLC after transfer to the LLC. The amount of the taxable gift is the difference between the value of the general partnership interest immediately prior to the transfer, and the value of the interest in the partnership held by the LLC immediately after the transfer.

The transfer of the general partnership interest to the LLC did not constitute a lapse or termination of voting rights under Code Sec. 2704(a)(2) because the general partner's voting rights in the LLC were created prior to October 8, 1990, the effective date of Code Sec. 2704(a). The general partnership agreement was created before that date, and not amended after October 8, 1990.

9752002-9752005 FICA Taxes for Religious LLC

A member of a Code Sec. 501(d) religious organization who works under a vow of poverty, in an enterprise conducted and owned by the organization, is not subject to employment taxes if the duties are required by the religious order. The member must have taken a vow of poverty and have no rights to the organization's assets when he leaves the organization. The transfer of a tax-exempt religious organization's unincorporated commercial enterprises to a limited liability company owned by the organization does not change this result.

Appendix C

9751048 Publicly Traded LLCs; Investment LLCs; Distribution of Units by Corporation to Shareholders

A parent corporation and its subsidiary transferred investment assets to an LLC. The LLC was not a publicly traded partnership within the meaning of Code Sec. 7704 since its income consisted entirely of interest, dividends and gains from the sale of stock or securities.

The transfer of the investment assets to the LLC did not result in taxation under Code Sec. 721(b) as a contribution to an investment company since the LLC was not an investment company for purposes of the rule. The subsidiary corporation contributed no more than one percent of the total fair market value of the contributed assets to the LLC. Therefore, the subsidiary's contribution was considered insignificant and the nonidentical assets were disregarded in determining whether the LLC's assets were diversified. Since the transfer did not result in diversification, there was no transfer of property to a partnership that would be treated as an investment company if it were incorporated.

The transfer of the investment assets to the LLC was non-taxable under Code Sec. 721(a) if the net reduction in the member's liabilities as a result of the LLC's assumption of those liabilities did not exceed the member's adjusted basis in the contributed assets.

The corporation recognized gain on the distribution on membership interest in the LLC to its shareholders. The distribution was treated as if the LLC sold the membership units to its shareholders at fair market value.

The corporation's distribution of the membership units to its shareholders constituted a transfer under Code Sec. 743. Therefore, the LLC was required to adjust the basis of its assets under Code Secs. 742 and 755.

The corporation's distribution of the membership units to its shareholders constituted an exchange causing the LLC to terminate under Code Sec. 708(b)(1)(D).

9751012 Like-Kind Exchanges

A parent corporation may transfer property in a like-kind exchange to an intermediary (accommodation party) and then have the intermediary transfer the replacement property to an LLC formed by the parent corporation. The LLC is treated as the same entity as the parent corporation assuming the LLC has not filed an election to be classified as a corporation.

9750004-9750008 LLC Ownership of Stock in S Corporation

An LLC that is classified as a partnership for federal tax purposes may not own stock in an S corporation. An LLC's acquisition of stock in an S corporation will terminate the S corporation election.

The IRS may grant relief from inadvertent termination as a result of the LLC's acquisition of stock in the S corporation if all of the following apply:

- The S corporation's election was terminated under Code Sec. 1362(d)(2) or (3).
- The IRS determines that the termination was inadvertent.
- The parties take steps to make the corporation a qualifying S corporation no later than a reasonable period of time after discovery of the events resulting in the termination.

- The corporation, and each person who was a shareholder of the corporation at any time after termination and prior to corrective steps, agree to make such adjustments consistent with the treatment of the corporation as an S corporation that the IRS requires. In such cases, the corporation is treated as continuing to be an S corporation during the period specified by the IRS.

9745017 LLC Ownership of Stock in S Corporation

An LLC may own the stock in an S corporation if all of the following apply:

- The LLC is a single member LLC
- The LLC is disregarded as an entity separate from its owner (rather that classified as a corporation) under the federal check-the-box classification rules
- The owner of the LLC is a permitted S corporation shareholder

An LLC owned by an individual or qualified trust may own the stock in an S corporation.

9741037 Applicability of Code Sec. 1491 in Merger of Two LLCs

The merger of two Delaware LLCs did not result in a transfer to a foreign partnership subject to former Code Sec. 1491. Under Code Sec. 1491, there was a 35 percent excise tax on transfers of property by U.S. persons to an LLC that was classified as a corporation or partnership.

9741021 Merger of General and Limited Partnerships into LLC; At-Risk Limitations

If a general partnership and limited partnership with identical ownership interests convert or merge into an LLC, the LLC is treated as the continuation of the largest partnership. The LLC retains the employer identification number of the largest partnership. None of the partners, partnerships or LLC recognizes gain or loss on the exchanges of their partnership interests for interests in the LLC or on the merger of the partnerships into the LLC.

If the requirements for qualified nonrecourse financing are met, the at-risk limitations will not apply to the losses generated by the properties held by the LLC.

9741018 Merger of General and Limited Partnerships into LLC; At-Risk Limitations

If a general partnership and limited partnership with identical ownership interests convert or merge into an LLC, the LLC is treated as the continuation of the largest partnership. The LLC retains the employer identification number of the largest partnership. None of the partners, partnerships or LLC recognizes gain or loss on the exchanges of their partnership interests for interests in the LLC or on the merger of the partnerships into the LLC.

If the requirements for qualified nonrecourse financing are met, the at-risk limitations will not apply to the losses generated by the properties held by the LLC.

9740001 Relief from Unforeseen Consequences of an LLC Election

In appropriate cases, the IRS may grant relief from unforeseen consequences of a LLC election. The parent corporation merged a first and second-tier subsidiary into itself. The parent corporation received a favorable ruling from the IRS that the merger of the subsidiaries into the parent constituted a tax-free liquidation. In order to obtain the favorable ruling, the parent corporation was required to represent that the liquidation of the two subsidiaries would not be preceded by or followed by a reincorporation of any of the businesses or assets of either of the subsidiaries.

Subsequently, the parent corporation transferred certain assets acquired in the merger to a limited liability company that was classified as a partnership for federal tax purposes and as a corporation for state tax purposes. The IRS issued a favorable ruling that the LLC would be classified as a partnership for federal tax purposes and that the prior favorable ruling on the merger would not be adversely affected. The parent corporation was required to reaffirm its prior representations, including the representation that it had no intention to reincorporate any of the businesses or assets that it acquired in the subsidiary corporation.

Later, the state amended its laws so that the LLC would be classified as a partnership rather than as a corporation for state tax purposes. This created a problem for the LLC, which would have lost its prior exemption from the state's personal property tax. The IRS permitted the LLC to restore its prior favorable tax treatment by electing to be taxed as a corporation for federal income tax purposes. The election by the LLC to be classified as a corporation was a reincorporation of the business and assets acquired in the prior merger and a potential violation of the representations made in connection with the prior letter rulings. However, the IRS granted relief because there were no plans or intentions, at the time of the merger, to reincorporate any of the business or assets acquired by the parent in the merger of the subsidiaries. The IRS ruled that the LLC's election to be taxed as a corporation would not adversely affect the prior favorable rulings that the mergers were tax free distributions and complete liquidation.

9739036-039 Tax-Exempt Hospitals

A tax-exempt hospital may form an LLC with two for-profit subsidiaries of two other tax-exempt hospitals for the purpose of providing diagnostic laboratory services for the patients of each of the hospitals, and expanding diagnostic laboratory services available to the general public. The contribution of cash and diagnostic laboratory equipment to the LLC in exchange for membership units, and the LLC's provision of diagnostic laboratory services to patients of each of the three hospitals and the general public, will not adversely affect the tax-exempt status of any of the three hospitals. The transaction will not adversely affect the non-private-foundation status of any of the three hospitals. The income received will not be treated as unrelated business income.

9739014 LLC Ownership of Stock in S Corporation

The owner of a single-member LLC may own stock in an S corporation if the LLC is classified as a disregarded entity for federal tax purposes and the member of the LLC otherwise qualifies as an S corporation shareholder. The transfer of S corporation shares to a single-member LLC does not terminate the S corporations election.

9738013 Merger of Limited Partnerships into LLC; At-Risk Limitations

If two limited partnerships with identical ownership interests convert or merge into an LLC, the LLC is treated as the continuation of the largest limited partnership. The LLC retains the employer identification number of the largest limited partnership. None of the limited partners, limit partnerships or LLC recognizes gain or loss on the exchanges of their partnership interests for interests in the LLC or on the transfer of assets from the limited partnerships to the LLC.

If the requirements for qualified nonrecourse financing are met, the at-risk limitations will not apply to the losses generated by the properties held by the LLC. The debt may be qualified nonrecourse financing even though the LLC is liable for repayment.

9736043 Unrelated Business Income

An exempt organization that provided prepaid group dental services to subscribers did not have unrelated business income on its allocable share of income from an LLC that provided financing to subscribers for the prepaid group general services.

9736004 Minority and Marketability Valuation Discounts

The IRS disallowed minority and marketability discounts for membership interests donated to family members under the sham transaction doctrine and Code Secs. 2703 and 2704. The Service noted the following:

- The member's transfer of property to the LLC and the gifts of membership interests occurred shortly before the member's death.
- The death beneficiaries received from the LLC the same assets that they would have received from the decedent if the assets had not been funneled through the LLC.
- The only ascertainable purpose for organizing the LLC was to depress the value of the assets that were transferred to the LLC. Nothing of substance was intended to change as a result of the transactions. The death beneficiaries retained control over the assets, and their management rights did not change as a result of the transactions.
- All of the transactions, including the transfer of assets from the decedent to the LLC and the subsequent gifts of membership interests to the family members should be viewed as a single testamentary transaction occurring at the decedent member's death.

9720008-9720013 Formation of LLC; Merger of LLCs into Limited Partnership

A member's basis in the LLC membership interest equals the amount of money and the adjusted basis in property contributed to the LLC.

The LLC's basis in the contributed assets equals the members' adjusted basis in the assets immediately before the contribution.

LLCs may merge into a limited partnership, after which the members of the LLC are limited partners. The tax consequences are as follows:

- If the members of one of the merging LLCs own more than 50 percent of the limited partnership after the merger (the majority LLC), the limited partnership will be treated as the continuation of the majority LLC.
- The other merging LLCs (the minority LLCs) are treated as contributing their assets and liabilities to the limited partnership in exchange for limited partnership interests. The minority LLCs are then deemed to terminate, and their taxable years close.

Appendix C

- No gain or loss is recognized by the LLCs or members on the contribution of assets by the minority LLCs and the members of the majority LLC to the limited partnership in exchange for limited partnership interests.
- The limited partnership's basis in the contributed assets equals the contributors' basis in the assets at the time of contribution.
- The minority LLCs and the members of the majority LLC have a basis in their limited partnership interests equal to the amount of money and adjusted basis of other property contributed to the limited partnership at the time of contribution.
- Immediately after the merger, the minority LLCs are deemed to have distributed the limited partnership interests received in the merger to the members of the LLC in liquidation of each member's interest in the minority LLCs. The basis of a limited partnership interest received by a member in liquidation of the LLC is the adjusted basis of the member's interest in the LLC, reduced by any money distributed in the same transaction.
- If no member of the minority LLCs receives money, unrealized receivable or inventory as a result of the liquidating distributions, no gain or loss is recognized by the minority LLCs or any of their members on the distributions of partnership interests to the members in the liquidations of the minority LLCs.
- The limited partners and general partners may recognize gain if the transfer of liabilities from the LLC to the partnership results in a net decrease in an LLC member's share of liabilities. The transfer of nonrecourse liabilities from the LLC to the partnership may result in a net decrease in a member's share of liabilities. A liability is nonrecourse as to the members of an LLC if no member currently bears the economic risk of loss for the liability. These liabilities are allocated to all the members in the LLC based on their share of profits. Thus, a member's basis is increased by the amount of nonrecourse liabilities multiplied by the member's percentage interest in profits. The nonrecourse liabilities normally become recourse liabilities when they are transferred to a limited partnership in a merger because a general partner is personally liable for all partnership liabilities. Recourse liabilities are allocated to the partners who are personally liable. All of the recourse liabilities are allocated to the general partner if no limited partner is currently liable for such debts after the merger. A member/limited partner is treated as receiving a distribution of money from the limited partnership to the extent of the decrease in his allocable share of liabilities. The deemed distribution of money reduces the limited partner's basis in the partnership interest. The limited partner recognizes gain to the extent the deemed distribution of money exceeds the limited partner's basis in the partnership.
- The transfer of recourse liabilities from the LLC to the partnership does not result in a deemed distribution of money or taxation to members if the members who were personally responsible for the liabilities prior to the merger continue to be personally liable after the merger.
- The transfer of encumbered property from the LLC to the partnership is subject to the disguised sale rules of Code Sec. 707(a)(2)(B). However, no gain or loss is recognized to the merging LLCs or its members under the disguised sale rules if the liabilities transferred are "qualified liabilities." The liabilities are qualified liabilities if the loan proceeds have been utilized to fund capital

improvements or for the ordinary and necessary expenses of operating the properties and if the debts are longstanding in duration.

   • Code Sec. 704(c) applies to the transfer of appreciated property by the LLC to the partnership.

9719019-9719029 Formation of LLC; Merger of LLCs into Limited Partnership

A member's basis in the LLC membership interest equals the amount of money and the adjusted basis in property contributed to the LLC.

The LLC's basis in the contributed assets equals the members' adjusted basis in the assets immediately before the contribution.

LLCs may merge into a limited partnership, after which the members of the LLC are limited partners. The tax consequences are as follows:

   • If the members of one of the merging LLCs own more than 50 percent of the limited partnership after the merger (the majority LLC), the limited partnership will be treated as the continuation of the majority LLC.

   • The other merging LLCs (the minority LLCs) are treated as contributing their assets and liabilities to the limited partnership in exchange for limited partnership interests. The minority LLCs are then deemed to terminate, and their taxable years close.

   • No gain or loss is recognized by the LLCs or members on the contribution of assets by the minority LLCs and the members of the majority LLC to the limited partnership in exchange for limited partnership interests.

   • The limited partnership's basis in the contributed assets equals the contributors' basis in the assets at the time of contribution.

   • The minority LLCs and the members of the majority LLC have a basis in their limited partnership interests equal to the amount of money and adjusted basis of other property contributed to the limited partnership at the time of contribution.

   • Immediately after the merger, the minority LLCs are deemed to have distributed the limited partnership interests received in the merger to the members of the LLC in liquidation of each member's interest in the minority LLCs. The basis of a limited partnership interest received by a member in liquidation of the LLC is the adjusted basis of the member's interest in the LLC, reduced by any money distributed in the same transaction.

   • If no member of the minority LLCs receives money, unrealized receivable or inventory as a result of the liquidating distributions, no gain or loss is recognized by the minority LLCs or any of their members on the distributions of partnership interests to the members in the liquidations of the minority LLCs.

   • The limited partners and general partners may recognize gain if the transfer of liabilities from the LLC to the partnership results in a net decrease in an LLC member's share of liabilities. The transfer of nonrecourse liabilities from the LLC to the partnership may result in a net decrease in a member's share of liabilities. A liability is nonrecourse as to the members of an LLC if no member currently bears the economic risk of loss for the liability. These liabilities are allocated to all the members in the LLC based on their share of profits. Thus, a member's basis is increased by the amount of nonrecourse liabilities multiplied by the member's percentage interest in profits. The nonrecourse liabilities normally become recourse liabilities when they are transferred to a limited partnership in a merger because a general partner is personally liable for all partnership liabilities. Recourse liabilities are allocated to the partners who are personally liable. All of the recourse liabilities are allocated to the general partner if no limited partner is currently liable for such debts after the merger. A member/limited partner is treated as receiving a distribution of money from the limited partnership to the extent of the decrease in his allocable share of liabilities. The deemed distribution of money reduces the limited partner's basis in the partnership interest. The limited partner recognizes gain to the extent the deemed distribution of money exceeds the limited partner's basis in the partnership.

• The transfer of recourse liabilities from the LLC to the partnership does not result in a deemed distribution of money or taxation to members if the members who were personally responsible for the liabilities prior to the merger continue to be personally liable after the merger.

• The transfer of encumbered property from the LLC to the partnership is subject to the disguised sale rules of Code Sec. 707(a)(2)(B). However, no gain or loss is recognized to the merging LLCs or its members under the disguised sale rules if the liabilities transferred are "qualified liabilities." The liabilities are qualified liabilities if the loan proceeds have been utilized to fund capital improvements or for the ordinary and necessary expenses of operating the properties and if the debts are long standing in duration.

• Code Sec. 704(c) applies to the transfer of appreciated property by the LLC to the partnership.

9719015 Formation of LLC; Merger of LLCs into Limited Partnership

A member's basis in the LLC membership interest equals the amount of money and the adjusted basis in property contributed to the LLC.

The LLC's basis in the contributed assets equals the members' adjusted basis in the assets immediately before the contribution.

LLCs may merge into a limited partnership, after which the members of the LLC are limited partners. The tax consequences are as follows:

• If the members of one of the merging LLCs own more than 50 percent of the limited partnership after the merger (the majority LLC), the limited partnership will be treated as the continuation of the majority LLC.

• The other merging LLCs (the minority LLCs) are treated as contributing their assets and liabilities to the limited partnership in exchange for limited partnership interests. The minority LLCs are then deemed to terminate, and their taxable years close.

• No gain or loss is recognized by the LLCs or members on the contribution of assets by the minority LLCs and the members of the majority LLC to the limited partnership in exchange for limited partnership interests.

• The limited partnership's basis in the contributed assets equals the contributors' basis in the assets at the time of contribution.

• The minority LLCs and the members of the majority LLC have a basis in their limited partnership interests equal to the amount of money and adjusted basis of other property contributed to the limited partnership at the time of contribution.

- Immediately after the merger, the minority LLCs are deemed to have distributed the limited partnership interests received in the merger to the members of the LLC in liquidation of each member's interest in the minority LLCs. The basis of a limited partnership interest received by a member in liquidation of the LLC is the adjusted basis of the member's interest in the LLC, reduced by any money distributed in the same transaction.

- If no member of the minority LLCs receives money, unrealized receivable or inventory as a result of the liquidating distributions, no gain or loss is recognized by the minority LLCs or any of their members on the distributions of partnership interests to the members in the liquidations of the minority LLCs.

- The limited partners and general partners may recognize gain if the transfer of liabilities from the LLC to the partnership results in a net decrease in an LLC member's share of liabilities. The transfer of nonrecourse liabilities from the LLC to the partnership may result in a net decrease in a member's share of liabilities. A liability is nonrecourse as to the members of an LLC if no member currently bears the economic risk of loss for the liability. These liabilities are allocated to all the members in the LLC based on their share of profits. Thus, a member's basis is increased by the amount of nonrecourse liabilities multiplied by the member's percentage interest in profits. The nonrecourse liabilities normally become recourse liabilities when they are transferred to a limited partnership in a merger because a general partner is personally liable for all partnership liabilities. Recourse liabilities are allocated to the partners who are personally liable. All of the recourse liabilities are allocated to the general partner if no limited partner is currently liable for such debts after the merger. A member/limited partner is treated as receiving a distribution of money from the limited partnership to the extent of the decrease in his allocable share of liabilities. The deemed distribution of money reduces the limited partner's basis in the partnership interest. The limited partner recognizes gain to the extent the deemed distribution of money exceeds the limited partner's basis in the partnership.

- The transfer of recourse liabilities from the LLC to the partnership does not result in a deemed distribution of money or taxation to members if the members who were personally responsible for the liabilities prior to the merger continue to be personally liable after the merger.

- The transfer of encumbered property from the LLC to the partnership is subject to the disguised sale rules of Code Sec. 707(a)(2)(B). However, no gain or loss is recognized to the merging LLCs or its members under the disguised sale rules if the liabilities transferred are "qualified liabilities." The liabilities are qualified liabilities if the loan proceeds have been utilized to fund capital improvements or for the ordinary and necessary expenses of operating the properties and if the debts are long standing in duration.

- Code Sec. 704(c) applies to the transfer of appreciated property by the LLC to the partnership.

9716007 S Corporation Ownership of LLC

An S corporation could own membership interests in an LLC classified as a partnership for federal tax purposes. The LLC could in turn own stock in another corporation. Before 1997, an S corporation was also prohibited from directly owning 80 percent of the stock in another corporation. However, it could own the stock indirectly through an LLC that was classified as a partnership for federal tax purposes.

An S corporation may not own stock in a foreign corporation.

9713007 Transfer of Business from Limited Partnership to LLC

A partnership may transfer some of its lines of business to an LLC to limit the liability of the partners with respect to that business. Generally, no gain or loss is recognized to the LLC or the members on the transfer of business or contribution of assets to the LLC under Code Sec. 721.

9701032 Conversion of Subsidiary into LLC

A parent corporation may convert a subsidiary corporation into a LLC by liquidating the subsidiary and contributing the assets received on liquidation to a newly formed LLC. The merger the subsidiary corporation into the parent corporation qualifies as a nontaxable liquidation under Code Sec. 332. The contribution to the LLC by the parent corporation of assets received from the subsidiary in exchange for membership units is nontaxable under Code Sec. 721. Neither the parent corporation, subsidiary corporation nor LLC recognizes gain as a result of the contribution of assets to the LLC.

9701029 Merger of C Corporation into LLC

The merger of a C corporation into an LLC is treated as a transfer of assets by the corporation to the LLC in exchange for the assumption of liabilities by the LLC and the corporation's receipt of LLC membership interests, followed by the corporation's distribution of the membership interests in the LLC to the shareholders of the corporation in complete liquidation.

The corporation and the LLC will not recognize gain or loss on the transfer of assets to the LLC in exchange for the membership interests.

The corporation recognizes gain or loss on the corporation's distribution of the ownership interests in the LLC to the LLC members in the complete liquidation of the corporation. Gain or loss is recognized to the same extent as if the corporation were to sell the distributed membership interests for their fair market value to the members.

The corporation's shareholders recognize capital gain or loss on the deemed distribution of the LLC membership interests from the corporation to its shareholders. The distribution is treated as full payment in exchange for their stock in the corporation.

If the LLC made an election under Code Sec. 754 before the merger, the distribution of the membership interests to the shareholders will constitute a transfer under Code Sec. 743. The LLC must then adjust the basis of its assets under Code Secs. 743 and 755.

The corporation's distribution of membership interests to the shareholders constitutes an exchange which causes the LLC to terminate under Code Sec. 708(b)(1)(B). The termination results in a deemed distribution of the LLC's assets to the shareholders, and a deemed immediate recontribution of those assets to a new LLC by the members.

9647028-032 Classification of Indiana LLC

An LLC organized under the laws of Indiana is classified as a partnership for federal income tax purposes.

9644059 Classification of Iowa LLC

An LLC organized under the laws of Iowa is classified as a partnership for federal income tax purposes.

9640010 Conversion of Subsidiary Corporation to LLC; Ownership by S Corporation of Subsidiary Indirectly Through LLC

A parent corporation may convert a subsidiary corporation into an LLC by forming an LLC and transferring the assets of the subsidiary corporation to the LLC in exchange for membership units. The subsidiary corporation is then liquidated. The membership units in the LLC owned by the subsidiary are transferred to the parent corporation in the liquidation. Neither the subsidiary nor the LLC recognize gain or loss as a result of the transfer of assets to the LLC. The liquidation of the subsidiary corporation and the transfer of the LLC membership units to the parent corporation qualify as a complete liquidation under Code Sec. 332.

Before 1997, an S corporation was also prohibited from directly owning 80 percent of the stock in another corporation. However, it could own the stock indirectly through an LLC that was classified as a partnership for federal tax purposes.

9639055 Classification of LLC

An LLC organized under the laws of State B is classified as a partnership for federal income tax purposes.

9637033 Classification of LLC; S Corporation Ownership

An LLC formed under the laws of Country N is classified as a partnership for federal tax purposes.

An S corporation may own a foreign LLC that is classified as a partnership for federal tax purposes.

9637030 Conversion from General Partnership to LLC; Cash Method of Accounting

There is no tax to the general partnership, LLC or the members if a general partnership converts into an LLC, except as provided under Code Sec. 752. There is no termination of the general partnership. The LLC is treated as the continuation of the partnership. The taxable year of the partnership will not close for any of the partners.

An LLC organized for the landscaping and nursery business must continue to use the cash method of accounting after conversion from a general partnership unless it seeks permission from the IRS to change its accounting method.

9636007 Conversion of S Corporation to LLC Taxed as S Corporation

An S corporation may convert to an LLC that is classified as a corporation. The conversion is treated as an F reorganization. The IRS will not issue an advance ruling on whether the transaction qualifies as an F reorganization. The reorganization does not terminate the corporation's election as an S corporation. The LLC is classified as an S corporation after the conversion.

Appendix C

9633021 Conversion from Limited Partnership to LLC; Employer Identification Number

There is no tax to the partners if a limited partnership converts into an LLC. There is no termination of the limited partnership. The partnership does not need to close its tax year. The LLC is treated as a continuation of the partnership.

An LLC is not required to obtain a new employer identification number after the conversion from a limited partnership.

9633014 Classification of LLC

An LLC formed under the laws of State B is classified as a partnership for federal tax purposes.

9626031 S Corporation Ownership of Stock Through an LLC

An S corporation may not own 80 percent or more of the stock in any other corporation, such as a domestic or foreign corporation. An S corporation may own more than 80 percent of the stock in any U.S. or foreign corporation if it owns the stock indirectly through an LLC. The Code only prohibits an S corporation from directly owning more than 80 percent of the stock in another corporation.

9625022-023 Life Insurance Transferred to LLC; Classification of Kansas LLC

Gross income does not include amounts paid under a life insurance contract that are paid by reason of the death of the insured. The exclusion is limited if the policy is transferred for valuable consideration. However, there is no limitation on the exclusion if the policy is transferred to the insured, a partner of the insured, a partnership in which the insured is a partner, or to a corporation in which the insured is a shareholder or officer. An LLC that is classified as a partnership for federal tax purposes is treated as a partnership for purposes of this rule. A Kansas LLC is classified as a partnership for federal tax purposes.

9625013-018 Life Insurance Transferred to LLC; Classification of Kansas LLC

Gross income does not include amounts paid under a life insurance contract that are paid by reason of the death of the insured. The exclusion is limited if the policy is transferred for valuable consideration. However, there is no limitation on the exclusion if the policy is transferred to the insured, a partner of the insured, a partnership in which the insured is a partner, or to a corporation in which the insured is a shareholder or officer. An LLC that is classified as a partnership for federal tax purposes is treated as a partnership for purposes of this rule.

A Kansas LLC is classified as a partnership for federal tax purposes.

9623016 Classification of LLC; Conversion from General Partnership to LLC

An LLC organized under the laws of State B for the practice of law is classified as a partnership for federal tax purposes.

There is no tax to the general partnership, LLC or the members if a general partnership converts into an LLC, except as provided in Code Sec. 752. There is no termination of the general partnership. The LLC is treated as a continuation of the general partnership.

9622007 Classification of Louisiana LLC

An LLC organized under the laws of Louisiana is classified as a partnership for federal income tax purposes.

9618023 Conversion from General Partnership to LLC; Basis in LLC; Employer Identification Number

There is no tax to the general partnership, LLC or the members if a general partnership converts into an LLC except as provided by Code Sec. 752. There is no termination of the general partnership. The LLC is treated as a continuation of the general partnership.

The basis of each member's interest in the LLC immediately after the conversion is the same as the basis of that member's interest in the general partnership immediately prior to the conversion except as provided by Code Sec. 752.

An LLC is not required to obtain a new employer identification number after the conversion from a general partnership. The tiered partnership rules do not apply.

9618022 Conversion from General Partnership to LLC; Basis in LLC; Employer Identification Number

There is no tax to the general partnership, LLC or the members if a general partnership converts into an LLC except as provided by Code Sec. 752. There is no termination of the general partnership. The LLC is treated as a continuation of the general partnership.

The basis of each member's interest in the LLC immediately after the conversion is the same as the basis of that member's interest in the general partnership immediately prior to the conversion except as provided by Code Sec. 752.

An LLC is not required to obtain a new employer identification number after the conversion from a general partnership. The tiered partnership rules do not apply.

9618021 Conversion from General Partnership to LLC; Basis in LLC; Employer Identification Number

There is no tax to the general partnership, LLC or the members if a general partnership converts into an LLC except as provided by Code Sec. 752. There is no termination of the general partnership. The LLC is treated as a continuation of the general partnership.

The basis of each member's interest in the LLC immediately after the conversion is the same as the basis of that member's interest in the general partnership immediately prior to the conversion except as provided by Code Sec. 752.

An LLC is not required to obtain a new employer identification number after the conversion from a general partnership. The tiered partnership rules do not apply.

9617020 Investment LLC

There is no tax on the transfer of appreciated marketable securities to an LLC if each member transfers a diversified portfolio of marketable securities that satisfies the 25 and 50 percent tests under Code Sec. 368(a)(2)(F)(ii).

9617018 Investment LLC

There is no tax on the transfer of appreciated marketable securities to an LLC if each member transfers a diversified portfolio of marketable securities that satisfies the 25 and 50 percent tests under Code Sec. 368(a)(2)(F)(ii).

Appendix C

9617017 Investment LLC

There is no tax on the transfer of appreciated marketable securities to an LLC if each member transfers a diversified portfolio of marketable securities that satisfies the 25 and 50 percent tests under Code Sec. 368(a)(2)(F)(ii).

9615025 S Corporations and Passive Rental Income

A corporation's election as an S corporation is terminated if the corporation has Subchapter C earnings and profits at the close of each of three consecutive taxable years, and has gross receipts for each of such years that are more than 25 percent of which are passive investment income. The receipt by an S corporation of a distributive share of rental income from an LLC is not passive income for such purposes if the corporation provides significant services or incurs substantial costs in the rental business.

9611041 Classification of Connecticut LLC

An LLC organized under the laws of Connecticut is classified as a partnership for federal income tax purposes.

9611008 Classification of LLC

An LLC organized under the laws of State X is classified as a partnership for federal income tax purposes.

9610006 Classification of Foreign-Owned LLC

An LLC organized in the United States that is owned by foreign persons is classified as a domestic partnership.

9609029 Classification of Delaware LLC

A Delaware LLC is classified as a partnership for federal tax purposes.

9607006 Classification of LLC; Conversion from Limited Partnership to LLC

An LLC organized under the laws of State B is classified as a partnership for federal tax purposes.

There is no tax if a limited partnership converts to an LLC. There is no termination of the partnership. The basis of each member's interest in the LLC is the same as that member's interest in the partnership before the conversion. The LLC is treated as a continuation of the partnership.

9606006 Classification of Louisiana LLC

A Louisiana LLC is classified as a partnership for federal tax purposes.

9604014 Formation of LLC; Contribution to LLC by Trust; Distribution of Membership Interests by Trust

No gain or loss is recognized on contribution of property to an LLC assuming the LLC is not an investment company.

A trust may contribute its assets to an LLC in exchange for membership interests and then distribute the membership interests to the trust beneficiaries. No gain or loss is recognized to the trust or the LLC on contribution of assets to the LLC. No gain or loss is recognized to the trusts on distribution of membership interests to the beneficiaries if the trusts do not elect to recognize gain or loss on the distributions under Code Sec. 643(e)(3)(B).

9602018 Conversion from General Partnership to LLC; Cash Method of Accounting

There is no tax to the general partnership, LLC or the members if a general partnership converts into an LLC. There is no termination of the general partnership.

An LLC organized for the practice of law may continue to use the cash method of accounting after conversion from a general partnership.

9602012 Classification of Delaware LLC

A Delaware LLC is classified as a partnership for federal tax purposes.

9552015 Classification of LLC

An LLC organized under the laws of State B is classified as a partnership for federal tax purposes.

9551032 Classification of Texas Limited Banking Association

A Texas Limited Banking Association is not a limited liability company, and is therefore classified as a corporation for federal tax purposes.

9547020 Classification of LLC

An LLC organized under the laws of State B is classified as a partnership for federal tax purposes.

9543023 Merger of C Corporation into LLC

The merger of a C corporation into an LLC is treated as an asset transfer in exchange for LLC membership interests, followed by the liquidation of the corporation. No gain or loss is recognized in the merger.

9543017 Merger of S Corporation into LLC

The merger of an S corporation into an LLC is treated as an asset transfer in exchange for LLC membership interests, followed by the liquidation of the S corporation. No gain or loss is recognized in the merger.

9538036 Classification of LLC

An LLC organized for a medical practice is classified as a partnership for federal income tax purposes.

9538022 Conversion from General Partnership to LLC; Cash Method of Accounting; Basis of Assets and Membership Interests

There is no tax to the general partnership, LLC or the members if a general partnership converts into an LLC. There is no termination of the general partnership.

An LLC organized for the practice of law must continue to use the cash method of accounting after conversion from a general partnership.

The LLC will take a carryover basis in the assets, and the members will take a carryover basis in their membership interests.

9536008 S Corporations and Rental Income

An S corporation's share of rental income from an LLC is not passive income under Code Sec. 1362(d)(3)(D)(i), but is passive income under Code Sec. 469. The LLC rented property subject to franchise agreements. As a limited partner in the franchises, the LLC provided significant services and incurred substantial costs in the rental business.

9536007 S Corporations and Rental Income

An S corporation's share of rental income from an LLC is not passive income under Code Sec. 1362(d)(3)(D)(i), but is passive income under Code Sec. 469. The LLC rented property subject to franchise agreements. As a limited partner in the franchises, the LLC provided significant services and incurred substantial costs in the rental business.

9535036 Conversion of General Partnership Interests in Limited Partnership to LLC; Cash Method of Accounting; Classification of LLC

The general partners of a limited partnership may convert into an LLC without taxation.

A limited partnership may continue to use the cash method of accounting after the general partners of the limited partnership convert their general partnership interests to membership interests in an LLC.

An LLC organized under the laws of State N is classified as a partnership for federal income tax purposes.

9533011 Classification of LLC

An LLC organized under the laws of State X is classified as a partnership for federal income tax purposes.

9532008 LLC Owned by S Corporation

An S corporation may own an LLC during the period of time that the LLC is classified as a partnership for federal tax purposes.

9529015 Classification of LLC

An LLC organized under the laws of State B is classified as a partnership for federal income tax purposes.

9526029 Classification of Brazilian LLC

A Brazilian *limitada (Sociedade por Quotas de Responsabilidade Limitada)* is classified as a partnership for federal tax purposes.

9525065 Conversion from General Partnership to LLC; Cash Method of Accounting; Employer Identification Number

There is no tax to the general partnership, LLC or the members if a general partnership converts into an LLC. There is no termination of the general partnership. The LLC is treated as a continuation of the general partnership. There is no close of the partnership's taxable year.

An LLC organized for the practice of accounting may continue to use the cash method of accounting after conversion from a general partnership.

An LLC is not required to obtain a new employer identification number after the conversion from a general partnership.

9525058 Conversion from General Partnership to LLC; Cash Method of Accounting; Self-Employment Taxes

There is no tax to the general partnership, LLC or the members if a general partnership converts into an LLC. There is no termination of the general partnership.

An LLC organized for the practice of law may continue to use the cash method of accounting after conversion from a general partnership.

The members are subject to self-employment taxes after the conversion.

9524022 Classification of French SAS

A *Societe par actions simplifiee* (SAS) is classified as a partnership for federal tax purposes if the SNC does not possess more corporate characteristics than noncorporate characteristics.

9520046 Classification of Texas LLC

A Texas LLC is classified as a partnership for federal income tax purposes.

9520036 Classification of Texas LLC; LLC Owned by Two Subsidiaries of Common Parent

A Texas LLC that is owned by two foreign subsidiaries of a foreign parent corporation is classified as a partnership for federal tax purposes.

9511033 Classification of LLC; Conversion from General Partnership to LLC

An LLC organized under the laws of State S is classified as a partnership for federal tax purposes.

There is no tax to the general partnership, LLC or the members if a general partnership converts into an LLC, except as provided in Code Secs. 731 and 752. There is no termination of the general partnership. The LLC is treated as a continuation of the general partnership.

9511023 Classification of Foreign LLC

A foreign LLC is classified as a partnership for federal income tax purposes.

9510037 Classification of Texas LLC

A Texas LLC is classified as a partnership for federal income tax purposes even though the LLC was owned by two wholly owned subsidiaries of a common parent.

9507004 Classification of Delaware LLC

A Delaware LLC is classified as a partnership for federal income tax purposes even though the LLC was owned by a parent and a subsidiary.

9501033 Classification of Maryland LLC; Conversion from General Partnership to LLC; Cash Method of Accounting

A Maryland LLC is classified as a partnership for federal tax purposes.

There is no tax to the general partnership, LLC or the members if a general partnership converts into an LLC. There is no termination of the general partnership. The LLC is treated as a continuation of the general partnership. There is no close of the partnership's taxable year.

An LLC organized for the practice of law may continue to use the cash method of accounting after conversion from a general partnership.

Appendix C

9452024 Conversion from General Partnership to LLC; Cash Method of Accounting

There is no tax to the general partnership, LLC or the members if a general partnership converts into an LLC. There is no termination of the general partnership. The LLC is treated as a continuation of the general partnership.

An LLC organized for the practice of medicine may continue to use the cash method of accounting after conversion from a general partnership.

9443024 Classification of Utah LLC; Conversion of Limited Partnership to LLC

A Utah LLC is classified as a partnership for federal tax purposes.

There is no tax if a limited partnership converts to an LLC. There is no termination of the partnership. The LLC is treated as a continuation of the partnership.

9443018 Classification of Florida LLC

A Florida LLC is classified as a partnership for federal tax purposes.

9436019 Classification of LLC; Taxes on Foreign Members of LLC

An LLC organized under the laws of State B is classified as a partnership for federal tax purposes.

If an LLC is engaged in a U.S. trade or business, all foreign members of that LLC will be treated as engaged in a U.S. trade or business. If an LLC has a permanent establishment in the United States, each of the LLC's members will be treated as having a permanent establishment in the United States.

9434027 Classification of LLC; Conversion from General Partnership to LLC; Cash Method of Accounting

An LLC is classified as a partnership for federal tax purposes.

There is no tax to the general partnership, LLC or the members if a general partnership converts into an LLC. There is no termination of the general partnership. The LLC is treated as a continuation of the general partnership.

An LLC organized for the practice of management consulting may continue to use the cash method of accounting after conversion from a general partnership.

9433088 Classification of LLC; Related Members; Free Transferability of Interests; Continuity of Life

An LLC will have the corporate characteristics of free transferability, even if there are restrictions on transfer, if the LLC is owned by related members. In such cases, the restrictions on transfer are not meaningful.

An LLC will not have the corporate characteristic of continuity of life, even if all members are related, if the operating agreement provides for dissolution on the death, bankruptcy, dissolution or withdrawal of a member unless the remaining members agree to continue the LLC.

9433023 Classification of LLC

An LLC organized under the laws of State B is classified as a partnership for federal tax purposes.

9433008 Classification of LLC; LLC Owned by S Corporation

An LLC organized under the laws of State A is classified as a corporation for federal tax purposes.

If an LLC owned by an S corporation is reclassified by the IRS as a corporation, the S corporation's election as an S corporation will be terminated unless the S corporation obtains a ruling from the IRS that the termination was inadvertent.

9432018 Classification of LLC; Conversion from General Partnership to LLC; Cash Method of Accounting; Self-Employment Taxes

An LLC is classified as a partnership for federal tax purposes.

There is no tax to the general partnership, LLC or the members if a general partnership converts into an LLC. There is no termination of the general partnership. The LLC is treated as a continuation of the general partnership.

An LLC organized for the practice of law may continue to use the cash method of accounting after conversion from a general partnership.

The members of an LLC are liable for self-employment taxes on their distributive shares of LLC income attributable to a trade or business carried on by the LLC.

9426037 Conversion from General Partnership to LLC

There is no termination of the partnership if a New York general partnership reorganizes as a Delaware LLC.

9426030 Conversion from General Partnership; Cash Method of Accounting

An LLC organized for the practice of law must continue to use the cash method of accounting after conversion from a general partnership.

9425013 Classification of North Dakota LLC

A North Dakota LLC is classified as a partnership for federal tax purposes.

9423040 Conversion from General Partnership to LLC; Accounting Methods After Conversion

There is no termination of the partnership if a general partnership reorganizes as a Delaware LLC.

The LLC must continue to use the same method of accounting as the general partnership until it receives permission to change its accounting methods or until the IRS challenges the method on examination.

9423037 Conversion from General Partnership to LLC

There is no termination of the partnership if a general partnership reorganizes as a Delaware LLC.

9422034 Classification of Indiana LLC; Conversion from General Partnership to LLC; Cash Method of Accounting; Tax Shelter Classification; Professional LLC

An LLC organized under the laws of Indiana is classified as a partnership for federal tax purposes.

There is no tax to the general partnership, LLC or the members if a general partnership converts into an LLC. There is no termination of the general partnership. The LLC is treated as a continuation of the general partnership. The LLC must continue to use the same taxable year as the LLP.

An LLC organized for the practice of accounting may continue to use the cash method of accounting after conversion from a general partnership.

Appendix C

9421025 Classification of LLC; Conversion from General Partnership to LLC; Depreciation Recapture; Cash Method of Accounting

An LLC is classified as a partnership for federal tax purposes.

There is no tax to the general partnership, LLC or the members if a general partnership converts into an LLC. There is no depreciation recapture under Code Sec. 1245. There is no termination of the general partnership. The LLC is treated as a continuation of the general partnership.

An LLC organized for the practice of law may continue to use the cash method of accounting after conversion from a general partnership.

9420028 Conversion from General Partnership to LLC

There is no termination of the partnership if a general partnership reorganizes as a Delaware LLC.

9417009 Conversion from Limited Partnership to LLC

There is no tax if a limited partnership converts to an LLC. There is no termination of the partnership. The LLC is treated as a continuation of the partnership. There is a carryover of basis in the partnership interests and partnership assets. The holding period of the membership interests includes the holding period of the partnership interests. The LLC's basis in the assets is the same as the basis of those assets in the partnership immediately prior to the conversion.

9416029 Classification of LLC; Conversion from Limited Partnership to LLC

An LLC organized under the laws of State B is classified as a partnership for federal tax purposes.

There is no tax if a limited partnership converts to an LLC. There is no termination of the partnership. The LLC is treated as a continuation of the partnership.

There is a carryover of basis in the partnership interests and partnership assets. The holding period of the membership interests includes the holding period of the partnership interests. The LLC's basis in the assets is the same as the basis of those assets in the partnership immediately before the conversion.

9416028 Classification of LLC; Conversion from Limited Partnership to LLC

An LLC organized under the laws of State B is classified as a partnership for federal tax purposes.

There is no tax if a limited partnership converts to an LLC. There is no termination of the partnership. The LLC is treated as a continuation of the partnership.

There is a carryover of basis in the partnership interests and partnership assets. The holding period of the membership interests includes the holding period of the partnership interests. The LLC's basis in the assets is the same as the basis of those assets in the partnership immediately prior to the conversion.

9416026 Classification of Delaware LLC

A Delaware LLC is classified as a partnership for federal tax purposes.

9416025 Classification of Delaware LLC

A Delaware LLC is classified as a partnership for federal tax purposes.

9415005 Classification of LLC; Conversion from General Partnership to LLC; Cash Method of Accounting

A Delaware LLC is classified as a partnership for federal tax purposes.

An LLC organized for the practice of law may continue to use the cash method of accounting after conversion from a general partnership.

9412030 Classification of LLC; Conversion from LLP to LLC; Cash Method of Accounting; Tax Shelter Classification; Professional LLC

An LLC organized under the laws of State J is classified as a partnership for federal tax purposes.

There is no tax to the LLP, LLC or the members if an LLP merges into an LLC. There is no termination of the LLP. The LLC is treated as a continuation of the LLP. The LLC must continue to use the same taxable year as the LLP.

An LLC organized for the practice of accounting may continue to use the cash method of accounting after conversion from an LLP.

9409016 Classification of Louisiana LLC; Merger of Corporation into LLC

A Louisiana LLC is classified as a partnership for federal tax purposes.

The merger of a subsidiary corporation into a related LLC is non-taxable. It is treated as a transfer of corporate assets to the LLC and the liquidation of the subsidiary.

9409014 Classification of Louisiana LLC; Merger of Corporation into LLC

A Louisiana LLC is classified as a partnership for federal tax purposes.

The merger of a subsidiary corporation into a related LLC is non-taxable. It is treated as a transfer of corporate assets to the LLC and the liquidation of the subsidiary.

9407030 Classification of LLC; Conversion from General Partnership; Cash Method of Accounting; Tax Shelter Classification; Professional LLC

An LLC organized under the laws of State B is classified as a partnership for federal tax purposes.

There is no tax if a general partnership converts to an LLC. There is no termination of the partnership. The LLC is treated as a continuation of the partnership.

An LLC organized for the practice of law may continue to use the cash method of accounting after conversion from a general partnership.

9404021 Classification of Louisiana LLC; Merger of Corporation into LLC

A Louisiana LLC is classified as a partnership for federal tax purposes.

The merger of a subsidiary corporation into a related LLC is non-taxable. It is treated as a transfer of corporate assets to the LLC and the liquidation of the subsidiary.

9350003 Classification of LLC; Conversion from General Partnership; Cash Method of Accounting; Tax Shelter Classification; Professional LLC

An LLC organized under the laws of State Z is classified as a partnership for federal tax purposes.

Appendix C

There is no tax if a general partnership converts to an LLC. There is no termination of the partnership. The LLC is treated as a continuation of the partnership.

An LLC organized for the practice of law may continue to use the cash method of accounting after conversion from a general partnership.

9343036 Stock Bonus Plan Established by LLC

An LLC may establish a qualified stock bonus plan for distribution of stock of a corporate partner and its parent corporation. A corporate employer may transfer plan assets consisting of employer securities to a plan maintained by an LLC. The stock of the corporate employer will continue to constitute "employer securities" until distributed by the LLC's plan to the plan participants.

9341018 Classification of German GmbH; Free Transferability of Interests

A German GmbH is classified as a partnership for federal tax purposes.

The GmbH lacked the corporate characteristic of free transferability of interests and modified free transferability where the governing documents provided that the owner must first offer the shares to the company and then to the existing shareholders and no transfers could be made to third parties without the consent of the other members.

9335063 FICA Taxes on Work Outside the United States; Classification of Foreign LLC

An "American employer" is required to withhold FICA taxes on wages paid to citizens or residents of the United States who perform services as an employee outside of the United States. A U.S. or foreign LLC that is classified as a partnership is an "American employer" for withholding purposes if two-thirds or more of the partners are residents of the United States.

An LLC organized under the laws of Country Y is classified as a partnership for U.S. tax purposes.

9335062 FICA Taxes on Work Outside the United States; Classification of Foreign LLC

An "American employer" is required to withhold FICA taxes on wages paid to citizens or residents of the United States who perform services as an employee outside of the United States. A U.S. or foreign LLC that is classified as a partnership is an "American employer" for withholding purposes if two-thirds or more of the partners are residents of the United States.

An LLC organized under the laws of Country Y is classified as a partnership for U.S. tax purposes.

9335032 Classification of Delaware LLC

A Delaware LLC is classified as a partnership for federal tax purposes.

9333032 Classification of Illinois LLC

An Illinois LLC is classified as a partnership for federal tax purposes.

9331049 S Corporations; China LLC

An S corporation election will be terminated if it organizes a limited liability company in China. The China LLC was apparently classified as corporation for U.S. tax purposes. The Service granted relief from termination under Code Sec. 1362(f).

9330009 S Corporations; Investment LLCs

An S corporation may organize an LLC without creating a second class of stock that would disqualify S corporation election.

An LLC may be used as an investment vehicle. There is no personal holding company tax even if all of the passive income is retained in the LLC.

9331010 Classification of LLC; Formation of LLC

An LLC formed under the laws of State Z is classified as a partnership for federal tax purposes.

No gain or loss is recognized on contribution of property to an LLC assuming the LLC is not an investment company. There is a carryover basis in the assets. The LLC members have a basis in their membership interests equal to the amount of money and adjusted basis of assets contributed to the LLC.

9328005 Cash Method of Accounting

A Utah LLC, previously classified as a partnership, may use the cash method of accounting.

9326035 Classification of LLC; Majority Consent for Continuation of LLC

An LLC will lack the corporate characteristic of continuity of life if it may by continued on loss of a member by the unanimous consent of all managers and the majority consent of members.

9325048 Classification of LLC

An LLC owning working interests in oil and gas wells is classified as a partnership for federal tax purposes.

9325039 Classification of Illinois LLC; Majority Consent for Continuation of LLC

An Illinois LLC is classified as a partnership for federal tax purposes. The ruling was withdrawn for reconsideration because a majority in number rather than a majority in interest was required to vote for continuing the LLC after withdrawal of a member.

9321070 Conversion from General Partnership; Classification of Utah LLC; Centralized Management

If a general partnership transfers selected assets directly to an LLC owned by the partners, the assets will be treated as distributed to the partners and then contributed to the LLC.

An LLC formed under the laws of Utah (referred to as State C) is classified as a partnership for federal tax purposes.

An LLC formed by an individual and a corporation of which she was the sole director lacked centralized management.

Appendix C

9321047 Classification of Arizona LLC; Conversion from General Partnership; Cash Method of Accounting; Tax Shelter Classification; Professional LLC

An LLC formed under the laws of Arizona (referred to as State O) is classified as a partnership for federal tax purposes. An Arizona LLC lacks the corporate characteristic of continuity of life even if only a majority of the remaining members must agree to continue the business after withdrawal of a member.

There is no tax if a general partnership converts to an LLC. There is no termination of the partnership. The LLC is treated as a continuation of the partnership.

An LLC organized for the practice of law may use the cash method of accounting.

9320045 Classification of Utah LLC; Centralization of Management

An LLC formed under the laws of Utah (referred to as State B) and that owned working interests in oil and gas wells is classified as a partnership for federal tax purposes.

There is no centralization of management if the LLC reserves management to members.

9320019 Classification of Utah LLC

An LLC formed under the laws of Utah (referred to as State B) and that owned working interests in oil and gas wells is classified as a partnership for federal tax purposes.

9318011 Classification of LLC

An LLC formed under the LLC laws of an unspecified state is classified as a partnership for federal tax purposes.

9313009 Classification of Utah LLC; Formation of LLC

An LLC formed under laws of Utah (unspecified state in the ruling) is classified as a partnership for federal tax purposes.

There is no tax on the contribution of oil and gas working interest to the LLC in exchange for membership interest.

9308039 Classification of West Virginia LLC

A West Virginia LLC is classified as a partnership for federal tax purposes.

9308027 Classification of Delaware LLC

An LLC formed under the laws of Delaware (referred to as State A) is classified as a partnership for federal tax purposes.

9306008 Classification of United Kingdom LLC

A United Kingdom LLC is classified as a partnership for federal tax purposes. It lacks free transferability of interests if there are restrictions on at least 20 percent of all LLC interests.

9242025 Classification of Texas LLC

A Texas LLC is classified as a partnership for federal tax purposes if it lacks at least two corporate characteristics.

9227033 Classification of Nevada LLC

A Nevada LLC is classified as a partnership for federal tax purposes.

9226035 Conversion from General Partnership to LLC

There is no tax if a general partnership converts to an LLC. There is no termination of the partnership. The LLC is treated as a continuation of the partnership.

9219022 Classification of Utah LLC

An LLC formed under the laws of Utah (referred to as State Z) is classified as a partnership for federal tax purposes.

9218078 Classification of Texas LLC

A Texas LLC is classified as a partnership for federal tax purposes if it lacks at least two corporate characteristics.

9216004 Classification of Foreign LLC

A foreign LLC organized under the laws of Country A is classified as a partnership for federal tax purposes.

9210039 Classification of Foreign LLC

A foreign LLC organized under the laws of Country A is classified as a partnership for federal tax purposes.

9210019 Classification of Texas LLC; Merger of Limited Partnership into LLC

A Texas LLC is classified as a partnership for federal tax purposes if it lacks at least two corporate characteristics. The LLC lacked the corporate characteristic of free transferability where only the consent of the manager was required for transfers of interests.

There is no tax if a limited partnership merges into an LLC. There is no termination of the partnership. The LLC is treated as a continuation of the partnership.

9215009 Classification of Foreign LLC

A foreign LLC organized under the laws of City X in Country Y is classified as a corporation.

9152009 Classification of United Kingdom LLC; Continuity of Life

A United Kingdom LLC is classified as a partnership for federal tax purposes.

A United Kingdom LLC lacks the corporate characteristic of continuity of life even though dissolution is not automatic and requires further shareholder action. This ruling was distinguished from Letter Ruling 9002056 because the organizational documents for the LLC in this ruling required the shareholders to meet and to vote for dissolution on bankruptcy of the LLC.

9147017 Classification of LLC

An LLC formed under the laws of State Y is classified as a partnership for federal tax purposes.

Appendix C

9119029 Classification of Florida LLC; Conversion from Limited Partnership to LLC

A Florida LLC is classified as a partnership for federal tax purposes.

There is no tax if a limited partnership converts to an LLC. There is no termination of the partnership. The LLC is treated as a continuation of the partnership.

9052039 Classification of LLC

An LLC formed under the laws of State Z is classified as a partnership for federal tax purposes.

9030013 Classification of Florida LLC

A Florida LLC is classified as a partnership for federal tax purposes.

9029019 Classification of Florida LLC; Conversion from General Partnership to LLC

An LLC formed under the laws of Florida (referred to as State Z) is classified as a partnership for federal tax purposes.

There is no tax if a general partnership converts to an LLC. There is no termination of the partnership. The LLC is treated as a continuation of the partnership.

9010028 Classification of German GmbH

A German GmbH lacked the corporate characteristic of free transferability of interests where the articles prohibited transfers without the consent of the other partners, which consent could not be unreasonably withheld. In addition, the owner was required to first offer the shares to the other owners before selling to a third party. The IRS later withdrew Letter Ruling 9035041.

9010027 Conversion from General Partnership to LLC; Centralization of Management

There is no tax if a general partnership converts to an LLC. There is no termination of the partnership. The LLC is treated as a continuation of the partnership.

There is no centralized management if a Florida LLC reserves management to members in proportion to membership interests.

9002056 Classification of United Kingdom LLC; Continuity of Life

A United Kingdom LLC is classified as a partnership for federal tax purposes.

A United Kingdom LLC lacks the corporate characteristic of continuity of life if the memorandum and articles of association require the shareholders to meet and vote in favor of dissolution after a dissolution event.

8937010 Classification of Florida LLC

A Florida LLC is classified as a partnership for federal tax purposes.

8908035 Conversion from LLC to Unlimited Liability Company

There is no tax on the conversion from an LLC organized under the laws of a foreign country into an unlimited liability company.

8828022 Classification of Foreign LLC

An LLC organized under the laws of a foreign country is classified as a corporation.

8809073 Conversion from LLC to Unlimited Liability Company

There is no tax on the conversion from an LLC organized under the laws of a foreign country into an unlimited liability company.

8436030 Classification of German GmbH

The IRS declined to rule on the classification of a German GmbH.

8401001 Classification of Brazilian LLC

A Brazilian *limitada* is classified as a corporation for federal tax purposes.

8309062 Classification of German GmbH

A German GmbH is classified as a partnership for federal tax purposes.

8304138 Classification of Foreign LLC

A foreign LLC organized under the laws of Country Z is classified as a corporation.

8304138 Classification of Foreign LLC

A foreign LLC organized under the laws of Country X is classified as a partnership for federal tax purposes.

8221136 Classification of German GmbH

A German GmbH is classified as a partnership for federal tax purposes.

8114095 Classification of German GmbH

A German GmbH is classified as a corporation for federal tax purposes.

8106082 Classification of Spanish Limitada; Liquidating Distributions; Formation of LLC

A Spanish *limitada* is classified as a partnership for federal tax purposes.

No gain is recognized on a liquidating distribution except to the extent that the money received exceeds a member's basis in his LLC interest.

8104129 Classification of Foreign LLC

A foreign LLC organized under the laws of Country X is classified as a partnership for federal tax purposes.

8029031 Contribution of Property to Foreign LLC

LLC shareholders do not recognize gain or loss on the contribution of property to a foreign LLC under Code Sec. 351, whether or not additional shares are issued. There is a carryover basis in assets.

8023109 Merger of LLCs

The merger of a subsidiary LLC into a parent LLC is treated as a Code Sec. 332 liquidation if the LLCs are classified as corporations for federal tax purposes.

Appendix C

8019112 Classification of Brazilian LLC

One Brazilian *limitada* was classified as a partnership for federal tax purposes and the other *limitada* was classified as a corporation.

8012080 Classification of Foreign LLC

A foreign LLC organized under the laws of Country X is classified as a partnership for federal tax purposes.

8007029 Classification of Saudi Arabian LLC

A Saudi Arabian LLC is classified as a partnership for federal tax purposes.

8006068 Classification of Saudi Arabian LLC

A Saudi Arabian LLC is classified as a corporation for federal tax purposes.

8004010 Classification of LLC

An LLC organized under the laws of State X is classified as a partnership for federal tax purposes. There is no centralization of management if all of the major management and policy decisions of the LLC are made by its partners.

8003072 Classification of Brazilian LLC

A Brazilian *limitada* is classified as a partnership for federal tax purposes.

8002076 Reincorporation of LLC

The reincorporation of an LLC is a nontaxable F reorganization.

7952027 Classification of German GmbH

A German GmbH is classified as a corporation for federal tax purposes.

7950044 Non-divisive D Reorganization

The transfer of assets, liabilities and stock between related German LLCs is a non-divisive D reorganization.

7948066 Non-divisive D Reorganization

There was a non-divisive D reorganization where a corporation merged into an LLC. The LLC did not issue shares in the merger since LLCs did not issue stock under applicable laws. The corporation and the LLC were owned equally by two unrelated corporations (or their affiliates).

7947048 Non-divisive D Reorganization

There was a non-divisive D reorganization where an LLC merged into a corporation. The LLC and the corporation were both owned by the same corporation.

7941054 Classification of Brazilian LLC

A Brazilian *limitada* is classified as a corporation for federal tax purposes.

7937054 Classification of German GmbH; Formation of LLC

A German GmbH is classified as a corporation for federal tax purposes.

No gain or loss is recognized on the contribution of assets and liabilities to an LLC on formation of the LLC.

7936050 Classification of Chilean Limitada

A Chilean *limitada* is classified as a corporation for federal tax purposes if it possesses more corporate characteristics than noncorporate characteristics.

7935046 Classification of Hong Kong LLC; Formation of LLC

No opinion was expressed on whether a Hong Kong LLC is classified as a corporation for federal tax purposes.

No gain or loss is recognized on the contribution of assets and liabilities to an LLC on formation of the LLC except to the extent of boot received.

7928063 Classification of Brazilian LLC

A Brazilian *limitada* is classified as a corporation for federal tax purposes.

7926034 Classification of Saudi Arabian LLC

A Saudi Arabian LLC is classified as a corporation for federal tax purposes.

7921079 Classification of Saudi Arabian LLC

A Saudi Arabian LLC is classified as a partnership for federal tax purposes.

7911065 Conversion of Corporation into LLC

The conversion of a corporation into an LLC is a nontaxable exchange under Code Sec. 1036.

7908027 Drop-Down of Assets from Parent to Subsidiary LLC

The drop-down of assets and liabilities by a parent LLC into a newly formed subsidiary LLC followed by the transfer of stock in the subsidiary LLC from the parent LLC to its parent corporation is a non-divisive D reorganization.

7908004 Classification of German GmbH

A German GmbH is classified as a corporation for federal tax purposes.

7907066 Conversion of LLC to Corporation

The conversion of an LLC to a corporation by charter amendment is a nontaxable exchange under Code Sec. 351.

7852111 Non-divisive D Reorganization

There was a non-divisive D reorganization where a corporation merged into an LLC. The LLC and the corporation apparently had common shareholders.

7843099 Transfer of Property to LLC

The transfer of property to an LLC that is classified as a corporation is a nontaxable transaction under Code Sec. 351.

7843006 Classification of Greek LLC

A Greek LLC is classified as a corporation for federal tax purposes if it has more corporate characteristics than noncorporate characteristics.

Appendix C

7841008 Classification of Italian SRL

A *societa a responsabilit limitata* (SRL) is classified as a corporation for federal tax purposes if it possesses more corporate characteristics than noncorporate characteristics.

7836019 Conversion of Corporation into LLC

The conversion of a corporation into an LLC is a nontaxable exchange under Code Sec. 1036.

7833112 Formation of LLC

No gain or loss is recognized on the contribution of assets and liabilities to a foreign LLC on formation of the LLC except for gain on the transfer of inventory.

7831021 Classification of Brazilian LLC; Conversion from Corporation to LLC

A Brazilian *limitada* is classified as a corporation for federal tax purposes.

The conversion of a Brazilian corporation to an LLC is a nontaxable exchange under Code Sec. 1036.

7826023 Classification of Portuguese LLC

A Portuguese LLC is classified as a corporation for federal tax purposes.

7821084 Transfer of LLC Interest to Subsidiary LLC

The transfer by a parent company of LLC shares from one subsidiary LLC to another subsidiary LLC (where both LLCs are classified as corporations) is a nontaxable exchange under Code Sec. 351.

7817129 Classification of Brazilian LLC

A Brazilian *limitada* is classified as a partnership for federal tax purposes.

7814012 Classification of Brazilian LLC

A Brazilian *limitada* is classified as a corporation for federal tax purposes.

7810072 Conversion from Corporation to LLC

The conversion of a corporation to an LLC is a nontaxable F reorganization.

7747089 Classification of One-Person GmbH

A one-person GmbH is classified as a sole-proprietorship for federal tax purposes.

7741040 Conversion from LLC to Corporation

There is no tax on the conversion from an LLC organized under the laws of Greece into a corporation.

7729058 Conversion from Corporation to LLC

The conversion of a corporation to an LLC is a nontaxable F reorganization.

7716015 Change in LLC Ownership to Related Subsidiary

A parent corporation's transfer of LLC stock to a subsidiary is a nontaxable contribution under Code Sec. 351.

7203140670A Drop-Down of Assets into Subsidiary LLC

The drop-down of assets and liabilities into a subsidiary LLC is a nontaxable exchange under Code Sec. 351.

7111100730A Conversion from Corporation to LLC

The conversion of a corporation to an LLC is a nontaxable F reorganization.

7108110470A Classification of Mexican Limitada

A Mexican *sociedade de responsabilidad limitada* is classified as a partnership for federal tax purposes if it does not possess more corporate characteristics than noncorporate characteristics. The IRS determined that the *limitada* lacked the corporate characteristics of free transferability and continuity of life, and was thus classified as a partnership for federal tax purposes.

6707214880A Classification of Foreign LLC

An LLC formed under the laws of a foreign country is classified as a partnership for federal tax purposes.

PART 2.
GENERAL COUNSEL MEMORANDUM

39798 Classification of LLC

The lack of personal liability of members of an LLC will not preclude the IRS from classifying an LLC as a partnership.

35294 Classification of Columbian SRL

A Columbian *Sociedad de Responsabilidad Limitada* (SRL) is classified as a corporation for federal tax purposes if it possesses more corporate characteristics than noncorporate characteristics. The SRL was treated as a separate jurisdictional entity taxed as a corporation.

Table of Internal Revenue Code Sections

Table of Treasury Regulations

References are to paragraph (¶) numbers.

Table of Internal Revenue Service Releases

References are to paragraph (¶) numbers.

Notices

Technical Advice Memoranda

Treasury Decisions

Table of Cases

References are to paragraph numbers.

Index

References are to paragraph (¶) numbers.